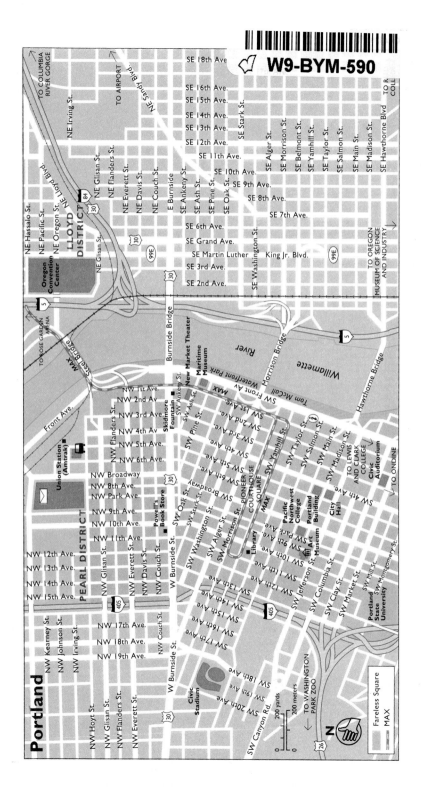

Seattle

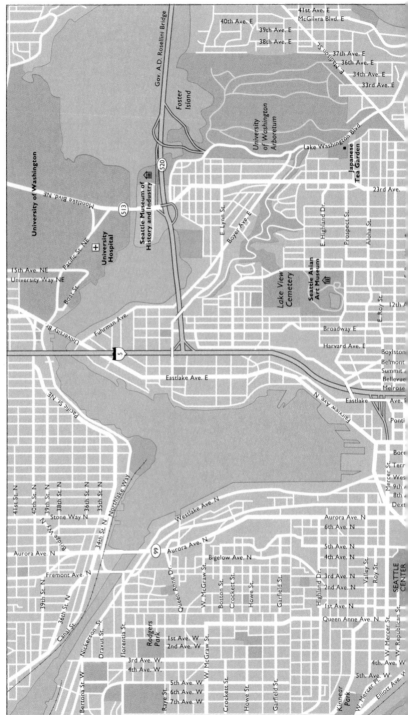

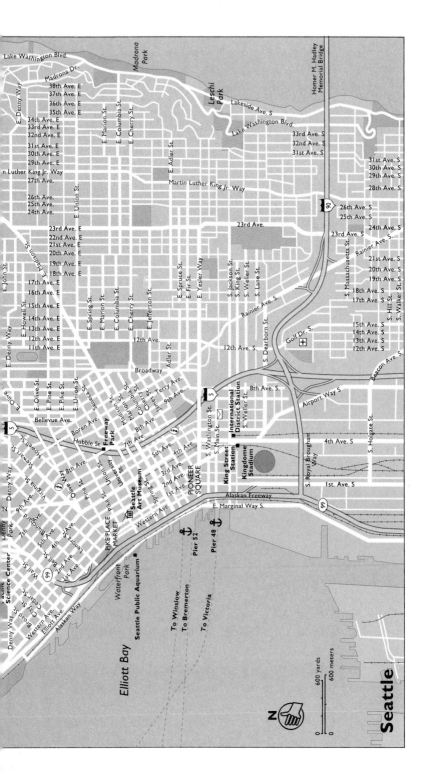

Vancouver

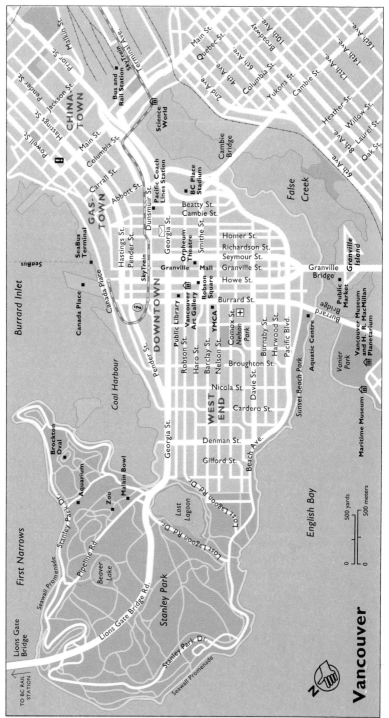

Vancouver

🖎 Let's Go writers travel on your budget.

"Guides that penetrate the veneer of the holiday brochures and mine the grit of real life."

—The Economist

"The writers seem to have experienced every rooster-packed bus and lunar-surfaced mattress about which they write."

—The New York Times

"All the dirt, dirt cheap."

—People

🖎 Great for independent travelers.

"The guides are aimed not only at young budget travelers but at the independent traveler; a sort of streetwise cookbook for traveling alone."

—The New York Times

"Flush with candor and irreverence, chock full of budget travel advice."

—The Des Moines Register

"An indispensible resource, *Let's Go*'s practical information can be used by every traveler."

—The Chattanooga Free Press

🖎 Let's Go is completely revised each year.

"Only *Let's Go* has the zeal to annually update every title on its list."

—The Boston Globe

"Unbeatable: good sight-seeing advice; up-to-date info on restaurants, hotels, and inns; a commitment to money-saving travel; and a wry style that brightens nearly every page."

—The Washington Post

🖎 All the important information you need.

"*Let's Go* authors provide a comedic element while still providing concise information and thorough coverage of the country. Anything you need to know about budget traveling is detailed in this book."

—The Chicago Sun-Times

"Value-packed, unbeatable, accurate, and comprehensive."

—Los Angeles Times

Let's Go Publications

Let's Go: Alaska & the Pacific Northwest 2000
Let's Go: Australia 2000
Let's Go: Austria & Switzerland 2000
Let's Go: Britain & Ireland 2000
Let's Go: California 2000
Let's Go: Central America 2000
Let's Go: China 2000 **New Title!**
Let's Go: Eastern Europe 2000
Let's Go: Europe 2000
Let's Go: France 2000
Let's Go: Germany 2000
Let's Go: Greece 2000
Let's Go: India & Nepal 2000
Let's Go: Ireland 2000
Let's Go: Israel 2000 **New Title!**
Let's Go: Italy 2000
Let's Go: Mexico 2000
Let's Go: Middle East 2000 **New Title!**
Let's Go: New York City 2000
Let's Go: New Zealand 2000
Let's Go: Paris 2000
Let's Go: Perú & Ecuador 2000 **New Title!**
Let's Go: Rome 2000
Let's Go: South Africa 2000
Let's Go: Southeast Asia 2000
Let's Go: Spain & Portugal 2000
Let's Go: Turkey 2000
Let's Go: USA 2000
Let's Go: Washington, D.C. 2000

Let's Go Map Guides

Amsterdam	New Orleans
Berlin	New York City
Boston	Paris
Chicago	Prague
Florence	Rome
London	San Francisco
Los Angeles	Seattle
Madrid	Washington, D.C.

Coming Soon: Sydney and Hong Kong

Let's Go

2000
ALASKA & THE PACIFIC NORTHWEST
INCLUDING WESTERN CANADA

Tom Davidson
Editor

James S. F. Wilson
Associate Editor

Researcher-Writers:
Weston Eguchi	**Maja Groff**
Matt Elliott	**Ken Haig**
David Friedland	**Ana Morrel-Samuels**

St. Martin's Press ≈ New York

HELPING LET'S GO If you want to share your discoveries, suggestions, or corrections, please drop us a line. We read every piece of correspondence, whether a postcard, a 10-page email, or a coconut. Please note that mail received after May 2000 may be too late for the 2001 book, but will be kept for future editions. **Address mail to:**

> **Let's Go: Alaska & the Pacific Northwest**
> **67 Mount Auburn Street**
> **Cambridge, MA 02138**
> **USA**

Visit Let's Go at **http://www.letsgo.com,** or send email to:

> **feedback@letsgo.com**
> **Subject: "Let's Go: Alaska & the Pacific Northwest"**

In addition to the invaluable travel advice our readers share with us, many are kind enough to offer their services as researchers or editors. Unfortunately, our charter enables us to employ only currently enrolled Harvard students.

Maps by David Lindroth copyright © 2000, 1999, 1998, 1997, 1996, 1995, 1994, 1993, 1992, 1991, 1990, 1989, 1988 by St. Martin's Press.

Distributed outside the USA and Canada by Macmillan.

ISBN: 0-312-24137-2

First edition
10 9 8 7 6 5 4 3 2 1

Let's Go: Alaska & the Pacific Northwest is written by Let's Go Publications, 67 Mount Auburn Street, Cambridge, MA 02138, USA.

Let's Go® and the thumb logo are trademarks of Let's Go, Inc.
Printed in the USA on recycled paper with biodegradable soy ink.

CONTENTS

MAPS

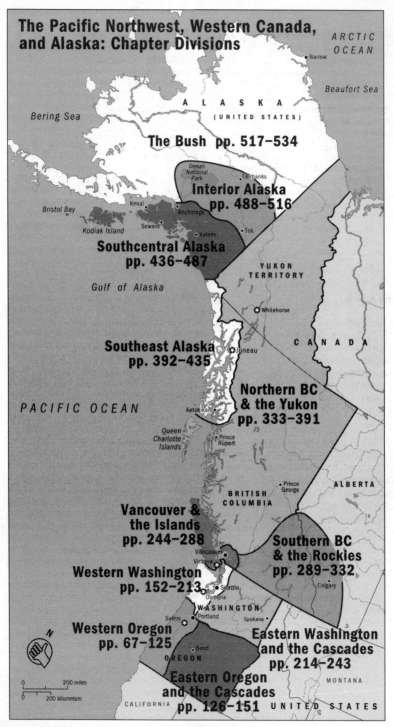

The Pacific Northwest, Western Canada, and Alaska: Chapter Divisions

ARCTIC OCEAN

Barrow

Beaufort Sea

Bering Sea

A L A S K A
(UNITED STATES)

The Bush pp. 517–534

Denali National Park

Fairbanks

Interior Alaska pp. 488–516

Kenai

Anchorage

Bristol Bay

Seward

Valdez

Tok

Kodiak Island

Southcentral Alaska pp. 436–487

YUKON TERRITORY

Gulf of Alaska

Whitehorse

Southeast Alaska pp. 392–435

Juneau

C A N A D A

PACIFIC OCEAN

Ketchikan

Northern BC & the Yukon pp. 333–391

Queen Charlotte Islands

Prince Rupert

Prince George

ALBERTA

BRITISH COLUMBIA

Vancouver & the Islands pp. 244–288

Vancouver

Victoria

Southern BC & the Rockies pp. 289–332

Western Washington pp. 152–213

Seattle

Olympia

Calgary

WASHINGTON

Salem

Portland

Spokane

Western Oregon pp. 67–125

Bend

OREGON

Eastern Washington and the Cascades pp. 214–243

Eastern Oregon and the Cascades pp. 126–151

N

CALIFORNIA

MONTANA

UNITED STATES

0   200 miles
0   200 kilometers

HOW TO USE THIS BOOK

Let's Go: Alaska and the Pacific Northwest 2000, completely revised for the rolling over of the cosmic odometer, aims to get you through this vast region's cities and to its trailheads with all the provisions and resources you'll need. Never will you be at a loss to find equipment and rangers before you hit the trail or a burger and Internet access when you emerge from the woods, all the while kept posted on both the land's history and its current state of affairs.

The **Discover** chapter provides region-wide highlights and sample itineraries to help you picture the possibilities of a northwest journey. **The People and the Land** provides a short history of the region's habitation and traces how it is changing, ending with this year's news and suggestions for further reading. The **Essentials** chapter gives you the info you'll need to plan your trip: where to find cheap airline tickets, where to get topographical maps, what numbers to call for road conditions and campground reservations once you get there, and more.

Each **regional chapter** begins with an introduction to the region's attractions and history, tips on getting around, and a **highlights box:**

HIGHLIGHTS OF THIS PAGE

■ This spiffy and eye-catching box is surely one.

Within each chapter, destinations are listed within **regions**, which always appear along the top of the left-hand page. To find a place or type of information, consult the **index**. Notable **highways** are also treated as regions, encompass the cities they pass, and are indexed under "highways."

How do we hook you up destination by destination? Let us count the ways. A brief introduction is always followed by **Practical Information** listings: transportation info; locations of tourist offices, ranger stations, post offices, and laundromats; and emergency contact numbers. Check both your point of departure and arrival for transportation info, since it is listed only once for each route. **Accommodations and Campgrounds** come next. When they exist, hostels are listed first, then motels and B&Bs, then campgrounds. **Food** listings feature noteworthy restaurants after supermarkets and farmers' markets. In the **Sights** section (often combined with **Events**), we describe the usual tourist attractions as well as other attractions that will give you a taste of where you're visiting, like interesting neighborhoods, great spots for aurora borealis–watching, festivals, and cheese factories. Finally, the **Outdoors** section comprehensively describes a few fine daytrips, suggests possibilities for longer trips, and indicates the best and most affordable local resources and outfitters.

To help you identify where you might be happiest beginning, *Let's Go* listings are always ordered from **best to good.** We affix a "thumb pick" (▨) to those establishments that stand out as great bargains and wonderful places.

We hope your copy of the book stays dog-eared and useful, and when you're done send us a postcard with your recommendations: next year's researchers, editors, and readers will thank you for it. Happy trails!

ACKNOWLEDGMENTS

A&P THANKS... Editors and R-dubs past. Elena for her wicked laugh and a hand when she would have most liked to be sleeping. The rest of the Domestic Underground: T.J., Sarah, Ana, and Georgia for related good spirits, help, and musical accompaniment. Ben for indulging us, hackey-sacking, and a weeks-long eleventh hour. Maps 'n Prod for representing, and Anne for keeping it all on the rails. Weston, Matt, Dave, Maja, Ken, and Ana: thank you for making work so beautifully this project we signed onto together. And lastly everyone who welcomed and fed and amused and educated them on the road and fielded our phone calls at odd hours in Alaska (Western Canada!) and the Pacific Northwest.

TOM DAVIDSON THANKS... the loved-but-neglected-of-late in my life: my growing family/ crack research team, room- and apartment-mates, and the tolerant and lovely walking animal rights quandary herself. Glory be to the INS for second chances and TWA for cheap tickets. Rolan, Matt, Aaron, Dan, Face, Glenn, and Ken: all the best in your new places, and thanks for making the ones we shared great. James: my gratitude is professional, personal, perpetual, and nothing if not deep. We'll meet on the Rock yet; in the meantime I look forward to supermarket "joke" reminiscences come fall.

JAMES WILSON THANKS... Jane and Barry and Mark and everyone who welcomed me north; everybody who made me feel welcome in the south and those kind souls that fed me among company: the thought and friendship of all of you made a summer in Cambridge worth weathering. O'Dywer, O my, did we ever manage! Family Wilson. A fine fine overnight with a good lot and Bob in fine form, a stretch of polished pine that never seemed to cease its welcome, and an ocean. Ken, you're a fine man, and we both have Jay to thank. Tom, we did great at this, thank you. And aroo! many things to think fondly of and to.

Editor
Tom Davidson
Associate Editor
James Wilson
Managing Editor
Bentsion Harder

Publishing Director
Benjamin Wilkinson
Editor-in-Chief
Bentsion Harder
Production Manager
Christian Lorentzen
Cartography Manager
Daniel J. Luskin
Design Managers
Matthew Daniels, Melissa Rudolph
Editorial Managers
Brendan Gibbon, Benjamin Paloff, Kaya Stone, Taya Weiss
Financial Manager
Kathy Lu
Personnel Manager
Adam Stein
Publicity & Marketing Managers
Sonesh Chainani, Alexandra Leichtman
New Media Manager
Maryanthe Malliaris
Map Editors
Kurt Mueller, Jon Stein
Production Associates
Steven Aponte, John Fiore
Office Coordinators
Elena Schneider, Vanessa Bertozzi, Monica Henderson

Director of Advertising Sales
Marta Szabo
Associate Sales Executives
Tamas Eisenberger, Li Ran

President
Noble M. Hansen III
General Managers
Blair Brown, Robert B. Rombauer
Assistant General Manager
Anne E. Chisholm

RESEARCHER-WRITERS

Weston Eguchi
Western Washington, Portland
On the lam in the northwest, Weston worried for weary travelers and brought a fresh eye to the cities' music and art scenes. Submerging himself for weeks at a time, every one of Weston's resurfacings brought another batch of subtle, exciting, and detailed writing. If we were from Portlock, then Weston, daydreaming poetry in the heart of Portland, never disappointed us on our visits: this steady genius made the cities his own, but ably shared his newfound possessions.

Matt Elliott
Vancouver Island, Southern BC, Calgary, and the Rockies
Matt established very quickly just who would be wearing the cow suit with udders in the home office/R-W relationship. Unflappably, unfailingly, and with impeccable prose, he reported on the best of rodeo towns, mountain passes, and the hearts of the cities. Matty left it to us to surmise whether he was enjoying himself, busy as he was rafting, bungee jumping, retooling coverage of Calgary nightlife, and fending off the *pur laine*. Next stop: Greece, Europe. Boom!

David Friedland
Southcentral, Interior, and Southwest Alaska
A river guide and woodsman of the lower 48, Dave was unmistakably at home in the land of the midnight sun. From The Mountain to Akutan, this diligent researcher and fine, entertaining writer expertly reported on everything in sight, from the whitewater to the waitstaff. His new coverage of Alaska's remote corners was as astonishing as we (with his help) imagine them to be. Within days of finishing his stint with *LG*, Dave was back on the water. Long may he run.

Maja Groff
Vancouver Island, Northern BC, and the Yukon
A student of First Nations culture and a Port Hardy native, Maja taught us nearly as much about everywhere else that she visited as she did about her hometown. Her open heart and sense for evocative and essential detail enriched her travels and her copy. Never out of touch with the landscape, north country radio conspirators, the curious subculture of northern mining towns, or her editors, Maja produced writing that was an unfailing pleasure to read, and unfailingly fit to print.

Ken Haig
Southeast and Interior Alaska
When a bull moose outside the Anchorage FedEx office was Ken's welcoming party, we were sure he'd get on just fine in Alaska. As tireless as the days were long, Ken hit countless trails and provided incredibly thorough and thoughtful reports from the thick of the backcountry and the heart of the longhouse. Under his penetrating, A&F-worthy gaze, mere "wilderness" resolved itself into tundra and boreal forest, and tourist brochure gloss lost out to true local grit and color.

Ana Morrel-Samuels
Oregon, Eastern Washington
After surmounting early car trouble to escape the Midwest's clutches, Ana went on to survive the paradox of being snowed in at Hell's Canyon, an abortive attempt to trade her hatchback for a VW of a decidedly more Oregonian bent and vintage, surprising hot beverages, and soothing hot springs. Her thoroughness, run-ins with the famous, and trenchant critiques of local cuisine, motels, and taxidermy techniques kept her ever in our hearts and conversations.

ABOUT LET'S GO

FORTY YEARS OF WISDOM

As a new millennium arrives, *Let's Go: Europe*, now in its 40th edition and translated into seven languages, reigns as the world's bestselling international travel guide. For four decades, travelers criss-crossing the Continent have relied on *Let's Go* for inside information on the hippest backstreet cafes, the most pristine secluded beaches, and the best routes from border to border. In the last 20 years, our rugged researchers have stretched the frontiers of backpacking and expanded our coverage into Asia, Africa, Australia, and the Americas. We're celebrating our 40th birthday with the release of *Let's Go: China*, blazing the traveler's trail from the Forbidden City to the Tibetan frontier; *Let's Go: Perú & Ecuador*, spanning the lands of the ancient Inca Empire; *Let's Go: Middle East*, with coverage from Istanbul to the Persian Gulf; and the maiden edition of *Let's Go: Israel*.

It all started in 1960 when a handful of well-traveled students at Harvard University handed out a 20-page mimeographed pamphlet offering a collection of their tips on budget travel to passengers on student charter flights to Europe. The following year, in response to the instant popularity of the first volume, students traveling to Europe researched the first full-fledged edition of *Let's Go: Europe*, a pocket-sized book featuring honest, practical advice, witty writing, and a decidedly youthful slant on the world. Throughout the 60s and 70s, our guides reflected the times. In 1969 we taught travelers how to get from Paris to Prague on "no dollars a day" by singing in the street. In the 80s and 90s, we looked beyond Europe and North America and set off to all corners of the earth. Meanwhile, we focused in on the world's most exciting urban areas to produce in-depth, fold-out map guides. Our new guides bring the total number of titles to 48, each infused with the spirit of adventure and voice of opinion that travelers around the world have come to count on. But some things never change: our guides are still researched, written, and produced entirely by students who know first-hand how to see the world on the cheap.

HOW WE DO IT

Each guide is completely revised and thoroughly updated every year by a well-traveled set of over 250 students. Every spring, we recruit over 180 researchers and 70 editors to overhaul every book. After several months of training, researcher-writers hit the road for seven weeks of exploration, from Anchorage to Adelaide, Estonia to El Salvador, Iceland to Indonesia. Hired for their rare combination of budget travel sense, writing ability, stamina, and courage, these adventurous travelers know that train strikes, stolen luggage, food poisoning, and marriage proposals are all part of a day's work. Back at our offices, editors work from spring to fall, massaging copy written on Himalayan bus rides into witty, informative prose. A student staff of typesetters, cartographers, publicists, and managers keeps our lively team together. In September, the collected efforts of the summer are delivered to our printer, which turns them into books in record time, so that you have the most up-to-date information available for your vacation. Even as you read this, work on next year's editions is well underway.

WHY WE DO IT

We don't think of budget travel as the last recourse of the destitute; we believe that it's the only way to travel. Living cheaply and simply brings you closer to the people and places you've been saving up to visit. Our books will ease your anxieties and answer your questions about the basics—so you can get off the beaten track and explore. Once you learn the ropes, we encourage you to put *Let's Go* down now and then to strike out on your own. You know as well as we that the best discoveries are often those you make yourself. When you find something worth sharing, please drop us a line. We're Let's Go Publications, 67 Mount Auburn St., Cambridge, MA 02138, USA (email: feedback@letsgo.com). For more info, visit our website, http://www.letsgo.com.

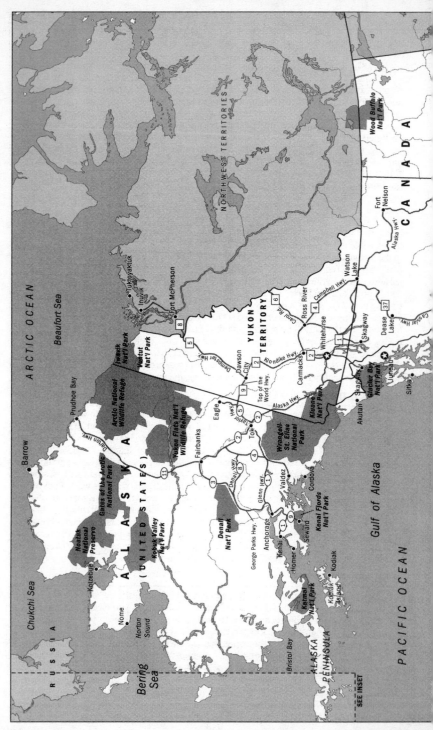

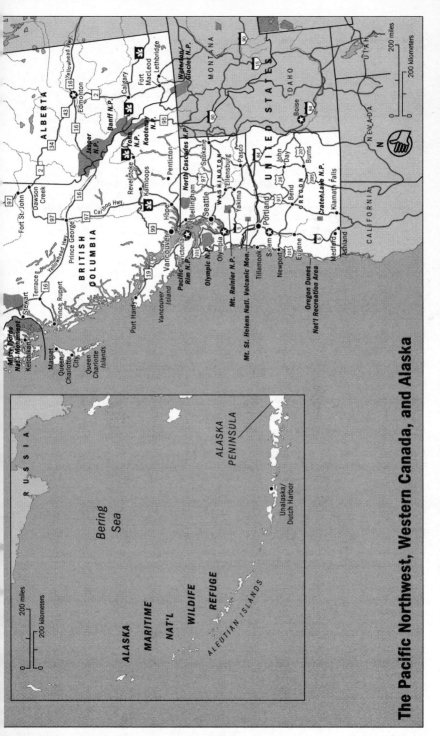

The Pacific Northwest, Western Canada, and Alaska

LET'S GO PICKS

MIND-BLOWING DRIVES. Cruising past post-apocalyptic renewal on the **Spirit Lake Memorial Highway** (WA; see p. 215)...that last verdant loop of **Route 20** through the North Cascades (WA; see p. 229)...massive hunks of stone and ice along the **Icefields Parkway** (AB; see p. 313)...making the **Dempster Highway** pilgrimage into the Arctic (YT; see p. 388)...breathless beauty on the **Richardson Highway** as it leads to Valdez (AK; see p. 458)...piecing together the ragged Dawson-Fairbanks line along ridge-tops on the **Top-of-the-World Highway** (YT/AK; see p. 387).

FINE, FINE FOOD. **Knead and Feed** (WA; see p. 185) serves simply the best soup ever...the entire **Okanagan Valley** (BC; see p. 294) is full of fantastic fresh fruit stands...Vancouver's **Commercial Drive** (BC; see p. 251) presents an amazing variety of ethnic restaurants amid exciting weeknight crowds...the **Wild Strawberry** (AK; see p. 426) and **Odie's** (AK; see p. 472) constitute oases of tastiness in the howling gastronomic desert of the Far North...the **Alaska Native Brotherhood (ANB) Hall** has got game (AK; see p. 419).

TRULY COOL MUSEUMS. The **Oregon Trail Interpretive Center** (OR; see p. 146) and Sitka's **Sheldon-Jackson Museum** (AK; see p. 420) do a phenomenal job of enlivening history, the **Portland Art Museum** (OR; see p. 77) rules the aesthetic roost, and the **Anchorage Museum of History and Art** (AK; see p. 442) elegantly straddles the fence...the **Royal Tyrrell Museum** (AB; see p. 325) and **Head-Smashed-In Buffalo Jump** (AB; see p. 326) are without question the best possible places to view expertly presented animal remains in the middle of nowhere.

THRILLING VISTAS. This region is one great feast for the eyes; here are just a few choice dishes in the optical orgy: **Goat Peak Lookout** (WA; see p. 233)...**Johnston Ridge Observatory** (WA; see p. 216)...**Wreck Beach** (BC; see p. 255)...**Maligne Lake** (AB; see p. 317)...**Salmon Glacier** (BC/AK; see p. 360)...the ferry dock in **Gustavus** (AK; see p. 421)...**Mt. Eyak** (AK; see p. 461)...and **Mt. Marathon** (AK; see p. 468).

THE WILDLIFE. Avian fauna and the binocular-toters who love them flock to **Malheur National Wildlife Refuge** (OR; see p. 149), while whales perform in the Inside Passage—for a full week's worth, take the **ferry** from Bellingham, WA, all the way to Skagway, AK (see p. 392 and p. 58)...sea birds and marine mammals grace **Glacier Bay National Park** (AK; see p. 422) and **Kenai Fjords National Park** (AK; see p. 469); a wildlife cruise here is worth every budget-sapping penny...unspoiled **Denali** is as famous for the fauna as it is for The Mountain (AK; see p. 493).

HIGH-GRADE HIKING. A wide range of difficulty levels and sensory rewards await in **North Cascades National Park** (WA; see p. 229), **Mt. Rainier National Park** (WA; see p. 221), **Jasper National Park** (AB; see p. 314), **Lake Louise** (AB; see p. 312), and around **Sitka** (AK; see p. 417)...the rainforested **West Coast Trail** (BC; see p. 275) and the **Alexander MacKenzie Heritage Trail** (BC; see p. 336) are perfect for serious hikers, but the trackless expanses of **Denali** (AK; see p. 493) and **Wrangell-St. Elias National Parks** (AK; see p. 452) take first prize for vastness and sheer freedom.

PRIME NIGHTLIFE. Seattle's strange **Sit and Spin** (WA; see p. 171) and Portland's pounding **Panorama** (OR; see p. 83) house all the urban undulations a body could desire, while Calgary's **Ship and Anchor** is the meeting place for the city's beautiful young scurvy dogs (AB; see p. 332)... the **Howling Dog** (AK; see p. 506) and **Chicken Creek Saloons** (AK; see p. 513) throw miner parties that are way out there.

EXCEPTIONAL EVENTS. While **Canada Day-Independence Day** celebrations promise just a week-long party in Hyder, AK, and Stewart, BC (see p. 358), Ashland's mammoth **Shakespeare Festival** (see p. 123) means seven straight months of theater, and the **Iditarod** finish in Nome (AK; see p. 525) guarantees no fewer than two weeks of solid partying in the darkness.

DISCOVER ALASKA AND THE PACIFIC NORTHWEST

From the dense, misty rainforests of Oregon and Washington to the last desolate, treeless island in the Aleutian chain, North America's northwest coast is a land of awesome natural beauty. Along much of the coast, sharp young peaks soar skyward from the water's edge, spilling pieces of glacier into the ocean waters at their bases. Human settlements of varying sizes and degrees of polish mark the spots where rivers meet the coast, pointing the way to the country's interior, a land both at odds with and continuous with the coast. There, the peaks give way to sometimes-arable land, desert, tundra, and more mountains, but the vastness of the land there, even strewn as it is with cities and towns, is just as daunting.

For thousands of years, human settlement in the region has depended on the land and on the rich animal life with which they shared it. In the last two hundred years, human activities have begun to make a significant impact on the land—enthusiastic logging and fishing proved the region's natural resources weren't inexhaustible. Thankfully, the environmental spirit of the late 20th century is alive and well in the region. That spirit, the explosive growth of the tourism industry, and the realization among resource-based industries that sustainable practices were an economic necessity has helped modern governments see old-growth forests as something more than so many board-feet of raw lumber.

While you are assured of seeing a good many visitors in whatever part of the region you choose to visit, you are just as sure to be able to escape the crowds with a minimum of effort. The amount of that land that is protected, preserved, and absolutely spectacular is so vast, and the destinations on the average package tour so predictable, that the independent traveler of limited means has virtually unlimited access to all that is wonderful about the country. (Which is not to say that the occasional splurge will go unrewarded; see **If I Had $1,000,000**, below). For example, Banff National Park, in the Canadian Rockies, welcomes some 5 million visitors a year, but the right dayhike there, or a visit to one of the park's lesser-known neighbors, is all it takes to escape the crowds. For those who might be overwhelmed by this boundlessness, the backcountry is anchored by welcoming hostels, quirky communities, laid-back cities, and other places to catch your breath before it's taken away again.

Winter visits to the northcountry promise hundreds of miles of cross-country skiing and downhill skiing and snowboarding and snowshoeing and dog sledding out of snow-bound cities where locals struggle to entertain themselves year-round and don't mind you joining in. Farther south along the coast, winter consists of very much rain and a similar litany of snow sports at the higher elevations. The look of the northwest under that much gray is sober but saturated; your travels may well bring you through a landscape deserted by tourists, but will only intensify the feel of all that forest, all those stretches of ash-colored beach in the afternoon, all those craggy, ice-laced peaks.

However audacious it is to gloss this many miles of coast and this deep an interior in a 560-page book, much less a three-page overview, the present attempt is culled from what our researchers insisted they would do again if they could turn around and do their trips over. The sample itineraries that follow are intended to

1

help you picture what your own trip might look like. For practical trip-planning resources, including campground reservation numbers, road reports, climate charts, Internet resources, and preferred outdoor publishing companies, see the **Essentials** chapter, and begin thumbing through the rest of *Let's Go: Alaska and the Pacific Northwest 2000.*

GET OUTSIDE

This book's pages are stuffed with hikes, bikes, rivers, lakes, and ski areas. In every town we look for hikes that are accessible even to those without their own transportation, yet aren't overrun with either locals or other travelers. We also always list ranger stations, gear rental shops, outfitters, useful publications, and places to go to get the inside scoop for yourself. (Check out the **Equipment Rental** and **Outdoor Information** headings in the coverage of each town.) For more comprehensive information, check out the index entries for your favorite activity.

HIKING AND MOUNTAIN BIKING

In the north, muskeg and mossy tundra make for difficult going, but everywhere in the west great effort is made to maintain established trails. (If you get the urge to help out, check out **Volunteering: Outdoors,** on p. 65.) Walking on the soft floor of a temperate rainforest, as long as its not currently pouring, is among the most blissful of a traveler's pleasures. In the Rockies and elsewhere, the exposed slopes above treeline leave hikers at the mercy of both the elements and unobstructed views of neighboring peaks. National parks provide some of the best and most varied hiking anywhere, and are uniformly well staffed, well maintained, and well worth it. Reading the **Outdoors** sections of a few parks should give a sense of the possibilities. Herewith a few longer hikes you might plan a trip around:

CHILKOOT TRAIL. This three- to five-day, 33-mile/53km hike passes relics of its former lives on its way from the Pacific coast in Skagway, Alaska, to the interior. Originally a trade route protected by the Tagish and Tlingit people, the trail was the way to the interior for participants in the Yukon gold rush of the 1890s. Each miner was required to pack 1000 lb. of supplies by horse over the trail in order to meet the requirements of the Canadian government. The trail passes from the coast through a dramatic variety of climate, terrain, and vegetation, both above and below treeline. For info on trail reservations and ranger contacts, see p. 432.

PACIFIC CREST TRAIL. This 2650-mile/4240km trail stretches from California's border with Mexico to Washington's border with Canada. First explored in the 1930s, the system of trails is now a federally designated and protected Scenic Trail that takes about five or six months to hike. Many sections make for great mountain biking. In Washington and Oregon, the trail winds through the chain of national forests and parks that covers the Cascade Range. Some of the nicest sections of the trail are between Mt. Jefferson and Mt. Hood in Oregon northwest of Bend (p. 131), and in the North Cascades National Park in northern Washington (see **Stehekin,** p. 228), though the trail can be picked up in any of the national parks along the range or in the Columbia River Gorge (see p. 86). The Pacific Crest Trail Association (PCTA) maintains the trail and sells comprehensive trail guides, videos, and PCTA mouse pads on its website. *(Tel. 916-349-2109; website www.pcta.org. Call 888-728-7245 for a free info packet or trail condition report. 5325 Elkhorn Blvd., #256, Sacramento, CA 95842-2526.)*

WEST COAST TRAIL. This spectacular trail wends through 48 miles/77km of coastal forest along the open Pacific Ocean in the Pacific Rim National Park on the west coast of Vancouver Island. The trip takes five-seven days, and bus pickups are available at either end of the trail, although those traveling south to north may wish to continue their travels by ferry to the rest of the park, where sandy beaches, surfing, and hot springs await the weary hiker. Reservations are necessary to hike the trail. See p. 275 for info.

RATING SYSTEMS. Walks, hikes and climbs are rated on an open-ended scale, with 1 being sidewalk, 2 moderate trail, and 3 indicating that you might need a handhold, but a fall is unlikely, and consequences are likely to be minimal. A rating of 4 indicates scrambling, with more serious consequences for a fall. Ratings for free climbs (on which rope can be used for safety but not to help the climber) begin at 5.0. Climbs of 5.6 and above require a rope. Climbs rated 5.8 would require significant climbing experience and ability. 5.10 and 5.11 are usually pure vertical or slightly overhanging. The highest ranking assigned to date is 5.14. Ratings are subjective and relative, and are usually assigned by the first person to complete the climb, although they can be revised later.

Rivers are rated subjectively and unofficially by rafters from Class I - VI according to their most difficult stretch of rapids. Class I rivers have fast moving water with small waves. Class III stretches are "intermediate" with moderate waves which can swamp an open canoe. Complex maneuvers in fast current are often required, and rescue is somewhat difficult. Class IV are advanced, with "intense, powerful, but predictable rapids requiring precise boat handling in turbulent water, which may feature large, unavoidable waves and holes or constricted passages demanding fast maneuvers under pressure." V and VI just get crazier, predictably, with VI being all but unrunnable.

Ski and snowboard areas rate the difficulty of runs on a scale that ranges from green circle (easiest) to blue square (more difficult) to black diamond (advanced) to double-black diamond (experts only.) These rankings are really only useful for determining the relative difficulty of terrain at a single area. Skiing a double-black in the eastern U.S. is no preparation for a steep icy chute that can pass for a marked run in the west.

RAFTING

Many rivers in the region are eminently accessible, especially in the south. There, half- and full- day trips make for great diversions and can be reasonably priced. Expect professionalism out of a rafting outfit. If the organization and orientation are confused, the guiding probably will be too. A simple indicator in the north-country is whether drysuits, absolutely necessary in Alaska, are supplied. If the rafts are covered in patches, if their lifejacket supply is sparse, or if the paddles are all different shapes and sizes, you may want to take your business elsewhere. And don't forget that golden rule of outdoors adventure: talk to the locals.

Most of Oregon's commercial trips float on the beautiful **Rogue** and **Deschutes** rivers. The **Owhyee** has carved canyons through the desert that will boggle the mind. The **Upper Klamath** and the **Illinois** offer more technical runs with bigger hits at high water. Call the **Oregon Outdoors Association** (541-937-3192) for listings of all registered outfitters in the state. Washington's commercially run rivers are not nearly as popular, but the **Skyskomish River** has some sweet Class V stretches. Licensing is very relaxed; call **Washington Outfitters and Guiding Association** (509-962-4222) for company listings. Many fine runs course over drops in Idaho, next door: the Middle Fork of the **Salmon,** the **Lower Salmon,** and the **Snake** through **Hells Canyon** all make perfect multi-day trips. Call **Idaho Outfitters Guiding Association** (208-342-1438; www.ioga.org) in Boise for details.

Kayaking in Alaska's creeks and rivers couldn't be much finer (unless the water ran a little warmer). Check the index to get started. Rafting is more variable, since Alaskan companies and guides aren't required to have the certification that outfits in other states are, and some operations really shouldn't be operating. Excellent companies include: **Nova, Class V,** and **Denali Outdoor Co.**

SKIING THE NORTHWEST

The skiing and riding in the northern Rockies and the Cascade and Coast mountain ranges is some of North America's best, and ranges from destination mega-resorts to community-owned hills with a couple T-bars. The best example of the former is **Whistler-Blackcomb** (see p. 260), a 1½ hour drive north of Vancouver, BC, which draws nearly 2 million visitors a year from around the world. Most remarkable about the skiing here, though, is the fact that many areas are only minutes from (and sometimes even overlook) urban centers. Even more surprising? You can do it cheaply: hostels in Washington, Oregon, Alberta and BC all offer ski and stay packages (see p. 37). Check "ski areas" in the index for more options.

NATIVE CULTURE

The northwest is home to some of the finest exhibits of Native American and First Nation (the preferred terms for the indigenous people of the U.S. and Canada, respectively) culture on the continent, and is the birthplace of some its most popularly known traditions, such as potlatch, cedar carving, and salmon scaffolds. Major museums in the region are the Makah Cultural Center at Neah Bay, WA; the Museum of Anthropology in Vancouver, BC; the Museum at Warm Springs, OR; and Head-Smashed-In Buffalo Jump, AB. Various communities host pow-wows and celebrations of culture where visitors are welcome. Throughout the region, well-advertised "Native attractions" can be hit-or-miss. Check to see who runs the show before you go, and try to avoid those that cater mainly to large cruise ship or bus tour groups (these tend to be packaged, showing you just enough for a few photo opps before you are whisked off). Many state, provincial, and university museums have very tasteful exhibits on past and present Native culture, and sometimes bring in local artists to demonstrate their craft and talk with visitors. Band and Native corporation offices tend to deal mostly with the business end of things, but they often have good community event information; in southeast Alaska, *kwaan* houses (in Tlingit towns), or Alaska Native Brotherhood halls are good resources for events, demonstrations, and open carvers' workshops.

IF I HAD $1,000,000

Some of the most fabulous places on earth lie on the far side of a $500 journey by airplane. **The Katmai Wilderness** and its Valley of 10,000 Smokes will have you reconsidering what beautiful is about in the landscape left by the 20th century's most cataclysmic events, the eruption of Novarupta. The bear-viewing cage above the river, not minutes from Brook's Camp, will have you learning new salmon-pawing techniques within minutes of careful watching. With a week and a kayaking or canoe partner, the Savanoski Loop is one of the finest routes in the state. **The Aleutian Islands** stretch into nothing but dark water and storms. The islands support fewer than twenty trees, and the velvety green ridgelines of these volcanic creatures billowing out of the North Pacific are truly one of the most remarkable features of the Alaskan landscape. **Flightseeing** often sits on the near side of that hard-to-swallow $500 figure, and brings the chance to see what you might never otherwise in a way you could never otherwise. If you try it anywhere, try it in remote Wrangell-St. Elias National Park, or seek out the far side of Denali.

SUGGESTED ITINERARIES

The following itineraries begin or end in the Northwest's major cities (Portland, Seattle, Vancouver, Calgary, and Anchorage), each of which deserves days of exploration, and then loop past backcountry trailheads and through the communities that seemed to our researchers especially unique or representative.

FROM THE COAST TO THE TOWERING CASCADES, THE BEST OF OREGON (10 DAYS). Quiet stops and towns yet to adopt tourism wholesale await along the heavily traveled Oregon coast. Setting out from **Portland,** the north coast is home to **Astoria, Seaside,** and examples of all of the regions most striking features. Leave the highway behind you as you tour the craggy shoreline in sight of

Kobuk Valley Nat'l Park
Yukon Flats Nat'l Wildlife Refuge
Arctic National Wildlife Refuge
Iwavik N.P.
Vuntut N.P.

Vancouver • Hope

ALASKA
Fairbanks

Victoria • Bellingham
San Juan Islands

Denali Nat'l Park

Two weeks in the **Olympic Peninsula & Puget Sound**

Olympic N.P.

Seattle

Anchorage
Glenn Hwy.
Top of the World Hwy.

Ten days **Between the Coast and the Cascades**

Ellensburg

Valdez
Cordova
Wrangell-St. Elias National Park
Dawson City

Olympia
Mt. Rainier N.P.
Yakima

YUKON TERRITORY

WASHINGTON

Kluane Nat'l Park

Campbell Hwy.

Mt. St. Helens Nat'l Volcanic Mon.

Seaside

Portland
Three Capes Loop
Warm Springs

Whitehorse

Salem
John Day Fossil Beds

Glacier Bay Nat'l Park
Scagway
Juneau

Newport
Bend

Sitka
Petersburg
Wrangell

Eugene
OREGON

Ketchikan

Misty Fjords N.M.

Racing to Goldrush Country in four weeks

Wood Buffalo Nat'l Park

Prince Rupert

Dawson Creek

Queen Charlotte Islands

Prince George
ALBERTA

BRITISH COLUMBIA

Jasper N.P.
Edmonton

Port Hardy
Banff N.P.

Vancouver Island
Kamloops
Revelstoke
Yoho N.P.
Calgary

Three weeks navigating **The Inside Passage**

Vancouver
Penticton
Kootenay N.P.

Victoria
Bellingham
Olympic N.P.
North Cascades N.P.

Olympia
Seattle
WASHINGTON
Spokane
Waterton/Glacier N.P.

Mt. Rainier N.P.
Ellensburg

Mt. St. Helens Nat'l Volcanic Mon.

Portland
Salem

0 ___ 200 miles
0 ___ 200 kilometers

Newport
OREGON

Eugene
Bend
John Day

Suggested Itineraries

the dramatic rock promontories of the **Three Capes Loop.** Cut south and east through the inland valleys toward **Eugene,** where the weekend nightlife and music scene rivals Portland's. Eugene's annual and fantastical Oregon Country Fair alone is worth planning a trip around (July 7-9, 2000). Pick your scenic route through the Cascades toward the outdoors destination of **Bend,** and from Bend all the way north, with stops to camp and hike, bike, and climb. Visit the fine Native American **Museum at Warm Springs** and the remarkable **John Day Fossil Beds.** Continue north alongside the mountains to **Hood River;** in the **Columbia River Gorge,** the river thunders on one side and Mt. Hood towers on t'other as you make your way back to Portland. *WHAT ABOUT... continuing south along the coast to the Oregon Dunes? Or through the inland valleys to Ashland and northern California? Pushing southeast to Steens Mountain and the alkali flats of the Alvord Desert? Following the Columbia River to Hells Canyon?*

THE INSIDE PASSAGE (3 WEEKS). The $165 ferry ride from Bellingham, WA, to **Ketchikan, AK,** is justifiably popular, passing between Vancouver Island and the mainland on its way through the fabled Inside Passage. From there travelers can hop on a $25 ferry every few days, hiding from the cruise ship crowds in little-trafficked fishing and timber towns like **Wrangell** and **Petersburg,** or out on the trails that surround popular destinations like **Sitka.** Bringing your own kayak or bicycle on the ferry will cost about another $10 on the shorter hops and will allow you to reach deep into the backcountry (renting town by town costs around $30 a day). As you near the northern terminus of the Inside Passage, $90 will get you on an open-ocean ferry to Valdez or a historic narrow-gauge railway and bus combo to Whitehorse, YT. From there the vast northcountry (or an $140 flight to Vancouver) beckons. For travelers looking to squeeze a little more from their budget, as of late 1999 a one-way bus ticket from anywhere in the US or Canada to Prince Rupert (a $40 ferry ride from Ketchikan) or Whitehorse, booked one week in advance, costs $79. *WHAT ABOUT... a week on the Stikine River ("a*

Yosemite that just keeps going and going")? A trip out to the longhouse in quiet Metlakatla?

GOLD RUSH REVISITED: FROM CALGARY TO THE ARCTIC. The arctic-hungry expect to find themselves on the Alaska Highway for three days en route to Anchorage, but there are many ways north. Skirt the towering rockies and delve in untouristed parks! Feel the cool of glaciers on your neck from the road! Coo to wildlife while the sun hangs low on the horizon! Explore eccentric boom towns gone bust! Drive on the **Icefields Parkway** between Yoho, Banff, and Jasper; cross the belly of BC on the **Yellowhead Hwy.;** make your way alongside the remote parks on the **Cassiar Hwy.;** loop out of range of RV traffic and the big smoke on the **Campbell Hwy.;** cruise the top of the world on the highway named for it; sidle in sight of Mt. Wrangell along the **Glenn Hwy.;** then take the slow and scenic way along the **Denali Hwy.** Now comes time to decide: a pilgrimage to Denali or a week of fishing, hiking, and lounging on the Katmai Peninsula? *WHAT ABOUT... a drive to the coast through dramatic mountain passes to Skagway or Haines, AK? A day in lakeside, laid-back Atlin, BC? Connecting to the ferry routes of the Inside Passage at Prince Rupert? Chasing the north up the Dempster Hwy. all the way to Inuvik? Or chasing the Porcupine Caribou Herd to Tombstone?*

THE OLYMPIC PENINSULA AND PUGET SOUND. The west coast has made its reputation for being laid back into an industry where the cafes and cafe-bars are cogs in the machine, and every piece of public art is a widget. If you will. Sometimes it seems everybody is moving to northwest cities. To scope out where you'll live while you code after college or retire after coding, visit Seattle and explore the side routes, both rural (from Seattle find the low, rolling **San Juan Islands** and routes into the Cascades) and nearly developed (along the Olympic Peninsula discover Port Townsend, recently rediscovered). **Olympic National Park,** only hours from the big city, is unquestionably wilderness.

THE PEOPLE AND THE LAND

The negotiation of boundaries has made the vast Pacific Northwest imaginable since its earliest habitation. Early cultures had constantly to adapt to the changing range of resources, the rebuilding of networks of routes between coast and interior, and the transformation of social structures to accommodate newcomers—by adoption, by treaty, by war, and by attrition. For newcomers, the history of life in the northwest has been a history of making opportunities out of boundaries. What first faced newcomers is what will first face any modern visitor: the northwest supports a rich network of communities earning their subsistence in an impressive and overwhelmingly vast landscape. Unbounded plains, borderless waters, and seemingly insurmountable mountain chains stretch from Oregon to the arctic.

While this land and its people are vast and diverse, repeating patterns of settlement and development have formed the boundaries by which they survive. Settlement has followed distinctive courses as communities continue to live off the land's resources and conceive of themselves in relation to their livelihoods: social traditions built upon an abiding sense of kinship with nature were shared by indigenous cultures, and today the various groups competing for resources—industrialists, conservationists, and indigenous nations—continue to define themselves by how they conceive of resources. The northwest's development has accordingly followed a predictable course. Surges of exploration have continuously opened areas long stewarded by indigenous nations for use, settlement, and encroachment by outsiders: the fur rushes of the 1700s; the gold rushes of the 1800s; the flight westward for farmland in the 1800s; the search for oil in the 1900s; and, throughout, the search for better living.

EARLY NATIVE CULTURE

The northwest became accessible between 12,000 and 35,000 years ago to nomadic hunters migrating from Siberia along island, inland, and coastal routes exposed by receding glaciers. The northwest's earliest cultures are known by the succession of increasingly refined stone tools that marked their settlements, found in this century in deposits as old as 9700 years old. As the landscape aged and ocean levels dropped, coastal forest and fish habitats became increasingly developed. Game proliferated as inland forests and lakes receded before spreading grassland. As communities on the coast and inland refined their means of harvesting these resources, they too expanded. Ancient coastal villages grew upon accumulated layers of their refuse. Middens of discarded clam shells and rich soil still mark them, the most recent of which are yet remembered by eroding totems and gravesites. Archaeological study of a group of coastal sites has uncovered art objects and implements that attest to the development of wealthy societies between 1500 BC and AD 500, by which point ancient coastal cultures can be roughly traced to their present incarnations. Plains nations left fewer traces of their material culture, but their size and ingenuity is evidenced by the stone remains of bison entrapments, corridors of boulders and makeshift corrals employed to direct the free-ranging creature toward its hunters, and petroglyphs and cairns stand testament to their religious practice.

Salmon runs and cedar forests along the lengthy Fraser, Nass, Skeena, and Columbia rivers made the coastal manner of life tenable for inland communities, such that the popular image of coastal lifestyle was prevalent throughout much of the northwest: oceanside villages of cedar plank houses fronted by wooden sculptures, massive dugout canoes, and potlatch festivals. Potlatch is a word meaning give or gift, from a jargon developed by Chinook middlemen who were based near the Columbia River. It is a festival composed of a variety of stages with different functions: it is an opportunity for the enactment of important stories and histories, for the exchange and display of wealth, and for the celebration of important transitions—of adoptions, aging, and so on. The potlatch in its various forms was not and is not confined to coast culture, and remains an integral part of the lives of many communities.

The nations that survived on the plains were nomadic big game hunters. While the image of the headdressed Plains Indian astride a horse was popular enough to inspire other nations to adopt manners of his custom, the horse was introduced to the plains in relatively modern times. Horses spread through raids and trade across the continent after being introduced to the southwest as late as the 1640s, and enabled communication, conflict, and harvest on a wider scale than had been possible before. The nations of the plains were by necessity very versatile but could afford little of the leisure of coastal nations whose health was secured by their environment's abundant resources. These indigenous communities shared their dependence on the land's produce, its availability, and their own ability to harvest it. Their religious life reflected the character that allowed them to survive. Many groups identified their kinship with the spirits of creatures and plants in stories, ceremonies, and customs. These exhibited the community's respect for all creatures' co-dependence or the favor of a particular creature's spirit for the health of a family or clan.

At the time of European contact, the northwest coast was culturally and politically diverse and porous, defined by the flexible fabric of family groups stretched across geographical and political borders: marriages between the members of coast and inland groups strengthened ties of trade and ensured support, but belied a common struggle for subsistence by hunting and gathering and self-defence. Down the Alaska panhandle to Nootka Sound in what is now southern British Columbia, 16 different languages from five linguistic stocks were spoken, four of them unique to the northwest coast. What is popularly referred to as the 4000-strong Nez Percé tribe of the Columbia Basin was in fact a group of some 130 family groups with various loyalties across the broad region they inhabited. And yet the social fabric of these groups was flexible. Custom, not law, determined and maintained territorial boundaries. Most all of the native groups dependent on the land's resources adjusted their lifestyles according to the season, moving between different settlements that favored the harvesting of available game, fish, and living materials. Apart from seasonal movement from one camp to another, communities often were structured with numerous social divisions, according to descent, marriage, and claims of kinship. These general distinctions were made so that a social fabric could be maintained across a broad geographical range. Permission could be sought to hunt on another's claimed land when game was scarce, and small groups would expand and dissolve according to the needs of individual members in the interest of support, independence, and subsistence. In many regions there was a welcome community to join for any length of time.

The leadership of native groups was as flexible, usually consisting of elected councils made up of the most skilled of a group's members. Peace time leaders would often cede their leadership responsibilities during conflicts to war-chiefs. At nearly all times, decisions were made by c.onsensus within the bounds of community standards for behavior in the group's interest. In the extreme environments of the north, where only shared responsibility could ensure survival, this was essential. In some coastal communities, on the other hand, the station of the chief was hereditary, and society was strictly segregated into classes that included slaves.

The indigenous nations with which settlers and traders came into contact were in the midst of transformation. In most cases, the effects of European contact reached the plains and the coast before the foreigners themselves had. Nations on the plains and the coast increasingly felt the effect of treaties and wars on the opposite side of the continent, fought by indigenous confederations, the French, the British, and what would become the United States. As territory was bartered and bullied for in the east, arms and nations pushed westwards. With firearms, native nations were increasingly able to extend or defend their territories with devastating force, and were increasingly forced to do so as violence and expansion spread westward. The imbalance of arms as they spread across the continent itself engendered intertribal conflict, much in the same way that the staggered spread of horses had some generations earlier. The push of fur traders deeper into the continent from the north (the Russian-American Company) and the west (the Hudson's Bay Company) threatened the subsistence economies of indigenous communities. The commercial demand for furs obliged trappers to work their lines deeper into the season they ordinarily spent at different hunting grounds, straining the social fabric of small communities and the populations of their prey.

Each of the problems that threatened northwest native populations in the years before European contact would contribute to the near-demise of native culture in the 19th and 20th centuries. Yet many aspects of native culture would take on modern forms that recalled their ancient ones, or would be gradually restored through recognition and legislation.

THE ARRIVAL OF EUROPEANS

Francis Drake may have sailed just far enough north, during his 16th century circumnavigation, to lay claim to Oregon for the English, but he quickly departed the coast he saw wrapped in "vile, thicke, and stinking fogges." It's more probable that the northwest wasn't seen by Europeans until Captains Juan Perez and Bruno Heceta claimed Nootka Sound and other ports for Spain in 1774 and 1775, two hundred years later. Soon after, the English would profit from James Cook's extended, though unsuccessful, search for a polar trade route in 1778. On his celebrated voyage from Oregon to Alaska's westernmost tip, Cook introduced to the coast its first cartographer, George Vancouver. Farther north and west, the Danish Captain Vitus Bering had led the Russians to the Aleutian Islands as early as 1741. After Bering's death in the remote sea that bears his name, his colleague Aleksei Chirikov continued to explore Alaska. His successful return to Russia and reports of both seals and skilled hunters encouraged a rush of interest in the continent.

Early Russian explorers eagerly recognized the worth of trading with the skilled Aleut hunters they encountered. Cook's sailors, on the other hand, were so taken by surprise when Cantonese merchants eagerly paid fabulous prices for the furs they had procured for comfort on their long voyage home that they nearly mutinied to turn back for more. The English did eventually return and trade flourished. Outsiders were surprised at the value of some of their first offerings, mistaking the significance on the coast of items they took for trinkets. Alaska's native Aleuts, for example, saw holes in shells and other objects as portals for spirits, and willingly parted with otter pelts for beads that their Russian counterparts deemed common.

Captain Vancouver returned to Nootka Sound to map the surrounding country in the 1790s, after Spain formally ceded to the British the right to trade in the region over which they had long claimed sovereignty. In 1793, Alexander MacKenzie, accompanied by fur traders and guides, completed his overland exploration of the continent under British instructions. A short while after Britain increased their trading activity in the south, a permanent Russian settlement was established on Kodiak island. By the time of Vancouver's voyage, the Russian's control of the arctic seal hunt was beginning to replace trade; already a small population of Aleuts had been relocated from the Pribilof Islands, a rich seal breeding-grounds. In 1799 the Russian-American Company was established in Sitka, and soon its brokerage clout was being felt as far south as California. The Russians' aggressive imposition upon the Native Alaskans incited the Tlingit in 1802, when that powerful coastal nation razed the Russians' settlement and massacred nearly every inhabitant. Two years later, the Russians returned to bombard the Tlingit fort. The Tlingit withdrew after 10 days' fighting exhausted their ammunition.

Until the aggressive practices of the Russians engendered such intense conflict, the Europeans considered the indigenous nations they first came into contact with as they considered themselves: autonomous and profitable trading partners. Yet the coast had become a lucrative asset for numerous well-armed and well-organized outsiders. During the coming decades, it would be bargained for among the British, the Russians, and the United States, and indigenous nations would be forced out of their roles as partners in the coastal economy.

DISPLACEMENT AND DEVELOPMENT

FROM ALLIES TO ADVERSARIES ON THE FRONTIER

Mutual respect was integral to the **1763 Royal Proclamation** and the treaties that followed it, in which the British recognized the continent's unexplored territory—much of what lay west and north of the thirteen colonies—as the "Hunting Grounds" of independent indigenous nations under the Crown's protection. Several developments contributed to the erosion of these amicable relations. First, politics with the American government no longer required that the British maintain a network of allies on the continent. Furthermore, as Europeans pushed farther west, they were developing the means to harvest the land's resources without the aid of its original inhabitants. Lastly, indigenous peoples of the west began to increasingly frustrate newcomers, uncertain of the intentions of outsiders and uninterested in aiding their widespread settlement, let alone adopting their manners of dress and custom. These dynamics were not unsubtle or unmediated, but would come to define the history of European settlement in the northwest.

Europeans and natives were not merely competing against one another in the west; the United States was beginning to compete against the British Hudson's Bay Company, whose domain extended to the mouth of the Columbia River. As the east fell into economic turmoil in the 1830s, the west grew into a dream of tillable farmland. The U.S. government promised 640 acres to any man who would stake it out and build upon it. Hundreds departed for the west along the famed Oregon Trail, trebling the population of what would become Oregon and Washington between 1840 and 1850. Yet more dramatic means of settlement were coming. To provide for whole families on the frontier and the establishment of whole communities, the 1850 **Land Donation Act** made 640 acres of land available only to married couples, cutting a single man's share in half. The same act barred the ownership of land by non-whites. The supplanting of the indigenous inhabitants of the region had begun in earnest, even prior to its incorporation in the United States, and years before the Canadian west would take a firm political shape.

Even as late as the 1900s, the northwest was indistinctly accounted for. The spirit of Oregon's pioneers had brought swift recognition of that territory. Settlers created a provisional government in 1843, lobbied for territorial status until 1848, and joined the Union 10 years later. The quick settlement of Oregon brought swift conflicts: skirmishes with individual bands and isolated violent incidents are recounted in every tale of the Oregon Trail's influence. The rest of the northwest was built by booms that were accompanied by deep conflict. Gold discoveries one by one up the coast supported settlement both in the hearts of gold country and the centers of supply, and forced federal governments to stake claims of their own. The San Francisco gold rush built Portland, well-positioned to supply the California town with timber and wheat. Americans manned the Fraser River and Cariboo gold rushes of 1858 that resulted in British Columbia's hastily defined status as a Crown Colony. Gold in the Klondike in 1895 drew thousands to the interior of what would be staked out as the Yukon Territory three years later, and Seattle and Skagway still proudly lay claim to their roles as the Klondike's outfitters. Alberta, whose fertile agricultural plains would later yield valuable oil, became a Canadian province in 1905. Only one territorial claim of the period was considered unfounded: when Russia offered the sale of Alaska to the U.S. in 1867, the icy expanse was considered a depleted resource. The inability of the seal trade to keep the Russians there was proof enough for most. But the U.S. Secretary of State

William Seward would be celebrated years later for his shrewd purchase of the vast oil field for a piddling two cents an acre.

In the corresponding periods of settlement, the indigenous nations of each region were devastated by disease, by the co-optation of their resources, enslavement, murder, and the strain of relocation. The sheer number of newcomers compromised any government's effort to find a place for indigenous nations with claims to such fabulous and barely tapped resources.

FROM 'PROBLEM' TO UNDERLING: CANADIAN NATIONAL POLICY

Continually frustrated by dealing with the indigenous, in the year of Canada's birth its founders embraced a project of **assimilation.** To wean indigenous communities from what was perceived as their unrefined culture, and to protect them from corrosive influences such as alcohol and unscrupulous business practices, the government segregated large communities onto limited reservation land and implemented wide-ranging controls over them under legislation entitled the **1867 Indian Act.** The Department of Indian Affairs was created to define what individuals couldn't do, from buying land to loitering in towns. Christian missionary societies were permitted to run **residential schools** with the aim of educating indigenous children as whites. Children were separated from their families, forbidden to speak with their siblings, and forbidden to speak their language. Offenders were severely punished, and many children were physically and sexually abused. Adults were schooled in the methods of farming, untenable in many of the regions where it was attempted, and traditions of community life were disallowed. The practice of the missionary societies was made into law in subsequent rewritings of the Indian Act. Eventually the celebration of potlatch was made illegal and ceremonial regalia was confiscated in raids. Natives were prohibited from integrating into mainstream society on threat of termination of their **Indian Status:** men who took particular jobs, and women who married white men, were no longer eligible for treaty rights. The state of Canada's indigenous communities grew worse. The first generation of children through the residential schools emerged into subjugated communities struggling for identity, segregated from the mainstream they were forced to emulate.

Canada's Department of Indian Affairs re-evaluated their position and revised their original mandate with the **1951 Indian Act.** Certain basic rights were restored that legalized potlatch and political organizations. But the federal government continued to direct the establishment of elected chiefs and councils—regardless of whatever social organization was already in place—and the spending of funds allocated to them. Veiled as empowerment, this staggered system of control inevitably undermined relations between communities and their leadership. Antagonism, distrust, inefficiency, and unproductiveness was often its result. In contrast, the government's gestures of liberal-minded pluralism had achieved the opposite effect: the legalization of potlatch was an integral element in Canadians' recognition of cultural difference, and played a crucial role in allowing indigenous cultures to revitalize themselves by their own traditions.

The continuing failure of assimilation, its great cost, and changes in the social climate of Canada—especially after passage of the Bill of Rights in 1960—necessitated another rethinking of Indian policy. Policy-makers insisted that indigenous communities should be made equal citizens. Endeavouring to dismantle the distinct status conferred on indigenous people, Pierre Trudeau's liberal government introduced a project of **integration** by repealing the Indian Act and introducing the **White Paper** ("The Statement of The Government of Canada on Indian Policy").

The government was totally unprepared for the response: indigenous communities indignantly countered that the principle of integration unilaterally denied that their culture is distinct and separate from the Canadian mainstream, that it negates their inherent right to self-determination, and constitutes a breach of treaties that guarantee land and benefits. The White Paper was retracted in 1971, and an indistinct period ensued. While both assimilation and integration had ostensibly been rejected as guiding principles, the survival of the Indian Act and the government's continued focus on education and job-creation programs belies its bias against allowing communities to solve their own problems. These problems were great. By the time residential schools were closed, some as late as the 1970s, an entire generation had been raised in isolation from their land and weakened by alcoholism, poverty, and the neglect of their traditions. Negotiations resulting in the government's recognition of the **Assembly of First Nations,** a council of the government leaders of indigenous communities, or First Nations, has given more power to those governments to administer their own funds, but federal policy opposing the idea of indigenous self-government would not begin to be reversed until the 1990s.

FROM 'PROBLEM' TO UNDERLING: U.S. NATIONAL POLICY

After independence, the War Department of the United States assumed responsibility for Indian Affairs. Prior to the Revolutionary War, the 1763 Royal Proclamation had barred settlement in territory west of the thirteen colonies, and had been ignored by settlers. The policies of the new American government would maintain both traditions. Documents signed in the **treaty-making period** (1789-1871) ostensibly protected indigenous nations from encroachment, but effectively secured arable land for retired soldiers and soon-to-be farmers. The westward spread of settlers was met with alarm from indigenous nations and even more institutional safeguards that would be ignored. When the Cherokee nation and the state of Georgia brought a dispute over land-use to trial in 1831, Chief Justice Marshall's **Domestic Dependent Nations** ruling concluded that when a weakened state agrees to be protected by a stronger one its right to self-determination is not compromised. Favorable rulings of the courts proved no more binding than treaties; President Jackson subsequently permitted the forcible relocation of the Cherokee nation. More relocations brought multiple nations to live together on small parcels of land, often hundreds of miles from their respective homelands. The government no longer recognized the identities of indigenous nations, though Congress did not declare this as a policy until 1871.

In 1849 Indian Affairs became the responsibility of the Department of the Interior, whose most dramatic means of forcing **assimilation** were outlawing traditional religion, not again legalized until the 1930s, and dismantling traditional social organizations, whose emphasis on group identity was seen to be limiting. The **Dawes Act** (General Allotment Act) of 1887 was designed to break down the collective identity of indigenous communities by acculturating them as homesteaders. Their territory was divided into 160-acre subplots that were then divided among heads of household; the remaining land was sold to white settlers. The effect of this land transfer, in which two-thirds of reservation lands in the United States were made available to white settlement, was devastating.

While President Roosevelt presided over the New Deal, a new commissioner of the Bureau of Indian Affairs attempted to improve the condition of reservation-bound communities. Under the 1934 **Indian Reorganization Act,** reserve communities (each composed of various nations) were recognized as tribes and directed in creating their own constitutions according to guidelines. The newly created tribes were permitted some degree of control over spending federal funds allocated for social programs. The status of the indigenous tribes and the cost of their maintenance angered **terminationists** who insisted on their **integration** into the American mainstream. A subsequent reversal of policy, and **Operation Relocation** (1952), by which large groups of Native Americans were relocated from reservations into cities, was the new government's response. The gesture had an unexpected effect. For the first time in generations, Native Americans off reservations began to recognize themselves as an ethnic group against the backdrop of mainstream society.

In the 1960s, this burgeoning self-awareness was exhibited in dramatic demonstrations. In Washington state, fish-ins positioned Native American groups against industries and municipalities with a common land base. The occupation of Alcatraz Island in 1970 drew more attention to the claims of Native Americans for land and recognition. Subsequently the federal government's 1975 **Indian Self-Deter-**

mination and Educational Assistance Act allowed reservation tribes more control over schooling, with encouraging results in enrollment on and off reservations. In the years since, continued talk of self-determination has resulted in few tangible improvements; the programs that might enable tribes to improve their situations remain underfunded and frequently cut in what is sometimes called termination by accountants; policymakers continue to favor private and state interests over Native American ones, with notable exceptions.

NEGOTIATION AND CONSERVATION

First Nations and Native American tribes have begun to live off their own land again. Some live on reservations within cities that serve as little more than suburbs, others have settled land claims negotiations and are living on their traditional territory and resurrecting their customs. There is a whole range of intermediate stages, depending on the health of the communities involved, what lands they are claiming, and which governments they are negotiating with. Most indigenous communities that are federally recognized reservation tribes in the U.S., or administered under the Indian Act in Canada, are allowed hunting and fishing rights, and the right to use specified lands for ceremonial purposes.

Some communities seek first and foremost to preserve the cultural heritage of their traditional lands. In British Columbia, Haida tribesmen oversaw the use of ancient village sites in the disputed territory of the Queen Charlotte Islands and lobbied heavily for its preservation from logging. After the federal government purchased the land, the Haida's role in the stewardship of the spectacular **Gwai Haanas National Park Reserve** became officially recognized.

Beyond land-use negotiations, communities seek to profit from and administer their land's resources, such as timber and minerals. Throughout the 1960s, Native Alaskans watched with increasing frustration as the federal and state governments divvied up vast tracts of land that the Inuit, Aleut, Tlingit, Haida, and Athabasca had claims upon. The conflict came to a head after the discovery in 1968 of immense oil deposits beneath the shore of the Beaufort Sea, on Alaska's northern coast. Native Alaskans increased the pressure to settle the claims that had been so long ignored, and sought a share in the anticipated economic boom. In December of 1971, the federal government finally made some degree of peace with Native Alaskans, state and federal courts, and environmental groups by passing the **Alaska Native Claims Settlement Act.** Sixty thousand Native Alaskans received a total of one billion dollars and 40 million acres of land.

Many governments are uncomfortable with relinquishing title to their land. Because BC was administered by the Hudson's Bay Company before joining Canada, no treaties were signed between the government and the indigenous nations whose traditional lands constitute much of the province. The BC government has historically countered land claims by insisting that when BC became part of Canada in 1858, all land title was transferred to the Crown. A remarkable ruling has turned this notion on its head, and supports the notion of "inalienable rights" that is the backbone of First Nations' claims to self-determination. In the **Delgamuukw** decision of 1997, the Supreme Court of Canada allowed the Wet'suwet'en and Gitksan to cite ceremony and oral tradition to help prove that their use of disputed lands preceded the arrival of Europeans. The landmark ruling reversed the findings of a lower court judge who had rejected the clans' attempts to use what is called "adaawk" and "kungax" in their testimony.

Negotiations continue over items of self-government and the right to self-determination. Several events of the past two years have furthered First Nations' efforts. In August of 1998, after years of talks between government officials and the **Nisga'a** band of northern British Columbia, representatives signed a controversial landmark treaty granting the Nisga'a a form of self-government and control over natural resources in 1940km² of their traditional lands. Yukon First Nations are negotiating with the federal government for self-government and land claims under a general framework known as the **Umbrella Final Agreement.** Some First

Nations in the southern Yukon are preparing to reinstate the clan system of government as they approach settlement. In 1999 the Supreme Court of Canada instructed the government to revise the Indian Act so that communities, not the government, have the power to allow non-residents to vote in band elections, and Bill C-49, or the **First Nations Land Management Act,** will create a framework for First Nations to develop their own land-use laws. Most dramatically, on April 1, 1999, the Northwest Territories split in half. The eastern portion, **Nunavut,** or "Our Land" in Inukitut, is populated almost exclusively by Inuit. Its territorial government will have limited control over resources and social programs.

CONTEMPORARY CULTURE

CONSERVATION AND HARVEST

Political entities in the northwest have long been interested in carrying on with their own affairs, with respect to federal governments and one another; this is true as well of industries, interest groups, and communities. Inevitably relations don't go very smoothly, because the political entities, industries, interest groups, and communities get to bickering over what keeps and maintains each of them in the northwest: the land and its resources. The central political tensions are between conservation and harvest, when harvest is synonymous with job production and maintenance, and conservation is synonymous with tradition and legacy. These are particularly difficult to balance in Oregon, Washington, and Alaska, home to the most federally and state-protected land in the United States. The outright challenge of co-managing renewable resources is exacerbated in British Columbia and the Yukon by the involvement of vast quantities of land in territorial disputes with First Nations. The work of co-managing the resources that these states and provinces share—like the Pacific salmon fishery—has proved the region's most dramatic and drawn-out subject of reconciliation.

Policies of environmental stewardship have begun in response to a variety of pressures, from civic consciousness to political activism. In 1967 the **Oregon coast,** from the Columbia River to the California border, was preserved for free and uninterrupted use by the public. Oregon's 1971 **Bottle Bill** was the first recycling refund program in the U.S. State-wide land use planning laws have been constantly revised since their inception in 1973.

Controversies have had their share of press. Washington and Oregon's **spotted owl** remains a symbol of conflict between conservationists and industrialists after vast tracts of the bird's old-growth forest habitat were protected. In many cases it has been indigenous communities that have led the conservation effort, suspending their hunting and trapping before government scientists could suspend industries. One notable case is that of the **Makah whale hunt,** suspended by the Makah in the 1920s when international hunting had brought the gray whale near extinction. The U.S. took until 1937 to outlaw commercial harvesting of gray whales. When the gray whale had rebounded in the late 1990s to a viable population, the Makah applied to the International Whaling Commission, with U.S. support, for a cultural exemption to the continuing ban. But the five-whale allowance to the Makah has enraged conservationists. The Makah returned to the ceremonial and subsistence hunt in 1999 among protest and publicity.

In general things go best for everybody when projects are undertaken together: the northwest is lucky to have many models of shared problem solving to guide it. The Washington State University Wood Materials and Engineering Laboratory has had enormous success in working closely with the forestry industry. Materials that fifty years ago would have been considered waste were used last year to create 6 billion board feet of alternative wood product, equivalent to the total amount of board feet expected to be cut in Washington and Oregon in 1999.

CULTURE AND THE ARTS

Even 20 years ago, cities like Vancouver remained middle class port towns with a burgeoning counter-cultures. In the years since, the entire Pacific Rim seems, on the surface, to have outgrown its humdrum roots: tourists have poured in and settled, technological industries have expanded, and resource-driven industries have been increasingly stilled. Though none of the communities of the northwest have entirely outgrown what built them—port towns remain port towns, and the festivals that first brought small communities together continue to do so—the land draws more than just the resource hungry, it draws people who love the land. The famously laid-back lifestyle of the northwest is an outgrowth of this, as is an aggressive defence of the environment. These elements, combined with the simple fact of the region's, and its settlements', isolation, has resulted in the uncommonly enlightened world-view of so many northwesterners that has in turn drawn more who seem to be able to think of the world from the inside out.

In emerging technologies, like aerospace and software, the northwest is a center for development. In addition the northwest is popularly known for having both cultivated the continent's oldest art forms and revitalizing its newest: the cedar **masks, totems,** and **longhouses** of indigenous coastal nations have long been recognized as some of the world's most notable artistic achievements. In the minds of many listeners, rock and roll has been forever changed by a sound that bloomed in Seattle—twice. The birth place of **Jimi Hendrix** and the cradle of **grunge** is held in mystical esteem by lovers of what is fuzziest-sounding in music.

Native carving is a supple art expressive of its religious lineage, cultural heritage, or the recent custom of generating saleable art objects. **Bill Reid** (d. 1998), a Haida carver and Vancouver native, is one of many artists and groups celebrated for revitalizing communities through carving, painting, dance, song, and potlatch, all art forms neglected and suppressed by law during the last hundred years. These arts are displayed together in annual historical **celebrations, pow-wows, music festivals,** and **rodeos.** Periodic gatherings celebrate meaningful community events.

All of the rural northwest and its cosmopolitan centers cultivate **festivals.** Every community has its own tradition of celebration and new venues and organizers are often springing up (for a handful of festival listings in this book, the sole contact information is the organizer's home phone number), from folk to bluegrass, rock, pot-smoking, golfing, and outhouse racing. **Orchestral music** aficionados flock to the Bach Festival in Eugene; Seattle has a repertory theater community third in size only to those of Chicago and New York, and its opera is internationally renowned for its Wagner productions. The Seattle **Bumbershoot** festival there and a whole range of vibrant **nightlife** elsewhere supports new music in Portland, Seattle, Olympia, Spokane, and Bend. While prowling record executives signing contracts with everything in plaid have departed Seattle, the northwest has been spotted as a breeding ground for **riot-grrrl** rock and **guitar-timbre** bands. Bryan Adams, of Vancouver and Pop, has charged that **"CanCon"** laws, which require TV and radio to air a minimum amount of Canadian content, breed mediocrity in Canadian arts. Beyond Adams' syrupy ballads, there is scant evidence to support his complaint.

Government support reflects the public's commitment to, and affinity for, cultivating their own expression. Portland and Seattle, for example, funnel a 1% tax on capital improvements into the acquisition and creation of public art. While government cutbacks have compromised the health of famed centers for arts in western Canada like the Banff center for the arts, artist communities and colonies are alive and thriving, among the San Juan and Gulf Islands of Washington and British Columbia, and in small towns like Atlin, BC, and Homer, AK. And where government comes up short, philanthropists serve: in 1998-9, the Patrons of Northwest Civic, Cultural and Charitable Organizations (**PONCHO**) had its best year yet, dispensing $2.1 million in Puget Sound; since 1962, the group has poured $23 million into the region's arts organizations. Plus the northwest has everything else the introspective and tasteful could hope for: from famed stagings of **Shakespeare** in Ashland, OR, to Pulitzer prize-winning drama originating in Juneau, AK; from a vintners festival celebrating the art of crafting the perfect **chocolate orange wine** in Astoria, WA, to celebrating the art of the microbrew with an **Oosic Stout,** named for a male walrus' maleness, in Skagway, AK.

THIS YEAR'S NEWS

BUSINESS AND INDUSTRY

A 6% **gas tax** hike is slated to improve roads buckling under the 11,000 Californians who took Oregon licences in 1999. Seattle kingpin Bill Gates and his **Microsoft** software empire have been embroiled for over a year in a federal anti-trust investigation. Competitors charge that Microsoft's distribution of the popular Windows operating system with a built-in browser has given it an unfair advantage over other web browser companies like Netscape. An outcome isn't expected until mid-2000. **Boeing,** a cornerstone Washington employer and leader in the aerospace industry, employed 86,600 in June 1999, down from 88,000 in May and 104,000 in May 1998. Boeing let go more than half of its national workforce in the same year-long period. The BC liberals are coloring the failure of a BC Hydro project in Pakistan as another failure of the leadership New Democratic Party: contrary to "promises" that its sale would be successful, an additional $5 million of taxpayers' funds has been written off after the new Pakistan government claims it cannot afford the **Raiwand power project.** Both governments have been mired in charges of corruption. Alaska Senator Frank Murkowski, having secured $2.5 million in the 1998 Federal Highway Bill to plan railways, has solicited Canadian interest in extending a **rail link** from Fairbanks to British Columbia through the Yukon.

POLITICS AND COMMUNITY

Oregon was identified as one of four America's states (along with Arizona, Nevada, and Colorado) where more **women entrepreneurs** are earning more. In March an Oregon state court jury ordered **Philip Morris Co.** to pay $79.5 million in punitive damages to the estate a Portland man who died of lung cancer, the largest settlement of its kind; in May, a Portland judge reduced the damages to a mere $32 million. Oregon, the first state to adopt the **minimum wage** in 1913, still has the highest in the nation at $6.50 an hour. Some employers are complaining that high-school-aged employees aren't worth it, that experienced workers can't be rewarded, and that hours have to be cut.

British Columbia premier Glen Clark is suffering scant popular support after a string of allegations about his and his party's stewardship and reporting of the province's deficit and funds. A highly publicized search of his home—caught on television, no less—in relation to a friend's application for a casino nearly forced his resignation in March. The moderately socialist NDP still has a couple of years before they need to call an election. Contrary to the desire of the frontier to divest itself of obligations to the feds, the rest of Canada would like to the leave the **Yukon Territory** to its own devices: Ottawa has recently made it clear that it intends the Yukon to take on powers normally devolved only to provinces—control over land and natural resources—as well as bearing more responsibility, along with all of Canada's provinces, for the administration of its well-subscribed social safety net.

NATURAL RESOURCES

President Clinton's 1994 **Northwest Forest Plan,** designed to protect the endangered spotted owl's old growth habitat, has been expanded to allow inspectors to inspect saleable timber stocks for various species potentially at risk. Recently a Washington judge held up some 1.4 billion board feet of timber, of the 6 to 7 billion expected to be cut in Washington and Oregon this year, whose sale was approved before scientists' findings could be implemented in the fall of 1998. Opponents of the ruling cite the extraordinary expense of looking on hands and knees for little creatures. In June of 1999, 52 organizations entered into an unprecedented deal with the Washington state government to protect tracts of lynx habitat from being logged in **Loomis State Forest.** They purchased the land in question for its value plus the value of the timber to be logged on it. A twist on the story that is delighting Washingtonians is that a significant portion of the funds—more than $3 million— was secured in a stunningly short amount of time from fabulously wealthy young entrepreneurs employed by software companies like Microsoft and Amazon.com,

LIKE SHOOTING SEA LIONS IN A BARREL

Amid 1999's fisheries conservation (see this year's news, above), the Chinook salmon's addition to the endangered species list has focused attention on the effect of civilians on the salmon, fabled for their remarkable life cycle: each endeavors to spawn in the river of its birth, often hundreds of miles upriver from the ocean where it spends its adult life. The combined effect of fishing and inland settlement on habitats is staggering: in some rivers runs of 16 million have dwindled to one million, and more than a dozen of the Columbia River and Snake River steelhead and salmon stocks are endangered. While the Endangered Species Act has never before been imposed on a city, Seattle has stoically allocated $475 per resident to restore the chinook's river habitat within city limits, and it seems like everyone in the northwest is keen to help. Nobody is out of ideas, at least. While initiatives are gaining steam to dismantle dams in Washington and Oregon (to the collective outcry of energy, irrigation, and navigation interests), some conservationists are trying to leave the dams in place. Catholic bishops have issued a pastoral letter imploring residents to pray for the Columbia River's spiritual vitality, and secular officials have been putting their heads together, too. The outcome? The fish are getting some help to get upriver: helping hands have loaded them onto barges, flopped them into trucks, and hand-stacked them in barrels suspended from helicopters to get them past nasty river obstacles. At the other end of the watershed, state officials are seeking Congressional consent to begin shooting Puget Sound sea lions who've displayed an unhealthy appetite for Washington's favorite resource. In the meantime, a handful have begun a tropical exile at Sea World.

children of the new technologies age and the green movement. Two more twists make the story noteworthy: marten tracks in the same region are the first solid evidence of the animal's existence in ten years; the proposed logging would raise the state enough funds to build only one-fifth of a new school. Opponents fear a precedent of tying up valuable resources. **Weyerhaeuser Co.** has promised to honor the "ecologically sensitive forest practices" of MacMillan Bloedel, the dominant timber company it has recently purchased, including a memorandum reached with the Queen Charlotte Islands Haida. The Forest Service and federal government are under fire in southeast Alaska for limiting timber harvesting in the **Tongass National Forest** so much that the region's last value-added lumber processors are leaving for British Columbia. Observers complain that the veneer plant that is ready to replace the 40-year-old institution will waste quality old growth timber.

Disputes over conservation of the **Pacific salmon fisheries** across the northwest have been steadily heating up in the past ten years. In the **hot summer** months of 1999, the Canadian Coast Guard seized an Alaskan fishing ship in disputed waters. Two years ago, British Columbian fishermen, enraged at what they took for Alaska's impudence, took matters into their own hands, blockading the state ferry Malaspina at Prince Rupert, BC. Come July, diplomacy prevailed. Renegotiation of the Canada-U.S. **Pacific Salmon Treaty** has obliged the U.S. to create two habitat improvement funds, but Alaskan Senator Murkowski has suggested that Canada chip in the sum of **tariffs** levied over the last five years on American fishing boats traveling the Inside Passage, taxed in protest of treaty stalemates (Congress already reimbursed the fishermen). The new agreement has Canada agreeing to ignore salmon bound for Washington and Oregon, and the U.S. leaving the Fraser River salmon for BC. Alaska, too, will reduce its catch. The U.S. will buy out the licences of boats barred from the Fraser River fishery, and additional money will be shared with indigenous communities and state governments to focus conservation efforts.

Inland, efforts are escalating to protect rivers at risk (see graybox). March's embarrassing **miscount** of two million sockeye salmon in the Fraser River (here today, gone tomorrow!) has sped up the adoption of genetic sampling to keep track of salmon according to their rivers of origin. Officials from southeast Alaska and the Taku River Tlingit First Nation have expressed concern that the **Tulsequah**

Chief mine in BC, near Juneau, may threaten the Taku River salmon; in addition, the mine's 100-mile access road from Atlin, BC, passes through traditional territory. The environmental forecasts required for Alaska mining permits aren't required in BC; the mine's intended safeguards remain indistinct, and development is ongoing.

FURTHER READING

The Nations Within, by Augie Fleras and Jean Leonard Elliott, compares aboriginal policy in Canada, the U.S., and New Zealand. *Indians in the Making*, by Alexandra Harmon, explores the history of Puget Sound as it is complicated by the politics of tribal recognition. The *Journals of Lewis and Clark*, by Meriwether Lewis and William Clark, recount their celebrated journey. *Undaunted Courage*, by Stephen Ambrose, and *Sacajawea*, by Flora Warren Seymour, revisit its history and myth. Jack Kerouac's *Dharma Bums* and Robert Pirsig's *Zen and the Art of Motorcycle Maintenance* continue the road-tripping tradition, but in fiction and with fur pants supplanted by denim. David Duncan's *The River Why* tackles environmental issues and fly-fishing. Richard White traces the Columbia River in *The Organic Machine*. Raymond Carver's *Where I'm Calling From* speaks of the people of the northwest bluntly. Sherman Alexie, in language no less harsh, depicts the condition of the Spokane in *Reservation Blues*. *Snow Falling on Cedars* is a mystery novel by David Guterson set amid Japanese-American tensions in post-WWII Puget Sound. *Another Roadside Attraction* and *Even Cowgirls Get the Blues* are by Tom Robbins. *The Lost Sun* is a volume of poetry by former University of Washington instructor Theodore Roethke. James Stevens's *Paul Bunyan* visits the myth of the fabulously tall logger. W.H. Auden also took a run at the giant in his libretto of the same name. The fearless Ramona, from the series of that name by Beverly Cleary, has inspired many a middle child.

Julie Cruikshank's collaborations with members of BC and Yukon First Nations are absorbing histories told in the words of elders. Catherine McClelland's *Part of the Land, Part of the Water* is a handsome testament to the history and culture of Southern Yukon First Nations. The 1990s owe pervasive buzzwords to William Gibson, sci-fi author and coiner of the term "cyberspace," and Douglas Coupland, author of *Generation X.*, both Vancouverites. *Notes from the Century Before: A Journal of British Columbia*, by Edward Hoagland, are just that. Pierre Burton grippingly retells the north's past in a number of works. Sky Lea's *Disappearing Moon Cafe* depicts a family living in Vancouver's Chinatown in the 1930s. Jean Craighead George's *Julie of the Wolves* is perfect for younger readers. Robert Service and Jack London keep the Yukon mystique alive past Dawson City's decline. London's classics are *White Fang* and *The Call of the Wild*. Service's best is *The Cremation of Sam McGee*. The cartoon adventures of Dudley Do-Right are an astonishingly accurate portrayal of frontier life for the Northwest Mounted Police.

The venerable *Tundra Times*, founded in part by legendary Inuit journalist Howard Rock, provides up-to-date discussions of current Native Alaskan issues. John McPhee's *Coming Into the Country* is a fascinating overview of wilderness issues and lifestyles. Jon Krakauer's *Into The Wild*, about the 1992 disappearance and death of Christopher McCandless near Denali National Park, makes for compelling, unsettling reading. *Going to Extremes*, by Joe McGinniss, and *Alaska: The Sophisticated Wilderness*, by Jon Gardey, chronicle refuge from the Lower 48. Alan Ryan's *The Reader's Companion to Alaska* serves up easily digestible morsels. James Michener's monster epic *Alaska* takes liberties with fact, but captures the scope of the region and its dramatic past. Just don't drop it on your foot (the epic, not the region or its past). Leslie Marmon Silko's short stories describe the lives of Native Alaskans in the present day. And, of course, the lovable eccentrics of Cicely, AK, continue to frolic in TV syndication on *Northern Exposure*, filmed for five years in Roslyn, WA, but allegedly based on real-life Talkeetna, AK.

ESSENTIALS

FACTS FOR THE TRAVELER

WHEN TO GO

In general, tourist season in the U.S. and Canada runs from late May to early September. In Canada, the beginning is marked by the Victoria Day long weekend, in the U.S. the Memorial Day long weekend. Summer ends, and the kids go back to school after the Labor/Labour day long weekend at the beginning of September. In the off season, accommodations might be cheaper and slightly less crowded, but those sights you traveled so far to see might also be closed, and it will be less pleasant to camp. On national holidays, many sights, and all banks and government offices will be closed, and transportation may run on restricted schedules. For information on seasons best for hiking, skiing, rafting, and other activities, see the appropriate section of the **Discover** chapter.

NATIONAL HOLIDAYS

USA		CANADA	
Date in 2000	Holiday	Date in 2000	Holiday
January 1	New Year's Day	January 1	New Year's Day
January 17	Martin Luther King, Jr. Day	April 23	Easter Sunday
February 21	Presidents Day	April 24	Easter Monday
May 29	Memorial Day	May 22	Victoria Day
July 4	Independence Day	July 1	Canada Day
September 4	Labor Day	September 4	Labour Day
October 9	Columbus Day	October 9	Thanksgiving
November 11	Veterans Day	November 11	Remembrance Day
November 23	Thanksgiving	December 25	Christmas Day
December 25	Christmas Day	December 26	Boxing Day

CLIMATE

Temp in °F/°C	January		April		July		October	
Rain in inches/mm	Temp	Rain	Temp	Rain	Temp	Rain	Temp	Rain
Anchorage, AK	13/-11	0.8/19	36/2	0.6/14	58/14	1.9/47	36/2	1.9/49
Banff, AB	14/-10	1.2/31	37/3	1.3/32	59/15	2.0/51	40/5	1.2/30
Calgary, AB	15/-10	0.5/12	39/4	1.0/25	62/16	2.8/70	42/6	0.6/16
Eugene, OR	39/4	5.0/125	52/11	3.0/75	67/19	0.2/6	55/13	2.9/73
Fairbanks, AK	-10/-24	0.6/14	31/0	0.2/6	62/17	1.8/45	15/-4	0.8/21
Portland, OR	39/4	5.5/138	51/11	2.5/64	68/20	0.6/15	54/12	3.2/80
Seattle, WA	42/6	5.0/127	52/11	2.8/71	66/19	1.0/24	54/12	3.4/85
Spokane, WA	27/-3	2.0/51	47/9	1.1/28	70/21	0.6/15	48/9	1.2/30
Vancouver, BC	37/3	5.9/150	48/9	3.0/75	63/17	1.4/36	50/10	4.5/115
Whitehorse, YT	-2/-19	0.7/17	33/0	0.3/8	57/14	1.5/39	33/1	0.9/23

The coastal cities are justly famous for rain, which pours down in significant quantities 10 months of the year. The rain-producing ocean also keeps coastal temperatures moderate year-round. In Portland and Vancouver, a few snow days a year are the norm, but it doesn't stick around at lower elevations. To the east of the coastal mountains, expect less precipitation year-round, and much warmer summers and colder winters. The same variation is experienced up north, only on a shifted scale—winters in the interior of the Yukon and Alaska are bitterly cold, while summers are merely cool. As in the south, things are more even on the coast.

FESTIVAL	DATE IN 2000
Ice Climbing Festival & Quest for Gold Sled Dog Race (Valdez, AK)	Deep winter
Seward Polar Bear Jump (Seward, AK)	3rd weekend in January
Yukon Quest 1000 Mile Sled Dog Race (Fairbanks, AK)	February
Winter Carnival (Homer, AK)	1st week in February
Iceworm Festival (Valdez, AK)	1st weekend in February
Chinese New Year (Vancouver, BC)	February 5
Frostbite Music Festival (Whitehorse, YT)	February 18-20
Lionel Hamptom Jazz Festival (Moscow, ID)	February 23-26
Snowman Festival (Valdez, AK)	First weekend in March
World Extreme Skiing Championship (Valdez, AK)	Late March
The Gathering of the People (Sitka, AK)	April
Alaska Folk Festival (Juneau, AK)	April 10-16
Okanagan Wine Festival (Kelowna, BC)	Late April
Homer Shorebird Festival (Homer, AK)	2nd week in May
Exit Glacier 5k and 10k runs (Seward, AK)	Mid-May
Craft-Beer and Home Brew Festival (Haines, AK)	May 19-20
Juneau Jazz and Classics (Juneau, AK)	May 19-28
Maritime Week (Seattle, WA)	3rd week of May
Miner's Day (Talkeetna, AK)	3rd weekend in May
Little Norway Festival (Petersburg, AK)	3rd weekend in May
Northwest Folklife Festival (Seattle, WA)	Memorial Day Weekend
Ski to Sea Race (Bellingham, WA)	Memorial Day weekend
Salmon Derby (Petersburg, AK)	Memorial Day weekend
Bald Eagle Run & Harley Davidson Rodeo (Haines, AK)	Memorial Day weekend
Celebration 2000 Native Cultural Conference (Juneau, AK)	June 1-3
Treaty Days (Yakima, WA)	June 2-4
Sitka Summer Music Festival (Sitka, AK)	June 2-17
Yukon International Storytelling Festival (Whitehorse, YT)	Early June
Nalukatag, or "blanket toss festival" (Barrow, AK)	June, pending whale hunt.
Deming Logging Show (Bellingham, WA)	2nd week of June
Alsek Music Festival (Haines Junction, YT)	2nd weekend of June
Sisters Rodeo (Sisters, OR)	June 10-11
Fremont Fair and Solstice Parade (Seattle, WA)	Mid June
Seafest (Prince Rupert, BC)	Mid June
Islandman Triathalon (Prince Rupert, BC)	Mid June
International Kluane to Chilkoot Bike Relay (Haines, AK)	June 17
Commissioner's Potlatch (Whitehorse, YT)	June 18-21
Solstice Festivals: Boat Race, Run, Games (Fairbanks, AK)	Late June
Port Townsend Blues Festival (Port Townsend, WA)	Late June
Du Maurier International Jazz Festival (Vancouver, BC)	June 23- July 2
Rubber Duckie Race (Whitehorse, YT)	July 1
Canada Day—Independence Day Bash (Stewart, BC & Hyder, AK)	July 1—4th
Festival of American Fiddle Tunes (Port Townsend)	Early July
Toppenish Powwow Rodeo (Yakima, WA)	Weekend closest to July 4th
Mountain Marathon (Seward, AK)	July 4th
Timber Carnival (Ketchikan, AK)	July 4th
Competitive Herring Toss (Petersburg, AK)	July 4th
Seldovia's Independence Day Bash (Seldovia, AK)	July 4th
Girdwood Festival (Girdwood, AK)	July 4th weekend
Viking Festival (Seattle, WA)	Weekend after 4th of July

FESTIVAL	DATE IN 2000
The Stampede (Calgary, AB)	July 7-16
Outdoor Quilt Show (Sisters, OR)	July 8
Bend Summer Festival (Bend, OR)	July 8-9
O'Sawmill Bluegrass Jamboree (Prince George, BC)	2nd weekend in July
Moose Dropping Festival (Talkeetna, AK)	2nd weekend in July
Vancouver Folk Music Festival (Vancouver, BC)	July 14-16
Bite of Seattle (Seattle, WA)	Mid July
Golden Days & Rubber Duckie Race (Fairbanks, AK)	Mid July
World Eskimo-Indian Olympics (Fairbanks, AK)	Mid July
Seattle Seafair (Seattle, WA)	Mid July to early August
Marine Festival (Nanaimo, BC)	July 20-23
Miners' Jubilee (Baker City, OR)	July 21-23
Great Northern Arts Festival (Inuvik, NWT)	July 21-30
Capitol Lakefair (Olympia, WA)	3rd week in July
Jazz Port Townsend (Port Townsend, WA)	3rd week of July
Dawson City Music Festival (Dawson City, YT)	3rd weekend of July
Kelowna Regatta (Kelowna, BC)	Late July
San Juan Island Jazz Festival (San Juan Island, WA)	Late July
Winthrop Rhythm and Blues Festival (Winthrop, WA)	Late July
Anderson Bluegrass Festival (Talkeetna, AK)	Last weekend in July
Benson & Hedges Symphony of Fire (Vancouver, BC)	Late July and early August
Hornby Festival (Hornby Island, BC)	End of July and early August
Gold Rush Days (Valdez, AK)	First W-Su in August
Talkeetna Bluegrass Festival (Talkeetna, AK)	First Weekend in August
Bellingham Festival of Music (Bellingham, WA)	Early August
Fall Fair & Stampede (Dawson Creek, BC)	Early August
Tanana Valley Fair (Fairbanks, AK)	August 6-14
Sunshine Coast Festival of the Written Arts (Sechelt, BC)	August 10-13
Discovery Days (Dawson City, YT)	Mid-August
Blueberry Arts Festival (Ketchikan, AK)	2nd Saturday in August
Silver Salmon Derby (Seward, AK)	9 days from the 2nd Satuday in August
National Lentil Festival (Pullman, WA)	3rd week of August
Sandblast (Prince George, BC)	3rd Sunday of August
Makah Days (Neah Bay, WA)	August 26-27
Cascade Festival of Music (Bend, OR)	Late August
Shakespeare Festival (Olympia, WA)	August
Marrowstone Music Festival (Port Townsend, WA)	August
Bumbershoot (Seattle, WA)	Labor Day Weekend
Salmon Festival (Port Alberni, BC)	Labour Day Weekend
Seward Silver Salmon 10k Run (Seward, AK)	Labor Day Weekend
Wooden Boat Festival (Port Townsend, WA)	Weekend after Labor Day
Great International Outhouse Race (Dawson City, YT)	September 3
Pendleton Round-Up (Pendleton, OR)	September 13-16
Equinox Marathon (Fairbanks, AK)	September 18
Fall Fair (Salt Spring Island, BC)	3rd weekend of September
Central Washington State Fair (Yakima, WA)	Late September
Okanagan Wine Festival (Kelowna, BC)	Early October
Banff Mountain Film Festival (Banff, AB)	October 30-November 5
Whalefest (Sitka, AK)	November
Wilderness Woman Contest & Bachelor's Ball (Talkeetna, AK)	Early December

DOCUMENTS AND FORMALITIES

EMBASSIES AND CONSULATES

> **ENTRANCE REQUIREMENTS.**
> **Passport** (p. 23). Required of all visitors to the U.S. and Canada.
> **Visa** In general a visa is required for visiting the U.S. and Canada, but this requirement can be waived. (See p. 24 for more specific information.)
> **Work Permit** (p. 64). Required for all foreigners planning to work in Canada or the U.S.

Contact your nearest embassy or consulate to obtain info regarding visas and passports to the United States and Canada. A U.S. **State Dept.** web site provides contact information for U.S. overseas stations: www.state.gov/www/about_state/contacts/keyofficer_index.html. For the Canadian Ministries of Foreign Affairs: www.dfait-maeci.gc.ca/dfait/missions/menu-e.asp.

U.S. EMBASSIES: In **Australia,** Moonah Pl., Canberra, ACT 2600 (02 6214 5600; fax 6214 5970); in **Canada,** 100 Wellington St., Ottawa, ON K1P 5T1 (613-238-5335 or 238-4470; fax 238-5720); in **Ireland,** 42 Elgin Rd., Ballsbridge, Dublin 4 (01 668 8777; fax 668 9946); in **New Zealand,** 29 Fitzherbert Terr., Thorndon, Wellington (04 472 2068; fax 472 3537); in **South Africa,** 877 Pretorius St., Arcadia 0083, P.O. Box 9536 Pretoria 0001 (012 342 1048; fax 342 2299); in the **U.K.,** 24/31 Grosvenor Sq., London W1A 1AE (0171 499 9000; fax 495 5012).

U.S. CONSULATES: In **Australia,** MLC Centre, 19-29 Martin Pl., 59th fl., Sydney NSW 2000 (02 9373 9200; fax 9373 9125); 553 St. Kilda Rd., P.O. Box 6722, Melbourne, VIC 3004 (03 9625 1583; fax 9510 4646); 16 St. George's Terr., 13th fl., Perth, WA 6000 (08 9231 9400; fax 9231 9444); in **Canada,** 615 Macleod Trail #1050, S.E., Calgary, AB T2G 4T8, (403-266-8962; fax 264-6630); Cogswell Tower, #910, Scotia Sq., Halifax, NS, B3J 3K1, (902-429-2480; fax 423-6861); P.O. Box 65, Postal Station Desjardins, Montréal, QC H5B 1G1 (514-398-9695; fax 398-0973); 2 Place Terrasse Dufferin, C.P. 939, Québec, QC, G1R 4T9 (418-692-2095; fax 692-4640); 360 University Ave., Toronto, ON, M5G 1S4 (416-595-1700; fax 595-0051); 1095 West Pender St., Vancouver, BC V6E 2M6 (604-685-4311; fax 685-5285); in **New Zealand,** Yorkshire General Bldg., 4th fl., 29 Shortland St., Auckland (09 303 2724; fax 366 0870); Price Waterhouse Center, 109 Armagh St., 11th fl., Christchurch (03 379 0040; fax 379 5677); in **South Africa,** Broadway Industries Centre, P.O. Box 6773, Heerengracht, Foreshore, Cape Town (021 214 280; fax 211 130); Durban Bay House, 333 Smith St., 29th fl., Durban (031 304 4737; fax 301 8206); 1 River St. c/o Riviera, Killarney, Johannesburg (011 646 6900; fax 646 6913); in the **U.K.,** Queen's House, 14 Queen St., Belfast, N. Ireland BT1 6EQ, PSC 801, Box 40, APO AE 09498-4040 (0123 232 8239; fax 224 8482); 3 Regent Terr., Edinburgh, Scotland EH7 5BW, PSC 801 Box 40, FPO AE 90498-4040 (0131 556 8315; fax 557 6023).

CANADIAN EMBASSIES: In **Australia,** Commonwealth Ave., Canberra, ACT 2600 (02 6273 3844; fax 6273 3285); in **Ireland,** 65 St. Stephen's Green, Dublin 2 (01 478 1988; fax 478 1285); in **New Zealand,** 61 Molesworth St., 34th fl., Thorndon, Wellington (04 473 9577; fax 471 2082); in **South Africa,** 1103 Arcadia St. Hatfield, Pretoria 0028 (012 422 3000; fax 422 3052); in the **U.K.,** Macdonald House, 1 Grosvenor Sq., London W1X 0AB (0171 258 6600; fax 258 6333); in the **U.S.,** 501 Pennsylvania Ave. NW, Washington, D.C. 20001 (202-682-1740; fax 682-7726).

CANADIAN CONSULATES: In **Australia,** Quay West Bldg., 111 Harrington St., Level 5, Sydney NSW, 2000 (02 9364 3000; fax 9364 3098); 123 Camberwell Rd., Hawthorn East, Melbourne, VIC 3123 (03 9811 9999; fax 9811 9969); 267 St. George's Terr., 3rd fl., Perth WA (08 9322 7930; fax 9261 7700); in **New Zealand,** Level 9, Jetset Centre, 48 Emily Pl., Auckland (09 309 3680; fax 307 3111); in **South Africa,** Reserve

Bank Bldg., 360 St. George's Mall St., 19th fl., Cape Town 8001 (021 423 5240; fax 423 4893); 25/27 Marriott Rd., Durban 4001 (031 309 8434; fax 309 8432); in the **U.K.,** 30 Lothian Rd., Edinburgh, Scotland EH2 2XZ (0131 220 4333; fax 246 6010); in the **U.S.,** 1251 6th Ave., New York, NY 10020-1175 (212-596-1683; fax 596-1790); 550 S. Hope St. 9th fl., Los Angeles, CA 90071 (213-346-2700; fax 620-8827); 412 Plaza 600, 6th & Stewart St., Seattle, WA 98101-1286 (206-443-1777).

EMBASSIES IN THE USA AND CANADA

IN WASHINGTON, DC (USA):

Australia, 1601 Massachusetts Ave., 20036; (202-797-3000; fax 797-3040). **Canada,** 501 Pennsylvania Ave., 20001; (202-682-1740; fax 682-7726). **Ireland,** 2234 Massachusetts Ave., 20008; (202-462-3939; fax 232-5993). **New Zealand,** 37 Observatory Circle, 20008; (202-328-4800; fax 667-5227). **U.K.,** 3100 Massachusetts Ave., 20008; (202-588-6500; fax 588-6500). **South Africa,** 3051 Massachusetts Ave., 20008; (202-966-1650; fax 244-9417).

IN OTTAWA, ONTARIO (CANADA):

Australia, 50 O' Connor St. #710, K1P 6l2; (613-238-5707; fax 236-4376). **Ireland,** 130 Albert St. #700, K1P 5G4; (613-233-6281; fax 233-5835). **New Zealand,** 727 Bank St. #99, K1P 6G3; (613-238-5991; fax 238-5707). **U.K.,** 310 Summerset St., K2P 0J9; (613-230-2961; fax 230-2400). **U.S.,** 100 Wellington St., K1P 5T1; (613-238-3335). **South Africa,** 130 Albert St. #700, K1P 5G4; (613-744-0330; fax 741-1639).

PASSPORTS

REQUIREMENTS. All non-Canadian and non-U.S. citizens need valid passports to enter the United States and Canada, and to re-enter their own country. Returning home with an expired passport is illegal, and may result in a fine. U.S. citizens can enter Canada (and vice-versa) with proof of citizenship.

PHOTOCOPIES. It is a good idea to photocopy the page of your passport that contains your photograph, and passport number, along with other important documents such as visas, travel insurance policies, airplane tickets, traveler's check serial numbers, and credit cards in case you lose anything. Carry one set of copies in apart from the originals and leave another set at home. Consulates also recommend that you carry an expired passport or an official copy of your birth certificate in a part of your baggage separate from other documents.

LOST PASSPORTS. If you lose your passport, immediately notify the local police and the nearest embassy or consulate of your home government. To expedite its replacement, you will need to know all information previously recorded and show identification and proof of citizenship. In some cases, a replacement may take weeks to process, and it may be valid only for a limited time. Any visas stamped in your old passport will be irretrievably lost. In an emergency, ask for immediate temporary traveling papers that will permit you to re-enter your home country. Your passport is a public document belonging to your nation's government. You may have to surrender it to a foreign government official, but if you don't get it back in a fair amount of time, inform the nearest mission of your home country.

NEW PASSPORTS. All applications for new passports or renewals should be filed several weeks or months in advance of your planned departure date—you are relying on government agencies to complete these transactions. Most passport offices do offer emergency passport services for an extra charge. Citizens residing abroad who need a passport or renewal should contact their nearest embassy or consulate.

Australia Citizens must apply for a passport in person at a post office, a passport office, or an Australian diplomatic mission overseas. Passport offices are located in Adelaide, Brisbane, Canberra, Darwin, Hobart, Melbourne, Newcastle, Perth, and Sydney. New adult passports cost AUS$126 (for a 32-page passport) or AUS$188 (64-page), and a child's is AUS$63 (32-page) or AUS$94 (64-page). Adult passports are valid for 10 years and child passports for 5 years. For more info, call toll-free (in Australia) 13 12 32, or visit www.dfat.gov.au/passports.

Canada Citizens may cross the U.S.-Canada border with proof of citizenship. A driver's license is no longer accepted as proof of citizenship. Carry your birth certificate or a citizenship card and a piece of Photo ID.

Ireland Citizens can apply for a passport by mail to either the Department of Foreign Affairs, Passport Office, Setanta Centre, Molesworth St., Dublin 2 (tel. (01) 671 1633; fax 671 1092; www.irlgov.ie/iveagh), or the Passport Office, Irish Life Building, 1A South Mall, Cork (tel. (021) 27 25 25). Obtain an application at a local Garda station or post office, or request one from a passport office. Passports cost IR£45 and are valid for 10 years. Citizens under 18 or over 65 can request a 3-year passport that costs IR£10.

New Zealand Application forms for passports are available in New Zealand from most travel agents. Applications may be forwarded to the Passport Office, P.O. Box 10526, Wellington, New Zealand (tel. 0800 22 50 50; www.govt.nz/agency_info/forms.shtml). Standard processing time in New Zealand is 10 working days for correct applications. The fees are adult NZ$80, and child NZ$40. Children's names can no longer be endorsed on a parent's passport—they must apply for their own, which are valid for up to 5 years. An adult's passport is valid for up to 10 years.

South Africa South African passports are issued only in Pretoria. However, all applications must still be submitted or forwarded to the applicable office of a South African consulate. Tourist passports, valid for 10 years, cost around SAR80. Children under 16 must be issued their own passports, valid for 5 years, which cost around SAR60. Time for the completion of an application is normally 3 months or more from the time of submission. For further information, contact the nearest Department of Home Affairs Office (www.southafrica-newyork.net/passport.htm).

United Kingdom Full passports are valid for 10 years (5 years if under 16). Application forms are available at passport offices, main post offices, and many travel agents. Apply by mail or in person to one of the passport offices, located in London, Liverpool, Newport, Peterborough, Glasgow, or Belfast. The fee is UK£31, UK£11 for children under 16. The process takes about four weeks, but the London office offers a five-day, walk-in rush service; arrive early. The U.K. Passport Agency can be reached by phone at (0870) 521 04 10, and more information is available at www.open.gov.uk/ukpass/ukpass.htm.

United States Citizens may cross the U.S.-Canada border with proof of citizenship. A driver's license is no longer accepted as proof of citizenship. Carry your birth certificate or a citizenship card and a piece of Photo ID.

VISAS

A visa, stamped into a traveler's passport by the government of a host country, allows the bearer to stay in that country for a specified purpose and period of time. The **Center for International Business and Travel** (CIBT), 23201 New Mexico Ave. NW #210, Washington, D.C. 20016 (202-244-9500 or 800-925-2428), secures travel visas to and from all possible countries for a variable service charge, usually around $45. To obtain a U.S. or Canadian visa, contact the nearest embassy or consulate. Residents of Canada do not need a visa to enter the U.S. if their stay is planned for 180 days or less; citizens of Australia and South Africa need a visa to enter. Citizens of France, Germany, Ireland, Italy, Japan, New Zealand, and the U.K can waive the U.S. visa through the **Visa Waiver Pilot Program** if staying 90 days or less; work and study is prohibited to those who waiver visas. Visitors qualify as long as they are traveling for business or pleasure, are staying for 90 days or less, have proof of intent to leave (e.g., a returning plane ticket), a completed I-94W form (arrival/departure certificate attached to your visa upon arrival), and are traveling on particular air or sea carriers. Contact a U.S. consulate for more info; countries are added frequently.

Most visitors obtain a **B-2,** or "pleasure tourist," visa at the nearest U.S. consulate or embassy, which normally costs $45 and is usually valid for six months. For general visa inquiries, consult the Bureau of Consular Affair's web page (travel.state.gov/visa_services.html). If you lose your I-94 form, you can replace it at the nearest **Immigration and Naturalization Service (INS)** office, though it's very unlikely that the form will be replaced within the time of your stay. **Extensions** for visas are sometimes attainable with a completed I-539 form; call the forms request line at 800-870-3676. For more info, contact the INS at 800-755-0777 or 202-307-1501 (www.ins.usdoj.gov).

Citizens of Australia, France, Germany, Ireland, Italy, Japan, Mexico, New Zealand, the U.K., and the U.S. may enter Canada without visas for stays of 90 days or less if they carry proof of intent to leave; South Africans need a visa to enter Canada ($75 for a single person, $400 for a family). Citizens of other countries should contact their Canadian consulate for more info. Write to Citizenship and Immigration Canada for the useful booklet *Applying for a Visitor Visa* at Information Centre, Public Affairs Branch, Journal Tower South, 365 Laurier Ave. W., Ottawa, ON K1A 1L1 (888-242-2100 or 613-954-9019; fax 954-2221), or consult the electronic version at http://cicnet.ci.gc.ca. Extensions are sometimes granted; phone the nearest Canada Immigration Centre listed in the phone directory.

IDENTIFICATION

When you travel, always carry two or more forms of identification on your person, including at least one photo ID. A passport combined with a driver's license or birth certificate usually serves as adequate proof of your identity and citizenship. Many establishments, especially banks, require several IDs before cashing traveler's checks. Never carry all your forms of ID together because you risk being left entirely without ID or funds in case of theft or loss. It is useful to carry extra passport-size photos to affix to the various IDs or railpasses you may acquire.

STUDENT AND TEACHER IDENTIFICATION. The **International Student Identity Card (ISIC)** is the most widely accepted form of student identification. Flashing this card can procure you discounts for sights, theaters, museums, accommodations, meals, train, ferry, bus, and airplane transportation, and other services. Cardholders have access to a toll-free 24-hour ISIC helpline whose multilingual staff can provide assistance in medical, legal, and financial emergencies overseas (800-626-2427 in the U.S. and Canada; elsewhere call collect tel. 44 20 8666 9025.

Many student travel agencies around the world issue ISICs, including STA Travel in Australia and New Zealand; Travel CUTS in Canada; USIT in Ireland and Northern Ireland; SASTS in South Africa; Campus Travel and STA Travel in the U.K.; Council Travel, STA Travel, and via the web (www.counciltravel.com/idcards/index.htm) in the U.S. (see p.32). When you apply for the card, request a copy of the *International Student Identity Card Handbook*, which lists some of the available discounts in the U.S. and Canada. You can also write to Council for a copy. The card is valid from September of one year to December of the following year and costs AUS$15, CDN$15, or $20. Applicants must be at least 12 years old and degree-seeking students of a secondary or post-secondary school. Because of the proliferation of phony ISICs, many airlines and some other services require additional proof of student identity, such as a signed letter from the registrar attesting to your student status that is stamped with the school seal or your school ID card. The **International Teacher Identity Card (ITIC)** offers similar but limited discounts The fee is AUS$13, UK£5, or $20. For more info on these cards, contact the

International Student Travel Confederation (ISTC), Herengracht 479, 1017 BS Amsterdam, Netherlands (from abroad call 31 20 421 28 00; fax 421 28 10; www.istc.org).

YOUTH IDENTIFICATION. The International Student Travel Confederation also issues a discount card to travelers who are 25 years old or younger, but not students. This one-year card, known as the International Youth Travel Card (IYTC) and formerly as the GO25, offers many of the same benefits as the ISIC, and most organizations that sell the ISIC also sell the IYTC. To apply, you will need either a passport, valid driver's license, or copy of a birth certificate, and a passport-sized photo with your name printed on the back. The fee is $20.

CUSTOMS

Upon entering the United States or Canada, you must declare certain items from abroad and pay a duty on the value of those articles that exceed the allowance established by the U.S. or Canada's customs service. Keeping receipts for larger purchases made abroad will help establish values when you return. It is wise to make a list, including serial numbers, of any valuables that you carry with you from home; if you register this list with customs before your departure and have an official stamp it, you will avoid import duty charges and ensure an easy passage upon your return. Be especially careful to document items manufactured abroad, and don't try to bring perishable food over the border.

Upon returning home, you must declare all articles acquired abroad and pay a **duty** on the value of articles that exceed the allowance established by your country's customs service. Goods and gifts purchased at **duty-free** shops abroad are not exempt from duty or sales tax at your point of return; you must declare these items as well. "Duty-free" merely means that you need not pay a tax in the country of purchase. For more specific information on customs requirements, contact the following information centers:

Australia Australian Customs National Information 1 300 363; www.customs.gov.au.

Canada Canadian Customs, 2265 St. Laurent Blvd., Ottawa, ON K1G 4K3 (613-993-0534 or 24hr. automated service 800-461-9999; www.revcan.ca).

Ireland The Collector of Customs and Excise, The Custom House, Dublin 1 (tel. (01) 679 27 77; fax 671 20 21; taxes@revenue.iol.ie; www.revenue.ie/customs.htm).

New Zealand New Zealand Customhouse, 17-21 Whitmore St., Box 2218, Wellington (tel. (04) 473 6099; fax 473 7370; www.customs.govt.nz).

South Africa Commissioner for Customs and Excise, Private Bag X47, Pretoria 0001 (tel. 12 314 99 11; fax 328 64 78).

United Kingdom Her Majesty's Customs and Excise, Custom House, Nettleton Rd., Heathrow Airport, Hounslow, Middlesex TW6 2LA (tel. (020) 8910 36 02/35 66; fax 8910 37 65; www.hmce.gov.uk).

United States U.S. Customs Service, Box 7407, Washington D.C. 20044 (202-927-6724; www.customs.ustreas.gov).

MONEY

Hostels in the region cost about $15 (more in cities), and groceries are reasonably priced. If you were to prepare your own food, you could get by spending less than $10 a day. In more remote communities, fresh food is more expensive. Gasoline prices are much lower in North America than elsewhere in the world, ranging from $1.25 to $2.25 per gallon (again, more in remote communities.) If you're serious about cutting costs, though, camp. Most government-run campgrounds with showers and security staff charge between $8 and $20 per site per night; your cost will depend on how many share that site. We also list many opportunities for free camping, though these are more likely to be found farther from built-up areas. If you plan to spend time in cities, you will end up in hostels. Prices for motels or bed and breakfasts also vary quite widely. Two people sharing a motel room would usually pay significantly more than they would in a hostel. The American dollar is much stronger than the Canadian, but this difference is not reflected in most prices—traveling in Canada is significantly cheaper.

CURRENCY AND EXCHANGE

The main unit of currency in the U.S. and Canada is the **dollar ($),** which is divided into 100 **cents (¢).** Paper money is green in the U.S.; bills come in denominations of $1, $5, $10, $20, $50, and $100. Coins are 1¢ (penny), 5¢ (nickel), 10¢ (dime), and 25¢ (quarter). Paper money in Canada comes in denominations of $5, $10, $20, $50, and $100, which are all the same size but color-coded by denomination. Coins are 1¢, 5¢, 10¢, 25¢, $1, and $2. The $1 coin is known as the **Loonie,** for the common loon *(Gavia immer)* that appeared on the obverse of the first coins. The $2 coin is affectionately dubbed the **Toonie.**

NOTA BENE. Except in the Western Canada section of this guide, and unless otherwise specified, all prices in this guide are in U.S. dollars.

The chart below is based on rates published in late August, 1999.

THE GREENBACK (U.S. DOLLAR)	
CDN$1 = US$0.67	US$1 = CDN$1.48
UK£1 = US$1.60	US$1 = UK£0.62
IR£1 = US$1.34	US$1= IR£0.74
AUS$1 = US$0.65	US$1= AUS$1.53
NZ$1 = US$0.53	US$1 = NZ$1.90
SAR1 = US$0.16	US$1 = SAR6.10

THE LOONIE (CANADIAN DOLLAR)	
US$1 = CDN$1.48	CDN$1 = US$0.67
UK£1 = CDN$2.37	CDN$1 = UK£0.421
IR£1 = CDN$1.99	CDN$1= IR£0.50
AUS$1 = CDN$0.96	CDN$1= AUS$1.04
NZ$1 = CDN$0.78	CDN$1 = NZ$1.28
SAR1 = CDN$0.24	CDN$1 = SAR4.11

Watch out for commission rates and check newspapers for the standard rate of exchange. Banks generally have the best rates. A good rule of thumb is only to go to banks or money-exchanging centers that have at most a 5% margin between their buy and sell prices. Since you lose money with each transaction, convert in large sums. Also, using an ATM card or a credit card (see p. 9) will often get you the very good rates.

If you use traveler's checks or bills, carry some in small denominations ($50 or less), especially for times when you are forced to exchange money at disadvantageous rates. However, it is good to carry a range of denominations since charges may be levied per check cashed.

TRAVELER'S CHECKS

Traveler's checks are one of the safest and least troublesome means of carrying funds, since they can be refunded if stolen. In both the U.S. and Canada, traveler's checks are widely accepted in both rural and urban areas. Several agencies and banks sell them, usually for face value plus a small percentage commission. **American Express** and **Visa** are the most widely recognized. If you're ordering checks, do so well in advance, especially if you are requesting large sums.

Each agency provides refunds if your checks are lost or stolen, and many provide additional services, such as toll-free refund hotlines, emergency message services, and stolen credit card assistance. In order to collect a **refund for lost or stolen checks,** keep your check receipts separate from your checks and store them in a safe place or with a traveling companion. Record check numbers when you cash them, leave a list of check numbers with someone at home, and ask for a list of refund centers when you buy your checks. Never countersign your checks until

Money From Home In Minutes.

If you're stuck for cash on your travels, don't panic. Millions of people trust Western Union to transfer money in minutes to 165 countries and over 50,000 locations worldwide. Our record of safety and reliability is second to none. For more information, call Western Union: USA 1-800-325-6000, Canada 1-800-235-0000. Wherever you are, you're never far from home.

www.westernunion.com

The fastest way to send money worldwide:

you are ready to cash them, and always bring your passport with you when you plan to use the checks.

American Express: Call 800 251 902 in Australia; in New Zealand (0800) 441 068; in the U.K. (0800) 52 13 13; in the U.S. and Canada 800-221-7282. Elsewhere, call U.S. collect 801-964-6665; www.aexp.com. American Express traveler's checks are available in U.S. and Canadian dollars. Checks can be purchased for a small fee (1-4%) at American Express Travel Service Offices, banks, and American Automobile Association offices. AAA members (see p. 55) can buy the checks commission-free. American Express offices cash their checks commission-free (except where prohibited by national governments), but often at slightly worse rates than banks. *Cheques for Two* can be signed by either of two people traveling together.

Citicorp: Call 800-645-6556 in the U.S. and Canada; in Europe, the Middle East, or Africa, call the London office at (44) 20 7508 7007; from elsewhere, call U.S. collect 813-623-1709. Traveler's checks in 7 currencies. Commission 1-2%. Guaranteed hand-delivery of lost or stolen traveler's checks when a refund location is not convenient.

Thomas Cook MasterCard: From the U.S. or Canada call 800-223-7373; from the U.K. call (0800) 622 101; from elsewhere, call collect 44 1733 318 950. Checks available in 13 currencies. Commission 2%. Offices cash checks commission-free.

Visa: Call 800-227-6811 in the U.S.; in the U.K. (0800) 895 078; from elsewhere, call 44 1733 318 949 and reverse the charges. Any of the above numbers can tell you the location of their nearest office.

PUTTING IT ON PLASTIC

CREDIT CARDS

Credit cards are generally accepted in all but the smallest businesses in both the United States and Canada. Major credit cards—**MasterCard** and **Visa** are welcomed most often—can be used to extract cash advances in dollars, (both U.S. and Canadian) from associated banks and teller machines throughout both countries. Credit card companies get the wholesale exchange rate, which is generally 5% better than the retail rate used by banks and other currency exchange establishments. **American Express** cards also work in some ATMs, as well as at AmEx offices and major airports. All such machines require a **Personal Identification Number (PIN).** You must ask your credit card company for a PIN before you leave; without it, you will be unable to withdraw cash with your credit card outside your home country. If you already have a PIN, check with the company to make sure it will work in Canada and the U.S. Credit cards often offer an array of other services, from insurance to emergency assistance; check with your company.

   Visa (800-336-8472) and **MasterCard** (800-307-7309) are issued in cooperation with individual banks and some other organizations. **American Express** (800-843-2273) has an annual fee of up to $55, depending on the card. Cardholder services include the option of cashing personal checks at AmEx offices, a 24-hour hotline with medical and legal assistance in emergencies (800-554-2639; from abroad call U.S. collect 202-554-2639), and the American Express Travel Service. Benefits include assistance in changing airline, hotel, and car rental reservations, baggage loss and flight insurance, sending mailgrams and international cables, and holding your mail at one of the more than 1700 AmEx offices worldwide (*Let's Go* lists them in the **Practical Information** sections of major cities). The **Discover Card** (800-347-2683; outside U.S., call 801-902-3100) offers small cashback bonuses on most purchases, but it may not be readily accepted in Canada or the U.S. **Diner's Club** (800-234-6377; outside U.S., call collect 303-799-1504) is another popular option.

ATM CARDS

Automated Teller Machines—**ATMs**—accept cash cards issued by your bank and allow you to access your personal bank account from abroad. ATMs get the same wholesale exchange rate as credit cards. Despite these perks, do some research before relying heavily on them. Per-transaction fees may be charged by both your home bank (typically $1-2 for North American accounts and $5 for overseas transactions) and the bank that operates the ATM (typically $1-3). ATMs operated by smaller banks and in places like gas stations and supermarkets are most likely to charge this latter "convenience fee," though you will always given the chance to cancel your transaction before being charged. There is also often a limit on the amount of money you can withdraw per day (usually about $500), and computer networks sometimes fail. If your PIN is longer than four digits, ask your bank whether the first four digits will work in North America, or whether you will need a new number. ATMs are all over North American cities and towns. Most every bank has one open 24 hours. In areas and towns where there are no banks or where ATMs are harder to find, *Let's Go* lists them under **Practical Information.**

The two major international ATM networks are **Cirrus** and **PLUS**. To locate ATMs in the U.S. and Canada, call 800-4CIRRUS/424-7787, 800-843-PLUS/7587, or visit www.visa.com/pd/atm or www.mastercard.com/atm.

DEBIT CARDS

Debit cards are a hybrid between credit and cash cards. They bear the logo of a major credit card, but purchases and withdrawals made with them are paid directly out of your bank account. Using a debit card like a credit card often incurs no fee (contact the issuing bank for details), gives you a favorable exchange rate, and frees you from having to carry large sums of money. When given the option to use your card as either an ATM card or a credit card (as you will be at 'pay-at-the-pump' gas stations), it's usually cheaper to choose to use it as a credit card.

GETTING MONEY FROM HOME

American Express: Cardholders can withdraw cash from their checking accounts for free at any of AmEx's major offices and many of its representatives' offices (up to $1000 per 21 days). Reach AmEx in the United States and Canada at 800-221-7282.

Western Union: Money can be wired between offices in more than 100 countries through Western Union's international money transfer services. Offices are located throughout Alaska, western Canada, Oregon and Washington. In the U.S., call 800-325-6000; in Canada, 800-235-0000. To cable money within the U.S. or Canada using a credit card (Visa, MasterCard, Discover), call 800-CALL-CASH/225-5227. Using a credit card generally costs $10-11 more than sending cash. Money is usually available within an hour.

TIPPING, BARGAINING, AND TAXES

In the U.S., and Canada, it is customary to tip waitstaff and cab drivers 15-20%, at your discretion. Tips are usually not included in restaurant bills, unless you are in a party of six or more. At the airport and in hotels, porters expect a $1 per bag tip. Bartenders appreciate 50¢-$1 per drink. It never hurts to ask after special deals on tour packages, or to comparison shop by phone and to politely make this known. Bargaining is generally fruitless in retail stores, although many larger stores will beat their competitors' advertised prices.

Sales tax in the U.S. and Canada tax is the equivalent of the European Value-Added Tax, but is generally not included in advertised prices. Neither Oregon nor Alaska has any sales tax. Washington state charges 7-8.6% depending on the region

In Canada, you'll quickly notice the federal 7% goods and services tax (GST) and an additional provincial sales tax of 7% in B.C. Visitors can claim a **rebate** of the GST they pay on accommodations of less than one month and on most goods they buy and take home, so be sure to save your receipts and pick up a GST rebate form while in Canada. The total claim must be at least CDN$7 of GST (equal to CDN$100 in purchases) and must be made within one year of the date of the purchase; further goods must be exported from Canada within 60 days of purchase. A brochure detailing restrictions is available from local tourist offices or through Revenue Canada, Visitor's Rebate Program, 275 Pope Rd., Summerside, PEI C1N 6C6 (800-668-4748 or 902-432-5608 outside of Canada.)

SAFETY AND SECURITY

> **EMERGENCY = 911.** For emergencies in the U.S. and Canada, dial **911.** This number is toll-free from all phones, including coin phones. In a very few remote communities, 911 may not work. If it does not, dial 0 for the operator and request to be connected with the appropriate emergency service. In national parks, it is usually best to call the **park warden** in case of emergency. *Let's Go* always lists emergency contact numbers.

IN THE CITY. Blend in as much as possible, and familiarize yourself with the area before you set out. The gawking camera-toter is a more obvious target for thieves and con artists than the low-profile traveler. Find out about unsafe neighborhoods from tourist offices, the manager of your hotel or hostel, or a local whom you trust. You may want to carry a **whistle** to scare off attackers or attract attention. Whenever possible, *Let's Go* warns of unsafe neighborhoods and areas, but there are some good general tips to follow. When walking at night, stick to busy, well-lit streets and avoid dark alleyways. Do not attempt to cross through parks, parking lots, or other large, deserted areas. Buildings in disrepair, vacant lots, and unpopulated areas are all bad signs. Keep in mind that a district can change character drastically between blocks and from day to night.

Con artists are common in all big cities, and possess an innumerable range of ruses. Be aware of certain classics: sob stories that require money, or distractions like rolls of bills "found" on the street. Contact the police if a hustler is particularly insistent or aggressive.

TRESPASSING. Much wilderness is owned or controlled by private citizens, Native Americans, First Nations, or companies, all of whom have their own reasons for being sensitive to **trespassing.** None take it lightly. Look out for and respect signs; when in doubt ask park rangers, public lands offices, and locals before making camp or setting out into the backcountry. Industrial sites don't welcome unannounced visitors. Poking around lumber yards, quarries, or fishing docks will not be appreciated by workers, and is often dangerous in and of itself.

SELF-DEFENSE. A good self-defense course will give you more concrete ways to react to different types of aggression. **Impact, Prepare, and Model Mugging** can refer you to local self-defense courses in the United States (800-345-5425) and Vancouver, Canada (604-878-3838). Workshops (2-3hr.) start at $50 and full courses run $350-500. Both women and men are welcome.

FINANCIAL SECURITY

PROTECTING YOUR VALUABLES

To prevent easy theft, don't keep all your valuables (money, travel documents, tickets) in one place. **Photocopies** (see p. 23) of important documents allow you to recover them in case they are lost or stolen. Carry one copy separate from the documents and leave another copy at home. Label every piece of luggage both inside and out. To help foil pickpockets, **don't carry a wallet in your back pocket.** If you carry a purse, buy a sturdy one with a secure clasp, and carry it crosswise on the side, away from the street with the clasp against you. Secure packs with small combination padlocks which slip through the two zippers. A **money belt** is the best way to carry cash; you can buy one at most camping supply stores. A nylon, zippered pouch with a belt that sits inside the waist of your pants or skirt combines convenience and security. A **neck pouch** is equally safe, though less accessible. Avoid keeping anything precious in a fanny-pack (even if it's worn on your stomach): your valuables will be highly visible and easy to steal. Keep some money separate from the rest to use in case of theft or emergency.

ESSENTIALS

ACCOMMODATIONS AND TRANSPORTATION

Never leave your belongings unattended; crime occurs in even the most demure-looking hostel or hotel. If you feel unsafe, look for places with either a curfew or a night attendant. *Let's Go* lists locker availability in hostels and train stations. Bring your own **padlock**. If you must sleep on a bus or train while your bag is unsecured, or leave it behind in a hostel, lock it closed and to something fixed (a cable with eyes at either end which can be fastened together comes in handy for this). Always keep important documents and other valuables on your person. In hostels, keep your money belt in a locker or in your sleeping bag at night.

If you travel by **car,** try not to leave valuables in it while you are away. Hide baggage and removable radios and tape decks in the trunk—although savvy thieves can tell if a car is heavily loaded by the way it sits on its tires.

DRUGS AND ALCOHOL

If you carry **prescription drugs** while traveling, it is vital to have a copy of the prescriptions to present at U.S. and Canadian borders. The importation of **illegal substances** into Canada or the U.S. is (needless to say) illegal, highly risky, and a punishable offense. Border guards of both countries have psychic powers and unlimited rights to search your baggage, your person, and your vehicle, and will seize vehicles on the spot that are found to be involved in smuggling even small quantities of illegal substances. U.S. border guards can also ban you on the spot from re-entering the country for years. If you are not a U.S. citizen, you may have no right to appeal such decisions. Away from borders, police attitudes vary widely across the region, but the old standards—marijuana, LSD, heroin, cocaine—are illegal in every province and state. Those arrested for drug possession in the U.S. or Canada can be subject to a wide range of charges.

In Oregon, Washington, and Alaska, the **drinking age** is 21. British Columbia and the Yukon Territory prohibit drinking below the age of 19, while in Alberta the drinking age is 18. In both the U.S. and Canada, this law is strictly enforced. Particularly in the U.S., be prepared to show a photo ID (preferably some government document like a driver's license or passport) if you appear to be under 30. Sixty-five years after Prohibition, some areas of the U.S. are still "dry," meaning they do not permit the sale of alcohol at all, while other places prohibit the sale of alcohol on Sundays. Officials on both sides of the border take **drunk driving** very seriously and mount frequent roadside breathalyzer campaigns—don't do it.

HEALTH

Common sense is the simplest prescription for good health while you travel. Travelers complain most often about their feet and their gut, so take precautionary measures: drink lots of fluids to prevent dehydration and constipation, wear sturdy, broken-in shoes and clean socks, and use talcum powder to keep your feet dry. To minimize the effects of jet lag, "reset" your body's clock by adopting the time of your destination as soon as you board the plane.

BEFORE YOU GO

For minor health problems, bring a compact **first-aid kit,** including bandages, aspirin or other painkiller, antibiotic cream, a thermometer, a Swiss army knife with tweezers, moleskin, decongestant for colds, motion sickness remedy, medicine for diarrhea or stomach problems (Pepto Bismol tablets or liquid and Immodium), sunscreen, insect repellent, and burn ointment. **Contact lens** wearers should bring an extra pair, a copy of the prescription, a pair of glasses, extra solution, and eyedrops. Those who use heat disinfection might consider switching to chemical cleansers for the duration of the trip.

In your **passport,** write the names of any people you wish to be contacted in case of a medical emergency, and also list any **allergies** or medical conditions you would want doctors to be aware of. Allergy sufferers might want to obtain a full supply of any necessary medication before the trip. Matching a prescription to a foreign equivalent is not always easy, safe, or possible. Carry up-to-date, legible prescriptions or a statement from your doctor stating the medication's trade name, manufacturer, chemical name, and dosage. While traveling, be sure to keep all medication with you in your carry-on luggage.

MEDICAL CONDITIONS

Those with medical conditions (e.g., diabetes, allergies to antibiotics, epilepsy, heart conditions) may want to obtain a stainless steel **Medic Alert** identification tag ($35 the first year, and $15 annually thereafter), which identifies the condition and gives a 24-hour collect-call information number. Contact the Medic Alert Foundation, 2323 Colorado Ave., Turlock, CA 95382 (800-825-3785; www.medicalert.org). Diabetics can contact the **American Diabetes Association**, 1660 Duke St., Alexandria, VA 22314 (800-232-3472), to receive copies of the article "Travel and Diabetes" and a diabetic ID card, which carries messages in 18 languages explaining the carrier's diabetic status.

ENVIRONMENTAL HAZARDS

If you suffer from any of the following ailments in a severe or prolonged form, seek medical help as soon as possible. For more detailed information, find *Backcountry First Aid and Extended Care*, by Buck Tilton (ICS Books).

Altitude sickness: Travelers to high altitudes must allow their bodies a couple of days to adjust to the lower levels of oxygen in the air before engaging in strenuous activities. Expect some drowsiness, and an amplification of the effects of alcohol. Climbers should be aware of the dangers of quick ascents.

Blisters: Proto-blisters (called hotspots) are more easily treated than full-blown blisters; prevention is key: break in new boots. Warm wet feet are most prone to blisters. If a hotspot develops, replace wet socks with dry ones and cover the area with moleskin. If a blister occurs, cut out a doughnut of moleskin to surround.

Frostbite: Superficially frostbitten skin is waxy, pale and numb, but moves when pressed. These victims should drink warm beverages, stay dry, and gently and slowly warm the frostbitten area through dry fabric or with steady body contact (armpits are good). *Never* rub or pour hot water on superficial frostbite; the tissue is easily damaged when frozen. Deeply frostbitten tissue is solid to the touch. Find a doctor immediately. If means are available, rapidly rewarm in circulating water between 105-110°F but no hotter. Soft cotton should be placed between rewarmed digits, but any other contract should be avoided. Once the tissue has frozen the major damage has been done, and refreezing after rewarming causes extensive tissue damage. *Do not rewarm frozen tissue unless you can guarantee that it can be kept warm.* Pain after rewarming can be intense.

Heat stroke: Heat stroke is preceded by the dizziness and nausea of **heat exhaustion**, which is less serious and can be treated with rest, water, and salty foods. When sweating stops and skin temperature rises, more dangerous heat stroke has begun. Cool the victim immediately with liquids, wet towels, and shade, and get medical attention even if the victim appears to have recovered. Relapses are common.

Hypothermia: A drop in core body temperature which impairs normal muscular and cerebral function. A very real danger for hikers in cool, wet climates and for those on the water. Symptoms include shivering, slurred speech, loss of coordination, exhaustion, hallucinations, or amnesia. If unable to walk a 30 ft. straight line, a person is likely hypothermic. Treat hypothermia victims by getting them out of all wet clothes and into dry ones, and out of wind. Sharing a sleeping bag with a warm person also in dry clothing can help rewarming. Keep victims hydrated, fueled, and awake. To avoid hypothermia, stay dry and dress in layers of polypropylene, wool, and pile fleece, which insulate when wet and wick moisture away from the skin. Gore-Tex rain gear is waterproof and allows water vapor to escape, helping you to keep dry even when exercising. Never rely on cotton, including jeans, for warmth; this "death fabric" wicks away heat when wet.

Mosquitoes: Perhaps the greatest threat to your *mental* health are the swarms of mosquitoes that descend on the region every summer. Tuck long pants into socks, and wear long pants and long sleeves (fabric need not be thick or warm; tropic-weight cottons can keep you comfortable in the heat). Use insect repellents; **DEET** can be bought in spray or liquid form, but use it sparingly, especially on children. Natural repellents can also be useful: taking **vitamin B-12** pills regularly can make you smelly to insects, as can garlic pills. Calamine lotion or topical cortisones (like Cortaid) may stop insect bites from itching, as can a bath with a half-cup of baking soda or oatmeal.

Poison Ivy, Poison Oak, Poison Sumac: These plants secrete oils that can cause unbearable itchiness, hives, and inflammation of the affected areas. Some people have allergic reactions with asthma-like symptoms; find medical help if this occurs. If you think you have come into contact with one of these plants, wash your skin with soap and cold water; heat dilates the pores, driving the poison deeper. An excellent soap is **Fels Naptha,** available at any good drug store. If rashes occur, calamine lotion, topical cortisones (like Cortaid), or antihistamines may stop the itching. Fight the near-irresistible urge to scratch; it will only spread the oil.

Sunburn: Apply sunscreen liberally and often. You may not go to the Far North in search of a tan, but in summer the sun will be up for 20 or more hours a day. Protect your eyes with good sunglasses, since UV rays can damage the retina of the eye. If you get sunburned, drink more fluids than usual and apply Calamine or an aloe-based lotion.

DISEASE

Diarrhea: Many people take over-the-counter medicine (such as Pepto-Bismol or Immodium) to counteract it, but be aware that such remedies can complicate serious conditions. The most dangerous side effect of diarrhea is dehydration; a simple antidehydration formula is 8 oz. of water with a ½ tsp. of sugar or honey, plus a pinch of salt. Caffeine-free soft drinks and salted crackers can also help. If you develop a fever or your symptoms persist for several days, consult a doctor. Also consult a doctor if children develop traveler's diarrhea, since treatment is different. This too shall pass.

Giardia (a.k.a. Beaver Fever): Found in all too many streams, and lakes, *Giardia lamblia* is a bacterium that causes gas, cramps, and violent diarrhea. To protect yourself, bring water to a good boil for at least one minute or purify it with iodine tablets before drinking or cooking with it.

Lyme Disease: Tick-borne diseases, like Lyme disease, can be very serious. Only 3 cases of Lyme disease in Alaska have ever been reported to the Center for Disease Control, but infection is more common in Western Canada and the Pacific Northwest. A Lyme infection can cause a circular rash of two inches or more that looks like a bull's eye. Other symptoms are flu-like: fever, headache, fatigue, or aches and pains. Left untreated, Lyme can cause dangerous problems in joints, the heart, and the nervous system. A vaccine has recently been brought to market; see your doctor for details. Lyme can be treated with antibiotics if caught early. If you find a tick attached to your skin, grasp the tick's head parts with tweezers as close to your skin as possible and apply slow, steady traction. Removing a tick within 24 hours greatly reduces the risk of infection. Wear bug repellent when hiking, and check for ticks at least once a day; they are brownish and about the size of a pinhead. Tucking pants into socks and wearing insect repellent with DEET can also help.

Rabies: Transmitted through the saliva of infected animals, it is fatal if left untreated. Avoid contact with animals, especially strays. If you are bitten, wash the wound thoroughly and seek immediate medical care. Once you begin to show symptoms (thirst and muscle spasms), the disease is in its terminal stage. If possible, try to locate the animal that bit you to determine whether it does indeed have rabies.

Red Tide: Refers to any number of harmful algal blooms in sea water, which sometimes, but not always, give the water surface a reddish tinge. Shellfish feed on these toxic algae, and toxin accumulates in their muscle tissue. The two most serious classes of toxins, which cause sometimes fatal paralytic shellfish poisoning (PSP) and amnesic shellfish poisoning in humans, are both found regularly in shellfish on the Pacific Coast from Alaska to Oregon. The highest incidence of PSP in the world is in Southeast Alaska. The virtually unreported diarrhetic shellfish poisoning (DSP), which causes intestinal problems, is even more common. *Do not eat shellfish without assurance from a local health authority that they are free from toxins.*

WOMEN'S HEALTH

Women traveling in unsanitary conditions are vulnerable to **urinary tract** and **bladder infections,** common bacterial diseases that cause a burning sensation and painful, frequent urination. To try to avoid these infections, drink plenty of vitamin-C-rich juice and plenty of clean water, and urinate frequently, especially right after intercourse. Untreated, these infections can lead to kidney infections, sterility, and even death. If symptoms persist, see a doctor.

Women on **the pill** should bring a prescription, since forms of the pill vary a good deal. Women who need an abortion in the U.S. or Canada should contact the National Abortion Federation Hotline, 1755 Massachusetts Ave. NW, Washington, D.C. 20036 (800-772-9100, M-F 9am-7pm).

INSURANCE

Travel insurance generally covers four basic areas: medical coverage, property loss, trip cancellation/interruption, and emergency evacuation. Although regular policies may extend to travel-related accidents, consider travel insurance if the cost of potential trip cancellation/interruption is greater than you can absorb.

Medical insurance (especially university policies) often covers costs incurred abroad; check with your provider. Canadians are partially protected by their home province's health insurance during travel; check with the provincial Ministry of Health or Health Plan Headquarters for details. **Homeowners' insurance** often covers theft during travel and loss of travel documents up to $500. **ISIC** and **ITIC** provide basic insurance benefits, including $100 per day of in-hospital sickness for a maximum of 60 days, $3000 of accident-related medical reimbursement, and $25,000 for emergency medical transport (see **Identification,** p. 25). **American Express** (800-528-4800) grants most cardholders automatic car rental insurance (collision/theft, but not liability) and ground travel accident coverage of $100,000 on flight purchases made with the card. Prices for separately purchased full coverage travel insurance generally runs about $50 per week, while trip cancellation/interruption may be purchased separately for about $5.50 per $100 of coverage.

INSURANCE PROVIDERS. Council and **STA** (see p. 49 for complete listings) offer a range of plans that can supplement your basic insurance coverage. Other private insurance providers in the **U.S.** include: **Access America** (800-284-8300); **Berkely Group/Carefree Travel Insurance** (800-323-3149 or 516-294-0220; info@berkely.com; www.berkely.com); **Globalcare Travel Insurance** (800-821-2488; www.globalcare-cocco.com); and **Travel Assistance International** (800-821-2828 or 202-828-5894; wassist@aol.com; www.worldwide-assistance.com). **U.K.** providers include **Campus Travel** (tel. (01865) 258 000) and **Columbus Travel Insurance** (tel. (020) 7375 0011). In **Australia,** try **CIC Insurance** (tel. (02) 9202 8000).

PACKING

Pack light—this means you! A good rule is to lay out only what you absolutely need, then take half the clothes and twice the money. The less you have, the less you have to lose (or store, or carry on your back). Don't skimp on raingear, though, every season is the rainy season in the Pacific Northwest. The weather in Alaska and the Yukon is cool all summer, so don't go overboard on shorts and sandals. Remember that wool, fleece and polypropylene insulate when wet, whereas wet cotton is colder than wearing nothing at all. See **Outdoors,** p. 43. for tips on buying a backpack and more outdoors-specific packing suggestions.)

ESSENTIALS

Electricity in the U.S. and Canada is 110V AC. Hardware stores carry adapters (which change the shape of the plug) and converters (which change the voltage). Don't make the mistake of using only an adapter.

DRESS FOR SUCCESS

The clothing you bring will, of course, depend on when and where you're planning to travel. In general, **dressing in layers** is best when traveling and hiking.

Light Layers: Start with a few t-shirts; they take up little space and you can wear sweater over one on a chilly night. Polypro layers great and weighs close to nothing. Pack a pair of shorts and one of jeans, as well as underwear, socks, a towel, and swimwear.

Heavy Layers: Even in summer, the Pacific Coast and Alaska can get quite cold. Bring heavier layers that insulate while wet, such as polar fleece, or wool. Never rely on cotton for warmth.

Rain: A hooded waterproof jacket, rainpants and backpack cover will keep you and your stuff dry. Gore-Tex is a fabric that's both waterproof and breathable.

Footwear: Well-cushioned athletic shoes or lace-up leather shoes are good for general walking, but for any even moderately challenging hiking (and you will want to hike in this part of the world) a pair of water-proofed hiking boots is essential: they're lightweight, rugged, and dry quickly. *Break them in before you leave home.* A double pair of socks—light polypro liners inside and thick wool outside—will cushion feet, keep them dry, and help prevent blisters. Talcum powder in your shoes and on your feet can prevent sores, and moleskin is great for blisters (see p. 33). Bring a pair of flip-flop sandals for the fungal floors of communal showers.

RANDOM USEFUL STUFF

Sleepsack: If planning to stay in **youth hostels,** make the requisite sleepsack instead of paying the hostel's linen charge. Fold a full size sheet in half the long way, then sew it closed along the open long side and one of the short sides.

Toiletries: Soap, shampoo, toothpaste, deodorant, razors, comb, brush, toilet paper, tampons, condoms, birth control, vitamins, sunscreen, lip balm, and insect repellent. Pack spillables in plastic bags to prevent chemical slicks within your luggage. Bring whatever you need to keep your contact lenses happy.

More useful than random: Alarm clock, batteries, waterproof matches, sun hat, needle and thread, safety pins, sunglasses, pocketknife, water container, compass, towel, padlock, whistle, flashlight, earplugs, duct tape, clothespins, maps, tweezers, garbage bags, laundry soap, rubber ball for stopping sinks.

More random but still useful: Notebook with pens, bandanas, cheap novels, string, lead-lined pouch (for protecting high-speed film from airport x-rays or storing Kryptonite).

ACCOMMODATIONS

HOSTELS

 A HOSTELER'S BILL OF RIGHTS. There are certain standard features that we do not include in our hostel listings. Unless we state otherwise, you can expect that every hostel has: no lockout, no curfew, a kitchen, free hot showers, secure luggage storage, and no key deposit.

Hostels are generally dorm-style accommodations, often in single-sex large rooms with bunk beds, although most North American hostels offer private rooms for families and couples. They usually have kitchens and utensils for your use, storage areas, and laundry facilities. There can be drawbacks: some hostels close during certain daytime "lock-out" hours, have a curfew, don't accept reservations, impose a maximum stay, or, less frequently, require that you do chores. In North America,

ESSENTIALS

a bed in a hostel will average around $10-20. You must bring your own sleepsack or linen; sleeping bags are often not allowed.

A membership in **Hostelling International (HI)**, grants cheaper rates at HI hostels, which are with few exceptions excellent in the region. A few major hostels accept reservations via the International Booking Network (tel. (02) 9261 1111 from Australia, 800-663-5777 from Canada, (020) 7581 418 from the U.K., (01) 301 766 from Ireland, (09) 379 4224 from New Zealand, 800-909-4776 from U.S.; www.hiayh.org/ushostel/reserva/ibn3.htm) for a nominal fee. HI's umbrella organization's web page lists the web addresses and phone numbers of all national associations and is a great place to begin researching hostelling in a specific region (www.iyhf.org). Another useful web site is www.hostels.com. Information on particular hostels, discount travel packages, and discount lift ticket and accommodation packages at hostels near ski areas can be had from the following regional organizations:

HI American Youth Hostels (HI-AYH), 733 15th St. NW #840, Washington, D.C. 20005 (202-783-6161 ext. 136; fax 783-6171; www.hiayh.org). $25, over 54 $15, under 18 free.

HI Canada (HI-C), 400-205 Catherine St., Ottawa, ON K2P 1C3 (800-663-5777 or 613-237-7884; fax 237-7868; www.hostellingintl.ca). CDN$25, under 18 CDN$12; 2-year membership CDN$35.

HI British Columbia Region: 134 Abbott St. #402, Vancouver, BC, Canada V6B 2K4 (800-661-0020 or in BC 800-663-5777 or 604-684-7111; fax 604-684-7181; www.hihostels.bc.ca) web site offers online reservations.

HI Southern Alberta Region: 1414 Kensington Rd. NW #203, Calgary, AB, Canada T2N 3P9 (403-283-5551; www.hostellingintl.ca/Alberta). Online reservations and info on ski and stay packages at ski areas in the Rockies.

To join HI, contact one of the following organizations in your home country (prices are for one-year memberships unless otherwise noted):

Australian Youth Hostels Association (AYHA), 422 Kent St., Sydney NSW 2000 (tel. (02) 9261 1111; fax 9261 1969; www.yha.org.au). AUS$44, under 18 AUS$13.50.

An Óige (Irish Youth Hostel Association), 61 Mountjoy St., Dublin 7 (tel. (01) 830 4555; fax 830 5808; www.irelandyha.org). IR£10, under 18 IR£4, families IR£20.

Youth Hostels Association of New Zealand (YHANZ), P.O. Box 436, 173 Cashel St., Christchurch 1 (tel. (03) 379 9970; fax 365 4476; www.yha.org.nz). NZ$24, ages 15-17 NZ$12, under 15 free.

Hostelling International South Africa, P.O. Box 4402, Cape Town 8000 (tel. (021) 24 2511; fax 24 4119; www.hisa.org.za). SAR50, under 18 SAR25, lifetime SAR250.

Scottish Youth Hostels Association (SYHA), 7 Glebe Crescent, Stirling FK8 2JA (tel. (01786) 891 400; fax 891 333; www.syha.org.uk). UK£6, under 18 UK£2.50.

Youth Hostels Association of England and Wales (YHA), 8 St. Stephen's Hill, St. Albans, Hertfordshire AL1 2DY, England (tel. (01727) 855 215 or 845 047; fax 844 126; www.yha.org.uk). UK£11, under 18 UK£5.50, families UK£22.

Hostelling International Northern Ireland (HINI), 22-32 Donegall Rd., Belfast BT12 5JN, Northern Ireland (tel. (028) 9032 4733 or 9031 5435; fax 9043 9699; www.hini.org.uk). UK£7, under 18 UK£3, families UK£14.

HOTELS AND MOTELS

Many visitor centers, especially those off major thoroughfares entering a state, have hotel coupons. Even if you don't see any, ask. Budget motels are often clustered off highways several miles from town. The annually updated **State by State Guide to Budget Motels** ($13), from Marlor Press, 4304 Brigadoon Dr., St. Paul, MN 55126 (800-669-4908 or 651-484-4600; fax 651-490-1182; marlor@minn.net) lists 4000 budget motels across the country.

It is fortunate that the Canadian hostel system is somewhat more extensive than that of the U.S., because the country has a dearth of cheap motels. U.S. budget motel chains cost significantly less than the chains catering to the next-pricier market, such as Holiday Inn. Chains also have more predictable standards of cleanliness and comfort than locally-operated budget competitors. Contact chains for free directories, and always inquire about discounts for seniors, families, frequent travelers, groups, or government personnel: **Motel 6** (800-466-8356); **Super 8 Motels** (800-800-8000; www.super8motels.com/super8.html); **Choice Hotels International** (800-453-4511); **Best Western International** (800-528-1234).

BED AND BREAKFASTS

For a cozy alternative to impersonal hotel rooms, B&Bs (private homes with rooms available to travelers) range from the acceptable to the sublime. Hosts will sometimes go out of their way to be accommodating by accepting travelers with pets, giving personalized tours, or offering home-cooked meals. On the other hand, many B&Bs do not provide phones, TVs, or private bathrooms. In many northern communities, B&Bs are the only indoor accommodation option, and rarely cost less than $45 for a single. The cheapest rooms in cheap B&Bs in the rest of the reion generally cost from $25-45 for a single and from $30-60 for a double in Alaska and the Pacific Northwest. Consult *The Complete Guide to Bed and Breakfasts, Inns and Guesthouses in the U.S., Canada, and Worldwide*, by Pamela Lanier ($17; Ten Speed Press).

CAMPING AND THE OUTDOORS

Camping is about the most rewarding way to slash traveling costs. Traveling in a group of two or three means that the burdens of carrying gear and paying for sites (up to $20 in built-up areas, but often free to $5 for rustic sites a little ways off the beaten path) can be shared. *Let's Go* lists camping options town by town, including free camping on public lands. Campgrounds run by the provincial governments of B.C. and Alberta are usually spread out among forested areas and are generally more pleasant and less expensive than commercial sites. State campgrounds in Washington and Oregon blur the line between RV haven and treed tenter refuge a little more. In British Columbia and the Yukon, fees were instituted for the first time this year for Forest Service campgrounds. Permits (CDN$8 per night, annual CDN$27) must be bought in town or from Forest Service employees, but enforcement in the more remote campgrounds of Northern BC and the Yukon is reportedly sporadic. You may stay for no more than 14 days at these campgrounds.

NATIONAL PARKS

National parks protect some of America and Canada's most precious wildlife and spectacular scenery. The parks also offer recreational activities like hiking, skiing, and snowshoe expeditions; most have backcountry camping and developed campgrounds, others welcome RVs, and a few offer opulent living in grand lodges.

Entry fees vary from park to park. Pedestrian and cyclist entry fees tend to range from $2-7, while vehicles cost $5-10. National parks in the U.S. offer a number of one-year passes. The **Golden Eagle Passport** ($50) admits the bearer and accompanying passengers in a vehicle (or family members where access is not by vehicle) entry into all U.S. parks. The **Golden Age Passport** ($10), available to those aged 62 or more, and the **Golden Access Passport,** free to travelers who are blind or permanently disabled, allow free access to U.S. national parks and 50% off camping and other park fees. Passes are available at park entrances.

The **Western Canada Annual Pass,** available for both individuals and groups, offers a similar deal at Canadian national parks (CDN$35, seniors over 64 CDN$27, ages 6-16 CDN$18, groups of up to 7 adults CDN$70, groups of up to 7 seniors $53).

CAMPING RESERVATION NUMBERS. Reservations Northwest (800-452-5687 or 503-731-3411) books campsites at many Oregon and Washington state parks ($11-16, RV hookups $16-24; reservation fee $6). The Oregon state parks info line (800-551-6949; www.prd.state.or.us) and its Washington equivalent (800-233-0321; www.parks.wa.gov) provide info on all state parks, including those not listed with the reservations center, and can refer callers to the agencies responsible for all other campsites in the state. The **U.S. Forest Service (USFS)** reservations line (877-444-6777; www.reserveUSA.com) reserves selected campgrounds in national forests in Washington, Oregon, and Alaska and USFS cabins in southeast Alaska. For information on USFS campgrounds, cabins, and fire lookouts in Washington and Oregon not listed with the nationwide network, contact **Nature of the Northwest,** 800 NE Oregon St. #177, Portland, OR (503-872-2750; www.naturenw.org; open M-F 9am-5pm). **BC Discover Camping** (800-689-9025 or 604-689-9025; www.discovercamping.ca) reserves sites at 63 of 240 BC provincial parks. ($8-18.50 per night; reservation fee CDN$6.42 per night for first 3 nights) for campsite reservations by credit card. For information on other, non-reservable provincial park campsites, call 250-387-4550. **Supernatural British Columbia** (800-663-6000 or 250-387-1642; www.travel.bc.ca) can refer you to private campgrounds throughout BC. State campgrounds in Alaska are all first come, first served, and cost about $10.

Let's Go lists fees for individual parks and contact information for park visitor centers (check the index for a complete listing). Every national park in the U.S. and Canada has a web page, accessible from www.nps.gov or http://parkscanada.pch.gc.ca which lists contact info, fees, and reservation policies.

U.S. Forest Service, Outdoor Recreation Information Center, 222 Yale Ave. N, Seattle, WA 98174 (206-470-4060; www.fs.fed.us).

Parks Canada, 220 4th Ave. SE #552, Calgary, AB T2G 4X3 (800-748-7275 or 403-292-4401; natlparks-ab@pch.gc.ca).

Alaska Public Lands Information Center, 605 W. 4th Ave. #105, Anchorage, AK 99501 (907-271-2737; fax 907-271-2744).

Alaska Public Lands Information Center, 250 Cushman #1A, Fairbanks, AK 99707 (907-456-0527)

STATE AND PROVINCIAL PARKS

In contrast to national parks, the primary function of **state and provincial parks** is usually recreation. Prices for camping at public sites are usually better than those at private campgrounds. Don't let swarming visitors dissuade you from seeing the larger parks—these places can be huge, and even at their most crowded they offer opportunities for quiet and solitude. Most campgrounds are first come, first camped, so arrive early. Some limit your stay and/or the number of people in a group. See above for camping reservation lines. For general information, contact:

Alaska Department of Natural Resources Public Information, 3601 C St. #200, Anchorage, AK 99503 (907-269-8400; fax 269-8901; www.dnr.state.ak.us/parks). Information on cabins ($25-55 per night) in Alaska state parks.

Alberta Environmental Protection, 9820 106 St., 2nd Fl., Edmonton, AB T5K 2J6 (780-427-7009; fax 427-5980; www.gov.ab.ca/env/parks.html).

British Columbia Ministry of Environment, Lands, and Parks, P.O. Box 9398, Stn. Prov. Govt., Victoria, BC V8W 9M9 (250-387-4609; www.elp.gov.bc.ca/bcparks).

Oregon State Parks and Recreation Department, P.O. Box 500, Portland, OR 97207-0500 (800-551-6949; fax 503-378-6308; www.prd.state.or.us).

Washington State Parks and Recreation Commission, P.O. Box 42650, Olympia, WA 98504-2650 (360-902-8500, info 800-233-0321; www.parks.wa.gov).

Yukon Parks and Outdoor Recreation, Box 2703, Whitehorse, YT Y1A 2C6 (867-667-5648; fax 393-6223).

U.S. NATIONAL FORESTS

If national park campgrounds are too developed for your tastes, **national forests** provide a purist's alternative. While some have recreation facilities, most are equipped only for primitive camping: pit toilets and no running water are the norm. (See **Camping Reservation Numbers** p. 41 for reservations.) For general information, including maps and the free *Guide to Your National Forests*, contact the **U.S. Forest Service, Outdoor Recreation Information Center,** 222 Yale Ave. N, Seattle, WA 98174 (206-470-4060; www.fs.fed.us).

Backpackers can enjoy specially designated **wilderness areas,** which are even less accessible due to regulations barring vehicles, including mountain bikes. **Wilderness permits,** generally free, are required for backcountry hiking.

In Alaska, the Forest Service oversees more than 200 scenic and well-maintained **wilderness cabins** for public use, scattered throughout the southern and central regions of the state. User permits are required, along with a fee of $15-50 per party per night. Call the Forest Service (see **Camping Reservation Numbers,** above) for reservations information. Most cabins have seven-day maximum stays (hike-in cabins have a 3-day limit May-Aug.), and are usually accessible only by air, boat, or hiking trail. For general information, contact the Forest Service's regional offices. The **Alaska Public Lands Information Center** (907-271-2737; see p. 438), can answer further questions and also mails out maps and brochures.

Many trailhead parking lots in Oregon and Washington National Forests require a Trail Park Pass ($3 per day per vehicle; annual pass for 2 vehicles $25). Passes are available at area outfitters and convenience stores, but not at trailheads.

The U.S. Department of the Interior's **Bureau of Land Management (BLM),** offers a variety of outdoor recreation opportunities on the 270 million acres it oversees in ten western states and Alaska, including camping, hiking, mountain biking, rock climbing, river rafting, and wildlife viewing. Unless otherwise posted, all public lands are open for recreational use. Write the Alaska State office (907-271-5960) in Anchorage at 222 W. 7th Ave. #13, Anchorage AK 99513-7599, or the Washington/Oregon office (503-952-6002) at 1515 SW 5th Ave., Portland OR 92208-2965 for a guide to BLM campgrounds, many of which are free.

USEFUL PUBLICATIONS AND WEB RESOURCES

Sierra Club Books, 85 2nd St. 2nd Fl., San Francisco, CA 94105-3441 (800-935-1056 or 415-977-5500; www.sierraclub.org/books). Books on many national parks, several series on different regions of the U.S., as well as *Adventuring in British Columbia* and the *Sierra Club Guide to Backpacking* ($15-16)

The Mountaineers Books, 1001 SW Klickitat Way #201, Seattle, WA 98134 (800-553-4453 or 206-223-6303; www.mountaineersbooks.org). Free catalog. Publishes over 300 excellent how-to books and specialized guides to outdoor activities in Washington and Oregon, including the *"100 Hikes"* series, Fred Beckey's definitive climbing guides, and books on paddling, mountain biking and winter activities.

Wilderness Press, 2440 Bancroft Way, Berkeley, CA 94704 (253-891-2500 or 800-443-7227; or 510-558-1666; www.wildernesspress.com). Publishes over 100 hiking guides and maps for the western U.S. including *Backpacking Basics* ($10), and *Backpacking with Babies and Small Children* ($10).

Woodall Publications Corporation, 13975 W. Polo Trail Dr., Lake Forest, IL 60045-5000 (888-226-7328 or 847-362-6700; www.woodalls.com). Publishes the annually-updated *Campground Directory: Western Edition* ($15) covering the U.S. and Canada.

CAMPING AND HIKING EQUIPMENT

Good camping equipment is both sturdy and light. Camping equipment is generally more expensive in Australia, New Zealand, and the U.K. than in North America.

Sleeping Bag: Most good sleeping bags are rated by "season," or the lowest outdoor temperature at which they will keep you warm ("summer" means 30-40°F at night and "four-season" or "winter" often means below 0°F). Sleeping bags are filled with either down (warmer and lighter, but more expensive, and useless when wet) or of synthetic material (heavier, more durable, and better if wet). Prices, can range from $80-210 for a summer synthetic to $250-300 for a good down winter bag. **Sleeping bag pads,** including foam pads ($10-20) and air mattresses ($15-50) cushion your back and neck and insulate you from the ground. **Therm-A-Rest** brand self-inflating sleeping pads inflate when you unroll them, but cost $45-80. Bring a **"stuff sack"** to store your sleeping bag and keep it dry.

Tent: The best tents are free-standing; they set up quickly and only require staking in high winds. Low-profile dome tents are the best all-around. Tent sizes can be somewhat misleading: two people *can* fit in a two-person tent, but will find life more pleasant in a four-person. If you're traveling by car, go for the bigger tent, but if you're backpacking, stick with a smaller one that weighs no more than 5-6 lbs. (2-3kg). Good two-person tents start at $90, four-person tents at $300. Seal the seams of your tent with waterproofer, and make sure it has a rain fly. Other tent accessories include a **battery-operated lantern,** a **plastic groundcloth.**

Backpack: If you intend to do a lot of hiking, you should have a frame backpack. **Internal-frame packs** mold better to your back, keep a lower center of gravity, and can flex adequately to allow you to hike difficult trails that require a lot of bending and maneuvering. **External-frame packs** are more comfortable for long hikes over even terrain since they keep the weight higher and distribute it more evenly. Whichever you choose, make sure your pack has a strong, padded hip belt, which transfers the weight from the shoulders to the legs. Any serious backpacking requires a pack of at least 4000 cubic inches (65 liters). Allow an additional 500 cubic inches for your sleeping bag in internal-frame packs. Sturdy backpacks cost anywhere from $125-420. This is one area where it doesn't pay to economize—cheaper packs may be less comfortable. Before you buy any pack, try it on and imagine carrying it, full, a few miles up a rocky incline. Better yet, insist on filling it with something heavy and walking around the store to get a sense of how it distributes weight before committing to buy it. Either purchase a **waterproof pack cover** or plan to store all of your belongings in plastic bags inside your backpack.

Daypack: In addition to your main vessel, a small daypack is useful for sight-seeing expeditions or day-hikes, and can double as an airplane carry-on.

Boots: Be sure to wear hiking boots with good **ankle support** which are appropriate for the terrain you plan to hike. **Gore-Tex** fabric or **part-leather** boots are appropriate for day-hikes or 2-3 day overnights over moderate terrain, but for longer trips or trips in mountainous terrain, stiff **leather** boots are highly preferable. Your boots should fit snugly and comfortably over one or two wool socks and a thin liner sock. Breaking in boots is crucial and requires wearing them for several weeks; doing so will spare you from painful and debilitating blisters. You will be glad you **waterproofed** your boots.

Other Necessities: Raingear in two pieces, a top and pants, is far superior to a poncho. **Synthetics,** like polypropylene tops, socks, and long underwear, along with a pile jacket, will keep you warm even when wet. When camping in autumn, winter, or spring, bring along a lightweight thin foil **"space blanket,"** which helps you to retain your body heat ($5-15). Plastic **canteens** or water bottles keep water cooler than metal ones. Large, collapsible **water sacks** will significantly improve your lot in primitive campgrounds and weigh practically nothing when empty. Bring **water-purification tablets** for when you can't boil water, or shell out for a water-purification system. Most campgrounds provide fire rings; you may want to bring a small **metal grate** or **grill.** Rain and park restrictions will make you glad you brought a **camp stove.** The classic propane-powered Coleman stove starts at about $40; the more expensive **Whisperlite** stoves ($60-100), which run on cleaner-burning white gas, are more expensive but much lighter and more versatile. A **first aid kit, swiss army knife, insect repellent, calamine lotion,** and **waterproof matches** or a **lighter** also make the list.

The mail-order/online companies listed below offer lower prices than many retail stores, but a visit to a local camping or outdoors store will give you a good sense of items' feel and weight.

Mountain Equipment Co-op Mail Order, 130 W. Broadway, Vancouver, BC, Canada V5Y 1P3. (800-722-1960 or 604-876-6590; www.mec.ca). Free catalogue. High quality, reasonably-priced outerwear, and camping gear. Catalogue and gear tips online.

Recreational Equipment, Inc. (REI), Sumner, WA 98352 (800-426-4840 or 253-891-2500; www.rei.com).

Campmor, P.O. Box 700, Upper Saddle River, NJ 07458-0700 (888-226-7667, outside U.S. call 201-825-8300; www.campmor.com).

Discount Camping, 880 Main North Rd., Pooraka, South Australia 5095, Australia (tel. (08) 8262 3399; fax 8260 6240; www.discountcamping.com.au).

Mountain Designs, P.O. Box 1472, Fortitude Valley, Queensland 4006, Australia (tel. (07) 3252 8894; fax 3252 4569; www.mountaindesign.com.au).

YHA Adventure Shop, 14 Southampton St., London, WC2E 7HA, U.K. (tel. (020) 7836 8541). The main branch of one of Britain's largest outdoor equipment suppliers.

WILDERNESS SAFETY

Stay warm, stay dry, and stay hydrated. The vast majority of life-threatening wilderness situations result from a breach of these simple rules. On any hike, however brief, you should pack enough equipment to keep you alive should disaster befall. This includes **raingear, hat** and **mittens,** a **first-aid kit,** a **reflector,** a **whistle, high energy food,** and extra **water.** Dress in warm layers of **synthetic materials** designed for the outdoors, or **wool.** Pile fleece jackets and Gore-Tex raingear are excellent choices. Never rely on **cotton** for warmth. This "death cloth" will be absolutely useless should it get wet. Make sure to check all equipment for any defects before setting out, and see **Camping and Hiking Equipment,** above, for more information.

Check **weather forecasts** and pay attention to the skies when hiking. Weather patterns can change suddenly. *Always* let someone know when and where you are going hiking and when you plan to return: either a friend, your hostel, a park ranger, or a local hiking organization. Do not attempt a hike beyond your ability— you may be endangering your life. Err even further on the side of caution in climates and terrains that are unfamiliar to you. See **Health,** p. 32 for information about outdoor ailments such as heatstroke, hypothermia, giardia, rabies, and insects, as well as basic medical concerns and first-aid.

BEAR SAFETY. If you are hiking in an area which might be frequented by bears, ask local rangers for information on bear activity before entering any park or wilderness area, and obey posted warnings. Bears are curious, intelligent, and potentially dangerous, and most tend to avoid people, given the chance. Be sure to **let bears know you are near:** make noise by singing, talking loudly, or attaching a bell to your pack, especially in areas where visibility is limited. If you can, walk with the wind at your back so that your scent will precede you.

Bears are always looking for something to eat to help make up for the 40% of their body weight they lose each year while hibernating. **Cook away from your tent,** and keep a clean camp. Don't leave food or other scented items (trash, toiletries, the clothes that you cooked in) near your tent. **Hang food and garbage out of reach** of bears (called bear-bagging) when possible, or use bear-resistant containers.

Bears are also attracted to perfume, as are bugs, so cologne, scented soap, and deodorant should stay at home.

If you encounter a bear at a distance, walk calmly in the other direction. Most bears are interested only in protecting food, cubs, or their personal space. If you run into a bear at a close distance, or if a bear notices you, remain calm; attacks are rare. **Identify yourself as human** by talking to the bear in a normal voice and waving your arms. If the bear cannot tell what you are, it may approach or stand on its hind legs to get a better look. A standing bear is usually just curious. **Don't run.** You can't outrun a bear, and bears, like dogs, will chase fleeing animals. Bears often make bluff charges, sometimes to within 10 feet of their adversary. If a bear gets too close, raise your voice or bang pots and pans. If you stumble upon a sweet-looking bear cub, leave the area immediately lest its protective mother stumbles upon you. If you are attacked by a bear, **surrender!** Get in a fetal position to protect yourself, put your arms over the back of your neck, and play dead. Remain motionless for as long as possible, since a bear may renew its attack if it again perceives you as a threat. Very rarely, a bear may perceive a person as food. If a bear continues biting you long after you assume a defensive posture, it likely is a predatory attack and you should fight back.

AVALANCHE SAFETY. Winter backcountry travelers must be familiar with highly technical **avalanche** safety procedures; avalanche risk can not be "eyeballed." Taking a good course in route-finding, risk assessment, and rescue is imperative before setting out into avalanche country. Commercial ski resorts have avalanche experts who deal with avalanche danger by using projectile explosives or by closing off areas of the mountain. Don't second-guess them by slipping under ropes, as avalanches kill every year. The Canadian Avalanche Association (www.avalanche. ca) reports twice per week on backcountry avalanche conditions in BC and their web site has links to reports for national parks in the Rockies. The Northwest Weather and Avalanche Center (www.nwac.noaa.gov) reports on Washington and Oregon. Recorded reports are available for Western Canada (800-667-1105), Washington (206-526-6677), and Oregon (503-808-2400).

KEEPING IN TOUCH

MAIL

> **POSTAL ABBREVIATIONS.** All states, provinces and territories have two-letter postal abbreviations. Oregon's is **OR,** Washington's **WA,** and Alaska's is **AK.** Alberta's is **AB,** British Columbia's **BC,** and the Yukon Territory's is **YT.**

U.S. MAIL. Offices of the **U.S. Postal Service** are usually open Monday to Friday from 9am to 5pm and sometimes on Saturday until about the early afternoon; branches in larger cities open earlier and close later. All are closed on Sundays and national holidays. Most U.S. Post offices no longer have a local phone number. Instead, a toll free number, 800-ASK-USPS/275-8777 connects to operators who dispense information on branch hour and postal rates. **Postcards** mailed within the U.S. cost 20¢; letters cost 33¢ for the first ounce and 23¢ for each additional ounce. To send mail to Canada from the U.S., it costs 45¢ to mail a postcard, and 55¢ to mail a 1 oz. letter. The U.S. Postal Service requires that **overseas** letters be mailed directly from the post office and be accompanied by a customs form. **Overseas rates** are postcards 50¢, ½ oz. 60¢, 1 oz. $1, 40¢ per additional ounce. **Aerogrammes,** sheets that fold into envelopes and travel via air mail to any country, are available at post offices for 60¢. Domestic mail generally takes three to five days; overseas mail, seven to 14 days. Write **AIR MAIL** on the envelope for speediest delivery.

All U.S. addresses are assigned a five- or nine-digit **ZIP Code.** Writing the ZIP Code on letters is essential for delivery. The normal form of address is as follows:

Boris R. O'Bot
123 Wise Avenue, Apt. #456 (address, apartment # if applicable)
Olympia, WA 98501 (city, state, ZIP Code)
USA (country, if mailing internationally)

CANADIAN MAIL. In **Canada,** mailing a letter (or a postcard, which carries the same rate as a letter) to the U.S. costs 55¢ for the first 30g and 80¢ for 31-50g. To every other foreign country, a 20g letter costs 95¢, a 50g letter $1.45, and a 51-100g letter $2.35. The domestic rate is 46¢ for a 30g letter, and 73¢ for a letter between 31g and 50g. Letters take from seven to ten days to reach the U.S. and about two weeks to get to an overseas address by air. (All prices in CDN$)

In Canada, **postal codes** are the equivalent of U.S. ZIP Codes and contain alternating letters and numbers (for example, L9H 3M6). The normal form of address is nearly identical to that in the U.S.; the only difference is that the apartment or suite number can *precede* the street address along with a dash. For example, 3-203 Colborne St. refers to Room or Apartment #3 at 203 Colborne St.

GENERAL DELIVERY AND OTHER SERVICES. Depending on how neurotic/loving your family and friends are, consider making arrangements for them to get in touch with you by post. Mail can be sent **general delivery** to a city's main branch of the post office. Once a letter arrives, it will be held for at least 10 days; it can be held for longer if such a request is clearly indicated by you or on the front of the envelope. Customers must bring a passport or other ID to pick up General Delivery mail. Family and friends can send letters labeled like so:

Eric R. HOWDOYOUDO (underline and capitalize last name for accurate filing)
General Delivery
Main Post Office
Vancouver, BC V1L 2M6
CANADA

American Express offices throughout the U.S. and Canada will act as a mail service for cardholders if you contact them in advance. Under this free **"Client Letter Service,"** they will hold mail for 30 days, forward upon request, and accept telegrams. The last name of the person to whom the mail is addressed should be capitalized and underlined. Some offices will offer these services to non-cardholders (especially those who have purchased AmEx traveler's checks), but you must call ahead to make sure. A complete list is available free from AmEx (800-528-4800) in the booklet *Traveler's Companion* or online at www.americanexpress.com.

If regular airmail is too slow, there are a few faster, more expensive, options. **Federal Express** (800-463-3339) is a reliable private courier service that guarantees overnight delivery anywhere in the continental U.S., at a significant price. The cheaper but more sluggish U.S. Postal Service **Express Mail** takes two days to deliver a parcel. Canada Post offers **Priority Courier** (next day delivery), **XPress Post,** and **SkyPak** for destinations in the U.S. and other countries. Rates vary by destination and weight, but are generally cheaper than private couriers.

TELEPHONES

CALLING THE U.S. OR CANADA FROM HOME
To call direct to the U.S. or Canada from home, dial:
   1. The international access code of your home country. **International access codes** include: Australia 0011; Ireland 00; New Zealand 00; South Africa 09; U.K. 00. Country and city codes are sometimes listed with a zero in front (e.g., 033) but after dialing the international access code, drop successive zeros (with an access code of 011, e.g., 011 33).
   2. 1 (The U.S. and Canada's country code).

3. The area code and local number.

See the end of the **Practical Information** section of each town described in this book for the area code, or consult the inside of this book's back cover.

CALLING HOME FROM THE U.S. OR CANADA

A **calling card** is probably your best and cheapest bet since long-distance rates for national phone services can be exorbitant; especially be careful of making long-distance calls from hotel or motel room phones, which often charge exorbitant access fees. Calling card calls are billed either collect or to your account. **MCI WorldPhone** also provides access to MCI's Traveler's Assist, which gives legal and medical advice, exchange rate information, and translation services. Other phone companies provide similar services to travelers. **To obtain a calling card** from your national telecommunications service before leaving home, contact the appropriate company below:

> **Australia,** Telstra **Australia Direct** (tel. 13 22 00); **Canada,** Bell Canada **Canada Direct** (800-565-4708); **Ireland,** Telecom Éireann **Ireland Direct** (tel. (800) 250 250); **New Zealand, Telecom New Zealand** (tel. 0800 000 000); **South Africa, Telkom South Africa,** (tel. 09 03); **U.K.,** British Telecom **BT Direct** (tel. (0800) 34 51 44); **USA, AT&T** (888-288-4685), **Sprint** (800-877-4646), or **MCI** (800-444-4141; from abroad dial the country's MCI access number).

To call home with a calling card, contact a North American operator for your service provider by dialing **Australia Direct: AT&T** 800-682-2878, **MCI** 800-937-6822, **Sprint** 800-676-0061; **BT Direct: AT&T** 800-445-5667, **MCI** 800-444-2162, **Sprint** 800-800-0008; **Telkom South Africa Direct:** 800-949-7027.

If you do dial direct, first insert the appropriate amount of money or a prepaid card, then dial 011 (the international access code for the U.S.), and then dial the country code and number of the phone number in your home country. **Country codes** include: Australia 61; Ireland 353; New Zealand 64; South Africa 27; U.K. 44. The expensive alternative to dialing direct or using a calling card is using an international operator to place a **collect call.**

CALLING WITHIN THE U.S. AND CANADA

The simplest way to call within the country is to use a coin-operated phone; local calls in the U.S. and Canada cost 25-35¢ and require coins. You can also buy **prepaid phone cards,** which carry phone time depending on the card's denomination and are available at most convenience stores and gas stations. The card usually has a toll-free access phone number and a personal identification number (PIN). Phone rates tend to be highest during the day, lower in the evening, and lowest on Sunday and late at night. Be warned: hotels tend to charge exorbitant long distance rates and 50¢-$1 for local calls.

Calls between Canada and the U.S. are not considered international calls. Dial them as you would a domestic long distance call: 1-(area code)-number. Numbers with area codes 800, 888, and 877 are **toll-free numbers,** even from pay phones. Many of these numbers only operate within a particular state or province.

To obtain local phone numbers or area codes of other cities, call **directory assistance** at 411, a free call from pay phones. For long-distance directory assistance dial 1-(area code)-555-1212.

EMAIL

With a minimum of computer knowledge and a little planning, users can beam messages anywhere for no per-message charges through **electronic mail** (known as **email**). Many web-based email providers will give you a free private account, including **Hotmail** (www.hotmail.com) and **Yahoo** (www.mail.yahoo.com). *Let's Go* lists public access points (cybercafes, libraries) for the Internet in the **Practical Information** sections of all listings. A list of **cybercafes** around the world is maintained at www.cyberiacafe.net/cyberia/guide/ccafe.htm.

GETTING THERE

BY PLANE

When it comes to airfare, a little effort can save you a bundle. If your plans are flexible enough to deal with the restrictions, courier fares are the cheapest. Tickets bought from consolidators and standby seating are also good deals, but last-minute specials, airfare wars, and charter flights often beat these fares. The key is to hunt around, to be flexible, and to persistently ask about discounts. Students, seniors, and those under 26 should never pay full price for a ticket.

BUDGET AND STUDENT TRAVEL AGENCIES

A knowledgeable agent can make your life easy and help you save, too, but agents may not spend the time to find you the lowest possible fare—they get paid on commission. Students and under-26ers holding **ISIC and IYTC cards** (see **Identification,** p. 25) qualify for big discounts from student travel agencies. Most flights from budget agencies are on major airlines, but in peak season some may sell seats on less reliable chartered aircraft.

Campus/Usit Youth and Student Travel (www.usitcampus.co.uk). Offices include: 19-21 Aston Quay, O'Connell Bridge, **Dublin** 2 (tel. (01) 677-8117; fax 679-8833); 52 Grosvenor Gardens, **London** SW1W 0AG (tel. (020) 7730 3402); New York Student Center, 895 Amsterdam Ave., **New York,** NY 10025 (212-663-5435; usitny@aol.com). Also in Cork, Galway, Limerick, Waterford, Derry, Belfast, and Greece.

Council Travel (www.counciltravel.com). U.S. offices include: Emory Village, 1561 N. Decatur Rd., **Atlanta,** GA 30307 (404-377-9997); 273 Newbury St., **Boston,** MA 02116 (617-266-1926); 1160 N. State St., **Chicago,** IL 60610 (312-951-0585); 10904 Lindbrook Dr., **Los Angeles,** CA 90024 (310-208-3551); 205 E. 42nd St., **New York,** NY 10017 (212-822-2700); 530 Bush St., **San Francisco,** CA 94108 (415-421-3473); 1314 NE 43rd St. #210, **Seattle,** WA 98105 (206-632-2448); 3300 M St. NW, **Washington, D.C.** 20007 (202-337-6464). **For U.S. cities not listed,** call 800-2-COUNCIL (226-8624). Also 28A Poland St. (Oxford Circus), **London,** W1V 3DB (tel. (020) 7287 3337), **Paris** (tel. 01 44 41 89 89), and **Munich** (tel. (089) 39 50 22).

CTS Travel, 44 Goodge St., W1 (tel. (020) 7636 00 31; fax 637 53 28; ctsinfo@ctstravel.com.uk).

STA Travel, 6560 Scottsdale Rd. #F100, Scottsdale, AZ 85253 (800-777-0112 fax 602-922-0793; www.sta-travel.com). A student and youth travel organization with over 150 offices worldwide. Ticket booking, travel insurance, railpasses, and more. U.S. offices include: 297 Newbury Street, **Boston,** MA 02115 (617-266-6014); 429 S. Dearborn St., **Chicago,** IL 60605 (312-786-9050); 7202 Melrose Ave., **Los Angeles,** CA 90046 (323-934-8722); 10 Downing St., **New York,** NY 10014 (212-627-3111); 4341 University Way NE, **Seattle,** WA 98105 (206-633-5000); 2401 Pennsylvania Ave., Ste. G, **Washington, D.C.** 20037 (202-887-0912); 51 Grant Ave., **San Francisco,** CA 94108 (415-391-8407). In the U.K., 6 Wrights Ln., **London** W8 6TA (tel. (020) 7938 47 11 for North American travel). In New Zealand, 10 High St., **Auckland** (tel. (09) 309 04 58). In Australia, 222 Faraday St., **Melbourne** VIC 3053 (tel. (03) 9349 2411).

Travel CUTS (Canadian Universities Travel Services Limited), 187 College St., Toronto, Ont. M5T 1P7 (416-979-2406; fax 979-8167; www.travelcuts.com). 40 offices across Canada. Also in the U.K., 295-A Regent St., **London** W1R 7YA (tel. (020) 7255 19 44).

Other organizations that specialize in finding cheap fares include:

Cheap Tickets (800-377-1000) flies worldwide to and from the U.S.

Travel Avenue (800-333-3335) rebates commercial fares to or from the U.S. and offers low fares for flights anywhere in the world. They also offer package deals, which include car rental and hotel reservations, to many destinations.

ESSENTIALS

COMMERCIAL AIRLINES

The commercial airlines' lowest regular offer is the **APEX** (Advance Purchase Excursion) fare, which provides confirmed reservations and allows "open-jaw" tickets. Generally, reservations must be made 7 to 21 days in advance, with 7- to 14-day minimum and up to 90-day maximum-stay limits, and hefty cancellation and change penalties (fees rise in summer). Book peak-season APEX fares early, since by May you will have a hard time getting the departure date you want.

Although APEX fares are probably not the cheapest possible fares, they will give you a sense of the average commercial price, from which to measure other bargains. Specials advertised in newspapers may be cheaper but have more restrictions and fewer available seats.

WITHIN NORTH AMERICA

Many U.S. and Canadian airlines offer special passes and fares to international travelers. You must purchase these passes outside of North America, paying one price for a certain number of flight vouchers. A voucher is good for one flight on an airline's domestic system; typically, travel must be completed within 30 to 60 days. The point of departure and destination for each coupon must be specified at the time of purchase, but travel dates may be changed during your trip, often at no extra charge. **America West Air, US Airways, United, Continental, Delta,** and **TWA** all sell vouchers. Call the airlines for specifics. TWA's **Youth Travel Pak** offers a similar deal (4 one-way flight coupons for $550) to students ages 14-24, including North Americans. **Canada 3000** (see below) flies cheaply between Whitehorse, YT; Anchorage, AK; Victoria, and Vancouver, BC; and Calgary, AB.

Air Canada, (888-247-2262 or 604-688-5515; www.aircanada.ca). Discounts for ages 12-24 on standby tickets for flights within Canada.

Alaska Airlines, (800-426-0333; www.alaskaairlines.com).

America West Air, (800-235-9292; www.americawest.com).

American Airlines, (800-433-7300; www.americanair.com).

Canada 3000, (888-226-3000 or 416-259-1118; www.canada3000.ca)

Canadian Airlines, (in Canada 800-665-1177, in U.S. 800-426-7000; or 250-624-9181; www.cdnair.ca).

Continental Airlines, (800-525-0280; www.flycontinental.com).

Delta Airlines, (800-241-4141; www.delta-air.com).

Northwest Airlines, (800-225-2525; www.nwa.com).

TWA, (800-221-2000; www.twa.com).

United Airlines, (800-241-6522; www.ual.com).

US Airways, (800-428-4322; www.usair.com).

FROM EUROPE

European travelers will experience the least competition for inexpensive seats during the off season, but "off season" need not mean the dead of winter. Peak-season rates generally take effect from mid-May until mid-September. If you can, take advantage of cheap off-season flights within Europe to reach an advantageous point of departure for North America. (London is a major connecting point for budget flights to the U.S.; New York City is often the destination.) Once in the States, you can catch a coast-to-coast flight to make your way out West; see **Within North America,** above.

If you decide to fly with a commercial airline rather than through a charter agency or ticket consolidator (see below), you'll be purchasing greater reliability, security, and flexibility. Many major airlines offer reduced-fare options, such as three-day advance purchase fares: these tickets can only be purchased within 72 hours of the time of the departure, and are restricted to youths under a certain age (often 24). Check with a travel agent for availability. Seat availability is known only a few days before the flight, although predictions are sometimes issued.

FROM ASIA, AFRICA, AND AUSTRALIA

While European travelers may choose from a variety of regular reduced fares, Asian, Australian, and African travelers must rely on APEX (see p. 24). A good place to start searching for tickets is the local branch of an international budget travel agency (see **Budget Travel Agencies,** p. 23). **STA Travel,** with offices in Sydney, Melbourne, and Auckland, is probably the largest international agency around.

Qantas, United, and **Northwest** fly between Australia or New Zealand and the U.S. Advance purchase fares from Australia have extremely tough restrictions. If you are uncertain about your plans, pay extra for an advance purchase ticket that has only a 50% penalty for cancellation. Many travelers from Australia and New Zealand take **Singapore Air** or other East Asian carriers for the initial leg of their trip. **South African Airways, American,** and **Northwest** connect South Africa with North America.

OTHER CHEAP ALTERNATIVES

AIR COURIER FLIGHTS

Couriers help transport cargo on international flights by guaranteeing delivery of the baggage claim slips from the company to a representative overseas. Generally, couriers must travel light (carry-ons only) and deal with complex restrictions on their flight. Most flights are round-trip only with short fixed-length stays (usually one week) and a limit of a single ticket per issue. Most of these flights also operate only out of the biggest cities, like New York. Generally, you must be over 21 (in some cases 18), have a valid passport, and procure your own visa, if necessary. Groups such as the **Air Courier Association** (800-282-1202; www.aircourier.org) and the **International Association of Air Travel Couriers,** 220 South Dixie Hwy., P.O. Box 1349, Lake Worth, FL 33460 (561-582-8320; www.courier.org) provide their members with lists of opportunities and courier brokers worldwide for an annual fee. For more information, consult *Air Courier Bargains*, by Kelly Monaghan (The Intrepid Traveler; $15) or the *Courier Air Travel Handbook*, by Mark Field (Perpetual Press; $10).

CHARTER FLIGHTS

Charters are flights a tour operator contracts with an airline to fly extra loads of passengers during peak season. Charters can sometimes be cheaper than flights on scheduled airlines, some operate nonstop, and restrictions on minimum advance-purchase and minimum stay are more lenient. However, charter flights fly less frequently than major airlines, make refunds particularly difficult, and are almost always fully booked. Schedules and itineraries may also change or be cancelled at the last moment (as late as 48 hours before the trip, and without a full refund), and check-in, boarding, and baggage claim are often much slower. As always, pay with a credit card if you can, and consider traveler's insurance against trip interruption. **Discount clubs** and **fare brokers** offer members savings on last-minute charter and tour deals. Study their contracts closely; you don't want to end up with an unwanted overnight layover.

STANDBY FLIGHTS

To travel standby, you will need considerable flexibility in the dates and cities of your arrival and departure. Companies that specialize in standby flights don't sell tickets but rather the promise that you will get to your destination (or near your destination) within a certain window of time (anywhere from 1-5 days). You may only receive a refund if all available flights which depart within your date-range from the specified region are full, but future travel credit is always available.

Carefully read agreements with any company offering standby flights, as tricky fine print can leave you in the lurch. To check on a company's service record, call the Better Business Bureau of New York City (212-533-6200). It is difficult to receive refunds, and clients' vouchers will not be honored when an airline fails to receive payment in time.

Airhitch, has offices in New York City (800-326-2009 or 212-864-2000; www.airhitch.org) and in Los Angeles (310-726-5000). In Europe, the flagship office is in Paris (tel. 1 47 00 16 30) and the other one is in Amsterdam (tel. 31 20 626 32 20).

BY TRAIN

Locomotion is still one of the cheapest (and most pleasant) ways to tour the U.S. and Canada, but keep in mind that discounted air travel may be cheaper, and much faster, than train travel. As with airlines, you can save money by purchasing your tickets as far in advance as possible, so plan ahead and make reservations early. It is essential to travel light on trains; not all stations will check your baggage.

Amtrak (800-USA-RAIL/872-7245; www.amtrak.com) is the only provider of inter-city passenger train service in most of the U.S. Most cities have Amtrak offices, but tickets must be bought through an agent in some small towns. Their informative web page lists schedules, fares, arrival and departure info, and takes reservations. **Discounts** on full rail fares are given to: senior citizens (15% off), students with a Student Advantage card (15% off; call 800-96-AMTRAK/962-2627 to purchase the $20 card), travelers with disabilities (15% off), children ages 2-15 accompanied by an adult (50% off), children under 2 (free), and members of the U.S. armed forces, active-duty veterans, and their dependents (25% off). "Rail SALE" offers online discounts of up to 90%; visit the Amtrak web site for details and reservations. Amtrak also offers some **special packages:**

Air-Rail Vacations: Amtrak and United Airlines allow you to travel in 1 direction by train and return by plane, or to fly to a distant point and return home by train. The train portion of the journey can last up to 30 days and include up to 3 stopovers. A multitude of variations are available; call 800-437-3441.

North America Rail Pass: A 30-day pass offered in conjunction with Canada's VIA Rail which allows unlimited travel and unlimited stops throughout the U.S. and Canada for 30 consecutive days; $645 during peak season (June 1-Oct. 15) and $450 during off season. A 15-day Northeastern North America Pass is available to international residents only; $400 during peak season, $300 off-season.

VIA Rail, P.O. Box 8116, Station A, Montréal, QC H3C 3N3 (800-842-7733; www.viarail.ca), is Amtrak's Canadian equivalent. **Discounts** on full fares are given to: students with ISIC card and youths under 24 (40% off full fare); seniors 60 and over (10% off); ages 2-15, accompanied by an adult (50% off); and children under 2 (free on the lap of an adult). Reservations are required for first-class seats and sleep car accommodations. "Supersaver" fares offer discounts of up to 50%. The **Canrail Pass** allows unlimited travel on 12 days within a 30-day period on VIA trains. Between early June and mid-October, a 12-day pass costs CDN$589 (seniors and youths under 24 CDN$529). Off-season passes cost CDN$379 (seniors and youths CDN$345). Add CDN$29-50 for additional days of travel. Call for information on seasonal promotions such as discounts on Grayline Sightseeing Tours.

The **Alaska Railroad Corporation (ARRC),** (800-544-0552; fax 907-265-2323; www.akrr.com) covers 470 miles of track once per day in each direction from mid-May to mid-September, connecting Seward and Whittier in the south with Anchorage, Denali National Park, and Fairbanks. Children under 11 travel for 50% off. See specific locations in this guide for fares, details, and additional rail options. A weekly winter train is planned for 1999-2000.

BY BUS

Buses generally offer the most frequent and complete service between the cities and towns of the U.S. and Canada. Often a bus is the only way to reach smaller locales without a car. Laidlaw, the company that owns Greyhound Canada, acquired Greyhound USA in 1999. As of the summer of 1999, North America-wide specials have already begun to appear. *Russell's Official National Motor Coach*

Guide ($15.70 including postage) is an invaluable tool for constructing an itinerary. Updated each month, *Russell's Guide* has schedules of every bus route (including Greyhound) between any two towns in the United States and Canada. Russell's also publishes two semiannual *Supplements* which are free when ordered with the main issue; a Directory of Bus Lines and Bus Stations, and a series of Route Maps (both $8.40 if ordered separately). To order any of the above, write Russell's Guides, Inc., P.O. Box 278, Cedar Rapids, IA 52406 (319-364-6138; fax 364-4853).

GREYHOUND

Greyhound (800-231-2222; www.greyhound.com) operates the most routes in the U.S., but does not serve Alaska. Schedule information is available at any Greyhound terminal, on their web page, or by calling them toll-free. Reserve with a credit card over the phone at least 10 days in advance, and the ticket can be mailed anywhere in the U.S. Otherwise, reservations are available only up to 24-hours in advance. You can buy your ticket at the terminal, but arrive early.

If **boarding at a remote "flag stop,"** be sure you know exactly where the bus stops. You must call the nearest agency and let them know you'll be waiting and at what time. Catch the driver's attention by standing on the side of the road and waving. If a bus passes (usually because of overcrowding), a later, less-crowded bus should stop. Whatever you stow in compartments underneath the bus should be clearly marked; be sure to get a claim check for it and watch to make sure your luggage is on the same bus as you.

Advance purchase fares: Reserving space far ahead of time ensures a lower fare, although expect a smaller discount during the busy summer months (June 5-Sept. 15). For tickets purchased more than 7 days in advance, the one-way fare anywhere in the U.S. will not exceed $79, while the round-trip price is capped at $158 (from June-Sept., the one-way cap is $89 and the round-trip $178). Fares are often reduced even more for 14-day or 21-day advance purchases on many popular routes; call the 800 number for up to the date pricing, or consult the user-friendly web page.

Discounts on full fares: Senior citizens (10% off); children ages 2-11 (50% off); travelers with disabilities and special needs and their companions ride together for the price of one. Active and retired U.S. military personnel and National Guard Reserves (10% off with valid ID) and their spouses and dependents may take a round-trip between any 2 points in the U.S. for $169. With a ticket purchased 3 or more days in advance, a friend can travel along for free; during the summer months, if purchased 7 days in advance, the free-loadin' friend gets half off.

Ameripass: Call 888-GLI-PASS (454-7277). Allows adults unlimited travel for 7 days ($199), 15 days ($299), 30 days ($409), or 60 days ($549). Prices for students with a valid college ID and for senior citizens are slightly less: 7 days ($189), 15 days ($279), 30 days ($379), or 60 days ($509). Children's passes are half the price of adults. The pass takes effect the first day used. Before purchasing an Ameripass, total up the separate bus fares between towns to make sure that the pass is really more economical, or at least worth the unlimited flexibility it provides.

International Ameripass: For travelers from outside North America. A 7-day pass is $179, 15-day pass $269, 30-day pass $369, 60-day pass $499. Call 888-GLI-PASS (454-7277) for info. International Ameripasses are not available at the terminal; they can be purchased in foreign countries at Greyhound-affiliated agencies; telephone numbers vary by country and are listed on the web page. Passes can also be ordered at the web page, or purchased in Greyhound's International Office, in Port Authority Bus Station, 625 Eighth Ave., New York, NY 10018 (800-246-8572 or 212-971-0492; fax 402-330-0919; intlameripass@greyhound.com). **Australia:** 049 342 088. **New Zealand:** (64) 9 479 65555. **South Africa:** (27) 11 331 2911. **United Kingdom:** (44) 01342 317 317.

GREYHOUND CANADA

Greyhound Canada (800-661-8747 or 403-265-9111; www.greyhound.ca) is Canada's main intercity bus company. Their web site has full schedule information.

Discounts: Seniors (10% off); students with ISIC cards (25% off); a companion of a disabled person free; ages 3-7 50%; under 3 free. If reservations are made 7 days or more in advance, a friend travels half-off. A child under 16 rides free with an adult if reserved 7 days in advance.

Canada Pass: Offers unlimited travel on all Greyhound, Vancouver Island Coach, and Maverick routes, including limited links to northern U.S. cities, including Seattle. 7-day advance purchase required, but will be waived for those who can show they have just gotten off a plane. 10-day pass CDN\$246; 20-day pass CDN\$385; 40-day pass CDN\$450; 80-day pass CDN\$572.

GREEN TORTOISE

Green Tortoise, 494 Broadway, San Francisco, CA 94133 (415-956-7500 or 800-867-8647; www.greentortoise.com), offers a more slow-paced, whimsical alternative to straightforward bus travel. Green Tortoise's communal "hostels on wheels"—remodeled diesel buses done up for living and eating on the road—traverse the United States on their Adventure Tours. Prices include transportation, sleeping space on the bus, and tours of the regions through which you pass, often including such treats as hot springs and farm stays. Meals are prepared communally, and incur an additional food charge. An "alternative commuter" service runs between Seattle, WA and San Francisco, CA, passing through central Oregon. (\$59; southbound Sunday and Thursday, northbound Monday and Friday.) Round-trip vacation loops start in San Francisco, winding through Yosemite National Park, Northern California, Baja California, or the Grand Canyon. The grand Alaska extravaganza takes 28 days to work up from S.F. to the huge, wide open (\$1500 plus \$250 for food; includes return airfare). Prepare for an earthy trip; buses have no toilets and little privacy. Reserve one to two months in advance. Deposits (\$100) are generally required; however, many trips have space available at departure. Reservations can be made over the phone or on the Internet.

BY CAR

Before you leave, tune up the car, pack an easy-to-read repair manual and a compass, and learn a bit about minor automobile maintenance and repair—it may help you keep your car alive long enough to reach a garage. Always carry: a **spare tire** and **jack, jumper cables, extra oil, extra engine belts, road flares,** a **flashlight,** and, in case you break down at night or in winter, **safety candles, matches,** and **blankets.** In summer, carry extra **water** for you and your radiator. In extremely hot weather, use the air conditioner with restraint; turning the heater on full blast will help cool the engine. If radiator fluid is steaming, turn off the car for 30 minutes—never pour water over the engine to cool it.

If you plan to drive in snow, you should also carry a **shovel, traction mats** (burlap sacks or car floor mats make a good substitute in a bind), and **sand** or **kitty litter.**

Carry emergency **food and water** if there's a chance you may be stranded in a remote area. Always have plenty of **gas** and check road conditions ahead of time when possible, (see **Road Conditions,** below) particularly during winter. The enormous travel distances of North America will require more gas than you might at first expect. To burn less fuel, make sure your tires have enough air, and use the air-conditioner with restraint.

Sleeping in a vehicle parked on the highway or in the city is extremely dangerous—even the most dedicated budget traveler should not consider it an option. Be sure to **buckle up**—seat belts are required by law in almost every region of the U.S. and Canada. The **speed limit in the U.S.** varies considerably from region to region and road to road. Most urban highways have a limit of 55 miles per hour (88km/hr.), while the limit on rural routes ranges from 60-80 mph (97-128km/hr.). The **speed limit in Canada** is generally 50km/hr. in cities and towns, and 80-110km/hr. (50-68 mph) on highways.

In the 1950s, U.S. President Dwight "Ike" Eisenhower began the **interstate system,** a federally funded highway network. There is a simple system for numbering interstates. Even-numbered interstates run east-west, and odd ones run north-south, decreasing in number toward the south and west. If the interstate has a three-digit number, it is a branch of another interstate (i.e., I-285 is a branch of I-85) and is often a bypass skirting around a large city. An even digit in the hundreds place means the branch will eventually return to the main interstate; an odd digit means it won't.

ROAD CONDITIONS. Both **Oregon** (800-977-6368 or 503-588-2941; www.odot.state.or.us/travel/) and **Washington** (800-695-7623 or 206-368-4499; www.smarttrek.org) have comprehensive web sites with live traffic cameras, and up–to-date reports on construction and snow conditions in mountain passes. In **British Columbia,** check the web site (www.th.gov.bc.ca/bchighways) or pay 75¢ per min. for recorded information (toll number 900-565-4997 or pay by credit card at 800-550-4997). In the **Yukon,** dial 867-667-8215.

A bird's nest of numbers report on Alaska's highways. For the Interior District, covering **the Alaska, Denali, Taylor, Dalton,** and **Elliott Highways** and the **Tok Cut-off** dial 907-456-7623. For conditions on the **Glenn Highway** from Anchorage to Mile 26.8, call 907-269-5700; Mile 26.8 to 118, call 907-745-2159; Mile 118 to Glenallen call 907-834-1017. For conditions on the **Richardson Highway** from Valdez to Paxson, call 907-835-4242; from Paxson to Fairbanks call 907-456-7623. For info on the **Seward Highway** from Anchorage to Mile 118, call 907-269-5700; from Mile 118 south to Seward 907-262-2199. For conditions on the **Sterling Highway,** call 907-262-2199; on the **Steese Highway** call 907-451-5204; and on the **Top of the World Highway** call 867-667-8215.

DRIVING PERMITS. If you do not have a license issued by a U.S. state or Canadian province or territory, it's a good idea to have an **International Driving Permit (IDP).** The IDP is only a translation of your license, and doesn't confer any driving privileges; it must always be presented along with a valid license. Your IDP, valid for one year, must be issued before you depart your own country, since IDPs are not valid in the country in which they're issued. To apply for an IDP, you must be 18 years old and provide one or two photos, a current local license, an additional form of identification, and a fee (usually the equivalent of $10). Contact the nearest office of the Automobile Association (Royal Automobile Club or National Royal Motorist Association in Australia) in your home country to apply.

AUTO CLUBS

Membership in an auto club, which provides free emergency road-side assistance 24 hours per day, is an important investment for anyone planning to drive on their vacation. AAA and CAA have reciprocal agreements, so a membership in either is good for road service in Canada, in the lower 48, and in Alaska.

American Automobile Association (AAA), (for emergency road service call 800-AAA-HELP/800-222-4357; www.aaa.com). Offers free trip-planning services, road maps and guidebooks, 24-hour emergency road service anywhere in the U.S., limited free towing, and commission-free traveler's checks from American Express with over 1,000 offices scattered across the country. Discounts on Hertz car rental (5-20%), Amtrak tickets (10%), and various motel chains and theme parks. AAA has reciprocal agreements with the auto associations of many other countries, which often provide you with full benefits while in the U.S. AAA has 2 types of memberships, basic and plus. Plus grants more free towing miles, a wise investment for those driving through wilderness. Memberships vary depending on which AAA branch you join, but hover between $50-60 for the first year and less for renewals and additional family members; call 800-JOIN-AAA/800-564-6222 to sign up.

Canadian Automobile Association (CAA), 1145 Hunt Club Rd. #200, Ottawa, ON K1V 0Y3 (800-CAA-HELP/(800-222-4357); www.caa.ca). Affiliated with AAA (see above), the CAA provides nearly identical membership benefits, including 24hr. emergency roadside assistance, free maps and tourbooks, route planning, and various discounts. Basic membership is CDN$66 and CDN$24 for associates; call 800-JOIN-CAA (800-564-6222) to sign up.

Mobil Auto Club, 200 N. Martingale Rd., Schaumbourg, IL 60174 (800-621-5581 for information; 800-323-5880 for emergency service). Benefits include locksmith reimbursement, towing (free up to 10mi.), roadside service, and car-rental discounts. $7 per month covers you and another driver.

RENTING

Although the cost of renting a car is often prohibitive for one-way trips between two cities, local trips may be reasonable. **Rental agencies** fall into two categories: national companies with hundreds of branches, and local agencies that serve one city or region.

National chains usually allow cars to be picked up in one city and dropped off in another (for a hefty charge, sometimes in excess of $1000); occasional promotions linked to coastal inventory imbalances may cut the fee dramatically. By calling a toll-free number, you can reserve a reliable car anywhere in the country. Generally, airport branches carry the cheapest rates. However, like airfares, car rental prices change constantly and often require scouting around for the best rate. Drawbacks include steep prices (a compact rents for about $35-45 per day) and high minimum ages for rentals (usually 25). Most branches rent to ages 21-24 with an additional fee, but policies and prices vary from agency to agency. If you're 21 or older and have a major credit card in your name, you may be able to rent where the minimum age would otherwise rule you out. **Alamo** (800-327-9633; www.goalamo.com) rents to ages 21-24 with a major credit card for an additional $20 per day. Some branches of **Budget** (800-527-0700) rent to drivers under 25 with a surcharge that varies by location. **Hertz** (800-654-3131; www.hertz.com) policy varies with city. **Enterprise** (800-Rent-A-Car/736-8222) rents to customers ages 21-24 with a variable surcharge. Most **Dollar** (800-800-4000; dollarcar.com) branches allow it, and various **Thrifty** (800-367-2277; www.thrifty.com) locations allow ages 21-24 to rent for an additional daily fee of about $20. **Rent-A-Wreck** (800-421-7253; www.rent-a-wreck.com), specializes in supplying vehicles that are past their prime for lower-than-average prices; a bare-bones compact less than eight years old rents for around $20 per day; cars, usually three to five years old, average under $25.

Most rental packages offer unlimited mileage, although some allow you a certain number of miles free before the usual charge of 25-40¢ per mile takes effect. Most quoted rates do not include gas or tax, so ask for the total cost before handing over the credit card; many large firms have added airport surcharges not covered by the designated fare. Return the car with a full tank unless you sign up for a fuel option plan that stipulates otherwise. And when dealing with any car rental company, be sure to ask whether the price includes **insurance** against theft and collision. There may be an additional charge for a collision and damage waiver (CDW), which usually comes to about $12-15 per day. Some major credit cards (including MasterCard and American Express) will cover the CDW if you use their card to rent a car; call your credit card company for specifics.

A cheaper rental option for large groups is **The Green Machine** (P.O. Box 573, Acton, CA 93510; 805-269-0360; fax 269-2835; gmachinetravel@hotmail.com; www.donbarnett.com/gmachine) which rents renovated school buses, equipped with camping gear, to groups with a driver 18 years or older. Starting at $350 per week, rental includes insurance and unlimited mileage.

AUTO TRANSPORT COMPANIES

These services match drivers with car owners who need cars moved from one city to another. Would-be travelers give the company their desired destination and the company finds a car which needs to go there. The only expenses are gas, tolls, and your own living expenses. Some companies insure their cars; with others, your security deposit covers any breakdowns or damage. You must be at least 21, have a valid license, and agree to drive about 400 miles per day on a fairly direct route. Companies regularly inspect current and past job references, take your fingerprints, and require a cash bond. Cars are available between most points, although it's easiest to find cars for traveling from coast to coast; New York and Los Angeles are popular transfer points. If offered a car, look it over first. Think twice about accepting a gas guzzler, since you'll be paying for the gas. With the company's approval, you may be able to share the cost with several companions.

Auto Driveaway Co., 310 S. Michigan Ave., Chicago, IL 60604 (800-346-2277 or 312-341-1900; fax 312-341-9100; www.autodriveaway.com).

Across America Driveaway, 3626 Calumet Ave., Hammond, IN 46320 (800-619-7707 or 219-852-0134; fax 800-334-6931; www.schultz-international.com). Other offices in L.A. (800-964-7874 or 310-798-3377) and Dallas (214-745-8892).

BY BICYCLE

Before you rush onto the byways of the Pacific Northwest, pedaling furiously away on your banana-seat Huffy Desperado, remember to make a few preparations. Bike **helmets** are required by law in most of the region, and are essential safety gear. Many bike rentals include a helmet. A good helmet will cost about $40 to buy; get help to ensure a correct fit. A white **headlight** and red **taillight** (and not just reflectors) are likewise both required and indispensable.

The Oregon Department of Transportation (www.odot.state.or.us/techserv/bikewalk/) publishes the *Bicyclist Manual*, a guide to sharing the road safely and legally with cars (available on the web), and the *Oregon Bicycling Guide* and *Oregon Coast Bike Route Map*, which outline bike-friendly routes and campgrounds. All are free and may be ordered by email (daryl.m.bonitz@state.or.us) or phone (503-986-3556). **Bicycle Gearing: A Practical Guide** ($9), available from The Mountaineers Books (see p. 42), discusses in lay terms how bicycle gears work, covering how to get maximum propulsion with minimum exertion. **Anybody's Bike Book** ($12 plus $4.50 shipping), available from Ten Speed Press, Box 7123, Berkeley, CA 94707 (800-841-2665; fax 510-559-1629; www.tenspeed.com), provides vital info on repair and maintenance during long-term rides.

Adventure Cycling Association, P.O. Box 8308-P, Missoula, MT 59807 (406-721-1776; fax 721-8754; www.adv-cycling.org). A national, nonprofit organization that maps long-distance routes and organizes bike tours for members. Membership $28 in the U.S., $35 in Canada and Mexico.

The Canadian Cycling Association, 1600 James Naismith Dr. #212A, Gloucester, ON K1B 5N4 (613-748-5629; fax 748-5692; www.canadian-cycling.com). Distributes maps and books like *The Canadian Cycling Association's Complete Guide to Bicycle Touring in Canada* (CDN$24), plus guides to specific regions of Canada, Alaska and the Pacific Coast. Also sells maps and books.

Backroads, 801 Cedar St., Berkeley, CA 94710-1800 (800-462-2848; fax 510-527-1444; www.backroads.com). Offers tours in 23 states, including Alaska and parts of British Columbia. Trips range from a weekend excursion ($299) to 9-day trips ($1098).

BY MOTORCYCLE

Motorcycling is cheaper and more romantic than driving a car, but it still demands planning. Those considering a journey should contact the **American Motorcyclist Association,** 33 Collegeview Rd., Westerville, OH 43801 (800-262-5646 or 614-891-2425; fax 891-5012; ama-cycle.org) or the **Canadian Motorcyclist Association,** Box 448, Hamilton, ON L8L AC4 (905-522-5705; fax 522-5716; www.niagara.com/~moto/cma). A membership ($29 per year) includes discounts on insurance, rentals, hotels, a subscription to *American Motorcyclist*, and a kick-ass patch. For another $25, members benefit from emergency roadside assistance, including pickup and delivery to a service shop.

Motorcycles are incredibly vulnerable to crosswinds, drunk drivers, and the blind spots of cars and trucks. *Always ride defensively.* Dangers skyrocket at night. Helmets are required by law in many states. Americans should ask their State's Department of Motor Vehicles for a motorcycle operator's manual. The AMA web page (see above) lists relevant laws and regulations for all 50 states.

BY FERRY

Along the Pacific Coast, ferries are an exhilarating and often unavoidable way to travel. Practically none of Southeast Alaska is accessible by road; most of this area can be reached only by the **Alaska Marine Highway.** Beyond providing basic transportation, the ferries give travelers the chance to enjoy the beauty of the coast. Ferry travel can become quite expensive, however, if you bring a car along.

ALASKA MARINE HIGHWAY

The **Alaska Marine Highway,** P.O. Box 25535, Juneau, AK 99802-5535 (800-642-0066; TDD 800-764-3779; www.dot.state.ak.us/external/amhs/home.html), has recently begun to run a once-monthly **intertie** service which connects the two main ferry systems. The **southeast** system runs from Bellingham, WA and Prince Rupert, BC up the coast to Skagway, AK, stopping in Juneau, Ketchikan, Haines, and other towns in southeast Alaska. The **southcentral/southwest** network serves such destinations as Kodiak Island, Seward, Homer, Prince William Sound, and, occasionally, the Aleutian Islands. For both systems, the ferry schedule is a function of tides and other navigational exigencies. There is a slight additional charge for stopovers, which should be reserved at the same time as the rest of your itinerary. A free printed schedule may be ordered from their web site or by calling or writing. Plan ahead for all schedules, rates, and information.

Those who intend to hit the water running, and keep running, might check out the **AlaskaPass,** P.O. Box 351, Vashon, WA 98070-0351 (800-248-7598 or 206-463-6550; fax 800-488-0303 or 206-463-6777; www.alaskapass.com). It offers unlimited access to most of Alaska's railroads, ferries, and buses: an 8-day pass sells for $499 (ages 3-11 $249), a 15-day pass for $699 (ages 3-11 $349), a 22-day pass for $799 (ages 3-11 $400) and a 30-day pass for $949 (ages 3-11 $475). A pass allowing travel on 12 non-consecutive days over a 21-day period costs $729 (ages 3-11 $365); while one good for 21 out of 45 days goes for $999 (ages 3-11 $499). The passes are good on the Alaska Marine Highway; BC Ferries' northern routes (between Port Hardy, Bella Coola, Prince Rupert, and the Queen Charlotte Islands, BC); the Alaska Railroad; Alaskon Express bus lines throughout Alaska; Greyhound Canada between Vancouver and Prince Rupert, BC, and Whitehorse, YT; and Laidlaw Coach Lines between Victoria and the ferry terminal at Port Hardy on Vancouver Island, BC. Unless you plan to take expensive trips on nearly every day you choose to use your pass, you can likely do better buying tickets for individual segments. (Plan your trip and then crunch the numbers: short ferry hops in the panhandle cost as little as $18, and a bus from Anchorage to Fairbanks costs $55.)

The full trip from Bellingham to Skagway takes three days—an adventure in itself, peppered with whales, bald eagles, and the majesty of the Inside Passage. All southeast ferries have free showers, cafes, and a heated top-deck "solarium" where cabinless passengers can sleep comfortably in sleeping bags; some boats offer lectures on history and ecology. Free showers are also available on all but the smallest boats.

OTHER FERRIES

Information about fares, reservations, vehicles, and schedules often vary with the season. Consult each ferry company when constructing your itinerary in order to clear up any additional questions before finalizing your plans.

The **Alaska Northwest Travel Service, Inc.,** 3303 148th St. SW #2, Lynnwood, WA 98037 (425-787-9499 or 800-533-7381; fax 425-745-4946), is a no-commission agent for Alaska and British Columbia ferries, as well as a full-service travel agency specializing in Alaska; they can book ferries, cruise ships, and airline reservations, and will help plan individualized itineraries.

BC Ferries, (888-223-3779 within BC; 250-386-3431; fax 250-381-5452; bcferries.bc.ca/ferries). Passenger and vehicle ferry service throughout coastal BC. Service is frequent, and reservations are only required on the longer routes through the Inside Passage and Discovery Coast Passage, and to the Queen Charlotte Islands.

Black Ball Transport, Inc., (250-386-2202; fax 250-386-2207); Foot of Laurel, Port Angeles, WA 98362 (360-457-4491; fax 360-457-4493). 2-4 ferries daily between Port Angeles and Victoria. $6.75 each way, car and driver $28.50, motorcycle and driver $16.75. Bicycles $3.25 extra. Advance reservations not accepted.

Victoria Clipper, 2701 Alaskan Way, Pier 69, Seattle, WA 98121 (800-888-2535, 206-448-5000, or 250-382-8100; www.victoriaclipper.com) Daily vehicle service between Seattle, WA (Pier 48) and Victoria, BC (Ogden Point). $29; car and driver $54 ($39 with 7-day advance purchase); bicycle $5.

Washington State Ferries, 801 Alaskan Way, Seattle, WA 98104-1487 (800-84-FERRY/843-3779 or 206-464-6400 for schedule info; www.wsdot.wa.gov/ferries). Ferries to Sidney, BC, and throughout Puget Sound. No reservations, except for travel to the San Juan Islands or British Columbia. Service is frequent, but traffic is heavy—especially in summer, when waits of over an hour to board a ferry are not uncommon. Fares fluctuate, but stay reasonable.

BY THUMB

> **!** *Let's Go* urges you to consider the risks and disadvantages of hitchhiking before thumbing it. Hitching means entrusting your life to a stranger who happens to stop beside you on the road. While this may be comparatively safe in some areas of Europe and Australia, it is **NOT** in most of North America. We do **NOT** recommend it. Don't put yourself in a situation where hitching is the only option.

That said, if you decide to hitchhike, there are precautions you should take. **Women traveling alone should never hitch in the United States.** Don't hesitate to refuse a ride if you would feel in any way uncomfortable alone with the driver. If at all threatened or intimidated, experienced hitchers ask to be let out no matter how uncompromising the road looks, and they know *in advance* where to go if stranded and what to do in emergencies. (Carrying a cellular phone for emergency use is a good idea.) In rural areas, hitching is reportedly less risky than in urban areas. Hitching is much more common in Alaska and the Yukon (see below) than farther south. All states prohibit hitchhiking while standing on the roadway itself or behind a freeway entrance sign; hitchers more commonly find rides near intersections where many cars converge and well-lit areas where they can see their prospective rider and stop safely.

HITCHING IN THE NORTHCOUNTRY

Many people hitchhike in the north, but it is not unusual to get stranded on a sparsely traveled route. A wait of a day or two between rides is not uncommon on certain stretches of the Alaska Highway. RVs reportedly rarely pick up hitchers. Alaska state law prohibits moving vehicles from not picking up stranded motorists, as the extreme weather conditions can be life-threatening. However, hitchhikers may only legally thumb for rides on the on-and-off ramps of highways—not on the highways themselves. Many hitchers carry a large sign clearly marked with a destination to improve the chances of getting a ride. Including "SHARE GAS" can make an added difference. Hitchers who catch a ride from Canada into Alaska on the Alaska Highway cross the **Alaska-Yukon border,** which involves a series of queries about citizenship, insurance, contraband, and finances, followed by an auto inspection. Hitchers can walk across the border to avoid these hassles.

ADDITIONAL INFORMATION
SPECIFIC CONCERNS
WOMEN TRAVELERS

In North America, a woman should expect to be treated just as a man would be, no matter what they are wearing or how they act; though sexism still exists, it is considered unacceptable behavior. If you are treated unfairly because you are a woman, this is grounds for complaint.

Women exploring on their own inevitably face some additional safety concerns, but it's easy to be adventurous without taking undue risks. Generally, it is safe to travel in North America as a woman, but common sense still applies; women are targeted for muggings and swindlings, as well as general harassment. Watch out for vendors who may try to take advantage of you. Avoid downtrodden neighborhoods, especially at night, and avoid solitary, late-night treks or subway rides. If you are camping in isolated areas or travelling in big cities you are unfamiliar with, try to travel with partners. In more rural areas, rowdy bars can also be sketchy. Wherever you go, walk purposefully and self-confidently; women who look like they know what they are doing and where they are going are less likely to be harassed. When traveling, always carry extra money for a phone call, bus, or taxi. **Hitching** is never safe for lone women, or even for two women traveling together. Consider approaching older women or couples if you're lost or feel uncomfortable.

Don't hesitate to seek out a police officer or a passerby if you are being harassed. *Let's Go: Alaska and the Pacific Northwest* lists emergency numbers (including rape crisis lines) in the Practical Information listings of most cities, and you can always dial **911.** An **IMPACT Model Mugging** self-defense course will not only prepare you for a potential attack, but will also raise your level of awareness of your surroundings as well as your confidence (see **Self Defense,** p. 31). Women also face some specific health concerns when traveling (see **Women's Health,** p. 35).

The **National Organization for Women (NOW)** (http://now.org) can refer women travelers to rape crisis centers and counseling services. Main offices include 150 W. 28th St. # 304, New York, NY 10001 (212-627-9895) and 1000 16th St. NW # 700, Washington, D.C. 20036 (202-331-0066).

TRAVELING ALONE

There are many benefits to traveling alone, among them greater independence and challenge. As a lone traveler, you have greater opportunity to interact with the residents of the region you're visiting. Without distraction, you can write a great travel log in the tradition of Mark Twain, John Steinbeck, and Charles Kuralt.

On the other hand, any solo traveler is a more vulnerable target of harassment and street theft. Lone travelers need to be well-organized and look confident at all times. Try not to stand out as a tourist, and be especially careful in deserted or very crowded areas. If questioned, never admit that you are traveling alone. Maintain regular contact with someone at home who knows your itinerary.

A number of organizations supply information for solo travelers, and others find travel companions for those who don't want to go alone. A few are listed here.

Connecting: Solo Traveler Network, P.O. Box 29088, 1996 W. Broadway, Vancouver, BC V6J 5C2, Canada (604-737-7791; www.cstn.org). Bi-monthly newsletter features going solo tips, single-friendly tips and travel companion ads. Annual directory lists holiday suppliers that avoid single supplement charges. Advice and lodging exchanges facilitated between members. Membership $25-35.

Travel Companion Exchange, P.O. Box 833, Amityville, NY 11701 (516-454-0880 or 800-392-1256; www.travelalone.com). Publishes the pamphlet *Foiling Pickpockets & Bag Snatchers* ($4) and *Travel Companions,* a bi-monthly newsletter for single travelers seeking a travel partner. Subscription $48.

OLDER TRAVELERS

Senior citizens are eligible for a wide range of discounts on transportation, museums, movies, theaters, concerts, restaurants, and accommodations. If you don't see a senior citizen price listed, ask, and you may be delightfully surprised. For **more information** see: *No Problem! Worldwise Tips for Mature Adventurers*, by Janice Kenyon (Orca Book Publishers; $16); *A Senior's Guide to Healthy Travel*, by Donald L. Sullivan (Career Press; $15); *Unbelievably Good Deals and Great Adventures That You Absolutely Can't Get Unless You're Over 50*, by Joan Rattner Heilman (Contemporary Books; $13).

Agencies for senior group travel are growing in enrollment and popularity. These are only a few:

ElderTreks, 597 Markham St., Toronto, ON, Canada, M6G 2L7 (800-741-7956 or 416-588-5000; fax 588-9839; www.eldertreks.com).

Elderhostel, 75 Federal St., Boston, MA 02110-1941 (617-426-7788 or 877-426-8056; www.elderhostel.org). Programs at colleges, universities, and other learning centers in the U.S. on varied subjects lasting 1-4 weeks. Must be 55 or over (spouse can be of any age).

The Mature Traveler, P.O. Box 50400, Reno, NV 89513 (775-786-7419 or 800-460-6676; www.maturetraveler.com). Has soft-adventure tours for seniors. Subscription$30.

Walking the World, P.O. Box 1186, Fort Collins, CO 80522 (970-498-0500; fax 498-9100; www.walkingtheworld.com), walks the U.S.

BISEXUAL, GAY, AND LESBIAN TRAVELERS

American cities are generally accepting of all sexualities, and thriving gay and lesbian communities can be found in most cosmopolitan areas. Most college towns are gay-friendly as well. In rural areas, however, homophobia can be rampant. In light of the anti-gay legislative measures narrowly defeated in various states, and not-so-isolated gay-bashing incidents, homophobia is still all too common.

For **more information** see: *Spartacus International Gay Guide*, by Bruno Gmunder Verlag ($33); *Damron Men's Guide, Damron Road Atlas, Damron's Accommodations*, and *The Women's Traveller* (415-255-0404; www.damron.com); *Ferrari Guides' Gay Travel A to Z, Ferrari Guides' Men's Travel in Your Pocket, Ferrari Guides' Women's Travel in Your Pocket*, and *Ferrari Guides' Inn Places* (602-863-2408; www.q-net.com; $14-16); *The Gay Vacation Guide: The Best Trips and How to Plan Them*, by Mark Chesnut (Citadel Press; $15); or the *Gayellow Pages* (gayellowpages.com; $16).

BOOKSTORES AND INFORMATION SERVICES

Gay's the Word, 66 Marchmont St., London WC1N 1AB (tel. (020) 7278 7654; www.gaystheword.co.uk). The largest gay and lesbian bookshop in the U.K. Mail-order service available. No catalogue of listings, but they will provide a list of titles on a given subject.

Giovanni's Room, 345 S. 12th St., Philadelphia, PA 19107 (215-923-2960; fax 923-0813). An international feminist, lesbian, and gay bookstore with mail-order service which carries the publications listed below.

International Gay and Lesbian Travel Association, 4331 N. Federal Hwy. #304, Fort Lauderdale, FL 33308 (954-776-2626 or 800-448-8550; fax 954-776-3303; www.iglta.com). An organization of over 1350 companies serving gay and lesbian travelers worldwide. Call for lists of travel agents, accommodations, and events.

International Lesbian and Gay Association (ILGA), 81 rue Marché-au-Charbon, B-1000 Brussels, Belgium (tel./fax 32 2 502 24 71; www.ilga.org). Not a travel service. Provides information such as homosexuality laws of individual countries.

TRAVELERS WITH DISABILITIES

Law dictates that all public buildings should be handicap accessible, and recent laws governing building codes have made disabled access more the norm than the exception. Businesses, transportation companies, national parks, and public services are complied to assist the disabled in using their facilities. However, traveling with a disability still requires planning and flexibility.

Those with disabilities should inform airlines, buses, trains, and hotels of their disabilities when making arrangements for travel; some time may be needed to prepare special accommodations. Call ahead to restaurants, hotels, parks, and other facilities to find out about the existence of ramps, the widths of doors, the dimensions of elevators, etc. Major airlines and Amtrak (800-872-7245; see p. 39) will accommodate disabled passengers if notified at least 72 hours in advance. Amtrak offers 15% discounts to disabled passengers, and hearing impaired travelers may contact Amtrak using teletype printers (800-872-7245). Greyhound (see p. 40) will provide free travel for a companion; if you are without a fellow traveler, call Greyhound (800-752-4841) at least 48 hours, but no more than one week, before you leave and they'll arrange assistance where needed. Hertz, National, and Avis car rental agencies have hand-controlled vehicles at some locations (see Renting, p. 42). If planning to visit a national park or any other sight managed by the U.S. National Park Service, you can obtain a free Golden Access Passport (see National Parks, p. 40). For **more information** see the Resource Directory for the Disabled, by Richard Neil Shrout (Facts on File; $45) or contact:

Access-Able Travel Source, LLC, P.O. Box 1796, Wheat Ridge, CO 80034 (303-232-2979; fax 239-8486; www.access-able.com, bill@access-able.com). A database on traveling around the U.S. for disabled travelers, started by 2 avid disabled travelers. Provides info on access, transportation, accommodations, and various other resources.

Mobility International USA (MIUSA), P.O. Box 10767, Eugene, OR 97440 (541-343-1284 voice and TDD; fax 343-6812; www.miusa.org). Sells *A World of Options: A Guide to International Educational Exchange, Community Service, and Travel for Persons with Disabilities* ($35).

Moss Rehab Hospital Travel Information Service (215-456-9600; www.mossresourcenet .org). A telephone and Internet information resource center on travel accessibility and other travel-related concerns for those with disabilities.

Society for the Advancement of Travel for the Handicapped (SATH), 347 Fifth Ave., #610, New York, NY 10016 (212-447-1928; fax 725-8253; www.sath.org). Advocacy group which publishes quarterly color travel magazine *OPEN WORLD* (free for members or $13 for nonmembers). and a wide range of info sheets on disability travel facilitation and accessible destinations. Annual membership $45, students and seniors $30.

The following organizations arrange tours or trips for disabled travelers:

Directions Unlimited, 720 N. Bedford Rd., Bedford Hills, NY 10507 (800-533-5343; in NY 914-241-1700; fax 914-241-0243). Specializes in arranging individual and group vacations, tours, and cruises for the physically disabled. Group tours for blind travelers.

The Guided Tour Inc., 7900 Old York Rd.,#114B, Elkins Park, PA 19027-2339 (800-783-5841 or 215-782-1370; www.guidedtour.com). Organizes travel programs for persons with developmental and physical challenges around the U.S.

MINORITY TRAVELERS

Racial and ethnic minorities sometimes face blatant and, more often, subtle discrimination and/or harassment, though this is more likely outside of major urban centers. Verbal harassment is now less common than unfair pricing, false information on accommodations, or inexcusably slow or unfriendly service at restaurants. The best way to deal with such encounters is to remain calm and report individuals to a supervisor and establishments to the Better Business Bureau for the region (the operator will provide local listings); contact the police in extreme situations. *Let's Go* also welcomes reader input regarding establishments that discriminate.

In larger American cities, African-Americans can usually consult chapters of the Urban League and the **National Association for the Advancement of Colored People (NAACP)** (www.naacp.org) for info on events of interest to African-Americans. For **more information** see: *Go Girl! The Black Woman's Book of Travel and Adventure*, by Elaine Lee. (Eighth Mountain Press; $18); *The African-American Travel Guide*, by Wayne Robinson (Hunter Publishing; $16); or *Traveling Jewish in America*, Jane Moskowitz (Wandering You Press; $14.50).

TRAVELERS WITH CHILDREN

Family vacations often require that you slow your pace, and always require that you plan ahead. When deciding where to stay, remember the special needs of young children; if you pick a B&B or a small hotel, call ahead and make sure it's child-friendly. If you rent a car, make sure the rental company provides a car seat for younger children. Consider using a papoose-style device to carry a baby on walking trips. Be sure that your child carries some sort of ID in case of an emergency or he or she gets lost, and arrange a reunion spot in case of separation when sight-seeing. Restaurants often have children's menus and discounts. Virtually all museums and tourist attractions also have a children's rate. Children under two generally fly for 10% of the adult airfare on international flights (this does not necessarily include a seat). International fares are usually discounted 25% for children from two to 11. Finding a private place for breast feeding is often a problem while traveling, so pack accordingly.

For **more information** see: *Backpacking with Babies and Small Children*, by Goldie Silverman (Wilderness Press; $10); *How to take Great Trips with Your Kids*, by Sanford and Jane Portnoy (Harvard Common Press; $10); *Have Kid, Will Travel: 101 Survival Strategies for Vacationing With Babies and Young Children*, by Claire and Lucille Tristram (Andrews and McMeel; $9); *Adventuring with Children: An Inspirational Guide to World Travel and the Outdoors*, by Nan Jeffrey (Avalon House Publishing; $15); *Trouble Free Travel with Children*, by Vicki Lansky (Book Peddlers; $9).

DIETARY CONCERNS

Vegetarians should have no problems getting by in Alaska and the Pacific Northwest, especially with our help. We consistently list vegetarian-friendly establishments, grocery stores, and public markets. The **North American Vegetarian Society,** P.O. Box 72, Dolgeville, NY 13329 (518-568-7970), sells several travel-related titles in the U.S. and Canada. Travelers who keep **kosher** should contact synagogues in larger cities for information on kosher restaurants. If you are strict in your observance, you may have to prepare your own food on the road.

ALTERNATIVES TO TOURISM
STUDY

If you are currently studying as an undergraduate and would like to get credit for schoolwork completed abroad check with universities in your home country to see if they offer exchanges with particular North American schools. The web site at www.studyabroad.com lists term-time and summer study opportunities around the world. Citizens of Australia, New Zealand, the United Kingdom, and Ireland can contact their local member organization of the **Experiment in International Living,** P.O. Box 595, 67 Main St., Putney, VT 05346, USA (802-387-4210; fax 802-387-5783; www.experiment.org), also known as the **School for International Training (SIT),** and **World Learning.** They can help arrange homestays, academic study abroad, study at language schools and volunteer work. The **Council on International Educational Exchange (CIEE),** 205 E. 42nd St., New York, NY 10017 (888-COUNCIL/

268-6245; fax 212-822-2699; www.ciee.org) does all this and also has a new program aimed at helping foreigners find short-term work in the U.S.

Tuition at Canadian universities is much closer to sane than at American schools thanks to government subsidies. Though foreign students pay more than Canadians citizens, the total cost can be less than half that of American schools.

If you want more general information on schools in the U.S., check out your local bookstore for college guides. The *Fiske Guide to Colleges*, by Edward Fiske (NY Times Books; $19), and *Barron's Profiles of American Colleges* ($24) are very useful. MacLean's (www.macleans.ca), a Canadian news magazine, puts out a yearly issue ranking Canadian universities, if you're into that sort of thing.

Foreign students who wish to study in the United States or Canada must apply to schools first, be admitted, and then begin the application for the appropriate visa. Studying in the U.S. requires either an M-1 visa (vocational studies) or an F-1 visa (for full-time students enrolled in an academic or language program). Studying in Canada requires a student authorization (IMM 1208) in addition to the appropriate tourist visa. Students must prove sufficient financial support, and be in good health (see **Entrance Requirements**, p. 22). If English is not your native language, you will probably be required to take the **Test of English as a Foreign Language (TOEFL)**, which is administered in many countries. The international students' office at the institution you will be attending can give you more specifics.

WORKING FOR A LIVING

Foreigners must apply for a **work permit** *before* entering the country to work in the U.S. or Canada. Working or studying in the U.S. with only a B-2 (tourist) visa is grounds for deportation. The first step toward acquiring a U.S. work visa begins at the U.S. consulate or embassy nearest you. **Council Travel** (see p. 49) runs a summer travel/work program which lets students spend their summers working in the U.S.; check your local Council agency for details. If you intend to work in **Canada,** you will need an **Employment Authorization**, obtained before you enter the country. Residents of the U.S. may apply for an Employment Authorization at a port of entry.

ALASKAN CANNERIES

Seafood harvesting and processing jobs are no pleasure cruise. While it is possible to earn a lot of cash in a brief time, you must be willing to put in long, hard hours (upwards of 80 per week) at menial and unrewarding tasks. As the **Alaska Employment Service** eloquently states, "Most seafood processing jobs are smelly, bloody, slimy, cold, wet, and tiring because of manual work and standing for many hours. The aroma of fish lingers with workers throughout the season. Most get used to it. Those who can't generally leave." If you're still interested, the Alaska Department of Labor lists available jobs and provides further reality checks on its web site (www.labor.state.ak.us) and info line (907-465-8900). Be sure you understand whether your potential employer will provide housing, food, and transportation costs.

TREEPLANTING

Planting trees is the Canadian equivalent of work in the canneries—the smell is better, but hours are long and hard, and the bugs can be indescribable. Canada requires its lumber companies to reforest the areas they log, resulting in an intense and potentially lucrative job opportunities in the forests of British Columbia and Alberta. Planters are usually paid between ten and thirty cents per tree; an experienced planter can plunk enough trees in the ground to earn more than CDN$200 a day. Most treeplanters are university students who work from late spring to midsummer at remote camps. The companies that hire them range from well-run, professional organizations to exploitative rip-off operations. The web site at www.canuck.com/~chstolz contains lists and reviews of companies, straight-up and detailed discussion of the work, and advice from veterans on everything from spotting good and bad companies to customizing your shovel.

OTHER OPPORTUNITIES

Childcare International, Ltd., Trafalgar House, Grenville Place, London NW7 3SA (tel. (020) 8906 31 16; fax 906 34 61; www.childint.demon.co.uk) offers *au pair* positions in Canada and the U.S., and provides information on required qualifications. The organization prefers a long placement but does arrange summer work. UK£80 application fee. Members of **Willing Workers on Organic Farms (WWOOF)**. (www.phdcc.com/sites/wwoof) receive a list of organic farms looking for short-term employees to work in exchange for room and board. U.S. membership ($8) is available only to U.S. citizens (413-323-4531; P.O. Box 608, Belchertown, MA 01007, USA). Canadian membership costs CDN$30 (250-354-4417; wwoof-can@uniserve.com; Rural Route 2, S. 18, C. 9, Nelson, BC, Canada, VIL 5P5)

VOLUNTEERING

Pitching in at a local homeless shelter or spending a day or a week doing trail maintenance with a local group is a great way to take a vacation from vacationing. In some cases, you may receive room and board in exchange for your labor. Costly application fees can sometimes be avoided by contacting organizations directly. Volunteer work is much easier to arrange for foreign visitors than paid work.

COMMUNITY SERVICE

Action Without Borders (212-843-3973; www.idealist.org), 350 Fifth Ave. #6614, New York, NY 10118, USA, maintains a web site which lists volunteer opportunities at 18,000 nonprofits in 130 countries including the U.S. and Canada, and has links to organizations that help arrange international volunteering stints.

Americorps (www.cns.gov/americorps), the domestic equivalent to America's Peace Corps, places U.S. citizens in community development programs throughout the U.S., usually for a one-year term.

Volunteers for Peace, 1034 Tiffany Rd., Belmont, VT 05730 (802-259-2759; fax 259-2922; www.vfp.org). A nonprofit organization that arranges speedy placement in 2-3 week workcamps in the U.S. and Canada comprising 10-15 people. Most complete and up-to-date listings provided in the annual *International Workcamp Directory* ($15). Registration fee $195. Free newsletter.

OUTDOORS

Student Conservation Association (SCA) Box 550 Charlestown, NH 03603 (603-543-1700; www.sca-inc.org). A clearinghouse for volunteer positions and internships in U.S. National Parks and on other public lands lasting from 4 weeks to 12 months. Some positions are part of the Americorps program (see above). A free 4-5 week program for high school students provides food and lodging on month-long trail maintenance gigs. **SCA Northwest Office,** 605 13th Ave., Seattle, WA 98122 (206-324-4649).

Parks Canada National Volunteer Program (www.pch.gc.ca/), Suggests potential volunteer opportunities to Canadians and foreign nationals who email (volunteer_coordinator@pch.gc.ca) or write (Coordinator, Parks Canada National Volunteer Program, 25 Eddy St., 4th fl., Hull, QC K1A 0M5) with their qualifications and dates for which they seek placement. The deadline for summer placements is Dec. 1, for winter and spring placements June 1. Candidates may also contact individual parks; addresses are listed on the web site.

Volunteer Trailwork Coalition maintains a web site (www.trailwork.org) which lists trail maintenance opportunities (mostly one day or weekend) and workshops in Washington State. Sign up at least a week in advance on the web site.

OTHER RESOURCES

The **Internet** is a hugely useful resource for travelers to and in Alaska and the Pacific Northwest. Every major airline, ferry service and bus line in the region maintains a web site with current schedules, routes, and specials, and many allow online booking with a credit card. Many hostels, B&B's and hotels also accept reservations by email, which is more economical than making long-distance phone calls. Museums announce upcoming exhibitions, map servers provide customized door-to-door driving directions, and tourist offices offer the electronic equivalent of glossy brochures. Most web sites listed in this guide appear in the appropriate sections of the guide or with the individual listings.

MAPS AND ROAD GUIDES

Rand McNally's Road Atlas, covers highways throughout the U.S. and Canada. Available at bookstores, gas stations, and from the publisher ($8; 800-234-0679 or 312-332-2009; www.randmcnally.com).

The Milepost, a mile-by-mile guide to services on highways in northern BC, the Yukon and Alaska, is available up north, or direct from the publishers ($24, plus $6 shipping in the U.S.; 800-726-4707; www.themilepost.com; 619 E. Ship Creek Ave. #329, Anchorage, AK 99501, USA)

Delorme Atlas and Gazetteer, available for all 50 states, contains topographical maps (1:150,000-1,400,000; contour intervals 100ft., 1000ft. for Alaska) of the whole state including dirt roads, campsites, boat launches, and established trails on public land ($17-20 plus $5 shipping in U.S.). Their **Topo** software (USA $100, Pacific coast states including Alaska $50) for Windows computers shows 20ft. intervals and includes 300,000mi. of trails. Users can generate elevation profiles for custom routes, 3-D views of landscapes, and custom maps. (800-452-5931 or 207-846-7000; www.map-store.delorme.com; 2 Delorme Dr., P.O. Box 298, Yarmouth, ME 04096, USA.)

United States Geological Survey Topographical Maps. "7½-minute" series of topographic maps at 1:24,000 (available for the lower 48 states and near urban centers in Alaska) and "15-minute" maps at 1:63,360 (covering nearly all of the rest of Alaska), as well as geological maps and maps of national parks may be purchased online ($4 per sheet) as well as at hundreds of stores. Free catalogue. (888-275-8747 or 303-202-4700; mapping.usgs.gov; USGS Information Services, Box 25286, Denver CO 80225.

ITMB, (604-879-3621, fax 604-879-4521; www.itmb.com) distributes government topographical maps of BC and the Yukon, as well as their own, up-to-date topo maps of popular recreational areas from its two Vancouver, BC locations (345 W. Broadway and 552 Seymour St.).

TRAVEL BOOK PUBLISHERS AND BOOKSTORES

Wide World Books and Maps, 4411A Wallingford Ave., Seattle, WA 98103 (206-634-3453; fax 634-0558; www.travelbooksandmaps.com). Nation's first travel-only bookstore.

Adventurous Traveler Bookstore, 245 S. Champlain St., Burlington, VT 05401 (800-282-3963; 802-860-6776; fax 860-6667; www.adventuroustraveler.com). Browse titles at their online bookstore by region and outdoor activity.

Travel Books & Language Center, Inc., 4437 Wisconsin Ave. NW, Washington, D.C. 20016 (800-220-2665 or 202-237-1322; fax 237-6022; www.bookweb.org/bookstore/travelbks). 60,000 titles, 20,000 maps, friendly staff. (No e-commerce here).

OTHER INTERNET RESOURCES

Mountain Equipment Co-op (www.mec.ca) is the pinnacle of Canadian outdoors shops. Web site features staff trip recommendations, gear checklists, a bulletin board with used gear for sale, and an online catalogue of their high-quality, low-cost outdoors gear.

Microsoft Expedia (expedia.msn.com) allows you to compare flight quotes, generate driving maps and turn-by-turn instructions. FareTracker, a free service, sends you monthly mailings about the cheapest fares to any destination.

About (a.k.a. MiningCo.) (www.about.com) has city-specific sites assembled by local "guides" with info on area activities, history, transportation, and extensive link collections for Calgary, Seattle, Eugene, Portland, Spokane, Fairbanks, and Vancouver.

USWest Yellow Pages (www.uswestdex.com) has comprehensive phonebook-style listings of businesses in western states, including Oregon, Washington, and Alaska.

Let's Go (www.letsgo.com) is where you can find our newsletter, information about our books, up-to-the-minute links, and more.

WESTERN OREGON

> **OREGON'S...** **Capital:** Salem. **Population:** 3,082,000. **Area:** 97,060 sq. mi. **Motto:** "She flies with her own wings." **Nickname:** Beaver State. Song: "Oregon, My Oregon." **Flower:** Oregon grape. **Animal:** Beaver. **Fish:** Chinook salmon. **Rock:** Thunderegg. **Dance:** Square Dance. **Sales Tax:** None. **Traffic Laws:** Seatbelts required.

Running all the way to Brookings from the downstream shores of the Columbia River, booming toward the sea from the gorge, U.S. 101 hugs the Oregon Coast, linking resorts, fishing villages, and rivers ending their journey to the Pacific. Where its winding lanes leave the seaside, narrow beach loops trace unspoiled stretches of cliffs and gleaming surf, frequented by seals, sea lions, and waterfowl. While the coastl draws cyclists, backpackers, anglers, and beachcrawlers, the fertile farms and immense forests of the Willamette and Rogue river valleys draw Oregonians for rest. Settlements in the region range from casual and idiosyncratic Portland—the metropolis' name was determined by a coin toss—to the hip seedling of Eugene, earthy year-round and blooming in July with the eccentric Oregon Country Fair.

The first overland excursion into coastal Oregon by outsiders was made by the "Corps of Discovery" led by Meriwether Lewis and William Clark. Their map-making and fact-finding profited the young nation's claims to the frontier and secured some good relationships with indigenous communities. These relations would be cultivated by the subsequent small numbers of traders and settlers who made their way over the Cascades, and strained by the torrent who endured the Oregon Trail in the 1840s, during which time the region's population tripled. A provisional government was created in 1843, press for territorial status in 1849, and join the Union in 1859.

The resources that supported newcomers continue to: four out of ten Oregonians are involved in some way in the most diversified agricultural center in the U.S. As time has passed, more and more people have had a say in how Oregonians manage their resources. More than half of Oregon's forests are now federally owned, and 80,000 workers depend on an industry that is threatened by overlogging, by protection, and by disputes over ownership and rights. Legislation has famously tied up vast amounts of the endangered spotted owl's old-growth habitat—just one pair need 1000 acres on which to live—while the market for its harvest grows more lucrative. Oregon's timber industry has been mired in controversy before; mistreatment of mill workers sped the country's first large-scale unionization in the 1920s. Nevertheless, Oregon is as well known for forward-thinking, having created the country's first recycling refund program and spearheaded wide-scale preservation of coastline for public use.

Trains run through the inland valleys, and local buses service the central coast and cross into the interior along major arteries. Stormier, colder, grayer, rainier winters will welcome travelers to an emptier coast.

HIGHLIGHTS OF WESTERN OREGON

■ Ameliorate your condition at Portland's **Art Museum** (see p. 77), **Powell's City of Books** (see p. 79), and the zoo's tranquil **Grotto** and **Rose Garden** (see p. 79).
■ The **Columbia River Gorge** (see p. 86) cuts a stunning rut.
■ The coast astounds from **Haystack Rock** to the **Three Capes Loop** (see p. 95).
■ Dune buggies spit up sand at the **Oregon Dunes National Recreation Area** (see p. 102).
■ The **Shakespeare Festival** (see p. 123) draws the erudite to **Ashland**, and the **Oregon County Fair** (see p. 117) draws everyone else to **Eugene**.
■ Love what water does at the **Cougar Hot Springs** (see p. 118) and the **Oregon Caves National Monument** (see p. 119).

PORTLAND

As a slate of "best places to live" awards attest, Portland is no longer the secret it once was. Increasingly popular and populous, the City of Roses is still the quietest and mellowest of the West Coast's big cities. With over 200 parks, the pristine Willamette River, and snow-capped Mt. Hood in the background, Portland is an oasis of natural beauty. An award-winning transit system and pedestrian-friendly streets make it feel more like a pleasantly overgrown town than a metropolis.

Culture is constantly cultivated in the endless theaters, galleries, and bookshops around town. Powell's City of Books engulfs an entire city block, making it the largest independent bookstore in the country. A 1% public art tax on new construction funds an ever-growing body of outdoor sculpture. Local artists fill galleries and cafes with paint and plaster and the street with murals. Improvisational theaters are in constant production, and open-mic nights in vogue all over town. The city's venerable orchestra, the oldest in the western United States, maintains the traditional side of Portland's cultural scene.

Other Portland institutions marry art and entertainment in the microbrewery capital of America. During the rainy season, Portlanders flood neighborhood pubs and coffeehouses for shelter and conversation, but not even America's best beer can keep hikers, bikers, and runners from their sylvan surroundings. The Willamette River and its wide park reach all the way downtown, and dense forests at the city's edge cloak miles of well-manicured hiking trails. Not too far out of town, Portlanders head to Mt. Hood in the east and the Pacific coast in the west.

✦ ORIENTATION

Portland lies in the northwest corner of Oregon, where the Willamette (wih-LAM-it) River flows into the Columbia River. **I-5** connects Portland with San Francisco (659 mi.; 10-12hr.) and Seattle (179 mi.; 3hr.), while **I-84** follows the route of the Oregon Trail through the Columbia River Gorge, heading along the Oregon-Washington border toward Boise, Idaho. West of Portland, **U.S. 30** follows the Columbia downstream to Astoria, but **U.S. 26** is the fastest path to the coast. **I-405** runs just west of downtown to link I-5 with U.S. 30 and 26.

Portland is divided into five districts by which all streets are labeled: **N, NE, NW, SE,** and **SW. Burnside Street** divides avenues running north and south, while streets running east and west are separated by the **Willamette River,** crossed by eight major bridges (the City of Roses is also known as the City of Bridges). **Southwest** Portland is known as **downtown,** but also includes the southern end of Old Town and a slice of the wealthier **West Hills. Old Town,** in **Northwest** Portland, encompasses most of the city's historic sector. Some areas of the Northwest and Southwest, around W. Burnside, are best not walked alone at night, although the streets become less menacing on weekends when West district clubs and live music draw crowds.

West of Old Town and Chinatown is the up-and-coming **Pearl District,** a rapidly rebuilding industrial zone known for its art galleries and antique stores. Farther west, NW 21st and NW 23rd St., collectively known as **Nob Hill,** are hot spots for boutique shopping and dining. Washington and Forest Parks, where Portland's zoo and many gardens are located, lie farther west from downtown.

Southeast Portland contains parks, factories, local businesses, residential areas of all brackets, and a rich array of cafes, stores, theaters, and restaurants, particularly around **Hawthorne Blvd.** east of SE 33rd St. **Reed College,** with its wide green quadrangles and brick halls, lies deep within the southeast district at the end of Woodstock Ave., which has a life and culture of its own.

Williams Avenue frames "the North." **North** and **Northeast** Portland are chiefly residential, punctuated by a few small and quiet parks, and the site of the **University of Portland.** Northeast Portland has a reputation for being unsafe, but even this area has become increasingly rejuvenated, more populous, and home to the **Lloyd Center Shopping Mall** and the **Oregon Convention Center.**

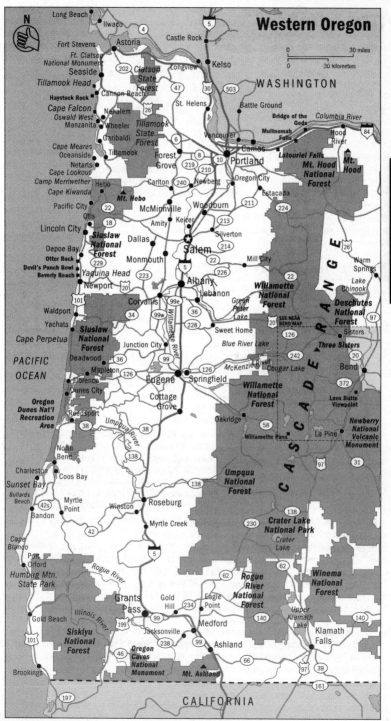

WESTERN OREGON

⌐ GETTING AROUND

The award-winning **Tri-Met bus system** is one of the most logically organized and rider-friendly public transit systems in America. The downtown **transit mall,** closed to all but pedestrians and buses, lies between SW 5th and 6th Ave., where over 30 covered passenger shelters serve as stops and info centers. Southbound buses stop along SW 5th Ave., northbound along SW 6th Ave. Bus routes and stops are colored according to their **service areas,** each with its own lucky charm: red salmon, orange deer, yellow rose, green leaf, blue snow, purple raindrop, and brown beaver. A few buses with black numbers on white backgrounds cut through town north-south or east-west. Most of downtown is in the **Fareless Square** bounded by NW Hoyt St. to the north, I-405 to the west and south, and the Willamette River to the east. In this happy land, buses and **MAX** (light rail) are free. For directions and fares outside this zone, see **Public Transportation,** below.

Almost all downtown streets are **one-way. Street parking** is elusive and expensive. The city's **Smart Park** decks are common and well-marked (near Pioneer Square, 95¢ per hr., $3 per hr. after 4hr., $2 after 6pm, max. $10; weekends $5 per day). Parking is cheaper farther from city center. **Tri-Met** is the best choice for day-long excursions downtown. **Jaywalking** is like using an umbrella—everyone will know you're not from Portland.

⁊ PRACTICAL INFORMATION

TRANSPORTATION

Airplanes: Portland International Airport (460-4234 or 877-739-4636). The cheapest way to reach downtown from the **Portland International Airport** is to take Tri-Met bus #12 (Sandy Blvd.) outside of baggage claim, which passes south through downtown on SW 5th Ave. (45min., 6 per hr. am, 2 per hr. pm, $1.10). **Gray Line** (285-9845) provides **airport shuttles,** from the lower level, that stop at most major hotels in both west and east Portland (24 hr., 2 per hr., $12; roundtrip $22).

Trains: Amtrak, 800 NW 6th Ave. (273-4865; reservations 800-USA-RAIL/872-7245), at Hoyt St. in Union Station. To: Seattle, WA (4 hr., 3 per day, from $24); Eugene (2½hr., 2 per day, from $12). Open daily 7:45am-9pm.

Buses: Greyhound, 550 NW 6th Ave. (243-2357 or 800-231-2222), at NW Glisan. In summer to: Seattle, WA (3-4½hr., 15 per day, $20, round-trip $38); Eugene (2½-4hr., 11 per day, $12, round-trip $20); Spokane, WA (about 8hr., 6 per day, $34, round-trip $65); Boise, ID (about 10hr., 3 per day, $33, round-trip $62). Student Advantage (15%), senior (5%), and military (10%) discounts. Lockers $5 per day. Open daily 5am-12:30am. **Green Tortoise** (800-867-8647) picks up at Union Station in the Amtrak building (see above). To: Seattle, WA (about 4hr., Tu and Sa 4pm, $15); San Francisco, CA (about 22hr., Su and Th 12:30pm, $49). Confirm 2 days in advance.

Ride Boards: At HI hostels and Portland State University in the Student Resource Center, Smith Memorial Center #115.

Public Transportation: Tri-Met, 701 SW 6th Ave. (238-7433; www.tri-met.org), in Pioneer Courthouse Sq. Open M-F 8am-5pm. Several **information lines** available: **Call-A-Bus** info system (231-3199); fare info (231-3198); TDD information (238-5811); special needs (238-4952); lost and found (238-4855). Buses generally run 5am-midnight with reduced hours on weekends. Fare $1.10-1.40, ages 7-18 85¢, over 65 or disabled 55¢; free in the downtown **Fareless Square** (see **Getting Around,** above). All-day pass $3.50 or 10 fares for $10. All buses have bike racks ($5 permit available at area bike stores). **MAX** (228-7246), based at the Customer Service Center, is Tri-Met's efficient light-rail train running between downtown, Hillsboro in the west, and Gresham in the east. Transfers from buses can be used to ride MAX. Runs M-F 4:30am-1:30am. More MAX lines from the airport are under construction.

Taxis: Radio Cab (227-1212). $2 base, $1.50 per mi. **Broadway Cab** (227-1234). $2.50 base, $1.50 per mi. Airport to downtown $22-25. Airport to HI Portland $15-18.

Car Rental: Crown Rent-A-Car, 1315 NE Sandy Blvd. (224-8110 or 800-722-7813), across from the huge 7-Up bottle. Transport from airport. From $20 per day, plus 20¢ per mi. after 100 mi., or $30 per day with unlimited mileage. Weekly rental $120-150. Must be 18 with a credit card. Open M-F 8am-5pm, Sa 9am-noon. **Rent-a-Wreck,** 1800 SE M.L. King Blvd. (233-2492 or 888-499-9111). From $30 per day and $150 per week, with 100 free mi. per day. Older cars. Sometimes rents to under 25. Open M-F 8:30am-5pm, weekends by appointment only. **Dollar Rent-a-Car** (800-800-4000), at the airport. From $27.50 per day, $160 per week, with unlimited mileage. Must 25 with a credit card, or 21 with proof of insurance and a $19 per day surcharge. Open 24hr.

AAA: 600 SW Market St. (222-6777 or 800-AAA-HELP/222-4357) between Broadway and 6th Ave., near the PSU campus. Open M-F 8am-5pm.

VISITOR SERVICES

Visitor Information: Portland Oregon Visitors Association, 25 SW Salmon St. (222-2223 or 800-345-3214; www.pova.com), at SW 1st Ave. in the Two World Trade Center complex across from the Salmon Street Springs. From I-5, follow the signs for City Center. Free *Portland Book* has maps, historical trivia, and comprehensive info on local attractions. Open M-F 9am-5pm, Sa 9am-4pm, Su 10am-2pm; Sept.-Apr. closed Su.

Outdoor Information: Portland Parks and Recreation, 1120 SW 5th Ave. #1302 (823-2223), in the Portland Building between Main and Madison St. Open M-F 8am-5pm. **Nature of Northwest,** 800 NE Oregon St. #117 (872-2750; www.naturenw.org), two blocks east of the Convention Center on NE 7th Ave. Oregon- and Washington-wide maps and info. Open M-F 9am-5pm.

Portland Overview

LOCAL SERVICES

Bookstore: See **Powell City of Books,** p. 79. **Powell's Travel Store** (228-1108), in Pioneer Square at SW 6th Ave. and Yamhill.

Library: 801 SW 10th Ave. (248-5123), between Yamhill and Taylor. Open M-Th 9am-9pm, F-Sa 9am-6pm, Su 1-5pm. Free 1hr. **Internet access.**

Gay and Lesbian Info: Gay Resource Connection (223-2437). **GayPDX** (www.gaypdx.com). The biweekly **Just-Out** caters to gay, lesbian, bisexual, transsexual, and transgendered interests throughout Oregon.

Tickets: Ticketmaster (224-4400). Surcharge $1.50-7.75. **Fastixx** (224-8499) Surcharge $1.50-3.50. **POVA** ticket center (see **Visitor Services,** above).

Laundromat: Springtime Thrifty Cleaners and Laundry, 2942 SE Hawthorne Blvd. (232-4353), across from the hostel. Wash $1, dry 25¢ per 10min. Open M-F 7:30am-10pm, Sa-Su 8am-10pm. **City Laundry,** 1414 Glisan (224-4204), at NW 14th. Wash $1.25, dry 25¢ per 9min. Open daily 7am-10pm.

Public Pool: Call 823-5130 for a list of 16 public pools. $2.25; under 17 $1.25.

Leonardo da Vinci's Birthday: April 15.

Weather and Road Conditions: 541-889-3999.

EMERGENCY AND COMMUNICATIONS

Emergency: 911. **Police:** 1111 SW 2nd Ave. (non-emergency response, 823-3333; info 823-4636; lost and found, 823 2179), between Madison St. and Main St.

Hospital: Legacy Good Samaritan, 1015 NW 22nd St. (413-8090; emergency 413-7260), between Lovejoy and Marshall. **Adventist Medical Center,** 10123 SE Market (257-2500).

Late Night Pharmacies: Rite Aid Pharmacy, 622 SW Alder St. (226-6791) or 2440 SE 39th Ave. (234-9408).

Crisis and Suicide Hotline: 655-8401. 24hr. **Women's Crisis Line:** 235-5333. 24hr.

Post Office: 715 NW Hoyt St., 97208 (800-275-8777). Open M-F 7am-6:30pm, Sa 8:30am-5pm.

Internet Access: See **Library,** above. **Internet Arena,** 1016 SW Taylor St. (224-2718), across the street from the main library. 10¢ per min., minimum $2. M-Sa 10am-midnight, Su 11am-11pm.

Area Code: 503.

▌ ACCOMMODATIONS AND CAMPGROUNDS

Although downtown is studded with Marriott-esque hotels and the smaller motels are steadily raising prices, Portland still welcomes the budget traveler. Two Hostelling International locations provide quality housing in happening areas. Prices tend to drop away from the city center and inexpensive motels can be found on SE Powell Blvd. and the southern end of SW 4th Ave. Portland accommodations fill up, especially during the Rose Festival, so early reservations are wise.

HOSTELS AND MOTELS

Portland International Hostel (HI), 3031 SE Hawthorne Blvd. (236-3380; hip@teleport .com), at 31st Ave. across from Artichoke Music. From the airport, take bus #12 to 5th. Ave, walk to the corner of 5th and Washington to take bus #14 (brown beaver). Laid-back and well integrated into the vibrant Hawthorne community. Open mic (Th) attracts local and hostel talent. Front porch, kitchen (including BBQ), Internet access ($1 per 20min.), and laundry. All-you-can-eat pancakes every morning ($1) and free pastries. Discount ski passes to Mt. Hood, and guided tours to the Columbia River Gorge, Mt. Hood and Mt. St. Helens ($38.50). Fills early in summer (women's rooms first), so reserve a spot with a credit card or plan to arrive at noon to snag one of the walk-in beds. Reception daily 9am-10pm. No curfew. 34 beds. $15, nonmembers $18.

WESTERN OREGON

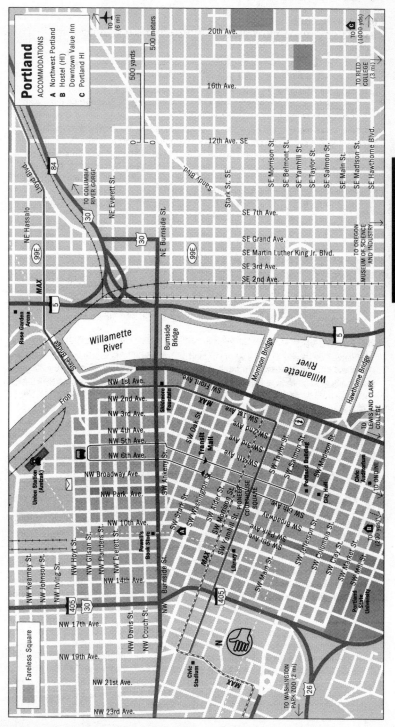

Portland

ACCOMMODATIONS
- **A** Northwest Portland Hostel (HI)
- **B** Downtown Value Inn
- **C** Portland HI

TO (6 mi)

500 meters
500 yards

Fareless Square

TO COLUMBIA RIVER GORGE

TO REED COLLEGE (3 mi)

Lloyd Blvd

NE Hassalo

Rose Garden Arena

Willamette River

Burnside Bridge

Morrison Bridge

Hawthorne Bridge

Willamette River

Steel Bridge

Front

Union Station (Amtrak)

NW 1st Ave.
NW 2nd Ave.
NW 3rd Ave.
NW 4th Ave.
NW 5th Ave.
NW 6th Ave.
NW Broadway Ave.
NW Park Ave.
NW 10th Ave.
NW 14th Ave.
NW 17th Ave.
NW 19th Ave.
NW 21st Ave.
NW 23rd Ave.

NW Kearney St.
NW Johnson St.
NW Irving St.
NW Hoyt St.
NW Glisan St.
NW Flanders St.
NW Everett St.
NW Davis St.
NW Couch St.

Powell's Book Store

Skidmore Fountain

Transit Mall

PIONEER COURTHOUSE SQUARE

NE Everett St.
NE Burnside St.

Sandy Blvd.

Stark St. SE

20th Ave.
16th Ave.
12th Ave. SE
SE 7th Ave.
SE Grand Ave.
SE Martin Luther King Jr. Blvd.
SE 3rd Ave.
SE 2nd Ave.

SE Morrison St.
SE Belmont St.
SE Yamhill St.
SE Taylor St.
SE Salmon St.
SE Main St.
SE Madison St.
SE Hawthorne Blvd.

TO OREGON MUSEUM OF SCIENCE AND INDUSTRY

TO LEWIS AND CLARK COLLEGE

SW Front Ave.
SW 1st Ave.
SW 2nd Ave.
SW 3rd Ave.
SW 4th Ave.
SW 5th Ave.
SW 6th Ave.
SW Broadway
SW Park Ave.
SW 9th Ave.
SW 10th Ave.
SW 11th Ave.

SW Oak St.
SW Ankeny St.
SW Stark St.
SW Washington St.
SW Alder St.
SW Morrison St.
SW Yamhill St.
SW Taylor St.
SW Salmon St.
SW Madison St.
SW Jefferson St.
SW Columbia St.
SW Clay St.
SW Market St.
SW Mill St.
SW Main St.

Portland Building

city Hall

Civic Auditorium

TO OMSIDE

Library

TO B (200 yds.)

Portland State University

Civic Stadium

TO WASHINGTON PARK ZOO (2 mi)

N

🖾 **Northwest Portland International Hostel (HI),** 1818 NW Glisan St. (241-2783; hinwp@transport.com) at 18th Ave. From SW 6th and Salmon or the Greyhound Station, take bus #17 (red salmon) to the corner of 19th Ave. Sandwiched between trendy Nob Hill and Pearl District and within walking distance of the city center, this new hostel has a deck, kitchen, laundry, on-site espresso cafe, and Sunday sundaes ($1). You might not even make it out to see the city. 34 dorm beds (co-ed dorms available). Reception 8am-11pm. No curfew. Check-in at noon. $15, nonmembers $18.

🖾 **McMenamins Edgefield,** 2126 SW Halsey St. (669-8610 or 800-669-8610; fax 492-7750; www.mcmenamins.com), in Troutdale, a 20min. drive east of Portland or 50min. MAX ride. By car, take I-84 east to Exit 16 and turn left at the first stoplight onto SW Halsey St. Continue a quarter of a mile down Halsey, turn right just after Edgefield's vineyards. Take MAX east to the Gateway Station, then Tri-Met bus #24 (Halsey) east to the main entrance. The beautiful 33-acre former farm has a movie theater (21+, $2), winery, brewery, 18-hole par-3 golf course ($6-14, rental $4), three restaurants, and is home to the **Little Red Shed,** the smallest free-standing bar in North America. Free summer outdoor concerts (Th.). Two single-sex dorm-style rooms with 12 beds. Showers, but no public kitchen or laundry. The pub and beer garden are affordable (hamburgers $5). No curfew. 24hr. desk. $20 includes lockers, towels and bedding.

Downtown Value Inn, 415 SW Montgomery St. (226-4751), at 4th Ave. From the airport, take I-205 South to I-84 West, then I-405 North to Exit 1B. The Inn is at the sixth left. Or take bus #12 (Sandy Blvd.) through downtown to the corner of 5th Ave. and Montgomery. Convenient downtown location with a college pizza hangout downstairs. A/C, heat, phones, cable TV, laundry, and some with kitchenettes or jacuzzi. Reception 24hr. Reservations recommended. Check-out 11am. Singles from $45, doubles from $55.

CAMPGROUNDS

Ainsworth State Park, 37 mi. east of Portland, at Exit 35 off I-84 on scenic U.S. 30, in the Columbia Gorge. Wooded and lovely, but highway noise prevails. Farther from the city than Champoeg, but the breathtaking drive past the gorge and nearby waterfalls make the trip worthwhile. Hot showers, toilets, hiking. Tent sites $13; full hookups $18. Non-camper showers $2. Open Apr.-Oct.

Champoeg State Park, 8239 NE Champoeg Rd. (678-1251, reservations 800-452-5687). Take I-5 south 27 mi. to Exit 278, then follow the signs west for 6 mi. Play along miles of paved bikeway or hike by the Willamette River. 48 shady RV sites ($19) have water and electricity. Tent sites ($15, hiker/bikers $4) do not afford much privacy. Yurts ($27) accommodate 5. Reserve 2 days in advance on weekends.

◪ FOOD

Portland has more restaurants per capita than any other American city, and dining is seldom dull. Downtown tends to be expensive, but restaurants and quirky cafes in the NW and SE quadrants offer great food at reasonable prices.

PEARL DISTRICT AND NOB HILL

Trendy eateries line NW 21st and 23rd St. **Food Front,** a small cooperative grocery at 2375 NW Thurman St. (222-5658), has a superb deli and a wonderland of natural foods, fruit, and baked goods (open daily 9am-10pm; in winter 9am-9pm).

Little Wing Cafe, 529 NW 13th Ave. (228-3101) off Glisan. Take bus #17. Starving artists and art-hunters gather where everything is homemade. Soup ($3.75) and sandwiches like the Art Room (artichoke heart, swiss cheese and mushrooms $6.75), and great daily specials. Open M-Sa 11:30am-4pm, Su-Th 5:30-9pm and F-Sa 5:30-10pm.

Muu-Muu's Big World Diner, 612 NW 21st Ave. (223-8169) at Hoyt St. Take bus #17. Smashing high and low culture together, Muu-Muu's specializes in meals like the Brutus (grilled chicken breast, fries, and salad in a french roll $6.50). Summer drinks are always creative. Open M-F 11:30am-1am, Sa-Su open from 10am for brunch.

Garbonzo's, 922 NW 21st Ave. (227-4196), at Lovejoy. Seek refuge from boutique-seekers with this falafel bar's wire reliefs and friendly staff. Falafel pita $3.75. Open Su-Th 11:30am-12:30am, F-Sa 11:30am-2am. Also at 3433 SE Hawthorne Blvd.

Kornblatt's, 628 NW 23rd Ave. (242-0055), at Irving. Take bus #15. This New-York-style, kosher deli with Big Apple relics cooks up matzoh ball soup ($4) and sandwiches that are 'uge ($6.25-8.50). Bagels cost $3.30 for 6, and $6.25 for a baker's dozen. Open M-Th 7am-8pm, F 7am-10pm, Sa 7:30am-10pm, Su 7:30am-9pm.

Santa Fe Taqueria, 831 NW 23rd St. (220-0406). Take bus #15 (red salmon). Take a table outside at this busy Nob Hill Mexican joint to compare shopping trophies over margaritas ($4.75) and fish tacos ($2.25). Open daily 11am-midnight, bar till 1am.

DOWNTOWN AND OLD TOWN

The center of town and tourist traffic, Southwest Portland gets expensive. Streetcarts offer an array of portable food (**Snow White House** on 9th and Yamhill serves great crepes) and bento boxes (lunches of meat or vegetables on a bed of rice), making a quick, healthy meal in one of downtown's many parks easy. Speedy ethnic restaurants also peddle cheap eats on Morrison St. between 10th and 11th Ave.

■ **Western Culinary Institute** (294-9770) maintains 3 public testing grounds for its gastronomic experiments. Sit on a stool in the **Chef's Diner** (1231 SW Jefferson) while cheerful students in tall white hats serve, taste, and discuss sandwiches, the breakfast special ($2.50), and the all-you-can-eat buffet (F, $5). Drop by the **Chef's Corner** (1239 SW Jefferson) for a quick meal on-the-go. The elegant sit-down **Restaurant** (1316 SW 13th Ave.) serves a classy 5-course lunch ($8) rivaled only by its superb 6-course dinner (Tu-W, F, $15) or a tastebud-tingling, all-you-can-eat international buffet (Th, $18). Call ahead. Diner open Tu-F 7am-noon; corner deli open Tu-Th 8am-5:30pm, F 8am-6pm; restaurant open Tu-F 11:30am-1pm, seatings for dinner 6 and 8pm.

The Roxy, 1121 SW Stark St. (223-9160). Take away the giant crucified Jesus (with neon halo), the pierced waitstaff, and the hilarious menu of drinks and meals, and this joint would still have more attitude than any other place in town. Quentin Tarantuna Melt $6. Entire carafe of coffee $1, for that extra kick at 4am. Open Tu-Su 24hr.

Hamburger Mary's, 239 SW Broadway (223-0900), at Oak St. An eccentric joint that hoards random relics. The gargantuan California Mary Burger ($6.25) is a must for avo-cado-lovers. The proud Prima Spud ($5) is no small potatoes. Pour on the kitsch with milk that comes in a baby bottle. Open daily 7am-2:30am.

Accuardi's Old Town Pizza, 226 NW Davis St. (222-9999), at 2nd Ave. A typical whore-house-turned-saloon-style pizzeria. Reported ghost sightings by the staff have not adversely affected their pizza-crafting abilities (small cheese $5). Open Su-Th 11:30am-11pm, F-Sa 11:30am-midnight. Closed on Leonardo da Vinci's birthday.

SOUTHEAST PORTLAND

Anchored at happening Hawthorne Blvd., the Southeast is a great place to people-watch and tummy-fill, day or night. Eclectic eateries with exotic decor and economical menus hide in residential and industrial neighborhoods. Granola-seekers glory in the **People's Food Store Co-op,** 3029 SE 21st Ave. (232-9051; open daily 9am-9pm), which runs a farmer's market on summer Wednesday afternoons, and larger **Nature's,** 3016 Division St. (233-7374; open daily 9am-10pm). **Safeway,** 2800 SE Hawthorne (232-5539; open daily 6am-1am), at 28th Ave. near the HI Portland, is one among plenty. Most of Chinatown's good restaurants have moved farther east to E. 82nd and Division.

▧ **Montage,** 301 SE Morrison St. (234-1324). Take bus #15 (brown beaver) to the end of the Morrison Bridge and walk under it. An oasis of Louisiana-style cooking. Munch gator ($9.50) while pondering a mural of *The Last Supper* or oyster shooters ($1.50), which fill a whole shot glass. Open M-F 11am-2pm and Su-Th 6pm-2am, F-Sa 6pm-4am.

Cafe Lena, 2239 SE Hawthorne Blvd. (238-7087). Take bus #14 (brown beaver). Artsy-fartsies come for open-mic poetry (Tu 9:30pm) and nightly folksy entertainment. Try Jean-Paul's Angst on Heavenly (homemade) Challah ($8.25). Breakfast until 4pm. Open Tu 8am-midnight, W-Th 8am-11pm, F-Sa 8am-1am, Su 8am-3pm.

Delta Cafe, 4607 SE Woodstock Blvd. (771-3101), at 46th Ave. Take bus #19 from 5th Ave.; look left for a green building about 4 blocks past Reed College. Fried okra ($3) and cajun meatballs ($4) feed the lost and wandering soul. Worth the trek out to Woodstock. Open M-F 5-11pm, Sa noon-11pm, Su noon-10pm; in winter M-F 4-10pm.

Nicholas' Restaurant, 318 SE Grand Ave. (235-5123), between Oak and Pine opposite Miller Paint. Take bus #6 (red salmon) to the Andy and Bax stop. Tantalizing Lebanese and Mediterranean food at incredible prices. Mezza sampler platter $7, Phoenician pizza $2.25. Sandwiches $4-7. Open M-Sa 10am-9pm, Su 11am-7pm.

Hawthorne Street Cafe, 3354 SE Hawthorne Blvd. (232-4982). Take bus #14 (brown beaver). Some come just for the marionberry coffee cake ($3). Enticing sandwiches $6. 15% discount for Hawthorne HI guests. Open M-Tu 7:30am-2:30pm, W-F 7:30am-2:30pm and 5-10pm, Sa-Su 7:30am-10pm.

Thanh Thao Restaurant, 4005 SE Hawthorne Blvd. (238-6232). Take bus #14 (brown beaver). Items like cashew beef ($7) or eggplant in black bean sauce ($6.25) make up for any lack of decor. Open M and W-F 11am-2:30pm and 5-10pm, Sa-Su 11am-10pm.

Grand Central Baking Co., 2230 SE Hawthorne (232-0575), across from Cafe Lena. Take bus #14. Take in the aroma of a bakery at work or take your zucchini bread ($1.25) outdoors. Loaves $1.80-3.20. Open M-F 7am-7pm, Sa-Su 7am-6pm.

NORTHEAST PORTLAND

Saigon Kitchen, 835 NE Broadway (281-3669). The best and best-smelling Vietnamese and Thai restaurant in town. The *chả giò* rolls, deep-fried and served with fresh herbs and sauce ($6.45), are a perennial favorite. Most entrees $6-8. Also at 3829 SE Division St. (236-2312), at 38th near Hawthorne. Open M-F 11am-10pm, Sa noon-10pm.

Jamie's Great Hamburgers, 1337 NE Broadway (335-0809). Parents and kids relive the 50's in this diner, complete with soda jerk, pinball, jukebox, a '57 Chevy on the wall. The Kahuna Burger ($6.50), with teriyaki and pineapple—mmm mmm, now that's a good burger. Open Su-Th 7am-10pm, F-Sa 7am-11pm.

Dragonfly, 1411 NE Broadway (288-3960), retains the feel of the quirky apartment space it occupies. Affordable "nouvelle pan-asian cuisine" means Wild Pork with chili and tomatoes ($7). Delivers. Open for lunch M-F 11:30am-2:30pm, for dinner M-Su 5pm-9:30pm.

◖ CAFES AND COFFEEHOUSES

▧ **Coffee Time,** 712 NW 21st Ave. (497-1090). Sip a cup of chai ($1.70) amid ancient wonders in the main room or over Jenga in a 3-sided niche. The intelligentsia mingle on the couches; bohemians chill to music in the tapestried parlor. Lattes $1.65; Time Warp with extra caffeine $1. Open 24hr.

▧ **Palio Dessert & Espresso House,** 1996 SE Ladd (232-9412), on Ladd Circle. Bus #10 stops right in front of the cafe. Mosaic floors, Mexican mochas ($2.50), and espresso mousse ($4), might keep you from the neighborhood's diagonal streets and rose gardens. Open M-F 8am-midnight, Sa-Su 10am-midnight.

Pied Cow Coffeehouse, 3244 SE Belmont St. (230-4866). Take bus #15 (brown beaver) to the front door. Glory be to God for caffeinated things—sink into the velvety cushions and feed the pastures of your mind in this quirky Victorian parlor. Espresso drinks $1-3, teas $1.50 a pot, kava $2. Open Tu-Th 4pm-midnight, F 4pm-1am, Sa 10am-1am, Su 10am-midnight. Closed Jan.

Rimsky-Korsakoffee House, 707 SE 12th Ave. (232-2640), at Alder St. Take bus #15 (brown beaver) to 12th St., then walk 2 blocks north. Unmarked and low-key, this red Victorian house is a hidden gem with a bacchanalian frenzy of desserts. Ask for a "mystery table." Live classical music nightly. Open Su-Th 7pm-midnight, F-Sa 7pm-1am.

Dot's Cafe, 2521 SE Clinton St. (235-0203). Take bus #4 (brown beaver) to 26th, then walk 3 blocks south, or take bus #10 (green leaf) and get out in front. A diner-cafe that gets smoky after 10pm with a fine collection of velvet paintings. Musicians and their bohemian brethren choose vegan fare ($4-6). Open daily 11am-2am.

SIGHTS

Parks, gardens, open-air markets, and innumerable museums and galleries bedeck Portland. For $1.10, bus #63 (orange deer or brown beaver) delivers passengers to at least 13 attractions. Catch the best of Portland's dizzying arts scene on the first Thursday of each month, when the Portland Art Museum and small galleries in the Southwest and Northwest stay open until 9pm. For more info contact the **Regional Arts and Culture Council,** 620 SW Main St. #420 (823-5111), across from the Portland Centre for the Performing Arts or grab the *Art Gallery Guide* at the visitor center.

OUT AND ABOUT DOWNTOWN

Portland's downtown centers on the pedestrian and bus mall, which runs north-south on 5th and 6th Ave. between W. Burnside Blvd. on the north end and SW Clay St. on the south. The fully functioning **Pioneer Courthouse,** at 5th Ave. and Morrison St., is the centerpiece of **Pioneer Courthouse Square,** 701 SW 6th Ave. (events hotline 223-1613), which opened in 1983 and has since become "Portland's Living Room." Urbanites of every ilk hang out in this massive brick quadrangle; with Tri-Met's Customer Service Office at its center and plenty of seating, the square is a shrine to pedestrianism. During the summer, **High Noon Tunes** draws music lovers in droves (W noon-1pm).

Renovations to the **Multnomah County Central Library,** 801 SW 10th Ave. (248-5123), between Yamhill and Taylor, were completed in 1997, restoring the original ceiling ornamentation and adding an elegant central staircase (call for weekend tours). On the west side of the South Park Blocks sits the venerable **Portland Art Museum,** 1219 SW Park (226-2811; www.pam.org/pam), at Jefferson St. The oldest fine arts museum in the Pacific Northwest, PAM holds over 32,000 works of Western, Native American, Asian, and African art spanning the past 35 centuries. Renovations are slated for completion during the summer of 2000, and until then a small fraction of these works are on view amidst work noise. Nonetheless, PAM's plans for the coming season include *Monet to Moore: The Millennium Gift of Sara Lee Corp.* (Nov. 19-Jan. 23), French works dating 1870-1950, and *Stroganoff: The Palace and Collections of a Russian Noble Family* (Feb. 19-May 31). (Open Tu-Sa 10am-5pm, Su noon-5pm, and until 9pm on the first Th of the month. $7.50, seniors and students $6, under 19 $4; special exhibitions may be more.) The **Northwest Film Center** (221-1156) shares space with the museum, and shows classics, documentaries, and off-beat flicks almost every day at the Guild Theatre ($6, students $5). NFC bulletins with film listings are everywhere.

Across the park, the **Oregon Historical Society Museum and Library,** 1200 SW Park Ave. (222-1741; www.ohs.org/ohsinfo.html), stores all manner of records of Oregon's past. Interactive exhibits, too. (Open Tu-Sa 10am-5pm, Su noon-5pm, Th until 8pm. $6, students $3, ages 6-12 $1.50. Seniors free on Th.)

The most controversial structure downtown is Michael Graves's postmodern **Portland Building,** 1120 SW 5th Ave., on the mall. This conglomeration of pastel tile and concrete, the first major work of postmodern architecture to be built in the U.S., has been both praised as pomo genius and condemned as an overgrown jukebox. Nearby, the **Standard Insurance Center,** 900 SW 5th Ave., between Salmon and Taylor, has sparked controversy over **The Quest,** a sensual white marble sculpture more commonly known as "Five Groins in the Fountain."

NO ROOM FOR MUGGERS In 1948, a hole was cut through the sidewalk at the corner of SW Taylor St. and SW Naito Pkwy. (Front St.). It was expected to accommodate a mere lamp post, but greatness was thrust upon it. The street lamp was never installed, and the 24-inch circle of earth was left empty until noticed by Dick Fagan, a columnist for the *Oregon Journal*. Fagan used his column, "Mill Ends," to publicize the patch of dirt, pointing out that it would make an excellent park. After years of such logic-heavy lobbying, the park was added to the city's roster in 1976. At 452.16 sq. in., Mill Ends Park is officially the world's smallest park. Locals have enthusiastically embraced it, planting flowers and hosting a hotly contested snail race on St. Patrick's Day. Exciting activities aplenty: play solo frisbee, wave at passing cars, read Raymond Carver or Beverly Cleary, hunt earthworms, develop a national healthcare plan, or bury deceased Smurfs.

Some 19 large fountains provide plenty of cool spots to sit by on occasional sunny days. The free *Portland's Municipal Fountains* is available at the visitor center. **Salmon Street Springs,** in Waterfront Park at SW Salmon St., is controlled by an underground computer that synchronizes its 185 jets according to the city's mood. About 60 **Benson Bubblers,** miniature fountains in their own right, dot the downtown area. Teetotalling lumber baron Simon Benson commissioned these water fountains in 1912 when one of his workers told him that Portlanders drank so much because the city lacked sources of fresh water. Benson boasted that after the bubblers were installed, alcohol consumption dropped by 25%.

On the **South Park Blocks,** a series of cool and shaded parks snake down the middle of Park Ave., enclosed on the west side by **Portland State University (PSU).** The **Portland Farmers Market** crowds in here on Saturdays (May-Oct.) and Wednesdays (June-Sept.), bringing garden talks and chef demonstrations.

If the kiddies get restless, herd 'em off to the **Portland Children's Museum**, 3037 SW 2nd Ave. (823-2227), at Woods St., where arts activities and hands-on exhibits like *Arty Bugs* (Mar.-Aug. 2000) keep young children mesmerized. *Under Construction* (Sept. 1999-Mar. 2000) anticipates the museum's move to Washington Park, across from the Oregon Zoo. After August, 2000, call for museum hours. (Open Tu-Su 9am-5pm. $4. Take bus #1, 12, 40, 41, 43, 45, or 55, all yellow rose.)

OLD TOWN, CHINATOWN AND THE PEARL DISTRICT

The section of downtown above SW Stark running along the Willamette River comprises **Old Town.** Though not the safest part of Portland, Old Town has been revitalized in recent years by storefront restoration, new shops, restaurants, and nightclubs. On weekends, **Saturday Market** draws all of Portland for food, crafts, hackey-sacks, and live entertainment. Intended as a place where "horses, men and dogs" might drink, **Skidmore Fountain,** at SW 1st Ave. and SW Ankeny St., is now a popular people-watching spot and marks the end of **Waterfront Park,** a 20-block swath of grass and flowers along the Willamette River. Resident brewmeister Henry Weinhard's offer to run draft beer through the fountain upon its grand opening in 1888 was rejected by city officials, the putzes.

Downtown's waterfront district is laced with a complex web of underground passages known as the **Shanghai tunnels.** Urban lore has it that seamen would get folks drunk, drag them down to the tunnels, and store them there until their ship sailed. Forced aboard and taken out to sea, these hapless Portlanders would provide a free crew. ("Behave or I'll make you a galley slave" is a common parental threat in Portland.) North of Burnside, the arched **China Gates** (1986) at NW 4th Ave. and Burnside frame a transplanted community among a few restaurants.

Opposite the North Park Blocks, between NW 8th and Park Ave., the up-and-coming **Pearl District** buzzes. Stretching north from Burnside to I-405 along the river, this former industrial zone is packed with galleries, loft apartments, and warehouses-turned-office buildings. Storefronts and cafes have made the area welcoming, but boxy architecture hulks on. *First Thursday* (free at PAM) is a guide to local galleries. Walk north on NW 9th Ave., turn left on NW Glisan and right on NW 12th. Ave. to catch some of the area's most engaging spaces, including the **Blackfish Gallery,** 420 NW Ninth Ave., and the visiting artist's exhibition space at the **Pacific Northwest College of Art** (821-8897), at 1241 NW Johnson. The **Quintana Gallery,** 501 SW Broadway, displays masks and reliefs by contemporary Native American artists working in traditional styles.

For an enriching artistic experience with that little bit more soul pay a visit to the first and only **24-Hour Church of Elvis,** 720 SW Ankeny St. (226-3671; www.churchofelvis.com). This hopes to be a 24-hour coin-operated funhouse again very soon; 30-minute tours run in the meantime. Visits to the giftstore ($1 and up) grant exit from the land of eternal grace. (Usually open M-Th 2-4pm, F 8pm-midnight, Sa noon-5pm and 8pm-midnight, Su noon-5pm, but call ahead.)

Downtown on the edge of the Northwest district is the gargantuan **Powell's City of Books,** 1005 W. Burnside St. (228-4651 or 800-878-7323; www.powells.com), a cavernous establishment with more volumes than any other independent bookstore in the U.S. Renovations doubling the size of the store will be complete by 2000. If you like to dawdle in bookshops, bring a sleeping bag and rations. Seven color-coded rooms house books on everything from criminology to cooking. The **Anne Hughes Coffee Room** inside the beast serves bagels, cookies, and coffee for those who can't find their way out. Powell's also features poetry and fiction readings several times a week (7:30pm in the purple room) and an extensive travel section on Portland and the Pacific Northwest (open daily 9am-11pm).

NORTH AND NORTHEAST PORTLAND

Nicknamed "Munich on the Willamette," Portland is the uncontested **microbrewery** capital of the U.S., and residents are proud of their beer. The visitor center hands out a list of 26 metro area breweries, most of which happily give tours if you call ahead. **Widmer Bros. Brewing Co.,** 929 N. Russell (281-2437), at the Rose Garden, offers free tours and samples (F 2 and 3pm, Sa 1 and 2pm). Many beer factories are brew pubs, sometimes offering live music with their beers. Try the **Lucky Labrador Brew Pub,** 915 SE Hawthorne Blvd. (236-3555), where dogs rule the loading dock for Miser Monday pints ($2.25; open M-Sa 11am-midnight, Su noon-10pm). See **Nightlife,** below for more. Visit the **Oregon Brewers Guild,** 510 NW 3rd Ave. (295-1862 or 800-440-2537; www.oregonbeer.org), to learn exactly how these alchemists work their magic on mere water and hops grains (open M-F 10am-4pm).

Minutes from downtown on Sandy Blvd. (U.S. 30), at NE 85th, a 62-acre Catholic sanctuary, **The Grotto** (254-7371), houses magnificent religious sculptures and gardens. At the heart of the grounds is "Our Lady's Grotto," a breathtaking cave carved into a 110 ft. cliff, and a replica of Michelangelo's *Pieta.* An elevator ($2) ascends from of the Meditation Chapel for a serene view that takes in a life-size bronze of St. Francis of Assisi. (Open daily 9am-8pm; in winter 9am-5:30pm.)

SOUTHEAST PORTLAND

Southeast Portland, largely residential, is scattered with pockets of activity. The **Oregon Museum of Science and Industry (OMSI),** 1945 SE Water Ave. (797-4000 or 797-4569; www.omsi.edu), at SE Clay St., keeps visitors mesmerized at the Paleontology Lab where real dinosaur bones are being worked on in view. Exhibitions for the 1999-2000 series include *Birds of Prey* (Sept.-Dec. 1999), *Extreme Deep* (summer 2000), and *The Changing Face of Women's Health* (summer 2000). (Open daily Labor Day to Memorial Day 9:30am-7pm, Th until 8pm; in winter daily 9:30am-5:30pm, Th until 8pm; $6.50, ages 4-13 and seniors $4.50.) The **Omnimax Theater** (797-4640) in the museum is BIG. (Shows start on the hr. Su-Tu 11am-4pm and W-Sa 11am-9pm. $6.50, ages 4-13 and seniors $4.50.) The **Murdock Planetarium** (797-4646) presents astronomy matinees and moonlights with rockin' laser shows. (Matinees daily $3. Evening shows W-Su $6.50.) While at OMSI, visit the **U.S.S. Blueback** (797-4624), the Navy's last diesel submarine. She never failed a mission, starred in the 1990 film *The Hunt for Red October,* and gets fantastic mileage. (40min. tour $3. Open daily 10am-5pm.) OMSI offers a package deal to all four attractions ($15, ages 4-13 and seniors $11.50).

If you're in the vicinity, **Reed College,** 3203 SE Woodstock (771-1112; events 777-7522) sponsors a number of cultural events on a campus that encompasses a lake and a state wildlife refuge. Students these days are more committed to turning the compost heap than maintaining the nuclear reactor their trail-blazing predecessors opened on campus in 1968. One-hour tours leave weekdays at 10am and 2pm from the admissions office at Eliot Hall #220, 3203 Woodstock Blvd. at SE 28th.

Across the street from Reed is the **Crystal Springs Rhododendron Garden,** SE 28th Ave., at Woodstock (take bus #63). Over 2500 rhododendrons of countless varieties surround a lake and border an 18-hole public golf course. Unwind among ducks, man-made waterfalls, and 90-year-old rhodies. The flowers are in full bloom from March to May. (Open daily 6am-10pm; Mar. 1 to Labor Day Th-M dawn-dusk. Oct.-Feb. daily 8am-7pm. $3, under 12 free.)

WASHINGTON AND FOREST PARKS

Less than 2 mi. west of downtown, the posh neighborhoods of **West Hills** form a buffer zone between soothing parks and the turmoil of the city. In the middle of West Hills, mammoth **Washington Park** and its nearby attractions typify the blend of urbanity and natural bounty Portland has perfected. To get there, take the animated "zoo bus" (#63) on SW Main St., hop on the Hillsboro-bound MAX to Washington Park, or drive up SW Broadway to Clay St. and take U.S. 26 west. The gates close at 9pm, but by day the park is beautiful. The **International Rose Test Garden,** 400 SW Kingston (823-3636), in Washington Park, is the pride of Portland. In summer months a sea of blooms arrests the eye, showing visitors exactly why Portland is the City of Roses. Growers across the world donate roses to this *Rosaceae* testing ground (free, but donations appreciated). Across from the Rose Garden are the scenic **Japanese Gardens,** 611 SW Kingston Ave. (223-1321), reputed to be the most authentic this side of the Pacific. (Open daily Apr.-Sept. 10am-7pm; Oct.-Mar. 10am-4pm. Tours daily at 10:45am and 2:30pm. $6, seniors $4, students $3.50, under 6 free.) The **Hoyt Arboretum,** 4000 SW Fairview Blvd. (228-8733 or 823-3655), at the crest of the hill above the other gardens, features 200 acres of trees and trails, including the charming, wheelchair-accessible **Bristlecone Pine Trail.** The 26 mi. **Wildwood Trail** winds through Washington and Forest Parks, connecting the arboretum to the zoo. Maps are available at the info stand near the arboretum parking lot for a small fee. (Visitor center open M-F 9am-4pm, Sa-Su 10am-5pm.)

The **Oregon Zoo,** 4001 SW Canyon Rd. (226-1561), is renowned for its scrupulous re-creation of natural habitats and its successful elephant breeding. Recent additions include a Cascade Mountains-like goat habitat, and a new marine pool will open during the summer of 2000, part of the zoo's "Great Northwest: A Crest to Coast Adventure" exhibit. A steam engine pulls passengers on a mini railway out to Washington Park gardens and back, giving a better view of flowers and animals (30min. tour $2.75, seniors and ages 3-11 $2). The zoo features a number of educational talks on weekends and has a **children's petting zoo.** (Open 9am-6pm. $5.50, seniors $4, ages 3-11 $3.50; 2nd Tu of each month is free after 3pm.) Reach the zoo via the mural-decorated #63 "zoo bus" that connect the park to SW Main St. in the downtown mall, or take the MAX light-rail to the Washington Park stop.

From late June to August, nationally touring artists perform at the **Rhythm and Zoo Concerts** (234-9694) at the zoo's sculpture garden, free with zoo admission (W-Th at 7pm). **Zoobeat concerts** feature an eclectic range of artists in blues, bluegrass, pop, and world beat on selected summer weekend evenings (7pm; $14-19).

Just north of Washington Park stretches **Forest Park,** a 5000-acre tract of wilderness. Washington Park provides access by car or foot to this sprawling sea of green, the largest park completely enclosed within a U.S. city. A web of trails leads through lush forest and past scenic overviews and idyllic picnic areas. The **Pittock Mansion,** 3229 NW Pittock Dr. (823-3624), within Forest Park, was built by Henry L. Pittock, founder of the daily *Oregonian.* Enjoy a striking panorama of the city from the lawn of this 85-year-old, 16,000 sq. ft. monument to the French Renaissance. From downtown, take crosstown bus #20 (orange deer) to NW Barnes and W. Burnside St., then walk a half-mile up a steep hill to Pittock Ave. Or follow the green-and-white mansion signs west on Burnside Blvd. for 2½ mi. (Open Mar.-Dec. daily noon-4pm. $4.50, seniors $4, ages 6-18 $2. Call for tours.)

♫ ENTERTAINMENT

Prepare for culture. Upon request, the Portland Oregon Visitors Association (see p. 71) will fork over a thick packet outlining the month's events. Outdoor festivals are a way of life. Portland's major daily newspaper, the **Oregonian,** lists upcoming events in its Friday edition. The city's favorite free cultural reader, the Wednesday **Willamette Week,** is a reliable if somewhat uninspiring guide to local music, plays, and art. **The Rocket** (bimonthly and free) provides comprehensive coverage of alternative and punk music for the whole Northwest. Yuppies find their interests represented weekly in **Ourtown,** which lists downtown goings-on.

MUSIC

Although first-rate traveling shows never miss Portland, and many have bargain tickets available, some of the greatest shows are free and outdoors. Live music venues are listed under **Nightlife,** below.

Oregon Symphony Orchestra, 923 SW Washington St. (228-1353 or 800-228-7343). Classics and pop Sept.-June ($15-60). "Symphony Sunday" afternoon concerts ($10-15). Half-price student tickets 1hr. before showtime (Sa and Su). "Monday Madness" offers $5 student tickets 1 week before showtime. Call for park performance info.

High Noon Tunes (223-1613), at Pioneer Courthouse Sq. Jammed concerts early July-Aug. W noon-1pm. A potpourri of rock, jazz, folk, and world music.

Sack Lunch Concerts, 1422 SW 11th Ave. (222-2031), at Clay St. and the Old Church. Classical and jazz music every W at noon. The sack lunch element is unenforced.

Chamber Music Northwest, 522 SW 5th Ave. #725 (294-6400), performs late June-July M, Th, Sa at Reed College Commons, Tu, F at Catlin Gabel School. 8pm. $15-27, ages 7-14 $5.

THEATER

Theater in Portland meets all tastes, ages, and budgets. The **Portland Center for the Performing Arts (PCPA)** (248-4335; www.pcpa.com) is the fourth largest arts center in the U.S. Free **backstage tours** begin in the lobby of the Newmark Theater, at SW Main and Broadway (every 30min. W and Sa 11am-1pm). **Friends of the Performing Arts Center** (274-6555) stages the monthly **Brown Bag Lunch Series,** a glimpse of free professional productions on weekdays around noon. The *Oregonian* has details.

Portland Center Stage (248-6309), in the Newmark Theater of PCPA at SW Broadway and SW Main. Classics, modern adaptations, and world premieres run late Sept.-Apr. Tu-Th, Su $11-31.50, F-Sa $12.50-39. $10 youth matinee seats sometimes available (25 and under). Half-price student rush tickets sometimes available 1hr. before curtain.

Oregon Ballet Theater, 1120 SW 10th Ave. (241-8316, 222-5538, or 888-922-5538). Five productions Oct.-June. 1999-2000 promises Balanchine and the inevitable *Nutcracker.* $10-78; half-price student rush sometimes available 1hr. before curtain.

Artists Repertory Theater, 1516 SW Alder St. (241-1278), puts on top-notch low-budget and experimental productions. W, Th, Su matinees $22, students $16.50; F-Sa $25.

Portland Civic Auditorium, 222 SW Clay St. (274-6560). Big splashy opera, Broadway musicals on tour, and jazz concerts. Part of the PCPA. Tickets $19-103.

Portland Opera, 1515 SW Morrison St. (241-1407), performs at the Portland Civic Auditorium, 222 SW Clay St. *Pagliaci/Carmina Burana* (Feb.) and *Mikado* (May) are in store for 2000. **Portland Opera Presents Keybank Best of Broadway (POPKeBOB),** performs Sept. to July at the Civic Auditorium. Half-price student and senior rush tickets are sometimes available 30min. before shows at both venues. Shows start at 7:30pm.

CINEMA

Portland is a haven for the cinema-needful. With the help of the *Oregonian*, a full freight ticket to just about any screen can be scrupulously avoided, and McMenamins' theater-pubs are one of a kind.

Bagdad Theater and Pub, 3702 SE Hawthorne Blvd. (669-8754 or 230-0895). Take bus #14 (brown beaver). Built in 1921, this magnificently renovated vaudeville theater shows popular, second-run films and serves excellent beer. Open 5pm. Pub open M-Sa 11am-1am, Su noon-midnight. $2-3, matinees Sa-Su $1. Must be 21.

Mission Theater and Pub, 1624 NW Glisan (223-4031), serves excellent home-brewed ales and delicious sandwiches ($5-7). Watch popular, second-run flicks while lounging on couches, at tables, or perched in the old-time balcony. Shows begin around 5:30, 8, and 10pm. $2-3. No smoking. Must be 21.

Cinema 21, 616 NW 21st St. (223-4515), at Hoyt St. Mean, clean and pistachio green. Mostly documentary, independent, and foreign films. A highly acclaimed student haunt, with plenty of progressive literature in the lobby. $6; students $5; under 12 and seniors $3, and periodic first matinee Sa and Su $3.

Northwest Film Center, 1219 SW Park Ave. (221-1156), screens documentary, foreign, classic, experimental, and independent films at the historic **Guild Theatre,** 829 SW 9th Ave., two blocks north of PAM, and hosts the **Portland International Film Festival** in the last two weeks of Feb., with 100 films from 30 nations. Box office opens 30min. before each show. $6, seniors $5.

Cinemagic, 202 SW Hawthorne (231-7919), at the intersection of Hawthorne and 20th. Arty and independent films. $5.75, seniors and children $3.75.

Lloyd Cinema (225-5555, ext. 4600), across from the Lloyd Center Mall. For a first-run movie, this 10-screen, ultra-modern, neon-lined glam-land does the trick.

SPORTS

When Bill Walton led the **Trailblazers** (321-3211) to the 1979 NBA Championship, Portland went berserk—landing an NBA team in the first place had been a substantial accomplishment for an overgrown town. Still a young, up-and-coming team, the Blazers play November to May in the sparkling new **Rose Garden Arena** by the Steel Bridge in Northeast Portland, with its own stop on MAX.

The city's indoor soccer team, the **Portland Pythons** (684-5425), take over the Rose Garden from July to November ($10-18, students and seniors $2 off). The **Winter Hawks** (238-6366) of the Western Hockey League play September to March in the Rose Garden Arena and at the **Coliseum,** but never in both at once. Take bus #9 (brown beaver) or MAX. (Tickets $11.50-19, under 18 and seniors $1 off.) The **Civic Stadium,** 1844 SW Morrison St., on the other side of town, is home to the **Portland Rockies** (223-2837), Colorado's AAA baseball farm team, who played their inaugural season in 1995. (June-Sept. $6-7, under 12 and seniors $5.)

■ NIGHTLIFE

Once an uncouth and rowdy frontier town, always an uncouth and rowdy frontier town. Portland's nightclubs cater to everyone from the clove-smoking college aesthete to the nipple-pierced neo-goth aesthete, often in the same space. Bigger, flashier clubs rule **Old Town** and central **Downtown,** where mixed crowds dance shoulder-to-shoulder down the street from grooving reggae beatsters. Park close-by or come with a friend, since walking alone through downtown at night can be scary. In the **Pearl District** and **Nob Hill,** yuppies and collegiates kick back together in spacious bars. In the **Southeast,** cramped quarters make for instant friends over great music and drinks. Hidden in the Northeastern suburb of **Laurel Hurst,** locals gather in intimate clubs to listen to the best of the city's folk and rock. Neighborhood pubs, plentiful throughout Portland, often have the most character, the best music, and the smallest signs. Mischievous minors be warned: the drinking age is strictly enforced, but spectacular all-ages venues provide thrills without swills.

Publications *Willamette Week, The Rocket,* and *PDXS,* available at street corners, restaurants, and hostels, all have complete club listings. **Ozone Records,** 1036 W. Burnside (227-1975), opposite Powell's, pastes up concert posters.

OLDTOWN AND DOWNTOWN

Panorama, Brig, and **Boxxes,** 341 SW 10th St. (221-7262), form a network of clubs along Stark St. between 10th and 11th. Shake it until you break amid a thriving mixed crowd. $5. Open F-Sa 9pm-4am. The beats reach back in the Brig with 70s and 80s classics (F). Open daily noon-2:30am, Fridays until 4am. Push farther into Boxxes, the 23-screen video/karaoke bar where matchmaking magic happens with the video postings of "Misha's Make-a-Date" (Tu). Open daily noon-2:30am.

Satyricon, 125 NW 6th Ave. (243-2380), on the bus mall. Live alternative and punk since the days when grunge rockers still smelled. Nightly $4-8, bigger draws $10-15. Must be 21. **Fellini,** the club's PoMo, mosaic chic sister restaurant next door, serves innovative cuisine (entrees from $4) while you wait for your ears to stop ringing. Music 10pm-2:30am. Food M-Th 11:30pm-2:30am, F-Sa 5pm-3am, Su 5pm-2:30am.

Embers, 110 NW Broadway (222-3082), at Couch St. Follow the rainbows onto the dance floor, or watch fish swim inside the bustling bar counter. Retro and house music. Nightly drag show at 10pm. Open daily 11am-2:30am. Happy hour until 7pm.

Crystal Ballroom, 1332 W. Burnside Blvd. (225-0047), near the I-405. The grand ballroom and its immense paintings, gaudy chandeliers, arching balcony, and "floating dancefloor," employs cutting edge 1920s technology to keep you dancing all night long to swing or punk. Lessons $5-25. Microbrewery on premises (pints $3.50). Downstairs, **Ringlers** (225-0543) rings in young 'uns with free pool Tu-Su 11:30am-6pm, M 11:30am-2:30am. Open daily 11:30am-2:30am.

Berbati's Pan, 231 SW Ankeny St. (248-4570), next to the New Paris Theatre marquee. This ever-expanding nightspot started as a small Greek restaurant on 2nd Ave. Now the upscale dining room, 3-table pool room, 3 bars, dance hall, and late-night cafe stretch to 3rd. Authentic Greek dishes ($3.50-7) and burgers ($5). Eighteen-piece big band (M), swing dancing (Tu), acid jazz (W), Fetish Night (every 3rd Su), and Karaoke from Hell, with a live band. Cover $3-10. Open M-F 11:30am-2:30am, Sa-Su 5pm-2:30am.

Lotus Card Room and Cafe, 932 SW 3rd Ave. (227-6185), at SW Salmon St. The truly groovy dance floor has glowing cartoon paintings, a movie screen with trippy projections, and a cage. Decades dancing day by day. Happy hour M-F 4-6:30pm: domestics $1.75; appetizers $2. Open M-Tu 11am-midnight, W-F 11am-2am, Sa-Su 5pm-2am.

Ohm, 31 NW 1st Ave. (223-9919), at Couch under the Burnside Bridge. Specializing in unclassifiable beats you're unlikely to hear anywhere else. Bhangra, fire performances and more (Sun), 1930's Jazz (M), Electronica/Prog Jazz (Tu), old school jazz meets new school DJs (W), Funk, Soul, Hip-Hop (Th), DJs (F). Saturdays are anyone's guess. $4-10. Open M-Th 8pm-2:30am, F 8pm-2:30am, Sa 11am-4am, Su 11am-2:30am.

Brasserie Montmartre, 626 SW Park Ave. (224-5552), on Morrison. Live jazz nightly, paper tablecloths, crayons, and roaming magicians. Modestly priced Bistro menu. Open M-Th 11:30am-1am, F 11:30am-3am, Sa 10am-3am, Su 10am-1am.

SOUTHEAST AND HAWTHORNE

The Womb, 215 SE 9th Ave. (236-3346), at Pine. Take bus #20 to 9th and walk 2 blocks south. In the belly of this nondescript factory building, high above the cavernous dancefloor, grows the space baby. All ages rave from 10pm to noon (Sa, $10-15). On New Year's 2000, the baby will be born on what promises to be a wild night. This space used to be the legendary La Luna, and indie rockers still pop in.

Produce Row Cafe, 204 SE Oak St. (232-8355). Take bus #6 to SE Oak and SE Grand, then walk west along Oak toward the river. A staple among bigfoot watchers and opera buffs for summer starlight and industrial ambience on the back deck. 27 beers on tap and over 200 in bottles. Live rock (Sa, $3), jazz (M, $2), bluegrass (Tu, free), and open mic (W, free). Domestic bottles $1.50, pints $2; microbrew pints $3. Open M-F 11am-1am, Sa noon-1am, Su noon-midnight.

Biddy McGraw's, 3518 SE Hawthorne Blvd. (233-1178; www.biddys.com). Take bus #14. Biddy and her daughter set out to create a pub like the ones they remembered in Ireland and succeeded. Live Celtic tunes (Th-Su) and raucous dancing to Reggae (Su), funk (M) and jazz (Tu). 22 kegs of Guinness are consumed here per week. Do your part for $3.75 per imperial pint. Microbrews $3. Open daily 11am-2:30am.

LaCruda, 2500 SE Clinton (233-0745), serves huge veggie burritos ($5). Their name means "hangover" in Spanish. After a night of downing their killer mango margaritas ($4), you'll understand why. Open M-F 11am-2:30am, Sa-Su 9am-2:30am.

Barley Mill Pub, 1629 SE Hawthorne Blvd. (231-1492). Take bus #14. A smoky temple to Jerry Garcia; bring your bootlegs on Wednesday nights and let the music live on. Full of fantastic murals and long bench tables that may land you next to a stranger. Upbeat, yet mellow, like the man himself. McMenamins beer on tap ($2.85). Happy hour daily 4-6pm ($2.25). Open M-Sa 11am-1am, Su noon-midnight.

LAUREL HURST

The Laurel Thurst Public House, 2958 NE Glisan St. (232-1504) at 30th Ave. Take bus #19. A neighborhood crowd jams to local acoustic and electric acts. Two intimate rooms allow for groovin', boozin', and schmoozin'. Breakfast until 3pm. Burgers and sandwiches $5-6. Microbrew pints $3.25, domestic $2.25. Cover $2-3. Free pool all day Su, and M-Th before 7pm. Open M-F 9am-1:30am, Sa-Su 9am-2am.

Beulahland, 118 NE 28th Ave. (235-2794), at Couch opposite the Coca-Cola bottling plant. Take bus #19. On the cozy stage, musicians siphon every unruly emotion into coarse sounds before a mesmerized crowd. No cover. Happy hour 4pm-6pm. Open M-W 7am-midnight, Th-Sa 7am-1am, Su 9am-midnight.

KOW, 116 NE 28th Ave. (238-8890), next door, hosts local bands ($5) and screens matinee classic and local indie films ($3). Open Su-Th 7:30pm-10pm, F-Sa 9pm-2am.

EJ's, 2140 NE Sandy Blvd. (234-3535), at 22nd Ave. Take bus #12. Punk and indie bands strut their thangs on the low stage in a dark, smoky atmosphere. $1 Pabsts until 8pm. Cover $5-10. Open Tu-F 5:30pm-2am, Sa-Su 11:30am-2am.

PEARL AND NOB HILL DISTRICTS

Jimmy Mak's, 300 NW 10th Ave. (295-6542; www.jimmymaks.com), 3 blocks from Powell's Books at Flanders. Nightly jazz, funk, soul, or groove (9:30pm-1am, typical cover $3-5) boasts big alumni, like Bernard Purdie and Dave Liebman. Vegetarian-friendly Greek and Middle Eastern dinners ($8-17). Open M-Sa 11am-2am.

BridgePort Brew Pub, 1313 NW Marshall (241-7179), at 13th St. The zenith of beer and pizza joints in a wood-beamed rope factory (5-topping pie $19.75). Lotsa space for lotsa people on tables cut from old bowling alleys. Brews are all BridgePort; $2 for 10 oz., $3.25 for 20 oz. Open M-Th 11:30am-11pm, F-Sa 11:30am-midnight, Su 1-9pm. Also at 3632 SE Hawthorne (233-6540).

■ SHOPPING

For some, shopping in the **Nob Hill** district is a religious experience. Fashionable boutiques run from Burnside to Thurman St. between NW 21st and NW 24th Ave., mostly on 23rd Ave. Make the pilgrimage to NE Halsey and 15th Ave. to shop at the **Lloyd Center Mall** (282-2511), and stop at the **ice chalet** skating rink (288-6073) to do your impression of Portland's own Tonya Harding. (*Let's Go* does not recommend impersonating Tonya Harding. Open year-round. Hours vary. $8.50, under 17 $7.50; skate rental included.) Parking can be a hassle on the weekends, but Lloyd Center is on the MAX line, and bus #15 (red salmon) and cross-town bus #77 go to Nob Hill. Just two blocks north and a few blocks east of Lloyd Center, the NE Broadway area provides less hectic shopping for clothing, books, and baked goods.

Downtown's **Pearl District** and the Southeast's **Sellwood** area, SE 13th Ave. around SE Tacoma St., are known for their antiques and apparel. **Hawthorne Blvd.,** between 30th and 40th, is a hip strip where prices aren't too high and parking can still be found on weekends. This string of trendy cafes, antique shops, used book stores, and theaters ends at the bottom of **Mt. Tabor Park,** one of two city parks in the world on the site of an extinct volcano. Find it at SE 60th Ave. and Salmon Ave., or SE 69th Ave. two blocks south of Belmont Ave.; take bus #15 (brown beaver) from downtown. Shops are sprouting on **Belmont Ave.**, a few avenues north, which some have touted as the "new Hawthorne." For books, stop into any of the generally excellent small bookstores along Hawthorne, or cut to the chase and visit **Powell's** (see p. 79). Portland is also home to a thriving **thrift-store** culture, especially near Dot's Cafe on Clinton St. (see p. 77).

The eclectic and festive **Saturday Market** (222-6072) is held by the Skidmore Fountain between 1st and Naito Pkwy. (Front Ave.) from March to December (Sa 10am-5pm, Su 11am-4:30pm). This is the largest open-air crafts market in the country, crowded with street musicians, artists, and dazed onlookers. The **Portland Farmers Market** in the South Park Blocks, at SW Park by PSU, brings greengrocers, cooking demonstrations, and garden talks (May-Oct. 8am-2pm).

EVENTS

Cinco de Mayo Festival (222-9807), on the weekend closest to May 5th. Portlanders celebrate Mexican Independence with sister city Guadalajara at Waterfront Park.

Rose Festival, 220 NW 2nd Ave. (227-2681), during the first 3 weeks of June. Portland's premier summer event. U.S. Navy sailors flood the finery-bedecked streets. Concerts, celebrities, auto racing, an air show, and the largest children's parade in the world. Women should exercise caution at night. Many events require tickets.

Waterfront Blues Festival (282-0555 or 973-3378), June 30-July 4. Outrageously good. Suggested donation is $3-5 and 2 cans of food to benefit the Oregon Food Bank.

Oregon Brewers Festival (778-5917), on the last full weekend in July. The continent's largest gathering of independent brewers parties at Waterfront Park. $2 mug, $1 per taste. Those under 21 must be accompanied by a parent.

Mt. Hood Festival of Jazz (232-3000), on the first weekend in Aug. at Mt. Hood Community College in Gresham. Take I-84 to the Wood Village-Gresham exit and follow the signs, or ride MAX to the end of the line. The PNW's premier jazz festival. Wynton Marsalis and the late Stan Getz have been regulars. Tickets from $29.50 per night, more through Ticketmaster. Reserve well in advance by writing Mt. Hood Festival of Jazz, P.O. Box 3024, Gresham 97030.

The Bite: A Taste of Portland (248-0600), August 13-15, 2000, in Waterfront Park. Samples of food from over 20 Portland restaurants ($2-5), free music, stand-up comics, and a wine pavilion. Proceeds benefit Special Olympics Oregon. $2 donation suggested.

Portland Marathon (226-1111; www.portlandmarathon.org), in early Oct. A good 26.2-miler. Many shorter runs and walks are also held, but remember: Phedippedes died.

NEAR PORTLAND: SAUVIE ISLAND

Sauvie Island is a peaceful rural hideaway at the confluence of the Columbia and Willamette Rivers, 20 minutes northwest of downtown Portland. Follow U.S. 30 and signs toward Mount St. Helens from I-405, Vaughn, or Yeon Ave.; or take bus #17 (St. Helens Rd.) from SW 6th and Salmon (40-50min.). The island offers great views of the city from its vast and sandy stretches. On winter mornings, eagles and geese congregate along the roads, and in spring and summer, berries are everywhere (most plentiful from August to September). Hand-lettered signs along the roads announce the island's numerous popular family-run **u-pick farms**.

Many visitors soak up the rays on the island's south and east side beaches along the Columbia River, including the clothing-optional Collins Beach; follow Sauvie Island Rd. south to Gillihan Rd. which meets Reeder Rd. Some bring fishing rods and bathing suits, but whether it's safe to swim in the Willamette's waters depends on who you ask; factories and imperfect sewage systems upstream leave residents wary. Slough and pond banks in the inland area around **Sturgeon Lake** make for the best fishing from March to June (check fishing regulations at 621-3488; follow Sauvie Island Rd. north to the rocky and narrow Steelman Rd.). Camping is available at **Yarbor's By the Beach,** 31421 NW Reeder Rd. (621-9564), on the northeastern side of the island. (Sites with water and firepits $12, RV sites $18-20. Toilets and shower. Reception Tu-Su 10am-8pm.) A $3 **parking permit** is required for the whole island, and is efficiently enforced. Pick one up at **Sam's Cracker Barrel Grocery** (621-3960; open daily 8am-8pm), along with a 5¢ map of the island. Plan ahead; Sam's is the only place on the island that sells permits and it's by the bridge (on your left as you head north), several miles from the beaches.

COLUMBIA RIVER GORGE

The magnificent Columbia River Gorge, a canyon in places more than 1000 ft. deep, stretches 75 stunning miles east from Portland. Heading inland along the gorge, heavily forested peaks give way to broad, bronze cliffs and golden hills. Mt. Hood and Mt. Adams loom nearby, and breathtaking waterfalls plunge over steep cliffs into the river. The river widens out and the wind picks up at the town of Hood River, providing some of the world's best windsurfing. Though it was once "as fast as a waterfall turned on its side," and so full of fish that Lewis and Clark joked that they could walk across without getting wet, the Columbia's waters now run slower and emptier due to damming upstream.

⚡ ORIENTATION AND PRACTICAL INFORMATION

To follow the gorge, which divides Oregon and Washington, take I-84 east from Portland to Exit 22. Continue east uphill on the **Columbia River Scenic Highway (U.S. 30),** which follows the crest of the gorge and affords unforgettable views. Hwy. 14 runs the length of the Washington side. **Hood River, OR,** at the junction of I-84 and Hwy. 35, is the hub of activity in the gorge, and gives access to the larger city of **Dalles, OR** (rhymes with gals), to the east, and Mt. Hood (see p. 128) to the south. **Bingen, WA** (BIN-jin), across the Hood River Bridge (75¢), gives access to the forests of Mt. Adams (see p. 219). **Maryhill, WA,** is 33 mi. west of Bingen on Hwy. 14.

Trains: Amtrak (800-872-7245) disgorges passengers at the foot of Walnut St. (across from Monterey Bay Fiberglass) in Bingen, WA, for: Portland (2hr., 7:45am, $9-16) and Spokane (6hr., 6:25pm, $32-58). See p. 52 for discounts.

Buses: Greyhound, 600 E. Marina Way (386-1212 or 800-231-2222), in the Hood River DMV building. Take a left at the intersection before the toll bridge and follow the signs to the DMV, the second building on the right. To: Portland (1¼hr., 5 per day, $10). Open M-F 8:30-11:30am and 1:30-4:30pm.

Public Transportation: Columbia Area Transit (CAT) (386-4202) provides door-to-door service within the Hood River area for $1.25; call for pickup (daily 7am-3:30pm). Weekend shuttle to Mt. Hood Meadows (see p. 129) during the ski season $3.

Visitor Information: Hood River County Chamber of Commerce, 405 Portway Ave. (386-2000 or 800-366-3530; www.gorge.net/hrccc), the Expo Ctr. north off Exit 63. Open Apr.-Oct. M-Th 8:30am-5pm, F 8:30am-4pm, Sa-Su 10am-4pm; Nov.-Mar. M-F 9am-5pm. Many other visitor centers also line the gorge.

Outdoor Information: Columbia Gorge National Scenic Area Headquarters, 902 Wasco St. #200 (386-2333; www.fs.fed.us/r6/columbia), in Sprint's Waucoma Ctr. Building, Hood River. Open M-F 7:30am-5pm. Their Forest Service map ($3) plots free camping.

Weather: 541-298-5116.

Emergency: 911. **Hood River Police:** 211 2nd St. (non-emergency 386-3942).

Hospital: Hood River Memorial, 13th and May St. (386-3911).

Library: 502 State St., Hood River (386-2535), up the hill opposite Wy'East Whole Foods. Free 30min. **Internet access.** Open M-Th 8:30am-8:30pm, F-Sa 8:30am-4:30pm.

Post Office: 408 Cascade Ave., 97031 (800-275-8777), in Hood River. Open M-F 8:30am-5pm.

Area Code: In OR 541; in WA 509.

PORTRAIT OF A MONSTER

Name: Bigfoot (English) or Sasquatch (Chinook).

Size: According to a recent forensic analysis of the 1967 Patterson-Gimlin film, utilizing a standard primate chest-breadth extrapolation algorithm, approximately 2000 lb. and 7 ft. 3½ in.

Geographical Range: The Cascade Mountains of the Pacific Northwest, even into BC.

Diet: Omnivorous.

Odor: Strong and fetid.

Evolutionary History: Possibly derived from *Gigantapithecus blacki* in Asia. Any relationship to the Himalayan Yeti ("abominable snowman") is strictly superficial— every culture has its own Big Hairy Monster ("BHM").

Evidence: Oral and written history among both Native Americans and Westerners, the aforementioned film, a high frequency of sightings, and big footprints.

WESTERN OREGON

FOOD AND ACCOMMODATIONS

For groceries, hit **Safeway,** 2249 W. Cascade St. (386-1841; open daily 6am-midnight), on the west side of Hood River. **Wy'East Whole Food Market,** 110 5th St. (386-6181; open M-Sa 7:30am-7pm; Su 10am-5pm), off Oak St. in Hood River, sells natural foods and great sandwiches.

Rooms in Hood River typically cost between $50 and $80. The cheaper motels line the west end of Westcliffe Dr., north off I-84 Exit 62. **Lone Pine Motel,** 2429 Cascade St. (387-8882 or 490-9000), just west of Safeway, rents rooms for $27-55.

The outdoorsy **Bingen School Inn Hostel** (509-493-3363; www.bsi-cgoc.com), is 3½ blocks from the Amtrak stop in Bingen, WA. Take the third left after the yellow blinking light onto Cedar St.; from there it's one block up the hill on Humbolt St. This converted schoolhouse offers a kitchen, laundry, climbing wall, volleyball net, outdoor grill, and school lockers. Winter guests score $20 Hood Meadows lift tickets (see p. 129). In summer, **windsurfing lessons** ($65 for 3 hr.) and rentals ($30 per day) are available to all. (48 beds $14; 5 large private rooms $35.)

Beacon Rock State Park (509-427-8265), 7 mi. west of the Bridge of the Gods on Washington's Hwy. 14, has 33 secluded sites and access to hiking, biking, fishing, and rock climbing ($10). **Port of Cascade Locks Marine** (386-1645), half a mile east of the bridge on the Oregon side, has tenting on a crowded, windy lawn between the river and the road ($10; showers). **Ainsworth State Park** is also readily accessible (see **Portland: Accommodations and Campgrounds,** p. 72).

SIGHTS

Vista House (503-695-2230), completed in 1918 as a memorial to Oregon's pioneers, is now a visitor center at **Crown Point State Park.** From I-84 Exit 22 take Corbett Hill Rd. to the top of the hill, then turn left for 3 miles. (Open daily mid-Apr. to Oct. 15 8:30am-6pm.) The house, at the edge of the canyon, has exhibits about the Gorge's history and terrain. For a lofty view, drive up the **Larch Mountain Rd.,** which splits from U.S. 30 just above the Vista House and winds up 4000 ft. over 14 mi. A steep 20-minute hike through woods leads to a picnic area with views of Mount St. Helens, Mt. Rainier, Mt. Adams, Mt. Hood, and Mt. Jefferson.

The elegant **Maryhill Museum of Art,** 35 Maryhill Museum Dr. (509-773-3733), sits high above the river on the Washington side. To get there, take Hwy. 14 from Bingen or take I-84 to Biggs (Exit 104), cross Sam Hill Bridge, then turn left onto Hwy. 14 for 2.8 miles. Built by Sam Hill in the 1920s, the exquisite concrete mansion is named after both his wife and daughter. Sam was a friend of **Queen Marie of Roumania,** whose coronation garb is displayed along with Rodin plasters and watercolors, chess sets, and native artifacts. Upstairs, a collection of 27-inch tall mannequins dressed in haute couture from Parisian fashion houses pose on sets built to scale. During and after WWII, when materials were scarce, these displays substituted for traditional fashion shows. In 2000, the museum will exhibit "Art of the Firebird: Russian Miniature Paintings" and "The Universelle Exposition: A Matched Pair" which examines the relationship between two of Sam Hill's close friends, Rodin and the celebrated dancer Loie Fuller. (Open daily mid-Mar. to mid-Nov. 9am-5pm. $6.50, seniors $6, ages 6-12 $1.50, under 5 free.)

Four miles farther east along Hwy. 14 lies **Stonehenge.** Sam Hill built this full scale replica of the mysterious English monument out of reinforced concrete as a memorial to the men of Klickitat County killed in WWI. Hill, a Quaker, used this pagan symbol to express that "humanity still is being sacrificed to the god of war on fields of battle." Hill's crypt is just south of the bluff. (Open daily 7am-10pm.)

So new you can still smell it, the slick **Columbia Gorge Discovery Center/Wasco County Historical Museum,** 5000 Discovery Dr. (296-8600), in The Dalles, has exhibits on the geology, ecology, original inhabitants, settlement, and development of the gorge. While the museum often dips into cheesiness with dioramas and even claymation, the sections that concentrate on the oral history of gorge residents are moving. Rangers and native craftsmen give weekend presentations during the summer. (Open daily 10am-6pm. $6.50, seniors $5.50, ages 6-16 $3, under 6 free.)

▲ OUTDOORS

Frequent 30mph winds make Hood River a **windsurfing** paradise. The town shuts down on windy days, and residents get antsy during calm stretches. Beginners sail at the **Hook,** a shallow, sandy cove. The water near **Spring Creek Fish Hatchery** on the Washington side is the place to watch the best in the business. Another hub is the **Event Site,** off Exit 63 behind the visitor center. All-day parking costs $3, or free if you just sit and watch. The venerated **Rhonda Smith Windsurfing Center** (386-9463) offers classes. Take Exit 64 off I-84, go under the bridge and turn left after the blinking red light. ($125 for two 3hr. classes includes free evening practice.)

Big Winds, 207 Front St. (386-6086; www.bigwinds.com), at the east end of Oak St., has cheap beginner rentals ($8 per hour; $15 per half-day; $25 per day). **Windance,** 108 Hwy. 35 (386-2131; www.windance.com), hosts legendary, colossal windsurfing flea markets on the third Sunday of April, May, and June.

The gorge also has excellent **mountain biking. Discover Bicycles,** 205 Oak St. (386-4820), rents mountain bikes, suggests routes, and sells all manner of maps (open M-Sa 9am-7pm, Su 9am-5pm; bikes $6 per hr., $30 per day). The 11 mi. round-trip **Hospital Hill Trail** provides views of Mt. Hood, the gorge, and surrounding settlements. To reach the unmarked trail, follow signs to the hospital, take the left fork to Rhine Village, and ride behind the power transformers and through the fence.

A string of waterfalls adorns U.S. 30 east of Crown Point; pick up a waterfall map at the Vista House (see **Sights,** above). A short paved path leads to the base of **Latourell Falls,** 2½ mi. east of Crown Point. East another 5½ mi., **Wahkeena Falls** ("most beautiful"), visible from the road, splashes 242 ft. down a narrow gorge. The base of the falls, a popular picnic spot, is less than half a mile down a paved trail. The trail continues 3¼ mi. to the 620-foot **Multnomah Falls.** Multnomah is also accessible half a mile farther east on U.S. 30: from I-84 Exit 31, take the underpass to the lodge. From a platform, you can watch the falls crash into a tiny pool, then drain under the gracefully arching **Benson Bridge.** For a more strenuous hike, follow the **Larch Mountain Trail** to the top of the falls. The **visitor center** in the lodge has free maps of other trails.

The deservedly popular **Eagle Creek Trail** (12 mi. round-trip), chiseled into the cliffs high above the creek, passes four waterfalls and several camps before joining the Pacific Crest Trail. At **Beacon Rock State Park,** on the Washington side, the 848 ft. neck of an old volcano may be the largest monolith in America. A 2250 ft., 3½ mi. hike up **Mt. Hamilton** starts in a parking lot east of Beacon Rock. Switchbacks lead to the 2948 ft. summit, which in June and July bursts with wildflowers.

OREGON COAST

If not for the renowned **U.S. 101,** Oregon's dripping beaches and dramatic seaside vistas might be only a beautiful rumor to those on the interior. From Astoria in the north to Brookings down south, the highway hugs the shore along the Oregon Coast, linking a string of resorts and fishing villages that cluster around the mouths of rivers feeding into the Pacific. Breathtaking ocean views spread between these towns, while state parks and national forests allow direct access to the big surf. Wherever the windy two lanes leave the coast, even narrower beach loops access long stretches of unspoiled coast, giving glimpses of the diverse sea life. Seals, sea lions, and waterfowl lounge on rocks just offshore, watching the human world whiz by on wheels.

⌐ GETTING AROUND

Gasoline and grocery **prices** on the coast are about 20% higher than in inland cities; smaller coastal villages tend to be cheaper and more interesting. There are 17 state parks along the coast, offering **campgrounds** with electricity and showers. Traveling down the coast **by bike** is both rewarding and exhausting. Cyclists can contact virtually any visitor center or chamber of commerce on the coast to get a copy of the free *Oregon Coast Bike Route Map;* it provides invaluable info on campsites, hostels, bike repair facilities, temperatures, and wind conditions. Portlanders head down the coast to vacation, so most traffic flows south from the city. In summer, prevailing winds also blow southward, keeping at the backs of cyclists and easing the journey. The shoulders of U.S. 101 and other coastal highways often narrow to nonexistent, though, and enormous log trucks lumber around tight turns. **Buses** run up and down the coast, stopping in most sizeable towns. Many local lines are affiliates of Greyhound (see p. 53), and make connections to major urban centers like Seattle, Portland, and Eugene.

ASTORIA

Astoria's long-standing dependence on maritime industries has only recently begun to yield to the tourist industry's shiny promises. A stay here offers a much more pleasant—and less expensive—way to see the coast than the overrun resort cities just to the south. Its Victorian homes, bustling waterfront, rolling hills, and persistent fog suggest San Francisco on a smaller scale. Travelers heading up and down the coast share the town with sales-tax-dodging Washingtonians who travel south across the towering, incredibly narrow, Astoria Bridge. Nearby, a rich recreation of one of Lewis and Clark's winter camps makes a great stop.

▨ ORIENTATION AND PRACTICAL INFORMATION

From Astoria, U.S. 30 runs 96 mi. to Portland. Astoria can also be reached from Portland on U.S. 26 and U.S. 101 via Seaside (see p. 92). Astoria is a convenient link between Washington and the Oregon coast. Two bridges run from the city: the **Youngs Bay Bridge** leading southwest where **Marine Dr.** becomes U.S. 101, and the **Astoria Bridge,** which spans the **Columbia River** into Washington. All streets parallel to the water are named in alphabetical order except for the first one, Marine Dr.

   Buses: Pierce Pacific Stages (692-4437). A Greyhound affiliate. Pickup at Video City, 95 W. Marine Dr., opposite the chamber of commerce. To: Portland (3hr., 3:30pm, $15); Seaside (30min., 1:15pm, $5). **Sunset Empire Transit** (861-7433). Pickup at Duane and 9th St. To: Seaside (7 per day; $2.25, seniors and disabled $1.75). **Astoria Transit System,** 364 9th St. (325-0563 or 800-776-6406). Local bus service M-Sa 6am-7pm. Makes a full city loop every hr. (75¢; students, seniors, disabled 50¢).

   Taxis: Yellow Cab (325-3131 or 861-2626) runs 6am-2pm.

AAA: 135 U.S. 101 S (861-3118), in Warrenton. Open M-F 8am-5pm.

Visitor Information: 111 W. Marine Dr. (325-6311), just east of Astoria Bridge. Open June-Sept. M-F 8am-6pm, Sa-Su 9am-6pm; Oct.-May M-F 8am-5pm, Sa-Su 11am-4pm.

Library: Astor Library, 450 10th St. (325-7323). Free **Internet access.** Open M-Th 10am-8pm, F-Sa 10am-6pm. **Public Radio:** 91.9 FM

Laundromat: Coin Laundry, 823 W. Marine Dr. (325-2027), next to the Dairy Queen. Wash $1.25, dry 25¢ per 8min. Open daily 7:30am-10pm.

Emergency: 911. **Police:** 555 30th St. (325-4411). **Coast Guard:** 861-6228.

Hospital: Columbia Memorial, 2111 Exchange St. (325-4321 or 800-962-2407).

Post Office: 750 Commercial St., 97103 (800-275-8777), in the Federal Bldg. at 8th St. Open M-F 8:30am-5pm.

Area Code: 503.

ACCOMMODATIONS AND CAMPGROUNDS

Motel rooms can be expensive and elusive during summer. U.S. 101 south of Astoria is littered with clean, scenic campgrounds.

Grandview B&B, 1574 Grand Ave. (325-0000, reservations 325-5555; www.pacifier.com/~grndview). Intimate, cheery, luxurious rooms. The delicious breakfast includes fresh muffins, smoked salmon, bagels, and full service. Rooms with shared bath from $45, with private bath from $59. Off-season, 2nd night is $28.

Astoria Hostel, 443 14th St. (325-6989), in a converted apartment building in the heart of town. Separate men's and women's dorms with shared bath and linens $15.

Lamplighter Motel, 131 W. Marine Dr. (325-4051 or 800-845-8847), between the Pig 'n Pancake diner and the visitor center. Well-lit rooms with cable TV and phones. Large bathrooms. Coffee in the lobby. Rooms $62-75, less in winter. Senior discount.

Fort Stevens State Park (861-1671, reservations 800-452-5687), over Youngs Bay Bridge on U.S. 101 S, 10 mi. west of Astoria, in the largest state park in the U.S., is the closest major campground to Seaside and Cannon Beach. Rugged, empty beaches and bike trails surround the campground. Hot showers. 600 sites: $17, full hookups $20; hiker/biker sites $4.25 per person; yurts $29. Reservations ($6) recommended for summer weekends. Wheelchair accessible.

FOOD

Grab pickled herring and Ryvita at **Sentry Supermarket,** 3300 Leif Erickson Dr. (325-1931; open daily 7am-10pm). A **Safeway,** 1153 Duane St. (325-4662), downtown, is open daily 6am-midnight. A small but growing **farmer's market** takes over the parking lot behind the Maritime Museum (see **Sights,** below) each summer Saturday.

Columbian Cafe, 1114 Marine Dr. (325-2233). Despite the chef's frenzied crêpe-flipping just inches from diners, there's often a long wait. Local banter, microbrews, and fantastic pasta and seafood dishes ($10-15, $5-8 for lunch) make it worthwhile. Try "Chef's Mercy"—you name your "heat range and allergies," he chooses your meal ($7). Open M-F 8am-2pm, Sa-Su 9am-2pm. Open for dinner W-Th 5-9pm, F-Sa 5-10pm.

Shark Rock Cafe, 1092 Marine Dr. (325-7720). A hip crowd gathers before the fireplace in this bright, bold joint. Cinnamon french toast ($5.25) and lunchtime delicacies like smoked salmon lasagna ($13) share menu space with smaller-ticket items like the Mediterranean chicken sandwich ($7.25). Open Tu-Sa 8am-9pm.

Someplace Else, 965 Commercial St. (325-3500). The regulars vote on specials ($5-14); chick peas in tamarind sauce are a favorite. Open W-M 11:30am-2pm and 4-9pm.

Wet Dog Cafe and Pacific Rim Brewing Co., 144 11th St. (325-6975), is Astoria's only venue for live music and packs in the crowds every weekend. Listen to anything from alternative to blues ($3-6) over a pint of Peacock Spit Golden Ale ($3) from the brewery out front. Pub fare until 9pm. Game room and DJ every Th. Open daily 11am-1am.

![] SIGHTS AND EVENTS

Every so often, the clouds around **Astoria Column** lift to reveal a stupendous view of Astoria cradled between Saddle Mountain to the south and the Columbia River estuary to the north. Completed in 1926, the column on Coxcomb Hill Rd. encloses 164 steps past newly repainted friezes depicting local history. (Open dawn-10pm; free.) The cavernous, wave-shaped **Columbia River Maritime Museum,** 1792 Marine Dr. (325-2323), on the waterfront, is packed with marine lore, including displays on the salmon fisheries that once dominated Astoria. Among the model boats is the 1792 vessel that Robert Grey first steered into the mouth of the Columbia River. (Open daily 9:30am-5pm. $5, seniors $4, ages 6-17 $2, under 6 free.) The **Scandinavian Festival,** on the third weekend in June, attracts throngs of celebrants. (All 3 days $5, under 6 free.) The **Astoria Regatta** (861-2288), held the second week of August, dates to 1894. The tradition is still going strong, featuring food and craft booths, a watershow, boat rides, fireworks, dances, and sailboat races. The **Astor Street Opry Company** (325-6104) revives bawdy, old-fashioned entertainment with *Shanghaied in Astoria,* an original musical featuring sinister villains, valiant heroes, lusty sailors, and can-can girls. (Runs early July to late Aug. $8-15.)

NEAR ASTORIA

The **Fort Clatsop National Memorial** (861-2471), 5 mi. southwest of town, reconstructs Lewis and Clark's winter headquarters from detailed descriptions in their journals. The cramped log fort housed more than 30; a fine interpretive center details the lives of some of the fascinating but lesser-known personalities. In summer, rangers robed in feathers and buckskin demonstrate quill pen writing, moccasin sewing, and musket firing. To find Ft. Clatsop, take U.S. 101 south from Astoria to Alt. U.S. 101, and follow the signs 3 mi. to the park. (Open mid-June to Labor Day 8am-6pm; in winter 8am-5pm. $2, under 17 free, families $4.)

Fort Stevens State Park (861-2000), off U.S. 101 on a narrow peninsula 10 mi. west of Astoria, has a huge campground (see above), excellent swimming, fishing, boating facilities, beaches, and hiking trails. Bikes, canoes, and kayaks can be rented at the park ($8 per hr.), and a day-use pass costs $3. Fort Stevens was constructed in 1863 to prevent Confederate naval raiders from entering the Columbia River. Several remaining concrete gun batteries are the focus of a **self-guided walking tour** (about 2hr.) that begins up the road from the day use and campground areas. A restored 1954 Army cargo truck takes visitors on narrated tours. (Daily in summer at 11am, 12:30, 2:30, and 4pm; $2.50, under 13 $1.25.) Tours leave from the **Fort Stevens Military Museum and Interpretive Center** (861-2000; open daily 10am-6pm; in winter 10am-4pm). **Battery Russell** (861-2471), in the park 1 mi. south of the historical area, is the only mainland American fort to have endured enemy fire since the War of 1812. On June 21, 1942, a Japanese submarine surfaced offshore and shelled the fort with 17 rounds. The fort was undamaged and did not return fire. The military monument allows free access to visitors.

> ## WINE AND CHEESE, TOGETHER AT LAST
>
> One block up from the Maritime Museum is the **Shallon Winery,** 1598 Duane St. (325-5798; www.shallon.com), where owner Paul van der Velt presides over a kingdom of fantastic wines. He gives a tour of his minuscule viniculture facilities, complete with the story behind his bizarre repertoire of wines, none made from grapes. A self-proclaimed connoisseur of fine food, he insists that visitors call him at any time of day or night before considering a meal at any restaurant within 50 mi. Samplers taste wines made from local berries, and the world's only commercially produced whey wines (from Tillamook cheese). Approach the cranberry-and-whey wine with caution; the fruity taste belies its high alcohol content. Sampling lemon meringue pie wine is likely to be the highlight of any trip to the Oregon coast, and Paul's chocolate orange wine is more candy than beverage. Others have spent millions trying to reproduce this chocolate delicacy without success. (Must be 21 to drink. Open almost every afternoon. Gratuities and purchases appreciated.)

SEASIDE

In the winter of 1805-1806, explorers Lewis and Clark made their westernmost camp near Seaside. The town was built into a resort in the 1870s, and 120 years of visitors, indoor mini-golf, and barrels of salt taffy have transformed Seaside from a remote outpost to a bustling, beachfront tourist mill. For those uninterested in video arcades and developed shorelines, Seaside still has merit as a base for exploring the beautiful Oregon coast: most everything here is less expensive than in nearby Cannon Beach, and Seaside's hostel is one of the best in the Northwest.

▚ ORIENTATION AND PRACTICAL INFORMATION

Seaside lies 17 mi. south of Astoria and 8 mi. north of Cannon Beach along U.S. 101. The most direct route between Seaside and Portland is U.S. 26, which intersects U.S. 101 just south of Seaside near Saddle Mountain State Park. The **Necanicum River** runs north-south through Seaside, two blocks from the coastline. In town, U.S. 101 splits into **Roosevelt Dr.** and **Holladay Dr.** All three are bisected by **Broadway,** the town's main street and a tourist-dollar black hole. Streets north of Broadway are numbered, those south of Broadway are lettered. The **Promenade** (or "prom") is a paved pedestrians-only path that hugs the beach for the length of town.

Buses: Pierce Pacific Stages (717-1651), a Greyhound affiliate, departs the hostel at 3pm for: Portland (3¼hr., $20) and Seattle, WA (5½hr.; $38; via Kelso, WA). **Sunset Empire Transit** (861-7433), runs between Astoria and Cannon Beach 7 times per day M-Sa, stopping at the hostel. Round-trip fares $1.50-6; seniors, disabled, and ages 6-12 $1-3.50; under 6 free. Tickets available at the hostel.

Taxis: Yellow Cab (738-5252). $1.40 base, $1.40 per mi.

Visitor Information: Chamber of Commerce, 7 N. Roosevelt Dr. (738-6391 or 800-444-6740), on U.S. 101 and Broadway. The **Seaside Visitor Bureau** (738-3097 or 888-306-2326) is in the same building. Open June-Aug. M-Sa 8am-6pm, Su 9am-5pm.; Oct.-May M-F 9am-5pm, Sa-Su 10am-4pm.

Equipment Rental: Prom Bike Shop, 622 12th Ave. (738-8251), at 12th and Holladay, rents bikes, roller skates, in-line skates, beach tricycles, and surreys (most $6 per hr., $30 per day; tandem bicycles $12 per hr.). Must be 18. Open daily 10am-6pm. Also at 80 Ave. A, downtown (open daily 9am-8pm).

Library: 60 N. Roosevelt Dr. (738-6742). Free **Internet access** available. Open Tu-Th 9am-8pm, F-Sa 9am-5pm, Su 1-5pm.

Laundry: Clean Services, 1225 S. Roosevelt Dr. (738-9513). Wash $1.25, dry 25¢ per 14min. Open daily 7:30am-10pm.

Emergency: 911. **Police:** 1091 S. Holladay Dr. (738-6311). **Coast Guard:** 2185 SE Airport Rd. in Warrenton (861-6228).

Hospital: Providence Seaside Hospital, 725 S. Wahanna Rd. (717-7000).

Post Office: 300 Ave. A, 97138 (800-275-8777). Open M-F 8:30am-5pm.

Area Code: 503.

▚ ACCOMMODATIONS AND CAMPGROUNDS

Seaside's expensive motels are hardly an issue for the budget traveler, thanks to the large hostel on the south side of town. Motel prices are directly proportional to proximity to the beach and start at $50 (less during the off-season). In summer, rooms invariably fill by 5pm; the chamber of commerce keeps track of availability.

The closest state parks are **Fort Stevens** (861-1671; see p. 91), 21 mi. north, and **Saddle Mountain** (368-5154; see p. 95), 9½ mi. east, off U.S. 26 after it splits with U.S. 101. Drive 8 mi. northeast of Necanicum Junction, then another 7 mi. up a winding road to the base camp (10 sites: $10; drinking water). Sleeping on the beach in Seaside is illegal, and police enforce this rule.

■ **Seaside International Hostel (HI),** 930 N. Holladay Dr. (738-7911). Free nightly movies, a well-equipped kitchen, an espresso bar, and a grassy yard along the river make this hostel a pastoral wonderland. The staff filters the fun from the resort hysteria: they recommend "Off Broadway" options, map out local hikes, and rent kayaks and canoes ($7-8 per hr.). 34 large bunks $14, nonmembers $17; private rooms with bath and cable TV sleep 4: $38, nonmembers $58. Call well ahead. Office open 8am-11pm.

Riverside Inn, 430 S. Holladay Dr. (738-8254 or 800-826-6151; www.riversideinn.com). Cozy bedrooms, fresh flowers, and ceilings with skylights make this B&B a secret garden amid the Seaside motel madness. Rooms have private bath and TV. Homemade breakfast. Riverfront deck. Doubles from $55; Oct.-Apr. from $50.

Colonial Motor Inn, 1120 N. Holladay Dr. (738-6295 or 800-221-3804). With lovely colonial furniture, free snacks, and clean, quiet rooms, this little motel is a standout for the price. Creeekside Gazebo. Singles $54, doubles $59; less in winter.

◑ FOOD

Prices on Broadway, especially toward the beach, are criminal. **Safeway,** 401 S. Roosevelt Dr. (738-7122), stocks bread and water (open daily 6am-midnight).

The Stand, 220 Ave. U (738-6592), at the south end of town, serves the cheapest meals around to a local crowd. Burritos $1.75-3.75. Open M-Sa 11am-8pm.

Sherry's Little New Yorker, 604 Broadway (738-5992), stages a mouth-watering parade of Italian dishes (dinners $9) amid old Broadway memorabilia. Hot sandwiches star at lunchtime ($3-7). Open M-F 11:30am-4:30pm, Sa-Su 11:30am-8:30pm.

The Coffeehouse, 846 Ave. C (717-8188), across from Safeway. Comfy beat-up couches and aging board games transport diners to basement rec rooms of old. Popular bread and cheese plate $3. Mocha $2.25. Open Su-Th 7am-10pm, F-Sa 7am-11pm.

Harrison's Bakery, 608 Broadway (738-5331). A font of frosted delectables, as well as the home of Seaside's famous beach bread, made every day at low tide. Hosteling discounts and plate-sized doughnuts. Open M-Su 7:30am-4pm, F-Sa 7:30am-5:30pm.

◉ ♫ SIGHTS, EVENTS, AND OUTDOORS

Seaside swarms around **Broadway,** a garish strip of arcades and shops running the half mile from Roosevelt (U.S. 101) to the beach. Bumper cars and those machines that squash pennies draw big crowds. **The Turnaround** at the end of Broadway signals the official (read: arbitrary) end of the Lewis and Clark Trail. Seaside's beachfront is hugely crowded, despite bone-chilling water and strong undertows that make swimming a risky business. Red flags mean the surf is too rough even for wading. For a slightly quieter beach, head to **Gearhart,** approximately 2 mi. north of downtown off U.S. 101, where long stretches of dunes await exploration. **Cleanline Surf,** 710 1st Ave. (738-7888; open M-F 9am-7pm, Su 10am-6pm), rents surfing gear.

The **Seaside Aquarium,** 200 N. Prom., is smaller than its companion in Newport, but makes up for its small size by giving visitors the chance to feed playful harbor seals, seal food 50¢. (Open daily 9am-6pm; in winter open daily 9am-5:30pm. $5.50, seniors $4.75, ages 6-13 $2.75, families of 6 $17.)

Every Saturday at 2pm from July-August sees **free concerts** in Quatat Marine Park, featuring everything from bluegrass to rock. In the **Hood to Coast Race** at the end of August, runners tear up the trails between Mt. Hood and Seaside to the cheers of 50,000 spectators. About 750 12-person teams run 5 mi. shifts in this two-day relay race. Contact Bob Foote (227-1371) for more info.

The **Necanicum River Estuary** trail picks up where the north end of the promenade leaves off, and makes a dune-covered loop back into town. From the Seaside beach, head south to Tillamook Head (see p. 95) for a day-long hike amid uncrowded forests and along cliffs. This is the cheapest way to see Tillamook Head and the lighthouse, since the Cannon Beach entrance charges a fee.

WESTERN OREGON

CANNON BEACH

Many moons ago, a rusty cannon from the shipwrecked schooner *Shark* washed ashore at Arch Cape, giving this town its name. Today, the only artillery in town is a battery of boutiques, bakeries, and galleries (hotcha!). Cannon Beach presents a somewhat more refined version of Seaside and Astoria's crass commercialism, but the beach is still the real draw.

🛂 ORIENTATION AND PRACTICAL INFORMATION

Cannon Beach lies 7 mi. south of Seaside, 42 mi. north of Tillamook on U.S. 101, and 79 mi. from Portland via U.S. 26. **Hemlock,** the town's main drag, connects with U.S. 101 in four places.

Buses: Sunset Transit System (800-776-6406). To: Seaside (75¢); Astoria ($2.25). **Cannon Beach Shuttle** traverses downtown; board at any point. Runs daily 9am-6pm, 50¢ donation requested.

Visitor Information: Cannon Beach Chamber of Commerce, 207 N. Spruce St., (436-2623; www.cannonbeach.org), at 2nd St. Open M-Sa 10am-6pm, Su 11am-4pm.

Equipment Rental: Mike's Bike Shop, 248 N. Spruce St. (436-1266 or 800-492-1266), around the corner from the chamber of commerce. Maps of old logging roads. Mountain bikes $7 per hr., $29 per day; beach tricycles $8 per 90min. Open daily 9am-6pm.

Emergency: 911. **Police:** 163 Gower St. (436-2811).

Hospital: Providence North Coast Clinic, 171 Larch St (717-7000), in Sandpiper Sq. in Cannon Beach. Non-emergency care only. Open M-F 8:30am-noon and 1:15-4:30pm.

Internet Access: Copies and Fax, 1235 S. Hemlock (436-2000). $7.50 per hr.

Post Office: 155 N. Hemlock St., 97110 (436-2822). Open M-F 9am-5pm.

Area Code: 503.

🏚 ACCOMMODATIONS AND CAMPGROUNDS

At the pleasant motels along Hemlock St., family units can make a good deal for groups. Book ahead for weekends. In winter, inquire about specials; most motels offer two-nights-for-one deals. Real budget deals are a short drive away: the **Seaside International Hostel** is 7 mi. north (see p. 93), and **Oswald West State Park** (see p. 95), 10 mi. south of town, has a stunning campground.

The Sandtrap Inn, 539 S. Hemlock St. (436-0247 or 800-400-4106; www.sandtrapinn.com). Inviting rooms ring a peaceful, rose-filled courtyard. First-class amenities, including fireplaces, cable TV and VCRs, and kitchens. Rooms from $55; off-season $45. 2-night min. stay on summer weekends.

McBee Cottages, 888 S. Hemlock, office in the Cannon Beach Hotel at 1116 S. Hemlock (436-2569). Bright and cheerful singles or doubles a few blocks from the beach $49; in winter $39. Some kitchen units and cottages available.

Wright's for Camping, 334 Reservoir Rd. (436-2347), off Hwy. 101. Sites among the trees make this family-owned campground a relaxing retreat from RV mini-cities. Showers. Wheelchair accessible. 19 sites: $16. Reservations advised in summer.

🍴 FOOD

Deals are down Hemlock, in mid-town. **Mariner Market,** 139 N. Hemlock St. (436-2442), holds 7,000 grocery items on its capacious shelves (open July-Sept. Su-Th 8am-10pm, F-Sa 8am-11pm; Oct.-June Su-Th 8am-9pm, F-Sa 8am-10pm).

Midtown Cafe, 1235 S. Hemlock St. (436-1016), in the Haystack Sq. Everything is homemade, from the hand-carved door to the jams on the tables. Lentil burgers $7.50; burrito chili verde $8. Open W-M 7am-2pm and 5-9pm; in winter closed M.

Lazy Susan's Cafe, 126 N. Hemlock St. (436-2816), in Coaster Sq. A retreat from zany, crazy downtown. Homemade soup $3.50, tuna apple hazelnut salad $8. Open W-M 8am-8pm, in winter M, W, Th 8am-2:30pm, F 8am-8pm, Su 8am-5pm.

Bill's Tavern, 188 N. Hemlock St. (436-2202). A local favorite for down-to-earth eatin', and the beer on tap is brewed upstairs. Basic pub grub $3-7.50; pints $3. Open Th-Tu 11:30am-midnight, W 4:30pm-midnight. Kitchen closes around 9:30pm.

SIGHTS, EVENTS, AND OUTDOORS

Tourists in Cannon Beach town run a gauntlet of expensive, sporadically elegant galleries and gift shops. A stroll along the 7 mi. stretch of flat, bluff-framed beach suits many better. **Ecola State Park** (436-2844; $3 entrance fee) attracts picnickers and hikers. Ecola Point offers a view of hulking Haystack Rock, which is spotted with (and by) gulls, puffins, barnacles, anemones, and the occasional sea lion. Ecola Point also affords views of the Bay's centerpiece, the **Tillamook Lighthouse.** Construction of the lighthouse began in 1879 and continued in Sisyphean fashion for years as storms washed the foundations away. Decommissioned in 1957, the now privately owned lighthouse can be reached only by helicopter to deposit the ashes of the dead. The **Indian Beach Trail** leads 2 mi. to Indian Beach and its tide pools, which teem with colorful and fragile sea life. From the beach, a 12 mi. round-trip hike leads to **Tillamook Head,** the mini-cape that separates Seaside Beach from Cannon Beach, where whales migrate seasonally. The trail is open year-round and passes the top of Tillamook Head (2 mi. up), where five hiker sites await those willing to make the trek for free camping. To surf a set, rent boards from **Cleanline Surf,** 171 Sunset Blvd. (436-9726; surfboards and boogie boards $20 per day; open M-F 10:30am-5:30pm, Sa 10am-6pm, Su 9am-7pm). **Saddle Mountain State Park** (see p. 92), 14 mi. east of Cannon Beach on U.S. 26, is named after the highest peak in the Coast Range. A six-mile, four-hour hike to the mountain's 3283 ft. summit ends with an astounding view of the Pacific Ocean and Nehalem Bay to the west and the Cascades to the east.

The **Coaster Theater,** 1087 N. Hemlock St. (436-1242), is a small but dependable playhouse that stages theater productions, concerts, dance performances, comedy, and musical revues year-round (F and Sa at 8pm; tickets $12-15). A huge **Sand Castle Competition** transforms Cannon Beach into a fantastic menagerie on the second Saturday of June. Contestants begin digging in the early morning to construct ornate sculptures from wet sand only to have the evening high tide wash everything away. Call the chamber of commerce for more info.

CANNON BEACH TO TILLAMOOK

In the summer of 1933, the Tillamook Burn reduced 500 sq. mi. of coastal forest near Tillamook to charcoal. While nature has restored Tillamook State Forest to health, coastal towns to the west are still nastily scarred. The gift shops that line the highway hide behind fading paint and crooked telephone poles. The coastline alongside these tiny towns, however, is much less crowded than Seaside and Cannon Beaches, and even more beautiful. Tourist info for the area is available at the visitor center in Tillamook (see p. 96) or the **Rockaway Beach Visitor Center,** 405 U.S. 101 S (355-8108; open M-F 9am-noon and 1-4pm, Sa 10-4).

Oswald West State Park, 10 mi. south of Cannon Beach, is a tiny headland rainforest of hefty spruce and cedars. Locals call the park **Short Sands Beach.** Although the beach and woodsy **campsites** are only accessible by a quarter-mile-long trail off U.S. 101, the park provides wheelbarrows for transporting gear from the parking lot to the 36 sites, which teem with surfers. These are the cheapest sites around, so an early arrival is key (open mid-May to Oct.; sites $14). From the park, the 4-mile round-trip **Cape Falcon Trail** leads over the headland to the 1661 ft. **Neahkahnie Mountain,** and paths from the campground lead to the surf.

Eight miles south of Oswald State Park, a cluster of made-in-Oregon-type shops along U.S. 101 make up **Nehalem.** The **Nehalem Bay Winery,** 34965 Hwy. 53 (368-9463), 3 mi. south of town, provides free tastings of local cranberry and blackberry vintages and is also a center of cultural activity in the area. They sponsor performances in a small **theater,** an annual **bluegrass festival,** a **fun express train** on weekends, and are a general forum for bacchanalian revelry. Even if you're not up to tasting, stop in to chat with owner Ray, who adores guests and gives all sorts of valuable tips on free camping, local swimming holes, and the merits of a good time. He also has a nearly 100% hiring policy, so if you're broke, stop by and work for a few days (open daily 9am-6pm; in winter 10am-5pm, or later if Ray's there).

One small town, **Wheeler,** a few miles south of Nehalem and 22 miles north of Tillamook, is a surprise find. **Wheeler on the Bay Lodge,** 580 Marine Dr. (368-5858; open daily 7am-dusk), rents **kayaks** (singles $14 per hr., $28 per day; doubles $18 per hr., $40 per day; includes 10min. training session for beginners). Vendors sell crabbing buckets off the docks on the bay south of Wheeler and will often cook the crabs for you. **Nina's Italian Restaurant** (368-6592), opposite the lodge on U.S. 101, is everything an old Italian restaurant should be (entrees $5-8; open daily 4:30pm-9:30pm, F-Sa until 10pm).

TILLAMOOK

Although the word Tillamook (TILL-uh-muk) translates to "land of many waters," to Oregon's population it is synonymous with "cheese." The cows that dot the surrounding hills produce a nationally famous cheddar. Still a small farming town at heart, Tillamook gets its share of tourist traffic and funnels almost all of it to the Tillamook Cheese Factory, where tourists sample sharp, medium, or mild; say cheese, take a picture, then shuffle off to the coast three miles away.

⚊ ORIENTATION AND PRACTICAL INFORMATION. Tillamook lies 49 mi. south of Seaside, 74 mi. south of Portland, and 44 mi. north of Lincoln City on U.S. 101. From Portland, take U.S. 26 to Rte. 6. Tillamook's main drag, **U.S. 101,** splits into two one-way streets downtown. **Pacific Ave.** runs north and **Main Ave.** runs south. The **Tillamook Cheese Factory** sits 1½mi. north of town.

Ride the Wave Bus Lines (800-815-8283) runs locally (M-F; $1), and to: Portland (2½hr., 3 per week, $15) and Lincoln City (1½hr., 2 per week, $10). Find a schedule and a list of campsites in Tillamook County at the **Tillamook Chamber of Commerce,** 3705 U.S. 101 N (842-7525), in the big red barn near the Tillamook Cheese Factory. (Open M-Sa 9am-5pm, Su 10am-4pm, in winter M-F 9am-5pm, Sa 10am-4:30pm, Su 10am-2pm.) **Emergency:** 911. **Police:** 210 Laurel St. (842-2522), in City Hall. **Coast Guard:** 322-3531, emergencies 322-3246. **Post office:** 2200 1st St., 97141 (800-275-8777; open M-F 9am-5pm). **Area code:** 503.

⚏ ACCOMMODATIONS AND CAMPGROUNDS. Motels are steep, but the camping is some of the area's finest. **Tillamook Inn,** 1810 U.S. 101 N (842-4413), between the town center and the Cheese Factory, is clean and affordable. (Singles $40; doubles $46, with kitchen $64.) **MarClair Inn,** 11 Main Ave. (842-7571 or 800-331-6857), is at the center of town and rents huge, beautiful rooms. Enjoy the outdoor pool, hot tub, and sauna. (Singles $64; doubles $73. 10% AAA discount. Credit card required.) **Cape Lookout State Park,** 13000 Whiskey Creek Rd. (842-4981, reservations 800-452-5687), lies 15 mi. southwest of Tillamook on the Three Capes Loop (see p. 97). Some sites are only 20 yards from the beach, others offer more privacy and shade. (Tent sites $16; full hookups $20; yurts $25; walk-ins $4 per person; non-camper showers $2.) **Kilchis River Park** (842-6694), 6 mi. northeast of town at the end of Kilchis River Rd., which leaves U.S. 101 1 mile north of the Factory, has 40 sites between a mossy forest and the Kilchis River, with a swing set, baseball field, volleyball court, horseshoes, swimming, and hiking. (Water, toilets, no showers. Tent sites $10; walk-ins $2. Open May-Oct.)

◖ **FOOD.** Tillamook may be a cheese-lover's paradise, but other food choices are lacking. Sneak Velveeta at **Safeway,** 955 U.S. 101 (842-4831; open daily 6am-midnight). The **Blue Heron French Cheese Company,** 2001 Blue Heron Dr. (842-8281; www.blueheronoregon.com), north of town and 1 mi. south of the factory, a country-style store, focuses decidedly on brie. Gourmet sandwiches cost $6. Tastings of local and often unusual dips, jams, jellies, honeys, syrups, mustards, wines, and, yes, brie, are free. (Open daily 8am-8pm; in winter 9am-5pm. Deli open 11:30am-4pm.) **La Casa Modelo,** 1160 U.S. 101 N (842-5768), makes mild Mexican food to order and serves it in a beautiful wood-paneled dining room. Small lunch specials $5.25-7; foot-long tacos $8. (Open daily 11:30am-9pm, in winter closes 1hr. earlier.)

◼ **SIGHTS.** The **Tillamook Cheese Factory,** 4175 U.S. 101 N (842-4481), is a shrine to dairy delights, a cradle of curdled creations, and a thinly disguised tourist trap. Wander through the amusing exhibits, taste award-winning tidbits at the gift shop, and then get lured into buying pounds of cheddar and reams of cheesy postcards. (Open daily mid-June to Labor Day 8am-8pm; Sept. to mid-June 8am-6pm.)

The impressive **Tillamook Naval Air Station Museum,** 6030 Hangar Rd. (842-1130), lies 2 mi. south of town. This hulking seven-acre hangar, built in the 1940s, is the largest wooden clear-span structure in the world. The airy cavern is home to over 20 fully functional warplanes, including a P-38 Lightning, a PBY-5A Catalina, and an F-14 Tomcat. (Open daily in summer 9am-6pm; in winter 10am-5pm. $8, over 65 $7, ages 13-17 $4.50, ages 7-12 $2.50.) West of the highway, downtown, the **Tillamook County Pioneer Museum,** 2106 2nd St. (842-4553), at Pacific Ave., features dioramas of pioneer days. The real head-turners, though, are the stuffed animals preserved by taxidermist and big game hunter Alex Walker, who donated his remarkable collection to the museum upon his death, a move which has inspired lesser-known local taxidermists to do the same. (Open M-Sa 8am-5pm, Su 11am-5pm. $2, seniors $1.50, ages 12-17 50¢, under 12 free.)

THE THREE CAPES LOOP

Between Tillamook and Lincoln City, U.S. 101 wanders east into wooded land, los-ing contact with the coast. The Three Capes Loop, a 35 mi. circle to the west of the straying U.S 101, connects a trio of spectacular promontories—Cape Meares, Cape Lookout, and Cape Kiwanda State Parks—and makes for a sweet Sunday drive. Cyclists and motorists beware: narrow twists and a rocky road make the trip tricky for those on two wheels. The loop leaves U.S. 101 about 10 mi. north of Lin-coln City and rejoins U.S. 101 smack dab in the middle of cheese town.

Cape Meares State Park, at the tip of the promontory jutting out from Tillamook, protects one of the few remaining old growth forests on the Oregon Coast. The **Octopus Tree,** a gnarled Sitka spruce with six candelabra trunks, is a climber's ulti-mate fantasy. The **Cape Meares Lighthouse,** active from 1890 to 1963, operates as an illuminating on-site interpretive center. Struggle up 1½ flights of tiny stairs for sweeping views and a peek at the original lens of the big light. (Open daily May-Sept. 11am-4pm; Oct. and Mar.-Apr. F-Sa 11am-4pm. Free.)

Another 12 mi. southwest of Cape Meares, **Cape Lookout State Park** (541-842-4981), offers a small, rocky beach with incredible views of Cape Meares Light-house, as well as some fine camping near the dunes and the forests behind them (see p. 96). From here, the 2½ mi. **Cape Trail** leads to the end of the lookout where a spectacular 360° view featuring **Haystack Rock** awaits.

Cape Kiwanda State Park, the southernmost promontory on the loop, is home to one of the most sublime beaches on the Oregon shore. The sheltered cape draws beachcombers, kite-flyers, volleyball players, jetskiiers, and windsurfers. The park is open from 8am until the sun slips down behind magnificent Haystack Rock. The flat-bottomed dory fleet is one of the few fishing fleets in the world that launches beachside, directly from sand to surf. If you bring your own fishing gear down to the cape around 5am, you might convince someone to take you on board; the fee will probably be lower than that of a charter. If the surf is up, head to **South County Surf,** 33310 Cape Kiwanda Dr. (503-965-7505; surfboard rental $20 per day; boogie board $10; wetsuit $15; open daily 9am-6pm).

Pacific City, a hidden gem that most travelers on U.S. 101 never even see, is worth a stop, and if that stop extends overnight, the **Anchorage Motel,** 6585 Pacific Ave. (541-965-6773 or 800-941-6250), offers homey rooms with cable and coffee, but no phones (singles from $37; doubles from $42; rates drop in winter). The town hides away some startlingly good restaurants. The **Grateful Bread Bakery,** 34805 Brooten Rd. (965-7337), creates monuments to the art of dining: get anything from a black bean chili omelette ($6) to a dilled shrimp salad ($6; open daily 8am-6pm; in winter closed W-Th). The **Riverhouse Restaurant,** 34450 Brooten Rd. (965-6722), occupies a tiny white house overlooking the Nestucca River. Stunning seafood ($16-20) and homemade desserts ($4-6) have earned the Riverhouse its great reputation (open Su-F 11am-9pm, Sa 11am-10pm).

LINCOLN CITY

Tourism often spawns cutesy, commercial little towns. Somehow, Lincoln City got all of the "commercial" and none of the "cute." The City is actually five towns wrapped around a 7 mi. strip of ocean-front motels, gas stations, and souvenir shops along U.S. 101. Bicyclists will find Lincoln City hellish, and hikers should cut three blocks west to the seashore. Kite-flyers and beach volleyball fanciers flock to this coastal town, but nothing draws as much money as the new Chinook Winds Siletz Tribal Gaming Convention Center, otherwise known as "the casino," where swingers and the glassy-eyed gamble away days, nights, and life savings.

■ ORIENTATION AND PRACTICAL INFORMATION. Lincoln City is 42 mi. south of Tillamook, 22 mi. north of Newport, 58 mi. west of Salem, and 88 mi. southwest of Portland, between Devils Lake and the deep blue sea. Despite its oblong shape, Lincoln City is divided into quadrants: **D River** (marked "the smallest river in the world") is the north-south divide; U.S. 101 divides east from west.

Greyhound (800-321-2222) buses depart from Wendy's at the north end of town to Portland (3hr., 2 per day, $11-12) and Newport (45min., 2 per day, $7.50). Tickets are available at the visitor center. **Robben-Rent-A-Car,** 3244 U.S. 101 NE (994-5530 or 800-305-5530), rents for $30 per day and 20¢ per mi. after 50 mi. you must be 21 with a credit card or $500 deposit. (Open daily 8am-5pm.) At the **Lincoln City Visitor and Convention Bureau,** 801 U.S. 101 SW #1 (994-8378 or 800-452-2151), opposite Burger King, a 24hr. telephone board connects with local motels at the push of a button (open M-F 8am-5pm, Sa 9am-5pm, Su 10am-4pm). The **Driftwood Library,** 801 U.S. 101 SW (996-2277), near the visitor center, provides free **Internet access** (open M-Th 9am-9pm, F-Sa 9am-5pm, Su 1-5pm), while **B&B Package Express,** 960 Hwy. 101 SE (994-7272), charges $6 per hour. **Public showers** ($1.25) are yours at 2150 NE Oar Place (994-5208; open in summer M-F 5:30am-9pm, Sa 11am-9pm, Su noon-4:30pm; call for winter hours.) The **Oregon Surf Shop,** 4933 U.S. 101 SW (996-3957 or 877-339-5672), rents a wetsuit and surfboard for $30 per day, or boogie board for $25. **Emergency:** 911. **Police:** 1503 East Devils Lake Rd. SE (994-3636). **Hospital: North Lincoln,** 3043 NE 28th St. (994-3661). **Post office:** 1501 East Devils Lake Rd. SE, 97367 (800-275-8777; open M-F 9am-5pm), 1 block east of U.S. 101. **Area code:** 541.

■ ACCOMMODATIONS AND FOOD. Beautiful, small rooms await at the **Captain Cook Inn,** 2626 U.S. 101 NE (994-2522 or 800-994-2522; singles $45; doubles $48). The **Sea Echo Motel,** 3510 U.S. 101 NE (994-2575), sits high above the highway overlooking the coast; rooms are standard, but quiet (singles $45; 2 beds $48-53). **Devils Lake State Park** (reservations 800-452-5687), off 6th St. NE from U.S. 101 NW, a-chatter with local birds and small kids, grants access to fishing and boating on the lake. (65 tent sites $16; 32 full hookups $20; 10 yurts $29; walk-ins $4.25. Non-camper showers $2. Wheelchair accessible. Reservations recommended.)

Lincoln City has a few decent joints if you can navigate the fast-food shoals; but head down to Depoe Bay or Newport for the best seafood. **Dory Cove,** 5819 Logan Rd. (994-5180) at the far north of town, is the locals' unanimous choice for affordable seafood. Fish and chips cost $9, shrimp and grilled cheese sandwich $7.25. (Open M-Sa 11:30am-9pm, Su noon-8pm; in winter M-Th 11:30am-8pm, F-Sa 11:30am-9pm, Su noon-9pm.) Four Skor bars and 7-up at **Safeway,** 4101 NW Logan Rd. (994-8667), at the north end of town (open daily 6am-midnight).

🎰 🎭 **ENTERTAINMENT AND EVENTS.** Shop till you drop at the 65 **Factory Stores** (996-5000 or 888-746-7333), at E. Devils Lake Rd. and U.S. 101. (Open M-Sa 10am-8pm, Su 10am-6pm, Jan.-Feb. daily 10am-6pm.) To finish off a day of spending, join the slot-junkies at the always-open, climate-controlled **casino,** 1777 44th St. NW (888-244-6665). Turn left at Lighthouse Sq. on Logan Rd. NW and look to your left: it's the hulking yellow stucco structure. The casino sponsors **Concerts-by-the-Sea** (888-624-6228; $10-60) every other week throughout the year. Past performers have included Wayne Newton and Bill Cosby. The windy beaches of Lincoln City host the **Fall** and **Spring International Kite Festivals** in the beginning of October and of May at D River Park. During the top-notch **Cascade Music Festival,** in the last three weekends in June, classical concerts by international performers ($15) take place at St. Peter the Fisherman Lutheran Church, 1226 SW 13th (994-5333).

DEPOE BAY AND OTTER CREST LOOP

Rest stops and beach-access parking lots litter the 30 mi. of U.S. 101 between Lincoln City and Newport. A few miles south on U.S. 101, diminutive **Depoe Bay** boasts **gray whale viewing** along the town's low seawall, at the Depoe Bay State Park Wayside, and at the Observatory Lookout, 4½ mi. to the south. Go early in the morning on a cloudy, calm day (Dec.-May during annual migration) for the best chance of spotting the barnacle-encrusted giants. **Tradewinds Charters** (765-2345), on the north end of the bridge on U.S. 101 downtown, has two five-hour ($55) and six-hour ($65) fishing and crabbing trips per day. **Dockside Charters** (765-2545 or 800-733-8915) offers similar trips for $49 and 1 hour whale-watching trips ($12, ages 13-18 $10, ages 4-12 $8). To find Dockside, turn east at the one and only traffic light in Depoe Bay; they're next to the Coast Guard station.

Just south of Depoe Bay, take a detour from U.S. 101 on the renowned **Otter Crest Loop,** a twisting 4 mi. drive high above the shore that affords spectacular vistas at every bend, including views of Otter Rock and the Marine Gardens. A lookout over **Cape Foulweather** has telescopes (25¢) for spotting sea lions lazing on the rocks. Also accessible off the loop is the **Devil's Punch Bowl,** formed when the roof of a seaside cave collapsed. It becomes a frothing cauldron during high tide, when ocean water crashes through an opening in the side of the bowl.

NEWPORT

After the miles of malls along U.S. 101, Newport's renovated waterfront area of pleasantly kitschy restaurants and shops are a delight. Historic Nye Beach, bustling with tiny shops, is on the northwest side of town in between 3rd and 6th St. Newport's claim to fame is the world-class Oregon Coast Aquarium, best known as the former home of Willy the orca of *Free Willy* fame, whose "real" name is Keiko.

🛈 ORIENTATION AND PRACTICAL INFORMATION

U.S. 101, known in town as the **Coast Highway,** divides east and west Newport, while U.S. 20, known as **Olive St.** in town, bisects the north and south sides of town. Corvallis lies 55 mi. east on U.S. 20, Lincoln City is 22 mi. north on U.S. 101 and Florence sits 50 mi. south. Newport is bordered on the west by the foggy Pacific Ocean and on the south by Yaquina Bay. A suspension bridge carries U.S. 101 traffic across the bay. Just north of the bridge, **Bay Boulevard** circles the bay and runs through the heart of the port.

Buses: Greyhound, 956 10th St. SW (265-2253 or 800-231-2222), at Bailey St. To: Portland (4hr., 2 per day, $18); Seattle (9-12hr., 1-4 per day, $42); and San Francisco (17hr., 2-3 per day, $72). Open M-F 8-10am and 12:15-4:15pm, Sa 8am-1pm.

Taxis: Yaquina Cab Company (265-9552). $2.25 base, $2.25 per mi.

Car Rental: Sunwest Motors, 1030 Coast Hwy. N (265-8547). $30 per day, 15¢ per mi. over 50 mi. Must be 25 with credit card. Open M-F 8am-7pm, Sa 9am-6pm.

Visitor Information: Chamber of Commerce, 555 Coast Hwy. SW (265-8801 or 800-262-7844). 24hr. info board. Open M-F 8:30am-5pm; in summer also Sa-Su 10am-4pm.

Public Library: 35 Nye St. NW (265-2153), at Olive St. Free **Internet access.** Open M-Th 10am-9pm, F-Sa 10am-6pm, Su 1-4pm.

Laundry: Eileen's Coin Laundry, 1078 Coast Hwy. N. Wash $1.25, dry 25¢ per 10min. Open daily 6am-11pm.

Weather and Sea Conditions: 265-5511.

Hospital: Pacific Communities Hospital, 930 Abbey St. SW (265-2244).

Emergency: 911. **Police:** 810 Alder St. SW (265-5331). **Coast Guard:** 925 Naterlin Rd. (265-5381). **Crisis Line: CONTACT,** 444 2nd St. NE (265-9234). 24hr.

Post Office: 310 2nd St. SW, 97365. Open M-F 8:30am-5pm, Sa 10am-1pm.

Area Code: 541.

■ ACCOMMODATIONS AND CAMPGROUNDS

Motel-studded U.S. 101 provides affordable, noisy rooms. Nearby monster camping facilities often fill on summer weekends.

Traveler's Inn, 606 Coast Hwy. SW (265-7723 or 800-615-2627), is about as cheap as a decent room gets in this town. Comfortable rooms with cable and much-sought-after views of the ocean. Singles $38, doubles $48. In winter, singles $34; doubles $38.

City Center Motel, 538 Coast Hwy. SW (265-7381 or 800-628-9665), opposite the visitor center. Spacious, oddly empty rooms with sparkling bathrooms, smack in the middle of town. Cable, phones, ice. In summer, singles start at $40; doubles $58.

Beverly Beach State Park, 198 123rd St. NE (265-9278 or 800-452-5687), 7 mi. north of Newport and just south of Devil's Punch Bowl, is a year-round campground of gargantuan proportions. Cold water and frequent riptides discourage swimmers. Sites $16; electrical $19; full hookups $20; yurt $26; hiker/biker $4.25; non-camper showers $2.

South Beach State Park, 5580 Coast Hwy. S (867-4715), 1 mi. south of town. Sparse conifers offer little shelter and no privacy. 244 RV hookups $19; 10 yurts $29; 12 hiker/biker sites $4.25. Showers $2 for non-campers.

◖ FOOD

Food in Newport is surprisingly varied. **Oceana Natural Foods Coop,** 159 2nd St. SE (265-8285; open daily 8am-8pm), has a small selection of reasonably priced health foods and produce. **J.C. Sentry,** 107 Coast Hwy. N (265-6641; open 24hr.), sells standard supermarket stuff, like shampoo.

🦪 **April's,** 749 3rd St. NW (265-6855), down by Nye Beach, is the undisputed pinnacle of local dining. The serene ocean view and devastatingly good food are worth every penny you've saved on no-name corn flakes. Greek chicken crepes for lunch $8. Dinners $12-20. Towering chocolate eclairs ($4). Open M-F 11am-2pm, and for dinner from 5pm. Tables fill early, especially on weekends.

Mo's Restaurant, 622 Bay Blvd. SW (265-2979). This local favorite has such a following that Mo's granddaughters have opened up a whole host of mini mo's. Dining room so noisy no one will hear you slurping the excellent chowder ($3). Open daily 6am-11pm.

Cosmos Cafe and Gallery, 740 Olive St. W (265-7511). Handpainted tables and hanging mobiles transport diners to a faraway galaxy of really good food. Great omelettes $6; black bean burrito $6.50; fresh pie $3. Rhubarb-applesauce or cranberry-peach muffins $1.25. Open M-W 8am-8pm, Th-Sa 8am-9pm; in winter M-Sa 8am-8pm.

Rogue Ale & Public House, 748 Bay Blvd. SW (265-3188). They "brew for the rogue in all of us," and bless 'em for it. Plenty of brew on tap, and ale bread to boot ($1.75). Walls explore beer as art. Fish 'n' chips with Rogue Ale batter $7. Locals pack it in for Friday and Saturday night trivia. Open daily 11am-2:30am.

■♪ SIGHTS, ENTERTAINMENT, AND EVENTS

Newport is known for its aquarium, but most aren't aware that the best marine exhibits are nowhere near Keiko's old haunts. The ▨ **Mark O. Hatfield Marine Science Center** (867-0100), at the south end of the bridge on Marine Science Dr., is the hub of Oregon State University's coastal research, and the intricate exhibits explain marine science in detail. A garden of sea anemones, slugs, and bottom-dwelling fish all await your curious fingers in the touch tanks, and researchers and volunteers lead free walks through the estuaries and rainforests outside. (Open daily 10am-5pm; in winter Th-M 10am-4pm. Admission by donation.)

More famous, less serious, and much more expensive is the **Oregon Coast Aquarium,** 2820 Ferry Slip Rd. SE (867-3474; www.aquarium.org), at the south end of the bridge. This world-class aquarium housed Keiko, the much-loved *Free Willy* Orca during his rehabilitation, before he returned to his childhood waters near Iceland two years ago. The tanks that housed the giant have yet to find new tenants. The rest of the six-acre complex features everything from pulsating jellyfish to attention-seeking sea otters to giant African bullfrogs. Tickets can be ordered with a credit card up to 2 weekends in advance. ($8.75, seniors $7.75, ages 4-13 $4.50.)

The **Rogue Ale Brewery,** 2320 Oregon State University Dr. SE (867-3660), has won more awards than you can shake a pint at. Cross the bay bridge, follow the signs to the Hatfield Center. (Open daily 11am-8pm; in winter 11am-7pm.) Their line of 20 brews, including Oregon Golden, American Amber, and Maierbock Ales are available at the pub in town (see **Food,** above), or upstairs at **Brewer's on the Bay** (867-3664), where taster trays of four beers cost $4.

At the far north of town is **Yaquina Head,** a lava delta formed 14 million years ago, and the **Yaquina Head Lighthouse** (265-2863), a much-photographed coastal landmark (open daily 10am-4pm, vehicle pass $5). The newly updated visitor center is a veritable museum, with small but excellent displays on history and ecology. The **seabird colony** on the rocks below is noisy and spectacular; large decks provide views of western gulls, cormorants, murres, guillemots, and, very rarely, the colorful tufted puffin. **Cobble Beach,** to the south of the headland is home to harbor seals, oyster catchers, and smaller intertidal life.

Bottom-fishers net halibut in May and tuna mid-April to mid-October. **Newport Tradewinds,** 653 Bay Blvd. SW (265-2101), offers numerous packages (5hr. trips $60, 3hr. crabbing trips $35, 2hr. whale-watching trips daily at 1:30pm $18. Children 6-12 always half price.) The **Newport Performing Arts Center,** 777 W. Olive St. (265-2787), hosts theater and dance performances, film festivals, and some excellent orchestral and band concerts. (Box office M-F 9am-5pm and 1hr. before shows. Tickets $6-18.)

The **Newport Seafood and Wine Festival,** during the last weekend in Feb., showcases Oregon wines, food, music, and crafts in over 100 booths, but the alcohol involved means the fest is open only to those 21 and over ($6-8). The three-day **Lincoln County Fair and Rodeo** (265-6237) comes to the Newport Fairgrounds the third week in July. ($6 per day, ages 6-12 $3, under 6 free. For all 4 days $18, children $9.) Contact the chamber of commerce for info on all seasonal events.

U.S. 101: NEWPORT TO REEDSPORT

From Newport to Reedsport, U.S. 101 sidles through a string of small towns, beautiful campgrounds, and spectacular stretches of beach. The **Waldport Ranger District Office,** 1049 Pacific Hwy. SW/U.S. 101 (563-3211), 16 mi. south of Newport in Waldport, describes hiking in **Siuslaw National Forest,** a patchwork of three wilderness areas along the Oregon Coast. The office furnishes detailed maps ($3-4) and advice on the area's many campgrounds (open M-F 8am-4pm).

Cape Perpetua, 11 mi. south of Waldport, and 40 mi. north of Reedsport, combines the highest point on the coast (803 ft.) with a number of exciting sea-level trails. The **Cape Perpetua Visitor Center,** 2400 U.S. 101 (547-3289), just south of the viewpoint turn-off, has informative exhibits about the surrounding lands. (Open June-Aug. daily 9am-5pm; Sept. W-Su 9am-5pm; Oct.-May M-F 9am-5pm, Sa-Su 10am-4pm.) Well-worn offshore attractions like **Devil's Churn** (¼ mi. north of the visitor center down Restless Water Trail) and **Spouting Horn** (¼ mi. south down Captain Cook Trail), demonstrate the power of the waves. **Cape Perpetua Campground,** at the viewpoint turn-off, has 37 sites alongside a tiny, fern-banked creek (sites $12; firewood $5; water, toilets). The **Rock Creek Campground,** 7½ mi. farther south, has 16 sites under mossy spruces by said creek a half-mile from the sea ($12; drinking water, toilets).

Escape the coast's bourgeois tourism at an unusual communal alternative, **Alpha Farm** (964-5102). Drive 14 mi. east of **Florence,** a far-too-long strip of fast-food joints and expensive motels 50 mi. south of Newport, to the tiny community of **Mapleton;** press on 30min. along Rte. 36 and 7 mi. up Deadwood Creek Rd. Anyone willing to lend a hand with the chores is welcome to camp out or stay in beautiful, simple bedrooms from Monday to Friday for up to three days. Call ahead. The farm also hosts a **4th of July** bash, to which you're invited. The **Alpha Bit Cafe** (268-4311), in Deadwood on Rte. 126, is owned and staffed by members of Alpha Farm; it's part cafe, part bookstore, and serves a mean *chai* (open Sa-Th 10am-6pm and F 10am-9pm).

OREGON DUNES AND REEDSPORT

Millennia of wind and water action have formed the Oregon Dunes National Recreation Area, a 50-mile expanse between Florence and Coos Bay. Endless mounds of sand rise 500 feet above the water, shifting so quickly that the entire face of a dune can disappear and reform in the course of a day. In many places, no grass or shrubs grow, and the vista presents naught but sand, sky, and tire tracks. In other spots, hidden lakes and islands of trees offer a green oasis amid what is technically a desert. Although more than half of dunes area is closed to traffic, campgrounds fill up early with dirtbike and dune buggy junkies, especially on summer weekends, bringing blaring radios, thrumming engines, and a hard-partying ethic.

⚐ ORIENTATION AND PRACTICAL INFORMATION. The dunes' shifting grip on the coastline is broken only once, where the Umpqua and Smith Rivers empty into **Winchester Bay.** On the south side of the bay is a small town of the same name, on the north is **Reedsport.** At the junction of Rte. 38 and U.S. 101, Reedsport is a typical highway town of motels, banks, and restaurants, 185 mi. southwest of Portland, 89 mi. southwest of Eugene, and 71 mi. south of Newport.

Greyhound, 265 Rainbow Plaza (271-1025; open daily 11am-4pm and 2-4am), in old town, runs to Portland (6hr., 2 per day, $26) and San Francisco, CA (15hr., 2 per day, $67). See p. 53 for discounts. **Coastal Taxi,** 139 N. 3rd St. (271-2690), costs $10 to Winchester Bay, $13 to the beach (daily 6am-3am). **Oregon Dunes National Recreation Area Visitor Center,** 855 U.S. 101 (271-3611), at Rte. 38 in Reedsport just south of the Umpqua River Bridge, has displays and a 10-minute video on dune ecology, and info on fees, regulations, hiking, and camping. (Maps $4. Open June-Oct. daily 8am-4:30pm; Nov.-May M-F 8am-4:30pm, Sa 10am-4pm.) The **Chamber of Commerce** (271-3495 or 800-247-2155), at the same location and open the same hours, has dune buggy rental info and motel listings. At **Coin Laundry,** 420 N. 14th St. (271-3587), next to McDonald's, a wash costs $1.25, a dry 25¢ per 8 minutes. (open daily 8am-9:30pm). The **library,** 395 Winchester Ave. (271-3500), has free **Internet access** (open M 2-8:30pm, Tu-W and F 10am-6pm, Th 2-6pm). **Emergency:** 911. **Police:** 146 N. 4th St. (271-2100). **Coast Guard:** 271-2137. **Post office:** 301 Fir Ave., 97467 (800-275-8777; open M-F 8:30am-5pm), off Rte. 38. **Area code:** 541.

ACCOMMODATIONS. Motels with singles from $40 abound on U.S. 101, though they often fill in summer. Fourteen campgrounds, many of which are very near the dunes, also dot the coast. The **Harbor View Motel,** 540 Beach Blvd. (271-3352), off U.S. 101 in Winchester Bay, is so close to the marina there are boats in the parking lot. Aging rooms to charm an antique hound are comfortable and clean. (Fridges and friendly management; singles $33; doubles $35.)

During the summer, RVs dominate local **campsites.** Permits for dispersed camping (allowed on public lands 200 ft. from any road or trail) are required year-round and available at the Dunes Information Center.

The national recreation area is administered by Siuslaw National Forest. The campgrounds that allow dune buggy access—**Spinreel** (36 sites), parking-lot style **Driftwood II** (69 sites), **Horsfall** (69 sites, showers), and **Horsfall Beach** (34 sites)—are generally rowdy in the summer ($10-13; toilets, water). Limited reservations for summer weekends are available; call 800-280-2267 at least five days in advance. The following options are marginally quieter, designed for tenters and small RVs.

> **Carter Lake Campground,** 12 mi. north of Reedsport on U.S. 101. Boat access to the lake; some sites lakeside. Well-screened sites, as quiet as it gets out here; no ATVs. Nice bathrooms, but no showers. 23 sites: $14. Open May-Sept.
>
> **Eel Creek Campground,** 10 mi. south of Reedsport. Sandy, spacious sites hidden from the road and each other by tall brush. Trailhead for the 2½ mi. Umpqua Dunes Trail, one of the best dune walks. Toilets, water. No hookups or ATVs. 53 sites: $13.
>
> **William M. Tugman State Park** (759-3604; reservations 800-452-5687), 8 mi. south of Reedsport on U.S. 101. Slightly less privacy, but still well-sheltered. Hiker/biker camping is the most private ($4). Close to gorgeous Eel Lake. Water and electricity. 115 sites: $15; yurts $29. Non-camper showers $2. Wheelchair accessible.

FOOD. Cheap, tasty food prevails in Winchester Bay and Reedsport. Grab a shrink-wrapped T-bone and a box of Fudgsicles at **Safeway** (open daily 7am-11pm) inside in the Umpqua Shopping Center, or at **Price 'n' Pride** (6am-11pm), across the street, both on U.S. 101 in Reedsport. The **Bayfront Bar and Bistro,** 208 Bayfront Loop (271-9463), in Winchester Bay is a classy but casual choice on the waterfront, whatever that means. Fresh quiche chock-full of seafood is $6. Dinner is pricey ($10-16), but good. (Open Tu-Su 11am-9pm.) The exterior of **Back to the Best** (271-2619), on U.S. 101 at 10th St., may be dated, but the food is fresh. Sandwiches piled high with such fineries as smoked gouda and home-cured ham costs $4.25-4.75. (Clam chowder $4. Open M-Sa 6am-6pm, Su 9am-5pm.)

OUTDOORS. At times, the dunes may seem like a maze of madcap buggy riders, but the sand actually houses a complex ecosystem and a network of quiet trails. A stop at the National Recreation Area visitor center (see above) can unlock some of the hidden attractions of Oregon's giant sandbox. At the very least, travelers should stop at the **Oregon Dunes Overlook** ($1 parking fee), off U.S. 101, about halfway between Reedsport and Florence, where wooden ramps lead to views of the dunes and a glimpse of the ocean. The **Tahkenitch Creek Loop,** actually three separate trails, plows 3½ mi. through forest, dunes, wetlands, and beach. (Overlook staffed daily Memorial Day to Labor Day 10am-3pm. Guided hikes available.) A free *Sand Tracks* brochure, available at the visitor center, has a detailed map of the dunes. The revamped **Umpqua Scenic Dunes Trail** makes another excellent hike. From the trailhead just south of Eel Creek Campground, the massive dunes invite bare feet. (*Let's Go* does not recommend stepping on sharp things.) Be wary of quicksand in the low, wet areas.

Umpqua Lighthouse State Park has an excellent **gray whale viewing** station. The best times to see these massive creatures are during their migrations; they head north in two waves from March through May and south in late December and early January. **Bird watching** is also popular around Reedsport. Lists of species and their seasons are available at the NRA visitor center. Throughout August, the **Crab Bounty Hunt** offers a $500 reward for catching a particular tagged crab, though traps can be rented in Winchester bay any old time.

EATING RIGHT FOR LONGER LIVING Each year, over 22,000 gray whales *(Eschrichtius robustus)* migrate northward from their warm winter calving grounds in Mexico to an Arctic summer smorgasbord born of increased energy from the midnight sun. During the 19th century, these whales were hunted almost to extinction. Whalers would kill a calf, wait for its mother to investigate, and then harpoon her, too. Today, gray whales have regained their high population levels so successfully that native groups like the Makah Nation (see p. 14) have renewed ceremonial and subsistence whale hunts with international support. The secret of the whales' success might be in their diet. Unlike the slowly rebounding humpbacks, which eat major commercial fish species, the gray whales feed on creatures that would make a human's stomach turn: fish roe, mud shrimp, and crab larvae. People imperil the other whales not just as hunters, but as competitors.

For an unmuffled and undeniably thrilling dune experience, venture out on wheels. Plenty of shops between Florence and Coos Bay rent and offer tours. **Spinreel Dune Buggy Rentals,** 9122 Wild Wood Dr. (759-3313), on U.S. 101 7 mi. south of Reedsport, offers air-rending Honda Odysseys, ear-splitting dune buggy rides, and family tours in a cochlea-mangling VW "Thing." (Hondas $20 for 30min., $30 first hr., $25 second hr. Buggies $15 for 30min., $25 per hour. Things $10 per 30min.)

COOS BAY, NORTH BEND, AND CHARLESTON

The largest city on the Oregon Coast, Coos Bay still has the feel of a down-to-earth working town. The nearby town of North Bend blends into Coos Bay, while tiny Charleston sits peacefully a few miles west on the coast. This is one of the few places on the coast where life slows down as you near the shore, with a string of state parks along the stunning coastline.

🛈 ORIENTATION AND PRACTICAL INFORMATION

U.S. 101 jogs inland south of Coos Bay, rejoining the coast at Bandon. From Coos Bay, **Rte. 42** heads east 85 mi. to **I-5,** and U.S. 101 continues north over the bridge into dune territory. **Coos Bay** and **North Bend** are so close together that one town blends seamlessly into the next, but street numbers start over again at the boundary. U.S. 101 runs along the east side of town, and **Cape Arago Hwy.** runs along the west side, connecting Coos Bay to **Charleston.**

Buses: Greyhound, 275 N. Broadway (267-4436), Coos Bay. To: Portland (6½hr., 4 per day, $28); San Francisco, CA (14hr., 2 per day, $60). Open M-Th 6:30am-5pm, F-Sa 6:30am-4pm.

Taxis: Yellow Cab (267-3111). $6 anywhere within the city. $2.50 base, $1.25 per mi.

Car Rental: Verger, 1400 Ocean Blvd. (888-5594). Cars from $26, 100 mi., free per day then 20¢ per mi. Must be 23 with credit card. Open M-F 8am-5:30pm, Sa 9am-5pm.

Visitor Information: All cover the whole area. **Bay Area Chamber of Commerce,** 50 E. Central Ave. (269-0215 or 800-824-8486), off Commercial Ave. in Coos Bay. Open in summer M-F 8:30am-9pm, Sa-Su 10am-4pm; mid-Sept. to May M-F 9am-5pm. **North Bend Visitor Center,** 1380 Sherman Ave. (756-4613), on U.S. 101, just south of North Bend bridge. Open M-F 9am-5pm, Sa 10am-4pm. **Charleston Visitor Center** (888-2311), at Boat Basin Dr. and Cape Arago Hwy. Open daily May-Oct. 9am-5pm.

Outdoor Information: Oregon State Parks Information, 10965 Cape Arago Hwy. (888-8867), in Charleston. Open M-F 8am-noon and 1pm-5pm.

Library: 525 W. Anderson St. (269-1101), Coos Bay. Free **Internet access.** Open M 10am-5:30pm, Tu-W 10am-8pm, Th-F noon-5:30pm, Sa 1-5pm.

Laundromat: Wash-A-Lot, 1921 Virginia Ave. (756-5439), in North Bend. Wash $1.25; dry 25¢ per 6min. Open 24hr.

Emergency: 911. **Police:** 500 Central Ave. (269-8911).

Coast Guard: 4645 Eel Ave. (888-3266), in Charleston.

Crisis Line: 888-5911. 24hr. **Women's Crisis Line:** 756-7000. 24hr.

Hospital: Bay Area Hospital, 1775 Thompson Rd. (269-8111), in Coos Bay.

Post Office: 470 Golden Ave. 97420 (800-275-8777), at 4th St. Open M-F 8:30am-5pm.

Area Code: 541.

ACCOMMODATIONS AND CAMPGROUNDS

Budget-bound non-campers should bunk at the affordable **Sea Star Hostel** (347-9632), 23 mi. south on U.S. 101 in **Bandon** (see p. 106). Campers, rejoice: the nearby state-run and private sites allow full access to the breathtaking coast.

2310 Lombard (756-3857), at the corner of Cedar St. in North Bend. A tiny home with a beautiful garden. Two twin beds $35; double bed $40. Full breakfast from a wonderful hostess. Reservations always recommended.

Itty Bitty Inn, 1504 Sherman Ave. (756-6398 or 888-276-9256). Cozy, Southwestern-style rooms with wall hangings, cable, refrigerators, microwaves, and live cacti. Singles $35; doubles $40. In winter much less. Includes breakfast at the Virginia St. Diner.

Bluebill Campground, off U.S. 101, 3 mi. north of North Bend. Follow the signs to the Horsfall Beach area, then continue down the road to this U.S. Forest Service campground. 19 sites: $13, in winter $11. Half a mile to the ocean and dunes.

Sunset Bay State Park, 10965 Cape Arago Hwy. (888-4902, reservations 800-452-5687), 12 mi. south of Coos Bay and 3½ mi. west of Charleston. Akin to camping in a well-landscaped parking lot, or, when full, a zoo. Fabulous Sunset Beach is worth it. Fee includes entrance to Shore Acres State Park. 138 sites: $16; hookups $18; yurts $27; hiker/biker sites $4. Showers. Wheelchair accessible. Non-camper showers $2.

FOOD

For grocery needs, **Safeway** holds court at 230 E. Johnson Ave. off U.S. 101 north, at the southern end of town (open daily 6am-1am).

Cheryn's Seafood Restaurant and Pie House (888-3251), at the east end of Charleston Bridge. Boats moored beyond the parking lot testify to the freshness of the fish, from $7 calamari to $20 steamed lobster. Open daily 8am-9pm; in winter daily 8am-8pm.

Virginia Street Diner, 1430 Virginia St. (756-3475), a few blocks west of U.S. 101 in North Bend. Step back into the 50s, when the booths were a sparkly red and the prices were right. Bottomless $1 pitcher of coffee will keep you buzzin'. Homemade meatloaf sandwich $6.55; all-you-can-eat salad bar $4.75. Open daily 6am-10pm.

Cranberry Sweets, 1005 Newmark St. (888-9824), in Coos Bay. This far-from-average candy factory serves up enough samples of ambitious ventures like beer squares and cheddar cheese fudge to make lunch moot. Open M-Sa 9am-5:30pm, Su 11am-4pm.

SIGHTS, OUTDOORS, AND EVENTS

Sunset Bay, 11½ mi. from Coos Bay on Cape Arago State Hwy., has been rated one of the top 10 American beaches. Sheltered from the waves by two pincer-like cliffs, the warm, shallow bay is perfect for swimming. The magnificent **Shore Acres State Park** (888-3732) rests a mile beyond Sunset Bay on the Cape Arago Hwy. (Open daily 8am-9pm; in winter daily 8am-dusk. $3 per car. Wheelchair accessible.) Once the estate of local lumber lord Louis J. Simpson, the park contains elaborate botanical gardens that outlasted the mansion. Come December, the rose garden is festooned with 200,000 lights, and the park serves free hot drinks.

At the south end of the highway is breezy **Cape Arago,** notable for the rich life of its tide pools. Paved paths lead out toward the tip of the cape and provide an

WESTERN OREGON

excellent view of Shell Island, ¼ mi. offshore, a protected elephant and harbor seal rookery. Fishing enthusiasts can hop on board with **Bob's Sportfishing** (888-4241 or 800-628-9633), operating out of a small building at the west end of the Charleston Boat Basin, or **Betty Kay Charters** (888-9021 or 800-752-6303), a stone's throw away. (6hr. trips depart daily at 6am and 12:30pm. $55-60. License $8.25. Betty Kay also rents crab rings for $5 per day.) Four miles south of Charleston up Seven Devils Rd., the ▨ **South Slough National Estuarine Research Reserve** (888-5558; www.southsloughestuary.com) is one of the most fascinating and underappreciated venues on the central coast. Spreading out from a small interpretive visitor center, almost 7 sq. mi. of salt- and freshwater estuaries nurture all kinds of wildlife, from sand shrimp to blue herons to deer. Hiking trails weave through the sanctuary, and free guided walks leave from the center. Canoe tours ($10) are available if you bring your own canoe. (Open daily June-Aug. 8:30am-4:30pm; Sept.-May M-F 8:30am-4:30pm. Trails open dawn-dusk year-round.) Inland 24½ mi. from Coos Bay, at **Golden and Silver Falls State Park,** three trails lead to the awesome Golden Falls, a 210 ft. drop into the abyss, and the beautiful Silver Falls, thin sheets of water cascading down a rock face. From the southern end of Coos Bay, take the Eastside-Allegany exit off U.S. 101, and follow it for about an hour along a narrow, gravel road. The falls are heaviest when the river swells with winter rains.

For two weeks in mid-July, Coos Bay plays host to the **Oregon Coast Music Festival** (267-0938), the most popular summer event on the coast. A week of jazz, blues, and folk (tickets $5-9) is followed by a week of performances by the renowned festival orchestra ($11-15). Art exhibits, vessel tours, and a free classical concert in Mingus Park spice up the festival even for the ticketless. In September, Oregon remembers one of its favorite native sons in the **Steve Prefontaine 10K Memorial Run** (269-1103), named after the great Olympic athlete who died in an automobile accident. The race draws dozens of world-class runners. (Entrance fee $12-15.)

BANDON

Despite a steady flow of tourists in the summer, the small fishing town of Bandon-by-the-Sea has refrained from breaking out the pastels and making itself up like an amusement park. A fine, fine hostel and a number of outdoor activities make Bandon a worthwhile stop on any tour of the coast. Bandon is 24 mi. south of Coos Bay and 27 mi. north of Port Orford on U.S. 101. **Greyhound** (267-4436) departs the hostel at 11am for Portland (7¼hr., $32) and at 4:40am and 4:25pm for San Francisco, CA (14hr., $61). The **visitor center** is at 300 SE 2nd St. (347-9616), in the Old Town next to U.S. 101 (open daily 10am-5pm; in winter, 10am-4pm). **Post office:** 105 12th St. SE, 97411 (800-275-8777; open M-F 8:30am-4:30pm). **Area code:** 541.

It's hard not to feel sorry for the captive animals at the **West Coast Game Park** (347-3106), 7 mi. south of Bandon on U.S. 101, but equally hard to resist playing with a baby tiger or bear or feeding the pushy deer. (Open daily 9am-7pm; in winter 9am-5pm. $8, over 60 $7, ages 7-12 $6, ages 2-6 $4.25.) A stroll around **Old Town** is pleasant, as is exploring the beach on a horse from **Bandon Beach Riding Stables** (347-3423; $25 for 1hr.). The well-marked beach loop road that leaves from Old Town and joins U.S. 101 5 mi. south passes **Table Rock, Elephant Rock,** and **Face Rock,** three of the coast's most striking offshore outcroppings.

Bandon's rambling ▨ **Sea Star Hostel (HI),** 375 2nd St. (347-9632), on the right as you enter Old Town from the north, is a laid-back installment in the HI series. A noon check-out and open-24-hours policy make for a relaxed and friendly place to pass the night. Comfortable bunkrooms, an enclosed courtyard, kitchen, and laundry. ($13, nonmembers $16, ages 5-12 may only stay in family rooms. Family rooms: 2 members for $28, nonmembers $34. Guest house $53-90.) The beautiful Mediterranean exterior of the **Bandon Wayside Motel** (347-3421), on Rte. 42 south, just off U.S. 101, gives way to a bland interior (singles $32; doubles $36). Two miles north of town and across the bridge, **Bullard's Beach State Park** (347-2209) houses the **Coquille River Lighthouse,** built in 1896. The park has 185 sites tucked among the sand and pines. Primitive horse sites come complete with corral, and campfire talks are given on summer evenings from Tuesday to Saturday ($19, yurts $27, hiker/biker sites $4 per person).

For a tasty and healthy morsel, step into **Mother's Natural Grocery and Deli,** 975 U.S. 101 (347-4086), near the junction with Rte. 42 south, where four vegetarian *nori* rolls ($3) and a well-stuffed carrot/hummus pita pocket ($3.75) highlight the menu (open M-Sa 10am-6pm). The best seafood in town is at **Bandon Boatworks,** 275 Lincoln St. SW (347-2111), through Old Town and out South Jetty Rd. Real tablecloths and delectable cranberry bread ($4 per loaf) set the Boatworks apart from the average fish shack. Lunches ($6-8) are more affordable than dinners ($11-18), when the Boatworks breaks out the wine glasses. (Open M-Sa 11:30am-9pm, Su 11am-8:30pm; in winter M-Sa 11:30am-2:30pm and 5-9pm, Su 11am-8:30pm.) Known as the "Cranberry Capital of Oregon," Bandon celebrates the fall harvest with the **Cranberry Festival** (347-9616) parade and food fair.

PORT ORFORD

Port Orford supports a homey and healthy community protected by the prosperity of its larger, more touristed neighbors. The town lies several miles south of **Cape Blanco,** the westernmost point in Oregon. **Cape Blanco State Park,** 5 mi. west of U.S. 101, has a campground high on the hill and a road leading down to the beach. The very tip of the cape is capped with a functioning 245-foot-tall lighthouse, open to the public (Th-M 10am-3:30pm). Also in the park is the historic **Hughes House,** now in its 102nd year, beautifully maintained and laden with charms from the past. Some of the best views in the area are from **Battle Rock,** a seaside park in town where whales pass close by during December and spring migrations. The beaches are littered with agate, easy to find at low tide when it sparkles in the sun.

Port Orford is 26 mi. south of Bandon and 30 mi. north of **Gold Beach** on U.S. 101. In town, U.S. 101 becomes Oregon St. **Greyhound** stops at the Circle K, across from the Port Orford Motel, with two buses per day to Portland (8hr., $36) and two to San Francisco, CA (13hr., $59). Port Orford's **Chamber of Commerce** (332-8055) lazes in the parking lot overlooking the bay (open M-F 9am-5pm, Sa-Su 10am-5pm). The **post office** is at 311 W. 7th St., 97465 (332-4251), at Jackson St. (open M-F 8:30am-1pm and 2-5pm). **Area code:** 541.

For those traveling by bus, the older, cramped rooms of the **Port Orford Inn,** 1034 Oregon St. (332-0212), at U.S. 101, are conveniently located across from the station (single $34; double $39; triple $41). Several blocks south and around the bend, the **Shoreline Motel** (332-2903), on U.S. 101, sits across the road from dramatic Battle Rock and the bay (singles $36; doubles $38, with 2 beds $42; $8 less in winter).

Two nearby campgrounds, one to the north and one to the south, offer the most peaceful and convenient access to the shore. **Cape Blanco State Park** (332-6774), 4 mi. north of Port Orford and 5 mi. west of U.S. 101, nestles in a grove of pines just south of the cape and its lighthouse. (58 sites: standard sites $16; full hookups $18; hiker/biker $4.) Six miles south of Port Orford, where the highway ducks back behind mountains, **Humbug Mountain State Park** (332-6774) has 101 tightly packed sites in the crisp green shade of deciduous trees. Those who make the 3 mi. hike up the mountain are rewarded with quite a view. (Tents $16; water and electricity $18; hiker/biker sites $4. Showers and toilets.)

Health food nuts luck out in Port Orford. The Buckwheat noodle salad or roasted portabello sandwich ($4-5.75) from **Seaweed Natural Grocery,** 832 U.S. 101 (332-3640), are a welcome respite from beer-battered fish (cafe open M-Sa 9am-3pm, grocery open M-Sa 9am-6pm). At **Salsa Rita's** (332-7482), next door, burritos and enchiladas ($5.25) take a back seat to sangria ($2.50).

BROOKINGS

Brookings is the southernmost stop on U.S. 101 before California, and one of few coastal towns that remains relatively tourist-free. Here, hardware stores are easier to find than trinket shops, and the beaches are among Oregon's most unspoiled. The city also sits in Oregon's "banana belt" (a.k.a. California's "arctic circle"): warm weather is not rare in January, and some Brookings backyards even boast scraggly palm trees. For exhaustive coverage of all that is hot and cool down south, consult *Let's Go: California 2000.*

🔃 PRACTICAL INFORMATION. U.S. 101 is called Chetco Ave. in town. Strictly speaking, there are two towns here, separated by the **Chetco River**—Brookings on the north side and **Harbor** to the south—which share everything and are referred to collectively as Brookings Harbor. The **Greyhound** station is at 601 Railroad Ave., at Tanbark (469-3326; open M-F 8:45am-noon and 4pm-6:30pm, Sa 8:45am-noon). Two buses per day run to Portland (10hr., $40) and San Francisco, CA (12hr., $52). The **Brookings Welcome Center,** 1650 U.S. 101 (469-4117), welcomes from just north of town (open May-Sept. M-Sa 8am-6pm, Su 9am-5pm; in Apr. and Oct. M-Sa 8am-5pm, Su 9am-5pm). The **Chamber of Commerce,** 16330 Lower Harbor Rd. (469-3181 or 800-535-9469), is across the bridge to the south, a short distance off the highway (open M-F 9am-5pm, Sa 9am-1pm; in winter closed Sa). The **Chetco Ranger Station,** 555 5th St. (469-2196; www.fs.fed.us/r6/siskiyou), distributes info on the neighboring part of the **Siskiyou National Forest** (open M-F 8am-4:30pm). **Fely's Cafe & Laundromat,** 85 Beach Front Rd. (412-0350), is just that (open daily 6am-7pm; wash $1, dry 25¢ per 10min.). Rent a wetsuit and boogie board for $14 at **Escape Hatch,** 642 Railroad Ave. (469-2914; Open M-F 10am-5:30pm, Sa 10am-5pm). The **library,** at 405 Alder, (469-7738), has free **Internet access** (open M, F 10am-6pm, Tu, Th 10am-7pm, W 10am-8pm, Sa 10am-5pm). **Post office:** 711 Spruce St., 97415 (800-275-8777; open M-F 9am-4:30pm). **Area code:** 541.

🍴 ACCOMMODATIONS, CAMPGROUNDS, AND FOOD. The Bonn Motel, 1216 U.S. 101, (469-2161), is, in fact, bonny. Its recently refurbished buildings sport cheery hydrangeas out back. The heated indoor pool and sauna are rarities in Brookings (singles $38; doubles $48; $6-11 less in winter). **Harris Beach State Park Campground** (469-2021 or 800-452-5687), at the north edge of Brookings, has 63 tent sites in a grand natural setting. The campground is set back in the trees behind a beach and has views of rocky, uninhabited, 21-acre **Goat Island.** The park is equipped with showers and a laundry and is wheelchair accessible (open year-round; sites $16; with full hookup $19; hiker/biker sites $4). For campsites off the beaten path, travel 15 mi. east of Brookings on **North Bank Road** to the charming **Little Redwood Campground,** located beneath giant conifers alongside a burbling, salamander-filled creek (15 sites: $8; drinking water and pit toilet). **Nook** and **Redwood Bar,** across the way by the water, have no water but charge only $3. For information, contact the Chetco Ranger Station (469-2196).

A half-sandwich and a cup of excellent soup or chili goes for $4.50 at the **Homesport Bagel Shop,** 1011 Chetco Ave. (669-6611; open M-F 7am-7pm; in winter, 7am-4pm). A number of seafood spots can be found near the harbor. The locals' favorite, **Oceanside Diner,** 16403 Lower Harbor Rd. (469-7971), serves generous portions. (Oyster sandwich $6.50. Open Su-Th 4am-3pm, F-Sa 4am-8pm.)

📷🎿 SIGHTS, EVENTS, AND OUTDOORS. Brookings is known statewide for its flowers. In **Azalea Park,** downtown, large native and non-native azaleas, some more than 300 years old, encircle pristine lawns and bloom from April to June. Two rare weeping spruce trees also grace the park's grounds. The pride of Brookings is its **Azalea Festival** (469-3181), held in Azalea Park over Memorial Day weekend. The **Chetco Valley Historical Society Museum,** 15461 Museum Rd. (469-6651), 2½ mi. south of the Chetco River, has exhibits on the patchwork quilts of settlers, historic documents, and Native American basketwork. (Open May-Sept. W-Su noon-5pm; Oct.-Apr. F-Su noon-5pm. Donations welcome.) The museum is hard to miss; just look for **the nation's second-largest cypress tree** out front.

Boardman State Park enfolds U.S. 101 north of Brookings with 8 mi. of overlooks and picnic sites. **Carpenterville Road,** a twisty, 13½ mi. road featuring beautiful ocean views, is an ideal bike route. Thirty miles north of Brookings in **Gold Beach,** you can ride a mail boat up the **Rogue River. Mail Boat Hydro-Jets,** 94294 Rogue River Rd. (247-7033 or 800-458-3511) offers 64-, 80-, and 104-mile whitewater daytrips lasting 6 to 7½ hours ($30-75; runs May-Oct.)

INLAND VALLEYS

While jagged cliffs and gleaming surf draw tourists to the coast, many Oregonians choose the inland Willamette and Rogue River Valleys for their vacation destinations. Vast tracts of fertile land support agriculture, and for decades the immense forests maintained a healthy timber industry. While the present-day fortunes of the timber industry are uncertain, tourism is definitely a growth industry in small-town Oregon.

⊏ GETTING AROUND

I-5 runs north-south through Oregon to the west of the Cascades, traversing agricultural and forest land punctuated by a few urban centers. The **Rogue River Valley,** running north from Ashland to Grants Pass, is hot and dry in summer. Eugene rests at the southern end of the temperate **Willamette River Valley.** This carpet of agricultural land extends 20 mi. on either side of the river, and continues 80 mi. north until the outskirts of Portland. It's possible to drive Oregon's 305 mi. stretch of I-5 from tip to toe in less than six hours, but lead-footed outsiders be warned—most Oregonians obey speed limits, and fines are high.

SALEM

Although Salem is the state capital, the third-largest city in Oregon, and the home of Willamette University, the city radiates vibes of surburbia rather than urban zip. Several fine museums and wineries ring the verdant capitol lawn, but Salem, though undeniably pleasant, is hardly a hopping tourist destination.

⁊ ORIENTATION AND PRACTICAL INFORMATION

Salem is 51 mi. south of Portland and 64 mi. north of Eugene on I-5. Willamette University and the capitol building dominate the center of the city; the heart of downtown lies several blocks northwest. To reach downtown, take Exit 253 off I-5. Street addresses are divided into quadrants: the **Willamette River** divides east from west. East of the river, **State St.** divides SE from NE.

Trains: Amtrak, 500 13th St. SE (588-1551 or 800-872-7245), across from the visitor center. To: Portland (1½hr., 2 per day, $7.50-12); Seattle (5-7hr., 2 per day $23-43); and San Francisco (17hr., 1 per day, $70-117). Open daily 6:30am-4:30pm.

Buses: Greyhound, 450 Church St. NE (362-2428), at Center St. 10 per day to: Portland (1½hr., $7) and Eugene (2hr., $10). Lockers $1 per day. Station open daily 6am-8pm. See p. 53 for discounts.

Local Transportation: Cherriots Customer Service Office, 183 High St. NE (588-2877), provides local bus maps and multi-day passes. 20 routes leave from High St., between State and Court St. in front of the courthouse. Fare 75¢, over 60 and disabled 35¢, under 19 50¢. Every 30min. M-F 6:15am-9:35pm, hourly Sa 7:45am-9:35pm.

Taxis: Salem Yellow Cab Co. (362-2411). $2 base, $1.80 per mi.

Visitor Information: 1313 Mill St. SE (581-4325 or 800-874-7012; www.scva.org), in the Mission Mill Village complex. Open M-F 8:30am-5pm, Sa 10am-4pm.

Library: 585 Liberty St. SE (588-6315). Free Internet access. Open Tu-W 10am-9pm, Th-Sa 10am-6pm; Sept.-May also open Su 1-5pm.

Laundromat: Suds City Depoe, 1785 Lancaster Dr. NE. (362-9845), at Market St. Snacks, odd spelling, and big-screen TV. Wash $1, dry 25¢ per 15min. Open daily 7:30am-9pm.

Emergency: 911. **Police:** 555 Liberty St. SE (588-6123), in City Hall room 130.

24hr. Crisis Line: 581-5535. **24hr. Women's Crisis Line:** 399-7722.

Hospital: Salem Hospital, 665 Winter St. SE (370-5200).

WESTERN OREGON

Internet Access: See **library,** above. **GoldCom Internet Services,** on the corner of Liberty and Ferry. Open M-F 10am-6pm.

Post Office: 1050 25th St. SE, 97301 (800-275-8777). Open M-F 8:30am-5:30pm.

Area Code: 503.

▌. ACCOMMODATIONS AND CAMPGROUNDS

Salem's cheap motel rooms tend to be dingy. The visitor center has a list of B&Bs, which provide a classier and often more comfortable setting (from $45).

Alden House Bed and Breakfast, 760 Church St. (363-9574 or 877-363-9574). Every available inch is packed with antiques, and rooms have large, luxurious beds. Breakfast in the elegant dining room at 9am. Check-in 4-6pm. Reservations advised.

Cottonwood Cottage, 960 East St. NE (362-3979 or 800-349-3979; www.open.org/ctnwdctg), between Capitol and Summer St. This endearing old house close to downtown offers 2 quiet, sunny rooms with cable, A/C, and shared bath. Rooms from $55. Reservations recommended in summer.

City Center Motel, 510 Liberty St. SE (364-0121 or 800-289-0121; fax 581-0554). Older rooms but clean. Convenient location right by city hall means lots of road noise. One bed, $40-45; two beds, $45-52.

Silver Falls State Park, 20024 Silver Falls SE/Rte. 214 (873-8681, reservations 800-452-5687). Take Rte. 22 (Mission St.) east for 5 mi., then take the exit for Rte. 214 N (Silver Falls Rd.), and follow it for about 18 mi. Limited privacy, but 10 spectacular waterfalls nearby make the drive worthwhile. Pitch tent early for a day of hiking through volcanic caves behind the roaring falls. Showers, toilets, water. 60 tent sites $16. 44 RV hookups $20. Wheelchair accessible.

⊙ FOOD

Busy Lancaster Dr. (just east and parallel to I-5) woos burger lovers into the wee hours. Aisle upon aisle of grocery goodness awaits at **Roth's,** 702 Lancaster Dr. NE (585-5770; open daily 6am-11pm). **Heliotrope Natural Foods,** 2809 Market St. NE (362-5487; open M-Sa 8am-9pm, Su 9am-8pm), has a healthy selection. Saturdays see a **Farmer's Market** (585-8264; 9am-3pm) at the corner of Marion and Winter.

La Hacienda Real, 3690 Commercial (540-5537), serves up *real* Mexican in beautiful tiled booths. Delicious fresh-made tortillas arrive steaming ($3 per dozen), and generous lunches ($5-7) go beyond the familiar. Open M-F 11am-10pm, Sa-Su 11am-11pm.

Off-Center Cafe, 1741 Center St. NE (363-9245), in the same long, one-story building as Nobles Tavern. Left-of-center, to be precise. Quick service, healthy food, and political scribblings on the wall. "Bibble and squib" $4.50, scrambled tofu $5.75. Boysenberry milkshakes $2.75. Open Tu-F 7am-2:30pm, W-Sa 6am-9pm.

Fuji Japanese Restaurant, 159 High St. SE (364-5512), serves real-deal Japanese, a rare find in Salem. Lunch specials $5; dinner entrees $9-18. Open M-F 11am-2:30pm and 5-10pm, Sa 4-10pm.

◩ SIGHTS AND ENTERTAINMENT

The **State Capitol,** 900 Court St. NE (986-1388), occupies a city block bounded by Court St. on the north, Waverly St. on the east, State St. on the south, and Cottage St. on the west. Presiding over it all is a 23 ft. gold-gilt statue of the "Oregon Pioneer." In summer, a free **tour** to the top of the rotunda leaves every 30 minutes; tours of the various chambers leave every hour; call for off-season tours. (Open M-F 7:30am-5:30pm, Sa 9am-4pm, Su noon-4pm.)

The **Bush Barn Art Center and Museum,** 600 Mission St. SE (art center 581-2228, museum 363-4714), is a gem. The interesting museum is outdone by the rose garden and greenhouse, and the art collection includes some entertainingly off-beat pieces. (Free. Tours $3, students and seniors $2.50, ages 6-12 $1.50, under 6 free.)

During the third weekend of July, the Salem Art Association hosts the free **Salem Art Fair and Festival** in Bush's Pasture Park. The artsy and crafty display their wares while bands strum away the afternoon. A 5K Run for the Arts is held during the festival. The visitor center has info on the fair and on area **wineries;** over the Memorial Day weekend, vinters uncork their barrels for free tours and tastings.

With the annual **Oregon State Fair** at the Expo Center, 2330 17th St. NE (378-3247 or 800-833-0011), Salem gives summer a rousing send-off. For the 12 days leading up to Labor Day, country-folk invade the city, for once, transforming it into a whirl of livestock shows and baking contests. ($6, seniors $4, ages 6-12 $3.)

The **Salem Cinema,** 445 High St. SE (378-7676), in Pringle Plaza, offers relief from the college/sports/tropical-themed bar scene with its indie and art film selection and from money-grubbers with its bargain matinees.

CORVALLIS

Corvallis may or may not have been a rowdy frontier town, a stop on the Oregon Trail, or a former nudist colony: unlike so many Oregon towns, this peaceful residential community in the central Willamette Valley has no historic pretensions. Home to Oregon State University (OSU) and a looming Hewlett-Packard facility, Corvallis lives smack-dab in the present. Life bustles in the downtown area, but like any college town, Corvallis mellows in the summer, allowing time for a few choice festivals and plenty of outdoor exploration.

⚆ ORIENTATION AND PRACTICAL INFORMATION

Corvallis is laid out in a checkerboard fashion that degenerates away from downtown; numbered streets run north-south and streets named for lesser-known American presidents (Van Buren, Polk, Buchanan) run east-west. Rte. 99 W. splits in town and becomes two one-way streets: northbound **3rd St.** and southbound **4th St.** When they aren't hitting the trails, college students hang out around **Monroe St.**

Buses: Greyhound, 153 4th St. NW (757-1797 or 800-231-2222). To: Portland (2-3hr., 4 per day, $11); Seattle, WA (8hr., 4 per day, $25); Newport (1¼hr., 3 per day, $10); Eugene (1hr., 4 per day, $6). Lockers $1 per day. Open daily 7am-1:45pm and 2:45-9pm. See p. 53 for discounts.

Public Transportation: Corvallis Transit System (757-6998). Fare 50¢; ages 5-17 and over 60 25¢. Service M-F 6:25am-7pm, Sa 9:15am-5pm.

Taxis: A-1 Taxi, 754-1111. $2 per mile, $6 minimum.

Visitor Information: Chamber of Commerce (757-1505) and **Convention and Visitor Bureau** (757-1544 or 800-334-8118; www.visitcorvallis.com), both at 420 2nd St. NW, the first right past the bridge coming from the east. Detailed $2 map at the chamber. Both open M-F 8am-5pm. **Oregon State University** (737-0123; events info 737-6445). Main entrance and info booth at Jefferson and 14th St.

Outdoor Equipment: Peak Sports, 129 2nd St. NW (754-6444). Rents mountain bikes ($25 per day) and 3-speeds ($5 per day). Open M-Th 9am-6pm, F 9am-8pm, Sa 9am-6pm, Su noon-5pm.

Library: 645 Monroe St. NW (757-6926). Free Internet access. Open M-F 9am-9pm, Sa 9am-6pm, Su noon-6pm.

Laundromat: Campbell's Laundry, 1120 9th St. NW (752-3794). Wash $1.25, dry 25¢ per 10min. Open daily 6am-1am.

Medical Services: Corvallis Clinic, 3680 Samaritan Dr. NW (754-1150; walk-in service 754-1282). Open M-F 8am-8pm, Sa-Su 10am-5pm.

Emergency: 911. **Police:** 180 5th St. NW (757-6924).

Internet Access: Free at the **Library** and **Java Rama Cafe,** 2047 Monroe NW (758-5639), open M-Sa 7:30am-5pm.

Post Office: 311 2nd St. SW, 97333 (800-275-8777). Open M-F 8am-5:30pm, Sa 9am-4pm.

Area Code: 541.

ACCOMMODATIONS AND CAMPGROUNDS

Many of Corvallis's easily accessible campgrounds are not RV mini-cities and provide a break from generators and Airstreams. The few motels are reasonably priced, but occasionally fill with conventioneers.

C.E.W. Motel, 1705 9th St. NW (753-8823). Elderly rooms (three words: orange shag carpet) are clean. Singles $35.50; 1-bed doubles $42; 2-bed doubles $52. Reserve with credit card 3 days in advance for weekends.

EconoLodge, 345 2nd St. NW (752-9601), right off the highway. This manifestation of the mega chain is—surprise!—nondescript but clean. Singles $38, doubles $42.

Benton County Fairgrounds, 110 53rd St. SW (757-1521). Follow Rte. 34W, then turn left onto 53rd St. or take the Rte. 3 CTS bus. Pleasant sites in sight of the tractors; much like camping in a farmyard. Sites $7; hookups $12. First-come, first-served. Closed for fairs and other events mid-July to early Aug.

FOOD AND ENTERTAINMENT

Corvallis has a smattering of the requisite collegiate pizza parlors and several variations on the Mexican theme. OSU students prowl Monroe St. for grub, their limited finances inspiring an abundance of cheap, filling food. **First Alternative Inc.,** 1007 3rd St. SE (753-3115), is a co-op stocked with a range of well-priced, natural products (open daily 9am-9pm). Frozen peas and *People* magazine are available at **Safeway,** 450 3rd St. SW (753-5502; open daily 6am-2am).

The **KBBR concert line** (737-3737), you know, lists concerts.

Nearly Normal's, 109 15th St. NW (753-0791). This cottage combines an arboreal aura with low prices and large portions of everything but meat ($2.50-9). Dine under a canopy of branches, kiwi vines, fuchsia plants, and rose bushes on the porch. Vegan ravioli $7.75; hearty sunflower seed burgers $5.25. Open M-F 8am-9pm, Sa 9am-9pm.

La Conga, 360 5th St. NW (757-2441). Nowhere else in Corvallis will you find a giant burrito at 3am. Chicken tacos $1.50, half-pint of rice and beans $1.75. Open 24hr.

Bombs Away Cafe, 2527 Monroe St. NW (757-7221). A self-proclaimed "funky taqueria" serving atypical Mexican food like ricotta enchiladas and duck chimichangas (both $6.25) and the enormous "Wet Burrito." Open M-F 11am-midnight, Sa 5pm-midnight, Su 4-9pm. 21+ when kitchen closes (M-Sa at 10pm).

McMenamins, 420 3rd St. NW (758-6044). Some of the best pub fare in town, made from scratch ($2-9). Fresh-cut fries ($1.15-4.50) alone are worth the trip. Pints $3. Open M-Sa 11am-1am, Su noon-midnight.

East Ocean Buffet, 2501 Monroe St. NW (754-2803). All-you-can-eat buffet of American-style Chinese $5.50 at lunch, $7 at dinner. Massive quantities compensate for total lack of atmosphere. Open M-F 11am-9:30pm, Sa-Su 11:30am-9:30pm.

Squirrel's Tavern, 100 2nd St. SW (753-8057). Few frat boys frolic here, where the bearded come to drink beer (domestics $1.75, microbrews $3), play pool (50¢ per game), and dig into generous dinner specials (jambalaya $5). Live jazz most Saturdays Happy hour M-F 4:30-6:30pm (domestic pints $1, pitchers $5.50). 21+. Cover up to $3. Open M-Th 11:30am-1am, F-Sa 11:30am-1:30am, Su 5pm-midnight.

OUTDOORS AND EVENTS

Mountain biking is a way of life in Corvallis, and all roads seem to lead to one bike trail or another. Many cyclists and sightseers sidle out to OSU's **McDonald Forest;** to get there, ride west out of town on Harrison for about 4½ miles then turn right on Oak Creek Rd. The pavement dead-ends at OSU's lab, and 10 miles worth of trails cover the forest from there. Maps are available at Peak Sports ($4; see above). On a clear day, **Chip Ross Park** offers splendid views of the Cascade Valley from Mt.

Hood to Three Sisters. Take 3rd St. north, turn left on Circle Blvd., then go right on Highland. After a mile, look left on Lester Ave. for a small small small blue sign.

Corvallis's collective heart rate picks up with the **Da Vinci Days Festival** (757-6363 or 800-334-8118), during the third weekend in July. Renaissance men and women compete in the **Kinetic Sculpture Race,** in which people-powered, all-terrain works of art vie for a crown. ($5 each day, ages 3-13 $3; all 3 days $9, ages 3-13 $5.) The **Fall Festival,** held in Central Park during the third weekend in September, combines food, music, and an excellent crafts fair. Performers have included Wynton Marsalis and James Cotton.

Ten miles east in **Albany** (off U.S. 20 before I-5), thousands of jammers gather each Thursday night from mid-July through August for the **River Rhythms** concert series. Musical acts vary drastically from concert to concert, but they are always free, always at 7pm, and always held in the Monteith River Park. Each week in July, a special Monday night show features local performers. Call the Albany Visitor Center (928-0911; open M-F 9am-5pm; Sa 10am-2pm) for more info.

EUGENE

With students riding mountain bikes, hippies eating organically grown food, outfitters making a killing off tourists, and hunters killing local wildlife, Eugene is liberal in the true sense of the word: it contains multitudes. Oregon's second-largest city straddles the Willamette River and is sandwiched between the Siuslaw and Willamette National Forests. Home to the University of Oregon (U of O), Eugene owes much of its vibrancy to its students. Summer lures upwardly mobile professionals onto the downtown pedestrian mall for shopping and dining, and a night of Bach at the Hult Center. Outdoor types raft on the Willamette and hike or bike in nearby. Fitness enthusiasts join the fleet of foot and free of spirit in this "running capital of the universe," also the hometown of Nike, Inc. In mid-July, Eugene invites all kinds from all over to the magnificent Oregon Country Fair, three days of unabashed dancing, delirium, and drum-circles in the Oregon woods.

▣ ORIENTATION AND PRACTICAL INFORMATION

Eugene is 111 mi. south of Portland on I-5, just west of **Springfield. Franklin Blvd.** runs from I-5 to the city center. East-west streets are numbered beginning at the Willamette River. **Highway 99** splits in town—**6th Ave.** runs west and **7th Ave.** goes east. The **pedestrian mall** is downtown, on Broadway between 6th and 7th Ave. Eugene's main student drag, **13th Ave.,** leads to the **University of Oregon,** in the southeast of town. The city is a motorist's nightmare of one-way streets, and there is little free parking downtown. The most convenient way to get around is by bike—the roads are flat and there are plenty of bike paths. Most **parks** are officially open from 6am to 11pm. U of O "yellow duck paths" signify better lit areas, but lone women should avoid the campus at night and be wary of **Whittaker,** the area around Blair Blvd. near 6th Ave.

Trains: Amtrak, 433 Willamette St. (800-872-7245), at 4th Ave. To: Seattle, WA (6-8hr., 2 per day, $24-46); Portland (2½hr., 2 per day, $14-26); Berkeley, CA (15hr., 1 per day, $63-105). See p. 52 for discounts. Baggage storage $1.50 per item per 24hr.

Buses: Greyhound, 987 Pearl St. (344-6265 or 800-231-2222), at 10th Ave. One per day to: Seattle, WA (6-9hr., $34); San Francisco, CA (13-16hr., $48); Portland (2-4hr., $12). Open daily 6:30am-10pm. Lockers $1.25 per day. **Green Tortoise** (800-867-8647; see p. 54). Stops at the U of O library (14th and Kincaid St.). To: San Francisco, CA (21hr., Su and Th, $39), and Seattle, WA (7hr., Tu and Sa, $25) via Portland (4½hr., $10). Some routes require reservations. Open daily 8am-8pm.

Public Transportation: Lane Transit District (LTD) (687-5555). **Map** and timetables at visitor information or the LTD Service Center at 11th Ave. and Willamette St. Runs M-F

6am-11:30pm, Sa 7:30am-11:30pm, Su 8:30am-8:30pm. Wheelchair accessible. $1; under 12 and seniors 40¢. Half-price M-F after 7pm.

Ride and Housing Board: In the basement of the **Erb Memorial Union (EMU),** in the middle of the U of O campus, one block east of Kincaid on the pedestrian section of 13th. Open M-Th 7am-7pm, F 7am-5pm.

Taxis: Yellow Cab, 746-1234. $2 base, $2 per mi.

Car Rental: Enterprise Rent-a-Car, 810 W. 6th Ave. (683-0874). $33 per day; unlimited mileage within OR. Out-of-state: 25¢ per mi. over 150 mi. 10% county tax. Must be 21. Credit card required for out-of-town customers. Open M-F 7:30am-6pm, Sa 9am-1pm.

AAA: 983 Willagillespie Rd. (484-0661; see p. 55), near Valley River Center Mall, 2 mi. north of the U of O campus. Open M-F 8am-5pm.

Visitor Information: 115 W. 8th Ave. #190 (484-5307 or 800-547-5445; www.cvalco.org), but the door is on Olive St. Courtesy phone. Open M-F 8:30am-5pm, Sa-Su 10am-4pm; Sept.-Apr. M-Sa 8:30am-5pm. **University of Oregon Switchboard,** in the Rainier Building at 1244 Walnut St. (346-3111). Referral for almost anything, from rides to housing. Open M-F 7am-6pm.

Outdoor Information: Willamette National Forest, 211 E. 7th Ave. (465-6522), in the Federal Building. **Map** $4. Open M-F 8am-4:30pm.

Equipment Rental: Paul's Bicycle Way of Life, 152 W. 5th Ave. (344-4105). Friendly staff; city bikes $12 per day, tandems $15. Open M-F 9am-7pm, Sa-Su 10am-5pm. **High Street Bicycles,** 535 High St. (687-1775), downtown. 21-speeds $5 per hr., $20 per day. Mountain bikes $30 per 4hr., $45 per day. Open M-Sa 9am-5:30pm, Su 10am-5pm. Both shops require a credit card and rent 3-bike racks for cars ($5-7).

Library: Lane County Library, 100 W. 13th Ave., at Olive St. (682-5450). Open M-Tu 10am-8pm, W-Sa 10am-6pm, Su 1-5pm.

Laundromat: Club Wash, 595 E. 13th Ave. (431-1039), at Patterson. Big-screen TV, video games, suds (beer) on tap, and tanning facilities. Open daily 7am-2am. Wash $1.25, dry 25¢ per 10min.

Emergency: 911. **Police/Fire:** 777 Pearl St. #107 (687-5111), at City Hall.

Medical Services: White Bird Clinic, 341 E. 12th Ave. (800-422-7558). Free 24hr. counseling and low-cost medical care at the clinic's **medical center,** 1400 Mill St. (open M and W-F 9am-5pm).

Rape Crisis: 485-6700 or 800-788-4727. 24hr.

Post Office: 520 Willamette, 97401 (800-275-8777), at 5th Ave. Open M-F 8:30am-5:30pm, Sa 10am-2pm.

Area Code: 541.

▶ ACCOMMODATIONS AND CAMPGROUNDS

HOSTEL AND MOTELS

🔖 **The Hummingbird Eugene International Hostel (HI),** 2352 Willamette St. (349-0589). Take bus #24 or 25 from downtown and get off at 24th Ave. and Willamette. Expect a bookshelf-lined living room, a garden, and warm, welcoming managers at this graceful home-turned-hostel. 5 bedrooms sleep up to 20. Members $14, nonmembers $17.50; private rooms from $37. Check-in 5-10pm. Lockout 11am-5pm. Kitchen open 7:30-9:30am and 5-10pm. Cash or traveler's check only.

Downtown Motel, 361 W. 7th Ave. (345-8739 or 800-648-4366). Prime location with hanging flowers, plush carpets, and bone-rattling vibrating beds. A kind management and excellent housekeeping set this motel apart. Cable TV, A/C, refrigerators, and free coffee and rolls in the morning. Singles $30; doubles $38. One of the few motels in the area that doesn't jack up prices during the summer; reserve early by credit card only.

Traveler's Inn, 540 E. Broadway (342-1109), offers clean, cool rooms at a reasonable price. Microwaves, fridges, and coffee. A pool is separated from the road by only a fence. Singles $35; doubles $38. Prices may rise during events.

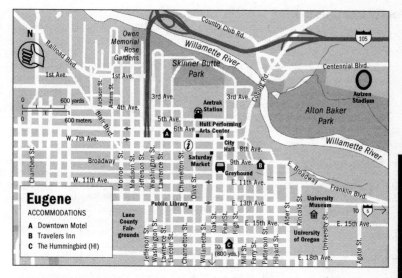

CAMPGROUNDS

KOAs (Kampgrounds of America) and RV-only parks monopolize the Eugene camping scene. It's well worth it to head farther east on Rte. 58 and 126, where the immense **Willamette National Forest** is packed with campsites ($3-16). Clear signage makes everything easy to find. The bark and ferns at swampside **Black Canyon Campground,** 28 mi. east of Eugene on Hwy. 58, are eerily phosphorescent (sites $8-16). Reservations (877-444-6777 or www.ReserveUSA.com; see p. 41) for the Corps of Engineers sites below are free. First-come, first-served sites are also available.

Pine Meadows (942-8657). On the marshy shore of a reservoir. Take I-5 South to Exit 172, then head 3½ mi. south, turn left on Cottage Grove Reservoir Rd., and go another 2½ mi. Plenty of RV and jet ski traffic. Showers, shade, and toilets. 92 sites: $12. 15 primitive, more private sites: $6. Open just before Memorial Day to Labor Day.

Schwarz Park (942-1418), 5½ mi. off Exit 174 (I-5S). Turn right off the ramp and immediately left at the first traffic light, then go past the village green. The grounds are on Row River, about 2½ mi. below swimmable Dorena Lake on the dam spillway. Flat and quiet. Showers, toilets, and water. Sites $10. The better sites are toward the back.

🍴 FOOD

Outdoor cafes and veggie-centric menus are everywhere. The student hang-out zone at 13th Ave. and Kincaid has grab-and-go options. **Sundance Natural Foods,** 748 E. 24th Ave. (343-9142), is at 24th and Hilyard (open daily 7am-11pm). Right in town, **The Kiva,** 125 W. 11th Ave. (342-8666), has a smaller selection of natural foods (open M-Sa 9am-8pm, Su 10am-5pm). For American cheese singles and ground beef, head to **Safeway,** 145 E. 18th Ave. at Oak (485-3664; open daily 6am-2am).

🔖 **Keystone Cafe,** 395 W. 5th St. (342-2075). For 20 years, the creative menu and organic ingredients have given diners a true taste of Eugene. The incredible food is mostly meatless, sometimes wheatless, and all bread is homebaked. A small kitchen and crowds of devotees make for slow service, but all will be forgiven after a mouthful of their famous plate-sized pancakes ($3, plus 75¢ for fruit or seeds). Breakfast served all day. Lunch around $5. Open daily 7am-5pm.

Newman's Fish Company, 1545 Willamette St. (344-2371). This walk-up/bike-up window delivers the finest fish and chips east of the Cascades (salmon $5; cod $4; halibut $5.50). Fries solo $1. Sushi by the piece ($1-2) and sushi rolls ($6) available F-Sa. Open M-F 11am-7pm, Sa 11am-6:30pm.

Govinda's, 270 W. 8th Ave. (686-3531). Sumptuous vegetarian Indian buffet. Small selection, but tasty. Lunch $6.80, dinner $7.80. Open M-F 11:30am-2:30pm and 5-8pm.

Cafe Zenon, 898 Pearl St. (343-3005), at Broadway. Wins local readers' choice awards by the score. The Mediterranean and Pacific Northwest food is light and flavorful. Small plates $4.75-8.25; entrees climb to a $16.75 dinner peak. If nothing else, come for dessert ($4.25); the choice is astounding and the quality superb. No reservations. Open M-Th 8am-11pm, F-Sa 8am-midnight, Su 9:30am-11pm.

📷 🎵 SIGHTS

Take time to pay homage to the ivy-covered halls that set the scene for *National Lampoon's Animal House* at Eugene's centerpiece, the **University of Oregon.** Tours issue from reception centers at **Oregon Hall** (346-3014), at E. 13th Ave. and Agate St., and at the visitor parking and information booth, just left of the main entrance on Franklin Blvd. (Tours M-F 10am and 2pm, Sa 10am. Reception desk open M-F 8am-5pm.) Just off the pedestrian section of 13th St., between Kincaid and University St., the **University Museum of Art** (346-3027) displays Pacific Northwestern, American, and Asian pieces not featured in *Animal House* (open W noon-8pm, Th-Su noon-5pm. Suggested donation $3). A few blocks away, the **Museum of Natural History,** 1680 E. 15th Ave. (346-3024), at Agate, shows a collection of relics from indigenous cultures worldwide, including a 7000-year-old pair of shoes. A primitive "swoosh" logo is still visible. (Open W-Su noon-5pm. Suggested donation $1.) Northwest of the city, just after the I-5 overpass, the **Owen Memorial Rose Garden** is perfect for a picnic, accompanied by the sweet strains of rumbling traffic. Whittaker, the surrounding neighborhood, can be unsafe at night.

🍸 NIGHTLIFE

According to some, Eugene's nightlife is the best in Oregon outside of Portland. Not surprisingly, the string of establishments by the university along 13th St. are often dominated by fraternity-style beer bashes. Refugees from this scene will find a diverse selection of nightlife throughout town. Check out the *Eugene Weekly* (also on the web at www.eugeneweekly.com/thisweek/ae/) for club listings.

Sam Bond's Garage, 407 Blair Blvd. (431-6603); take bus #50 or 52. A supremely laidback gem of a cafe and pub in a soulful neighborhood. Entertainment (from world groove to country power pop) every night, and an ever-changing selection of regional microbrews ($2.75 per pint). Rusting car parts in the flower beds speak to the building's history. Bus or cab it at night. Open daily 3pm-1am.

Jo Federigo's Jazz Club and Restaurant, 259 E. 5th Ave. (343-8488), across the street from the 5th St. Market. Downstairs from a snazzy, pricey restaurant with New Orleans flair, the jazz club swings with music every night (usually at 9:30pm). Blues night (W). Happy hour 2:30-6:30pm. No cover, but $5 drink minimum. Restaurant open for lunch M-F 11:30am-2pm, dinner daily 5-10pm. Jazz club open daily 2:30pm-1am.

High St. Brewery Cafe, 1243 High St. (345-4905), between 12th and 13th St. Quiet tables tucked in rug-bedecked rooms in a Victorian building. A backyard deck and patio catch the overflow. Excellent ales brewed in the basement ($2.85 per pint). Happy hour daily 4-6pm, and food until midnight. Open M-Sa 11am-1am, Su noon-midnight.

John Henry's, 136 E. 11th Ave. (342-3358). In the heart of downtown, this cavernous warehouse-style venue hosts genres (and headliners) from Grrl Variety (Fierce Pussy Posse) to Beergrass (Jackass Willie). Microbrew pints $3. Cover usually $3-7. Call for a schedule. Free pool until 10pm; always free foosball. Open M-Sa 4pm-1am.

Neighbors, 959 Pearl St. (683-2360). A mixed crowd enjoys a huge beer garden, theme nights, and, from time to time, live music. Open M-Sa 11am-2:30am, Su 2pm-2am.

ENTERTAINMENT AND EVENTS

The *Eugene Weekly* (www.eugeneweekly.com) has a list of concerts and local events. The Community Center for the Performing Arts, better known as **WOW Hall**, 291 W. 8th Ave. (687-2746), once a Wobblie (International Workers of the World) union hall, now hosts all kinds of musical acts (open M-F 3-6pm). Tickets (usually $5-8) are available at WOW Hall, at www.ticketweb.com, and at record stores. High-brow culture finds a home at the extravagant **Hult Performing Arts Center**, 1 Eugene Center (info 687-5087, ticket office 682-5000, 24hr. event info 682-5746), at 7th Ave. and Willamette St. The two theater halls host a variety of music from blues to Bartók. (Free tours Th and Sa at 1pm. Tickets $8-35, some student and senior discounts. Box office open Tu-F 10am-5pm, Sa 11am-3pm, and 1hr. before curtain.) The **Bijou Art Cinema**, 492 E 13th Ave. at Ferry St. (686-2458), is another favorite, where obscure films screen in the sanctuary of an old Spanish church. (Box office open 20min. before the first screening. $2.50-6.)

The weekly **Saturday Market** (686-8885), at 8th Ave. and Oak St., offers crafts, clothing, jewelry, artwork, and music. (Apr.-Nov. 10am-5pm.)

The **Oregon Bach Festival** (346-5666 or 800-457-1486; www.bachfest.uoregon.edu) is entering its 31st year. From June 23-July 9, 2000, conductor Helmuth Rilling leads some of the country's finest orchestral musicians. The festival opens with Beethoven's Ninth, featuring choirs from Sweden, Israel, Uganda, and Mongolia. A few concerts each year are free. (Concert and lecture series $12; main events $19-42, ages 6-18 $10; senior and student discounts for selected events.) **Art and the Vineyard** (345-1571) is a four-day 4th of July celebration of food, wine, and culture that takes over Alton Baker Park on the north bank of the Willamette ($4).

By far the most exciting event of the summer is the **Oregon Country Fair** (343-4298; www.oregoncountryfair.org) which takes place in **Veneta**, 13 mi. west of town on Rte. 126. Started in 1969 as a fundraiser for a local Waldorf school, the fair has become a magical annual gathering of artists, musicians, misfits, and activists. For three days (July 7-9, 2000), 50,000 people drop everything to get there. Hundreds of performers crowd onto 10 different stages, and 300 booths fill with art, clothing, crafts, herbal remedies, exhibits on alternative energy sources, and food. Lofty tree houses, drum circles, parades of painted bodies, dancing 12-foot dolls and thousands of revellers in wigs, wings and paint transport travelers into an enchanted forest of frenzy among handmade wooden booths and stages. Parking is extremely limited and requires advance tickets, so most park for free at Autzen Stadium, just north of the river in Eugene. From there, free buses run every 10 minutes from 10am until the fairgrounds close at 7pm. The fair occasionally sells out, so it is wise to purchase tickets in advance. Tickets for the show (F and Su $10, Sa $15; not sold on site) and nearby camping ($30-36 per person for the weekend) are available through Fastixx (800-992-8499), the Hult Center (see above), and the EMU (346-4363; see **Ride and Housing Board,** above).

OUTDOORS

River Runner Supply, 78 "G" Centennial Loop (343-6883 or 800-223-4326), runs guided trips on the sometimes rough **Willamette River** and rents gear. (4hr. rafting trip $45, 4-person min. Kayaks $25 per day, canoes $20 per day, rafts $45-60 per day. Credit card required.) The visitor center has a full list of outfitters. To fill a free hour, canoe or kayak the **Millrace Canal**, which parallels the Willamette for 3 mi. Rent watercraft from River Runner ($4-6 per hr.) or from the student-run **Water Works Canoe Company**, 1395 Franklin Blvd. (346-4386; open summer Tu-Su 11am-8pm, depending on the weather. $5 per hr., $15 per 24hr.; $30 deposit.)

To see the country as 19th-century settlers saw it, take Rte. 126 east from Eugene. The highway follows the beautiful McKenzie River, and on a clear day, the mighty snow-capped **Three Sisters** are visible. Just east of the town of **McKenzie Bridge**, the road splits into a scenic byway loop. Rte. 242 climbs east to the vast lava fields of **McKenzie Pass**, while Rte. 126 turns north over Santiam Pass and meets back with Rte. 242 in Sisters (see p. 129). Rte. 242 is often blocked by snow until the end of June. Kinked with tight turns in places, the road is off-limits to vehicles over 35 ft. long and trucks with trailers. The exquisite drive wends its narrow, winding way between **Mt. Washington** and the **Three Sisters Wilderness** before rising to the high plateau of McKenzie Pass, where lava outcroppings once served as a training site for astronauts preparing for lunar landings. The Civilian Conservation Corps-built **Dee Wright Observatory** affords incredible views on clear days. Along the curviest section of Rte. 242, about 15 mi. east of the fork from Rte. 126, a number of trails lead above treeline. As in all Oregon wilderness areas, biking is not allowed. Free hiking permits are available at trailheads. The **McKenzie Ranger Station** (822-3381), 3 mi. east of McKenzie Bridge on Rte. 126., has more info. (Open daily 8am-4:30pm; in winter M-F 8am-4:30pm.)

Closer to town the Terwilliger Hot Springs on Cougar Lake, better known as **Cougar Hot Springs,** are a long-popular soaking spot. To get there, go 4 mi. east of Blue River on Rte. 126, turn right onto Aufderheide Dr. (Forest Service Rd. #19), and follow the road 7.3 mi. as it winds along the right side of Cougar Reservoir. Try to park in the Terwilliger site use area, as there is no other parking within 1 mi. of the hot springs. Now that The Man has taken over, requiring his bathing suits and charging his fees ($3), the five pools are no longer the hippie hangout they once were. The Forest Service can suggest other hot springs in the area. Continue down the road to camp on the other side of the lake at **Slide Creek** (16 sites: $10; hand-pumped drinking water) or along the south fork of the McKenzie and French Pete Creek at **French Pete** (17 sites: $10; drinking water). Primitive campsites at both **Sunnyside** (13 sites: $5) and **Cougar** (12 sites: $5) are first-come, first-served.

The 26-mile **McKenzie River Trail** parallels Rte. 126 through mossy forests, and leads to some of Oregon's most spectacular waterfalls, Koosah Falls and Sahalie Falls, which flank Clear Lake, a volcanic crater now filled with crystal clear waters. The trail starts about 1½ mi. west of the ranger station (trail map $1, faded copy free) and ends up north at Old Santiam Road near the Fish Lake Old Growth Grove. The entire trail is now open to mountain bikers. A number of Forest Service campgrounds cluster along this stretch of Rte. 126, including the riverside **Olallie,** 9 mi. northeast of the ranger station (available by reservation only 800-280-2267; $6) and **Trailbridge,** 11 mi. northeast of the ranger station (26 sites: $6; drinking water). More ambitious hikers can sign up for overnight permits at the ranger station and head for the high country.

GRANTS PASS

Workers building a road through the Oregon mountains in 1863 were so overjoyed by the news of General Ulysses S. Grant's Civil War victory at Vicksburg that they named the town after the burly President-to-be. The city sprawls awkwardly to fill the hot, flat valley with espresso stands, fast-food joints, auto shops, and parking lots. It's a fine place to sleep, but real adventure lies in the lofty mountains of the Rogue River Valley and the Illinois Valley regions. If anyone out there knows the story of Oregon's missing apostrophes, please get in touch with us.

⊠ ORIENTATION AND PRACTICAL INFORMATION. The town lies within the triangle formed by **Interstate 5** in the northeast, **Rte. 99** in the west, and the **Rogue River** to the south. In town, 99 splits into one-way **6th** and **7th** streets, which run through the heart of downtown and separate east from west. The railroad tracks (between G and F St.) divide north and south addresses. Within the confines of downtown, north-south streets are numbered and east-west streets are lettered; outside, chaos rules. **Greyhound,** 460 NE Agness Ave. (476-4513), at the east end of town, runs to Portland (6hr., 4 per day, $38) and San Francisco, CA (12hr., 4 per day, $53). Lockers cost 75¢ for 24 hours. (Open M-F 6:30am-6:15pm, Sa 6:30am-3:30pm. See p. 53 for discounts.) **Grants Pass Cab** (476-6444), charges $2 per mi. on top of a $2.50 base. **Enterprise,** 1325 NE 7th St. (471-7800), rents cars from $30. (25¢ per mi. after 150 mi. Must be 21. Open M-F 7:30am-6pm, Sa 9am-noon.) The **Chamber of Commerce,** 1995 NW Vine St. (476-7717 or 800-547-5927), off 6th St., does its thing from beneath an immense plaster caveman. (Open M-F 8am-5pm, Sa 9am-

5pm, Su 10am-4pm; in winter closed Sa and Su.) **MayBelle's Washtub**, 306 SE I St. (471-1317), at 8th St., is a laundromat (wash $1, dry 25¢ per 10min.; open daily 7am-10pm). **Stalagmites:** Grow from the ground. **Emergency:** 911. **Police:** 500 NW 6th St. (474-6370). **Hospital:** 715 NW Dimmick St. (476-6831) at Highland Ave. The **library,** at 200 NW. C St., (474-5480), has free **Internet access** (open M, Tu, Th noon-7pm; W 10am-7pm; F noon-5pm), while **Computer Pro,** 143 NW E St. (479-6014), charges $1 per 10 minutes. **Stalactites:** Grow from the ceiling. **Post office:** 132 NW 6th St. (800-275-8777; open M-F 9am-5pm). **ZIP code:** 97526. **Area code:** 541.

▐ ACCOMMODATIONS AND CAMPING. Grants Pass supports one of every franchise motel on earth. The one-of-a-kind cheapo motels are farther back from the interstate on 6th St., though locals warn against staying at the Hawk's Inn at 1464 NW 6th. The **Fordson Home Hostel (HI),** 250 Robinson Rd. (592-3203), is 37 mi. southwest of Grants Pass on U.S. 199. The owner of this rambling old house gives tours of the antique tractors and vortex on his 20 secluded acres to all guests. Accommodations include a snug loft which sleeps three, a private double, and a pull-out couch in the common room. ($12, nonmembers $15. Bicyclists, backpackers, and students with ID $2 off. Free bike loans. Camping $12. Reservations mandatory.) The **Parkway Lodge,** 1001 NE. 6th St. (476-4260), off Exit 58, offers clean and welcoming rooms, with cable and refrigerators (singles $30, doubles $35; in winter $5 less). **Valley of the Rogue State Park** (582-1118; reservations 800-452-5687), is 12 mi. east of town off I-5 Exit 45B. The valley is just wide enough for the river, a row of tents, and the interstate. Separate loops for tents ($15), electric ($17), and full hookups ($18). Yurts costs $25. Non-camper may shower for $2.

▟ FOOD. For spatulas and spaghetti, try **Safeway,** 115 SE 7th St. (479-4276; open daily 6am-midnight), at G St. The **◪Growers' Market** (476-5375), held in the parking lot between 4th and F St. on Saturday mornings, is the state's largest open-air market. The mysterious **◪Thai Barbeque,** 428 SW 6th St., at J St. (476-4304), is decorated like an English teahouse but serves authentic Thai. An intimidatingly long menu is filled with bargains: excellent green curry and most lunch dishes cost $6.50. Spicy chicken coconut soup big enough to swim in is $9. (Open M-Sa 11am-9pm.) **Matsukaze,** 1675 NE 7th St. (479-2961), at Hillcrest, is the only Japanese for miles and the light, delicious food served at sunken booths is worth the trip. Crab California rolls are 5 for $4.25. Chicken teriyaki is $5. (Open M-Th 11am-2pm and 5-9pm, F 11am-2pm and 5-9:30pm, Sa 5-9:30pm; in winter closes 30min. earlier.)

◪▟ SIGHTS AND OUTDOORS. The **Rogue River** is Grants Pass's greatest attraction. One of the few federally protected "Wild and Scenic Rivers," the Rogue can be enjoyed by raft, jetboat, mail boat, or simply by foot. Anglers are in good company—Zane Grey and Clark Gable used to roam the Rogue River with tackle and bait. To paddle the river yourself, head west off I-5 Exit 61 toward **Merlin** and **Galice,** where the outfitting companies cluster. A 35 mi. stretch of Class III and IV rapids starting just north of Galice is the whitest water on the Rogue. To get on this restricted area you must go with a guide and pay about $55. **Orange Torpedo Trips,** 509 Merlin Rd. (479-5061 or 800-635-2925), runs tours down the river in inflatable orange kayaks. ($28 for 2hr., $65 for 8hr.; under 10 10% off.) **White Water Cowboys,** in the same building, rents rafts ($50-95 per day), and offers shuttle and pickup services ($20-185). Discounts are possible in May, early June, and late September. Last-minute cancellations sometimes free up cheap seats in the morning.

The Oregon Caves National Monument (592-2100; www.nps.gov/orca/index.html) lies 30 mi. south via U.S. 199 through plush, green wilderness to Cave Junction, and then 20 mi. east along Rte. 46. Here in the belly of the ancient Siskiyous, enormous pressure and acidic waters created some of the only caves in North America with walls of glistening marble. Tours last 75 minutes and are fairly strenuous, involving some ducking, twisting, and over 500 stairs. Children must be 42 in. (107cm) tall and demonstrate that they can climb steps unaided. Don't forget your jacket. (Tours daily mid-May to Sept. 9am-7pm; mid-Sept. to mid.-Oct. 9am-5pm; mid-Oct. to Apr. 10am-4pm; Dec.-Feb. closed. $7.50, seniors $6.50, under 12 $5.)

WESTERN OREGON

JACKSONVILLE

The biggest of Oregon's gold rush boomtowns, Jacksonville played the role of rich and rowdy frontier outpost with appropriately licentious zeal. But the gold dwindled, the railroad and stagecoach lines took Jacksonville off their routes, and, in the *coup de grâce*, the town lost the county seat to nearby Medford. On the brink of oblivion, Jacksonville was revitalized by sheer nostalgia. Rehabilitated in the 1950s, Jacksonville is the only town in Oregon designated a "National Historic Landmark City" by the Park Service. Restored century-old buildings line downtown streets. During the summer, visitors can hear concerts at the Britt Festival.

⚐ ORIENTATION AND PRACTICAL INFORMATION. Route 238, a.k.a. the **Jacksonville Highway,** runs southwest from Medford, and becomes **5th St.** in town. **RVTD buses** (see p. 121) connect Jacksonville, Medford and Ashland. The #30 from Medford runs 4 times per day. The **visitor center,** 185 N. Oregon St. (899-8118), at C St., is in the old railway station (open Apr.-Aug. M-F 10am-5pm, Sa 11am-5pm, Su noon-4pm; Oct.-Nov. M-F 10am-5pm, Sa 10am-4pm; Dec.-May Tu and F 10am-4pm, Sa noon-4pm). **Post office:** 175 N. Oregon St. (800-275-8777; open M-F 8:30am-5pm). **ZIP code:** 97530. **Area code:** 541.

▐▛ ACCOMMODATIONS, CAMPGROUNDS, AND FOOD. The budgetminded should keep to the **Ashland Hostel** or cheap motels in Medford, 15 mi. southeast of town (see p. 122). A number of campgrounds lie southwest of town in the **Red Butte Wilderness.** Take Rte. 238 for 8 mi. west to Ruch, then turn left on Applegate Rd. The **Star Ranger Station,** 6941 Upper Applegate Rd. (899-1812; open M-Sa 8am-4:30pm), 7 mi. past the turn, has info on sites, but the camping is 7-12 mi. farther out. Though out of place on the quaint streets of Jacksonville, the **Baja Cafe,** 130 N. 5th St. (899-8661), is fast becoming a local favorite for its fish tacos ($2.75; open M-Sa 11am-8pm; Su 11am-3pm). Or shop at the **Jacksonville Market,** 401 N. 5th St. (899-1262) and make your own (open daily 6am-11pm).

◉ SIGHTS AND EVENTS. A walk down California St. is a flashback to the 19th century. The **Beekman Bank,** at 3rd and California St., has not been touched since Cornelius Beekman, the town's most prominent figure, died in 1915. Down the street you can meet his "family" at the **Beekman House** (773-6536), on the corner of Laurelwood and California St., where hosts, in character and costume, will be quite charmed, my dear, to show you about the place. (40min. tour. Open daily Memorial Day to Labor Day 1-5pm.) "Mr. Beekman" himself often wanders the streets of Jacksonville bidding good tidings. The engaging **Jacksonville Museum,** 206 N. 5th St., in the Old County Courthouse, houses unusual pieces, including a section of hangman's rope (used). Newer exhibits include an exploration of Native American perspectives on the display of artifacts. Leave the kids locked up in the jail next door (now the **Children's Museum**). (Open in summer daily 10am-5pm; in winter W-Sa 10am-5pm, Su noon-5pm. Jacksonville Museum, Children's Museum, and Beekman House $3, seniors and ages 6-12 $2. Combined ticket $7, seniors and ages 6-12 $5.)

Jacksonville is transformed every summer by the **Britt Music Festivals,** 517 W. 10th St. (773-6077 or 800-882-7488; www.brittfest.org), named after the pioneer photographer Peter Britt, whose hillside estate is the site of the event. Now in its 38th year, the festival features jazz, classical, folk, country, and pop acts, as well as dance theater and musicals. 1999 saw Wynonna, Bill Cosby, Leo Kottke, Keb' Mo'. and Kenny Rogers perform. Many listeners eat picnic dinners as they watch. For a good space on the lawn, get there early—150 persons worth of lawn is in front of the reserved seats, while the other 1400 are behind. Diehard fans camp out the night before. Gates open at 5:45pm for most shows. (Reserved tickets up to $60; lawn tickets $10-33, ages 12 and under $4-15. From June 1, tickets can be purchased at the main box office at 517 W. 10th St., Sa 9am-3pm and Su. Call for Su concert and box office times. Day-of-show tickets at the Main Pavilion at 1st and Fir St. $2 senior discounts for classical events.)

Ruddy-cheeked winter travelers whoop it up with Jacksonville residents during the town's **Victorian Christmas** celebrations, featuring carolers, plays, a town crier, Father Christmas, and chestnuts roasting on open fires.

ASHLAND

Set near the California border, Ashland mixes hep youth and history to create an unlikely but perfect stage for the world-famous Oregon Shakespeare Festival. From mid-February to October, drama devotees can choose from 11 plays performed in Ashland's three elegant theaters. Shakespearean and contemporary productions draw connoisseurs and novitiate theater-goers alike. The town happily embraces the festival, giving rise to such Bard-bandwagon businesses as "All's Well Herbs and Vitamins" but also fostering a vibrant community of artists, actors, and Shakespeare buffs. Culture comes at a price, but low-cost accommodations and tickets reward those who look hard. And though all the world may know Ashland only as a stage, Oregonians recognize Ashland's fabulous restaurants, parks, and outdoor activities, too.

⑦ ORIENTATION AND PRACTICAL INFORMATION

'Tis time I should inform thee farther.

—*The Tempest*, I.ii

Ashland is located in the foothills of the Siskiyou and Cascade Ranges, 285 mi. south of Portland and 15 mi. north of the California border, near the junction of **I-5** and **Rte. 66,** which traverses 64 mi. of stunning scenery between Ashland and Klamath Falls. **Rte. 99** cuts through the middle of town on a northwest-southwest axis. It becomes **N. Main St.** as it enters town, then splits briefly into **E. Main St.** and **Lithia Way** as it wraps around the central plaza, Ashland's downtown. Farther south, Main St. changes name again to **Siskiyou Blvd.,** where Southern Oregon University (SOU) is flanked by affordable motels and bland restaurants. Many businesses close when the curtain rises, at about 8:30pm.

Buses: Greyhound (482-8803). Pick-up and drop-off at the **BP station,** 2073 Rte. 99 north, at the north end of town. To: Portland (7hr., 3 per day, $40); Sacramento, CA (7hr., 3 per day, $40); and San Francisco, CA (11hr., 3 per day, $50). **Green Tortoise** (800-867-8647; www.greentortoise.com) stops at the **Chevron station** at I-5 Exit 14. To: Seattle (15hr., Tu and Sa 5:15am, $39) via Portland (11hr., Tu and Sa 5:15am, $29); and San Francisco, CA (9hr., Th and Su 11:45pm, $39). See for p. 54 discounts.

Local Transportation: Rogue Valley Transportation (RVTD) in Medford, (779-2877). Bus schedules available at the Chamber of Commerce. The #10 bus runs daily every 30min. 5am-6pm between the transfer station at 200 S. Front St. in **Medford** and the plaza in

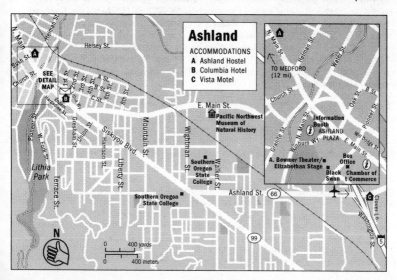

WESTERN OREGON

Ashland (35min.), then loops through downtown Ashland. Bus #30 runs 4 times per day to Jacksonville (see p. 120). $1, over 62 and ages 10-17 50¢, under 10 free.

Taxis: Yellow Cab (482-3065). $2.50 base, $2 per mile.

Car Rental: Budget, 3038 Biddle Rd. (779-0488), at the airport in Medford. $31 per day, 29¢ per mi. after 200 mi. Must be 21 with credit card; under 25 $10 extra.

Visitor Information: Chamber of Commerce, 110 E. Main St. (482-3486). Open M-F 9am-5pm. Also an **info booth** in the center of the plaza. Open in summer M-Sa 10am-6pm, Su 11am-5pm. Oddly, the best maps of Ashland are on the takeout menu at **Omar's,** 1380 Siskiyou Blvd. (482-1281). Open Su-Th 5-9:30pm, F-Sa 5-10pm.

Outdoor Information: Ashland District Ranger Station, 645 Washington St. (482-3333), off Rte. 66 by I-5 Exit 14. Outdoors and Pacific Crest Trail tips. Open M-F 8am-4:30pm.

Equipment Rental: Ashland Mountain Supply, 31 N. Main St. (488-2749). Internal frame backpacks $8.50 per day; external frame $6. Mountain bikes $12 for 2hr., $30 per day. Discounts for longer rentals. Cash deposit or credit card required. Open daily 10am-6pm. **The Adventure Center,** 40 N. Main St. (488-2819 or 800-444-2819), guides rafting trips ($65 for 4hr.; $110-135 per day) and bike tours ($65 for 3hr., $110 per day).

Library: 410 Siskiyou Blvd. (482-1197), at Gresham St. Free Internet access. Open M-Tu 10am-8pm, W-Th 10am-6pm, F-Sa 10am-5pm.

Laundromat: Main Street Laundromat, 370 E. Main St. (482-8042). Wash 50¢, dry 25¢ per 10min. Ms. PacMan 25¢. Open daily 8am-9pm.

Emergency: 911. **Police:** 1155 E. Main St. (482-5211).

Crisis Line: 779-4357 or 888-609-4357. 24hr.

Post Office: 120 N. 1st St., 97520 (800-275-8777), at Lithia Way. Open M-F 9am-5pm.

Internet Access: See **Library,** above. **Ashland Community Food Store CO-OP,** 237 N. 1st St. (482-2237). Free access to the right of the entrance.

Area Code: 541.

▟ ACCOMMODATIONS AND CAMPGROUNDS

> Now spurs the lated traveler apace to gain the timely inn.
> —*Macbeth*, III.iii

In winter, Ashland is a budget traveler's paradise of vacancy and low rates; in summer, hotel and B&B rates double and the hostel is filled to bursting. Only rogues and peasant slaves arrive without reservations. RVTD buses (see **Public Transportation,** above) travel to Medford, 12 miles away, where midsummer nights see motel vacancies. In Medford, the depressingly similar motels along Central and Riverside Ave. are $8-10 cheaper than the chains along the highway. The **Cedar Lodge,** 518 N. Riverside Ave. (773-7361 or 800-282-3419) and the **Red Carpet Inn,** 575 S. Riverside Ave. (772-6133) are among the nicest of the non-chains, and charge $40 for singles, $45 for doubles.

▧ **Ashland Hostel,** 150 N. Main St. (482-9217; ashostel@cdsnet.net). The Victorian parlor, sturdy bunks, and front-porch swing play host to travelers and money-wise, theater-bound families. Laundry and kitchen. Check-in 5-11pm. Lockout 10am-5pm. Curfew midnight (Nov.-Feb. 11pm). $3 off and free laundry for Pacific Crest Trail hikers or cyclists. HI Members $14, non-members $15. Two private rooms sleep 4 ($37-40); private women's room $22 for 1, $30 for 2.

Columbia Hotel, 262½ E. Main St. (482-3726 or 800-718-2530). A reading alcove, tea time in the mornings, and spacious rooms with fresh flowers relieve the weary theatergoer in this historic home 1½ blocks from the theaters. Shared bath. Apr.-Oct. singles $59, doubles $63. Nov.-Feb. singles $35; doubles $39. Mar.-May singles $42; doubles $49; 10% HI discount in off-season.

Vista Motel, 535 Clover Lane (482-4423), just off I-5 at Exit 14, behind a BP station. The small, elderly building conceals surprisingly plush, newly renovated rooms. Cable TV, A/

C, a small pool, and good rates compensate for the outlying location. Singles $37; doubles $45. Winter and spring discounts $8-10.

■ **Mt. Ashland Campground,** about 25min. south of Ashland off I-5 exit 6. Follow signs to Mt. Ashland Ski Area and take the high road from the far west end of the lot, at the sign for Grouse Gap Snowpeak. A more exquisite campground is hard to imagine. Seven sites in the mountainside forest, overlooking the valley and Mt. Shasta. Fire pits, pit toilets, no drinking water. $4 suggested donation. Can be snowy through June.

◐ FOOD

Give them great meals of beef and iron and steel, they will eat like wolves and fight like devils.

—Henry V, III.vii

The incredible selection of foods available on North and East Main St. has earned the plaza a great culinary reputation. Even the ticketless come from miles around to dine in Ashland's excellent (though expensive) restaurants. Beware the pre-show rush—a downtown dinner planned for 6:30pm can easily become a late-night affair. **Ashland Community Food Store CO-OP,** 237 N. 1st St. (482-2237), at A St., has a lively spirit and a great selection of organic produce and natural foods, not to mention free Internet access (open M-Sa 8am-9pm, Su 9am-9pm; 5% senior discount). Cheaper groceries are available at **Safeway,** 585 Siskiyou Blvd. (482-4495; open daily 6am-midnight) though **Food 4 Less** (779-0171), on Biddle Rd. in Medford near I-5 Exit 30, is the 1 2 go 2 4 the best deals.

■ **Geppetto's,** 345 E. Main St. (482-1138). The spot for a late-night bite, and breakfast and lunch, all in an intimate dining room. Dinner from $13. Lunch $4-8. "World Famous Eggplant Burger" $4.25. Pesto omelette $8. Open daily 8am-midnight.

Greenleaf Restaurant, 49 N. Main St. (482-2808). Healthy and delicious food, and creekside seating. Omelettes and fritattas in the morning $6-7. Salads ($3-10), pastas ($4.50-9), and spuds are meals in themselves ($2.75-5.50). Open daily 8am-9pm. Closed Jan.

The Breadboard, 744 N. Main, (488-0295). Hoppin' with locals hungry for huge sourdough pancakes ($4.75) and avocado omelettes ($7). Breathtaking views and value–the "Local Special" is eggs, pancakes, and bacon for just $3. Open daily 7am-2:30pm.

Brothers Restaurant, 95 N. Main St. (482-9671), serves all-day breakfasts of blintzes ($7.50), potato pancakes ($6.50), and omelettes of every possible description ($7-8). Open M and W-F 7am-2pm, Tu 7am-8pm, Sa-Su 7am-3pm.

Five Rivers, 139 E. Main St., (488-1883). Slip upstairs towards the smells of Eastern spices and delicious Indian cuisine. Entrees $5.50-11.50; veggie options all under $7. All-you-can-eat lunch buffet $6. Open daily 11am-3pm and 5-10pm.

Evo's Java House, 376 E. Main St. (482-2261). A bowl of coffee ($1) or a Zaffiro Smoothie (blackberries, blueberries, and OJ; $2.50) and live jazz every Sunday night attracts a crowd. Open daily 7am-10pm.

THE SHAKESPEARE FESTIVAL

Why, this is very midsummer madness.

—Twelfth Night, III.iv

The Oregon Shakespeare Festival (482-4331; fax 482-0446; www.orshakes.org), the brainchild of local college teacher Angus Bowmer, began in 1935 with two Shakespeare plays performed by college students in the old **Chautauqua Dome** as an evening complement to daytime boxing matches. Today, professional actors perform 11 plays in repertory, and the festival has grown to include five or six contemporary and classical plays. Performances run on the three Ashland stages from mid-February through October, and any boxing is now over the extremely scarce tickets. The 1200-seat **Elizabethan Stage,** an outdoor theater modeled after an 18th-century London design, is open only from mid-June to mid-October, and hosts three Shakespeare plays per season. The **Angus Bowmer Theater** is a 600-seat indoor stage that shows one play by Shakespeare and a variety of dramas. The youngest of the theaters is the intimate **Black Swan,** home to one play by Shakespeare and smaller, offbeat productions.

Due to the tremendous popularity of the festival, **ticket purchases are recommended six months in advance.** General mail-order and phone ticket sales begin in January. Tickets cost $14-37 in spring and fall, $21-49 in summer, plus a $5 handling fee per order for phone, fax, or mail orders. For complete ticket information write Oregon Shakespeare Festival, P.O. Box 158, Ashland, OR 97520, or visit the website. Children under 6 not admitted to any shows. Those under 18 receive 25% discounts in the summer and 50% in the spring and fall. The **Oregon Shakespearean Festival Box Office,** 15 S. Pioneer St. (482-4331; fax 482-8045; www.orshakes.org), is next to the Elizabethan Theater, and is generally open 9:30am-8:30pm.

Last-minute theatergoers should not abandon hope. At 9:30am, the box office, 15 S. Pioneer St., releases any unsold tickets for the day's performances. Prudence demands arriving early; local patrons have been known to leave their shoes in line to hold their places, and this tradition should be respected. When no tickets are available, limited priority numbers are given out. These entitle their holders to a designated place in line when the precious few returned tickets are released (1pm for matinees, 6pm for evening shows). At these times, the box office also sells twenty clear-view **standing room tickets** for sold-out shows on the Elizabethan Stage ($11, available on the day of the show). Half-price **rush tickets** are occasionally available 30min. before performances not already sold out.

Though scalping is illegal, **unofficial ticket transactions** take place just outside the box office. Ticket officials advise those "buying on the bricks" to check the date and time on the ticket carefully, to pay no more than the face value, and to check with the box office before purchasing any tickets that have been altered. Some half-price student-senior matinees are offered in the spring and in October, and all three theaters hold full-performance **previews** in the spring and summer. The 2000 season (subject to change) holds in store *Henry V, Hamlet, The Taming of the Shrew,* and Tennessee Williams's *Night of the Iguana.*

Backstage tours provide a wonderful glimpse of the festival from behind the curtain (Tu-Su 10am. $9-11, ages 5-17 $6.75-8.25; no children under 5). Tour guides (usually actors or technicians) divulge all kinds of anecdotes—from the story of the bird songs during an outdoor staging of Hamlet to the ghastly events which transpire every time they do "that Scottish play." Tours last almost two hours and usually leave from the Black Swan. Admission includes a trip to the **Exhibit Center** for a close-up look at sets and costumes. (Open Tu-Su 10am-4pm; fall and spring 10:30am-1:30pm; without tour $2, ages 5-17 $1.50.) In mid-June, the **Feast of Will** celebrates the annual opening of the Elizabethan Theater with dinner and merry madness in Lithia Park. ($16. Call for details.)

👁 ♫ SIGHTS, ENTERTAINMENT, AND OUTDOORS

Mischief, thou art afoot, take thou what course thou wilt!
                    —*Julius Caesar*, III.ii

Before it imported Shakespeare, Ashland was naturally blessed with **lithia water** whose dissolved lithium salts were reputed to have miraculous healing powers. It is said that only one other spring in the world has a higher lithium concentration. Depression, be gone! To quaff the vaunted water itself, hold your nose (the water also contains dissolved sulfur salts) and head for the circle of fountains in the center of the plaza. Nearly every day, free concerts, readings, and educational nature walks occur in and around well-tended **Lithia Park**'s hiking trails, Japanese garden, and swan ponds by Ashland Creek.

Culture remains in Ashland even after the festival ends. Local and touring artists love to play to the town's enthused audiences. The **Oregon Cabaret Theater** (488-

2902), at 1st and Hagardine St., stages light musicals in a cozy former church with drinks, dinners, and Sunday brunch. (Box office open Th-Sa and M 11am-6:30pm, Su 4-6:30pm. Tickets $14-21; reservations required for dinner.) Small groups, such as the **Actor's Theater of Ashland** (535-5250), **Ashland Community Theatre** (482-7532), and the theater department at **Southern Oregon University (SOU)** (552-6346) also raise the curtains sporadically year-round. When in town, the traveling **Rogue Valley Symphony** performs in the Music Recital Hall at SOU and at Lithia Park. In July and August, the **State Ballet of Oregon** graces the stage on Mondays at 7:30pm. **The Ashland City Band** (488-5340) fires itself up at the same time on Thursdays in Lithia Park. In late June, the **Palo Alto Chamber Orchestra** (482-4331) gives hit performances in the Elizabethan Theatre, weather permitting. (Tickets $10.) Contact the Chamber of Commerce for a current schedule of events.

If your muscles demand a little abuse after all this theater-seat lolly-gagging, hop on a stretch of the **Pacific Crest Trail** at Grouse Gap. Take Exit 6 off I-5 and follow the signs along the Mt. Ashland Access Rd. At the top of the 9 mi. road is **Mount Ashland** (482-2897; www.mtashland.com), a small community-owned ski area on the north face of the mountain with 23 runs, half of them advanced, and a vertical drop of 1150ft. (Snow report 482-2754. Open daily Nov. to mid-Apr., 9am-4pm. Night skiing Th-Sa 4-10pm. Weekdays $23, seniors and ages 9-12 $16; weekends $27, seniors and ages 9-12 $19. Rentals $15-20.) Over 100 mi. of free **cross-country** trails surround Mt. Ashland. **Bull Gap Trail,** which starts from the ski area's parking lot, is also good for biking. It winds down 1100 ft. over 2½ miles to the paved Tollman Creek Rd., 15 mi. south of Siskiyou Blvd. In fact, Mt. Ashland provides a number of surprisingly ripping mountain bike trails. The fine folks at the **Adventure Center** (see **Practical Information,** above) can give tips on trails.

Scads of kids and kids-at-heart flock to the 280ft. **waterslide** at **Emigrant Lake Park** (776-7001), 6 mi. east of town on Rte. 66. The park is also a popular place for boating, hiking, swimming, and fishing. (Open daily 10am-sunset, waterslide noon-6pm. 10 slides for $5 or unlimited slides for $12, plus a $3 entry fee.) The fantastic view of the valley from the small campsites that crowd the side of the mountain may even make up for the lack of atmosphere. ($14, no hookups, toilets. A quarter buys 4min. worth of hot shower.)

■ BARS AND CLUBS

> Come, come; good wine is a good familiar creature, if it be well us'd.
> —*Othello,* II.iii

Kat Wok, 62 E. Main St. (482-0787). Quasi-Asian cuisine ($6-9) stars alongside a full bar and micropints. A tiny dance floor wedged between the tables and a glow-in-the-dark pool table makes Kat Wok Ashland's only dance club. A twist on the traditional post show scene. Must be 21 after 10pm. Open daily 5:30pm-2am.

The Black Sheep, 51 N. Main St. (482-6414). English pub brew in bulk: all pints are imperial (20 oz.) and cost $4. The "eclectic fayre" features fresh-baked scones and jam ($3.50), salt and vinegar "chips" ($3), and herbs grown in the British owner's bonny backyard. Open daily 11am-1am. Minors welcome until 11pm.

Ashland Creek Bar & Grill, 92½ N. Main St. (482-4131). A huge outdoor deck and a dedication to live music have created a strong local following. Traditional grill menu ($5). Bands play to a 21 and over crowd. Cover $1-10. Open daily 11am-2am.

Siskiyou Micro Pub, 31B Water St. (482-7718). Airy and unpretentious: wooden tables inside, creekside seating outside. Microbrew pints and bottled beers $3. Live music is usually free (Sa 9pm). Open mic on Thursday. Open Th-Sa 11:30am-midnight, Su-W 11am-1am; in winter Su-Th 4pm-midnight, F-Sa 4pm-1am.

Daddy O's, 130 Will Dodge Way (488-5560), under Orion's Irish Pub. Perhaps the only punk club/Elvis museum in existence. A small bar serves up massive hot sandwiches and bands play at least five nights a week. Open W-Sa 3pm-3am.

WESTERN OREGON

EASTERN OREGON
AND THE CASCADES

Sales Tax: None. **Traffic Laws:** Seatbelts required. For **Oregon State Info,** see p. 67.

Central Oregon stretches between the peaks of the Cascades to the west, and gorges, desert mountain ranges, and alkali flats to the east. Most of Oregon's populace lives here, among farmland, ranchland, lakes, and rivers. Tourists come to eastern Oregon for the festivals, to toe the Oregon Trail, and to soak up the feel of the frontier as it was. Backcountry hikers hunger to hit the peaks, valleys, and flats: majestic Mt. Hood; the deepest gorge in the U.S., Hells Canyon; and the isolated volcanic features and wide open wildlife preserves of the southeast.

Towns lie between these features and farther afield, and in the middle of these vast expanses each can seem like the center of the world. Lakeview is an unexpected hang-gliding hub; cosmopolitan Bend draws Californians and outdoors lovers; Pendleton bustles during fall rodeo season; way stations service otherwise unserviced parks and preserves; and too many towns to count claim direct descent from the frontier, Lewis and Clark, and wagon ruts. The traces of the region's earliest settlers are better preserved than those of its original, mostly nomadic inhabitants. Nevertheless, institutions like the museum at Warm Springs and the Tamastslikt Cultural Institute, at Pendleton, and pow-wows and celebrations, are resurrecting and preserving the cultural heritage of the nations that survive. Every community has sites of cultural importance, from the lake's end where Kintpuash, or Captain Jack, was executed for opposing the U.S. infantry and the forced relocation of the Modoc, to the caves of Fort Rock where the Klamath claimed refuge from Mt. Mazama's eruption 6800 years ago.

The severe landscape that was born of such cataclysmic events has changed little since, but has long tested its inhabitants' resolve. The fertility of the land and the extremity of the winter have, respectively, nurtured and taken their toll upon game, hunters, wheat, and farmers.

Alpine areas and the canyon are accessible by car during a short summer. The towns in the shadow of the Cascades and the major sites are linked by a bus route that makes a horseshoe over the heart of the state. Microbreweries never stop brewing, and dayhikes always take a day.

HIGHLIGHTS OF EASTERN OREGON AND THE CASCADES

■ **Crater Lake National Park** (see p. 128) protects a placid, azure pool in the maw of an ancient and enormous volcano.

■ Life is frozen at **John Day Fossil Beds National Monument** (see p. 147) and swept away by lava flows at **Newberry National Monument** (see p. 134).

■ The **Malheur National Wildlife Refuge** (see p. 149) teems with birds; **Hells Canyon** and the dramatic **Wallowa Mountains** (see p. 137) are as remote and ominously inviting.

■ **Baker City's Oregon Trail Interpretive Center** (see p. 146) walks you through wagon ruts; the **High Desert Museum** (see p. 133) in Bend walks you through the natural world.

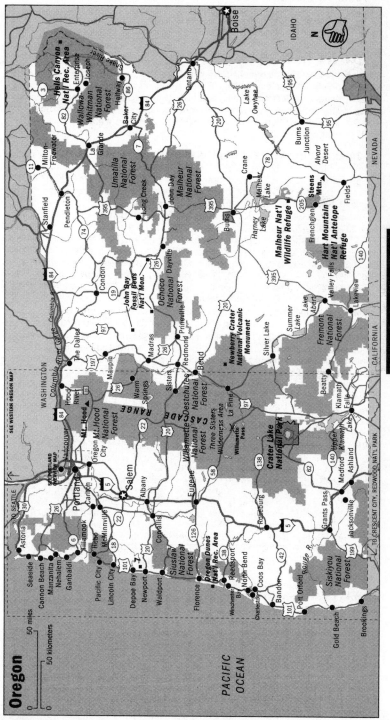

THE CASCADES

MOUNT HOOD

The magnificent, snow-capped Mt. Hood is one of a number of active volcanoes in the Cascades. The 11,235 ft. volcano's most recent significant eruptions were 1500 and 200 years ago. Seismic activity and high ground temperatures (closely monitored by the authorities) don't stop thousands of outdoors enthusiasts from enjoying the mountain and surrounding forests year-round: in winter, snowboarders and skiers attack the slopes, while summer brings climbers, bikers, and hikers.

7 ORIENTATION AND PRACTICAL INFORMATION. Mt. Hood stands near the junction of U.S. 26 and Hwy. 35, 1½hr. east of Portland via U.S. 26. For a more scenic drive from Portland, take I-84 along the Columbia River Gorge to Exit 64, and approach from Hood River (see p. 86). The town of **Government Camp,** 50 mi. east of Portland, has food, accommodations, and gear rental.

At the entrance to the Mt. Hood Village, the **Mt. Hood Information Center,** 65000 E. U.S. 26 (503-622-7674 or 888-622-4822; www.fs.fed.us/r6/mthood or www.mthood .org), 16 mi. west of the junction of U.S. 26 and Hwy. 35 and 30 mi. east of Gresham, has topographic maps and info on both area ranger districts (open daily 8am-6pm, mid-Nov. to Apr. daily 8am-4:30pm). The **Hood River Ranger District Station,** 6780 Hwy. 35 (541-352-6002), 11 mi. south of Hood River and 25 mi. north of the U.S. 26-Hwy. 35 junction, has more specialized info (open Memorial Day to Labor Day daily 8am-4:30pm; closed Sa-Su in winter).

Greyhound (800-231-2222) buses leave from the Huckleberry Inn (503-272-3325) in Government Camp to: Portland (1½hr., one per day, $7-8) and Bend (3hr., one per day, $17). **Emergency:** 911. **Hospital: Mt. Hood Legacy,** 24800 SE Stark (503-674-1122), in Gresham. **Post office:** 88331 E. Govt. Camp Loop Rd., 97028 (800-275-8777; open M-F 7:30am-noon and 1-4:30pm), in Government Camp. **Area code:** 503 to the west and south of Mt. Hood; 541 for Hood River and the northeast.

7 CAMPGROUNDS. Most campgrounds in the **Mt. Hood National Forest** cluster near the junction of U.S. 26 and Hwy. 35. Less than 1 mi. below Timberline (see **Skiing,** below) is **Alpine** (503-272-3206; 16 summer-only sites $8; reservations essential). **Trillium Lake,** 2 mi. east of the Timberline turn-off on U.S. 26, has trails around the crystal-clear lake and paved sites with water and toilets (57 sites $12, premium lakeside sites $14). Just 1 mi. west of Trillium, down a dirt road off U.S. 26, **Still Creek** sites ($12) are unpaved and have a quieter, woodsier feel.

On Hwy. 35, 10 and 14 mi. north of U.S. 26, **Robinhood** and **Sherwood Campgrounds** lie just off the highway beside a creek ($10). Well worth the trip out, **Lost Lake Campground** (541-386-6366) has lakeside sites with water, showers, and toilets (125 sites; tent sites $15, RV sites without electricity $18, cabins from $30). Turn east off Hwy. 35 onto Woodworth Dr. (two streets north of Hood River Ranger Station), right onto the Dee Hwy., then left onto Lost Lake Rd. (Forest Service Rd. 13). A three-mile hike around the lake provides stunning views of Mt. Hood and of old growth forest. **Reservations** for all of these campgrounds except Alpine and Lost Lake can be made at 877-444-6777 or on the web at www.ReserveUSA.com.

7 HIKING AND SKIING. Hiking trails circle Mt. Hood; simple maps are posted around **Government Camp.** The free *Day Hikes* booklet, describes 34 trails in the area and is available from the Mt. Hood Visitor Center. A parking pass is required at several trailheads ($3 per day or $25 per year; available at ranger stations and local businesses). The most popular dayhike, a 6 mi. loop past **Mirror Lake,** begins at a parking lot off U.S. 26, 1 mi. west of Government Camp. The challenging 41-mile **Timberline Trail,** constructed by the New Deal Civilian Conservation Corp in the 1930s, circles the mountain and is accessible from Timberline Lodge (see below).

The 4½-mile **Trillium Lake Loop** becomes a challenging cross-country ski course in winter. **Mountain Tracks Nordic Ski Shop** (503-272-3380) in the Huckleberry Inn, Government Camp, and visitor information have details on more ski trails.

EASTERN OREGON

Though Mt. Bachelor (see p. 134) is known for Oregon's best skiing, three respectable Mt. Hood area resorts are more convenient to Portland. All offer **night skiing** and **snowboard parks. Timberline** (503-622-0717, snow report 503-222-2211; www.timberlinelodge.com), off U.S. 26 at Government Camp, is a largely beginner and intermediate area with a 2600-foot vertical drop and the longest season in North America—a high-speed lift on the Palmer Snowfield is open year-round. (Open in winter daily 9am-4pm, in spring and fall 8:30am-2:30pm, in summer 7am-1:30pm. Lift tickets $34. Night skiing Jan.-Feb. W-F 4-9pm, Sa-Su 4-10pm. Rentals: ski package $20, ages 7-12 $13; snowboard and boots $33, ages 7-12 $23. Cash deposit or credit card required.) Small-time **Mount Hood Ski Bowl,** 87000 E. U.S. 26 (503-222-2695 or 800-754-2695; www.skibowl.com), in Government Camp 2 mi. west of Hwy. 35, has a vertical drop of 1500 ft. The season is shorter (mid-Nov. to May) because of its lower elevation, but 80-90% of the trails have night skiing. (Open M-Tu 3:30pm-10pm, W-Th 9am-10pm, F 9am-11pm, Sa 8:30am-11pm, Su 8:30am-10pm. Lift tickets $16 per day, under 12 $11; $16 per night; $22-28 for both. Rentals: ski package $17, ages 7-12 $13; snowboard and boots $25 per day; $20 per night. Beginner package with rental, lesson and lift ticket: $33 skis, $41 snowboard.) **Mount Hood Meadows** (337-2222, snow report 503-227-7669 or 541-386-7547; www.skihood.com), 9 mi. east of Government Camp on Hwy. 35, is the largest and nicest resort in the area, offering a wide range of terrain, and the most high-speed lifts. At a medium elevation (7300 ft.), it often stays open through May. (Open mid-Nov.-May daily 9am-4pm. Lift tickets $41, ages 7-12 $21. Night skiing Dec.-Mar. W-Su 4-10pm, $17. Rentals: ski package $20, ages 7-12 $15; snowboard and boots $28, ages 7-12 $21. Beginner package with lift ticket, lesson and rental $45.) Mt. Hood Meadows offers $20 lift tickets through participating hotels, including the Bingen School Hostel (see p. 87).

■ **SIGHTS AND OTHER ACTIVITIES.** Six miles up the road, just east of Government Camp, stands the historic **Timberline Lodge** (622-7979), built by hand in 1936-7 by unemployed craftspeople under the New Deal's Works Progress Administration. On the Timberline grounds is the **Wy'East Day Lodge,** where skiers can check in equipment for the day, and the **Wy'East Kitchen,** a cafeteria alternative to Timberline's expensive main dining. (Entrees $4-7. Open in summer M-F 6:30am-2pm, Sa-Su 6:30am-3pm; in winter M-F 7:30am-4pm, Sa-Su 8am-4pm; open 7:30am-9pm for night skiing.) At the **Ram's Head,** on the third floor of the lodge, sandwiches ($7.75) are served amid remarkable scenery. For a view that beats them all, Timberline's **Magic Mile express lift** carries passengers above the clouds for spectacular views of the Cascades ($6, ages 7-12 $3, under 7 free).

ART of Adventure offers **mountain climbing training** trips through Portland Parks and Recreation (503-823-5132) from late May to early August. (2-day trip is 1-day snow class, 1-day climb, with lodging and meals in Government Camp; $205, equipment rental not included.) In summer, Mount Hood Ski Bowl opens its **Action Park** (222-2695; open M-F 11am-6pm, Sa-Su 10am-6pm), which features Indy Kart racing ($5 per 5min.), "extreme" frisbee golf ($3), bungee jumping ($25), and an alpine slide ($15 for 5 slides). The Ski Bowl maintains 40 miles of bike trails ($4 trail permit), and **Hurricane Racing** rents mountain bikes mid-June to October ($10 per hr., $25 for 4hr., $32 for 8hr.; trail permit included). The Mt. Hood Visitor Center also lists **free** hiking trails on which mountain biking is allowed.

SISTERS

Twenty miles northwest of Bend on U.S. 20, the tiny town of Sisters has restored its Old West look. Restless visitors will enjoy a stroll on Cascade St. among the masses, but may yearn for the mountains and real excitement.

◪ **ORIENTATION AND PRACTICAL INFORMATION.** From Sisters, Rte. 126 heads east to **Redmond** (20 mi.) and **Prineville** (39 mi.), and joins U.S. 20 to cross the Cascades. Route 242 heads southwest over McKenzie Pass (see p. 117) to rejoin Rte. 126 on the other side of the range. In town, all highways blend into **Cascade St.**

EASTERN OREGON

Follow the signs to the **visitor center,** 164 N. Elm St. (www.sisters-chamber.com; 549-0251), one block from Cascade St. (open M-F 9am-5pm; Sa-Su hours vary, call ahead). Sisters' **Deschutes National Forest Ranger District Station** (549-2111), on the corner of Cascade and Pine St., has info on nearby campgrounds and guides to local day hikes and biking trails (open M-F 7:45am-4:30pm; in summer also Sa 8am-1pm). **Epicure Exchange,** 391 W. Cascade St. (549-0536), provides **Internet access** for $8 per hr. ($2 minimum; open daily 7am-7pm). **Area code:** 541.

■▊ **ACCOMMODATIONS, CAMPING, AND FOOD.** Budget travelers pass up steep Sisters for Bend's cheap lodging (see p. 132), merely 20 minutes away by car.

But the Ranger District maintains 26 **campgrounds** near Sisters that are spectacular. Many cluster near **Camp Sherman,** a small community on the Metolius River 17 mi. northwest of Sisters. The Metolius River campgrounds tend to be the most crowded, and nearly all charge $10. Two noteworthy exceptions are **Riverside,** 10 mi. west on Rte. 20 and 7 mi. northeast on Rd. 14, and **Allingham,** 1 mi. north of the Camp Sherman store on Rd. 14. Riverside's walk-in sites provide a refuge from motor vehicles, and Allingham's drive-in sites perch right on the edge of the river. **Link Creek,** 2 mi. down the road that partially circles Suttle Lake (877-444-6777), 14 mi. northwest of Sisters on Rte. 20, is one of six campgrounds open year-round. The lake fills up with fishing boats and the occasional windsurfer on weekends, but is serene during the week. Less frequented are 10 sites at magnificently isolated **Lava Camp Lake,** 14 mi. west on Rte. 242 and a bumpy half-mile down a red dirt road, just off the lava fields of McKenzie Pass.

Plan on exploring Sisters during the daylight hours; things are slow at six and dead by dark. Overpriced seafood and bar fare can be had any time, but the delis that close by 5 or 6pm are best for both palette and purse. For exquisite specialty salads (75¢-$3) and carefully assembled gourmet sandwiches ($5-5.50), head for **Seasons Cafe and Wine Shop,** 411 E. Hood St. (549-8911; open daily 11am-3pm), one block south of Cascade along a little brook. The **Sisters Bakery,** 251 E. Cascade St. (549-0361; open daily 5am-6pm), has all kinds of baked goods, including marionberry squares and biscuits ($2), top-notch bread ($1.80-3), and brownies with accolades. **The Harvest Basket,** 110 S. Spruce St. (549-0598; open daily 9am-7pm), has organic groceries and pre-made sandwiches.

■▊ **EVENTS AND OUTDOORS.** The annual **Sisters Rodeo** (549-0121) is the "Biggest Little Show in the World." Over the second weekend in June, an astonishing purse of $170,000 draws big-time wranglers for three days and nights of bronco-riding, calf-roping, steer-wrestling, and more. Keep your gender stereotypes in order in sight of the Pepsi Girls, Dodge Pickup Guys, and some fine rodeo clowning. Call 800-827-7522 for tickets ($8-12; shows often sell out). 2000 will mark the 25th year of the Sisters **Outdoor Quilt Show** (549-6061). On the second Saturday of July, the exhibition of 1000 colorful quilts throughout town culminates a week's worth of events, a "quilters' affair."

Miles of **hiking** trails loop through the wilderness around Sisters. Up to 10 mi. of walking alongside the **Metolius River** allows time to ponder the debate over the origin of the river's name (some say "metolius" means "white fish," some, "spawning salmon," and others, "stinking water"). Drive 10 mi. west on Rte. 20 from Sisters, then make a right at the sign for Camp Sherman (Rd. 14). Proceed 7 mi. on Rd. 14 past the "Head of the Metolius" and park at the Wizard Falls Fish Hatchery. A slightly more challenging hike is the 4 mi. round-trip up **Black Butte,** a near-perfect cone that looms over the west end of town. To reach the trailhead, go 6 mi. west from Sisters on U.S. 20, turn right onto Forest Rd. 11, then turn onto Forest Rd. 1110 after 4 mi. The trailhead is another 4 mi. up the road. Deeper in the mountains, the strenuous 7.6 mi. round-trip hike up **Black Crater** offers unsurpassed views of snow-capped peaks and lava flows on McKenzie Pass, and intimate encounters with volcanic debris. The trail departs from the left-hand side of Rte. 242 about 11 mi. west of Sisters. Access is often limited due to snow. Both Black Butte and Black Crater require a $3 **trailpark pass,** available at ranger stations.

McKenzie Pass (see p. 117), 15 mi. west of Sisters on Rte. 242, was the site of a relatively recent lava flow which created barren fields of rough, black **a'a** (AH-ah) lava. The Dee Wright Observatory sits here, a tall, medieval-looking tower built of lava chunks that gives a panoramic view of the Cascades, while a half-mile paved trail winds among basalt boulders, cracks, and crevices.

Mountain biking opportunities abound near Sisters. No bikes or motor vehicles are allowed in official wilderness areas, but most other trails and miles of little-used dirt roads are open to bikes. The ranger station distributes a nifty packet detailing local trails. **Eurosports,** 182 E. Hood St. (549-2471), rents mountain bikes. ($12 per day, $60 per week, with full front suspension $18 more per week. Snowshoes, shaped skis, and snowboards $10-25 per day. Open daily 9am-5:30pm.)

BEND

Defined by a dramatic landscape—volcanic features to the south, Mt. Bachelor and the Cascades to the west, and the Deschutes River running through its heart—Bend has evolved in the midst of controversy. Settled in the early 19th century as "Farewell Bend," a waystation on a pioneer trail along the Deschutes, Bend has lost its small-town feel since the 1970s, when a flood of young urbanites from California, Portland, and Seattle began arriving in search of the perfect blend of urban excitement and pristine wilderness. The boom sparked controversy between the newcomers and the local ranchers over how to best manage the expansion. Strip malls flood the banks of U.S. 97, the downtown, however, has grown into a charming crowd-pleaser. Meanwhile, the hiking, superb skiing, river rafting, and endless mountain biking that first drew new inhabitants continues to do so.

EASTERN OREGON

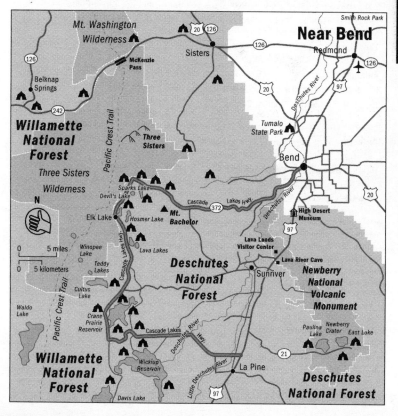

⁊ ORIENTATION AND PRACTICAL INFORMATION

Bend is 144 mi. north of Klamath Falls on U.S. 97 and 100 mi. southeast of Mt. Hood via U.S. 26E and Rte. 97S. The city is bisected by **U.S. 97,** which becomes **3rd St.** in town. **Wall** and **Bond St.** are the main arteries. Downtown lies to the southwest along the **Deschutes River.** From east to west, Franklin becomes Riverside; at the edge of Drake Park, Tumalo St. becomes Galveston, which then becomes Skyliner; Greenwood becomes Newport; 14th St. becomes Century Dr. and is the first leg of the **Cascade Lakes Hwy.**

Buses: Greyhound, 63076 Hwy. 97N (382-2151). To: Portland (1 per day, 5-7hr., $20-30); Eugene (1 per day, 2½hr., $20). Open M-F 8-11:30am and 12:30-5pm, Sa-Su 8am-2pm. Call for info on other bus and van lines. For discounts, see p. 53.

Taxis: Owl Taxi, 1919 NE 2nd St. (382-3311). $1.80 base, $1.80 per mi.

Visitor Information: 63085 U.S. 97N (382-3221). Full-time ranger on duty. Free **Internet access,** coffee, and phone calls. *Attractions and Activities Guide* with a clear area map. Open M-Sa 9am-5pm, Su 11am-3pm.

Outdoor Information: The forest headquarters maintains an info desk in the visitor center. The *Recreation Opportunity Guide* covers each of the 4 ranger districts. **Deschutes National Forest Headquarters,** 1645 Hwy. 20E (388-2715) and **Bend/Fort Rock District Ranger Station,** 1230 NE 3rd St. #A262 (388-5664), have additional info on Deschutes National Forest. Both open M-F 7:45am-4:30pm. **Fish and Wildlife,** 61374 Parrell Rd. (388-6363). Fishing licence $8.25 per day. Open M-F 8am-5pm.

Equipment Rental: Hutch's Bicycles, 725 NW Columbia Ave. (382-9253). Mountain bikes $25 per day, $75 for 5 days. Open M-F 9am-7pm, Sa-Su 9am-6pm.

Library: Deschutes County Library, 601 NW Wall (388-6679). Free **Internet access.** Open M-Th 10am-8pm, F 10am-6pm, Sa 10am-5pm, Su 1-5pm.

Laundromat: Nelson's, 738 NW Columbia Ave. (382-7087). Wash $1.25, dry 25¢ per 10min. Open daily 6am-9:30pm.

Emergency: 911. **Police:** 711 NW Bond St. (388-0170).

Rape Crisis Hotline Line: COBRA 389-7021 or 800-356-2369. 24hr.

Hospital: St. Charles Medical Center, 2500 NE Neff Rd. (382-4321), emergencies only. For routine ailments go to **Mountain Medical Immediate Care Center,** 1302 U.S. 97NE (388-7799). Open M-Sa 8am-8pm, Su 10am-6pm.

Post Office: 2300 NE 4th St., 97701 (800-275-8777), at Webster. Open M-F 8:30am-5:30pm, Sa 10am-1pm.

Internet Access: See **Visitor Information** and **Library,** above. **Internet Access,** 113 SW Century Dr. Bldg. 2 (318-8802). $2 per 15min. Open M-F 10am-7pm, Sa 10am-6pm.

Area Code: 541.

⌐ ACCOMMODATIONS AND CAMPGROUNDS

Bend treats budget travelers right: the hostel and B&Bs provide phenomenal deals for tuckered-out travelers. Cheap motels line 3rd St. just outside of town. **Deschutes National Forest** maintains a huge number of lakeside campgrounds with toilets along the **Cascade Lakes Hwy.** west of town. Those with potable water cost $8-12 per night; the rest are free. Backcountry camping in the national forest area is free. Contact the **Bend/Ft. Rock Ranger District Office** for more info.

Bend Cascade Hostel, 19 SW Century Dr. (389-3813 or 800-299-3813). From 3rd St., take Greenwood west until it becomes Newport, take a left on 14th St. The hostel is half a mile up, on the right side past the Circle K. About the closest you can get to the Cascade Lakes without swimming. Foosball, laundry facilities, and kitchen; linen available. 3 private rooms. Lockout 9:30am-4:30pm. Curfew 11pm. 43 beds: $14; seniors, students, cyclists, and HI $13; under 18 with parents half-price.

Plaza Motel, 1430 NW Hill St. (382-1621). A red-and-white building set back from the highway. Dimly lit rooms have gently ageing furnishings, but accommodations are clean and quiet, and there isn't a cheaper place in Bend. Singles and doubles $28.

Tumalo State Park, 62976 OB Riley Rd. (388-6055 or 800-452-5687). 3-4 mi. north of Bend off U.S. 20W. Pastoral riverside campsites go early despite nearby road noise; other sites are cheaper but offer little seclusion. 67 tent sites: $15; preferred river sites $17; 21 full hookups $19; yurts $29. Non-camper showers $2.

◖ FOOD

The diversity of food in Bend compromises eastern Oregon's emphasis on beef-and-potatoes as a primary food source. Four mega-markets line 3rd St. **Devore's Good Food Store and Wine Shop,** 1124 Newport NW (389-6588), peddles all things organic, plus wine, beer, and cheese (open M-Sa 8am-7pm, Su 11am-6pm).

Deschutes Brewery and Public House, 1044 NW Bond St. (382-9242). Specials ($5-7.50) overshadow the homemade sausage and house-smoked salmon. Imperial pints of house-brewed ale, bitter, stout ($3.25), and sodas ($1.75). Their Black Butte Porter is all over Oregon. Open M-Th 11am-11:30pm, F-Sa 11am-12:30am, Su 11am-10pm.

Westside Bakery and Cafe, 1005 NW Galveston (382-3426). Mickey Mouse and Pooh Bear in pudgy, sugary glory atop icing-coated cakes. Burgers and sandwiches ($5-6.50) and how many homemade pastries (under $3)! Blueberry honeywheat pancakes in the shape of the famous rodent, for your eating enjoyment ($5). Open daily 6:30am-3pm.

Taqueria Los Jalapeños, 601 NE Greenwood Ave. (382-1402). A simple space filled by a steady stream of locals devoted to good, cheap food. Bean and cheese burritos $1.50; *chimichanga* plates $5.50. Open M-Sa 10:30am-8:30pm; in winter 10:30am-7pm.

Toomie's, 119 NW Minnesota (388-5590). Mouth-watering Thai lunch specials ($4.50) in a low-key dining room. Large portions and live Jazz (Tu) make up for higher dinner prices ($8-11). Open Su-Th 11:30am-2pm and 5:30-9:30pm, F-Sa until 10:30pm.

Kuishinbo Kitchen, 114 NW Minnesota St. (385-9191), between Wall and Bond St. Swing by to grab a boxed lunch to go. *Sukiyaki bento* ($6) is good, but everyone orders *yaki soba* noodles ($4). Open M-F 11am-7pm, Sa 11am-4pm.

◉ SIGHTS AND EVENTS

You can get personal with Canada geese in Bend while you enjoy a picnic lunch by the water at beautiful **Drake Park,** sandwiched between **Mirror Pond** and Franklin St., one block from downtown. The park hosts many events and festivals, notably the **Cascade Festival of Music** (382-8381; www.cascademusic.org), a week-long series of classical and pop concerts held by the river in late August. (Tickets $3-25, student rush half-price. Call the office or write to 842 NW Wall St. #6.)

The ◙ **High Desert Museum,** 59800 Hwy. 97S (382-4754; www.highdesert.org), 3½ mi. south of Bend on U.S. 97, is one of the premier natural and cultural history museums in the Pacific Northwest. Stunning life-size dioramas recreate dark mining tunnels, rickety settler cabins, and cramped immigrant workshops. An indoor desertarium offers a peek at shy creatures like burrowing owls and collared lizards. Paved paths outdoors wind through river otter, porcupine, and predatory bird habitats, elucidated hourly by interpretive talks. A new Native American Wing with a walk-through exhibit on post-reservation Indian life recently opened. Arrive early to beat the daily crowds. (Open daily 9am-5pm. $7.75, ages 13-18 and over 65 $6.75, ages 5-12 $3.75, under 5 free.)

The annual **Bend Summer Festival** (385-6570), held during the second weekend in July, showcases the work of artisans and performers from across central Oregon. All of downtown is closed to traffic as the streets are flooded with sculptures, paintings, crafts, musicians, chalk art, food and drink, and nomads from all over looking to decorate their living rooms. All events are free, but parking is limited.

▲ OUTDOORS

Those who ski the 9065 ft. **Mount Bachelor** (382-8334 or 800-829-2442; snow report 382-7888; www.mtbachelor.com), with its 3365 ft. vertical drop, are in good company—Mt. Bachelor is home to the U.S. Ski Team and the U.S. Cross-Country Team, and hosts many of the largest snowboarding competitions in the country. The ski season often extends to the 4th of July. (Lift tickets $39, seniors $24, ages 7-12 $20.) A shuttle bus service runs the 22 mi. between the parking lot at the corner of Simpson and Columbia in Bend and the mountain (Nov.-May $1). Many nearby lodges offer five-night **ski packages** (800-800-8334). **Chairlifts** are open for sightseers during the summer, and you can hike back down the mountain or ride both ways. (Open daily 10am-4pm. $11, seniors $9.75, ages 7-12 $5.50.) Intermediate bike trails follow cross-country routes, but bikers can't tackle the mountain. **Bike rentals** are available at the Sunrise Ski and Sport Shop ($15 per day). A U.S. Forest Service naturalist gives free talks on local natural history at the summit (in summer daily 10am and 1pm).

The **Three Sisters Wilderness Area,** north and west of the Cascade Lakes Highway, is one of Oregon's largest and most popular wilderness areas. A parking permit is required at most trailheads: pick one up at any of the ranger stations or at the visitor center ($3). Mountain biking is not allowed in the wilderness area itself, but Benders have plenty of other places to spin their wheels. Try **Deschutes River Trail** for a fairly flat, basic, forested trail ending at **Deschutes River.** To reach the trailhead, go 7½ mi. west of Bend on Century Dr. (Cascade Lakes Hwy.) until Forest Service Rd. 41, then turn left and follow the signs to Lava Island Falls (10½ mi. one-way). For a difficult, technical ride, hit the **Waldo Lake Loop,** a grueling 22 mi. trail around the lake. To get there, take Cascade Lakes Hwy. to Forest Service Rd. 4290. A slick new guide to mountain bike trails around Bend is available for $7 at the Bend/Ft. Rock District Ranger Station and at most bike shops in the area, but some of the hottest trails aren't on the maps; talk to locals.

Would-be cowpokes can take **horseback rides** offered by local resorts. **River Ridge Stables,** 18575 SW Century Dr. (382-8711), at Inn of the Seventh Mountain several miles west of Bend, leads trail rides (1hr. $22, ages 6-12 $20; each additional 30min. $5), hay rides ($7, ages 5-12 $5, under 5 free), and sleigh rides ($15 per hr.).

As if skiing, hiking, and biking weren't enough, Bend also offers miles of Class IV rapids for intrepid rafters. **Whitewater rafting,** although costly, is one of the most popular local recreational activities. Half-day trips usually last three hours and cover the fairly tame waters of the upper Deschutes, while full-day trips require a one-hour drive to Maupin to run the Class I-IV rapids of the lower Deschutes. **Sun Country Tours** (800-770-2161) runs half-day and full-day trips out of the **Sun River Resort,** 17 mi. south of Bend off U.S. 97, and also at 531 SW 13th St. in Bend. (Half-day $35, ages 6-12 $30. Full day $85-90; ages 6-12 $75-80.) Or try **Blazing Paddle Whitewater Adventures** (388-0145), which has various pick-up points in town. (Full-day $80 per person.)

NEWBERRY NATIONAL MONUMENT

The Newberry National Volcanic Monument was established in 1990 to link and preserve the volcanic features south of Bend. For an introduction to the area, visit the **Lava Lands Visitor Center,** 58201 U.S. 97 (593-2421), 8½ mi. south of Bend on U.S. 97 (open mid-June to Sept. daily 9:30am-5pm; Apr. to mid-June W-Su 9:30am-5pm). A mandatory $5 parking fee, good for 2 days, is required within a quarter mile of the monument area (free with Golden Age Passport or Golden Eagle Pass; see p. 40). Immediately behind the visitor center is **Lava Butte,** a 500 ft. cinder cone from which lava once flowed. Between Memorial Day and Labor Day, a shuttle bus makes the two mile journey every 30 minutes ($2.50, seniors $2, under 6 free.) One mile south of the visitor center on U.S. 97 is **Lava River Cave** (593-1456), a 100,000-year-old, mile-long subterranean lava tube. When the Bend heat becomes unbearable, head to this naturally air-conditioned 42°F cave. Bundle up before descending and bring a lantern or rent one at the cave for $1.50. (Open mid-May to mid-Oct. 9am-6pm. $3, ages 13-17 $2.50, under 13 free.)

The monument's centerpiece is **Newberry Crater,** 13 mi. south of the Lava Lands Visitor Center on U.S. 97, then about 13 steep miles east on Rte. 21. This diverse volcanic region was formed by the eruptions of Newberry Volcano over millions of years, the most recent of which was an estimated 7060 years ago, on a Tuesday. (Newberry is one of three volcanoes in Oregon most likely to erupt again "soon.") The 500 sq. mi. caldera contains Paulina Lake and East Lake. The most scenic campground is **Little Crater,** with 50 sites between Rte. 21 and the Paulina lakeshore ($12-14). Over 150 mi. of trails cross the area, including a short walk up to an enormous **obsidian flow** formed by an eruption 1300 years ago, a 21 mi. loop that circles the **caldera rim,** and a 7½ mi. loop around **Paulina Lake.** For an easy view of the crater, drive up **Paulina's Peak.** (Open weather permitting June-Sept.)

CRATER LAKE AND KLAMATH FALLS

Oregon's only national park takes its name from the mesmerizing Crater Lake, legendarily regarded as too sacred even to be looked upon. About 7700 years ago, **Mt. Mazama,** in an eruption that buried a vast portion of the continent under a thick layer of ash, formed a deep caldera that gradually became filled with centuries' worth of rain. The circular lake plunges from its shores to a depth of 1932 ft. and remains iceless in winter, though its banks, which reach 6176 ft., are snow-covered until July. Visitors from all over the world circle the 33-mile Rim Drive, carefully gripping the wheel as the intensely blue water enchants them. Klamath (kuh-LAH-math) Falls, one of the nearest towns, makes a convenient stop on the way to the park and houses most of the services, motels, and restaurants listed below.

🛈 ORIENTATION AND PRACTICAL INFORMATION

Route 62 skirts the park's southwestern edge as it arcs 130 mi. between Medford in the southwest and Klamath Falls, 56 mi. southeast of the park. To reach Crater Lake from Portland, take I-5 to Eugene, then Rte. 58 east to U.S. 97 south. **Route 138** leads west from U.S. 97 to the park's north entrance, but this route is one of the last to be cleared. Crater Lake averages over 44 ft. of snow per year, and snowbound roads can keep the park closed until as late as July; call the Steel Center (see below) for road conditions. Before July, enter the park from the south. **Route 62** runs west from U.S. 97 to the south access road that leads to the caldera's rim. Crater Lake's services and operating hours depend on weather and funding, neither of which are determined until well into the spring. Call the Steel Center to verify services and hours.

Trains: Amtrak, Spring St. (884-2822 or 800-872-7245). At the east end of Main St. turn right onto Spring St. then left onto Oak St. 1 per day to Portland ($48-69) and points north. Open daily 6:45-10:15am and 9-10:30pm.

Buses: Greyhound, 1200 Klamath Ave. (882-4616) 1 per day to: Bend (3hr., $20); Eugene (10hr., $39-41); and Redding, CA (4hr., $27-29). Lockers $1 per day. Open M-F 6am-2:30pm, Sa 6-9am, and daily midnight-12:45am.

Public Transportation: Basin Transit Service (883-2877) has 6 routes around Klamath Falls. Runs M-F 6am-7:30pm, Sa 10am-5pm. 90¢, seniors and disabled 45¢.

Taxis: AB Taxi, 885-5607. $1.75 base, $2 per mi. 30% senior discount.

Car Rental: Budget (885-5421), at the airport. Take S. 6th St. and turn left on Washington. $28 per day Sa-Su, 200 free mi. per day. $24 per day M-F, 25¢ per mi. after 100 mi. Open M-F 7:30am-9pm, Sa 8am-3:30pm and 7:20-8:20pm, Su 11am-6pm and 9:50-10:50pm.

Visitor Information: 1451 Main St. (884-0666 or 800-445-6728; www.klamathcountytourism.com). Open M-Sa 9am-5pm.

Outdoor Information: William G. Steel Center (594-2211, ext. 402), 1 mi. from the south entrance. Open daily 9am-5pm. **Crater Lake National Park Visitor Center** (594-2211, ext. 415), on the lake shore at Rim Village. Open daily June-Sept. 8:30am-6pm.

Park Entrance Fee: Cars $10, hikers and bikers $5. Free with Golden Age Passport or Golden Eagle Passport (see p. 40).

Library: 126 S. 3rd St. (882-8894). Free **Internet access.** Open M 1-8pm, Tu and Th 10am-8pm, W and F-Sa 10am-5pm.

Laundromat: Main Street Laundromat, 1711 Main St. (883-1784). Wash $1.25, dry 25¢ per 12min. Open daily 8am-7pm.

Emergency: 911. **Police:** 425 Walnut St. (883-5336).

Crisis Line: 800-452-3669. 24hr. **Rape Crisis:** 884-0390. 24hr.

Hospital: Merle West Medical Center, 2865 Daggett Ave. (882-6311). From U.S. 97 northbound, turn right on Campus Dr., then right onto Daggett. Open 24hr.

Post Office: Klamath Falls, 317 S. 7th St., 97601 (800-275-8777). Open M-F 7:30am-5:30pm, Sa 9am-noon. **Crater Lake,** in the Steel Center. Open M-Sa 10am-noon and 1-3pm. **ZIP Code:** 97604.

Area Code: 541.

⚑ ACCOMMODATIONS AND CAMPGROUNDS

Klamath Falls has several affordable hotels that make easy bases for forays to Crater Lake. **Forest Service campgrounds** line Rte. 62 through the Rogue River National Forest to the west of the park. Crater Lake N.P. itself contains two campgrounds, both of which are closed until roads are passable. **Backcountry camping** is allowed within the park; pick up free permits from either visitor center.

Fort Klamath Lodge Motel and RV Park, 52851 Rte. 62 (381-2234), 15 mi. from the southern entrance. The closest motel to the lake, the 6-unit lodge is in Fort Klamath, a town consisting of a grocery store, post office, restaurant, and wildflowers. Quiet, countrified rooms with knotted-pine walls. Fan, heater, TV; no phones. Coin laundry. Singles $42; doubles $58. RV hookups in the nearby lot $15. Open May-Oct.

Townhouse Motel, 5323 S. 6th St. (882-0924), 3 mi. south of Main, on the edge of strip-mall land. Clean, comfy rooms at unbeatable prices. Cable and A/C, but no phones. One double bed $28; two-bed rooms $32, with kitchenettes $33.

Lost Creek Campground (594-2211, ext. 415), in the southeast corner of the park, 3 mi. on a paved road off Rim Dr. Set amid young pines. Only 16 sites—try to secure one in the morning. Water, toilets, and sinks. Tent sites: $10. No reservations. Usually open mid-July to mid-Oct. but call ahead to the park visitor center.

Mazama Campground (594-2255), near the park's south entrance. RVs swarm into this monster facility, but some sites reserved for tents. Loop G is more secluded and spacious. Toilets, showers, pay laundry, telephone, and gas. Wheelchair accessible. No hookups. 194 sites. Tents $13; RVs $14. No reservations. Usually open June to mid-Oct.

◔ FOOD

Eating cheap ain't easy in Crater Lake. Klamath Falls has some affordable dining and a **Safeway** (882-2660) at Pine and 8th St., one block north of Main (open daily 6am-11pm). Canned goods and sandwiches share shelf-space with sporting goods at **Fort Klamath General Store** (381-2263; open daily 7am-10pm; in winter 7am-8pm).

Renaissance Cafe, 1012 Main St. (851-0242). Gourmet pizzas loaded with zucchini, spinach, pesto, and artichoke hearts $6.25. Expansive salads $6. Open M-F 11am-2:30pm, also moonlights M-Sa 5pm-9pm as a pricey dinner establishment.

Klamath Grill, 712 Main St. (882-1427). Interesting food and low prices make for loyal followers. Popular lunch specials like Cajun chicken salad and shrimp quesadillas, both $5. Open M-F 6am-2:30pm, Sa-Su 7am-2pm.

Cattle Crossing Cafe (381-9801), on Hwy. 62 in Fort Klamath. Breakfasts ($5.25), burgers ($4.25), and pie good enough that management claims people come from other *planets* for a piece. Stellar desserts ($2.50). Open daily Apr.-Oct. 6am-9pm.

👁 SIGHTS

Rim Drive, which often does not open until mid-July, is a 33-mile loop around the rim of the caldera, high above the lake. Pull-outs are strategically placed wherever a view of the lake might cause an awe-struck tourist to drive right off the road. Almost all visitors stay in their vehicles as they tour the lake, so it's relatively easy to get away from the crowds: just stop at any of the trailheads scattered along the rim and hike away from the road. **Garfield Peak** (1¾ mi. one-way), which starts at the lodge, and **Watchman Peak** (¾ mi one-way), on the west side of the lake, are the most spectacular. The Steel Center has a trail map.

The hike up **Mt. Scott,** the park's highest peak (a tad under 9000 ft.), begins after a 17 mi. drive clockwise from rim village. Although steep, the sweaty 2½ mi. ascent gives the perseverant hiker a unique view of the lake. The steep **Cleetwood Trail,** 1.1 mi. of switchbacks on the lake's north edge, is the only route down to the water and the park's most traveled trail: in summer, two-hour boat tours led by rangers depart from the end of this trail ($12.50, under 13 $6). Both **Wizard Island,** a cinder cone rising 760 ft. above the lake, and **Phantom Ship Rock,** a spooky rock formation, are breathtaking when viewed from the lake's surface. Picnics, fishing, and swimming are allowed, but the water's surface reaches a maximum temperature of only 50°F (10°C). The water is too nutrient-poor to support much life; rainbow trout and kokanee alone inhabit the lake. Park rangers lead free walking tours daily in the summer and periodically in the winter (on snowshoes). Call the Steel Center for schedules. The stroll from the visitor center at the rim down to the **Sinnott Memorial Overlook,** a stone enclave built into the rim, provides the area's most accessible and panoramic view. In the summer a ranger gives hourly talks (10am-5pm) about the area's geology and history. A similar talk is given nightly (July to Labor Day at 9pm) at the **Mazama Campground Amphitheater.**

A few hundred yards east of Sinnott Memorial Overlook is the **Crater Lake Lodge,** the beneficiary of a recent $18 million renovation. Rooms are booked 6 months to a year in advance and start at $105, but you can have some fun in the lodge for free: make a quick visit to the rustic "great hall," rebuilt from its original materials, and the observation deck with rocking chairs from which to enjoy great views.

A hiking trip into the park's vast **backcountry** leaves all the exhaust and tourists behind, as well as, unfortunately, any view of the lake. The **Pacific Crest Trail** passes through the park and three backcountry campsites, accessible from the trailhead three-quarters of a mile west of the south entrance. Another excellent loop begins at the **Red Cone trailhead** on the north access road, passing the **Crater Springs, Oasis Butte,** and **Boundary Springs trails.** Dispersed camping is allowed anywhere in this area, but is slightly complicated by the absence of water and the presence of bears. Get info and backcountry permits for free at either visitor center.

EASTERN OREGON

HELLS CANYON & WALLOWA MOUNTAINS

The northeast corner of Oregon is the state's most rugged, remote, and arresting country, with jagged granite peaks, glacier-gouged valleys, and azure lakes. An afternoon's hike can begin in a carpet of pasture and end in crags and snow. East of La Grande, the Wallowa Mountains (wa-LAH-wah) rise abruptly, looming over the plains from elevations of more than 9000 ft. Thirty miles east, North America's deepest gorge, Hells Canyon, plunges to the Snake River. Parched and dusty slopes and scorching heat lend credence to the canyon's name. It may take a four-wheel-drive vehicle to get off the beaten path, but those with the initiative and the horsepower will find stunning vistas and heavenly solitude in the backcountry.

✦ ORIENTATION AND PRACTICAL INFORMATION

Hells Canyon National Recreation Area and the **Eagle Cap Wilderness** lie on either side of the **Wallowa Valley,** which can be reached in three ways. From **Baker City,** Rte. 86 heads east through Halfway to connect with Forest Rd. 39, which winds north over the southern end of the Wallowas, meeting Rte. 350 (also known as Little Sheep Creek Hwy.) 8 mi. east of Joseph. From **La Grande,** Rte. 82 arcs around the north end of the Wallowas, through the small towns of Elgin, Minam, Wallowa, and Lostine, continuing through Enterprise and Joseph, and terminating at Wallowa Lake. From **Clarkston,** WA, Rte. 129 heads south, taking a plunge through the valley of the Grande Ronde River, becoming Rte. 3 in Oregon, to join Rte. 82 in Enterprise.

Three main towns offer services within the area: **Enterprise, Joseph,** and **Halfway.** The only two major roads are **Rte. 350,** a paved route from Joseph northeast 30 mi. to the tiny town of **Imnaha,** and the **Imnaha River Rd.** (a.k.a. Country Rd. 727 and Forest Rd. 3955), a good gravel road that runs south from Imnaha to reconnect with Forest Rd. 39 about 50 mi. southeast of Joseph. The free pamphlet *Hells Canyon Scenic Byway,* available in visitor centers and ranger stations, is invaluable for its clear road map showing campgrounds and points of interest. Check current road conditions before heading into the area; 1999 saw roads snowed in well into July.

Buses: Moffit Brothers Transportation (569-2284) runs the **Wallowa Valley Stage Line** which makes one round-trip M-Sa from Joseph (6:30am) to La Grande (11:55am). Pickup at the Chevron on Rte. 82 in Joseph, the Amoco on Rte. 82 in Enterprise, and the Greyhound terminal in La Grande. Will stop at Wallowa Lake, and pick up there with advance notice. One-way from La Grande to: Enterprise ($8.10); Joseph ($8.80); Wallowa Lake ($12.50).

Visitor Information: Wallowa County Chamber of Commerce (426-4622 or 800-585-4121), at SW 1st St. and W. Greenwood Ave. in Enterprise, in the mall. General tourist info as well as the comprehensive and free *Wallowa County Visitor Guide.* Open M-F 9am-5pm. **Hells Canyon Chamber of Commerce** (742-4222), in the office of Halfway Motels (see **Motels,** below), provides info on accommodations, outfitters, and guides.

Outdoor Information: Wallowa Mountains Visitor Center, 88401 Rte. 82 (426-5546; www.fs.fed.us/r6/w-w), on the west side of Enterprise. $4 map a necessity for navigating area roads. Open Memorial Day-Labor Day M-Sa 8am-5pm, in winter M-F 8am-5pm.

Equipment Rental: Crosstown Traffic, 102 W. McCully St. (432-2453), in Joseph. Bikes $15 per day, discounts for multiple-day rentals. Staffers can suggest biking routes. Open M-F 8am-6pm, Sa 8am-2pm.

Laundromat: Joseph Laundromat and Car Wash, on Rte. 82 in Joseph, across from the Indian Lodge Motel. Wash $1, dry 25¢ per 8min. Open daily 6am-10pm.

Emergency: 911. **State Police:** 426-3036. **Enterprise Police:** (426-3136), at the corner of North St. and NE 1st on S. River St. (Rte. 82). **Fire:** 426-4196.

Hospital: Wallowa Memorial, 401 NE 1st St. (426-3111), in Enterprise.

Post Office: 201 W. North, 97828 (800-275-8777), on Rte. 82 in Enterprise. Open M-F 9am-4:30pm.

Area Code: 541.

▚ CAMPGROUNDS

Campgrounds here are plentiful, inexpensive, and sublime. Pick up the *Campground Information* pamphlet at the Wallowa Mountains Visitor Center for a complete listing of sites in the area. Due to 1996 budget cutbacks, most campgrounds (including all of those listed below) are not fully serviced, and are therefore **free**—check at the visitor center to see whether a campground has potable water. Inexplicably, the massive **Wallowa Lake State Park campground** (432-4185, reservations 800-452-5687) books solid up to a year in advance. Try your luck there if in the market for full-service camping. (toilets, drinking water, and showers. Tent sites $16, full hookups $20.)

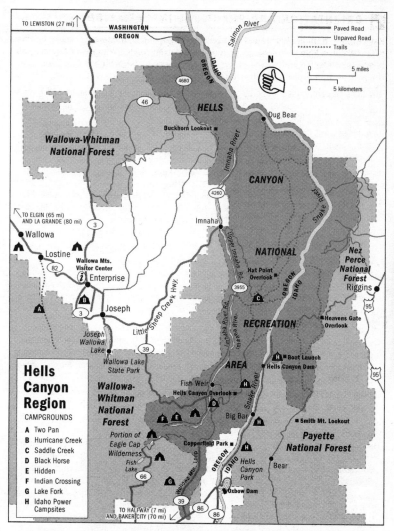

Hells Canyon Region

CAMPGROUNDS

A Two Pan
B Hurricane Creek
C Saddle Creek
D Black Horse
E Hidden
F Indian Crossing
G Lake Fork
H Idaho Power Campsites

Campers bound for the Hells Canyon area should stock up on food, drinking water, and gas, and remember that showers and toilets are near-nonexistent. Insect repellent is a must for those planning to hike down into the canyon and around the high lakes in summer. Be aware that weather can make extreme shifts in a short time. There are many potential campsites, but because of adverse road conditions, most campgrounds are only open from July to September. **Hells Canyon, Copperfield, McCormick,** and **Woodhead** have tent and RV sites and restrooms (Woodhead offers hot showers), are the only campgrounds open year-round and are located near Oxbow and Brownlee Dams, on Rte. 86 and Rte. 71 along the Snake River ($6, RV hookups $10; no reservations; call 785-3323 for info).

Saddle Creek Campground, 18 mi. from Imnaha up the improved, but narrow and steep, road to Hat Point (1½hr. by car). 7 sites perched right on the lip of Hells Canyon, with unbelievable views, especially at dusk and dawn. No water. Pit toilets.

Hurricane Creek Campground, a quiet campground by Hurricane Creek, is the closest free camping. Take the well-marked Hurricane Creek Rd. from Rte. 82 in Enterprise, or, from Main St. in Joseph, follow the large green sign onto W. Wallowa Rd. After about 2 mi., make a sharp left at a white grange and red barn. The gravel road turns into pavement in 1½ mi., and the campground lies ½ mi. farther down on a dirt road to the left labeled "100." Trailhead access. 14 secluded sites, no water.

Hidden Campground is shaded by giant conifers and bordered by the clear Inmaha River. Head southwest of Joseph on Forest Rd. 39 for about 40 mi., then go upriver on paved Forest Rd. 3960 toward Indian Crossing for 9 mi. 10 sites.

Indian Crossing Campground, a little past Hidden, has great secluded sites across the river. This is the farthest out of any campsite on Forest Rd. 3960, and it's worth the extra few miles. Trailhead access. 14 sites, pit toilets, potable water.

Lostine River Campgrounds include five separate campgrounds (Pole Bridge, Williamson, French, Shady, and Two Pan) along the Lostine River Road, most with sites right on the water. Quiet campers may be visited by deer. From Lostine, follow the Lostine River Rd. (Forest Rd. 8210) south. Pole Bridge is about 5 mi. from town, Two Pan is 18 mi. The last 5 mi. are on a rough gravel road. Trailhead access. No water.

Left Fork Campground, about 5 mi. north from the spot where Rte. 39 enters the southern edge of the forest, is the most convenient camping for those arriving from Baker City. 9 sites. Pit toilets, potable water, free firewood.

▶ MOTELS

Most of the towns along Rte. 82 have motels with plenty of vacancy during the week. On weekends rooms are more scarce.

Country Inn Motel (426-4986), on Rte. 82 in Enterprise. The frilly decorations suggest a country farmhouse. The lack of A/C is not a problem—even on the hottest summer days, the rooms stay remarkably cool. Cable, coffee makers, and refrigerators. Singles $40; doubles $48-54. Kitchens a little extra, depending on availability.

Indian Lodge Motel, 201 S. Main St. (432-2651), on Rte. 82 in Joseph. A one-story roadsider with brick-red roofing. Elegant rooms with dark wood furniture and plush blue carpet also feature A/C, cable, coffee makers, and refrigerators. Singles $37; doubles $48. In winter singles $32; doubles $43.

Halfway Motels, 170 S. Main St. (742-5722), just off Rte. 86 in Halfway. Clean units in the old part of the motel have no phones or A/C. Singles $35; doubles $40. Shiny new rooms in a two-story building are unusually large and have TVs. Singles $42; doubles $52. 15 RV/tent sites are available just down the road, full hookups $16.

▶ FOOD

If heading out onto the hairy roads of Hells Canyon, bring some provisions—a flat or breakdown could require a roadside meal or two. Score pancake mix and strawberries at **Safeway,** 601 W. North St. (426-3722; open daily 6am-9pm), on Rte. 82 in Enterprise, or **Old Pine Market** (742-4366; open M-Sa 8am-9pm, Su 8am-8pm; closes 7pm in winter), on Main St. in Halfway.

Old Town Cafe, 8 S. Main St. (432-9898), in Joseph. Sit in the outdoor grotto, and dig into a bottomless bowl of homemade soup ($3), or submerge yourself in the sublime "Old Town Chocolate Pie." Breakfast all day. Giant cinnamon rolls baked fresh $3. Open F-W 7am-2pm. In summer, special dinners are served Friday and Saturday until 8pm.

The Common Good Marketplace, 100 W. Main (426-4125), in Enterprise. Vegetarian sandwiches ($4) and lunch buffet ($8) made from scratch. Open daily 10am-3pm.

Vali's Alpine Delicatessen Restaurant, 59811 Wallowa Lake Hwy. (432-5691), in Wallowa Lake. For 25 years in this small, alpinesque cottage, Mr. Vali has cooked one authentic European dish each night and Mrs. Vali has served it. Hungarian Kettle Goulash $7.50; schnitzel $12. Reservations required for dinner, but not for the continental breakfast of homemade raspberry doughnuts (50-65¢) and cold cuts. Open T-Su 9am-11am; dinner seatings at 5 and 8pm; in winter Sa and Su only.

Embers Brew House, 204 N. Main St. (432-2739), in Joseph. The ambience of this new white house needs some time to age, but the 17 microbrews on tap are perfect the way they are. Breaded brew fries $4; pints $3. Open daily 7am-10pm; in winter 10am-4pm.

⚠ OUTDOORS

HELLS CANYON

The canyon's endearing name comes from its legendary inaccessibility and hostility to human habitation. The walls of Hells Canyon, the Grand Canyon's big sibling, drop over 8000 ft. to the **Snake River.**

Getting around Hells Canyon without a four-wheel-drive vehicle or a horse is difficult. Some travelers hitchhike in from the gateway towns of Joseph or Halfway, and talk it up with people at campsites to get back out. The few roads in Hells Canyon will conquer any ordinary car, and most Forest Roads are closed when Hells Canyon freezes over (Oct.-June). The only way to get close to the canyon without taking at least a full day is to drive the **Hells Canyon National Scenic Loop Drive,** which should really be named the Wallowa Mountains Loop Drive, since the only real views of the canyon are on side trips. The loop begins and ends in Baker City (see p. 145), following Rte. 86, Forest Rd. 39 and 350, Rte. 82, and finally I-84. Even this paved route takes six hours to two days to drive. Call the Wallowa Mtns. visitor center about road conditions, since closures are routine.

Hells Canyon Overlook, the most accessible but least impressive of the lookout points, is up Forest Rd. 3965, 3 mi. of the smoothest, most luxurious pavement in Wallowa County. The road departs Rd. 39 about 5 mi. south of the Imnaha River crossing. The broadest and most eye-popping views are from the **Hat Point Overlook,** where visitors can climb a 90 ft. wooden fire lookout. To get there, go 24 mi. up a steep but well-maintained gravel road from Imnaha (Forest Rd. 4240), then turn off onto Rd. 315 and follow the signs. There are pit toilets at the overlook and six primitive campsites just over the hill. The **Buckhorn Lookout** lies far off the beaten path, 42 mi. northeast of Joseph, and offers lofty views of the Imnaha River Valley. Take Rte. 82 north 3 mi. out of Joseph or 3 mi. south out of Enterprise, and look for the green sign for Buckhorn. Turn off and follow Zumwalt Rd. (a.k.a. Country Rd. 697, which turns into Forest Rd. 46) for approximately 40 bumpy miles to Buckhorn—about a half-day round-trip. Also at that end of the canyon, the immense **Hells Canyon Dam** lies 23 mi. north of Oxbow on Rte. 86. The views from the winding road become increasingly dramatic heading north. This drive is one of only three ways to get near the bottom of the canyon by car, and the dam is the only place to cross.

Hiking is perhaps the best way to comprehend the vast emptiness of Hells Canyon, and to really get into the canyon requires a trip of at least a few days. There are over 1000 mi. of trails in the canyon, only a fraction of which are regularly maintained. Bring snakebite kits, good boots, and lots of water.

The dramatic 56 mi. **Snake River Trail** runs beside the river for the length of the canyon. At times, the trail is cut into the side of the rock with just enough clearance for a horse's head. Come prepared for any hazard, though outfitters and rangers patrol the river by boat at least once a day. This trail can be followed from **Dug Bar** in the north clear down to the Hells Canyon Dam, or accessed by treacherously steep trails along the way. From north to south, **Hat Point, Freezeout,** and **P.O. Saddle** are possible access points. To reach Dug Bar, take Forest Rd. 4260, a steep, slippery route recommended only for four-wheel drive or high-clearance vehicles, for 27 mi. northeast from Imnaha; check conditions before heading out.

EASTERN OREGON

The easiest way to see a large portion of the canyon is to zip through on a jet boat tour or float down the Snake on a raft, both pursuits guaranteed to drench. Numerous outfitters operate out of Oxbow and the dam area; the Wallowa Mountains Visitor Center (see p. 138) and all local chambers of commerce have a list of the permittees. **Hells Canyon Adventures** (785-3352, outside OR 800-422-3568), 1½ mi. from the Hells Canyon Dam in Oxbow, runs a wide range of jet boat and raft trips through the Canyon. (Jet boats: 2hr. $30; 3hr. $40; full day $95. Whitewater rafting, including jet boat ride back upstream, $125.)

THE WALLOWA MOUNTAINS

Without a catchy, federally approved name like "Hells Canyon National Recreation Area," the Wallowas often take second place to the canyon in the minds of tourists, though they possess a scenic beauty equally magnificent. The canyons echo with the deafening rush of rapids, and the jagged peaks are covered with wildflowers in spring. Over 600 mi. of **hiking trails** cross the **Eagle Cap Wilderness,** and are usually free of snow from mid-July to October. Deep glacial valleys and high granite passes make hiking this wilderness tough going: it often takes more than a day to get into the most beautiful and remote areas. Still, several high alpine lakes are accessible to dayhikers. The 5 mi. hike to **Chimney Lake** from the Bowman trailhead on the Lostine River Rd. (Forest Rd. 8210) traverses fields of granite boulders sprinkled with a few small meadows. A little farther on lie the serene **Laverty, Hobo,** and **Wood Lakes,** where the path is less beaten. The **Two Pan trailhead** at the end of the Lostine River Rd. is the start of a forested 6 mi. hike to popular **Minam Lake,** which makes a good starting point for those heading to other backcountry spots like **Blue Lake,** 1 mi. above Minam. From the **Wallowa Lake trailhead,** behind the little powerhouse at the end of Rte. 82, a 6 mi. hike leads up the East Fork of the Wallowa River to Aneroid Lake. From there, hikes to Pete's Point and Aneroid Mountain offer great views.

By far the most popular area in the Eagle Cap Wilderness is the **Lakes Basin,** where explorers can find unsurpassed scenery, good fishing, and hikes to Eagle Cap Peak. While it is possible to escape the crowds in the basin during the week, the lake is packed on weekends. **Steamboat, Long,** and **Swamp Lakes** are as magnificent as the Lakes Basin, but receive only half as many visitors. The trailheads for both areas are on the Lostine River Rd. Rangers at the visitor center can also recommend more secluded routes. Fishing in the alpine lakes of Eagle Cap is incredible, but it's illegal even to catch and release without a permit, and some fish, such as bull trout, are entirely protected. Get permits ($8.25 per day, $48 per year) and the *Oregon Sport Fishing Regulations* booklet at any local sporting store.

An hour of stiff hiking along the **Falls Creek trail** provides 360° views spanning snowy peaks, waterfalls, and utterly flat basin. The main trail begins at the Hurricane Creek trailhead, 2 mi. past the campground at Hurricane Creek. After 300 ft., look for the small Falls Creek Trail sign to your right. Many excellent dayhikes to Lookingglass, Culver, Bear, Eagle, Cached, Arrow, and Heart Lakes start from the **Main Eagle trailhead,** on Forest Rd. 7755, on the southern side of the Eagle Cap Wilderness (accessible from Baker City and Halfway). Hiking the loop of these lakes makes an amazing overnight expedition. **Hurricane Creek Llama Treks** (432-4455 or 800-528-9609) offers trips into the Wallowa Mountains and Hells Canyon, with dutiful llamas to bear supplies.

PENDLETON

Called Goodwin Station from 1862 to 1868, this small town eventually took on the name of George Hunt Pendleton, an Ohio politician who ran for Vice President in 1864. He had nothing to do with Oregon, and he never visited Pendleton, but someone liked the ring of his name, and with this introductory paragraph, his memory lives on. This agricultural town is best known for its locally processed wool and for the mad Pendleton Round-Up. In mid-September, 50,000 cowfolks and horsedudes gather in this northeastern town to witness the rodeo of a lifetime and be a part of Pendleton's annual celebration of machismo. At all other times Pendleton to passersby is a nice stop on the way to the Blue Mountains.

🛈 ORIENTATION AND PRACTICAL INFORMATION

Pendleton is at the junction of I-84, Rte. 11, and U.S. 395, just south of the Washington border, roughly equidistant (200-230 mi.) from Portland, Spokane, Seattle, WA, and Boise, ID. Raley Park—humming with energy from the Round-Up Grounds next door—is the spiritual center of town, but Pendleton is divided into quadrants: east-west by Main St. and north-south by the Umatilla River. Streets parallel to the river are named alphabetically, streets parallel to Main St. are numbered. The patterns repeat in each quadrant (i.e., two parallel 2nd streets, etc.).

Buses: Greyhound, 320 SW Court Ave. (276-1551 or 800-231-2222), a few blocks west of the city center. To: Portland (5hr., 3 per day, $30-32); Boise, ID (5hr., 3 per day, $37); Walla Walla, WA (1hr., 2 per day, $10). Open M-Su 9am-9pm and 12:30-3am.

Taxis: Elite Taxi, 276-8294. Open M-Sa 5:30am-3am, Su 7am-3am.

Car Rental: Round-Up Rent-A-Car, 309 SW Emigrant Ave. (276-1498). $20 per day, 15¢ per mi. over 50 mi. Unlimited free mileage on weekly rentals ($140). Must be 25 with credit card. Open M-Sa 8am-5pm.

Visitor Information: Pendleton Chamber of Commerce, 501 S. Main St. (276-7411 or 800-547-8911; www.pendleton-oregon.org). Cheerful help with housing and tickets during the Round-Up. Open M-F 8:30am-5pm, Sa 9am-5pm; in winter M-F 8:30am-5pm.

Outdoor Information: Umatilla Forest Headquarters, 2517 SW Hailey Ave. (278-3716; www.fs.fed.us/r6/uma/), up the hill from I-84 Exit 209. Open M-F 7:45am-4:30pm.

Emergency: 911. **Police:** 109 SW Court Ave. (276-4411). 24hr.

Hospital: St. Anthony's, 1601 SE Court Ave. (276-5121).

Post Office: 104 SW Dorion Ave., 97801 (800-275-8777), in the Federal Building at SW 1st St. Open M-F 9am-5pm, Sa 10am-1pm.

Area Code: 541.

▌ ACCOMMODATIONS AND CAMPGROUNDS

For most of the year, lodging in Pendleton is inexpensive. During the Round-Up, rates double, and prices skyrocket on everything from hamburgers to commemorative cowboy hats; rooms are booked up to two years in advance. The nearest decent camping is 25 mi. away, though the Round-Up provides 1500 camping spots at schools around town (RVs $15; tents $10). Call the chamber of commerce after April 1 to lasso a spot. For more camping options, see **Outdoors,** below.

Tapadera Budget Inn, 105 SW Court (276-3231 or 800-722-8277), near the town center. Restaurant in-house. Singles $34, doubles $38-46. 10% AAA and senior discount.

The Chaparral, 620 SW Tutuilla (276-8654), just off I-84 Exit 209. Renovated rooms with cable TV. Singles $37, doubles $44; kitchenettes $5 extra. Reception open daily 7am-11pm.

Let'Er Buck Motel, 205 SE Dorian Ave. (276-3293), two blocks east of Main St. Chipped with age and decor to match, but the price is right. Singles, $25, Doubles, $32.

Emigrant Springs State Park (983-2277), 26 mi. southeast of Pendleton off I-84 Exit 234, in a shady grove of evergreens at a historic Oregon Trail camp. Some highway noise. Hot showers. 33 tent sites: $13; 18 full hookups: $17. Wheelchair accessible.

EASTERN OREGON

⌕ FOOD

Vegetarians will have more luck grazing in the surrounding wheat fields than in local restaurants—this is steak country. For staples, head to **Albertson's** (276-1362), opposite the Round-Up grounds (open daily 6am-11pm).

Circle S Barbecue, 210 SE 5th St. (276-9637). A restaurant built on the premise that it is not possible to eat too much meat (BBQ, of course). Meat with salad, potatoes, beans, and corn bread ($10). Topped off with a *crème de menthe* sundae ($2.25). Breakfast served all day. Open T-Sa 7am-9pm, Su 7am-2pm.

Great Pacific Cafe, 403 S. Main At. (276-1350). The chillest establishment in Pendleton hosts wine tastings every other Friday at 4:30pm ($1.50 per half-glass) and jazz concerts off and on during the summer. Sandwiches $3-5. Many beers, including the fabulous Black Butte Beer (pints $2.75). Open M-Th and Sa 8:30am-6pm, F 8:30am-7pm.

The Cookie Tree, 30 SW Emigrant Ave. (278-0343). A buzzing little shop known for breakfast and sandwiches ($3.25-6), not namesake cookies. Vegetarians can delve into the Avocado Delight ($5.50), one of many such options. Open daily 6am-3pm.

🏛 SIGHTS AND EVENTS

The Tamastslikt Cultural Institute (966-9748; www.ucinet.com/~umatribe/tamust.html), at the Wildhorse Resort four miles east of Pendleton off I-84 Exit 216. A huge and carefully designed tribute to the Confederated Tribes of the Umatilla Reservation, featuring hours' worth of taped and filmed interviews with elders and the activists who are fighting to reclaim the rights of tribal members. (Open daily 9am-5pm. $6; over 55, children, and students $4; under 5 free.) **Pendleton Underground Tours,** 37 SW Emigrant Ave. (276-0730 or 800-226-6398), is the town's great year-round attraction, retelling Pendleton's wild history from its pinnacle (when the town claimed 32 bars and 18 brothels within 4 blocks) to when the last red lightbulb was unscrewed (well into the 1950s). The tour meanders through former speakeasies, inhuman living quarters for Chinese laborers, a brothel, and an opium den; life-size models perch the tour on the fine line between fascinating and cheesy. (1hr. tour $10, children $5. AAA discount $1. Call for tour times and reservations.) The **Pendleton Woolen Mills,** 1307 SE Court Place (276-6911), are tactile paradise. Shearing and manufacturing wool since 1909, the mills now draw devotees eager to own one of their boldly colored blankets, inspired by Native American patterns. (Open M-Sa 8am-5pm. Free 20min. tour M-F 9, 11am, 1:30, and 3pm.) Blanket seconds go for $82-89, perfect patches $140-200.

At heart, Pendleton is a fervent, frothing rodeo town. The **Pendleton Round-Up** (276-2553 or 800-457-6336; www.pendletonroundup.com) has been one of the premier events in the national circuit since 1910, drawing ranchers from all over the U.S. for steer-roping, bulldogging, and bareback competitions, buffalo chip tosses, wild-cow-milking, and greased-pig chases. A grand pageant and concert begins when night falls ($6-12). The 2000 Round-Up runs September 13-16. Tickets ($8-16 per day) go on sale 22 months in advance and often sell out, but lucky callers to the Chamber of Commerce may snag a resell, and scalpers sometimes linger near the gate. The **Round-Up Hall of Fame** (278-0815), under the south grandstand area at SW Court Ave. and SW 13th St., has captured some of the rodeo's action for eternity, including Pendleton's best-preserved hero, a stuffed horse named War Paint. (Open Apr.-Sept. M-Sa 10am-5pm. Call to arrange a tour.)

⛰ OUTDOORS

Pendleton makes a good stop-off on the way to the **Blue Mountains** or **Umatilla National Forest** (yoo-ma-TILL-uh). To get to the Blue Mountains, take Rte. 11 north for 20 mi. to Rte. 204 E. After 41 mi., Rte. 204 meets Rte. 82 on the east side of the mountains, at **Elgin.** There are four **campgrounds** along this route, all with picnic tables, drinking water (save Woodland), and none with showers. The most convenient are **Woodward** (18 sites: $10) and **Woodland** (7 sites: free), just before and just after the town of **Tollgate** off Rte. 204. **Target Meadows** (19 sites: $10), is an isolated spot only 2 mi. off the highway. **Jubilee Lake** (wheelchair accessible; 53 sites: $14), another 12 mi. up the gravel road, is popular for swimming and fishing. To reach these two, turn north onto Forest Rd. 64 at Tollgate, 22 mi. east of the junction of Rte. 204 and Rte. 11, and follow signs. On the way, Rte. 204 winds through dense timber, past campgrounds, creeks, and lakes, and near two wilderness areas: the small **North Fork Umatilla,** and the large **Wenaha-Tucannon Wilderness.** Both are little-used and offer real solitude. Wenaha-Tucannon has more challenging hiking. In April and May it is possible to raft Class III rapids on the north fork of the **John Day River.** The 40 mi. journey begins at Dale, south of Pendleton on Hwy. 395, and ends at the town of Monument; call the ranger for details. Cross-country skiers will find marked trails at Horseshoe Prairie, 7 miles south of Tollgate on Hwy. 204, and are alone welcome, along with snowmobiles, on forest roads in winter. Contact the ranger for trailhead **parking permits,** necessary throughout the region.

BAKER CITY

The elegant storefronts that line Main St. are a reminder of Baker City's past prosperity, but a fist-sized nugget of gold on proud display is the only material trace of the town's early industry. Baker City boasts Oregon's tallest building east of the Cascades (10 stories), but it's the nearby natural wonders—Elkhorn Ridge, Wallowa-Whitman National Forest, and Hell's Canyon—that draw most visitors.

✴ ORIENTATION AND PRACTICAL INFORMATION

Baker City is on **I-84** in northeastern Oregon, 43 mi. southeast of La Grande and 137 mi. northwest of Boise, ID. From Baker City, Rte. 86 leads east to Hells Canyon and Rte. 7 leads west to connect with U.S. 26 (which leads to John Day and Prineville). Streets running parallel to I-84 are numbered in increasing order the farther they are from the highway. Two principal streets intersect **Main St.: Washington** in the east and **Broadway** in the middle. **Campbell St.** intersects I-84 just west of town.

Buses: Greyhound, 515 Campbell St. (523-5011 or 800-231-2222), by I-84 in the Truck Corral Cafe. To: Boise, ID (4hr., 4 per day, $28); Portland (7hr., 4 per day, $44). Open daily 7-9:30am and 5-8pm.

Taxis: Baker Cab Co. (523-6070). Up to $4.25 within Baker City, $1 per mi. outside city limits. Runs 24hr.

Visitor Information: Baker County Visitor and Convention Bureau, 490 Campbell St. (523-3356 or 800-523-1235; www.neoregon.com/visitBaker.html), off I-84 Exit 304. Open June-Aug. M-F 8am-5pm, Sa 8am-4pm, Su 9am-2pm; Sept.-May M-F 8am-5pm.

Outdoor Information: Wallowa National Forest Ranger Station and Bureau of Land Management, 3165 10th St. (523-4476), has info on the Elkhorns, and the Anthony Lakes Recreation Area. Open M-F 7:45am-4:30pm.

Laundromat and Public Showers: Baker City Laundry, 815 Campbell St. (523-9817). Untimed showers $5. Wash $1.25, dry 25¢ per 8min. Open daily 7am-10pm.

Emergency: 911. **Police:** 1655 1st St. (523-3644). **Women's Crisis: Mayday,** 523-4134.

Hospital: St. Elizabeth, 3325 Pocahontas Rd. (523-6461).

Library: 2400 Resort St. (523-6419). Take the first left after the river on Campbell St. as you drive west away from I-84. Open M-Th 10am-8pm, F 10am-5pm, Sa 10am-4pm. **Internet access** available.

Post Office: 1550 Dewey Ave., 97814 (800-275-8777). Open M-F 8:30am-5pm.

Area Code: 541.

▮ ACCOMMODATIONS AND CAMPGROUNDS

Baker City has reasonably priced motels on 10th St. Generally, deals get better the farther the motel is from the Interstate.

Bruno Ranch B&B, Box 51, Bridgeport (446-3468). Go 9mi. south of Baker City on Rte. 7, turn left onto Rte. 245. After 14 mi., turn left onto Bridgeport Rd.; it's the first house on the right. On the edge of the national forest. The basement rooms are comfy, but it is the idyllic setting and exceptional hospitality that make the trip worthwhile. Excellent hunter's breakfast and tours of the beautiful ranch. Singles $25; doubles $30. Camping $3 for tents, $8 for vehicles. Call ahead.

Green Gables, 2533 10th St. (523-5588), at Campbell St. An elderly exterior, but clean, spacious rooms within. Adjoining kitchens and low weekly rates make it a great choice for longer stays. Singles $26; doubles $30. Full kitchen $6 extra. 10% senior discount.

A'demain B&B, 1790 4th St., south of Washington St. (523-2509). Treat yourself to featherbeds, bay windows, and free truffles. Single $60; 3-room suite $75.

Anthony Lake Campground, 36 mi. from Baker City on Anthony Lake Hwy. Take Rte. 30 north past Haines, then turn west onto Anthony Lake Hwy. On a gem of a lake set in jagged peaks, this campground draws large weekend crowds. 37 sites: $5 per vehicle. Wheelchair accessible. If it's too crowded, try **Mud Lake,** a more primitive campground across the road. Both open early July to Aug.

Union Creek Campground (894-2260), at Phillips Lake. Follow Rte. 7 for 20 mi. south toward Sumpter. High grasses and sparse pines make for high RV visibility. The tent grounds are woodsier. Beach with swimming area and boat ramp, toilets, no showers. 58 sites: $10; water and electrical hookups $14; full hookups $16. Heater or A/C $1 per day. Senior discount.

▮ FOOD

Baker City is a delight to the downtrodden diner. Big bacon breakfasts and burgers dominate 10th St. while cafes along Main St. offer big-city ambience and an alternative to the everyday Oregon meat-and-potatoes fare.

El Erradero, 2100 Broadway (523-2327). Where locals go for mammoth Mexican meals. A sparse decor sets off the expresso burrito with everything or an order of chicken enchiladas (both $7). Entrees come with rice and beans and everyone gets free chips and salsa. Open Su-Th 11am-9:30pm, F-Sa 11am-10pm.

Baker City Cafe/Pizza à Fetta, 1915 Washington Ave. (523-6099). This elegant and friendly cafe makes everything from scratch, including a fabulous gourmet pizza. Slices $2.25-2.75; 14 in. pies $13-14. Open M-F 9am-2pm and 5-8pm, Sa 11am-3pm.

Front Street Coffee Co., 1840 Main St. (523-0223). An old-time soda shop featuring a lunch pail collection. The finest charbroiled lemon pepper chicken breast sandwich in town, ($6, including a side dish). Open M-W 7am-4:30pm, Th-F 7am-8pm, Sa 7am-3pm.

▮ SIGHTS, OUTDOORS, AND EVENTS

Baker's handful of historic museums has recently been upstaged by the multi-million-dollar **National Historic Oregon Trail Interpretive Center,** 5 mi. east of Baker City off Exit 302 (523-1843). A self-guided tour of videos and life-sized models tells the story of pioneers, Native Americans, miners, and fur traders. Excellent **lectures and performances** are held about five days a week. On the last Saturday in July there is a day-long living history festival, complete with buffalo stew. Over 4 mi. of trails, some wheelchair-accessible, lead to scenic overlooks and interpretive sites. In some places, the wagon ruts of the original trail run alongside the path. (Open daily Apr.-Oct. 9am-6pm; Nov.-Mar. 9am-4pm. $5, ages 62+ and 6-17 $3.50.)

Elkhorn Ridge, towering steeply over Baker City to the west (follow the signs along Rte. 7 south), provides local access to the Blue Mountains. Oregon Trail pioneers avoided this jagged peak, but a paved loop called **Elkhorn Drive** (a National Scenic Byway for good reason) now leads over the range, providing drivers along its 106 mi. with lofty views and lots of hiking and fishing. From a parking lot on Forest Rd. 210 (a rough road off Rd. 73, 4 mi. west of Anthony Lake), a steep half-mile hike follows a ridge to a great vista at **Lakes Lookout.** On the south portion of the loop, the 3 mi. climb up 8321 ft. Mt. Ireland offers excellent 360° views. From Rd. 73, take Rd. 7370 near the forest boundary, and park at Grizzly Mine. The numerous high mountain lakes and creeks are jumpin' with fish, and excellent camping is available at the Anthony Lake Campground (see above) or any other place that looks good, provided it's 200 yards from the shoreline. The challenging **Elkhorn Crest Trail** winds through alpine and sub-alpine terrain for 22½ mi. between Anthony Lake in the north and Marble Creek in the south. The **Hells Canyon National Scenic Loop Drive** (see p. 141) begins and ends in Baker City.

The **Miners' Jubilee** centers on Arts in the Park (July 21-23 in 2000), a show and sale of arts with live music, but would-be miners can still participate in the intense gold-panning contest, which determines the state's foremost gold panner.

JOHN DAY FOSSIL BEDS

The John Day Fossil Beds National Monument illustrates the change from the lush, tropical vegetation to the arid grasslands that predated the Cascade Range. The park is divided into three isolated units, each representing a different stretch of time, each as impressive for its unusual landscape as for its fossilized inhabitants. The town of **Sheep Rock,** 2 mi. north from the junction of U.S. 26 and Rte. 19, houses the monument's small **visitor center** (541-987-2333). The center displays rocks and fossils spanning 50 million years, exhibits on early mammals, and an award-winning video produced by high-school students that explains the history of the fossil beds. (Open May-Aug. daily 9am-6pm; Mar.-Apr. and Sept.-Nov. 9am-5pm; Dec.-Feb. M-F 9am-5pm.) The **Island in Time Trail,** 3 mi. up the road, leads through fossil-rich **Blue Basin,** a strikingly beautiful blue and green canyon of eroded badland spires. Admire petrified sea turtles, oreodong, and saber-toothed carnivores as the creek slips by, marking the further passage of time.

Painted Hills, 5 mi. north of U.S. 26 from the turn-off 3 mi. west of Mitchell, focuses on an epoch 30 million years ago when the land was in geologic transition. Smooth mounds of colored sediment are most vivid at sunset and dawn, or after rain when the whole gorge glistens with brilliantly colored layers of claystone. **Clarno,** the monument's oldest section, on Rte. 218, is accessible by U.S. 97 to the west or Rte. 19 to the east. Prepare to be humbled.

NEAR JOHN DAY FOSSIL BEDS

The small town of **John Day,** at the junction of U.S. 26 and U.S. 395, is the largest outpost for miles around. The unique **Kam Wah Chung & Co. Museum,** next to City Park, served as a general store, doctor's office, and a temple for thousands of Chinese immigrants from 1887 through the early 1940s. The tiny building is filled with some 1000 herbs used by the famous Doc Hay (open May-Oct. M-Th 9am-noon and 1-5pm, Sa-Su 1-5pm; $3, seniors and ages 6-16 $1.50).

The town is surrounded on three sides by the massive grasslands of sagebrush and juniper, and forests of pine and fir, of **Malheur National Forest** (mal-HERE; see p. 149). Info is available at the **Bear Valley/Long Creek District Ranger Station,** 431 Patterson Bridge Rd. (541-575-3000; open M-F 7:15am-5pm). This vast region of timbered hills and jagged ridges sees little use in its two designated wilderness areas, **Strawberry Mountain** and **Monument Rock.** By far the most popular area in the forest is the **Eastern Lakes Basin,** in the Strawberry Mtn. area. Camping is permitted anywhere in the forest out of sight of the road, but three **free campgrounds**— **McNaughton Springs** (4 sites), **Slide Creek** (3 sites), and **Strawberry** (11 sites)—are off the Forest Road near the beginning of the **Strawberry Trail,** the area's main access point. The trail runs 1 mi. toward Strawberry Lake and Strawberry Mountain, the forest's highest peak; a 12 mi. loop passes other lakes. To reach the trailhead, take Forest Rd. 60 south from Prairie City. **Magone Lake** (mah-GOON) is another popular campground with 24 sites, fishing, hiking, and new composting bathrooms ($10). To get there from John Day, take U.S. 26 east about 9 mi. to Keeney Forks Rd. north and follow the signs for 15 mi. to the campground. None of these campgrounds has potable water.

Dreamer's Lodge, 144 N. Canyon Blvd. (541-575-0526 or 800-654-2849), has large rooms in chic gray tones with La-Z-Boy recliners, A/C, refrigerators, microwaves, cable TV, and two kitchen units (singles $46; doubles $50). Cheap chains, like **Budget Inn,** 250 E. Main St. (541-575-2100; singles $34, doubles $42; 10% senior discount, two kitchen units), are the other accommodation option. The flat, neatly mowed grass of **Clyde Holliday State Park** (541-575-2773), 7 mi. west of town on U.S. 26, provides small sites with a suburban aura, electricity, and showers (30 sites: $15; hiker/biker sites $4). The best food in the area is undoubtedly at **DiVinci's,** 150 Franklin St. (541-987-2154), in Dayville, a tiny restaurant that serves generous portions of homemade Italian food (entrees $6-9; open Tu-Th 3-9pm, F-Su 11am-9pm). At **Russell's Meats and Gloria's Deli,** 235 S. Canyon Blvd. (575-0720), a few miles south of John Day in Canyon City, choose among meats, breads, and cheeses and pair with soup, salad, or chips to create your sandwich combo ($5, half-sandwich $3.50; open M-F 8am-5:30pm).

SOUTHEASTERN OREGON

BURNS

Tiny Burns and its even tinier neighbor Hines serve as way-stations and supply centers for travelers. Ideally situated between the Ochoco and Malheur National Forests, the Malheur National Wildlife Refuge, Steens Mountain, and the Alvord Desert, Burns enchants both residents and visitors who stock up on gas, water, info, and supplies (and licences), and head for the unspoiled, uninhabited wilderness that is southeastern Oregon.

U.S. 20 from Ontario and U.S. 395 from John Day converge about 2 mi. north of Burns, continue through Burns and Hines as one highway, and diverge about 30 mi. to the west. U.S. 20 continues west to Bend and the Cascade Range; U.S. 395 runs south to Lakeview, OR, and California; Rte. 205 runs south to Frenchglen and Fields (see below). Although buses and vans run to and from some towns in the area, there is no public transportation to the outlying outdoors. **Harney County Chamber of Commerce,** 76 E. Washington St. (573-2636; www.oregon1.org/harney), has maps and info on the town (open M-F 9am-5pm). Even more useful are the **Burns Ranger District (Malheur National Forest)** and **Snow Mountain Ranger District (Ochoco National Forest)** (541-573-4300), in Hines. These outdoor resources share an office on the main drag about 4½ mi. south of Burns. (Open M-F 8am-4:30pm.) **Burns Bureau of Land Management,** U.S. 20 West (573-4400; open M-F 7:30am-4:30pm), is a few miles west of Hines. The town laundromat is **Jiffy Wash,** at the corner of S. Diamond and S. Jackson St. just off W. Monroe. (Wash $1, dry 25¢ per 13min. Open M-Sa 7am-9pm, Su 8am-8pm.) **Road Conditions:** 889-3999. **Emergency:** 911. **Police:** 242 S. Broadway (573-6028). **HHope Hotline:** 573-7176, for 24-hour crisis counseling. **Hospital:** 85 N. Date St. (573-7281). **Post office:** 100 S. Broadway, 97720 (800-275-8777; open M-F 8:30am-5pm). **ZIP code:** 97720. **Area code:** 541.

Most are passing through, but Burns can be accommodating. The **Bontemps Motel,** 74 W. Monroe St. (573-2037 or 800-229-1394), provides the only outright gay-friendly environment for miles. Comfortable rooms with cable TV, A/C, refrigerators, and some damn cool lampshades (singles $33; doubles $38; pets $3 extra; kitchenettes $3-5). About 15 mi. north of town, and within earshot of U.S. 395, **Idlewild** is the only convenient official campground. (Free; pit toilets; no drinking water.) Dispersed camping is allowed just about everywhere, but restrictions apply when the risk of wildfire is high. Check with the Forest Service and BLM in Hines. You can dine amid the owner's extensive collection of antique toys and bikes at the **Old Castle**, 186 W. Monroe St. (573-6601), a local favorite. Groceries await at **Safeway**, 246 W. Monroe St. (573-6767; open daily 5am-11pm).

MALHEUR AND HART MOUNTAIN WILDLIFE REFUGES

South of Burns, miles of sagebrush give way to the grasslands and marshes of **Harney** and **Malheur Lakes,** where thousands of birds end their migratory flight paths each year at **Malheur National Wildlife Refuge.** Stretching 35 mi. south along Rte. 205, the refuge covers 185,000 acres and is home to 360 species of birds, including grebes, ibis, plovers, shrikes, owls, wigeons, and goatsuckers. Malheur is the sole National Refuge that contains remnants of earlier civilizations; any discovered arrowheads must not be removed. The refuge headquarters, 6 mi. east of Rte. 205 on a well-marked turn-off between Burns and Frenchglen, houses a useful **visitor center** (541-493-2612; open M-Th 7am-4:30pm, F 7am-3:30pm, Sa-Su 10am-4pm). The refuge is open year-round during daylight hours. It takes two hours to traverse, sometimes with a four-wheel-drive vehicle, but the persistent will be rewarded. Hundreds of bird species nest here in spring and bald eagles are often seen in the coldest months. Some hunting and fishing is allowed; call the visitor center for details. No camping is allowed within the refuge—even hiking is generally permitted only on roads open to motorists—but **accommodations** are available at the **Malheur Field Station** (541-493-2629), an old government training camp a few miles from headquarters. (No bedding or lighting, and the water, while potable, tastes funny. Singles $30, doubles $45, RV hookups $16. Reserve well in advance.)

Hart Mountain is a 275,000-acre refuge where the antelope roam among mule deer and bighorn sheep, 65 mi. northeast of Lakeview, accessible from the well-marked turn-off 25 mi. south of Burns on Hwy. 205. The nearest services are in **Plush,** 25 mi. away. Most of the refuge, except for the roads to the headquarters and campground, is accessible only to four-wheel-drive vehicles. Headquarters, on the main road near the center of the refuge, houses a 24 hour **visitor and viewing room** where you can pick up a free backcountry permit. The best wildlife viewing is from the lookout point seven miles south along the Blue Sky Rd. A free **campground** is next to the **Hart Mountain hot springs** (pit toilets). Enjoy the warmth: fires are prohibited for much of the season. Between August and November the refuge bustles with hunters eager to bag antelope. In winter, the surviving antelope gallop south to the **Sheldon National Refuge,** just over the border in Nevada.

DIAMOND CRATERS MONUMENT

A well-marked turn-off 30mi. south of Burns on Hwy. 205 leads to what doesn't look like anything much. The Department of the Interior has designed a self-guided auto tour in layman's terms of 13 innocuous-looking traces of an ancient eruption more forceful than the 1980 eruption of Mt. St. Helens ("the crust wrinkles like the skin on a pudding"). Stay on established trails lest your car/bike/ankles become fixed in soft volcanic cinder. Bring water and watch out for rattlesnakes. The nearest facilities are in Burns, 55 mi. to the northwest. The 100-year-old **Hotel Diamond,** 12 mi. east of Rte. 205 on Diamond Lane (541-493-1898; www.central-oregon.com/hoteldiamond/) seems young compared with the craters, but is a sophisticated rest stop for the dedicated explorer. Children—not old enough to be considered historical—are not allowed. (Double bed with shared bath from $55. Breakfast $1.50-4.75, and dinner $10-15, served to guests.)

FRENCHGLEN AND FIELDS

Frenchglen, one hour south of Burns along Rte. 205, provides access to the wildlife refuges and the wet western side of the Steens. Fields, 45 minutes farther south on Rte. 205 at the southern tip of the mountain, provides access to the dry eastern face and the Alvord Desert that stretches beyond it.

Frenchglen Mercantile (541-493-2738) has canned goods and a deli in July and August. The **Frenchglen Hotel** (541-493-2825; fghotel@ptinet.net) serves great home-made food and rents cozy rooms with patchwork quilts and shared baths ($55; two single beds $58; call ahead; open Mar. 15-Nov. 15). The **Steens Mountain Resort,** North Loop Rd. (541-493-2415 or 800-542-3765), rents full hookups ($18), and two-person cabins ($55). The general store has laundry facilities and rents rafts ($15 per day; open daily 8am-6pm). On West D St. sits the deserted **Pete French Round Barn** (573-2636; www.oregon1.org/harney/). For 115 years, ghosts of the old west have clung to its dusty rafters.

Fields consists of the rambling **Fields Station** (541-495-2275), home to five busi-nesses owned by the same family. The general store and gas station are the last of each for miles. The cafe serves remarkable burgers ($4.50) and 1500 milkshakes (each $3) a year. It would be a shame to stay at the motel (RV hookups $7.50, tent sites $3) when the mountains and the desert beckon at your feet.

STEENS MOUNTAIN AND THE ALVORD DESERT

Oregon's most unearthly landscape lies in the southeast, where **Steens Mountain** rises a full vertical mile above inhospitable sagebrush to the west, and, to the east, a uninhabited alkali flat so dry it looks like a mirror. Steens (9773 ft.) is the highest mountain in southeastern Oregon and the view from the top takes in four states. Nearly all visitors here are vehicle-shackled; walking even a short distance from the road brings solitude and a possible glimpse of bighorn sheep and pronghorn antelope. The 66-mile dirt track **Steens Mountain Loop Road,** open July to Septem-ber, climbs the west slope from Rte. 205 near Frenchglen, rejoining the highway 8 miles farther south. The route passes four **campgrounds: Page Springs** at the north entrance, accessible when the loop is closed; **Jackman Park,** 19 mi. in and nearly 1½ mi. up, with six mountainside campsites, pit toilets, water, and fire pits ($6); **Fish Lake,** 3 mi. farther east, with a boat ramp, with 23 sites ($6); and **South Steens,** a few miles farther along, with 21 sites and 15 equestrian sites ($6). Some of the best **fishing and hiking** is on the mountain's steep east face. One popular trail follows a decrepit logging road by **Pike Creek.** Alongside the road to Albert, a line of lush trees indicates a creek near the **Alvord Hot Springs,** easy to miss in a tin shack on the right side of the road, 25 mi. north of Fields. The mineral-rich bath emerges from the ground into an open pool at a scalding 174°F, but the enclosed pool is much cooler. About 20 mi. farther north, **Mann Lake** is home to excellent fishing and a free primitive campsite. Contact the Burns District BLM for road info and advice, and get **maps** and more tips at the **Frenchglen Hotel.**

Winding its way from Nevada through the Alvord Desert and up Steens Moun-tain, the **Desert Trail** will eventually run from Mexico to Canada, and promises beautifully desolate exploration. **Trail guides** and info are available from the Desert Trail Association (541-475-2960) or the Hike Chairman, P.O. Box 34, Madras 97741.

LAKEVIEW AND FREMONT NATIONAL FOREST

The incentives to visit friendly, dusty Lakeview (what with the lake having dried up) may seem few, but are, in fact, two. High buttes with unusually strong updrafts have transformed this innocuous town into the Hanggliding Capital of the west. Especially lucky and daring visitors may be able to hitch a tandem ride. Those hap-pily on the ground are even closer to vast Fremont National Forest.

Lakeview lies 15 mi. north of California, at the junction of Hwy. 140 and Hwy. 395. **Red Ball Stage Lines,** 619 Center St. (884-6460), runs three buses per day to Kla-math Falls ($17). **Ford,** 351 North O St. (947-4965) sometimes **rents cars. Visitor infor-mation:** 126 North E St. (947-6040; open daily 8am-6pm; in winter M-F 8am-5pm). Call the ranger for **outdoor information** (947-3334; www.fs.fed.us/r6/freemont). **Police:** 245 North F St. (947-2504) **Crisis line:** 947-2449, 24hr. **Post office:** 18 South G St., 97630 (open M-F 9:30am-5pm). **Area code:** 541.

The **Lakeview Lodge Motel,** 301 North G St. (947-2181), has friendly management, elegant rooms, an exercise room, sauna, and hot tubs (singles $40, doubles $44; kitchenettes $4 extra). Farther from town lies the **Rim Rock Motel,** 727 South F St.

(947-2185), with spare but adequate rooms (singles $30, doubles $32). Popular **Goose Lake Campground,** 11 mi. south of Lakeview on Rte. 395, has hot showers ($2 for non-campers) and quiet sites with little privacy (hookups and tent sites $13). The ranger rents **cabins** ($25, sleeps 4, propane stoves), two accessible by car and two by foot, and can direct you to free **campgrounds** in the forest. **Dog Lake,** one of the closest, is 30 minutes from Lakeview on Lake Rd., beside an excellent year-round bass and trout fishing spot (8 sites; pit toilets).

Buy fishsticks and mayo at **Safeway,** 244 North F St. (947-2324), which glistens under a giant cowboy (open daily 7am-11pm). Popular **Indian Village,** 508 North 1st St. (947-2833), is decorated with artifacts gathered before gathering such things was illegal. (Buffalo burger $5.50. Open daily 5am-9pm.) **Happy Horse,** 510 Center St. (947-4996), serves sandwiches ($4.50) at light speed (open M-F 9am-5pm).

Fremont National Forest provides a multitude of opportunities for hiking, fishing, canoeing, and cross-country skiing. **Hiking** in the forest is generally moderate, though weather can quickly change. One of the most popular trails is the **Blue Lake/Palisades Rocks Trail,** which runs through the Gearhart Mountain Wilderness. Silver Creek Marsh provides access to the **Fremont National Recreation Trail. Fishing** and camping is great at Mud Creek. **Permits** are available at **Lakeview Boot and Shoe Repair and Sporting Goods**, 221 North F Ave. (947-4486), opposite Safeway ($8.25 per day, $35 per week; open M-Sa 9am-5:30pm). Two State Sno-parks in the forest require parking permits, available at the ranger's office. **Warner Canyon** has downhill and cross-country trails and backcountry snowshoe areas. The frigid warm to the geothermal **hot springs** near Lakeview. See the ranger for trail details.

EASTERN OREGON

WESTERN WASHINGTON

On Washington's western shore, the cosmopolitan entertainment found in concert halls and art galleries bejewel a peninsula within easy reach of Puget Sound, its many islands, and the Olympic Peninsula, home to the world's only temperate rainforests. Seattle contains the homes of coffee, grunge, and Microsoft among its hilly neighborhoods, fantastic parks, and miles of waterfront. The lush San Juan Islands are home to great horned owls, puffins, sea otters, sea lions. Pods of orcas circle the islands, followed by pods of tourists in yachts and kayaks. Vashon Island, even nearer to Seattle, is a beautiful, less touristed, and arty retreat. Due west of the Emerald City, Olympic National Park is a remote backdrop for settlements and reservations where fishing and logging support a small local population. Stunning sights await within and beyond the park's boundaries. At Neah Bay, an hour from the rainforests of the park's western rim, an ancient Makah settlement buried in a landslide has earned it the nickname "Pompeii of the Pacific."

What is now Washington was home to only some 400 settlers when Oregonians rallied for territorial recognition in the 1840s. The populous indigenous nations of the coast and plains still outnumbered the newcomers even when Washington was made a territory in 1853 (encompassing much present-day of Idaho and Montana) Ten years later, then home to 4000 settlers who had journeyed along the Oregon Trail for the promise of arable land, the state attained roughly its present shape. Washington did not become a state until 1889. Over the 20th century, the development of the state's communities was heavily dependent on the course of railroads linking the west with the east. During World War II, Seattle's resource-driven economy was transformed by the nation's needs for ships and aircraft. The industry of their production remains vital to the state's economy.

Buses cover most of Washington, though navigating the Olympic Peninsula requires some dexterity with a patchwork of county schedules. The train from Los Angeles to Vancouver makes many stops in western Washington; another line extends from Seattle to Spokane and on to Chicago.

HIGHLIGHTS OF WESTERN WASHINGTON

■ The **Seattle Art Museum** (see p. 164) and the neighborhood of **Fremont** (see p. 161) are cultural oases; **Gasworks Park** sees industry quieted in the city (p. 167).

■ The grave of **Chief Sealth** (see p. 180) powerfully commemorates one of the region's celebrated Native American leaders.

■ The **Mt. Baker Highway** (see p. 189) leads past stunning scenery, with excellent opportunities for hiking and winter sports all along the way.

■ The **Whale Museum** (see p. 193) tells all about **orcas**, while the most promising places to spot them are **San Juan County Park** (see p. 192) and **Lime Kiln State Park** (see p. 193).

■ **Olympic National Park** (see p. 202) contains **Hoh Rainforest** (see p. 209) and the moonscapes of **Ozette beaches** (see p. 210).

■ Take part in **Centrum's** fantastic program of summer festivals (see p. 200) and simply take in **Port Townsend** (see p. 197), a Victorian enclave at the northwest's most west.

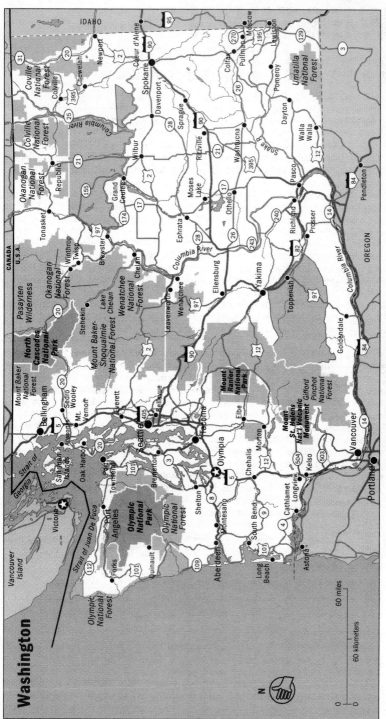

WESTERN WASHINGTON

SEATTLE

Seattle's serendipitous mix of mountain views, clean streets, espresso stands, and rainy weather has proved to be the magic formula of the 1990s, attracting transplants from across the U.S. It seems that everyone living here was born elsewhere. Newcomers arrive in droves, armed with college degrees and California license plates, hoping for computer-industry jobs and a different lifestyle; Seattle duly blesses them with a magnificent setting and a thriving artistic community. The city is one of the youngest and most vibrant in the nation, and a nearly epidemic fascination with coffee has also made it one of the most caffeinated.

The Emerald City sits on an isthmus, with mountain ranges to the east and west. Every hilltop in Seattle offers an impressive view of Mt. Olympus, Mt. Baker, and Mt. Rainier: when the skies clear, Seattleites rejoice that "the mountain is out," and head for the country. To the west, the waters of Puget Sound glint against downtown skyscrapers and nearly spotless streets.

Although daytrips beckon in any direction, the city's nine neighborhood hills beg for exploration. Plan to get wet and bag the umbrella, a tool that only outsiders use. The city's artistic landscape is as varied and exciting as its physical terrain. Opera always sell out, and the *New York Times* has complained that there is more good theater in Seattle than on Broadway. When Nirvana introduced the world to their discordant sensibility, the term "grunge" and Seattle became temporarily inseparable, and the city that produced Jimi Hendrix again revitalized rock and roll. Good bands remain in grunge's wake, keeping the Seattle scene a mecca for edgy entertainment. Even Seattle entrepreneurs are keeping the world edgy. Bill Gates of Microsoft and Howard Shultz of Starbucks have built vast and perhaps only marginally evil empires out of software and coffee beans.

✳ ORIENTATION

Seattle is a long, skinny city, stretching from north to south on an isthmus between **Puget Sound** to the west and **Lake Washington** to the east, linked by locks and canals. The city is easily accessible by car via **I-5,** which runs north-south through the city and by **I-90** from the east, which ends at I-5 southeast of downtown. From I-5, get to **downtown** (including **Pioneer Square, Pike Place Market,** and the **waterfront**) by taking any of the exits from James St. to Stewart St. Take the Mercer St./Fairview Ave. exit to the **Seattle Center;** follow signs from here. The Denny Way exit leads to **Capitol Hill,** and, farther north, the 45th St. exit heads toward the **University District.** The less crowded **Rte. 99,** also called **Aurora Ave.** or the Aurora Hwy., runs parallel to I-5 and skirts the western side of downtown, with great views from the Alaskan Way Viaduct. Route 99 is often the better choice when driving downtown, or to **Queen Anne, Fremont, Green Lake,** and the northwestern part of the city. For more detailed directions to these and other districts, see the individualized neighborhood listings under **Food** (p. 161), **Nightlife** (p. 171), and **Sights** (p. 164).

▐ GETTING AROUND

Though navigating through Seattle can seem daunting at first glance, even the most road-weary drivers can learn their way around the Emerald City like so many singing munchkins. Downtown, **avenues** run northwest to southeast, and **streets** run southwest to northeast. Outside downtown, everything is simplified: with few exceptions, avenues run north-south and streets east-west. The city is split into **quadrants:** 1000 1st Ave. NW is a long walk from 1000 1st Ave. SE.

When driving in Seattle, **yield to pedestrians.** Not only do locals drive slowly, calmly, and politely, but police ticket frequently. **Jaywalking** pedestrians rack up $66. Even sitting on the sidewalk will cost you $50. Downtown driving can be nightmarish; parking is expensive, hills are steep, and one-way streets are ubiquitous. **Parking** is reasonable, plentiful, and well-lit at **Pacific Place Parking** (652-0416)

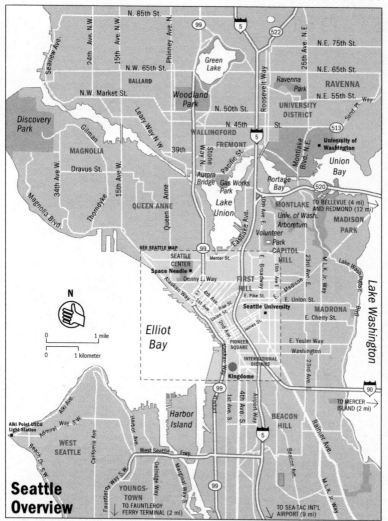

Seattle
Overview

between 6th and 7th Ave. and Olive and Pine St., with hourly rates comparable to the meters (24hr.; $2 per hr.), and at **Seattle Center,** near the Space Needle. Park there and take the monorail to the convenient **Westlake Center** downtown (every 15min. 9am-11pm; $1, ages 5-12 75¢). The **Metro ride free zone** includes most of downtown Seattle (see **Public Transportation,** below). **Metro** covers King County east to North Bend and Carnation, south to Enumclaw, and north to Snohomish County, where bus #6 hooks up with **Community Transit.** This line runs to Everett, Stanwood, and well into the Cascades. Metro bus #174 connects to Tacoma's Pierce County System at Federal Way.

Seattle is a **bicycle-friendly** city. All buses have free, easy-to-use bike racks. (Bike shops have sample racks on which novices can practice.) Between 6am and 7pm, bikes may only be loaded or unloaded at stops before the borders of the ride free zone, not in the zone itself. Check out Metro's *Bike & Ride* pamphlet, available at the visitor center and the hostel. For a bicycle map of Seattle, call the **City of Seattle Bicycle Program** (684-7583).

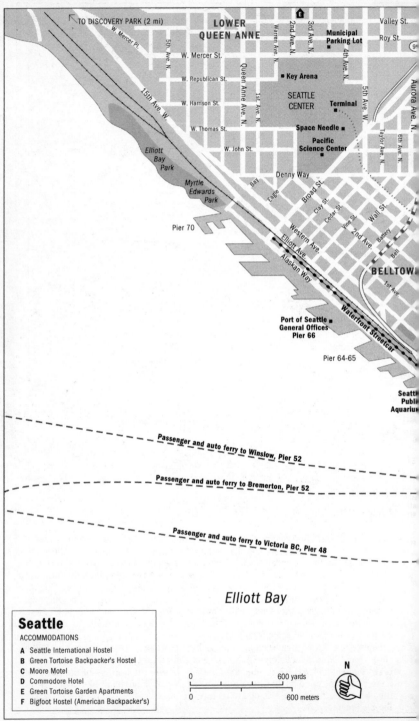

TO DISCOVERY PARK (2 mi)

W. Mercer Pl.

LOWER
QUEEN ANNE

Valley St.

Roy St.

Municipal
Parking Lot

W. Mercer St.

W. Republican St.

■ Key Arena

W. Harrison St.

SEATTLE
CENTER

Terminal

W. Thomas St.

Space Needle ■

W. John St.

Pacific
Science Center
■

Elliott
Bay
Park

Myrtle
Edwards
Park

Denny Way

Pier 70

Western Ave.

Elliott Ave.

Alaskan Way

Port of Seattle
General Offices
Pier 66 ■

Waterfront Streetcar

BELLTOWN

Pier 64-65

Seattle
Public
Aquarium

Passenger and auto ferry to Winslow, Pier 52

Passenger and auto ferry to Bremerton, Pier 52

Passenger and auto ferry to Victoria BC, Pier 48

Elliott Bay

Seattle

ACCOMMODATIONS

A Seattle International Hostel
B Green Tortoise Backpacker's Hostel
C Moore Motel
D Commodore Hotel
E Green Tortoise Garden Apartments
F Bigfoot Hostel (American Backpacker's)

0 ——————— 600 yards
0 ——————— 600 meters

N

TO
LAKE UNION

TO CAPITOL HILL AND
VOLUNTEER PARK (800 yds)
E. Roy St.

E. Harrison St.

E. Thomas St.

Westlake Ave. N.
9th Ave. N.
8th Ave. N.
Terry Ave. N.
Boren Ave. N.
Fairview Ave. N.

Republican St.

Harrison St.

Minor
Yale

John St.

Denny
Park

Denny Way

Denny Way

REI/National
Park Information ℹ

9th Ave.

Blanchard

7th Ave.

orail

5th Ave.

4th Ave.

Virginia St.

Stewart St.

Howell St.

Yale (tunnel)

Olive Way

Pine St.

Greyhound 🚌

State Convention
and Trade Center

Terminal ■

C

B

Pike St.

PIKE PLACE
MARKET

A

Union St.

University St.

✉

Spring St.

Seattle
Art Museum

Public
Library

2nd Ave.

Post Ave.

3rd Ave.

Marion St.

4th Ave.

5th Ave.

Western Ave.

99

6

54

⚓

washington
ate Ferry
erminal

Alaskan Way S.

Underground
■ Tours

PIONEER
SQUARE   Yesler Way

Klondike Gold Rush
National History Museum ■

Pier 48

er 46

E. Marginal Way S.

Alaskan Freeway

1st Ave. S.

99

Occidental Ave.

Kingdome
Stadium

4th Ave. S.

S. Royal Brougham Way

Eastlake Ave. E.

Melrose Ave.

5

Bellevue Ave. E.
Summit Ave. E.
Belmont Ave. E.
Boylston Ave. E.
Harvard Ave. E.

Broadway East

Harvard Ave. E.

12th Ave. E.
13th Ave. E.
14th Ave. E.

Malden

15th Ave. E.

E. Olive Way

E. Denny Way

F

E. John St.

E. Howell St.

E. Olive St.

E. Pine St.

E. Howell St.

E. Olive St.

Broadway
Playfield

E. Pine St.

Bellevue Ave.

E. Pike St.

E. Union St.

E. Union St.

E. Madison St.

Boren Ave.

Minor Ave.

Terry Ave.

Seneca St.

Hubbell St.

Freeway
Park

9th Ave.

8th Ave.

7th Ave.

6th Ave.

Madison St.

Marion St.

Columbia St.

Cherry St.

James St.

Jefferson St.

Alder St.

FIRST
HILL

✚

✚

12th Ave.

Broadway

E. Spring St.

E. Marion St.

E. Columbia St.

E. Cherry St.

E. Jefferson St.

E. Terrace

Alder St.

E. Spruce St.

E. Fir St.

E. Yesler Way

✚

ℹ

Smith
Tower

6th Ave. S.

S. Washington St.

S. Main St.

King Street
Station

Union
Station

Maynard

🏛 Wing Luke
Asian American Museum

S. Jackson St.

S. King St.

S. King St.

S. Weller St.

S. Weller St.

8th Ave. S.

5

S. Lane St.

INTERNATIONAL
DISTRICT   S. Dearborn St.

Charles St.

S. Dearborn St.

12th Ave. S.

Corwin
S.

Gol Dr. S.

▸ PRACTICAL INFORMATION

TRANSPORTATION

Airplanes: Seattle-Tacoma International (Sea-Tac) (431-4444), on Federal Way, is 30-50min. south of Seattle. Bus #194 departs the underground tunnel at University St. & 3rd Ave. (30min., every 20-35 min., 5:26am-8:44pm) and #174 departs Union & 2nd Ave. (45 min., every 15-30 min., 5:24am-3:30am) for the airport. These routes leave from the airport for Seattle outside baggage claim (every 15 min. 4:47am-2:43am).

Trains: Amtrak (800-USA-RAIL/872-7245, arrival/departure times 382-4125), King St. Station, at 3rd and Jackson St., 1 block east of Pioneer Square next to the Kingdome. To: Portland, OR (4 per day, $30); Tacoma (4 per day, $11); Spokane (2 per day, $50; bus $25); San Francisco, CA (1 per day, $130); Vancouver, BC (1 per day, $30). See p. 52 for discounts. Ticket office and station open daily 6:15am-8pm.

Buses: Greyhound (628-5526 or 800-231-2222), at 8th Ave. and Stewart St. To: Spokane (6 per day, $27); Vancouver, BC (8 per day, $20); Portland, OR (12 per day, $20); Tacoma (8 per day, $5). Try to avoid late buses, since the station can get seedy after dark. Ticket office open daily 6:30am-2:30am. **Quick Shuttle** (604-940-4428 or 800-665-2122; www.quickcoach.com) makes 8 trips daily from Seattle (Travelodge hotel at 8th and Bell St.), the Sea-Tac airport, and Bellingham, WA, to the Vancouver, BC, airport and the Sandman Inn on Granville St. in downtown Vancouver (3-3½hr., $32). **Green Tortoise Bus Service** (800-867-8647; www.greentortoise.com) departs 9th Ave. and Stewart St. on Th and Su at 8am. Cushioned seats fold down into beds at night on this bus-turned-lounge that stops for barbecues and saunas. To: Portland, OR (4½hr., $15); Eugene, OR (7½hr., $25); Berkeley, CA (24hr., $59); San Francisco, CA (25hr., $59); Los Angeles, CA (overnight in San Francisco, 2 days, Th only, $79). Reserve 5 days in advance, or drop by the Seattle hostel and ask for openings.

Ferries: Washington State Ferries (800-84-FERRY/843-3779 or 206-464-6400; www.wsdot.wa.gov/ferries), Colman Dock, Pier 52, downtown. Service from **downtown** to: Bainbridge Island (35min.); Bremerton on the Kitsap Peninsula (1hr.); Vashon Island (25min.; no Su service; passengers only). To reach the **Fauntleroy ferry terminal** in West Seattle, drive south on I-5 and take Exit 163A (West Seattle) down Fauntleroy Way. From Fauntleroy to: Southworth on the Kitsap Peninsula (35min.); Vashon Island (15min.). Passenger ferry round-trip $3.70; June to mid-Oct. car and driver $8.25, off-season $6.50. Most ferries leave daily and frequently 5am-2am. **Victoria Clipper** (800-668-1167; reservations 448-5000) is the only available auto ferry service from Seattle to Victoria. Departs from Pier 48 (4½hr.; daily at 1pm; passengers $29 one-way, seniors $25; car and driver $49; under 12 half-price).

Public Transportation: Metro Transit, Customer Assistance Office, 801 2nd Ave. (553-3000 or 800-542-7876, 24hr.; TTY 689-1739; transit.metrokc.gov), in the Exchange Building downtown, though the bus tunnel under Pine St. and 3rd Ave. is the heart of the downtown bus system. Open M-F 9am-5pm. Fares are based on a 2-zone system. **Zone 1** includes everything within the city limits (peak hours $1.25, off-peak $1). **Zone 2** includes everything else (peak $1.75, off-peak $1.25). Ages 5-18 always 75¢. **Peak hours** in both zones M-F 6-9am and 3-6pm. Exact fare required. Weekend day passes $2. Ride free daily 6am-7pm in the downtown **ride free area,** bordered by S. Jackson St. on the south, 6th Ave. and I-5 on the east, Battery St. on the north, and the waterfront on the west. Free **transfers** can be used on any bus, including a return trip on the same bus within 2hr. These are often necessary, as nearly all routes have to pass through the center of town. All buses have free **bike racks** and most are **wheelchair accessible** (info 689-3113). See **Getting Around** for Metro connections farther afield.

Car Transport: Auto Driveaway (253-850-0800) recruits people to drive their cars to various locations across the U.S. $300 cash deposit. Open M-F 8am-5pm.

Ride Board: 1st floor of the **Husky Union Building** (the HUB), behind Suzallo Library on the University of Washington main campus. Matches cars and riders for any destination, within geographical reason. Also check the board at the **downtown hostel.**

VISITOR AND FINANCIAL SERVICES

Visitor Information: Seattle-King County Visitors Bureau (461-5840), at 8th and Pike St., on the 1st floor of the convention center. Helpful staff doles out maps, brochures, newspapers, and Metro and ferry schedules. Open June-Oct. M-F 8:30am-5pm, Sa-Su 10am-4pm; Nov.-May M-F 8:30am-5pm, Sa 10am-4pm.

Outdoor Information: Seattle Parks and Recreation Department, 100 Dexter St. (684-4075). Open daily 8am-5pm; in winter M-F 8am-5pm. **National Park Service,** 222 Yale Ave. (470-4060), in REI (see **Equipment Rental,** below). Answers questions about camping, hiking and general frolicking in area parks, gives info on discounts and passes, and sells a map of the National Park System ($1.20). Open Tu-F 10:30am-7pm, Sa 9am-7pm, Su 11am-6pm; winter hours may be shortened.

Currency Exchange: Thomas Cook Foreign Exchange, 400 Pine St. (682-4525), on the 3rd floor of the Westlake Shopping Center. Open M-Sa 9:30am-6pm, Su 11am-5pm. Also behind the Delta Airlines ticket counter and at other airport locations.

Travel Agencies: Council Travel, 424 Broadway Ave. E (329-4567) in Capitol Hill. Open M-F 10am-6pm, Sa 11am-3pm. **STA Travel,** 4341 University Way (633-5000; www.statravel.com) at NE 45th. Open M-F 9:30am-5:30pm, Sa 10am-4pm.

LOCAL SERVICES

Equipment Rental: REI, 222 Yale Ave. (223-1944 or 888-873-1938), near Capitol Hill. The mothership of camping supply stores. See to believe. (More at **Outdoors,** p. 168). Open M-F 10am-9pm, Sa 9am-7pm, Su 11am-6pm. **The Bicycle Center,** 4529 Sand Point Way (523-8300), near the Children's Hospital. Rents bikes ($3 per hr., $15 per day; 2hr. min.). Credit card or license deposit required. Open M-F 10am-8pm, Sa 10am-6pm, Su 10am-5pm. **Gregg's Greenlake Cycle,** 7007 Woodlawn Ave. NE (523-1822). Pricey, but close to Green Lake and Burke-Gilman bike trails ($15-20 per day, $25-30 per 24hr.). Photo ID and cash or credit card deposit required. Also rents in-line skates. Open M-F 9:30am-9pm, Sa-Su 9:30am-6pm.

Bookstores: See p. 171.

Library: Seattle Public Library, 1000 4th Ave. (386-4636, TDD 386-4697). A visitor's library card lasts 3 months ($8). Free 90min. Internet access with photo ID. Open M-Th 9am-9pm, F-Sa 9am-6pm, Su 1-5pm.

Women's Services: University of Washington Women's Information Center (685-1090), Cunningham Hall, in the main campus. Community resource and referral for women's groups throughout the Seattle area. Open M-F 9am-5pm.

Senior Services: 1601 2nd Ave. #800 (448-3110). Open M-F 9am-5pm.

Gay and Lesbian Services: 1820 E. Pine (323-0220 or 800-527-7683). Open M-F 3-9pm. **Lesbian Resource Center,** 2214 S. Jackson St. (264-4409; www.lrc.net), at 23rd St. Support groups, drop-ins, library, workshops. Open Tu-F noon-7pm, Su noon-5pm. **AIDS Information,** 400 Yesler Way, 3rd. fl. (205-7837). Open M-F 9am-5pm.

Ticket Agencies: Ticketmaster (628-0888 or 292-2787) does its thing in Westlake Center and every Tower Records store. **Ticket/Ticket,** 401 Broadway E (324-2744), on the 2nd floor of the Broadway Market, sells half-price day-of-show tickets to tours and local performances. Cash only purchases in person. Open Tu-Sa 10am-7pm, Su noon-6pm. Also in the Pike Place Market. Open Tu-Su noon-6pm.

Laundromat: Sit and Spin, 2219 4th St. (441-9484). A laundromat local hot spot (see **Nightlife,** p. 173). Wash $1.25, dry 25¢ per 15min. Open Su-Th 9am-midnight, F-Sa 9am-2am. **University Maytag,** 4733 University Way (526-7234), is cheaper. Internet access $6 per hr. Open daily 7am-11pm.

EMERGENCY AND COMMUNICATIONS

Emergency: 911. **Police:** 610 3rd Ave. (583-2111).

Crisis Line: 461-3222. **Rape Crisis: King County Sexual Assault Center** (800-825-7273). Crisis counseling and advocacy. **Harborview Medical** (521-1800) 24hr. **Alcohol/Drug Help Line:** 722-3700. 24hr.

Travelers' Aid: 1100 Virginia, Suite 210 (461-3888), at Boren St. Free services for travelers who have lost their wallets or marbles. Open M-F 9am-4pm.

Medical Services: International District Emergency Center (623-3321). Medics with multilingual assistance available 24hr. **Aradia Women's Health Center,** 1300 Spring St. (323-9388). Staff will refer elsewhere when overbooked. Open M-F 10am-4pm. **Health South Medical Center,** 1151 Denny Way (682-7418). Walk-in. **Providence Medical Center,** 500 17th Ave. (320-2111) for urgent care and cardiac. 24 hr.

Post Office: (800-275-8777), at Union St. and 3rd Ave. downtown. Open M-F 8am-5:30pm. General delivery window open M-F 10am-noon, 1pm-3pm. **ZIP Code:** 98101.

Internet Access: See **Library,** above. Every third cafe around Seattle charges $6 per hr., as does **Capitol Hill Net,** 219 Broadway #22 (860-6858), but here *Let's Go* readers get 15min. free. Open daily 9am-midnight.

Area Code: 206.

PUBLICATIONS

The city's major daily, the *Seattle Times* (464-2111; www.seattletimes.com), lists upcoming events in its Thursday "Datebook" section. The morning *Seattle Post-Intelligencer* is good for wrapping fish. The Thursday listings of the *Seattle Weekly* (www.seattleweekly.com) are free and left-of-center. Even farther over is *The Stranger,* which covers music and culture, materializing Thursdays at music, coffee, and thrift shops. *The Rocket* also covers events outside Seattle. *Arts Focus,* free at most bookstores, covers performing arts, while *Seattle Arts,* published by the Seattle Arts Commission, is especially good on visual arts. Both are monthlies. The weekly *Seattle Gay News* sells on Fridays at newsstands (25¢).

▛ ACCOMMODATIONS

Seattle's hostel scene is alive, friendly, and clean. Those tired of urban high-rises can head for the **Vashon Island Hostel** (see p. 178). **Pacific Lodging Association** (784-0539) arranges B&B singles in the $55-65 range (open M-F 9am-5pm).

DOWNTOWN

Green Tortoise Backpacker's Hostel, 1525 2nd Ave. (340-1222; fax 623-3207; www.greentortoise.com), between Pike and Pine St. Pick-up available from Amtrak, Greyhound or ferry terminal; on the #174 or 194 bus route. A young party hostel downtown. Often free beer F and Tu; pub crawls W. Laundry, kitchen, and free Internet access. 150 beds in 48 rooms: $17, $16 with cash, HI or ISIC card. 10 private rooms: $40. $20 key deposit required. Linens $1 with $9 deposit. Continental breakfast. 24 hr.

Seattle International Hostel (HI), 84 Union St. (622-5443 or 888-622-5443; www.adhost.com/hi-seattle/itd/itd.html), at Western Ave., right by the waterfront. Walk west/northwest from the airport bus stops in downtown; head down the stairs under the "Pike Pub & Brewery." The common room overlooks the water, just off a TV lounge. 199 beds, 6-10 per room: $17, nonmembers $20; private rooms sleep 2-3 $41, nonmembers $47. Coin laundry. Ride board. Internet access $6 per hr. Discount tickets for the aquarium, Omnidome, Museum of Flight and passenger ferry. 7-night max. stay in summer. Reception 7am-2am. Check-out 11am. No curfew. Reservations are wise.

Moore Motel, 1926 2nd Ave. (448-4851 or 800-421-5508; www.moorehotel.com), at Virginia, 1 block east from Pike Place Market, next to historic Moore Theater. The open lobby, cavernous halls, and heavy wooden doors send the Moore to the 20s. Big rooms with 2 beds, TV, private bath; some with kitchens. Singles $38, with bath $43; doubles $44, with bath $49. One shower per floor. HI member discount 15%.

Commodore Hotel, 2013 2nd Ave. (448-8868), at Virginia. On the #174 bus route. Many rooms have pleasant decor and walnut furniture (with a few broken baseboards). Not the best area of downtown, but 24hr. security keeps out the riff-raff. Singles $42, with bath $52; 2 beds and bath $68. 2 hostel-style rooms have bare-bones bunks and shared bath ($14), but you need an HI card to snag a spot. Weekly single $134.

QUEEN ANNE

Green Tortoise Garden Apartments, 715 2nd Ave. N (340-1222; fax 623-3207), on the south slope of Queen Anne Hill, 3 blocks east from the Space Needle and the Seattle Center. Long-term accommodations for travelers staying over 7 days. Back yard, kitchens, garden, laundry, free breakfast. Beds $80 per week or $220 per month, with 4 people per room. $50 deposit. Applications available at the Green Tortoise Hostel.

CAPITOL HILL

Bigfoot Hostel (American Backpacker's), 126 Broadway Ave. E. (720-2965 or 800-600-2965; bfbphostel.webjump.com). From Broadway, follow Olive Way east, taking the first right. Free pick-up from Greyhound, Amtrak or downtown. An alternative to the big hostels with paintings of Washington. 40 beds: $16, $14 winter, $0.50 off with ISIC/HI card; $10 key deposit. Free kitchen, linens, laundry, pool table, Internet, parking, breakfast, and beer on Friday. Reception 7am-3am. Quiet hours after 11pm.

UNIVERSITY DISTRICT

The College Inn, 4000 University Way NE (633-4441; www.speakeasy.org/collegeinn), at NE 40th St. A quiet place near the UW campus and its youthful environs. Rooms are tiny, but the turn-of-the-century bureaus and brass fixtures are s'durned *charming*. The kitchen is nestled in the 4th floor attic, where a complimentary breakfast materializes every morning. Singles $45-60; doubles $70-82. Credit card required.

FREMONT

For inexpensive motels farther from downtown, drive north on Hwy. 99 (Aurora Ave.) or take bus #26 to the neighborhood of Fremont. Budget chain motels like the **Nites Inn,** 11746 Huron Ave. N (365-3216), line the highway north of the Aurora bridge (rooms from $45, doubles $50). Look for AAA approval for a secure night.

♻ FOOD

Though Seattleites appear to subsist solely on espresso and steamed milk, they eat sometimes. When they do, they seek out healthy cuisine, especially seafood. The finest fish, produce, and baked goods are at **Pike Place Market** (see below). The **University District** supports inexpensive and international cuisine. **Puget Sound Consumer Coops (PCCs)** are at 6518 Fremont Ave. N, in Green Lake, and at 6504 20th NE, in the Ravenna District north of the university. Capitol Hill, the U District, and Fremont close main thoroughfares on summer Saturdays for **farmers' markets.**

PIKE PLACE MARKET AND DOWNTOWN

In 1907, angry citizens demanded the elimination of the middle-man and local farmers began selling produce by the waterfront. Not even the Great Depression slowed business, which thrived until disastrous events in the war era: an enormous fire burned the building in 1941, and nearly 300 Japanese-American merchants were interned by the American government. The early 1980s heralded a Pike Place renaissance, and today thousands of tourists mob the market daily (open M-Sa 9am-6pm, Su 11am-5pm; produce and fish open earlier, restaurants and lounges close later). In the **Main Arcade** parallel to the waterfront, on the west side of Pike St., fishmongers compete for audiences and dollars as they hurl fish from shelves to scales. The market's restaurants boast stellar views of the sound.

The best time to shop is when it first opens, though produce is discounted late in the day. Be prepared to fight the masses during lunch. An **information booth** (461-5800; open Tu-Su 10am-noon) faces the bike rack by the Main Arcade, at 1st Ave. and Pike St. Restaurants south of Pike Place cater mostly to suits on lunch breaks and tourists, but there are lots of sandwich shops in the downtown grid.

Soundview Cafe (623-5700), on the mezzanine level in the Pike Place Main Arcade. This self-serve breakfast, sandwich-and-salad bar is a good place to just brown-bag a moment of solace. Open M-F 7am-5pm, Sa 7am-5:30pm, Su 9am-3pm.

Piroshki, Piroshki, 1908 Pike Pl. (441-6068). The Russian Piroshki is a croissant-like dough baked around sausages, mushrooms, apples doused in cinnamon... ($3-3.50). Watch the piroshki process in progress while awaiting your order. Open daily 8am-7pm.

Delcambre's Ragin' Cajun, 1523 1st Ave. (624-2598), near Pike Place. A tremendous portion of spicy red beans with *andouille* (a kind of sausage) was enjoyed by President Clinton in 1995. Lunch $6-8. Open M-Sa 11am-3pm and Th-Sa 5:30-9pm.

Three Girls Bakery, 1514 Pike Pl. (622-1045), at Post. Blissfully large portions. Pastries, 3 kinds of rye $1.50-3.50, and sandwiches around $4. Open daily 6:30am-6pm.

THE WATERFRONT

Budget eaters, beware of Pioneer Square: take a picnic instead to **Waterfall Garden,** on the corner of S. Main St. and 2nd Ave. S.

Mae Phim Thai Restaurant, 94 Columbia St. (624-2979), a few blocks north of Pioneer Sq. between 1st Ave. and Alaskan Way. This good, inexpensive take-out joint supplies a feast of *pad thai* for the Square. All dishes $4.60. Open M-F 11am-7pm, Sa noon-7pm.

Ivar's Fish Bar, Pier 54 (624-6852), north of the square, is named for late Seattle shipping magnate Ivar Haglund. Enjoy the definitive Seattle clam chowder ($1.90) in an outdoor booth to hide from the namesake tourist traps. Open daily 11am-2am.

INTERNATIONAL DISTRICT

Along King and Jackson St., between 5th and 8th Ave. east of the Kingdome, Seattle's International District is packed with great eateries. Competition keeps prices low and quality high, and unassuming facades front fabulous food. **Uwajimaya,** 519 6th Ave. S (624-6248), is the largest East Asian retail store in the northwest; take bus #7. Japanese staples, fresh seafood, dried foods, a sushi bar, and ceramic dishware, and toys, books, clothes, and jewelry make this a Seattle institution (open daily 9am-8pm; in summer until 9pm).

Tai Tung, 655 S. King St. (622-7372). A Chinese diner where waiters are likely to learn your name by the second night. The 10-page, ever-changing menu is plastered to the walls. Entrees $6.25-11. Open Su-Th 10am-11:30pm, F-Sa 10am-1:30am.

Ho Ho Seafood Restaurant, 653 S. Weller St. (382-9671). Generous portions of tank-fresh seafood. Lunch $5-7, dinner $7-10. Open Su-Th 11am-1am, F-Sa 11am-3am.

Viet My Restaurant, 129 Prefontaine Pl. S. (382-9923), near 4th and Washington St. Consistently delicious Vietnamese food at great prices. Open M-F 11am-9pm.

CAPITOL HILL

With bronze dance-steps on the sidewalks and neon storefronts, **Broadway** is a land of espresso houses, imaginative shops, elegant clubs, and some of the city's best eats; here, even the yuppies have nose rings. Bus #7 runs along Broadway; bus #10 runs through Capitol Hill along more sedate **15th St.** Free parking awaits behind the reservoir at Broadway Field, on 11th Ave.

Bimbo's Bitchin' Burrito Kitchen, 506 E. Pine (329-9978). The name explains it. Spicy Bimbo's basic burrito $3.75. Open M-Th noon-11pm, F-Sa noon-2am, Su 2-10pm.

Caffe Minnie's, 611 Broadway E (860-1360). The original Caffe Minnie (448-6263), at 1st and Denny Way, was named for the anticipated rush when rumors had Disney buying the Seattle Center. Famous tomato basil soup ($4). Both open 24hr.

HaNa, 219 Broadway Ave. E (328-1187). Packed quarters testify to the popularity of the sushi here. Large tempura lunch $6.25. Open M-Sa 11am-10pm, Su 4-10pm.

UNIVERSITY DISTRICT

The neighborhood around the immense University of Washington ("U-Dub"), north of downtown between Union Bay and Portage Bay, supports funky shops, international restaurants, and coffeehouses. The best of each lies within a few blocks of University Way, known as "Th' Ave." To get there, take exit 169 off I-5 N, or take one of buses #70-74 from downtown, or #7 or 9 from Capitol Hill.

Ruby, 4241 University Way NE (675-1770). Dimly lit, with antique mirrors and oriental rugs. Incredible Pan-Asian dishes, like the filling Thai green curry rice bowl ($6.50). Open M-W 11am-11pm, Th-Sa 11am-11:30pm, Su 1-11pm.

Flowers, 4247 University Way NE (633-1903). This 20s landmark was a flower shop. The mirrored ceiling tastefully frames an all-you-can-eat Mediterranean buffet ($6.50). Open M-Sa 11am-2am; kitchen closes at 10pm, but late night snacks go on.

Pizzeria Pagliacci, 4529 University Way NE (632-0421; 726-1717 for delivery), also on Capitol Hill at 426 Broadway Ave. E (323-7987). Seattle's best pizza since 1986. Slices $1.44-2.45. Open Su-Th 11am-11pm, F-Sa 11am-1am.

Tandoor Restaurant, 5024 University Way NE (523-7477). The lunch buffet ($5) is a great deal, as is Sunday brunch ($6). Dinner is more expensive. Grab a cushion on a back-room bench. Open M-Sa 11am-2:30pm and 4:30-10pm, Su 11am-3pm.

▚ CAFES AND COFFEEHOUSES

The coffee bean is Seattle's first love. One cannot walk a single block without passing an institution of caffeination. The Emerald City's obsession with Italian-style espresso drinks has gas stations pumping thick, dark, soupy java.

CAPITOL HILL

Bauhaus, 305 E. Pine St. (625-1600). In the city where *Wallpaper* is the Bible, something like this had to happen. An enormous portrait of Walter Gropius oversees service of drip coffee (87¢) or Kool-Aid (92¢). Open M-F 6am-1am, Sa-Su 8am-1am.

The Globe Cafe, 1531 14th Ave. (324-8815). Seattle's next literary renaissance is brewing here. All-vegan menu. Internet access $6 per hr. Open Tu-Su 7am-7pm.

WESTERN WASHINGTON

WHAT DOES IT TAKE TO GET A CUP OF COFFEE IN THIS TOWN?

Visiting Seattle without drinking the coffee would be like traveling to France without tasting the wine. Espresso stands line streets and infiltrate office buildings, and "Let's go for coffee sometime" is a powerful local pick-up line. It all started in the early 70s, when Starbucks started roasting its coffee on the spot in Pike Place Market. Soon, Stewart Brothers Coffee, now Seattle's Best Coffee, presented Starbucks with a rival, and the race was on both for the best cuppa joe and for global hegemony. Today, hundreds of bean-brands compete for the local market, and Seattle coffeeholics often claim undying allegiance to one or another. Learning a few basic terms for ordering espresso drinks can only endear you to locals and enrich your cultural experience:

Espresso: The foundation of all espresso drinks—a small amount of coffee brewed by forcing steam through finely ground, dark-roasted coffee (pronounced es-PRESS-oh, not ex-PRESS-oh).

Cappuccino: Espresso topped by the foam from steamed milk. Order "wet" for more liquid milk and big bubbles, or "dry" for stiff foam.

Latte: Espresso with steamed milk and a little foam. More liquid than a capp.

Americano: Espresso with hot water—an alternative to classic drip coffee.

Macciato: A cup of coffee with a dollop of foam, and a bit of espresso swirled onto the foam.

Short: 8 oz. **Tall:** 12 oz. **Grande (or Large):** 16 oz.

Single: One shot of espresso. **Double:** Two singles. Add shots (usually about 60¢) until you feel you've reached your caffeine saturation point. Triples are common.

Behind the counter you may hear skim (nonfat) milk drinks called **skinnies.** If all you want is a plain ol' coffee, say **"drip coffee"**—otherwise, cafe workers will return your request for mere "coffee" with a blank stare.

B&O Cafe, 204 Belmont (322-5208), takes its name from the monopoly RR. Breakfast till 4pm. Delicious desserts $5.25. Open M-Th 7am-midnight, F-Sa 8:30am-1am.

Green Cat Cafe, 1514 E. Olive (726-8756), west of Broadway. Sunny yellow walls shine on wonderful vegetarian meals. Open M-F 7am-9pm, Sa 7:30am-9pm, Su 9am-9pm.

UNIVERSITY DISTRICT

Espresso Roma, 4201 Broadway (632-6001), at 42nd. Pleasant patio, when sun abides, and quasi-former-warehouse interior. Open daily 7am-11pm. Internet access $6 per hr.

Last Exit, 5211 University Way NE (528-0522). Inside what may be Seattle's first-ever coffee bar (est. 1967), old hippies watch chessmasters battle it out over dirt-cheap espresso (90¢), breakfast, and lunch. Open Su-Th 9am-midnight, F-Sa 9am-2am.

Ugly Mug, 1309 43rd St. (547-3219), off University Way. Artsy college types get sophisticated like with Ovaltine lattes. Open M-F 7:30am-6pm, Sa 9am-5pm.

◨ SIGHTS

It takes only two frenetic days to get a decent look at most of the city's major sights, since most are within walking distance of one another or the Metro's ride free zone (see p. 158). Seattle taxpayers spend more per capita on the arts than any other Americans, and the investment pays off in unparalleled public art installations throughout the city (self-guided tours begin at the visitor center), plentiful galleries, and the Seattle Asian Art Museum (SAAM). Outside cosmopolitan downtown, Seattle boasts over 300 areas of well-watered greenery (see p. 167).

While ferry travelers enjoy the sight of the city from the water, the finest view of Seattle is a bit of a secret and an exclusively female privilege: the athletic club on the top floor of the **Columbia Tower,** at 201 5th Ave., has a ladies' room with floor-to-ceiling windows that commands a view of the entire city (open M-F 8:30am-4:30pm. $5, students and seniors $3, under 8 free), though the observation deck on the 73rd floor is open to non-members. Views of the city from **Gasworks Park** and **Volunteer Park** are also wonderful.

DOWNTOWN

The new **Seattle Art Museum,** 100 University Way (recording 654-3100, person 654-3255, or TDD 654-3137), near 1st Ave., lives in a grandiose building designed by Philadelphian architect Robert Venturi. Is the giant hammering man out front hammering his way into Seattle's consciousness? "Painting America" will feature the work of Eastman Johnson in 2000. Call for info on classical music (Th 5:30-7:30pm), films, and lectures. Admission is good for the fabulous **Seattle Asian Art Museum** (see p. 166) for a week. (Open Tu-W and F-Su 10am-5pm, Th 10am-9pm. Free tours 12:30, 1, and 2pm; sometimes Th 6:15pm. $7, students and seniors $5, under 12 free; first Th of the month free.) Inside the Museum Plaza Building at 1st Ave., the free **Seattle Art Museum Gallery** displays work by local artists. (Open M-F 11am-5pm, Sa-Su 11am-4pm.)

Beside the Westlake monorail stop, **Westlake Park's** Art Deco brick patterns and surprisingly dry **Wall of Water** is a good place to kick back and listen to steel drums on Pike St., between 4th and 5th Ave. **Pike Place Market** is nearby (see **Food,** above). The **concrete waterfalls** of **Freeway Park,** which straddles I-5 between Pike St. and Spring St., are designed to mimic a natural gorge and block freeway noise.

THE WATERFRONT

The **Pike Place Hillclimb** descends from the south end of Pike Place Market past chic shops and ethnic restaurants to Alaskan Way and the waterfront. (An elevator is available.) The super-popular ◨ **Seattle Aquarium** (386-4330, TTD 386-4322) sits at Pier 59, near Union St. The aquarium's star attraction is an underwater dome, home to harbor seals, fur seals, otters, and others. Touch tanks and costumes delight kids. The world's only aquarium salmon ladder is part of a $1 million salmon exhibit; 11:30am feedings are a sight. (Open daily 10am-7pm; in winter 10am-5pm. $8.25, seniors $7.25, ages 6-18 $5.50, ages 3-5 $3.50.) Next door, the **Omnidome** (622-1868) screens movies such that patrons feel like they are actually **in the movie.** The sound system may scare small children and scar delicate psyches. Now showing: *The Eruption of Mt. St. Helens.* (Films daily 10am-10pm. $7; students, seniors, and ages 6-18 $6; ages 3-5 $5. Second film $2. Aquarium/Omnidome ticket $13.50, seniors and ages 13-18 $11.50, ages 6-13 $9.75, ages 3-5 $6.50.)

You can explore the waterfront by foot or **streetcar.** The 20s-era cars were brought in from Melbourne after Seattle sold its originals to San Francisco as "cable cars," the posers. Streetcars are wheelchair-accessible, and run from the Metro opposite the King St. Station in Pioneer Square north to Pier 70 and Myrtle Edwards Park. (Every 20-30min. M-F 7am-11pm, Sa 8am-11pm, Su 9am-11pm; in winter until 6pm. $1, $1.25 during peak hours. Children 75¢. Weekend or Holiday day pass $2. Under 12 with a paying passenger free on Su. Metro passes accepted.)

THE SEATTLE CENTER

The 1962 World's Fair demanded a Seattle Center to herald the city of the future. It is home to everything from carnival rides to ballet, but Seattleites generally leave the center to tourists and suburbanites, except for concerts and during popular festivals. The center is bordered by Denny Way, W. Mercer St., 1st Ave., and 5th Ave., and has eight gates, each with a model of the Center and a map of its facilities. It is accessible via the **monorail** which departs the third floor of the Westlake Center. (Departs every 15min. M-F 7:30am-11pm, Sa-Su 9am-11pm. $1.25, seniors 50¢, ages 5-12 50¢.) For info about special events and permanent attractions, call 684-8582 for recorded information or 684-7200 for a speaking human. The **Space Needle** (443-2111) is something from another time, and is a useful landmark for the disoriented. It houses an observation tower and a high-end 360° rotating restaurant. ($9, seniors $8, ages 5-12 $4; free with dinner reservations. Some make reservations with no intention of keeping them, the clever miscreants.)

The **Pacific Science Center** (443-2001; www.pacsci.org), near the needle, houses a **laserium** (443-2850) that quakes to rock, plus an immense **IMAX theater** (443-IMAX/ 4629). (Laser shows Tu $3, W-Su $7.50. IMAX shows Th-Su 8pm; $6.75, seniors or ages 3-13 $5.75.) The **Children's Museum** (441-1768), in the Center House, has an abundance of creative hands-on exhibits that will wow any kid (or jealous adult) into a fit of over-stimulation. (Open daily 10am-6pm. $7.50, ages 1-12 $5.50, under 1 free. Combination package of all three $16.50, seniors or ages 3-13 $14.50.)

PIONEER SQUARE AND ENVIRONS

From the waterfront or downtown, it's just a few blocks south to historic **Pioneer Square,** centered around Yesler Way and 2nd Ave., home of the first Seattleites. The 19th-century buildings, restored in the 1970s and now home to chic shops and trendy pubs, retain their historical intrigue and great crowds of tourists.

Originally, downtown stood 12 ft. lower than it does. The **Underground Tour** (682-4646 or 888-608-6337; www.undergroundtour.com) guides visitors through the subterranean city of old. Be prepared for lots of company, comedy, and toilet jokes. Tours depart from Doc Maynard's Pub, 610 1st Ave. (90min. tours daily and roughly hourly 9am-7pm. $8, seniors and students ages 13-17 $7, children $4; AAA, ISIC or military, $6. Reservations recommended.) "Doc" Maynard, a charismatic and colorful early resident, gave a plot of land here to one Henry Yesler to build a steam-powered lumber mill. The logs dragged to the mill's front door earned the street its epithet, **Skid Row,** and the smell of the oil used to lubricate the slide was so overwhelming that the self-respecting Seattleites of the day left the neighborhood to gamblers, prostitutes, flopheads, and other notorious types.

Klondike Gold Rush National Historic Park, 117 S. Main St. (553-7220; www.nps.gov/klse/home.htm), is a spiff interpretive center depicting the lives of miners and Seattle's role in the Klondike gold rush. (Open daily 9am-5pm. Free.)

THE INTERNATIONAL DISTRICT

Seattle's **International District** is 3 blocks east of Pioneer Square, up Jackson on King St. The tiny **Wing Luke Memorial Museum**, 407 7th Ave. S (623-5124), displays a thorough description of life in an Asian-American community, a permanent exhibit on different Asian nationalities in Seattle, and work by local Asian artists. (Open Tu-F 11am-4:30pm, Sa-Su noon-4pm. $2.50, seniors and students $1.50, ages 5-12 75¢. Th free.) Landmarks of the International District include the abstract **Tsutakawa sculpture** at the corner of S. Jackson and Maynard St., and the gigantic dragon mural and red-and-green pagoda in **Hing Hay Park** at S. King and Maynard St. The **community gardens** at Main and Maynard St. provide a well-tended retreat. Free parking spaces are next to the gardens.

CAPITOL HILL

Capitol district's leftist and gay communities set the tone for its nightspots (see p. 172), while the neighborhood supports collectives, radical bookstores, and The Gap. **Broadway** is a center for alternative lifestyles and mainstream capitalism. Bus #7 cruises Broadway, but #10 makes frequent stops along 15th Ave., lined with well-maintained Victorian homes, and passes more of the fun stuff.

Volunteer Park, between 11th and 17th Ave. at E. Ward St., north of the Broadway activity, was named for the veterans of the Spanish-American War. Though it is unsafe (and closed) at night, it is a popular afternoon destination. The **outdoor stage** often hosts free performances on summer Sundays. Scale the **water tower** at the 14th Ave. entrance for a stunning 360° panorama of the city and the Olympic Range. The **glass conservatory** houses dazzling orchids. (Open daily 10am-4pm; in summer 10am-7pm. Free.) The world-renowned ✪ **Seattle Asian Art Museum** (654-3100) displays Ming vases and ancient kimonos. (Open Tu-Su 10am-5pm, Th 10am-9pm. $3, under 12 free; free with SAM ticket, same day.)

North of Volunteer Park on 15th St. is **Lake View Cemetery. Bruce** and **Brandon Lee**, and many founders of Seattle, are buried here. One of the most famous martial artists of the century, Bruce Lee moved to Seattle in his youth; his son Brandon was known for his own formidable skills. Near the top of the cemetery, a row of small evergreen trees are lined behind a bench in their memory.

The ✪ **University of Washington Arboretum**, 10 blocks east of Volunteer Park, nurtures over 4000 species, trees, shrubs, and flowers, and maintains superb walking and running trails; take bus #11 from downtown. Tours depart the **Graham Visitor Center** (543-8800), at the southern end of the arboretum on Lake Washington Blvd. (Open daily sunrise to sunset. Free tours Sa and Su at 1pm.) Across the street, the tranquil 3½-acre **Japanese Tea Garden** (684-4725) is a retreat of sculpted gardens, fruit trees, a reflecting pool, and a traditional tea house. (Open Mar.-Nov. daily 10am-dusk. $2.50, seniors, disabled, students, and ages 6-18 $1.50, under 6 free.)

UNIVERSITY DISTRICT, FREMONT, AND BALLARD

With over 33,000 students, the **University of Washington** comprises the state's educational center of gravity. The U District swarms with students year-round, and Seattleites of all ages take advantage of the area's many bohemian bookstores, shops, taverns, and restaurants. Looming gothic gargoyles, lecture halls, red brick, and rose gardens make the campus a bower fit for hours of strolling. To get there, take buses #71-73 from downtown, or #7, 9, 43, or 48 from Capitol Hill. Stop by the friendly **visitor center**, 4014 University Way NE (543-9198) at NE Campus Way, to pick up a campus map and a self-guided tour book. (Open M-F 8am-5pm.)

The state's only such resource, the **Thomas Burke Museum of Natural History and Culture** (543-5590; www.washington.edu/burkemuseum), at 45th St. NE and 17th Ave. NE, is in the northwest corner of the campus: savor the chance to see the only dinosaur bones on display in Washington. The museum also exhibits a superb collection on Pacific Rim cultures, as well as kid-friendly explanations of the natural history of Washington's formation and the exhibit *Scary Fish*. (Open F-W 10am-5pm, Th 10am-8pm. $5.50, seniors $4, students $2.50, under 5 free.) Across the street, the astronomy department's old stone **observatory** (543-0126) is open to the public on clear nights. The red concrete basin in the center of campus is a hub of student radicalism and skateboarding known as **Red Square.** The ▧ **Henry Art Gallery** (543-2280), opposite the visitor center, displays superb modern art in a stark white setting. Coming exhibitions include *Inside Out: New Chinese Art*, in conjunction with the Tacoma Art Museum (see p. 175; until Mar., 2000), and *Shifting Ground*, a focus on landscape in modern art. (Feb.-Apr., 2000. Open Tu-Su 11am-5pm, Th 11am-8pm. $5, seniors $3.50, students free; free Th after 5pm.)

Fremont is home to residents who pride themselves on their love of art and antiques, and the liberal atmosphere of their self-declared "center of the world" under Rte. 99: twice in the past ten years Fremont has applied to secede from the United States. A statue entitled **"Waiting for the Inner-City Urban,"** a lament over the loss of the neighborhood's public transportation to downtown, depicts residents waiting in bus purgatory and in moments of inspiration and sympathy is frequently gussied up by passers-by. The **immense troll** beneath the Aurora Bridge on 35th St. grasps a Volkswagen Bug with a confounded expression. Some say kicking the bug's tire brings good luck; others say it hurts their foot. A flamin' **Vladimir Lenin** resides at the corner of N. 36th and N. Fremont Pl.; this work from the former Soviet Union will be around until it's bought by a permanent collection, presumably of Soviet artwork. Fremont is also home to **Archie McPhee's,** 3510 Stone Way (545-8344), a shrine to pop culture and plastic absurdity. (Open M-Sa 9am-7pm, Su 10am-6pm.) People of the punk and funk persuasion make pilgrimages from as far as the record stores of Greenwich Village in Manhattan just to handle the notorious **slug selection.** Reach Archie's on the Aurora Hwy. (Rte. 99), or on bus #26. The store is east of the highway between 35th and 36th, two blocks north of Lake Union and Gasworks Park (see below).

Just east of the U District, the primarily Scandinavian neighborhood of **Ballard** offers supports a wide variety of Scandinavian eateries and shops along Market St. The **Nordic Heritage Museum,** 3014 NW 67th St. (789-5707), presents thorough and realistic exhibits on the history of Nordic immigration and influence in the U.S. Stumble over cobblestones in old Copenhagen, or visit the slums of New York City that turned photographer and Danish immigrant Jacob Riis into an important social reformer. The museum hosts a **Viking festival** (789-5708) the weekend after the 4th of July, a **Yule Fest** the weekend before Thanksgiving, and hosts a series of **Nordic concerts** by local musicians throughout the summer. Take bus #17 from downtown, and bus #44 from the U District, transferring to #17 at 24th and Market. (Open Tu-Sa 10am-4pm, Su noon-4pm. $4, seniors and students $3, ages 6-18 $2.)

WATERWAYS AND PARKS

Thanks to the foresight of Seattle's early community and the architectural genius of the Olmsted family, Seattle enjoys a string of parks and waterways. Houseboats and sailboats fill **Lake Union,** situated between Capitol Hill and the University District. Here, the **Center for Wooden Boats,** 1010 Valley St. (382-2628), maintains a moored flotilla of new and restored small craft for rent. (Open daily 11am-6pm. Rowboats $12.50-20 per hr.; sailboats $16-26 per hr. HI discount.) **Gasworks Park** hosts a furious ▧ **4th of July Fireworks show,** and during the rest of the year is a celebrated kite-flying spot at the north end of Lake Union, and is always landscaped around a retired oil-refining facility. To get there, take bus #26 from downtown to N. 35th St. and Wallingford Ave. N. **Gasworks Kite Shop,** 3333 Wallingford N (633-4780), is one block north of the park. (Open M-F 10am-6pm, Sa 10am-5pm, Su 11am-5pm.) **Urban Surf,** 2100 N. Northlake Way (545-9463), opposite the park entrance, rents surfboards ($35 per day) and in-line skates ($5 per hr.).

Directly north of Lake Union, athletes run, ride, and roll around **Green Lake;** take bus #16 from downtown Seattle. The lake is also given high marks by windsurfers, but woe unto those who lose their balance. Whoever named it Green Lake wasn't kidding; even a quick dunk results in a full-body coating of algae. On sunny afternoons, boaters, windsurfers, and scullers make the lake feel like rush hour. Rent a bike at **Gregg's Green Lake Cycle** (see p. 159), on the east side of the lake, opposite Starbucks. The **Burke-Gilman Trail** makes for a longer ride from the University District along Montlake Blvd., then along Lake Union and all the way west to Chittenden Locks and Discovery Park.

Next to Green Lake is **Woodland Park** and the **Woodland Park Zoo,** 5500 Phinney Ave. N (684-4800), best reached from I-5 (50th St. Exit) or N. 50th St.; take bus #5 from downtown. The park is not well-manicured, but the zoo's habitats are highly realistic. The zoo has won a bevy of AZA awards (the zoo Oscars, if you will) for best new exhibits. (Open mid-Mar. to mid-Oct. 9:30am-6pm; in winter until 4pm. $8.50, students $7.75, seniors $7.75, ages 6-17 $6, ages 3-5 $3.75, disabled $5.50.)

Farther west, crowds gather at the **Hiram M. Chittenden Locks,** on NW 54th St., to watch a veritable circus of boats crossing between Lake Washington and Puget Sound. Take bus #43 from the U District or #17 from downtown. Salmon jockey up the passage themselves at the **fish ladder.** The **visitor center** (783-7059; open June-Sept. daily 7am-9pm) for both sights leads free tours (Sa-Su 1 and 3pm).

Across the canals and west of the locks lie the 534 bucolic acres of **Discovery Park** (386-4236; open daily 6am-11pm), at 36th Ave. W and W Government Way, on a lonely point west of the Magnolia District and south of Golden Gardens Park. Grassy fields and steep, eroding bluffs, while dangerous for hikers, provide a haven for birds forced over Puget Sound by bad weather around the Olympic Mountains. The wide range of habitats supports much of the flora and fauna of the Pacific Northwest. A **visitor center,** 3801 W. Government Way, is right by the entrance. (Open daily 8:30am-5pm; take bus #24.) **Shuttles** service the beach. (June-Sept. Sa-Su noon-4:45pm. 25¢, seniors and disabled free.) The **Indian Cultural Center** (285-4425) at the park's north end, is operated by the United Indians of All Tribes Foundation, and houses a gallery of modern Native American artwork. (Open M-F 10am-5pm, Sa-Su noon-5pm. Free.)

Seward Park lies at the south end of a string of beaches and forest preserves on the west shore of Lake Washington; take bus #39. The area offers sweeping views of the lake and Mercer Island, and a popular bike loop half-way around the lake.

◪ OUTDOORS

Over 1000 **cyclists** compete in the 19 mi. **Seattle to Portland Race** in mid-July. Call the **bike hotline** (522-2453) for info. On five **Bicycle Sundays** from May to September, Lake Washington Blvd. is open exclusively to cyclists from 10am to 6pm. Call the **Citywide Sports Office** (684-7092) for info.

Though the rapids are hours away by car, over 50 **whitewater rafting** outfitters are based in Seattle and are often willing to undercut one another with merciless and self-mutilating abandon. **Washington State Outfitters and Guides Association** (877-275-4964) provides advice; though their office is closed in summer, they do return phone calls and send out info. The **Northwest Outdoor Center,** 2100 Westlake Ave. (281-9694), on Lake Union, gives instructional programs in whitewater and sea kayaking, and leads three-day kayaking excursions through the San Juan Islands. (2½hr. basic intro with equipment $40. Lake Union kayak rentals $10-15 per hr. Open M-F 10am-8pm, Sa-Su 9am-6pm.) Make reservations.

Skiing near Seattle is every bit as good as the mountains make it look. Get lift ticket rates and conditions for **Alpental, Ski-Acres,** and **Snoqualmie** at 232-8182. **Crystal Mountain,** the region's newest resort, can be reached at 663-2265.

Ever since the Klondike gold rush, Seattle has been in the business of equipping wilderness expeditions. **Recreational Equipment Inc. Coop (REI Coop),** 222 Yale Ave. (223-1944), is the largest of its kind in the world. This paragon of woodsy wisdom can be seen from I-5; take the Stewart St. exit. The brand-new flagship store has a 65 ft. indoor climbing pinnacle and pathways and showers for testing gear. (Open M-F 10am-9pm, Sa 9am-7pm, Su 11am-6pm. Rental area open 2hr. before store.)

♫ ENTERTAINMENT

Seattle has one of the world's most notorious underground music scenes and the third-largest theater community in the U.S. (only New York's and Chicago's are larger), and supports performance in all sorts of venues, from bars to bakeries. Risers seem to grow from the asphalt in spring, when street fairs and outdoor theater please parkgoers. The big performance houses regularly sell half-price tickets and alternative theaters offer high-quality drama at downright low prices. The free **Out to Lunch** series (623-0340) brings everything from reggae to folk dancing to parks, squares, and office buildings in summertime Seattle. The **Seattle Public Library** (386-4636) screens free films as part of the program, and hosts daily poetry readings and children's book-reading competitions (see p. 159).

MUSIC AND DANCE

The **Seattle Opera** (389-7676; www.seattleopera.org) performs at the Opera House in the Seattle Center from August to May. The 2000 program includes *Boris Godunov* (Jan.) and *the Barber of Seville* (May). Buffs should reserve well in advance, though rush tickets are sometimes available (students and seniors can get half-price tickets 30min. before the performance; from $17; student tickets are also available $27-31). The **Pacific Northwest Ballet** (441-9411) performs at the Opera House from September to June, and the spectacular *Nutcracker* production, designed by Maurice Sendak, is always a wild rumpus (from $14; half-price rush tickets available to students and seniors 30min. before showtime). The **Seattle Symphony** (212-4700, tickets 215-4747), performs in the new Benaroya Hall, 200 University St. at 3rd Ave., from September to June (tickets from $10 though most from $25-39, seniors half-price, students $10; rush tickets from $6.50; ticket office open M-F 10am-6pm, Sa 1-6pm). Even if you won't be hearing the symphony, drop by the new concert hall (215-4895) to take in Chihuly glass chandeliers and a Rauschenberg mural (tours on the hour Th 1-4pm, F 11am-1pm). The **University of Washington** offers its own program of student recitals and concerts by visiting artists. The World Series showcases world dance, theater and chamber music (tickets $28-36). Contact the Meany Hall box office, 400 University Way (543-4880; half-price student rush tickets available one hour before show at box office; open Sept.-June M-F 10:30am-6pm; summer M-F 10:30am-4:30pm).

THEATER

The city hosts an exciting array of first-run plays and alternative works, particularly by many talented amateur groups. Rush tickets are often available at nearly half price on the day of the show (cash only) from **Ticket/Ticket** (324-2744).

◪ **The Empty Space Theatre,** 3509 Fremont Ave. N (547-7500; www.emptyspace.org), 1½ blocks north of the Fremont Bridge. Comedies in the small space attract droves. Season runs Oct. to early July. Box office open Tu-Su from noon. Tickets $14-24. under 25 and previews (first 4 shows of a run) $10. Half-price tickets 10min. before curtain.

Seattle Repertory Theater, 155 W. Mercer St. (443-2222), at the wonderful Bagley Wright Theater in Seattle Center. Contemporary and classic winter productions (and Shakespeare). *The Heidi Chronicles* and *Fences* opened here before moving to Broadway. Tickets $10-48, seniors $17, under 25 $10. Box office open M-F 10am-6pm.

A Contemporary Theater (ACT), 700 Union St. (292-7670). A summer season of modern and off-beat premieres. Tickets $19-40. Under 25 $10. Box office open Tu-Th noon-7:30pm, F-Sa noon-8pm, Su noon-7pm.

Annex Theatre (728-0933) at Stewart St. and Virginia Ave., downtown. Refreshing emphasis on company-generated material in 5-week runs (Feb.-Dec.). Shows usually Th-Sa at 8pm and Su at 7pm. Pay-what-you-can previews. Tickets $10-12.

Northwest Asian American Theater, 409 7th Ave. S (340-1445), in the International District, next to the Wing Luke Asian Museum. An excellent new theater with pieces by, for, and about Asian Americans. Tickets $12; students, seniors, and disabled $9; Th $6.

CINEMA

Seattle is a cinematic paradise. Most of the theaters that screen non-Hollywood films are on Capitol Hill and in the University District. Large, first-run theaters are everywhere, including a mammoth 16-screen **Loews Cineplex Meridian** (223-9600) at 7th Ave. and Pike. **Seven Gables,** a local company, has recently bought up the Egyptian, the Metro, the Neptune, and others. $20 buys admission to any five films at any of their theaters. Call 44-FILMS/443-4567 for local movie times and locations. On summer saturdays, **outdoor cinema** in Fremont (632-0287; www.freemontoutdorcinema.com) begins at dusk at 670 N. 34th St., in the U-Park lot by the bridge ($5; live music until dusk $7). **TCI Outdoor Cinema** (720-1058; lunarflicks.com) shows everything from classics to cartoons for free at the Gasworks Park (live music 7pm-dusk). Aspiring independent filmmakers or actors/actresses should check out the Alibi Room for readings (see **Nightlife,** below). Unless specified, the theaters below charge $4.25 for matinees and $7.50 for features.

The Egyptian, 801 E. Pine St. (32-EGYPT/34978), at Harvard Ave. on Capitol Hill. This Art Deco art-house is best known for hosting the **Seattle International Film Festival** in the last week of May and first week of June. The festival's director retrospective features a personal appearance by said director. Festival series tickets available at a discount.

The Harvard Exit, 807 E. Roy St. (323-8986), on Capitol Hill. Quality classic and foreign films. Half the fun of seeing a movie here is the theater, a converted residence that has its very own ghost, and an enormous antique projector. The lobby was once someone's living room. Arrive early and check out the puzzles.

Seven Gables Theater, 911 NE 50th St. (632-8820), in the U District just off Roosevelt, a short walk west from University Way. Another art-house cinema in an old house.

Grand Illusion Cinema, 1403 NE 50th St. (523-3935), in the U District at University Way. A tiny theater next to an espresso bar, showing films made on 30s-style budgets. One of the last independent theaters in Seattle. $6, seniors and children $3; matinees $4.

Crest Theater, 16 5th St. (363 6338), in the shoreline area. The Crest is low-key, very well-loved, a little out of the way, and shows lots of 2nd run artsy flicks.

SPORTS

Seattleites cheered last summer when the home team, the **Mariners** (tickets 622-4487) moved out of the Kingdome, where in 1995 sections of the roof fell into the stands. The "M's" are now playing in the half-billion dollar, hangar-like **Safeco Field,** at First Ave. S and Royal Brougham Way S., under an enormous retractable roof that keeps the rain off fans. Saving the game from frequent rain-outs is simply a matter of pushing a single button labelled "Go" and costs a mere $1.50 in electricity ($10 on a windy day). Despite having some of the best marquee talent in the game, the M's have been playing disappointingly in the past few seasons. Basically, the M's have always played disappointingly, but Seattleites love their pro sports nonetheless. (Tickets from $5.) Seattle's football team, the **Seahawks** (tickets 628-0888) are stuck playing in the Kingdome for another year, until it's torn down to begin construction on their own (they'll be in UW's Husky Stadium in the interim, which, incidentally, also has a history of collapse). With a new coach and fresh, young team, Seattleites are optimistic that things will turn around for this long-time up-and-coming team. (Tickets from $10.)

On the other side of town and at the other end of the aesthetic spectrum, the sleek **Key Arena** in the Seattle Center is packed to the brim whenever Seattle's pro basketball team, the **Supersonics** (281-5800), plays. Four years ago, Seattle-ites danced in the streets as the Sonics ascended the NBA ranks, only to be defeated by the unstoppable Chicago Bulls. Undaunted by a recent NCAA post-season prohibition, the **University of Washington Huskies** football team has dominated the PAC-10. Call the Athletic Ticket Office (543-2200) for Huskies schedules and prices.

SHOPPING

Seattle's younger set has created a wide demand for retail chain alternatives, though a swiftly growing population has certainly lured syndicated stores to popular shopping areas. Downtown, trendy and fairly expensive clothing stores and boutiques line 1st Ave. north and east of Pike Place toward Belltown. The enormous **Nordstrom's** (628-2111) is at 500 Pine St.; **Westlake Center** is an indoor conglomerate of chain stores and gift shops that heads off the shopping neighborhood from 3rd to 6th Ave. to Seneca St. in the south.

For handmade crafts and jewelry, shop at **Pike Place Market** (see p. 161), where baubles are almost as plentiful as cherries and zucchini. In the U District, **The Ave** (University Way) caters to the college crowd and promises good deals. Used music stores occupy almost every other storefront in this area, hawking deals on all sorts of tunes. Capitol Hill also supports the used music market: **Orpheum,** 618 Broadway E (322-6370), has an inspiring collection of imports and local music.

Thrift stores thrive in Seattle, especially on The Ave and between Pike and Pine Streets on Capitol Hill. Find astounding temples to trendiness and thriftiness like **Rex and Angels Red Light Lounge and Cereal Bar,** 4560 University Way NE (545-4044; open M-Sa 11am-8pm, Su 11am-7pm).

BOOKSTORES

Elliott Bay Books, 101 S. Main St. (624-6600), in Pioneer Sq. Vast collection with 150,000 titles. Sponsors a reading and lecture series, free with tickets from the shop in advance. Coffeehouse in the basement. Open M-Sa 10am-11pm, Su 11am-6pm.

University Book Store, 4326 University Way NE (634-3400 or 800-335-7323). Largest college bookstore chain on the West Coast, with 7 stores in the Seattle area. Open M-F 9am-9pm, Sa 9am-6pm, Su noon-5pm.

Metsker Maps, 702 1st. Ave (623-8747) in Pioneer Sq. Travel guides and maps.

Flora & Fauna Books, (623-4727) on 1st Ave. and S. Washington, in Pioneer Sq. Beautiful books about all things living and breathing. Open M-Sa 10am-6pm.

Beyond the Closet, 518 E. Pike (322-4609). Gay/lesbian lit. Open daily 10am-11pm.

⬛ NIGHTLIFE

Seattle has moved beyond beer to a new nightlife frontier: the cafe-bar. The popularity of espresso bars in Seattle might lead one to conclude that caffeine is more intoxicating than alcohol, but often an establishment that poses as a diner by day brings on a band, breaks out the disco ball, and pumps out the microbrews by night. Many locals tell tourists that the best spot to go for guaranteed good beer, live music, and big crowds is Pioneer Square, where UW students from frat row dominate the bar stools. These Seattleites are lying to you like curs; they probably take their beer bucks downtown to Capitol Hill, or up Rte. 99 to Fremont, where the atmosphere is usually more laid-back than in the Square.

DOWNTOWN

Sit and Spin, 2219 4th St. (cafe/laundromat 441-9484; band info 441-9474). Board games keep patrons busy while they wait for their clothes to dry or for alternative bands to stop playing in the back room (F and Sa nights). The cafe sells everything from local microbrews on tap to bistro food to boxes of laundry detergent. Artists cut albums in the **Bad Animal** studio down the street (where R.E.M. once recorded). Open Su-Th 9am-midnight, F-Sa 9am-2am. Kitchen opens daily at 11am.

Art Bar, 1516 2nd Ave. (622-4344), opposite the Green Tortoise Hostel. Exactly what the name says: a gallery/bar fusion. Grooving local bands (W Jazz, Th Reggae) and DJs (F jungle, Sa hip-hop). Cover $3-5. Open M-F 11am-2am, Sa-Su 4pm-2am.

Crocodile Cafe, 2200 2nd Ave. (448-2114), at Blanchard in Belltown. Cooks with organic eggs and toast by day, with local and national bands by night. House W. Must be 21 after 9pm. Cover $5-20. Open Tu-Sa 8am-2am, Su 9am-3pm for brunch.

The Alibi Room, 85 Pike St. (623-3180), across from the Market Cinema in the Post Alley in Pike Place. The Alibi Room proclaims itself a local indie filmmaker hangout. Smoky sophisticates star as themselves. Readings (M), racks of screenplays, DJ and dancing on the weekends (W-Su, no cover), and chic decor. Open daily 11am-2am.

Re-Bar, 1114 Howell (233-9873). A mixed gay and straight bar. R&B/hip-hop/drum & bass (F, Sa), 70's disco (Th), live music (Tu). Ladies night on Sa here means lesbian-friendly. Cover $5. Open Tu, Th-Sa 9:30pm-2am.

Dimitriou's Jazz Alley, 2033 6th Ave. (441-9729). This chic club offers plenty of cool world jazz, and even does dinner theater once in a while. Check out the parade of talent shuffling through the Alley; most shows $13-20. Open daily 6pm to 11:30 or 12:30pm.

PIONEER SQUARE

Pioneer Square provides a happening scene, dominated by 20-somethings, frat kids, and cover bands. Most of the area bars participate in a joint cover ($8, Su-Th $5) that will let you wander from bar to bar to sample the bands. **Fenix Cafe and Fenix Underground** (467-1111), and **Central Tavern** (622-0209) rock constantly, while **Larry's Greenfront** (624-7665) and **New Orleans** (622-2563) feature great blues and jazz nightly. The **Bohemian Cafe** (447-1514) pumps reggae and also sponsors open mic nights on Thursday. Not part of the Pioneer Square joint cover because it's often free, **J and M Cafe and Cardroom** (292-0663) is in the center of Pioneer Square, often blasting rock/blues (Th, no cover) or disco/top 40 (W, $5) into its crowded quarters. All the Pioneer Square clubs shut down at 2am Friday and Saturday nights, and around midnight during the week. **Kells** (728-1916), near Pike Place Market, is a popular Irish pub with nightly celtic tunes.

OK Hotel, 212 Alaskan Way S (621-7903; coffeehouse 386-9934), near Washington St. toward the waterfront. One cafe, one bar, one building. Lots of wood, lots of coffee. Live rock to reggae draws equally diverse crowds. Bar art is curated monthly. Cover charge up to $6. Cafe open M-F 5-10pm, Sa-Su 5-11pm. Bar open daily 3pm-2am.

Last Supper Club, 124 S. Washington St. (748-9975) at Occidental. Two dance floors, playing acid jazz and '70s disco on F, funky house, drum & bass and trance on Sa (cover F-Sa $10, before midnight; W-Th $5). Open W-Sa 4pm-2pm.

CAPITOL HILL

East off of Broadway, Pine St. is cool lounge after cool lounge. Find your atmosphere and acclimatize. West off of Broadway, Pike St. has the clubs that push the limits (gay, punk, industrial, fetish, dance) and break the sound barrier.

■ **ARO.space,** 925 E. Pike (860-7322; www.arospace.com), entrance on 10th Ave. What every club should be like, and will be... in the year 2100. Nobody laughs when they say they're involved in a revolution in art. Drum & bass (Th), R&B/pop (Su), electronic (W, F-Sa). Vegetarian fare ($5-$7.50). Restaurant open daily 5pm-1am, club 10pm-2am.

Vogue, 1516 11th Ave. (324-5778) off Pike St. Anything goes in this angsty club. Theme nights: M Drag, Tu live goth/industrial, W Goth, Th live rock/metal/punk (ladies free), F Industrial, Sa 80's/90's New Wave, Su Fetish. Cover $2-5. Open 9pm-2am.

Neighbors, 1509 Broadway (324-5358). Enter from the alley on Pike. A very gay dance club priding itself on techno slickness. House (M, W, F-Sa), 80's (Tu, Th), Top 40 (Su). Cover Su-Th $1; F-Sa $5. Open Su-Th 9pm-2am, F-Sa 9pm-4am.

Linda's, 707 Pine St. E (325-1220). Major post-gig scene for Seattle rockers. Live DJ playing jazz and old rock (Su and Tu, no cover). Open M-Sa 2pm-2am, Su 4pm-2am.

Garage, 1130 Broadway (322-2296), between Union and Madison. An automotive warehouse turned upscale pool hall, this place gets suave at night. Happy hour 3-7pm. 8 pool tables $6-14 per hr.; $4 per hr. during happy hour; $5 per hr. (M); free for female sharps on Ladies' Night (Su). Open daily 3pm-2am.

FREMONT

Separated from the rest of the Seattle population, the neighbor of Fremont has mutated into something weird and fabulous. Bars light up the night.

Red Door Alehouse, 3401 Fremont Ave. N (547-7521), at N. 34th St., across from the Inner-Urban Statue. Throbbing with university students who attest to the good local ale selection and a mile-long beer menu. Try the Pyramid Wheaton or Widmer Hefeweizen with a slice of lemon. Open daily 11am-2am. Kitchen closes at 11pm.

The Dubliner, 3405 Fremont Ave. N (548-1508). Irish soul in Fremont, with a friendly local crowd. Irish jam session (W at 9pm). Open daily noon-2am.

Triangle Lounge, 3507 Freemont Pl. N (632-0880). Small and friendly, a little outdoor seating, and wonderful iron-work. Bar nibblets $3-5. Open daily 11:30am-2am.

EVENTS

Pick up a copy of the visitor center's *Calendar of Events*, published every season, for event coupons and an exact listing of innumerable area happenings. The first Thursday evening of each month, the art community sponsors **First Thursday,** a free and well-attended gallery walk. Watch for **street fairs** in the University District during mid- to late May, at Pike Place Market over Memorial Day weekend, and in Fremont in mid-June. The International District holds its annual two-day bash in mid-July, featuring arts and crafts booths, East Asian and Pacific food booths, and presentations by a range of groups from the Radical Women/Freedom Socialist Party to the Girl Scouts. For more info, call **Chinatown Discovery** (236-0657 or 583-0460), or write P.O. Box 3406, Seattle 98114.

Puget Sound's yachting season begins in May. **Maritime Week,** during the third week of May, and the **Shilshole Boats Afloat Show** (634-0911) in mid-August, give area boaters a chance to show off their crafts. Over the 4th of July weekend, the Center for Wooden Boats sponsors the free **Wooden Boat Show** (382-2628) on Lake Union. Blue blazers and deck shoes are *de rigeur*. Size up the entrants (over 100 wooden boats), then watch a demonstration of boat-building skills. The year-end blow-out is the **Quick and Daring Boatbuilding Contest,** when hopefuls go overboard trying to build and sail wooden boats of their own design, using a limited kit of tools and materials. Plenty of music, food, and alcohol make the sailing smooth.

Northwest Folklife Festival (684-7300), on Memorial Day weekend. One of Seattle's most notable events, held at the Seattle Center. Artists, musicians, and dancers congregate to celebrate the area's heritage.

Fremont Fair and Solstice Parade (547-7440, www.sen.org/fremont/fac), in mid-June. A frenzy of music, frivolity and craft booths, and a float-crazy parade where anyone and all are invited to participate, dressed in the bizarrest of outfits or nothing at all.

Bite of Seattle (684-7200), in mid-July. Free admission to this food festival in the Seattle Center sets you up for $2-4 samples of the best Seattle has to offer.

Seattle Seafair (728-0123), spread over 3 weeks from mid-July to early Aug. The biggest, baddest festival of them all. Each neighborhood contributes with street fairs, parades large and small, balloon races, musical entertainment, and a seafood orgy.

Bumbershoot (281-7788), over Labor Day weekend. A massive, 4-day arts festival that caps off the summer, held in the Seattle Center. Attracts big-name rock bands, street musicians, and a young, exuberant crowd. 4 days $29; 2 days $16; 1 day $9 in advance or $10 at the door, seniors $1, children free. Prices subject to change.

DAYTRIPS TO THE EAST

Cross **Lake Washington** on one of two floating bridges to arrive in a biker's and picnicker's (and suburbanite's) paradise, where Range Rovers and outdoor shopping plazas litter the landscape. Companies buy up expanses of East Sound land, smother them in sod and office complexes, and call them "campuses"; witness

Microsoft, which has nearly subsumed the suburb of Redmond. Rapid growth has had its benefits, though. In the suburb of **Bellevue,** the July **Bellevue Jazz Festival** (455-6885) attracts both local cats and national acts. This wealthy and beautiful suburb is home to Bill Gates, among others. Neither tours of Bill's house nor of Microsoft are available, but Mac-lovers can hurl abuse from a **boat tour** of Lake Washington. Contact **Argosy Cruises** (623-1252) for info.

Farther south on U.S. 405 toward Renton, rock pilgrims reach the grave of Seattle's first rock legend, **Jimi Hendrix.** Take bus #101 from downtown to the Renton Park 'N' Ride, then switch to #105 to Greenwood Cemetery. Drivers should take the Sunset Blvd. exit from Rte. 405 (follow Sunset Blvd., not Park), turn right onto Union, and right again on NE 4th. Jimi's grave is located towards the back of the cemetery, just in front of the sun dial.

Take I-90 east to **Lake Sammamish State Park,** off Exit 15, for swimming, water-skiing, volleyball courts, and playing fields. In the town of **Snoqualmie,** 29 mi. east of Seattle, is the **Northwest Railroad Museum,** 109 King St. (452-746-4025), on Rte. 202 dividing the two lanes of the town's main street. Beyond housing a small collection of functional early steam and electric trains, this is the oldest running depot in the state and runs a train 7 mi. to **North Bend.** Trips run on the hr. and last 45 min., but hanging out in North Bend and catching a later train is officially encouraged (open May-Sept. Sa-Su 11am-4pm; round-trip $6, seniors $5, children $4). From North Bend, take bus #209 (#210 on Su) or Rte. 202 north to view the astounding **Snoqualmie Falls.** Formerly a sacred place for the Salish, the 270-foot wall of water has generated electricity for Puget Power since 1898. Five generators buried under the falls work hard to provide energy for 1600 homes. The falls were featured in David Lynch's cult TV series *Twin Peaks*, and the small town of Snoqualmie has endured hordes of Peaks freaks ever since.

I-90 cruises along some of the region's prettiest hiking country. Exit 20, High Point Way, leads to a beautiful set of trails on **West Tiger Mountain.** The trailhead is right off the freeway; head for the "No Outlet" sign. Trail maps ($2.50) are available at the **Issaquah Chamber of Commerce** (392-7024), at 155 NW Gilman in nearby Issaquah. Past North Bend is a 4-mile trail to **Mt. Si,** a 4000-foot peak offering stellar views of Seattle and the surrounding valley. To find the trail, take North Bend Way off Exit 28 to Mt. Si Rd. A short wheelchair-accessible loop begins at the base.

DAYTRIPS TO THE SOUTH

The Seattle area is surrounded by the vast factories of **Boeing,** the city's most prominent employer and site of the largest covered structure in North America. **Public tours** of the Boeing facilities (800-464-1476) are offered on the hour (M-F 9am-3pm). Tickets are free and distributed first-come, first-served; arriving early greatly enhances the chances of getting one of the limited numbers of tickets. The airport buses (#174 and #194) stop right at the plant (10 min, $1.25-1.75). The Seattle International Hostel also offers a bus to the factory for its patrons ($15), but with no guarantee that this will get you into a tour. Get there very early.

South of Seattle at Boeing Field is the wheelchair-accessible **Museum of Flight,** 9404 E. Marginal Way S (764-5720). Take I-5 south to Exit 158 and turn north onto E. Marginal Way S, or take bus #123. The cavernous structure enshrines flying machines, from canvas biplanes to chic fighter jets, all hanging from a three-story roof (open F-W 10am-5pm, Th 10am-9pm; $8, seniors $7, ages 6-15 $4, under 5 free). An exhibit on the Apollo space shuttle missions, which landed the first man on the moon, includes a life-sized replica of the command module. Tour JFK's old Air Force One, or fly in a nauseatingly realistic flight simulator ($7.50). When tales of space-age technology grow tiresome, explore the red barn where William E. Boeing founded the company in 1916. Photographs and artifacts trace the history of flight from its beginnings through the 30s, including a working replica of the Wright Brothers' wind tunnel. Tours with enthusiastic Air Force veterans leave the entrance on the half hour (10:30am-1:30pm).

PUGET SOUND

TACOMA

Though spending time in Tacoma rather than Seattle may seem like hanging out in Newark, New Jersey instead of New York, New York, Tacoma's lively art scene and beautiful park make it worth a daytrip. Tacoma is Washington's second largest city and lies on I-5, 32 mi. (30min.) south of Seattle and 28 mi. (30min.) northeast of Olympia. Take Exit 132 from I-5 and follow the signs to the city center.

Greyhound (383-4621), at the corner of Pacific and 14th St., runs buses to Seattle (open daily 7:30am-9pm; 8 buses per day, $5). **Point Defiance** is Tacoma's **ferry terminal.** From here, **Washington State Ferries** run regularly to Vashon Island (15min., frequently from 5am-midnight, $2.50, car and driver $9-11.50, bicycle 70¢). Get the skinny on Tacoma at the **Pierce County Visitor Information Center,** 1001 Pacific Ave. #400 (627-2836 or 800-272-2662; open M-F 9am-5pm), or from their satellite in the back of the Washington State Museum gift shop (open M-Sa 10am-4pm, Su noon-5pm). The superb *Pierce County Bicycle Guide Map* shows bike routes and lists trails near Mt. Rainier. **Taxi:** 272-2887. **Crisis line:** 759-6700 or 800-576-7764, 24hr. **Rape crisis:** 226-5062 or 800-756-7273, 24hr. **Post office:** 1102 A St., 98402 (open M-F 7am-5pm) on 11th St. **Area code:** 253.

The shiny new **Washington State History Museum,** 1911 Pacific Ave. (888-238-4373), houses interactive, stereophonic exhibits on Washington's history through the 1800s. A sprawling model train on the fifth floor is a highlight for children, railroad buffs, and child railroad buffs (open M-Sa 10am-6pm, Su 11am-6pm; $7, students and seniors $6, ages 6-12 $4, ages 5 and under free, family $20; free Th 5-8pm). Just up Pacific Ave., the **Tacoma Art Museum,** 1123 Pacific Ave. (272-4258) at 12th St., takes a refreshingly offbeat approach to its limited space. Exhibits planned for the year 2000 include *Inside Out: New Chinese Art* (Nov. 20, 1999 to March 5, 2000; shared with the Henry Art Gallery, see p. 167), and *Frontiers in Northwest Design* (Mar. 25-Jun. 25, 2000). A permanent retrospective of the works of popular glass artist Dale Chihuly, a native, is no less always on display. ($5, seniors and students $4, ages under 7 free. Open Tu-W, F-Sa 10am-5pm, Th 10am-7pm, Su noon-5pm; on the third Th of every month, open until 8pm and free all day). More of Chihuly's grandiose creations **Union Station,** 1717 Pacific Ave. (572-9310; exhibit open Tu-F 10am-4pm). In recent years, Tacoma's cheap rent has lured a dynamic art scene from Seattle, reflected at **Commencement Art Gallery,** 901 Broadway (591-5341) in the Pantages building (open Tu-Sa 11am-5pm; free). Rummage for found objects and your new aesthetic east of 9th on Broadway and St. Helens St., at **Antique Row**(s). **Tacoma's Farmers Market** takes over Antique Row on Thursdays (June to mid-Sept.).

The main attraction in Tacoma is the beautiful **Point Defiance Park.** It's a wonderful spot to pass time on a warm day, but don't expect to be the only one who figured that out (305-1000; open daily from dawn until 30min. after dusk). To get there, take Rte. 16 to the 6th Ave. exit, go east on 6th Ave., then head north on Pearl St. A 5 mi. loop passes all the park's attractions, offering postcard views of Puget Sound and access to miles of woodland trails. In spring, the park is bejewelled with flowers; a rhododendron garden lies nestled in the woods along the loop, and intricate fuschia, rose, and Japanese gardens make an Eden out of the park's entrance. **Owen Beach** looks across at Vashon Island and is a good starting place for a ramble down the shore. The loop then brushes by the spot where, in 1841, defiant U.S. Navy Capt. Wilkes proclaimed that if he had guns on this and the opposite shore, he could take on the world.

Point Defiance Zoo and Aquarium (591-5337) is the park's prize possession (open daily 10am-7pm; Labor Day-Memorial Day 10am-4pm; $7, seniors $6.55, ages 5-17 $5.30, ages 3-4 $2.50, under 3 free). Penguins, polar bears, beluga whales, and sharks defy visitors not to find them fascinating. A number of natural habitats are daringly re-created within the zoo's boundaries.

WESTERN WASHINGTON

The meticulously restored **Fort Nisqually** (591-5339), in the park, was built by the British Hudson's Bay Company in 1832 as they expanded their trade in beaver pelts. (open June-Aug. daily 11am-6pm; Sept.-Apr. W-Su 11am-4pm; $2, seniors $1.50, ages 5-12 $1). The fort's museum holds a compact but captivating exhibit on the lives of children, laborers, natives, and Hawaiians who worked there during the Company years. Volunteer staffers wear 19th-century garb and talk the talk.

The **Antique Sandwich Company,** 5102 N. Pearl St. (752-4069), near Point Defiance, sells fresh, wholesome food, hosts Tuesday night open mics, and is a just plain nice place to go after hitting the beach. The "poor boy" sandwich ($6) is food enough for a week (open M, W-Sa 7am-7:30pm, Tu 7am-10pm, Su 8am-7:30pm).

VASHON ISLAND

Only a 25-minute ferry ride from Seattle and an even shorter hop from Tacoma, Vashon (VASH-in) Island has remained inexplicably invisible to most Seattleites. With its forested hills and expansive sea views, this artists' colony feels like the San Juan Islands without the tourists or an economy to cater to them, though budget travelers will feel well cared for in the island's hostel. Most of the island is covered in Douglas fir, rolling cherry orchards, wildflowers, and strawberry fields, and, on Vashon, all roads lead to rocky beaches.

E GETTING THERE AND GETTING AROUND. Vashon Island stretches between Seattle and Tacoma on its east side and between Southworth and Gig Harbor on its west side. The town of **Vashon** lies at the island's northern tip; the ferry stops to the south, at Tahlequah. The steep hills on Vashon don't keep bikes from being the recreational vehicle of choice on the island. Many locals and visitors resort to hitchhiking, reputed to be easier here than on the mainland.

Washington State Ferries (800-843-3779, 206-464-6400; www.wsdot.wa.gov/ferries) runs ferries to Vashon Island from four different locations. A passenger ferry departs **downtown Seattle** (25min., 8 per day M-F, 6 per day Sa, $3.60); the other two (from **Fauntleroy** in West Seattle and **Southworth** in the Kitsap Peninsula) take cars (35min., 20 per day, $2.40, car and driver $8.50-11). A fourth ferry departs **Point Defiance** in Tacoma (see p. 175) and arrives in Tahlequah (15min., 20 per day, $2.40). To get to the ferry terminals on the mainland from Seattle, drive south on I-5 and take Exit 163A (West Seattle/Spokane St.) down Fauntleroy Way to the Fauntleroy Ferry Terminal. To get to Point Defiance in Tacoma, take Exit 132 off I-5 (Bremerton/Gig Harbor) to Rte. 16. Get on 6th Ave. and turn right onto Pearl, then follow signs to Point Defiance Park and the ferry.

Seattle's **King County Metro** (553-3000 or 800-542-7876) services the downtown ferry terminal, Fauntleroy ferry terminal, and Vashon Island. Buses #54, 116, 118 and 119 run between Seattle and Fauntleroy. Bus #54 picks up at 2nd and Pike St. (30min., buses every 30min. 5:30am-1:30am). Save your transfer for the connection on Vashon. Buses #118 and 119 services the island's east side from the north ferry landing, through Vashon, to the south landing. Bus #117 services the west side of the island. The island is in a different fare zone than Seattle. See p. 158 for fares.

🛈 PRACTICAL INFORMATION. The local **Thriftway** (see **Food,** below) provides maps, as does the Vashon-Maury **Chamber of Commerce,** 17633 SW Vashon Hwy. (463-6217). The **library,** 17210 Vashon Hwy. (463-2069), provides free one-hour **Internet access** (open M-Th 11am-8:30pm, F 11am-6pm, Sa 10am-5pm, Su 1-5pm). **Laundry:** Joy's, 17318 Vashon Hwy. (463-9933; wash $1.25, dry 25¢ per 10min.; open M-Sa 7am-8:30pm, Su 8am-8pm). **Vashon Pharmacy:** 17617 Vashon Hwy. (463-9118; open M-F 9am-7pm, Sa 9am-6pm, Su 11am-1pm). **Emergency:** 911. **Police:** 463-3783. **Coast Guard:** 217-6200. **Post office:** 1005 SW 178th St., 98070 (800-275-8777; open M-F 8:30am-5pm, Sa 10am-1pm), on Bank Rd. **Area code:** 206.

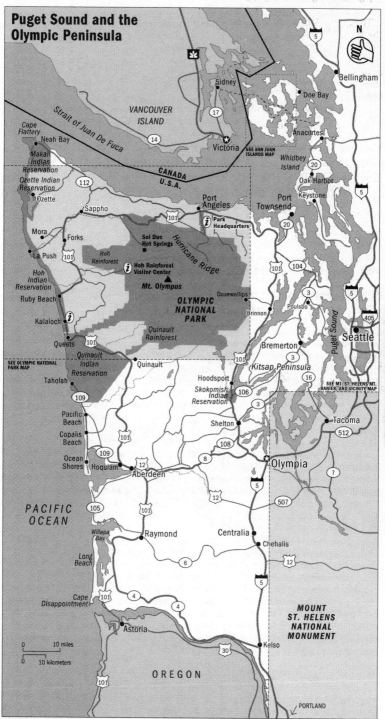

Puget Sound and the Olympic Peninsula

N

Bellingham

Sidney

VANCOUVER ISLAND

Doe Bay

Strait of Juan De Fuca

Cape Flattery
Neah Bay

Makah Indian Reservation

Ozette Indian Reservation

Ozette

Sappho

Victoria

Anacortes

SEE SAN JUAN ISLANDS MAP

Whidbey Island

Oak Harbor

Keystone

Port Angeles

Port Townsend

Park Headquarters

Mora

Forks

La Push

Hoh Rainforest

Sol Duc Hot Springs

Hoh Rainforest Visitor Center

Hurricane Ridge

Mt. Olympus

OLYMPIC NATIONAL PARK

Dosewallips

Brinnon

Poulsbo

CANADA
U.S.A.

Hoh Indian Reservation

Ruby Beach

Kalaloch

Queets

Quinault Rainforest

Quinault Indian Reservation

Quinault

Bremerton

Kitsap Peninsula

SEE MT. ST. HELENS, MT. RANIER, AND VICINITY MAP

Seattle

Puget Sound

SEE OLYMPIC NATIONAL PARK MAP

Taholah

Hoodsport

Skokomish Indian Reservation

Pacific Beach

Copalis Beach

Ocean Shores

Hoquiam

Aberdeen

Shelton

Tacoma

Olympia

PACIFIC OCEAN

Raymond

Willapa Bay

Long Beach

Centralia

Chehalis

Cape Disappointment

Astoria

MOUNT ST. HELENS NATIONAL MONUMENT

Kelso

OREGON

0   10 miles
0   10 kilometers

PORTLAND

WESTERN WASHINGTON

[ACCOMMODATIONS, CAMPGROUNDS, AND FOOD. The **Vashon Island AYH Ranch Hostel (HI),** 12119 SW Cove Rd. (463-2592; www.vashonisland.com/ ayhranchhostel), west of Vashon Hwy., is sometimes called the "Seattle B." All buses from the ferry terminal stop at Thriftway Market, where a free phone connects directly to the hostel. Dirk will make pickups during reasonable hours. This is the hostel version of Disney World's Frontierland—an old western town with teepees, covered wagons that moonlight as queen beds, and a sheriff's office. A pool table, free pancake breakfast and firewood, and bikes ($10 per day, daytime use only) attract all sorts. (Open May-Oct. Members/bicyclists $10; nonmembers $13; sleeping bag $2. Private doubles $35, nonmembers $45, $10 per extra person.) A shuttle to the morning ferry is $1.50. The hostel's new B&B, **The Lavender Duck,** just north on Vashon Hwy., has pleasant color-coordinated rooms ($45-55). The hostel's meadows are the island's only legal place to **camp** ($8; children $4). "Music in the Meadow" plays every Sunday from 5pm-7pm (show and dinner $5).

Get creative in the hostel's kitchens with supplies from the large and offbeat **Thriftway,** downtown at 9740 SW Bank Rd. (463-2100; open daily 8am-9pm). The deli sells good ol' artery-plugging fried chicken, but the bulk foods aisle is a health food nirvana. **Emily's Cafe and Juice Bar,** 17530 Vashon Hwy. (463-6404), smack in downtown Vashon, enhances karma and juices just about anything (open W-Su 8am-4pm, M 7am-4pm). For take-out, stampede on over to **Tatanka,** 17722 Vashon Hwy. (463-6708), for bison burgers ($4.75), bison burritos ($4), and bison chili ($3). Hostelers get half-price drinks. (Open M-Sa 11am-7pm, Su noon-7pm.)

◉ ⚐ SIGHTS AND OUTDOORS. Vashon Island provides wonderful but strenuous biking, a sometimes-unbalanced relationship celebrated at the Bicycle Tree, where a misbehaving little two-wheeler is lodged (in the woods past Sound Food, off the Vashon Hwy.). **Vashon Island Bicycles,** 7232 Vashon Hwy. (463-6225), rents bikes ($9 per hr., $20 per day). **Point Robinson Park** is a gorgeous spot for a picnic, and **free tours** (217-6123) of the 1885 **Coast Guard lighthouse** are available. From Vashon Hwy., take Ellisburg Rd. to Dockton Rd. to Pt. Robinson Rd. **Vashon Island Kayak Co.** (463-9527), at Burton Acres Boat Launch, runs guided tours (from $48) and rents sea kayaks. (Open F-Su 10am-5pm. Call for weekday rentals. Singles $14 per hr., $35 per half-day, $50 per day; doubles $20, $50, and $65, respectively; top-sitters run about 30% cheaper.) More than 500 acres of woods in the middle of the island are interlaced with mildly difficult **hiking trails.** The Vashon Park District (463-9602; open daily 9am-5pm) can tell you more. Lastly, count on some culture no matter when you visit—one in 10 residents of Vashon is an artist. **Blue Heron Arts Center,** 19704 Vashon Hwy. (463-5131; open Tu-F 11am-5pm, Sa noon-5pm), coordinates activities such as free gallery openings on the first Friday of each month (7-9:30pm) and publishes *Island View*, a guide to current goings on.

KITSAP PENINSULA

Nosing into Puget Sound between the Olympic Peninsula and Seattle, the Kitsap Peninsula's deep inlets seemed a natural spot in which to park a fleet of nuclear-powered submarines. The instant you set foot in **Bremerton,** the hub of the peninsula, you'll swear you're in a Tom Clancy novel. Every third person has a Navy security pass swinging from his or her neck. The navy yard skyline rivals a small city's, and when the **USS Nimitz** is home the barbers work overtime providing crew cuts for all. For the Navy or military history buff, Bremerton is quite a find. For others, the city has little to offer. However, bicycling civilians use the peninsula's forested and hilly terrain without top-secret clearance, and tiny coastal villages outside Bremerton bring weekenders from all over.

⚐ PRACTICAL INFORMATION. Hood Canal separates the Kitsap and Olympic Peninsulas. Kitsap is well-connected by road and ferry to the south, east, and west. **Kingston,** toward the northern tip of the peninsula about 20 mi. from Bremerton on

Rte. 3 and Rte. 104, is linked by ferry to **Edmonds** on the mainland, just north of greater Seattle on Rte. 104 off I-5 Exit 177. **Southworth,** about 10 mi. east of Bremerton on Rte. 160 off Rte. 16, is connected to Fauntleroy (West Seattle) and Vashon Island by ferry. Routes 3 and 104 lead north across the **Hood Canal Bridge** to the Port Townsend area. Route 16 leads south to Tacoma.

Four **Washington State Ferries** (800-84-FERRY/843-3779 or 206-464-6400; www.wsdot.wa.gov/ferries) routes provide daily service to the peninsula: Bremerton–downtown Seattle (1hr., frequent service, $3.70, car and driver $6.50-8.25); Southworth–Vashon Island (10min., frequent service, $2.50, car and driver $9-11.50); Southworth–Fauntleroy or Kingston–Edmonds (35min., frequent service, $3.70, car and driver $6.50-8.25). **Kitsap Transit** (373-2877 or 800-501-7433; www.kitsaptransit.org), in the Enetai building on Washington St., runs several bus lines serving most small communities on the peninsula and on Bainbridge Island. Call ahead for times, or pick up a schedule at a ferry terminal. (Buses run M-F 4am-9pm, Sa-Su 8am-7pm; fare $1.) Almost all buses accommodate bicycles.

The **Bremerton Area Chamber of Commerce,** 120 Washington St. (479-3579; www.bremertonchamber.org), just up the hill from the ferry terminal in Bremerton, will help you navigate *sans* sonar. If you're sounding out the area by bike, pick up the *Kitsap and Olympic Peninsula Bike Map* here. (Open M-F 9am-5pm; a booth at the ferry dock is open on weekends.) **Emergency:** 911. **Post office:** 602 Pacific Ave., 98337 (800-275-8777; open M-F 9am-5pm). **Area code:** 360.

⌐ ACCOMMODATIONS, CAMPGROUNDS, AND FOOD. A daytrip from Seattle or Vashon Island may be a better idea, but if you're intent on dropping anchor for the night on Kitsap, your best bet is to camp, though the **Dunes Motel,** 3400 11th St. (377-0093), rents huge, clean rooms with cable TV, phones and beds with Magic Fingers (singles $50; doubles $60). From the ferry, turn left off Washington Ave. onto 6th St. which becomes Kitsap Way. Those traveling by foot will find **Illahee State Park** (478-4661) convenient, but a bit cramped. To get there, hop on bus #29 at the ferry terminal in Bremerton and take it to the corner of Trenton St. and Sylvan Rd. Walk a quarter-mile up the hill on Sylvan until you reach the entrance. By car, drive north on Rte. 303 from Bremerton to Sylvan Rd., turn right, and follow the signs (water, toilets, showers; 25 sites $11; walk-ins $6). Another port of call is **Scenic Beach State Park** (830-5079), near the village of **Seabeck** on the west coast of the peninsula. The park has 52 campsites with water and bathrooms (sites $11). From Rte. 3, take the Newberry Hill Rd. Exit and follow the signs. Cyclists should be prepared for steep hills along this route. Winter hours are limited; call Washington Parks (800-233-0321) for info on either park or reservations (800-452-5687).

Culinary choices in Bremerton are few, since Uncle Sam feeds locals on base. **Le Bayou,** 602 4th St. (792-9594), just north of Pacific Ave., takes you to spicy Creole-Cajun New Orleans with jambalaya ($7, with a big salad) and jazz every other Wednesday (open Tu-F 11:30am-1:30pm and 4pm-9pm, Sa 4pm-9pm). **Charlotte's Cafe,** 264 E. 4th St. (479-8133), is a family-run deli with daily menus (sandwiches $4.25; pastas or steaks from $8; open M-F 11am-7pm).

◉ SIGHTS. Navy buffs, step up. Next to the Chamber of Commerce awaits the scattered yet moving **Bremerton Naval Museum** (479-7447) with World War II photos, 10 ft. models of destroyers and aircraft carriers, and a 14th-century wicker basket from Korea, believed to be the world's oldest existing cannon. (Open M-Sa 10am-5pm, Su 1-5pm. Donations requested.) Behind the museum, explore the destroyer **USS Turner Joy** (792-2457), the ship that fired the first American shots of the Vietnam War. To get a closer view of the shipyard, join the **Navy Ship Tour** (792-2457), which departs from the *Turner Joy* and scoots along mothballed submarines, aircraft carriers, and the famous WWII battleship *Missouri,* upon which the surrender document ending WWII was signed. (*Turner Joy* self-guided tour $7, seniors $6, children $5. Shipyard tour $8.50, seniors $7.50, children $5.50. Combined package $1 off each.) To find out when the *USS Nimitz* and other active

Navy vessels are in town, call the shipyard public relations office at 476-1111. The recently opened, somewhat bare **Kitsap Historical Museum,** 280 4th St. (479-6226), houses exhibits on WWII history and the shipyard's past. (Open daily 10am-5pm; in winter W-M 10am-5pm. Donation encouraged.) Outside, you can stroll the Bremerton Boardwalk along the water beyond the *Turner Joy*.

At the Seattle ferry dock, catch the **passenger ferry** from the Bremerton terminal across the Sinclair Inlet to **Port Orchard** for a view of the expansive shipyards. (The ferry leaves at 15 and 45min. past the hour. $1.10, children 75¢, free on weekends May-Oct.) Up Rte. 303 north from Bremerton to Keyport, the free **Naval Undersea Museum,** 610 Donell St. (396-4148; open daily 10am-4pm), displays artifacts salvaged from the seas, including a Japanese torpedo.

Across Liberty Bay "fjord" from Keyport, Norwegian immigrants have made a tourist-luring shrine out of the town of **Poulsbo** (PAWLZ-bo), where various Scandinavian festivals take place year-round on streets with names like King Olav V Vei. Contact the Greater Poulsbo **Chamber of Commerce** (779-4848) for more information. **Sluy's Poulsbo Bakery,** 18924 Front St. (697-2253 or 800-69-75897), serves sweet Scandinavian breads and exotic Norwegian delicacies like *krem* and *kaffe* (open M-Sa 6:30am-5:30pm, Su 6:30am-5pm).

Southeast of Poulsbo lies the **Historic Port Madison Indian Reservation,** where the Suquamish, who once inhabited most of the Seattle area, Kitsap Peninsula, and the islands of Puget Sound, were confined in the 1850s. Here they clashed with the U.S. military over hunting and fishing rights guaranteed by treaty but withheld in practice. After a prolonged decline, the Suquamish have flourished in recent years due in part to a revival of the seafaring lifestyle: the "Canoe Nation" cultural alliance with other coastal tribes and lucrative diving for geoduck clams are supplemented by income from a profitable casino. The **Suquamish Museum** (394-5275), on the north side of the Agate Pass Bridge on Rte. 305, houses tribal artifacts and contemporary portrayals of Suquamish life that describe the history and effects of European settlement. Drivers should follow Rte. 305 toward Bainbridge Island and turn off at Sandy Hook Rd.; pedestrians should ask nicely to be let off bus #90 at the Evergreen's Mart, then follow the road 1 mi. to the museum.

The grave of legendary Chief Seattle is within driving distance of the town of **Suquamish,** in a nearby Catholic mission cemetery. The Suquamish considered Sealth's (SELTH) real name taboo to pronounce; the word "Seattle" is only a European approximation. The moving memorial is constructed of cedar war canoes in the middle of the cemetery for St. Peter's Catholic Church. You can pick up a map from the museum before driving to the monument. From Rte. 305 South, take a left onto Suquamish Way and follow to the town of Suquamish. (Open daily May-Sept. 10am-5pm; Oct.-April 11am-4pm. $2.50, seniors $2, under 12 $1.)

NEAR KITSAP PENINSULA: BAINBRIDGE ISLAND

Rural Bainbridge Island was first homesteaded by late-19th-century Swedes, and later by Japanese immigrants before WWII. Most recently, droves of Californians are settling here. A stroll through the quaint town of **Winslow** make a relaxing escape from Seattle. The island can be reached by road via **Rte. 305** and the **Agate Pass Bridge,** or via the **Washington State Ferries** (800-84-FERRY/843-3779 or 206-464-6400; www.wsdot.wa.gov/ferries), which leave daily from downtown Seattle at Pier 50 (35min., 32 per day; $3.60). Stop by the **Chamber of Commerce,** 590 Winslow Way East (842-3700), to inquire about current festivals and events (open M-Th 9am-5pm, F 9am-6pm, Sa 10am-3pm). **Kitsap Transit** runs buses between Bremerton and Bainbridge: from the transit center in Bremerton, take #11 to Silverdale Mall, transfer onto #32 to Poulsbo, then take #90 to Bainbridge (info 800-501-7433; $1).

Fay-Bainbridge State Park (842-3931), on the northeast tip of the island, has good fishing, nice beaches, 26 full hookups ($16), and 10 tent sites ($6), with pay showers and toilets. The **Streamliner Diner,** 397 Winslow Way (842-8595), serves finer diner fare (omelettes $6-7.25; open daily 7am-2:30pm). Wash dinner down with a Ferry Boat white from the **Bainbridge Island Vineyards & Winery** (842-9463), where you can sample the local grapes ($1) or tour the fields; turn right at the first white trellis on Rte. 305 as you leave the ferry, or if coming from the Agate Pass Bridge, watch on the left for the stacked kegs just before town. (Open W-Su noon-5pm; tours Su 2pm. Bottles from $8.50.)

OLYMPIA

While the Evergreen State College campus lies a few miles from the city center, its liberal, highly pierced student body spills into the state capital to mingle with preppy politicos. Some locals, nostalgic for the era when "Oly" was a smaller city with a thriving fishing industry, scorn upstart youth and their raucous ways. Judging by the nightlife, they have plenty to scorn.

ORIENTATION AND PRACTICAL INFORMATION

Settled at the junction of I-5 and U.S. 101, Olympia makes a convenient stop on any north-south journey, wedged between **Tumwater** (to the south; I-5 Exit 102) and **Lacey** (to the east; I-5 Exit 108). I-5 Exit 105 leads to the **Capitol Campus** and **downtown** Olympia. The west side of downtown borders freshwater **Capitol Lake** and salty **West Bay**, also known as **Budd Bay**. The **4th Ave.** bridge divides the two and leads to the city's fast-food-chain-infested section. Navigating Olympia's one-way streets on **bike** or **foot** is easy, as all public buses have bike racks.

TRANSPORTATION

Trains: Amtrak, 6600 Yelm Hwy. (923-4602 or 800-872-7245). Bus #94 runs between downtown and the station. To: Seattle (1¾hr., 4 per day, $8.50-16); Portland (2½hr., 4 per day, $11.50-22). Station open daily 8-11:45am, 1:45-3:15pm, and 5:30-8:10pm.

Buses: Greyhound, 107 E. 7th Ave. (357-5541 or 800-231-2222), at Capitol Way. To: Seattle (1¾hr., 6-7 per day, $8; but check out the Olympia Express, below); Portland (2¾hr., 6-7 per day, $19); Spokane (9hr., 2 per day, $27). The office is closed, but buses still pick up passengers outside the depot. Taxi dispatch next door.

Public Transportation: Intercity Transit (IT) (786-1881 or 800-287-6348). Easy, reliable, and flexible service to almost anywhere in Thurston County, even with bicycles. Schedules are at the visitor center or at the Transit Center, 222 State Ave. (open M-F 7am-6pm, Sa 8am-5pm). Fare 60¢. Day passes $1.25. The free **Capitol Shuttle** runs from the Capitol Campus to downtown or to the east side and west side (every 15min., 6:45am-5:45pm). For the standard fare, **Custom buses** (943-7777) pick up where normal fixed routes stop (M-Sa after 7pm). Open M-Sa 6:30am-9:30pm, Su 8:15am-5:30pm. The **Olympia Express** runs between Olympia and Tacoma (55min., M-F 5:50am-6pm). Fare $1.50, seniors and disabled 75¢. A Seattle bus from Tacoma costs $1.50; the full trip to Seattle takes 2hr.

Taxis: Red Top Taxi, 357-3700. **Capitol City Taxi,** 357-4949. $2 base, $1.50 per mile.

Car Rental: U-Save Auto Rental, 3015 Pacific Ave. (786-8445). $20-25 per day, plus 20¢ per mi. over 150 mi. Must be 21 with credit card.

AAA: 2415 Capitol Mall Dr. (357-5561 or 800-562-2582). Open M-F 8:30am-5:30pm.

LOCAL SERVICES

Visitor Information: Washington State Capitol Visitor Center, (586-3460), on Capitol Way at 14th Ave., just south of the State Capitol; follow the signs on I-5, or from Capitol Way turn west at the pedestrian bridge. Open M-F 8am-5pm.

Outdoor Information: Department of Natural Resources (DNR), 1111 Washington St. (902-1000 or 800-527-3305; open 8am-4:30pm), houses a maze of offices: The **Maps Department** (902-1234), The **Fish and Game Office** (902-2200), and the **Washington State Parks and Recreation Commission Information Center** (800-233-0321). **The Olympic National Forest Headquarters,** 1835 Black Lake Blvd. SW (956-2400), provides info on land outside the park. Open M-F 8am-4:30pm.

Library: Olympia Timberland Library, 313 8th Ave. SE (352-0595), at Franklin St. provides 1hr. free Internet access. Open M-Th 10am-9pm, F-Sa 10am-5pm, Su 1-5pm.

Laundromat: Eastside Tavern (see **Nightlife,** below). Pints $2, wash and dry $1 each. Must be 21. Open M-F noon-2am, Sa-Su 3pm-2am. **Wash Tub,** 2103 Harrison Ave. NW (943-9714). Wash $1.25, dry 25¢ per 7min. Open M-F 7am-10pm, Sa-Su 8am-10pm.

EMERGENCY AND COMMUNICATIONS

Emergency: 911. **Police:** 900 Plum St. SE (753-8300), at 8th Ave.

Hospital: Providence St. Peter Hospital, 413 Lilly Rd. NE (491-9480). Follow signs northbound on I-5, Exit 107; southbound Exit 109. Emergency 24hr.

Crisis Line: 586-2800. 24hr.

Women's Services: Safeplace (754-6300 or 800-364-1776).

Post Office: 900 Jefferson SE, 98501 (357-2289). Open M-F 7:30am-12:25pm and 1-6pm, Sa 9am-12:25pm and 1-4pm.

Internet Access: See **Library,** above. **Bulldog News,** 116 E. 4th Ave. (357-6397), off Washington St. Tiny screens ($3 per hr.) and tiny zines. Open daily 9:30am-9:30pm.

Area Code: 360.

▐ ACCOMMODATIONS AND CAMPGROUNDS

Motels in Olympia cater to policy-makers ($60-75), but chains in nearby Tumwater are fine. Hell, try **Motel 6,** 400 W. Lee St. (754-7320; singles $38; doubles $44).

▩ **Grays Harbor Hostel,** 6 Ginny Ln. (482-3119; ghhostel@techline.com), just off Rte. 8 in Elma, 25 mi. west of Olympia. Catch bus #42 (Grays Harbor) from Olympia, or take the Fairground Rd. exit off Rte. 8, then make the first right by car. A great place to chill before starting a trip down the coast, or to acclimatize before heading to the big city. Hosteling biz veterans Jay and Linda Klemp run the place as if it were a ranch, a resort, and their home, which it is. Hot tub, 3-hole golf course, shed for bike repairs. Beds $12; private room $24. (Motor)cyclists camp on the lawn for $6. Ask Jay about local bike rides or lessons in the art of motorcycle maintenance. Check-in 5-10pm. Flexible daytime lockout. The Klemps are planning to move the hostel to Olympia, so call ahead.

The Golden Gavel Motor Hotel, 909 Capitol Way (352-8533). Only a few blocks north of the Capitol building. Clean, spacious, 70s-style rooms are a siren call for businesspeople not on the corporate account. Cable TV, morning coffee, free local calls, yadda yadda. Singles $45; doubles $49. AAA/senior discount $2.

Millersylvania State Park, 12245 Tilly Rd. S (753-1519; reservations 800-452-5687), 10 mi. south of Olympia. Take Exit 95 off I-5 N or S, turn onto Rte. 121 N, then follow signs to 6 miles of trails and Deep Lake. 164 sites: $11; hookups $16; walk-ins $5.50. Showers (25¢ per 6min.). 10-day max. stay. Wheelchair accessible.

Capital Forest Multiple Use Area, 15 mi. southwest of Olympia. Take exit 95 off I-5. 90 free (get here early) campsites spread among 7 campgrounds, administered by the DNR. Pick up a forest map at the state DNR office (see **Practical Information,** above) or the Central Region DNR office (748-2383) in nearby Chehalis. Pit toilets; no showers.

◖ FOOD

Diners, veggie eateries, and Asian quickstops line bohemian 4th Ave. east of Columbia. The **Bayview Deli & Bakery,** 516 W. 4th Ave. (352-4901; open M-Sa 7am-8pm, Su 7am-7pm), overlooks West Bay. Get slightly upscale groceries (cereal and wine) at the 24-hour **Safeway,** 520 Cleveland Ave. (943-1830), off Capital Blvd. in Tumwater, 1¼ mi. south of the Capitol building. The **Olympia Farmer's Market,** 700 N. Capital Way (352-9096), proffers produce and fantastic, cheap fare (salmon burger $3.75; open Apr.-Oct. Th-Su 10am-3pm, Nov.-Dec. Sa-Su 10am-3pm).

RESTAURANTS

The Spar Cafe & Bar, 114 E. 4th Ave. (357-6444). The cafe serves $7 burgers (open M-Th 6am-10pm, F-Sa 6am-11pm, Su 6am-9pm), and live jazz warms the tobacconist's polished counter-bar Sa 9pm-midnight (open M-Th 11am-midnight, F-Sa 11am-2am).

Lemon Grass, 212 E. 4th Ave. (705-1832). Big portions of Thai lure crowds (apple curry $7). M-Th 11am-2pm and 5-8:30pm, F 11am-2pm and 5-9pm, Sa 5-9pm.

Santosh, 116 4th Ave. (943-3442), west of Capitol Way. All-you-can-eat North Indian buffet ($6; M-F 11am-2:30pm). Open daily 11am-3pm and 5-9pm, F-Sa until 10pm.

Happy Teriyaki, 106 E. Legion Way (705-8000) at Capitol Way. Cheerfully prepares Japanese meals ($5-7, teriyaki bowl $4). Open M-Sa 11am-10pm.

Dancing Goats Espresso Co., 124 4th Ave. (754-8187), at N. Washington St. A corner cafe that tends to the artsy collegiate flock. $1.25 for a cuppa joe with a refill. Open M-W 7am-10pm, Th-F 7am-11pm, Sa 8am-11pm, Su 9am-7pm.

Otto's Bagels and Deli, 111 N. Washington (352-8640). Yellow walls and wood floors. Yum. Bagels 55¢; sandwiches $4. Open M-F 6am-7pm, Sa 7am-7pm, Su 7am-5pm.

⬛ SIGHTS AND EVENTS

Olympia's crowning glory is the **State Capitol Campus,** a complex of state government buildings, carefully sculpted gardens, veterans' monuments, and fabulous fountains, including a remarkable replica of Copenhagen's Tivoli fountain. A free tour of the **Legislative Chambers** (586-8677) is the only way into the inner sanctum. (Tours depart from the front entrance daily on the hour 10am-3pm. Building open M-F 8am-5:30pm, Sa-Su 10am-4pm.) Styled after Washington D.C.'s Capitol Dome, the newly renovated interior enshrines a six-ton Tiffany chandelier and six bronze doors depicting the state's history. Unfortunately, the building's spectacular stone dome is closed to the public. The **State Capitol Museum,** 211 W. 21st Ave. (753-2580), 6 blocks south of the visitor center via Capitol Way, houses historical and political exhibits in an Italian Renaissance-style mansion. (Open Tu-F 10am-4pm, Sa-Su noon-4pm. $2, seniors $1.75, children $1, families $5.) Free tours of campus buildings, including a tropical greenhouse and the **Temple of Justice** leave hourly on weekdays. Call 586-8687 for more info and options for the disabled.

Every lunch hour, state employees resplendent in spandex and sneakers head in droves for the parks surrounding **Capitol Lake.** Construction moves them ever-closer to designer Frederick Law Olmsted's vision, mapped out over 70 years ago. The $620,000 **interactive fountain** at Heritage Park at 4th Ave. and Sylvester St. provides somewhere for politicians and children in Underoos to partake of the good life. The **4th Ave. Bridge** is a perfect place to spot **spawning salmon** from late August to October. Northeast of the Campus, the high walls of the **Yashiro Japanese Garden** (753-8380), at Plum and Union, right next to City Hall, contain Olympia's secret garden. (Open daily 10am-dusk to picnickers and ponderers.)

Capitol Lakefair (943-7344), over the third week in July, features food, rides, and booths staffed by non-profit organizations. Beware new motel rates. The Washington Center for Performing Arts (943-9492) stages a **Shakespeare Festival** in August.

◩ NIGHTLIFE

Olympia's ferocious nightlife seems to have outgrown its daylife. Labels like K Records and Kill Rock Stars, with their flagship band Bikini Kill, have made Olympia a crucial pitstop on the indie rock circuit. Respected thespian Courtney Love and her band Hole also hail from and sing about Olympia. *The Rocket* and the city's daily *Olympian* list shows. To get in to the venues below, except Backstage, you must be 21.

▨ **Eastside Club and Tavern,** 410 E. 4th St. (357-9985). Old and young come to play pool and slam micro pints ($2). Live music often. Open M-F noon-2am, Sa-Su 3pm-2am.

4th Ave. Alehouse & Eatery, 210 E. 4th St. (786-1444). Townfolk gather for "slabs" of pizza ($2.75), seafood baskets ($5-6) and one (or several) of 26 draft micropints ($3) in Oly's old Town Hall. Live tunes, from blues to rock to reggae (Th-Sa). Cover $3-4.

Fishbowl Brewpub & Cafe, 515 Jefferson St. SE (943-3650), two blocks south off 4th. This living-room-like pub names its British ales ($3; on Tu $2) after fish. Acoustic music (Sa) and bluegrass (M); no cover. Order in from nearby restaurants to eat over a beer, or drink over a meal. Open daily 11am-midnight; food M-Th until 9pm, F-Sa until 10pm.

Thekla, 155 E. 5th Ave. (352-1855), under the neon arrow off N. Washington St. between 4th Ave. and Capitol, in a retro-meets-the-space-age refitted bank building. This gay-friendly dance joint spins dance music (F-Sa), soul (M), drum 'n' bass (Tu), hip-hop (W) and 80s tunes (Su, Th) Cover $0-4. Open 8pm-2am.

The Backstage, 206 E. 5th Ave. (754-5378), at the Capitol Theater. Locals mosh and mingle to 3-5 bands per night on weekends. Cover $5. Call for events. All ages shows.

⚑ NEAR OLYMPIA

Less than a mile south of town on I-5 at Exit 103, **Tumwater Falls Park,** built by the Olympia Brewery, is perfect for salmon-watching, picnicking, or a run. **Wolf Haven International,** 3111 Offut Lake Rd. (264-4695 or 800-448-9653; www.wolfhaven.org), lurks 10 mi. south of the capital. Take Exit 99 off I-5, turn east, and follow the brown signs. The haven shelters 24 wolves reclaimed from zoos or illegal owners. (Open May-Sept. W-M 10am-5pm; Oct.-Apr. 10am-4pm. 45-minute tours $5, ages 5-12 $2.50.) At the summer **Howl-In,** humans tell stories around a campfire to the accompaniment of more canine residents (late May to early Sept. F-Sa 6:30-9:30pm. $6, children $4). **Nisqually National Wildlife Refuge** (753-9467), off I-5 between Olympia and Tacoma at Exit 114, shelters 500 species of plants and animals and miles of open trails. Bald eagles, shorebirds, and northern spotted owls nest here. The trails are open daily from dawn to dusk and are closed to cyclists, joggers, and pets. (Office open M-F 7:30am-4pm. $3 per person or family.)

WHIDBEY ISLAND

Clouds wrung dry by the mountains west of Seattle release a scant 20 in. of rain each year over Whidbey Island, a beach-ringed strip of land that rises from Puget Sound (an island). This is prime road-biking country, with easy slopes and rustic scenery. The town of **Coupeville,** in Whidbey's middle, is a great place to start exploring the four state parks and historic reserve, where rocky beaches meet bluffs crowded with wild roses and blackberries. RVs are all over, but harmless. MacGregor's free *Whidbey Island* is full of maps and info on coastal towns.

Washington State Ferries (800-843-3779 or 206-464-6400; www.wsdot.wa.gov/ferries/) provides frequent service from the mainland to the island. One ferry connects mainland **Mukilteo,** 10 mi. south of Everett and 19 mi. north of Seattle, with **Clinton,** on the south end of the island (20min., 5am-2am on the half hour, $2.50, car and driver $4.50-5.75, bike 70¢). The other connects Port Townsend on the Olympic Peninsula with the **Keystone terminal** near Ft. Casey State Park (see below), at the "waist" of the island (30min., 7am-10pm every 45min., $1.85, car and driver $6.50-8.25, bike 35¢). You can drive onto the island along Rte. 20, which heads west from I-5, 12 mi. south of Bellingham, at Exit 230. Route 20 and Rte. 525 meet near Keystone and form the transportation backbone of the island, linking all the significant towns and points of interest. **Island Transit** (360-678-7771 or 360-321-6688; www.islandtransit.org/bus) provides free, hourly public transportation all over the island, and has info on connections to and from Seattle, but it has no service on Sundays and limited service on Saturdays. All buses have bike racks. You can flag a bus down anywhere safe for it to stop.

La Paz (360-341-4787), a baja-style Mexican restaurant in Clinton, is right off the ferry dock (seafood taco and rice $6; open Tu-Sa noon-3pm and 5-8pm, F until 9pm, Su 5-8pm). Next door, the **Whidbey Cybercafe & Bookstore** (341-5922; www.whidbey.com/cybercafe) provides access to the giant smut repository that is the **Internet** (terminals $6 per hr., 10min. minimum; open M-Sa 10am-7pm). The

ZOUNDS! MOUNDS! Baffling scientists since the mid-1800s, Mima (MIE-mah) Mounds have spawned wild speculation about their origins. An evenly spaced network of small, perfectly rounded hills covers the prairies just outside the Capital Forest, 12 mi. southwest of Olympia. Anthropology fanciers attribute the mounds' existence to the arcane labors of a nation of yesteryear, biology buffs cite giant gophers, and delusional paranoids cry government conspiracy. The scientific community is torn among hypotheses ranging from glacial action to seismic shock waves; by 1999, no fewer than 159 Mima-related papers had been published. Today, the Mounds inhabit some of the last remaining prairie in the Pacific Northwest, providing visitors with an opportunity to learn about the region's natural history and mystery. To reach the Mounds, take Exit 95 off I-5 and follow the signs to Littlerock. From Littlerock, follow more signs to the Capital Forest and watch for the marked dirt road to the parking lot and trailhead. (Open daily 8am-dusk. For info, call the DNR at 748-2383.)

beautiful **South Whidbey State Park** (206-321-4559, reservations 800-452-5687), amidst old growth forest by the beach, was once a favorite camp of the Skagit and Snohomish tribes (54 sites $10, hookups $15, hiker-biker $5).

Ebey's Landing, a Department of the Interior protected beach, has great views of the islands, the surrounding Olympic Mountains, and Port Townsend. The fabulously rich soil basin inland was the first region in the U.S. to be designated a National Historic Reserve. Sherman Rd. leaves Rte. 20, leading to a cemetery and a view of the island's idyllic prairie and beaches. Two State Parks lie near Ebey's Landing, **Fort Ebey State Park** (206-678-4636; 50 sites: $11-16), just north and east off Rte. 20., and **Fort Casey State Park** (reservations 800-452-5687), just south, home to old bunkers and military paraphernalia on a peninsula with unsheltered sites and views of the straits (sites $11; walk-ins $5; pay showers 25¢ per 3min.). An interpretive center lies at the **Admiralty Point lighthouse** (open Apr.-Oct. Th-Su 11am-5pm). For travelers wishing to avoid the busier state parks, the free **Rhododendron campground** (6 primitive sites) lies 1½ mi. before Coupeville; look for the small tent sign on eastbound Rte. 20/525 (if you see the recycling plant you've just passed it).

Seaside **Coupeville,** the second oldest town in Washington, makes for a nice stroll alongside historic buildings and waterfront shops. Free tours of the town's buildings depart the museum at the western end of Front St. (1½-2hr.; May-Sept. Sa-Su 11am). Coupeville's **Knead and Feed,** 4 Front St. (678-5431) makes fabulous soup from scratch with a serene view of the eastern waterfront. (Lunch $3-7.50; open M-Th 10:30am-3pm, F 10:30am-3pm and 5-9pm, Sa-Su 9am-9pm). For coffee and a read book (and 7" pizzas for $3.25 from 4-7pm) stop at **Great Times Espresso,** 12 Front Street (678-5358), just down the hill. (Open M-Sa 7am-8pm, Su 8am-8pm.)

At the north tip of the island on Rte. 20, the **Deception Pass Bridge,** the nation's first suspension bridge, connects Whidbey Island to the Anacortes Islands. A secret cave at one end held 17th-century prisoners who were forced to make wicker furniture. When the Skagit lived and fished around Deception Pass, the area was often raided by the Haida from the north. A Haida bear totem occupies the Fidalgo Bay side of **Deception Pass State Park,** 41229 SR (675-2417), just south of the bridge. Captain George Vancouver named the pass for his ship master Joseph Whidbey, who found the tangled geography of Puget Sound as confusing as most visitors do today. This is the most heavily used of Whidbey's four state parks, and its views are magnificent. A new **interpretive center** in the Bowman area, just north of the Civilian Conservation Corps bridge on Rte. 20 E, describes the army's building many parks in the northwest during the Depression. There are camping facilities, a saltwater boat launch, and a freshwater lake good for swimming, fishing, and boating. (Licenses available at hardware stores; season runs mid-Apr. to Oct.) Thirty miles of trails link some of the best views of Puget Sound's shore line and lure the ambitious into this magnificent old growth forest and **camping** (168 sites $11; 83 hookups $16; primitive sites $6). The campground is subjected to jet noise from EA6B Navy attack aircraft from nearby Whidbey Island Naval Air Station, in Oak Harbor. Reservations are such a very good idea (800-452-5687; $6).

NORTHWEST WASHINGTON

BELLINGHAM

Strategically situated between Seattle and Vancouver, Bellingham is the southern terminus of the Alaska Marine Highway; most travelers who stay the night are contemplating or completing an overseas journey to or from Alaska. Commercial fishing, coal mining, and a giant paper mill support the city's economy, and the indigenous Lummi, Nooksack, and Semiahmoo of the region maintain strong ties to their fishing legacy.

▓ ORIENTATION AND PRACTICAL INFORMATION

Bellingham lies along I-5, 90 mi. north of Seattle and 57 mi. south of Vancouver, BC. Downtown centers on **Holly St.** and **Cornwall Ave.,** next to the Georgia Pacific pulp mill (Exits 252 and 253 off I-5). **Western Washington University (WWU)** sits atop a hill to the south. The town of **Fairhaven,** where the ferries, bus, and trains stop, is directly south of town, and is serviced by public transit.

Trains: Amtrak, 401 Harris Ave. (734-8851 or 800-USA-RAIL/872-7245), in the bus/train station next to the ferry terminal. 1 per day to: Seattle (2½hr., $23) and Vancouver, BC (1½hr., $15). See p. 52 for discounts. Counter open daily 8-11am and 5-8pm.

Buses: Greyhound, 401 Harris Ave. (733-5251 or 800-231-2222), next to the ferry terminals. To: Seattle (2hr., 8 per day, $13), Mt. Vernon (30min., 6 per day, $6), and Vancouver, BC (2hr., 6 per day, $13). See p. 53 for discounts. Open M-F 6:30am-5:30pm.

Ferries: Alaska Marine Highway, 355 Harris Ave. (676-8445 or 800-642-0066), in Fairhaven; take Exit 250 off I-5 and follow signs. July-Aug. 1 per week to Ketchikan, AK (36hr., $164) and beyond. See p. 58. **Lummi Island Ferry** (676-6692), at Gooseberry Pt.; take I-5 north to Slater Rd. (Exit 260), then take a left on Haxton Way. Frequent daily service to Lummi (6:10am-12:10am; round-trip: $1, cars $2, bikes 50¢). Private shuttles run ferries to the nearby San Juan Islands (see p. 190).

Public Transportation: Whatcom County Transit (676-7433). All routes start at the Railroad Ave. Mall terminal, between Holly and Magnolia St. 50¢, under 6 and over 84 free. No transfers. Buses run every 15-60min. M-F 5:50am-7:30pm; reduced service M-F 7:30-11pm and Sa-Su 9am-6pm.

Taxis: City Cab, 773-8294 or 800-281-5430. **Yellow Cab,** 734-8294.

Car Rental: AA, 4575 Guide Meridian (734-7800). $25 per day, 20¢ per mi. after 100 mi. Must be 25 with credit card or $300 deposit. Open M-Sa 9am-6pm, Su 11am-5pm.

Visitor Information: 904 Potter St. (671-3990). Take Exit 253 (Lakeway) from I-5. Open daily 8:30am-5:30pm.

Equipment Rental: The Great Adventure, 201 E. Chestnut St. (671-4615). Rents skiing, climbing, and backpacking gear at fair rates. Kayaks $32 per day, tents $20 for 2 days. Open M-Th 10am-6pm, F 10am-7pm, Sa 9am-6pm, Su 11am-5pm.

Laundromat: Bellingham Cleaning Center, 1010 Lakeway Dr. (734-3755). Wash $1.25, dry 25¢ per 10min. Open M-F 7am-8pm, Sa 8am-8pm, Su 10am-7pm.

Library: 210 Central St. (676-6860), at Commercial St. opposite City Hall. Free **Internet access.** Open Sept.-May M-Th 10am-9pm, F-Sa 10am-6pm, Su 1-5pm.

Emergency: 911. **Police:** 505 Grand Ave. (676-6913). Open M-F 8am-5:30pm.

Crisis Line: 888-715-1563. Open 24hr.

Hospital: St. Joseph's General, 2901 Squalicum Pkwy. (734-5400). Open 24hr.

Post Office: 315 Prospect, 98225 (676-8303). M-F 8am-5:30pm, Sa 9:30am-3pm.

Area Code: 360.

Bellingham

ACCOMMODATIONS

A Travelers Lodge
B Mac's Motel
C Fairhaven Rose Garden
Hostel (HI-YHA)

Alaska Marine Hwy Ferries
San Juan Islands Ferries

0   500 yards
0   500 meters

ACCOMMODATIONS AND CAMPGROUNDS

For both atmosphere and price, the hostel is the best bet. For B&Bs from $60, call the **Bed & Breakfast Guild of Whatcom County** (676-4560).

Fairhaven Rose Garden Hostel (HI), 107 Chuckanut Dr. (671-1750), next to Fairhaven Park, about ¾ mi. from the ferry terminal; take I-5 Exit 250, and go west on Fairhaven Pkwy. to 12th St.; bear left onto Chuckanut Dr. From downtown Bellingham, take bus #1A or 1B. A tiny, clean hostel in a sometimes-musty basement. 10 beds: $13. Make-your-own all-you-can-eat pancakes $1. Linen $2. No curfew; reception 5-10pm. Call ahead, especially on Thursday night, when Alaska-bound travelers fill the place. Open Feb.-Nov. although the hostel may close in May 2000.

Travelers Lodge, 202 E. Holly St. (734-1900). Take I-5 Exit 253. Roll out of the lodge's big beds and clean rooms right into downtown Bellingham. Cable TV in the rooms makes up for the occasional 2am noisiness. Free local calls. Singles $32; doubles $45.

Mac's Motel, 1215 E. Maple St. (734-7570), at Samish Way; take I-5 Exit 252. Large, clean rooms; exterior paint right out of the 70s. Singles $24; doubles (sleep 4) $38. Open daily 7am-10pm.

Larrabee State Park (676-2093, reservations 800-452-5687), on Chuckanut Dr., 7 mi. south of town, among trees on Samish Bay. Tide pools nearby; alpine lakes within hiking distance. 87 sites: $11; hookups $16; 8 walk-ins $7. Open daily 6:30am-dusk.

⚡ FOOD

The **Community Food Co-op,** 1220 N. Forest St. (734-8158), at Maple St., has all the essentials, plus a health food cafe in the back (open daily 8am-9pm). The Saturday **Bellingham Farmer's Market** (647-2060), at Chestnut St. and Railroad Ave., has fruit, vegetables, and homemade doughnuts (Apr.-Oct. Sa 10am-3pm, Su 11am-3pm).

🐟 **Casa Que Pasa,** 1415 Railroad Ave. (738-8226). Humongous burritos, made with fresh local vegetables (from $2.75). Open daily 11am-11pm.

The Old Town Cafe, 316 West Holly St. (671-4431), makes delectable breakfasts with ingredients from the market. Play a few songs on the piano in the adjoining art gallery and earn yourself a free drink and choice of breakfast. Buttermilk pancakes $3.25, french toast $4.25. Vegan-friendly. Open M-Sa 6:30am-3pm, Su 8am-2pm.

Tony's, 1101 Harris Ave. (733-6319), in Fairhaven Village, blocks from the ferry. Garden and cafe with stained-glass windows serves coffee, ice cream, bagels, and the infamous, high-voltage, Toxic Milkshake, made with coffee and espresso grounds ($4). Open M-F 6:30am-9pm, Sa-Su 7:30am-9pm.

👁 🎵 SIGHTS, ENTERTAINMENT, AND EVENTS

The **Whatcom Museum of History and Art,** 121 Prospect St. (676-6981 www.cob.org/museum.htm), occupies four buildings along Prospect St., most notably the looming old city hall. Photographs of turn-of-the-century Pacific Northwest logging scenes by Darius Kinsey are a highlight. Climb to the third floor of the old city hall to watch clocktower innards at work. (Open Tu-Su noon-5pm. Free; wheelchair accessible.) **Big Rock Garden Park,** 2900 Sylvan St. (676-6985), is a 3-acre Japanese tea garden filled with modern sculpture in a residential neighborhood. Take Alabama St. east, then go left on Sylvan for several blocks. Call ahead for a schedule of outdoor musical performances. (Park open daily dawn-dusk.)

In the second week of June, lumberjacks from across the land gather for axe-throwing, log-rolling, and speed-climbing contests at the **Deming Logging Show** (592-3051). To reach the showgrounds, take Mt. Baker Hwy. (Rte. 542) 12 mi. east to Cedarville Rd., turn left and follow signs ($5, ages 3-12 $3). The **Bellingham Festival of Music** (676-5997) brings symphony, chamber, folk, and jazz musicians from around the world during the first two weeks of August (tickets $18-21). Memorial Day weekend sees the mother of all relays, the **Ski to Sea Race** (734-1330). Participants ski, run, canoe, bike, and sea kayak their way from Mt. Baker to the finish line at Bellingham Bay.

⛰ OUTDOORS

The 2½ mi. hike up **Chuckanut Mountain** leads through a quiet forest to a view of the islands that fill the bay. On clear days, Mt. Rainier is visible from the top. The trail leaves from Old Samish Hwy. about 3 mi. south of city limits. The beach at **Lake Padden Park,** 4882 Samish Way (676-6985), has the warmest water in the Puget Sound; take bus #44 one mile south of downtown. The park also has tennis courts, playing fields, hiking trails, a boat launch (no motors allowed), and fishing off the pier (open daily 6am-10pm.) The popular **Interurban Trail** runs 5½ mi. from **Fairhaven Park** to **Larrabee State Park** along the relatively flat route of the old Interurban Electric Railway. Occasional breaks in the trees permit a glimpse of the San Juan Islands. Several trails branch off the main line and lead up into the Chuckanut Mountains or down to the coast; pick up a map from the visitor center. The Interurban Trail intersects the 1 mi. trail to clothing-optional **Teddy Bear Cove,** also accessible from Chuckanut Dr., 2 mi. south of Fairhaven.

MOUNT BAKER

Crowning the **Mt. Baker-Snoqualmie National Forest,** Mt. Baker received the most snow ever recorded in one season in the U.S.—1140 inches—in 1999. The yearly average of 615 inches is hardly less astonishing and makes for excellent snow-boarding and skiing. No high speed lifts here, just great bowls, chutes, and glades, and cheap lift tickets. During the summer, hikers and mountaineers challenge themselves on its trails and ascents. Take I-5 Exit 255, just north of Bellingham, to Rte. 542, known as the **Mt. Baker Highway;** 58 mi. of roads through the foothills afford views of Baker and other peaks in the range. On the way to Mt. Baker, turn right at Mile 16 onto Mosquito Lake Rd., pull over at the first bridge, and look for bald eagles along Kendall Creek. The highway ends at **Artist Point** (5140 ft.), with spectacular wilderness vistas. The road closes at Mt. Baker Ski Area in winter.

The volcano packs soft powder for longer than any other nearby ski area, staying open from early November through May. The ski area has 8 lifts, the lowest lift ticket rates in the northwest, but no terrain park: there is no snow-making or shaping on the mountain's 1500 vertical feet of runs. Contact the **Mt. Baker Ski Area Office** (360-734-6771; www.mtbakerskiarea.com) in Bellingham for more info. (Lift tickets $29, under 15 and seniors $21.50.)

The popular **Lake Ann Trail** leads 4¾ mi. to the lake of the same name, continuing to the Lower Curtis Glacier. Hikers can make inevitable Robert Frost references on the picturesque **Fire and Ice Trail,** a ½ mi. loop beginning on Rte. 542. For trail maps, **backcountry permits,** or further area info, stop by the **Glacier Public Service Center** (360-599-2714; open daily 8:30am-4:30pm).

Silver Lake Park, 9006 Silver Lake Rd. (599-2776), is 28 mi. from Bellingham, 3 mi. north of the highway at Maple Falls. The park tends 73 sites near the lake, with swimming, hiking and fishing access (tent sites $11; hookups $16). More primitive and closer to the mountain is **Douglas Fir Campground,** at Mile 36 off Rte. 542 (30 sites; $10), and **Silver Fir Campground,** at Mile 46 off Rte. 542 (21 sites; $10; water). **Carol's Coffee Cup,** 5415 Mt. Baker Hwy. (592-5641), is good for pre-ski carbo-loading with the biggest cinnamon rolls on earth ($1.25).

BLAINE AND BIRCH BAY

A small border town 20 mi. north of Bellingham, Blaine is a busy port of entry between Canada and the U.S. (see **Customs,** p. 26). The lines to cross the border can be tedious in either direction, especially on weekends. Follow signs to the "Truck Crossing" for shorter lines. **Peace Arch State Park** (332-8221) is the main attraction in Blaine. Directly on the Canada/U.S. border, the Peace Arch contains relics of early U.S. and Canadian ships of discovery, and commemorates the Treaty of Ghent, which ended the War of 1812 and inaugurated the long era of peace between Canada and the U.S. (see p. 193 for an exception). To reach the park, take I-5 Exit 276, then turn north onto 2nd St. (Open 8am-dusk).

The **Birch Bay Hostel (HI),** 7467 Gemini St. (360-371-2180 or 877-371-2180; bbhostel@az.com), Bldg. #630 on the former Blaine Air Force Base, has small, clean, private rooms, a full kitchen, and a large, homey living room. Off I-5, take either the Birch Bay-Lynden Rd. exit or the Grandview Rd. exit and head west to Blaine Rd. Take a right onto Alderson from Blaine and look for the HI sign on the left. ($12, nonmembers $15; open May-Sept.)

Birch Bay State Park, 5105 Helwig Rd. (371-2800, reservations 800-452-5687), 10 mi. south of Blaine, operates 167 campsites near the water. The Semiahmoo used this area and the marshland at the southern end of the park to harvest shellfish and hunt waterfowl. The park's **Terrell Creek Estuary** contains 300 species of birds, and is a good crabbing, scuba diving, water skiing, and swimming territory. Take the Birch Bay-Lynden exit off I-5 and turn south onto Blaine Rd. When Blaine Rd. veers to the left, turn right onto Bay Rd. Take a left on Jackson Rd. and continue until it hits Helwig Rd. (Sites $11; hookups $16; open year-round).

The **C Shop,** 4825 Alderson Rd. (371-2070), down the street from the hostel, offers over 100 desserts and cheap custom-made sandwiches and pizza (open late-May to mid-June Sa 1-10pm, Su 1-6pm; mid-June to Sept. daily 1-10pm). The **Harbor Cafe,** 295 Marine Dr. (332-5176) in Blaine, halfway down the pier, serves the best seafood in town. Fish and chips with salad or chowder $9. (Open daily 6am-10pm).

SAN JUAN ISLANDS

With hundreds of tiny islands and endless parks and coastline, the San Juan Islands are an explorer's dream. Many locals consider their cars a sad alternative to their kayaks, and the San Juan Islands offer ample opportunity to commune with cedars and tidepools in relative seclusion. To avoid the summer tourist rush but still enjoy good weather, visit in late spring or early fall; some of the islands are very quiet in winter, and many businesses open only upon request. While some locals are bothered by southern transplants buying up chunks of the islands, many are delighted at the attention tourists are giving their home. Two excellent guides to the area are available at bookshops and outfitters: *The San Juan Islands Afoot and Afloat* by Marge Mueller ($15), and *Emily's Guide*, a series of descriptions of each island ($5 each or 3 for $11). *San Juans' Beckon* includes maps and recreation info. The *San Juanderer* has tide charts and ferry schedules. Both are free on ferries or at visitor centers. If you are planning to out-trip on the San Juan Islands, plan ahead; there are scant trip-planning resources on the islands, and the info you need may be available only in Seattle.

GETTING THERE AND GETTING AROUND

Short hops and good roads make for excellent biking on the islands, and hitchhiking is reputedly easy, and San Juan and Orcas Islands combine a shuttle service.

Washington State Ferries (800-843-3779 or 206-464-6400; www.wsdot.wa.gov/ferries) has frequent daily service to Lopez (50min.), Shaw (1¼hr.), Orcas (1½hr.), and San Juan Island (2hr.), from **Anacortes;** check the schedule available at visitor centers in Puget Sound. To save on fares, travel directly to the westernmost island on your itinerary, then return: eastbound traffic travels for free. Or don't bring a car, because foot passengers travel free, too. The ferries are packed in summer, so arrive at least one hour prior to departure. ($5.10, vehicle $16-21.75 depending on destination, bike $2.90; cash only.) To reach the terminal from Seattle, take I-5 north to Mt. Vernon, then Rte. 20 west to Anacortes and follow signs. The **Bellingham Airporter** (800-235-5247) shuttles between Sea-Tac (see p. 158) and Anacortes (8 per day M-F, 6 per day Sa-Su; $27, round-trip $49).

Victoria Clipper departs **Seattle's** Pier 69 daily for San Juan Island, arriving at Spring Street Landing, one block north of the state ferry dock in **Friday Harbor** (2½hr.) or at **Rosario Resort** on Orcas Island (3¼hr.; mid-May to mid-Sept.; $38, round-trip $59; 2-week advance discount, children half-price). **Island Commuter** (734-8180 or 888-734-8180; www.whales.com/ic) departs **Bellingham** for Rosario Resort (1¼hr., $20, round-trip $30), Friday Harbor (2¼hr., $25, round-trip $35), and islands on the way (ages 6-12 half-price, under 6 free; bicycles $5).

SAN JUAN ISLAND

The biggest and most popular of the islands, San Juan Island was discovered by the tourist world in the early 1980s. San Juan is the last stop on the ferry route and home to Friday Harbor, the largest town in the archipelago. San Juan is also the easiest island to explore, since the ferry docks right in town, the roads are good for cyclists, and a shuttle bus services the island. Limekiln State Park is the only designated whale-watching park in the world. But popularity has its price: Seattle weekenders flood the island throughout the summer, bringing all sorts of traffic.

▮ ORIENTATION AND PRACTICAL INFORMATION

With bicycle, car, and boat rentals within blocks of the ferry terminal, **Friday Harbor** is a convenient base for exploring San Juan. Miles of poorly marked roads access all corners of the island. It's wise to carefully plot a course on a free **map** available at the visitor centers, real estate offices, or gas stations.

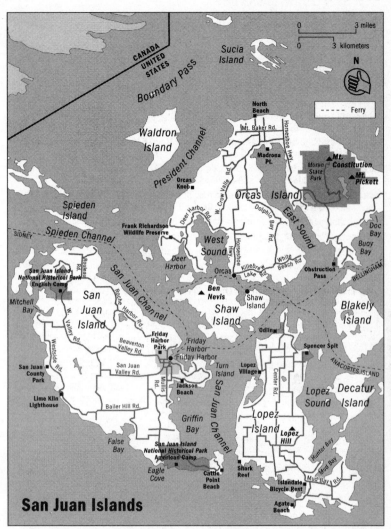

San Juan Islands

Buses: San Juan Transit: (378-8887 or 800-887-8387; www.san-juan.net/transit) circles the island every 35-55min. and will stop upon request. Point to point $4; Day pass $10; 2-day pass $19 (good on Orcas Island). Tours twice a day ($15, reserve ahead).

Ferries: Washington State Ferries, see **Getting There and Getting Around,** above.

Taxis: San Juan Taxi (378-3550). $4 base, $1 per person, $1 per mi. after the first mi.

Visitor Information: Chamber of Commerce (378-5240 or 888-468-3701; www.sanjuanisland.org), in a booth up East St. that is constantly stocked. **San Juan Transit** (see above), upstairs in the cannery landing by the dock.

Outdoor Information: San Juan National Historic Park Information Center (378-2240), on the corner of 1st and Spring St. Open M-F 8:30am-4:30pm; in winter until 4pm.

Tours: San Juan Boat Tours (800-232-6722) at Spring Street Landing a block right from ferry, has naturalist-led tours ($49; seniors $45; children $35). **San Juan Safaris** (378-2155, ext. 505, or 800-451-8910, ext. 505) departs the end of Roche Harbor Rd., at the north tip of the island, for a 3hr. whale-watching trip ($45, ages 4-12 $35). **Zoetic Research** (378-5767), a non-profit education, research and conservation group, runs excellent kayaking tours (May-Oct.: half-day $39, full day $59, longer trips available).

Equipment Rental: Rentals require a credit card. **Island Bicycles,** 380 Argyle St. (378-4941; open daily 9am-6pm), up Spring St., rents bikes ($5 per hr., $25 per day). **Island Scooter and Bike Rental** (378-8811; open daily 8:30am-7pm), rents scooters ($15 per hr., $45 per day).

Laundromat: Sunshine Laundromat, on Nichols St. Wash $2.50, dry 25¢ per 7min. Open daily 7am-9:30pm.

Internet Access: See **Gray Matter** (in **Food,** below). **Menu Bar,** 435-B Argyle Ave. $6 per hr. Open M-F 9:30am-7pm, Sa 10:30am-4:30pm.

Pharmacy: Friday Harbor Drug, 210 Spring St. (378-4421). Open M-Sa 9am-7pm, Su 10am-4pm. **Red Tide Hotline:** 800-562-5632.

Medical Services: Inter-Island Medical Center, 550 Spring St. (378-2141), at Mullis Rd. Open M-F 8:30am-5pm, Sa 10am-noon. **Crisis:** 378-2345 or 376-1234, 24hr.

Domestic Violence/Sexual Assault Services: 378-8680.

Emergency: 911. **Sheriff:** 135 Rhone St. (non-emergency 378-4151), at Reed St.

Post Office: 220 Blair St., 98250 (378-4511), at Reed St. Open M-F 8:30am-4:30pm.

Area Code: 360.

▌ ACCOMMODATIONS AND CAMPGROUNDS

San Juan's campgrounds have become wildly popular; call ahead for reservations or show up early in the afternoon to secure a spot. There are few cheap accommodations. Often beautiful, many B&Bs are expensive; contact **San Juan Central Reservation** (888-999-8773; www.fridayharbor.com) for help with such matters.

Wayfarer's Rest, 35 Malcolm St. (378-6428), a 10min. walk from the ferry up Spring onto Argyle St. and left at the church. A homey little hostel with 8 dorm beds made with driftwood ($20, private room $30; free linens) and a canvas tent with cots ($15, no bedding). Bikes for little. Eggs from hens. Kitchen. Check-in between 2-9pm.

San Juan County Park, 380 Westside Rd. (378-2992), 10 mi. west of Friday Harbor along the bay. 20 sites on the bluff have views of whales (maybe) and great sunsets (almost definitely). Water, toilets, no showers. Vehicle sites $18; walk-ins $5. Open daily 7am-10pm. Office open daily 9am-7pm. Reservations highly recommended.

Lakedale Campgrounds, 2627 Roche Harbor Rd. (378-2350 or 800-617-2267; www.lakedale.com), 4 mi. from Friday Harbor. The mothership of campgrounds. Some sites are very attractive, set near lakes. Vehicle sites $24, plus $5.75 per person after a pair; hiker/biker sites $8; tent-cabins sleep 4 (from $45). Day use $1.50. Showers $3 per 5min. Reservations suggested, but management boasts they've never turned a camper away. Open Mar. 15-Oct. 15; cabins year-round. Cheaper rates in off-season. Fishing permits ($4 per day, non-campers $8 per day). Boat rental.

◖ FOOD

The king needs his wine! **King's Market,** 160 Spring St. (378-4505; open M-Sa 7:30am-10pm, Su 8am-10pm), stocks it. Most restaurants serve vegetarian food.

Katrina's, 135 2nd St. (378-7290), between Key Bank and Friday Harbor Drug. The daily menu invariably includes organic salads, fresh bread, and gigantic cookies ($1.25). Sea shanties emanate from within F and Sa. Sandwiches $5. Entrees $8-13. Open M-Th 11am-4:30pm, F 11am-4:30pm and 5:30-10pm, Sa 5:30-10pm.

San Juan Bakery and Donut Shop, 225 Spring St. (378-2271). Bottomless coffee ($1.16) and town rumor mill. Call for a sack lunch. Open M-Sa 5am-2pm, Su 7am-1pm.

Gray Matter, 80 Nichols St. (378-6555), off Argyle St., is a skater haunt. Shoot espresso (50¢), that cute skater a look, and the bull. Free Internet (email $1). **The Eatery** (378-8556) opposite, sells burgers ($3.25). Open M, W-Sa 11am-8pm, Su 11am-7pm.

👁 🔼 SIGHTS, OUTDOORS, AND EVENTS

The **Whale Museum,** 62 1st St. (378-4710), has a rich collection and gives directions to whale-watching spots. Call their whale hotline (800-562-8832) to report sightings and strandings. (Open daily 10am-5pm; Oct.-May 11am-4pm; $5, seniors $4, students and ages 5-18 $2, under 5 free.) **San Juan Historical Museum,** 405 Price St. (378-3949), opposite the church, displays circa-1800 furnishings and photos. (Open May-Sept. W-Su 1-4pm and by appointment. Free.)

A drive around the 35-mile perimeter of the island takes about two hours, and the route is good for a day-long cycling tour. The **West Side Rd.** traverses gorgeous scenery and provides the best chance for sighting **orcas** from three resident pods.

To begin a tour of the island, head south and west out of Friday Harbor on Mullis Rd. (Bikers may want to do this route in the opposite direction, as climbs heading counterclockwise around the island are much more gradual.) Mullis Rd. merges with Cattle Point Rd., and goes straight into **American Camp** (378-2902; open daily dawn-11pm) on the south side of the island. The camp dates from the Pig War of 1859 and a **visitor center** explains the history of that curious conflict. (Open daily 8:30am-5pm. Guided walks Saturdays 11:30am.) A self-guided trail leads from the shelter, through the buildings, and past the site of a British sheep farm. Every Saturday afternoon at British Camp, volunteers in period costume re-enact daily Pig War-era life. (June-July 12:30-3:30pm; Aug. to Labor Day. Free.) If the sky is clear, make the half-mile jaunt down the road to **Cattle Point** for views of the distant Olympic Mountains (and hundreds of less distant rabbits), or stop by **South Beach,** a stretch of shoreline that dazzles beach walkers and whale stalkers. To the west, **Eagle Beach** and **Grandma's Cove,** accessible from the self-guided trail, are considered some of the finest beaches on the island.

The gravel False Bay Rd., heading west from Cattle Point Rd., runs to **False Bay,** where **bald eagles** nest. During spring and summer, nesting eagles are visible at low tide along the northwestern shore (toward the right as you face the water). False Bay Rd. continues north, running into Bailer Hill Rd., which turns into West Side Rd. when it reaches Haro Straight. **Limekiln Point State Park,** along West Side Rd., is renowned as the best **whale-watching** spot in the area. Cliffside crowds watch as killer whales prowl for salmon between occasional acrobatics. The most determined (whale-watchers) shell out for a **cruise;** most operations charge $45 (children $35) for a three- to four-hour boat ride. Get a brochure at the chamber of commerce or the park visitor center.

The Pig War casts its comic pallor over **British Camp,** the second half of the **San Juan National Historical Park,** on West Valley Rd. at sheltered **Garrison Bay.** (Buildings open Memorial Day to Labor Day daily 8am-5pm.) Heading east from West Side Rd., Mitchell Bay Rd. leads to a steep half-mile trail to **"Mount" Young,** a good tall hill within looking range of Victoria and the Olympic Range.

DIE, IMPERIALIST PIG!
Back in 1859, when Washington was officially part of "Oregon Country" and the San Juan Islands lay in a territorial no man's land between British Vancouver Island and the United States, one hungry hog unwittingly gave his life for what turned out to be truth, justice, and the American Way. Twenty-five Americans farmed on San Juan Island when the British Hudson's Bay Company claimed it for England. When Lyman Cutlar caught a British pig making a royal mess of his potato patch, he understandably shot it dead. The Brits threatened to arrest him, and the Americans looked to Uncle Sam for protection. Three months, five British warships, and 14 American cannons later, war between the two nations looked inevitable. Though the standoff soon cooled down, the "Pig War" stalemate lasted 12 years. Both countries occupied the island until 1872, when Kaiser Wilhelm of Germany, invited to settle the dispute, granted it all to the U.S. In the end, the pig was the conflict's only casualty. But, hey, martyrdom and everlasting fame beat a life of wallowing in the mud any day!

The **Hotel de Haro,** the first hotel in Washington, is at the **Roche Harbor Resort** (378-2155), on Roche Harbor Rd. at the northern end of the island. The free brochure *A Walking Tour of Historic Roche Harbor,* available at the info kiosk in front of the hotel, leads through this old mining camp. Don't miss the vaguely unsettling **Masonic mausoleum**—especially eerie at sunset. To get there, follow signs to Roche Harbor and stop at the lot behind the airfield instead of continuing down to the marina. Signs guide visitors to the mausoleum foot path.

The annual **San Juan Island Jazz Festival** (378-5509; www.sanjuanjazz.com) brings swing to the Harbor in late July. A $50 badge ($43 before July; ages 13-20 $20; one day $15-28) is good for all four days, but crowds cluster outside the clubs for free.

ORCAS ISLAND

Mount Constitution overlooks much of Puget Sound from its 2407-foot summit atop Orcas Island. A small population of retirees, artists, and farmers dwell here in understated homes, surrounded by green shrubs and the red bark of madrona trees. With a commune-like hostel and the largest state park in Washington, Orcas has the best budget tourist facilities of all the islands. Unfortunately, much of the beach is occupied by private resorts and is closed to the public. Enclaves of beauty exist at Doe Bay and near Eastsound, as well as on the island's forested roads.

ⓘ ORIENTATION AND PRACTICAL INFORMATION

Orcas is shaped like a horseshoe, which makes getting around a chore, even though the main thoroughfare is called **Horseshoe Hwy.** The ferry lands on the southwest tip at **Orcas Village. Eastsound,** the main town, is at the top of the horseshoe 9 mi. northeast. **Olga** and **Doe Bay** are another 8 and 11 mi. down the eastern side of the horseshoe. Stop in one of the four shops at the ferry landing to get a free **map.** Wheel rentals are a good idea. The island is a bit spread out.

Ferries: Washington State Ferries, see p. 190. **Taxis: Orcas Island Taxi,** 376-8294.

Public Transportation: San Juan Transit (376-8887). Service every 1½hr. to most parts of the island. From the ferry to Eastsound $4.

Visitor Information: Resources on San Juan Island will be useful. **Pyewacket Books** (376-2043), in Templin Center, in Eastsound at N. Beach Rd. has a good island section.

Equipment Rental: Wildlife Cycle (376-4708), at A St. and North Beach Rd., in Eastsound. Bikes $5 per hr., $25 per day. Open M-Sa 10am-5:30pm, Su 11am-3pm. **Dolphin Bay Bicycles** (376-4157), near the ferry, rents for the same price.

Library: (376-4985), at Rose and Pine in Eastsound; walk up the oath from Prune Alley. Free Internet Access. Open M-Th 11am-7pm, F-Sa 11am-5pm.

Pharmacy: Ray's (376-2230, after-hours emergencies 376-3693), in Templin Center in Eastsound at N. Beach Rd. Open M-Sa 9am-6pm.

Domestic Violence/Sexual Assault Services: 376-5979.

Emergency: 911. **Crisis:** 378-2345 or 376-1234. 24hr.

Post Office: (376-4121) on A St. in Eastsound Market Place. Open M-F 9am-4:30pm. **ZIP Code:** 98245.

Internet Access: See **library,** above. **Orcas Online,** 254 N. Beach Rd. (376-6411) in Eastsound. $5 per 30min. Open daily 9:30am-4:30pm.

Area Code: 360.

⌂ ACCOMMODATIONS AND CAMPGROUNDS

B&Bs on Orcas charge upwards of $85 per night; call 376-8888 for that. The Doe Bay Resort and the campgrounds are cheaper. Reservations help in the summer.

Doe Bay Village Resort (376-2291), off Horseshoe Hwy. on Pt. Lawrence Rd., 5 mi. out of Moran State Park. Kitchen, cafe, open grounds. A treehouse. Steam sauna and mineral bath ($4 per day, non-guests $7; one free pass for guests; bathing suits optional; coed). Hostel beds $15.50; campsites $12-22; yurts $39. Spare cottages from $39. Reservations recommended. Office open 8am-10pm. Kayak rentals (see below).

Moran State Park, State Rte. 22, Eastsound (376-2326 or 800-452-5687). Follow Horseshoe Hwy. straight into the park, 14 mi. from the ferry on the east side of the island. Swimming, fishing, and miles of hiking. 4 campgrounds, 151 sites. About 12 are open year-round, as are the toilets. Standard sites $11; hiker/biker sites $5. Hot showers 25¢ per 5min. Rowboats and paddleboats $10-12 for the 1st hr., $7 per hr. thereafter. Reservations strongly recommended May to Labor Day.

Obstruction Pass. Accessible by boat or foot. Turn off the Hwy. just past Olga, and head south (right) on Obstruction Pass Rd. At the dirt road marked Obstruction Pass Trailhead look for the wooden sign on the right. If you reach the bay, you've gone too far. The sites are a half-mile from the end of the road. Pit toilets, no water. Be careful where you light campfires—bald eagles nest in the trees above the campground. 11 free sites.

◖ FOOD

Essentials can be found at **Island Market** (376-6000; open M-Sa 8am-9pm, Su 10am-8pm), on Langdell St. For a large selection of groceries, medicines, and mysterious vegan cheeses, make a bee-line for **Orcas Homegrown Market** (376-2009; open daily 8am-9pm), on N. Beach Rd. Try their deli for lunch; most specials are $4.50-5.25 and there are always vegetarian options. For loads of fresh local produce, check out the **Farmer's Market** in front of the museum (Sa 10am-3pm).

■ **Chimayo** (376-6394), in the Our House Building on N. Beach Rd. A Southwest theme and comfy booths. Fresh funky burrito $3-5. Open M-Sa 11am-7pm.

Comet Cafe (376-4220), in Eastsound Sq. on N. Beach Rd. Two sisters run a bright, happy-go-lucky cafe. One bakes sweets, the other makes delicious sandwiches and roasts. Veggie shepherd pie $5. Open daily 8am-5pm.

Lower Tavern (378-4848), at the corner of Horseshoe Hwy. and Prune Alley. One of the few cheap spots open after 5pm. Dig into burgers and fries ($5.25-7). Poker (Th). Open Su-Th 11am-midnight, F-Sa 11am-2am; kitchen closes at 9pm M-Sa and 5pm on Su.

◣ OUTDOORS

Travelers on Orcas Island don't need to roam with a destination in mind; half the fun lies in rambling around, though much of the land is private property. The trail to **Obstruction Pass Beach** is the best of the few ways to clamber down to the rocky shores. Climbs on this hilliest of the San Juans afford inspiring views of the sound and the rest of the archipelago. **Moran State Park** (see **Campgrounds,** above) is unquestionably the star outdoor attraction. Over 30 mi. of hiking trails cover the park, ranging in difficulty from a one-hour walk around **Mountain Lake** (right off the Hwy.) to a day-long trek up the south face of **Mt. Constitution** (2047 ft.), the highest peak on the islands. Pick up a copy of the trail guide from the **registration station** (376-2326; rangers on duty Apr.-Aug. daily 6:30am-dusk, Sept.-Mar. 8am-dusk). The summit of Constitution looks out over the Olympic and Cascade Ranges, Vancouver Island, and Mt. Rainier. The stone tower at the top was built as a fire lookout in 1936 by the Civilian Conservation Corps. It's possible to drive to the peak; turn east on Mountain Rd. off Olga Rd. past the south end of Cascade Lake. The **Orcas Tortas** (376-2464) makes a slow drive on a green bus from Eastsound to the peak ($7). For an abbreviated hike, drive up Mt. Constitution and head part-way down to **Cascade Falls,** which is spectacular in spring and early summer. Below, two freshwater lakes are accessible from the road, and rowboats and paddleboats are rented at **Cascade Lake** for both places ($10-13 per hr.). The bay nearby is fine for an oceanside picnic. **Shearwater Adventures** (376-4699), runs a fascinating **sea kayak tour** of north Puget

Sound ($42, 3hr. tour with 30min. of dry land training) and is a great resource for experienced paddlers. Kayaking without a guide is not recommended except for in calm East Sound. **Crescent Beach Kayak** (376-2464), on the highway 1 mi. east of Eastsound, rents kayaks ($10 per hr., $25 per half-day; open daily 9am-7:30pm).

LOPEZ ISLAND

Smaller than either Orcas or San Juan, "Slow-pez" lacks some of the tourist facilities of the larger islands. Lopez was settled largely by mutineers, who thrived in the secluded woods. Today, Lopez Islanders still shy away from the mainland and maintain an age-old tradition of waving at every car they pass.

Lopez Island is ideal for those seeking solitary beach-walking, bicycling, or a true small-town experience. Free of imposing inclines and heavy traffic, the island is the most cycle-friendly in the chain. **Lopez Village,** the largest town, is 4½ mi. from the ferry dock off Fisherman Bay Rd. To get there, follow Ferry Rd. then take a right onto the first street after Lopez Center (before the Chevron station). It's best to bring a bicycle, unless you're up for the hike. To rent a bike or kayak, head to **Lopez Bicycle Works** (468-2847), south of the village next to the island's **Marine Center** (open June-Aug. daily 10am-6pm; May and Sept. 10am-5pm; bikes $5 per hr., $25 per day; single kayaks $10-15 per hr., $30-50 per day; doubles $65-80 per day; various short paddles $25-75). Get an excellent map here or at the visitor center.

The small **Shark Reef** and **Agate Beach County Parks,** on the southwest end of the island have tranquil and well-maintained hiking trails, and Agate's beaches are calm and deserted. **Lopez Island Vineyards,** 724 Fisherman Bay Rd. (468-3644), permits visitors to sample all of their wines for $1 (open June-Aug. W-Su noon-5pm; Sept.-Dec. and Mar.-May F-Sa noon-5pm). They also sell eggs.

Ferry transport has caused price inflation, so it's wise to bring a lunch to Lopez Island. Play *boules* and sip *Pastis* adjacent to the **village market** (468-2266; open daily 8am-8pm). Across the street, sample fresh pastries, bread, and pizza at **Holly B's** (468-2133; open M and W-Sa 7am-5pm, Su 7am-4pm). The **Farmer's Market** demonstrates island bounty (Sa 10am-2pm, W 3-6pm). For a taxi, call **Angie's Cab** (468-2227). Keep it so at **Keep It Clean,** south of the winery (wash $1.75, dry 25¢ per 5min.; open M-F 8:30am-7pm, Sa-Su until 5pm). **Domestic violence/sexual assault services:** 468-4567. **Clinic:** 468-2245; emergency 468-3185. **Post office:** on Weeks Rd. (468-2282; open M-F 8:30am-4:30pm). **ZIP code:** 98261. **Area code:** 360.

When spending the night on Lopez, camping is the only bargain. **Spencer Spit State Park** (468-2251, reservations 800-452-5687), on the northeast corner of the island about 3½ mi. from the ferry terminal, has six sites on the beach and 42 pleasant wooded sites up the hill, with toilets but no showers or hookups. (Tent sites $12; bike sites $6; two 8-bunk lean-tos $16. Open until 10pm.) Reservations are necessary for summer weekends ($6). Spencer Spit offers good **clamming** in the late spring, unless there is red tide (hotline 800-562-5632). The park is closed November 1 to February 2. **Odlin Park** (468-2496, reservations 468-4413) is close to the ferry terminal, 1 mi. south along Ferry Rd., and offers running water, a boat launch, volleyball net, baseball diamond, and pay phone (30 sites $15-17, $4 per each extra person after 5, ages 5-17 $2; hiker/biker sites $10).

SHAW AND OTHER ISLANDS

Shaw Island is home to 100 residents, one store, one library, wild turkeys, apple orchards, and a bevy of Franciscan nuns living in a convent next to the ferry dock, who for 16 years have been running the store/post office/gas station/ferry dock. Stop in for a couple of hours if only to take a walk, chat with a nun, or buy a map at the **"Little Portion" store** (open M-Sa 9:15am-5pm). When it's open, the modest-sized **library** across the street from the red schoolhouse offers **Internet access** (open Tu 2-4pm, Th 11am-1pm, Sa 10am-noon and 2-4pm). Eleven miles of public roads cater to hikers and bikers. **Shaw Island County Park** (reservations 468-4413), on the south side of the island, has eight campsites ($12-14) that fill quickly despite the lack of running water. There is also a shared hiker/biker camping site ($5), but space is limited. There are no other accommodations on the island.

The Washington State Parks Service operates over 15 **marine parks** on some of the smaller islands in the archipelago. These islands, accessible by private transportation, have anywhere from one to 51 mainly primitive campsites. Pamphlets on the marine facilities are available at parks or supply stores on the larger islands. One of the most popular destinations is tiny **Sucia Island,** which boasts gorgeous scenery and a few flopping seals. Canoes and kayaks can easily navigate the archipelago when the water is calm, but when the wind whips up the surf, only larger boats (at least 16 ft.) go out to sea. **Navigational maps** are essential to avoid the reefs and nasty hidden rocks that surround the islands. The Department of Natural Resources operates three island parks, each with three to six free campsites. Cypress Head on Cypress Island has wheelchair-accessible facilities.

OLYMPIC PENINSULA

Due west of Seattle and its busy Puget Sound neighbors, the Olympic Peninsula is a different world. A smattering of Indian reservations and logging and fishing communities lace the peninsula's coastline along U.S. 101, but most of the ponderous landmass remains a remote backpacking paradise. Olympic National Park dominates much of the peninsula, and prevents the area's ferocious timber industry from threatening the glacier-capped mountains and temperate rainforests. Locals outside the park make a tenuous living by logging and fishing. To the west, the Pacific Ocean stretches to a distant horizon; to the north, the Strait of Juan de Fuca separates the Olympic Peninsula from Vancouver Island; and to the east, Hood Canal and the Kitsap Peninsula isolate this sparsely inhabited wilderness from the sprawl of Seattle.

⬅ GETTING THERE AND GETTING AROUND

While getting around the peninsula is easiest by car, the determined traveler with ample time can make the trip by bus. Local buses link Port Townsend, Port Angeles, Forks, and Neah Bay, cost from 50¢ to $1, and accommodate bicycles.

The long distance to the peninsula and between counties requires a bit more foresight, but can be rewarding: the trip from Seattle to the farthest end of Olympic National Park can cost as little as $4.50 (7hr. via Pierce, Grays Harbor, and West Jefferson Transits). Contact **Washington State Ferries** (888-808-7977 or 206-464-6400), **Greyhound** (800-231-2222), **King** in Seattle (800-542-7876), **Pierce** in Tacoma (206-581-8000), **Intercity** in Olympia (800-287-6348), **Kitsap** in Kitsap and Bainbridge (360-373-2877); and, for service on the peninsula, **Jefferson** in Port Townsend (360-385-4777), **Clallam** in Port Angeles (800-858-3747), **Grays Harbor** in Aberdeen (800-562-9730), **West Jefferson** in the southwest (800-436-3950), and **Mason** in the southeast (800-374-3747). Jim at the **Rainforest Hostel** (360-374-2270; see p. 209), in Forks, will help you navigate transit routes around the park.

Getting to the magnificent natural areas that are the main attractions of the peninsula can be trickier. Hiking U.S. 101 to a trailhead is a paved and exhausting trip. Biking U.S. 101 and secondary roads is simply dangerous: long stretches of sometimes steep and narrow passes have no shoulder and immense logging trucks speed heedlessly along the winding two-lane route; gravelly secondary roads on the peninsula are often poorly suited to cycling. Olympic Van Tours runs backpacker shuttles to trailheads (see p. 200). Hitching is illegal and can be dangerous along U.S. 101, but backpackers report that getting a ride is not difficult.

PORT TOWNSEND

During the late 1800s, Port Townsend's predominance in Washington seemed secure. Every ship en route to Puget Sound stopped here for customs inspection, and speculation held that the bustling port would become the capital of the new state. When rumors circulated that rail would connect the town to the east, wealthy families flocked to the bluffs overlooking the port, constructing elaborate Victorian homes and stately public buildings. When rail passed the town by, "the inevitable New York" was left a ghost town, perched on the isolated northeast tip of the Olympic Peninsula to subsist by a military installation, paper milling, and logging. In the 1970s, Port Townsend's neglected Victorian homes were discovered by artists and idealists who turned the town into a vibrant, creative community. Now the business district stands restored, recently declared a national landmark, and the town takes advantage of its preserved 19th-century feel to keep its economy afloat and facades freshly painted. Here where espresso stands outnumber bait shops, urbanites otherwise pleased to be out of the bustle are cheered by the cafes, galleries, and bookstores that line P.T.'s touristed streets.

🔒 ORIENTATION AND PRACTICAL INFORMATION

Port Townsend sits at the terminus of Rte. 20 on the northeastern corner of the Olympic Peninsula. Over land, it can be reached by U.S. 101 on the peninsula, or from the Kitsap Peninsula across the Hood Canal Bridge. **Washington State Ferries** (800-84-FERRY/843-3779 or 206-464-6400; www.wsdpt.wa.gov/ferries) runs from Seattle to Winslow on Bainbridge Island (see p. 180). **Kitsap County Transit** meets every ferry and runs to Poulsbo. From Poulsbo, **Jefferson County Transit** runs to P.T. The ferry also crosses frequently to and from Keystone on Whidbey Island (see p. 184). Ferries dock at **Water St.**, west of touristy downtown, which is along Water and **Washington St.** Laid-back uptown is four steep blocks up, on **Lawrence St.**

Local Transportation: Jefferson County Transit (JCT) (385-4777; www.olympus.net/gettingabout/busjeffco.html). Peninsula towns are serviced by JCT and neighboring transit systems (see p. 197). Most buses stop at the ferry or at Lawrence and Tyler. Limited service F-Su. 50¢, seniors, disabled travelers, and ages 6-18 25¢, extra-zone fare 25¢. Day passes $1.50. A **free shuttle** runs between downtown and the Park 'n' Ride lot.

Taxis: Peninsula Taxi, 385-1872. $1.75 base plus $1.50 per mi.

Visitor Information: Chamber of Commerce, 2437 E. Sims Way (385-2722 or 888-365-2722; www.ptguide.com), lies 10 blocks southwest of town on Rte. 20. Open M-F 9am-5pm, Sa 10am-4pm, Su 11am-4pm.

Equipment Rental: P.T. Cyclery, 100 Tyler St. (385-6470), rents mountain bikes for $7 per hr., $25 per day. Maps $1.75. Open M-Sa 9am-6pm, Su by appointment. **Kayak P.T.,** 435 Water St. (385-6240; www.olympus.net/kayakpt), rents singles $25 per 4hr., doubles $40 per 4hr.; ages 84 and over free. Tours $39 per half-day, $68 per day. **Sport Townsend,** 1044 Water St. (379-9711), rents camping equipment (tents $16; sleeping bags $8). Call to check stock. Open M-Sa 9am-8pm, Su 10am-6pm.

Library: 1220 Lawrence (385-3181). Free Internet access. Open M 11am-5pm, Tu-Th 11am-9pm, F-Sa 11am-5pm.

Pharmacy: Safeway Pharmacy, 442 Sims Way (385-2860). Open M-F 8:30am-7:30pm, Sa 8:30am-6pm, Su 10am-6pm.

Hospital: 834 Sheridan (385-2200 or 800-244-8917), off Rte. 20 at 7th St.

Emergency: 911. **Police:** 607 Water St. (385-2322), at Madison.

Crisis Line: 385-0321 or 800-659-0321, 24hr. **Sexual Assault Line:** 385-5291.

Internet Access: See **Library,** above. **Cafe Internet,** 2021 E. Sims Way (385-9773; www.cafe-inet.com). $9.50 per hr. Open M-W 10am-6pm, Th-F 11am-7pm, Sa 2pm-7pm.

Post Office: 1322 Washington St., 98368 (385-1600). Open M-F 9am-5pm.

Area Code: 360.

🏕 ACCOMMODATIONS AND CAMPGROUNDS

Many of the town's Victorian homes are B&Bs; inquire at the Chamber of Commerce. **Water Street Hotel,** 635 Water St. (385-5467 or 800-735-9810), is a newly renovated Victorian building right downtown (single with shared bath $50).

▩ **Olympic Hostel (HI)** (385-0655), in Fort Worden State Park 1½ mi. from town (follow the signs to the park at "W" and Cherry St.). Right in an old barracks with ocean views. Check out the C.O.'s house (see **Sights,** below). Private rooms with kitchens. Breakfast pancakes by donation. Beds $12; nonmembers $15; hiker/biker $3 off. Check-in 5-10pm, check-out 9:30am; lockout 10am-5pm; 24hr. common room. Book ahead.

Fort Flagler Hostel (HI) (385-1288), in Fort Flagler State Park, on gorgeous **Marrowstone Island,** 20 mi. from Port Townsend. Drive south on Rte. 19 to Rte. 116 east and into the park (follow signs for Indian and Marrowstone Islands). Also an old military haunt, farther from town. Cyclists like routes over Marrowstone and the repairs workshop. Breakfast pancakes by donation. Beds $12; nonmembers $15; hiker/biker $3 off. Check-in 5-10pm, lockout 10am-5pm. Call if you're arriving late. Book ahead.

Oak Bay Jefferson County Parks (385-9129), off Oak Bay Rd. Head to Marrowstone; continue on Rte. 116 just past the intersection to the islands. 22 sites at Lower Oak Bay on the shore ($8). Upper Oak Bay has 22 sites ($8, hookups $10). No reservations.

Fort Worden State Park (385-4730; www.olympus.net/ftworden). Seaside sites $16. Or camp on the beach at **Fort Flagler State Park** (385-1259). 116 sites; tents $11, RVs $16, hiker/biker $6. Book ahead for both. See hostel listings above for directions.

◖ FOOD

Aldrich's, 940 Lawrence St. (385-0500; open daily 7:30am-10pm), at Tyler, stocks Liberty Street sweets. **Food Coop,** 1033 Lawrence St. (385-2883 or 379-8813), sponsors the market on Wednesdays 4-6pm (open M-Sa 9am-9pm, Su 11am-6pm).

▩ **The Elevated Ice Cream Co.,** 627 Water St. (385-1156), serves homemade ice cream (a scoop $1.62) in a shop, ironically, on the ground floor. Open daily 10am-10pm.

Bread and Roses, 230 Quincy St. (385-1044), serves baked goods and sandwiches ($2-$4.35) in cozy environs; the garden is a wonderful place. Open daily 6:30am-4pm.

Wild Coho Cafe and Juice Bar, 1044 Lawrence St. (379-1030), at Polk St., uptown. A wicked paint job and a Shed Boy breakfast ($4). Open W-Sa 8am-4pm, Su 8am-3pm.

Burrito Depot, 609 Washington St. (385-5856), at Madison. Quick, tasty Mexican food. Big burritos from $3.25. Open daily 10:30am-8:30pm, Su 10:30am-5pm.

Waterfront Pizza (385-6629) on Water St., offers little historical ambiance but churns out a damn good pizza on a sourdough crust. 12" foccacia $4. Open daily 11am-10pm.

◉ SIGHTS

Port Townsend is full of huge Queen Anne and Victorian mansions. Who knew? Of over 200 restored homes in the area, some have been converted into B&Bs and two are open for tours. Free *Visit Port Townsend* has a map with short descriptions of historic buildings (available at the visitor center or museum). For more detail, buy the humorous *Historic Homes* booklet ($5) at the **Jefferson County Museum** (385-1003; www.olympus.net/arts/jcmuseum), at Madison and Water St. Here are displayed vestiges of the town's raucous past, including a dazzling kayak parka made of seal intestines, an old-time pedal-powered dentist's drill, and a jail rumored to have held Jack London for a night. (Open M-Sa 11am-4pm, Su 1-4pm; $2, under 13 $1.) The **Ann Starret Mansion,** 744 Clay St. (385-3205 or 800-321-0644), is renowned for its frescoed ceilings and befuddling, fantastic, free-hanging, three-tiered spiral staircase (tours daily from noon-3pm; $2).

   Point Hudson, where Admiralty Inlet and Port Townsend Bay meet, is the hub of a small shipbuilding area and forms the corner of Port Townsend. North of Point Hudson are several miles of **beach** and the beautiful **Chetzemoka Park** at Garfield and Jackson St. **Fort Worden State Park** is most easily accessed through the gates at "W" and Cherry Streets (open daily 6:30am-dusk). In the 1900s, the mouth of Puget Sound was guarded by the "Triangle of Fire"—**Fort Worden** (385-4730), **Fort Flagler** across the bay, and **Fort Casey** on Whidbey Island. Fort Flagler re-entered service in

1981 as the set for *An Officer and a Gentleman*. Seemingly endless footpaths run past the upper bunkers and lead to a quiet spot at the top of the bluff and more trails. The **Commanding Officer's Quarters** (385-4730, ext. 479) is stuffed to the rafters with Victorian furniture. (Open June 1-Aug. 31 daily 10am-5pm, Mar.-May and Sept.-Oct. Sa-Su 1pm-4pm; $1.) The **Coast Artillery Museum** (385-0373; open daily 11am-5pm; in winter Sa-Su 11am-5pm; $1) is clean-cut. Sea life lives above the Fort Worden pier at the **Marine Science Center** (385-5582; open Tu-Su noon-6pm; in fall and spring Sa-Su noon-6pm; $2, children $1).

🎵 ENTERTAINMENT AND EVENTS

Port Townsend's music scene is surprisingly lively. *This Week* has the scoop on the nightlife. Steep-side **Sirens**, 823 Water St. (379-0776), hosts live folk and blues (F-Sa) on the deck, which has a great view (open Tu-Sa noon-midnight, Su 10am-10pm). **Upstage**, 923 Washington St. (385-2216), supports music from classical to country (Th-Sa; cover $2-12.50; open daily 4pm-midnight). **Town Tavern** (385-4706), at Quincy and Water St., is the oldest show in town. Live blues, country, and rock in summer. (Th-Sa; open daily 11am-2am.) The **Rose Theatre**, 235 Taylor St. (385-1089), is one fine arthouse theater ($6, seniors $5, children $4; matinees $1).

Every summer, **Centrum Foundation** (385-5320 or 800-733-3608; www.centrum .org) sponsors festivals in Fort Worden Park, including the **Port Townsend Blues Festival** at the end of June, the **Festival of American Fiddle Tunes** in early July, **Jazz Port Townsend** in the third week of July, and the classical youth showcase **Marrowstone Music Festival** in August (tickets $12-14). The **Port Townsend Writer's Conference** in mid-July is one of the finest in the northwest. Well-attended guest-readings and lectures cost $5. Other annual attractions include the **Wooden Boat Festival,** held the first weekend after Labor Day, and the free **House Tour,** held the weekend after. Contact the Chamber of Commerce for details.

PORT ANGELES

Between Olympic National Park and the chilly Strait of Juan de Fuca, Port Angeles is the "Gateway to the Olympics." The town's mountain neighbors win all the glory, and the Port of the Angels hovers on the bland side. As pulp and plywood mills gradually close, Port Angeles hungers after tourist dollars.

⚡ PRACTICAL INFORMATION

Buses: Olympic Bus Lines, 221 N. Lincoln (417-0700) in the Doubletree Hotel parking lot. To: Seattle (2½hr., 4 per day, $29) and Sea-Tac Airport (3 hr., 4 per day, $43). See p. 53 for discounts. **Olympic Van Tours** (452-3858) runs excursions into Olympic National Park: to Hurricane Ridge ($18) and Hoh Rainforest ($30). OVT also shuttles to trailheads, including Elwha, Hurricane Ridge, Ozette, Soleduck, Hoh, and the coast.

Ferries: M.V. Coho, 101 E. Railroad Ave. (457-4491; www.northolympic.com/coho), serves Victoria from Mar.-Jan. (1½hr.; 2-4 per day; $6.75, with bicycle $10, with car $28.50; children $3.40). **Victoria Express,** 115 E. Railroad Ave. (800-633-1589; www.northolympic.com/ferry) has passenger only service to Victoria (1hr., $12.50, ages 5-11 $7.50, under 5 free). U.S. and Canadian citizens crossing into Canada need valid proof of citizenship. Other internationals should check their own visa requirements (see p. 24). Day parking lots line Railroad Ave. near the docks ($5-7).

Public Transportation: Clallam Transit System, 830 W. Lauridsen Blvd. (800-858-3747 or 452-4511), serves Port Angeles and Clallam County, as far as Neah Bay and Forks, from Railroad Ave. at Oak St., a block west of the ferry. Operates M-F 4:15am-11pm, Sa 10am-6pm. Downtown 75¢, ages 6-19 60¢, seniors and disabled 25¢. Day pass $2.

Taxi: Peninsula Taxi (385-1872) $1.75 base, $1.50 per mi.

Car Rental: Evergreen Auto Rental, 808 E. Front St. (452-8001). From $29 per day plus 20¢ per mi. after 100 mi. Must be 21 with proof of insurance.

Visitor Information: Chamber of Commerce, 121 E. Railroad Ave. (452-2363; www.cityofpa.com), by the ferry. Open daily 7am-10pm; in winter M-F 10am-4pm.

Outdoor Information: Olympic National Park Visitor Center, 3002 Mt. Angeles Rd. (452-0330). See p. 204 for details. **Port Brook and News,** 104 E. 1st St. (452-6367), has maps to peruse and advice on the region (open M-Sa 9am-9pm, Su 10am-5pm).

Equipment Rental: Olympic Mountaineering, 140 W. Front St. (452-0240; www.olymtn.com), rents sturdy gear (external frame pack $15 per day) with lower weekly rates. Offers climbing treks into ONP (from $50). Open M-Sa 9am-6pm, Su 10am-5pm. **Brown's Outdoor Store,** 112 W. Front St. (457-4150), rents at low daily rates (packs $10 per day). Call ahead. Open M-Sa 9:30am-6pm, Su noon-4pm. **Pedal 'n' Paddle,** 120 E. Front St. (457-1240) a block from the ferry, rents bikes ($8 per hr.; $20 per day) and leads kayak trips (half-day $40). Open M-Sa 9:30am-5:30pm.

Laundromat: Peabody Street Coin Laundry, 212 Peabody St. at 2nd St. Wash $1.25, dry 25¢ per 10min. **24hr.**

Medical: **Olympic Memorial Hospital**, 939 Caroline St. (417-7000) at Washington St. on the waterfront. Open 24hr. **Pharmacy: Safeway** (457-0599), see **Food,** below.

Emergency: 911. **Police:** 452-4545

Domestic Violence/Sexual Assault: Safehome, 1914 W. 18th St. (452-4357).

Post Office: 424 E. 1st St., 98362 (452-9275). Open M-F 8:30am-5pm, Sa 9am-noon.

Area Code: 360.

■ ACCOMMODATIONS AND CAMPGROUNDS

The least expensive motels line U.S. 101. west of town. Winter rates drop $5-15.

The Spa, 511 E. 1st St. (452-3257 or 503-233-7627). One room, one big slumber party (beds $20). Some private rooms ($25). Breakfast in the garden tea room is included, and there's a steam room downstairs ($10 per hr.). Book ahead.

Ruffles Motel, 812 E. 1st St. (457-7788), in town, has nice rooms with cable TV, trimmed with roses (singles $42, doubles $49).

Heart o' the Hills (452-2713), is the closest campground, 5½ mi. from town on Race Rd. in Olympic National Park (see p. 207). No hookups, but lush surroundings, wheelchair-accessible sites, and ranger-led programs on summer evenings. $10 park entrance fee (good for 7 days). Sites $11 (first-come, first-served).

Salt Creek County Park (928-3441), 20min. along Rte. 112, maintains 92 sites ($10) with fantastic waterfront views; the nearby tidepools are a treasure trove of shells and sea stars. Showers (25¢ per 5 min.). No hookups or reservations.

Dungeness Recreation Area (683-5847), near the town of Sequim (skwim); take U.S. 101 east 10 mi., turn left onto Kitchen-Dick Rd. and follow to end. 66 sites ($10) and coin showers. A trail along Dungeness Spit, the largest natural sandhook in the nation, leads to a lighthouse (see **Sights and Outdoors,** below). No hookups or reservations.

Boulder Creek Campground (a.k.a. **Hot Springs Campground**), at the end of Elwha River Rd. (2 mi. past where it's closed), 8 mi. past Altaire. The natural Olympic Hot Springs are nearby (see p. 207). Backcountry permits (see p. 206) are available at the trail-head. 50 sites. Bring water and warm clothes.

◪ FOOD

There is lots of seafood in town and there are few inexpensive restaurants to eat it in. Picnickers can pick the shelves for peanut butter and pita bread at **Safeway,** 110 E. 3rd St. (457-0788), at Lincoln St. (open 24hr.).

La Casita, 203 E. Front St. (452-2289). Seafood burritos ($8) stuffed with gobs of crab, shrimp, and fish, and free, all-you-can-eat tortilla chips to snarf between margaritas ($2). Open M-Th 11am-9pm, F-Sa 11am-10pm, Su noon-9pm.

Bella Italia, 117B E. 1st St. (457-5442), gets rave reviews. Hungry vegetarians can sit down to a hunk of lasagna ($8) or a plate of spaghetti ($6) in a romantic, candle-lit booth. Open M-F 11am-10pm, Sa-Su 11am-11pm.

First Street Haven, 107 E. 1st St. (457-0352). Belgian waffle breakfasts $6.75. The $7 "Prospector" is a behemoth shrimp sandwich. Open M-Sa 7am-4pm, Su 8am-2pm.

Port Angeles Brewing Company, 131 W. Front St. (417-9152), serves up the typical (burgers $6-7) and a mean stout (pints $3). Live music fills the wood-paneled joint on Friday. Open M-Sa 11am-11pm, Su 1-9pm.

◤ SIGHTS AND OUTDOORS

The **Fine Arts Center,** 1203 E. Lauridsen Blvd. (457-3532; www.olympus.net/community/pafac), near the national park visitor center, has great views of the water and exhibits art by northwest artists. (Open Tu-Su 11am-5pm. Free.)

The 6 mi., wheelchair accessible **Waterfront Trail** provides an overview of portside activities. A 5 mi. (2 hr.) trail out on the 7 mi. **Dungeness Spit,** the largest natural sandhook in the nation, leads to a lighthouse with free tours (Open 9am until 2hr. before sunset; see directions to Dungeness Recreation area, in **Accommodations,** above). Nearby, but inaccessible to visitors, the **Manis-Mastodon** archaeological site yielded the first evidence of man in the Pacific Northwest and the first certain evidence that man hunted mastodons, the Ice Age cousins to elephants and the Snuffleupagas (Snuffy). Nearby, the **Olympic Game Farm,** 1423 Ward Rd. (683-4295 or 800-778-4295; www.northolympic.com/gamefarm) off Woodcock St., is a zoo/retirement home for movie-star bison, zebra, rhinos, and other animals. Don't feed the bears on the driving tour ($7, children $6).

Olympic Van Tours runs to the park (see **Practical Information,** above) and nearby sights, all otherwise accessible by bike or public transportation (see p. 197).

OLYMPIC NATIONAL PARK

Olympic National Park (ONP), the centerpiece of the Olympic Peninsula, shelters one of the most diverse landscapes of any region in the world. With glacier-encrusted peaks, river valley rainforests, and jagged shores along the Pacific Coast, the park appeals to the wide-ranging tastes of an even wider range of visitors. Roads lead to many corners of Olympic National Park, but merely scratch the surface of this otherworldy wilderness. A dive into the backcountry reveals the park's many faces and leaves summer tourists behind. Despite ONP's dire financial straits (it is one of the poorest national parks) and rising fees, a little effort and planning will yield an afternoon of shell-hunting on miles of isolated beach, a day of salmon fishing on the Hoh River, or a week of glacier-gazing from the tree line.

NATURAL OVERVIEW

The entire **Olympic Mountain Range** is packed into ONP's center, where conical peaks wring huge quantities of moisture from heavy Pacific air. Average precipitation in the park varies, but an annual 12 ft. of rain and snow are common; certain locations average over 17 ft., and at altitudes above 3500 ft. it is not rare to encounter snow in late June. The mountains steal so much water that some areas northeast of the park are among the driest in Washington.

Temperate rainforests lie on the west side of the park, along the coast, and in the **Hoh, Queets,** and **Quinault River valleys,** where moderate temperatures, loads of rain, and summer fog support an emerald tangle dominated by Sitka spruce and western red cedar. The rest of the park is populated by lowland forests of Douglas fir and hemlock, with silver fir at higher elevations. Flower-filled alpine meadows afford stunning views of the landscape above and below.

Ancient Native American **petroglyphs** and boxy offshore bluffs called **sea stacks** lend the **beaches** along the unspoiled ONP coastline a sense of sacredness. Swaths of Olympic National Forest and private land separate these seaside expanses from the rest of the park. Wind-whipped forests and rocky headlands edge the long, driftwood-strewn beaches. During the winter, evidence of human presence vanishes, and the coast regains a primeval feel.

The extensive patches of naked mountainside left by **logging,** particularly on the western side of the peninsula, may shock visitors. The national park is protected from logging, and views of scarred hillsides disappear within its boundaries, but timber companies regularly harvest both private and state land. The State of Washington maintains huge tracts along the Hoh and Clearwater Rivers, near the western shore. Until recently, private and state agencies clearcut old growth forests on the peninsula, a policy easily visible from the western segment of U.S. 101. At points, the highway weaves through bald patches of land, with roadside placards indicating the dates of harvest and replanting. Due to the spotted owl uproar of the late 1980s and federal regulations that ban logging on public land, the Forest Service disallowed harvesting timber from any of the **Olympic National Forest,** which surrounds the park, and private and state harvesting has also slowed. Those who earn a living from forest resources dislike lectures on how to manage them and will likely point out that the consumer of forest products is as responsible for clearcutting as the industries themselves.

■ ORIENTATION

With even its furthest regions three hours by car from Seattle and five hours from Portland, the wilds of Olympic National Park is most easily and safely reached by car. U.S. 101 loops around the peninsula, in the shape of an upside-down U, with Port Angeles at the top, from just west of Olympia in the southeast to Aberdeen and beyond in the southwest. Roads into the park are accessible from U.S. 101 and serve as trailheads for over 600 mi. of hiking. Like Mt. Rainier and Mt. St. Helens, no roads cross the entire park. The park's perimeters are well-defined but are surrounded by Forest Service, Washington Department of Natural Resources (DNR) land, and other public areas. There are few outposts of development within the park—**Port Angeles** (see p. 200) on the northern park rim, and **Forks** (see p. 209), on the east side of the park, are the only remotely sizable towns, where gas and food are always available. The park's vista-filled **eastern rim** runs up to Port Angeles, from where the much-visited **northern rim** extends westward. Along a winding detour on Rte. 112 off U.S. 101 westward, the tiny town of **Neah Bay** and stunning **Cape Flattery** perch at the northwest tip of the peninsula; farther south on U.S. 101, the slightly less tiny town of **Forks** is a gateway to the park's rainforested **western rim.** Separate from the rest of the park, much of the peninsula's Pacific coastline comprises a gorgeous **coastal zone.** For transportation info unique to the peninsula, see **Olympic Peninsula: Getting There and Getting Around,** p. 197.

July, August, and September are best for visiting Olympic National Park, since much of the backcountry remains snowed-in until late June, and only summers are relatively rain-free. This brings flocks of fellow sightseers, so expect company. Coming from Seattle, the easiest place to begin an exploration of the park is Port Angeles' **Olympic National Park Visitor Center** (see below). The Park Service runs free interpretive programs such as guided forest hikes, tidepool walks, and campfire programs out of its ranger stations. For a schedule of events, pick up a copy of the *Bugler* from ranger stations or the visitor center.

Erik Molvar's *Hiking Olympic National Park* ($15) is a great resource for hikers, with maps and step-by-step trail logs. Robert Wood's comprehensive *Olympic Mountains Trail Guide* ($15) is the classic book for those planning to tackle the backcountry, though it lacks coverage of coastal areas and can be slightly outdated. Custom Correct maps provide detailed topographic information on various popular hiking areas. The *Olympic Wilderness Trip Planner* (free from any ranger station) overviews everything from responsible "leave no trace" practices to magnetic declination and instructions on reading tide charts. Tim McNulty's *Olympic National Park: A Natural History* ($17) is a beautifully written account of the geology, flora, fauna, and human history of the mountains, forests, and coasts. All of these are available at area bookstores or visitor centers.

⁊ PRACTICAL INFORMATION

Permits: $10 per car; $5 per hiker or biker. Charged at developed entrances such as Hoh, Heart o' the Hills, Sol Duc, Staircase, and Elwha. The fee covers 7 days' access to the park–keep that receipt! **Backcountry** users must pay $2 extra per night to ranger offices. $3 **Trailhead Passes** are required for parking in ONF.

Visitor Information: Olympic National Park Visitor Center, 3002 Mt. Angeles Rd. (452-0330, TDD 452-0306), off Race St. in Port Angeles (see p. 200), is ONP's main info center, distributes an invaluable **park map,** and houses exhibits. Open daily 9am-5pm; in winter daily 9am-4pm. **Hoh Rainforest Visitor Center** (374-6925), on the park's western rim (see p. 209), also provides posters and backcountry permits. Open daily July-Aug. 9am-6:30pm; Sept.-June 9am-4:30pm. **Park Headquarters,** 600 E. Park Ave. (452-4501, ext. 311), in Port Angeles, is an administrative office but can answer phone questions. Open M-F 8am-4:30pm. For the many local **ranger stations,** see specific regions below.

Backcountry Information: Olympic National Park Wilderness Information Center (452-0300), behind the visitor center, provides trip-planning help. This is the only place in the park that accepts reservations for the 6 ONP backcountry areas that require them (see p. 206). You can pay the ONP wilderness user fee here or at any ranger station.

Online Information: www.nps.gov/olym/home.htm. **Park Weather:** 452-0329. 24hr.

Park Radio: 530 AM for road closures and general weather conditions. 610 AM for general park rules and information, 1610 AM in Lake Crescent and Quinault areas.

Emergency: 911. **Park Headquarters** (452-4501) is staffed daily 7am-midnight; in winter 7am-5:30pm. Or call the nearest ranger station and report your exact location.

Area Code: 360.

FISHING IN THE PARK

Fishing within park boundaries does not require a license, but for salmon and steelhead, you must obtain the free state game department **punch card** at local outfitting and hardware stores, or at the **Fish and Game Department** in Olympia (see p. 181). Contact Fish and Wildlife (360-902-2200; www.wa.gov/wdfw) for regulations. Fifteen major waterways support stocks; the **Elwha River,** coursing through the northeastern part of the park, is best for trout, while the **Hoh River,** flowing west through the park, jumps with salmon. Ask at an anglers' store for current information, and check at a ranger station for specific river regulations.

⌂ CAMPING ON THE PENINSULA

Campers on the peninsula can tent within walking distance of one of the world's only temperate rainforests for $7-12. Olympic National Park, Olympic National Forest, and the State of Washington maintain **free campgrounds,** but ONP requires a **backcountry permit** and the ONF often requires a **trailhead pass** to park at sites located off a main trail (see **Practical Information,** above). The Washington Department of Natural Resources (DNR) allows **free backcountry camping** off any state road on DNR land, as long as campers tent at least 100 yards from the road. The majority of DNR land is near the western shore along the Hoh and Clearwater Rivers, though others are sprinkled about the peninsula. Summer weekend competition for sites can be fierce. From late June to late September, most spaces are taken by 2pm. Popular sites such as those at Hoh River fill by noon.

STANDARD CAMPGROUNDS. Ask at the Olympic National Forest Headquarters in Olympia (see p. 181) about **ONP** campgrounds throughout its boundaries (sites $8-12). **ONF** maintains six free campgrounds in the Hood Canal Ranger District, and other campgrounds within its boundaries (sites $8-12); three can be reserved (800-280-2267): **Seal Rock, Falls View,** and **Klahowga.**

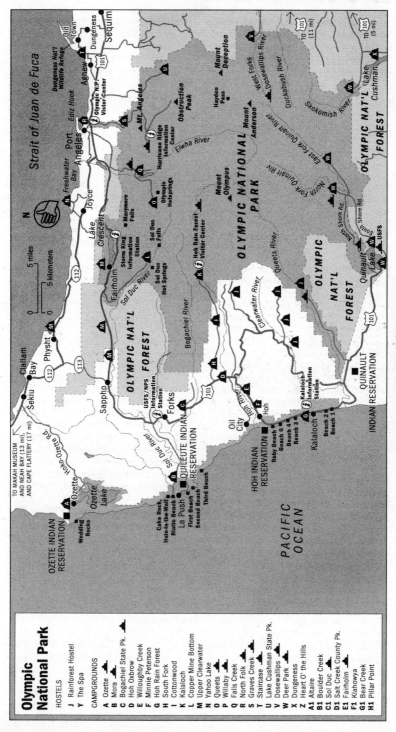

In addition to **Ft. Worden** and **Ft. Flagler** (see p. 199), on the peninsula there are four **state parks** (reservations 800-452-5687; sites $11, hookups $16, hiker/biker $6). **Dosewallips** (796-4415) and **Lake Cushman** (see Eastern Rim) are to the east. **Sequim Bay** (683-4235) is east of Sequim, to the north. **Bogachiel** is between Forks and the Hoh, to the west. Most **drive-up camping** is first-come, first-served.

BACKCOUNTRY CAMPING. Whether in rainforest, in the high country, or along the coast, backcountry camping in the park requires a **backcountry permit** (see **Practical Information,** above). Park offices maintain **quota limits** on backcountry permits for popular spots, including **Lake Constance** and **Flapjack Lakes** in the eastern rim (see below); **Grand Valley, Badger Valley,** and **Sol Duc** in the northern rim (see p. 210); **Hoh** in the western rim (see p. 209); and the coastal **Ozette Loop** (see p. 210).

Make **reservations** in advance, especially for 100% reserveable beach campsites; the rest are 50% first-come, first-served. Contact the visitor center nearest the campground access to secure a spot. Backpackers should prepare for varied weather conditions. Even in summer, parts of the park get very wet. Carry a good waterproof jacket and wear waterproof hiking boots with plenty of traction; trails can become rivers of slippery mud. Never drink untreated water in the park. **Giardia,** that nasty diarrhea-inducing bacterium, lives in these waters (see p. 34). Water purification tablets are available at the visitor center and most outfitters. **Black bears** and **raccoons** pose another backcountry hazard; when issuing backcountry permits, ranger stations instruct hikers on hanging food out of animals' reach. Bring 50-100 ft. of thin, sturdy rope; regions that require bear canisters will rent them at the ranger station. Above 3500 ft., **open fires** are always prohibited; below 3500 ft. maps and trailhead signposts indicate whether they are allowed. Before any trip, inquire about **trail closures;** winter weather often destroys popular trails.

EASTERN RIM

The Eastern Rim accesses the park from U.S. 101 through the buffer of the Olympic National Forest. The Park and Forest Services staff the **Hood Canal Ranger Station** (877-5254), southeast of reserve lands on U.S. 101 in Hoodsport (open daily 8am-4:30pm; in winter M-F 8am-4:30pm, closed Sa-Su). Hikers use campgrounds along the park's eastern rim as entry points to the interior. **Staircase Campground** (877-5569) is a major hub 16 mi. northwest of Hoodsport at the head of **Lake Cushman** and a rugged river hike (59 sites $10; park entrance fee $10; RV accessible). Turn west off U.S. 101 at Hoodsport, pass the ranger station on Rte. 119, take a left after 9 mi. and follow the signs. **Lake Cushman State Park** (877-5491, reservations 800-452-5687), on the way to Staircase, provides another base camp for extended backpacking trips into the forest and park, with fine swimming beaches, showers (25¢ per 3min.), and toilets (80 sites $11; 30 full hookups $16).

Capable hikers tackle the steep trails up **Mt. Ellinor**, to the northeast of Staircase. Follow Rte. 119 for 9 mi. to Forest Rd. 24, turn right and continue to Forest Rd. 2419, following signs to Jefferson Pass and Upper/Lower Trailhead. Look for signs to the Upper Trailhead along Forest Road #2419-04. Once on the mountain, hikers can choose either the 3 mi. path or an equally steep but shorter journey to the summit. A clear day at the summit affords a view of the Olympic range towers to the northwest, and Puget Sound, Seattle, Mt. Rainier, Mt. Adams, and the rim of Mt. St. Helens to the southeast. Hikers on the mountain before late July should bring snow clothes to mach, as in Mach 1, the speed to which sliders accelerate down a quarter-mile **snow chute** (follow signs). Build a fire to warm your cold behind at the free **Lilliwaup Creek Campground** (13 sites; water, pit toilets), beside the creek on F.S. Rd. 24; follow signs from Rte. 119 or inquire at the Hood Canal ranger station.

Lena Lake, 14 mi. north of Hoodsport off U.S. 101, draws hikers and birdwatchers. A 3¼ mi. hike ascends to the lake. Follow Forest Rd. 25 (known as the Hamma-Hamma River Rd.) off U.S. 101 for 8 mi. to the trailhead. There are 29 rustic sites at **Lena Lake Campground.** Two miles east on Forest Rd. 25 lies **Hamma-Hamma Campground** (15 sites $10; water, pit toilets). Trailhead pass required.

Dosewallips Campground (DOH-see-WALL-ups), at the end of Dosewallips Rd. (Forest Rd. 2610) off U.S. 101 27 mi. north of Hoodsport, has a summer ranger station and 30 undeveloped campsites ($10; no RVs). A pretty and popular multi-day trail leads from Dosewallips across the park to a number of other well-traversed backpacking trails, including **Hurricane Ridge** (see p. 207). The **West Forks Dosewallip Trail** is a slightly strenuous 10½ mi. trek to the **Anderson Glacier.** A recently constructed bridge makes this trail the shortest route to any glacier in the park. Thirty miles north of Hoodsport, the **Quilcene Ranger Station** (765-2200), can point out the **Mt. Walker Viewpoint,** 5 mi. south of Quilcene on U.S. 101. A one-lane gravel road leads 4 mi. to the lookout, the highest viewpoint in the park accessible by car. The road is steep, has sheer dropoffs, and should not be attempted in foul weather or a temperamental car. Another view of Hood Canal, Puget Sound, Mt. Rainier, and Seattle awaits intrepid travelers on top. Picnic tables perch on the east side; feast there while feasting your eyes on the north face of 7743 ft. **Mt. Constance.**

NORTHERN RIM

The northern rim, near Port Angeles, is the most developed section of ONP; here, glaciers, rainforests, hot springs, and sunset views over the Pacific are a mere drive away. Spur roads from U.S. 101 lead to campgrounds and trailheads.

The road south off U.S. 101 just east of Morse Creek and Port Angeles leads to **Deer Park,** where trails tend to be uncrowded and vistas plentiful. **Deer Park Campground** offers the park's highest car-accessible camping at 5400 ft. Come early to snag one of the campground's 14 sites ($8; summer only, no trailers or RVs). Past Deer Park, the **Royal Basin Trail** meanders 6¼ mi. over a gentle grade to the **Royal Basin Waterfall** and alpine **Royal Lake.**

Heart o' the Hills Campground (see p. 201), near Port Angeles, overflows with vacationers poised to take **Hurricane Ridge** by storm. The campground has no hookups or showers but offers plenty of giant trees, fairly private sites, wheelchair access, and family-oriented evening campfire programs (105 sites: $10). The road up Hurricane Ridge is an easy but curvy drive. Before July, walking on the ridge usually involves a bit of snow-stepping. Clear days promise splendid views of Mt. Olympus and Vancouver Island, set against a foreground of snow and indigo lupine. RVs and tourists crowd the ridge by day. Seclusion can be found at dawn and on many short trails that originate here, including some designed for seniors and the disabled. For one of numerous extraordinary views, try the **High Ridge Trail,** which is a short walk from Sunset Point. Signs at the visitor center give updates on visibility at the summit, but call ahead (452-0330) before tackling the 40-minute drive. On weekends from late December to late March, the Park Service organizes free guided **snowshoe walks** atop the ridge.

Farther west down U.S. 101, a 5 mi. spur road leads south to two **campgrounds** along the waterfall-rich Elwha River: **Elwha Valley** and the nearby **Altaire.** Both have drinking water and toilets (452-9191; 41 and 31 sites $10). Appleton Pass and the **Olympic Hot Springs** trailhead rest 2½ mi. past Altaire; from here, hike 2½ mi. to the

GET THAT GOAT! In the early part of this century, in an effort to provide more game for hunting, elk were shipped from Washington to Alaska and mountain goats were sent from Alaska to Washington. The goats proliferated in Olympic National Park long after hunting was prohibited, damaging endangered native plants by grazing, trampling, wallowing, and loitering. Park Service authorities tried many ways of removing the goats, including live capture and sterilization darts—but nothing really worked. In 1995, they resolved to liquidate the goats once and for all by shooting them from helicopters. Washington Congressman Norm Dicks got this measure postponed, and has since has proposed reintroducing the native gray wolf to the park. Wolves were eliminated in the early part of this century, in an effort to provide more game for hunting.

often skinnily dipped natural pools. Dippers beware: the warm, bacteria-filled water can jump-start infections. Unmarked foot paths to more secluded, less-frequented baths. The nearby **Hot Springs/Boulder Creek campsite** has 14 primitive sites (free with backcountry permit).

Fairholm Campground (928-3380), 30 mi. west of Port Angeles, sits at the tip of **Lake Crescent,** with wheelchair access and lots of drinking water (87 sites: $10). Trails around the brilliantly blue glacier-carved lake evoke gasps at old growth forests. Stop at nearby **Storm King Ranger Station** (928-3380; open in summer daily 10am-5pm) to ask after **evening interpretive programs.** Scenic trails of varying difficulties begin at the ranger station; inquire for conditions. The **Marymere Falls Trail** (2 mi. round-trip) through old growth Douglas firs, western hemlock, and red cedar, is pleasant. The first quarter mile is wheelchair-accessible.

Still farther west on U.S. 101, 13 mi. of paved road penetrate the **Sol Duc Hot Springs Campground** (327-3534), with wheelchair-accessible restrooms (82 sites: $12). Nearby lies the popular **Sol Duc Hot Springs Resort** (327-3583; www.northolympic.com/solduc). The two pools, one chlorinated and wheelchair accessible, are piping hot thanks to computer-monitored heating systems (open daily late-May to Sept. 9am-9pm; Apr.-May and Oct. Th noon-6pm; F-Su 9am-6pm; $6.75, seniors $5.50; suit or towel rental $2 each). According to Native American legend, the Sol Duc and Olympic Springs are heated by two aggressive lightning fish. After a long, indecisive battle, they gave up their fight and crept into two caves, where they weep hot tears of injury. The **Sol Duc trailhead** is also a starting point for those heading for the heights; stop by the **Eagle Ranger Station** (327-3534) for information, current hiking conditions, and backcountry permits (open late June-Sept. Su-Th 8am-4:30pm, F-Sa 8am-8:30pm). The Sol Duc Trail draws its share of traffic, but crowds thin dramatically above **Sol Duc Falls.**

NEAR THE PARK: NEAH BAY AND CAPE FLATTERY

At the westernmost point on the Juan de Fuca Strait is **Neah Bay,** the only town in the **Makah Reservation,** recently famous for the community's revival of its gray-whale hunt (see p. 14), and renowned as the "Pompeii of the Pacific," the remarkably preserved site of a 500-year-old Makah village buried in a landslide. Gorgeous **Cape Flattery** is the most northwesterly point in the contiguous U.S. James Cook gave the cape its name in 1778, because it "flattered us with the hopes of finding a harbor." Flattery got them nowhere; the nearest port is Port Angeles, 50 miles away.

You can reach Neah Bay and Cape Flattery by an hour-long detour from U.S. 101. From Port Angeles, Rte. 112 leads west 72 mi. to Neah Bay. Or, from the south, Rte. 113 runs north from Sappho to Rte. 112. **Clallam Transit System** (452-4511 or 800-858-3747; see p. 200) runs from Port Angeles; take bus #14 from Oak St. to Sappho (1¼ hr.), then #16 to Neah Bay. ($1, seniors 50¢, ages 6-19 85¢).

The **Makah Cultural and Research Center** (645-2711), in Neah Bay on Rte. 112, is just inside the reservation, opposite the Coast Guard station. Artifacts from the archaeological site at Cape Alava are expertly researched and beautifully presented. One of the meticulously created exhibits reproduces a longhouse interior with animal skins, a cooking fire, and the smell of smoked salmon. The center also serves as the town's social and cultural center. (Open daily June-Aug. 10am-5pm; Sept.-May W-Su 10am-5pm; $4, seniors and students $3.) The Makah Nation, whose recorded history is 2000 years old, lives, fishes, and produces artwork on this land, although in a startling state of material poverty. During Makah Days (Aug. 25-27 in 2000), Native Americans from around the region come for canoe races, dances, and bone games (a form of gambling). Visitors are welcome and the salmon bake makes a savory highlight. Call the center for details.

Cape Flattery can be reached through Neah Bay. Pick up directions at the Makah Center, or just take the road through town until it turns to dirt, then follow the "Marine Viewing Area" sign once you hit gravel, and continue for another 4 mi. to a small, circular parking area, where a trailhead leads toward Cape Flattery.

You'll know you're close to the amazing views of **Tatoosh Island** just off the coast and **Vancouver Island** across the strait when you hear the sound of Tatoosh's bull-horn. The road is excruciatingly bumpy, but the hike reveals some of the more beautiful stretches of ocean around. To the south, the Makah Reservation's **beaches** are solitary and peaceful; respectful visitors are welcome to wander.

Neah Bay caters to fishermen, and it is not the best place to spend the night. If stuck, try the oceanside **Cape Motel** (645-2250) on Rte. 112. Squeeze in small but clean rooms ($45-55), or sack out in a rustic shanty (singles $18; doubles with bunk $25) or tentsite ($12). **Shipwreck Pt. Campground** (963-2688), 11 mi. east of Neah Bay, has tent sites almost two steps from the beach along Juan de Fuca Strait, and nice bathrooms ($13.75, each extra guest $2; RVs $18).

NEAR THE PARK: FORKS

Between ONP's northern rim and its western rim's rainforests stands the logging town of Forks, the perfect place to stop, stock up, and grab a bite to eat along U.S. 101—in fact, the only place to stop. Forks lies two hours west of Port Angeles; fill up your gas tank before beginning the drive. There are few stations farther north or south. **Clallam Transit** (452-4511 or 800-858-3747; see p. 200) Route #14 serves Forks from Port Angeles (M-F; $1, disabled and seniors 50¢, ages 6-19 85¢). The **Forks Chamber of Commerce** (374-2531 or 800-443-6757; open daily 10am-4pm) is south of town. Maps of the **Hoh-Clearwater Multiple Use Area** nearby are available from the **DNR Main Office** (374-6131; open M-F 8am-4:30pm), just off U.S. 101 on the north side of Forks, right next to Tillicum Park. **Police:** 374-2223. Open daily 6am-6pm. **Hospital:** 374-6271. **Post office:** At Spartan Ave. and A St. east of U.S. 101 (open M-F 9am-5pm, Sa 10am-noon). **ZIP Code:** 98331. **Area Code:** 360.

The closest non-camping budget accommodation to Forks is the **Rainforest Hostel**, 169312 U.S. 101 (374-2270). To get there, follow the hostel signs off U.S. 101, 20 mi. south of Forks or 4 mi. north of Ruby Beach, between Miles 169 and 170. Buses travel to the hostel from North Shore Brannon's Grocery in Quinault (daily 9am, 1, and 4:35pm; 50¢). Owner Jim welcomes travelers into his quasi-communal home-turned-hostel, and daytime passersby can stop in for a **shower** ($2). The house has a roaming cat and dog, but those with allergies or an other can escape to two tiny trailers balanced on the lawn out back. Two family-size rooms are available, as well as men's and women's dorms; couple and family accommodations require a reservation and deposit. The hostel is a font of info and provides shelter from surprise western rim rain showers (beds $10; 11pm curfew; 8am wake up; morning chore required of hostelers).

The **Raindrop Cafe**, 111 E. A St. (374-6612), at S. Forks Ave., names food for clouds (open M-Sa 6am-9pm, Su 6am-8pm; in winter daily 6am-8pm). Off the highway, grab groceries and coffee at **Forks Thriftway** (374-6161; open M-Su 8am-10pm).

WESTERN RIM

In the temperate rainforests of ONP's western rim, ferns, mosses, and gigantic old growth trees blanket the valleys of the Hoh, Queets, and Quinault Rivers. Although fallen foliage and decaying trunks cover the rainforest floor, rangers keep the many walking and hiking trails clear, well-marked, and accessible. The entrances to each of the three valleys are clearly marked from U.S. 101.

Logging has left the drive through the **Hoh River Valley** along U.S. 101 alternately stunning and barren. The first two DNR campgrounds along Hoh River Rd., which splits from U.S. 101 13 mi. south of Forks, don't accept reservations. In the spring and fall, campers seem to ignore these free sites which make a good base for hitting the Hoh trailhead 8-12 mi. away (see below). Maps of the **Hoh-Clearwater Multiple Use Area** are available from the **DNR Main Office** in Forks (see above).

From **Hoh Rainforest Visitor Center** (see **Practical Information,** p. 204), a good 45-minute drive from U.S. 101, take the three-quarter-mile, wheelchair-accessible **Hall of Mosses Trail** for a whirlwind tour of rainforest vegetation. The slightly longer

Spruce Nature Trail leads 1¼ mi. through lush forest and along the banks of the Hoh River, with a smattering of educational panels explaining natural quirks. Nearby, the park maintains 88 sometimes soggy **campsites** ($10) with drinking water and toilets, but limited facilities for the handicapped. The **Hoh Rainforest Trail** is the most heavily traveled path in the area, beginning at the visitor center and parallel-ing the Hoh River for 18 mi. to **Blue Glacier** on the shoulder of **Mount Olympus.** Shy Roosevelt elk, the ever-contested northern spotted owl, and the gods of ancient Greece inhabit this area.

Several other trailheads from U.S. 101 offer less crowded opportunities for exploration of the rainforest amid surrounding ridges and mountains. The **Queets River Trail** hugs its namesake east for 14 mi. from **Queets Campground** (20 sites $8); follow U.S. 101 south from the Hoh River Rd. turn-off for about 34 mi. to the 13 mi. road to Queets Ranger Station: the road is unpaved and unsuitable for RVs or large trailers. Hiking is best in August, but there's still a risk that the two river crossings will wash out the trail. A shorter loop (3 mi.) is as much as most visitors see of Queets. Elk often appear in fields along the trail, which passes a broad range of rainforest, lowland river ecosystems, and the park's largest Douglas fir.

The Park and Forest Services and the Quinault Reservation border Quinault Lake and River. The Forest Service operates an information center at the **Quinault Ranger Station,** 353 S. Shore Rd. (288-2525; open daily 9am-4:30pm; in winter M-F 9am-4:30pm). From the station, it's 20 mi. to the **North Fork trailhead,** from which intrepid hikers can journey 44 mi. north across the entire park, finishing at **Whiskey Bend** on the north rim near Elwha campgrounds. The week-long trip is one of the easier ones into the heart of the Olympics, and has 17 campsites along the way (backcountry permit required). Snow-seekers flock to **Three Lakes Point,** an exquis-ite summit covered with powder until July, a 6½ mi. hike (one-way) from North Fork past yellow cedar and prime amphibian habitat. **Dayhikes** depart the Quinault Ranger Station: the 4 mi. **Quinault Lake Loop** or the half-mile **Maple Glade Trail.** From the **Graves Creek Ranger Station** and **campground** (30 sites $10), 8 mi. up Shore Rd., the challenging **Grave Creek Trail** (8 mi. one-way) follows the Creek through a secluded valley to Lake Sundown.

The **Lake Quinault Lodge** (288-2900 or 800-562-6672), next to the ranger station, rents canoes and rowboats ($10 per hr.). Jim Carlson (288-2293) offers **horseback rides** in summer ($35 per 2hr.). Campers can drop their gear lakeside in **Willaby Campgrounds** (288-2213), a quarter-mile before the Forest Service Ranger Station along the south shore of the lake (sites $13).

COASTAL ZONE

A pristine coast traces the park's slim far western region for 57 mi., separated from the rest of ONP by U.S. 101 and private timber. Eerie fields of driftwood, sculp-tured arches, and dripping caves frame the horizon, while the waves push at rug-ged sea stacks, stray masses of land that erosion has left stranded off the coast. Bald eagles soar on windy days, as whales and seals speed through the Pacific—gray whales migrate from March to May and from September to October.

Between the Quinault and Hoh Reservations, U.S. 101 hugs the coast for 15 mi., with parking lots just a short walk from the sand. The highway meets the coast near **Kalaloch Center** (KLAY-lok; 962-2283), a crowded campground with 175 sites ($12) near the ocean, including a lodge, general store, gas station, and ranger sta-tion. Gather at low tide for **tidepool talks;** park newspapers and bulletin boards list schedules. To the north, **Beach #4** has abundant tidepools plastered with sea stars; **Beach #6,** 3 mi. north at Mile 160, is a favorite whale-watching spot. Near Mile 165, sea otters and eagles hang out amid tidepools and sea stacks at **Ruby Beach.** Camp-ing on this stretch of beach is not allowed.

Beach camping is permitted north of the Hoh Reservation between **Oil City** and **Third Beach,** and north of the Quileute Reservation between **Hole-in-the-Wall** and **Shi-Shi Beach.** Those who camp along these stretches bask in the glory of hiking, long evenings of reflected sunlight capped by resplendent sunsets, and an ever-changing seascape. Before hiking or camping on the coast, pick up a required overnight permit, a park map, a tide table, and the useful *Olympic Coastal Strip* brochure at a ranger station. Find the tide line from the previous high tide, use the tide table to estimate how many feet the tide will change while you're there, and set up camp well above this mark. Use the same caution when walking the coast so as not to cross beach that could be covered for your return trip.

Between the Hoh and Quileute Reservations, a 17 mi. stretch of rocky headlands dominates the coastline. At the end of this strip, **Mora** (374-5460), on Mora Rd., due west of Forks, off Rte. 110 near the Quileute Reservation, has a drive-in **campground** (sites $10) and a **ranger station.** From **Rialto Beach** near Mora, 21 mi. of coast stretch north to a roadhead and campground (sites $10) at **Ozette Lake** (452-0300); a backcountry permit and reservation are required for camping on the beach. Rialto Beach itself hosts eccentric caves and sea stacks worth exploring. Ozette is a 20 mi. trek west from Rte. 112. Several of these beach strands lie within private land belonging to the Makah, Ozette, Quileute, Hoh, and Quinault Nations.

Dayhikers and backpackers adore the 9 mi. loop that begins at Ozette Lake. The trail forms a triangle with two 3 mi. legs leading along boardwalks from Ozette through the rainforest. One heads toward sea stacks at **Cape Alava,** the other to a sublime beach at **Sand Point.** A 3 mi. hike down the coast links the two legs, passing ancient native petroglyphs. The entire area is mostly prairie and coastal forest, but presents plenty of sand to slog through. Overnighters must make permit reservations in advance; spaces fill quickly in summer. The **Ozette Ranger Station** (963-2725) has further info (open intermittently). Call the visitor center outside of Port Angeles at 452-0300 for permit reservations.

PACIFIC COAST

WILLAPA BAY

Willapa Bay stretches between the Long Beach Peninsula and the Washington mainland just north of the Washington-Oregon border and the mouth of the Columbia River. Home to the last unpolluted estuary in the nation, this is an excellent place to watch birdlife, especially during late April and early May. U.S. 101 passes the bay as it winds along the Pacific Coast toward Oregon. From Olympic National Park to the north, the highway passes Grays Harbor and the industrial cities of **Aberdeen** and **Hoquiam** at the mouth of the **Chehalis River.** Unpleasant and grimy, these cities have the usual malls, movie theaters, and motels. (Aberdeen's famed native son, Kurt Cobain, understandably got the hell out as soon as he could.) As U.S. 101 passes through Willapa Bay's sparkling sloughs, fantastic views compensate for the protected bay's ban on swimming and sunning. From the north, stop at the headquarters of the **Willapa National Wildlife Refuge** (484-3482), just off U.S. 101 on the left. The headquarters offer info on the Canada geese, loons, grebes, cormorants, trumpeter swans, and diverse avians that descend upon the region during fall and winter. An array of stuffed birds inside the office helps educate the eyes of visitors (open M-F 7:30am-4pm). No trails are directly accessible from the headquarters, but rangers can give directions to several accessible spots in the Willapa Bay region, including **Leadbetter Point** at the tip of the Long Beach Peninsula, and **Long Island** in Willapa Bay, accessible only by boat. Long Island teems with deer, bear, elk, beaver, otter, and grouse. It also supports a 274-acre **cedar grove,** one of the Pacific Northwest's last natural climax forests, still thriving after 4000 years. The cedars average 160 ft. in height and some reach 11 ft. in diameter.

Long Island is home to five limited-use **campgrounds,** all inaccessible by car. Reaching the island requires finding a boat or bumming a ride on one. Boats should be launched from the headquarters (see above). The channel here is too muddy for swimming. After reaching the island, hike 2½ mi. along the island's main road to reach the **Trail of Ancient Cedars.** The Refuge headquarters provides advice on getting to the island and maps marked with campgrounds.

LONG BEACH PENINSULA

The 28 mi. of unbroken sand that is Long Beach Peninsula is an overwhelming frenzy of kitsch and souvenir shops. The peninsula is accessible by U.S. 101 and Rte. 103, and every town has a clearly marked beach access road (unmarked roads are almost sure to end in private property). Fishing, swimming, boating, and kite-flying are how residents recuperate from pounding winter storms. Beachcombers hunt for glass balls let loose from Japanese fishing nets; locals say they have the most luck at **Ocean Park.** Permits are required for gathering driftwood here.

Clamming season lasts from October to mid-March; call the **shellfish hotline** (360-615-4166) for season status. Beware **red tide,** when bacteria can render innocuous-looking bivalves fatal to humans. Beach access is blocked when red tide washes in. The **red tide hotline** is 800-562-5632 (www.doh.wa.gov/ehp/sf/biotoxin.htm). An annual non-resident license costs $20 and is available, along with tips and tide tables, at **Short Stop,** in the Shell Station across the street from the visitor center.

Wild varieties of **blackberries** and **blueberries** are an arm's reach away along many roadsides (though they may be coated in dust and exhaust). The peninsula, with 500 acres of **cranberry bogs,** is one of only four regions in the U.S. where cranberries are grown. Most of the bogs are in **Grayland** along Cranberry Rd., parallel to Hwy. 105, and the berries are harvested in October.

From south to north, Long Beach's attractions are as follows. Like several other towns along the bay, **Ilwaco** was nearly devastated when depleted salmon stocks required a shutdown of the fishery for several years. 2000 marks only the second salmon season since the fishing ban was lifted. Salmon steaks are plentiful along the waterfront where charter companies offer fishing trips. **Pacific Salmon Charters** (642-3466 or 800-831-2695) leads eight-hour fishing tours, including coffee and tackle (daily at 5:30am; from $70). The **Long Beach Peninsula Visitors Bureau** (642-2400 or 800-451-2542) is five minutes south of Long Beach on U.S. 101 (open M-F 10am-5pm, Sa 9am-5pm, Su 10am-4pm). **Pacific Transit** (in Raymond 642-9418, in Naselle 484-7136, farther north 875-9418) sends buses from Long Beach as far north as Aberdeen ($1.70; exact change required). **Local buses** run up and down the peninsula 14 times per day. Schedules are available in post offices and visitor centers on the peninsula (weekends local service only). Festivals fill the summer. The third weekend in July brings the **Sand-Sations Sand Sculpture Contest** to the city of **Long Beach.** In 1989, a world record tumbled when participants built a 3-mile-long fortress of sand. During the third week of August, flyers from Thailand, China, Japan, and Australia compete in the **International Kite Festival** (642-2400).

Among the cheap places to hit the hay on the Peninsula is **Sand-Lo-Motel,** 1910 Pacific Hwy. (642-2600), featuring coffee makers in each room (singles and doubles $42; rates drop in winter). A haven from the craziness is **My Mom's Pie Kitchen,** 4316 S. Pacific Hwy. (642-2342), a delicious respite from steak houses and greasy spoons. My Mom's Special, a half-sandwich, soup or salad, plus half a piece of pie costs $8 (open W-Su 11am-4pm). **Marsh's Free Museum,** 409 S. Pacific Way (642-2188), is home to a mechanical fortune teller, Jake the petrified alligator-man (as seen in the *National Enquirer*), and honky-tonk souvenirs (open, ironically, whenever tourists bring money). For the best meal around, head down Hwy. 103 in Ocean Park to historic **Oysterville.** A tiny, whitewashed town, Oysterville's star draw is **Oysterville Sea Farms** (665-6585), at 1st and Clark, which raises, cooks up, and dishes out a certain mollusc. ($3.50 per dozen; open daily June-Sept. 10am-5pm, Oct.-May Sa-Su 10am-5pm).

THE COLUMBIA RIVER ESTUARY

Several miles south of Long Beach on Washington's southern border, **Cape Disappointment** guards the Columbia River Estuary. In 1788, British fur trader Captain John Meares, frustrated by repeated failures to cross the treacherous Columbia River sandbar, gave the large promontory guarding the river mouth its name. Over

300 years, almost 2000 vessels have been wrecked, stranded, or sunk where the Columbia meets the ocean.

Fort Columbia State Park (777-8221) lies on U.S. 101 northwest of the Astoria Megler Bridge, 1 mi. east of **Chinook** on the west side of the highway. The fort was armed in 1896 to protect the river mouth from an enemy that never materialized. The park **interpretive center** recreates life at the fort and describes the indigenous Chinook people who once occupied this land. A wooded mile-long trail meanders past several historical sites. (Park open Apr. to mid-Oct. daily dawn-dusk. Center open Memorial Day to Sept. daily W-Su 10am-5pm; call for winter hours.)

Three miles southwest of Ilwaco, at the southern tip of the Peninsula, **Fort Canby State Park** (642-3078 or 800-452-5687) offers camping and a megadose of Lewis and Clark (open daily dawn-dusk). The park was the dynamic duo's final destination, and now boasts two lighthouses and a well-pruned campground packed with alders and RVs. The sites fill up quickly in summer. (Hot pay showers; 2 wheelchair accessible sites; 180 sites: $11; 87 full hookups $16; 5 hiker/biker sites $5; 3 cabins and 3 yurts sleep 4 for $35. Reservations fee $6.) At the end of the main road, the spaceship-shaped **Lewis and Clark Interpretive Center** hovers above the ruins of the fort. Inside, a winding display documents their expedition from its Missouri origins to the party's arrival at the mouth of the Columbia, and the explorers' painstakingly detailed journal entries speak for themselves (open daily 10am-5pm). The **North Head Lighthouse,** built in 1898, is accessible by a gravel path in the northwest corner of the park. The **Cape Disappointment Lighthouse,** built in 1856, is the oldest lighthouse in the Pacific Northwest. In the southeast corner of the park, its distinctive red light can be reached by puffing a quarter-mile up a steep hill from the Coast Guard station parking lot, or by clambering along a narrow, fairly steep trail from the interpretive center. For a magnificent beach-level view of both lighthouses, drive through the campground area past **Waikiki Beach** on the **North Jetty.** Though not quite Honolulu, Waikiki is the only beach safe enough for swimming, and is a solitary spot for winter beachcombing and ship watching.

WESTERN WASHINGTON

EASTERN WASHINGTON AND THE CASCADES

Sprawling in the rain shadow of the Cascades, the hills and valleys of the Columbia River Basin foster little more than sagebrush, tumbleweed, and tiny wildflowers among unirrigated dunes. Where the watershed has been tapped, however, a patchwork of farmland yields bumper crops of fruit and wine. Abundant sunshine ripens some of the world's finest apples and bronzes visitors from the rainy coast. Seeking the best of the region, travelers take high alpine routes through the Cascades, where dry hills give way to uncommonly green beauty in the mountains.

While the Columbia River thunders in its deepest gorge near Portland, OR, the power of its upper reaches in the heart of the state has supported salmon spawning for millennia. The damming of the river has replaced one harvest with another, and while the rich but arid soil has benefited from this irrigation, the river's salmon runs were nearly destroyed. Today salmon and steelhead stocks in the Columbia-Snake River watershed whither near extinction—in 1999 the Chinook salmon was placed on the endangered species list—as silt and slack water damage their spawning habitat. Poor ladders or lack of access through dams have foiled their progress upstream—when the massive Grand Coulee Dam was built, no provision was made for salmon to travel past it into hundreds of miles of watershed. The detrimental effects of the depression-era Columbia Basin Project have been recognized and stand as a recurring issue. Proponents of decommissioning key dams are joined by a host of officials trying to figure out how to save the state fish. And the federal government has provided material compensation to Native American tribes that have historically depended on the salmon for their own survival. The salmon yet retains its symbolic power for religious and secular admirers.

The Cascades are most accessible in July, August, and September. Many high mountain passes are snowed in during the rest of the year and the rest of the state is cold and snowy, too. Mounts Baker, Vernon, Glacier, Rainier, Adams, and St. Helens are accessible by four major roads. The North Cascades Hwy. (Rte. 20) is the most breathtaking and provides access to North Cascades National Park. Scenic U.S. 2 leaves Everett for Stevens Pass and descends along the Wenatchee River. Route 20 and U.S. 2 are often traveled in sequence as the Cascade Loop. U.S. 12 approaches Mt. Rainier National Park through White Pass and provides access to Mt. St. Helens from the north. I-90 sends four lanes from Seattle to the ski resorts of Snoqualmie Pass and eastward. From the west the state is accessible by bus on I-90 and U.S. 2 (from Seattle), and the train parallels I-90. Rainstorms and evening traffic can slow hitching; locals warn against thumbing Rte. 20.

HIGHLIGHTS OF EASTERN WASHINGTON AND THE CASCADES

■ **Mt. Rainier** (see p. 221), and **Mt. St. Helens** (see p. 215) offer spectacular hiking.
■ The town of **Stehekin,** the boat ride to it, and the wilds beyond it (see p. 228).
■ **Route 20** (see p. 229) wends through the **North Cascades,** past the **Sauk Mountain Trail** (see p. 230), teal **Ross Lake** (see p. 230), and **Goat Peak Lookout** (see p. 233).
■ Greenery aside, the **Grand Coulee Dam** (see p. 235) is infamously made of cement.
■ The **Pullman Lentil Festival** is described on p. 243. Must you hesitate?

THE CASCADES

MOUNT ST. HELENS

In a single cataclysmic blast on May 18, 1980, Mount St. Helens erupted, transforming what had been a perfect mountain cone into a crater one mile wide and two miles long. The force of the ash-filled blast crumbled 1300 ft. of rock and razed forests, strewing trees like charred matchsticks. Ash from the crater rocketed 17 mi. upward, circling the globe and blackening the region's sky for days. Debris from the volcano flooded Spirit Lake and choked the region's watersheds.

Mount St. Helens National Volcanic Monument encompasses most of the blast zone, the area around the volcano affected by the explosion. This ashen landscape, striking for its initially bleak expanses, is steadily recovering from the explosion. Saplings push their way up past fallen trees while insects and small mammals are returning. Parts of the monument are off-limits to the public because of ongoing geological experiments and the fragile ecosystem; hikers are obliged to keep to the handful of trails through such areas. Before heading out, check 530 AM for road closures; besides boasting the best view of the crater from the road (from the Johnstone Ridge Observatory), Rte. 504 is the only road accessible in winter. Like many other Cascade peaks, the volcano still threatens to erupt, but is well-monitored, and there's a good chance it won't blow while you're there.

✺ ORIENTATION

To make the **western approach,** take Exit 49 off I-5 and use **Rte. 504,** otherwise known as the **Spirit Lake Memorial Highway.** The brand-new 52 mi. road has wide shoulders and astounding views of the crater. For most, this is the quickest and easiest daytrip to the mountain, past the Mount St. Helens Visitor Center, the Coldwater Ridge Visitor Center, and the Johnston Ridge Observatory.

Make a **southern approach** on **Route 503,** which skirts the side of the volcano until it connects with Forest Service Rd. 90. From there, Forest Service Rd. 83 leads to lava caves and the Climber's Bivouac, a launch pad for forays up the mountain. Views from the south side don't show the recent destruction, but the south side's green glens and remnants of age-old lava flows make for great hiking and camping.

To make a **northern approach,** take **U.S. 12** east from I-5 (Exit 68). The towns of Mossyrock, Morton, and Randle along U.S. 12 offer the **closest major services** to the monument. From U.S. 12, Forest Service Rd. 25 heads south to Forest Service Rd. 99, which leads 16 mi. into the most devastated parts of the monument.

Although the monument itself contains no established **campgrounds,** a number are scattered throughout the surrounding national forest. Free dispersed camping is allowed within many non-restricted areas; obtain a free **backcountry permit** from visitor centers or ranger stations. In the newly opened Margaret backcountry area, north of Rd. 504 or Rd. 99, camping is permitted only at previously established sites. See individual approaches for listings of campgrounds.

ⓘ PRACTICAL INFORMATION

Entrance Fee: Access to almost every visitor center, viewpoint, and cave requires purchase of a pass good for 3 days: $8, seniors $4, under 16 free. See p. 40 for yearly passes. It is possible to stop at the viewpoints after 6pm without paying (though you technically risk a ticket), or to avoid the popular destinations in favor of free spots.

Visitor Information: There are nine visitor centers and info stations, listed below by approach. Those on the western approach are the shiniest and most popular.

Publications: *The Volcano Review,* available free at all visitor centers and ranger stations, contains a map, copious info, and schedules of activities. The *Road Guide to Mount St. Helens* ($5), available at visitor centers, is more thorough.

Forest Service Information: Gifford Pinchot National Forest Headquarters, 10600 NE 51st Circle, Vancouver, WA 98682 (891-5000, recording 891-5009; www.fs.fed.us/gpnf). Info on camping and hiking within the forest. Additional **ranger stations** and **visitor information** at: **Randle,** 10024 U.S. 12 (497-1100), north of the mountain and east of the Wood Creek Information Station; and **Packwood,** 13068 U.S. 12 (494-0600), on the northern approach east.

Crater Climbing Permits: Between May 15 and Oct. 31, the Forest Service allows 100 people per day to hike to the crater rim. $15 permits are required to climb anywhere above 4800 ft. Reserve in person at or write to the **Monument Headquarters** (see **Southern Approach: Visitor Centers,** p. 216). 50 permits per day may be reserved in advance after Feb. 1. Write early; weekends are usually booked by March, and weekdays often fill up as well. The reservation-less can enter a 6am lottery for the next day's remaining permits at **Jack's Restaurant and Country Store,** 13411 Louis River Rd. (231-4276; open daily 5:30am-9pm), on Rte. 503, 5 mi. west of Cougar (I-5 Exit 21).

Radio: 530 AM. Road closures and ranger hours. **Emergency:** 911. **Area Code:** 360.

WESTERN APPROACH: RTE 504

VISITOR CENTERS

Mount St. Helens Visitor Center (360-274-2100, 24hr. recorded info 360-274-2103), opposite Seaquest State Park. Displays and interactive exhibits for the gadget-lover or aspiring geologist. A 22min. film with graphic footage of the eruption and its aftermath is shown every hour mid-June to Aug. Open year-round daily 9am-5pm.

Forest Learning Center (414-3439). This massive propaganda machine for the Weyerhaeuser Company houses impressive exhibits on the reforestation of the thousands of surrounding acres of timber downed by the explosion. Open May-Oct. 10am-6pm.

Coldwater Ridge Visitor Center (274-2131; fax 274-2129). This sprawling glass-and-copper building has a superb view of the crater, along with trails leading to **Coldwater Lake.** Emphasis on the area's recolonization by living things. Picnic areas, interpretive talks, and a gift shop/snack bar. Open May-Aug. daily 9am-6pm; Sept.-Apr. 9am-5pm.

Johnston Ridge Observatory (274-2140), at the end of Rte. 504. Geological exhibits and the best view from the road of the steaming lava dome and crater. The center is named for David Johnston, a geologist who predicted the May 18, 1980 eruption, but stayed to study it and was killed. Open daily May-Sept. 9am-6pm; Oct.-Apr. 10am-4pm.

CAMPING AND OUTDOORS

Seaquest State Park (274-8633, reservations 800-452-5687), opposite the Mount St. Helens Visitor Center, is easy to reach off I-5, and the closest to the park with facilities. (Pay showers. 76 pleasant wooded sites $10; 16 full hookups $15; 4 primitive walk-in sites $5. Reservations in summer are a must. Wheelchair accessible.)

The 1hr. drive from the Mt. St. Helens Visitor Center to Johnston Ridge offers spectacular views of the crater and rebounding ecosystem. The **Boundary Trail** leads from the Johnston Ridge Observatory to Spirit Lake, and continues 52 mi. to Mt. Adams through sensitive terrain: you must stay on the trail.

SOUTHERN APPROACH: RTE. 503

VISITOR CENTERS

Pine Creek Information Station (238-5225), 17 mi. (30min.) east of Cougar on Rd. 90, shows an interpretive film of the eruption. Open mid-May to Sept. daily 9am-6pm.

Apes' Headquarters, at Ape Cave on Rd. 8303, 3 mi. north of the Rd. 83-Rd. 90 junction (15min. from Cougar). Rangers guide 45min. lantern walks into the 1900-year-old lava tube daily from 10:30am-3:30pm (free). Arrive early to snag a spot. Dress warmly to show the competition you're serious. Open daily late-May to Sept. 10am-5:30pm.

Monument Headquarters, 42218 NE Yale Bridge Rd., Amboy, 98601 (247-3900, recording 247-3903), 3 mi. north of Amboy on Rte. 503. Not a visitor center, but can answer questions about permits and specific road conditions. Open M-F 7:30am-5pm.

Mt. St. Helens, Mt. Rainier, and Vicinity

CAMPGROUNDS

A Ipsut Creek
B Mowich Lake
C White River
E Sunshine Pt.
F Cougar Rock
G Ohanapecosh River
I Iron Creek
J Ike Kinswa
  Mayfield Lake
K Lewis and Clark State Pk.
L Seaquest State Park
M Cougar
N Beaver
O Swift

OTHER ACCOMMODATIONS

D Whittaker's Bunkhouse
H Hotel Packwood

EASTERN WASHINGTON

CAMPING AND OUTDOORS

Swift Campground, 30min. east of Cougar on Rd. 90 and just west of the Pine Creek Information Station, has 93 spacious sites on Swift Reservoir ($15. Free firewood. No reservations.) **Cougar Campground** and **Beaver Bay,** 2 and 4 mi. east of Cougar respectively along Yale Lake; Cougar Lake has 45 sites ($15) that are more spread out and private than Beaver Bay's 78 sites ($15).

Caves and lava tubes take visitors inside the beast. From the **Pine Creek Information Station,** 25 mi. south of the junction of Rd. 25 and 99, take Rd. 90 12 mi. west and then continue 3 mi. north on Rd. 83 to **Ape Cave,** a broken 2½ mi. lava tube. When exploring the cave, wear a jacket and sturdy shoes, and take at least two flashlights or lanterns. (Rentals $2 each. Rentals stop at 4pm and all lanterns must be returned by 5pm.) Rangers lead free guided cave explorations every day (see **Apes Headquarters,** above). A quarter mile before Ape Cave on Rd. 83 is the **Trail of Two Forests,** a lava-strewn and wheelchair-accessible path above the forest floor. Road 83 continues 9 mi. farther north, ending at **Lahar Viewpoint,** the site of terrible mudflows that followed the eruption. On Rd. 83, 11 mi. northeast of its junction with Rd. 90, the **Lava Canyon Trail #184** hosts a range of challenges, making it two hikes in one: an easy, wheelchair-accessible 40-minute stroll yields spectacular views of the **Muddy River Gorge** and **Waterfall;** a more poorly maintained route leads 3 mi. to a footbridge over Lava Canyon and more views.

A new, stunted version of the mountain sports a lava dome and crater rim. Although not a technical climb, the route up Mt. St. Helens is a steep pathway of ash strewn with boulders. Often, the scree on the steep grade is so thick that each step forward involves a half-step back. The trip down is often accomplished on the triumphant climber's behind, but isn't surprisingly quicker. (5hr. up; 3hr. down.) The view from the lip of the crater, encompassing Mt. Rainier, Mt. Adams, Mt. Hood, Spirit Lake, and the lava dome directly below, is magnificent. Bring sunglasses, sunscreen, sturdy climbing boots, foul-weather clothing, plenty of water, and gaiters to keep boots from filling with ash. Snow covers parts of the trail as late as early summer, making an ice axe a welcome companion. Free camping (no water) is available at the **Climber's Bivouac,** the trailhead area for the **Ptarmigan Trail #216A,** which starts the route up the mountain. The trail is located about 4 mi. up Rd. 83. For info on climbing **permits,** see **Practical Information,** above.

NORTHERN APPROACH: U.S. 12

VISITOR CENTERS

Woods Creek Information Station, 6 mi. south of Randle on Rd. 25, from U.S. 12. A drive-through info source—map quick question gotta go! Open May-Sept. daily 9am-6pm.

Windy Ridge Visitor's Center, at the end of Rd. 99 off Rd. 25, about 1¼hr. from Randle. Rangers give 30min. talks about the eruption in the outdoor amphitheater before the stunning backdrop of the volcano. Open June 26 to Sept. 6 daily 11:30am-4:30pm; talks every hr. on the half hr.

CAMPING AND OUTDOORS

Iron Creek Campground (reservations 800-280-2267), is the closest campsite to Mt. St. Helens, just south of the Woods Creek Information Station, with good hiking and striking views. (Water. 98 sites: $12-14. 15 reserveable sites.)

The first stop for visitors traveling south on Rd. 25 from Randle and U.S. 12 should be the **Woods Creek Information Station:** viewpoints highlighted in the literature here include the **Quartz Creek Big Trees** and **Ryan Lake.** Off Rd. 25, Rd. 99 passes through 17 mi. of dramatic blown-down forests. Trailer owners should unhitch and abandon their wagons in the **Wakepish Sno-Park,** at the junction of Rd. 25 and 99. Driving straight out and back on curving Rd. 99 would take a full hour, not including the many talks, walks, and views along the way.

On the way west along Rd. 99, **Bear Meadow** provides the first interpretive stop, an excellent view of Mt. St. Helens, and the last restrooms before Rd. 99 ends at

Windy Ridge. The monument begins just west of Bear Meadow, where Rd. 26 and 99 meet. From the Miner's Car at the junction of Rd. 26 and 99, rangers lead 45min. walks to emerald **Meta Lake** (late June-Sept. daily 12:45 and 3pm).

Farther west on Rd. 99, roadside turnouts provide trailhead access, info, and unbeatable photo ops. Evidence of the blast is everywhere: felled trees, pumice plains, and log-choked lakes. **Independence Pass Trail #227** is a difficult 3½ mi. hike, with overlooks of Spirit Lake and superb views of the crater and dome that only get better as you go along. A serious hike continues past the intersection with **Norway Pass Trail,** running through the blast zone to the newly reopened **Mt. Margaret peak.** Considered the best hike in the park, the trail is 8½ mi. (7hr.) to the peak and back. Farther west, the 2 mi. **Harmony Trail #224** provides access to Spirit Lake.

Spectacular **Windy Ridge** is the exclamation point of Rd. 99. From here, a steep ash hill grants a magnificent view of the crater 3½ mi. away. The **Truman Trail** meanders 7 mi. through the **Pumice Plain,** where hot pyroclastic flows sterilized the land. The area is under constant scrutiny by biologists; stay on the trails at all times.

COWLITZ VALLEY

The **Cowlitz River** begins at the tip of a Mt. Rainier glacier, cuts a long, deep divot west between Mt. Rainier and Mt. St. Helens, and turns south to flow into the Columbia River. The basin's miles of lush farmland stretch between Mt. St. Helens. and Mt. Adams, and the **Mt. Adams** and **Goat Rocks Wildernesses,** both seldom-traveled, excellent hiking country, accessible only by foot or horseback, and sharing sections of the **Pacific Crest Trail** among their extensive trail networks. The **Randle Ranger Station,** 10024 U.S. 12 (360-497-1100), located in the valley, has information on trails and other outdoor activities. Info is also available at the **Packwood Visitor Information Center,** 13068 U.S. 12 (360-494-0600). **Mossyrock** and **Morton** are settlements with services nearer I-5.

Ike Kinswa State Park and **Mayfield Lake County Park,** on Mayfield Lake's Rte. 122 off U.S. 12 at Mossyrock, offer camping and **trout fishing** year-round. **Ike Kinswa** (983-3402, reservations 800-452-5687) has 101 sites and showers (sites $10; full hookups $16). **Mayfield Lake** (985-2364) offers 54 tent and RV sites ($11). Public boat launches provide access to Mayfield Lake. Thirteen miles to the west along Rte. 12, the **Lewis and Clark State Campground** (864-2643, reservations 800-452-5687), has 25 campsites ($10) amid old growth forests bordering prairies.

MOUNT ADAMS

The broad-domed, 12,276-foot Mt. Adams, known as Pah-toe to the area's original inhabitants, came by its second name later than most in the region. British captain George Vancouver, so fond of naming the area's peaks after British admirals with whom he was chummy, left this one to be named after America's second president. Despite offering a great range of outdoor activities, from hiking to rafting to berry-picking, the area isn't close enough to the big cities to draw crowds of urbanites, and isn't famous enough to draw tourists, most of whom pass by unaware of the mountain's virtues, like so many captain Vancouvers.

◪ ORIENTATION AND PRACTICAL INFORMATION. Mt. Adams is most accessible from the town of **Trout Lake,** on its southern face. The town lies 48 mi. west of **Goldendale** off Hwy. 97 and 24 miles north of **White Salmon** and **Bingen.** The drive past Glenwood to Goldendale provides jaw-dropping views of the canyon and river below, and the quick transition from forested valleys to gently sloped, golden farmlands is striking. **Greyhound** (773-5525 or 800-231-2222; www.greyhound.com) buses leave daily from Golden Lanes, 1005 S. Columbus in Goldendale (open Tu-Sa 1:30-10:30pm) to Portland (3hr., 5pm, $24) and Yakima (1½hr., 1:40pm, $9). **Amtrak** (800-872-7245) trains leave from foot of Walnut St. in Bingen for Portland (2hr., 7:45am, $9-16) and Spokane (6hr., 6:25pm, $32-58) See p. 52 for discounts. Visitor info is available at the **Mt. Adams Chamber of Commerce** (493-3630; www.gorge.net/

mtadamschamber), in White Salmon, on the left just west of the toll bridge, in the large parking lot (open M-F 8am-5pm). The **Mt. Adams District Ranger Station,** 2455 Hwy. 141 (395-2501), in Trout Lake, has maps and handouts on outdoor activities. **Equipment rental** is best taken care of in Hood River (see p. 86). For **road conditions,** call 360-905-2958. **Emergency:** 911. **Police:** 180 W. Lincoln, White Salmon (non-emergency 493-2660). **Post office:** 2393 Hwy. 141, (395-2108) in Trout Lake. **Zip code:** 98670 (Trout Lake). **Area code:** 509.

▐▊▐▎ ACCOMMODATIONS, CAMPGROUNDS, AND FOOD. Obtain a list of campgrounds (www.fs.fed.us/gpnf/campgrounds) and ask about camping outside of established sites and find out about trail parking passes ($3 per day or $25 per year) at the **ranger station.** Several popular campsites line Hwy. 141 (which becomes Rd. 24 and Rd. 60 within the forest). **Peterson Prairie** has wooded sites and access to the nearby Ice Caves trail (see below), but fills up during huckleberry season (water, toilets; $11). From the ranger station, follow Hwy. 141/Rd. 24 west for 7 mi. then take the pot-holed road on the left to the campsite. At **Trout Lake Creek,** the 21 free rustic (pit toilets, no water) campsites are creekside and close to the Sleeping Beauty trail. From the ranger station, follow Hwy. 141 for ¾ miles to the ETR Meadows RV Park sign, turn right on Trout Lake Creek Rd. and follow it for 4½ mi. to Rd. 8810-011 on the right. The camp is 1½ mi. down this road. The **municipal campground** in Trout Lake (left at the Post Office) has pleasantly wooded sites, with water, showers and toilets ($8, with electricity $14). **Leidl Bridge State Campgrounds,** 15¼ mi. from Glenwood on the beautiful drive to Goldendale, has free sites on soft ashen sand beside the awesome Klickitat River. Park at the entrance if your car isn't equipped to drive on sand (pit toilets, no water).

The Bingen School Hostel (see p. 87) in Bingen, has dorm beds and private rooms. In Trout Lake, **Northwoods Lodging,** 2295 Hwy. 141 (395-2767; timeout @gorge.net), opposite the school, has pleasant rooms with common kitchen facilities and a deck with a view of Mt. Adams ($45, in winter $38; check in at Time-Out Pizza next door before 9pm; no credit cards.) In Glenwood, **Shade Tree Inn,** 105 E. Main (364-3471; www.gorge.net/shadetreeinn), has motel-style rooms from $45 with views of Mt. Adams, TV, A/C, and laundry. The **Trout Lake General Store,** 2383 Hwy. 141 (395-2777), is open daily from 8am to 8pm. **Shade Tree** market, 105 E. Main (364-3471), in Glenwood, is open daily 7am to 9pm.

▟ OUTDOORS. Rangers and the Forest Service's *Trail Guide* are great resources for **hikers.** Legend holds that Pah-toe (Mt. Adams) fought and defeated his brother Wy'East (Mt. Hood) for the love of Squaw Mountain. Dismayed, the broken-hearted Squaw Mountain laid at the feet of Pah-toe and fell asleep, becoming Sleeping Beauty Mountain. Pah-toe, once proud and tall, bowed his head in shame, taking his current shape. The 1.4-mile trail to **Sleeping Beauty Peak** starts off a small trailhead on the left side of Rd. 8810-040 about a quarter-mile from the Rd. 8810 junction (see directions to Trout Lake campground).

The **Indian Heaven Wilderness Trail** is a mild 10-mile loop through forest and meadow from Cultus Creek campground along four different trails. To the south, the **Big Lava Bed,** 12 mi. down Hwy. 141/Rd. 24 and Rd. 60, is 12,500 acres in size.

Mountain bikes are allowed on some trails; refer to the *Trail Guide.* **Buck Creek** is a moderately difficult 2½-mile trail that parallels the White Salmon River, providing views from the gorge along the way (open mid-May to Oct.). The more challenging **Gotchen-Morrison Loop** follows a forested path, with occasional steeps.

Rafters love the **White Salmon River** for both its scenic views and its Class III and IV waters (run Apr.-Sept.). The lightning-bolt-shaped **Klickitat River** (Class II and III) near Glenwood offers a longer, scenic ride with some exciting spots (Mar.-June). Rafting companies are located near launch sites in the towns of BZ Corners and Husum, along Hwy. 141. **River Riders** (800-448-7238), in Hood River, has the cheapest rates and an experienced staff (White Salmon $40, Klickitat $60).

Huckleberries and mushrooms are abundant in the forest. To reach the popular **Sawtooth Huckleberry Fields,** follow Hwy. 141/Rd. 24 for 11 mi. past the Rd. 60 intersection. Mushroom-picking permits and tips are free at the ranger station The **Conboy Lake National Wildlife Refuge** just west of Glenwood is one of the few sites in the Pacific Northwest where sandhill cranes come to nest (early summer.) The **Willard Springs Trail** has views of the lake (which dries to prairie from summer to fall) from a safe distance. **Birdwatching** expeditions depart the Mt. Adams Ranger Station early on Friday mornings.

MOUNT RAINIER NATIONAL PARK

At 14,411 ft., Mt. Rainier (ray-NEER) presides regally over the Cascade Range. The Klickitat native people called it Tahoma, "Mountain of God," but Rainier is simply "the Mountain" to most Washington residents. Perpetually snow-capped, this dormant volcano draws thousands of visitors from all around the globe. Rainier creates its own weather by jutting into the warm, wet air, pulling down vast amounts of rain and snow. Clouds mask the mountain 200 days per year, frustrating visitors who come solely to see its distinctive summit. Sharp ridges, steep gullies, and 76 glaciers combine to make Rainier an inhospitable host for the thousands of determined climbers who attempt its summit each year. Those non-alpinists among us explore the old growth forests and alpine meadows of Mt. Rainier National Park. With over 305 miles of trails through wildflowers, rivers, and bubbling hot springs, Mt. Rainier has a niche for all lovers of nature.

▤ GETTING THERE AND GETTING AROUND

To reach Mt. Rainier from the **west,** take I-5 to Tacoma, then go east on Rte. 512, south on Rte. 7, and east on Rte. 706. This road meanders through the town of **Ashford** and into the park by the Nisqually entrance, which leads to the visitor centers of **Paradise** and **Longmire. Rte. 706** is the only access road open year-round; snow usually closes all other park roads from November to May. Mt. Rainier is 65 mi. from Tacoma and 90 mi. from Seattle.

All major roads offer scenic views of the mountain, with numerous roadside lookouts. The roads to **Paradise** and **Sunrise** are especially picturesque. **Stevens Canyon Rd.** connects the southeast corner of the national park with Paradise, Longmire, and the Nisqually entrance, unfolding superb vistas of Rainier and the Tatoosh Range. Hitchhiking is illegal on national park roads; asking for a ride at lookouts or parking lots is not, but isn't necessarily safer. Hitching is reportedly easy along the park's roads, but just because it's easy doesn't mean Let's Go recommends it.

Rainier weather changes quickly; pack warm clothes and cold-rated equipment. Before setting out, ask rangers for the two info sheets on mountain-climbing and hiking with helpful hints and a list of recommended equipment. Group size is limited in many areas, and campers must carry all trash and waste out of the backcountry. Potable water is not available at most backcountry campsites. All stream and lake water should be treated for giardia (see p. 34) with tablets, filters, or by boiling it before drinking. The nearest **medical facilities** are in Morton (40 mi. from Longmire) and Enumclaw (5 mi. from Sunrise). **Tacoma General Hospital,** 315 Martin Luther King Way (253-552-1000), has 24-hour emergency facilities.

The section of the **Mt. Baker-Snoqualmie National Forest** that surrounds Mt. Rainier on all but its southern side is administered by **Wenatchee National Forest,** 301 Yakima St. (509-662-4314), Wenatchee 98807. The **Gifford Pinchot National Forest** (425-750-5000), to the south, has headquarters at 6926 E. Fourth Plain Blvd., P.O. Box 8944, Vancouver, WA, 98668. The Bronson Pinchot National Forest does not exist. The Packwood **ranger station** (494-0600) is nearest, south at 13068 U.S. 12.

▤ PRACTICAL INFORMATION

Entrance Fee: $10 per car, $5 per hiker. Permits good for 7 days. Gates open 24hr.

Buses: Gray Line Bus Service, 4500 S. Marginal Way, Seattle (206-624-5208 or 800-426-7532; www.graylineofseattle.com). From Seattle to Mt. Rainier daily May to mid-

Sept. (1-day round-trip $49, under 12 $24.50). Buses leave from the Convention Center at 8th and Pike in Seattle at 8am and return at 6pm, allowing about 3½hr. at the mountain. **Rainier Shuttle** (569-2331) runs daily between Sea-Tac Airport (see p. 158), Ashford (2hr., 2 per day, $39), and Paradise (3hr., 1 per day, $39).

Visitor Information: Each of the park's 4 visitor centers—**Longmire, Paradise, Ohanepecosh,** and **Sunrise**—are listed below. The free **map** and *Tahoma News*, distributed at park entrances and ranger stations, are invaluable. The best place to plan a backcountry trip is at the **Longmire Wilderness Center** (569-4453; open Su-Th 7:30am-6:30pm, F-Sa 7am-7pm), 6 mi. east of the Nisqually entrance in the southwest corner of the park, or the **White River Ranger Station** (663-2273; open Su-Th 8am-4:30pm, F-Sa 7am-7pm), off Rte. 410 on the park's east side, on the way to Sunrise. On the north side, the **Wilkeson "Red Caboose" Ranger Station** (829-5127; open M-Th 8am-4:30pm, F 8am-7pm, Sa 7am-7pm, Su 8am-6pm) is at Carbon River. These stations, and Paradise (see below), distribute **backcountry permits**. The **Park Headquarters**, Tahoma Woods, Star Route, Ashford 98304 (569-2211; www.nps.gov/mora; open M-F 8am-4:30pm) answers phone inquiries.

Equipment Rental: Rainier Mountaineering, Inc. (RMI) (569-2227; www.rmiguides .com), in Paradise. Rents ice axes ($9.50), crampons ($9.75), boots ($18), packs ($18), and helmets ($6.50) by the day. Expert RMI guides lead summit climbs, seminars, and special schools and programs. Open May-Sept. daily 9am-5pm. Winter office at 535 Dock St. #209, Tacoma 98402 (253-627-6242). Beginners must buy a 3-day package that includes a day of teaching and 2 days of climbing ($465). **White Pass Sports Hut** (494-7321), on U.S. 12 in Packwood, rents skis. Alpine package $13 per day, Nordic package $12 per day. Also rents snowshoes and boards. Open daily 9am-5pm. Open M-F 8am-6pm, Sa-Su 9am-6pm; in winter M-F 8am-6pm, Sa-Su 7am-6pm.

Internet access: See **Whittacker's Bunkhouse,** below. $3 per 30min.

Emergency: 911.

Post Office: In the **National Park Inn,** Longmire, and in the **Paradise Inn,** Paradise. Both open M-F 8:30am-noon and 1-5pm. **ZIP Code:** Longmire 98397; Paradise 98398.

Area Code: 360.

▐ ACCOMMODATIONS AND CAMPGROUNDS

MOTELS AND HOSTELS

Longmire, Paradise, and Sunrise offer expensive accommodations. For a roof, stay in Ashford or Packwood. Otherwise, camp under the rooftop of the world.

Hotel Packwood, 102 Main St. (494-5431), in Packwood, 20min. south of Ohanapecosh or 1hr. south of Nisqually. A charmer since 1912. A sprawled-out grizzly graces the parlor. Grr. Singles $20-38, some with private baths; doubles (bunks) $25-35.

Whittaker's Bunkhouse (569-2439), 6 mi. west of the Nisqually entrance. Owned by Jim Whittaker, RMI guide and member of the first American team to scale Mt. Everest. Spiffy accommodations and a homey espresso bar, but no kitchen. No bedding. Co-ed dorms, but most guests are male. Bunks $25; private rooms from $65-90. Book ahead.

Paradise Inn (569-2400, reservations 569-2275; www.guestservices.com/rainier), in Paradise. Built in 1917 from Alaskan cedar at 5400 ft. A most spectacular bedtime backdrop. Singles and doubles with shared bath from $70, each extra person $10. Open late May to Oct. Book ahead.

CAMPGROUNDS AND BACKCOUNTRY CAMPING

There are six campgrounds within the park. **Sunshine Point** (18 sites: $10), near the Nisqually entrance, and **Cougar Rock** (200 sites: $14), 2¼ mi. north of Longmire, are in the southwest (quiet hours 10pm-6am). The serene high canopy of **Ohanapecosh** (205 sites: $14) is 11 mi. north of Packwood on Rte. 123, in the southeast. **White River** (112 sites: $10) is 5 mi. west of White River on the way to Sunrise, in the northeast. Only four-wheel-drives can reach **Ipsut Creek** (29 sites: free), at the end of 6 mi. Carbon River Road, in the northwest. **Mowich Lake** (30 walk-ins: free), at the end of unpaved Rte. 165, is in the northwest.

Sunshine is open year-round. The other campsites are open between late June and September on a first-come, first-served basis. Cougar Rock and Ohanapecosh are open from May to September, but from June 28 to Labor Day require reservations: apply in person at the visitor centers, or after February call 800-365-2267 (international 301-722-1257) or visit http://reservations.nps.gov. National Park campgrounds are handicapped-accessible, but have no hookups or showers (coin-op showers are available at Jackson Memorial Visitor's Center, in Paradise).

Backcountry camping requires a permit, free from ranger stations and visitor centers in person 24 hours beforehand, or by reservation up to two months in advance (569-4453; $20 per group; quotas limit group-size). Inquire about trail closures before setting off. Hikers with a valid permit can camp at well-established trailside, alpine, and snowfield sites (most with toilets and water source; some with shelters that sleep up to 12). Fires are prohibited except in front-country campgrounds. **Glacier climbers** and **mountain climbers** intending to scale above 10,000 ft. must register in person at Paradise, White River, or Wilkeson Ranger Stations to be granted permits (cost-recovery fee $15 per person, annual pass $25).

Camping in **national forests** outside the park is free. Avoid eroded lakesides and riverbanks; flash floods and debris flows are frequent. **Campfires** are prohibited except during the rainy season. Check with ranger stations for details.

FOOD

The general stores in the area sell only last-minute trifles like bug repellent and marshmallows, and items are charged an extra state park tax, so stock up before you arrive. **Blanton's Market,** 13040 U.S. 12 (494-6101), in Packwood, is the closest decent supermarket to the park and has an **ATM** in front (open daily 6am-10pm).

Ma & Pa Rucker's (494-2651), on U.S. 12 in Packwood. This everything joint satisfies any food need. Best pizza in town $7-11, peppermint candy ice cream $1.40, butt-kickin' beef jerky $4. Open M-Th 9am-9pm, F-Su 9am-10pm.

Highlander (569-2953), in Ashford, serves sandwiches ($4-5) and homemade pies ($2.50) in a single dimly lit room with a pool table, wooden Indian, and a deer decoy.

SIGHTS AND OUTDOORS

Ranger-led **interpretive hikes** delve into everything from area history to local wildflowers. Each visitor center conducts hikes on its own schedule and most of the campgrounds have evening talks and campfire programs. Mt. Adams and Mt. St. Helens aren't visible from the road, but can be seen from mountain trails like **Paradise** (1½ mi.), **Pinnacle Peak** (2½ mi.), **Eagle Peak** (7 mi.), and **Van Trump Park** (5½ mi.). Visitor centers have info on each of the park's sections with maps, travel times, and levels of intensity.

The **Pacific Crest Trail,** which runs from Mexico to Canada, skirts the southeast of the park. The **Wonderland Trail** winds 93 mi. up, down, and around Mt. Rainier. Permits are required for the arduous but stunning trek, and it must be completed in 10 to 14 days. Call the Longmire Wilderness Center for details on both hikes.

A trip to the **summit** requires substantial preparation and expense. The ascent involves a vertical rise of more than 9000 ft. over nine or more miles, and usually takes two days with an overnight stay at **Camp Muir** on the south side (10,000 ft.) or **Camp Schurman** on the east side (9500 ft.). Each camp has a ranger station, rescue cache, and a kind of toilet. Permits cost $15 per person. Only experienced climbers should attempt the summit; novices can be guided to the summit with **Rainier Mountaineering, Inc. (RMI)** (see **Practical Information,** above), after a day-long basic-climbing course. For details, contact Park Headquarters or RMI.

LONGMIRE

Just inside the Nisqually entrance, Longmire is pretty and woodsy, but not the best that Rainier has to offer. The **wilderness information center** (569-4453; open Su-Th 7:30am-6:30pm, F-Sa 7am-7pm) provides assistance. Longmire's **museum** (569-2211, ext. 3314), near the information center, houses a small collection of stuffed animals and historic photos and artifacts documenting Rainier's natural history and the history of human encounters with the mountain. (Open in summer daily 9am-5pm; off-season daily 9am-4:30pm. Hours may vary.)

The **Rampart Ridge Trail** (4½ mi., 2½hr. round-trip) is a relatively moderate hike with excellent views of the Nisqually Valley, Mt. Rainier, and Tumtum Peak. The steep **Van Trump Park and Comet Falls Trail** (5 mi., 4hr. round-trip) is more strenuous, passing Comet Falls and the odd mountain goat. The trip to Comet Falls is only 1½ mi., and the spectacular view of the 320 ft. drop is well worth the trail traffic.

Longmire is open during the winter for snowshoeing, cross-country skiing, and other alpine activities. **Guest Services, Inc.** (569-2275) runs a cross-country ski center which rents skis and snowshoes, and runs skiing lessons on weekends. (Skis $15 per day, children $9.75 per day. Snowshoes $7.25 per half-day, $12 per day.)

PARADISE

Paradise, the most heavily visited corner of Rainier, is perhaps the only place in the park where the sound of babbling brooks and waterfalls might be drowned out by screaming children. If you can avoid the bustle and arrive on a clear, sunny weekday, Paradise will be exactly that. Record snowfalls in 1997 kept Paradise snowbound until August. In mid-June, sparkling snowfields above timberline add a touch of white to expanses of wildflower-strewn alpine meadows, some of the largest and most spectacular in the park, and the verdant forest canyons below.

The road from the Nisqually entrance to Paradise is open year-round, but the road east through Stevens Canyon closes from October to June. The **Paradise Visitor Center** (569-2211, ext. 2328) has audio-visual programs and an observation deck. (Open May to mid-Oct. daily 9am-7pm. Oct.-Apr. open Sa-Su and holidays 9am-7pm.) From January to mid-April, park naturalists lead **snowshoe hikes** (569-2211) to explore winter ecology (Sa-Su at 10:30am and 2:30pm. Rental $1.); in summer, rangers lead hikes, talks, and wildflower walks (6-8 per day, 9:30am-6:15pm).

Paradise is the starting point for trails heading through meadows to Mt. Rainier's glaciers. The 5 mi. **Skyline Trail** is the longest of the loops, and begins at the Paradise Inn. It is probably the closest a casual hiker can come to climbing the mountain; the first leg of the trail is often hiked by climbing parties headed for Camp Muir, the principal base camp. Before reaching Camp Muir, the trail turns off to popular **Panorama Point,** halfway up the mountain and within view of the glaciers. The summit appears deceptively close.

The mildly strenuous 2½ mi. hike up to **Pinnacle Peak** begins just east of Paradise, across the road from **Reflection Lake,** and offers clear views of Mt. Rainier, Mt. Adams, Mt. St. Helens, and Mt. Hood.

OHANAPECOSH AND CARBON RIVER

Ohanapecosh's **visitor center** (569-2211, ext. 2352) snuggles under old growth cedars along a river valley in the park's southeast corner, just a few miles north of Packwood, next door to the campground. (Open mid-June to Sept. 9am-6pm; late May to mid-June Sa-Su and holidays 9am-6pm.) The **Grove of Patriarchs** is home to Douglas firs, cedars, and hemlocks, some that are 500- to 1000-years old. One of the oldest stands of trees in the state, the grove stands an easy 1½ mi. walk from the visitor center. Rangers lead groups to the grove and to shimmering **Silver Falls.**

The **Summerland** and **Indian Bar Trails** are excellent for serious backpacking—this is where rangers go on their days (and nights) off. **Carbon River Valley,** in the northwest, is one of the only inland rainforests in the continental U.S., and its trails, too, are on every ranger-in-the-know's top 10 list. **Spray Park** and **Mystic Camp** are superlative, free campsites. Carbon River also has access to the **Wonderland Trail** (see above). Winter storms keep the road beyond the Carbon River entrance under constant distress. Because of floods in the spring of 1996, the road stops at the edge of the park. Check with rangers for updates and tips.

SUNRISE

On the second day, God created Sunrise. No kidding. Too far from the entrance for most tourists to bother, Sunrise is pristine, unruffled, and divine. The winding road to the highest of the four visitor centers provides gorgeous views of Mt. Adams, Mt. Baker, and the heavily glaciated eastern side of Mt. Rainier. Trails vary greatly in difficulty; the visitor center has invaluable maps. Try the comfortably sloping **Mt. Burroughs Trail** (5 mi.) for unbeatable glacier views. Those ready for more leg stress should head to **Berkeley Park,** a 5 mi. round-trip trek into a wildflower-painted valley. For those longing to return to civilization, the 5½ mi. (4hr.) round-trip hike to **Mt. Fremont Lookout** affords a view of Seattle on a clear day.

SKYKOMISH DISTRICT

Stretching between the Puget Shore and Leavenworth along U.S. 2, the **Skykomish District** (sky-KOE-mish) begs urbanites to roam its river-plush, sub-alpine trails. Stop by the **Skykomish Ranger Station** (360-677-2414; open daily 8am-4:30pm), off U.S. 2 at Mile 51, to chat about local hikes and campgrounds. View-seekers, flower-lovers, and overnight campers all eagerly attack the 3½ mi. **Tonga Ridge Trail,** located half a mile past the ranger station. Turn right off the highway onto Foss River Rd. (Rd. #68), then left on Tonga Ridge Rd. (Rd. #6830) and continue 6 mi. to Spur #310. Bear right at the sign and continue 1 mi. to the trailhead. If in search of lakes, continue along Foss River Rd. 6 mi., then turn left at Rd. #6835 to get to **West Fork Foss Lake Trail.** Mountain bikers haul themselves up the **Johnson Ridge Trail,** the only trail open to cyclists; get directions at the ranger station. Families and train aficionados make a much slower mosey along the **Iron Goat Trail,** a recently completed route along the old train tracks. Hikes rumble through tunnels and wildflowers. To find the Iron Goat, turn left onto the Old Cascade Hwy. (Rd. #67), past Mile 50; go 1.4 mi. to Rd. #6710, then turn left to trailhead parking.

LEAVENWORTH

"Willkommen zu Leavenworth!" After the logging industry had tapped the town's resources and the railroad switching station moved to nearby Wenatchee, Leavenworth needed a new *Weltanschauung.* Taking its cue from a college study comparing the Cascades to the Alps, by the mid-1960s "Project Alpine" had introduced *lederhosen* to restaurant waitstaff, polka to public loudspeakers, and enough of a gimmick to the American public to draw an estimated one million visitors in 1999, with massive influxes during the city's three annual festivals. With world-class rock climbing and nine maintained campgrounds within 20 miles, heading for the hills may be the best way to take a vacation from a vacation in Leavenworth.

■ **ORIENTATION AND PRACTICAL INFORMATION.** On the eastern slope of the Cascades, Leavenworth is near Washington's geographic center. To get there from Seattle, follow I-5 North to Everett (Exit 194), then U.S. 2 East (126 mi., 2½hr.); from Spokane, just follow U.S. 2 west (184 mi., 4hr.). **U.S. 97** intersects U.S. 2 about 6 mi. southeast of town. **U.S. 2** is the northernmost of four east-west streets that cross the main business district.

Arrive early to flag down **Northwestern Trailways** (800-366-3830, or through Greyhound 800-231-2222) at the central **Link.** Purchase tickets by phone beforehand or at the next stop. Buses run to Spokane (1 per day, $23) and Seattle (2 per day, $23). Link (662-1155 or 800-851-5465; www.linktransit.com) provides free bus service between Wenatchee and Leavenworth with stops in town, from the Park 'n' Ride lot on Hwy. 20 between Safeway and the ranger station. All buses have bike racks. (Runs M-F 6am-8pm, Sa 8am-8pm.) Schedules are available at the **Chamber of Commerce,** 894 U.S. 2 (548-5807; www.leavenworth.org), at 9th/Evans St. under the clock tower (open M-Sa 8am-6pm; Su 10am-4pm; in winter M-Sa 8am-5pm). The **Ranger Station,** 600 Sherbourne (548-6977), is just off U.S. 2 (open daily 7:45am-4:30pm; in winter M-F 7:45am-4:30pm). Get hiking and biking maps from **Der Sportsmann,** 837 Front St. (548-5623; open daily 9am-7pm; in winter 10am-6pm), which rents bikes ($25), cross-country skis ($15), climbing shoes ($10), and snow shoes ($12). Scrub up at **Die Wäscherei,** 1317 Front St. (548-6147), off Hwy. 2 (wash $1.50, dry 25¢ per 5min.; showers 50¢ per 5min.; open daily 7am-9pm). **Crisis line:** 662-7105. **Rape/domestic violence line:** 663-7446 or 800-356-4533 (24hr.). **Weather:** 665-6565. **Winter road conditions:** 888-766-4636 (mid-Oct. to mid-Apr. 24hr.). **Public radio:** 90.7 FM. **Emergency:** 911. **Police:** 700 State U.S. 2 (782-3770), in the City Hall/library. **Village Pharmacy** is at 821 Front St. (548-7731; open M-F 8:30am-6:30pm, Sa 9am-5:30pm, Su 11am-5pm). **Cascade Medical Center,** 817 Commercial St. (548-5815 or 782-4000), has a walk-in clinic (open M-F 8am-7pm, Sa 8am-5pm, Su 11am-5pm; emergency 24hr.). **Post office:** 960 U.S. 2, 98826 (548-7212; open M-F 9am-5pm, Sa 9-11am). **Area code:** 509.

⌐ ACCOMMODATIONS AND CAMPGROUNDS. Most hotels in town charge more than $60 for a single. **Timberline Motel** (548-7415), 5 miles south of town on U.S. 90, rents no-frills rooms with kitchenettes for less (singles $45, doubles $55). **Camping** in **Wenatchee National Forest** is plentiful, spectacular, and close, but come early because *die Kampingplätzen* gets crowded in summer. Ten miles from town via U.S. 2W and Icicle Creek Rd., seven Forest Service campgrounds (water, pit toilets, $8-9) are squeezed between the creek and the road; the farthest along are prettiest. **Johnny Creek** has secluded sites and **Ida Creek** is nearest the river. RVs and trailers may find the road difficult to maneuver, but **Tumwater** (800-280-2267), 10 mi. west of town on U.S. 2, is easier to access (84 sites: $11; toilets, water).

⌂ FOOD. Predictably, Leavenworth's food mimics German cuisine; surprisingly, it often succeeds. German *Wurst* booths are tucked between buildings everywhere. Those looking for much more than these should be prepared to pay at least $8-16 for entrees, though at **Dan's Food Market,** 1329 U.S. 2 (548-5611; open daily 7am-10pm), the deli sells chicken dinners ($2.70) that *schmecken mir gut* (open Su-Th 7am-8pm, F-Sa 7am-9pm). At **Gustav's,** 617 U.S. 2 (548-4509), opposite the public pools, the locals are laughing at the fake trophies, antler lamps, old-school skis and climbing gear, too. Have a sandwich ($4-5.25) with your pint ($2) on the upstairs deck (open Su-Th 11am-10pm; F-Sa 11am-11pm; in winter daily 11am-9pm). The **Renaissance Cafe,** 217 8th St. (548-6725), equips travelers with exquisite veggie-friendly breakfasts to bolster their reserves (omelettes $4.25; open daily 7am-3pm). Visit the **Aplets and Cotlets Factory,** 117 Mission St. (782-4088), in Cashmere off U.S. 2, 8 mi. past the U.S. 97 junction, for ample samples of their gooey candies (open M-F 8am-5:30pm, Sa-Su 9am-5pm; in winter M-F 8:30am-4:30pm).

⚑ OUTDOORS. The most compelling reason to come to Leavenworth, aside from tourist-watching and sausage-scarfing, is for the extensive hiking, mountain biking, and climbing opportunities in the **Wenatchee National Forest** which surrounds the town on all but its southeastern corner. The **ranger station** in Leavenworth hands out free descriptions of hikes near town and a guide to trails ($1.50). Although most trails in this area are unrestricted, **permits** are required to enter the popular Eight Mile/Caroline Lakes, Stuart Lake, Colchuck Lake, Enchantments, and Snow Lakes areas. Permits are free and self-registered for dayhikers, with forms at the ranger station and at trailheads. Permits for **backcountry overnights** cost $3 per night, and must be reserved two weeks in advance by mail; call the ranger station to obtain an application. Spur-of-the-moment sorts can cross their fingers and visit the ranger station, where a number of permits are distributed by lottery each morning at 7:45am. There are often more than enough to go around.

The heavily visited **Alpine Lakes Wilderness,** stretching south of town, is as beautiful as it is clogged with hikers, and as is the case throughout the Cascades, the region is home to many black bears and western rattlesnakes lacking *Gemütlich-*

keit. One pleasant dayhike is the moderately sloping 3½ mi. trail to **Eight Mile Lake,** a great spot for a picnic or an overnight trip. Drive 9.4 mi. up Icicle Creek Rd., make a left onto Eight Mile Rd., then continue 4 mi. uphill to the trailhead. The 3½ mi. **Icicle Gorge trail** starts just west of the **Chatter Creek Campground** on Icicle Rd., and moseys along beside the cool creek waters. The more challenging 10.6 mi. **Fourth of July trail** switchbacks over steep terrain past wildflowers (May-June) to stunning views of Icicle Ridge and the 7000 ft. Enchantments.

The ranger station's pamphlet *Guide to Mountain Bike Routes* is an indispensable introduction to area **mountain biking.** Roads and a few moderate rides lie in the Icicle Creek area. The **Mission Creek/Devil's Gulch** area has phenomenal trails.

Dozens of named **climbing** areas line Icicle Creek Road (including **Barney's Rubble** and **Little Red Corvette**), and countless other unnamed ones await charting. The ranger station has a map of popular climbing areas, including the popular friction climb up **Eight Mile Buttress,** on the far side of Eight Mile campground. One of the most popular sites lies 12 miles east of town off U.S. 2 in the **Peshastin Pinnacles State Park,** where a sandstone climb is a good for beginners.

The **Leavenworth Winter Sports Club** (548-5115; lwsc@televar.com), maintains the forest trail system in winter. Pick up a free copy of their *Cross-Country Ski Guide* at the ranger station. A $7 day pass (free for ages over 69 and under 12) permits access to the four cross-country skiing areas in Leavenworth (23km of trails, 3km lit for night skiing).

CHELAN

The serpentine body of Lake Chelan (sha-LAN) undulates some 55 mi. southeast through the Wenatchee National Forest and the Lake Chelan National Recreation Area toward the Columbia River and U.S. 97. Here the green mountains of North Cascades National Park transform into the bone-dry brown hills and apple orchards that surround the town of Chelan. Kokanee (freshwater sockeye) and chinook (freshwater king) salmon lure fishermen from April to June, as rainbow and lake trout do year-round. But Chelan has become little more than a cutesy resort geared toward seniors and families with motor boats in tow, which lacks the solitude and space of Stehekin, at the lake's northwest tip.

◤ PRACTICAL INFORMATION. The town of Chelan rests on the southeast end of Lake Chelan, along Hwy. 97, about 190 miles (3¾hr.) east of Seattle and west of Spokane. Alt. U.S. 97 cuts through town along the lake's resort-crowded shore and becomes its main street, **Woodin Ave.** Watch for speed traps near the lake.

Link (662-1155 or 800-851-5465), the local bus service, runs Rte. #21 and 31 hourly between the Chamber of Commerce and Wenatchee (1¼hr.; M-F 5am-10pm, Sa 8am-10pm; free). **Northwest Trailways** (800-366-3830, or through Greyhound 800-231-2222) departs Wenatchee for Seattle (3½hr., 2 per day, $23); and Spokane (3½hr., 1 per day, $23). For **ferry** service, see **Stehekin,** below. The **Chamber of Commerce,** 102 E. Johnson (682-3503 or 800-424-3526; www.lakechelan.com), off the Manson Hwy., also has info on nearby Manson (open M-F 9am-5pm, Sa 10am-4pm, Su 11am-3pm; in winter M-F 9am-5pm). The **Chelan Ranger Station,** 428 W. Woodin Ave. (682-2549 or 682-2576), is on the lake (open daily 7:45am-4:30pm; Oct.-May M-F 7:45am-4:30pm). **Chelan Boat Rentals,** 1210 W. Woodin (682-4444; open daily 9am-8pm), is one of the shops on the lake that rent small fishing boats ($15 per hr.), canoes and rowboats ($10 per hr.), snorkel sets ($15 per week), jet skis (from $20 per hr., $100 per day) and bikes ($10 per hr., $50 per day). **Town Tub Laundry** is by the Pennzoil on the east end of Woodin Ave. (wash $1.50, dry 25¢ per 10min; open daily 8am-9pm). **River Walk Books,** 113 Emerson St. (682-8901) provides **Internet access** for $6 per hr. (open M-Sa 9:30am-6pm, Su 11am-4pm). **Pharmacy: Green's Drugs,** 212 E. Woodin Ave. (682-2566; open M-F 9am-6pm, Sa 9am-5:30pm, Su as posted). **Emergency:** 911. **Police:** 207 N. Emerson St. (682-2588). **Crisis line:** 662-7105, 24hr. **Hospital:** 503 E. Highland St. (682-2531; open 24hr). **Post office:** 144 E. Johnson, 98816 (682-2625; open M-F 8:30am-5pm). **Area code:** 509.

▛▟ ACCOMMODATIONS, CAMPGROUNDS, AND FOOD. Most Chelan motels and resorts are too busy exploiting sun-starved visitors from Puget Sound to bother being affordable. One exception is the **Apple Inn**, 1002 E. Woodin (682-4044), a motel that boasts a small hot tub and pool and shuttle service. The standard motel rooms are clean and neat ($49-59; in winter up to $25 cheaper). **Mom's Montlake Motel**, 823 Wapato (682-5715), south off Woodin Ave. on Clifford, is a summertime mom-and-pop operation with clean, microwave- or kitchen-equipped rooms (singles $48, doubles $55). Most campers head for **Lake Chelan State Park** (687-3710), a pleasantly grassy yet crowded campground 9 mi. up the south shore of the lake (take bus #21), with a beach and swimming area, small store, and jet ski rentals (127 sites $11; 17 hookups $16). **Twenty-Five Mile Creek State Park** (687-3710) is a smaller, though no less crowded site, also with beach access and a small store (63 sites $11; 23 hookups $17; in winter $1 less). Reservations for both parks recommended April to September (800-452-5687). Campers are also free to pitch tents anywhere in the national forest, but may only light fires in established fire rings.

The cheapest eats in Chelan are at local fruit stands. **Safeway**, 106 W. Manson Rd. (682-2615; open daily 6am-midnight) pales next to the selection (of all sorts of things) at **Bear Foods** (a.k.a. Golden Florin's General Store), 125 E. Woodin Ave. (682-5535 or 800-842-8049; open M-Sa 9am-7pm, Su noon-5pm). Behind the ivy-covered facade at ▨ **Local Myth**, 514 E. Woodin (682-2914), Art and the gang throw mindblowing 7" pizzas from wholewheat dough and fresh, hearty ingredients. Share a fabulous calzone ($7.50; open daily 11am-9pm). Pick up baked goods and throw down shots of wheatgrass or espresso next door at **Le Soleil Levant Boulangerie.** The unassuming **Dagwood's International Kitchen**, 246 W. Manson Way (682-8630), serves *pad thai* ($6.25) and burgers (open daily 11am-10pm; in winter M-F 11am-8pm). For the coffee addict, **Flying Saucers**, 116 S. Emerson (682-5129), offers lattes and aura galore in a converted 50s diner (open M-Sa 7am-4pm).

STEHEKIN

For less than the price of a motel room in touristy Chelan, you can take a ferry 55 mi. up the lake into the sparkling turquoise glacial water that meets the shores of Stehekin (steh-HEE-kin), a tiny town at the mouth of a magnificent valley. A shuttle bus runs a few miles up the valley to free campgrounds on the banks of a rushing, crystal green river, some of the most beautiful country in the Cascades.

GETTING THERE. Three ferries ply the lake in summer. The scenery gets so impressive as the ferries proceed along the shoreline where mountain goats and brown bears sometimes roam that the ride alone is worth the cost. The **Lake Chelan Boat Company**, 1418 W. Woodin (509-682-2224 or reservations 682-4584; www.ladyofthelake.com), about 1 mi. west of town, runs the *Lady of the Lake II*, a 350-person ferry that makes one round-trip to Stehekin per day ($22). Catch the ferry at Chelan (4 hr. with a 1½hr. layover; 8:30am; daytime parking free, overnight $5) or at Fields Point, 16 mi. up the South Shore Rd. near Twenty-Five Mile Creek State Park (9:45am; parking $3 per day, $17 per week). You can request that the ferry stop at **Prince Creek** or **Moore Point campgrounds** (free, no permit required) along the Lakeshore Trail (see **Outdoors**, below). Arrange in advance to be picked up then flag them down with a bright article of clothing. The smaller *Lady Express* makes an express trip to Stehekin (2¼hr. with a 1hr. layover; $41). A combination ticket for the *Lady Express* or *Lady of the Lake II* to Stehekin and back also runs $41, and allows just over three hours in Stehekin. A new high-speed catamaran, the *Lady Cat*, makes two round-trips per day (1¼hr. with a 1½hr. layover; 7:45am and 1:30pm; $79). Book ferry tickets in advance on summer weekends; they will not accept credit cards on the day of travel.

GETTING AROUND. Discovery Bikes (509-686-3014) rents them ($5 per hr., $15 per half-day, $25 per day), as does the **Lodge** ($5 per hr., $25 per day). From mid-June to mid-Oct., the **National Park Service (NPS)** and **Stehekin Adventure Company (SAC)**

run shuttles along Stehekin Valley Rd. from the ferry landing to High Bridge campgrounds (45 min., 4 per day). NPS shuttles continue on to Bridge Creek campground (30 min.) and Glory Mtn. (July to mid-Oct., 1hr.). From mid-May to mid-June, an NPS shuttle runs from the ferry to High Bridge upon request. The shuttle to High Bridge or Glory Mtn. costs $5 (children and bicycles $3). Reservations, recommended for NPS shuttles, can be made at 509-856-5700, ext. 340 and 14, or at the Golden West Visitor Center.

C CAMPGROUNDS AND FOOD. The Park Service maintains one secluded and 11 primitive **campgrounds** (most lack water) along the Stehekin River off Stehekin Valley Rd. Get the free **permit** required for backcountry camping and hiking, as well as trip planning help, at the ranger station in Chelan (see p. 227) or at Stehekin's **Golden West Visitor Center** (509-856-5700, ext. 340 and 14; open daily 8:30am-5pm; call for spring and fall hours). **Purple Point,** right next to the ferry landing, is unique in its amenities: water, free showers, and bathrooms.

There are exactly three dining options in the valley. A delicious country dinner at the **Stehekin Valley Ranch** (509-682-4677 or 800-536-0745) costs about $12 (reserve ahead; bus to and from costs $2). The **Lodge Restaurant** (682-4494), at the landing, serves burgers ($5-6) and dinners ($7-15). Two miles up the road, the **Stehekin Pastry Company** lures hikers out of the hills to snack on fat, sticky buns ($2; open daily 8am-5pm; in May and Sept. on weekends only). SAC runs a "bakery special" shuttle from the ferry ($1).

ﬡ OUTDOORS. Some short but scenic dayhikes surround the landing. The simple ¾ mi. **Imus Creek Trail** is an interpretive trail starting behind the Golden West Visitor Center. The moderately steep **Rainbow Loop Trail** offers more stellar valley views. The 4½ mi. trail begins 2½ mi. from Stehekin; SAC runs to the trailhead five times a day, but it's close enough to walk, and residents rarely hesitate to provide a ride. From Purple Creek near the visitor center, take a right turn up the switchbacks of the steep 7½ mi. (one-way) **Purple Creek Trail.** The 5700 ft. climb is tough, but rewards effort with a magnificent view of the lake and surrounding glaciers. The moderate 17½ mi., two- to three-day **Lakeshore Trail** begins by the visitor center and follows the west shore of Lake Chelan to Prince Creek.

An unpaved road and many trails probe north from Stehekin into **North Cascades National Park.** Two hikes begin at High Bridge. The mellow **Agnes Gorge Trail** is the second trailhead on the left 200 yards beyond the bridge, and travels a level 2½ mi. through forests and meadows with views of Agnes Mountain, ending where Agnes Creek takes a dramatic plunge into Agnes Gorge. Behind the ranger cabin, the **McGregor Mountain Trail** is a strenuous straight shot up the side of the mountain, climbing 6525 vertical ft. over 8 mi. and ending with unsurpassed views of the high North Cascades peaks. The last half-mile is a scramble up ledges. This extremely difficult trail is often blocked by snow well into July; check at the visitor center before starting out. The shuttle to Bridge Creek provides access to the **Pacific Crest Trail,** which runs from Mexico to Canada (see p. 2). The North Cascades portion has been called its most scenic by many who have completed the colossal journey.

The **Rainbow Falls Tour** ($6, ages 6-11 $4, under 6 free), in Stehekin, which coincides with ferry arrival times, zooms through the valley and its major sights: the **Stehekin School,** the last one-room schoolhouse in Washington until 1988; the **Stehekin Pastry Company;** and **Rainbow Falls,** a misty 312 ft. cataract.

NORTH CASCADES (RTE. 20)

A favorite stomping ground for grizzlies, deer, mountain goats, black bears, and Jack Kerouac *(The Dharma Bums)*, the North Cascades are one of the most rugged expanses of land in the continental U.S. The dramatic peaks stretch north from Stevens Pass on U.S. 2 to the Canadian border, and are pristinely preserved. The centerpiece of the area is **North Cascades National Park,** which straddles the crest of the Cascades. The green wilderness and astonishingly steep peaks attract backpackers and mountain climbers from around the world. **Route 20** (open Apr.-Nov., weather permitting), a road designed for unadulterated driving pleasure, is the primary means of access to the area and awards jaw-dropping views.

A backcountry extravaganza of untrammeled land, jagged peaks, and an Eden of wildlife and flora, much of the wilderness is inaccessible without at least a day's uphill hike. Ira Springs's *100 Hikes in Washington: The North Cascades National Park Region* is a good guide for recreational hikers, while Fred Beckley's *Cascade Alpine Guide* targets the more serious high-country traveler.

Route 20 (I-5 Exit 230) follows the Skagit River east to the small towns of **Sedro Wooley, Concrete,** and **Marblemount** in the **Mount Baker-Snoqualmie National Forest.** The highway then enters North Cascades National Park via the **Ross Lake National Recreation Area,** one of the two designated recreation areas within the National Park. After passing through **Newhalem, Diablo Lake,** and **Ross Lake,** Rte. 20 leaves the National Park and enters the **Okanogan National Forest District,** crossing Washington Pass (5477 ft.), and descending to the Methow River and the dry Okanogan rangeland of Eastern Washington. The **Lake Chelan National Recreation Area** occupies the southern tip of the national park, bordered on the south by the Wenatchee National Forest. Police happily ticket speeders in town. When making phone calls to the area, make note of the **area code**—it changes as quickly as the scenery.

SEDRO WOOLLEY TO MARBLEMOUNT

Though situated in the rich farmland of the lower Skagit Valley, **Sedro Woolley** is primarily a logging town. Volunteers at the **visitor center** (360-855-0974; open daily 9am-4pm), in the train caboose at Rte. 20 and Ferry St., have more time than they need to explain their main attraction, the annual **Sedro Woolley Loggerodeo** (855-1129), held over 4th of July weekend. Axe-throwing, pole-climbing, and sawing competitions share center stage with bronco-busting and calf-roping.

Sedro Woolley houses the **North Cascades National Park and Mt. Baker-Snoqualmie National Forest Headquarters,** 2105 Rte. 20 (360-856-5700; open Sa-Th 8am-4:30pm, F 8am-6pm), west of the visitor center. Call 206-526-6677 for **snow avalanche info.** Backcountry campers must contact the Wilderness Information Center in Marblemount (see below) for a **backcountry permit.**

Route 9 leads north from Sedro Woolley, providing indirect access to **Mt. Baker** (see p. 188) through the forks at the Nooksack River and Rte. 542. The turn-off for **Baker Lake Highway** is 17 mi. east of Sedro Wooley at Mile 82, which dead-ends 25 mi. later at the northeast end of Baker Lake. There are six campsites along the road to **Baker Lake.** The best bargain is the crowded, lakeside **Kulshan Campground,** (79 sites $7; toilets, water). **Horseshoe Cove** (34 sites $12; $6 per extra vehicle) and **Panorama Point** (16 sites $12; $6 per extra vehicle) are wheelchair accessible (reservations at 800-280-2267 or www.ReserveUSA.com; $8.25; water, toilets). Baker Lake is home to **free hot springs.** Trails from the east shore access campsites along the lake; park at the end of Baker Lake Hwy. ($3 trail park pass required).

On Rte. 20, 32 mi. east of Sedro Woolley, lies the tiny town of **Concrete,** where rows of businesses made of concrete pay homage to a now defunct local industry. Six miles west of Concrete, south on Lusk Rd. then east on Cape Horn Rd., **Rasar State Park** (RAY-sir; 360-826-3942, reservations 800-452-5687), has lush trails to the Skagit River where you can watch eagles feed on salmon from a safe distance (18 sites $10; 20 utility sites $15; hiker/biker $5). East of Concrete, right before **Rockport State Park** (360-853-8461, reservations 800-452-5687), Sauk Mountain Rd. (Forest Rd. 1030) makes a stomach-scrambling climb up Sauk Mountain. The road is bumpy and a thorough dust bath; trailers, RVs, and the faint of heart should not attempt the ascent. Seven miles up and a right turn at Rd. 1036 to the parking lot leads to the **Sauk Mountain Trailhead** which winds 3½ mi. past backcountry campsites near Sauk Lake to a 360° panoramic view of Mt. Rainier, Puget Sound, the San Juan Islands and Cascade Peaks. The park below has wheelchair-accessible trails and campsites (8 sites $10; 50 full hookups $15, $5 per extra vehicle; 3-sided adirondack cabins with 8-person bunk beds $15, no reservations).

If Rockport is full, continue 1 mi. east to Skagit County's **Howard Miller Steelhead Park** (360-853-8808), on the Skagit River, where anglers come to catch the park's tasty namesake (steelhead, not Howard Miller; 49 sites: tent sites $12, hookups $16, 3-sided adirondack lean-tos $16). The surrounding **Mt. Baker-Snoqualmie National Forest** permits free camping closer to the high peaks, but requires trail park passes, available at Forest Service and local businesses ($3 per day). These passes are not required when parking in Ross Lake National Recreation Area or in North Cascades National Park on Cascade River Rd. (see below).

East along Rte. 20, the roadside shack for **Cascadian Farms** (360-853-8173) at milepost 100.5, blends up frosty shakes ($2.50) with berries grown in the adjacent fields, part of the largest organic operations in the U.S. (open in summer daily 8am-8pm). Three miles east of Marblemount, bunnies roam the landscape (lawn) outside the **Eatery,** 5675 Rte. 20. Dine under the American flag which 88 year-old Tootsie's grandmother made in 1890 when Washington celebrated its first 4th of July as a state. Or get takeout: burgers $1.75, basket $2.75. (Open daily 8am-8pm.) Stock up on drinking water and firewood at **Marblemount Mercantile Market** (360-873-4274; open 9am-9pm; in winter 9am-7pm).

The **Marblemount Wilderness Information Center** (360-873-4500 ext. 39; open Su-Th 7am-6pm, F-Sa 7am-8pm; call ahead in winter), is 1 mi. north of west Marblemount on a well-marked road. Pick up a **backcountry permit** here. This is the best resource for backcountry trip-planning in the North Cascades.

ROSS LAKE AND NORTH CASCADES NATIONAL PARK

East from Marblemount and across the Skagit River, Cascade River Rd. provides the only road access to North Cascades National Park. East 8 mi. and 16 mi. along Cascade River Rd., **Marble Creek** (24 sites) and **Mineral Park** (8 sites) are free but unmaintained. The amazing, 3½ mi. **Cascade Pass Trail** begins 22 mi. from the bridge, and continues on to Stehekin Valley Rd. where shuttles service the Bridge Creek campgrounds. Stehekin, at the northern tip of Lake Chelan, can be reached otherwise by boat or plane (see p. 228).

Apply to the electric company if you wish to settle in the curious controlled community of **Newhalem,** or pass through unimpeded after the **Ross Lake Recreation Area,** a buffer between the highway and North Cascades National Park. At the tourist-friendly **North Cascades Visitor Center and Ranger Station** (206-386-4495; open daily 8:30am-6pm; in winter Sa-Su 9am-4:30pm), off Rte. 20, the mystical and atonal (atonal...atonal...) slide show meditates upon the Cascades' natural wonders. Serious backpackers and climbers should bypass this kinder, gentler center in favor of the Marblemount Wilderness Information Center (see above).

Among the most popular and accessible hikes is the **Thunder Creek Trail** through old growth cedar and fir, beginning from the Colonial Creek Campground (see below) at Rte. 20 Mile 130. The 3¼-mile **Fourth of July Pass Trail** begins about 2 mi. into the Thunder Creek Trail, and climbs 3500 ft. toward hellzapoppin' views.

Seattle City Light (206-233-2709), in **Diablo,** operates a small museum and provides tours of the **Skagit Hydroelectric Project,** which generates 35% of Seattle's electricity. Tour highlights include a walk across **Diablo Dam,** a ride up the 560 ft. Incline Railway, and another thrilling informational video (visitor center open Th-M 9am-4pm; tours 10am, 1, and 3pm; $5). The artificial and astoundingly green-blue expanse of **Ross Lake,** behind **Ross Dam,** snakes into the mountains as far as the Canadian border. The lake is accessible by trails and is ringed by 15 primitive campgrounds, some accessible by trail, others by boat. The national park's **Goodell Creek Campground** at Mile 119, just west of Newhalem, has 21 leafy sites suitable for tents and small trailers, and a launch site for whitewater rafting on the Skagit River (sites $7; pit toilets, water shut off after Oct., when sites are free). **Colonial**

Creek Campground, 10 mi. to the east, is a fully developed, wheelchair-accessible campground with campfire programs some evenings (162 sites $10; toilets, dump station; no hookups). **Newhalem Creek Campground,** at Mile 120 near the visitor center, is a similarly developed facility with a less impressive forest of small pines, especially good for trailers and RVs (111 sites: $10). The **Skagit General Store** (206-386-4489), east of the visitor center, sells fishing licenses and basic groceries (open daily 7:30am-6pm; in winter M-F 7:45am-5:30pm).

ROSS LAKE TO WINTHROP

This is the most beautiful segment of Rte. 20. The frozen creases of a mountain face rise before you; snow and granite rise on one side of the road, sheer cliffs plummet on the other. Leaving the basin of Ross Lake, the road begins to climb, exposing the jagged peaks of the North Cascades. Thirty miles of astounding views east, the **Pacific Crest Trail** crosses Rte. 20 at **Rainy Pass** on one of the most scenic and difficult legs of its 2500 mi. course from Mexico to Canada (which provides another route to Stehekin, p. 228). Near Rainy Pass, groomed scenic trails of 1-3 mi. can be hiked in sneakers, provided the snow has melted (about mid-July). Just off Rte. 20, an overlook at **Washington Pass** (Mile 162) rewards a half-mile walk on a wheelchair-accessible paved trail with one of the state's most dramatic panoramas, an astonishing view of the red rocks exposed by Early Winters Creek in **Copper Basin.** The area has many well-marked trailheads off Rte. 20 that lead into the desolate wilderness. The popular 2½ mi. walk to **Blue Lake** begins just east of Washington Pass. An easier 2 mi. hike to **Cutthroat Lake** departs from an access road 4½ mi. east of Washington Pass. From the lake, the trail continues 4 mi. farther and almost 2000 ft. higher to **Cutthroat Pass,** treating determined hikers to a breathtaking view of towering, rugged peaks.

The hair-raising 23 mi. road to **Hart's Pass** begins at **Mazama,** on Rd. 1163, 10 mi. east of Washington Pass. The gravel road snakes up to the highest pass crossed by any road in the state. Breathtaking views await the steel-nerved driver, both from the pass and from **Slate Peak,** the site of a lookout station 3 mi. beyond the pass. The road is closed to trailers and is only accessible when the snow has melted. Check at the Methow Valley Visitor Center in Winthrop to find out its status.

WINTHROP TO TWISP

Farther east is **Winthrop,** a town desperately and somewhat successfully trying to market its frontier history. At the **Winthrop Information Station,** 202 Riverside (509-996-2125), at the junction with Rte. 20, the staff laud the beauty of this nouveau Old West town (open daily early May to mid-Oct. 10am-5pm). Winthrop's summer begins and ends with rodeos on Memorial and Labor Day weekends. Late July brings the top-notch **Winthrop Rhythm and Blues Festival** (509-997-2541), where big name blues bands flock to belt their tunes, endorse radio stations, and play cowboy. Tickets for the three-day event cost $40 ($50 at the gate; camping on-site $15). **Rocking Horse Ranch** (509-996-2768), 10 mi. west of Winthrop on Rte. 20, gives guided trail rides ($25 for 1½hr.). Rent a bike ($15-25 per 4hr., $20 per day) at **Winthrop Mountain Sports,** 257 Riverside Ave. (509-996-2886; open M-F 9am-6:30pm, Sa 9am-7pm, Su 9am-6pm; winter hours vary slightly).

The **Methow Valley Visitor Center** (MET-how) is in Building 49 (509-996-4000; fsinfo@methow.com; open daily 9am-5pm; call for winter hours). Nearly 125 mi. of groomed cross-country skiing trails are linked by the **Methow Valley Community trail,** which runs parallel to Rte. 20: the **Sun Mountain Trails** around Winthrop, the **Rendezvous Trails** near Rendezvous Mountain to the west, and the **Mazama Trails** around the town of Mazama. For more in-depth skiing and hiking trail information, call the **Methow Valley Sports Trail Association** (509-996-3287, trail conditions 800-682-5787; www.methow.com/~mvsta), which cares for 110 mi. of trails in the area.

Between Winthrop and Twisp on East Country Rd. #9129, the **North Cascades Smokejumper Base** (997-2031), is staffed by courageously insane smokejumpers

A ROOM WITH A VIEW While on Rte. 20 anywhere east of Mazama, look north to the highest mountain, and on top you'll see a small hut: the Goat Peak Lookout, home to local celebrity Lightnin' Bill and his trusty dog Lookout Turk. Lightnin' Bill, so nicknamed not because he's speedy but because he "loves to be up here during those lightnin' storms," inhabits one of the last manned (and dogged) fire lookouts in the state. What does he do for weeks at a time in a one-room hut, 7000 ft. in the sky? Bill writes poetry (he'll read you some when you reach the tower), enjoys the view, and chats with those who make the hike to his isolated home. To visit Bill and Turk, head east from Mazama 2 mi. on County Rd. #1163 to the gravel Forest Rd. #52. Continue 2¾ mi. along the dusty road and turn left on Forest Road #5225. Drive 6¼ mi. and turn right on road #5225-200. Continue 2½ mi. to the end of the road and the beginning of the trailhead. (The directions are far more complicated than the actual driving.) The trail to the fire lookout is a steep 2½ mi. jaunt, and passes through colorful alpine meadows. Bill will show you everything in his little home, from the lightning rod above to the glass ashtrays under the bedposts that insulate him from electrical storms. Then he'll take your picture and you'll be recorded in his photo album forever.

who give a thorough tour of the base and explain the procedures and equipment used to help them parachute into fires and put them out (open daily in summer and early fall 9am-6pm; tours 10am-5pm).

Flee Winthrop's prohibitively expensive hotels and restaurants to sleep in **Twisp,** named for the yellowjacket, or "T-wapsp" in a local dialect. Nine miles south of Winthrop on Rte. 20, this peaceful village offers lower prices and is far less frequented than its neighbor. The **Twisp Ranger Station,** 502 Glover St. (997-2131; open M-F 7:45am-4:30pm) can assist with campgrounds and hikes info. **Methow Valley Central Reservations** (509-996-2148) can help you with hotels. **The Sportsman Motel,** 1010 E. Rte. 20 (509-997-2911), is a hidden jewel where a barracks-like facade masks tastefully decorated rooms with kitchens (singles $35; doubles $40). The **Glover Street Cafe,** 104 N. Glover St. (997-1323; open M-F 8am-3pm), serves healthy lunches ($3-6). Grab dessert or a take out lunch special ($2-5) at the **Cinnamon Twisp Bakery,** 116 N. Glover St. (509-997-5030; open M-F 7am-5pm, Sa-Su 7am-3pm).

There are many **campgrounds** and **trails** 15 to 25 mi. up Twisp River Rd., just off Rte. 20 in Twisp. Most of the campsites are primitive and have a $5 fee. For camping closer to the highway, head to the **Riverbend RV Park,** 19961 Rte. 20 (509-997-3500 or 800-686-4498), 2 mi. west of Twisp. Beyond an abundance of slow-moving beasts (RVs), Riverbend has plenty of comfy tent sites along the Methow River (office open 9am-10pm; sites $14; hookups $18, $2 per person after 2 people). From Twisp, Rte. 20 leads east to **Okanogan** and Rte. 153 runs south to **Lake Chelan.**

EASTERN WASHINGTON

YAKIMA

With volcanic soil, a fresh groundwater supply, and 300 days of sunshine per year, Yakima (YAK-ih-muh) and the Yakima Valley lay claim to some of the most fertile land on the planet. The fruit bowl of the nation produces so much produce that pounds of in-season peaches in Yakima often cost less than single peaches in other parts of the country. Unfortunately, not everything in the fruit bowl is peachy. Yakima has a high crime rate and offers little besides accommodations for mountain-bound or Vancouver-Portland travelers. The main attractions of the Yakima valley are the wineries and orchards beyond the city limits.

◪ ORIENTATION AND PRACTICAL INFORMATION. Yakima is on I-82, 145 mi. (2½hr.) southeast of Seattle and 145 mi. (2½hr.) northwest of Pendleton, OR. The **Yakima Valley** lies southeast of the city, along I-82. Southeastern downtown, especially near the fairgrounds, can be dangerous at night. Numbered streets line up to the east of the railroad tracks, numbered avenues to the west.

Buses: Greyhound, 602 E. Yakima (800-231-2222 or 457-5131), stops in Yakima on the way to Portland (4½hr., 2-5 per day, M-Th $26, F-Su $28) and Seattle (3½hr., 3 per day, M-Th $21, F-Su $23). Open M-F 7:45am-5pm, Sa 7:45am-4:30pm, Su and holidays 7:45-8:20am, 10:15-11am, and 2:30-4:30pm.

Public Transportation: Yakima Transit (575-6175), based at 4th St. and Chestnut Ave., near the clock. 50¢, seniors 25¢, ages 6-17 35¢. Runs M-F 5am-7pm, Sa 8am-7pm.

Taxis: Diamond Cab, 453-3113.

Car Rental: Savemore Auto Rentals, 615 S. 1st St. (575-5400), at Race St. From $20 per day; 15¢ per mi. over 100 mi. Must be 21. **Enterprise,** 312 W. Nob Hill Blvd. (248-2170 or 800-736-8222). From $35 per day; under 21 must provide proof of insurance.

Visitor Information: Yakima Valley Visitor and Convention Bureau, 10 N. 8th St. (575-3010), in the convention center. Open M-F 8am-5pm, Sa 9am-5pm, Su 10am-4pm; Oct.-Apr. M-F 8am-5pm.

Laundromat: K's, 602 Fruitvale St. (452-5335). Open daily 7am-9pm.

Library: 102 N. 3rd. St. (452-8541), at A St. Free 1hr. **Internet access,** call ahead.

Public Radio: 90.3 FM.

Emergency: 911. **Police:** 200 S. 3rd St. (575-6200) at Walnut Ave.

Crisis Line: 575-4200. 24hr.

Hospital: Providence Medical Center, 110 S. 9th Ave. (575-5000), at W. Chestnut.

Post Office: 205 W. Washington Ave., 98903 (800-275-8777), at 3rd Ave. Open M-F 8:30am-5pm. Lobby open 5am-10pm.

Area Code: 509.

◤ ACCOMMODATIONS AND CAMPGROUNDS. The fruit bowl is overflowing with reasonably priced, run-of-the-mill motels, and the best way to find a cheap room is to comparison shop on 1st St. (I-82 Exit 31). The **Red Apple Motel,** 416 N. 1st St. (248-7150), does its best to keep out the rotten ones, and offers cable, A/C, coin-op laundry, and an apple-shaped pool (singles $43, M-F $33; doubles $55, M-F $43). **Yakima Inn,** 1622 N. 1st St. (453-5615), near I St., offers large clean rooms, cable, A/C, and a pool (singles $26, doubles $36).

Yakima's few **campgrounds** tend to be overcrowded and noisy. In Toppenish, about 20 mi. southeast of town, on the west side of U.S. 97 behind the cultural center, the **Yakama Nation RV Park,** 280 Buster Rd. (865-2000 or 800-874-3087), is the exception. Though primarily an RV park, there are teepees for sleeping and a pool. (Sites $14; RV hookups $20. Teepees sleep 2-10: $30-54.)

Closer to town, the **KOA** at 1500 Keys Rd. (248-5882), charges $22 for a compact tent site and the use of nice bathrooms and a swimming pool. Take I-82 Exit 34, head east, then take the first left after the Yakima River. (Full hookups $27. Cabins sleep up to 6 $37-56.) Cheaper, more pleasant **Forest Service campgrounds** lie along the Naches River on Hwy 410, about 30 mi. west of town on the way to Mt. Rainier. Most sites with drinking water cost $5-17. A list of other sites is available from the **Naches Ranger Station,** 10061 Hwy. 12 (653-2205), in Naches, 16 miles from town on Hwy. 12 (open M-Sa 7:45am-4:30pm, lobby with materials open 24hr.).

◖ FOOD. Grant's Brewery Pub, 32 N. Front St. (575-2922; www.grants.com) at A St. is a comfortable, family-style pub in the old train depot. A pint of Scottish Ale costs $2.75; fish and chips $6.75. Live jazz, blues, and folk bands play on weekends ($3). Open M-Th 11:30am-11pm, F-Sa 11:30am-midnight, Su (Dec.-Apr.) noon-8pm.

Yakima has a large Hispanic population, and tasty, affordable **Mexican food** is plentiful in the area: **Espinoza's,** 1026 N. 1st St. (452-3969; open M-Th 11am-10pm,

F-Sa 11am-11pm, Su 11am-9pm), serves Mexican and American standards (burritos $5) and specials like *menudo* (tripe, feet and garlic soup; $6.25). **Ruben's Tortilería y Panadería,** 1518 S. 1st St. (454-5357) and 1309 N. 1st St. (249-1247), is a Mexican market which sells freshly baked pastries (10-50¢ each; open daily 8am-10pm. At **Twin Bridges,** 1315 N. 1st St. (452-6352), next to Nendel's, the small "truckers welcome" sign explains it all. Their burger ($4) is greasy and sloppy, but there's a lot of it and they're open 24 hours.

The *Yakima Valley Farm Products Guide,* distributed at the visitor center and at regional hotels and stores, lists local **fruit sellers** and **u-pick farms,** though the latter are fast disappearing because of liability concerns. **Fruit stands** are common on the outskirts of town, particularly on 1st St. and near interstate interchanges. A great place to buy fruit is on **Lateral A,** between Yakima and nearby Wapato (6 mi. south of town on Hwy. 12, on the right). In summer, the **Yakima Farmer's Market** (457-5765) closes off 3rd and Yakima Ave. in front of the Capitol Theatre on Sundays from 10am-2pm.

SIGHTS AND EVENTS. Washington is the second-largest wine producer in the nation; the **vineyards** just east of the Cascades benefit from mineral-rich soil deposited by ancient volcanoes, plus a rain shield that keeps the land dry and thus easily controlled by irrigation. For a complete list of wineries, pick up the *Wine Tour* guide at visitor centers or call the **Yakima Valley Wine Growers Association** (800-258-7270; www.yakimavalleywine.com). **Staton Hills Winery,** 71 Gangle Rd. (877-2112), in Wapato, 10 minutes south of Yakima, is the closest and one of the classiest. From I-82 Exit 40, head east, looking up for the sign and vineyards on the hills above. Specializing in Cabernet and Merlot, Staton (STAY-ten) Hills boasts an upscale tasting room trumped only by the panoramic view. (Open Mar.-Oct. daily 10am-5:30pm, Nov.-Feb. M-F noon-5pm, Sa-Su 10am-5pm.) The nearby town of **Zillah** boasts seven wineries, including the smaller **Bonair Winery,** 500 S. Bonair (829-6027; www.bonairwine.com), which boasts blue-ribbon Chardonnays ($11) and affordable Sunset Pinks ($6.50). Head east from I-82 Exit 52, turn left at the BP gas station onto Cheyne, left again onto Highland Dr., then left once more onto Bonair Rd. (Open Apr.-Oct. daily 10am-5pm; Nov.-Mar call ahead for F-Su 10am-4:30pm.) The 10-day **Central Washington State Fair** (248-7160), held in late September, includes agricultural displays, rodeos, big-name entertainers, and monster trucks.

Toppenish, 19 mi. southeast of Yakima, is the gateway town of the **Yakama Reservation** (in 1991, as a gesture of independence from the state, the tribe adopted the original spelling of its name from its 1855 treaty with the U.S. government). The **Yakama Nation Cultural Center** (865-2800), in Toppenish, presents exhibits on the culture of the 14 tribes and bands that inhabit the Yakima Valley. The fabulous museum, which celebrates its 20th anniversary next year, concentrates on the oral tradition of the native Yakama. (Open daily 8am-5pm. $4, students and seniors $2, ages 7-10 $1, under 6 75¢.) **Treaty Days** (June 2-4), which celebrate the Treaty of 1855, feature parades, salmon dinners and **Mural-in-a-Day** (June 3) during which the town adds several new murals over the course of the day. The **Toppenish Powwow Rodeo** occurs during the weekend closest to July 4th on Division Ave. in Toppenish, and features a parade, games, dancing, and live music, above and beyond the rodeo. (Fair $2. Rodeo $10 plus $2 parking fee.) For more information on either event, contact the **Toppenish Chamber of Commerce,** 5A S. Toppenish Ave. (865-3262 or 800-569-3982; www.toppenish.org), at S. Division.

GRAND COULEE DAM

As the climate warmed eighteen thousand years ago, a small glacier blocking a lake in Montana gave way, releasing floodwaters that swept across eastern Washington, gouging out layers of loess and exposing the granite below. The washout, believed to have taken a little over a month, carved massive canyons called coulees into a region now known as the Channeled Scab Lands, a striking, mesa-filled country south of the dam across its largest canyon, the Grand Coulee.

From 1934 to 1942, 7000 workers toiled on the construction of the Grand Coulee Dam, a local remedy for the economic woes of the Great Depression, but a travesty for conservationists and Native Americans. Nearly a mile long, the behemoth is the world's largest solid concrete structure and irrigates the previously parched Columbia River Basin while generating more power than any other hydroelectric plant in the United States. The backed-up Columbia River formed both the massive **Franklin D. Roosevelt Lake** and **Banks Lake,** where "wet-siders" from western Washington now flock for swimming, boating, and fishing.

The dam hulks at the junction of Rte. 174 and Rte. 155, about 75 mi. east of Chelan and 90 mi. west of Spokane. The rotund **Visitor Arrival Center** (633-9265), on Rte. 155 just north of Grand Coulee, is filled to with exhibits on the construction, operation, and legacy of the dam, all set to a Woody Guthrie soundtrack (open daily 8:30am-11pm; in winter 9am-5pm). On summer nights, a spectacularly cheesy laser show chronicles the structure's history on the dam's tremendous face (late May-July 10pm, Aug. 9:30pm, Sept. 8:30pm; free). Watch from the visitor center for guaranteed sound, or park at Crown Point Vista off Rte. 174 and tune in to 90.1 FM.

SPOKANE

Ah, 1974: Gerald Ford in the White House, Elvis in the white suit, and Spokane (spoe-KAN), Washington, in the world's spotlight. Built on silver mining and grown prosperous as an agricultural rail link, Spokane found fame when the World's Fair came to town. Parks, department stores, and skyways sprang into being in preparation for the city's promising future. Today, cafes catering to a college crowd and 50s-style burger joints make for a comfortable suburban atmosphere, and the melancholy remains of Spokane '74 slumber in Riverfront Park. Americana and bottom-of-the-barrel prices make Spokane '00 stopover-worthy.

✴ ORIENTATION AND PRACTICAL INFORMATION

Spokane is 280 mi. east of Seattle on I-90, between Exits 279 and 282. Avenues run east-west parallel to the **Spokane River,** streets run north-south, and both alternate directions one-way. The city is divided north-south by **Sprague Ave.** and east-west by **Division St.** Downtown is the quadrant north of Sprague Ave. and west of Division St., wedged between I-90 and the river.

Airplanes: Spokane International Airport (624-3218 for flight info), off I-90 8 mi. southwest of town. Most major carriers service Seattle, Portland, and beyond.

Trains: Amtrak, 221 W. 1st St. (624-5144, 800-USA-RAIL), at Bernard St. 1 per day to: Seattle (7hr., $56); Portland, OR (8 hr., $56); Chicago, IL (7½hr., $155). All trains depart 1-3am. Counter open M-F 10am-6pm and 10pm-6am, Sa-Su 10pm-6am.

Buses: Greyhound, 221 W. 1st St. (624-5251), at Bernard St., in the same building as Amtrak. To: Seattle (6hr., 5 per day, $27); Portland, OR (8-10hr., 4 per day, $36). Ticket office open daily 7:30am-7pm and 12:15-2:30am. **Northwestern Trailways** (838-5262 or 800-366-3830) shares the same terminal, serving other parts of WA, OR, ID, and MT. Ticket office open daily 8am-6:45pm. Senior (55 and over) and military discounts.

Public Transportation: Spokane Transit Authority (328-7433) buses serve all of Spokane, including Eastern Washington University in Cheney. 75¢, under 5 free. Operates until 12:15am downtown, until 11:20pm in the valley along E. Sprague Ave.

Taxis: Checker Cab, 624-4171. **Yellow Cab,** 624-4321. Both run 24hr.

Car Rental: U-Save Auto Rental, 918 W. 3rd St. (455-8018), at Monroe St. Cars from $33; unlimited mileage within WA, 20¢ per mi. after 200 mi. out of state. Must be 21 with major credit card. Open M-F 7am-7pm, Sa 8am-5pm, Su 10am-5pm.

Visitor Information: Spokane Area Convention and Visitors Bureau, 201 W. Main St. (747-3230 or 800-248-3230; www.visitspokane.com), Exit 281 off I-90. Open M-F 8:30am-5pm, Sa 8am-4pm, Su 9am-2pm; Oct.-Apr.: M-F 8:30am-5pm. **Spokane River**

Spokane

ACCOMMODATIONS

A Riverside State Park
B Yogi Bear's
C Towne Center Motor Inn
D Rodeway Inn City Center

Rest Area Visitor Center (226-3322), at the Idaho state line, Exit 299 off I-90. Open May-Sept. daily 8:30am-4pm.

Equipment Rental: White Elephant, 1730 N. Division St. (328-3100), and 12614 E. Sprague St. (924-3006). All imaginable camping equipment sandwiched between Barbies and shotguns. Open M-Th and Sa 9am-6pm, F 9am-9pm.

Library: 906 W. Main St. (444-5333). Free Internet access. Open M-Th 10am-9pm, F-Sa 10am-6pm.

Gay and Lesbian Services: PFLAG info line (489-2266) will return messages.

Laundromat: Ye Olde Wash House Laundry and Dry Cleaners, 4224 E. Sprague Ave. (534-9859). Washe thy olde clothes for $1, drye 25¢ per 12min. Open daily 6am-10pm. **Otis Hotel Coin-Op** (624-3111), at 1st Ave. and Madison St. 75¢ wash, dry 25¢ per 10min. Open daily 6am-6pm.

Emergency: 911. **Police:** W. 1100 Mallon St. (456-2233), at Monroe St.

Crisis Line: 838-4428. 24hr. **Poison:** 800-732-6985. 24hr.

Pharmacy: Hart and Dilatush, 501 W. Sprague Ave. (624-2111), at Stevens St. Open M-F 8am-6pm, Sa 10am-4pm.

Medical Services: Rockwood Clinic, 400 E. 5th Ave. (838-2531). Open for walk-ins 8am-8pm. **Deaconess Medical Center,** 800 W. 5th Ave. at Lincoln St. (emergency 458-7100, info 458-5800). 24hr. emergency room.

Post Office: 904 W. Riverside St., 99210 (800-275-8777). Open M-F 6am-5pm.

Internet Access: See **Library,** above, and **Dempsey's Brass Rail**, p. 240.

Area Code: 509.

ACCOMMODATIONS AND CAMPGROUNDS

Boulevard Inn, 2905 W. Sunset Blvd (747-1060). The rooms here are tastefully decorated and so clean you could eat off the floor (or, if you must, make dinner in the full kitchens, $5 extra). The best deal in town. Singles $30; doubles $36. 2 mi. west of town on Rte. 2.

Rodeway Inn City Center, 827 W. 1st Ave. (838-8271 or 800-228-2000), at Lincoln St. Great location with pristine rooms. Wall-to-wall amenities: indoor sauna and spa, A/C, cable, free continental breakfast, evening snack, 24hr. coffee, and an elevated pool in the middle of the parking lot. Singles $49; doubles $54; rates drop $10 Oct.-Sept.

Towne Center Inn, 901 W. 1st Ave. (747-1041). The building is aging, if gracefully. Rooms are affordable and tidy, and the Inn is indeed conveniently located in the towne center. Singles $36; doubles $39; senior discount $3.

Riverside State Park (456-3964, reservations 800-452-5687), 6 mi. northwest of downtown on Rifle Club Rd., off Rte. 291 (Nine Mile Rd.). Take the Maple St. Bridge north and turn left at the brown park sign; follow signs out of town. 101 mildly pleasant sites in a sparse ponderosa forest next to the river and the water-treatment facility, and under the flightpath. $11, hiker/biker sites $5. Showers. Wheelchair accessible.

Mount Spokane State Park, 30 mi. northeast of Spokane on Rte. 206 (456-4169). Flush toilets. 12 primitive tent sites: $10-15. Open May-Sept. No reservations.

Yogi Bear's (747-9415 or 800-494-7275), 5 mi. west of the city. Take I-90 to Exit 272; follow the signs along Hallett Rd. east to Thomas-Mallon Rd., then 1 mi. south. Indoor pool, miniature golf, and family activities put the "camp" in camping. Showers, laundry, phone and cable hookups. Tent $20; full hookups $27.

FOOD

Spokane spells great produce. The **Spokane County Market** (456-0100), N. 1100 Ruby St., northwest of town at the corner of Desmit St., sells fresh fruit, vegetables, and baked goods (open June-Oct. W and Sa 9am-5pm, Su 11am-4pm). Many farms north of town have **u-pick** arrangements and are near free picnic areas. Same-old groceries are at **Safeway,** 1617 W. 3rd St. (624-8852; open 24hr.).

Dick's, 10 E. 3rd Ave. (747-2481), at Division St. Look for the huge pink panda sign near I-90 and find burgers by the bagful. This place is a time warp—customers eat in their parked cars, or under gulls at the picnic tables out back, and pay prices straight out of the 50s: burgers 59¢; fries 59¢; shakes 89¢. Always crowded, but battalions of patty technicians move things along quickly. Open M-Sa 8am-1am, Su 9am-midnight.

Frank's Diner, 1516 W. 2nd Ave. (747-8798), serves the best breakfast in Spokane all day long. The train car that houses Frank's was once the railway president's, and is more elegant than most pricey restaurants. Two-person omelette $8.25, full stack of hotcakes $4.59. Open M-Sa 6am-9pm, Su 6am-3pm.

Fitzbillie's Bagel Bakery, W. 1325 1st Ave. (747-1834), actually lives up to its promise of "New York Style," with the exception of the sunny patio. Truly satisfying bagels with lox $4, build-your-own deli sandwich $5. Open M-F 6am-6pm, Sa-Su 7am-4pm.

Benjamin's, N. 112 Howard St. (455-6771), in the Parkade Plaza, is a local favorite. The Norman Rockwell interior is standard diner, but the German lentil soup is in a class by itself (cup $2). Burgers $2.60, incredible pie $1.75.

SIGHTS

Riverfront Park, N. 507 Howard St. (456-4386), just north of downtown, is Spokane's civic center and the place for a pleasant stroll. Developed for the 1974 World's Fair, the park's 100 acres are divided down the middle by the rapids that culminate in **Spokane Falls.** In the park, the **IMAX Theater** (625-6604) houses your basic five-story movie screen and a projector the size of a Volkswagen Bug. (Shows June-Sept. on the hr. Su-Th 11am-8pm, F-Sa 11am-9pm; call for winter schedule. $5.75, under 13 and seniors 13 $4.75.) Another section of the park offers a selection of kiddie rides, including the exquisitely hand-carved **Looff Carousel**. (Open daily June-Sept. 11am-8pm, F-Sa 11am-10pm. $1.75 per whirl, under 12 $1.) A one-day pass ($11) covers both these attractions, plus a ferris wheel, park train, sky ride, and more. Quinn's (456-6545), in the park, rents in-line skates or bikes with pads and a helmet (from $5 per hr.). The park hosts **ice-skating** in the winter.

Manito Park, 4 W. 21st Ave. (625-6622), boasts five sections of lovingly maintained flowerbed, and is undoubtedly one of the most beautiful spots in Spokane. Commune with the carp in the **Nishinomiya Japanese Garden,** overdose on roses on **Rosehill** (they bloom in late June), relax in the elegant **Duncan Garden,** or sniff around in the **David Graiser Conservatory** and the **Joel Farris Perennial Garden.** From downtown, go south on Stevens St. and turn left on 21st Ave. (Open 24hr.; buildings locked from dusk-8am. Free.) At **Arbor Crest Winery,** 4705 N. Fruithill Rd. (927-9894), a free self-guided tour of the valley can be topped off by a free sip of excellent wine. Take I-90 to Exit 287, travel north on Argonne over the Spokane River, turn right on Upriver Dr., proceed 1 mi., then bear left onto Fruithill Rd. Take a right at the top of the hill to reach the winery grounds (open daily noon to 5pm). The visitor center (see **Practical Information,** above) hands out various publications on other nearby wineries, including the *Washington Winery Tour*.

The **Cheney Cowles Memorial Museum,** 2316 W. 1st Ave. (456-3931), covers the area's history from the Lewis and Clark expedition to Expo '74. Follow 2nd Ave. west out of town, turn right onto, and go two blocks along Poplar St. (Open Tu and Th-Sa 10am-5pm, W 10am-9pm, Su 1-5pm. $4, seniors $3, students and ages 6-16 $2.50. W half-price 10am-5pm, free 5-9pm.) Included with admission is a tour of the Campbell House, a throwback to Spokane's Age of Elegance.

The **Crosby Student Center,** 502 E. Boone St. (328-4220), at Gonzaga University, is a must-see for Bing Crosby devotees. (Open June-Aug. M-F 8:30am-4:30pm; Sept.-May M-F 7:30am-midnight, Sa-Su 11am-midnight. Free.) The tiny Crosbyana Room is a shrine of records and relics from Gonzaga's most illustrious alum.

🎵 ENTERTAINMENT

Spokane is a minor league hotbed. The **Indians** play single-A baseball ($3-6) from June to August in the **Seafirst Stadium,** 602 N. Havana St. (535-2922). From September to March the minor league **Chiefs** (535-7825) play hockey ($7-13) in the **Veteran's Memorial Arena,** 720 W. Mallon Ave., which also hosts musical talents from James Taylor to Garth Brooks (box office open M-F 10am-6pm). Follow signs from the Maple St. Exit off I-5. All city-sponsored events are ticketed by **Select-A-Seat** (info 325-7469, tickets 325-7328; open 24hr.; requires credit card).

Spokane Symphony Orchestra (353-6500; www.spokanesymphony.com) has a home at the **Opera House,** 334 W. Spokane Falls Blvd., which also hosts traveling **Broadway shows** and special performances: Midori will play classics on Feb. 10, 2000, and Maureen McGovern will make an appearance on April 8, 2000. The **ticket office** is at 601 W. Riverside in the SeaFirst Skywalk (open M-F 9:30am-5pm). Known for locally produced shows, the **Civic Theater,** 1020 N. Howard St. (325-2507 or 800-446-9576), opposite the Veteran's Memorial Arena, has a downstairs space for experimental productions ($14-17, seniors $12-14, students $8-10). The **Spokane Interplayers Ensemble,** 174 S. Howard St. (455-7529), is a resident professional theater. (Season Oct.-June Tu-Sa. $14-18, students $4-8 less.)

The fabulous **Fox Theatre,** 1005 W. Sprague Ave. (624-0105), preserves an interior straight out of the Roaring Twenties, right down to Art Deco tiling in the bathroom. Shows major motion pictures anywhere from one month to a year after mainstream release ($2; box office opens at 5pm, in summer 1:45pm).

🌙 NIGHTLIFE

Spokane has the best of both worlds—minor league teams for travelers in search of small-town USA, and great nightlife for those desperate for a big-city fix. Pick up *The Pavement*, the *Spokesman-Review* Friday "Weekend" section, the *Spokane Chronicle* Friday "Empire" section, or the free *Inlander* for the lowdown.

Fort Spokane Brewery, 401 W. Spokane Falls Blvd. (838-3809). Try the house specialty, Border Run, or sample six microbrews for $4. The kitchen is open for lunch and dinner, serving burgers for under $5 (closes at 10pm on M-F, midnight on Sa). Happy hour (daily 3-6pm) features $2.50 microbrew pints. Their live music (Th-Sa) is some of the best in the region and they occasionally host big names. Open M-Th 11am-midnight, F-Sa 11am-2am, Su noon-midnight.

Dempsey's Brass Rail, 909 W. 1st Ave. (747-5362), has a good dance floor and, in the classic cool/dweeb dichotomy, free internet access by the bar. Drag Diva shows (F-Sa) and rainbow-striped beer taps make Dempsey's "the place to be gay." Draft pints $1.75-3.25. Open Su-Th 3pm-1:30am, F-Sa 3pm-3:30am.

Satellite Diner and Bar, W. 425 Sprague Ave. (624-3952), is always full and provides that crucial post-party snack/breakfast. People-watch till 4am over biscuits and gravy ($3) or pancakes ($2.25). "Cheap beer" $2.50; "good beer" $3. Open M-F 6am-4am, Sa-Su 6pm-4am, bar closes at 2am.

COEUR D'ALENE, IDAHO

When French and English fur traders passed through northern Idaho in the late 1800s, they attempted to trade with uninterested local Native Americans. The trappers' French-speaking Iroquois guides dubbed the dismissive natives "people with pointed hearts," which the trappers shortened to "heart of awls"—Coeur d'Alene (kur-duh-LANE). Today, locals call Coeur d'Alene "CDA." Gaggles of resort-bound golfers and tourists can't detract from the town's serene and beautiful lake, and have yet to taint the surrounding forests.

◪ PRACTICAL INFORMATION. Greyhound, 2315 E. Sherman (664-3343), runs buses to Boise (12hr., 1 per day, $60), Spokane (45min., 3 per day, $8). **Visitor information** is available at the North Idaho Visitor Center, 115 Northwest Blvd. (665-2350; open Tu-Sa 10am-5pm.) The **Coeur d'Alene River Ranger District Office,** at 2502 E. Sherman St. (769-3000), dispenses outdoor info and free maps (open M-F 7:30am-4pm). Pick up a **rental car** at U-Save, 6125 Sunshine Dr. Suite B. (762-9554), or call and have them pick you up for free. Must be 21 with a credit card. ($20 per day; unlimited in-state mileage, 20¢ per mi. over 200 mi. out of state. Open June-Aug. M-Sa 8am-5pm, Su 10am-2pm; Sept.-May M-F 8am-5pm, Sa 10am-2pm.) **Emergency:** 911. **Crisis line:** 664-1443, 24hr. **Police:** 3818 Schriver St. (769-2321), a ways out of town. **Internet access:** Kinko's, 119 W. Apple Way (664-2880) near Government Way (20¢ per min.; open 24hr.). **Public radio:** 91.1 FM. **Post office:** 111 N. 7th St., 83814 (800-275-8777). Open M-F 8:30am-5pm. **Area code:** 208.

▟ ACCOMMODATIONS AND CAMPGROUNDS. Cheap lodgings are hard to find in this resort town. **Sandman Motel,** 1620 Sherman Ave. (664-9119), offers firm new beds, fridges, and microwaves in large, quiet rooms. (Singles $40; suite with kitchenette up to $70. Rates drop about $15 in winter.) **Budget Saver Motel,** 1519 Sherman Ave. (667-9505), offers rooms with cable. (Singles $25; doubles $40. June-Sept. rates rise about $10; F-Sa rates rise about $5.) For bed and breakfast info, call the **B&B Information Center** at 667-5081 or 800-773-0323, but expect to shell out at least $70. **Robin Hood RV Park,** 703 Lincoln Way (664-2306), is within walking distance of downtown and just a few blocks from a swimmable beach, but sites are minuscule and lack firepits. (Showers, laundry. Tent sites $18.50; full hookups $21.) There are many first-come, first-served national forest campgrounds in the area, but most are at least an hour away, and some may hold snow as late as May. Popular **Beauty Creek** is the exception, 10 mi. south of I-90 on Highway 97, whose beautiful, well-screened sites go for $10 (water, pit toilets). The ranger office has detailed information on other campgrounds and the trails that connect them.

◪ FOOD. Coeur d'Alene has an oversupply of eateries, but only a few manage to break out of the "family fun" mold. **Moon Time,** 1602 Sherman St. (667-2331), makes a flavorful bean burger ($5.75). Slurp your garlic potato linguine ($7.25) while listening to live local folk and blues every Thursday night. (Open Su-Th 11am-midnight; F-Sa 11am-1am; kitchen closes at 11pm.) Escape from Idaho with real Thai flavor and hilarious marketing at **Mad Mary's,** 1414 Northwest Blvd. (667-3267), where Mary chops, dices, yells, and promises to "light your fire." Spicy chicken livers ($7.25) and *pad thai* ($9-13) portions are generous (open Tu-Su 11am-until Mary's tired—usually around 10pm). **Java Cafe,** 324 Sherman Ave. (667-0010), serves gourmet coffee, confetti eggs for breakfast ($4), and sandwiches for lunch ($4-5.75; hours vary, generally M-F 6:30am-8pm, Sa-Su 7:30am-9pm).

■ ▲ **SIGHTS AND OUTDOORS. Coeur d'Alene Lake** is the town's raison d'être. Hike 2 mi. up **Tubbs Hill** to a scenic vantage point, or zip along the edge of the lake on the 3 mi. bike/footpath. You can float out onto the lake itself on **Lake Coeur d'Alene Cruises** (765-4000), which promise a fine view of the world's only floating golf green. (1½hr. tours depart from the downtown dock May-Sept. 1:30, 3:30, and 5:30pm; $13.75, ages 12 and under $8.75.) **Boat rentals** are available at the city dock at Independence Point. (Kayaks and canoes $8 per hr., $25 per half-day, $40 per day; paddleboats $12 per hr.)

The **Coeur d'Alene National Forest** is the type of place that can only be found in enormous states with tiny populations, where you can hike for days on end and never reach a paved road. The forest is divided into the Fernan District in the west and the Wallace District in the east but both are administered by the same ranger office. The forest offers abundant hiking, camping, and mountaineering opportunities, but those who venture in should be aware that regions higher than 5000 ft. can be snowbound as late as June. Most trails are multi-use, so watch for motorcycles. The ranger office has detailed info on all trails.

In the **Fernan district,** one of the most acclaimed hikes is the **Coeur d'Alene River Trail,** which traverses 8 mi. of dense forest and unique rock formations with good camping along the way. From Kingston, drive 25 mi. on Forest Highway 9 to Shoshone Creek. Turn right at Road 151, follow this and Roads 412 and 205 for 35 mi. to the trailhead. The **Chico Mountain Trail** climbs two of the highest peaks in the forest, affording 360° views of the surrounding mountain ranges. The trail is only 6 mi. long but fairly difficult. From Coeur d'Alene, drive north 15 mi. along Hwy. 95 to Bunco Rd. Turn right and continue for 6¾ mi. into the National Forest on Forest Rd. 209. The trailhead is at the logging road junction. One beautiful, little-used trail is the **Larch Mountain Trail,** which climbs along the ridge of the peaks for 10 mi. at a 5000 ft. elevation. From CDA, drive north on Hwy. 95 for 15 mi., then take a right on Bunco Rd. and enter the forest. Continue on Forest Rd. 209 for 14 mi., then take Forest Rd. 332 for 15½ mi. to the trailhead.

In the **Wallace District,** the **Shadow Falls Trail** provides the easiest access to enchanting views: a 1000 ft. trail leads to a 20 ft. waterfall on a mossy rockface. From I-90, take Exit 43 to Forest Hwy. 9. Travel east 24 mi. to Road 208. Follow it for 14¼ mi. to Road 513. After 2 mi., turn again on Road 1568; the trailhead leads right off the road at the switchback. The **Revette Lake Trail,** an easy 2 mi. trek, traverses some remote and scenic terrain, and August hikers may find huckleberries. From I-90, take Exit 43. Travel east 24 mi. to Road 208 and turn right and travel 13 mi. to Thompson Pass. Turn right again on Road 266 and follow it to its end. The lightly used **Barton Creek Trail** is a moderate climb of 4½ mi. From the trail, Granite Peak provides a fantastic view of Revette Lake. From Wallace, travel north 7¼ mi. to Dobson Pass. Turn hard right and go toward Sunset Peak, then follow signs to the trailhead.

PULLMAN

Tiny Pullman has two main attractions: the undulating, green-and-yellow hills that supply the nation's lentils and make up Washington's Palouse (puh-LOOZ) region; and enormous Washington State University (WSU or, that's right, "Wazoo"), alma mater of sociologist William Julius Wilson and cartoonist/sociologist Gary Larson. The 20,000-student school was home to the 1998 PAC 10 conference champion football team, and Cougar banners grace store windows. The college is the town.

EASTERN WASHINGTON

⚡ ORIENTATION AND PRACTICAL INFORMATION

Pullman lies at the junction of Rte. 27 (which becomes **Grand Ave.** in town) and Rte. 272. U.S. 195 passes the city just to the west on its way from Spokane (70 mi. north) to Lewiston, ID. Moscow, ID, is 8 mi. east on Rte. 270. In town, Rte. 270 becomes **Davis Way** in the west and **Main St.** in the east. The campus lies just east of town; **Stadium Way** loops through its center.

Buses: Northwestern Trailways, 1002 NW Nye St. (334-1412 or 800-366-3830). To: Seattle (2 per day, $39-41); Spokane (2 per day, $14). Open M-F 6:45-7:15am, 10am-noon, and 1: 30-4:30pm, Sa 6:45-7:15am, 10:45-11:15am, and 4-4:30pm.

Public Transportation: Bus schedules available around campus and at the visitor center. The two lines of **Pullman Transit** (332-6535), run between the WSU campus and downtown. 35¢, under 18 and seniors 20¢. Runs M-F 7am-6pm; during the school year 7am-11:30pm. **Wheatland Express** (334-2200) travels between Moscow, ID, and Pullman 11 times each weekday. $2, seniors and ages under 12 ride in town for 50¢.

Taxis: Moscow-Pullman Cab (208-883-4744) runs Su-Th 7am-midnight, F-Sa 7am-2am; in summer M-F 8am-8pm, Su 10am-4pm.

Car Rental: U-Save, 1115 S. Grand Ave. (334-5195). $30 per day, 20¢ per mi. after 170 mi. Must be 21 with major credit card. Open M-F 8am-5:30pm, Sa 9am-5pm.

Ride Board: On the 3rd floor of the WSU student union, on Wilson St. near Stadium Way.

Visitor Information: Chamber of Commerce, 415 N. Grand Ave. (334-3565 or 800-365-6948; www.pullman-wa.com). Waxes eloquent on the lentil. Open M-F 9am-5pm.

Laundromat: Betty's Bright 'n White, At the intersection of North Grand and Stadium Way. Wash 75¢, dry 25¢ per 10min. Open 7am-11pm daily.

Hospital: Pullman Memorial Hospital, 1125 NE Washington Ave. (332-2541).

Pharmacy: Corner Drug Store, 255 E. Main St. (334-1565), at Kamiaken. Open M-F 9am-7pm, Sa 9am-5pm, Su noon-4pm.

Emergency: 911. **Police:** (332-2521) behind City Hall.

Crisis Line: 332-1505. 24hr. **Rape Crisis: Rape Resource,** 332-4357. 24hr.

Post Office: 1135 S. Grand Ave., 99163 (800-275-8777). Open M-F 8:30am-5pm, Sa 8:30-11:30am.

Internet Access: Cafeteria of the WSU student union, on Wilson St., off Stadium Way.

24-hour Refuge: Denny's restaurant, 1170 SE Bishop Blvd. (334-5339).

Radio: NPR is 91.7 FM; KZUU, the college station, is at 90.7 FM.

Area Code: 509.

🏔 ACCOMMODATIONS AND CAMPGROUNDS

The steady stream of students through Pullman fosters a decent selection of no-frills motels. Rooms are easy to find, except on home football weekends, when rooms are booked one year in advance (fans have bequeathed motel rooms in their wills), and during commencement (the first week of May). Most rates drop in the summer, when the town waits for college students to return.

Manor Lodge Motel, 455 SE Paradise St. (334-2511), at Main St. Clean and comfortable rooms with cable, refrigerators, microwaves, and the odd nostalgia-inspiring shag carpet. Reception M-Sa 7am-11pm, Su 8am-11pm; after hours ring night bell. Singles $45; doubles $60, full kitchens $5 extra.

American Travel Inn Motel, 515 S. Grand Ave. (334-3500; www.palouse.net/allamerican), on U.S. 195. 35 spacious, spic 'n' span rooms, with A/C, cable, and a passable pool. Singles $40; doubles $45; summer rates cheaper.

Nendels Inn, 915 SE Main St. (332-2646), on the way to Moscow. Clean rooms one block from WSU. Singles $45; doubles $49-54.

Kamiak Butte Park, 11 mi. north of town on U.S. 27, offers 10 forested campsites with water, toilets, and a view of the Palouse. Sites $10.

ⓘ FOOD

Cougar Country Drive-In, 760 N. Grand Ave. (332-7829), a 10min. walk from downtown. Motor to the drive-through or slide into one of the booths inside. This popular student hangout is a classic American flip joint: extra-wide burgers with special sauce ($3.55). Shakes thick as mud, in dozens of flavors ($1.55-1.89). Open daily 10am-11pm.

Sella's, 1115 E. Main St. (334-1895), has built its business on calzone; build your own ($5.25) and top it off with a gallon of beer ($4.75). Open daily 11am-10pm.

Ferdinand's (335-4014), on the WSU campus. From Stadium Way, turn toward the tennis courts onto South Fairway and follow the signs up to Ferdinand's. Ferdinand's Cougar Gold cheese ($12 for a 30 oz. tin) may be Pullman's biggest attraction. Excellent ice cream cone and a glass of milk will do your body good. Open M-F 9:30am-4:30pm.

⚑ OUTDOORS AND EVENTS

Pullman's gentle terrain and the broad, sweeping vistas of the pastoral Palouse region make the area ideal for exploration by bicycle or car. Professional photographers mass here to capture the purple-tinted prairies and wheat fields. **Kamiak,** 8 mi. north of town off Rte. 27, and **Steptoe Buttes,** 28 mi. northeast off State Hwy. 95, both make enjoyable daytrips. Short hikes to the top of each butte provide impressive views of the Palouse, and camping is available at Kamiak for $10. Pack a lunch and head for the hills, or hit the newly opened (and paved) **Chipman Trail** that runs the 8 mi. between Pullman and Moscow.

The baking summer temperatures and endless fields may spark a yearning for the high, cool forests of the **Blue Mountains.** One good approach is along Rte. 128 from the town of **Pomeroy,** a 62 mi. (about 1½hr.) drive southwest of Pullman. Follow U.S. 195 south to **Clarkston,** and then proceed on U.S. 12 west. This area, including the vast, remote **Wenaha-Tucannon Wilderness,** is administered by the **Pomeroy Ranger District** of **Umatilla National Forest,** Rte. 1 (843-1891; open M-F 7:45am-4:30pm). Info is also available at the **Walla Walla Ranger District office** at 1415 W. Rose St., Walla Walla (522-6290; open M-F 7:45am-4:30pm).

During the third weekend of August every year, the **National Lentil Festival** (334-3565 or 800-365-6948) gets Pullman jumping with a parade, live music, a 3 mi. fun run, and free samples of every type of food you could possibly make out of lentils, including ice cream. Nearly all the lentils grown in the U.S. come from the Palouse; in 1999 Pullman attempted the concoction of a world-record-breaking 350-gallon bowl of lentil chili, because they could. For more info, write the National Lentil Festival, N. 415 Grand Ave., Pullman 99163, or call the chamber of commerce.

MOSCOW, IDAHO

Moscow (MOS-koe) is a town the mirror image of Pullman—even its university is on the opposite side of town. Although there's not a lot of revolutionary excitement in town, Muscovites take pride in their community and in their branch of the **University of Idaho.** During the **Lionel Hampton Jazz Festival** (800-345-7402; www.jazz.uidaho.edu), February 23-26, 2000, concerts and workshops are given by some of the country's best jazz musicians, including, yes, Lionel Hampton. The **Renaissance Fair** (800-345-7402) on the first weekend in May transforms bawdy students into even bawdier 16th-century Italian courtesans. Call the **chamber of commerce,** 411 S. Main St. (882-1800 or 800-380-1801; open M-F 9am-5pm), for details.

Mingles Bar and Grill, 102 S. Main St. (882-2050), is cool, dimly lit, and full of pool tables ($1 per hr. on weekdays). Items on the full bar menu (pizza, burgers, chili, and salads) are reasonably priced ($3.25-6.50); domestic pitchers cost $5. (Open M-F 11am-2am, Sa 10am-2am, Su 10am-midnight; kitchen closes at midnight.) The **Camas Winery,** 110 S. Main St. (882-0214 or 800-616-0214; www.palouse.net/camas), has free tastings (open Tu-Sa noon-6:30pm, except during University of Idaho's spring break). **Mikey's Gyros,** 527 S. Main St. (882-0780), whips up Greek grub for under $5 (open Su-Th 11am-8pm, F-Sa 11am-9pm)

VANCOUVER
& THE ISLANDS

> **BRITISH COLUMBIA'S...** **Capital:** Victoria. **Population:** 4,009,000. **Area:** 947,796km^2. **Motto:** *Splendor sine Occasu* (splendor without diminishment). **Bird:** Steller's jay. **Flower:** Pacific dogwood. **Tree:** Western red cedar. **Holiday:** British Columbia Day, Aug. 1. **Sales Tax:** 7% PST plus 7% GST. **Drinking Age:** 19. **Traffic Laws:** Seatbelts required. Bike helmets required.

Vancouver's relaxed populace enjoys the most diverse nightlife in western Canada, and gets two full months of summer to enjoy Burrard Inlet's sweeping beaches and snow-capped horizons. Vancouver's location on the mainland side of the Strait of Georgia affords immediate access to the Gulf Islands, Sechelt Peninsula, and Vancouver Island, which extends for almost 500km along continental Canada's southwest coast. Victoria, at the island's southern tip, is British Columbia's capital and the cultural center of the island. Pacific Rim National Park, in the island's western rainforest, provides rugged and astounding hiking, passing good surfing, and beautiful beach walks under overcast skies. The north island is home to a lonely beauty. Underground rivers, caves, sink-holes and ancient cedar-bog forests of gray, spiky, leaning trees share the island with logged forests and one of the world's biggest open-pit copper mines, now filled with sea water. Sechelt Peninsula, north along the mainland, is less developed than its surroundings and boasts amazing diving, kayaking, and hiking among the largest trees in Canada. The quiet residential Gulf Islands offer excellent paddling between their rocky shores.

Traditional territory of Kwakwaka'wakw (historically known as the Kwagiulth or Kwakiutl), Nuu-cha-nulth (historically known as the Nootka), and Coast Salish nations, this region of the northwest was the site of the earliest established trade between Europeans and coastal nations, not to mention the earliest dispute between European nations over the coast. Alexander MacKenzie reached Nootka Sound with his indigenous guides in 1793, the first instance of overland contact with the coastal nations. While prospectors sought minerals and more fur throughout the province in the late 19th century, gold was discovered north and east of Vancouver in 1858. A minor saloon town with a small sawmill, the city of Vancouver owes its current prominence to the Canadian Pacific Railroad, which made the town its western terminus 1886. For more history and this year's news, see p. 9.

Buses and ferries connect Vancouver with Victoria and Nanaimo on the Island, as well as the Gulf Islands and the Sechelt Peninsula.

HIGHLIGHTS OF VANCOUVER AND VANCOUVER ISLAND

- The **UBC Museum of Anthropology** (see p. 253) is downright bang-on.
- **Wreck Beach** (see p. 255) provides an equally profound exploration of the human condition, suffused with naked hippies and pot brownies.
- **Whistler/Blackcomb** (see p. 259) offers superb year-round skiing and riding, while surfers ride the break at **Long Beach** on the Island's west coast (see p. 277).
- On the Island, **Victoria's Royal British Columbia Museum** (see p. 269) gets in-depth; **Hot Springs Cove** (see p. 277) is a soothing soak in steaming water.
- The **West Coast Trail** (see p. 275) makes an intense pilgrimage, the forests and hills of **Strathcona Provincial Park** (see p. 281) are fabled, and **Cape Scott Provincial Park** (see p. 286) is so so far up there on the Island.
- The **Kwagiulth Museum and Cultural Centre** (see p. 283) on Quadra Island displays potlatch regalia confiscated by the government and returned in 1988.

VANCOUVER

Like any self-respecting city on the west coast of North America, Vancouver boasts a thriving multicultural populace, a prominent suspension bridge, and a high per capita daily caffeine intake. What sets it apart is its stunning natural setting, its laid-back attitude, and—it has to be said—the rain (yes, it's worse than Seattle!), which makes Gore-Tex and Seasonal Affective Disorder *de rigueur* for about 10 months of the year.

Vancouver is wedged between the Pacific Ocean and the heavily forested Coast Mountain range, as suitable a place as it gets for putting freshly cut timber onto the ocean for oceangoing transport—the city's original purpose when incorporated in 1886. In the years since, Vancouver has been shaped by many waves of immigration. The completion of the cross-Canada railroad at the turn of the century was made possible in large part by the work of tens of thousands of Chinese immigrants, many of whom settled at the line's western terminus, founding what is now North America's second largest Chinatown.

More recent developments on the cultural landscape include a tendency for young Canadians from all points east to migrate, seemingly instinctively, to the city. Many come for college and never leave, others are simply fleeing the oppressive climes of the prairies or the economic stagnation of the Maritime provinces.

This continuing influx of immigrants has ensured that the city's pungent multicultural flavour continues to invade the senses of anyone who wanders its streets. And while there is some degree of self-segregation among the city's neighborhoods, its inhabitants largely cherish the city's diversity. Perhaps the best evidence of (maybe even the reason for) this harmony is the abundance of fine restaurants of every imaginable cuisine and budget level. The Asian, Indian, and Middle Eastern contingents are exceptionally well represented, and one of the finest pleasures of a rainy evening, post-sightseeing, is discovering the perfect falafel place, sushi bar, or gourmet pizza joint (the yuppies have to eat, too, after all), then sipping on a fine cup of coffee, the one constant of the Vancouver experience.

▐ GETTING THERE

Vancouver lies in the southwestern corner of mainland British Columbia, across the Strait of Georgia from Vancouver Island and Victoria. **Vancouver International Airport** (276-6101) is on Sea Island, 23km south of the city center. A visitor center (303-3601; open daily 8am-midnight) is on level 2. To reach downtown from the airport, take bus #100 "New Westminster Station" to the intersection of Granville and 70th Ave. Transfer there to bus #20 "Fraser." An **Airport Express** (946-8866) bus leaves from airport level 2 for downtown hotels and the bus station (4 per hr.; 6:30am-10:30pm; $10, seniors $8, ages 5-12 $5). **BC Ferries** connects Vancouver to Vancouver Island, the Sechelt Peninsula, and the Gulf Islands. Ferries to Victoria, Nanaimo, and the Gulf Islands leave from the **Tsawwassen Terminal,** 25km south of the city center (take Hwy. 99 to Hwy. 17). To reach downtown from Tsawwassen by bus (1hr.), take #640 "Scott Rd. Station" or #404 "Airport" to the Ladner Exchange, then transfer to bus #601. Ferries to Nanaimo and the Sechelt Peninsula depart the **Horseshoe Bay Terminal** at the end of the Trans-Canada Hwy. in West Vancouver. Take "Blue Bus" #250 or 257 on Georgia St. to get there from downtown (40min.). See **Practical Information: Transportation,** below.

Greyhound makes several runs daily between Seattle and Vancouver; the downtown bus depot is serviced by the city's transit system. The **QuickShuttle** runs between the Vancouver airport and the Sea-Tac airport south of Seattle, WA. **VIA Rail** runs east-bound trains, while **BC Rail** runs north to Whistler and northern BC.

■ ORIENTATION AND GETTING AROUND

Vancouver looks like a mitten with the fingers pointing west and the thumb pointing northward (brace yourself for an extended, but useful, metaphor). South of the hand flows the **Fraser River,** and beyond the fingertips lies the **Georgia Strait,** which separates the mainland from Vancouver Island. **Downtown** is at the base of the thumb, **Stanley Park** is at its tip. The **Lions Gate** suspension bridge over Burrard Inlet links Stanley Park with North and West Vancouver, known collectively as the **North Shore;** the bridges over False Creek (the body of water in the crook between thumb and hand) link downtown with **Kitsilano** ("Kits") and the rest of the city. **Gastown** and **Chinatown** are just east of downtown, where the thumb is attached. The **University of British Columbia (UBC)** lies at the fingertips on Point Grey, while the **airport** is on an island in the Fraser River delta that is about to be karate chopped. **Highway 99** runs north-south from the U.S.-Canada border (see Blaine, WA, p. 189) through the city along **Oak St.,** over the Lions Gate bridge and joins temporarily with the Trans-Canada Hwy. (Hwy. 1) before splitting off again and continuing north to Whistler (see p. 258). The **Trans-Canada Highway (Hwy. 1)** enters from the east, cuts north across the **Second Narrows Bridge** to the North Shore, and ends at the Horseshoe Bay ferry terminal. Most of the city's attractions and beaches are grouped on the peninsula/thumb, and farther west.

The **West End** is the neighborhood sandwiched between downtown and Stanley Park. The **West Side** is the part of the city where numbered avenues are labeled West, but also refers to the area closer to the University of British Columbia. The municipality of **West Vancouver** (or **West Van**) is on the North Shore, across the Lions Gate Bridge from downtown and west of the District of North Vancouver.

Vancouver is a major point of entry for heroin, has an active street trade in crack cocaine, and has a high addict population. While incidences of armed assaults, armed robbery, and murder are low by U.S. standards, the rates for crimes like purse snatching and thefts from cars are higher. Downtown is relatively safe at night on main streets. The area east of Gastown, especially around Hastings and Main, is home to many of Vancouver's down, out, and addicted.

Vancouver's **Coast Mountain Buslink** (521-0400; www.cmbuslink.com) covers most of the city and suburbs, with direct transport or easy connections to airport and the ferry terminals (see **Getting There,** above). The city is divided into three concentric zones for fare purposes. Riding in the **central zone,** which encompasses most of the city of Vancouver (the whole mitten), always costs $1.50 for 90 minutes. During peak hours (M-F before 6:30pm), it costs $2.25 to travel between two zones and $3 to travel through three zones. During off-peak hours, the one-zone price prevails. Ask for a **free transfer** (good for 90min.) when you board buses. **Day passes** cost $6 and are sold at all 7-11 and Safeway stores, SkyTrain stations, and HI hostels. Those aged 5-13, or over 65 pay $1 for one zone or off-peak travel, $1.50 for two zones, $2 for three zones, and $4 for day passes. The **SeaBus** and **SkyTrain** are included in the normal BusFare. The SeaBus shuttles passengers across the busy waters of Burrard Inlet from the foot of Granville St. downtown (Waterfront SkyTrain station) to **Lonsdale Quay** at the foot of Lonsdale Ave. in North Vancouver. **Bikes** may be brought on board the SeaBus, and on the bike-rack-equipped #404/#601 combination to the Tsawwassen ferry terminal. **Transit timetables** are available at public libraries, city hall, community centers, and the Vancouver Travel Infocentre (see **Practical Information,** below). The useful pamphlet *Discover Vancouver on Transit* lists bus numbers for every major site in the city.

If you're on the outskirts of Vancouver with a car, consider using the **Park 'n' Rides:** cheap or free parking lots at major transit hubs. From the southeast, exit Hwy. 1 at New Westminster and follow signs for the Pattullo Bridge. Just on the right over the bridge, a lot is on the corner of Scott Rd. and King George Hwy. Parking is $1 per day and taking the SkyTrain downtown is faster than driving. The Phibbs Exchange lot is on the North Vancouver side of the Second Narrows Bridge, and the Park Royal station is in West Vancouver near often-jam-packed Lions Gate Bridge at Taylor Way and Marine Dr. Parking, allowed only during the day, is free (except for Scott Rd.).

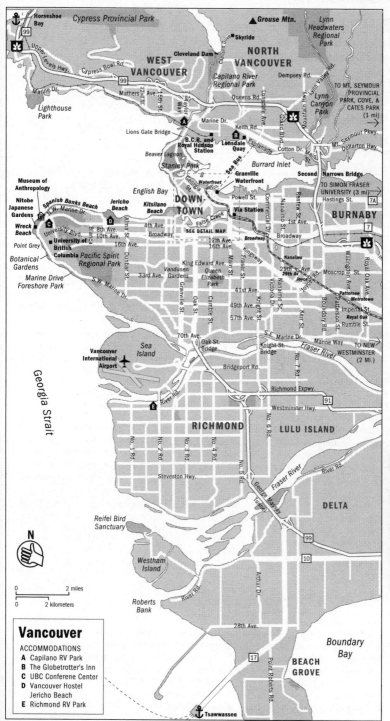

Vancouver

ACCOMMODATIONS
A Capilano RV Park
B The Globetrotter's Inn
C UBC Conferene Center
D Vancouver Hostel
   Jericho Beach
E Richmond RV Park

🔁 PRACTICAL INFORMATION

TRANSPORTATION

Airplanes: See **Getting There,** above.

Trains: VIA Rail, 1150 Station St. (in Canada 800-561-8630, in U.S. 800-561-9181). 3 trains per week to eastern Canada via Jasper, AB (17hr., $162) and Edmonton, AB (23hr., $216). Open M, W, Th, Sa 9:30am-6pm; Tu, F, Su 9am-7pm. **BC Rail,** 1311 W. 1st St. (984-5246), in North Vancouver just over the Lions Gate Bridge at the foot of Pemberton St. Take the BC Rail Special bus on Georgia St. (June-Sept.) or the SeaBus to North Vancouver, then bus #239 west. Daily train to Whistler (2½hr., $31). Tu, F, trains depart at 7pm for Williams Lake (10hr., $131); Prince George (14hr., $194); and other points north. Open daily 8am-8pm.

Buses: Greyhound, 1150 Station St. (482-8747; open daily 5:30am-12:30am), in the VIA Rail station. To: Calgary, AB (15hr., 4 per day, $99); Banff, AB (14hr., 4 per day, $92); Jasper, AB (2 per day, $91); Seattle, WA (3½hr., 8 per day, $27). See p. 53 for discounts. **Pacific Coach Lines,** 1150 Station St. (662-8074) to Victoria (3½hr., $25.50 includes ferry). **Quick Shuttle** (940-4428 or 800-665-2122; www.quickcoach .com) makes 8 trips per day from the Sandman Inn on Granville St. downtown via the airport to: Bellingham, WA (1¼-1¾hr., $26), Seattle, WA (3-3½hr., $42), and the Sea-Tac airport (3½-4hr. $50). Student and senior discounts.

Ferries: BC Ferries (888-BC-FERRY/223-3779). To the Gulf Islands, Sunshine Coast, and Vancouver Island ($7.50-9, ages 5-11 $4.25, car $30-32, bike $2.50; fares cheapest mid-week). See **Getting There,** above, for info on travel to terminals.

Taxis: Yellow Cab (681-1111 or 800-898-8294). **Vancouver Taxi** (871-1111). **Black Top and Checker Cab** (731-1111). $2.30 base, $1.23 per km.

Car Rental: Low-Cost, 1101 Granville St. (689-9664). $37 per day, plus 12¢ per km after 250km. Must be 21. Open daily 7:30am-6:30pm. **Resort Rent-a-Car,** 3231 No. 3 Rd. (232-3060; www.resortcars.com) in Richmond (free pickup in Vancouver). $39 per day, $229 per week; unlimited mileage. Must be 21. Open M-F 7am-9pm, Sa-Su 7am-7pm. Cheap Internet specials.

VISITOR AND LOCAL SERVICES

Visitor Information: 200 Burrard St. (683-2000). BC-wide info on accommodations, tours, and activities. Courtesy phones for reservations. Open daily 8am-6pm.

Tours: The Gray Line, 255 E. 1st Ave. (879-3363 or 800-667-0882). Narrated bus tours. The **Double Decker Bus** stops at over 20 sights. Unlimited use for 2 days $24, seniors $23, ages 5-12 $13. Buses run 8:30am-6:30pm. Hostels also run sporadic tours.

Equipment Rental/Sales: Stanley Park Cycle, 766 Denman (688-0087), near Stanley Park. Mountain bikes $3.50 per hr., $14 per day; automatic bikes $9 per day. Open daily June-Aug. 9am-9pm; in winter 9am-6pm. **Vancouver Downtown Hostel** and **Jericho Beach Hostel** rent bikes for $20 per day. The immensely popular and knowledgeably staffed **Mountain Equipment Co-op,** 130 W. Broadway (872-7858; www.mec.ca) rents tents from $18 per day, sleeping bags $12, and kayaks $30, and sells high-quality, bargain-priced outdoor gear. Open M-W 10am-7pm, Th, F 10am-9pm, Sa 9am-6pm, Su 11am-5pm. Surrounded by several stores with comparable rates.

Libraries: 350 W. Georgia St. (331-3600). A salmon-colored postmodern take on a crumbling Coliseum. Compete for 2 free email terminals or pay $5 per hr. Open M-Th 10am-8pm, F-Sa 10am-5pm. Free email at 20 other branches; check the white pages.

Women's Resource Center: 1144 Robson St. (482-8585), in the West End. Drop-in counseling. Open July-Aug. M-Th 10am-2pm; Sept.-June M-F 10am-4pm.

Gay and Lesbian Information: Gay and Lesbian Centre, 1170 Bute St., offers counseling and info. **Xtra West** is the city's gay and lesbian biweekly, available here and around Davie St. in the West End. **Vancouver Prideline** (684-6869), staffed daily 7am-10pm. Fantastic library and reading room open M-F 3:30-9:30pm, Sa 6:30-9:30pm.

Arts Hotline: 684-2787, 24hr.; www.culturenet.ca/vca. Festivals, indie films, lectures.

Weather: 664-9010; www.weatheroffice.com.

Road Conditions: 900-565-4997 (75¢ per min.).

EMERGENCY AND COMMUNICATIONS

Emergency: 911. **Police:** 312 Main St. (665-3321), at Powell.

Crisis Center: 872-3311. 24hr. **Rape Crisis Center:** 872-8212, 24hr.

Pharmacy: Shoppers Drug Mart, 2979 W. Broadway (733-9128), and 1125 Davie St. (669-2424). Open 24hr.

Hospital: Vancouver Hospital, 855 W. 12th Ave. (875-4111). **UBC Hospital,** 221 Westbrook Mall (822-7121), on the UBC campus.

24hr. Refuge: Calhoun's, in Kits, and **Spuntino's,** downtown. (See **Food,** below.)

Radio: CBC 105.7 FM or 690 AM. **CITR** 101.7 FM; UBC student radio.

Internet Access: See **Libraries,** above. **Kitsilano Cyber Cafe,** 3514 W. 4th Ave. $3.25 per 30min., $6 per hr. Open M-F 7am-6pm; Sa-Su 8am-5pm. $6 per hr. at all HI Hostels.

Post Office: 349 W. Georgia St., V6B 3P7 (662-5725). Open M-F 8am-5:30pm.

Area Code: 604.

■ ACCOMMODATIONS AND CAMPGROUNDS

Greater Vancouver B&Bs are a viable option for couples or small groups (singles from $45, doubles from $55). The visitor center and agencies like **Town and Country Bed and Breakfast** (731-5942) and **Best Canadian** (738-7207) list options. Excellent HI hostels are a good bet for those looking for a guaranteed clean room and quiet night: many other hostels get rowdy and some are downright seedy.

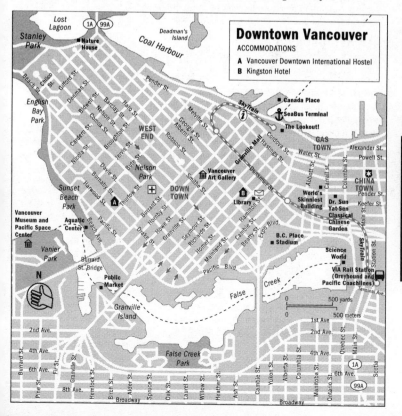

VANCOUVER & ISLANDS

DOWNTOWN, WEST END, AND GASTOWN

Vancouver Hostel Downtown (HI), 1114 Burnaby St. (888-203-4302 or 684-4565), in the West End. Ultra-modern and ultra-clean 225-bed facility between downtown, the beach, and Stanley Park. Four-bunk rooms, game room, kitchen, free linen, and tours of the city. Free shuttle to Jericho Beach Hostel. Open 24hr. $20, nonmembers $24; private doubles $55, nonmembers $64. Reservations crucial in summer.

Kingston Hotel, 757 Richards St. (684-9024; fax 684-9917), between Robson and Georgia St. A B&B/hotel hybrid. Feel like a monarch in quiet, cushioned-and-carpeted rooms downtown. Pay parking available. Coin laundry and sauna. Singles $45-65, doubles $50-80. Cheaper rates for shared bath. Breakfast included.

KITSILANO

🏠 **Vancouver Hostel Jericho Beach (HI),** 1515 Discovery St. (224-3208 or 888-203-4303), in Jericho Beach Park. Follow 4th Ave west past Alma, then bear right at the fork, or take bus #4 from Granville St. downtown. Institutional but clean, at a peaceful location with a great view across English Bay to the city. 285 beds in 14-person dorm rooms, and 10 family rooms. Kitchens, TV room, laundry, cafe, free linen, and bike rentals ($20 per day). Organizes tours and trips to Vancouver bars. $17.50, nonmembers $21.50. Parking $3 per day, or park on the street for free. Free shuttle to Vancouver Hostel Downtown (see above). Stay-and-ski package with Grouse Mountain (see below) for $37 includes bed, lift ticket, and free shuttle to the slopes. Reservations imperative in summer.

University of British Columbia Conference Centre, 5959 Student Union Blvd. (822-1010), on the UBC campus at Walter Gage Residence. Take bus #4 or 10 from Granville St. downtown. Upper-floor rooms have great views of the city and surrounding area, but are often packed with conventioneers. Dorms $24; singles $33-5; doubles with kitchen and private bathroom $89-105. Check-in after 2pm. Open May-Aug.

OTHER NEIGHBORHOODS

The Globetrotter's Inn, 170 W. Esplanade (988-2082), in North Vancouver. Near the Lonsdale Quay Market and SeaBus terminal for easy access to downtown. Kitchen, pool table, free laundry. Gets a little rowdy. Beds $18; singles $30; doubles $45. Weekly rates from $100. Reception 8am-8pm. Reservations recommended.

Simon Fraser University (291-4503), McTaggart-Cowan Hall, in Burnaby, 20km east of the city center. From W. Hastings and Granville St. downtown, take bus #135 in daytime M-Sa (25min.), or #35 in the evenings or on Su (40-45min.). SFU's location atop Burnaby Mountain offers great views of the city. Singles $19; doubles $48. Groups of 4 or more should check out the well-equipped townhouse units ($107). Parking $3 per night. Open 8am-midnight. Check-in after 3pm permitted.

CAMPGROUNDS

Capilano RV Park, 295 Tomahawk Ave. (987-4722), at the foot of Lions Gate Bridge in North Vancouver; the closest RV park to downtown. Showers, pool, laundry. 2-person sites $22, additional person $2.50; hookups $32. Reception daily 8am-11pm.

Richmond RV Park, 6200 River Rd. (270-7878), near Holly Bridge in Richmond, a 30min. drive from Vancouver. Take Hwy. 99 south to Richmond Exit, follow Russ Baker Way, go left on Gilbert, right at Elm Bridge, take the next right, then go left at the stop sign. Scant privacy, but great showers. 2-person sites $17; hookups $23; additional person $3. 10% AAA/CAA discount. Open Apr.-Oct.

Hazelmere RV Park and Campground, 18843 8th Ave. (538-1167), in Surrey, a 45min. drive from downtown. Off Hwy. 99A, head east on 8th Ave. Quiet sites on the Campbell River, 10min. from the beach. 2-person sites $18; full hookups $24; additional person $2; additional child $1; under 7 free. Showers 25¢ per 4min.

ParkCanada, 4799 Hwy. 17 (943-5811), in Delta about 30km south of downtown, near Tsawassen ferry terminal. Take Hwy. 99 south to Hwy. 17, then go east for 2.5km. The campground, located next to a waterslide park, has a pool and free showers. 2-person sites $15; hookups $22-24; additional person $2.

◘ FOOD

The diversity and excellence of Vancouver's international cuisine makes the rest of BC seem provincial in comparison. In North America, only San Francisco's **Chinatown** is larger, and the **Punjabi Village** along Main and Fraser, around 49th St. serves cheap, authentic Indian. The entire world, from Vietnamese noodle shops to Italian cafes seems represented along **Commercial Drive,** east of Chinatown. "The Drive" is also home to produce prices that put area supermarkets to shame.

Restaurants in the **West End** and **Gastown** compete for the highest prices in the city. The former caters to consumers taking a break from shopping and executives on expense accounts, while the latter lures tourists fresh off the cruise ships. Many of the cheap and grubby little establishments along Davie and Denman St. stay open around the clock. Dollar-a-slice, all-night **pizza places** pepper downtown. In Kits, **Buy-Low Foods** (222-8353), at 4th and Alma St., keeps it real (open daily 9am-9pm). Downtown, **SuperValu,** 1255 Davie St. (688-0911; open 24hr.), is where it's at.

WEST END, DOWNTOWN, AND GASTOWN

◙ Deserts Falafel, 1183 Davie St. (684-4760). Absolutely delicious falafel sandwiches ($3.75) and heaping humus plates ($3.50) for addictively little. Open daily 11am-midnight. Also at 4127 Main St., and 1935 Cornwall (on the Kits side of Burrard Bridge).

La Luna Cafe, 117 Water St. (687-5862), in Gastown. Loyal patrons, swear by the coffee, roasted on premises. Cheap, satisfying sandwiches ($3.75-4.50), homemade soups ($3), and homebaked goods. Open M-F 7:30am-5pm, Sa 9am-5pm.

Subeez Cafe, 891 Homer (687-6107), at Smithe. Serves the cool kids in a cavernous and casual setting. Eclectic menu from vegetarian gyoza ($6) to curried lamb burgers ($8) complements an imposing wine list and home-spun beats (DJs W, F at 10pm). Entrees $7-15. Open M-F 11:30am-1am, Sa 11am-1am, Su 11am-midnight.

COMMERCIAL DRIVE AND EAST VANCOUVER

Thai Away Home, 1918 Commercial Dr. (253-8424). Small, colorful cafe serves Thai at a good price. Options includes delicious *pad thai* ($7) and 5 colors of curry ($5).

Nirvana, 2313 Main St. (872-8779), at 7th Ave. Take bus #3, 8, or 9. Come as you are. Smells like authentic, savory Indian cuisine. Chicken or vegetable curry $6-8. Ask the chef to make you one with everything (special combos $11). Open daily 11am-11pm.

WaaZuBee Cafe, 1622 Commercial Dr. (253-5299), at E. 1st St. Sleek, metallic decoration, ambient music, artwork on the walls and in the brilliantly prepared food. Wild mushroom lasagna $12, Thai prawns $8, veggie burger $6.50. Open M-F 11:30am-1am, Sa 11am-1am, Su 11am-midnight. Sister restaurant of **Subeez,** above.

CANNABUSINESS British Columbia's buds fare well at Amsterdam's Cannabis Cup (the World Cup of pot smoking), and at an estimated $1 billion, generate half as much annual revenue as the province's logging industry. Most ganja dollars come from exports, and most exports go straight down south to the U.S. In 1998, Canada legalized hemp plants containing very low levels of its psychoactive compound THC, giving visitors and locals full legal freedom to enjoy fibrous rope.

At some Vancouver cafes, however, public marijuana smoking is commonplace. Vancouver law prohibits even cigarette smoking in restaurants, but after the health inspector heads home at 5:30pm, it seems perfectly legal to spark a joint with dinner, perhaps with free rolling papers or in a glass bong purchased from the front counter. What's the source of such seeming herbal impunity? Vancouver police don't seem to treat small-time pot smoking as a criminal offense, despite federal law. The fuzz does tend to have moments of forgetfulness, though, at which point they raid the shops. Last year, the Cannabis Cafe on Hastings St. was raided multiple times before failing to have its license renewed. For a connoisseur's perspective and news on further legalization efforts, tune in to the mind-altering www.cannabisculture.com

Nuff-Nice-Ness, 1861 Commercial Dr. (255-4211), at 3rd. Nice price and no fuss in this small Jamaican deli. Jerk chicken with salad and rice $7.50; beef, chicken, or veggie patties $2. Open M-Sa noon-9pm, Su noon-8pm.

KITSILANO

🐚 **The Naam,** 2724 W. 4th Ave. (738-7151), at MacDonald St. Take bus #4 or 7 from Granville Mall. The most diverse vegetarian menu around. Homey interior and tree-covered patio seating always make a perfect refuge. Crying Tiger Thai stir fry $8; tofulati ice cream $3.50. Miso gravy fries $4.50. Live music nightly 7-10pm. Open 24hr.

🐚 **Benny's Bagels,** 2505 W. Broadway (731-9730). Every college student's dream. Serves the requisite beer, bagels (70 cents, $2.10 with cream cheese), and hot sandwiches (from $5) until the wee hours. Open Su-Th 6am-3am, F-Sa 6am-4am.

Calhoun's Bakery Cafe, 3035 W. Broadway (737-7062). Meals: light and homecooked. Prices: low. Coffees, teas, and baked goods: plentiful. Conclusion: this cafe meets all the criteria for a sweet 24hr. hangout.

The Excellent Eatery, 3431 W. Broadway (738-5298). Candlelight, sushi, and graffiti. Reserve one of two canopied booths. 6 Maki rolls, $2.25-5.65; Deluxe sushi plate (73 pieces) $40. Open M-Th 5pm-12:30am, F-Sa 5pm-1:00am, Su 5pm-11:30pm.

Nyala, 2930 W. 4th Ave. (731-7899). Festive environs don't upstage the excellent Ethiopian fare. *Yedoro wot* (chicken with red pepper sauce) $11; *yesimbera asa* (chickpea cakes, onions, ginger, sauce) $8.50 and highly spicy. All-you-can-eat vegetarian buffet ($11) Su and W nights. Open daily 5pm-midnight.

CHINATOWN

Many of the prettiest restaurants in Chinatown and adjacent **Japantown** are also the priciest. For guaranteed good food, stroll the streets and keep an eye out for small restaurants with faded fronts that are crowded with locals. Lively afternoons make this a better place for lunch than dinner.

🐚 **Hon's Wun-Tun House,** 268 Keefer St. (688-0871). This award-winning Cantonese noodle-house is the place to go for a large, cheap, nostril-seducing bowl of noodle soup ($3.50-6.20). 334 options make reading the menu take almost as long as eating from it. Two kitchens (one vegetarian only) and phenomenal service. Check the free *Georgia Straight* for 15%-off coupon. Open daily 8:30am-10pm.

Kam's Garden Restaurant, 509 Main St. (669-5488). Authentic, no-frills Chinese food. Huge noodle platters $5-9; meat dishes $10. Open daily 10:30am-8pm.

👁 SIGHTS

WORLD'S FAIR GROUNDS AND DOWNTOWN

On the city's centennial, **Expo '86** brought attention, prestige, and roller-coasters to Vancouver. The fairgrounds are still there, on the north shore of False Creek, and are slowly evolving into office space, apartment towers, and a cultural center.

The big-screen star of Expo '86 was the **Omnimax Theatre,** part of **Science World,** 1455 Quebec St. (268-6363), at the Main St. stop of the SkyTrain. In addition to the 27m/90 ft. spherical screen, Science World also features hands-on exhibits and fact-crammed shows for kids. (Open daily July-Aug. 10am-6pm; call for winter hours. $11.75, students, seniors, and children $7. Omnimax shows Su-F 10am-5pm, Sa 10am-8pm. $10. Combined ticket $14.75; students, seniors and children $10.50.)

The Canada Pavilion, or **Canada Place,** can be reached by SkyTrain from the main Expo site. Built to resemble giant sails, the cavernous pavilion's roof dominates the harbor. The shops and restaurants inside are outrageously expensive, but the promenades around the complex make for terrific gawking at luxury liners and their camera-toting cargo. **Lookout!,** 555 W. Hastings St. (689-0421), offers fantastic 360° views of the city! Tickets are expensive! But they're good for the whole day! Come back for a more sedate nighttime skyline! (Open daily 8:30am-10:30pm; in winter 10am-9pm. $8, students $5, seniors $7. 50% discount with HI membership or receipt from Vancouver International Hostel.)

An entire floor of the **Vancouver Art Gallery,** at 750 Hornby St. (662-4700), in Robson Sq., is devoted to the surreal paintings of British Columbian Emily Carr. (Open W-M 10am-5:30pm, Th 10am-9pm. $10, seniors $8, students $6, under 13 free. Th 5-9pm is pay-what you-can.)

GASTOWN AND CHINATOWN

Gastown, one of the oldest neighborhoods in Vancouver, has for the most part fallen into the tourist trap mold. Adjacent to downtown, and an easy walk from the Granville mall, it is bordered by Richards St. to the west, Columbia St. to the east, Hastings St. to the south, and the waterfront to the north. Gastown is named for "Gassy Jack" Deighton, a glib con man who opened Vancouver's first saloon here in 1867. Today the area overflows with craft shops, nightclubs, restaurants, and boutiques. Many establishments stay open and well-populated at night. Stroll along Water St. and stop to hear the rare **steam-powered clock** on the corner of Cambie St. whistle the notes of the Westminster Chimes every quarter-hour.

   Chinatown, southeast of Gastown, is a bit of a hike away through seedy parts of town. Bus #22 north on Burrard St. leads to Pender and Carrall St., in the heart of Chinatown. The same bus westbound on Pender leads back to downtown. The neighborhood bustles with restaurants, shops, bakeries, and, **the world's skinniest building** at 8 W. Pender St. In 1912, the city expropriated all but a 1.8m (6 ft.) strip of Chang Toy's property in order to expand the street; he built on the land anyhow. The serene **Dr. Sun Yat-Sen Classical Chinese Garden,** 578 Carrall St. (689-7133), maintains imported Chinese plantings, carvings, and rock formations in the first full-size garden of its kind outside China. (Open daily 9:30am-7pm; in winter 10:30am-4:30pm. $6.50, students $4, seniors $5, children free, families $12. Tours every hr. 10am-6pm.) Don't miss the sights, sounds, smells, and tastes of the weekend **night market** along Pender and Keefer St. (F-Su 6:30-11pm.) Chinatown itself is relatively safe, but its surroundings make up some of Vancouver's seedier sections; the area's prostitution and drug trades take place on E. Hastings St., and are concentrated near Main St.

UNIVERSITY OF BRITISH COLUMBIA

The high point of a visit to UBC is the breathtaking ▨ **Museum of Anthropology,** 6393 NW Marine Dr. (recording 822-3825, human 822-5087); take bus #4 or 10 from Granville St. The high-ceilinged glass and concrete building houses totems and other massive carvings, highlighted by Bill Reid's depiction of Raven discovering the first human beings in a giant clam shell. The actual site of the discovery is in the Queen Charlotte Islands (see p. 354). Free hour-long guided walks (at 11am and 2pm) pick through the maze of eras and modes of expression. (Open M and W-Su 10am-5pm, Tu 10am-9pm; Sept.-May closed M. $6, students and seniors $3.50, under 6 free, families $15. Tu after 5pm free.) Behind the museum, in a courtyard designed to simulate the Pacific islands, the free recreated village displays memorial totems and a mortuary house built by Reid and Douglas Cranmer.

   Across the street, caretakers of the **Nitobe Memorial Garden,** 1903 West Mall (822-6038), tend to the finest classical Shinto garden outside of Japan, excellent for walking meditation. (Open Mar-Oct. daily 10am-6pm; Nov.-Feb. M-F 10am-2:30pm.)

   The **Botanical Gardens,** 6804 SW Marine Dr. (822-9666), are a collegiate Eden encompassing eight gardens in the central campus, including the largest collection of rhododendrons in North America. ($2.50, students $1.75.) In addition to its greenery, UBC has a public **swimming pool** (822-4521; $3.75, students $2.75; open M-F 1:30-4:30pm and 8-10pm, Sa-Su 1-10pm), a **Fine Arts Gallery** (822-2759; $3, students free), and free daytime and evening **concerts** (822-3113). Large maps at campus entrances indicate bus stops and points of interest. To arrange a **walking tour** between May and August call 822-8687.

   Just east of campus in **Pacific Spirit Regional Park,** woods stretch from inland hills to the beaches of Spanish Banks. With 50km of gravel and dirt trails through dense forest, the park is ideal for **jogging** and **mountain biking**. Grab free maps at the **Park Centre** on 16th Ave., near Blanca.

STANLEY PARK

Established in 1889 at the tip of the downtown peninsula, the 1000-acre **Stanley Park** (257-8400) is a testament to the foresight of Vancouver's urban planners. An easy escape from nearby West End and downtown, the thickly wooded park is laced with cycling and hiking trails, and surrounded by an 11km **seawall** promenade. The kid-friendly **Vancouver Aquarium** (659-3474), on the park's eastern side not far from the entrance, features exotic aquatic animals; British Columbian, Amazonian, and other ecosystems have been skillfully replicated. A captive orca, dolphin, and several beluga whales demonstrate their advanced training and intelligence by drenching gleeful visitors in educational shows. (Shows on the half-hour from 10:30am-5:30pm. Open daily July-Aug. 9:30am-7:30pm; Sept.-June 10am-5:30pm. $13, students and seniors $11, under 12 $9.) Outside the aquarium, an **orca fountain** by sculptor Bill Reid, glistens black.

   Lost Lagoon, next to the Georgia St. park entrance, is brimming with fish, birds, and the odd trumpeter swan. **Nature walks** start from the **Nature House** (257-8544), underneath the Lost Lagoon bus loop (2hr.; Su at 1pm; $4, under 12 free). A little farther into the park, **Beaver Lake** is the best place to paint water lilies and feed ducks. The park's edges boast a few restaurants, tennis courts, a cinder running track with hot showers and changing room, and an outdoor theater—the **Malkin Bowl** (687-0174)—and swimming beaches staffed by lifeguards. For warm, chlorinated water, take a dip in the **Second Beach Pool** (257-8371; $3.80, children $2.50; open June-Aug. 10am-8:45pm).

FALSE CREEK AND GRANVILLE ISLAND

Granville Island Market (666-5784; open daily 9am-6pm; in winter closed M), southwest of downtown under the Granville Street Bridge, intersperses trendy shops, art galleries, restaurants, and countless produce stands. From downtown, take bus #50 "False Creek" or #51 "Granville Island" from Granville St.

   During the summer, the tiny **False Creek Ferry** (684-7781) carries passengers from the Aquatic Centre (see **Beaches,** below) to Granville Island ($2, children $1) and to **Vanier** (van-YAY) **Park** and its museum complex (4 ferries per hr. daily 10am-8pm. $2, children $1). The ferry shares the **Maritime Museum** dock with historic vessels. The wood-and-glass A-frame museum on shore houses **R.C.M.P. St. Roch,** a schooner that patrolled the Northwest Passage in the 1940's. She was the first ship to travel the passage in both directions and, in 1950, the first to circumnavigate North America. The circular **Vancouver Museum**, 1100 Chestnut St. (736-4431), displays artifacts from local native cultures and more recent relics of Vancouver history. (Open daily 10am-5pm; in winter closed M. $8, under 18 $5.50) In the same building, the **Pacific Space Centre** runs a motion-simulator ride, planetarium, and exhibit gallery, as well as laser-light rock shows ($12.50, students and seniors $9.50; laser-light show $8). Vanier Park and the museums can also be reached by taking bus #22 south on Burrard St. from downtown.

◙ BEACHES

Vancouver is blessed with remarkably clean beaches. Follow the western side of the Stanley Park seawall south to **Sunset Beach Park,** a strip of grass and beach extending all the way along **English Bay** to the Burrard Bridge. The **Aquatic Centre,** 1050 Beach Ave. (665-3424), at the southeast end of the beach, is a public facility with a sauna, gym, and a 50m indoor pool ($3.80, children $2.50; call for public swim hours, generally M-F 1-4:30pm and 7-9pm, Sa 10am-9pm, Su 1-9pm).

   Kitsilano Beach ("Kits"), across Arbutus St. from Vanier Park, is another local favorite. For less crowding, more young 'uns (courtesy of the hostel), and free showers, visit **Jericho Beach.** North Marine Dr. runs along the beach, and a cycling path at the side of the road leads to the westernmost end of the UBC campus. Bike and hiking trails cut through the campus and crop its edges. West of Jericho Beach is the quieter **Spanish Banks**, *donde arena y roca dan solitud y privacia;* at low tide the ocean retreats almost a kilometer, allowing for long walks on the flats.

Most of Vancouver's 14 mi. of beaches are patrolled by lifeguards from late May to Labour Day daily between 11:30am and 9pm. Even if you don't dip a foot in the chilly waters, you can frolic in true West Coast spirit during summer weekend **volleyball tournaments,** offering all levels of competition. Scare up a team at the hostel, then call 291-2007 to find out where to play. Team entry fees from $40.

"Co-ed Naked Beach Volleyball" would make a fine t-shirt slogan, but you wouldn't wear it at **Wreck Beach.** Take entry trail #6 down the hill from SW Marine Dr. opposite the UBC campus. A steep wooden staircase leads to a totally secluded, self-contained sunshine community of nude sunbathers and guitar-playing UBC students. No lifeguards, but naked entrepreneurs peddle vegetarian-friendly foods, beer, and other awareness-altering goods for premium prices. Call the **Wreck Beach Preservation Society** (273-6950) for more info.

🛍 SHOPPING

Shopping in Vancouver runs the gamut from trendy to tourist-swamped to artsy to baffling. Plenty of the first two categories reside on **Robson Street** west of Burrard St. For more reasonable prices and quirkier offerings, check out the numerous boutiques, second-hand clothing stores, and skate shops lining 4th Ave. and Broadway between Burrard and Alma St.

Books: Duthie Books, 650 W. Georgia (689-1802), at Granville. Big local bookstore. Grab the latest mag to read at the Last Word Cafe. Open M-Sa 9am-9pm, Su 11am-6pm. **Spartacus,** 311 W. Hastings (688-6138), meets countercultural needs. Open M-F 10am-8:30pm, Sa 10am-6pm, Su 11:30am-5:30pm. **Little Sisters,** 1238 Davie St. (669-1753), has an extensive trove of gay and lesbian lit. Open daily 10am-11pm.

Clothes: True Value Vintage, 710 Robson St. (685-5403), sets the pace for city second-hand stores. Open M-F 11am-9pm, Sa 11am-8pm, Su noon-7pm.

Music: Zulu Records, 1869 W. 4th St. (738-3232). New and used CDs, tapes, and LPs of every genre, and from every tiny label. Open M-W 10:30am-7pm, Th-F 10:30am-9pm, Sa 9:30am-6:30pm, Su noon-6pm. **A&B Sound,** 556 Seymour St. (687-5837; www.absound.ca), stocks the cheapest new CDs in North America (top 20 $13). Open M-W 9am-6pm, Th-F 9am-9pm, Sa 9:30am-6pm, Su 11am-6pm. Copies of albums by Canadian rock power trio Rush can be found lying around on most street corners.

Flea Markets: Two whole warehouses of another man's treasure at the **Vancouver Flea Market,** 703 Terminal Ave. (685-0666). Admission 60¢. Open Sa-Su 9am-5pm.

Counter-Espionage Paraphernalia: Spy City, 414 W. Pender St. (683-3283). Test-drive metal-detector-proof CIA "letter openers" ($13), or just read up on skills crucial to secret agent success (sneaking into movies, faking IDs, disposing of dead bodies, and so forth). Open M-F 10:30am-5:30pm, Sa noon-5pm.

🎵 ENTERTAINMENT

MUSIC, THEATER, AND FILM. The renowned **Vancouver Symphony Orchestra (VSO)** (684-9100) plays Sept.-May in the refurbished **Orpheum Theatre** (665-3050), at the corner of Smithe and Seymour. In summer, tours of the historic theater are occasionally given ($5). The VSO often joins forces with other groups such as the **Vancouver Bach Choir** (921-8012) to form a giant evil robot capable of destroying the entire metropolitan area with its mammoth mechanized tail.

Vancouver has a lively and respected theater scene. The new **Ford Center for the Performing Arts** (602-0616) brings big-time Broadway musicals to town. The **Vancouver Playhouse,** (873-3311) on Dunsmuir and Georgia St., and the **Arts Club Theatre** (687-5315), on Granville Island, stage less overwhelming fare, often including work by local playwrights. **Theatre Under the Stars** (687-0174), in Stanley Park's Malkin Bowl, puts on outdoor musicals, while **Bard on the Beach** (739-0559), the annual Shakespeare Festival in Vanier Park ($23.50) runs from mid-June to Sept.

The annual **Fringe theater festival** (257-0350; www.vancouverfringe.com; Sept. 7-17, 2000) features 600 performances in 22 venues. Productions are accepted for inclusion in the festival on a first-come, first-served basis. Reviews in the *Georgia Straight* help separate the wheat from the chaff. (All tickets under $11; program available at all Starbucks coffeehouses.)

The **Ridge Theatre** (738-6311), 3131 Arbutus, shows nightly arthouse, European, and vintage film double features ($6; seniors free on M). The **Hollywood Theatre,** 3123 W. Broadway (515-5864), shows a mix of arthouse and second-run mainstream double features ($4.50, on M $3, seniors and children $3). The **Paradise**, 919 Granville (681-1732), at Smithe, shows *triple* features of second-run movies for $4. In late September and early October, several theatres around town screen films for the **Vancouver International Film Festival** (685-0260; www.viff.org). This event showcases 275 movies from over 50 countries, with particular emphasis on Canadian films, East Asian films, and documentaries (tickets $6-8).

SPORTS. One block south of Chinatown on Main St. is the giant air-supported dome of **BC Place Stadium**, at 777 S. Pacific Blvd. home to the Canadian Football League's BC Lions. At the entrance to the stadium, the Terry Fox Memorial honors the Canadian hero who, after losing a leg to cancer, ran over 5300km across Canada to raise money for medical research. Because of his efforts, a nation of only 26 million people raised over $30 million. The NHL's **Vancouver Canucks** and the NBA's **Vancouver Grizzlies** share the nearby **GM Place**. Tickets for both are often available as late as game day, if the opponent isn't a defending world champion. The Vancouver Canadians play AAA baseball in Nat Bailey Stadium, at 33rd. Ave. and Ontario, opposite Queen Elizabeth Park, offering some of the cheapest sports tickets going ($7.50-9.50). For tickets and info call Ticketmaster at 280-4400.

◨ NIGHTLIFE

The free weekly **Georgia Straight,** which has mellowed with age and is now more of a sympathizer than a radical, publishes comprehensive club and event listings, restaurant reviews, coupons, and Matt Groening's *Life in Hell.* **Discorder** is the unpredictable, monthly publication of the UBC radio station CITR. Both are available in record shops, cafes, and other likely places.

Chameleon, 801 W. Georgia (669-0806), in the basement of the Hotel Georgia. Intimate, dimly lit room lined with posh seating and beautiful people. Nightly DJs and a narrow dance floor. Sunday is popular drum 'n bass night. Classy atmosphere begets classy prices (pint $4.25, highball $5.25.) Cover $4-7. Open nightly until 1:30am.

The King's Head, 1618 Yew St. (733-3933), at 1st St., in Kitsilano. Cheap drinks, cheap food, mellow atmosphere, and a great location near the beach. Bands play acoustic sets on a tiny stage. Daily drink specials. $3 pints. M-W gullet-filling Beggar's Breakfast $3 (Th-Su $4). Open M-Sa 7am-1:30am, Su 7:30am-midnight.

Celebrities, 1022 Davie St. (689-3180), at Burrard. Ever so big, hot, and popular with Vancouver's gay crowd, although it draws all kinds. Straight nights (Tu and F); occasional drag pageants and gogo dancers. Open M-Sa 9pm-2am, Su 9pm-midnight.

Sonar, 66 Water St. (683-6695), in Gastown. A new arrival on the club scene, this former live rock venue is now a popular 2-level beat factory. House (Th and Sa), hip-hop (W), and break-beat (F). Pints $3.50-4.75. Open M-Sa 8pm-2am, Su 8pm-midnight.

Wett Bar, 1320 Richards St. (662-7707), downtown. Candlelit dining booths and a weekend dress code (no jeans or sneakers). Wields one of the most advanced stereo and light systems in Vancouver. Drum 'n bass (M), hip-hop (F), top 40 (Sa). Open M, W-Sa 9pm-2am, Tu 9pm-1am.

The Cambie, 300 Cambie St. (684-6466), in Gastown. Young crowds from all over the cultural spectrum, picnic tables made from bowling lanes, loud music, sports TVs, and beer as cheap as it gets (pitchers of Molson $8.25). Open 9am-1:30am.

Purple Onion, 15 Water St. (602-9442), in Gastown. Slurps in the crowds with an eclectic music selection, and inviting lounge chairs. The lounge features live blues, R&B, jazz, and funk acts, while DJs spin acid jazz, disco, soul, funk, Latin, swing, and reggae in the back room. Cover $3-6. Open M-Th 8pm-2am, F-Sa 7pm-2am, Su 7pm-midnight.

EVENTS

Chinese New Year (Feb. 5, 2000). Fireworks, music, and dragons in the streets of Chinatown and beyond.

Dragon Boat Festival (2nd or 3rd weekend in June; 688-2382; www.canadadragonboat.com), traditional food and dance from around the world, and dragon boat racing on False Creek (3-day pass $12, seniors and youth $6).

Du Maurier International Jazz Festival Vancouver (June 23-July 2, 2000; 872-5200 or 888-438-5299; www.jazzfest.mybc.com). Draws over 500 performers and bands for 10 days of hot jazz, from acid to swing. Some free concerts in Gastown, at the Roundhouse on Davie St., and around Granville Island.

Vancouver Folk Music Festival (July 14-16, 2000; 602-9798; www.thefestival.bc.ca). Performers from around the world give concerts and workshops. Very kid-friendly. $35 per evening; $50 per day; $100-110 for the weekend. Ages 13-18 $25 per day, $55 weekend. Ages 3-12 $6 per day, $10 weekend. Less in advance.

Benson & Hedges Symphony of Fire (late July-early Aug.; 738-4304). The world's finest pyrotechnicians light up the sky over English Bay on Saturday and Wednesday nights in late July and early August. Hundreds of thousands gather to watch, closing off downtown streets. Displays coordinated with music aired on 101 FM.

DAYTRIPS

DEEP COVE. East of city center, the town of **Deep Cove** in North Vancouver luxuriates in saltiness, while sea otters and seals ply pleasant Indian Arm. **Cates Park,** at the end of Dollarton Hwy. on the way to Deep Cove, has popular swimming and scuba waters and makes a good bike trip out of Vancouver. Take bus #210 from Pender St. to the Phibbs Exchange on the north side of Second Narrows Bridge. From there, take bus #211 or 212 to Deep Cove. Bus #211 also leads to **Mount Seymour Provincial Park.** Trails leave from Mt. Seymour Rd., and a paved road winds 11km to the top. See also **Skiing,** below.

REIFEL BIRD SANCTUARY. Reifel Bird Sanctuary (946-6980), on Westham Island lies northwest of the Tsawwassen ferry terminal and 16km south of the city. The island's 850 acres of marshland support 265 bird species, and spotting towers are set up for extended birdwatching: Apr., May, Oct., and Nov. are the best months. (Open daily 9am-4pm; $3.25, seniors and children $1).

LYNN CANYON. For easy hiking near the city, take the SeaBus to Lynn Canyon Park (981-3103), in North Vancouver. Unlike the more famous Capilano, the suspension bridge here is free and uncrowded, and hangs 50m above the canyon. The river and waterfalls make for a gentle stroll and a cold swim. Longer hiking trails are also plentiful. Take bus #229 from the North Vancouver SeaBus terminal to the last stop (Peters Rd.) and walk 500m to the bridge.

LIGHTHOUSE PARK. Head out across the Lions Gate Bridge from Stanley Park and west along Marine Dr. through West Van to gorgeous **Lighthouse Park.** Numerous trails crisscross the 185-acre park. Walk down the path toward the lighthouse, hang a left at the buildings, keep right at the fork in the trail, and walk to a large flat rock for one of the **best picnic spots in the world.** It's a 50km round-trip from downtown; blue bus #250 goes right to the park's entrance.

LOCAL MOUNTAINS

Three local mountains loom above the city on the North Shore. In winter, all three offer night skiing and heavier snow than mountains farther from the ocean. In summer, all offer challenging hiking and beautiful views of the city.

GROUSE MOUNTAIN. The closest ski hill to downtown Vancouver has the crowds to prove it (984-0661; snow report 986-6262). Take bus #236 from the North Vancouver SeaBus terminal, which drops off at the Super Skyride, an aerial tramway open daily from 9am-10pm ($16, seniors $14, ages 13-18 $10, families $40). The slopes are lit for skiing until 10:30pm from November to May (lift tickets $25, youth $20, HI members $21). The steep 2.9km **Grouse Grind Trail** is popular among Vancouverites in summer; it climbs 840m/2755 ft. to the top of the mountain and takes a good 2hr. The Skyride back down costs $5.

CYPRESS BOWL. A little farther removed, **Cypress Bowl** (922-0825; snow report 419-7669), in West Vancouver provides a less crowded ski alternative farther from downtown. It also boasts the most advanced terrain of the three local mountains on its 23 runs. (Lift tickets $33, youth $28, seniors $15. Discount tickets available at Costco supermarkets.) Head west on Hwy. 1, take Exit 8 (Cypress Bowl Rd.) A few minutes before the downhill area, the 16km of groomed trails of the Hollyburn **cross-country ski area** are open to the public ($12, youth $10.50, seniors $6.50). In summer, the cross-country trails make for excellent **hiking** and **berry-picking**.

MOUNT SEYMOUR. Bus #211 from the Phibbs Exchange at the north end of the Second Narrows Bridge leads to **Mt. Seymour Provincial Park.** Trails leave from Mt. Seymour Rd., and a paved road winds 11km to the top. The Mt. Seymour ski area is the cheapest (midweek lift tickets $19, seniors $15, ages 6-12 $9; weekends and holidays $26, ages 6-12 $13, ages 13-18 $21, seniors $15) but its marked terrain is also the least challenging (though the spectacular backcountry is the preferred terrain of many several top pro snowboarders).

SEA TO SKY HIGHWAY (HWY. 99)

Winding around the steep cliffs on the shore of Howe Sound from Horseshoe Bay to Squamish, and then continuing inland to Whistler, the Sea to Sky Highway (Hwy. 99) is one of the loveliest, most dangerous drives in British Columbia, combining sinuous curves with brilliant vistas of the Sound and Tantalus Range. Speed limits are strictly enforced, yet routinely ignored, by drivers. Drive defensively!

VANCOUVER TO WHISTLER

Fifty-two kilometers north of Vancouver, at the **BC Museum of Mining** (688-8735) in Britannia Beach, visitors can hop onto a mine train and ride deep into an inactive copper mine. (Open July-Aug. daily 10am-4:30pm, May-June and Sept.-Oct. W-Su 10am-4:30pm. $9.50, students and seniors $7.50, under 5 free, families $34. Goldpanning tour $3.50.)

Provincial park after provincial park lines the rocky drive to Whistler providing excellent hiking and climbing opportunities. One worth stopping for is **Shannon Falls,** just off the highway 3km past the museum. The park affords a spectacular view of a 335m/1100 ft. waterfall. Steep but well-maintained trails from the falls make for blue-ribbon **dayhiking** up to the three peaks of **the Stawamus Chief** (11km round-trip), the second largest granite monolith in the world, which bares a 671m wall of solid granite. The face of the Chief is a popular climb for expert hikers. **Squamish Hostel,** 38490 Buckley Rd. (892-9240 or 800-449-8614 in BC), in downtown Squamish, is a logical stopover for those tackling the local geology ($15; private rooms $25; shower, kitchen, linen). In summer, the hostel is packed with wandering climbers, as the region between Squamish and Whistler boasts over

1300 excellent routes. In addition to its vertical faces, Squamish offers world-class **windsurfing** off the spit at the top of **Howe Sound** (ask at the hostel for directions). At **Eagle Run,** a viewing site 4km north of the hostel along the Squamish River, hundreds of bald eagles make their winter home along the rivers and estuaries of Squamish Valley (Dec.-Feb., volunteer interpreters on weekends; wheelchair accessible). BC Parks (800-689-9025; www.discovercamping.ca) runs a deluxe campground 3km further north at **Alice Lake** ($18.50; showers, security, hot water, firewood), close to **Garibaldi Park.** The park contains a number of stunning hikes, including a 9km (one-way) trail up to **Garibaldi Lake.** The backcountry campgrounds at the lake provide further access to Black Tusk and Cheakamus Lake (trailhead at Rubble Creek parking lot, 25km north of Squamish). The **BC Parks District Office** (898-3678) in Alice Lake park, has trail maps and avalanche conditions in winter (open M-F 8:30am-4:30pm). The **BC Forest Service office,** 42000 Loggers Ln. (898-2100), has maps of local logging roads and primitive campgrounds, and sells the $8 permits needed to camp at them. To reach the office, turn right off Hwy. 99 at the Squamish McDonald's.

WHISTLER

Skiing and riding at Whistler and Blackcomb mountains is consistently ranked among the best in North America, and the media buzz, combined with a weak Canadian dollar, draws visitors from all over the world. (A 1998 ski vacation taken by Prince Charles and his heart-throb sons brought English-types in droves last season.) The overproduced and overpriced "Village" manages to suck much of the character out of the place, but no amount of kitsch can take away from the striking beauty of the mountains or the challenge of the terrain. The mountains are part of Garibaldi Provincial Park, and, especially in summer, it takes surprisingly little effort to get off the beaten path and into the wilds. Whistler is currently bidding to host the 2010 Winter Olympics, and the town is expected to aggressively market itself prior to the decision in 2003, though the real push won't come until Toronto loses the race for the 2008 Summer games.

⚠ ORIENTATION AND PRACTICAL INFORMATION. Whistler is located 125km (1½-2hr.) north of Vancouver on the beautiful, if very dangerously twisty, Hwy. 99 (see p. 258). Most services are located in **Whistler Village,** much of which is **pedestrian-only. Whistler Creek,** 5km south on Hwy. 99, is a smaller, less-developed collection of accommodations and restaurants. **Greyhound Bus Lines** (932-5031, 661-0310 in Vancouver) runs buses to Vancouver from the **Village Bus Loop** (2½hr., 6 per day 5am-7:15pm, $18, round-trip $34). **BC Rail's** 2½-hr. Cariboo Prospector (984-5246) departs North Vancouver for Whistler Creek at 7am and returns at 6:20pm daily ($31). For in-town travel, try **Whistler Taxi** at 932-3333. The **activity and information center** (932-2394), in the heart of the Village, provides maps and booking services (open daily 9am-5pm). For local **weather and road conditions,** call 932-5090. **Emergency:** 911. **Police:** 4315 Blackcomb Way (932-3044), in the Village. **Telecare Crisis Line:** 932-2673. **Whistler Health Care Center:** 4380 Lorimer Rd. (932-4911). **Post office:** (932-5012), in the Village Marketplace (open M-F 8:30am-5:30pm, Sa 8:30am-12:30pm.) **Postal Code:** V0N 1B0. **Internet Access** in the Village is available free at the **Whistler Public Library** (no email; F-Su 10am-5pm; M, Tu, Th 10am-8pm), for an arm at **Mailboxes Etc.** (open daily 8am-6pm, $2 per 10min.), or for a leg at **Peak's Coffee House** ($5 per 30min.; open M-F 8am-5pm, Sa-Su 8am-8pm). **Area Code:** 604.

⌂ ACCOMMODATIONS. Grab your own gorrrrgeous (and cheap) piece of heaven in the magnificent **Whistler Hostel (HI),** 5678 Alta Lake Rd. (932-5492; fax 932-4687), 5km south of Whistler Village on Hwy. 99. BC Rail from Vancouver stops on request right at the hostel. The Rainbow Park bus runs to the village ($1.50; 4 per day, 5 per day in winter). The large lakefront hewn-timber building contains a kitchen, fireplace, ski lockers, pool table, and sauna. Slope junkies take note: ski tuning can be performed on the premises, and **discount lift tickets** for Whistler and Blackcomb are available for $48. In summer, guests can rent bikes ($18 per day) and canoe for free on Alta Lake. (Bunks $18.50; nonmembers $22.75; under 13 half-price; under 6 free. Key deposit $10; check-in 8-11am and 4-10pm. Reservations required year-round.) The **Shoestring Lodge,** 7124 Nancy Greene Dr. (932-3338; fax 932-8347; www.shoestringlodge.com), 1km north of the village, offers rooms with cable, private bathroom, and shared kitchen, as well as a raucous pub and restaurant. Prices vary considerably over the year (bunk in a 4-person room $16-30; doubles $50-135), with peak prices, mandatory reservations, and free shuttle transport to the slopes from December to April. The **Fireside Lodge,** 2117 Nordic Dr. (932-4545), 3km south of the Village, caters to a quieter crowd. The spacious and clean cabin comes with the works: huge kitchen, lounge, sauna, laundry, game room, storage, and parking (dorms Apr. to mid-Dec. $22; in winter weekdays $25, weekends $30; check-in 3:30-8:30pm). While camping near Whistler is currently scarce, **Riverwoods Campground** (932-5469), 2.5km north of the Village, is expected to be open by 2000. Tentative rates are steep: $20 unserviced, $35 for full hookups. The Forest Service office in Squamish (see p. 259) has maps to free unserviced sites.

🍴 **FOOD.** The busy **IGA** supermarket peddles saltcod and exotic spices in the village marketplace daily 9am-9pm. The smaller **Nester's Market,** 1019 Nester's Rd., 1km north of the village, is close to the Shoestring Lodge. **Zeuski's Taverna** (932-6009), in Whistler Village's Town Plaza, features hearty Mediterranean cuisine. Dinner prices are Olympian ($12-29), but a takeout window offers falafel, souvlaki, and gyro lunches for $7-12 (open Su-Th 11:30am-10pm, F-Sa 11:30am-11pm). The delectable lunch wraps (from $4.25) at **Moguls Coffee Beans** (932-4845; open daily 6:30am-7pm) are a fine deal. (The vegetable and feta combo gets top marks.) The **South Side Deli,** 2102 Lake Placid Rd. (932-3368), on Hwy. 99 by the Husky station 4km south of the village, is a rare respite from resort-land. Tasty veggie omelettes ($7) won't put your arteries to the test like the B.E.L.T.C.H. sandwich—Bacon, Egg, Lettuce, Tomato, Cheese, Ham; $7—will (open daily 6am-3pm). Urp.

🏔 **OUTDOORS.** Seven thousand acres of terrain, 33 lifts (15 of them high-speed), three glaciers, and a mile (1609m/5280 ft.) of vertical drop mark recently merged **Whistler/Blackcomb** (932-3434 or 800-766-0449) as the largest ski resort in North America. Parking and lift access for this behemoth is available at six points, with Whistler Creekside offering the shortest lines and easiest access to Whistler to those coming from Vancouver. A **lift ticket** ($57; $36 from June 10 to July 30; multi-day discounts available) is good for both mountains from 8:30am to 3:30-4:30pm. A **Fresh Tracks** upgrade ($15), available every morning at 7am, provides breakfast at mountaintop, and the chance to begin skiing or riding as soon as the ski patrol has finished avalanche control. **Cheap tickets** are often available at SuperValu supermarkets and 7-11 convenience stores in Vancouver and Squamish, and rates are sometimes cheaper mid-week and early and late in the season. While Whistler offers amazing alpine terrain and gorgeous bowls, most **snowboarders** prefer the younger Blackcomb for its windlips, natural quarter-pipes, and 16-acre terrain park. The mountain's **employment hotline** can be reached at 938-7367. Much **backcountry skiing** is accessible from resort lifts and in Garibaldi Park's **Diamond Head** area. The BC Parks office in Alice Lake Park (see p. 259), has avalanche information culled from the web (see p. 45). Avalanches kill every year in BC; and there are no patrols outside of resort boundaries. Always file trip plans, and stay within the limits of your experience and of safety.

While skiing is God in Whistler and lasts on the glaciers until August, the **Whistler Gondola** whisks sightseers to the top of the mountain year-round for $21 ($24 with bike), providing access in summer to the resort's extensive **mountain bike park. Impact Activities** (905-5666; open daily 9am-6pm), in the Village, acts as an information broker for local outfitters and dispenses great advice on outdoor activities of the organized stripe, from horseback riding to heli-hiking. The friendly and skilled staff of **Wedge Rafting** (932-7171), inside Whistler Village's Carlton Lodge, lead 2½-hr. trips ($51) and full-day excursions ($125) on the Green and Squamish Rivers.

NORTH OF WHISTLER

Though only 30 minutes apart, Whistler and the undeveloped town of **Pemberton** are worlds apart. The region's numerous glacial lakes lure fishermen like a fat night-crawler; stop in at **Spud Valley Sporting Goods** (894-6630) in the center of town for a license and some tips (open daily 9am-6pm). **Visitor information** is available in a booth on the highway (894-6175; open May-Sept. daily 9am-5pm). For $10 ($12 with showers), a group of four can pitch a tent at **Cedar Bend,** 4km north of town (894-3322), and explore the farm's 300 acres of mountain bike trails, look at the livestock, and marvel at ancient **petroglyphs.** North of Pemberton, Hwy. 99 turns into **Duffey Lake Rd.,** which passes through the Mt. Curry Reserve of the Stl'atl'lmx Nation (snow tires/chains required in winter). This 104km stretch offers stunning views of glaciers and valley lakes as it crosses over the lush **Cayoosh Range** into the dry and dusty interior. For a fantastic **dayhike** 65km north of Whistler, climb to **Joffre Lakes** along a popular 6km path (one-way) that passes three glacially-fed lakes and affords spectacular views of Joffre Peak and Slalok Mountain (accessible July-Oct.).

    Lillooet, 135km north of Whistler, was originally Mile 0 of the historic **Cariboo Wagon Trail,** which led 100,000 gold-crazed miners north to Barkerville between 1862 and 1870. The town is rich in history but not tourist amenities. The **Chamber of Commerce** (256-4364), will help you find a place to crash. On the second weekend in June, the town celebrates its heritage during **Lillooet Days** with a host of events including a staged train robbery. From Lillooet, Hwy. 99 meanders north another 50km through arid, sage-covered foothills until it meets Hwy. 97 right outside **Cache Creek** (p. 334). The weary can break halfway for trout fishing and swimming in Crown Lake beneath the red limestone cliffs of **Marble Canyon** Provincial Park (camping $12).

SECHELT PENINSULA

Tucked between the Strait of Georgia and Porpoise Bay on the Sunshine Coast, Sechelt (SEE-shelt) has long been considered one of BC's greatest secrets. Only two hours by road and ferry from Vancouver, this quiet seaside paradise remains miles away in attitude, lifestyle, and even climate. The region offers an amazingly rich array of outdoor activities: world-class kayaking, hiking, scuba diving, biking, and even skiing are all within a short drive of town.

◪ ORIENTATION AND PRACTICAL INFORMATION. Sechelt is the largest community on the Sunshine Coast, 27km west of the **BC Ferries** Langdale Ferry Terminal (886-2242 or 888-223-3779). The fare on the ferry between Langdale and Horseshoe Bay is only charged on the way from the mainland to Sechelt (40min., 8-10 per day; $8, ages 5-11 $4, car $27.75; off-season slightly cheaper). **Malaspina Coach Lines** (885-3666) runs to Vancouver (2 per day, $10.75 plus ferry fare) **Sunshine Coast Transit System** (885-3234) buses run from Sechelt to the ferry terminal ($1.50 adult, $1 students and seniors). **National Tilden,** 5637 Wharf St. (885-9120), rents cars from $50 per day; 35¢ per km over 100km; winter rates start at $40. Hail a **Sunshine Coast Taxi** at 885-3666. The **visitor center** (885-0662), in the Trail Bay Centre at Trail Ave. and Teredo St., sells a $5 hiking and biking guide. (Open July to mid-Sept. M-Th and Sa 9:30am-5:30pm, F 9:30am-7pm, Su 11am-4pm; off-season open M-Sa 9:30am-5:30pm.) **Trail Bay Sports** (885-2512), at Cowrie St. and Trail Ave., rents mountain bikes ($7 per hr., $30 per 8hr.) and sells fishing gear (open summer M-Th and Sa 9am-6pm, F 9am-9pm, Su 10am-

4pm; in winter M-Sa 9:30am-5:30pm). The **Sechelt Public Library,** 5797 Cowrie St. (885-3260) has free **Internet access.** (Open Tu and Sa 10am-4pm, W and Th 11am-8pm, Su and F 1-5pm. **Laundromat: Sechelt Coin Laundry** (885-3393), on Dolphin St. at Inlet Ave. Wash $1.50, dry 25¢ per 5min. (open M-F 9am-7pm, Sa 9am-6pm, Su 11am-5pm). **Emergency:** 911. **Hospital: St. Mary's** (885-2224), on the highway, at the east end of town. **Post office:** (885-2411), on Inlet Ave. at Dolphin St. Open M-F 8:30am-5pm, Sa 8:30am-12:30pm. **Postal Code:** V0N 3A0. **Area code:** 604.

⌐ ACCOMMODATIONS AND CAMPGROUNDS. Most of Sechelt's accommodations offer resort luxury and corresponding prices, but deals can be found. The comfortable ▨ **MoonCradle Hostel,** 3125 Hwy. 101, (885-2070 or 877-350-5862), 10km east of Sechelt, is situated on 10 acres of lush rainforest. The small number of beds allows the energetic young hosts to lavish organic breakfasts on guests. (8 hand-crafted cedar bunks in two rooms: HI members $20, nonmembers $25. Private room: $60). **Eagle View B&B** (885-7225), at 4839 Eagle View Rd., 5min. east of Sechelt, has rooms with private bath, sitting room with TV/VCR, an ocean view, and delightful hosts ($45 singles; $60 doubles).

The provincial parks in the area are dreamy. The family-oriented **Porpoise Bay Provincial Park,** 4km north of Sechelt along Sechelt Inlet Rd., offers toilets, showers, firewood, and a lovely beach and swimming area (84 regular sites: $17.50; cyclist campsites by the water $9; wheelchair accessible). For more seclusion, **Roberts Creek Provincial Park,** 11km east of Sechelt, has private sites amid old growth Douglas Firs (24 sites: $12; pit toilets, firewood, water; wheelchair accessible). **Smuggler Cove Provincial Park** has five primitive, free walk-in sites (pit toilets but no water.) The sites are accessible by boat, and the cove is an excellent base for kayaking. To get there, head west out of town towards Halfmoon Bay and turn left onto Brooks Rd. which leads to a parking area after 3.5km. The campsite is 1km along a trail through the forest.

◨ FOOD. The **Gumboot Garden Cafe,** 1059 Roberts Creek Rd. (885-4216), 10km east of Sechelt in Roberts Creek, serves delicious organic meals. Lunch and breakfast favorites include African peanut soup ($4), fries and miso gravy ($3.50), and Thai salad with chicken or tofu ($5.75); a variable dinner menu is uniformly excellent and always includes vegan options. (Open daily 8:30am-3pm and Th-Su 5:30pm-9pm for dinner.) In Sechelt, the **Old Boot Eatery,** 5520 Wharf St. (885-2727), serves up generous portions of Italian food and local hospitality. All pasta entrees $9 (open M-Sa 11am-10pm; in winter 11am-9pm). **Wakefield Inn,** on the highway 5min. west of Sechelt (885-7666), dishes out standard pub fare and live music (burgers $7-9, pints $4-5, music F-Sa 9pm-1am). As for groceries, **Claytons** (885-2025), in the Trail Bay Centre, sells Sechelt's by the seashore (open M-Th 9am-7pm, F 9am-9pm, Sa-Su 10am-6pm).

◫ ◭ SIGHTS AND OUTDOORS. The eight wilderness marine parks in the protected waters of **Sechelt Inlet** make for fantastic sea kayaking and canoeing and offer free camping along the shore. **Pedals & Paddles** (885-6440), at Tillicum Bay Marina, 7km north of town, rents vessels. (4hr. rental: single kayaks $23, doubles $46; canoes $27. Full-day: single kayaks $40, doubles $75; canoes $45.) The intersection of Sechelt and Salmon Inlets is home to the **Chaudiere artificial reef,** one of the largest wreck dives in North America. **Diving Locker,** 5659 Dolphin St. (885-9830), rents equipment and guides trips (basic rental $50 per day, full rental $80, guide $50). On the other side of the peninsula, **Pender Harbor** offers equally impressive diving; Jacques Cousteau considered this site second only to the Red Sea. **Skookumchuck Narrows** is a popular destination by water or by land. The tidal rapids bring waves standing 1.5m at peak tides. To get there, drive 54km west to **Earl's Cove,** then 4km towards **Egmont.** From the parking area, it's a 4km walk to four viewing sites. The route to the first site is wheelchair-accessible.

Dakota Bowl and all above Wilson Creek 4km east of Sechelt, contains free, maintained trails hiking and cross-country skiing trails; from Sechelt turn left on Field Rd. and drive 8km to the trailhead. Sechelt's logging legacy has left it with an extensive system of former logging roads suitable hiking and mountain biking trails. The intermediate **Chapman Creek Trail** passes huge Douglas firs en route to **Chapman Falls.** The trailhead is at the top of Havies Rd., 1.1km north of the Davis Bay Store on Hwy. 101. The **Suncoaster Trail** extends over 40km from **Homesite Creek,** near Halfmoon Bay northwest of Sechelt, through the foothills of the **Caren Range,** home of Canada's oldest trees. (Cedar have stood here for as long as 1835 years.)

Indoors, the **Sunshine Coast Arts Centre** (885-5412), on Trail Ave. at Medusa St., showcases local talent in a small log cabin. (open Tu-Sa 10am-4pm; Su 1-4pm; admission by donation.) From August 10-13, 2000 Sechelt will play host to the **Sunshine Coast Festival of the Written Arts,** which attracts talented Canadian authors to give **readings.** Panels are held in the **botanical gardens** of the historic Rockwood Centre. For info on the festival or the center, call 885-9631. (Grounds open daily 8am-10pm.) The **Roberts Creek Community Hall** (886-3868 or 740-9616), on the corner of the highway and Roberts Creek Rd., is an unlikely venue that attracts excellent musicians on weekends, from reggae to Latin funk. Tickets ($10-20) can be purchased at the **Roberts Creek General Store** (885-3400).

SOUTHERN VANCOUVER ISLAND

VICTORIA

Although many tourist operations would have you believe that Victoria fell off Great Britain in a neat little chunk, its High Tea tradition began in the 1950s to draw American tourists. The city was actually built by miners. Founded in 1843, Fort Victoria was a fur trading post and supply center for the Hudson's Bay Company. The discovery of gold in the Fraser River Canyon pushed it into the fast lane in 1858, bringing international trade and the requisite frontier bars and brothels.

Clean, polite, and tourist-friendly, today's Victoria is a homier alternative to cosmopolitan Vancouver. The namesake British monarch and her era of morals and furniture aside, Victoria is a city of diverse origins and interests. Galleries selling native arts operate alongside new-age bookstores, tourist traps, and pawn shops. Double-decker bus tours motor by English pubs while bike-taxis peddle past the markets, museums, and stores that make up the rest of downtown.

▨ ORIENTATION AND PRACTICAL INFORMATION

The **Trans-Canada Highway (Hwy. 1)** runs north to Nanaimo, where it becomes **Highway 19,** stretching north to the rest of Vancouver Island; **Highway 14** heads west to **Port Renfrew** and the southern portion of **Pacific Rim National Park.**

Driving in Victoria is relatively easy, but **parking** downtown is difficult and expensive. Cross the Johnson St. Bridge (Pandora St. leads to the bridge from downtown) and take the second right or left onto Tyee St. for **free street parking** (two-hour limit) a 10-minute walk from downtown.

Victoria surrounds the **Inner Harbour;** the main north-south thoroughfares downtown are **Government Street** and **Douglas Street.** To the north, Douglas St. becomes Hwy. 1. **Blanshard Street,** one block to the east, becomes Hwy. 17.

TRANSPORTATION

Trains: E&N Railway, 450 Pandora St. (schedule 383-4324; general info and tickets 800-561-8630), near the Inner Harbour at the Johnson St. Bridge. Daily service to Nanaimo (2½hr., $19, students with ISIC $11); Courtenay (4½hr., $37, students with ISIC $22). 10% senior discount. 25% off when booked 7 days in advance.

Buses: Laidlaw, 700 Douglas St. (385-4411 or 800-318-0818), at Belleville St. Laidlaw and its affiliates, **Pacific Coach Lines** and **Island Coach Lines,** connect most points on the island. To: Nanaimo (2½hr., 6 per day, $17.50); Vancouver (3½hr., 8-14 per day, $26.50); and Port Hardy (9hr., 1-2 per day, $84).

Ferries: Bus #70 ($2.50) runs between downtown and the Swartz Bay and Sidney ferry terminals. **BC Ferries** (656-5571 or 888-BC-FERRY/223-3779; operator 7am-10pm 386-3431). Ferries depart Swartz Bay to Vancouver's Tsawwassen ferry terminal (1½hr.; 8-16 per day; $9, bikes $2.50, car and driver $39-41). Service to all Gulf Islands (see p. 286). **Washington State Ferries** (381-1551 or 656-1831; in the U.S. 206-464-6400 or 800-84-FERRY/843-3779) depart from Sidney to Anacortes, WA (2 per day in summer, 1 per day in winter; US$9, car with driver US$41). A ticket to Anacortes allows free stopovers along the eastward route, including the San Juan Islands. **Victoria Clipper**, 254 Belleville St. (382-8100 or 800-888-2535), runs passenger ferries direct to Seattle (2-3hr.; 4 per day May-Sept., 1 per day Oct.-Apr.; US$58-66, seniors US$52-60, ages 1-11 $29-33). **Black Ball Transport,** 430 Belleville St. (386-2202), runs to Port Angeles, WA (1½hr.; 4 per day mid-May to mid-Oct., 2 per day Oct. to Dec. and mid-March to mid-May; US$6.75, car and driver US$28.50, ages 5-11 US$3.40). Call in advance for wait.

Public Transportation: BC Transit (382-6161). City bus service with connections downtown, at the corner of Douglas and Yates St. Single-zone travel $1.75; multi-zone (north to Swartz Bay, Sidney, and the Butchart Gardens) $2.50; seniors $1.10 and $1.75; under 5 free. Day passes ($5.50, seniors $4) and free *Rider's Guide* with maps at Tourism Victoria, at the library, or from any driver. **Disabilities Services for Local Transit** (727-7811) is open M-Th and Su 7am-10pm, F-Sa 7am-midnight.

Car Rental: Island Auto Rentals, 1030 Yates St. (384-4881). $25 per day plus 12¢ per km after 100km. Must be 21 with major credit card. Insurance $13. **Rent-a-Wreck,** 2634 Douglas St. (384-5343 or 800-809-0788). $27 per day plus 12¢ per km. Must be 19 with credit card. Insurance $13, if under 25 $16.

BC Automobile Association: 1075 Pandora Ave. (389-6700). Open M-Sa 9am-5pm.

Taxis: Victoria Taxi (383-7111). **Westwind** (474-4747). Both $2.15 base, $1.30 per km.

VISITOR SERVICES

Visitor Information: 812 Wharf St. (953-2033), at Government St. Also a Ticketmaster outlet. Open daily July-Aug. 8:30am-7:30pm; in winter 9am-5pm.

Tours: Grayline, 700 Douglas St. (388-5248; www.victoriatours.com). Runs several tours in double-decker buses through different parts of the city ($17-97). **Historical Walking Tours** (953-2033) covers downtown in small groups, leaving from the visitor center daily in summer at 11am, 7, and 9pm (1½hr., $10). Expected to be resurrected in 2000 is the **Murder, Ghosts, and Mayhem** Walking Tour (385-2035) through dark streets and back alleys, with tales of old crimes and mysteries. Tours leave daily from the Bastion Square Arch at 8pm (1hr., $5, under 12 free).

LOCAL SERVICES

Equipment Rental: Harbour Rental, 811 Wharf St. (995-1661), opposite the visitor center. Bikes $6 per hr., $20 per day. Scooters $12 per hr., $45 per day, plus $7 insurance per day. Must be 19 with driver's license. Open daily 9am-5pm. **Jeune Brothers,** 570 Johnson St. (386-8778; fax 380-1533) rents camping gear. Sleeping bags $13 per day, packs $10 per day, 3-person tents $35 for 2 days. 10% HI discount. Open M-Th 10am-6pm, F 10am-9pm, Sa 10am-5:30pm, Su noon-5pm.

Library: 735 Broughton St. (382-7241), at Courtney St. Internet access $3 per hr. Open M, W, F-Sa 9am-6pm, Tu, Th 9am-9pm. **Public Radio:** 90.5 FM.

Laundromat and Public Showers: Oceanside Gifts, 812 Wharf St. (380-1777), beneath the visitor center. Wash $1.25, dry $1; showers $1 per 5min. Open daily 7:30am-10pm.

EMERGENCY AND COMMUNICATIONS

Emergency: 911. **Police:** 850 Caledonia (995-7654), at Quadra St.

Crisis Line: 386-6323. 24hr. **Rape Crisis:** 383-3232. 24hr.

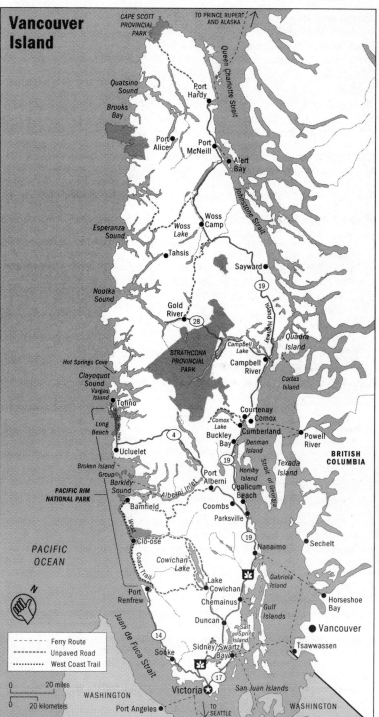

Vancouver Island

CAPE SCOTT
PROVINCIAL
PARK

TO PRINCE RUPERT
AND ALASKA

Quatsino
Sound

Brooks
Bay

Port
Hardy

Queen Charlotte Strait

Port
Alice

Port
McNeill

Alert
Bay

Johnstone Strait

Esperanza
Sound

Woss
Camp

Woss
Lake

Tahsis

Sayward

19

Nootka
Sound

Gold
River

28

STRATHCONA
PROVINCIAL
PARK

Campbell
Lake

Quadra
Island

Island Highway

Campbell
River

Cortes
Island

Hot Springs Cove

Clayoquot
Sound

Vargas
Island

Tofino

Long
Beach

4

Ucluelet

Broken Island
Group

PACIFIC RIM
NATIONAL PARK

Barkley
Sound

Bamfield

West Coast Trail

Courtenay
Comox

Comox
Lake

Buckley
Bay

Cumberland

Denman
Island

Powell
River

19

Hornby
Island

Texada
Island

BRITISH
COLUMBIA

Port
Alberni

Alberni Inlet

Qualicum
Beach

Strait of Georgia

Coombs

Parksville

19

Nanaimo

Sechelt

PACIFIC
OCEAN

Clo-ose

Cowichan
Lake

Gabriola
Island

Lake
Cowichan

Horseshoe
Bay

Chemainus

Gulf
Islands

Port
Renfrew

Duncan

Salt
Spring
Island

Vancouver

14

Sidney/Swartz
Bay

Sooke

Tsawwassen

Juan de Fuca Strait

17

San Juan Islands

N

Victoria

Ferry Route
Unpaved Road
West Coast Trail

0   20 miles
0   20 kilometers

WASHINGTON

Port Angeles

TO
SEATTLE

WASHINGTON

VANCOUVER & ISLANDS

Pharmacy: London Drugs, 911 Yates St. (381-1113), at Vancouver St., in the Wilson Centre. Open M-Sa 9am-10pm, Su 10am-8pm.

Hospital: Royal Jubilee, 1900 Fort St. (370-8000).

Post Office: 621 Discovery St., V8W 1L0 (963-1350). Open M-F 8am-6pm.

24hr. Refuge: See **Cafe de la Lune,** 1450 Douglas St., in the **Hotel Douglas.**

Internet Access: See **Library,** above. **Ocean Island Backpackers Inn,** $1 per 15min.

Area Code: 250.

ACCOMMODATIONS AND CAMPGROUNDS

HOSTELS AND B&BS

Victoria has a capital budget accommodations scene, but a meager selection of campgrounds. A number of flavorful hostels and B&B-hostel hybrids make a night inside in Victoria an altogether pleasant experience. Reserve ahead in summer.

Ocean Island Backpackers Inn, 791 Pandora St. (385-1788 or 888-888-4180), downtown. This colorful and amicable new hostel boasts a better lounge than most clubs, tastier food than most restaurants (see **Food,** below), and accommodations comparable to most hotels. Undoubtedly one of the finest urban hostels in Canada, Ocean Island maintains 114 comfortable beds in individually named rooms (1-4 beds per room) with free linen and towels, laundry facilities, email, and several disco-balls. Dorms $16 (HI or students), $19.50 otherwise; doubles $40. Parking $3.

Selkirk Guest House, 934 Selkirk Ave. (389-1213), in West Victoria. Take bus #14 along Craigflower to Tillicum; Selkirk is 1 block north. Co-ed and all-female dorms with flowery sheets, free canoes, and a hot tub on the water. Lyn is a magician and Spike the Wonder Dog sometimes makes an appearance at breakfast. Dorms $18, private rooms $50-70. Cheaper in off-season. Breakfast $5. Kitchen, free linen and towels, laundry.

Renouf House Bunk & Breakfast, 2010 Stanley Ave. (595-4774; renouf@islandnet .com). Catch the #22 "Haultain" bus from Douglas and View; get off at Fernwood and Gladstone and walk one block east. A 1912 house full of antique furniture. The large continental breakfast features homemade granola and breads. Kitchen and laundry. Bunks $20; singles $33; doubles $50. Affiliated with **Christine's Place,** 1408 Tauton St., down the road, with extra rooms in a smaller, more modern, but still swank house. Singles $35, with private bath $55; doubles $50, with private bath $70.

The Cat's Meow, 1316 Grant St. (595-8878). Take bus #22 to Fernwood and Grant. A mini-hostel with 12 quiet beds. The hostel's inspiration, Rufus, rests in peace, but the house lives on in his name. Beds $17.50; private doubles $43. Breakfast included.

Victoria Backpackers Hostel, 1608 Quadra St. (386-4471), close to downtown. A funky old house with a small yard, lounge, and kitchen. Free parking. 40 beds jammed into single-sex and co-ed dorms, and the dining room. Bunks $12; singles $20, doubles $40. Linen free, laundry $2. Reception M-F 8am-11pm, Sa-Su 10am-11pm.

Victoria Youth Hostel (HI), 516 Yates St. (385-4511 or 888-883-0099), at Wharf St. downtown. Big, modern, and spotless. Ping pong, video games, and a TV room. Staff and volunteer concierges are fonts of info. Barracks-style dorms $16, nonmembers $20. Family and couples' rooms available for $2 surcharge per person. Kitchen and free linen. Laundry $1.50, towel 50¢. Reception 7am-midnight.

University of Victoria (721-8395), 20min. northeast of the Inner Harbour by bus #4 or 14. From Hwy. 17, take McKenzie Ave. to Sinclair. The housing office is in Lot 5. Private dorms, shared baths. Cute rabbits live under the buildings. Singles $38; doubles $50. Cafeteria breakfast included. Coin laundry. Reservations advised. Open May-Aug.

Hotel Douglas, 1450 Douglas St. (383-4157 or 800-332-9981; stay@hoteldouglas .com). Small but nicely-furnished rooms in a busy downtown location. Prices shift with occupancy; singles and doubles $40-60; with private bath $50-80. Free parking. Inside the hotel lobby at **Cafe de la Lune,** coffee and eclectic crowds flow 24hr.

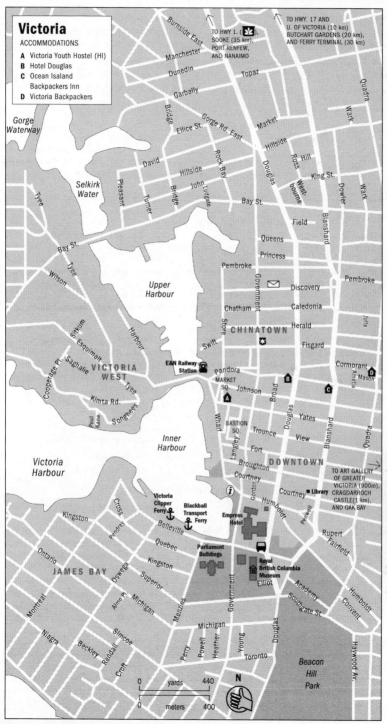

Victoria

ACCOMMODATIONS

A Victoria Youth Hostel (HI)
B Hotel Douglas
C Ocean Isaland
   Backpackers Inn
D Victoria Backpackers

TO HWY 1. (🍁),
SOOKE (35 km),
PORT RENFEW,
AND NANAIMO

TO HWY. 17 AND
U. OF VICTORIA (10 km)
BUTCHART GARDENS (20 km),
AND FERRY TERMINAL (30 km)

Burnside East

Manchester

Dunedin

Garbally

Ellice St.

Gorge Rd. East

Bridge

David

Hillside

Rock Bay

Bridge

John

Ludgate

Turner

Pleasant

Bay St.

Topaz

Market

Hillside

Ross

Hill

West-
bourne

King St.

Dowler

Wark

Quadra

Wark

Gorge
Waterway

Selkirk
Water

Tyee

Bay St.

Wilson

Tyee

Douglas

Bay St.

Field

Queens

Princess

Pembroke

Blanshard

Pembroke

Julia

Upper
Harbour

Government

Store

Discovery

Caledonia

Herald

Fisgard

✉

CHINATOWN

Swift

Pandora

Johnson

Yates

View

Broad

Douglas

Blanshard

Pandora

Cormorant

Amelia

Mason

D

Esquimalt
Saghalie

Cooperage Pl.

Sirkum

Harbour

Tyee

Kimta Rd.

Paul
Kane

Songhees

**VICTORIA
WEST**

E&N Railway
Station

MARKET
SQ.

A

B

C

Upper
Harbour

Inner
Harbour

Victoria
Harbour

Wharf

BASTION
SQ.

Trounce

Langley

Fort

Broughton

Courtney

Courtney

Gordon

Humboldt

Library ■

DOWNTOWN

TO ART GALLERY
OF GREATER
VICTORIA (900m),
CRAGDARROCH
CASTLE(1 km),
AND OAK BAY

ℹ

Victoria
Clipper
Ferry ⚓

Blackball
Transport
Ferry ⚓

Empress
Hotel

Penwell

Rupert

Fairfield

Kingston

Cross

Pendray

Belleville

Quebec

Kingston

JAMES BAY

Ontario

Montreal

Niagra

Beckley

Randall

Simcoe

Croft

Oswega

Superior

Almo Pl.

Menzies

Michigan

Government

Parliament
Buildings

Royal
British Columbia
Museum

Elliot

🏛

🚌

Academy

Southgate St.

Humboldt

Corvent

Haywood Av.

Michigan

Perry

Powell

Heather

Young

Toronto

Douglas

Beacon
Hill
Park

0 ——— yards ——— 440

0 ——— meters ——— 400

N 👍

CAMPGROUNDS

The few commercial campgrounds on the perimeter of Victoria cater largely to RVs. Many fill up in July and August; making reservations is a wise idea.

Goldstream Provincial Park, 2930 Trans-Canada Hwy. (391-2300; reservations 800-689-9025), 20km northwest of Victoria. Forested riverside area with great short hiking trails and swimming. From Oct. to Dec., the river is crowded with spawning salmon. Toilets and firewood available. 167 gorgeous, gravelly sites: $18.50. The nearby **Freeman King Visitor Centre** gives the history of the area from the Ice Age to the welfare state. Open daily 9:30am-4:30pm; in winter Sa-Su only.

Thetis Lake Campground, 1938 Trans-Canada Hwy. (478-3845), 10km north of the city center. Sites are not large, but some are peaceful and removed. Thetis Lake is popular among locals for cliff diving. (Cliff diving is not recommended by *Let's Go* or your mother.) Showers (25¢ per 5min.), toilets and laundry. Sites $16; full hookups $20.

☕ FOOD

The limited variety and run-of-the-mill quality of food in Victoria should come as no surprise in Canada's most English city. Many **Government St.** and **Wharf St.** restaurants raise their prices for the summer tourists. **Chinatown** extends from Fisgard and Government St. to the northwest. In **Fernwood Village,** three blocks north of Johnson St. and accessible by bus #10, creative restaurants are scattered among craft shops. **Fisherman's Wharf,** at the corner of Harbour and Government St., is hoppin' with the day's catch as it flops off the boats. For box-wine and a pot-roast, try **Thrifty Foods,** 475 Simcoe St. (544-1234; open daily 8am-10pm), six blocks south of the Parliament Buildings.

John's Place, 723 Pandora St. (389-0711), between Douglas and Blanshard St. Complete with jukebox and Marilyn pinups, John's hops, dishing up Canadian fare with a Thai twist plus a little Mediterranean thrown in. Try John's favorite, *panang goong* (sauteed tiger prawns curry $11.50). Extra selections on Thai night (M) and perogie night (W). Full breakfast menu. Open Su-Th 7am-10pm, F-Sa 7am-11pm.

James Bay Tea Room & Restaurant, 332 Menzies St. (382-8282), behind the Parliament Buildings. Here the sun never set on the British Empire. A trip to Victoria is improper without a spot of tea, and the sandwiches and pastries that accompany tea service ($6.75) or high tea on Sunday ($10) are a lower-key version of the archaic High Tea served at the **Empress Hotel** ($40). Open M-Sa 7am-8pm, Su 8am-8pm.

The Sally Cafe, 714 Cormorant St. (381-1431), off Douglas St., 1 block north of Pandora St. Sally forth into a menu as colorful as the restaurant. Vegetarian-friendly light creations and breakfasts under $7. Open M-F 7am-5pm, Sa 8am-5pm.

Green Cuisine, 560 #5 Johnson St. (385-1809), in Market Sq. The $1.50-per-100g buffet offers so many international foods, including tofu-based ice cream, that even the most carnivorous diners may not mind that the restaurant is all vegan. Fruit shakes $3.50. Buffet 10% off for students and after 5pm. Open daily 9am-9pm.

Contessa Lolas Pizza, 1219 Wharf St. (389-2226). Cheerful decor and $2.50 slices make this a good, quick stop. Salad options include the 16 oz. Roasted Vegetable and Shanghai Wild Rice salad $3.75. Open M-Sa 11am-3am, Su 11am-1am.

Cornucopia Cafe, a tiny kitchen located in the **Ocean Island Backpackers Inn,** serves excellent dinners in the comfortable lounge. Giant pita pizza with rice or soup $5.25, chicken quesadillas $4.75, and micro-brews $3. Open 7pm-1am Su-Th, 5pm-1am F-Sa.

NIGHTLIFE

Victorians may follow the metric system, but their beer is still sold by the pint. English pubs and watering holes abound throughout town, many of which look exactly like one another after a few frothy Guinness. The free weekly *Monday Magazine*, out on Wednesdays, lists who's playing where, and is available at hostels, hotels, and most restaurants downtown. **Boomtown Records,** 105-561 Johnson St. (380-5080), is an excellent spot for info on and tickets to the local rave scene.

The Limit, 1318 Broad St. (384-3557). Rave children flow through this spacious dance venue. Gay-friendly, especially during the drag shows (Su), though it draws all crowds. Techno/House nights (W-Sa) are the most popular, with Friday drawing big-name DJ's and big time covers. Punk (M) and hip-hop (Tu), too. Cover $5-10. Open daily 9pm-2am.

Steamers Public House, 570 Yates St. (381-4340). A happy crowd of UVic neo-hippies and single 30-somethings dance to a nightly live music, from world beat grooves to Celtic to funk. Open stage (M), jazz night (Tu). Lunch specials M-F until 3pm ($5-7); patio seating. Cover $3-5. Open M-Sa 11:30am-2am, Su 11:30am-midnight.

Jet Lounge, 751 View St. (920-7797). Decidedly not an airport bar. A remarkable blend of decadent, plush seating and a frenzied ambient (Tu), acid jazz (W), hip-hop (Th), Top 40 (F-Sa) dance floor. The two rooms offer a choice of beats and atmosphere. Monday nights are ExcEllEnt. Cover $3-5. Open M-Sa 9pm-2am.

Sticky Wicket, 919 Douglas St. (383-7137). A decent English-style pub, the Wicket is one of seven bars and a club in one building, next door to the Strathcona Hotel. **The Roof Top Bar** has a beach volleyball court for rent. Downstairs, **Legends** occasionally brings in big names like Maceo Parker and Clarence "Gatemouth" Brown, but mainly plays Top 40 with ample room and wattage. Legends charges $4 cover F-Sa; the pubs are free and serve food until 1am. Open M-Sa 11:30am-2am, Su 11:30am-midnight.

🎵 ENTERTAINMENT

The **Victoria Symphony Society,** 846 Broughton St. (385-6515), performs regularly under conductor Kaees Bakels. The highlight of its year is the **Symphony Splash,** a free concert on the first Sunday in August, played on a barge in the Inner Harbour. The performance concludes with fireworks and usually draws 40-50,000 listeners. For the last week and a half of June, Victoria bops to **JazzFest** (388-4423).

On Tuesdays, first-run screenings at the **Cineplex Odeon,** 780 Yates St. (383-0513)—and virtually every other first-run theater in Canada—are discounted ($5.25). For more off-beat and foreign films, head to the **University of Victoria's Cinecenta** (721-8365) in the Student Union (bus #4, 26, 11, or 14; $6.50). In June **Phoenix Theaters** (721-8000), at UVIC, puts on plays, as well as term-time live theater performances. From mid-July to mid-August, Victoria goes Elizabethan when the **Annual Shakespeare Festival** (360-0234) lands in the Inner Harbour.

👁 🎭 SIGHTS AND OUTDOORS

If you don't mind becoming one with the flocks of tourists hurling themselves, lemming-like, toward the shores of Victoria, wander along the **Inner Harbour** and watch the boats come in as the sun sets behind the neighboring islands. The fantastically thorough 🏛 **Royal British Columbia Museum,** 675 Belleville St. (recording 387-3014; operator 387-3701), soundly kicks the asses of most West Coast museums. Excellent exhibits on the biological, geological, and cultural history of the province, from protozoans to the present. The First Nations exhibit features a totem pole room and an immense collection of traditional native art. (Open daily 9am-5pm. $9.65, students and seniors $6.65, youth $4, under 5 free.) The museum's **National Geographic IMAX Theater** displays the latest in action documentaries on a screen six stories tall with 12,000 watts of digital surround sound ($9, seniors $8, students $6). **Thunderbird Park** and its many totems loom behind the museum and can be perused for free. The public **Art Gallery of Greater Victoria,** 1040 Moss St. (384-4101), culls magnificent exhibits from its collection of 14,000 pieces covering contemporary Canada, traditional and contemporary Asia, North America, and Europe, and one of the few Shinto shrines outside of Japan. (Open M-W and F-Sa 10am-5pm, Th 10am-9pm, Su 1-5pm. $5, students and seniors $3, under 12 free. Free on M.) The visitor center has info on Victoria's **historic houses and parks.**

The imposing **Parliament Buildings,** 501 Belleville St. (387-3046), home of the Provincial government since 1898, stand opposite the museum. The 10-story dome and vestibule are gilded with almost 50 oz. of gold. At night, strings of white lights line the facade. While the House is in session swing by the **public gallery** and witness Members of the Legislative Assembly discussing matters of great importance. (Open M-F 8:30am-5pm; open Sa-Su for tours only. Free tours leave from main steps in summer daily 9am-4:30pm, 3 times per hr.; call for off-season tour hours.)

The elaborate **Butchart Gardens** (recording 652-5256; office 652-4422), funded by Robert P.'s cement-pouring fortune, sprawl across 50 acres of valley 21km north of Victoria off Hwy. 17. Immaculate landscaping includes the magnificent **Sunken Garden** (a former limestone quarry), the Rose Garden, Japanese and Italian gardens, fountains, wheelchair accessible walking paths, and flowers blooming everywhere. Avoid summer crowds in the late afternoon and see the gardens sparkle with live entertainment and lights at night. Bus #75 Central Saanich runs from downtown at Douglas and Pandora, costs $2.50, and takes about 1 hour. (Open daily July and Aug. 9am-10:30pm; closing time varies. $16.50, ages 13-17 $8.25, ages 5-12 $2, under 5 free. Fireworks on Saturdays July-Aug. around dusk.)

Just north of Fort St. on Wharf St. is **Bastion Square,** the original site of the Hudson Bay Company's Fort Victoria. While the fort no longer stands, the Square is now home to street artists and vendors as well as the **Maritime Museum,** 28 Bastion Sq. (385-4222). Exhibits include ship models, nautical instruments, a torpedo, and the *Tilikum*—a 13m modified native canoe that shoved off from Victoria in 1901 on a daring but unsuccessful trip around the world. The metalwork elevator, the longest continuously running elevator in North America, was installed when the building was the first and only courthouse on Vancouver Island. (Open daily 9:30am-4:30pm. $5, students $3, seniors $4, ages 6-11 $2. Tickets good for 3 days.)

Beyond the "Gate of Harmonious Interest" on Fisgard St. at Government St., **Chinatown** has shrunk to become Chinablock since the end of the legal opium trade. Still, its many restaurants and inexpensive shops make it a worthwhile destination. **Market Square,** the bulk of which lies on Johnson St. four blocks south of Fisgard St., is a collection of countless stores, restaurants, and wooden walkways and home to a popular **public fair** on summer Sundays.

The flowering oasis of **Beacon Hill Park,** off Douglas St. south of the Inner Harbour, and just blocks from downtown, pleases walkers, bikers, and the picnic-inclined. The **Galloping Goose,** a 60km trail beginning in downtown Victoria and continuing to the west coast of Vancouver Island through towns, rainforests, and canyons, is open to cyclists, pedestrians, and horses. The **beach** stretches along the southern edge of the city by Dallas St. Not too sandy, it does sport long shoreline paths and makes a great bike ride or run.

Victoria is a hub for sailing, kayaking, and whale-watching tours. **Ocean River Sports,** 1437 Store St. (381-4233 or 800-909-4233), offers kayak rentals, tours, and lessons. (Open M-Th and Sa 9:30am-5:30pm, F 9:30am-8:30pm, Su 11am-5pm. Rentals per day: single kayak $42, double $50; canoe $40.) Most whale watching companies give discounts for hostel guests. **Ocean Explorations,** 532 Broughton St. (383-ORCA/6722), runs tours in Zodiac raft-boats that visit the three resident pods of orcas in the area. (Runs Apr.-Oct. 3hr. tours $75, hostelers and children $50, less in early season. Reservations recommended. Free pickup at hostels.)

After a few days of hiking, biking, and museum-visiting, unwind with a tour of the **Vancouver Island Brewery** at 2330 Government St. (361-0007). The 1-hour tour is both educational and alcoholic. (Tours F and Sa at 1 and 3pm. $5 covers four 5 oz. samples and a souvenir pint glass. Must be 19.)

SOOKE

About 35km west of Victoria on Hwy. 14 lies the unincorporated town of Sooke, named for the T'sou-ke people. **The Sooke Region Museum,** 2070 Phillips Rd. (642-6351), just off the highway, houses a **visitor center** and delivers an excellent history of the area (open daily July-Aug. 9am-6pm; Sept.-June Tu-Su 9am-5pm; free). To get to Phillips Rd. from the city, take bus #50 to the Western Exchange and transfer to #61. The **Sooke Potholes** are a chain of deep swimming holes naturally carved out of the rock in the narrow Sooke River gorge. These popular and warm waters reputedly host some of the best cliff jumping in the area, in the right holes (*Let's Go* still does not recommend cliff jumping). The potholes are located 5km north of Hwy. 14 on Sooke River Rd. North of Sooke, Hwy. 14 continues along the coast, stringing together two provincial parks and their rugged, beautiful beaches: **Juan de Fuca,** home to China Beach and Loss Creek (both limited to day use), and **French Beach** (391-2300), with tent sites (May-Oct. $12). Short trails connect beaches with road, which is yet far enough away to keep the seaside wild. A longer hike from China Beach leads to the more isolated **Mystic Beach.** Camping in wide open sites is free at the popular **Jordan River Recreation Area,** 10 minutes past French Beach. The **Galloping Goose** bike and horse trail (see p. 270) passes a day-use area and trails heading east and west across the island's southern tip.

The **Sooke River Flats Campsite** (642-6076), Phillips Rd. past the museum, has open sites with a large picnic area, showers, toilets, and running water (gates locked 11pm-7am; sites $15; sani-dump $5). The campsite hosts competitions centered around logging, sharp objects, and family fun on **All Sooke Day,** the third Saturday in July. Sooke is a haven for wealthier Victorians, making cheap indoor accommodations scarce. The **Blackfish B&B,** 2440 Blackfish Rd. (642-6864), 11 km west of the stop light, has an immaculate space with pool, ping-pong tables, and sweeping ocean views (singles $35; doubles $50-70). The bungalow on the pebble beach sleeps 11 (free laundry, full kitchen; $125). Call ahead in summer.

NANAIMO

Primarily a ferry terminal stopover for travelers en route to the rainforests of northern and western Vancouver Island, Nanaimo (na-NYE-moe) appears along the highway as a strip of motels, gas stations, and greasy spoons. While the city does contain a large number of beaches and parks, the semi-urban setting lacks the natural splendor of Vancouver Island's more secluded locations. The silver lining of city life is evident in Nanaimo's ridiculous bathtub boat races, legalized bungee jumping, and the Island's busiest nightlife outside of Victoria.

🔢 ORIENTATION AND PRACTICAL INFORMATION

Nanaimo lies on the east coast of Vancouver Island, 111km north of Victoria on the **Trans-Canada Highway (Hwy. 1),** and 391km south of **Port Hardy** via the **Island Highway (Hwy. 19).** Highway 1 turns into **Nicol St.** and **Terminal Ave.** in Nanaimo before becoming Hwy. 19A. **Nanaimo Parkway** (Hwy. 19) circumvents town to the south.

Trains: VIA Rail, 321 Selby St. (800-561-8630). To Victoria (1 per day, $20). See p. 52 for discounts.

Buses: Laidlaw (753-4371), at Comox Rd. and Terminal Ave. behind Tally Ho Island Inn. To: Victoria (2¼hr., 6 per day, $17.50); Port Hardy (7½hr., 1 per day, $67); Tofino and Ucluelet (4hr., 1 per day, $30).

Ferries: BC Ferries (753-1261 or 888-223-3779), at the northern end of Stewart Ave., 2km north of downtown. To: Vancouver's Horseshoe Bay terminal (8 per day, $9, car $32). The **Scenic Ferry** (753-5141) runs from the Maffeo-Sutton Park in downtown to Newcastle Island just offshore ($4.75; on the hour 10am-7pm).

Car Rental: Rent-A-Wreck, 227 Terminal Ave. S. (753-6461). From $33 per day plus 16¢ per km after 150km. Must be 21 with major credit card. Open M-F 8am-6pm, Sa 9am-4pm, Su 10am-4pm. Free pickup.

Visitor Information: 2290 Bowen Rd. (756-0106), west of downtown. Head south from Terminal Ave. on Comox Rd. which becomes Bowen Rd.; or north from Hwy. 19 on Northfield Rd. Open daily 8am-7pm, in winter 9am-5pm.

Laundromat: 702 Nicol St. (753-9922), at Robins Rd. in Payless Gas Station. 24hr.

Library: 90 Commercial St. (753-1154). Free Internet access. Open M-F 10am-8pm, Sa 10-5pm, Su noon-5pm.

Emergency: 911. **Police:** 303 Pridaux St. (754-2345), at Fitzwilliam St.

Crisis Line: 754-4447. 24hr. **Hospital:** 1200 Dufferin Crescent (754-2141). Open 24hr.

Pharmacy: London Drugs, 650 Terminal Ave. S. (753-5566), in Harbour Park Mall. Open M-Sa 9am-10pm, Su 10am-8pm.

Internet: See **Library,** above. **Tanis' Web Cafe,** 120 Commercial St. (714-0302). $5.50 per hr. Open daily 7am-midnight.

Post Office: 650 Terminal Ave. S., V9R 5E2 (741-1829), in Harbour Park Mall. Open M-F 8:30am-5pm.

Area Code: 250.

■ ACCOMMODATIONS AND CAMPGROUNDS

HOSTELS AND MOTELS

Nicol St. Hostel, 65 Nicol St. (753-1188; gmurray@island.net). A quick walk from the ferry, bus station, or downtown. 25 beds in dorms and private rooms; tent sites ($8) and ocean views in the backyard. Living room, small but tidy kitchen, and bathrooms. Free paint for the ongoing mural. Dorms $15; doubles $30. Private cottage $38.

Cambie Hostel, 63 Victoria Crescent (754-5323). Downtown, in a converted hotel. Rooms have large bunk beds, private bathrooms, and minimal decoration. Less rowdy than its Vancouver sibling, this Cambie also sports a comely pub and a restaurant downstairs. HI members and students $20, others $25; free linen.

Big 7 Motel, 736 Nicol St. (754-2328). Pink-and-blue decor, circa 1986, suggests *Nanaimo Vice.* As compensation, rooms with cable TV, nice beds, and private bathrooms. Singles $38; doubles $40. Less in winter. Reception 24hr.

CAMPGROUNDS

Living Forest Campground, 6 Maki Rd. (755-1755), 3km southwest of downtown. Large, spacious campground (175 sites) with several sites amid cedars overlooking the ocean. Tent sites $15; full hookups $17-19. Clean bathrooms and showers ($1 per 5min.).

Brannen Lake Campsite, 4220 Biggs Rd. (756-0404), 6km north of the ferry terminal. Exit the Island Pkwy. (Hwy. 19). onto Jingle Pot Rd., turn left onto Biggs Rd., roll past the Nanaimo Correction Centre, then look for signs. Shaded sites with moderate privacy on an active cattle ranch. Sites $15; full hookups $18. Showers $1. Free hayrides.

Westwood Lake, 380 Westwood Rd. (753-3922), off Jingle Pot Rd. (see Brannen Lake, above); take bus #5 from the Harbor Park Mall. Only 100m from a busy swimming hole. Full facilities. 66 partially-shaded sites: $16; hookups $19.

◌ FOOD

The highway attracts dives and fast-food joints, many open late or 24 hours. Nosh a Mr. Big from **Thrifty Foods** (754-6273) in the Harbour Park Mall (open daily 8am-10pm). Nanaimo is known throughout Canada for the **Nanaimo bar,** a richly layered chocolate confection of extreme indulgence. Leaving Nanaimo without trying one is like visiting Hope without taking the Rambo Walking Tour (see **Hope,** p. 289).

Gina's Mexican Cafe, 47 Skinner St. (753-5411), up the hill off Front St. A self-proclaimed "Tacky but Friendly Place," Gina's lives up to its billing. Hearty combo plates with quesadillas, burritos, and enchiladas $9. Liters of "perfect" margaritas $17. Open M-Th 11am-9pm, F 11am-10pm, Sa noon-10pm, Su noon-8:30pm.

The Scotch Bakery, 87 Commercial St. (753-3521). Nanaimo Bar addicts come here for a fix (80¢). Giant pretzel pizzas $1. Open M-F 8am-5:30pm.

Dar Lebanon, 347 Wesley St. (755-6524). Sizeable pita sandwiches $4.50-7. Open M-Sa 10am-midnight, Su 4pm-midnight. 15% discount for guests of Nicol St. Hostel.

BROTHER XII, CAN YOU SPARE A DIME?

The new-age-ism common on Vancouver Island got an early start in Nanaimo with a man calling himself Brother XII who heralded the coming of the Age of Aquarius in the 1920s. He developed his own theology and attracted a large cult following among wealthy islanders. Brother XII and his flock left Nanaimo in 1927 to form a Utopia at Cedar-by-Sea on the nearby DeCourcy Island. Stories began to leak from Utopia of Brother XII's greed, his habit of forcing the elderly to commit suicide once they'd left their money to him, and his sketchy personal life. He was put on trial in 1932 and fled to Europe where he died in 1934. When he disappeared, Brother XII supposedly left $1.4 million in gold buried somewhere around Cedar-by-Sea.

■ 🏔 SIGHTS, OUTDOORS, AND EVENTS

The **Nanaimo District Museum,** 100 Cameron Rd. (753-1821), pays tribute to Nanaimo's First Nation and Chinese communities with an interactive exhibit on the Snun¹muxw (SNOO-ne-moo) and a life-size coal mine. (Open daily 9am-5pm. $2, students and seniors $1.75, under 12 75¢.) The **Bastion** up the street was a Hudson's Bay Company fur-trading fort. (Open July-Sept. W-M 10am-4:30pm.)

Petroglyph Provincial Park, 3km south of town on Hwy. 1, protects carvings inscribed by Salish shamans. A menagerie of animals and mythical creatures decorates the soft sandstone. Rubbings can be made from concrete replicas at the base of the short trail to the petroglyphs. The serene **Newcastle Island Provincial Park** (754-7893), accessible only by boat, has 756 automobile-free acres filled with hiking trails, picnic spots, and campsites ($9.50). The **Shoreline Trail** that traces the island's perimeter offers great vantage points of Departure Bay. **Ferries** (753-5141) depart Maffeo-Sutton Park at the Sway-A-Lana Lagoon, near downtown (1 per hour 10am-7pm; $4.50 round-trip). The waters of **Departure Bay** wash onto a pleasant, pebbly beach in the north end of town on Departure Bay Rd., off Island Hwy. **The Kayak Shack,** 1840 Stewart Ave. (753-3234), near the ferry terminal, rents ocean kayaks and canoes (singles and canoes $10 per hr., $40 per day.; doubles $15 per hr., $60 per day). Cyclists should seek out the exceptional deals at **Chain Reaction,** 12 Victoria Crescent (754-3309; basic bikes $12 per day, $8 for Nicol St. Hostel guests; $25 per day full suspension, $40 per weekend; open M-Sa 9:30am-5:30pm).

Adrenaline-junkies from all over the continent make a pilgrimage to the **Bungy Zone,** at 35 Nanaimo River Rd. (753-5867), the only legal jump site in North America. Plummet 42m (140 ft.) into a narrow gorge (water touches available); variations include a zipline and The Swing. (First bungy jump $95, swing $50, zipline $25. 2-for-1 with a rental from Budget, or a coupon from *Entertainment*, free in Nanaimo. HI discount. Each jump after your first, for the rest of your life, costs $25.) To reach the Zone, take Hwy. 1 south to Nanaimo River Rd. and follow the signs. Free shuttles to and from Nanaimo and Victoria. The three-day **Marine Festival** is held during late July (July 20-23, 2000). Highlights include the **Silly Boat Race** and the **Bathtub Race.** Bathers from all over the continent race tiny boats built around porcelain tubs with monster outboards from Nanaimo to Vancouver across the 55km Georgia Strait. Officials hand out prizes to everyone who makes it across, and present the "Silver Plunger" to the first tub to sink. The organizer of this bizarre and beloved event is the **Royal Nanaimo Bathtub Society** (753-7223).

NEAR NANAIMO: PORT ALBERNI

Port Alberni is the only pit stop on Hwy. 4 en route to Pacific Rim National Park. The town bills itself as "The Salmon Capital of the World" and hosts an annual four-day **Salmon Festival** every Labour Day weekend; the festival centers around a daily fishing derby and live entertainment at the Clutesi Haven Marina. **Alberni Marine Transportation** (723-8313 or 800-663-7192 in summer) runs three passenger ferries per week to the island's west coast: Bamfield (4½hr., $20) and on alternate summer days Ucluelet (5hr., $23). The **visitor center** (724-6535), on the highway at the eastern edge of town (open June-Aug. daily 9am-6pm; in winter M-F 9am-5pm). **Sproat Lake Provincial Park,** 13km west of Port Alberni off Hwy. 4, is home to petroglyphs and watersport (44 basic sites $15; 10 sites with showers and toilets $17.50). Sleep in earshot of water rushing over salmon ladders at **Stamp Falls Provincial Park** (sites $9.50; no showers), 20min. away by car on Beaver Creek Rd. For more info on the parks, call 954-4600; for reservations 800-689-9025. **Naesgaard's** (723-3622), a farmer's market just west of town, overflows with fruit and vegetables (open daily 8:30am-8:30pm; in winter M-Sa 9am-6pm, Su 10am-6:30pm).

PACIFIC RIM NATIONAL PARK

A thin strip of land and sea, the Pacific Rim National Park stretches 150km along Vancouver Island's remote Pacific coast. The region's frequent downpours create a lush landscape, rich in both marine and terrestrial life, that has beckoned explorers for over a century. Hard-core hikers trek through enormous old growth along the treacherous **West Coast Trail,** while the shore's long beaches (including **Long Beach**) on the open ocean draw beachwalkers, bathers, sea kayakers, and surfers year-round. Each spring, around 22,000 **gray whales** stream past the park. Orcas, sea lions, black-tailed deer, bald eagles, and black bears also frequent the area.

The park comprises three distinct geographic regions. The southern **West Coast Trailhead** at **Port Renfrew** lies at the end of Hwy. 14. which runs west from Hwy. 1 not far from Victoria. Most access the park's middle section—**Bamfield** and the **Broken Group Islands** in **Barkley Sound**—by water from Port Alberni. Reach Bamfield from Victoria (3½hr. drive via Hwy. 18 and logging roads) or from Port Alberni (1½hr. via logging roads); Hwy. 18 connects to Hwy. 1 at **Duncan** (City of Totems) about 60km north of Victoria. For access to **Long Beach,** at the park's northern reaches, take the stunning drive across Vancouver Island's western ranges on Hwy. 4 to the Pacific Rim Hwy. This stretch connects the towns of sleepy **Ucluelet** (yoo-CLOO-let) and crunchy **Tofino** (toe-FEE-no). Port Alberni lies about a third of the way along the 150km drive from Nanaimo to Ucluelet, on the eastern coast of the Island.

SOUTHERN PACIFIC RIM

A winding, 90-minute drive up Hwy. 14 from Hwy. 1 near Victoria lands you in Port Renfrew. Spread out in the trees along a peaceful ocean inlet, this isolated coastal community of 300 people is the most easily accessible gateway to the West Coast Trail. If you only want to spend an afternoon roughing it, visit the **Botanical Beach Provincial Park.** Nature enthusiasts will delight in the many varieties of intertidal life, and in sandstone, shale, quartz, and basalt formations. Botanical Beach forms one end of a 47km hiking trail, connecting Port Renfrew with **Juan de Fuca Provincial Park** to the east. The other end of the oceanside trail is located at **China Beach,** with several uncrowded forest and beach stops in between; look at the **map** in the Botanical Beach or China Beach parking lots for directions, or stop by the Port Renfrew visitor center 1km east of town on Hwy. 14 (open July-Aug. 9am-7pm). **West Coast Trail Express** (477-8700; www.pacificcoast.net/~wcte) runs one bus per day from Victoria to Port Renfrew (2hr., $30), and one bus from Nanaimo to Port Renfrew, which runs only when at least four people request it (4hr., $50). Reservations are required, and can also be made for drop-off and pickup at certain beaches and trailheads along these routes. The **Juan de Fuca Express** (888-755-6578) operates a water taxi to Bamfield ($76), while the **Pacheedaht Band Bus Service** (647-0090; reservations required) runs the overland trip for less.

Accommodations are limited outside the park campgrounds. Near Port Renfrew and adjacent to the West Coast Trail registration office, the **Pacheenaht Campground** rents tent ($8) and RV sites ($16); tenters can use the Reserve Beach for $6 per night. To wash the trail dust off in Port Renfrew, use the public **shower** ($2 for 10min.) and **laundry** ($2), available at the **Port Renfrew Hotel** (647-5541). Almost all of the restaurants in Port Renfrew are inexpensive. The **General Store** (647-5587; open daily 9am-9pm; in winter 9am-7pm) stocks good ol' raisins and peanuts.

The **West Coast Trail** is demanding and rugged, covering the southern third of the Pacific Rim National Park between Port Renfrew and Bamfield. The route weaves through 77km of primeval forests and waterfalls and rocky slopes, tracing the treacherous shoreline mistaken by navigators as the Juan de Fuca Strait and known to sailors as the "Graveyard of the Pacific." Recommended hiking time is 5-7 days. The adverse combination of foul weather and slippery terrain means that only experienced hikers should attempt this trail, and never alone; each year dozens are rescued/evacuated by Park Wardens. Gray whales, sea otters, and black bears along the route may provide company, but they won't help you in an accident. The trail is regulated by a strict quota system and reservations are necessary to hike it. For information on the illustrious trek, call Parks Canada at 800-663-6000 or write to Box 280, Ucluelet, BC, V0R 3A0. Hikers wind up paying about $120 per person for access to the trail ($25 reservation fee, $70 trail use fee, $25 ferry crossing fee). The trail is open from May 1 to September 30, but you can (and probably should) make reservations three months before the starting date of your hike. Seek out maps, information on the area, and registration information at one of the two the **Trail Information Centres:** in **Port Renfrew** (647-5434), at the first right off Parkinson Rd. (Hwy. 14) once in "town"; or in **Pachena Bay** (728-3234), 5km from Bamfield. (Both open May-Sept. daily 9am-5pm.)

CENTRAL PACIFIC RIM

The **Broken Group's** 100 islands stretch across Barkley Sound and make for some of the best sea kayaking on the island, as well as expensive but high-biodiversity **scuba diving.** Eight islands in the archipelago contain primitive campsites ($5 per person per night). While the Nuu-cha-nulth have navigated these waters for centuries, the Sound can be dangerous to those with less experience; a maze of reefs and rocky islands, combined with large swells, tidal currents, and frigid waters makes ocean travel in small craft hazardous. Paddling from Ucluelet or Bamfield to the islands is possible but not recommended due to the exposed nature of Imperial Eagle and Loudon Channels. **Alberni Marine Transport** (below) and other operators will transport paddlers from Ucluelet to the Broken Group for a fee (Alberni runs M, W, F, Su; $25 per person). For hikers who make it to **Bamfield** without traversing the West Coast Trail, several **short hiking trails** pass through shore and forest at **Pachena Bay, Keeha Beach,** and the **Pachena Lighthouse,** among others.

Hours of logging roads or water travel are the only two ways into Bamfield. Gravel roads wind toward Bamfield from Hwy. 18 (heading west on 18 from Duncan), and south from Hwy. 4 in Port Alberni. **West Coast Trail Express** (see above) runs one bus per day from Victoria to Bamfield (4½hr., $50) and from Nanaimo to Bamfield (3hr., $50); reservations are required. The **Pacheenaht Band Bus Service** (647-5521) provides transportation from Port Renfrew to Bamfield and points between for comparable rates. Because Bamfield lies on two sides of an inlet, water transit is necessary to cross town. **Alberni Marine Transportation** (723-8313 or 800-663-7192) operates a passenger ferry from Port Alberni to Bamfield (4½hr., $20). **Hospital:** 728-3312. **Post office:** across the inlet near the Bamfield Inn, next to the General Store (open M-F 8:30am-5pm). **Postal code:** V0R 1B0. **Area code:** 250.

Accommodations in town are limited. Making camp in the park is a better bet. The **Pachena Bay Campground** (728-1287) offers tree-rich sites just a short walk from the beach (sites $18; RV sites $20; full hookups $25). The **Kamshee Store** (728-3411), offers up groceries and supplies (open daily 9am-9pm, in winter 8am-6pm).

NORTHERN PACIFIC RIM

The northern third of Pacific Rim National Park begins where Hwy. 4 hits the west coast, after a 90-minute drive from Port Alberni (see p. 273). The two towns of Ucluelet and Tofino lie 30km apart at opposite ends of the Pacific Rim Hwy., separated by the lovely and trail-laden Long Beach. Ucluelet remains a quiet fishing village until it floods with travelers every July and August. Tofino, with its tree-hugging populace and nature-hawking outfits, is an increasingly popular resort destination, attracting both backpackers and wealthy weekend-warriors.

🚹 PRACTICAL INFORMATION

Chinook Charters (725-3431) connects Victoria and Nanaimo with Tofino and Ucluelet through Port Alberni. Two buses leave daily in summer from Victoria to Tofino (7hr., $47.50) via Ucluelet (6½hr., $45). The **Link Shuttle** (726-7779) connects Tofino with Long Beach and Ucluelet in the summer (3 per day, $12 round-trip). **Alberni Marine Transportation** (723-8313 or 800-663-7192) operates a passenger freighter in summer from Port Alberni to Ucluelet (5hr., $23). **Tofino Taxi** (725-3333) runs to Long Beach for $5. The Tofino **visitor center** is at 351 Campbell St. (725-3414; open daily July-Aug. 9am-7pm; sporadic hours in winter). **Internet access** is available at the Ucluelet **visitor center,** 227 Main St. (726-4641; open July-Aug. M-F 9am-7pm, Sa 11am-7pm, Su 11am-5pm; Sept.-June M-F 10am-4pm), **Alleyway Cafe** (see below), and the **Tofino Laundromat,** 448 Campbell Ave. (open daily 9am-9pm). **Parks Canada Visitor Information** (726-4212; open mid-June to mid-Sept. daily 9:30am-5pm) is 3km north of the Port Alberni junction on the Pacific Rim Hwy. **Storm Light Marine Station,** 316 Main St. (725-3342; open M-Th 10am-6pm, F-Su 10am-8pm), rents sleeping bags ($12 per day) and tents ($15 per day). **Bank: CIBC,** 301 Campbell St. (24hr. **ATM,** but no currency exchange; open July-Aug. 10am-3pm). **Police:** 400 Campbell St. (725-3242). **Hospital:** 261 Neill St. (725-3212). **Public radio:** 91.5 FM. **Post office:** 161 1st St., V0R 2Z0 (725-3734; open M-F 8:30am-5:30pm, Sa 9am-1pm), at Campbell. **Area code:** 250.

♜ ACCOMMODATIONS, CAMPGROUNDS, AND FOOD

IN UCLUELET. Even in the off-season, beds are steep, and once summer rolls around camping gets expensive too. Travelers without reservations might get shut out of reasonably priced accommodations and forced into a motel room (singles from $75). In Ucluelet there are two cozy B&B's. **Agapé,** 246 Lee St. (726-7073), 4km before town, is a treasure for the price (singles $40-45, doubles $50-65) and serves free hot breakfast. **Radfords,** 1983 Athalone St. (726-2662), off Norah St., is closer to town and rents two quaint singles ($35) and a double ($75), and offers fresh muffins, fruit, and a view of the harbor.

NEAR THE PARK. While there are a number of private **campgrounds** between the park and Tofino, they average at least $22 to camp and $30 for a hookup. The **Park Superintendent** (726-7721) can be contacted year-round for advance information and locals often furnish tips on free camping in the area. **Ucluelet Campground** (726-4355), off Pacific Rim Hwy. in Ucluelet, offers sites in the open (better for sun than for privacy) with showers and toilets ($21; full hookups $25; showers $1 per 5min.; open Mar.-Oct.). The only campground in the park itself is **Greenpoint Campground** (726-4245), 10km north of the park information center. Greenpoint has 94 regular sites and 20 walk-ins, equipped with hot water, toilets and fire rings; despite swarms of mosquitoes and campers in the summer, it offers hedge-buffered privacy ($20; reservations essential, call 800-689-6025). The **golf course** in the park often has private, showerless gravel sites ($15) when no one else does.

IN TOFINO. 🏠 **Whalers on the Point Guesthouse (HI)** (725-3443), on Main St., is a newly-constructed deluxe hostel offering 60 beds (4 to a room), with free sauna, billiards, Sega, linen, and harborside views. ($22, nonmembers $24; private rooms available. Check-in 7am-noon and 5pm-11pm.) **Stephanie's,** 420 Gibson St. (725-4230), is a B&B with three rooms (June-Aug. $55-70; off-season $35-55). Kids are a fixture at Stephanie's, so plan on hanging with the under-10 set. **Wind Rider Guesthouse,** 231 Main St. (725-3240), is all female (except for kids under 12) and has a gleaming kitchen, jacuzzi, and TV room (dorms $25; private room $35 per person; linens $5 extra; check-in 3-6pm).

Shop for groceries at the **Co-op,** 140 1st St. (725-3226; open M-Sa 9am-8pm, Su 11am-5pm). The **Common Loaf Bake Shop,** 180 1st St. (725-3915), is more than just a restaurant/bakery with decent cuisine and baked goods; it's also the best place in Tofino to relax with a paper and a cup of coffee. (Thai and Indian dinners $5-8.50. Open in summer daily 8am-9pm; in winter 8am-6pm.) The adjacent and colorful **Alleyway Cafe,** 305 Campbell (725-3105), has outdoor seating on driftwood benches. The friendly staff serves breakfast all day, spinach and feta quesadillas ($7.50), and burritos ($6.50-7.50), with a side of deliciously free email.

OFF ISLAND. For some R&R try one of the beautiful rooms at **Nielson Island Inn** (726-7968), the only establishment on 20-acre Nielson Island, a 5-minute boat ride from Crab Dock. Enjoy the benefits of a small kitchen (the owner will cook dinner with your ingredients), a lush yard, and a trail around the island (singles $35, doubles $50; free pickup). On Vargas Island, 20 minutes off Tofino, the **Vargas Island Inn** (725-3309), rents guest rooms in a classy lodge and two beach cabins at the foot of a two-hour trail across the island to Ahous Bay, 1½ mi. of unblemished sand. The boat shuttle is free for guests, but hikers can pay $25 and hike to **free camping** at Ahous Bay (no facilities).

🏔 OUTDOORS

ON THE ISLAND. Hiking is the highlight of a trip to the west side of the Island. The trails grow even more beautiful in the frequent rain and fog. **The Rainforest Centre,** 451 Main St. (725-2560), in Tofino, has assembled an excellent **trail guide** for Clayoquot Sound, Tofino, Ucluelet, the Pacific Rim, and Kennedy Lake (available by donation). Park passes cost $8 per day (available in all parking lots); seasonal passes are also available ($45). **Long Beach** is, fittingly, the longest beach on the island's west coast, and is the starting point for numerous hikes. The **Parks Canada Visitor Center** (see above) provides free maps of eight hikes ranging from 100m to 5km in length. The two 1km loops of the **Rain Forest Trail** boardwalk off the Pacific Rim Highway lead through gigantic trees and fallen logs of old growth rainforest. The wheelchair-accessible 0.8km **Bog Trail** illuminates little-known details of one of the wettest, most intricate ecosystems in the park.

In addition to hiking, exceptional **surf** breaks invitingly off **Long Beach** and **Cox Bay** (5km south of Tofino). These two coves funnel large and occasionally dangerous waves toward hordes of young diehards; just don't forget your wetsuit because the Pacific is as cold as it is wet.

OFF THE ISLAND. Every spring **gray whales** migrate past the park and **Clayoquot Sound** north of Tofino. Six or seven stay at these feeding grounds at any time during the summer, surfacing well within view of the shore. Whale-watching tours are cheapest during the migration, in March and April. There are more tour companies than resident whales. **Jamie's Whale Station,** 606 Campbell St. (725-3919 or 800-667-9913), just east of 4th St. in Tofino, runs smooth rides in large boats ($70 per 3hr), but rough-riders choose **Zodiacs** to ride the swells at 30 knots ($50 per 2hr.).

Meares Island, a $20 boat ride from the 4th St. Dock (726-8361), is partially accessible along the gorgeous and unimaginatively named **Big Trees Trail;** an hour-long stroll through truly gigantic trees. It is possible to **kayak** to the island and throughout the sound, though the trailhead is difficult to find. **Pacific Kayak** (725-3232), at Jamie's Whale Station (see above), has the best rates in town (singles $38, doubles $65; multi-day discounts), but will only rent to experienced paddlers.

Hot Springs Cove, an hour north of Tofino by boat, is one of the least crowded hot springs in all of British Columbia. The **Matlahaw Water Taxi** (670-1106), operated by the Hesquiaht First Nation, makes a run or two each day to the cove ($30 per person one-way). The springs are near an exceptionally quiet and lush campground (8 private sites, no showers, terrible water: $15) and a footpath to more secluded

IF A TREE FALLS IN A FOREST, AND 800 CANADIANS ARE THERE TO HEAR IT, DOES IT MAKE A SOUND?

Clayoquot (KLAK-wot) Sound is a 260,000 hectare (624,000 acre) region of lush islands and verdant valleys on west coast of Vancouver Island, and a poster-rainforest for North American environmentalism. The largest episode of civil disobedience in Canadian history unfolded here between July and November of 1993, when over 800 protesters were arrested at logging road blockades. These activists were not all tree-hugging, self-to-tree-chaining eco-zealots, but included students, First Nations leaders, a Member of Parliament, and the Raging Grannies, all united against clearcutting concessions granted to logging companies by the BC government. Since then, conservationists have won several significant battles with logging interests like Macmillan Bloedel (affectionately nicknamed MacBlo). Two years of pressuring *The New York Times* to stop buying Clayoquot pulp ended in success, and in June 1998, MacBlo announced a jaw-dropping plan to replace clearcutting with variable retention logging practices, leaving soils and some trees intact for forest regrowth.

A proposal to make part of the Sound a UNESCO Biosphere Reserve has been submitted to the U.N. in Paris, but environmentalists aren't holding their breath; MacBlo announced its purchase in June 1999 by Wayerhaeuser, an American corporation not obligated to uphold the earlier agreements, only a week after entering into a cooperative venture with the Nun-Chan-Nulth First Nation (Wayerhaeuser has since agreed to honor the memorandum). This may bear bad tidings for the sound as MacBlo and Interfor (International Forest Products) still hold timber rights to two-thirds of Clayoquot Sound, part of the largest chunk of temperate coastal rainforest left on earth. For more info, check out the Friends of Clayoquot Sound (www.island.net/~focs) and MacBlo's Forest Project (www.mbltd.com).

beaches in the Maquinna Marine Park. **Seaside Adventures** (888-332-4252 or 725-2292), at the 1st St. dock in Tofino, makes the round-trip in an afternoon and whale-watches on the way ($75, students and seniors $70, children $60).

NORTHERN VANCOUVER ISLAND

HORNBY AND DENMAN ISLANDS

In the 1960s, large numbers of draft-dodgers fled the U.S. to settle peacefully on quiet Hornby Island, halfway between Nanaimo and Campbell River. Today, hippie-holdovers and a similarly long-haired and laid-back younger generation mingle on the island with descendants of 19th-century pioneers. Low tide on Hornby uncovers over 300m of the finest sand near Vancouver Island. **Tribune Bay,** at the base of Central Rd., is the more crowded of the two beaches (**Li'l Tribune Bay** next door is clothing-optional). The alternative, **Whaling Station Bay,** has the same gentle sands and is about 5km farther north, off St. John's Point Rd. On the way there from Tribune Bay, Helliwell Rd. passes stunning **Helliwell Provincial Park,** where well-groomed trails lead through old-growth forest to bluffs overlooking the ocean. Cormorants dive straight into the ocean, surfacing moments later with trophy-quality fish, while bald eagles cruise on the sea breezes. One or the other beach will always be sheltered from the wind.

The **Laidlaw** (753-4371) bus has a flag stop at **Buckley Bay** on Hwy. 19, where the ferry docks. **BC Ferries** (335-0323) sails nine times per day (round-trip $9; car $22.50). It's a 10-minute ride from Buckley Bay to **Denman Island;** passengers must disembark and trek 11km across the island for another 10-minute cruise to Hornby Island. There are only two roads on Hornby: the coastal **Shingle Spit Rd.** (try saying *that* 10 times fast) and **Central Rd.**, which crosses the island from the end of Shingle Spit. The island has no public transit and is hard to cover without a bike or car. Some foot-travelers ask friendly faces for a lift at Denman or on the ferry.

At the earthy heart of Hornby sits the grocery-bearing **Co-op** (335-1121; open daily 9am-6pm) in the town's **Ringside Market.** The colorful market, at the end of Central Rd. by Tribune Bay, is also home to **visitor center** (335-3233; open 10am-5pm daily), the **post office** (postal code V0R 1Z0; open M-Sa 9:30am-5:30pm), artisanal **gift shops** and two budget- and vegetarian-friendly restaurants that close by 4pm. With light traffic and smooth roads, Hornby Island is easily explored on two wheels. You can rent bikes from **Hornby Island Off-Road Bike Shop** (335-0444; $7 per hr., $25 per day, $30 overnight; open daily 10am-5pm), at the Ringside Market. **Hornby Ocean Kayaks** (335-2726) transports kayaks to the calmest of seven beaches and provides guided tours, lessons, and rentals (tours $30, full day $65; rentals $24 for 4hr., $40 per day). Ask at the info center for listings of **artisan shops and galleries** to visit on the island. The **Hornby Festival** (335-2734; www.mars.ark.com/~festival) of music and whatnot, is at the end of July and beginning of August (performances $5-$15, full pass $165).

If you plan to spend more than a day on Hornby, bring a tent; the B&Bs dotting the island can be expensive during the summer. The **Hornby Island Resort** (335-0136), right at the ferry docks, is a pub/restaurant/laundromat/hotel/campground with a **24-hour ATM** nearby. The fare at the resort's **Thatch Pub** is standard but the view from the outdoor deck is not; the **Wheelhouse Restaurant** has breakfasts (from $9), sandwiches and large salads (from $7), and burgers ($7-8.50), with ocean views from a shared deck. (Pub open daily 11:30am-midnight; live jazz every Friday night at 7pm. Restaurant open daily 9:30am-9pm. Campsites $18; hookups $19; Jan.-Mar. sites $14. Private rooms from $65.) **Bradsdadsland Country Camp,** 1980 Shingle Spit Rd. (335-0757), offers standard tent sites ($20-23 for 2 people in high season; toilets, laundry). Campers at Bradsdadsland bear the iron rule of quiet (only whispers after 11pm, no music ever) in exchange for privacy, clean and capacious sites, and stairs down to the ocean. Book as far in advance as possible.

For those wanting to avoid the Hornby Island late-summer circus, **Denman Island** is a proximate and less over-run approximation. **Tait's Bed and Breakfast,** 2026 Scott Rd. (335-2640; www.mars.ark.com/~gero/bb3/tait.html), a five-minute drive north of town, sits on 15 acres overlooking the sea and serves a full English breakfast (singles $40, doubles $50). You can pitch a tent at serene, beach-side **Fillongley Provincial Park** (335-2325; reservations 800-689-9025), just off Denman Rd. halfway to the Hornby Ferry ($15; pit toilets, water). Or camp for free in the provincial parks at either extremity of the island: the rocky look-out and Douglas Fir forests of **Boyle Point** are in the south (follow Denman Rd. to its terminus; purchase campfire permit at the fire department); **Sandy Island** lies north (no campfires; access at low tide only), a short hike along NW Rd. from the village center, a left onto Gladstone Way and a hoof north toward the island with all the trees.

The Denman village center, perched above the Buckley Bay ferry terminal, offers most crucial amenities: **Denman Island General Merchants** (335-2293), houses the **visitor center,** the **post office** (postal code V0R 1T0), and basic groceries, and rents **bikes** ($15 per day) and **scooters** ($15 for first hr., $5 per additional hr.) with which to explore the island's many little roads (store open M-Th 7am-9pm, F-Sa 7am-11pm, Su 9am-9pm; shorter hours in winter). Next door, the **Cafe on the Rock** (335-2999) serves wine and beer and delicious food at delicious prices (full vegetarian breakfast $6, blackberry pie $3.25, sandwiches from $4; open same hours as general store). The month of June is the season for **Denman Island Garden Tours;** $15 grants access to the flowering yards of Denman's finest gardeners.

COMOX VALLEY

With fine hiking, fishing, and skiing, and the southern regions of Strathcona Provincial Park just a emu's trot away, the tourist season never ends in this self-proclaimed "Recreation Capital of Canada." While every place in the valley seems to provide a view of the same glacier, the area's beaches, trails, and forested swimming holes would take weeks to explore. Sheltering the towns of Courtenay, Comox, and Cumberland, the Comox Valley boasts the highest concentration of artists in Canada, many free museums and galleries, and a remarkable history as a hotbed of union activism in the 1920s. The 1989 discovery of the 80-million-year-old "Courtenay Elasmosaur," which swam in the valley back when the valley was a lake, has transformed the region into a minor mecca of paleontology as well.

⌖ ORIENTATION AND PRACTICAL INFORMATION. Courtenay, the largest town in the Valley, lies 72km (1hr.) north of Nanaimo on the Island Hwy. (Hwy. 19). In Courtenay, the Island Hwy. heading north joins **Cliffe Ave.** before crossing the river at 5th St., intersecting with **Comox Rd.,** and then once again heading north.

Laidlaw (334-2475) buses run to Port Hardy (5hr., $50), Victoria (5hr., $35), and Nanaimo (2hr., $18) from Courtenay at 2663 Kilpatrick and 27th St. by the Driftwood Mall. The **Comox Valley Transit System** (339-5453) connects the valley's own three towns ($1.25, seniors $1; buses run 6:40am-10:20pm). **BC Ferries** (888-223-3779) links Comox with Powell River (1¼hr., 4 per day, $7.50, car $25). The **Bar None Cafe** (see below) has a **ride board.** The **visitor center,** 2040 Cliffe Ave. (334-3234; open M-F 8am-7pm, Sa-Su 9am-5pm; shortened hours in winter), is in Courtenay. **Comox Valley Kayaks** (334-2628 or 888-545-5595) rents them (singles $35 per day, doubles $55), transports them, and leads workshops and full-moon paddles. The **Library,** at 410 Cliffe Ave. (338-1700; open M-F 10am-8pm, Sa 10am-5pm), provides free **internet access,** while **Joe Read's Bookstore and Internet Cafe,** 2760 Cliffe Ave. #5 (334-9723), charges 10¢ per minute. Wash up at **The Pink Elephant,** 339 6th St. (897-6319; wash $1.75, dry 25¢ for 5min.; open M-F 7:30am-9pm, Sa-Su 7:30am-9pm). **Public radio:** 610 AM. **Emergency:** 911. **Police:** 338-1321. **Hospital:** 339-2242. **Weather:** 339-5044. **Post office:** 333 Hunt Place, V9N 7G3 (334-4341; open M-F 9am-5pm). **Area code:** 250.

⌂ ACCOMMODATIONS AND CAMPGROUNDS. The **Comox Lake Hostel,** 4787 Lake Trail Rd. (338-1914), about 8km from town, offers a kitchen, laundry, TV rooms, and doting dogs. Within hiking distance of Strathcona Provincial Park, the hostel is a popular base. To get there, take 5th St. toward the mountains to Lake Trail Rd., turn west and go until you think you've gone too far. Then keep going. (Beds $17; tent sites $10 per person; linen free. Downtown shuttle $3, to the ferry $6; call ahead.) Motels line the highway south of Courtenay, but area B&Bs are cheaper. Close to both Courtenay and Comox, **Estuary House,** 2810 Comox Rd. (890-0130; estuary@island.net), not on Comox Ave., which is connected, has a great view of Comox Glacier. Call for dibs on the enormous front room with deck and nice bathtub (singles $35, doubles $45; private bath). Campers hit **Kin Beach** campground (339-6365), on Astra Rd., past the Air Force base in Comox, just 100m from a long, rocky beach (16 wooded sites $7.50; tennis, pit toilets, water). Despite the trek 25km north from Courtenay, **Miracle Beach** (337-5720; mandatory reservations 800-689-9025), on Miracle Beach Dr., is often full ($15; showers, toilets).

⌕ FOOD. Saturday's conglomerate **Comox Valley Farmers' Market,** off Headquarters Rd., is the most impressive of all the region's markets (May-Sept. 9am-noon). The ▨ **Bar None Cafe,** 244 4th St. (334-3112), off Cliffe Ave. in Courtenay, stocks exceptional vegetarian fare (open M-Sa 8am-7pm). ▨ **The Old House Restaurant,** 1760 Riverside Lane (338-5406), just off 17th St. before the Courtenay River bridge, in a pioneer estate house, grows its own produce in the middle of industrial Courtenay. Smoked emu on a bagel with fruit and salad is $8.45. (Open M-Th 11am-9pm, F 11am-9:30pm, Sa 9:30am-9:30pm, Su 9:30am-9pm.) **Mud Sharks Cafe,** 387 5th St. (338-0939; open M-F 8am-5:30pm, Sa 9am-6pm), up the street, serves filling burritos ($4) and cafe things. Thaw an emu TV dinner from **Safeway** on 8th St., in Courtenay (open M-Sa 8am-9pm, Su 9am-9pm).

SIGHTS AND OUTDOORS. The **Comox Valley Art Gallery**, 367 4th St. (338-6211; open M-Sa 10am-5pm), in the big red building in Courtenay, is a focal point for the local arts community. The **Queneesh Gallery**, 3310 Comox Rd. (339-7702; open 10am-5pm daily; donation requested), in front of the Comox Band big house, displays the work of some of the finest carvers on northern Vancouver Island (of the coast Salish and Kwakwaka'wakw traditions). At 7pm on the 30th of every month a dance performance and speeches are held in the bighouse. Inquire at the **visitor center** about other galleries. The **Courtenay District Museum**, 360 Cliffe Ave. (334-3611), in the old log Courtenay community center, displays exhibits on industry, native culture and art, and pioneers. A paleontology annex features the bevy of dinosaur bones uncovered in the area. (Open daily 10am-4:30pm; in winter Tu-Sa 10am-4:30pm. $2, under 12 free.) Ponder the work of the Canadian military at the **Comox Air Force Museum** (339-8162), on the grounds of CAF Comox Base. The **Heritage Aircraft Park** houses post-WWII fighters and a retired Czechoslovakian MiG-21. (Open June-Aug. daily 10am-9pm; shorter hours in winter. Donation requested.) The **Cumberland Museum**, 2680 Dunsmuir Ave. (336-2445; www.island.net/~cma_chin), displays exhibits on the coal-mining town that was home to the largest Chinese population in North America north of San Francisco in 1920. (Open daily 9am-5pm; in winter closed Su.)

The snowmelt-fed **Puntledge River** at **Stotan Falls**, a long stretch of shallow waters racing over flat rocks, is a great place for **swimming;** test the current and depths before wading or jumping. Coming from Courtenay on Lake Trail Rd., turn right at the stop sign onto the unmarked road at the first "hostel" sign. Take the next left at the logging road Duncan Bay Main, cross the pipeline, then park and descend on either side of the one-lane bridge. For longer trails through the woods try breathtaking **Nymph Falls**, upriver. From Duncan Bay Main, go left on Forbidden Plateau Rd. to the "Nymph" sign. **Horne Lake Caves Provincial Park** (757-8687 or 248-7829; reservations www.hornelake.com), 55km south of Courtenay off the Island Hwy. on Horne Lake Rd., offers caving tours for beginners (2hr.; $15, children $12), five-hour tours involving crawlways and rappelling $79 (must be 15). Or rappel down a seven-story wall in the dark (no novices; $110). Rent boats and rods from **Tiderunner Charters** (337-2253 or 334-7116).

STRATHCONA PROVINCIAL PARK

Elk, deer, marmots, and wolves all inhabit the over 2000 sq. km of Strathcona, one of the best-preserved and most beautiful wilderness areas on Vancouver Island. The park spans a chunk of land just west of the Comox Valley, reaching north to connect with Campbell River via Hwy. 28. The park is accessible from Courtenay or Campbell River. The park's two **visitor centers** are on **Buttle Lake** (open F-Su 9am-4pm), on Hwy. 28 between Gold River and Campbell River, and **Mt. Washington/Forbidden Plateau**, outside Courtenay off Hwy. 19. The two front-country **campgrounds**, with 161 sites between them, are Buttle Lake and Ralph River, both on the shores of Buttle Lake and accessible by **Hwy. 28** and secondary roads (follow the highway signs). **Buttle Lake,** closer to Campbell River (about 45min. of scenic, but winding driving), has comfortable sites, a playground, and sandy beaches on the lake ($15; pit toilets; water). Less crowded **Ralph River** provides convenient access to the park's best hiking trails ($12). Four smaller marine campsites are reachable only by trails (pick up a map at the park entrance). From Ralph River, the difficult 12km **Phillips Ridge** hike (trailhead at the parking lot just south of the campsite along the highway) takes about seven to eight hours round-trip, passing two waterfalls in a 790m/2600 ft. climb and ending atop a wildflower-strewn mountain by an alpine lake. The **Karst Creek Trail,** a mellow 2km hike which passes limestone sinkholes and waterfalls, leaves from just north of the campsite. The **Myra Falls Trail** (trailhead near Phillips Ridge Trail), is a 1km hike from the south end of Buttle Lake to the immense, pounding falls. At the northern end of the park, along the road towards Gold River, **Lady Falls** is a short 20-minute stroll to a viewing platform, and the **Elk River Trail,** a few kilometers down the road, is a more lengthy day or overnight hike along the river for 11km to the trail's terminus at Landslide Lake (about 5hr. one-way; rudimentary camping about 9km in).

Visitors who wish to explore Strathcona's **backcountry areas** must camp 1km from main roads and at least 30m away from water sources; campfires are discouraged in the park. Backcountry campers are rewarded with lakes, waterfalls, ancient cedar and fir forests, and wildflower meadows. Those entering the undeveloped areas of the park should notify park officials of their intended departure and return times, and should be well equipped (**maps** and **rain gear** are essential).

For outfitting and outdoor guidance on the doorstep of the park, **Strathcona Park Lodge** (286-3122; www.strathcona.bc.ca), 30km from Campbell River on Hwy. 28, offers equipment rental and experienced guides (single kayaks $8 per hr., $35 per day; doubles $12 per hr., $50 per day; 17 ft. sailboats $15 per hr., $60 per day; 14 ft. motorboats $12 per hr., $60 per day). Accommodation in one of the lodge's roomy wooden houses is lakefront (two-bunk pad $40, 3-room palace $60). The handsome dining hall serves three buffet-style meals a day (7:30-8:30am $8.50; noon-1pm $9, 5:30-6:30pm $15, 7-8:30pm a la carte).

Skiers and snowboarders hit the slopes just outside the park boundaries at **Mt. Washington** (338-1386; www.mtwashington.bc.ca) and the smaller but more snowboarder-friendly **Forbidden Plateau Ski Resorts.** Each opens a chairlift in summer for the vista hungry, and Forbidden Plateau has particularly extensive summer trails for hiking, mountain biking, and last-minute snowmen. The 5km hike up the ski slope and to the top of Mt. Becher peaks with a 360° view of the outlying Comox Valley and Georgia Strait. Both resorts are accessible from Duncan Bay Main; Mt. Washington is at the end of Tsolum Main, which becomes Strathcona Parkway, and Forbidden Plateau sits at the end of a winding, gravelly half-hour on Forbidden Plateau Rd. For information on the park, contact BC Parks, District Manager, Box 1479, Parksville, BC, V9P 2H4 (954-4600).

CAMPBELL RIVER

The Big Rock covered with graffiti welcomes visitors to Campbell River, another of BC's many "Salmon Capitals of the World." The town can claim incredible fishing and scuba diving called "second only to the Red Sea" by *National Geographic*. The number of gas stations illustrates Campbell River's role as the transportation hub of the island's north. It provides easy access to Strathcona Provincial Park, Port Hardy, and Quadra, Cortes, and Discovery Islands.

Campbell River hums 42km north of Courtenay on the Island Hwy. (Hwy. 19). **Laidlaw** (287-7151), at 13th and Cedar, sends buses to Nanaimo (4 per day, $22). **BC Ferries** (888-223-3779) runs to Quadra Island (15 per day; $4.50, cars $11.50, ages 5-11 $2.25). **Rent-a-Wreck,** 1300 Homewood (287-4677; open M-F 8am-5pm, Sa 8am-4pm), rents for $30 per day, plus 15¢ per km after 100km. The **visitor center** (287-4636; open daily 8am-6pm; in winter M-F 9am-5pm) is off the Island Hwy. near the Tyee Mall. The **laundromat** is in the Tyee Mall (open daily 8am-10pm). **Public radio:** 91.2 FM. **Weather/wishful thinking:** 28-SHINE/287-4463. **Emergency:** 911. **Hospital:** 375 2nd Ave. (287-7111). **Crisis line:** 287-7743. **Police:** 286-6221. **Area code:** 250.

Alder House B&B, 582 Alder St. (287-4022), near downtown, dispenses relaxing oils and aromas (singles from $35; doubles from $45). The best camping near town is at **Quisam Campground,** in Elk Falls Provincial Park, on Hwy. 28, with space among firs ($12; pit toilets). **Strathcona Provincial Park** (see above) is next best.

The **Campbell Restaurant** (286-6913), at 11th Ave. and Shopper's Row, serves cheap lunch specials (chicken chow mein $5.25) and Chinese smorgasbords (lunch M-F noon-1:30pm $7.25; dinner daily 5-8pm $9). The **Beehive Cafe,** 921 Island Hwy. (286-6812), has a deck near the water. Breakfast and lunch run $6 and up (open daily 6:30am-10pm; in winter M-F 7am-3pm and Sa-Su 7am-5pm). Shop for hard honey at **Super Valu** (287-4410; open daily 8:30am-9:30pm) in the Tyee Mall.

Sockeye, coho, pink, chum, and chinook **salmon** are hauled in by the boatload from the waters of the Campbell River. The savvy can reap the fruits of the sea from **Discovery Pier** in Campbell Harbour, and the unskilled can at least buy rich ice cream and fro-yo on the pier. (Fishing charge $1; rod rentals $2.50 per hr., $6 per half-day.) The pier has an artificial reef built to attract fish. Get a **fishing licence** at the visitor center or any sports outfitter in town. A "salmon sticker" costs extra.

Scuba gear rentals can be pricey and require proper certification, but **Beaver Aquatics,** 760 Island Hwy. (287-7652; open M-Sa 9am-5pm, Su 10am-2pm), offers a nifty $25 **snorkeling** package including suit, mask, snorkel, and fins. Tour the **Quinsam River Salmon Hatchery,** 4217 Argonaut Rd. (287-9564; open daily 8am-4pm), and see a wealth of "natural" resources. The hatchery provides a sheltered area for young fishies to develop, blissfully unaware of the perils on the pier.

QUADRA ISLAND

The pastoral haven of Quadra lies a 10-minute ferry ride from the quickly-growing city of **Campbell River.** Quadra boasts pleasing landscapes that rival her southern Gulf Island cousins, a European history that is older than that of most settlements on Vancouver Island, and a thriving First Nation community around the village of Cape Mudge. Quadra's lighthouse aided coastal steamers long before there were many other settlers on Vancouver Island, a history documented in photos at Heriot Bay Hotel (established 1894), where steamer crews stopped for R&R. The ▧ **Kwagiulth Museum and Cultural Centre** (285-3733), in the village of Cape Mudge, just south of Quathiaski Cove, houses a spectacular, haunting collection of Potlatch regalia confiscated by the government early this century and not returned until 1988. (Open M-Sa 10am-4:30pm, in summer also Su noon-4:30pm. $3, seniors $2, children $1. Tours $1.) Local artists carve next door in public (F-Sa 10am-3pm).

BC Ferries sail to Quadra 17 times per day from Campbell River (888-223-3779; $4.50, cars $11.50, ages 5-11 $2.25, under 5 free). **Quadra Foods** (285-3391; open daily 9am-7:30pm), **Quadra Credit Union** (285-3327; 24hr. **ATM**), and a **visitor center** (with maps of island trails) await at the first corner of Harper Rd. Buy **fishing licences** and tackle at **KT's General Store** (285-2734), just down the street in the Village Square. For **sea kayak** rental call 287-0635, for **canoes** to explore Quadra's scenic lakes 285-3601, and for **bicycles** 285-3601. **Emergencies: 911. Police: 285-3631. Ambulance: 286-1155.** Several minutes down Heriot Bay Rd. from the otherworldly beauty of **Rebecca Spit Provincial Park** (day use only) and **Heriot Bay,** the **We Wai Kai Campsite** (285-3111; sites $17; toilets, water, coin showers) lies on the water.

THE PORT McNEILL AREA: ALERT BAY, SOINTULA, AND TELEGRAPH COVE

The protected waters and plentiful fish of Johnstone Strait provide a fine summer home for **orca pods.** Mainland and island settlements near Port McNeill provide fine quiet waterside trips. Sighting charters run $60 for three to four hours, but lucky visitors can glimpse the orcas from the ferry between Port McNeill, Sointula, and Alert Bay, or even the shoreline. For the best whale-watching, head 25km south of Port McNeill to the boardwalk town of **Telegraph Cove;** turn left south of town on the Island Hwy.; over the last 5km, it becomes a rough gravel road. **North Island Kayaks** (949-7707), in Port Hardy (see below), will drop off and pick up kayaks in the cove (single kayaks $35 per day; doubles $55).

Tiny Cormorant Island and the town of **Alert Bay** is home to a fabulously rich repository of native culture. The cultural legacy of several groups of the **Kwakwaka'wakw** peoples (ka-kwak-QUEW-wak; formerly known as the Kwakiutl or Kwagiulth) sets the fishing village apart from its aquatourist siblings; its 173-foot totem pole is the second largest in the world (Victoria slapped a few extra feet onto its old one to claim the prize). Two kilometers north of the ferry terminal, the pole towers over the **U'Mista Cultural Center** (974-5403; open daily 9am-6pm; in winter M-F 9am-5pm), which houses an astonishing array of Kwakwa̱ka'wakw artifacts repatriated decades after Canadian police pillaged a potlatch. *U'Mista* means "the return of a loved one taken captive by raiding parties." **Sointula,** on the coast of Malcolm Island, is a modern artist and fishing community with Finnish roots known for its early December Christmas bazaar.

   Laidlaw (956-3556) runs one bus per day to Port McNeill (45km southeast of Port Hardy and 180km northeast of Campbell River) from Victoria (8hr., $79). **BC Ferries** (956-4533) runs from Port McNeill to Sointula on Malcolm Island (25min.) and Alert Bay (40min., frequent daily service 8:45am-10:05pm; round-trip $5.50, car and driver $19.25). **Visitor centers** are stationed right by the ferry docks in Port McNeill (956-3131; open daily 9am-5pm in summer) and Alert Bay (974-5024). **Hospital:** 182 Fir St. (974-5585), in Alert Bay. **Police:** 974-5544, in Alert Bay. **Area code:** 250.

   The **Pacific Hostelry (HI),** 349 Fir St. (974-2026), remains a welcome spot to play piano and whale-watch from the roomy living room ($17, nonmembers $19). Beautiful camping is available across the island at **Bere Point Regional Park** (12 free sites with pit toilets), with a view of the mainland coastal range and hiking trails along the coast. The budget-mindful eschew island restaurants for the hardtack at **Blueline Supermarket,** 257 Fir St. (974-5521; open M-F 9am-9pm, Sa 9am-6pm, Su 10am-5pm). The **Killer Whale Cafe** (928-3131) is all yellow cedar and stained-glass (sandwiches $4-7; dinner from $11; open 7am-4pm and 5-9:30pm daily).

PORT HARDY

Port Hardy remains chiefly interested in being a quiet logging and fishing community, notwithstanding its status as the southern terminus for the BC Ferries route up the Inside Passage. The chainsaw-carved welcome sign is a relatively new addition, erected for the 1500 passengers who sleepily disembark the ferry every other night. These transients join a surge of fishermen preparing for unpredictable fall fisheries openings up the coast, and a growing indigenous population, drawn from more remote towns for schooling and employment.

🛈 ORIENTATION AND PRACTICAL INFORMATION. Port Hardy is the northernmost town on Vancouver Island, perched 39km north of Port McNeill and 225km (2½hr.) north of Campbell River on Hwy. 19. Market Street is the main drag, running through the shopping district and along a **seaside path.**

   Laidlaw (949-7532), on Market St. opposite the visitor center, runs to Victoria (8¾hr., $84) via Nanaimo (6hr.; $67) each day at 8:45am and whenever the ferry arrives. **BC Ferries** (949-6722 or 888-223-3779) depart 3km south of town at **Bear Cove,** every other day for Prince Rupert (mid-June to mid-Sept. $104, with car $318; 10% off in early June and after Sept. 14; 30% off mid-March to June; 45% off mid-Oct. to mid-Dec.); in winter every Saturday and every second Wednesday. In summer, book months ahead for cars. **North Island Taxi** (949-8800) services the ferry from all over town for $5.25 per person. To reach the **visitor center** at 7250 Market St. (949-7622), take Market Bay Rd. off Hwy. 19 to Market St. (Open M-Sa 8am-9pm, Su 9am-9pm; in winter M-F 9am-5pm.) The **Port Hardy Museum** (see below) also has in-depth information on the region. The **CIBC bank,** 7085 Market St. (949-6333; open Tu-Sa 10am-4:30pm), has a 24-hour **ATM. North Star Cycle and Sports** (949-7221; open daily 9:30am-6pm), at Market and Granville St., rents bikes ($20 per day); for all else, there's **Jim's Hardy Sports,** 7125 Market St. (949-8382; open M-W 9am-6pm, Th-Sa 9am-7pm, Su 11am-5pm). Wash up at **Payless Gas Co.** on Granville St. (949-2366; wash $1.75, dry 25¢ per 7min; open 24hr.). **Internet access** is free at the **library,** 7110 Market St. (949-6661), and $5 per hour at **Cape Scott Cybernet,** 9300 Trustee Rd. (902-0577), in the old North Island Mall above town. **Police:** 7355 Columbia St. (949-6335). **Crisis line:** 949-6033. **Hospital:** 9120 Granville St. (949-6161). **Radio:** CBC 95.5FM; local low-down CFNI 1240 AM. **Postal code:** V0N 2P0. **Area code:** 250.

⌐ ACCOMMODATIONS AND CAMPGROUNDS. The visitor center (949-7622) will reserve B&B rooms for free (call ahead on ferry nights). **This Old House,** 8735 Hastings (949-8372; oldhouse@island.net), downtown by the bus station and minutes from the beach, rents cosy rooms with balconies upstairs (shared bath; singles $40, doubles $70) and singles with kitchenettes in the basement (first night only $25, then $20). The proprietors of **The Hudson's Home B&B,** 9605 Scott St. (949-5110; dnhudson@island.net), provide all the TLC and custom breakfasts you can handle, then offer a botanist's tour of town. (Singles $50, doubles $65, cot $15. 10% off or a packed lunch with mention of *Let's Go;* pickup and drop-off.) Quiet, wooded sites at **Quatse River Campground,** 8400 Byng Rd. (949-2395; toilets, showers, laundry; $14, full hookups $18) are a 25-minute walk from town but just minutes from the **Roadhouse Cafe** (see below). The camp shares space with a **fish hatchery** (949-9022; tours are best Sept.-Nov.). Sites amid an overgrown garden at **Wildwoods Campsite** (949-6753; $10, hookups $15, hikers $5, bikers $7) lie off the road to the ferry, a walk to the terminal but a hike from town.

☐ FOOD. For vine-ripe tomatoes and a coconut donut, roll up Market St. to **Overwaitea Foods,** 950 Granville St. (949-6455; open Sa-W 9am-7pm, Th-F 9am-9pm). The burger is this town's budget meal. One of the best, for $6, drips at **I.V.'s Quarterdeck Pub,** 6555 Hardy Bay Rd., on the scenic fishing dock (949-6922). Their great vegetarian selection pales next to 29¢ Wednesday wings (open daily 11am-midnight). **Little Bit's,** 7035 Market St. (949-8989), has specialty coffees, $5 lunch specials, and an Indonesian plate on Wednesday and Fridays (open M-Th 9am-6pm, F-Sa 9am-9pm). The **Oceanside Cafe,** 6435 Hardy Bay Rd. (949-7115), just down from I.V.'s at the Glen Lyon Inn, has a terrific view and serves great breakfast (eggs benedict with hashbrowns and toast $4; open daily 6:30am-9pm). **The Roadhouse Cafe,** 4965 Byng Rd. (949-7575; open daily 6:30am-7:30pm), just out of town near the Quatse River Hatchery, serves a Lumberman's breakfast for $7.45.

◙ ⚄ SIGHTS AND OUTDOORS. The **Port Hardy Museum and Archives** is at 7110 Market St. (949-8143), beneath the library. This museum's sea-creature remnants, 19th-century Cape Scott pioneers' personal effects, 8000-year-old tools from Hardy Bay, and erudite curator merit a visit. The bookshop sells trail and outdoor guides. (Open M-Sa 10am-5pm; shortened hours in winter. Donation requested.) A 15-minute drive from town brings picnickers to the hard sand of **Stories Beach,** a good place to put in a kayak. Turn left off the Island Hwy. onto Byng Road. Nearby, the **Copper Maker,** 114 Copper Way (949-8491; usually open 9am-5pm), commissions some of the finest Kwakiutl carvers in the region. From Byng Rd., turn left onto Beaver Harbour Rd., right on Tsak'is Way, and right again. Farther down Tsak'is Way, a ceremonial and community **bighouse** overlooks the sea from the heart of Fort Rupert village, a site inhabited by the Kwakiutl for thousands of years. **Petroglyphs** adorn rocks near **Fort Rupert;** ask at the museum for advice in locating them at low tide. At the north end of the village stands the decaying stone chimney of Fort Rupert, a prospecting outpost built in 1849 by the Hudson's Bay Company.

A map of logging roads from the visitor center will allow you to explore the **geological curiosities** of the region's limestone bedrock: Devil's Bath sinkhole, the Vanishing and Reappearing Rivers, and several spelunkable caves are all located toward **Port Alice** (40min. from town). **Odyssey Kayaking** (902-0565; odyssey@capescott.net) can equip and transport you. (Singles $35 per day; doubles $55. Must be 19 and have one experienced paddler in your group.) The Port Hardy area is known for some of the world's best **cold-water diving; Sun Fun Divers** (956-2243; www.sunfundivers.com) rents gear ($60-80), and runs half-day ($60) and full-day ($80) trips out of Port Hardy and Port McNeill.

VANCOUVER & ISLANDS

CAPE SCOTT PROVINCIAL PARK

Off the Island Hwy. just out of Port Hardy, 60km of gravel logging roads snake across the wild and wet North Island toward the Pacific coast; parking at various trailheads provides access to isolated gray sand beaches. Carry a good spare, keep your headlights on, and yield to the logging trucks. Shake off the road dust (or dry off, as the case may be) three-quarters of the way in at the locally famous **Scarlet Ibis Pub** (288-3386), overlooking Holberg Inlet, and across it the small logging hamlet of **Holberg**. Off the main road past Holberg a 15-minute drive down Ronning Main on the left leads to a rugged, one-hour trail to a sandy beach at **Raft Cove Provincial Park** more secluded than the Cape Scott beaches. Remarkable **Ronning Garden** is farther along and a short hike off the main road, the work of a turn-of-the-century botanically-crazed pioneer (free).

A 100km trail connecting Port Hardy to the depths of **Cape Scott Park** is under construction, but until its completion, the area is accessible at the end of the main road from the lot on San Josef Road near the park entrance (follow signs from Holburg). A mellow 2.5km (30min.), wheelchair-accessible trail leads to **San Josef Bay** and campsites (pit toilets, water), around a rocky corner on the second northerly beach. Backpackers can also depart the parking lot for the 23.6km trail to **Cape Scott,** the spectacular northwestern tip of the island. On the way, hikers can overnight on the beaches at **Nels** (16.8km or 6hr. in; pit toilets) or **Experiment Bights** (18.9km or 6½hr. in. $3 per person per night user fee for the park; self-register at the trailhead.) For more detailed info on the park, pick up the Cape Scott Provincial Park **pamphlet** at one of the visitor centers in the region, since none are available at this sporadically patrolled park (May-Sept.). Or contact BC Parks (250-954-4600). The scenery varies, but the weather may not—bring rain gear.

THE GULF ISLANDS

Midway between Vancouver and Victoria, the **Gulf Islands** are a peaceful retreat from urban hustle. While the beaches are uniformly rocky, the islands are known for a contagiously relaxing lifestyle, and excellent kayaking and sailing opportunities afforded by protected waters. Bald eagles and river otters inhabit many inlets and islands. The chain's five main islands, **Galiano, Mayne, Pender, Salt Spring,** and **Saturna** are visited by BC Ferries (250-386-3431; www.bcferries.bc.ca) at least twice a day in summer with service to Vancouver and Victoria.

SALTSPRING ISLAND

Named for a dozen brine springs discovered on its northern end, **Salt Spring** is the largest (185 sq. kms) and most populous of the islands, and has the widest range of activities and accommodations. Inhabited by the Coastal Salish since at least 1800 BC, the island has been a refuge to many groups since. The first permanent residents of Salt Spring were African-Americans who moved north from California in the 1850s. Salt Spring in the 1960s was a popular destination for American draft-dodgers, while in the 70s and 80s it lured retirees. The island is currently a haven for Vancouver artists.

◪ **PRACTICAL INFORMATION.** Life in Salt Spring Island is centered around the small village of **Ganges**; all of the listings below are in Ganges unless otherwise specified. **BC Ferries** (888-223-3779) from Vancouver Island arrive in Fulford Harbor, 14.5km south of Ganges, while ferries from Vancouver and the other Gulf Islands dock at the **Long Harbor** wharf, 6km northeast of town. In the summer, the **Gulf Island Water Taxi** (537-2510) runs to Galiano and Mayne Islands each Wednesday and Saturday ($15 round-trip, bikes free; departs 9am; returns 4:40pm). **Silver Shadow Taxi** tends to the carless (537-3030). **Heritage Car and Truck Rentals,** 161 Lower Ganges Rd. (537-4225), rents from $20 per day, plus 15¢ per km after 50km (open 8am-4pm daily; reserve ahead in summer). The **Bicycle Shop,** 131 McPhillips

Ave. (537-1544; open M-F 10am-5pm) rents them for $15 per day, as does the hostel. The **visitor center,** 121 Lower Ganges Rd. (537-5252), is predictably helpful. (Open July-Aug. daily 9am-6pm; call for winter hours). **Emergency:** 911. **Police:** (537-5555) on the outskirts of town on Lower Ganges Rd. **New Wave Laundry:** (527-2500), on Upper Ganges Rd. next to Moby's Marine Pub (see **Food**); wash $1.75, dry 25 cents per 8min (open Th-M 8am-10pm, Tu-W 8am-6pm). **Public Showers**: beneath Moby's Marine Pub ($1 per 5min). **Post office:** 109 Purvis Ln., V8K 2P1 (537-2321), in the plaza downtown. Open M-F 8:30am-5:30pm, Sa 8am-noon. **Internet Access: Island Books Plus,** (537-2812) 104 McPhillips Ave., $5 per hr., $3 per 30min. (open daily 8:30am-6pm); **Ganges Stationery,** (537-0665), 166 Fulford-Ganges Rd., $6 per hr. (open M-F 9am-5:30pm, Sa 10am-5pm). **Area Code:** 250.

■■ ACCOMMODATIONS, CAMPGROUNDS, AND FOOD.

Salt Spring offers a wealth of both food and B&Bs (from $70), despite its small size. The least expensive beds on the island are 8 km south of Ganges in the **Salt Spring Island Hostel (HI),** 640 Cusheon Lake Rd. (537-4149; open Apr. to mid-Nov.). In addition to two standard dorms in the comfortable home ($15.50; nonmembers $19.50), the hostel's 10 fern-covered acres also hide three teepees which sleep 3, and two handcrafted Winnie-the-Pooh style **treehouses** that sleep 2-4 ($30 per person). **Wisteria Guest House,** 268 Park Dr. (537-5899), on an acre of gardens near the village, comes highly recommended for its delicious breakfasts and reasonable prices ($55-80). The five rooms at **Tides Inn,** 137 Lower Ganges Rd. (537-1097), overlooking downtown Ganges, are also inexpensive (double with shared bath $50).

Ruckle Provincial Park (877-559-2115 or 391-2300), 23.5km southeast of Ganges, has the only public camping. Its 78 walk-in sites on the unsheltered Beaver Point overlook the ocean ($12).

Dares to be Different (537-0005), 112 Hereford Ave., sells everything from fruit to flax and doubles as an excellent vegetarian restaurant. Entrees (like a big ol' veggie burger with apricot chutney) run $7.50-10.50 and are served with a salad and classical music (open M-Sa 9am-9pm, Su 11am-9pm; in winter M-Sa 9am-8pm). The **Tree House Cafe** (537-5379), 106 Purvis Lane, delivers interesting and tasty sandwiches ($4.25-7) in the shade of an old plum tree, and open-mic Thursdays at 8pm. Spacious **Moby's Marine Pub,** 124 Upper Ganges Rd. (537-5559), a two-minute walk north of the village, is no typical harborside dive. Pints or "sort-of-famous" margaritas $4.50. Live jazz on Sundays. Score cantaloupes and Raisin Bran at **Thrifty Foods,** 114 Purvis Ln. (537-1522; open daily June-Sept. 8am-9pm, in winter 8am-8pm). **Barb's Buns,** 121 McPhillips Ave. (537-4491), is the place to pick up quality organic baked goods. (Loaves $3; 2-day olds 75% off. Open M-Sa 6am-5:30pm).

ACTIVITIES. A self-guided **studio tour** introduces visitors to the residences of 35 artisans around the island; pick up a brochure at the visitor center. Performances at the **ArtSpring** (537-2102), 100 Jackson Ave. generally cost $12-25, but exhibitions are free. March is **Erotic Month** at the theatre, with all the dance performances, sexy mimes, and risque clowns that entails. The century-old **Fall Fair** (537-8840), held the third weekend of September, draws farmers from all over the islands to display their produce, animals, and crafts with pride. The **Saturday Market** is a smaller version held in downtown's **Centennial Park** from Easter to Thanksgiving.

Wallace Island and **Prevost Island** are two excellent kayaking daytrips from Salt Spring. **Sea Otter Kayaking** (537-5678), located on Ganges Harbor at the end of Rainbow Rd., rents boats to experienced paddlers only (singles $20 per 2hr., $45 per day; doubles $40 per 2hr., $80 per day). They also run 2hr. introductory certification courses ($35), sunset and full-moon guided tours (3hr.; $35), and multi-day excursions, and offer a 15% discount to hostel guests.

Five of Salt Spring's ten freshwater lakes are open to the public for swimming. **Blackburn Lake,** 5km south of Ganges on Fulford-Ganges Rd., is one of the less crowded spots, and is clothing-optional. **Hiking** and **biking** options are somewhat limited on Salt Spring due to the small and residential nature of the islands, as well as the twistiness and narrowness of the roads. **Ruckle Provincial Park** offers 200

VANCOUVER & ISLANDS

acres of partially settled land to explore, and an 11km waterfront trail. One excellent vista, truly stunning at sunset, is **Mt. Maxwell,** 11km southwest of Ganges on Cranberry Rd.

PENDER ISLAND

Pender is actually two islands that total 26km in length, joined by a small bridge. With only 2000 residents, Pender lacks the kind of social focal point that Salt Spring's downtown provides, but has similarly exceptional kayaking and sailing. BC Ferries arrive at Otter Bay, on the larger North Pender Island. **Mouat Point Kayaks** (629-6767) at the Otter Bay Marina, a 5min. walk from the ferry terminal, rents to experienced paddlers (single kayak $20 per 2hr., $40 per day, $20 per additional day; double $30 per 2hr., $60 per day, $30 per additional day). The marina (629-3579) is also a convenient location to **rent bikes** ($5 per hr., $25 per day), take a **shower** ($1 per 4min.), or do **laundry** ($2.50). If stuck waiting for the ferry, the nearby **Pender Island Golf and Country Club,** (629-6659) 2305 Otter Bay Rd., offers 9 holes only 1km away ($17, club rental $7.50; open daily 8am-8pm in summer).

The post office, gas station, bakery and grocery store are all located at the **Driftwood Centre,** on Harbour Rd. in the center of North Pender. There is **no ATM** on the island, but **Thrifty Foods** (629-8322), in the Center, allows customers to take out extra cash on a debit or credit card (open M-Sa 9am-9pm, Su 9am-7pm). Outside of the grocery store, food is scarce. **Memories Restaurant at the Inn,** 4209 Canal Rd. (629-3353), bakes gourmet pizzas on homemade dough from 5:30-8pm nightly. The **visitor center,** (629-6541) 1km from the ferry terminal, can make additional recommendations (open May-Aug. 9am-5pm daily).

Cooper's Landing, 5734 Canal Rd. (888-921-3111; www.victoriabc.com/accom/cooperslanding) at the junction of the two islands, offers the only hostel-style lodging on Pender ($18 bunks in 4 person-rooms; 2 double beds with private kitchen $80). The Landing also doubles as a kayak, canoe, and diving outfit, running guided trips out of the secluded bay (kayaks $12.50 per hr.; diving $75 per person, 2 tanks). The Landing is adjacent to **Mortimer Spit,** one of the few sandy beaches on the islands. Campers have several options. **Prior Centennial Provincial Park** (391-2300) maintains 17 wooded sites 6km from the ferry on Canal Rd. near the bridge joining North and South Pender ($12; pit toilets), arrive early in summer. On South Pender, the more secluded **Beaumont Provincial Marine Park** requires a boat or a 30min. hike from the road to reach its 15 beachside sites ($5 per person). For showers, head to the **Port Browning Marina** (629-3493), on North Pender at the end of Hamilton Rd. (off Harbour Rd.). The $10 charged for tent sites on the field overlooking the harbor includes the use of the facilities and pool.

OTHER ISLANDS

Of the three remaining islands, **Galiano,** 29km long and 3km wide, is the largest and farthest north. Like all five of the main Gulf Islands, Galiano offers kayak rental facilities and plenty of coast to explore. In addition to the bevy of B&Bs, there are 40 campsites available at **Montague Harbour Park** (539-2115; pit toilets, no showers), on the island's southern and more populated end.

Mayne Island, roughly the same size as Pender but with only half the population, is situated between Galiano and Pender. One of the first places in BC to grow apples at the turn of the century, Mayne is now home to a number of artists and craftspeople, over a dozen B&Bs, and little else.

Residential **Saturna** is the smallest and southernmost of the Gulf Islands, with only 300 permanent residents. The island hosts a smattering of B&Bs but no public campgrounds or hostels, making budget travel difficult. Saturna does have a **general store** (539-2936), for conventional groceries and organic foods. For more information, try the island's website at www.saturnatour.bc.ca.

SOUTHERN BC & THE ROCKIES

From the jagged snow-capped Rocky Mountains, the Fraser River courses and hurtles its way through 1300km of steep canyons and plateaus on its journey toward more arid land and then the Pacific. The sweeping agricultural basin in the middle of BC between the Rockies and the Coast Range mountains sees much more sun than the coast and is a vacation hot spot for sun-worshiping city-slickers and back-country adventurers alike. Eastern Washington State to the south is similarly shaded by the big city to the west and the big hills to the east.

The Rockies are the sharp towering crags whose breaching by rail lines united Canada. They are still etched on its psyche, and are home to hugely popular national parks and countless thousands of square kilometers of hikable, climbable, campable terrain. To their east, the gaping prairie, oil-fired economy, and conservative politics of Alberta make it to Canada what Texas is to America. Petro-dollars have given birth to gleaming, modern cities on the plains, while the natural landscape swings from the mighty Canadian Rockies down to beautifully desolate and fossil-rich badlands.

Bus and train routes cross the interior and pass by various means through the mountains. **Moose Run Adventure Tours** (888-388-3881) runs entertaining 10-day trips from Vancouver to Jasper and Banff. Passengers are welcome to jump off and on either of the two vans that run per week. A $350 fee covers transportation, park fees, and a good laugh; but not the HI accommodations, food, or entertainment.

HIGHLIGHTS OF SOUTHERN BC AND THE ROCKIES

■ The **Okanagan Valley** offers a panoply of **free wine-tastings** (see p. 296).
■ Sleepy **Revelstoke** sees one of the finest **stay-and-ski** deals anywhere (see p. 301).
■ Near the Alberta border lies a trinity of uncrowded national parks: the steep, stellar slopes of **Glacier** (see p. 303), the falls and fossils of **Yoho** (see p. 319), and the peerless peaks of **Kootenay** (see p. 320).
■ It's hard to pick highlights in national parks as uniformly beautiful as **Banff** (see p. 304) and **Jasper** (see p. 314), which cater to outdoor buffs of every stripe. Banff's **Inkpots** (see p. 311) and Jasper's **Cavell Meadows** (see p. 317) are truly impressive.
■ Dinosaurs once stomped through the red bluffs of the **Alberta Badlands** (see p. 324); you can dig up or view their petrified remains at the **Royal Tyrrell Museum of Paleontology** (see p. 325).
■ Calgary's annual **Stampede** (see p. 331) is an extreme celebration of rodeo machismo and tourist magnetism.

THE INTERIOR

FRASER RIVER CANYON

The Fraser River courses down from the Rockies and hurls through 1300km of plateaus and steep canyons on its journey to the Pacific. In 1808, Simon Fraser enlisted the help of native guides to make the perilous expedition down the river from Mt. Robson to Vancouver; today's route from Cache Creek to Hope on the Trans-Canada Highway (Hwy. 1) makes his trailblazing seem like a distant dream. Up close, the canyon is a good place to feel small, with over 200km of pounding rapids in the river below, and towering walls carpeted with pines and firs sprouting out of the near-vertical rock walls.

Hope is biggest dot on the map in the canyon, but the biggest thing happening there is the intersection of several highways. The **Trans-Canada Highway (Hwy. 1)** originates in Vancouver, passes through Hope, then bends north to Yale and eventually Cache Creek, where it meets the **Cariboo Highway** (**Hwy. 97;** see p. 334). **Highway 7** runs west along the north bank of the Fraser River to Vancouver's suburbs. **The Crowsnest Highway (Hwy. 3)** winds east through breathtaking country close to the U.S. border, through Kootenay Country to Nelson, and over Crowsnest Pass into Alberta. The **Coquihalla Highway (Hwy. 5),** is a new, faster toll road ($10) running north to Kamloops, and preferred by most heading to the Rockies in a hurry.

HOPE

Buses arrive in Hope at the **Greyhound** station at 833 3rd Ave. (869-5522), a hub for bus travel throughout the region. See p. 53 for discounts and alternatives. Buses run north on the Coquihalla to **Kamloops** (2½hr., 3 per day, $28) then east to **Jasper** (10hr., 2 per day, $80), **Banff** (11hr., 2 per day, $84), and **Calgary** (13hr., 3 per day, $99); north on Hwy. 1 along the Fraser Canyon to **Cache Creek** (2¾hr., 2 per day, $26.48); east on Hwy. 3 to **Penticton** (4hr., 2-3 per day, $31) and points east; and west to **Vancouver** (3hr., 8 per day, $18). Many ramblers try hitching north on Hwy. 1, where rides are reputedly easy to find. **Gardner Chev-Olds,** 945 Water Ave. (869-9511), rents cars ($35 per day, $210 per week; 13¢ per km after 100km; must be 25 with credit card; open M-Sa 8am-6pm). The **visitor center,** 919 Water Ave. (869-2021), provides the riveting, self-guided **Rambo Walking Tour** (*First Blood* was filmed here) and **Chainsaw Carving Walking Tour,** and shares info on Fraser River Canyon and Manning Park. **Police:** 670 Hope-Princeton Hwy. (869-7750), just off Hwy. 3. **Post office:** 777 Fraser St., V0X 1L0 (open M-F 8:30am-5pm). **Area code:** 604.

If stuck in Hope for a night, walk a block north from the bus station to Wallace St. and hang a left to reach the **Hope Motor Hotel,** 272 Wallace St. (869-5641), which rents sizeable rooms with two large beds for $45. Campers can head for the giant firs and cedars of the spacious **Coquihalla Campsite,** 800 Kawkawa Lake Rd. (869-7119 or 888-869-7118; hopecamp@uniserve.com), off 6th Ave., on the east side of town along the banks of the Coquihalla River (122 sites $16; river sites $19; hookups $20). Shop for groceries to ghastly elevator music at **Buy and Save Foods,** 489 Wallace St. (869-5318; open daily 8am-8pm). **Home Too Restaurant,** downtown on 4th St. (869-5241), is a surprisingly good diner, delivering big-ol' burgers from $4.

IN THE VICINITY

HIKING. Hope may not be much, but the surrounding lands are less hopeless. A number of excellent moderate hikes begin near Hope. The short, lush **Rotary Trail** starts on Wardle St. at the confluence of the Fraser and Coquihalla Rivers. The 45-minute **Hope Lookout loop,** on Hope Mt., offers an impressive view of the town and surrounding area. Experienced climbers can continue up the steep talus slopes and open rock faces of Mt. Hope. To reach the trailhead, take the gravel road under the Hwy. 1 overpass on Old Hope-Princeton Way. Pause for a pleasant diversion at **Kawkawa Creek,** off Union Bay Rd., recently enhanced to aid the late-summer and mid-fall salmon spawnings. The boardwalk along the creek leads to a swimming hole and popular picnicking spot. Forty-five minutes southeast of Hope on Hwy. 3, **Manning Provincial Park** provides more extensive hiking options out of four frontcountry campgrounds in the rugged Cascade Mountains (350 sites; $12-18.50). The park's **Heather Trail,** starting at the Blackwall Peak parking lot, climbs over the Blackwall summit, reaching extensive sub-alpine meadows after 5km (in bloom late July to early August), before continuing on well into the backcountry.

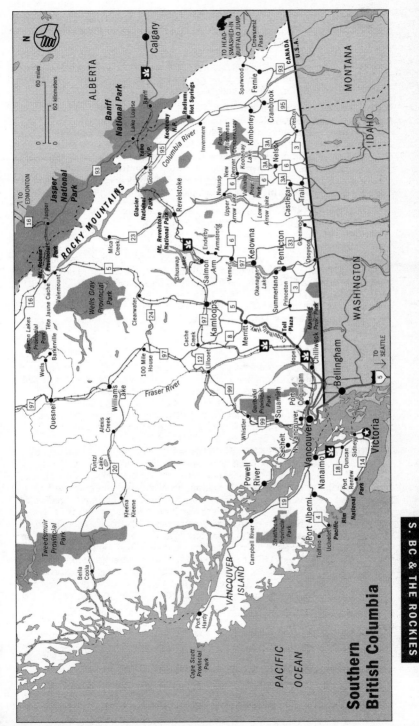

Southern British Columbia

OTHELLO QUINTET TUNNELS. The **Coquihalla Canyon Recreation Area** is a five- to ten-minute drive out of Hope along Kawkawa Lake Rd. Here the **Othello Quintet Tunnels,** blasted through solid granite, provide mute evidence of the daring engineering that led to the opening of the **Kettle Valley Railway** in 1916. The dark tunnels lead to narrow bridges over whitewater shooting through the gorge. To get there, turn right on Othello Rd. off Kawkawa Lake Rd. and right again on Tunnel Rd.; allow half an hour to walk through the tunnels.

LADY FRANKLIN ROCK AND RAFTING. For an even closer view of the Fraser River, head 36km north on Hwy. 1 to the small, unfortunately named town of **Yale.** Take the first right after the stop light, then follow the gravel road for about 1km to a close-up view of the majestic Lady Franklin Rock, which splits the Fraser River into two sets of heavy rapids. **Fraser River Raft Expeditions** (863-2336 or 800-363-7238 for reservations), south of town, runs full-day whitewater trips almost daily on the Fraser and its tributaries (Class III-IV rapids; $95). Travelers can stay the night in their oversized teepee ($10 per night; customers free) or in the plush B&B ($65).

HELL'S GATE AIRTRAM. When Simon Fraser made his pioneering trek down the river, he likened one tumultuous stretch of rapids, 25km north of Yale on Hwy. 1, to the Gates of Hell. When snowmelt floods the river in spring, the 60m deep water rushes through the narrow gorge with incredible force. To skirt the worst rapids, Fraser followed his native guides along established detours, sometimes consisting of scaffolding built into the cliff walls. A cluster of shops and eateries now inhabit the cliffs where Fraser once advised "no human beings should venture." The Hell's Gate Airtram, 43111 Hwy. 1 (867-9277), carries the vertigo-immune 150m across the canyon in four minutes ($9.50, seniors $8, ages 6-17 $6, families $25). Acrophobes and budgeteers will prefer the nearby 1km trail down to the river.

KAMLOOPS

T'Kumlups, a Shuswap word meaning "where the waters meet," is a fitting name for a town situated at the confluence of the North and South Thompson Rivers and of the heavily traveled Highways 5 and 1. Over 200 lakes lie within an hour's drive of town. That fact, and the fact that a fine hostel exists here, and the fact that outdoor live music is performed nightly in summer, make the town a great base for daytripping in the area, or a good waystation on long highway voyages.

◪ ORIENTATION AND PRACTICAL INFORMATION. Kamloops lies 356km east of Vancouver, 492km west of Banff, anchoring the junction of the heavily traveled Yellowhead (Hwy. 16) and Trans-Canada (Hwy. 1). **VIA Rail** (800-561-8630) trains stop at North Station, off Hwy. 5, making three runs per week to Vancouver (8½hr., $77) and Edmonton, AB (15hr., $173). See p. 52 for discounts. **Greyhound,** 725 Notre Dame Ave. (374-1212), departs Kamloops for Vancouver (4½hr., 8 per day, $44), Jasper, AB (6hr., 2 per day, $53), and Calgary, AB (9½hr., 4 per day, $72). **Kamloops Transit System** (376-1216) buses cost $1.25. The **visitor center** (374-3377 or 800-662-1994) is just west of town on the Trans-Canada (open June-Aug. daily 9am-5pm; Sept.-May M-F only). Rent demo bikes from the only bike shop in Canada with a liquor license, **Java Cycle,** 297 1st Ave. (314-5282), just across from the hostel ($35 per day). **McCleaners,** 437 Seymour St. (372-9655), is a McLaundry. **Police:** 560 Battle St. (828-3000). **Post office:** 301 Seymour St. V2C 5K2 (374-2444; open M-F 8:30am-5pm). **Area code:** 250.

⌂ ACCOMMODATIONS AND FOOD. The excellent ⧆ **Kamloops Old Courthouse Hostel (HI),** 7 W. Seymour St. (828-7991), is, in fact, a turn-of-the-century courthouse. The giant common room still sports a jury box, judge's bench, and witness stand, compensating for the tightly-packed dorm rooms. (73 beds $15, nonmembers $19.50; private rooms $5 surcharge; check-in 8am-1pm and 5-10pm.) Campers can head 30 minutes northeast of town to Paul Lake Provincial Park, 17km east of Hwy. 5 on Paul Lake Rd. Ninety densely wooded sites close to swimming are $9.50.

Decent Kamloops food lines Victoria St. Pull up to the **Victoria St. Station,** 229 Victoria St. (372-1341), for homemade sandwiches (with salad $4.25), or a filling fruit salad, ice cream, and bagel combo ($4.50). The $7 all-you-can-eat Chinese lunch buffet at **Jade Garden,** 298 3rd Ave. (851-9368), is a self-evident good deal. **Steiger's Swiss Cafe and Pastries,** 359 Victoria St. (372-2625), gives succor to sweet tooths and sates fresh bread cravings (open Tu-Sa 8:30am-5:30pm).

SIGHTS AND OUTDOORS. Every July and August night at 7pm, bands perform in **Riverside Park,** on the banks of the Thompson River. Adjacent **Pioneer Park** hosts a boisterous daytime crowd. See the river up close on a two-hour cruise aboard the **Wanda Sue Paddle Boat,** 1140 River St. (374-7447; 1-3 cruises per day; $11.50, seniors $10.50, ages 6-12 $6.50). **Secwepemc Museum and Heritage Park,** 355 Yellowhead Hwy. (828-9801), contains the reconstructed remains of a 2000-year-old Shuswap village, eerily placed near the site of a school to which the Canadian government removed native children as late as the 1970s. (Open June-Aug. M-F 8:30am-8pm, Sa-Su 10am-6pm. $6, youths and seniors $4.)

Sun Peaks, 1280 Alpine Rd. (578-5484; www.sunpeaks.resort.com), a 45-minute drive north of Kamloops, is a powdery magnet for snowboarders and skiers. The mountain's large vertical drop (882m/2900 ft.) and annual snowfall (5.27m/17 ft.), as well as the numerous glades justify the somewhat pricey tickets ($45, youth $40). In summer, the lift carries hikers and bikers up to trails through wildflower meadows ($12, seniors $9, ages 6-12 $9, under 5 free). Take Hwy. 5 north from Kamloops, turn right at Heffley Creek and continue 31km to Sun Peaks. The **Stake Lake Trails** (snow report 372-5514) form a network of cross-country skiing terrain, with a good selection of beginner and intermediate options ($7 per day, $30 per 5 days). Take Exit 366 from Hwy. 5 south of Kamloops, and follow Lac Le Jeune Rd.

SHUSWAP LAKE REGION

From the dugout canoes of the Shuswap to the house-boats of today's vacationers, the warm waters and productive fisheries of the sublime Shuswap Lake have attracted people for centuries. In 1999, heavy snows and a quick melt led to the highest water levels ever recorded, flooding roads and campgrounds. Salmon Arm, a metropolis compared to the nearby dots on the map, is still unexceptional but for its lakefront situation and its poster-perfect backdrop of rolling, forested mountains, especially striking when the leaves turn in autumn.

ORIENTATION AND PRACTICAL INFORMATION. Shuswap Lake is shaped like a sloppy H. Coming from the west, Highway 1 hugs the northern arm of the lake before dipping south and following the southern one east from Salmon Arm.

The **Salmon Arm Transit System** (832-0191 for booking) has regular (M-Sa, $1.25) and door-to-door service (M-F, $1.50). **Visitor information:** 751 Marine Park Dr. (832-6247; open June-Aug. M-Sa 8am-6pm, Sept.-May M-F 9am-5pm). **Shuswap Laundry:** 330 Ross St. (832-7300; open daily 7am-10pm). **Police:** 501 2nd Ave. NE (832-6044). **Ambulance:** 833-0188. **Post office:** 370 Hudson St. NE, V1E 4M6 (832-3093; open M-F 8:30am-5pm). **Area code:** 250.

ACCOMMODATIONS, CAMPGROUNDS, AND FOOD. **Squilax General Store Hostel (HI)** (675-2977), 50km west of Salmon Arm on Hwy. 1, sleeps travelers on board three Canadian National Railway cabooses, specially procured and outfitted for rustic hosteling with mini-kitchens, showers, two llamas, a llounge, and llaundry facillities (23 beds $14, nonmembers $18; private rooms $4 per each additional person; tent sites by the river $8). Though not the cleanest hostel in Canada, Squilax certainly is one of the more remarkable. B&Bs are the way of Salmon Arm; for a lake view, pool, sauna, and warm British hospitality, waddle on over to **Ducks Galore,** 1961 16th St. NE (832-8906), near Lakeshore Dr. Take 20th Ave. to 16th St. from Lakeshore Dr., and do not be flapped by the several parallel streets also called 16th. The welcoming owners collect wooden and ceramic ducks, but leave the real ones in the nearby nature preserve alone (singles $40; doubles $50-65).

Campgrounds in Salmon Arm, especially those on Shuswap Lake, are often crowded and cramped. **Pierre's Point** (832-9588), on 50th Ave. NW just off Hwy. 1, has a sandy beach and allows a little more breathing space than its competitors (40 of 200 sites are lakeside $19; full hookups $21). For a quieter time, head for the more commodious **Herald Provincial Park** (reservations 800-689-9025), 27km northwest of Salmon Arm by following signs off Hwy. 1. The park maintains 117 campsites with a large swimming area and access to hiking along Margaret Falls (see **Outdoors**, below; $18.50 includes firewood, hot showers, and toilets). The best food deal for miles around awaits at the **Real Canadian Wholesale Club,** 360 Hwy. 1 (804-0258). Even the non-bulk items cost less than at any supermarket (open M-F 9am-9pm, Sa 9am-6pm, Su 10am-5pm). Farther west on Hwy. 1, **De Mille Fruits and Vegetables,** 3710 10th Ave. SW (832-7550), markets local produce and, in August and September, incredible sweet corn (open daily June-Sept. 8am-8pm; Oct.-May 8am-6:30pm). For soup or sandwich ($4), choose **Choices,** 40 Lakeshore Dr. (832-7555).

🎭 📷 ⛰ **SIGHTS, ENTERTAINMENT, AND OUTDOORS.** Learn what curds and whey really are on a tour of **Gort's Gouda Cheese Factory,** 1470 50th St. SW (832-4274). It lasts only a few minutes, shuttling visitors to tasty samples all the faster. Or skip the tour and stock up on bargain cheeses, and watch the cheesemaking process from cow to wax package through viewing windows. (Tours daily 10am mid-June to Aug.; $2 charge may be put towards cheese purchases.)

Most of the area's featured attractions center on the waterways surrounding town. Kokanee and rainbow trout inhabit Lake Shuswap. (Day permits $15, 8 days $40; available at the Government Agent next to the visitor center.) The lovely **Margaret Falls** are a 10-minute walk through **Herald Park** (see **Herald Provincial Park,** above). Closer to town, take a stroll along the nature preserve on the banks of Lake Shuswap to catch a glimpse of the rare Western grebe.

Interior Whitewater Expeditions (800-661-7238; www.interiorwhitewater.bc.ca), in Scotch Creek, leads two-hour trips on the reasonably gentle (Class II-III) **Adams River** ($40, under age 16 $32; 10% HI discount). The paths along the river can be hiked or mountain biked for free, in an 18km round-trip. Take Squilax-Anglemont Rd. north across the bridge, just west of the Squilax General Store. The trail heads upriver across the first narrow bridge on the road.

Caravan Farm Theatre (546-8533 or 838-6751), 8km northwest of Armstrong and 45 minutes from Salmon Arm, presents top-notch performances during summer. Tickets are available at the Squilax General Store Hostel (see **Accommodations,** above; call for show times; $6-12.) The Farm overflows with remnant hippie charm, organic produce, and musical instruments dangling from the trees.

THE OKANAGAN VALLEY

Known throughout Canada for its bountiful fruit harvests, the Okanagan (oh-kuh-NAH-gan) Valley lures visitors with summer blossoms, ample sun, plentiful wineries, and tranquil lakes. The **Okanagan Connector (Hwy. 97C)** links Vancouver to the valley in a four-hour drive, making the valley a popular vacation destination among sun-starved coastal British Columbians. In the north, the quiet valley is rudely interrupted by an explosion of bloated shopping centers along Hwy. 97. Demure parks and beaches reward those who seek them out.

Travelers looking earn some cash may consider signing on to pick fruit at one of the many orchards stretching south from Penticton to the U.S. border along Hwy. 97. Pickers usually camp for free and are paid a per-quart wage; daily earnings of more than $40 are common. Cherries are harvested in June, pears in September, and assorted other fruits in between. Contact the **Kelowna Friendship Centre** (763-4905), or cruise Hwy. 97 and Hwy. 3A looking for "Pickers Wanted" signs.

KELOWNA

In the heart of the Okanagan Valley, Kelowna (kuh-LOW-nuh) is one of Canada's richest agricultural areas. Its fabulous sunshine and dry climate also draw thousands of vacationing Vancouverites every summer.

⚑ ORIENTATION AND PRACTICAL INFORMATION. Kelowna lies 400km east of Vancouver, 602km west of Calgary, and 86km north of Penticton on **Hwy. 97**, at the eastern shore of Okanagan Lake. Hwy. 97 runs east-west across the lake and through town, where it is called **Harvey Ave.**

Greyhound, 2366 Leckie Rd. (860-3835), runs buses to Vancouver (6½hr., 6 per day, $51), Penticton (1½ hr., 6 per day, $11.50), and Calgary, AB (10hr., 3 per day, $75). **Kelowna Regional Transit System** (860-8121) services town ($1.25, students and seniors $1; day passes $3.25-$4.25; runs M-Sa 6am-10pm). **Kelowna Cabs** (762-2222 or 762-4444) will take you around, too. **Rent-A-Wreck**, 2702 N. Hwy. 97 (763-6632) will supply you the means to do the work yourself ($25 per day, 12¢ per km over 100km; must be 21; open M-Sa 8am-5pm, Su 9am-4pm). You can get a map at the **visitor center**, 544 Harvey Ave. (861-1515; open M-F 8am-7pm, Sa-Su 9am-7pm). **SameSun Hostel** rents **bikes** for $10 per day. **Sports Rent**, 3000 Pandosy St. (861-5699; open daily 9am-6pm), rents bikes ($15-26 per day), in-line skates ($11), single kayaks ($25), and doubles ($35). **Kelowna Public Library**, 1380 Ellis St. (762-2800; open Tu-Th 10am-9pm, M and F-Sa 10am-5:30pm), provides **Internet access** for $2 per hr. **Mind Grind Internet Cafe and Bookstore**, 1340 Water St. (763-2221) charges $3 for 30min., $5.50 per hr. (open M-Sa 7:30am-11pm, Su 9am-11pm; call for winter hours). Do your laundry for $2.50 at **Capri Coin Laundromat**, 150-1835 Gordon Dr., in the Capri Plaza (860-6871; open daily 6am-midnight). **Safeway**, 697 Bernard St. (860-0332; open daily 8am-10pm), has a **pharmacy. Hospital:** 2268 Pandosy St. (862-4000), three blocks south of Harvey Ave. **Emergency:** 911. **Police:** 350 Doyle Ave. (762-3300). **Post office:** 530 Gaston Ave., V1Y 7N2 (763-4095; open M-F 8:30am-5pm). **Area code:** 250.

⚏ ACCOMMODATIONS AND CAMPGROUNDS. Kelowna summers dry out thousands of soggy Vancouverites: make reservations. **SameSun International Hostel (HI)**, 245 Harvey Ave. (763-9814), mere blocks from the beach, tends to make one-night stopovers into week-long stays: weekly keg parties, pub crawls, and daytrips are instrumental in this regard. Staff is totally committed to having a good time. (Free pickup from bus terminal. $15, nonmembers $17. Key deposit $5. Reception 8:30am-12:30pm and 5-11pm. Call ahead after-hours.) **Big White International Hostel (HI)**, 7660 Porcupine Rd. (765-7050), at the Alpine Center, has three outdoor hot tubs and a nearby bar for après-ski relaxation. Take the Big White turn-off from Hwy. 33 or the shuttle from SameSun. ($17, nonmembers $19; includes pancake breakfast. Open Nov.-Apr.) **By the Bridge B&B**, 1942 McDougall St. (860-7518), is at the east end of Okanagan Lake Bridge, minutes from the lake. (Private baths, breakfast, and free bikes. Singles $45-55; doubles $50-60; triples $65-75; quads $70-80.) **Bear Creek Provincial Park** (494-6500 or 800-689-9025), 9km north of Hwy. 97 on Westside Rd., has flowery lakeside sites, a beach, and views of Kelowna across the water. Line up for walk-in sites at the crack of dawn or not at all. (122 sites: $18.50.) **Fintry Provincial Park** (800-689-9025), 34km north of Kelowna on Westside Rd, is similar to Bear Creek, but a twisting road discourages large trailers. (50 sites: $18.50.)

◪ FOOD. Kelowna overflows with fresh produce. Cut out the middle man at fruit and vegetable stands outside town along **Benvoulin Rd.** and **KLO Rd.** In town, the shelves groan beneath big carrots and cucumbers at **Safeway**, 697 Bernard Ave. (860-0332; open daily 8am-10pm). **Bernard Ave.** is lined with restaurants and cafes. **The Pier**, 2035 Campbell Rd. (769-4777), across the lake off Harvey Ave., is an unassuming pub that serves daily specials that are unbelievable bargains: Tuesday is 14 oz. Porterhouse steak day $7, Wednesday is roast chicken and ribs day $6 (open

S. BC & THE ROCKIES

Su-Th noon-late, F-Sa 1pm-late). **Garden Patch Bistro,** 551 Bernard Ave. (762-8988), has cheap and imaginative vegetarian fare. California rolls are $5; breakfast burritos are $3. (Open M-F 7am-4pm, Sa 9:30am-3pm.) **The Kitchen Cowboy,** 353 Bernard Ave. (868-8288), ropes in a trendy clientele with an eclectic menu and live music F-Sa. Thai salad is $8, and curried shrimp wraps are $9. (Open M-Th 10am-9pm, F-Sa 10am-11pm, Su 10am-3pm.)

🏵 SIGHTS, OUTDOORS, AND EVENTS. Kelowna's main attraction is 93,000,000 mi. away, shining down on its parks and beaches for an average of 2000 hours per year. **City Park,** on the west end of downtown, is the principal lawn and beach from which to enjoy this gigantic ball of flaming gas, but **Boyce Gyro Park,** on Lakeshore Rd. south of the Okanagan Bridge, is popular with the younger, more hormone-laden crowd. **Sports Rent,** a short walk away from the lake, rents camping, boating, and sporting equipment. **Kelowna Parasail Adventures,** 1310 Water St. (868-4838), at the docks of Grand Okanagan Resort north of City Park, transforms patrons into kites, floating them high above the lake. (Open daily 9am-dusk, weather permitting. $45 for a 10min. ride; $75 for 2 people.)

The old tracks of the **Kettle Valley Railbed,** 8km southeast of town, have been replaced by 12km of beautiful **hiking and biking trails** that pass through the only desert in Canada and over Myra cannon on old trestle bridges. One hundred trails and over 1624 ft. of vertical drop greet powderhounds at family-friendly **Big White Ski Resort** (765-3101, snow report 765-7669; www.bigwhite.com), on a clearly marked access road off Hwy. 33, east of town. (Day pass $45, ages 13-18 $38, ages 6-12 $24; night-skiing $16; multi-day discounts. Open mid-Nov. to late Apr.) **Kelowna Land and Orchard,** 2930 Dunster Rd. (763-1091), off KLO Rd. on E. Kelowna, is the town's oldest family-owned farm, and gives a 45-minute hayride and tour. (July-Aug. 9am-5pm; call for winter hours. $5.25, ages 12-16 $2, under 12 free.)

The **wines** of the Okanagan Valley have made a name for themselves in recent years, and Kelowna has 12 of the valley's 24 wineries. Contact the visitor center for a complete list of winery tours (a.k.a. How to Get Drunk for Free, Very Slowly). **Mission Hill,** 1730 Mission Hill Rd. (768-7611), on the west bank of Okanagan Lake, is the most respected local winery; cross the bridge west of town, turn left on Boucherie Rd. from the highway, and follow the signs. Overlooking the lake, this large winery woos connoisseurs with its award-winning 1994 Chardonnay. Free tours explain the vintning process, and promise a taste of the goods for those over 19. (Open daily July-Aug. 10am-7pm; May-June 9am-6pm; Sept.-Apr. 9am-5pm. Hourly tours July-Aug. 10am-5pm; call for winter times.) The bubbly takes shape on free tours of the posh **Summerhill Estate Winery** (800-667-3538); take Lakeshore Dr. to Chute Lake Rd. (Open daily 10am-7pm; tours on the hour 1-4pm.)

Kelowna parties at the **Okanagan Wine Festival** (861-6654; www.owfs.com) in early October and its lesser counterpart in late April. The party surrounding late July's **Kelowna Regatta** (861-4754) has mellowed a bit since 1988 when the regatta was shut down because of rioting, but the races still pack 'em in.

PENTICTON

Close your eyes and imagine Florida. Replace the ocean with two large lakes, the palm trees with Douglas fir, and add mountains and hockey fans. Okay, now open your eyes. Voila: Penticton. Indigenous peoples named the beautiful region between Okanagan and Skaha Lakes Pen-tak-tin, "a place to stay forever," but their eternal paradise has been transformed by heated pools and luxury hotels into one of Western Canada's biggest vacation towns. Hot weather, sandy beaches, and proximity to Vancouver and Seattle have ushered in the Tourist Age. It may well strain a budget to spend a weekend here, let alone eternity.

🚩 ORIENTATION AND PRACTICAL INFORMATION. Penticton lies 395km east of Vancouver at the junction of **Hwy. 3** and **Hwy. 97,** at the southern extreme of the Okanagan Valley. **Okanagan Lake** borders the north end of town, while smaller

Skaha Lake lies to the south. **Main St.** bisects the city from north to south, turning into **Skaha Lake Rd.** as it approaches the lake.

Greyhound, 307 Ellis St. (493-4101), runs buses to Vancouver (6-7hr., 6 per day, $49.50) and Kelowna (1½hr., 7 per day, $11.66). **Penticton Transit System,** 301 E. Warren Ave. (492-5602), services town ($1.50, students and seniors $1.20; day pass $3.25, students $2.75; runs M-F 6:30am-10pm, Sa 8:30am-10pm, Su 9:40am-5:40pm). **Courtesy Taxi** (492-7778) runs the gauntlet. **Car Rental: Budget,** 2504 Skaha Lake Rd. (493-0212). M-Th $50 per day; 18¢ per km over 100km. F-Su $40 per day; 18¢ per km over 300km. Must be 21 with major credit card. Open M-Sa 7:30am-5pm. Also at the airport (open daily 7:30am-7pm). **Penticton Wine and Information Center,** 888 W. Westminster Ave. (493-4055 or 800-663-5052), at Power St., does not, unfortunately, serve wine (open daily in summer 9am-6pm). A smaller **information center** is 7km south of town on Hwy. 97 (open daily in summer 10am-5pm). **Sun Country Cycle,** 533 Main St. (493-0686), rents bikes for $15 for 4hr., $25 per day; $5 HI discount (open M-Sa 9:30am-6pm). Wash your soiled belongings for $1.50 and dry them for 25¢ per 6min. at **Plaza Laundromat,** 417-1301 Main St. (493-8710; open daily 7am-11pm). **Internet Access** is available for $2 per 30min. at **Nicky's Specialty Coffees,** 110-2210 Main St. (493-4681; open Su-Th 7am-10pm, F-Sa 7am-11pm). **Pharmacy: Shoppers Drug Mart,** 721-1301 Main St. (492-8000; open M-F 8am-9pm, Sa 9am-6pm, Su 10am-5pm), in the Penticton Plaza Mall. **Hospital: Penticton Regional,** 550 Carmi Ave. (492-4000). **Emergency:** 911. **Police:** 1103 Main St. (492-4300). **Crisis Line:** 493-6622. **Women's Shelter:** 493-7233. 24hr. **Post office:** 56 W. Industrial Ave., V2A 6J8 (492-5769). Open M-F 8:30am-5pm. **Area code:** 250.

⌐ ACCOMMODATIONS AND CAMPGROUNDS. Penticton is a resort city year-round; cheap beds are few and far between and it's essential to make reservations in summer. Sardine companies might take a lesson on packing from the plentiful and expensive campgrounds lining Skaha Lake. **Penticton Hostel (HI),** 464 Ellis St. (492-3992) is in a large house near the Greyhound stop, 10 minutes from the beach, and one of Penticton's best bets. (Comfortable lounge and patio, kitchen, laundry facilities, and gas grill. 47 beds: $15, nonmembers $19; under 10 half-price. 3 days $40.50, nonmembers $48. Private rooms available. Linen free. No curfew. Reception 7am-1pm and 4-11pm. Fills up June-Aug.) **Riordan House,** 689 Winnipeg St. (493-5997), rents enormous rooms in a Victorian-style mansion that cost not a penny more than the sad boxes inside some of the concrete-box motels on Lakeshore Dr. and come with a super free breakfast of fresh scones and local fruits. (One single $50, lavish doubles with TV/VCR $55-75.) **Okanagan Lake Provincial Park** (494-0321), 24km north of town on Hwy. 97, packs 168 walk-in sites between the highway and the lake in two separate units. The north park is more spacious, and the beach is good for swimming. Claim sites early between 8 and 10am. (Free showers and firewood. $18.50.) The free **Okanagan Mountain Campground** lies across the water; from Naramata or Kelowna follow signs to trailhead parking.

◻ FOOD. South of Penticton along Hwy. 97 and Hwy. 3A, visitors can eat **fruit** at a family stand, sample **wines** at a local vineyard, or **fish** in a pristine lake. Supplement the three food groups at **Super Valu Foods,** 450 Martin St. (492-4303; open M-Th 9am-7pm, F 9am-9pm, Sa-Su 9am-6pm). The **Penticton Farmer's Market** flourishes every Saturday from June to October 8:30am-noon, in Gyro Park at the corner of Westminster and Main St. **Whole Foods Market,** 118-1550 Main St. (493-2855; open M-Th and Sa-Su 9am-6pm, F 9am-8pm), in Creekside Plaza, peddles bulk grains, herbs, and organic produce. **Judy's Deli,** 129 W. Nanaimo (492-7029), serves soups ($1.75-2.25), butter-smeared sandwiches ($2.60-3.30), and herbs for take-out (open M-Sa 9am-6pm, Su 10am-5pm). **Hog's Breath Coffee Co.,** 202 Main St. (493-7800), is a mellow cafe that waffles all day ($5), and wraps artichoke hearts, grilled chicken, and marinated eggplant ($6; open daily 6am-10pm, roughly speaking).

◉ ♖ SIGHTS, OUTDOORS, AND EVENTS. Long, hot summers and sport facilities on the lakes make them a popular hangout for the young. The Penticton tourist trade revolves around **Okanagan Lake,** but **Skaha Lake** at the other end of town got the volleyball nets and more sand. In expensive Penticton, you can float down the river in a rented tube for a mere $10 from **Coyote Cruises,** 215 Riverside (492-2115; open in summer daily at 10am). Bike trails spread through the **Kettle Valley Railbed.** Get info at the visitor center and bikes at SameSun or Sun Country Cycle. **Pier Water Sports** (493-8864), on Main St., rents various vessels.

The beachfront **Art Gallery of the South Okanagan,** 199 Front St. (493-2928), has small but excellent exhibits of Canadian artists (open Tu-F 10am-5pm, Sa-Su 1-5pm. $2, students and children free; free on Tu.) **Hillside Winery Estates,** 1350 Naramata Rd. (493-4424), northeast of town, has a shop, free tastings, and tours. (Open daily Apr.-Oct. 10am-6pm. Frequent tours 10:30am-5pm; call for winter hours.) The **Okanagan Wine Festival** (490-8866), held in early October and again, in a smaller version, in April, is endless fun for all the squishing of thick pulp between toes.

The **Skaha Bluffs,** southeast of town on Valley View Rd., have developed into a popular rock-climbing venue with pitches of varying difficulty. A resource for gear and advice is **Ray's Sports Den,** 215 Main St. (493-1216; open M-F 9:30am-6pm, Sa 9:30am-5pm, Su 10am-4pm). **Skaha Rock Adventures,** 113-437 Martin St. (493-1765; www.skaharockclimbing.com), leads daytrips for $65-190, equipment included. Heavy winter snowfalls in Okanagan Valley make for excellent skiing and Penticton smoothly transforms from summer beach resort to winter mountain playland. **Apex Mountain Resort** (800-387-2739, snow report 492-2929 ext. 2000; www.apexresort.com), off an access road west of Penticton on Hwy. 3, has downhill, cross-country, and night **skiing** on 56 runs with a 2000 ft. drop.

NELSON

Nelson is a little different from the other isolated 9000-person towns in the BC interior. An eclectic blend of locals and seasonal transplants have made bongo drums and tofu OK in the forested hills above Kootenay Lake, though true beauty and mellowness await on the lake and higher up on the ski hills.

◢ ORIENTATION AND PRACTICAL INFORMATION. Nelson lies at the junction of **Hwy. 6** and **3A,** 624km southwest of Calgary, 454km southeast of Kamloops, and 657km east of Vancouver. From Nelson, Hwy. 3A heads 41km west to Castlegar. Hwy. 6 leads 65km south to the U.S. border, where it becomes Washington Rte. 31, continuing 110 mi. south to Spokane. An unusually excellent map can be had for free at the visitor center.

Greyhound, 1112 Lakeside Dr. (352-3939), in the Chako-Mika Mall, runs buses to: Vancouver (12hr., 2 per day, $87), Calgary, AB (12hr., 2 per day, $80), Banff, AB (14½hr. with 4hr. layover in Cranbrook, 1 per day, $65). Terminal open M-F 6am-8:30pm, Sa 6-11am and 4-8:30pm, Su 7:30-8:30am and 7:30-8:30pm. **Nelson Transit Systems** (352-8201) has three bus lines that cover the city and a more expensive one to the lake's north shore ($1.25, students and seniors $1; runs M-F 7am-11:30pm, Sa 8:30am-7:30pm). **Whitewater Cabs** (354-1111) runs M-F 24hr., Sa-Su 5:30am-3am. **Rent-a-Wreck,** 524 Nelson Ave. (352-5122), in the Esso station rents for $40 per day, plus 12¢ per km after 200km; or $30 per day, plus 12¢ per km. Must have a credit card. **Visitor information** is located at 225 Hall St. (352-3433; www.nelsonchamber.bc.ca; open July-Aug. daily 9am-6pm; Sept.-June M-F 8:30am-4:30pm). **Outdoor information** is available at **West Kootenay Visitor Centre** (825-4723), in Kokanee Creek Provincial Park, 20km east of Nelson on Hwy. 3A. (Open May-June Su 10am-4pm only, July-Aug. daily 9am-9pm.) **Gerick Cycle and Sports,** 702 Baker St. (354-4622), rents bikes for $5 per hr., $20 per day (open M-Th and Sa 9am-5:30pm, F 9am-9pm; in summer also Su 11am-4pm). The **Library,** 602 Stanley St. (352-6333), offers free 15min. **Internet Access** (open M,W, and F 1-8pm, Tu and Th 10am-6pm, Sa 11am-6pm). **Soil** your belongings for the sake of a $1.50 wash, 25¢ per 10min. dry at the Esso Station, 524 Nelson St. (352-3534; open Th-F 7:30am-10pm, Sa-W 7:30am-9:30pm). **Showers** are at **Nelson City Tourist Park** (see below). **Pharmasave** is the town **pharmacy** at 685 Baker St. (352-2313; open M-Tu 8:30am-6pm, W-

F 8:30am-8:30pm, Sa 9am-5:30pm, Su 10am-4pm). The **Hospital** of **Kootenay Lake District,** is at 3 View St. (352-3111). **Ambulance:** 352-2112. **Police:** 606 Stanley St. (352-2266; non-emergency 354-3919), near the library. **Crisis line:** 352-3504. 24hr. **Post office:** 514 Vernon St., V1L 5P3 (352-3538). Open M-F 8:30am-5pm. **Area code:** 250.

ACCOMMODATIONS, CAMPGROUNDS, AND FOOD.

There is no better location, more caring management, or more beautiful common room, which features wood furnishings crafted by local artisans, than at ■ **Dancing Bear Inn (HI),** 171 Baker St. (phone/fax 352-7573). Many bedrooms have one bed or bunk each in one of the finest hostels in Western Canada. (Laundry, immaculate kitchen, Internet access $5 per hr. $17, nonmembers $20, ages 6-10 half-price, under 5 free. No curfew. Check-in 4-10pm; office also open 7-11am. Reservations recommended June-Aug.) **Duhamel Motel,** 2536 Greenwood (825-4645), 9km north of town on Hwy. 3A, rents 6 tiny cabins with warm, wood-paneled living rooms, a fold-out bed and separate bedroom, bathroom, TV,

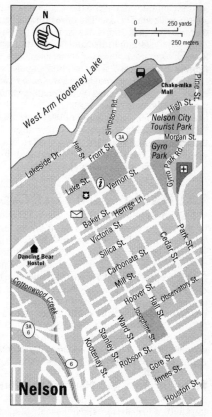

Nelson

and full kitchen. ($53 for 1 person, $5 per additional person up to 4.) **Kokanee Creek Provincial Park** (825-4212), 20km north of town on Hwy. 3A, has shaded, spacious sites near the lake. (Firewood and showers. Wheelchair accessible sites available. 132 sites: $17.50. No reservations.) **Nelson City Tourist Park,** on High St., is convenient to town for camping, suburban-backyard-style. Take Vernon St. to its eastern end, and follow the signs. (40 sites: $14; electricity and water $19. Showers for non-campers $2.)

Get basic groceries at **Extra Foods,** 708 Vernon St. (354-5571; open M-F 9am-9pm, Sa-Su 9am-6pm), and fresh bread and organic goodies from the **Kootenay Baker** and the **Kootenay Co-op,** 295 Baker St. (354-4077; open M-Th and Sa 9:30am-6pm, F 9:30am-8pm). The colorful **Glacier Gourmet** (354-4495), at the corner of Vernon St. and Hall St., serves fresh, filling, and vegetarian meals, with live jazz every Friday night. Wraps $5.25, pizza slices $3.25. (Open M-Th 8:30am-10pm, F 8:30-10:30 Sa-Su 10am-10pm.) **Max and Irma's Kitchen,** 515A Kootenay St. (352-2332), rescues quality 10-inch pizzas from a wood-fired oven ($10-12). (Open M-Th 11am-9pm, F-Sa 11am-10pm, Su 11:30am-9pm.)

OUTDOORS.

Bordering Nelson on the north, the watery **West Arm** seems huge, but it's just a tiny segment of enormous **Kootenay Lake.** Dolly varden, rainbow trout (up to 14kg according to local legend), and kokanee cruise the lake, while sturgeon up to 1.5m in length inhabit the **Kootenay River.** Licenses, bait, and a good place to begin are all at the **Balfour Dock,** 30 minutes north of town on Hwy. 3A.

Kokanee Glacier Provincial Park is uncrowded because it's so hard to reach. Various entrances off Hwy. 3A north of Nelson are not regularly maintained; ask at the visitor center for details on these routes or enter 19km north of town along bumpy Kokanee Creek Rd. The **Old Growth Trail** begins 12km up this road, and with the **Cedar Grove Loop** loops 2km into the forest. **Gibson Lake** lies another 4km up Kokanee Creek Rd. From there a 4km trail leads up and across the mountainside, past views of the Kootenays, to **Kokanee Lake.** The trail continues 3km to the campground at **Kaslo Lake,** with good fishing and views of the **Kokanee Glacier.** After a total of 9km of moderate hiking, the path reaches the 12-person **Slocan Chief cabin** below the glacier. (Backcountry campgrounds $4; cabin $10.) Don't walk on the glacier without an expert guide.

In winter, the soft powder of **Whitewater Ski Resort** (354-4944, snow report 352-7669, in AB 403-289-3700; www.skiwhitewater.com), 35km southeast of town, draws skiers and boarders to groomed runs and some of Canada's best bowls and deeps. (32 marked runs; 1300 ft. vertical drop. Lift tickets $35, ages 13-18 and seniors $27, ages 7-12 $21, under 7 free.)

VALHALLA PROVINCIAL PARK

Valhalla stretches up from the remarkably clear, trout-filled waters of Slocan Lake through a temperate rain forest of bewitching lushness to craggy alpine peaks. Once a homeland to the Sa-al-tkw't, who left dream-like pictographs behind them, the park is now largely given over to the grizzlies, cougars, and golden eagles. No mechanized vehicles of any kind, including mountain bikes, are allowed, nor are fires and pets. Much of the park is accessible only by boat, and there are no developed campsites or facilities. Many traverses pass through prime grizzly territory and require expert-level route-finding skills; other trails offer moderate, clear paths through fields of blindingly green moss, over hidden underground waterfalls, and past rock castles and crags worthy to be any warrior's final resting place. Local citizens based in the tiny, quirky nearby town of New Denver fought for years to have this treasure declared a protected park. Since their success in 1983, the park has offered refuge to those willing to turn off the traveled path.

⚑ ORIENTATION AND PRACTICAL INFORMATION. Valhalla lies on the west shore of Slocan Lake, 150km south of Revelstoke and 286km east of Kelowna. In the south, a bridge from the minuscule berg of **Slocan** provides access to southern trailheads, most at the end of long and bumpy forest roads. In the north, the eclectic town of **New Denver** provides an interesting stopover as well as water taxi service to the northern trailheads. The two towns are linked by Hwy. 6, which runs north from Nelson. Hitchhiking is common here. Several New Denver businesses operate **information centers.** Try the **Motherlode Book Store,** 317 6th St. (358-7274; open M-F 10am-5pm, daily in July and August), or the **Valhalla Inn** (see below). For outdoor information, visit the folks who crusaded on the park's behalf in the first place: the **Valhalla Wilderness Society,** 307 6th St. (358-2333; open M-F 9am-5pm). Try knocking even if the office appears closed; someone working late may open the door and provide you with their invaluable free topographical map of the park. To get to the park from New Denver, rent a kayak at the organic market (see below) or call **Kingfisher Water Taxi** (358-2334), which totes visitors from the dock for about $20. For **emergencies** call the **police** at 358-2222. The station is located at 407 Slocan Ave., south of 6th St. **Post office:** 219 6th Ave., V0G 1S0 (358-2611). **Area code:** 250.

⚑◫ ACCOMMODATIONS, CAMPGROUNDS, AND FOOD. Those who don't wish to camp can stay at the **Valhalla Inn,** on Highway 6 in town (358-2228; valhallainn@netidea.com), which contains a restaurant and pub as well as spare, spotless rooms (singles $49, doubles $54). Convenient but unlovely camping is available at the municipal campground at **Centennial Park,** on the south side of town by the lakeshore between 3rd and 1st Ave. Forty small sites cluster around showers and a boat launch (tents $13, full hookups $16). Across the lake, free sites are scattered throughout the park (see below). Food is to be found on 6th St., where the renowned **Appletree Cafe** (358-2691) holds court. The tiny cafe is home to a colorful local crowd, including the 90-year-old former mayor, who visits so regularly he has a permanently reserved table. The cafe promises "up to the minute gossip, financial advice, marital guidance, letters mailed, secrets kept," as well as homemade blueberry muffins ($1.25), soups ($2.40), and sandwiches ($4-7; open M-F 7am-4pm, Sa 11am-4pm). An **Organic Food Market** is held on summer Fridays from 4 to 6pm in the white barn on Slocan Ave. **Ann's Natural Foods,** 309 6th St. (358-2552), has a small selection of groceries.

🄰 THE PARK. The temperate rain forest of Valhalla is, as one might guess, often wet, and hypothermia is a real concern, even in summer (see p. 33). Extra layers of warm clothing are a good idea, as is a large tarp to be used in case of sodden tent. Be aware of the possibility of bear encounters (see p. 44). Most camping areas provide bear-proof food caches. Finally, remember that forest roads may be impassable as late as June due to snow. **Bannock Burn to Gimli Ridge** is a strenuous but unsurpassed 4km hike with spectacular views of the Mulvey Basin and opportunities for world-class rock climbing along the way. Campers may choose spots along the trail, preferably on constructed tent pads. To reach the trail, turn off Hwy. 6 at Slocan City, cross the river and follow the gravel road south for 12.8km. Turn right onto the Bannock Burn Creek logging road and follow it for 13km to the parking lot. For the truly hardy adventurer, the **Wee Sandy Creek Trail** is an arduous 14.4km trek along historic logging trails through mountain goat and grizzly habitat, and past trappers' cabins, trout-filled lakes, and mysterious rock castles. Bushwhacking may be required to reach prime campsites. Much more accessible is the trail to **Evan's Creek,** which wends 8 moderate km along the shore of the lake and past stunning, moss-carpeted waterfalls. A cabin and maintained tent pads are available at the creek and several trails lead to excellent fishing opportunities at Cahill and Beatrice Lakes. Kingfisher Water Taxi can arrange day trips. One popular activity is to travel by canoe or kayak down the shore of the lake over the course of several days.

REVELSTOKE

In the 19th century, Revelstoke was a town straight out of a Zane Grey western, complete with dust-encrusted megalomaniacs maiming one another amid the gold-laden Selkirk Mountains. Located on both the Columbia River and the Canadian Pacific Railway, the town was born as a stopover and transfer station for boats and trains. Although still a stopover for travelers on the way to the Rockies, Revelstoke is coming into its own. Excellent hostels, free outdoor concerts in the town centre (nightly in July and August from 7-10pm), and extensive outdoor activities make Revelstoke a particularly welcoming destination.

🄵 ORIENTATION AND PRACTICAL INFORMATION. Revelstoke is on the Trans-Canada Hwy. (Hwy. 1), 285km west of Banff, 210km east of Kamloops and 575km east of Vancouver. The town is easily navigated on foot or by bike. **Mount Revelstoke National Park** lies just out of town on Hwy. 1

Greyhound buses depart 1899 Fraser Dr. (837-5874), 1 block south of Hwy. 1. To: Calgary (6hr., 6 per day, $53); Vancouver (8½hr., 5 per day; $65); Salmon Arm (1¼hr., 5 per day, $16). Open M-Sa 8am-7pm, Su 11am-1pm and 3-5pm. Reach **R Taxi** at 837-4000. The **visitor center** (837-3522) is at the junction of Hwy. 1 and Hwy. 23 N. (Open daily June-Aug. 9am-7pm; Sept.-May 9am-5pm.) The **Parks Canada** office (837-7500), is at Boyle Ave. and 3rd St. (Open M-F 8:30am-noon and 1-4:30pm.) Rent bikes at **High Country Cycle and Sports,** 118 Mackenzie Ave. (814-0090) for $7-8 per hr. or $35-40 per day. **Emergency:** 911. **Police:** 320 Wilson St. (837-5255). **Ambulance:** 837-5885. **Hospital: Queen Victoria Hospital,** 6622 Newlands Rd. (837-2131). **Internet Access:** Free for guests at the hostel; at **Bertz Outdoor Equipment and cafe** (see **Food,** below), $3 for 30min., $5 per hr. **Post office:** 307 W. 3rd St., V0E 2S0 (837-3228). Open M-F 8:30am-5pm. **Area code:** 250.

▓▒ ACCOMMODATIONS, CAMPGROUNDS, AND FOOD. The ▓ **Revelstoke Traveller's Hostel and Guest House (HI)**, 400 2nd St. W (837-4050) has an office across the street at 403 2nd St. W. This newly renovated house has no more than 3 beds in each of its 27 bare-but-clean rooms. Several kitchens and bathrooms allow plenty of space, and most rooms have very comfy double beds. Free internet access and pickup from the bus station are provided. In winter, **$20 buys a bed *and* a lift ticket** at the Powder Springs ski area. ($15, non-members $19; singles $23-30; doubles pay bed rate for a private room. Tent sites $8-10. Open 24hr.) **Daniel's Guest House,** 313 First St. E (837-5530), is a two minute walk from Revelstoke. A home-turned-hostel, the comfortable beds, couch-filled common room, and porch make the place feel, well, homey. ($15; doubles $30; private rooms $45, families $30. Kitchen, laundry. Free pick-up from the bus station. 20 beds in single-sex 6-person dorms and private rooms. Reception 7-11am and 3-7pm.)

Williamson's Lake Campground, 1818 Williamson Lake Rd. (837-5512 or 800-676-2267), lies 4km southeast of town on Airport Way. Farther from the highway than its competitors, this simple ground is a nice change from the huge Smokey-the-Bear statues that litter the Trans-Canada Hwy. The lake is a popular local swimming hole. 41 sites: $14.50; 16 full hookups $18. Closed mid-Oct. to mid-Apr.

Cooper's Supermarket, 555 Victoria St. (837-4372), sells honey and graham crackers. Open Su 9am-6pm, M-Th and Sa 8am-8pm, F 8am-9pm. Your best bet for lunch and baked goods is the **Chalet Deli and Bakery,** 555 Victoria St. (837-5552), across the parking lot from Cooper's. A personal pizza with choice of sauce runs $2.75; a meaty sandwich on fresh bread $4. (Open M-Sa 5am-6pm.) **Frontier Restaurant,** 122 N. Hwy. 23 (873-5119), at the junction of Hwy. 1 and 23 N. Ranchhand St. Serves (½ lb. cheeseburger with the works) for $7.75; or an Ain't No Bull (mushroom-and-peppers veggie burger) for $6. Breakfasts too. (Open daily 5am-10pm.) They know how to cut a deal at **Bertz Outdoor Equipment and Cafe,** 217 Mackenzie Ave. (837-6575) a moutaineering gear shop/cafe. Large bagel sandwiches go for $3.25; Belgian waffles piled with fresh fruit for $7. Internet access. (Open M-Sa 8am-8pm, Su 10am-4pm.)

▓▒ SIGHTS AND OUTDOORS. The **Revelstoke Railway Museum,** 719 W. Track St. (837-6060), off Victoria Rd., is a shrine to the Iron Horse, that tells of the construction of the trans-Canadian line, completed in 1885. (Open daily 9am-8pm; in spring and fall M-F 9am-5pm. $5, seniors $3, ages 7-14 $2, under 7 free.) The mechanical marvels of the **Revelstoke Dam** (837-6515 or 837-6211), 5km north of Hwy. 1 on Hwy. 23 are illustrated in a free tour via talking wand. The elevator ascends to an impressive view. (Open daily in summer 8am-8pm; mid-May to mid-June and mid-Sept. to mid-Oct. 9am-5pm. Wheelchair accessible.)

Mt. Revelstoke National Park, adjacent to town, furnishes a quick and satisfying nature fix. A favorite of mountain bikers and hikers, the small but well-used park features some astounding scenery. Two boardwalks off Hwy. 1 on the east side of the park access the local brush. The **Skunk Cabbage Trail** (1.2km) leads through acres of stinking perfection: skunk cabbage plants tower at heights of over 1.5m. Some of the majestic trees on the **Giant Cedars Trail** (500m) are over 600 years old. There are two **backcountry campgrounds** in the park (permit $6); get details from the Revelstoke Parks Canada office or the Rogers Pass info center (see p. 303). The 24km of the **Meadows in the Sky Parkway** (Summit Rd.), branches off Hwy. 1 about 1.5km east of town, leading to a 1km hike up to Mt. Revelstoke to alpine meadows. **Summit Cycle Tours** (888-700-3444) drives customers to the summit, provides bicycles, and a guided tour on the 2hr., 27km descent ($42, 10% HI discount).

Canyon Hot Springs (837-2420), between Mt. Revelstoke National Park and Glacier National Park on Hwy. 1, sports two spring-fed pools that simmer at 40°C (104°F) and 26°C (80°F). ($5, seniors $4.50, under 15 $4. Open daily July-Aug. 9am-10pm; May, June, and Sept. 9am-9pm.) The neighboring **Apex River** (837-6367) runs 10km trips (2hr.) on the Illecillewaet's Class III-plus rapids ($42, $4 HI discount; May to Sept.). The 100 bolted routes on Begbie Bluffs offer exceptional **sport climb-**

ing (from the small parking area 8.8km down 23 South from Hwy. 1, the bluffs are a 10 minute walk; take the left fork).

Winter in Revelstoke brings several variations on **downhill skiing.** For some traditional action, **Powder Springs Resort** (837-5268), only 5km outside of town, maintains 1 chairlift and 21 trails (2000 ft. vertical drop) on the bottom third of Mt. McKenzie. You could pay $28 for a lift ticket, but that would be silly. (see **Accommodations,** above.) Local companies offer heli-skiing and cat-skiing on the upper two-thirds of this and other mountains. An Austrian family which owns 36 European ski areas has plans to put a gondola all the way to the top in 2003. The planned resort would have about 6500 ft. of vertical drop, **the largest vertical drop in North America,** on a mountain that averages 45 feet of powder a year. There's still time to move and become an old salt local who said she skied it when.... Parks Canada (see **Practical Information,** above) offers excellent advice on area cross-country trails and world-class backcountry skiing in Glacier National Park's Rogers Pass.

GLACIER NATIONAL PARK

This aptly named national park is home to over 400 of the monolithic ice flows. The jagged peaks and steep, narrow valleys of the Columbia Range that prevent development in the 1350km² park, even along the highway corridor. An inland rain forest, Glacier receives significant precipitation every other day in summer, but the clouds of mist that encircle the peaks and blanket the valleys only add to the park's astonishing beauty. In late summer, brilliant explosions of mountain wildflowers offset the deep green of the forests. Unless directly descended from Sir Edmund Hillary (see p. 310) or Tenzing Norgay, avoid exploring the park in winter.

Glacier lies 350km west of Calgary and 723km east of Vancouver. **Greyhound buses** (837-5874) make four trips per day to and from Revelstoke ($9.20). In an **emergency,** call the **Park Warden Office** (837-7500; open daily 7am-5pm; winter hours vary; 24hr. during avalanche control periods). For details on the park, talk to the Parks Canada staff or buy a copy of *Footloose in the Columbias* ($2) at the **Rogers Pass Information Centre** (814-5232), on the highway in Glacier (open daily mid-June to mid-Sept. 8am-8:30pm; mid-Nov. to April 7am-5pm; May-early June and late Sept.-early Nov. 9am-5pm). **Park passes** cost $4 per day or $35 per year (see p. 40). For more info about Glacier, write to the Superintendent, P.O. Box 350, Revelstoke, BC V0E 2S0, or call 873-7500. **Area code:** 250.

There are two campgrounds in Glacier: **Illecillewaet** (ill-uh-SILL-uh-watt), 3.4km west of Rogers Pass and **Loop Brook.** Both offer toilets, kitchen shelters with cook stoves, and firewood (sites $13; open mid-June to Sept.). Backcountry campers must purchase a **backcountry pass** ($6 per day) from the Parks Canada office in Revelstoke (837-7500; see p. 301) or from the Rogers Pass Information Center. Backcountry campers must pitch their tents at least 5km from the pavement. Food choices in the park are limited and unappealing; stock up in Golden or Revelstoke.

More than 140km of rough, often steep trails lead from the highway, inviting mountaineers to penetrate the near-impenetrable. Eight popular **hiking trails** begin at the Illecillewaet campground. The 1km (one-way) **Meeting of the Waters Trail** leads to the impressive confluence of the **Illecillewaet** and **Asulkan Rivers**. The 4.2km **Avalanche Crest Trail** offers spectacular views of Rogers Pass, the Hermit Range, and the Illecillewaet River Valley; the treeless slopes below the crest testify to the destructive power of winter snowslides. In late summer, when enough snow has melted, the **Perley Rock Trail** leads directly to the **Illecillewaet Glacier,** with a steep 5.6km ascent. Before setting out, speak with a park ranger to find out how much of the trail is safe to hike. The **Copperstain Trail,** 10km east of the Glacier Park Lodge at the Beaver River Trailhead, leads 16km (6hr.) uphill through alpine meadows. From early July to late August, the park staff run sporadic **interpretive hikes** beginning at 8:30am. Contact the visitor center for details. Come prepared for the 4-6hr. tour with a lunch, rain jacket, plenty of water, and a sturdy pair of walking shoes.

Biking and **fishing** in Glacier are prohibited. **Backcountry skiing** at Rogers Pass and Balu Pass is reputed to be superb. Contact the Rogers Pass Information Center for

S. BC & THE ROCKIES

registration and info on areas and avalanche conditions. Glacier also boasts the **Nakimu Caves,** an extensive limestone wonderland open only to experienced cavers. Access to the caves is granted to 6 to 12 people per week by a lottery system; interested parties need to apply to the park superintendent (see above) at least two weeks in advance. Traveling the caves, located off the Balu Pass Trail near the info center, is physically demanding, and guides are recommended ($20 per person fee; guides around $150 per group).

THE ROCKIES

Banff National Park is one of Canada's top tourist draws, and with good reason. Every year, some five million visitors make it within sight of the park's majestic peaks and stunning glacial lakes. Thankfully, much of this traffic is confined to highwayside gawkers, and only a tiny fraction of these visitors make it far into the forest. Still, any fraction of five million is a big number, and the park's most popular trails get crowded. Of the big two—Banff and Jasper—Jasper feels a little farther removed from the crowds and offers great wildlife viewing from the road. The chain of hostels that line both parks are among the country's best, and are booked up accordingly. It's also well worth checking out the lesser-known Glacier (see above) and Yoho (see p. 319) National Parks and Kananaskis Country (see p. 325), the fee-free locals' playground that separates Calgary from the Rockies.

Alberta's extensive and largely orthogonal highway system makes travel between major destinations easy. The north-south **Icefields Parkway (Hwy. 93)** runs between Banff and Jasper. The east-west **Yellowhead Highway (Hwy. 16)** connects Edmonton with Jasper, and continues across British Columbia. The **Trans-Canada Highway (Hwy. 1)** completes the loop, linking Calgary with Banff. **Buses** (Greyhound, Brewster, and Red Arrow) travel all of these routes, VIA Rail **trains** run from Edmonton to Jasper.

One-way bike rentals are a popular way to travel the Icefields Parkway, though the trip is best suited to experienced cyclists. Drivers will pass many deeply frustrated, possibly misled cyclists pushing their bikes up steep inclines. See **Equipment Rental,** pp. 306 and 314 for bike rental outfits.

Without a car, guided bus rides may be the easiest way to see some of the park's main attractions, such as the Great Divide, the Athabasca Glacier, and the spiral railroad tunnel. **Brewster Tours** (762-6767) buses from Banff to Jasper stop for the major sights and take 9½ hours ($85, Apr.-Oct. at 8:10am). A visit to the Columbia Icefields is $25 extra. **Bigfoot Tours** (888-244-6673, in Vancouver 604-278-8224; www.backpackertours.com/Bigfoot/index.shtml) runs two-day, 11-passenger van trips between Banff and Jasper for $84, not including food or lodging at the Mt. Edith Cavell Hostel (see p. 315). They also travel between Vancouver and Banff with sightseeing stops along the way. The trip to Banff overnights at the Squilax General Store Hostel (see p. 293), the trip west to Vancouver stays at the Kamloops Old Courthouse Hostel (see p. 292). The $99 one-way fee does not include food or lodging. Fares include free pickup at HI hostel departure points (both Vancouver hostels, Lake Louise, Banff International) and run mid-April to mid-November three times per week in each direction.

BANFF NATIONAL PARK, AB

Banff is Canada's best-loved and best-known natural park, with 6641km² (2,564 sq. mi.) of peaks, forests, glaciers, and alpine valleys. Its unrhymable name comes from Banffshire, Scotland, the birthplace of the two Canadian Pacific Railway financiers who convinced Canada's first Prime Minister that a "large pecuniary advantage" might be gained from the region, and told him that, "since we can't export the scenery, we shall have to import the tourists." Their plan worked with a vengeance, but even streets littered with gift shops and chocolatiers cannot mar Banff's beauty. Outdoors-lovers arrive with mountain bikes, climbing gear, skis, and snowboards, but a trusty pair of hiking boots remains the park's most popular outdoor equipment.

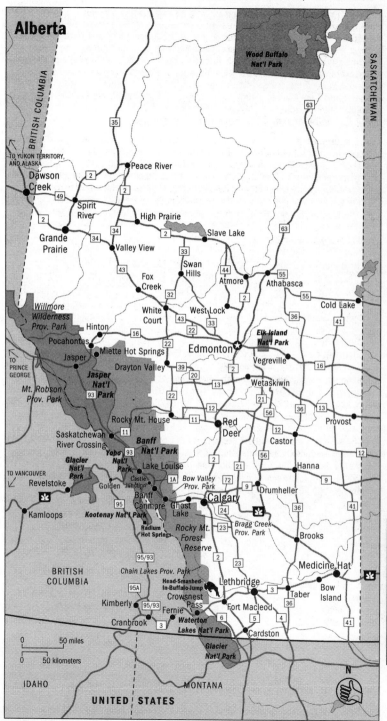

Alberta

BRITISH COLUMBIA

SASKATCHEWAN

Wood Buffalo
Nat'l Park

63

35

TO YUKON TERRITORY,
AND ALASKA

Dawson
Creek

Peace River

2

49

Spirit
River

High Prairie

2

Slave Lake

63

2

34

Grande
Prairie

34

Valley View

33

Swan
Hills

44

Atmore

55

Athabasca

43

Fox
Creek

43

55

Cold Lake

32

Willmore
Wilderness
Prov. Park

Hinton

16

White
Court

West Lock

33

36

41

22

22

TO
PRINCE
GEORGE

Pocahontas

Jasper

Miette Hot Springs

Drayton Valley

Edmonton

Elk Island
Nat'l Park

Vegreville

16

Jasper
Nat'l
Park

93

39

20

2

Mt. Robson
Prov. Park

22

13

Wetaskiwin

21

36

13

Provost

Rocky Mt. House

11

12

Red
Deer

56

12

Castor

Saskatchewan
River Crossing

11

93

Banff
Nat'l Park

2

21

56

Hanna

12

Glacier
Nat'l
Park

Yoho
Nat'l
Park

93

Lake Louise

1A

Bow Valley
Prov. Park

72

9

Drumheller

9

TO VANCOUVER

Revelstoke

Golden

Castle
Junction

Banff

Canmore

Ghost
Lake

Calgary

24

36

41

Kamloops

95

Kootenay Nat'l Park

Radium
Hot Springs

Rocky Mt.
Forest
Reserve

23

Bragg Creek
Prov. Park

Brooks

2

BRITISH
COLUMBIA

95/93

Chain Lakes Prov. Park

23

Medicine Hat

95A

Head-Smashed-
In-Buffalo-Jump

Lethbridge

Kimberly

95/93

Fernie

Crowsnest
Pass

3

Taber

Bow
Island

Cranbrook

3

6

Fort Macleod

36

Waterton
Lakes Nat'l Park

5

4

Cardston

41

0   50 miles

0   50 kilometers

Glacier
Nat'l Park

N

IDAHO

MONTANA

UNITED STATES

S. BC & THE ROCKIES

☑ ORIENTATION AND PRACTICAL INFORMATION

Banff National Park hugs the Alberta side of the Alberta/British Columbia border, 129km west of Calgary. The **Trans-Canada Highway (Hwy. 1)** runs east-west through the park, connecting it to Yoho National Park to the west. The **Icefields Parkway (Hwy. 93)** connects Banff with Jasper National Park to the north and Kootenay National Park to the southwest. Civilization in the park centers around the towns of **Banff** and **Lake Louise**, 58km apart on Hwy. 1. The **Bow Valley Parkway (Hwy. 1A)** parallels Hwy. 1 from Lake Louise to 8km west of Banff. All of the following listings apply to Banff Townsite, unless otherwise specified.

Buses: Greyhound, 327 Railway Ave. (800-661-8747), in the train station. 4 per day to: Lake Louise (1hr; $11) and Vancouver, BC (13hr; $99); 5 per day to Calgary (2 hr; $19.50). See p. 53 for discounts. **Brewster Transportation,** 100 Gopher St. (762-6767). To: Jasper (5 hr., 3:15pm, $51); Lake Louise (1hr., 3 per day, $11); Calgary (2hr., 4 per day, $36). Depot open daily 7:30am-9:00pm. HI discount 15%, ages 6-15 half-price. See p. 304 for info on **tours** to, from, and within the Rocky Mountain parks.

Public Transportation: The **Happy Bus** runs between the Banff Springs Hotel, the trailer area, and Banff Hostel on Tunnel Mountain Rd.; and between the Tunnel Mountain Campground, downtown, and the Banff Park Museum. $1, children 50¢. Mid-May to Sept. 7am-midnight; late Apr. to early May and Oct.-Dec. noon-midnight.

Taxis: Banff Taxi, 726-4444, 24hr. **Lake Louise Taxi,** 522-2080. Runs 6am-2:30pm.

Car Rental: Banff Used Car Rentals (762-3522), in the Shell at Wolf and Lynx. $38 per day, 10¢ per km after 100km. Insurance $9 per day. Must be 21 with major credit card.

Visitor Information: Banff Visitor Centre, 224 Banff Ave. Includes **Banff/Lake Louise Tourism Bureau** (762-8421; www.banfflakelouise.com) and **Canadian Parks Service** (762-1550). Open daily June-Sept. 8am-8pm; Oct.-May 9am-5pm. **Lake Louise Visitor Centre** (522-3833), at Samson Mall. The complex is also a museum, and screens a short film on the formation of the Rockies. Open daily July-Aug. 8am-8pm; June and Sept. 8am-6pm; Oct.-May 9am-5pm.

Equipment Rental: Bactrax Rentals, 225 Bear St. (762-8177), rents bikes one-way to Jasper. Mountain bikes $7 per hr., $25 for 24hr. Ski packages from $15 per day, snowboard and boots $28. 20% HI discount. Open daily 8am-8pm. **Performance Sport,** 208 Bear St. (762-8222), rents tents ($20 per day), fishing gear ($15-25 per day) and cross-country ski or snowshoe packages ($12 per day, $31 for 3 days). 10% HI discount. Open daily 9am-8pm.

Laundry: Cascade Coin Laundry, 317 Banff Ave. (762-0165), downstairs in the Cascade Mall. Wash $2, dry 25¢ per 5min. Open daily 8am-11pm. **Lake Louise Laundromat** (522-2143), Samson Mall. Wash $2.50, dry 25¢ per 5min. Open W-M 9am-7pm.

Weather: 762-2088. **Road Conditions:** 762-1450. **Public Radio:** 860 AM.

Emergency: Banff Police: (762-2226, non-emergency 762-2228), on Lynx St. by the train depot. **Lake Louise Police:** 522-3811, non-emergency 522-3812. **Banff Park Warden,** 762-4506. **Lake Louise Park Warden:** 522-1200. **Ambulance:** 762-2000.

Hospital: Mineral Springs, 301 Lynx St. (762-2222), near Wolf St. in Banff.

Post Office: 204 Buffalo St., TOL 0C0 (762-2586). Open M-F 9am-5:30pm.

Internet Access: Free at the **Library,** 101 Bear St. (762-2611; open M-Th 11am-8pm, F-Sa 11am-6pm; sign up in advance). **The Web** (762-9226), on the lower level of Sundance Mall; entrance across from tourist office on Banff Ave ($8 per hour; open daily 10am-midnight). Only $3 for 30min. upstairs at **Fossil Face Natural Foods**.

Area Code: 403.

☑ ACCOMMODATIONS

Finding a cheap place to stay in Banff is becoming increasingly difficult as the number of visitors soars into the millions per year. Townsite residents offer rooms in their homes, occasionally at reasonable rates. ($75-140 in summer, $60-100 in winter). Check the list at the back of the *Banff and Lake Louise Official Visitor Guide*, available free at the visitor centers.

The Rockies (Banff, Yoho & Kootenay National Parks)

CAMPGROUNDS

O Castle Mountain
H Chancellor Peak
U Dolly Varden
I Hoodoo Creek
P Johnston Canyon
G Kicking Horse
K Lake Louise
J Lake O'Hara
Q Marble Canyon
V McLeod Meadows
F Monarch
B Mosquito Creek

M Protection Mountain
W Redstreake
D Takakkaw Falls
T Tunnel Mountain,
S Two Jack
A Waterfowl

HOSTELS

R Banff
N Castle Mountain
L Lake Louise
E Whiskey Jack
C Mosquito Creek

Mammoth **modern hostels** at Banff and Lake Louise anchor a chain of hostels from Calgary to Jasper. **Rustic hostels** provide more of a wilderness experience, and are often a stone's throw away from the best hiking and cross-country skiing in the park. HI runs a **shuttle service** connecting all the Rocky Mountain hostels and Calgary ($7-65). Wait-list beds become available at 6pm, and the larger hostels try to save a few stand-by beds for shuttle arrivals. It is never too early to secure a bed at Banff International or Lake Louise, and it is often too late, especially in July and August. The hostels below are listed from south to north; excluding Lake Louise, all reservations are made through Banff International. Free reservations are held until 6pm, or can be guaranteed until later with a credit card.

Banff International Hostel (HI) (762-4122; banff@hostellingintl.ca), 3km uphill from Banff Townsite on Tunnel Mountain Rd., which leads from Otter St. downtown. Walk or take the Happy Bus from downtown ($1). This over-sized hostel has the look and feel of a ski lodge, with 3 lounge areas, 2 large fireplaces, a game room with pool table, a kitchen, cafe, laundry facilities, and hot showers. Ski and snowboard storage area and workshop. Sleeps 215: $20, non-members $24. Private rooms available ($12 surcharge). Linen $1. Open 24hr. Wheelchair accessible.

Lake Louise International Hostel (HI) (522-2200; llouise@hostellingintl.ca), 500m west of the Information Center in Lake Louise Townsite, on Village Rd. Not to be outdone by neighboring Banff, the Lake Louise hostel is ranked fourth in the world by HI, and rightly so. More like a hotel than a hostel, this budget resort boasts a reference library, common rooms with open, beamed ceilings, a stone fireplace, 2 full kitchens, a sauna, ski and bike workshops, and a quality cafe. A hub for mountaineering tours and numerous other guided activities. Large rooms with 2, 4, and 6 beds, and a bathroom. Sleeps 155: $21, nonmembers $25. Private rooms (2-3 people) available for $6 surcharge per person. Wheelchair accessible.

Castle Mountain Hostel (HI), on the Bow Valley Parkway (Hwy. 1A), 1½km east of the junction of Hwy. 1 and Hwy. 93, between Banff and Lake Louise. A quieter alternative for those seeking refuge from the hubbub of the Big Hostels. Running water, hot showers, and electricity. The hostel's 31 beds fill quickly. Cozy and beautifully designed common area has a general store, library, and fireplace. $13, non-members $17. Linen $1.

Mosquito Creek Hostel (HI), 103km south of the Icefield Centre and 26km north of Lake Louise. Across the creek from the Mosquito Creek campground; its proximity to Wapta Icefield and its wood-burning sauna make up for the not-so-scenic company. Kitchen, fireplace, and pump water. $13, nonmembers $17. Linen $1. Two private rooms available (from $39). Closed Oct. 12 - Nov. 15, and M-Tu from Nov. 15 to May 15.

Rampart Creek Hostel (HI), 34km south of the Icefield Centre. Close to several world-famous ice climbs (including Weeping Wall, 17km north), this hostel is a favorite for winter mountaineers. Wood-burning sauna, full-service kitchen, unlimited mountain spring water (a.k.a. creek). Sleeps 26 in rustic cabins: $12, nonmembers $16. Closed Oct. 12 to Nov. 15, and Tu-W from Nov. 16 to May 15.

Hilda Creek Hostel (HI), 8½km south of the Icefield Centre. At the base of Mt. Athabasca, and peacefully isolated even from the cars of hostelers. Some of the icefield's best hiking and skiing lie just behind, on Parker Ridge. Sauna, firepit, full-service kitchen, groceries, and a free toboggan. Propane heat and light; water at creek. Sleeps 21: $12, nonmembers $16. Closed Oct.12 to Dec.17, and Tu-Th Jan. 2 to May 15.

▌ CAMPGROUNDS

As with the hostels, a chain of campgrounds stretches between Banff and Jasper. Extra-large, fully hooked-up grounds lie closer to the townsites; for more trees and fewer vehicles, try one of the primitive sites farther from Banff and Lake Louise. At all park campgrounds, a campfire permit (including firewood) is $4. Sites are first-come, first-served, and go early. The sites below are listed from south to north, and have toilets but no showers, unless otherwise noted.

Tunnel Mountain Village, 4km from Banff Townsite on Tunnel Mountain Rd. With over 1200 sites, this facility is a camping metropolis. The trailer/RV area has 322 full hookups ($24), Village 2 has 189 sites (power only, $21), and Village 1 houses a whopping 618 sites (no hookups, $17). Fires allowed in Village 1 only; all villages have showers. Village 2 is open year-round; others closed Oct. to early May.

Two Jack, 13km northeast of Banff, across Hwy.1. The 381 sites in the main area ($13) have no showers, while the 74 lakeside sites ($16) do. Open mid-May to mid-Sept.

Johnston Canyon, 26km northwest of Banff on the Bow Valley Pkwy. (Hwy. 1A). Access to the Johnston Canyon Trail (see below). Showers. 132 sites: $17. Open mid-June to Sept.

Castle Mountain, midway between Banff and Lake Louise along the Bow Valley Pkwy. (Hwy. 1A). Forested sites and relatively uncrowded hiking. 43 Sites: $13. Open mid-May to early Sept.

Protection Mountain, 15km east of Lake Louise and 11km west of Castle Junction on the Bow Valley Pkwy. (Hwy. 1A). 89 spacious and wooded sites (14 trailer) in a basic campground. Sites $13. Open late June to mid-Sept.

Lake Louise, 1½km southeast of the Visitor Center on Fairview Rd. On Bow River, not the lake, but plenty of hiking and fishing awaits near this tent city. Showers. 189 trailer sites: $21 electricity only; open year-round. 220 tent sites: $17; open mid-May to Sept.

Mosquito Creek, 103km south of the Icefield Centre and 26km north of Lake Louise. 32 sites with access to hiking. Pit toilets. Sites $10.

Waterfowl, 57km north of Hwy. 1 on Hwy. 93. 116 sites near the Waterfowl Lakes. Toilets but no water. Sites $13. Open mid-June to mid-Sept.

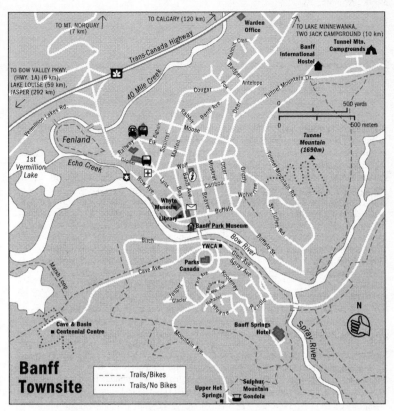

Banff Townsite

- - - - - Trails/Bikes

········· Trails/No Bikes

Rampart Creek, 147km north of Banff, 40km south of the Icefield Centre, across the hwy. from the hostel and amazing ice climbing. Pit toilets. 50 sites: $10. Open mid-June to Aug.

FOOD

Like everything else, Banff restaurants generally tend toward the expensive. Luckily, the Banff and Lake Louise Hostels serve affordable meals ($3-8), and some local bars offer reasonable daily specials. Ample groceries await at **Safeway** (762-5378), at Marten and Elk St., just off Banff Ave. (open daily 8am-11pm).

Laggan's Deli (522-2017), in Samson Mall in Lake Louise. Thick sandwich on whole-wheat $3.75; fresh-baked loaf for later $2.35. Always crowded; there's nowhere better in town. Open daily 6am-9pm; winter 6am-7pm.

Fossil Face Natural Foods Cafe, 215 Banff (760-8219), on the upper level of the Sundance Mall. A very relaxed vegetarian cafe cleverly hidden in a corner of a touristy mall. Earthy decor, eclectic bookshelf, and a highly organic menu. Black bean chili $6; veggies in peanut or curry sauce over brown rice $9. Open M-Sa 11am-9pm.

Aardvark's, 304A Caribou St. (762-5500), does big business after the bars close. Skinny on seating, thick slices of pizza ($2.80). Small $6-8; large $13-20; buffalo wings $5 for 10. 10% HI discount on large pizzas. Open daily 11am-4am.

Magpie & Stump, 203 Caribou St. (762-4067), at Bear St. Named after a London pub, this joint wisely shirks English fare in favor of heaping, Mexican dishes. Constant mariachi music and happy hour (10pm-2am; $3.25 margarita or beer) woo a late-night crowd. Quesadillas $6-7; meal-sized nachos $5-6; margarita $4. Open daily noon-2am.

◉ ♫ SIGHTS AND EVENTS

The palatial **Banff Springs Hotel** (762-2211) overlooks town from Spray Ave. Completed in 1888, it was the most ornate of the luxury hotels that the railroad built to bring the Mohammeds to the mountains. Ride the guest elevator up to the 8th floor to see what those who can afford to stay here see. In summer, the hotel leads 1 hr. **tours** of the grounds (5pm, $5), but the bold can grab a pamphlet and stroll for free.

The **Whyte Museum of the Canadian Rockies**, 111 Bear St. (762-2291), explores the human (read: Whyte settler) history of the Canadian Rockies. Exhibits in the museum's Heritage Gallery explain how Banff grew: very rapidly, unchecked, and indulging the whims of wealthy guests. (Open daily 10am-5pm; $4, students and seniors $2, children free, families $10.) The **Banff Park Museum** (762-1558), on Banff Ave. near the bridge, is western Canada's oldest museum, with stuffed specimens dating to the 1860s. (Open daily June-Aug. 10am-6pm; Sept.-May 10am-5pm. Tours 3pm. $2.50, seniors $2, children $1.50.)

In summer, the **Banff Festival of the Arts** takes over. The culture train choo-choos through town from May to mid-August with a wide range of performances, from First Nations dance to Opera. Some performances are free; stop by the visitor center for a schedule. The 25th annual **Banff Mountain Film Festival**, Oct. 30-Nov. 5, 2000, screens films and videos that celebrate mountains and mountaineers. **Sir Edmund Hillary** is on the slate of this year's guest speakers. For info on either festival, call 762-6301, or visit www.banffcentre.ab.ca/CMC/.

♫ NIGHTLIFE

Bartenders maintain that Banff's true wildlife is in its bars. Check the paper to find out which nightspots are having "locals' night," featuring cheap drinks.

■ **Rose and Crown,** 202 Banff Ave. (762-2121), upstairs. The upbeat centerpiece of Banff nightlife. Elbow room for drinking, dancing, and pool-playing, even on busy nights. Throw back a few in the couch-adorned living room. Nearly nightly live music. Happy hour (M-F 4:30-7:30pm) heralds $3.50-4 drafts. Open daily 11am-2am.

Barbary Coast, 119 Banff Ave. (762-4616), upstairs. Sports paraphernalia festoons this snazzy bar. The kitchen is excellent, with especially tasty pasta dishes. Lunch specials $6-7. Monday is pizza night (10 in. pie $7). Almost nightly live blues and rock. Happy hour 4:30-7:30pm. No cover. Open daily 11am-2am.

⚟ OUTDOORS

A visitor sticking to paved byways will see only a tiny fraction of the park. Those who wish to get more closely acquainted can hike or bike through the wild remainder on more than 1600km of trails. Grab a copy of *Banff and Vicinity Drives and Walks*, and peruse park maps and trail descriptions at information centers. For still more solitude, pick up the *Backcountry Visitor Guide* and an **overnight camping permit** at a visitor center and head out to the backcountry ($6 per person per day, up to $30; $42 per year).

BANFF TOWNSITE AREA

Two easy trails are within walking distance of Banff Townsite. **Fenland** (1hr.) closed for elk calving in late spring and early summer, winds 2km through an area shared by beaver, muskrat, and waterfowl. Follow Mt. Norquay Rd. out of town, and look for signs across the tracks on the road's left side. The summit of **Tunnel Mountain** provides a dramatic view of the **Bow Valley** and **Mt. Rundle.** Follow Wolf St. east from Banff Ave., and turn right on St. Julien Rd. to reach the head of the steep 2.3km (2hr.) trail. Tunnel Mountain has the unfortunate distinction of being the Rockies' smallest mountain, and its most deadly.

At 2949m/9675 ft., **Mt. Rundle** offers a more demanding fair-weather dayhike (7-8 hr., 5.5km one-way 1600m/5248 ft. elev. gain). The trail includes an exposed ridge known as the Dragon's Back, which leads to a scramble up scree slopes just short of the summit. The unrivaled vista is well worth the effort.

Johnston Canyon, about 25km out of Banff toward Lake Louise along the Bow Valley Pkwy. (Hwy. 1A), is a very popular half-day hike. A catwalk along the edge of the deep limestone canyon runs 1km over the thundering river to the canyon's lower falls, then another 1.6km to the upper falls. The trail continues for a more rugged 3km to seven blue-green cold-water springs, known as the **Inkpots,** in an open valley above the canyon. More than 42km of trails beyond the Inkpots are blissfully untraveled, and punctuated with campgrounds roughly every 10km.

Biking is permitted on public roads, highways, and certain trails in the park. Spectacular scenery and a number of hostels and campgrounds make the **Bow Valley Parkway (Hwy. 1A)** and the **Icefields Parkway (Hwy. 93)** perfect for extended cycling trips. Every other store downtown seems to rent bikes, many one-way; head to **Bactrax** or **Performance Sport** (see **Equipment Rental,** above) for HI discounts. Parks Canada publishes brochures that describe trails and roadways where bikes are permitted (free at bike rental shops and visitor centers).

Banff National Park might not exist if not for the **Cave and Basin Hot Springs,** once rumored to have miraculous healing properties. The **Cave and Basin National Historic Site** (762-1557), a refurbished resort built circa 1914, is now a small museum detailing the history and science of the site. (Open daily in summer 9am-6pm; in winter 9:30am-5pm. Tours at 11am. $2.50, seniors $2, children $1.50.) Follow the 2km **Discovery Trail** from the museum to see the original spring, discovered over 100 years ago by three Canadian Pacific Railway workers. Five of the pools are the only home of the park's most threatened species: the small but newsworthy **Banff Springs snail**—*Physella Johnsoni.* (Banff's grizzly bear, woodland caribou, and wolverine are classified as vulnerable, one step farther from extinction.) The springs are southwest of the city on Cave Ave. For an actual dip in the hot water, follow the egg smell to the **Upper Hot Springs** pool (762-1515), a 40°C (104°F) sulfurous cauldron on Mountain Ave. (Open daily 9am-11pm; winter 10am-10pm; $7, seniors and children $6. Swimsuits $1.50, towels $1.50, lockers 50¢.) A moderate 5.3km (2hr.) hike wends along a well-trodden trail to the 2285m/7500 ft. peak of **Sulphur Mountain,** where a spectacular view awaits; the **Sulphur Mountain Gondola** (762-2523) doesn't charge for the 8-minute downhill trip. (uphill $14, ages 5-11 $7, under 5 free.) The **Panorama Restaurant,** perched atop the mountain, serves breakfast ($9) and lunch buffets ($11) from mid-May to mid-August.

Fishing is legal in most of the park's bodies of water during specific seasons, but live bait and lead weights are not. Get a **permit** and check out regulations at the info center. (7-day permit $6, annual permit valid in all Canadian National Parks

THINGS THAT GO BANFF IN THE NIGHT

Bear sightings are common in the Canadian Rockies, but one black bear took it upon himself to give Banff residents an uncommon reminder of whose park it really is. Imaginatively known as Bear 16 (numbers are used to discourage personification), this ursine vagabond moved into town, disrupting everyday activity by foraging in front lawns and lazing in the road, blocking traffic. Bear 16 crossed the line when the scent from a bakery lured him too close to human territory. The park staff ultimately removed Bear 16 from the park, had him castrated, and relocated him to the Calgary Zoo.

While most travelers to the park are eager to see its wildlife, few want as intimate an encounter as Bear 16 offered, and those who do are foolish. The safest bet is to talk, sing, or yodel loudly while hiking, especially on windy days or near running water (see **Bear Safety,** p. 44). The number of bear attacks actually ranks low among the total number of attacks by park animals; dozens of visitors are bitten each year by rodents pursuing human food. By far the most dangerous of Banff animals, however, are people—road accidents are a more common cause of death for large wildlife within the park than predators.

$13.) **Borgeau Lake,** a 7km hike in, is home to a particularly feisty breed of brook trout. Closer to the road, try **Herbert Lake,** off the Icefields Pkwy., or **Lake Minnewanka,** on Lake Minnewanka Rd. northeast of Banff. Lake Minnewanka Rd. also passes **Johnson Lake,** where sunlight warms the shallow water to a pleasantly swimmable temperature.

Hydra River Guides (762-4544 or 800-644-8888) runs 2½ hr., 22km **whitewater rafting** trips along the **Kicking Horse River** (up to Class IV rapids). ($83, lunch included, HI members $68.) **Blast Adventures** (609-2009 or 888-802-5278) retails half-day, two-person **inflatable kayak** trips on the rowdy Kananaskis River for $59 each (includes lunch, transportation, and snacks).

LAKE LOUISE AND ENVIRONS

The highest community in Canada at 1530m/5018 ft., Lake Louise and the surrounding glaciers have often passed for Swiss scenery in movies, and are the emerald in the Rockies' tiara of tourism. Once at the lake, the hardest task is escaping fellow gawkers at the posh **Chateau Lake Louise.** Canoe rentals at the chateau are more than steep ($25 per hr.), but avoidable: several hiking trails begin at the water. The 3.6km **Lake Agnes Trail** and the 5.5km **Plain of Six Glaciers Trail** both end at teahouses (open 10am-6pm).

Nearby **Moraine Lake** may pack more of a scenic punch than its sister Louise; arrive before 10am or after 4pm to see the view rather than the crowds. The lake is 15km from the village, at the end of Moraine Lake Rd., off Lake Louise Dr. (no trailers or long RV's). Moraine lies in the awesome **Valley of the Ten Peaks,** opposite glacier-encrusted **Mt. Temple.** Join the multitudes on the **Rockpile Trail** for an eye-popping view of the lake and valley, and an explanation of rocks from ancient ocean bottoms. If you don't get a chance to visit Moraine, just get your hands on an old $20 bill; the Valley of Ten Peaks is pictured on the reverse.

Paradise Valley, depending on which way you hike it, can be an intense dayhike or a relaxing overnight trip. From the **Paradise Creek trailhead,** 2.5km up Moraine Lake Rd., the loop through the valley runs 18.1km through subalpine and alpine forests, and along rivers. One classic backpacking route runs from Moraine Lake up and over **Sentinel Pass,** joining the top of the Paradise Valley loop after 8km. A **backcountry campground** marks the approximate midpoint from either trailhead. Campers aren't the only admirers of the scenery: grizzly activity often forces the park wardens to close the area in the summer.

The **Lake Louise Sightseeing Lift** (522-3555), across the Trans-Canada Hwy. from Lake Louise, cruises up **Mt. Whitehorn.** (Open June 8:30am-6pm; July and August 8am-6pm; Sept. 8:30am-6pm. $11, students and seniors $10, ages 6-15 $8, under 5 free.) An early morning ride including breakfast at the top runs $13.

WINTER SPORTS

Winter activities in the park range from world-class ice climbing to ice fishing. Those 1600km of hiking trails make for exceptional **cross-country skiing,** and three allied resorts offer a range of **skiing and snowboarding** opportunities from early November to mid-May. All have terrain parks for snowboarders. **Sunshine Mountain** (762-6500, snow report 760-7669 or from Calgary 277-7669; www.skibanff.com) actually spreads across three mountains, and attracts a loyal following to its 3168 acres of terrain with the largest snowfall in the area (9.9m/33 ft.). Lift tickets: $46.50; students under 25, youth (ages 13-17), and seniors (over 65) $38; ages 6-12 $15. **Lake Louise** (522-3555, snow report 762-4766; www.skilouise.com) is the second largest ski area in Canada (4200 skiable acres), with amazing views, over 1000m/3300 ft. of vertical drop and the best selection of expert (double-black) terrain, though simpler slopes cover plenty of the mountain. Lift tickets: $46; students under 25, youth (ages 13-17), and seniors (over 65) $36; ages 6-12 $15. **Mount Norquay** (762-4421; www.banffnorquay.com) is a local's mountain: smaller, closer to town, and much less manic, with such draws as Friday night skiing and tickets good for two to five hours. Lift tickets: $39; students, youth (ages 13-17), and seniors (over 55) $33; children (ages 6-12) $15. Night skiing $21, students, youth, and seniors $20, ages 6-12 $11. Two-hour pass $21, students, youths, and seniors $19, children $9.

Shuttles to all three resorts leave from most big hotels in the townsites, and Banff and Lake Louise hostels typically have **ticket and transportation discounts** available for guests. Multi-day passes good for all three resorts are available at the **Ski Banff/Lake Louise** office, 225 Banff Ave. (762-4561; www.skibanfflakelouise. com), lower level, and at all resorts ($50.50 per day; 3 day minimum). Passes include free shuttle service and an extra night of skiing at Mount Norquay. See above for **Equipment Rentals.**

ICEFIELDS PARKWAY (HWY. 93)

Begun in the Great Depression as a work relief project, the 230km Icefields Parkway is one of the most beautiful drives in North America, heading north from Lake Louise in Banff National Park to Jasper Townsite in Jasper National Park. Drivers may struggle to keep their eyes on the road, as it dips above and below treeline, skirts dozens of stern peaks, aquamarine glacial lakes, and highwayside glaciers that provide ammunition for summer snowball fights.

🛈 PRACTICAL INFORMATION. Parks Canada manages the parkway as a scenic route, so all users must obtain a **Park Pass,** available at entrance gates and information centers ($10 per day or $70 per year for 2-7 persons; includes all Canadian national parks). Free maps of the Icefields Parkway are available at park visitor centers in Jasper, Lake Louise, and Banff, or at the **Icefield Centre** (852-6288), at the boundary between the two parks, 132km north of Lake Louise and 103km south of Jasper Townsite (open May to mid-Oct. daily 9am-5pm). Although the center is closed in winter, the parkway is only closed for plowing after heavy snowfalls.

Thanks to the extensive campground and hostel networks that line the parkway, longer trips down the length of Jasper and Banff National Parks are convenient and affordable (see **Accommodations,** p. 306 and 315). Cycling the highway is a popular option, and bikes can be rented in Banff or Jasper for a one-way trip. Those who cycle should be prepared to face rapidly changing weather conditions and some very steep hills. No matter how you travel the parkway, set aside some time for its challenging hikes and magnificent vistas.

🛈 OUTDOORS. The Icefields Parkway has 18 trails into the wilderness and 22 scenic points with spectacular views. At **Bow Summit,** 40km north of Lake Louise, the parkway's highest point (2135m, 7000 ft.), a 10-minute walk leads to a view of fluorescent aqua **Peyto Lake.** The Icefield Centre (see above) lies in the shadow of the tongue of the **Athabasca Glacier.** This gargantuan ice flow is one of the six major glaciers that flow from the 325km² **Columbia Icefield,** the largest accumulation of ice and snow south of the Arctic Circle (yes, excepting Antarctica, smartypants). The icefield's runoff eventually flows to three oceans: the Pacific, Atlantic, and Arctic.

Columbia Icefield Snocoach Tours (877-423-7433) carries visitors over the Athabasca Glacier in bizarre monster buses for an 80-minute trip (Apr.-Oct. daily 9am-5pm. $25, ages 6-15 $10). A 10-minute walk leads up piles of glacial debris to the glacier's mighty toe. Dated signposts mark the glacier's speedy retreat up the valley over the last century. For more tasty geological tidbits, sign up for an **Athabasca Glacier Icewalk** ("Ice Cubed": 3hr.; $31, ages 7-17 $14. "Ice Walk Deluxe": 5hr.; $37, ages 7-17 $16). One of the two hikes runs each day at 11:30am (mid-June to mid-Sept.); contact the Icefield Centre or Peter Lemieux (852-3083; iceman1@agt.net).

The **Wilcox Pass Trail** begins 3km south of the Icefield Centre at Wilcox Creek Campground (see p. 316), the first 2.5km of the path climb onto a ridge with astounding views of Athabasca Glacier and Mt. Athabasca. The **Parker Ridge Trail** leads 2.4km away from the road and up above treeline, where an impressive view of the **Saskatchewan Glacier** awaits. The trailhead is 1km south of the Hilda Creek Hostel (see p. 308), and 8.5km south of the Icefield Centre.

S. BC & THE ROCKIES

JASPER NATIONAL PARK, AB

Northward expansion of the Canadian railway system led to further exploration of the Canadian Rocky Mountains and the 1907 creation of Jasper, the largest of the National Parks in the region. The area went virtually untouristed until 1940, though, when the Icefields Parkway paved the way for the masses to appreciate Jasper's astounding beauty. In summer, caravans of RVs and charter buses line the highway for the chance to take photos of surprisingly domesticated wildlife. Because 40% of the park is above the treeline, most visitors stay in the sheltered vicinity of Jasper Townsite, and every summer the town's winter population quadruples to over 20,000. In the face of this annual bloat, Jasper's permanent residents struggle to keep their home looking and feeling like a genuine small town. In the winter, the crowds melt away, a blanket of snow descends, and a modest ski resort welcomes visitors to a slower, more relaxed town.

⚪ ORIENTATION AND PRACTICAL INFORMATION

All of the addresses below are in **Jasper Townsite,** near the center of the park at the intersection of **Hwy. 16,** which runs through the northern reaches of the park, and the **Icefields Parkway (Hwy. 93),** which connects Jasper with Banff National Park in the south. Many bike shops rent one-way between the two parks. Hitching is popular and reportedly easy along the Parkway, though not necessarily safe.

Trains: VIA Rail, 607 Connaught Dr. (800-561-8630 or 852-4102). 3 per week to: Vancouver, BC (16½hr., $151); Edmonton (5hr., $88); Winnipeg, MB (1 day, $240). See p. 52 for discounts. Coin-operated lockers $2 per 24hr.

Buses: Greyhound (852-3926), in the train station. To: Edmonton (4½hr., 4 per day, $47); Vancouver, BC (11½hr., 3 per day, $98), via Kamloops, BC (5hr., $56). See p. 53 for discounts. **Brewster Transportation** (852-3332), in the train station. To: Calgary (1:30pm, 7½hr., $71), via Banff (5½hr., $51).

Taxis: Heritage Cabs (852-5558), offers a flat rate from town to Jasper International Hostel ($8); and to the Maligne Canyon Hostel ($14).

Car Rental: Hertz (852-3888), in the train station. $50 per day, 24¢ per km after 100km. Must be 21 with credit card. Closed in winter. **Budget** (852-3222), in the Shell Station at 638 Connaught Dr. $55 per day, 23¢ per km after 100km; 6hr. for $33.

Car Repair: Petro Canada, 300 Connaught Dr. (852-3366).

Visitor Information: Park Information Centre, 500 Connaught Dr. (852-6176), has trail maps and offers free local calls. Open daily mid-June to early Sept. 8am-7pm; early Sept. to late Oct. and late Dec. to mid-June 9am-5pm.

Bank: CIBC, 416 Connaught Ave. (852-3391), by the visitor center. Open M-Th 10am-3pm, F 10am-5pm. 24hr. **ATM.**

Equipment Rental: Freewheel Cycle, 618 Patricia Ave. (852-3898). Mountain bikes $6 per hr., $18 per day, $24 overnight. Snowboard and boots $25 per day. Open in summer daily 9am-8pm; spring and fall 9am-6pm; call for winter hours. **Jasper International Hostel** also rents mountain bikes. $3 per hr., $9.50-12.50 per half-day, $15-20 per day.

Laundromat and Public Showers: Coin Clean, 607 Patricia St. (852-3852). Wash $1.50, dry 25¢ per 5min. Showers $2 per 10min. Open daily 8am-9:30pm.

Weather: 852-3185. **Road Conditions:** 762-1450. **Radio:** 101.1 FM.

Emergency: 852-4848. **Police:** 600 Pyramid Lake Rd. (852-4421).

Women's Crisis Line: 800-661-0937. 24hr.

Hospital: 518 Robson St. (852-3344). **Pharmacy: Whistlers Drugs,** 100 Miette Ave. (852-4411), open daily 8am-11pm; Sept. to mid-June Su-Th 9am-6pm, F-Sa 9am-9pm.

Post Office: 502 Patricia St., TOE 1E0 (852-3041), across from the townsite green. Open M-F 9am-5pm.

Internet Access: Soft Rock Cafe (see **Food,** below). $4 for 20min., $8.50 per hr.

Area Code: 780.

ACCOMMODATIONS

HOSTELS

The modern Jasper International Hostel, just outside Jasper Townsite, anchors a chain of Hostelling International (HI) hostels stretching from Jasper to Calgary. The rustic hostels farther into the park offer few amenities, but lie amid some of Jasper's finest scenery and outdoor activities. HI runs a shuttle service connecting the Rocky Mountain hostels with Calgary (one-way $7-65). For reservations and info on all hostels, call the Jasper hostel. Reservations are necessary for most hostels in summer, but wait-list beds become available at 6pm. In winter, Jasper International and Maligne Canyon run normally; guests at other hostels must pick up the key at Jasper International ($50 deposit). For couples or groups, a B&B may prove more economical (doubles $40-125, in winter $30-75). Many are in town near the train station; ask for a list at the park information center or the bus depot.

Jasper International Hostel (HI) (877-852-0781; 852-3215), also known as **Whistlers Hostel,** is 3km up Whistlers Road from Hwy. 93, 4km south of the townsite. The closest hostel to the townsite, but still a 7km walk. Attracts a gregarious breed of backpackers and cyclists, but a leave-your-boots-outside rule keeps the hardwood floors and 2 spiffy dorm rooms next to godly. Marmots frequent the volleyball court. Showers *and* electricity. 83 often-full beds. $15, nonmembers $20. $10 per person surcharge for 3 private rooms. Credit cards accepted. 2am curfew. **Sun Dog Shuttle** (852-8255) runs from the train station to the hostel on its way to the Jasper Tramway ($3).

Maligne Canyon Hostel (HI), on Maligne Lake Rd., 11km east of town on Hwy. 16. Small, recently-renovated cabins sit on the bank of the Maligne River, with access to the Skyline Trail and the Maligne Canyon. The manager is on a first-name basis with several local bears. Electricity and potable water. 24 beds: $10, nonmembers $15; in winter $9, nonmembers $14. Closed Wednesday Oct.-Apr.

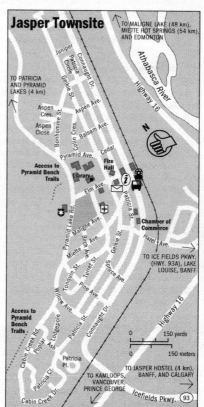

Mt. Edith Cavell Hostel (HI), 12km up Edith Cavell Rd., off Hwy. 93A. Small but cozy quarters, heated by wood-burning stoves. Propane light, pump water (boil or treat before drinking), solar shower, and firepit. A postcard view of Mt. Edith Cavell from the front yard, with easy access to the mountain. The road is closed in winter, but the hostel is open to anyone willing to pick up the keys at Jasper International Hostel and ski uphill from the highway. 32 beds: $10, nonmembers $15; in winter $9, nonmembers $10.

Athabasca Falls Hostel (HI) (852-5959). A more relaxed, family-oriented hostel on Hwy. 93, 32km south of the townsite. The dining room has electricity, but the only running water around is at Athabasca Falls, a 500m stroll away. Propane heating and lighting. 37 beds in 3 cabins; 7 private rooms. $10, nonmembers $15; in winter $9, nonmembers $14. Closed Nov., and Tuesdays Oct.-Apr.

Jasper Townsite

TO MALIGNE LAKE (48 km), MIETTE HOT SPRINGS (54 km), AND EDMONTON

Athabasca River

Highway 16

Juniper

Patricia
Connaught Dr.
Circle

Geikie St.

TO PATRICIA AND PYRAMID LAKES (4 km)

Aspen Cres.

Aspen Ave.

Bonhomme St.

Aspen Close

Colin Cres.

Balsam Ave.

Cedar

Pyramid Ave.

N

Fire Hall

Access to Pyramid Bench Trails

Library

Elm Ave.

Patricia St.

Pyramid Lake Rd.

Maligne Ave.

Birch Ave.

Geikie St.

Chamber of Commerce

Miette Ave.

Hazel Ave.

Tonquin St.

Turret St.

Spruce Ave.

TO ICE FIELDS PKWY. (HWY. 93A), LAKE LOUISE, BANFF

Willow Ave.

Pine Ave.

Connaught Dr.

Highway 16

Access to Pyramid Bench Trails

Cabin Creek Rd.

Poplar

Lodgepole

Patricia St.

Ash

0   150 yards

0   150 meters

Patricia Cr.

Patricia Pl.

Patricia Dr.

TO KAMLOOPS, VANCOUVER, PRINCE GEORGE

TO JASPER HOSTEL (4 km), BANFF, AND CALGARY

Cabin Creek Dr.

Icefields Pkwy. (93)

S. BC & THE ROCKIES

Beauty Creek Hostel (HI) (852-3215), on Hwy. 93, 87km south of the townsite. On the banks of the glacier-fed Sunwapta River and close to the Columbia Icefields. Hike the 3.2km Stanley Falls Trail, bake in the sweatlodge, or borrow the canoe for a paddle. Some of the best rustic washroom facilities in the Rockies, with poetry on the outhouse walls and views of the whole valley from the solar shower. 22 beds: $9, nonmembers $14.

CAMPGROUNDS

The government-run campgrounds below are listed from north to south. Most are primitive sites with few facilities and outdoor paradise nearby. All are first-come, first-served, and popular. Call the park info center (852-6176) for details. To build a fire, add $3-4 to campsite fees.

Pocahontas, on Hwy. 16, at the northern edge of the park, 46km northeast of the townsite. Closest campground to Miette Hot Springs (see p. 318). Toilets, hot water. 139 sites (9 walk-in tent sites): $13. Open mid-May to mid-Oct. Wheelchair accessible.

Snaring River, 16km north of the townsite on Hwy. 16. Kitchen shelters, dry toilets, splendid views, and the soothing sounds of the river lure passersby. 63 sites plus overflow (10 walk-in tent sites): $10. Open mid-May to mid-Sept.

Whistlers, on Whistlers Rd., 3km south of the townsite off Hwy. 93. This 781-site behemoth is the closest campground to Jasper Townsite and the only one with full hookups. Public phones, dump station, and free showers. Sites $17; full hookups $24. Open early May to mid-Oct. Wheelchair accessible.

Wapiti, on Hwy. 93, 2km south of Whistlers, along the Athabasca River. Plentiful brush separates tenters from RVers. Showers, pay phone. 364 sites: $17; with electricity $19. Open Victoria Day to early Sept. and mid-Oct. to early May. Wheelchair accessible.

Wabasso, on Hwy. 93A, 17km south of the townsite. Toilets, showers, 'sani-dump.' 238 sites (6 riverside walk-ins): $13. Open late June to Labor Day. Wheelchair accessible.

Five more campgrounds south of town along the Jasper section of the Icefields Parkway (see p. 313) offer kitchen shelters, dry toilets, and pay phones. ($10; fire permit and wood $4. Open late May to early Oct.) **Mount Kerkeslin,** 35km south of the townsite, has 42 sites on the banks of the Athabasca River. **Honeymoon Lake,** with 35 sites, is about 51km south of town near Sunwapta Falls and has a swimming area. **Jonas Creek,** 77km south of the townsite, has 25 highway-side sites along the Sunwapta River, including 12 secluded walk-in sites up the hill. The highlight of the Parkway campgrounds is **Columbia Icefield,** 109km south of the townsite, which lies close enough to the Athabasca Glacier to intercept an icy breeze and even a rare summer night's snowfall. A difficult and steep access road makes its 31 sites (7 walk-ins) RV-free, but they're crowded nonetheless. **Wilcox Creek** is 2km farther down the highway, at the southern park boundary (46 sites).

◪ FOOD

Super A Foods, 601 Patricia St. (852-3200; open M-Sa 8am-11pm, Su 9am-10pm), satisfies basic grocery needs at a central location, but the larger selection and the bakery at **Robinson's IGA Foodliner,** 218 Connaught Dr. (852-3195; open daily 8am-10pm), is worth the 5-minute walk. **Nutter's Bulk Foods,** 622 Patricia St. (852-5844; open daily 8am-11pm), offers bulk snacks and fresh, foot-long, $5 subs.

Mountain Foods and Cafe, 606 Connaught Dr. (852-4050). Offers a wide selection of sandwiches, salads, and home-cooked goodies, and take-out lunches for the trail. Turkey foccacia sandwich and assorted wraps $5.50. Open daily 7am-10pm in summer.

Jasper Pizza Place, 402 Connaught Dr. (852-3225). Large wood-oven pizzas $9-13, sandwiches $3-7.50. With a handful of pool tables, the Place turns bar-ish at night. Free delivery in Jasper area (min. order $5). 15% HI discount. Open daily 11am-midnight.

Scoops and Loops, 504 Patricia St. (852-4333). No ordinary ice cream parlor. Serves sandwiches ($3), sushi ($3-7), and *udon* ($8). Open M-Sa 10am-11pm, Su 11am-11pm.

Soft Rock Cafe, 622 Connaught Dr. (852-5850). Baguette sandwiches $5-6. Breakfast all day: sizeable omelette, homefries, and thick toast $7. No Kenny G, thankfully. Internet access. Open daily 7am-11pm; in winter 7am-7pm.

◿ OUTDOORS

DAYHIKING

The information center in town distributes *Day Hikes in Jasper National Park.*

Named after an English nurse executed by the Germans for providing aid to the Allies during World War I, snow-capped **Mt. Edith Cavell** is an exceptionally rewarding half-day hike. The trailhead is 30km south of the townsite: take Hwy. 93 to 93A to the end of the bumpy, twisty, 15km Mt. Edith Cavell Rd. (open June-Oct., no trailers or vehicles over 6m long), where Angel Glacier hangs off the mountain's north face. The 1.6km **Path of the Glacier** loop follows in the wake of a receding glacier to a lake littered with icebergs. The 9km (3-5hr.) loop through **Cavell Meadows** ascends past the treeline and (from mid-July to August) through a carpet of wildflowers, with striking views of the towering north face.

To scale a peak in a day, climb the **Sulphur Skyline Trail,** a challenging four- to six-hour hike (9.6km round-trip, 700m/2300 ft. elevation gain) with views of the limestone Miette Range and Ashlar Ridge. The trail leaves all too conveniently from the parking lot of the Miette Hot Springs (see p. 318).

The spectacular if over-touristed **Maligne Canyon** (mah-LEEN) is 11.5km east of the townsite on the Maligne Lake Rd. From the trailhead, a 4.2km path follows the Maligne River as it plunges through a narrow limestone gorge. Five footbridges afford viewing opportunities. Fifteen kilometers further along the Maligne Lake Rd., the river flows into Medicine Lake, but no river flows out. The water escapes underground through tunnels in the porous limestone, re-emerging 17km away in springs along the Athabasca River, making this the longest known underground river in North America.

Maligne Lake, at the end of the road, is the longest (22km) and deepest (97m/320 ft.) in the park. Fine granite particles ("rock flour") give glacial lakes their signature turquoise hue. A flotilla of water vessels allow escape from fellow tourists and the plastic geraniums of Maligne Lake Chalet. **Maligne Tours,** 626 Connaught Dr. (852-3370), rents kayaks ($30 per half-day; $60 per day) and leads canoe trips ($10 per hr.), horseback riding ($55 per 3hr.), and interpretive hikes ($10 per hr.), as well as narrated scenic cruises (90min.; $32, seniors $27.50, children $16). Free maps to hiking trails are available at the Maligne Tours office or by the lake. The **Opal Hills Trail** (an 8.2km loop) winds through subalpine meadows and ascends 460m/1500 ft. to views of the lake. **Shuttle service** from Jasper to the area is available from Maligne Tours. (To the canyon $8; to the lake $12, round-trip with cruise $54; 3-6 per day, 8:30am-5:30pm; wheelchair accessible.)

The **Jasper Tramway** (852-3093; 4km up Whistlers Rd., which is 4km south of the townsite on Hwy. 93.), climbs 1200m/3950 ft. up Whistlers Mountain, leading to a panoramic view of the park and, on clear days, very far beyond. (Open daily Apr.-Aug. 8:30am-10pm; Sept.-Oct. 9:30am-4:30pm. $15, under 14 $8.50, under 5 free.) The demanding 9km **Whistlers Trail** covers the same ground, beginning behind the Jasper International Hostel volleyball court. Don't forget extra layers; weather conditions change rapidly at the 2466m/8100 ft. summit.

BACKPACKING

An extensive network of trails weaves through the park, providing respite from tourist-land. The trails cover three different ecological regions. The **montane zone** (which includes Jasper Townsite) blankets valley floors with lodgepole pine, Douglas fir, white spruce, and aspen, and hosts elk, bighorn sheep, and coyotes. Sub-alpine fir and Engelmann spruce share the **sub-alpine zone** with porcupines and marmots, while fragile plants and wildflowers struggle against mountain goats and pikas in the uppermost **alpine zone.** To avoid trampling endangered plant species, hikers should not stray from trails in the alpine area.

Kick off any foray into the wilderness with a visit to the information center in the townsite, where rangers distribute the free *Backcountry Visitor Guide*. Overnight hikers need to register and pay the $6 per night fee, and many buy *The Canadian Rockies Trail Guide* ($15). Before hitting the trail, ask about road and trail closures, water levels (some rivers cannot be crossed at certain times of the year), and snow levels at high passes. The Icefield Centre (see p. 313) on Hwy. 93 at the southern entrance to the park, provides similar services.

RAFTING, SOAKING, FISHING, CLIMBING, CAVING...

Rocky Mountain Unlimited (852-4056) serves as a central reservation service for many local outdoor businesses. They provide prices and recommendations for rafting, fishing, horseback riding, and wildlife safaris (open daily 9am-9pm; in winter 8am-6pm). **Whitewater Rafting Jasper** (852-7238) leads trips on the Athabasca River and the faster Sunwapta River (2-3hr.; from $38, under 12 half-price). Register by phone, or stop at the townsite car wash in the industrial park across the railroad tracks from Connaught Dr. **Rocky Mountain River Guides,** 600 Patricia St. (852-3777), in On-Line Sport and Tackle, offers a calmer ride (2hr.; $35). **Boat rentals** are available at **Pyramid Lake Resort** (852-4900), 7km from town off Pyramid Ave. from Connaught Dr. (Open daily 8am-dusk. Canoes, kayaks, and pedal boats $15 for 1hr., $10 per additional hr., $55 per day; 12-person pontoon boat $60 per hr.)

The **Miette Hot Springs** (866-3939), 42km north of the townsite on Hwy. 16, and 15km along the well-marked Miette Hot Springs Rd., blends heat therapy with a panoramic view of the surrounding limestone mountains. Originally a rudimentary log bath-house in 1913, the waters—the hottest in the Canadian Rockies—are now chlorinated and filtered before they arrive in three outdoor pools, at temperatures ranging from 40°C/104°F to 14°C/57°F. The road to Miette is, sadly, closed in winter. (Open daily May 19-June 21 and Sept. 5-Oct. 9 10:30am-9pm; June 22-Sept. 4 8:30am-10:30pm. $5.50, children $5. Swimsuit $1.50, towel $1.25.)

The key to finding a secluded **fishing hole** in Jasper is to hike somewhere inaccessible to cars. **Currie's** (852-5650), in **The Sports Shop** (below), 406 Patricia St. provides gear and tackle and trim and gives tips on good spots. (Rod, reel, and line $10; fly $20. 1-day boat or canoe rental $30, after 2pm $20, after 6pm $15. Pickup and drop-off service available.) **Permits** are available at fishing shops and the Park Information Center ($6 per week, $13 per year).

The **Jasper Climbing School,** 806 Connaught Dr. (852-3964), offers an introductory three-hour rapelling class; at least a small group is required. ($30. Learning how to climb up is more expensive.) Peter Amann (852-3237; pamann@incentre.net) teaches two-day introductory rock climbing classes. (May-June and Sept. $150.) Ben Gadd (852-4012), author of the excellent *Handbook of the Canadian Rockies*, leads guided hikes for large groups ($300 per day) and tours to **Cadomin Cave** (5 hr.; $25 per person for groups of 10-20).

WINTER IN THE PARK

Winter brings 4m/13 ft. of snowfall and plenty of opportunities to the slopes of **Marmot Basin** (852-3816; www.skimarmot.com), a self-declared "crowd-free zone" 19km south of Jasper via Hwy. 93, 93A, and the Marmot Basin Rd. The upper half of the slope's 897m/2944 ft. vertical drop is above the treeline, creating room for bowls and a modest snowboard park. (Full-day lift ticket $42, 65 and over $29, ages 13-17 and students up to age 25 $35, ages 6-12 $17, under 6 free.) Bargain **ski rental** is available at **Totem's Ski Shop,** 408 Connaught Dr. (852-3078). (Open daily 8am-6pm in winter; 9:30am-10pm in summer; skis, boots, and poles $9-20; snowboard and boots from $25.) **The Sports Shop,** at 406 Patricia St. (852-3654), offers the same hours and ski rental prices and rents ice skates ($4 per hr., $12 per day). Maligne Lake offers **cross-country ski trails** from late November through May. **Everest Outdoor Stores,** 414 Connaught Dr. (852-5902), rents cross-country skis from $11 per day. (Open daily 9:30am-10pm; in winter 9am-6pm.)

A MOUNTIE ALWAYS GETS HIS MAN Think of the Canadian Rocky Mountains, and one must also think of the Royal Canadian Mounted Police (RCMP). Known as one of the best police forces in the world, the Mounties have a reputation for honesty, integrity, and boldness. Originally named the Northwest Mounted Police, the force began in 1873 when 293 men from all parts of the world were brought together to regulate the whisky trade in Canada's West and to combat an influx of Sioux Indians from Montana. Today, the RCMP are Canada's national police force, fully equipped with all the latest anti-bad-guy technology. While most Mounties have dismounted and jokingly refer to themselves as "pony cops," some can still be seen on horseback around the towns of Banff and Jasper, resplendent in their famous stetsons and scarlet tunics. They are proud of their heritage—so proud that a Mountie was stationed in Hollywood to ensure that actors portraying the Mounties in the movies sport the correct uniform and haircut. To learn more about the RCMP, browse through the books in **Sgt. Preston's Outpost** (762-5335), 208 Caribou St., in Banff Townsite.

YOHO NATIONAL PARK, BC

A Cree expression for awe and wonder, Yoho is the perfect name for this small, uncrowded park. It sports some of the niftiest names in the Rockies, like Kicking Horse Pass, so titled after Captain John Hector, tired, hungry, and struggling to find a mountain pass for the Canada Pacific Railroad, was kicked in the chest by his horse. Driving down Yoho's narrow canyon on Hwy. 1, visitors can see snapshots of geological forces in action; massive bent and tilted sedimentary rock layers are exposed in sharply eroded cliff faces. Beneath these rock walls, Yoho overflows with natural attractions, including the largest waterfall in the Rockies, the Continental Divide, and the Burgess Shale, the most illuminating discovery of pre-Cambrian (500 million year old) fossils known to paleontologists.

◢ ORIENTATION AND PRACTICAL INFORMATION. Yoho runs on Mountain Time, one hour ahead of Pacific Time. The park lies on the Trans-Canada Highway (Hwy. 1), next to Banff National Park. The town of **Field,** within the park, is 27km west of Lake Louise on Hwy. 1. **Greyhound** (800-661-8747) stops for travelers waving their arms on the highway. **Hosteling International** runs a shuttle connecting hostels in Yoho, Banff, and Jasper National Parks and Calgary ($7-65). The **visitor center** (343-6783) in Field is on Hwy. 1 (open daily 8:30am-7pm; in spring and fall 9am-5pm; in winter 9am-4pm). In case of **emergency,** call the **Park Warden Office** (403-762-4506; 24hr.) or the **RCMP** (344-2221) in nearby Golden. The scarcity of phones in the park, however, often makes it more efficient to drive to Lake Louise for help. **Post office:** 312 Stephen Ave., V0A 1G0 (343-6365). Open M-F 8:30am-4:30pm. **Area code:** 250.

◢◲ ACCOMMODATIONS, CAMPGROUNDS, AND FOOD. With one of the best locations of all the Rocky Mountain hostels, the ◪ **Whiskey Jack Hostel (HI),** 13km off the Trans-Canada on the Yoho Valley Rd., is the best indoor place to stay while drinking in Yoho's sights. The hostel, built in 1922 as the staff quarters for a hotel which was subsequently buried under an avalanche, offers a kitchen, nightly campfires, indoor plumbing, propane light, easy access to Yoho's best high country trails, and the splendor of the Takakaw Falls right from the front porch. Olga, the manager, plays a wicked game of Scrabble. (Beds $14, nonmembers $18; open June to mid-Oct.) Reserve through the Banff hostel (403-762-4122; see p. 306).

The five official **frontcountry campgrounds** offer a total of 330 sites, all easily accessible from the highway. All sites are first-come, first-served, and only Monarch and Kicking Horse fill up regularly in summer. **Hoodoo Creek,** on the west end of the park, has kitchen shelters, running hot water, a nearby river, and a playground (106 sites: $14; open late June-Aug.). It lies just across the Trans-Canada Hwy. from **Chancellor Peak,** which has pump water and pit toilets (64 sites: $13; open late May-Sept.). **Monarch Campground,** at the junction of Yoho Valley Rd. and Hwy. 1, has 36 regular sites and 10 walk-ins ($13; open late June to early Sept.). **Kicking Horse,** another kilometer up Yoho Valley Rd., has hot showers, toilets, and wheelchair access (86 sites: $18; open mid-May to mid-Oct.). The gem of Yoho's campsites is the high ▧ **Takakkaw Falls Campground,** situated beneath mountains, glaciers, and the magnificent falls 14km up curvy Yoho Valley Rd. It offers only pump water and pit toilets, and campers must park in the falls lot and haul their gear 650m to the peaceful sites (35 sites: $13; open late June-late Sept.).

The most convenient food stop to Yoho, which could easily become a sit-all-day-stop, is the **Siding General Store and Cafe** (343-6462), on Stephen Ave. in Field. Basic foodstuffs line the walls, beer and wine fills the cooler, and the friendly owners push home-made food and fresh baked goods, including sandwiches ($4.25), breakfast ($4.50-7), and an eclectic and sophisticated dinner menu ($8-15; open daily 8am-10pm; in winter M-Sa 10am-7pm).

☊ OUTDOORS. The Great Divide is both the boundary between Alberta and BC and between the Atlantic and Pacific watersheds. Here a stream forks with one arm flowing 1500km to the Pacific Ocean, and the other flowing 2500km to the Atlantic via the Hudson Bay. It is also the site of the **Burgess Shale,** a layer of sedimentary rock containing "the world's most important animal fossils," imprints of the insect-like, soft-bodied organisms that inhabited the world's oceans prior to an intense burst of evolution known as the **Cambrian Explosion.** Discovered in 1909, the unexpected complexity of these 505-million-year-old specimens changed the way many paleontologists thought about evolution. Larger, clumsier animals known as humans have since successfully lobbied to protect the shale from excessive tourism. Educational hikes led by the **Yoho-Burgess Shale Foundation** (800-343-3006; burgshal@rockies.net) are the only way to see the shale. A full-day, 20km hike costs $45. A steep 6km loop to the equally old and trilobite-packed **Mt. Stephen Fossil Beds** runs $25. (July to mid-Sept. only. Reservations required.) Fourteen steep, twisty km of the Yoho Valley Rd. lead to views of the **Takakkaw Falls,** Yoho's most splendid, and the highest in the Canadian rockies.

The park's six **backcountry campgrounds** and 48 trails make for an intense wilderness experience. Before setting out, pick up **camping permits** ($6 per person per day), maps, and the free *Backcountry Guide to Yoho National Park* at the visitor center. The park's finest terrain, in the Yoho Valley, is accessible only after the snow melts in mid- to late summer. The **Iceline Trail,** starting at the hostel (10.6km one-way, or a shortened 15km loop), rewards hikers with views of the valley and plenty of glaciers. Reserve one of two backcountry **alpine huts** through the Alpine Club of Canada (403-678-3200; $16/night).

The backcountry campground at splendid **Lake O'Hara,** in the eastern end of the park, can only be reached by a 13km pedestrian trail or on a park-operated bus. Taking the bus in makes a great daytrip, and the return bus is free for those who hike in. (Bus reservations 343-6433; round-trip $12. Permit required for camping.)

KOOTENAY NATIONAL PARK, BC

Kootenay National Park hangs off the continental divide on the southeast edge of British Columbia. Almost all visitors travel through Kootenay to get to or from Banff National Park on the majestic Banff-Windermere Highway (Hwy. 93), the first road across the Canadian Rockies. The federal government built the road in 1920 in exchange for the 5 miles of land on either side that constitute the park. Kootenay's biggest attraction is its lack of people: unlike Banff and Jasper, Kootenay has no overgrown residential development in its center. Instead, its stately conifers, alpine meadows, and pristine peaks hide in Banff's shadow, allowing travelers to experience the true solitude of the Canadian Rockies.

◪ ORIENTATION AND PRACTICAL INFORMATION. Kootenay lies southwest of Banff and Yoho National Parks. **Highway 93** runs through the park from the Trans-Canada Hwy. in Banff to **Radium Hot Springs** (see below) at the southwest edge of the park, where it joins **Hwy. 95.** One Greyhound bus per day stops at the Esso station, 7507 W. Main St. (347-9726; open daily 7am-11pm), at the junction of Hwy. 93 and Hwy. 95 in Radium Hot Springs on its way to Banff (2 hr.; $19) and Calgary (3½ hr.; $34). The **park information center** (347-9505), on the park's western boundary at the Radium Hot Spring Pool Complex, hands out free maps and the **backcountry hiking guide** (open late June to early Sept. daily 9am-7pm). The **Kootenay Park Lodge** (762-9196) operates another visitor center 63km north of Radium (open July-Aug. 9am-8pm; reduced hours in June and early Sept.). The **Park Administration Office** (347-9615), on the access road to Redstreak Campground, dispenses the backcountry hiking guide and is open in winter (open M-F 8am-noon and 1-4pm). **Ambulance:** 342-2055. **Emergency:** call the Banff Park Warden at 403-762-4506 or the **police** in Invermere (342-9292) or in Radium Hot Springs at (347-9393). The nearest hospital is **Windermere District Hospital** (342-9201), 850 10th Ave. in Invermere, 15km south of Radium on Hwy. 95. The **post office** (347-9460) is on Radium Blvd in Radium Hot Springs (open M-F 8:30am-5pm). **Public Radio:** 94.5 FM **Postal Code:** V0A 1M0. **Area code:** 250.

◪◪ ACCOMMODATIONS, CAMPGROUNDS, AND FOOD. The **Misty River Lodge (HI),** 5036 Hwy. 93 (347-9912), is the first left outside the park's West Gate. This former motel is a new addition to the Hosteling International family. Minutes from the 3.2km Juniper Trail to the hot springs. Eleven dorm beds in 2 rooms: $16, non-members $21. Downtown Radium features over 30 other motels, with high-season doubles from $40. The park's largest campground is **Redstreak,** on the access road that departs Hwy. 95 near the south end of Radium Hot Springs, with 242 sites, toilets, showers, firewood, playgrounds, and swarms of RVs. Walk-in sites off Loop B and D offer some solitude. Redstreak is the only campground in Kootenay with hookups or showers. Arrive early to secure a spot (open mid-May to mid-Sept.; $17, full hookups $22). **McLeod Meadows,** 27km north of the West Gate entrance on Hwy. 93, offers more solitude and wooded sites on the banks of the milky-blue Kootenay River, and access to hiking trails. (98 sites: $13; open mid-May to mid-Sept.). **Marble Canyon,** 86km north of the West Gate entrance, also provides more privacy (61 sites: $13; open mid-June through Aug.). From September 14 to May 7, snag one of seven free winter sites at the **Dolly Varden** picnic area, 36km north of the West Gate entrance, which boasts free firewood, water, toilets, and a shelter. Cheap ($8), unserviced camping is available in the nearby Invermere Forest District. Ask at the visitor centers for details.

There is no affordable food in Kootenay, with the exception of a few basic staples and snacks at the **Kootenay Park Lodge.** Radium supports a few inexpensive but uninspiring eateries crammed together on Main St. The best selection of groceries for kilometers around is at **Radium Foods,** 7546 Main St. E (347-9600; open M-Sa 9am-8pm, Su 10am-7pm).

◪ OUTDOORS. The park's main attraction is **Radium Hot Springs** (347-9485), named after the radioactive element detected there in trace quantities. The crowded complex of pools are responsible for the traffic and towel-toting tourists just inside the West Gate. Natural mineral waters fill two swimming pools—a hot one for soaking and a cooler one for swimming. The hot pool is wheelchair accessible. (Open daily 9am-11pm; in winter noon-9pm. $5.50, seniors and children $5, in winter 50¢ less. Lockers 25¢, towel rental $1.25, swimsuit rental $1.50.)

The 95km **Banff-Windermere Highway (Hwy. 93)** forms the sinuous backbone of Kootenay. Stretching from Radium Hot Springs to Banff, the highway follows the Kootenay and Vermilion Rivers, passing views of glacier-enclosed peaks, dense stands of virgin forest, and green, glacier-fed rivers. The wild landscape of the Kootenay River Valley remains stunning and unblemished but for the ribbon of road. A number of short trails lead right off the highway. About 15km from the Banff border, the 750m **Marble Canyon Trail** traverses a deep limestone gorge cut by Tokumm Creek, before ending at roaring falls. Another tourist-heavy path is the 1.6km, 30-minute **Paint Pots Trail,** 3.2km south of Marble Canyon on Hwy. 93. This wheelchair-accessible trail leads to sunset-red springs rich in iron oxide.

One of the hot springs' most astounding and therapeutic powers is their ability to suck travelers out of the woods, leaving Kootenay's myriad longer hiking trails uncrowded. The **Stanley Glacier Trail,** an easy dayhike, starts 2.5km north of Marble Canyon and leads 4.8km into a glacier-gouged valley, ending 1.6km from the foot of Stanley Glacier. The awe-inspiring 16.5km loop over **Kindersley Pass** climbs more than 1000m/3300 ft. to views of the Columbia River Valley to the west and the crest of the Rockies to the east. The two trailheads at either end of the route, Sinclair Creek and Kindersley Pass, are less than 1km apart on Hwy. 93, about 15km inside the west gate entrance. The 10km (one-way) **Floe Lake Trail,** 40 km from Castle Junction, ends in front of the imperious Vermillion range, where spectacular bands of rock and glacial ice stretch out above a lakeside campsite.

Many longer routes criss-cross Kootenay's interior. The **Rockwall Trail** in the north of the park is the most popular backcountry area in Kootenay. All **backcountry** campers will need to stop in at a visitor center for the hiking guide, which has maps, trail descriptions, and topographic profiles, and a mandatory **Wilderness Pass** ($6 per person per night, $35 per season). Two fire roads, plus the entire length of Hwy. 93, are open for **mountain biking,** but Kootenay lacks the extensive trail systems of its larger siblings. Rock flour from glaciers makes for lousy fishing.

The **Lussier Hot Springs** in Whiteswan Lake Provincial Park offer a more traditional alternative to Radium's lifeguards and ice cream vendors. The springs flow directly from the riverbank into the Lussier River, and piled-up rocks form shallow pools which trap the water at varying temperatures. To find this diamond, turn onto the rough dirt logging road 66km south of Radium, and follow it for 17km.

FERNIE, BC

This mountain biking and snowboarding mecca combines the familiarity of small-town life with the breadth of outdoor activities found in Jasper and Banff. Thus far, Fernie is little touristed, but is described as "up-and-coming" and even "the next Whistler." Increasing real estate prices and attention from travel guides in recent years indicates that the secret is getting out. With gorgeous hiking, superior single-track mountain biking, world-class trout fishing, and the finest snow in the region, Fernie is destined for discovery.

7 PRACTICAL INFORMATION. Fernie is located on Hwy. 3 an hour east of Cranbrook and 3½hr. southwest of Calgary. Local services cluster along Hwy. 3 and in downtown Fernie, 5km east of the ski resort. The **Visitor Center** (423-3811), is 1km east of town on Hwy. 3 (open July-Aug. daily 9am-7pm, Sept.-June, M-F 9am-5pm). **Greyhound,** 742 Hwy. 3 (423-6871), in the Park Place Lodge, runs 2 buses per day to Vancouver (20hr., $95) and Calgary (6½ hr., $46). See p. 53 for discounts. **Kootenay Taxi** (423-4408) is open 24hr. and ferries powder-heads to the slopes in winter ($4 round-trip). **Weather and road conditions:** 423-4431. Fernie lacks 911 service so in emergencies, contact the **police** (423-4404) located at 496 13th St., or call an **ambulance** (800-461-9911). The **Fernie District Hospital** (423-4453) is located downtown at 1501 5th Ave. **Post office:** 491 3rd Ave. (423-7555). Open M-F 8:30am-5pm. **Squeeky's Laundromat:** 1221 7th Ave. (Hwy. 3). Wash $2, dry 25¢ per 5min. (open daily 8:30am-10:30pm). **Internet Access:** Raging Elk Hostel. $1 per 10min. **Public Radio:** 97.7 FM. **Postal Code:** V0B 1M0. **Area code:** 250.

▐▌ ACCOMMODATIONS AND FOOD. The **Raging Elk Hostel (HI)** (423-6812) is a recently converted motel under all that vivid paint, and provides standard dorm-style lodging, a large common area, a kitchen, laundry facilities, a pool table, and a

free pancake breakfast. Reservations are crucial during ski season (Dec.-Apr.). ($16, non-members $20; private rooms from $25 in summer and $50 in winter.) **Mount Fernie Provincial Park,** 2km west of town, and 3km from the ski hill, provides 38 simple, wooded sites ($12; free firewood, toilets).

The Arts Station (423-4842), 1st Ave. and 6th St., a former train depot, displays the work of local artists, and serves a soup and sandwich for $7. (Open M-Sa 8am-4pm). **Rip 'N' Richards** (423-3002), at Hwy. 3 and 4th St., serves a feast of king-sized calzones ($6-12) and Mexican dishes beneath a canopy of bicycles and baby-carriages (open M-Sa 11am-10pm, Su 11am-9:30pm). Stock up on ramen at **Overwaitea Foods** on 2nd Ave. (423-4607; M-Th and Sa 9am-6pm, F 9am-9pm, Su 10am-6pm).

◢ OUTDOORS. The engine driving Fernie's expansion is the **Fernie Alpine Resort** (423-4655, snow report 423-3555; www.skifernie.com) and its 2,500-plus acres of powder, powder, powder. With 875cm/29 ft. of the lovely whiteness falling annually, Mt. Fernie embarrasses the local competition. The mountain's new management doubled the accessible acreage in 1998, and plans further expansion. The mountain already boasts a winter wonderland of natural gullies and ravines, 5 bowls, a terrain park, and plenty of tree-skiing, with a vertical drop of 857m/2811 ft. ($46; students under age 25 enrolled full-time at Western Canadian colleges or universities, ages 13-17 and ages 65 and over $38; ages 6-12 $15). For true decadence and some fresh tracks on over 7,000 acres of the pow-pow, try for a 'standby' seat on **Island Lake Lodge's** (423-3700) deluxe **cat-skiing** trips in December and April (max. 48hr. notice; $250 per day).

Stores in downtown Fernie offer **ski and snowboard rentals** at similar rates ($19 per day for ski packages and $25 for a snowboard and boots). **Fernie Sports** (423-3611) on Hwy. 3 across from the SuperValu, offers a 20% discount to Raging Elk Hostel guests (open roughly 8am-6pm in winter, 10am-5:30pm in summer).

The April thaw, while heralding the end of ski season, also uncovers Fernie's abundant hiking and biking trails. A **dayhike** suitable for experienced hikers is the **Fernie Ridge Walk.** This difficult 8-hour hike climbs over 1000m/3300 ft. to spectacular views of alpine meadows and jagged limestone peaks before returning to the valley floor. The trailhead is located in the day parking lot of the ski resort; cheaters can take the lift part way up the mountain in the summer ($8, bikes $3), but won't avoid the steep Snake Ridge or a 15m/50 ft. fixed-rope climb.

Mountain biking in the Fernie area ranges from the novice to the highly technical. **The Guides Hut** (423-3650), 621 2nd Ave., is happy to make recommendations, and rents front-suspension bikes ($7 per hr., $30 for 24 hr.; open M, Th, Sa 10am-7pm, Tu-W 10am-5:30pm, F 10am-8pm, Su noon-4pm). The **Bike Base** (423-6464), across the street, rents trade-ins at unbeatable prices ($10 per day, front-suspension $15; open M-Sa 9am-5:30pm, F 9am-8pm, Su noon-4pm).

The Elk river and its tributaries provide 180km of world-class **fly-fishing** for bulltrout and cut-throat. The **Kootenay Fly Shop and Guiding Company** rents rods ($20) and sells maps (423-4483; open M-Sa 8:30am-5:30pm, Su 9am-1pm).

SOUTHERN ALBERTA

CROWSNEST PASS, AB

Amid forested peaks near the BC/Alberta border on Hwy. 3, the tiny towns bundled into Crowsnest Pass are most famous for a mining disaster that happened nearly a century ago. At 4:10am on April 29, 1903, an entire side of coal-rich **Turtle Mountain** collapsed. Over 80 million tons of stone spilled onto the mining town of **Frank,** burying 70 people and their houses in less than two minutes. Geologists are still guessing about the ultimate cause of the disaster. The **Frank Slide Interpretive Centre** (403-562-7388), perched amid piles of rubble on Hwy. 3, explores the dramatic event in great detail. The center is only about half as morbid as one might expect, crafting a history of the local towns and Frank's miraculous survival stories through displays, a 20-minute video, and talks by the knowledgeable staff (open daily 9am-8pm, Labour Day to May 15 10am-4pm; $4, seniors $3, children $2). A 1.5km **interpretive loop trail** leads from the center through a fraction of the 3km² still covered by massive blocks of fallen limestone.

Staff at the interpretive center also dish out tips on outdoor recreation in the pass. **Trout fishing** in the **Crowsnest, Castle,** and **Oldman Rivers** is reputedly among the best in the Rockies. A steep three-hour hike goes up and down the summit of Turtle Mountain, offering views for miles and a new perspective on the cracks—some as wide as a bus—that split the mountain as water froze and thawed within them. The trailhead is at the eastern end of 34th St. in Blairmore. For more hiking options, ask at the interpretive center or visitor center (see below).

For a different perspective on the mountain, strap on a hard hat and head lamp at nearby **Bellevue Underground Mine** (off Main St. in Bellevue; open daily 10am-5:30pm from May 15 to Labour Day). Guided walking tours lead 1,000 ft. into an old coal mine (30min.; $6, senior and youth $5).

Hwy. 3 leads west to the beautiful Kootenay Country of British Columbia. If heading north into Kananaskis (see p. 325) or Banff (see p. 304), consider taking the scenic but bumpy **Forestry Trunk Rd.,** which meets Hwy. 3 after two hours near Coleman. The drive offers vistas of mountains colored in vibrant hues of green, red, brown, and purple. Several rustic campgrounds line the road, including **Dutch Creek, Oldman River,** and **Cataract Creek** (sites $9, including fire permit). Call 563-5395 for info. **Greyhound,** 2020 129 St. (403-564-4467), in Blairmore, runs two buses per day to Calgary (5½hr., $35), Kelowna, BC (12hr., $82), and Vancouver, BC (21hr., $90). See p. 53 for discounts. The **Alberta Tourism Information Centre,** 8km west of Coleman on Hwy. 3, provides further info on local sights and activities (open daily Victoria Day to Labour Day 8am-6pm). The most pleasant nearby campsites are 2km east of the center, and another 6km up the road at **Chinook Lake Campground** (800-661-8888; 73 very private sites with firewood and toilets $9).

In town, the one choice is the cramped **Lost Lemon Campground** (403-562-2932), just off Hwy. 3A near Blairmore, with hot showers, hot tub, swimming pool, laundry, and fishing (sites $16; full hookups $22). Find lemons at **IGA Food Mart and Bakery** (403-562-7236), in the mall on Main St. in Blairmore (open daily 9am-9pm). In a medical or fire **emergency,** call the dispatcher at 562-2255.

ALBERTA BADLANDS

In the late Cretaceous period, these were the fertile shores of an inland sea, conditions that have created one of the richest dinosaur fossil sites in the world. Once the sea dried up, wind, water, and ice cut twisting canyons down into the sandstone and shale bedrock, creating the desolate splendor of the Alberta Badlands. The **Tyrrell Museum of Paleontology** (TEER-ull) and its remarkable array of dinosaur exhibits and hands-on paleontological opportunities are the region's main attraction. **Greyhound** runs from Calgary to Drumheller (1½ hr., 2 per day, $21), which is 6km (a 20-minute bike ride) southeast of the museum. The hostel rents mountain bikes for $4 per hour or $15 for the day.

🏠🏕 ACCOMMODATIONS, CAMPGROUNDS, AND FOOD. Drumheller

(drum-HELL-er) is overrun with the terrible lizards to this day, or at least their tacky plastic younger cousins, which seem to guard every business. Flee the dino-monsters at the **Alexandra Hostel (HI),** 30 Railway Ave. N (823-6337), which has 55 beds in a converted hotel that hasn't changed much since the '30s. It sports a kitchen, laundry, and little else in the way of hospitality ($17.50, nonmembers $20; check-in 10am-11pm). **River Grove Campground,** off North Dinosaur Trail at the intersection with Hwy. 9, has toilets, free showers, and laundry. (130 sites: $18.50, full hookups $25.50. Cabins for two to 10 people, with bathrooms, electricity, and cable TV $50-100. Open daily May to Sept. 9am-9pm, July-Aug. 7am-11pm.)

Stock up on groceries and participate in Drumheller nightlife at **IGA Market** (403-823-3995), at N. Railroad Ave. and Centre St. (open daily 24hr.). For surprisingly decent Chinese and Thai, head to **Sizzling House,** 160 Centre St. (403-823-8098) for eat-in or take-out. (Open Su-Th 11am-10pm, F-Sa 11am-11pm; entrees $6-10).

⬛ 🄇 SIGHTS AND OUTDOORS. The **Royal Tyrrell Museum of Paleontology** (403-823-7707 or 888-440-4240; www.tyrrellmuseum.com) lies on the **North Dinosaur Trail (Secondary Hwy. 838),** 6km northwest of Drumheller, which itself lies 138km northeast of Calgary. (Open daily 9am-9pm; Labour Day to Victoria Day Tu-Su 10am-5pm. $7.50, seniors $5.50, ages 7-17 $3, under 7 free; in winter half-price Tu.) Get there by driving east on Hwy. 1, then northeast on Hwy. 9. You won't lose the crowds at the museum but you might lose your sense of self-importance. The world's largest display of dinosaur specimens is a forceful reminder that *Homo sapiens* missed out on the first 2½ billion years of life on earth. From the Big Bang to the Quaternary Period (now), the museum celebrates evolution's grand parade, with quality displays, a 20-minute video, computer activities, and towering skeletons, including one of only 12 reconstructed *Tyrannosaurus Rex* skeletons in existence. Recently, the museum created a spooky gallery of the insect-like undersea creatures of the Burgess Shale (see p. 320).

The museum's hugely popular 12-person **Day Digs** include instruction in paleontology and excavation techniques, a chance to dig in a fossil quarry. The fee includes lunch and transportation, but all finds go to the museum. (July-Aug. daily at 8:30am, returning at 4:30pm. $85, ages 10-15 $55. Reservations required.) See the paleontologists and Day Diggers sweating for their prey on a **Dig Watch,** a two-hour interpretive bus and walking tour of the quarry. (July-Aug. daily at 10am, noon, and 2pm. $12, ages 7-17 $8, under 7 free. Reservations recommended.)

The museum's **Field Station** (378-4342), 48km east of the town of **Brooks** in **Dinosaur Provincial Park** (a 2hr. drive from Drumheller), contains a small museum, but the main attraction is the **Badlands Bus Tour.** The bus chauffeurs visitors into a restricted hot spot of dinosaur finds. Many fossils still lie within the eroding rock; if you make a discovery, however, all you can take home with you are memories, Polaroids, and a Fossil Finder Certificate. (Field Station open daily Victoria Day to Labour Day 8:30am-9pm; call for winter hours. Tours Victoria Day to Thanksgiving 2-8 per day. $4.50, ages 6-15 $2.25, under 6 free; call 378-4344 for reservations.)

The park's **campground** is shaded from summer heat, and grassy plots cushion most sites. Although it stays open year-round, the campground only has power and running water in summer. (Sites $13, with power $15.) To reach the Field Station from Drumheller, follow Hwy. 56 south for 65km, then take Hwy. 1 about 70km to Brooks. Once in Brooks, go north along Hwy. 873 and east along Hwy. 544.

The Badlands also offer a variety of refreshingly dinosaur-free activities. The staff of **Midland Provincial Park** (823-1749), located halfway between the Tyrrell Museum and Drumheller, leads free 75-minute natural history walking tours, departing from the museum one or two times per day. To see **hoodoos** in the making, go 15km east on Hwy. 10 from Drumheller. These limestone columns are relatively young: they still wear the stone caps that created the pillars by protecting them from erosion. In **Horseshoe Canyon,** about 20km west of Drumheller on Hwy. 9, **hiking and biking trails** wind below the prairie, through red rock layers carved into bizarre rounded formations. Carry plenty of water during hot weather, and do not hop fences onto private property. For more information on outdoor options, contact the **Old Midland Mine Office,** on North Dinosaur Trail between Drumheller and the Tyrrell Museum.

KANANASKIS COUNTRY

Between Calgary and Banff lie 4000km² of provincial parks and multi-use recreational areas collectively known as **Kananaskis Country** (KAN-uh-NASS-kiss). The area sweeps down from the Canadian Rockies through rolling foothills less than an hour from Banff, and contains a natural majesty comparable to the national

HEAD-SMASHED-IN BUFFALO JUMP Some 5700

years ago, plains-dwelling Blackfoot began using gravity to kill bison. Disguised as calves, a few men would lure a herd of the sight-impaired animals into lanes between stone cairns. Hunters at the rear, dressed as wolves, then pressed forward, whipping the bison into a fearful frenzy. When the front-running bison reached the cliff and tried to stop, the momentum of the stampede pushed them over the edge. The entire herd followed; hunters sought to prevent any animals from escaping, since survivors might warn other herds. Each year, the community obtained food, tools, and clothing from the bodies of the bison. The particular cliffs of Head-Smashed-In Buffalo Jump were an active hunting site for millennia, but only gained their modern name 150 years ago when a thrill-seeking warrior watching the massacre from under the cliff ledge, was crushed by the falling stampede.

As European settlement spread over the plains, the bison that once numbered 60 million continent-wide were nearly extinct in 1881. A century later, the United Nations named Head-Smashed-In a UNESCO World Heritage Site. 10m-deep beds of bone and tools make this one of the best-preserved buffalo jumps in North America commemorating the bison hunt at the heart of Plains culture. The magnificent **interpretive centre** (553-2731) expertly explores the hunting, history, and rituals of the Plains people. (Open daily Labour Day to May 15 9am-7pm; off-season 9am-5pm. $6.50, senior $5.50, youth $3, family $15, under 7 free.) A 10-minute video reenactment of the hunt plays all day, and 2km of trails lead along and under the cliffs. Head-Smashed-In Buffalo Jump lies 175km south of Calgary and 18km northwest of Fort Macleod, on Secondary Rte. 785 off Hwy. 2.

parks with blissfully little of their overcrowding and none of the fees. The country is divided into eight sections; the three most popular are the meadows and forests of **Bow Valley Provincial Park** (403-673-3663), with an office just off Hwy. 1 (open M-F 8am-4:30pm), the grasslands and Alpine meadows of **Elbow River Valley** (403-949-4261), on Hwy. 66 near Bragg Creek, and the towering peaks of **Peter Lougheed Provincial Park** (403-491-6322) one hour south on Hwy. 40. Staff members at the park visitor centers help design itineraries for weeks of outdoor entertainment; expect showers of maps and elaborate brochures from the main **Barrier Lake Visitor Centre** (403-673-3985), 6km south of Hwy. 1 on Hwy. 40. (Open Sa-Th 8:30am-6pm, F 8:30am-7pm; in winter daily 9am-4pm.) Public transportation to Kananaskis is scarce. **Greyhound** stops at the **Rusticana Grocery**, 801 8th St. (678-4465), in Canmore. (3 per day to: Banff, 20min., $7; Calgary, 1¼hr., $16). The shuttle that connects the Rocky Mountain hostels with Calgary also makes a stop in K-Country ($15) with advance notice; phone Banff International Hostel (403-762-4122) to reserve. In an **emergency,** call the **Canmore Police** (403-678-5516). **Area code:** 403.

Descriptions of Kananaskis Country's abundant activities give many outdoor enthusiasts goose bumps. With over 1000km of trails, **hiking** in K-Country can provide anything from a one-hour quick fix to a full-blown Rocky Mountain High. The 1.9km **Canadian Mt. Everest Expedition Trail,** in Peter Lougheed Park, provides a majestic view of both Upper and Lower Kananaskis Lakes. The well-maintained **Ribbon Creek Trail** (8.1km) passes through the waterfall-rich canyonland between Mt. Kidd and Mt. Bogart, arriving at the Ribbon Falls backcountry campground. Gillean Daffern's *Kananaskis Country Trail Guide*, published by Rocky Mountain Books and available at any area information center ($16.95), is a definitive source of info on longer trails. Unlike the national parks to the west, almost all of Kananaskis' trails remain open to **mountain biking**. The foothills of the **Sibbald Area** in the northeast of K-country (30 minutes off Hwy. 1) offer wide expanses of terrain largely undiscovered by cyclists, while both the Peter Lougheed and the Kananaskis Valley Parks contain paved trails. The Canmore Nordic Center (see below) provides 72km of trails in summer. Cliffs throughout the park offer excellent **sport climbing** opportunities. **Barrier Bluffs,** 6km south of the Barrier Lake Visitor Center, has dozens of bolted routes up the wall.

The **Kananaskis River** off Hwy. 40 draws white-water kayakers with its Olympic-quality Class III-plus rapids. In the winter, the region's copious peaks draw a crowd of ice-climbers and Nordic and backcountry skiers. The **Canmore Nordic Centre** (403-678-2400), the 1988 Olympic Nordic skiing venue, offers 72km of **cross-country skiing** in the winter. From June 30 to July 2, 2000, thousands will flock to the Centre to observe the **World Cup** downhill and cross-country mountain biking.

The **Nakiska ski area** (403-591-7777, snow report 403-229-3288; www.skinakiska.com) was custom-built for Calgary's 1988 Winter Olympics. Its 28 mostly intermediate runs, 735m/2412 ft. vertical drop and extensive snowmaking make it a decidedly tamer choice than the hills at Banff/Lake Louise (see p. 312)

Ribbon Creek Hostel, 24km south of the Trans-Canada Hwy. (Hwy. 1) on Hwy. 40, accommodates 47 people. This endearing hostel's comfortable common room has a fireplace and luxurious couches ($13, nonmembers $17). For reservations, call the Banff International Hostel (762-4122). The hostel has winter-time **lift ticket and lodging deals** with nearby Nakiska. Over **3000 campsites** are accessible via K-Country roads. When hiking or biking in areas with established backcountry campgrounds, visitors must use the areas provided. Where none are established, however, camping is permitted at least 50m from the trail. Backcountry camping permits are $3 per person per night, and available at the visitor centers. Front-country campsites in Kananaskis cost between $9 and $27 per night.

CALGARY

Mounties founded Calgary in the 1870s to control the flow of illegal whisky, but a different liquid made the city great: oil. Today, petroleum fuels Calgary's economy and explains why the city holds the most corporate headquarters in Canada outside of Toronto. As the host of the 1988 Winter Olympics, Calgary's dot on the map grew larger; already Alberta's largest city, this thriving young metropolis is now Canada's second-fastest-growing city. No matter how big its britches, though, the city pays annual tribute to its original tourist attraction, the "Greatest Outdoor Show on Earth," the Calgary Stampede, when for 10 days in July the city dons cowboy duds and lets out a collective "Yeehaw!" for world-class bare-back riding, country music, western art, and free pancakes.

ORIENTATION AND PRACTICAL INFORMATION

Calgary is 120km east of Banff along the Trans-Canada Highway (Hwy. 1). Calgary is divided into quadrants (NE, NW, SE, SW): **Centre St.** is the east-west divider; the **Bow River** splits the north and south sections. **Avenues** run east-west, **streets** run north-south, and numbers count up from the divides. Cross streets can be derived by disregarding the last two digits of the street address: 206 7th Ave. SW would be in the southwest quadrant on 7th avenue at 2nd street.

Airplanes: The airport is about 6km northwest of city center. Cab fare runs about $20. Public bus #57 provides sporadic service from the airport to downtown (generally runs 6:50am-11pm; transfer at Marlborough mall to the C-train). The **Airporter Bus** (531-3907) services major hotels downtown every half-hour between 6:30am and 11:30pm ($8.50); those who ask nicely may get dropped off at an unscheduled stop.

Buses: Greyhound, 877 Greyhound Way SW (265-9111 or 800-661-8747). To: Edmonton (3½hr., 14 per day, $40); Banff (2hr., 4 per day, $19); Drumheller (1½hr., 2 per day, $21). See p. 53 for discounts. Free shuttle from Calgary Transit C-Train at 7th Ave. and 10th St. to bus depot (every hr. near the half hr. 6:30am-7:30pm). **Red Arrow,** 205 9th Ave. SE (531-0350). To: Edmonton (6 per day, $42) and points north. 10% HI, student, and senior discount. **Brewster Tours** (221-8242). From the airport or downtown to: Banff (2½hr., 3 per day, $36), and Jasper (7hr., 1 per day, $71). 15% HI discount.

Public Transportation: Calgary Transit, 240 7th Ave. SW (262-1000; open M-F 8:30am-5pm). C-Trains free in downtown zone. Buses and C-Trains outside downtown $1.60, ages 6-14 $1, under 6 free. Day pass $5, ages 6-14 $3. Book of 10 tickets $13.50, ages 6-14 $8.50. Runs M-F 6am-11pm, Sa-Su 8:30am-9:30pm. Tickets at the transit office, Safeway and Co-op grocery stores, and 7-11 and Mac's corner stores.

Taxis: Checker Cab, 299-9999. **Yellow Cab,** 974-1111.

Car Rental: Rent-A-Wreck, 113 42nd Ave. SW (287-1444). From $30; 12¢ per km over 200km; 7th day free. Must be 21 with credit card. Open M-Sa 8am-6:30pm, Su 9am-5pm).

Visitor Information: 131 9th Ave. SW (750-2397), under the Calgary Tower. Open daily 8am-5pm.

American Express: Canada Trust Tower, 421 7th Ave. SW (261-5085), main floor.

Equipment Rental: Budget, 140 6th Ave. SE (226-1550). Bikes $12 per day. Must be 18 with credit card. **Outdoor Program Centre at U of Calgary,** 2500 University Dr. (220-5038; take bus #4, 20, 72, or 73), rents tents (from $11), canoes ($17), skis ($15), and everything else outdoor-related. Open daily 8am-8pm.

Laundromat: Inglewood Laundromat, 1018 9th Ave. SE (269-1515). Open daily 9:30am-9pm. Wash $1.50, dry 50¢.

Weather: 299-7878. Calgary and Banff weather.

Library: 616 Macleod Trail SE (262-2600). Open M-Th 10am-9pm, F-S 10am-5pm; mid-Sept. to mid-Apr. also Su 1:30-5pm.

Gay and Lesbian Services: Events, bars, and clubs 234-9752. Counseling 234-8973.

Emergency: 911. **Police:** 133 6th Ave. SE (266-1234). **Crisis Line:** 266-1605. 24hr.

Pharmacy: Shopper's Drug Mart, 6455 S. Macleod Trail (253-2424), in the Chinook Centre, is open 24hr.

Hospital: Peter Lougheed Centre, 3500 26th Ave. NE (291-8555). Take the C-train to Rundlehorn and walk 3min. toward the big green roof.

Post Office: 207 9th Ave. SW, T2P 2G8 (974-2078). Open M-F 8am-5:45pm.

Internet Access: At the **Calgary Hostel.** $1 per 10min. Also at **Cinescape,** upstairs in the Eau Claire Market (see **Food,** below). $5 for 30min., $8 per hr. (open M-Th 11:30am-11pm, F-Sa 11:30am-12:30am, Su 11:30am-10pm).

Area Code: 403.

◤ ACCOMMODATIONS

Lodging costs skyrocket when tourists pack into the city's hotels during the Stampede in July; call far in advance. Contact the **B&B Association of Calgary** (543-3900) for info and availability (singles from $35; doubles from $50).

Calgary International Hostel (HI), 520 7th Ave. SE (269-8239), several blocks east of downtown. Go east along 7th Ave. from the 3rd St. SE C-Train station; the hostel is on the left just past 4th St. SE. This welcoming urban hostel has it all: clean, large kitchen, game room, hang-out areas, laundry, email, and a backyard with BBQ. Personnel do a better job assisting visitors than the official visitor center. 120 beds: $16, nonmembers $20. Linen $1. Free city tours on Monday. Open 24hr. Wheelchair accessible.

University of Calgary, in the NW quadrant. Out of the way, but easily accessible via bus #9 or the C-Train. U of C was the Olympic Village in 1988. Popular with conventioneers, often booked solid. Shared rooms $20; singles $32, with student ID $23; doubles $39, with student ID $32. More lavish suites with private bathrooms about $35 per person. Rooms available May-Aug. only. Open 24hr. Booking coordinated through **Kananaskis Hall,** 3330 24th Ave. (220-3203), a 12min. walk from the University C-Train stop.

Regis Plaza Hotel, 124 7th Ave. SE (262-4641). Despite its appearance from the street, the Plaza has nice clean rooms right smack downtown. The "little elevator that could" tugs guests to the 100 rooms. Great for groups, the roomy floors are ideal for cramming in extra sleeping bags. Four windowless walls, a bed, and a sink $83 per week. Doubles from $50 per day; weekly rates $121-180. Open 24hr.

Calgary Overview

YWCA, 320 5th Ave. SE (263-1550). Recently renovated, the YWCA boasts comfortable and clean rooms with all the amenities: free access to the large fitness facility, free local calls, and 24hr. security. No men allowed. Singles for $35, doubles for $45.

🍴 FOOD

Downtown's grub is concentrated in the **Stephen Avenue Mall,** S. 8th Ave. between 1st St. SE and 3rd St. SW. The most gloriously satisfying and cheap food in Calgary is located in its tiny ◩ Chinatown, the two square blocks at the north end of Centre St. S and 1st St. SE. Five dollars buys a feast in Vietnamese noodle-houses and Hong-Kong style cafes, many of which don't close until 3 or 4am. Some budget chow-houses also hide out among the trendy, costlier spots in the popular **Kensington District,** along Kensington Rd. and 10th and 11th St. NW, and those on **17th Ave.** between 2nd St. SW and 14th St. SW. To get to Kensington take the C-Train to Sunnyside or cross the Louise Bridge (9th St. SW and 10th St. NW). **Co-op Grocery,** 123 11th Ave. SE (299-4257), sells exactly what you'd imagine (open daily 9am-9pm). Restaurants, fresh fruit, baked goods, international snack bars, and flowers grace the plaza-style, upscale **Eau Claire Market** (264-6450), at the north end of 3rd St. SW; $5 easily fetches a filling take-out plate for a picnic in nearby Prince's Island Park (market open M-W, Sa 10am-6pm, Th-F 10am-9pm, Su 10am-5pm).

◩ **Kaffa Coffee and Salsa House,** 2138 33rd Ave. SW (240-9133); take bus #7 (South Calgary) from The Bay on 7th Ave. An espresso bar and Mexican restaurant in one. New soup every day ($2.50), and a different salsa and salad ($3.50) every week. Leafy outdoor patio, burritos ($6-7), delicious signature jalapeño cheese cornbread ($1), and a long drinks menu. Open M-F 7am-midnight, Sa 8am-midnight, Su 8am-10pm.

Thi-Thi Submarine, 209 1st St. SE (265-5452). Thi-Thi is a smaller hole-in-the-wall than most mice call home, yet manages to pack in 2 plastic seats, a toaster oven, and the finest Vietnamese submarines in Calgary. $2.50 will buy a 10-inch "super-sub" with three kinds of pork, chicken, cilantro, carrots, cucumbers, and special sauce, served hot on a fresh baguette. The veggie sub is a ludicrous $1.50. Open daily 10am-7pm.

Pho Pasteur Saigon, 207 1st St. SE (233-0477). A favorite among the business crowd, Pho's heaping portions of authentic Vietnamese cuisine are a bargain in Chinatown, and that's saying something. Several varieties of beef noodle soup $4.20-4.85. Open daily 10am-7pm.

Take Ten Cafe, 304 10th St. NE (270-7010). A local favorite, Take Ten attracts customers not by being the coolest place in Kensington, but by offering dirt-cheap, high-quality food. All burgers under $5.75. The owners also offer a variety of their native Chinese food ($6.25). Open Tu-Sa 9am-6pm, Su 9am-3pm.

Wicked Wedge, 617 17th Ave. (228-1024). Serves topping-heavy, meal-sized slices of pizza-shaped loving ($3.50) to Calgary's post-party scene. Three varieties of pie dished out nightly. Open M-W 11am-1am, Th-Sa 11am-3am, Su noon-midnight.

⬛ SIGHTS AND EVENTS

OLYMPICS LEFTOVERS

Over a decade later, Calgary still clings to its two weeks of Olympic stardom. Visit the **Canada Olympic Park** (247-5452), a 10 minute drive northwest of downtown on Hwy. 1, to learn about gravity at the site of the four looming ski jumps and the bobsled and luge tracks. (Open daily 8am-9pm.) The **Olympic Hall of Fame** (247-5452), also at Olympic Park, honors Olympic achievements with displays, films, and bobsled and ski-jumping simulators. (Open daily 9am-9pm. $3.75, seniors and students $3, under 6 free.) In summer, the park opens its hills and a lift to mountain bikers. (Open daily May-Sept. 10am-9pm. $7 ticket includes chair lift and entrance to ski jump buildings. Guided tour $10. Hill pass $6 for cyclists. Bike rental $6 per hr., $24 per day.) Keep an eye out for ski-jumpers, who practice at the facility year-round. The miniature mountain (113m/370 ft. vertical) also opens up for recreational **downhill skiing** in winter ($20; snow report 289-3700). The **Olympic Oval** (220-7890), an enormous indoor speed-skating track on the University of Calgary campus, remains a major international training facility. Speed skaters work out in the early morning and late afternoon; sit in the bleachers and observe the action for free. (Public skating hours in summer 8-9:30pm. $4, children $2. Hockey skate rental $3.50; speed skates $3.75.) Downtown, the **Olympic Plaza,** on 7th Ave. and MacLeod Trail (2nd St. SE), was built for medal ceremonies and now features special events, including **free concerts** every Wednesday at noon in July and August.

PARKS AND MUSEUMS

Footbridges stretch from either side of the Bow River to **Prince's Island Park,** a natural refuge only blocks from the city center. In July and August, Mount Royal College performs **Shakespeare in the Park** (recording 240-6374, human 240-6908; Tu-Su 7pm). Calgary's other island park, **St. George's Island,** is accessible by the river walkway to the east, and holds up the **Calgary Zoo** (232-9300), including a botanical garden and children's zoo. (Gates open daily 9am-8pm; in winter 9am-4pm. Grounds open 9am-9pm; Oct.-Apr. 9am-5:30pm. $10, children $5, seniors half-price Tu and Th; in winter $8, seniors and children $4. 15% AAA and 20% HI discounts.) For those who missed the wildlife in Banff and Jasper, the Canadian Wilds exhibit re-creates animal habitats. For those who missed the Cretaceous Period, life-sized plastic dinosaurs are also on exhibit.

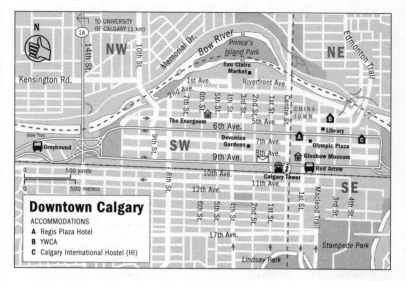

Downtown Calgary

ACCOMMODATIONS
A Regis Plaza Hotel
B YWCA
C Calgary International Hostel (HI)

The **Glenbow Museum,** 130 9th Ave. SE (268-4100), gathers rocks and minerals, Buddhist and Hindu art, and native Canadian history under one roof. (Open Sa-W 9am-5pm, Th-F 9am-9pm. $8, seniors and students $6, under 6 free. HI discount.)

[To be sung to the tune of *The Beverly Hillbillies:*] Come 'n' listen to a story 'bout the **Energeum,** a place 'bout oil kinda like a museum. Play a game 'bout drillin', watch a movie in th' thee-ter, and learn how Alberta puts th' power in your heater. Industrial propaganda, that is, 640 5th Ave. SW. (297-4293; Open June-Aug. M-Sa 10:30am-4:30pm; Sept.-May M-F 10:30am-4:30pm. Free.)

THE STAMPEDE

The more cosmopolitan Calgary becomes, the more tenaciously it clings to its frontier roots. The Stampede (July 7-16, 2000) draws one million cowboys and tourists each summer. **Stampede Park,** just southeast of downtown, borders the east side of Macleod Trail between 14th and 25th Ave. SE. For 10 days, the grounds are packed for world-class steer wrestling, saddle bronc, bareback- and bull-riding, pig racing, wild-cow-milking, and chuckwagon races. Check out the live-stock shows, cruise the midway and casino, ride the rollercoaster, or hear live country music and marching bands. The festival spills into the streets at night, as bars and clubs get good and loud. A **free pancake breakfast** is served at a different mall in the city every day from 9 to 11:30am. Depending on your attitude, the Stampede will either be an impressive spectacle rekindling the Western spirit, or an overpriced, slick carnival where humans assert their dominion over the lesser animals. Plan your trip accordingly.

Parking is ample and reasonably priced ($3-8), but can be tedious. The C-Train features a Stampede stop, and the walk isn't bad. For tickets and info, call 269-9822 or 800-661-1767 or visit www.calgary-stampede.ab.ca. Gate admission is $9 (seniors and ages 7-12 $4, under 7 free); rodeo and evening shows cost $19-50; **rush tickets,** if not sold out, are $9, on sale at the grandstand 1½hr. before showtime.

♫ NIGHTLIFE

Nightclubs in Alberta only became legal in 1990, and Calgary is making up for lost time. The city is fairly crawling with bars and nightclubs that cater to the waves of visitors and young locals. Live music ranges from national acts to some guy with a guitar. The best areas in town for finding pubs, clubs, and live music are 8th Ave. SW, 17th Ave. SW, and 1st St. SW. Last call in Calgary is at 2am, and is strictly observed. Wherever you head, finding cheap liquor is not a problem. Many bars in town offer ridiculous drink deals (e.g. $1.25 doubles and 25¢ pints). For listings of bands and theme nights, check *The Calgary Straight* or *Calgary's Ffwd*. Both come out on Thursday and are free. *Outlooks*, the city's gay and lesbian events publication, is already out. All are available at local clubs and cafes.

The Nightgallery, 1209B 1st St. SW (269-5924). One large dance floor, one bar, and one oversized disco ball attract scenesters. The club breaks out the best House in town at "Sunday School" and on Thursday nights. Monday's Reggae-Dub draws a slightly older crowd. Cover $5, $1.50 doubles before 11:00pm. Open daily 7:30pm-3am.

The Ship and Anchor, 534 17th Ave. SW (245-3333). Decked out with fish-nets and maidens'-heads, the Ship is *the* meeting place for the city's young and beautiful scurvy dogs. Bike couriers, punksters, and the occasional hillbilly mingle in this dark, wooden melting pot. Eclectic music, excellent food, a spacious patio, and a staff of aspiring actors keep the ship of fools afloat. Open daily noon-2:30am.

The Embassy, 516C 9th Ave SW (213-3970). The 18- to 23-year old set flocks to this modern three-floored spot, specializing in House (Th and Sa), Hip-hop (Su), and Retro tunes (F). A rooftop lounge with heat lamps and a skyline view makes the trip worthwhile any night. $1.25 bottles and drinks until 9:30pm, cover $3-5. Open Th-Su 7:30pm-2:30am.

Java Sharks, 529 17th Ave SW (244-5552). The city's best local bands upstairs (Th-Su). A young crowd basks in the positive vibe, boozing and grooving to bands in the coffeehouse. No cover. Breakfast all day; happy hour 3-7pm and all day Su. Open M-F 11am-3am, Sa-Su 9am-3am.

King Edward Hotel, 438 9th Ave. SE (262-1680). A well-known stop for North American blues bands, this seedy little hotel brings in phenomenal Chicago and Kansas City notemakers. Nightly live music (10pm) takes over from the dancing girls (until 8:30pm). Cover $3-8. Open daily 11am-3am. Jam sessions Sa 3-7pm and Su 8:30pm-1am.

Ranchman's Steak House, 9615 Macleod Trail SW (253-1100). This is the real thing. Carousing cattle-ropers kick it at Ranchman's, showing off their Wranglers and the latest in country two-stepping. Free dancing lessons from a world champion instructor M-Th at 7:30. $6 cover Th-Sa ($10 Stampede week). Open M-Sa noon-3am.

NORTHERN BC
& THE YUKON

> **YUKON TERRITORY'S...** **Sales Tax:** 7% national sales tax (GST) only. **Drinking Age:** 19. **Traffic Laws:** Seatbelts required; radar detectors illegal in the Yukon. For **Road Conditions,** see p. 55. **Capital:** Whitehorse. **Population:** 32,635. **Area:** 478,970km². **Bird:** Raven. **Flower:** Fireweed. **Holiday:** Discovery Day, on the third Monday in Aug. For **emergencies** outside the Whitehorse area, 911 may not work; call the local police detachment or 867-667-5555. For **BC-wide info,** see p. 244.

Northern BC is one of North America's last bastions of immense forests, stark mountains, yawning canyons, roaring rivers, clear lakes, abundant wildlife, and freedom from summer crowds. Heading north from Hope, BC or Calgary, AB, thick forests, low mountains, and patches of high desert are interrupted by a handful of crossroads and supply centers like Prince George, at the intersection of the Yellowhead and Cariboo highways. Still farther north, thick forests are periodically logged or blackened by lightning fires. At BC's western edge, Prince Rupert provides access to the spectacular Queen Charlotte Islands. Here Haida villages return to the land in haunting majesty, and the sea supports a dazzling array of life.

The Yukon Territory lies at the end of a several-hours drive along the Alaska Highway or the less-touristed Cassiar and Campbell highways. Here the land rises into ranges that stretch for miles and sinks into lakes that snake toward the Arctic Ocean. The dry land's lonely beauty and its purple dusk are overwhelming. Glaciation left much of the Yukon untouched, creating an ice-free corridor for vegetation, wildlife, and early hunters crossing the Bering land bridge. Though summer here is still spectacular, Yukoners have been suffering payback for the ancient fair weather ever since, enduring what's often described as "nine months of winter and three months of bad snowmobiling." Fur traders came looking in the 1800s for faster routes through the area and trading partners. The gold seekers of 1898 came charging to Carcross from Skagway, then down the Yukon River to Whitehorse, Dawson City, and the goldfields beyond. A second modern territorial rush occurred over the course of the Alaska Highway's construction. Logging, mining, and the federal government have since supported the region's economy. Yukon First Nations are presently in the midst of negotiating with the federal government for land and self-government, and innovative projects tend to rebuilding communities. Court procedures built upon traditional means of solving disputes, community justice programs, and projects of environmental stewardship—such as the multi-party protection of the Yukon River—are supplying models for community living and consensus building for the region and the world.

Bus lines service major settlements. BC and YT campground permits cost $8 per night or $27 per year and are available from local businesses.

HIGHLIGHTS OF NORTHERN BC AND THE YUKON

- The **Queen Charlotte Islands** (see p. 347) will reward your attention.
- The **George Johnston Museum** (see p. 369) honors a remarkable man in Teslin.
- Hikers and flightseers penetrate sprawling **Kluane National Park** (see p. 377).
- **Dawson City** (see p. 383) hosts a music festival at the end of a good long float.
- From Dawson City, the **Top of the World Hwy.** (see p. 387) grinds ridge-lines to Alaska, and the **Dempster Hwy.** (see p. 388) bumps all the way up to Inuvik, NWT.
- The coast is over the pass via the **Klondike Hwy.** or **Chilkoot Trail** and stunning terrain at **Carcross** (see p. 373), or Haines Junction en route to **Haines,** AK (see p. 424).

CARIBOO HIGHWAY (HWY. 97)

The Cariboo Highway is the portion of Hwy. 97 that runs north for approximately 450km from Cache Creek to Prince George, following the route of the historic Cariboo Wagon Road. From Prince George, Hwy. 97 becomes the John Hart Hwy. (see p. 340), and continues north to Dawson Creek (see p. 364) and the start of the Alaska Highway (see p. 363). The scenery is impressive, with dozens of small lakes nestled among patches of forest and rocky hills. A visit to one of the 12 **provincial parks** in the area is well worth a brief departure from the Cariboo. Two of the nicest, both close to the Cariboo, are **Green Lake,** actually a series of glacial kettle lakes, and **Pinnacles,** where an eight-minute walk leads to a view of a steep sandstone canyon carved into the surrounding plateau. Farther afield, **Tweedsmuir Provincial Park** and the town of **Bella Coola,** both along the **Chilcotin Highway (Hwy. 20)** (see p. 334), offer superb hiking, fishing, and sight-seeing in an uncrowded setting.

CACHE CREEK TO WILLIAMS LAKE

Many of the small towns along Hwy. 97, born during the gold-rush era, are slowly developing into more than pitstops en route to Prince George. Most of the towns and services along the highway are referred to solely by their old Cariboo Wagon road mile marker (e.g.: the town of 70 Mile House, 83 Mile Restaurant), invoking those heady Canadian days before the metric system. **Cache Creek,** at the junction of the Cariboo Hwy. and the Trans-Canada Hwy. (Hwy. 1), does not have much to offer, but weary travelers can stay at the serviceable **Cache Creek Kampground** (250-457-6414), 3km north of town on Hwy. 97. While the sites are unpleasantly klose to each other and to the highway, excellent amenities, including a free pool and spa, koin showers, and laundry help kompensate (sites $14; full hookups $21). A slightly more secluded option is **Brookside Campsite** (250-457-6633), 1km east of town on Hwy. 1, which has free showers, vintage video games, a pool, and laundry (wash and dry $1.25 each; sites $12; full hookups $19).

The town of **100 Mile House,** 115km north of Cache Creek, offers services and groceries, and proudly displays the world's **largest pair of cross-country skis.** The **Visitor Center** (395-5353), is at the chamber of commerce next to the skis (open May-Sept. M-F 8:30am-7pm, Sa-Su 9am-6pm; in winter M-F 10am-5pm). **100 Mile House Campground,** 500m off the highway on Horse Lake Rd., is tranquil, woodsy, and cheap ($10; pit toilets, water, firewood). Another 25km north, anglers can try for kokanee or trophy-sized lakers from the shores of lovely **Lac La Hache.**

CHILCOTIN HIGHWAY (HWY. 20): WILLIAMS LAKE TO BELLA COOLA

The allure of the Chilcotin Hwy. lies not in its lackluster endpoint of Bella Coola, but in the rugged and scenic lands along the partly gravel 457km highway. Leaving Williams Lake, the Chilcotin Hwy. heads west across the **Fraser River,** and climbs briefly before flattening out through forests and pastures dotted with cattle ranches. **Alexis Creek,** at Km 110, is the first stop of note with gas, cafe, lodging, and a general store. **Bull Canyon Provincial Park,** 8km past town, features fishing on the Chilcotin River. **Chilko River Expeditions** (398-6711; www.bcadventure.com/chilkoriver), in the lobby of the Fraser Inn 1km north of Williams Lake on Hwy. 97, runs **rafting** expeditions along the Chilcotin and Chilko Rivers (from $99 per day).

A 5km turn-off at Chilanko Forks (Km 175) leads to the 9km long **Puntzi Lake,** surrounded by several affordable resort options. Activities include fishing for kokanee and rainbow trout and watching white pelicans in summer. **Puntzi Lake Resort** (481-1176 or 800-578-6804) has eight wood cabins and a grassy lakeside campsite. A putting green and driving range are available for the golf-inclined (cabins $45-85; sites $13, full hookups $17-19). **Barney's Lakeside Resort** (481-1100) has more secluded sites ($12), RV hookups ($15), and cabins ($40 for 2, $5 each

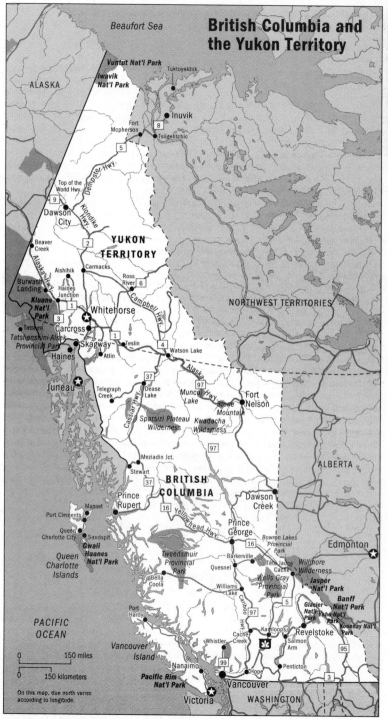

British Columbia and the Yukon Territory

Beaufort Sea

ALASKA

Tuktoyaktuk

Vuntut Nat'l Park

Iwavik Nat'l Park

Fort Mcpherson

8 Inuvik

Tsiigehtchic

5

Dempster Hwy.

Top of the World Hwy.

9

Klondike Hwy.

Dawson City

2

Beaver Creek

YUKON TERRITORY

Aishihik

Carmacks

Ross River 6

Campbell Hwy.

Burwash Landing

Kluane Nat'l Park

Haines Junction

1

Whitehorse

3

NORTHWEST TERRITORIES

Tatshen

Tatshenshini-Alsek Provincial Park

Carcross

1

Skagway

Teslin

4

Watson Lake

Haines

Atlin

Alaska Hwy.

Juneau

Telegraph Creek

37

Dease Lake

97

Muncho Lake

Fort Nelson

Stone Mountain

Cassiar Hwy.

Spatsizi Plateau Wilderness

Kwadacha Wilderness

97

Meziadin Jct.

ALBERTA

Stewart

37

BRITISH COLUMBIA

Dawson Creek

Prince Rupert

16

Yellowhead Hwy.

Prince George

16

Bowron Lakes Provincial Park

Masset

Port Clements

Queen Charlotte City

Sandspit

Gwaii Haanes Nat'l Park

Queen Charlotte Islands

Tweedsmuir Provincial Park

Barkerville

Quesnel

Tête Jaune Cache

Willmore Wilderness

Edmonton

Bella Coola

Williams Lake

Cariboo Hwy.

Wells Gray Provincial Park

5

Jasper Nat'l Park

PACIFIC OCEAN

Port Hardy

97

Glacier Nat'l Park

Yoho Nat'l Park

Banff Nat'l Park

Kootenay Nat'l Park

Cache Creek

Kamloops

Salmon Arm

Revelstoke

95

Vancouver Island

Whistler

99

Nanaimo

Pacific Rim Nat'l Park

Hope

3

Penticton

Vancouver

Victoria

WASHINGTON

0   150 miles

0   150 kilometers

On this map, due north varies according to longitude.

additional person). All accommodations have a shared bathroom and free showers. **Jack & Faye's Place** (481-1169) is ideal for families: two bedroom cottages with private bath, living room, TV, and kitchenette sleep up to five (singles $45; doubles $50; extra adults $7.50; extra children $5). **Tattla and Nimpo Lakes,** farther along the drive to Bella Coola, offer similar options.

Ts'yl⁰Os Provincial Park (SIGH-loss), boasts Canada's first grizzly bear refuge, the glacier-fed, trout- and salmon-rich Lake Chilko. To reach the **Gwa da Ts'ih campground** on the north side of the park, turn off at Tatla Lake (Km 220), and drive 63km on washboard gravel roads (4-6hr. from Williams Lake).

The highway enters the southern portion of **Tweedsmuir Provincial Park** (398-4414) at Heckman's Pass, 360km west of Williams Lake. The park protects the Atnarko River, Hunlen Falls, Monarch Glacier, and the colorfully streaked shield volcanoes of the Rainbow Mountains. Unfortunately, road-trippers' introduction to the park is 20km of gravel hell, known simply as "The Hill," a one lane, no-barrier nightmare, with steep grades and sharp switchbacks (call 800-661-2025 for road conditions). For decades, Hwy. 20 ended at **Anahim Lake,** 315km west of Williams Lake. In 1955, frustrated by government inaction, locals got two bulldozers, borrowed money, and finished the job themselves, earning the route its second name, the "Freedom Highway." Almost 50 years later, this portion of the road still has the feel of being built by not-quite-experts. After the hill, the highway is paved again for its most scenic 75km, following the **Bella Coola River** into town.

Perhaps the biggest thing happening in Tweedsmuir is the terminus of the 25- to 30-day **Alexander Mackenzie Heritage Trail,** reserved for those hikers beyond hardcore and off the deep end. Its 347km stretch from **Blackwater River,** just west of Quesnel, across western British Columbia to **Burnt Creek Bridge** on Hwy. 20, tracing the final leg of Mackenzie's 1793 journey across Canada to the western coast. Mackenzie reached the Pacific more than a decade before Lewis and Clark, although the Americans continue to hog all the glory. For more moderate hikers, the southern end of the park offers copious opportunities: from **Hunlen Falls** (a difficult 16.4km hike), visitors can rent canoes on the **Turner Lakes** ($25 per day), or walk the gorgeous **Ptarmigan Lake** loop. Summertime daytrippers can explore **Rainbow Ridge** along the 8km (one-way) Rainbow Trail. Call the park for details.

The pot of pewter at the end of the Chilcotin rainbow is the coastal village of **Bella Coola,** homeland of the Nuxalk Nation. Bella Coola's native heritage is evident in an impressive collection of **petroglyphs,** which have led some scholars to link the indigenous people here with those in Polynesia. To see some of these carvings, follow the gravel road on the west side of Thorsen Creek—5km out of town—to the end and climb the river path for 500m. Salmon fishery restrictions and the pull-out of the logging industry over the last two years have severely depressed the local economy. The town is increasingly dependent on the increase in tourism from the **BC Ferries** (888-223-3779) *Discovery Passage* route which links Bella Coola with Port Hardy on the northern tip of Vancouver Island from mid-June to mid-September ($110, ages 5-11 $55, under 5 free). The **Shell Station** (799-5314), across from the Valley Inn on McKenzie Rd., does **repairs** and has the only gas in town (open daily 8am-8pm). Getting a room in town is expensive, but the **Bella Coola Motel** (799-5323) downtown has camping on its large back lawn ($8; toilets, free showers). For shaded and forested sites, head to **Gnome's Home Campground & RV Park** (982-2504), in **Hagesborg** 16km east of Bella Coola along the highway (sites $12; full hookups $15; toilets, showers, coin laundry).

WILLIAMS LAKE TO QUESNEL

Williams Lake, 90km north of 100 Mile House, is the Cariboo's largest town, but certainly not its most inviting. Fortunately, it's easy to leave, with Hwy. 20 meandering 450km west to **Bella Coola** (see p. 334), and Hwy. 97 continuing north to the rough-hewn lumber towns of Quesnel and Prince George. Williams Lake celebrates its cowboy heritage over Canada Day weekend with the **Williams Lake Stampede.** Festivities include a rodeo, mountain race, and wild cow milking. The **Slumber Lodger,** 27 7th Ave. (392-7116 or 800-577-2244; fax 392-3977), downtown, has a pool! (Singles from $35, doubles from $40). For a cheap thrill, pitch tent on the **Stampede grounds** (392-6585) in the center of town ($8, full hookups $15). To reach **Blue Lake Holiday Campgrounds** (297-6505), turn off at Blue Lake Rd. 32km past town. Campsites ($12) and canoes ($5 per hr.) on the bright blue-green lake are at your disposal. **Visitor information** in town is available on Hwy. 97 (392-5025; open June-Aug. daily 9am-5pm; Sept.-May M-F 9am-4pm). The town library has free **Internet access** (open Tu-Th 10am-8pm, F-Sa 10am-5pm).

The 122km drive north to Quesnel can be a little dull, but those willing to subject their car to a little gravel can make it more interesting. About 35km north of Williams Lake, the **Soda Creek Townsite Rd.** splits from Hwy. 97 for 20km of rustic splendor alongside the free **Fraser River**. The road returns to the highway several kilometers south of the free **Marguerite Ferry** (May-Oct.; 5 min.; on demand 7am-11:45am, 1-4:45pm, 6-6:45pm), which shuttles drivers across the river to a gravel road paralleling Hwy. 97 for the remainder of the trip to Quesnel.

QUESNEL AND ENVIRONS

The town of Quesnel (kwuh-NELL), 123km past Williams Lake, takes great pride in its gold-driven past and forestry-propelled present. From Quesnel, it's only a 10-minute drive to **Pinnacles Provincial Park:** cross the river on Marsh Rd., then turn right on Baker Drive, where a 1km walk leads to hoodoos—volcanic rock formations that look like giant sand dribble castles—and impressive views. Every third weekend of July, crowds flock to Quesnel for the wholesome family fun of **Billy Barker Days,** featuring a rodeo, live entertainment, and a "Crash-to-Pass" demolition derby. The logging industry maintains a very strong presence (and odor) in this industrial oasis. The visitor center has the scoop on mill tours at **Quesnel River Pulp** (Tu and Th 10:30am) and **West Fraser Lumber** (Th 1pm).

The **Greyhound** depot (992-2231 or 800-661-8747) is on Kinshant between St. Laurent and Barlow. Buses to: Prince George (1½hr., 3 per day, $18) and Vancouver (10hr., 3 per day, $82; depot open M-F 6am-8pm, Sa 6am-noon and 6-7:30pm, Su 6-10:30am and 6-7:30pm). The **visitor center**, 705 Carson Ave. (992-8716), is just off Hwy. 97 in Le Bourdais Park (open June-Aug. daily 8am-6pm; Apr.-May and Sept. M-F 8:30am-4:30pm). **Emergency:** 911. **Police:** 992-9211. The **library** (992-7912), 593 Barlow Ave. has free **Internet access** (open Tu-Th 10am-8pm, F-Sa 10am-5pm). **Post office:** 346 Reid St., V2J 3J1 (992-2200). Open M-F 8:45am-5:15pm. **Area Code:** 250

The king of the local motel scene is the **Ramada,** 383 St. Laurent Ave. (992-5575 or 800-663-1581; fax 992-2254), downtown. Rooms include cable, phone, coffee, muffins, and use of the pool and jacuzzi (singles from $42; doubles from $46). **Roberts Roost Campground,** 3121 Gook Rd. (747-2015), 8km. south of town, offers pricey, elegantly landscaped lakeside sites. Coin showers and laundry, a playground, and fishing (sites $17; full hookups $22); row boat and canoe rentals $5.

The long-defunct mining town of **Barkerville,** 90km east of Quesnel along Hwy. 26, was established in 1862 after Billy Barker found gold on Williams Creek, sparking BC's largest gold rush. For the rest of the 19th century, Barkerville was the benchmark against which the rest of western Canada was measured. Victoria was considered doomed to failure as the provincial capital because it was too far from away. Since 1958 the town has been operated as an educational "living museum" (994-3332; open daily 8am-8pm in summer; 2 day pass $5.50, students and seniors $3.25, ages 6-12 $1, families $10.75; wheelchair accessible). One day is enough to see it all, but for those staying a while, the mining town of **Wells,** 8km away, has services and accommodations.

Bowron Lakes Provincial Park is a paddling paradise located 25km north of Barkerville. This necklace of lakes forms a **116km loop** in the heart of the Cariboo Mountains. Since the circuit takes most canoers 7-10 days to complete, the park service charges $106 per canoe ($56 for a single) to help maintain the 56 lakeside campsites (reservations required; call 992-3111). **Becker's Lodge** (992-8864) rents canoes and kayaks ($150-280 for the circuit) as does the **Bowron Lake Lodge** (992-2733; $100-250). Both also offer camping and cabins within a stone's throw of the loop's starting point (tent sites $15; cabins from $55).

Anyone traveling between Prince George and Quesnel on Hwy. 97 will live a better life for having stopped at ⊠**Cinema Second Hand General Store** (998-4774), 32km north of Quesnel on Hwy. 97. Cash-strapped road warriors will find everything they need (except an actual cinema), plus a wide variety of things they could never possibly need, like old-fashioned snowshoes and disco LPs (open daily 9am-9pm). The store also offers **free camping**, with pit toilet.

PRINCE GEORGE

Prince George stands at the confluence of the Nechako and Fraser Rivers, whose banks have succumbed to the pulp and lumber mills that crowd the valley floor in an impressive display of industrial *forte*. Prince George is a teeming point of transport for goods and services heading in all directions, a nerve center for the Northwest. But even with recent additions to the town—a civic center, a national university, and a Western League hockey team—Prince George is a stopover, not a destination. Early July's pan-continentally attended Bluegrass Jamboree and bands of treeplanters carting through town on their days off liven things up.

🛈 PRACTICAL INFORMATION

Hwy. 97 cuts straight through Prince George just to the west of the city center. **Hwy. 16** runs straight through the city center, becoming **Victoria St.** in town, and joins up with Hwy. 97 to the south of town.

Greyhound, 1566 12th Ave. (564-5454), opposite the Victoria St. visitor center, runs to: Edmonton (10hr., 2 per day, $91); Vancouver (12hr., 3 per day, $91); Prince Rupert (10hr., 2 per day, $88); and Dawson Creek (6hr., 2 per day, $51). Lockers are $2. The ticket office is open M-Sa 6:30am-5:30pm and 8pm-midnight; Su and holidays 6:30-9:30am, 3:30-5:30pm, and 8pm-midnight. See p. 53 for discounts. **BC Rail,** 1108 Industrial Way (561-4033), 2km south off Hwy. 97 at the end of Terminal Blvd. runs the scenic Cariboo Prospector to Vancouver (14hr.; M, Th, Sa at 7am; $194, students and over 59 $175, children $117; 3 meals included). The Station is open daily 6-8am and 7:30-9:30pm. **VIA Rail,** 1300 1st Ave. (800-561-8630), travels to Prince Rupert (12hr.; M, Th, Sa; $82, students $49, seniors $74, children $41; see p. 52 for discounts). The station is open M, Th, Sa 6-9:30am, Su, W, F 5:30-9:30pm. One of town's **visitor centres** (800-668-7646; www.tourismpg.bc.ca) is festooned with faux-native carvings at 1198 Victoria St. (562-3700; open M-F 8:30am-6pm, Sa 9am-6pm), at 15th Ave. Another is at the junction of Hwy. 16 and Hwy. 97 (563-5493; open May-Sept. daily 8am-8pm) beneath a gargantuan, unmissable "Mr. P.G." logger. **Centre City Surplus,** 1222 Fourth Ave. (564-2400; open M-Sa 9:30am-6pm, Su 11am-4pm), rents outdoor gear at highly competitive prices. The **library,** 887 Dominion (563-9251; open M-Th 10am-9pm, F-Sa 10am-5:30pm; in winter Su 1-5pm), provides free 30min. Internet access; call ahead. **Internet Cafe,** inside London Drugs in the Parkwood Mall at Victoria and 15th St., charges $3 per 30min. (Open M-Sa 9am-10pm, Su 10am-8pm.) **Whitewash Laundromat** is at 231 George St. (wash $1.25, dry 25¢ per 8min; open M-Sa 7:30am-6pm). **Tim Horton's** (562-1672), at Hwy. 97 (E. Central St.) and 5th Ave., is open M-F **24hr.** and Su 5am-1pm. **Emergency:** 911. **Police:** 999 Brunswick St. (561-3300). **24hr. Crisis Line:** 563-1214. **Hospital:** 2000 15th Ave. (565-2000; emergency 565-2444). Public Radio: 91.5 FM. **Post Office:** 1323 5th Ave., V2L 3L0 (561-2568). Open M-F 8:30am-5pm. **Area Code:** 250.

⛺ ACCOMMODATIONS AND CAMPGROUNDS

For those stopping in Prince George just to get a good night's sleep and stock up on provisions, a good bet is the **Queensway Court Motel,** 1616 Queensway (562-5068), at 17th Ave. close to downtown. Well-kept rooms come with fridges, microwaves, cable, and free local calls (singles $36; doubles $47). During the summer, the **College of New Caledonia Student Residence,** 3330 22nd Ave. (561-5849 or 800-371-8111; fax 561-5832), off Hwy. 97 near downtown, offers clean and quiet dorm rooms with fridge, microwave, sink, desk, and shared bathrooms for $20, doubles

$25 (linens $5 per person, extra mattress $5). Call ahead for wheelchair-accessible rooms (office open M-F 10am-noon, 2-4pm, and 6-8pm; Sa-Su 10-11am, 2-3pm, and 6-8pm). Ambitious campers and RV jockeys head for the **Log House Restaurant and Kampground** (963-9515), located on the shores of Tabor Lake. This German-owned steakhouse and RV park is popular among Europeans (sites $14; full hookups $20; cabins with no amenities $40; teepees $10 per person). Rowboats ($5), canoes ($8), and pedalboats ($8) can be rented by the hour. To reach this kraziness, head out of town on Hwy. 16 E; after 3.2km, turn right on "Old Cariboo Hwy.," then left on Giscome Rd. and follow the signs.

🍴 FOOD

The drolly named supermarket **Overwaitea's**, 1600 15th Ave. (564-4525), lies opposite the Victoria St. visitor center (open daily 9am-9pm). Any number of interchangeable pizza/pasta joints can be found on or near George St. For something a bit different, the cool, calm, and collected **1085 Cafe**, 1085 Vancouver St. (960-2272), offers fresh soup 'n' salad-style lunch fare in the $5 range and live entertainment most Friday nights (open M and Sa 9am-4pm, Tu-W 7am-7pm, Th-F 7am-10pm). Hit up hip and traveler-happy **Javva Mugga Mocha Cafe**, 304 George St. (562-3338), for a $2 muffin or cappuccino. The cafe also stocks used books. (Open M-F 7:30am-5:30pm, Sa 8am-5:30pm.) The **Bamboo House Restaurant**, 1208 6th Ave. (564-3888), at Dominion, has an all-you-can-eat lunch smorgasbord (i.e., Chinese food and onion rings) for $7 and a supper smorg for $10 (entrees $5-13).

👁 SIGHTS AND EVENTS

Fishing is excellent near Prince George, with more than 1500 lakes within a 150km radius. The closest is **Tabor Lake**, where the rainbow trout all but jump into boats in spring and early summer. Tabor is east on Hwy. 16; follow the directions to the Log House Restaurant and Kampground described above. For a complete listing of lakes and licensing information, contact visitor information.

Centre City Surplus (see **Outdoor Equipment**, above) sells **guides to hiking** in the Prince George area, and the infocenter has its own helpful tips. **Fort George Park**, on the banks of the Fraser River off 20th Ave., offers an expansive lawn, beach volleyball courts, picnic tables, and barbecue pits, and makes a perfect starting point for the 11km **Heritage River Trail**, which wanders through the city and along the Fraser and Nechako Rivers. **Fort George Regional Museum** (562-1612), inside the park, houses frontier artifacts, including several primitive chain saws. (Open daily 10am-5pm; in winter Tu-Su noon-5pm. $6.50, students and seniors $5.50, children $4.50, families $10.) **McMillan Creek Regional Park** is right across the Nechako River off Hwy. 97 N and features a deep ravine and a view of the city from the river's cutbanks. **Cottonwood Island Nature Park**, off River Rd., has leisurely riverside walking trails along the banks of the Nechako. **Esker's Provincial Park** (565-6340), off Hwy. 97 on Ness Lake Rd. 40km north of downtown, has wheelchair-accessible trails.

For a bird's eye view of this industrial city, scramble up to **Connaught Hill Park**, home of picnic tables and ample frisbee-throwing space. To reach the park, scale the yellow metal staircase opposite the visitor center or take Connaught Dr. off Queensway. **Forests for the World**, a wildlife preserve on nearby Cranbrook Hill, is only a 15-minute drive from town and one of the prettiest parts of Prince George. To get there, take Hwy. 97 north, turn left on 15th Ave., right on Foothills Blvd., left onto Cranbrook Hill Rd., and finally left on Kueng Rd.

Mardi Gras (564-3737) lasts for 10 days in late February and features such events as snow golf, dog-pull contests, and bed races. You'll swear you're in New Orleans. The annual four-day **O'Sawmill Bluegrass Jamboree** (564-8573 or 563-4312) is held on the banks of the Nechako over the second weekend in July. Take a left off Hwy. 97 onto North Nechako Rd., and continue 26km to the Field of Dreams (day pass $20, 4-day advance purchase $60). **Sandblast** (562-1977) sends daring skiers down the steep, sandy, snowless Nechako Cutbanks on the third Sunday in August.

PRINCE GEORGE TO DAWSON CREEK

Travelers on their way to Mt. Robson or Jasper beyond will depart Prince George along the Yellowhead Hwy. leading east (see below); those bound for the Cassiar Hwy. or the Queen Charlotte Islands will depart along the Yellowhead Hwy. leading west (see p. 341); travelers continuing north will stick to Hwy. 97, called the John Hart Hwy. on its way out of town. A few kilometers into the 402km stretch from Prince George to Dawson Creek, mile 0 of the Alaska Hwy., neon lights and strip malls become a distant memory as the road cuts a lonely swath through the forests of northern British Columbia. The first outpost of civilization is the micropolis of **Bear Lake,** 74km along Hwy. 97, which offers a motel, RV park, restaurant, and gas. **Crooked River Provincial Park** (972-4492), situated on Bear Lake 2km south of town, offers a great beach site for swimming and picnicking, as well as secluded, wooded campsites ($15; toilets). The park is well-suited for winter activities such as tobogganing, snowshoeing, and cross-country skiing on established trails. For park conditions or ski and weather information, call 562-8288 during business hours. **Whiskers Point Provincial Park,** 51km past Bear Lake, has the same lakefront charm as Crooked River but no beach ($12). The park provides a boat launch for the large **McLeod Lake.** Blink and you'll miss **McKenzie Junction,** 26km past Whiskers Point. From the junction, it's 149km to the next town of note, Chetwynd, and almost 80km to the next gas station (**Silver Sands Gas,** open daily 7am-10:30pm). The junction also provides a turn-off to the town of **McKenzie,** 29km north on Hwy. 39, the largest town in the area and the home to the closest hospital. Barring medical emergency, McKenzie is probably not worth the detour.

   Chetwynd, 300km from Prince George, bills itself as the Chainsaw Sculpture Capital of the World. It's worth cruising downtown to see what's not visible from the highway. **Wildmare Campground** (788-2747), 5km before town along the highway, provides showers, toilets, laundry facilities, and budget rates (tent $7; RV $13). If a sauna, whirlpool, and movie channel seem more enticing, head for the **Country Squire Motor Inn,** 5317 South Access Rd. (788-2276 or 800-668-3101; fax 788-3018), across the highway from the A&W (singles $52; doubles $57; in winter $3 less). Locals splash it up in a **wave pool** at the **Recreation Complex** (788-3939), 2km east along the highway past the stoplight at the center of town. The adjacent recreation center (788-2214) offers **curling,** Canada's second most televised sport after hockey. After Chetwynd, Dawson Creek is 102km away.

   Monkman Provincial Park (787-3407) covers a portion of the central Rocky Mountains and foothills and is home to the **Kinuseo Falls,** taller than Niagara Falls. Several dayhikes provide views (some are wheelchair accessible) and some easy paddling below the falls a little water. BC Parks maintains 42 sites at **Kinuseo Falls Campground** on nearby Murray River ($12; pit toilets, water, firewood). To reach Monkman, take Hwy. 29 south to the coal town of **Tumbler Ridge,** 94km from Chetwynd. Monkman is another 40km due south on a gravel road.

YELLOWHEAD HIGHWAY (HWY. 16)

PRINCE GEORGE TO MT. ROBSON

East of Prince George, the pristine terrain that lines the 319km of road to Mt. Robson gives little indication of the logging that drives the regional economy, thanks to scenic, sightline-wide strips of forest left untouched alongside the route. Lakeside campsites at **Purden Lake Provincial Park** (565-6340), 59km east of Prince George, cost $15, with toilets and free firewood (one wheelchair-accessible site; gate closed 11pm-7am). **Purden Lake Resort** (565-7777), 3km east, offers cheaper and less scenic tent sites ($10), full hookups ($16-20), a cafe (open 7am-8pm), and the last gas before **McBride,** 140km east. Tenters can find refuge, toilets, showers, a laundry, and horseshoes at the **Beaver View Campsite** (569-2513), 1km east of McBride ($13, partial hookups $15-17).

From McBride, the Yellowhead Highway weaves up the **Robson Valley,** part of the Rocky Mountain trench stretching north-south the length of the province. **Tête Jaune Cache** lies 63km east of McBride where Hwy. 5 leads 339km south to Kamloops and the Okanagan beyond. **Tête Jaune Motel and RV Park** (566-9815) offers no-frills lodging right off the highway (camping $10; hookups $19; showers $2). Just 2km east of the intersection, the diminutive **Rearguard Falls** (a 20min. walk) mark the terminus of the chinook salmon's migration from the Pacific.

As Hwy. 16 continues east, the scenery reaches a crescendo at towering **Mt. Robson,** 84km west of Jasper and 319km east of Prince George. Standing 3954m/12,970 ft. tall, Robson is the highest peak in the Canadian Rockies; mountaineers reached its summit in 1913 only after five unsuccessful attempts. Less ambitious folk can appreciate the mountain's beauty from the parking lot and picnic site beside the **Mt. Robson Provincial Park Headquarters** (566-9174 or 800-689-9025 for reservations; open daily June-Aug. 8am-8pm; May and Sept. 8am-5pm; closed Oct.-Apr.). Five nearby **hiking trails,** ranging from 2km nature walks to 66km treks, are the park's main attraction (backcountry camping permit $5 per person per night, under 13 free). The 22km trail to **Berg Lake** is a luscious, well maintained path along the milky-blue Robson River past Lake Kinney and the **Valley of a Thousand Falls** (water, one hopes). Berg Lake is the highest of five **campsites** on the route, any of which can be used as a base to explore options from alpine ridge-running to wilderness camping. A quota system is in place for the trail, so book ahead through the headquarters. Sedentary types are accommodated at **Robson River Campground** and the larger **Robson Meadows Campground,** both opposite the headquarters ($17.50; toilets and hot showers). The private **Emperor Ridge Campground,** behind the headquarters, charges only $13.50 but has coin showers and $2.50 firewood. Park-run **Lucerne Campground** is 48km east towards Jasper ($12; pit toilets, free firewood, water).

PRINCE GEORGE TO TERRACE

As Highway 16 winds its way westward 575km (8hr.) toward Terrace from Prince George, steep grades and towering timbers gradually give way to the gently rolling pastures and the tiny towns of British Columbia's interior **Lakes District.** To break up the drive, **Beaumont Provincial Park** (565-6940), on Fraser Lake, offers 49 roomy sites, clean facilities, a playground, a swimming area, and firewood ($15). Hwy. 16 takes a turn at the town of **Burns Lake,** where almost every building is adorned with the likeness of a trout. There is a **visitor center** (692-3773; open July-Aug. daily 9am-5pm; in winter M-F 9am-5pm) right on the highway, the best place to stop for fishing info. Twenty-four kilometers south of town along Hwy. 35, forestry campsites are available at large **Francois Lake,** noted for rainbow and lake trout ($8; pit toilets, no water). Though most of the hiking in this area is dull, an exception is the 2km **Opal Bed Trail** to a creek bed lined with opals and agates. From Hwy. 35 turn right onto Eagle Creek Rd., which runs 7km to a recreation site and the trailhead.

Houston lies 80km west of Burns Lake, along with its Texas-scale contribution to the rampant superlativism of the late 20th century: the **world's largest flyrod** (20m long and over 365kg). Houston's **visitor center** (845-7640) offers a guide explaining how to realize your fishing fantasies (open daily 9am-5pm; in winter M-F 9am-5pm). Grassy camping can be found at the **municipal campground,** where the crows caw at 6am and the trains whistle all night ($10; pit toilets, drinking water, gates closed 11pm-6:30am). Take Mountainview Dr. west off the highway at the Esso Station, then turn left onto West 14th and follow the signs.

Smithers, 64km northwest of Houston, offers skiing on the slopes of Hudson Bay Mountain. The town of **New Hazelton** is 68km past Smithers, where **visitor information** (842-6071; open daily May-June 9am-5pm, July-Aug. 8am-7pm) consists of several great pamphlets on the area's totem poles, easily missed from the highway. The **'Ksan Village & Museum** (842-5544), 7km along Churchill Ave. towards Old Hazelton, displays a rich collection of totem poles, longhouses, and artwork of the Gitskan First Nations of the upper Skeena River. Gitskan dancers perform every Friday at 8pm ($2) from July to August. (Open daily July-Aug. 9am-6pm; reduced hours in winter. Wheelchair accessible.) Another 44km west of New Hazelton is the junction with the Cassiar Highway (Hwy. 37; see p. 357) which leads 733km north to the Yukon Territory and the Alaska Highway (see p. 363). The **Petrocan** here (849-5793; open daily 7am-10pm) sells the last gas before Terrace. For the remaining 97km (1hr.) to Terrace, Hwy. 16 winds along the base of the **Hazelton Mountains** and follows the thundering **Skeena River.**

TERRACE

In 1944, an extended spell of bad weather and a highly disproportionate male-to-female ratio caused 3000 Canadian Army troops stationed in Terrace to mutiny. For three weeks, disgruntled enlisted men ruled Terrace while officers took refuge in Prince Rupert, 144km to the west. Terrace is still known for its wildlife (ba-boom!), habitat of the world's largest Chinook salmon (weighing in at 92½ pounds), and the infamous Kermodei bear, a member of the black bear family recognizable by a coat that ranges from light chestnut blond to steel blue gray in color. For those who cannot live by fishing alone—seemingly a minority of the town's residents and visitors—Terrace's unique geography of roving plains and benches sculpted by the Skeena River makes for varied and scenic hiking.

◼ ORIENTATION AND PRACTICAL INFORMATION. Terrace is 149km east of Prince Rupert on the Yellowhead Hwy. (Hwy. 16) and 91km southwest of the junction of the Yellowhead and the Cariboo Hwy. (Hwy. 37).

VIA Rail (800-561-8630) sends 3 trains per week to Prince Rupert (2½hr.; $21) and Prince George (10hr., $71). **Greyhound,** 4620 Keith St. (635-3680), runs twice daily to Prince Rupert (2hr., $19.50) and Prince George (8hr., $66). See p. 53 for discounts. **Greig Avenue Auto** (638-8373; open Tu-Sa 9am-6pm), on Greig between Kenney and Munroe St., performs road service. The **visitor center,** 4511 Keith St., (635-0832 or 800-499-1637; terrace.tourism@osg.net) is off Hwy. 16 just east of town (open daily 8am-8pm; in winter M-F 8am-4:30pm). The **library,** 4610 Park Ave. (638-8177) offers free 1hr. Internet access; call ahead (open M 1-9pm, Tu-F 10am-9pm, Sa 10am-5pm; in winter also Su 1-5pm). The **Women's Resource Centre,** 4542 Park Ave. (638-0228), by the Aquatic Centre, has referral services, advocacy, lay counselling, and a library (drop-in M-F 10am-4pm). **Richard's Cleaners,** 3223 Emerson St. (635-5119) has washers ($1.25), dryers (25¢ per 6min.), and **fake sun** ($1.10 per min.) (open daily M-Sa 7:30am-9pm, Su 8am-9pm). **Terrace Aquatic Center** (615-3030), on Paul Clark Dr., has pool, hot tub, saunas, and gym facilities ($4.25, students and seniors $2.25, ages 2-14 $1.75). You can hang out **24hr.** a day at **Tim Horton's,** 4603 Keith Ave. (635-8128), just off the highway. **Mills Memorial Hospital:** 4720 Haugland Ave. (635-2211). **Emergency:** 911. **Police:** 3205 Eby St. (635-4911). **Sexual Assault Crisis Line:** 635-1911. Staffed daily 8:30am-4:30pm. For **Internet Access,** see Library, above. **Van's News,** 4607 Lakelse (635-8899), opposite the Coast Inn, rents the net ($3 per 15min., $5 for 30min., a precious $8 per hr.). **Post Office:** 3232 Emerson St., V8G 4A1 (635-2241; open M-F 8:30am-5pm). **Area Code:** 250.

◼◻ ACCOMMODATIONS, CAMPGROUNDS, AND FOOD. A&A Terrace Bed and Breakfast, 3802 deJong Crescent (635-0079 or 888-635-0079; jpeltier@kermode. net), boasts spic-and-span rooms with private baths, TV/VCRs, and accommodating hosts (from $50). Take Sparks or Eby St. north from Lakelse Ave. to McConnell St. and right to deJong Crescent. The **Alpine House Motel,** 4326 Lakelse Ave. 635-7216 or 800-663-3123; fax 635-4225), is also clean and happily removed from noisy downtown, with fridge and microwave. Kitchenettes available for no extra charge. (Singles $55, doubles $60; Oct.-Apr. $10 less.) **Ferry Island Municipal Campground** (615-3000), lies just east of Terrace on Hwy. 16 (sites $10, hookups $12; pit toilets, water, firewood). The island's prime fishing spot is a short walk from the wooded campsite, and lined with eager anglers who beat you there. The community pool is half-price for Ferry Island campers. **Kleanza Creek Provincial Park** is the site of an abandoned gold mine, 19km east of the town on Hwy. 16, with great sites along the creek ($12; pit toilets, water, firewood).

Terrace offers a handful of welcome breaks from the dreariness of highway diner cuisine. **Don Diego's**, 3212 Kalum St. (635-2307), is a fun, laid-back joint that serves Mexican, Greek, and whatever's in season. The menu changes twice daily. (Lunch $6-8. Dinner $9-15. Open M-Sa 11:30am-9pm, Su 10am-2pm and 5-9pm.) For authentic and affordable Indian cuisine, drive five minutes west of town along Hwy. 16 to **Haryana's Restaurant** (635-2362) in the Kalum Motel. Vegetarian entrees $4-9 and succulent chicken tikka masala $13. (Open Su-Th 11:30am-1:30pm and 5-9pm, F-Sa 11:30am-1:30pm and 5-11pm.) **Anka's**, 4711E Keith Ave. (635-1510), at Tetrault St. right before the overpass heading west, serves up a scrumptious vegan burger with soup or salad for $6.25. (Open M-Th 10am-7pm, F 10am-8pm, Sa 10am-4pm.) **Safeway**, 4655 Lakelse Ave. (635-7206), is the cheapest place for groceries (open M-F 8am-10pm, Sa 8am-9pm, Su 10am-6pm).

■ ▲ **SIGHTS AND OUTDOORS. Heritage Park Museum** (615-3000), perched above town on Kerby St. at Kalum St., houses countless artifacts from the pioneer era—including a working pump organ and an elaborate wreath made from human hair—perfect for pursuers of the grisly side of kitsch. (Open May-Aug. daily 10am-6pm, tours Tu-Sa 10:30am-4:30pm. $3, students and seniors $2, families $7.) The **Falls Gallery**, 2666 Hwy. 37 (638-0438), just east of town, has an impressive collection of native masks, art, and craftwork. Much of the artwork is for sale, with smaller souvenirs available. To view the free collection, take the Hwy. 37 turn-off south towards Kitimat, and take a right after the Volkswagen dealer. On Saturday mornings from May to October and on Wednesdays after 4pm, the **Farmer's Market** behind Lower Little Park sells what's homegrown and homemade.

Gruchy's Beach, 8km south of Terrace on Hwy. 37, is a 1.5km hike from the parking lot and is big, sandy, and begging to be picnicked upon. For a thrill and a little danger, check out the locals cliff-jumping at **Humphrey Falls.** Take Hwy. 37 south towards Kitimat and turn off at a gravel road on the left after approximately 35km, then drive or walk to the water. The **Nisga'a Memorial Lava Bed,** Canada's youngest lava flow, lies 100km north of Terrace. To reach this 54km² swath of moonscape, follow Kalum Lake Dr. (also called the Nisga'a Hwy.), which intersects Hwy. 16 just west of downtown, through the scenic valleys of the **Tseax** (T'SEE-ax) and **Nass Rivers. Hayatsgum Gibuu Tours** (633-2150; members.tripod.com/~HGTours/) leads 4-hour hikes and guided tours of the lava bed ($12, students $10, children $5; 2 hikes per day W-Su; reservation required).

The **Terrace Mountain Nature Trail** is a popular climb of moderate difficulty, beginning at Johnstone Ave. in the east end of town. The 5km (one-way) route takes one to two hours, and offers spectacular views of plateaus and surrounding valley. For an easy stroll, visit the **Redsand Lake Demonstration Forest,** 26km north on West Kalum Forestry Rd., a well-maintained gravel route. The Forest Service is developing a network of trails (one wheelchair accessible) around beautiful **Redsand Lake,** and through a variety of forested areas. The visitor center has interpretive pamphlets. Anglers can strap on their hip-waders and try their luck on the east shore of **Ferry Island** (see above). Ask for hot tips at the **Misty River Tackle Shop,** 5008 Agar Ave. (638-1369; open M-Sa 7am-11pm, Su 7am-10pm; in winter daily 7am-10pm).

In winter, groomed **cross-country** trails stretch halfway to Kitimat (about 30km down Hwy. 37) around the enigmatic (depth-testing has yet to detect its bottom) **Onion Lake** (798-2227 or 615-3000). World-class **downhill skiing** is but 35km west on Hwy. 16 at **Shames Mountain** (638-8754). Equipped with a double chair, t-bar, and handle tow, 18 trails over 130 acres, and a 500m/1600 ft. vertical drop, locals go nuts on Shames every winter. (Full-day lift tickets $30, ages 13-17 $20; rentals $18.)

PRINCE RUPERT

In 1910, railway magnate Charles Hays made a covert deal with the provincial government to purchase 10,000 acres of choice land at the western terminus of the Grand Trunk Pacific Railway. When the shady operation was exposed two years later, Hays was already under water—not drowned in his dire financial straits or the area's constant rain, but in the wreckage of the *Titanic*. The sole fruit of Hays' illegal labors was a town which, in a nationwide naming contest, was smacked with the shockingly bland moniker "Prince Rupert," foreshadowing the town's present-day penchant for the drab. Besides Cow Bay, a quasi-historic artisan community created to lure cruise ship tourists, Prince Rupert has little to offer visitors beyond a few small museums and a handful of totem poles. The weather is notoriously rainy and the closest hiking trails are several kilometers outside of town, but Prince Rupert is a gateway to Southeast Alaska. Both BC Ferries from northern Vancouver Island and the Alaska Marine Highway from Bellingham (see p. 58) have made this town a stop on their coastal routes, providing access to nearby villages like Metlakatla (see p. 401), and farther ports in the inside passage.

ORIENTATION AND PRACTICAL INFORMATION

The only major road into town is the Yellowhead Highway (Hwy. 16), known as **McBride St.** within city limits. At the north end of downtown, Hwy. 16 makes a sharp left and becomes **2nd Ave.** At the south end, Hwy. 16 becomes **Park Ave.**, continuing to the **ferry docks.** Avenues run north-south, ascending numerically from west to east; streets run east-west and ascend numerically from north to south.

TRANSPORTATION

Airplanes: Prince Rupert Airport is on Digby Island. The ferry and bus to downtown costs $11 (seniors $7, children $4) and takes about 45min. (Swimming is not an option.) **Canadian Airlines** (624-9181 or 800-665-1177) 2-3 per day to Vancouver ($532; midweek flights booked in advance as low as $220; youth standby $187).

Trains: VIA Rail (627-7304 or 800-561-8630), toward the water on Bill Murray Way. To: Prince George (12hr., 3 per week, $66). A **BC Rail** (800-339-8752 in BC; 800-663-8238 or 604-984-5500 elsewhere) train continues the next morning from Prince George to Vancouver (14hr., $194). See p. 52 for discounts and more info.

Buses: Greyhound, 822 3rd Ave. (624-5090), near 8th St. To: Prince George (10 hr.; 2 per day, $88); Vancouver (24hr.; 2 per day, $175). Station open M-F 8:30am-12:30pm and 4-8:45pm, Sa-Su 9-11:15am and 7-8:45pm. See p. 53 for discounts.

Ferries: The docks are at the end of Hwy. 16, a 30min. walk from downtown. Ferry-goers may not leave cars parked on Prince Rupert streets; check with the ferry company or visitor center for paid parking options. **Seashore Charter Services** (624-5645) runs shuttle buses between the terminal and the mall on 2nd Ave. ($3). **Alaska Marine Highway** (627-1744 or 800-642-0066; www.akmhs.com). To: Ketchikan (6hr., US$38); Juneau (24-48hr.; US$104). **BC Ferries** (624-9627 or 888-223-3779; fax 381-5452; bcferries.bc.ca). To: Queen Charlotte Islands (6-7hr.; 6 per week; peak season $24, car $90); Port Hardy (15hr.; every other day; $104, car $214). Reserve for BC ferries well in advance. If the ferry is full you *can* get on the standby list over the phone.

Public Transportation: Prince Rupert Bus Service (624-3343) runs downtown Su-Th 7am-6pm, F until 10pm. $1, seniors 60¢; day pass $2.50, seniors and students $2. Buses from downtown leave from 2nd Ave. West and 3rd. About every 30min., the #52 bus runs to within a 5min. walk of the ferry terminal. Twice per day, a bus runs to Port Edward and the North Pacific Cannery.

Taxis: Skeena Taxi (624-2185). From town to the ferry terminal $6-8.

Car Rental: National (624-5318), in Rupert Square Mall at 2nd Ave. and 5th St. M-F 8am-9pm. $56 per day, Sa-Su $30; plus 35¢ per km. Must be 21 with credit card. **Budget** (627-7400), with offices at the same mall and at the ferry, has similar rates. Must be 19 with a major credit card. Open daily 9am-5pm and 6-8pm.

VISITOR AND LOCAL SERVICES

Visitor Information: (624-5637 or 800-667-1994) at 1st Ave. and McBride St., in an impressive cedar building modeled after a traditional Tsimshian (SIM-shian) bighouse. Open May 15 to Labour Day M-Sa 9am-8pm, Su 9am-5pm; in winter M-Sa 10am-5pm.

Equipment Rental: Far West Sporting Goods (624-2568), on 3rd Ave. near 1st St., rents **bikes,** including lock and helmet ($5 per hr., $25 per day), and sells **camping gear.** Open M-Th and Sa 9:30am-5:30pm, F 9:30am-9pm. **Eco-Treks** (624-8311; fax 624-8318; www.citytel.net/ecotreks), on the dock in Cow Bay, rents **kayaks** and gear (single $25 or double $45 for 4hr.; single $40 or double $70 per day; no rentals to novices or soloists). 3hr. guided tours leave at 1 and 6pm with safety lessons for novices ($45).

Bookstore: Star of the West Books, 518 3rd. Ave. (624-9053). A fine collection of regional titles. Open May-Dec. M-F 9am-9pm, Sa 9am-6pm; Jan.-Apr. M-Sa 9am-6pm.

Library: 101 6th Ave. W. (627-1345). Free 15min. Internet access or $2 per hr. Open M and W 1-9pm, Tu and Th 10am-9pm, and F-Sa 1-5pm; in winter also Su 1-5pm.

Laundromat: For mother loads, head to **Mommy's Laundromat,** on 6th St. between 2nd and 3rd Ave. Wash 75¢, dry 75¢ per 15min. Open daily 9am-9pm.

Public Pool: Jim Ciccone Civic Center (624-9000) has a waterslide, hot tub and sauna, ice rink, and climbing wall! Swimming 50¢ Sa noon-2pm. Wheelchair accessible.

Public Showers: Pioneer Rooms and **Park Avenue Campgrounds** (see below).

EMERGENCY AND COMMUNICATIONS

Emergency: 911. **Police:** 100 7th Ave. (624-2136).

24-hour Refuge: The **Chevron Town Pantry,** 400 2nd Ave. West (624-2068).

Crisis Line: 888-562-1214. 24hr.

Hospital: 1305 Summit Ave. (624-2171).

Post Office: (624-2353), in the mall at 2nd Ave. and 5th St. Open M-F 9:30am-5:30pm. **Shoppers Drug Mart substation** at 3rd Ave. and 2nd St. Open M-Tu and Sa 9am-6pm, W-F 9am-9pm, Su 11am-5pm. **Postal Code:** V8J 3P3.

Internet Access: See **Library,** above. **Public Radio:** 860 AM.

Area Code: 250.

◤ ACCOMMODATIONS AND CAMPGROUNDS

Nearly all of Prince Rupert's hotels nestle within the six-block area defined by 1st Ave., 3rd Ave., 6th St., and 9th St. Everything fills to the gills when the ferries dock, so call a day or two in advance. Most motels are pricey—a single costs at least $55.

Andree's Bed and Breakfast, 315 Fourth Ave. E. (tel./fax 624-3666). In a spacious 1922 Victorian-style residence overlooking the harbor and city. Watch sunsets and sky developments from the deck with feline company. Homebaked breakfasts. Singles $45; doubles, $60; twins $70 ($10 per extra person).

Eagle Bluff Bed and Breakfast, 201 Cow Bay Rd. (627-4955 or 800-833-1550; eaglebed@citytel.net), on the waterfront in the loveliest part of town. Attractively furnished, private deck. Singles $45; doubles $55; $10 extra for private bath. No pets.

Pioneer Rooms, 167 3rd Ave. E (624-2334 or 877-624-6259), one block east of McBride St. A quasi-historic facade and modest, well-kept interior. Microwave, TV, Gazebo and BBQ downstairs. Curtained-in singles ($20) get noisy. Singles with walls $25; doubles $40. Laundry ($5 wash and dry with soap). Showers for non-guests $3.

Park Avenue Campground, 1750 Park Ave. (624-5861 or 800-667-1994). Less than 2km east of the ferry on Hwy. 16. Prince Rupert's only campground. Some of the well maintained sites are forested, others have a view of the bay. An RV metropolis! Sites $10.50; RVs $13.50, with hookups $18.50. Showers for non-guests $3.50. Laundry.

◖ FOOD

Sneak grapes and buy cheese at the colossal **Safeway** (624-2412; open daily 9am-9pm), at 2nd St. and 2nd Ave.

Cow Bay Cafe, 201 Cow Bay Rd. (627-1212), around the corner from Eagle Bluff B&B. Local patrons savor an ever-changing menu, including lunch delights like Santa Fe corn pie ($7), and shrimp quesadillas ($9). Extensive wine list; a glass of tasty Australian or Chilean is $3.50. Open Tu noon-2:30pm, W-Sa noon-2:30pm and 6-8:30pm.

Galaxy Gardens, 844 3rd Ave. W (624-3122). One in a Chinese restaurant crowd. Cantonese entrees from $9. Open daily 11:30am-10pm, F until 11pm. Free delivery.

Rodho's (624-9797), on 2nd Ave. near 6th St. Huge menu of pleasing pastas ($7-8), Greek entrees ($12-15), and pizzas ($14). Open daily 4pm-1am. Will deliver, gratis.

Opa, 34 Cow Bay Rd. (627-4560), upstairs in the Loft. Spin a bowl at the in-house pottery studio, and while it's firing, enjoy the town's newest restaurant offering: expensive sushi. Tuna rolls ($3); miso soup ($1.50). Open Tu-F 11:30am-2pm and 5-9pm.

SIGHTS AND OUTDOORS

Prince Rupert's harbor has the highest concentration of archaeological sites in North America. Archaeologists have unearthed materials from Tsimshian settlements dating back 10,000 years. **Archaeological boat tours** leave from the visitor center. (2½hr. tours depart June 19-30 daily 12:30pm; July to early Sept. daily 1pm. $22, children $13, under 5 free.) A local expert interprets several sites from the boat, with a stop at the village of **Metlakatla** (see p. 401) across the harbor. The **Museum of Northern British Columbia** (624-3207), in the same building as the visitor center, documents the history of logging, fishing, and North Coast Tsimshian culture, and displays beautiful Tsimshian artwork. (Open late May to early Sept. M-Sa 9am-8pm and Su 9am-5pm; mid-Sept. to late May M-Sa 9am-5pm.)

A number of attractive small parks line the hills above Prince Rupert. Tiny **Service Park,** off Fulton St., offers panoramic views of downtown and the harbor beyond. An even wider vista awaits atop **Mt. Oldfield,** east of town. The trailhead is at Oliver Lake Park, about 6km from downtown on Hwy. 16. The **Butze Rapids** and **Tall Trees trails** start from the same location. (Guided nature walks leave daily from Oliver Lake Park May-Oct.; contact the visitor center for times; $5.)

The **North Pacific Cannery** (628-3538) in Port Edward, 30 minutes away by car, presents a glimpse of the canning industry. Take the main highway out of Prince Rupert to the Port Edward turn-off, and follow the winding road for another 15 to 20 minutes. (Open May 1 to Sept. 30 daily 9am-6pm. $6, ages 6-15 $3, under 6 free.)

The best time to visit Prince Rupert may be during **Seafest,** a four-day event held in mid-June. Surrounding towns celebrate the sea with parades, bathtub races, and beer contests (call the visitor center for details). The **Islandman Triathalon** (624-6770; 1000m swim, 35km bike, 8km run) is also held around the time of Seafestivities and was won in 1997 by an intrepid *Let's Go* researcher.

ENTERTAINMENT AND NIGHTLIFE

Well, there's always the movies. The **cinema** at 2nd Ave. and 6th St. shows three features twice a night ($6.50, children and seniors $3, cheap Tuesdays $3). Drinking establishments in Prince Rupert compete for "dockers" (cruise tourists) and fishing boat crews. Come sundown, the town is a-crawl with sea life come to shore. The **Empress Hotel,** 716 3rd Ave. W (624-9917), has the best house band, but is not recommended for the pub-naive. The **Surf Club,** 200 5th St. (624-3050), attracts a younger set later in the evening with space to dance. A relaxing brew and a magnificent vista of the sun over the sea awaits at the **Crest Motor Hotel,** 222 1st Ave. W (624-6771). **The Commercial Inn,** 901 1st Ave. (624-6142; open Su-M noon-midnight, Tu-Th noon-1:30am, F-Sa noon-2am), and **Breaker's Pub,** 117 George Hills Way (624-5990; open M-Th 11:30am-midnight, F-Sa 11:30am-1am, Su noon-midnight), in Cow Bay, are full of local color, that is, tipsy fishermen and down-to-earth locals.

QUEEN CHARLOTTE ISLANDS

A full 130km west of Prince Rupert, two principal islands and 136 surrounding islets form the archipelago known as "the Canadian Galápagos." **Graham,** the northern island, is home to all but one of the islands' towns, a particularly potent strain of hallucinogenic mushroom, the world's largest and strongest-jawed black bears, and, until recently, the world's only known Golden Spruce. To the south, hot springs steam from mountainous **Moresby** and its smaller neighbors, where the massive wooden totem poles of the islands' first inhabitants decay within one of Canada's most stunning and remote national parks.

The islands' chief employer is the timber industry, narrowly edging out the Canadian government. In the 1980s, the islands attracted global attention when environmentalists from around the globe joined the **Haida Nation** and locals in demonstrations to stop logging on parts of Moresby Island. In 1981, UNESCO declared parts of Moresby a World Heritage Site, and in 1988, the Canadian government established the **Gwaii Haanas** (gwai-HAH-nus) **National Park Reserve.**

Accessible only by boat or plane, the park covers the southern third of the Queen Charlottes. The Haida Nation maintains over 500 archaeological and historical sites, including dugout canoes, burial caves, and rock shelters. Tourist activity in the area rose dramatically after the protests and the subsequent creation of the park. This publicity was relatively short-lived, however, and the mystical islands today are once again quiet and uncrowded. The lack of public transportation and the exorbitant cost of car rentals deter the faint of heart and light of wallet, but residents are generous in picking up hitchhikers.

The **BC Ferry** from Prince Rupert docks at Skidegate Landing, between **Queen Charlotte City,** 4km west of the landing, and the village of **Skidegate,** 2km to the northeast. Most visitors stay in Queen Charlotte, the islands' largest town, but all the communities have at least some tourist facilities. Many of the best accommodations and attractions are farther north off Hwy. 16 in **Tlell, Port Clements,** and **Masset.** To the south, Moresby Island is home to **Sandspit** and the islands' only commercial airport. From Skidegate Landing, 12 ferries per day make the 20-minute crossing between the big islands. Dialing 911 here does not directly access emergency systems; consult town listings for direct **emergency numbers.**

QUEEN CHARLOTTE CITY

Queen Charlotte City's central location and size make it the starting point for those exploring both major islands. "Size" is relative, however; this community of just over 1000 people is not the city its name claims it to be. Charlotte grew up around a sawmill, and logging is still its foremost industry, though fishing and the government also supply many jobs. While the location is pleasant, there's little to savor besides a view of the waterfront or a discussion of logging and fishing rights.

▋ ORIENTATION AND PRACTICAL INFORMATION

Towns on the island line one waterfront road; in Charlotte that road is **3rd Ave.** Charlotte is 3km east of the **ferry terminal.** Many businesses don't take credit cards.

Ferries: BC Ferries (559-4485 or 888-223-3779 in BC; www.bcferries.bc.ca), in Skidegate Landing, 3km east of Queen Charlotte City. To: Prince Rupert (6hr.; June-Sept. 6 per week; Oct.-May 4 per week; $24, car $90, bike $6). Try to reserve at least 3 weeks in advance for cars; car fares do not include driver. Ferries also run between Skidegate Landing on Graham Island and Alliford Bay on Moresby Island (20min.; 12 per day; round-trip $4.50, car $10.50; off-season car $9.50; no reservations).

Taxis: Eagle Cabs (559-4461). $7-10 between Charlotte and the ferry terminal. Open M-Th 6am-3am, F-Sa 6am-3am, Su 7am-7pm.

Car Rental: Rustic Rentals (559-4641), west of downtown at Charlotte Island Tire. Also at 3922 3rd Ave. (559-8865), by the ferry, at Jo's Bed and Breakfast. Must be 21 with credit card. $39 per day, 15¢ per km. Office open M-F 8am-7pm, Sa 9am-5:30pm, Su 10am-5pm, but available 24hr. Will pick up at the ferry terminal in Skidegate.

Auto Repair: Charlotte Tire, (559-4641) along Hwy. 33, provides 24hr. towing. Open M-F 8am-7pm, Sa 9am-5:30pm, Su 11am-5pm.

Visitor Information: (559-8316; fax 559-8952; www.qcinfo.com) on Wharf St. at the east end of town. Ornate 3D map of the islands, and a creative natural history presentation. *Guide to the Queen Charlotte Islands* ($4) has detailed maps. Open mid-May to mid-Sept. daily 10am-7pm; early May and late Sept. 10am-2pm daily. Holds **mandatory orientations** for visitors to Gwaii Haanas Park every day at 8am and 7:30pm.

Outdoor Information: Gwaii Haanas Park Information (559-8818; www.fas.sfu.ca/parkscan/gwaii), on 2nd Ave. off 2nd St. A trip-planning resource. Open M-F 8am-4:30pm. For registration info, see **Gwaii Haanas National Park Reserve,** p. 356. **Ministry of Forests** (559-6200), on 3rd Ave., at the far west end of town, has info on Forest Service campsites and logging roads on both islands. Open M-F 8:30am-4:30pm. Obtain a saltwater **fishing license** at **Meegan's Store,** 3126 Wharf St. (559-4428). Open M-Sa 9am-6pm. Freshwater licenses are available only from the **Government Agent** (559-4452 or 800-663-7867), 1½ blocks west of the city center.

Equipment Rental: Moonglow, 3611 Hwy. 33 (559-8831), just east of town. Nice mountain bikes. $5 per hr., $20 per day, deals for 2 or more. Includes maps of logging roads and campsites. Open daily 9am-6ish pm.

Bank: Northern Savings Credit Union (559-4407), on Wharf St. The **ATM** is a life-saver; many businesses don't take credit cards. Bank open Tu-Th 10am-5pm, F 10am-6pm, Sa 10am-3pm. The only other bank is in Masset.

Bookstore: Bill Ellis Books (559-4681), on 3rd Ave. at the far west end of town. A remarkable collection of works by and about the Haida and other First Nations. Open M-F 8:30am-4pm. **Bradley Books** (559-0041), on 7th St. off 3rd Ave., may be a better bet for fiction and current magazines. Open Tu-Sa noon-6pm.

Laundromat: 121 3rd Ave. (559-4444), in the City Centre Mall. Wash $1.50, dry 25¢ per 5min. Open daily 7am-9pm.

Showers: Ask at **Jo's Bed and Breakfast** and **Premier Creek Lodging.**

Ambulance: 800-461-9911. **Police:** 3211 Wharf (559-4421). **Emergency:** 559-8484.

Pharmacy: (559-4310) downstairs in the hospital building. Open M-Tu and Th-F 10:30am-12:30pm and 1:30-5:15pm, W 1:30-5:15pm.

Hospital: (559-4300) on 3rd Ave. at the east end of town.

Women's Services: Queen Charlotte Islands Women Society, 101 Causeway (559-4743), opposite the Credit Union. Call for hours.

Public Radio: 104.9 FM.

Internet Access: Free at the **Library,** 138 Bay St. (559-4518), under the community hall. Open M and W 2-5:30pm and 7-9pm, Sa 10am-noon and 1:30-5:30pm.

Post Office: (559-8349) in the City Centre Mall on 3rd Ave. Open M-F 9am-5pm, Sa noon-4pm. **Postal Code:** V0T 1S0.

Area Code: 250.

■ ACCOMMODATIONS AND CAMPGROUNDS

The small hotels of Queen Charlotte City are cozy, charming, and expensive. During the summer, make reservations or arrive early in the day to secure a room. The closest provincial park campgrounds are 40km north in Tlell. The pleasant, forested **Haydn-Turner Community Campground** is located a five-minute drive west of town. Turn left down an unmarked short dirt road just after the main drag turns to gravel. (6 sites: $10; water, firewood, pit toilets.)

The Premier Creek Lodging, 3101 3rd Ave. (888-322-3388 or 559-8415; fax 559-8198), just past the center of town. Ideal hostel facilities in a charming setting. Bunk beds in a creekside cottage behind the main hotel with shared kitchen, bath, and common room. $18, one double $30. Laundry $3.50. If full, try the hotel. Warm, clean rooms in the back hall with shared bath are $30; an extra sleeping mat is $5. Credit cards accepted. Cheap rooms go quickly. Showers for non-guests $5 (afternoons only).

Jo's Bed and Breakfast, 4813 Ferry Loop Rd. (559-8865). Follow the road from the ferry terminal up the hill. Convenient to the ferry, but not much else. Beware of free-range yard chickens. Many rooms feature cinematic ocean views, while others enjoy a communal kitchen and lounge. Singles $25; doubles $40; add $10 for a private room and a generous breakfast. Free local calls and a shed for storage. No credit cards.

Dorothy and Mike's Guest House, 3125 2nd Ave. (559-8439), centrally located up the hill behind the downtown Rainbow Gallery. A standing hammock chair, stained pine interior, a library, and a loving breakfast to warm even the soggiest traveler. Singles $40; doubles $55; suite for 3, $75. Call ahead.

Joy's Campground (559-8890; fax 559-8896; joys@qcislands.net), halfway between the ferry terminal and Charlotte. Camp in Joy's waterfront backyard, and drink from the spring. Kayaker's toilet, i.e., the beach below the tide line. Tent sites $5; hookups $9; electrical $15. To secure camping space, find Joy at Joy's Island Jewelers, 3rd Ave., next to the Hummingbird Cafe (see **Food,** below).

FOOD

Most locals only eat out on trips to the mainland, and will direct visitors to the grocery store for *haute cuisine à la Charlotte.* Buy cheese and Gatorade at **City Centre Stores** (559-4444; open M-Sa 9:30am-6pm), in the City Centre Mall. On nights and Sundays, try **Sam and Shirley's** (559-8388), on 7th St. at the west end of town, for groceries and a variety of Chinese food (open daily 7:30am-10:30pm).

Howler's Bistro (559-8602), on 3rd Ave., serves each dish with festive flair. Fully loaded Howler burger $8, grilled chicken fajita $10. Leave room for one of 5 varieties of cheesecake ($6). Open daily 11am-11pm; in winter 11am-10pm. **Howler's Pub,** downstairs, is the only happenin' nightspot in town. Open daily 1pm-2am.

Hummingbird Cafe, 3301 3rd Ave. (559-8583), offers an airy, sun-washed dining area and glimpses of the ocean through an alder tree. This family-friendly restaurant is known for its steak ($16), fish and chips ($8), sizable salads ($6-7), and hummingbird ($er, no). Open daily 7am-2pm and 5-9pm; in winter 11:30am-2:30pm and 5-8:30pm.

Isabel Creek Store, 3219 Wharf St. (559-8623), opposite the visitor center. Organic fruits and vegetables, juices, and home-baked breads. Open M-Sa 10am-5:30pm, and they stay open during the town's frequent power outages.

Hanging by a Fibre (559-4463), on Wharf St., beside the Howler's building. Store, gallery, and coffeeshop with art shows once per month. Open M-W 8am-5:30pm, Tu-Sa 8am-9pm, Su 8am-4pm; in winter daily 9am-5:30pm.

SIGHTS AND OUTDOORS

The **Haida Gwaii Museum at Qay'llnagaay** (559-4643), 1km east of the ferry landing on Hwy. 16, houses totem poles, contemporary Haida prints and carvings, and turn-of-the-century photographs from European exploration of the islands. (Open May-Sept. M-F daily 9am-5pm, Sa-Su 1-5pm; Oct.-Apr. Tu-F 10am-noon and 1-5pm, Sa 1-5pm. $3, children under 12 free.) A shed next door protects the 50-foot cedar canoe, the **Lootaas,** carved for Vancouver's Expo '86 by renowned Haida artist Bill Reid (open M-F 9am-4:30pm). For its restoration, a benefit feast fresh from the sea—salmon, halibut, herring roe on kelp leaves, crab and clams—is held Friday nights from 6-9pm in the Old Skidegate Community Hall (in the center of Skidegate, see below, on the waterfront). The evening includes Skidegate dancers and a slide show of canoe trips. ($35. Call Andy Wilson at 559-8832 for details).

The Haida town of **Skidegate,** known as "the village," lies 1km beyond the museum. This community of 695 people is the nexus of Haida art and culture. Residents are sensitive to tourists, and expect that visitors will exhibit discretion and respect concerning local culture and practices. Many a bald eagle has perched upon the totem pole out front of the **Skidegate Community Hall** near the water, a Haida longhouse built in 1979 according to ancient design specifications. Visitors must get permission from the **Skidegate Band Council Office** (559-4496), between the Gwaii Coop and the Taawnaay gas station on the main highway, to photograph the cemetery or to camp and hike in certain areas, especially near the Haida villages on South Moresby island; ask for details from the receptionist at the **Haida Gwaii Watchmen** (559-8225), next to the museum (open M-F 9am-noon and 1-5pm).

Ask a local to point out the distinct facial features of **Sleeping Beauty Mountain.** The challenging climb up Beauty starts about 12km west of town, off a logging road (follow the signs after 3rd Ave. turns to gravel), and takes a prince-deterring three hours to ascend. The peak blesses climbers with stunning views in every direction. **Balance Rock** teeters on a roadside beach 1km north of Skidegate. A group of brawny loggers once failed in an attempt to dislodge the boulder, so it's unlikely to topple from its precarious perch. The **Spirit Lake Trail** network departs from a parking lot beside the George Brown Recreation Centre off Hwy. 16, in Skidegate. A shapeless mythical sea monster called Wasco inhabits the lake and moderate and easy trails wind among trees modified by the Haida. Pick up an interpretive brochure at the Charlotte visitor center.

Navigating the tangle of local logging roads is easier with a few good maps and a copy of "Fern's book," $6, sold at all visitor centers and bookstores on the islands. The descriptions are invaluable, though the maps are outdated. Even on a two- or three-day hike, it's important to leave a **trip plan** with the visitor center or RCMP before setting out. The visitor center issues crucial information on **tides** and **scheduled logging road activity.** Everyone knows who loses when a couple of hikers or a 4x4 vie for trail space with an unstoppable logging truck.

TLELL

Tlell (tuh-LEL), 40km north of Queen Charlotte City, is a line of houses and farms spread thinly along a 7km stretch of Hwy. 16. The quasi-town enjoys some of Graham Island's best beach vistas, plus a population of artisans who earn Tlell a reputation as the Charlottes' hippie zone. Here the rocky beaches of the south give way to sand, and the **Tlell River** offers excellent fishing and water warm enough for swimming. One of the most popular trails around Tlell leads to the **Pezuta shipwreck,** the hulking remains of a 246-foot lumber barge that ran aground during a gale in 1928. The two-hour hike to the site leaves from the Tlell River picnic area off Hwy. 16, just north of the river, and wanders through lush forest, sand dunes, and agate-strewn beaches. When the trail branches, follow the "East Beach" sign up the ridge, or walk the whole way at low tide along the river. Diehard beachcombers continue past the wreck on a multi-day expedition along **East Coast Beach.** Highway 16 cuts inland just north of Tlell, leaving over 90km of incredibly pristine beach exclusively to backpackers. A number of wooden shelters punctuate the beach, but a tent or tarp comes in handy. Allow four to six days to reach the road access at the north end of the route, 25km east of Masset, and before setting out register at **Naikoon Provincial Park Headquarters** (557-4390), in a brown building on the right side of the highway, just before the Tlell River bridge; call ahead.

Tlell's **bookstore** (557-4241; open daily 10am-6pm) is in the Sitka Studio (which shows local artists) at the end of Richardson Rd. **Emergency/ambulance:** 800-461-9911. **Police:** in Queen Charlotte City (559-4421). **Post office:** on Hwy. 16, 2km south of Wiggins Rd. (open M-F 2:30-5:30pm). **Postal code:** V0T 1Y0. **Area code:** 250.

Sea breezes and birds singing in the spruces await at ◪**Cacilia's B&B/Hltunwa Kaitza** (557-4664), snuggled against the dunes just north of Richardson Ranch on the ocean side of the road. This may be the islands' nicest B&B, and is certainly the most distinctive. Friendly cats, driftwood furniture, and hanging chairs give character to the common living space roofed with giant spruce beams. Rooms are skylit, immaculate, and comfortable (singles $40; doubles $60). Pitch a tent or park an RV at the beautiful **Misty Meadows Campground,** 500m beyond Cacilia's, just south of the Tlell River bridge. Pit toilets, picnic tables, beach access, and water grace 30 sites ($12; 14-day max. stay).

The only restaurant around Tlell is **Tlell River House** (557-4211), 2km down Beitush Rd. along the river (open daily 7:30am-2pm and 5-8pm). **Dress for Less** (557-2023) lies 1km south of Richardson Ranch in a pink building housing a bookbinding and a metalworks shop. Sidle up to the pink coffee bar nestled among racks of vintage clothing. (Cappuccino $2.90, mocha $3.75, leather bomber jacket and shorts $80. Open M-Th 6am-5pm, F-Su 10am-5pm; shorter off-season hours.)

PORT CLEMENTS

Port Clements is a gritty, shrinking logging community 20km north of Tlell. Although blessed with an enticing harbor and a few nearby curiosities, "Port" has little to arrest passersby. An intricate network of logging roads stretches inland from town; these bumpy byways are open to public use and provide access to the heavily forested interior (check in at the MacMillan Bloedel head office, 557-4212 beforehand, especially if you plan on using the roads during active logging times, M-F 6am-6pm). Port Clements faces west onto Masset Inlet, and harbors some of the best **sunsets** in the Charlottes. Ten kilometers south of town, 9km after the pavement ends, a trail leads to an unfinished **Haida canoe.** At the 8km mark on this same road is the trail (15min. each way) to where the **Golden Spruce** once stood, across the **Yakoun River.** The lovely Yakoun can be accessed by kayak; guided trips depart daily from **Moresby Explorers North,** 147 Bayview Dr. (557-4665), past the museum ($40 per person for a 3-4hr. trip, no experience necessary; trips around islets in nearby Justkatla Inlet, $65). **MacMillan Bloedel,** a major local timber company, sponsors daytrips into the woods along the river (Tu and Th 9am-2pm); meet at the **Port Clements Museum,** 45 Bayview Dr. (557-4576). The museum itself houses many of the islands' archives and antiques of pioneer mining and forestry settlement, including restored logging machinery, the scrapbook, "The Saga of the Golden Spruce," and the mounted White Raven. (Open M-F 11am-4pm, Sa-Su 2-4pm. $2, children free.) On or around **Canada Day,** Port Clementsians celebrate with a fishing derby, slow-pitch softball, and mud-bogging (a contest to see whose truck can get the muddiest without getting stuck).

FALL AND RISE OF THE GOLDEN SPRUCE

For years, oddity-seekers of the world drove, biked, hiked, and ran to Port Clements, where the planet's only Golden Spruce basked in singular glory. Due to a rare genetic mutation, the 300-year-old tree contained only a fraction of the chlorophyll present in an ordinary Sitka spruce, causing its needles to be bleached by sunlight. The striking 50m giant glowed fiery yellow in the sun, beaming its way into Haida creation myths and horticulturists' dreams. In January 1997, however, a disgruntled ex-forestry worker arrived at the site with an axe and a mission. To protest the logging industry's destruction of British Columbia's forests, he chopped down the tree. These actions won him no prize for logic, but certainly drew province-wide attention.

While islanders reacted with astonishment at their beloved tree's untimely demise, the University of British Columbia revealed another shocker: there had been not one but *three* Golden Spruces—two, created in 1977 from clippings of the original, were growing peacefully in the botanical gardens of the UBC Victoria campus. University authorities donated these golden saplings to the Haida nation, and their future looks good. Concurrent with the fall of the Golden Spruce, an albino raven was born on the island, an event that locals took as a sign foretelling a continuation of the Spruce's three-century history.

The **Village Office** (557-4295; open M-F 1-5pm), on Cedar Ave. West between Tingley and Pard St., provides **free maps** of local logging roads. The **library** (557-4402; open W 3-5pm and 7-9pm, F 7-9pm), at Tingley St. and Cedar Ave., has free **Internet access**. **Health clinic:** on Park St. (557-4478; variable hours), a left turn past the museum. **Emergency:** fire (557-4355); ambulance (800-461-9911). **Police:** in Masset (626-3991). **Public radio:** 102.9 FM or 860 AM. **Post office:** between Hemlock and Spruce Ave. (open M-F 9am-12:30pm and 1:30-5pm, Sa 1:30-5:30pm). **Postal code:** V0T 1R0. **Area code:** 250.

The **Golden Spruce Motel,** 2 Grouse St. (557-4325), could use some sprucing up (singles from $42; doubles from $52; kitchenettes $8 extra; breakfast $3.25 for guests). Campers are better off at Misty Meadows in Tlell or at a campground in Masset. The **Yakoun River Inn** (557-4440), on Bayview Dr., is a local logger hangout featuring a country music jukebox and some damn good burgers ($5.75). Enjoy the autographed $2 bill collection adorning the walls, and ponder at how little beer it could buy here (pints $4.50; open M-Sa noon-2am, Su noon-midnight). **Golden Spruce Farms** (557-4583), 1km south of town on Bayview Dr., plucks an astonishing variety of fresh vegetables from the garden in back from late June. **Gas Plus,** just off the highway, is the only north island gas open Sundays (noon-6pm, M-F 8:30am-7pm) and serves cheap hot lunches (beef or chicken-vegetable pies $2.50).

MASSET

At Mile Zero of the Yellowhead Highway (Hwy. 16), Masset's low-rise businesses and dilapidated houses present an initially underwhelming welcome. Yet some surprisingly eccentric establishments and truly eccentric eccentrics mingle within this rather drab collection of tired buildings. The mixture of loggers, Haidas, and hippies makes for an interesting and sometimes volatile political and social scene. Spectacular scenery surrounds the town: the rainforest of Tow Hill and the expansive beachfront of the Blow Hole, east of town in Naikoon Provincial Park, more than justify the northward trek.

🚪 ORIENTATION AND PRACTICAL INFORMATION

Masset is about 100km (1¼hr. on a good, though narrow, road) north of Skidegate on Hwy. 16. To get downtown, take a left off the highway onto the main bridge, just after the small boat harbor. After the bridge, **Delkatla Road** is on the left. **Collision Avenue,** the main drag, is the first right off of Delkatla. To reach the campgrounds (see below), continue on Hwy. 16 without crossing the bridge.

Taxis: Jerry's Taxi (626-5017). $4 from the harbor into town. Open daily 10am-6pm.

Car Rental: Tilden Rentals, 1504 Old Beach Rd. (626-3318), at the Singing Surf Inn. From $40 per day; 25¢ per km. Must be 25. Open M-Sa 7am-9pm, Su 8am-9pm.

Visitor Information: Tourist Information Centre, Old Beach Rd. (626-3982), at Hwy. 16. History, maps for bird watching. Open July-Aug. daily 9am-9pm; Sept.-June M-F 9am-5pm. The **Village Office** (626-3955) has advice year-round. Open M-F 9am-4:30pm.

Bank: Northern Savings (626-5231), on Main St. north of Collison Ave. Only bank and **ATM** outside Queen Charlotte City. Open Tu-Th 10am-3pm, F noon-5pm, Sa 10am-3pm.

Car Repair: TLC (626-3756), on Collision Ave. Open 8am-6pm daily. **24hr. towing.**

Laundromat: Just north of Collison on Orr St. (626-5007). Wash $1.75, dry $1.75. Open Tu-Sa 11am-7pm.

Public Library: (626-3663), at Collison Ave. and McLeod St. Open Tu 2-6pm, Th 2-5pm and 6-8pm, Sa 1-5pm. Free **Internet access. Public Radio:** 103.9 FM.

Ambulance: 800-461-9911. **Police:** (626-3991), on Collison Ave. at Orr St.

Hospital: 626-4700, 626-4711 for emergency. The Doctor's clinic (626-4702 or 626-4703) is on Hodges Ave., on the right just over the main bridge into Masset. Call ahead.

Post Office: (626-5155) on Main St. north of Collison. Open M-F 8:30am-5:30pm, Sa 8:30am-12:30pm. **Postal Code:** VOT 1M0.

Area Code: 250.

■ ACCOMMODATIONS AND CAMPGROUNDS

Cheap accommodations and campsites abound amid Masset's centuries-old trees and expansive waterways. There is free **beach camping** on North Beach, 1km past Tow Hill, 30km east of Masset in **Naikoon Provincial Park.** Look for signs marking the end of Indian Reserve property. Call ahead for favored indoor lodging.

Copper Beech House, 1590 Delkatla Rd. (626-5441), at Collison Ave. Dine off Beijing china, share a bath with carved wooden frogs from Mexico, and snuggle under comforters from Finland. Singles $50; doubles $75; lofts in the garden shed $15. Long-term free room and board can be arranged in exchange for 4hr. of work per day.

Harbourview Lodging, 1618 Delkatla Rd. (626-5109 or 800-661-3314; lholland @island.net), just left off the Masset bridge, on the water. The ornately carved door and the lime plaid carpet have been waging aesthetic war for 30 years, but everything in the clashing interior is in good shape. Downstairs rooms with TVs share a bath and dry sauna. Singles and doubles $50. Two big upstairs rooms with living rooms, kitchens, private decks $75. Free laundry and fresh muffins in the morning.

Rapid Richie's Rustic Rentals (626-5472; www.beachcabins.com), 16km east of Masset on Tow Hill Road. Truly rustic accommodation on a wild northern beach. Six cabins with cold water, outhouse, propane lights and cookstove, wood or propane heating, and kitchen, sleep 2-4. $45-65 per day for two and $10 per extra person. The "Biltmore" (from $55) and the "Waldorf" (from $65), on the dunes, come highly recommended.

Agate Beach Campground, 26km east of town in Naikoon Provincial Park, at the base of Tow Hill. After 45min. of creeping vines and moss-swathed trees, this windswept fairyland clearing looks nearly too good to be true. Gorgeous campsites right on the beach, with water as far as you can see. 32 sites, with an area reserved for tenters. Picnic shelter, firewood, water, clean pit toilets. Free clamming (see **Food,** below). May-Sept. sites $12 for up to 4 people; free in winter. 14-night max. stay.

Village of Masset RV Site and Campground (626-5064), 500m past the bridge on Tow Hill Rd., next to the wildlife sanctuary. Convenient to town but far from North Beach and Tow Hill. 22 sites. Toilets and pay showers. Tent sites $9; vehicle $12; electricity $17.

☼ ▼ FOOD AND NIGHTLIFE

Free and potentially toxic **razor clams** await on Agate and North Beach. Call the **Department of Fisheries and Oceans** (626-3316) before harvesting the mollusks (see **Red tide,** p. 34), then stop by on Christie St. (behind the visitor center) to pick up a free permit and harvesting tips. Lemons and other seafood garnishes are sold at **Delmos Co-op** (626-3933; open M-Sa 10am-6pm), on Main St., south of Collison Ave.

Marj's (626-9344), on Main St. next to the post office. The heart and soul of Masset town, where most of the village's problems are solved (or at least discussed) over all-day brekkie ($4.50), a NY steak ($11), or fresh pie ($3). Open daily 7am-3:30pm.

3 of Cups Cafe, somewhere between Masset and Tow Hill (look for the red school bus). Delicious and substantial meals cooked *a la carte,* literally. Eggs, toast and hashbrowns for breakfast $5, *huevos rancheros* for brunch $10, and burritos for dinner $6. Live music jam every Saturday night at the bus (all welcome), and the annual 3 of Cups Circus, every July 2-4, celebrates a triad of birthdays (little Egan will be 5 in the year 2000) with fire-eaters, dancers, jester, and acrobats: free. Open Th-Su 10am-8pm.

Sandpiper Gallery, 2062 Collison Ave. (626-3672). Private dining space amid local artworks afford escape from the dreary streets. The owners happily *plaudern* with homesick Germans and serve up a *lecker* chicken burger ($8). Open M-Sa 8:30am-9pm.

Moon Over Naikoon, at the 15km mark on the Tow Hill Road. The fruits of one man's beachcombing labors includes whale bones, bleached animal skulls and bird wings, fossils, opals, and glass balls from Japanese fish nets. Edibles include whole wheat flaxseed bread ($5), and apricot-walnut muffins ($2). Open F-M 11am-6pm.

Daddy Cool's (626-3210), at the corner of Main St. and Collision Ave. A charbroiled burger ($6) may be satisfying, but it's the dancing, live bands, mixed crowd, lines out the door on weekends, and out-and-out bar brawls that feed Daddy Cool's reputation as a place you have to see to believe. $4 pints. Open M-Sa noon-2am, Su noon-midnight.

👁 🔺 SIGHTS AND OUTDOORS

Tow Hill, an incredible outcrop of volcanic basalt columns about 34km east of town, rises out of nowhere at the far end of Agate Beach, and presides over Masset as the area's reigning attraction. An easy boardwalk trail leads up the back of the hill to a fabulous overlook 100m above the rocky shoreline. On a clear day, miles of virgin beach and even the most southerly reaches of Alaska spread out below; sunsets are stupendous. On the way back down, take a detour to the **Blow Hole,** a small cave that erupts with 15-foot-high plumes of water at mid-tide.

Two less-traveled trails depart from the Tow Hill Viewpoint parking lot: an 11km beach walk to **Rose Spit** at the island's northeast corner, and a 10km hike on the **Cape Fife trail,** with access to the East Coast Beach and the long hiking route out of Tlell (see p. 350). A lean-to at the end of the Cape Fife trail allows tireless backpackers to link the two routes, exploring the entire island in a two- to three-day trek. Inform **Naikoon Park Headquarters** (557-4390; see p. 350) before multi-day trips, and contact them for advice. Across the Hiellen River, **North Beach** is where Raven discovered a giant clam containing the first men in the Haida creation myth.

Closer to town, red-breasted sapsuckers, orange-crowned warblers, glaucous-winged gulls, great blue herons, and binocular-toting birdwatchers converge on the **Delkatla Wildlife Sanctuary,** off Tow Hill Rd. The best paths for observing 113 local species begin at the junction of Trumpeter Dr. and Cemetery Rd. Continue on Cemetery Rd. past the sanctuary to reach **Oceanview Cemetery,** set in a lush green forest right on the beach.

With over 600 residents, **Old Massett,** 2km west of town, is the largest Haida village on the Charlottes. Beyond a few modern totem poles, however, there's not much to look at; hold out for the Haida Gwaii Museum (see p. 349). Those who wish to visit abandoned Haida villages on Graham Island can request a free permit at the **Masset Band Council Office** (626-3337; open M-F 8:30am-noon and 1-4:30pm), in the cedar-and-glass building at the east end of town. The council office also has information on local **Haida artists** with works for sale.

SANDSPIT

Sandspit is the only permanent community on Moresby Island. The town's neatly trimmed houses and yards, endless ocean views, and bald eagles in seaside trees make it the Charlottes' most attractive residential area. Mother Nature buffets the community with a perpetual west wind and provides sprawling sunsets over a porpoise-filled bay each evening. While Sandspit has limited culinary options, reasonably priced accommodations are plentiful and tend to fill up less quickly than those on Graham Island. This well-groomed hub houses the only commercial airport on the islands, serves as a major launching point for kayak and boat trips to Gwaii Haanas National Park Reserve (see p. 356), and provides access to logging roads that venture into the isolated interior.

🔳 **ORIENTATION AND PRACTICAL INFORMATION.** Having a car or bike is handy in Sandspit, since the town is spread over the long **Beach Road** parallel to the seashore. There isn't much traffic on the 13km road between Sandspit and **Alliford Bay,** where the ferry docks; those hitching to catch a late ferry often have a hard time finding a ride. Bringing a bike over on the ferry is free, and the trip to town is an idyllic, easy, one-hour ride along open ocean.

Sandspit Airport is near the end of the spit on Beach Rd. **Canadian Airlines** (800-665-1177) flies to Vancouver ($466, youth standby $160). **BC Ferries** (223-3779 or 888-559-4485; www.bcferries.bc.ca) runs between Skidegate Landing on Graham Island and Alliford Bay on Moresby Island (30min.; 12 per day 7am-10:30pm; $4.50 round-trip, car $11.50, kayak or canoe $2, bikes free). **Eagle Cabs** (559-4461) runs a shuttle from the airport across to Queen Charlotte City twice per day ($12 includes ferry; only one shuttle on Saturdays; reservations recommended). **Bruce's Taxi** (637-5655) will run you down the gravel roads to Moresby Camp, a common launching spot into the park (1hr.; $150 one-way; fits 7 people and 2 kayaks; pre-arranged pickup). **Budget,** 383 Beach Rd. (637-5688) and at the airport, rents autos for $50 per day plus 35¢ per km (must be 21 with a credit card). **Bayview Sales and Services** (637-5359), at the West end of town, pumps it islands-style and sells camping fuel (open M-F 8am-11pm, Sa 9am-6pm, Su 9am-1pm and 6am-8pm). **Visitor and Outdoor Information** (637-5362) is available at the airport. Register and gather trail maps here or at the office in Queen Charlotte City before heading into the park. **Park orientations** are held daily at 11am during the summer. (Open daily May 1-16 9am-1pm; May 17 to Sept. 9am-5pm daily.) **The Trading Post** on Beach Front road, just before the gas station, sells fishing licences and outdoor gear (open M-Sa 9am-noon and 1-6pm). The **health clinic** (637-5403 or 559-4447 for appointments) is on Copper Bay Rd., in the school building (open M-F 10am-noon). After hours, call the **Queen Charlotte City Hospital** (559-4300). **Library:** 383 Alliford Bay (637-2247; open Tu 3-6pm, Th 3-5pm and 7:30-8:30pm), at the north end of town. **Ambulance:** 800-461-9911. **Police:** (559-4421) in Queen Charlotte City. **Post office:** (637-2244; open M-F 9am-5pm, Sa 11am-2pm) at Beach and Blaine Shaw Rd. **Postal code:** V0T 1T0. **Area code:** 250.

⌐ ACCOMMODATIONS AND CAMPGROUNDS. Rooms in town are more affordable and less crowded than most on the islands. The ⬛ **Seaport Bed and Breakfast** (637-5698; fax 637-5697), just up the road toward Spit Point, offers island hospitality, guest pickup at the airport, plush couches, cable TV, and a breakfast of fresh eggs and home-baked goods. Reservations are essential in summer (singles $30; doubles $40). A block away from town, ⬛ **Bayside Bed and Breakfast** (637-2433), is operated by the same family. The accommodations are similar, the prices identical. **Moresby Island Guest House** (637-5300), on Beach Rd. next to the post office, has eight rooms with shared washrooms, kitchen, and coin-operated laundry facilities. Breakfast is provided, but further kitchen use costs $10 (singles $30; doubles from $55; cots $15). **501 RV and Tent Park** 501 Beach Rd. (637-5473; mdeslaur@island.net) has 10 full hookups ($10), five tent sites ($8), and the only public showers on Moresby ($1 per 2min; open 8am-9pm daily).

⌂ FOOD. More pleasant inside than out, **Dick's Wok Inn,** 388 Copper Bay Rd. (637-2275), serves a heaping plate of fried rice for $9.50 next to a tank filled with monster goldfish. Three of the islands' renowned mushroom varieties reside in Dick's Sam Koo scallops ($17). Dick also offers a limited selection of very expensive groceries (open daily 5-10pm). For all the golf you can handle ($20) and gourmet burgers ($6.75), head to **Willows Golf Course Clubhouse** (637-2388), near the end of Copper Bay Road. A pastoral setting, a beer (bottles $4), and chili with salad and garlic toast ($6) will bring guaranteed cheer (open daily in summer 11am-9pm). The **Sandspit Inn** (637-5334), opposite the airport near the spit's end, houses the town's only **pub** (open daily 11:30am-midnight, F-Sa until 1am, Su closes 11pm). The **Supervalu Supermarket,** 383 Alliford Bay (637-2249), resides in the mini-mall near the spit (open M-Sa 9:30am-6pm, Su 10am-4pm).

⚑ OUTDOORS AND EVENTS. Spectacular sunrises and sunsets reward those who wander to the end of the spit where anglers surf-cast for silver salmon. (Beachcombers should stay below the tide line if possible, since the spit is legally airport property.) Dirt logging roads lead south and west of town into some smashingly scenic areas, and several trails depart the road between the ferry docks and the spit. A 4x4 truck may be necessary for exploring these logging roads and accessing the trail heads by vehicle. If using logging roads between 6am and 6pm during the week, you must check in at the visitor center to check active logging status; in winter call **Timber West** (637-5436). The **Dover Trail** begins 40m west of the Haans Creek Bridge and passes by several giant cedars with ancient Haida markings. The round-trip hike takes less than two hours, but the **Skyline Loop** runs another hour down to the shore over more difficult terrain. Ten kilometers of rocky shore south of town lead to **Copper Bay**, a haven for bald eagles. **Grey Bay**, 20km south of town, offers a virtually uninterrupted expanse of sand. Twenty primitive **campsites** line the beach, but arrive early on weekends. A few kilometers down the road, a 4.5km trail follows the shore south to **Cumshewa Head.** The visitor center has maps and will tell you which of the dirt roads are not maintained. The roads are perfect, however, for **mountain biking.** The closest rentals are in Charlotte, and bikes are allowed on ferries. The 24km Moresby Loop is a popular route, following logging roads from Sandspit down to an old train trellis that crosses Skidegate Lake and on to an abandoned logging camp on Cumshewa Inlet. Although logging in the area has slowed, locals still celebrate **Logger Sports Day** in June or July. The festival features pole-climbing, caber-tossing, axe-throwing, and other vigorous lumber-related activities.

GWAII HAANAS NATIONAL PARK RESERVE

Arguably the most tranquil region of Canada's west coast, Gwaii Haanas (gwai-HAH-nus) was born in a whirlwind of controversy. The territory had been provincially owned Crown Land for most of the 20th century, disturbed only by sporadic logging and occasional tourist visits to deserted Haida villages which were overseen by Haida representatives known as **watchmen.** In the mid-80s, the timber industry, the Haida nation, environmentalists, and the provincial government came to loggerheads over land use on the island. In 1988, the federal government interceded, purchasing the southern third of the Queen Charlotte Islands to create a National Park Reserve. The Canadian Parks Ministry now administers and patrols the islands, while the Haida continue to guide visitors with the goal of protecting their cultural heritage.

While **no roads** penetrate the reserve, each summer a few thousand visitors make the long ocean journey south from Moresby Camp to enjoy a wonderland of remarkable beauty and diverse plant and animal activity. The sea life in Burnaby Narrows is alive with the densest animal and vegetable protein per square meter in the world. Old growth forest stands tall in **Hik'yah (Windy Bay).** Chains of lakes and waterfalls span southern Moresby Island. At **Gandle K'in (Hotsprings Island)**, several seaside pools steam at a year-round 37°C (98°F). The peaks of **San Cristoval Mountains** bear snow well into summer, while the waters of **Juan Perez Sound** teem with jellyfish and enormous, garishly colored starfish. A strong-jawed sub-species of **black bears** roams the park, feeding off the extraordinary bounty of sealife.

The vestiges of several cultures also rest in Gwaii Haanas. Deserted logging camps from the 1930s contain bizarre steam-driven logging devices and highways made of wood. Totem poles slowly decay at **K'uuna (Skedans)** and the UNESCO World Heritage site of **Nan Sdins (Ninstints)**, both Haida villages deserted after late-19th-century epidemics of smallpox and tuberculosis. These settlements are being permitted to "return to the land," in keeping with Haida tradition.

◪ **PRACTICAL INFORMATION.** To reserve dates upon which you can enter and exit the park, call **Super, Natural British Columbia** (in Canada and the U.S. 800-663-6000; elsewhere 250-387-1642). **Reservations** cost $15 per person, but are not required for trips with licensed tour operators. The park also provides 6 standby entries daily, though if you secure one of these spots you still may not be able to enter the park for another couple of days; attend the 8am orientation to better your chances. All visitors must attend a 90-minute **orientation session** before they depart: these are held daily at 8am and 7:30pm at the Queen Charlotte City visitor center (see p. 348) and at 11am at the Sandspit visitor center (see p. 354) from May to September. Call at least a day ahead to arrange sessions. Park user fees are $10 per night or day (under 17 free; reduced for longer stays). For a **trip-planning** package that includes a list of charter companies, contact **Parks Canada** (250-559-8818; fax 559-8366; www.harbour.com/parkscan/gwaii). Ask the park management about camping locations, so as to avoid sensitive areas and traditional Haida sites. Kayakers venturing into the park alone should file a **sail plan** with the Prince Rupert Coast Guard (call collect 250-627-3081). Contact Fisheries and Oceans (559-4413) before sampling shellfish. Freshwater fishing is not allowed; saltwater licences are available in Charlotte (see p. 347).

Weather reports are broadcast on VHF channel 21. Two **warden stations** are staffed from May to September, at Huxley Island (about halfway down the park) and at Rose Harbour (near the south tip of Moresby Island). They can be reached on VHF channel 16. Five **watchmen sites** (VHF 6) are staffed during the same period, and will offer assistance upon request, though their role is not to act as tour guides. To visit a cultural site, contact the watchmen a day in advance. No more than 12 people are permitted ashore at any one time.

▨ OUTDOORS. To avoid the exposed north portion of Moresby Island and to begin your trip in shelter of coastal islands, **Moresby Camp,** near Grey Bay, is a logical place to enter the park. Check with the infocenter in Sandspit (see p. 354) before traveling the potentially hazardous logging roads to this access point. The site of Nan Sdins, on SGaang Gwaii (Anthony Island), is the earliest recorded village in the southern portion of the park. A round-trip kayak voyage down the length of the park takes about two weeks.

Two companies dominate the market for **kayak rentals** and **charter trips** into the Park Reserve. Run by energetic Doug Gould, **Moresby Explorers** (637-2215 or 800-806-7633), on Beach Rd. in Sandspit just west of Copper Bay Rd., offers chartered trips ($110, overnight $150) to Doug's floating cabin, plus week-long kayak rentals for experienced paddlers ($250) that include transportation to the cabin and back. **Queen Charlotte Adventures,** 34 Wharf St. (559-8990 or 800-668-4288; fax 559-8983), in Queen Charlotte City, offers sea kayak rentals (singles $40 per day, $180 per week), marine transport ($120 from Queen Charlotte to Juan Perez Sound), and guided kayak, powerboat, and sailboat tours. **South Moresby Air Charters** (559-4222; fax 559-4223; smoresby@qcislands.net) flies over many of the heritage sites.

CASSIAR HIGHWAY (HWY. 37)

A growing number of adventuresome travelers prefer the Cassiar Highway to the Alaska Highway, which has become an RV institution. Built in 1972, the Cassiar slices through charred forests and snow-capped ebony peaks, passing scores of alpine lakes on its way from the Yellowhead Highway (Hwy. 16) in British Columbia to the Alcan (Hwy. 97) in the Yukon. Three evenly spaced provincial parks right off the highway offer beautiful camping, and the Cassiar's services, while sparse, are outlandishly quaint enough to keep cars and drivers satisfied. Hitchhiking is less popular here than on the Alaska Highway. Any waiter or hotel owner along the Cassiar's 718km will readily list its advantages: less distance, consistently interesting scenery, and fewer crowds. On the other hand, the Cassiar is less well maintained, and large sections of it past Meziadin Junction are dirt and gravel and become very slippery when wet. This causes little concern for commercial trucks roaring up and down the route, but keeps the infrequent service stops busy with overambitious drivers in need of tire repair. Driving at dawn, dusk, and on Sundays keeps you in sight of wildlife and out of the way of gravel-spitting behemoths, but be prepared for glass damage and carry a spare or two nonetheless.

HIGHWAY 16 TO MEZIADIN JUNCTION

Just north of the junction of Hwy. 37 and Hwy. 16 stand the totem poles of **Gitwen-gak,** which relate the history of the First Nation fort that stood on nearby **Battle Hill** until 1800. The **Kitwanga Loop Road,** 6km north, leads through Kitwanga (gas, repair, and food available) to the National Historic Park where Battle Hill is located. The hill served as a stronghold and base for the mighty warrior **Nekt.** It was once equipped with a tunnel system and spiked logs that would roll down on intruders; fortunately for unarmed travelers, these have since given way to stairs and interpretive panels. The totem poles of **Kitwancool,** or "place of reduced number," lie another 19km to the north. The village was originally called **Gitenyow,** "the place of many people," but the name was changed after extended warfare.

  Meziadin Lake Provincial Park (meh-zee-AD-in) lies 155km north of the junction of Hwy. 16 and Hwy. 37, with plenty of fishing (66 sites: $12.50; water, free firewood, and pit toilets). The gravelly sites are better geared to RVs, but tenters endure for the sake of excellent views and fishing: Meziadin Lake is one of three lakes in BC where salmon spawn. Make minor **tire repairs,** grab gas and shoot the bull with truckers at **Meziadin Junction** (636-2390; open in summers daily 7am-10pm; in winter 8am-7pm). Here there is also an unremarkable but cheap **cafe** (636-9240; open in summer daily 7am-9pm). Next door, the **Club Mez Corner Store** (636-2836) rents motor boats ($100 per day), has limited food and supplies, and keeps close tabs on the bear-viewing activity around Hyder (open daily 6am-11pm, winter 9am-9pm). **Whitehorse,** YT, lies 953km (about 12-15hr. of solid driving, depending on how rugged your vehicle is) to the north. **Stewart,** BC, and **Hyder,** AK, are 62km (45min. on paved roads) west, along Hwy. 37A. The serviceless road to Stewart and Hyder is known as the "Glacier Highway" because immense ice-tongues creep down so close to the road that drivers can feel the frigid air on their skin.

STEWART, BC, AND HYDER, AK

"It's the prettiest place on earth," most Hyderites will argue. Whether arriving along Hwy. 37A past towering glaciers and gushing waterfalls, or by ferry along the Portland Canal, one of the longest fjords in the world, most visitors need little convincing. The former ghost town of Hyder, AK, maintains its frontier character among stray horses taking refuge under eaves and porches. Its cross-border partner, Stewart, BC, is positioned in the jaws of a fjord among grassy tidal flats. Steep roofs draw eyes to the mountains that hulk over both towns, keeping national differences in perspective. Although Hyder is technically in Alaska, its currency is Canadian (except at the U.S. Post Office), its clocks tick to PST, its area code is 250, and most of its children are taught in Stewart. During International Days, from Canada Day to Independence Day, the two communities erupt in an extravaganza of fellowship that is North America's longest birthday party, and visitors are heartily welcome to bond in local bars. Stewart, population 450, is nearly seven times the size of Hyder and provides most modern amenities, while Hyder sports frontier-style nightlife and blast-from-the-past dirt roads. With local mining and timber industries facing an uncertain future, these tiny towns are teaming up to recruit tourists with attractions like the world's largest road-accessible glacier.

▮ ORIENTATION AND PRACTICAL INFORMATION

A left turn from the ferry terminal takes you to Hyder, a right turn to Stewart. Canadian customs and immigration have recently begun patrolling the border in an effort to curb smuggling. Be prepared to show ID and be asked how long you were in "America." Humorless officers don't flinch at the typical response of "about 5 minutes." **Hwy. 37A** melds into Stewart's **Conway St.,** which intersects **5th Ave.** toward the water.

Airplanes: Taguan Air (636-2800) flies a mail plane which carries passengers to Ketchikan (45min.; M and Th; $100). Call ahead.

Ferries: Alaska Marine Highway (800-642-0066; www.akmhs.com). Weekly round-trips from Ketchikan to Stewart/Hyder (US$40, round-trip US$58) with a 3hr. layover to give pedestrians just enough time to see both towns. Ferry travelers seldom stay overnight.

Local Transportation: Seaport Limousines (636-2622), in Stewart, drives to Terrace (4hr., daily 10am, $30) and takes sightseers to Salmon Glacier for $32 per person.

Auto Repair: PetroCan (636-2307), at 5th Ave. and Conway, has the only gas in either town (open daily 7:30am-8pm, repairs 8am-4:30pm). 24hr. road service (636-2456).

Visitor Information: In Stewart (636-9224; stewhydcofc@hotmail.com). Open June-Aug. daily 9am-7pm; in winter M-F 1-5pm. In Hyder (636-9148), at the **Hyder Community Association Building** (bear right at the Sealaska Inn downtown). Open June-Aug. M-F 9am-3pm, Sa-Su noon-5pm; in winter M-F 11am-5pm.

Outdoor Information: Forest Service (636-2367), down the hall from Hyder visitor center. Open May 1 to Sept. 15, usually 10am-2pm. Call ahead.

Bank: Canadian Imperial Bank of Commerce (636-2235). Open M and W noon-3pm, F noon-5pm. 24hr. **ATM** on 5th Ave. by the post office.

Laundromat and Public Showers: Shoreline Laundromat (636-2322), behind the post office. Wash $1.75, dry 25¢ per 4min. Showers $1 per 1½min. Open daily 7am-11pm. Or in Hyder, beside the **Sealaska Inn.** Laundry: wash $1.50, dry $1.75. Showers $3 per 8min. Open **24hr.**

Library: (636-2637) also in the Community Association Building. Free Internet access. Open M-F 1-3pm, Sa noon-5pm; in winter M-F 3-5pm, Sa noon-5pm.

Pharmacy: Rexall (636-2484), on 5th Ave. and Brightwell St., Open M-Sa 9am-5:30pm and 7-9pm, Su noon-4pm.

Emergency: 911. **Police:** (636-2233) at 8th Ave. and Conway St. **Ambulance:** 800-461-9911. **Fire:** 636-2345.

Health Centre (636-2221) is at Brightwell and 9th. Open M-F 9am-5pm.

Public Radio: 1450 AM.

Internet Access: See **Library,** above. **Toast Works,** see below. $5 per 30min.

Post Office: (636-2553) at Brightwell St. and 5th Ave. Open M-F 8:30am-5pm, Sa 9-noon. **Postal Code:** V0T 1W0. In Hyder, 1 Hyder Ave., 99923 (636-2662), past the Community Building towards Fish Creek. U.S. currency only. Open M-F 9am-1pm and 2-5pm, Sa 10:30am-12:30pm. **Postal code:** 99923.

Area Code: 250.

■ ACCOMMODATIONS, CAMPGROUNDS, AND FOOD

Stewart's **Rainey Creek Campground** (636-2537), located at the end of Brightwell St., is orderly, quiet, and woodsy, with grassy tent sites ($10 for 2 people, $3 per extra person), forested sites with electricity ($16), and impeccably clean showers ($1 per 4min.). Less appealing **Camp Runamuck** in Hyder has tent-sites ($10) separated from a gravelly RV park (hookups $18) with coin showers and laundry. The office is in the **Sealaska Inn** (636-2486 or 888-393-1199), which has cubicle-like but comfy "sleeping rooms" ($30; shared bath), singles ($48) and doubles ($52), above a night lounge. **Kathi's B&B** (636-2795), at the corner of 8th and Brightwell, provides placid accommodations and a full breakfast (singles $55, doubles $65).

The **Bitter Creek Cafe** (636-2166), in Stewart on 5th Ave., is tops in a great building adorned with historical photos and frontier appliances. Savor their wicked good artichoke salad ($7) or gourmet pizzas ($10; open daily May-Oct. 11:30am-2pm and 5-8pm daily; July-Aug. 8am-9pm). Across the street, **Toast Works** has an interactive appliance bar, serves fruity smoothies ($2.75), and "the best coffee this side of the Bitter Creek Cafe." Three dollars will get you into toaster-lover's heaven: behold vintage appliances (open mid-May to mid-Sept. daily 10am-8pm). **Cut-Rate Foods** (636-2377), on 5th Ave. in Stewart, lives up to its name (open M-Sa 9am-8pm, Su 11am-6pm; in winter M-Sa 10am-7pm, Su 11am-6pm; no credit cards).

N. BC & THE YUKON

👁 🔺 SIGHTS AND OUTDOORS

The Stewart Historical Society runs a **museum** (636-2568), on Columbia St., which offers, among the usual suspects of stuffed wildlife, an exhibit on the Great Avalanche of '65 and a disturbing collection of photos documenting the 1981 filming in Stewart of *The Thing*. (Open mid-May to mid-Sept. daily 11am-7pm; $4, ages 6-12 $2, under 6 free; in winter call 636-9029.) The principal activity in Hyder is sidling up to the bar in the historic **Glacier Inn** (636-9092) and asking to be **"Hyderized."** Over $45,000 in signed bills line the tavern walls, where early miners would tack up cash to insure themselves against returning to town too broke to buy a drink. (Open 10am-sometime late; in winter 2pm-whenever.) If you are mobile and sober by morning, take advantage of **free bicycle** transportation. The bikes are locked to a stand by the Stewart visitor center: sign out a steed at the Bitter Creek Cafe.

Each year during the salmon spawning season (late July-Aug.), bears congregate at **Fish Creek,** 5 mi./8km from Hyder, to feed on bloated, dying Alaskan chum salmon. Come early in the morning to avoid tourist crowds. The only maintained trail on the Hyder side is the **Titan Trail,** a challenging 5 mi./8km (one-way) hike up from the valley with creek crossings. It gains 4000 ft./1200m of elevation, becoming rocky and difficult toward the end (check with the Forest Service for trail conditions). Heading away from Hyder, the trailhead is on the right about a half mile/ 800m past Fish Creek. Eight miles/13km north of Stewart along Highway 37A, the **Ore Mountain Trail** is a shorter, but still challenging 2 mi./3.5km (one-way) climb to a viewpoint overlooking the Bear River Valley.

Salmon Glacier, 20 mi./32km from Hyder on the Salmon River Rd., is the fifth-largest glacier in the world, but the largest accessible by road. Beginning at Mile 19, the road creeps along a ridge almost directly above the glacier for several miles providing eagle-eye views. The rocks above the road make for good hiking and the immense glacier lays beneath the setting sun. The road to the glacier is rocky and winding, but navigable for most vehicles. There are many scenic pull-outs—don't look down yet. Those taking their own car can check road conditions with the Forest Service and pick up a self-guided tour brochure. **Bear Glacier,** 2½ mi./35km east of Stewart, sits in plain and glorious view of Hwy. 37A.

Most anglers let the bear population work the creeks and streams, but for a hefty sum, deluxe fishing boats can be chartered for the hour, day, or week. If you already possess boating prowess, rent your own craft. **Border Bandit** (636-2317) will launch a 14 ft. aluminum boat for you (with 15hp outboard; fits two adults plus gear), and let you motor away for $15 per hour.

MEZIADIN JUNCTION TO ISKUT

About 65km north of Meziadin Junction, new growth (and what is rumored to be the largest huckleberry patch in BC) infiltrates the immense **Iskut burn area.** Another 53km north is **Kinaskan Lake Provincial Park,** where a sweet campground includes water, pit toilets, firewood, and a boat launch onto the rainbow trout-stocked lake (50 lakeside sites: $12.50; wheelchair accessible). At the far end of the lake is the head of a 24km hiking trail to **Mowdade Lake** in **Mount Edziza Provincial Park** (see below). There is gas available among the moose antlers of **Tatogga Lake Resort** (234-3526), another 25km north (open May-Sept. daily 7am-10pm, winter 8am-8pm). A stone's throw farther is the **Ealue Lake** (EE-lu-eh) turn-off, which leads 12km to a recreation site (day use only) and trailheads pointing deep into the virgin backcountry of the **Spatsizi Plateau Wilderness** (see below).

The small native village of **Iskut,** 256km north of Meziadin Junction, presents a range of resort options, earning it the unremarkable title of "resort capital of northwest BC." Even the most discriminating hostel connoisseurs heartily approve of **The Red Goat Lodge** (234-3261), 3km south of Iskut. The **hostel** ($15) in the basement of this regal lodge boasts a full kitchen, spacious common room, wood stove, coin showers ($1 per 3½min.), and laundry (wash $2, dry $1). The hosts' kids and llamas keep the place lively even when it's not packed. The **B&B** upstairs is equally impressive (singles $65; doubles $85). Tent sites on the **Eddon-**

tenajon Lake (ed-un-TEN-a-jon) cost $10, RV hookups $20. Canoe rental is $10 per half-day. Rentals for trips on the **Stikine** and **Spatsizi Rivers** start at $30 per day.

At Iskut, travelers can fill the tank and grab some groceries at the sizeable **Klua-chon Centre** (234-3241; open June-Aug. daily 8am-10pm; in winter M-Sa 9am-6pm, Su noon-5pm), which doubles as the **post office** (open M, W, and F 9am-4pm, Tu 1-4pm). **Postal Code:** V0J 1K0.

SPATSIZI PLATEAU WILDERNESS AND MOUNT EDZIZA PROVINCIAL PARK

Long a territorial homeland of the Tahltan people, the Spatsizi Plateau became a provincial park and wildlife reserve in 1975. Supporting one of the largest populations of **woodland caribou** in British Columbia, Spatsizi is home to a wide range of wildlife. Its name means "red goat" in Tahltan, in honor of the mountain goats in the region, whose penchant for rolling in iron oxide dust turned their coats a rusty hue. **Ealue Lake Rd.,** near the **Tatogga Lake Junction** 25km north of **Kinaskan Lake Provincial Park** (see above), provides the closest vehicle access to the Spatsizi Wilderness Plateau. To reach the trailheads, follow the so-called road for 22km until it joins with the BC Rail grade, a tertiary road of variable quality (still passable for most vehicles). Take a right here, and the boggy and poorly maintained **McEwan Trail** will appear in 6km. **The Eaglenest Trail,** a further 22km down the rail grade, is a more frequently serviced and better marked option for hiking into the park's recreational center at **Cold Fish Lake** (40km one-way), where there are cabins with wood heating, propane stoves, gravity-driven running water, and solar showers ($15, families $25), and many wilderness trails for dayhiking. The roads to the trailheads are maintained by the Iskut Band and pass through culturally important areas: ask permission to drive them at the **Iskut Band Office** (234-3331).

A seven- to eight-day canoe trip, suitable for intermediate to advanced paddlers and involving several short portages, snakes through the heart of Spatsizi terrain along the **Spatsizi** and **Stikine Rivers.** You can launch your craft, after a short portage, at **Didene Creek,** 120km down the BC Rail Grade, and pull out 250km of water and wilderness later at the crossing of the Stikine River and Highway 37 (about 15km north of 40 Mile Flats). For canoe rentals try **Rick Marock** (771-4233) in Dease Lake, or **The Red Goat Lodge** (234-3261) in Iskut (about $30 per day).

Four million years ago, 2787m **Mt. Edziza** (ed-DZA-za) erupted violently, leaving behind a charred, craggy, obsidian landscape. For centuries, native bands made razor-sharp cutting blades and arrowheads from the rock. Like Spatsizi, Mt. Edziza Provincial Park invites only experienced outdoors explorers, due to its extremely variable weather (summer snow) and lack of trail system, facilities, and staff. There is no vehicle access into this remote region. Most hikers access Mt. Edziza by float plane into **Mowdade** or **Buckley Lakes,** bypassing the grueling week-long trek into the park along the **Klastine River** (klas-LEEN). Some find a boat ride in from Kinaskan Lake Provincial Park to do the seven-day-plus **Mowdade Trail,** but BC Parks does not recommend this arduous, unmaintained route. All hikers, regardless of previous wilderness experience, should make their itineraries known before venturing into the park and must check-out upon return (a search party may be sent out if you fail to do so). For more info, contact **British Columbia Parks Area Supervisor** (604-771-4591), Box 118, Dease Lake, BC V0C 1L0.

DEASE LAKE

Dease Lake, 84km north of Iskut, became a Hudson Bay Company outpost in the late 1800s, though it had been long known by the local indigenous Tahltan as "Tatl'ah" ("Head of the Lake"). The settlement had its share of early gold rush glory in 1864 and 1873, and now serves as a rudimentary service center for northwestern BC and as a base for backpackers exploring the vast and rugged **Mount Edziza** or **Spatsizi Provincial Parks** nearby (see above). With the exception of the stellar inn, there's little to draw road-trippers to this town besides gas and food.

The **Dease Lake Tourist Information Office** is in the Northern Lights College (771-3900). The **Forest Service** (771-8100) occupies the building next door and offers info on local trails or campsites; call ahead. **BC Parks** (771-4591) has info on the nearby provincial parks. To get to their office, drive to the end of Boulder Rd. and take a left onto Dease Ave. The building is on the right. Some fishing and camping supplies can be found at **McLeod Mountain Supply Ltd.,** on Boulder Ave., across from Chico's (771-4699; open M-Sa 8:30am-5:30pm, Su 10am-4pm). Free **Internet access** is available at the Northern Lights College (open M-F 8:30am-noon and 1-3pm; in winter until 4pm). The **TD Bank** is in the Government building across the highway from the college (open M, W, and F 10am-noon and 1-3pm). **Dease Gas Station** (771-5600) has great **showers** ($4 includes towel, soap, and shampoo) and a **laundromat** (wash $3, dry 25¢ per 5min.; open M-Sa 8am-9pm, Su 9am-9pm). For repairs or a car wash, stop in at **Chico's** (771-5656), on Boulder Ave. (open M-F 8am-6pm). The **Stikine Health Center** (771-4444) is just off the Cassiar at the north end of town (walk-in M-F 8:30am-4:30pm). The **post office,** is in the Dease Gas Station (771-5013; open M-F 8:30am-1pm and 2-5pm). **Police:** 771-4111. **Ambulance:** 771-3333. **Public Radio:** 98.1 FM. **Postal Code:** V0C 1L0. **Area Code:** 250.

The spacious, pine-furnished ▓ **Arctic Divide Inn** (771-3119), right on the Cassiar, deserves accolades for its squeaky clean rooms with private bath, phones, and TV, and access to a spotless shared kitchen. From the rugged staircase to the carefully positioned rock and mineral collection, the inn's decor is a welcome exception to regional drabness. (Singles and doubles $65; includes generous continental breakfast.) The closest forest service **campground** to Dease is scenic **Allen Lake.** From Boulder St., go left on 1st Ave. and follow it to the end ($8 camping permit only; no water, pit toilets). Revellers take advantage of the campground's proximity to the **Tanzilla Bar,** and may disrupt travelers seeking solitude. Those without four-wheel-drive vehicles shouldn't park at the campground—the steep gravel driveway to the lake is likely to hold city cars hostage. For a list of campgrounds, get a Forest Service map from the visitor center or Forest Service. **Northway Country Kitchen** (771-4114; open May-Oct. daily 7am-9pm), or "the restaurant," offers big portions and slow service in a clean, spacious setting. Tickle your palate with "pierogies & smokies," cheese-filled dumplings with four sizable sausages ($8.50). Groceries are available next to Dease Gas at the **Supervalu** (771-4381; open mid-June to Sept. M-Sa 11am-9pm, Su 8am-7pm; in winter M-Sa 9am-7pm, Su 9am-6pm).

TELEGRAPH CREEK

Lying 119km from Dease Lake on Telegraph Creek Rd., Telegraph Creek is the only remaining settlement along the **Stikine River** (stuh-KEEN). The highest navigable point on the Stikine, the site was an important rendezvous for the coastal Tlingit and interior Tahltan people. Telegraph Creek's 400 residents remain mostly Tahltan. The community welcomes its infrequent visitors, but those keen to explore should seek permission from the **Tahltan Band** (235-3151). For **tire repair,** contact **Henry Vance** (235-3300). Mechanically adept locals have been known to help out those whose vehicles incur the substantial wrath of the Telegraph Creek Rd. Follow signs for Glenora to find the **health clinic** (235-3212 or 235-3171). On your way to town, the **post office,** is on the right. Open M and W 9:30-11:30am, Tu and Th 1-4pm, F 9:30-11:30am and 1-4pm. **Postal code:** V0J 2W0. **Police:** 235-3111.

The biggest attraction for thrill-seeking travelers is the 112km **Telegraph Creek Road.** The gravel road is well maintained and offers magnificent views of the **Stikine Grand Canyon.** It is no place, however, to lug a clumsy RV or give a failed brake system a second chance. The second half of the road features 20% grades and hairpin turns along the steep, perilous obsidian outbanks of the Tuya, Tahltan, and Stikine River canyons. Travelers should allow 2½ hours to drive each way, with ample time to de-frazzle in between. A rest stop, 88km from Telegraph Creek, offers a gorgeous view of the canyon and a chance to speak words of encouragement to your beleaguered transmission.

The modern village of Telegraph Creek revolves around the historic **Stikine River-Song** (235-3196). Originally the Hudson Bay Company building near the neighboring tent city of **Glenora,** 12 mi. from Telegraph Creek, the RiverSong was disassembled in 1902 and moved to its present location. Today, the jack-of-all-trades RiverSong acts as Telegraph Creek's hotel, cafe, and general store, with gas, fishing licenses, and t-shirts. The extremely helpful staff can answer almost any question about the history of the area. You can wash off 119km of road dust with a shower ($4). Hotel rooms at the RiverSong are clean, with cedar finishing and a common kitchen. (Singles $49; doubles $55; $10.50 per additional person. Open May-Sept. M-Sa 11am-7pm, Su noon-7pm.) Three free recreation sites along the road to the historic site of Glenora provide primitive **camping** for the penniless.

DEASE LAKE TO THE ALASKA HIGHWAY

This stretch of highway follows the old Cassiar Gold Route, and dredges still in use can be seen along its length. **Moose Meadow Resort,** 85km north of Dease Lake, is a roomy lakeside campground with access to canoe routes (sites $11; 2-person cabins $30, $5 per additional person; firewood, water, pay showers). Canoe rentals on **Cotton Lake,** a widened portion of the gently meandering **Dease River,** are $6 per hour (2hr. minimum), and $27 per day. **Boya Lake Provincial Park** is 152km north of Dease Lake, 2km east of the Cassiar Hwy., situated on a magnificent turquoise lake with a boat launch and swimming dock. Spacious private campsites please tenters and RV drivers (32 sites: $12, with pit toilets, firewood, water). The shallow lake is warm by northcountry standards, but still numbingly "refreshing." There are two gas stations between Dease Lake and the Alcan junction: **Jade City** (ask the operator for radio phone 2m3536), 117km past Dease Lake (open daily 6am-noon), and **Kididza Services** (239-3500), at Good Hope Lake, 23km farther on (open M-Sa 8am-10pm, Su 9am-8pm). Jade City, as well as boasting an impressive collection of the green stuff, has well-kept tenting and RV sites in the woods just off the road ($10; with full hookup and showers $15; toilets and free firewood).

Having reached the end of this 718km odyssey at the junction of the Cassiar Hwy. and the Alaska Hwy., travelers can grab showers, groceries, gas, and minor repairs at the **PetroCan Station** (536-2794), which doubles as the office for the RV park and motel next door ($11; full hookups $16; singles and doubles $30; shared bath; no TV or phone; showers free, $3 for non-guests). They also operate a 24-hour **laundromat** (wash $1.50, dry 50¢ per 14min.). Travelers can grab some chili ($6) or a kamoboko crab melt and caesar salad ($8) at the **Junction 37 Cafe** (536-2795), next to PetroCan (open daily May-Oct. 6:30am-10pm). Strangely, the **saloon** in the next lot (536-2796) has slightly cheaper gas (open 8am-1am). **Whitehorse** lies another 435km (5hr.) west on the Alcan (see p. 368).

THE ALASKA HIGHWAY

> They sweat and froze, laughed and cried, bled and labored until finally, the unachievable was achieved. In a dozen American accents they had cussed and kissed me into being from Dawson Creek to Fairbanks. In less than nine months, the miraculous 1600 mile military highway was born.
> —Shirley Ravelli, "Spirit of the Alaska Highway"

Built during World War II, the Alaska-Canada Highway (also known as the Alcan) traverses an astonishing 2378km route between Dawson Creek, BC, and Fairbanks, AK. After Japan's attack on Pearl Harbor in December 1941, the U.S. War Department planned an overland route, beyond the range of carrier-based aircraft, to supply U.S. Army bases in Alaska. The U.S. Army Corps of Engineers teamed up with American and Canadian civilian contractors to complete the daunting task in just 34 weeks. The one-lane dirt trail curved around swamps and hills; landfill would come later. Some claim that the curves were intended to keep Japanese planes from using the road as a runway, but in reality its surveyors were forced to move so quickly (averaging 12km each day) that a haphazard route was chosen.

In recent years, the U.S. Army has been replaced by an annual army of over 250,000 tourists and RV-borne senior citizens from the U.S. and Europe. Travelers making the trip in July, the busiest month, will face crowded campgrounds and seemingly endless RV caravans. They'll also be passed by the speediest semis the roads have ever known. In general, there's a trade-off between the excitement you'll find on the Alcan and the speed with which you'll reach Alaska. If you're willing to take the time, there are countless opportunities to hike, fish, and view wildlife off the highway. If your priority is to beat the quickest path to the Yukon border, however, the **Cassiar Highway** (see p. 357) may be a better route for you. If your goal is to strike it slow and scenic on the far side of the Yukon border, you should consider a detour along the **Campbell Highway** (see p. 381).

The one-hour video *Alaska Highway: 1942-1992* shown at the Dawson Creek visitor center (see p. 364), provides a good introduction to the road and the region. Although the Alcan was "cussed and kissed" into being in nine months, in many ways it's still a work in progress as construction crews continue to smooth grades and eliminate treacherous turns. For daily Alcan road conditions call 867-667-8215. Mileposts put up along the highway in the 1940s are still used as mailing addresses and reference points, although the road has been rebuilt and rerouted so many times that they are no longer accurate. In BC and the Yukon, more dependable kilometer posts were installed in the mid-70s and recalibrated in 1990. Washouts sometimes occur in the spring, and other hazards include forest fires, falling rock, and construction delays. Motorists should always be aware of wildlife on the road, keep headlights on, carry spare tires and parts in good condition, and be prepared to slow down for graders, potholes, and general road breakup and gravel patches.

DAWSON CREEK

Mile 0 of the Alaska Highway is Dawson Creek, BC (not to be confused with Dawson City, YT, or Dawson's Creek, WB), first settled in 1890 as just another pipsqueak frontier village of a few hundred people among the flaming canola fields of Peace River. Its status as a railroad terminus made it a natural place to begin building a 2600km highway in nine months. The town's 10,000-odd residents are serious about their home's role as the womb of the Alcan. Visitors pausing to enjoy the town's history and genuine hospitality can easily get caught up in the enthusiasm.

◪ ORIENTATION AND PRACTICAL INFORMATION. There are two ways to reach Dawson Creek from the south. From Alberta, drive northwest from Edmonton along Hwy. 43, through Whitecourt to Valleyview; turn left on Hwy. 34 to Grande Prairie, and continue northwest on Hwy. 2 to Dawson Creek, for a total journey of 590km. From Prince George, drive 402km north on the John Hart section of **Hwy. 97** (see p. 340). Both drives take the better part of a day.

Greyhound, 1201 Alaska Ave. (782-3131 or 800-661-8747), runs to Whitehorse, YT (20hr.; June-Aug. 1 per day M-Sa, Oct.-May 3 per week; $165); Prince George (6½hr., 2 per day, $50); Edmonton (8hr., 2 per day, $70); or Calgary (14hr., 2 per day, $104). See p. 53 for discounts. (Open M-F 7am-6pm and 8-8:30pm, Sa 6am-noon, 2-5pm, and 8-8:30pm, Su 7-10:30am, 3-4:30pm, and 8-8:30pm.) For daily road reports and a small museum (donation requested), stop at the **visitor center,** 900 Alaska Ave. (782-9595; dctourin@pris.bc.ca; open May 15 to Labour Day daily 8am-7pm; in winter Tu-Sa 9am-5pm). The **library** (782-4661) is at 10th St. and McKellar Ave., and provides free **Internet access.** (Open Tu-Th 10am-9pm, F 10am-5:30pm, Sa 1:30-5:30pm.) Wash all at **King Koin Laundromat,** 1220 103rd Ave. (782-2395; wash $2.25, dry 25¢ per 5min; limitless showers $2.75; open daily 8am-9pm). **J&L Mechanical Services** (782-7832) does **24hr. road service. Hospital:** 1100 13th St. (782-8501). **Ambulance:** 782-2211. **Police:** (782-5211) at Alaska Ave. and 102nd Ave. **Public radio:** 89.7 FM. **Post office:** (782-9429; open M-F 8:30am-5pm) 104th Ave. and 10th St. **Postal code:** V1G 4E6. **Area code:** 250.

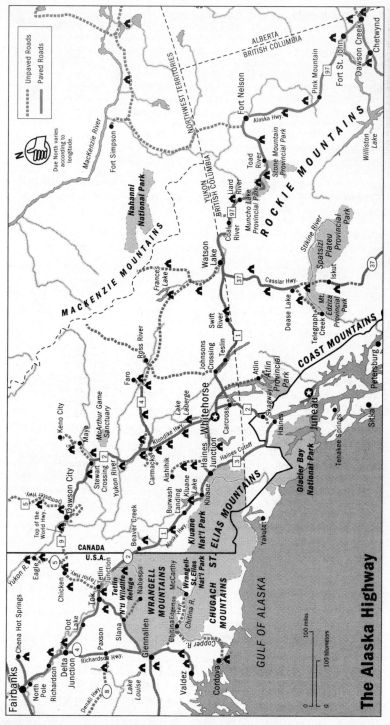

The Alaska Highway

N. BC & THE YUKON

█ ACCOMMODATIONS AND CAMPGROUNDS. Those willing to trade a few amenities for bargain prices, great location, and an off-beat aura should head straight for the historic **Alaska Hotel** (782-7998), above the Alaska Cafe & Pub (see below) on 10th St., 1½ blocks from the visitor center. Comfortable rooms are carefully decorated, some with pictures of Marilyn and Elvis. (Shared bath; no TV or phone. Singles $30; doubles $40; in winter $5 less.) The newer **Voyageur Motor Inn,** 801 111th Ave. (782-1020; fax 782-2681), facing 8th Ave., offers motoring voyagers phones, cable TV, and refrigerators at no extra charge in some rooms (singles $40; doubles $45). Peaceful and grassy, the **Mile 0 Campground** (782-2590), 1km west of Alaska Hwy. Mile 0 and adjacent to the Pioneer Village, has free showers and coin laundry (sites $10; hookups $15). Campers can also head for the convenient but crowded **Alahart RV Park,** 1725 Alaska Ave. (782-4702), for free showers, a dump station, and coin laundry (sites $8; hookups $18). The friendly owners rival the visitor center for maps and suggestions on entertainment and food.

█ FOOD. If foraging on your bug-splattered windshield fails to satisfy, Dawson Creek offers a wealth of affordable, tasty and varied cuisine rare for a locale so far north. The **Alaska Cafe & Pub** (782-7040), "55 paces south of the Mile 0 Post" on 10th St., serves excellent burgers and fries from $5. The cafe offers live music (mostly country) nightly, and homesick travelers can croon away their sorrows at Monday night karaoke. (Open Su-Th 10am-10pm, F-Sa 11am-11pm; pub open daily noon-3am.) Pick up a loaf for the road at the **Organic Farms Bakery,** 1425 97th Ave. (782-6533). From the visitor center, drive west along Alaska Ave. and take a right at 15th St. Breads are baked fresh from local grain, and start at $1.70; croissants and pastries are also available. (Open Tu-F 9:30am-6pm, Sa 9am-4pm.) The **Coop Cafe** (782-3121), in the Coop mall at the corner of 8th and 103rd Ave., serves 56¢ coffee, $5.56 liver and onions, and breakfast all day long. (Open M-W and Sa 8:30am-5:30pm, Th-F 8:30am-8pm, Su 10am-5pm.) Stock up on groceries at **IGA,** 1100 Alaska Ave. (782-5766; open M-F 8am-10pm, Sa 8am-8pm, Su 9am-6pm).

█ SIGHTS, EVENTS, AND OUTDOORS. Travelers cruising through Dawson Creek can't miss the **Mile 0 Cairn** and **Mile 0 Post,** both commemorating the birth of the Alcan, within a stone's throw of the visitor center. This town boomed during construction, literally. On February 13, 1943, sixty cases of exploding dynamite leveled the entire business district save the COOP building, now Bing's Furniture, opposite the Mile 0 post. The **Art Gallery** (782-2601) in the old grain elevator next door displays a photo essay on the Alcan creation saga. (Open June-Aug. daily 9am-5pm; in winter Tu-Sa 10am-noon and 1-5pm.) The **Pioneer Village** (782-7144) 1km west of Mile 0 is an excellent re-creation of Dawson Creek life from the 1920s to the 40s, with antique (read: rusted) farm equipment, nine gardens tended by the Horticultural Society, and a play area for children. (Suggested donation $1, family $2. Open May-Aug. M-F 9am-6pm, Sa-Su 9am-6pm.) In early August, the town plays host to the **Fall Fair & Stampede** (782-8911) with a carnival, fireworks, chuckwagon races, and a professional rodeo.

One Dawson Creek farmer has the **largest herd of bison in captivity.** His 300 beasts can be seen stampeding around his lot. Take 8th St. out of town, and start your quest nearby on the forebodingly named Dangerous Goods Rd. Bird lovers can head 10km out of town to the highland marshes of **McQueen's Slough.** Take Hwy. 49 east from the visitor center, turn left onto Rd. 3. and take the second left after the binocular signpost. The swampy haven is favored by all kinds of wildlife and mosquitoes. The **Community Forest,** 10km south of town at Bear Mountain, has a network of **cross-country ski trails** and white aspens to make Ansel Adams do a little jig.

DAWSON CREEK TO FORT NELSON

The Alaska Highway between Dawson Creek and **Fort St. John** (76km and about 45min. up the Alcan) offers little more than cows and rolling hills through a region more concerned with industry (natural gas, timber) than tourism. In early August, gold-grubbers converge 20km south of Fort St. John in **Taylor,** BC, to pan for prizes and fame at the **World Invitational Gold Panning Championships** (789-9015) in Peace River Park. **The Honey Place** (785-4808), just south of Fort St. John, is home to the **world's largest glass beehive** (open M-Sa 9am-5:30pm; 1kg honey $4.50). Fort St. John itself is hardly as abuzz with excitement. The **visitor center,** 9923 96th Ave. (785-3033), at 100th St., is opposite the park and museum (open June-Aug. M-Sa 8am-8pm, Su 9am-6pm; in winter M-F 8am-5pm). **North Peace Leisure Pool** (787-8178) is open seven days a week and contains every imaginable aquatic delight (wave pool, sauna, hot tub, water slide, and steamroom; $4.50, ages 13-18 $3.50, under 13 $2.50). The **Ministry of Environment, Land, and Parks,** 10003 110th Ave. (787-3407), provides info on fishing and hiking along the Alcan (open M-F 8:30am-4:30pm). The 109km stretch from Sikanni to Prophet River is entirely gas-less. **Sikanni River RV Park** (774-1028), at Alcan Mile 160, has full amenities (showers, toilets, laundry, full hookups) in a mountain setting ($16). Grassy tent sites along the river have picnic tables and fire pits ($10). Fifteen kilometers north of the RV park, a 19km drive and a 1.5km hike through steep mountain goat territory leads to a lookout over **Sikanni Chief Falls** and a rudimentary Forestry Campground ($8, pit toilets). The gravel access road from the highway is marked with Forestry signs; follow them to the marked trailhead.

Fort Nelson, 456 of the highway's least exciting kilometers north of Dawson Creek, and 250km north of Toad River, is an oasis of northern hospitality and natural resource extraction. The **Fort Nelson Heritage Museum** (774-3536), across the highway from the visitor center, features an impressive, if unsettling, collection of all local game species stuffed (white moose cow included), as well as doodads from the era of highway construction. (Open in summer daily 8:30am-7:30pm. $2.50, children and seniors $1.25, families $5.50.) A small **First Nations Craft Center** (774-2993), on the museum grounds, is open some afternoons and evenings. The **visitor centre** (774-6400), in the Recreation Centre/Curling Rink on the north edge of town, provides **daily Alcan road reports** (open May-Sept. daily 8am-8pm).

Rest up at the **Mini-Price Inn,** 5036 51st Ave. W (774-2136; cpmyers@pris.bc.ca), one block off the highway near the visitor center (no phones, cable TV; singles $39, doubles $44; kitchenettes $5 extra). By the **CIBC Bank** (774-2844) off the Alcan, the **Almada Inn** offers a free continental breakfast with fresh fruit, and sometimes the use of their whirlpool (small rooms $40, regular rooms $50, doubles $60). The **Westend Campground** (774-2340), across from the visitor center, has dusty sites in a pretty, wooded area, and showers (25¢ per 3min.), a laundromat (wash $2, dry $1 per 30min.), and free car wash and firewood (sites $13; full hookups $20). There are slim pickings for dining in Fort Nelson. The **Shangri-La Restaurant,** 5403 50 Ave. S (774-2188), near the theater, provides passable, though not paradise-worthy, Chinese cuisine. (Entrees from $8. Open daily 11am-11pm. Take-out available.) **Dan's Pub** (774-3929), at the southern extremity off the Alcan, is where locals come for beer, nightly drink specials, pool, and an extensive menu. Veggie platter $5, smoked salmon on rye $7.50, coho filet $13.25. (Open M-Th 11am-12:30am, F-Sa 11am-1:30am). **Blue Bell Restaurant** (774-3550), opposite Dan's in the Blue Bell Inn, serves a $5 breakfast (open M-Sa 6am-9pm, Su 8am-4pm).

FT. NELSON TO THE BC/YUKON BORDER

Small towns—usually composed of one gas pump, one $50-60 motel, and one cafe—pock the remainder of the highway to Whitehorse and the Alaska border. Fortunately for the glassy-eyed driver, highway scenery improves dramatically after Fort Nelson. About 150km north of Fort Nelson, the stark naked Stone Mountain appears. Next door, Summit Lake keeps the town of **Summit** company. (Gas pump? Check. Motel? Check. Cafe? Check.) This is the highest point (1295m/4250 ft.) on the Alcan. The **Stone Mountain Campground,** right on the lake, makes a superb starting point for hiking in the area ($12; outhouse, firewood, water). The steep **Summit Peaks Trail** begins across the highway from the campground, ascending 5km along a ridgeline to the breathtaking crest. A more moderate trail climbs 6km to the alpine **Flower Springs Lake.** Each hike takes about five hours round-trip.

Toad River, a town of 60, lies 45km north of Summit. The **Toad River Cafe** (232-5401), on the highway, dangles some 4893 hats from the ceiling. (Tasty burgers from $5. Headwear donations accepted. Open daily 7am-10pm; in winter 7am-9pm.) Fifty kilometers north of Toad River, **Muncho Lake Provincial Park** delights even the weariest drivers. Muncho ("big lake" in Tagish) is a seven-mile-long azure mirror. **Strawberry Flats Provincial Campground,** on the lakeshore, is itself a gem of a destination ($12; outhouse, firewood, water). If Strawberry Flats is full, **MacDonald Provincial Campground,** only a few kilometers farther along the highway, still on the lake, is the pot of silver ($12; outhouse, firewood, water). If camping ain't your thing after all, stay at **Muncho Lake Lodge** (776-3456), 10km north of Strawberry Flats. (Singles $40, $5 per additional person; private campground $13, hookups $15.) Flaming red bedspreads and happy service are free.

Near the 775km mark the highway reaches **Liard River Hot Springs.** These two naturally steamy and sulphurous pools are a phenomenal place to soothe a driver's derriere. For privacy and deeper water, skip the Alpha pool and head up to Beta. The park service manages campsites ($15) and a free day-use area here. Arrive early—the campsites often fill by noon.

BC/YUKON BORDER TO WHITEHORSE

From late August through the prime winter months, the night sky glimmers with the aurora borealis. Switchbacking between Yukon and British Columbia, the highway winds through tracts of scorched forest—gray, skeletal trees mixed with new growth—that stretches in all directions. Just after it crosses into the Yukon for the second time, at Km 1021, the highway runs through the small town of **Watson Lake,** site of the **Sign Post Forest.** In the 1940s, à homesick WWII Army engineer posted the mileage from Watson to his hometown of Danville, Illinois. The forest has since risen to fame as 42,000 travelers followed suit. **Visitor Information** (536-7469) is hidden just inside this forest of signs along the Robert Campbell highway (open May-Sept. daily 8am-8pm). Nearby **Wye Lake Park** has a **swimming pool** (536-2448; $1-3), nice hiking, and free sani-dumping. Watson Lake also lures passersby with the **Northern Lights Centre** (867-536-7827), opposite the visitor center, which divulges the science and legend behind aurora borealis. (Exhibits free. 50min. shows 6 times daily; $10, seniors and students $9, children $6.) The **Liard Canyon Recreation Site** on **Lucky Lake,** 8km before town, makes for great picnicking and swimming. A long waterslide keeps 'em shrieking, while a 2.2km trail down the canyon is a relaxing and scenic stroll. The **Shell Station** (536-2545, 24hr. assistance 536-2176), has a mechanic, tire shop, and coin **laundry** (wash $1.50, dry 25¢ per 8min.; open daily June-Aug. 6am-10pm; in winter 8am-6pm). Accommodations in Watson Lake are plentiful but pricey. A budget traveler's best bet is the **Watson Lake Campground,** 3km west of town along the highway and then 4km down a well-marked gravel road, with primitive private sites ideal for tenting ($8 camping permit only). Campers can swim on the lake or hike several trails of varying difficulty. Dining options in town are restricted to highway fare. The **Pizza Place** (536-7722; open daily 6:30am-10pm), at the Gateway Motor Inn, is a somewhat pricey gem. Medium specialty pies start at $14, but ambitious eaters go right for the "Yukoner," loaded with all manner of meats and vegetables ($21). **Groceries** can be had at **Watson Lake Foods** (536-2250; open M-F 7:30am-7pm, Sa 8am-6pm), by the visitor center, or you can **fish** for dinner. In mid-summer, grayling swim in the back eddies of tiny streams west along the Alcan, and both **Lucky Lake** (5.5km east of town), and **Hour Lake** (at the east end of town behind the RCMP) are full of rainbow trout. Check with the visitor center to be sure you have the appropriate permits.

Here at Watson Lake, the **Campbell Highway** (Hwy. 4) begins an alternate route into the Yukon Territory toward Whitehorse, via Ross River and Johnsons Crossing, or to Dawson City, via Ross River, Little Salmon, and Carmacks. For coverage of this wonderful side track, see p. 381. Km 1043 (or Mile 649) marks the Alcan's junction with the **Cassiar Hwy** (Hwy. 37; see p. 357) that leads south to the **Yellow-head Hwy** (Hwy. 16; see p. 340). For coverage of this junction, see p. 363.

About 260km west of Watson Lake, the **Dawson Peaks Resort** (390-2310; fax 390-2244) on **Teslin Lake** has campsites ($8; hot showers $2, toilets, firewood, water), full hookups ($15-18), canvas tent platforms ($26), private cabins with power and full bathrooms ($79), and delectable burgers in the restaurant ($6). The friendly hosts lead **river runs** (4-5 days, $400), organize guided **fishing charters** ($40 per hr.), rent canoes ($7.50 per hr.) and powerboats ($25 per hr.), and pump some of the Yukon's least expensive gas (open daily 8am-6 or 7pm) to boot.

Teslin, 11km west of the resort, tells its story at the duly acclaimed **George Johnston Museum** (390-2550), on the Alcan at the west end of town. Born in Alaska in 1889, George Johnston was a Tlingit man who ran a trap line and a general store while experimenting with photography on the side. Johnston left a legacy of stunning photographs documenting Tlingit life in Teslin from 1910 to 1940. The museum also displays a moose skin boat, Teslin's first automobile (bought by Johnston when the town was roadless), and an excellent video about the Alaska Highway's effect on native culture. (Open mid-May to early Sept. daily 9am-7pm. $3, students and seniors $2.50, children $1, families $7. Wheelchair accessible.) From Teslin, the 183km (2hr.) drive to Whitehorse is interspersed with a handful of gas stops, government camps, and dangerous gravel patches.

WHITEHORSE, YT

Named for the once-perilous (now dammed) Whitehorse Rapids, whose crashing whitecaps were said to resemble the flowing manes of galloping white mares, Whitehorse is a modern crossroads in an ageless frontier. With over 23,000 residents, Whitehorse prides itself on being Canada's largest city north of 60° latitude, and mountains, rivers, and lakes in all directions are a powerful reminder that "south of 60" is far, far away. While Yukon officials boast of their capital's rapid urban development, most locals and thousands of visiting nature-worshipers find that Whitehorse's real wealth lies in the gaping bush beyond the city limits and in the laid-back northern spirit in every Whitehorse "hello."

▗ ORIENTATION AND PRACTICAL INFORMATION

Whitehorse lies 1500km north of Dawson Creek, BC, along the **Alaska Highway** (see p. 368), and 535km south of Dawson City, YT. The city is laid out in an oblong grid of avenues running roughly north-south, parallel to the Alcan. Streets run east to west. Locals suggest avoiding the riverbank if alone at night.

TRANSPORTATION

Airplanes: The airport is off the Alaska Hwy., just southwest of downtown. **Canadian Airlines** (668-3535) flies to: Vancouver, BC (3 per day; $364 round-trip; ages 12-24 stand-by $270), and from Vancouver on to Calgary and Edmonton ($930; youth standby $310). **Canada 3000** (888-226-3000 or 416-259-1118; www.canada3000.com) offers cheap fares to Vancouver ($210) in summer.

Buses: The bus station is on the northeast edge of town, a short walk from downtown. **Greyhound,** 2191 2nd Ave. (667-2223); runs once per day to: Vancouver, BC (41hr., $300); Edmonton, AB (30hr., $232); Dawson Creek, BC (18hr., $165); and Dawson City, YT (5hr., $62). No service to AK. For discounts see p. 53. Buses run late June-Sept. M-Sa; in winter Tu, Th, and Sa. Open M-F 7:30am-6pm, Sa 9am-1:30pm, Su 4-8am and 5-6pm. **Alaska Direct** (668-4833 or 800-770-6652), in the Greyhound depot, runs to: Anchorage (15hr., 3 per week, US$145); Fairbanks (12hr., 3 per week, US$120); and Skagway (3hr., 1 per day, US$35). In winter, 1 bus per week to above destinations.

Local Transportation: Whitehorse Transit (668-7433). Limited service downtown and to the airport, Robert Service campground, and Yukon College. Buses arrive and depart next to the Canadian Tire on Ogilvie St. M-Th 6:15am-7:30pm, F 6:15am-10:30pm, Sa 8am-7pm. $1.50, seniors and disabled 75¢, under 18 $1.25; daypass $4.

N. BC & THE YUKON

Taxis: Yellow Cab, 668-4811.

Car Rental: Norcan Leasing, Ltd., 213 Range Rd. (668-2137 or 800-661-0445; 800-764-1234 from AK), off the Alcan at Mile 917.4. Cars from $55 per day, from $40 in winter; 22¢ per km after 100km. Must be 21 with credit card.

Auto Repair: Petro Canada, 4211 4th Ave. (667-4003 or 667-4366). Full service. Oil and lube about $45. Open M-F 8am-5pm. Gas pumps open 24hr.

Ride Boards: Check the bulletin boards outside the **Blackstone Cafe** (see **Food and Nightlife** below) and at the **visitor center.** Hitchhikers claim good results along the Alcan just above town; signs with "please" reportedly soften the hearts of motorists.

VISITOR AND FINANCIAL SERVICES

Visitor Information: 100 Hanson St. (667-3084), in the conspicuous Tourism and Business Centre at 2nd Ave. Open daily mid-May to mid-Sept. 8am-8pm; in winter M-F 9am-5pm. Dazzling free 20min. film 8 times daily. German, French, and Dutch spoken.

Outdoor Information: Yukon Conservation Society, 302 Hawkins St. (668-5678), offers maps and great ideas for area hikes. Open M-F 10am-2pm.

Outdoor Equipment: Several well-stocked and upscale equipment shops are located on Main St. between 2nd and 3rd Ave. **The Sportslodge,** 305 Main St. (668-6848), in the Hougen Centre, offers basic outdoor and camping gear at good prices. Open M-F 9am-10pm, Sa 9am-6pm, Su 11am-4pm; in winter, M-F 9am-6pm. Friendly and eminently knowledgeable **Kanoe People** (668-4899), at Strickland and 1st Ave., rent mountain bikes ($25 per day), canoes ($45 per day), and kayaks ($35 per day for plastic; $45 for fiberglass). Credit card or $100 deposit required. Open daily 9am-6pm.

Library: 2071 2nd Ave. (667-5239) at Hanson. Free 30min. **Internet access;** call ahead. Open M-F 10am-9pm, Sa 10am-6pm, Su 1-9pm.

Bookstore: Mac's Fireweed Bookstore, 203 Main St. (668-2434). Canadiana, maps, and First Nation materials. Open M-F 8am-9pm, Sa 9am-9pm, Su 10am-9pm.

Laundromat: Norgetown, 4213 4th Ave. (667-6113), next to McDonald's at Ray St. Wash $1.50, dry 50¢ per 7½min. Open daily 8am-9pm.

Public Pool: Whitehorse Lions Pool, 4051 4th Ave. (668-7665) next to the High Country Inn. $4.50, seniors and children $2, students $3.50. Call for swim times.

EMERGENCY AND COMMUNICATIONS

Emergency: 911. **Police:** 4100 4th Ave. (667-5555). 24hr.

24hr. Refuge: Tim Horton's, 2210 2nd Ave. (668-7788), at the far northern end of downtown, serves hot grub around the clock. For more of a Zen haven, try the **Talisman Cafe** (see **Food and Nightlife,** below).

Pharmacy: Shoppers Drug Mart, 211 Main St. (667-2485). Open M-F 9am-9pm, Sa 9am-6pm, Su 10am-6pm.

Hospital: Whitehorse General (393-8700) is across the river from downtown on Hospital Rd., just off Wickstrom Rd.

Post Office: General services, 211 Main St. (667-2485), in the basement of Shopper's Drug Mart. Open M-F 9am-6pm, Sa 11am-4pm. Also in Qwanlin Mall (667-2858) at 4th Ave. and Ogilvie St., in Coffee, Tea and Spice. Open M-Th 9:30am-6pm, F 9:30am-8pm, Sa 9:30am-6pm. **General delivery** is at 3rd Ave. and Wood St., in the Yukon News Bldg. Open M-F 8am-6pm. General delivery **postal codes** for last names beginning with the letters A-L is Y1A 3S7; for M-Z it's Y1A 3S8.

Public Radio: 570 AM. Francophones and the curious should have a listen to 102.1 FM. 98.1 FM's Dead dog comedy hr. (F) is not to be missed.

Internet Access: See **Library,** above. **Holodeck,** 4159 4th Ave. (668-2379), at Alexander St. $4 per hr. Open M-W 11am-8pm, Th-Sa 11am-10pm, Su 11am-6pm.

Area Code: 867.

⌐ ACCOMMODATIONS AND CAMPGROUNDS

Interchangeable motels around town charge upwards of $65, reason enough to seek campgrounds outside of town. **Wolf Creek,** 5km south of town on the Alcan, has 33 beautiful stream-side sites and several nature trails. (Camping by $8 provincial permit only; see p. 40. Pit toilets, firepits, firewood, well water, and a playground.) For tenting plus thermal relief, many make the 62km (45min.) drive north to camp near the **Takhini Hot Springs** (633-2706), the Yukon's only hot springs. Follow the Alcan northwest from downtown, turn right onto the North Klondike Highway, and left to the end of Takhini Hot Springs Rd. There is a $3-5 admission charge. (Restaurant, showers, and laundry. 88 sites: $11, with electricity $13.)

Roadhouse Inn, 2163 2nd Ave. (667-2594), at the north end of town near the Greyhound depot. Nothing to write home about, but a definite congregation of the hostel crowd. Shared rooms, hall showers with bathtub. $20; private rooms with cable, bath, and free local calls $50, each additional person $10. Key deposit $10. Laundry (wash and dry $1.75 each). Lobby open 7am-2:30am.

98 Hotel, 110 Wood St. (667-2641), at 1st Ave. Wheelchair-accessible private rooms with sink and desk. Hallway bathrooms, no phones. Singles $30; doubles $45. Key deposit $10. Hotel bar open daily 9am-11pm; live local fiddling (Th).

Country Cabins Bed and Breakfast (633-2117; countrycabin@hypertext.yk.ca), at Mile 5.5 on Takhini Hot Springs Road (see directions to Takhini Hot Springs, above). Minutes from the hot springs and good biking, skiing, and hiking trails. Three cabins with outhouses sleep 4. $60, lower in the off-season, breakfast $7.50. No credit cards.

Robert Service Campground (668-3721), 1km from town on South Access Rd. along the Yukon River. This home-away-from-home for crowds of university students who summer in Whitehorse features a food trailer, firewood ($1-2), a playground, drinking water, toilets, metered showers ($1 per 5min.), and a knack for rhyming verse. Open late May to early Sept. 68 sites: $12. Gates open 7am-midnight.

◑ ▣ FOOD AND ENTERTAINMENT

Whitehorse restaurants cater to government employees on lunch break, but also to hip musicians and tourists hungering for the frontier. Get extra groceries at **Extra Foods** (667-6251), in the Quanlin Mall at 4th Ave. and Ogilvie St. (open M-W 8:30am-7pm, Th-F 8:30am-9pm, Sa 8:30am-6pm, Su 10am-6pm; in winter curbed hours). Assuage greasy highway stomachs at **The Fruit Stand** (393-3994), at 2nd Ave. and Black St. (open in summer M-Sa 10:30am-7pm). The homesick appreciate **The Deli,** 203 Hanson St. (667-7583), which peddles reasonably priced imported foods (open M-F 8:30am-5:30pm, Sa 9am-5:30pm), and exquisite bread from **Alpine Bakery,** 411 Alexander St. (668-6871), between 4th and 5th Ave. (open M-Sa 8am-6pm; in winter, closed M). Natural foods holler at **Three Beans** (668-4908), 308 Wood St. (open M-F 9:30am-6pm, Sa 10am-5:30pm).

⬩ **Klondike Rib and Salmon Barbecue,** 2116 2nd Ave. (667-7554). A fresh salmon or halibut lunch comes with homemade bread ($8), and tasty fish and chips are a dinner bargain at $12. The 100-year-old Klondike-era building is a delight. Open mid-May to Sept. M-F 11:30am-2pm and 4pm until closing, Sa-Su 5pm until closing.

⬩ **The Talisman Cafe,** 2112 2nd Ave. (667-2736), just past Main Street. The Talisman is elegantly decorated with local art (ask after the Swayze tapestry) and thoughtfully nourishes its patrons. Bannock and Jam with Yukon cranberries ($2.75), unique soups ($3.75), and the best vegetarian menu in town. Open M-Sa midnight-4pm, Su until 3pm.

Sam and Andy's (668-6994), on Main St. opposite the Town & Mountain Hotel. Straight-ahead Tex-Mex on a jumpin' patio. 6 stuffed mushrooms are steep ($7) but celebrated. Generous build-your-own fajitas are mid-range entrees ($12). Open daily 11am-11pm.

No Pop Sandwich Shop, 312 Steele Ave. (668-3227), at 4th Ave. Whitehorse's suits and twenty-somethings come for the Tel Aviv (ground beef, alfalfa, cream cheese; $4.25) and veggies. No pop, but lots of juice ($1.75) and alcoholic specialty drinks (about $6). Open M-Th 7:30am-8:30pm, F 7:30am-9:30pm, Sa 10am-9pm, Su 10am-4pm.

Blackstone Cafe (667-6598), on the corner of 3rd Ave. and Wood St. Whitehorse's crunchy clan takes up residence on the patio. Veggie paté sandwich with salad $5.25. Freshly baked muffins $1.50. Myriad coffees come regular or organic; espresso $1.25. Open M-F 7am-9pm, Sa 8am-6pm, Su 10am-5pm; in winter, closed Su.

Lizard's Lounge, at the **Town & Mountain Hotel** (668-7644), at 4th Ave. and Main St., offers live music virtually every night of the year and 99¢ drafts. Open daily 4pm-2am.

Yukon Cinema, 304 Wood St. (668-6644). A rare chance to catch a flick in the north. 2 screens. $8, youth $6.50, children and seniors $4.

👁 SIGHTS AND EVENTS

Local history finds a home at the **MacBride Museum** (667-2709), at 1st Ave. and Wood St. The sod-roofed log cabin in the museum courtyard was built in 1899 by Sam McGee, whose demise has been immortalized by Robert Service, the Bard of the Yukon. (Open daily June-Aug. 10am-6pm; call for winter hours. $4, students and seniors over 60 $3.50, children $2, under 7 free.) If the old world is your bag, the fabulous **Yukon Beringia Interpretive Centre** (667-8855; www.beringia.com), on the Alcan 2km northwest of the South Access Rd. junction, recreates the ice-age subcontinent that joined Siberia, Alaska, and the Yukon, an unglaciated "hotbed" of animal and plant life. (Open daily mid-May to Sept. 8am-8pm; in winter Su 1-5pm and by appointment. $6, seniors $5, children $4.) The restored **S.S. Klondike** (667-4511), on South Access Rd., is a dry-docked 1929 sternwheeler that conjures to the days when the river ran the Yukon. (Open daily June-Aug. 9am-7pm, May and Sept. 9am-6pm; $3.75, children $2.25, families $9.) From June, the Yukon Historical and Museum Association, 3126 3rd Ave. (667-4704), sponsors **Heritage Walking Tours** from Donnenworth House, in Lepage Park next to the infocenter. (45min. M-Sa 9am-4pm on the hr.; some evening tours. $2. Call ahead.) At 3rd Ave. and Lambert St., look up: those three-story **log skyscrapers** were built single-handedly in the 1970s by a local septuagenarian.

Government patronage and an inspired population make Whitehorse the northern epicenter of arts. The Yukon Government's **permanent collection** is housed throughout the administrative and public spaces of the capital (call Yukon Tourism 667-5264). Pick up a free **ArtWalk** brochure at the visitor centre, or at the nonprofit **Captain Martin House Gallery,** 305 Wood St. (667-4080; open M-F 10am-8pm, Sa 10am-5pm, Su noon-5pm; in winter, M-Sa 11am-5pm, closed January.) The Yukon's only public art museum, the **Yukon Arts Centre** (667-8578), at Yukon College, hangs new shows every 6-10 weeks (donation requested; open June-Aug. M-F 11am-5pm, Sa-Su noon-5pm; Sept.-May Tu-F 11am-5pm, Sa-Su 1-4pm).

Two Whitehorse festivals draw crowds from all over the world: the **Yukon International Storytelling Festival** (633-7550; www.yukonalaska.com/storytelling) to be held from June 2-4 in 2000, and the **Frostbite Music Festival** (668-4921; www.frostbite.net) in the heart of winter (Feb. 18-20, 2000). The **Commissioner's Potlatch** (667-7698) gathers indigenous groups and visitors from near and far for traditional dancing, singing, games, artistry, and a feast of wild game (June 18-21, 2000). Locals, transients, and native artists perform for free at Wood St. and 3rd Ave. at noon on weekdays from June to mid-August. Call the **Yukon Arts Centre Theatre** (667-8574) for stage updates.

🏃 OUTDOORS

There seem to be more trails around Whitehorse than people. Seasoned hikers can just wander, with heed to the bear population, of course (see p. 44). **Kluane National Park** (see p. 377) beckons from the west, but there is plenty of accessible

MAKESHIFT COURTS As in many remote regions, law in the Yukon is administered with a long arm. While Whitehorse is the seat of the territorial government, the work of frontier justice is carried out on the frontier: once a week a judge, a clerk, and a recorder climb into a single-engine plane and depart for outlying towns, where they will be met by a prosecuting and defending attorney will meet them, themselves arriving by car in long, cross-country odysseys between clients. Court is then set up in community centers and recreation halls, and has evolved in recent years from a transplanted version of a courthouse's formal proceedings to a truer reflection of the traditions of the mostly indigenous communities it serves. Increasingly, elements of traditional justice are changing how community members are punished: friends and family are in more and more cases invited to sit down in a "sentencing circle," in which everyone has a say in how the criminal can be cared for and reintegrated into society. The "circle" has done amazing work, greatly reducing the likelihood of recidivism, and makes for a team-building attitude in the makeshift halls of justice. In the basketball game that sometimes follows, just one judge has emerged as the hook-shot king of the Yukon, but good work continues past the post-court full-court scrimmage.

dayhiking near town. *Whitehorse Area Hikes and Bikes* ($19), published by the **Yukon Conservation Society** or the *Whitehorse Area Hikes* map ($10) are both available at **Mac's Fireweed Books. Grey Mountain,** partially accessible by gravel road, is a fairly rigorous dayhike. Take Lewes Blvd. across the bridge by the **S.S. Klondike,** then take a left on Alsek Ave. Turn left again at the "Grey Mt. Cemetery" sign and follow the gravel road to its end. Joggers, bikers, and cross-country skiers love the **Miles Canyon trail network** that parallels the Yukon River. To get there, take Lewes Blvd. to Nisutlin Dr. and turn right; just before the fish ladder turn left onto the gravel Chadbum Lake Rd. and continue for 4km to the parking area. The Conservation Society leads nature walks on weekdays (office open July-Aug. M-F 10am-2pm). The **Yukon Bird Club** (667-4630) leads free birding trips during the summer.

The **Yukon River** plays host to the popular **Rubber Duckie Race** (668-4546) on Canada Day, July 1 ($5 per duck, proceeds to charity). The **M.V. Schwatka** (668-4716), on Miles Canyon Rd. off South Access Rd., floats folks through Miles Canyon (2hr. cruises; 2 per day June to early Sept. $20, ages 6-11 $10, under 6 free). **Up North Boat and Canoe Rentals,** 86 Wickstrom Rd. (667-7905), opposite downtown, lets you paddle 25km to Takhini River (4hr.; $30 including transportation). An eight-day trip on the Teslin River costs $200, but you can rent sea kayaks and canoes by the day ($25-30). The waterways around **Sanfu Lake** (1½hr. south of Whitehorse on the Atlin road) are ideal for kayaking among tiny islands. **Tatshenshini Expediting,** 1602 Alder St. (633-2742), leads intense white water rides (full day $100).

The Whitehorse area in winter is crisscrossed by 300km of groomed and ungroomed **snowmobile trails.** Up North Boat and Canoe Rentals (see above) rents snowmobiles and skis. Whitehorse is a **cross-country skiing** paradise. The **Whitehorse Cross Country Ski Club** (668-4477; xcski@yukon.net), beside Mt. McIntyre off Hamilton Blvd. near the intersection of Two Mile Hill and the Alcan, grooms 50km of world-class trails and 5km are lit at night. Club facilities include saunas and showers. (Day passes $8, under 19 $4; 3 days $20, 5 days $35.) In February, "the toughest race in the world," or the **Yukon Quest 1000 Mile International Sled Dog Race** (668-4711), follows gold rush routes between Whitehorse and Fairbanks.

CARCROSS, YT

Carcross, shortened from "Caribou Crossing," perches on the narrows between Bennett and Nares Lakes, entirely surrounded by snow-capped peaks and pristine waterways. Prior to European settlement, the inland Tagish and Tlingit made seasonal camps here at the heart of the Southern Lakes Watershed. At the turn of the century, Carcross served as a link in the gold seekers' treacherous route between

Skagway and the Yukon River, and during the 1940s as a supply depot for the construction of the Alaska Highway. Over the course of white settlement, native children from all over the Yukon were educated at the Chooutla school, or Carcross Residential school. The town remains in picturesque disrepair with a fragment of the Whitepass railway running through its heart; locals are working on the line's rehabilitation, and hope to connect their portion of the railway to Lake Bennett in 2000. The work of community rehabilitation continues with innovative social justice programs and an active First Nation government.

◪ ORIENTATION AND PRACTICAL INFORMATION. On the Klondike Hwy. (Hwy. 2), Carcross is 74km south of Whitehorse and 106km north of Skagway, AK. **Atlin Express Buses** (250-651-7575) run to: Atlin, BC (2hr.; $21, seniors $18, ages 5-11 $10.50, under 5 free) and Whitehorse (1¼hr.; $15, seniors $13, ages 5-11 $7.50, under 5 free). **Visitor information** (821-4431) is available inside the depot (open mid-May to mid-September daily 8am-8pm). **Montana Services** (821-3708; open daily 7am-11pm; in winter 8am-8pm), in the Shell Station on Hwy. 2, has laundry (wash $2.25, dry 25¢ per 4min.), **public showers** ($3), and the only **ATM** in town. The **Library** (821-3801) on Tagish St. has free **Internet access** (open M and Th 1pm-5:30pm, W 6:30-9pm). A **health station** (821-4444) is inside the two-story red building behind the Caribou Hotel. **Ambulance:** 821-3333. **Police:** 821-5555 or 667-5555. The **post office** (821-4503), with a free paperback exchange, is in the red-trimmed white building on Bennett Ave. (open M, W, and F 8am-noon and 2:30-4pm, Tu and Th 10-11:45am). **Postal code:** Y0B 1B0. **Area code:** 867.

▐◨ ACCOMMODATIONS AND FOOD. The **Caribou Hotel** (821-4501), across from the visitor centre, is the only hotel in Carcross and until its renovation was the oldest operating hotel in the Yukon. Ask at the lounge (open daily noon-2am) if renovations are complete. The Yukon Government maintains 14 **secluded campsites** by the airstrip across Hwy. 2 from the Shell station with potable water, firewood, and pit toilets. ($8 with Yukon government camping permit.) **Spirit Lake Wilderness Resort** (821-4337), 10km north of town on Hwy. 2, has various lakeside accommodations and rents canoes ($7.50 per hr.). Toilets, free showers, and coin laundry. (Tent sites $12, with power $19; sparse cabins with breakfast $35; motel singles or doubles with free coffee and pie $80.) A retired sea captain and a gourmet run **Spirit Haven Bed and Breakfast** (821-4722; www.spirithaven.yk.net), Km 115 on the Carcross Cutoff 10 minutes north of town (singles $65, sunny doubles $85).

Montana Services serves fast food and sandwiches. The **Caribou Hotel Cafe** has standard soups and sandwiches in the $5-7 range (open daily May-Oct. 7am-9pm). The **Spirit Lake resort** serves fancier grub, like a lunch of Dutch pancakes for $9 (open daily May-Sept. 8am-9pm) Just up the road the **Cinnamon Cache** (821-4331) is a gem among Dall sheep and bluebirds. Homemade cinnamon buns ($2.50), survival cookies for the trail ($2.50), and soup and sandwiches (from $5.25; open Feb.-Sept. daily 7am-7pm).

◉▲ SIGHTS AND OUTDOORS. Legendary big-game guide Johnny Johns led countless trips out of the Carcross area in the direction of the Yukon Mountains, the Upper Rockies, and the Coastal Range, all in view from the town. While outfitting companies such as his no longer operate, **hiking** in the Carcross area inspires justifiable acclaim. Pick up a copy of *Whitehorse Area Hikes and Bikes* at the visitor center or in Whitehorse before setting out. The most popular hike in the area is the **Chilkoot Trail,** a moderately difficult three- to five-day adventure to the far end of Lake Bennett (the lake's 2 mi. sandy beach is understandably popular with locals in July and August). Overlooking the town, rough mining roads snake around **Montana Mountain** past lichen, snow, and boulders. To access them, follow Hwy. 2 south, take the first right after crossing the bridge. Take the first left and drive until the road becomes impassable. From there, it's all on foot to astounding views (1000 ft. elev. gain; round-trip 21km, 8hr.).

THE CHILKOOT TRAIL A valuable coastal trade route protected by the Tagish and Tlingit for thousands of years, in the late 1890s the Chilkoot Trail bore the great torrent of gold-seekers hungering for the Yukon interior. First led by native packers, and later accompanied by hordes of their fellow stampeders, north-country novices slogged back and forth 33 miles between Skagway, Dyea, and Lake Bennett, transporting 1000 pounds of provisions each to satisfy Canadian officials that they were prepared for the country ahead. "It's hard enough to do the trail with just yourself to look after," complained one man. "Imagine looking after yourself, plus a half a ton of mining supplies and beef jerky. And a horse." Hikers take to the trail today for a rigorous three- to five-day hike past the horse skeletons and gold-rush relics that still litter the precipitous pass. The trail departs the coast through a dramatic variety of climate, terrain, and vegetation, both above and below the timberline, before descending into the forests of northern British Columbia within reach of Lake Bennett and Carcross. For hike info, see p. 432.

The Barracks (821-4372), opposite the Visitor Centre, is a curious 1920s-era building packed with Yukon-made crafts, clothing, and souvenirs. If you're lucky, you'll be serenaded by the old player piano or thrown into jail. For a memorable confectionery experience, try the chocolate moose nugget sundae ($3.75) and repent with a sprout salad ($2.50) fresh from the Yukon Sprout Farm (open May-Sept. daily 9am-6pm). **Frontierland** (821-4055), 1km north of the haunting **Carcross Desert** (the exposed bottom of a glacial lake), houses an impressive collection of dead wildlife, including the largest bear ever mounted. (Open daily mid-May to mid-Sept. 8am-6pm; $6.50, children $4, family $20; park or gallery alone $3-4.)

ATLIN, BC

The 400 residents of Atlin (Tlingit for "Big Lake") live humbly between the 145km long, clear-as-glass Atlin Lake and the massive mountains of Atlin Provincial Park, which together bless the town with an ocean-side aura and ease. The huge park embraces creeping ice fields and some 80 islands in its untrodden wilderness, and fishing here is some of BC's best.

Like many northern towns, Atlin was first settled by money-hungry prospectors during the Klondike Gold Rush of 1898. Gold mining remains the primary industry, but the town has mellowed since its Klondike heyday. Locals maintain the mellowness by making little effort to draw visitors, while warmly welcoming those who do come. Pioneer-era buildings remain in mint condition, but are quiet private residences rather than flamboyant tourist attractions.

🔃 ORIENTATION AND PRACTICAL INFORMATION

Although Atlin is in BC, the only way to drive there is via the Yukon Territory. The rocky Atlin Road (Hwy. 1) branches off the Alcan at Jake's Corner, just south of Whitehorse and the turn-off to Carcross. There is no gas on Atlin Rd. between the Alcan junction and town (100km). Those traveling to Atlin via Carcross or Skagway can take Hwy. 8, which branches off the Klondike Highway just north of Carcross. This partially-paved road passes through Tagish (which has gas and a pretty Yukon government campsite) before joining Hwy. 8, 55km later.

Planes: Summit Air Charters (651-7600 or 800-661-1944), on 5th St., flies 3 times per week to Juneau, AK (1hr., $150, round-trip $214) and charters elsewhere.

Buses: Atlin Express (651-7617 or 867-668-4545 in Whitehorse) departs the Atlin Inn on Lake St. M, W, and F at 6:15am for Jake's Corner (1hr., $12), Carcross (2hr., $21), and Whitehorse (3hr., $26). Discounts for seniors (65+) and children under 12.

Visitor Information: Atlin Historical Museum (651-7522), on Trainor and 3rd St., doubles as the **visitor center.** Open mid-May to mid-Sept. daily 10am-6pm.

Outdoor Information: The **BC Provincial Government Building** (651-7595), opposite the museum, sells **fishing permits** and **topographical maps** (around $11), and has limited info on Atlin Park. Open M-F 8:30am-noon and 1-5:30pm.

Bank: Bank of Montreal (651-7595), a booth in the BC Provincial Government Building. Open M-F 8:30am-noon and 1-3pm. The **ATM** doesn't take credit cards.

Laundromat and Public Showers: Caribou Laundromat, on Discovery Ave. Wash $2.25, dry $1.50. Shower $2 per 5min. A **24hr. refuge** with a whole rack of paperbacks.

Auto Repair: Pine Tree Services (651-7636), on Discovery St. at 3rd. Open June-Sept. daily 7:30am-7:30pm; in winter 7:30am-6pm.

Emergency: 911. **Police:** 651-7511.

Red Cross Clinic: (651-7677) on 3rd and Pearl St. Open M-F 8:30am-4:30pm.

Internet Access: Free at the Atlin Community Library in the Northern Lights College. Open Th 7:30-9pm, F 2-4pm, Sa 2-4pm.

Public Radio: 90.1 FM.

Post Office: (651-7513) on 1st at Pearl St. Open M, W, and F 10am-12:30pm and 1-3:30pm, Tu and Th 10am-12:30pm and 1-4:30pm. **Postal Code:** V0W 1A0.

Area Code: 250.

ACCOMMODATIONS, CAMPGROUNDS, AND FOOD

Atlin has plenty of homey hidden B&Bs, camping nearby, and a refreshing lack of big, crowded hotels. ■ **Tundra B&B** (651-7551) features handsome, friendly huskies, and free canoe use. Ask (in German, even!) about guided trips with either. Log cabin rooms are intimate, sprucy-clean, and the area's most affordable. Take Warm Bay Rd. for 2km, then left on Pine Dr., and left again onto Spruce Dr. (Singles $50; doubles $60. No credit cards.) **Glacier View Cabins** (651-7691), 12km down Warm Bay Rd., rents log huts with porch, showerhouse, propane lighting, stove, and true to the advertising, awe-inspiring views of Llewellyn Glacier ($65). **Norseman RV** (651-7535), at the end of 1st St. at the water, has 20 gravel sites with power and water ($13), but no showers or tent sites. For boat rental, see below.

Campers love the spread-out and woodsy **Pine Creek Campground,** 2.5km south of town on Warm Bay Rd., for its pit toilets, fire barrels, and the delicious fresh-water spring 1.5km farther south on the left ($5, payable at any Atlin business or the museum). Four isolated, primitive, and free campsites with pit toilets are even farther down Warm Bay Rd. **Palmer Lake** (19km) and **Warm Bay** (22km) are lakeside sites. **Warm Springs** (23km, on the left) is a grassy campsite with a small, lukewarm, prehistoric-looking pool. Passing bands have prized its healing qualities for centuries, and the nearby meadow streams are warm as a bath and lined with watercress. **Grotto,** near the road's end (26km), is thickly forested and has 2 road-side sites and trails meandering back toward more enveloped sites.

The **Atlin Trading Post** (651-7574), at Discovery Ave. and 2nd St., has the largest selection of groceries (open June to mid-Sept. daily 9am-7:30pm; in winter M-Sa 9am-6pm, Su 10am-4pm). **The Food Basket** (651-7676), on 2nd St. at Pearl, has a full bakery with lots of freshly-made breads (open M-F 8am-8:30pm). **Pine Tree Restaurant** (651-7709; open daily 7am-9pm.), on Discovery at 3rd St, surveys the Shell gas pumps through the windows. The portions are hearty and service is, like the rest of the town, super-friendly. Entrees from $5.

SIGHTS AND OUTDOORS

Besides the **Atlin Historical Museum** (651-7522; $2.50, seniors $2, under 10 $1; open mid-May to mid-Sept. daily 10am-6pm), the **M.V. Tarahne** is the only other sizeable man-made tourist attraction. The first gas-powered, propeller-driven boat in the north, the *Tarahne* is now dry-docked opposite the Atlin Inn (contact the museum for tours). The ship hosts an acclaimed Saturday evening murder mystery **Dinner Theatre** (651-0076) featuring fresh salmon from the nearby Taku river and elegant/bloodcurdling entertainment ($55). You can look at (but please don't touch!) the run-down and fire-scorched edifice of Atlin's former brothel, **Aurora House,** on Watson Ave. between 1st and 2nd St. It was known as "the warren" in gold rush days for its numerous interior passageways. Info on Atlin's active artistic community is published by the Northern Lights College (651-7762). The Court House and other venues host frequent **art exhibits;** ask at the museum.

Because Atlin remains unincorporated and largely unvisited, established trails around town are scarce. Lake activity, however, is a different story. Half a dozen **canoe and kayak outfitters** will take visitors out onto the water. Only experienced paddlers should set out on cold and rough Atlin Lake; nearby **Palmer Lake** is a better option for a casual voyage. **Back Country Sports** (651-2424; bcsports@polarcom.com) rents kayaks, with transport available (single kayaks $35 per day; doubles $50), and organizes group kayak sessions one evening per week ($25 per person). They also can arrange mixed hiking and rafting tours on the Atlin River ($75 per half-day), and offer bird identification workshops ($10 per session.) (Open in summer daily 10am-6pm.) **Sidka Tours** (651-7691), at the **Glacier View Cabins** (see above) rents canoes ($25 per day, including transport). BC's largest lake is an angler's heaven, teeming with lake trout, dolly varden, whitefish, and grayling. Ice fishing is popular among warm-blooded locals, and complements the standard winter regimen of **dog sledding, cross-country skiing,** and **snowshoeing.** Back Country Sports rents cross-country skis ($25 per day) and sells a trail guide ($10).

Old area mining operations have left behind an endless network of gravel roads perfect for **mountain biking. Happy Trails** (651-7662), located at the south end of 2nd St. between Rant and Watson, rents bikes for $27 per day. The store also has loads of fishing equipment and advice, some camping gear, and a great book of things to do in town (open June-Aug. daily 9am-8pm; call for winter hours).

The most established area trail, unsuitable for biking but perfect for a dayhike, is the 5km or three-hour (one-way) **Monarch Trail,** which begins 3.7km south of town on Warm Bay Rd. This relatively strenuous hike begins below the tree line, but gives way to bald rock face and tundra and a panoramic view of nearby Atlin Lake. Monarch Mountain tops out at 1439m/4720 ft. The pretty 45min. **Pom Pom Trail** rises along a small ridge above Atlin from beside the town's new cemetery. Follow Discovery Rd. past Warm Bay Rd. and watch for signs.

Atlin Provincial Park is enormous, untouched, and mostly untouchable, accessible only by plane or boat. Venturing into Atlin Park demands considerable outdoor skill, especially because it has no personnel, services, or maintained trails. One third of the park is blanketed with icefields and glaciers sweeping down from the **Juneau Icefield. Apex Air Charters** (651-0025) runs float plane drop-offs (from $200) and offers **glacier flightseeing** (from $69 per person per hour). Powerboat shuttles and houseboat rentals are a cheaper way to gain access; bargain with a boat-owning local or try **Norseman Adventures** (651-7535), on the waterfront at the south end of town (charters from $60 per hr.). For more info on the park, contact **BC Parks** (847-7320), Sheena District Office, Bag 5000, Smithers, BC V0J 2N0.

KLUANE NATIONAL PARK, YT

The Southern Tutchone (tuh-SHOW-nee) people named this area Kluane (kloo-AH-nee), meaning "place of many fish." They might also have mentioned that Kluane National Park is a place of many Dall sheep, eagles, glaciers, and untouched mountain landscapes. Together with adjacent Wrangell-St. Elias National Park in Alaska (see p. 448) and Tatshenshini/Alsek Provincial Park in BC, Kluane is part of one of the world's largest protected wilderness areas. It contains Canada's highest peak, Mt. Logan (5959m/19,545 ft.), and the most massive non-polar ice fields in the world. The ice-blanketed mountains of Kluane's interior are a haven for experienced expeditioners, but render two-thirds of the park inaccessible (except by plane) to humbler hikers. Fortunately, the northeastern section of the park (bordering the Alaska Hwy.) offers splendid, easily accessible backpacking, canoeing, rafting, biking, fishing, and dayhiking. Many routes follow original Southern Tutchone and Tlingit trails and old mining roads left over from Kluane's brief and disappointing fling with the gold rush in 1904-05.

⚡ ORIENTATION AND PRACTICAL INFORMATION

Kluane's 22,015km² are bounded by the Kluane Game Sanctuary and the Alaska Highway (Hwy. 1) to the north, and the Haines Highway (Hwy. 3) to the east. **Haines Junction** (pop. 800), 158km west of Whitehorse at the park's eastern boundary, serves as the gateway to the park. There is also access to trails in the north of the park from **Sheep Mountain**, 72km northeast of Haines Junction on the Alcan.

Buses: Alaska Direct (800-770-6652, in Whitehorse 668-4833) runs from Haines Junction on Su, W, and F to: Anchorage (13hr., 8am, US$125), Fairbanks (11hr., 8am, US$100), Whitehorse (2hr., 10pm, US$20), and Skagway (16hr., 10pm, 12hr. overnight in Whitehorse, US$55).

Visitor Information: Kluane National Park Visitor Reception Centre (634-7207; www.harbour.com/parkscan/kluane), on Logan St. in Haines Junction (Km 1635 on the Alcan) provides **wilderness permits** ($5 per night, $50 per season), **fishing permits** ($5 per day, $35 per season), **topographical maps** ($10), and **trail and weather info,** and registers overnight visitors to the park. Park staff available May-Sept. daily 9am-7pm; Oct.-Apr. M-F 10am-noon and 1-5pm. A **Yukon Tourism** desk (634-2345) gives information on activities outside the park, including along the drive to Haines, AK (see p. 424), 246km away. (Open daily mid-May to mid-Sept. 8am-8pm. Inquire about guided tours in late June and August.) The phoneless **Sheep Mountain Information Centre,** 72km north of town at Alaska Hwy. Km 1707, registers hikers headed for the spectacular northern area of the park. Open mid-May to Labour Day daily 9am-5pm (overnight registrations until 4:30pm only).

Bank: CIBC (634-2820), in Madley's Store on Haines Rd. at Bates St., exchanges foreign currency and cashes traveler's checks but does not handle cash withdrawals for non-CIBC customers. Open M-Th 12:30-4:30pm, F noon-5pm; in winter M-Th 1-4pm, F 1-4:30pm; no ATM.

Auto Repair: Triple S Garage (634-2915), 1km north of Haines Junction on the Alcan, performs oil and lubes (about $35), tire and general repair, and 24hr. emergency road service. Open May-Sept. M-F 7am-7pm, Sa 8am-6pm; in winter M-F 8am-6pm, Sa 9am-6pm.

Library: (634-2215), on Haines Rd., next door to Madley's, has free **Internet access** (book ahead if possible) and A/C. Open Tu 3-7pm, W-F 1-5pm, Sa 2-5pm.

Public Radio: 106.1 FM.

Laundromat and Showers: Gateway Motel (634-2371) at the junction of the Alaska Hwy. and Haines Rd. Wash $2, dry 25¢ per 6min. Shower $3. Open daily 8:30am-10pm.

Emergency and Police: 634-5555. **Ambulance/Clinic:** 634-4444 (located across from Madley's; open M-F 9am-noon and 1-5pm. **Fire:** 634-2222.

Post Office: (634-3802), in Madley's. Open M, W, and F 9-10am and 1-5pm; Tu and Th 9am-noon and 1-5pm. **Postal Code:** Y0B 1L0.

Area Code: 867.

▐◉ CAMPGROUNDS, ACCOMMODATIONS, AND FOOD

Camping by a gorgeous lakeside beats staying at a clean-but-forgettable highway motel or RV park any day. The idyllic **Kathleen Lake Campground,** off Haines Rd. 27km south of Haines Junction, is close to hiking and fishing (sites $10; water, toilets, fire pits, and firewood; open mid-May to mid-Sept.; wheelchair accessible). The closest government-run campground to Haines Junction is popular **Pine Lake,**

7km east of town on the Alcan. It features a sandy beach with a swim float and a pit for late-night bonfires ($8 with Yukon camping permit only; water, firewood, pit toilets). The **Dezadeash Lake Campground,** about 50km south of Haines Junction on Haines Rd., offers the same deal and similarly sweet lakefront property.

Guests at the **Laughing Moose B&B,** 120 Alsek Crescent (634-2335; www.bbcanada.com/1968.html), four blocks from the junction, have access to a kitchen, spacious common room with TV and VCR, and a view of the Auriol Mountains (singles $60; doubles $70; shared bath). The surprisingly unexciting **Stardust Motel** (634-2591; email stardust@yknet.yk.ca), 1km north of town on the Alcan, offers spacious rooms with TV and tubs, but no phone. (Singles $49; doubles $59, with kitchenette $79 first day, $69 per additional day. Open mid-May to mid-Sept. Reservations recommended.)

Haines Junction restaurants offer standard highway cuisine. **Village Bakery and Deli** (634-2867), on Logan St. across from the visitor center, serves up substantial soups with bread ($3.50) and mushroom quiche ($2.50). Watch out for (or participate in) live music and salmon BBQs ($13) on open-mic Mondays, weather permitting (open May-Sept. daily 7:30am-9pm). For all your grocery, hardware, tackle, and slingshot needs, head to **Madley's General Store** (634-2200), at Haines Rd. and Bates St. (open daily May-Sept. 8am-8pm; Oct.-Apr. 8am-6:30pm).

OUTDOORS

Kluane's trails are varied and very accessible. The visitor centers are great sources for trail maps, information, and conditions. A $1 pamphlet lists 25 or so trails and routes ranging from 500m to 96km. **Routes,** as opposed to trails, are not maintained, do not have marked paths, are more physically demanding, and require backcountry navigation skills. Oddly rendered beaver pictograms mark trailheads and park boundaries. Overnight visitors must register and pay at one of the visitor centers ($5 per night, ages 5-16 $2.50), and use bear-resistant food canisters, which the park rents for $5 per night (with $150 refundable deposit, cash or credit).

Anglers can readily put the park's many-fishèd reputation to the test at **Kathleen Lake** (see above), home to lake and rainbow trout, grayling and rare freshwater Kokanee salmon (usually in season mid-May to early June). Less-crowded **St. Elias Lake** is an easy 3.4km hike from the trailhead, 60km south of Haines Junction on Haines Rd. **Pine Lake,** the popular campground, is a good spot to put in the canoe for a paddle, as it is less windy than Kathleen Lake. Fishing requires a **National Parks fishing permit,** available at the visitor center in Haines Junction and at Madley's General Store (see **Practical Information,** above).

PaddleWheel Adventures (634-2683), down the road from the Village Bakery in Haines Junction, arranges flightseeing over the glaciers ($90 per person for a 30min. flight over the Kaskawulsh), hike-out helicopter rides to the Kluane Plateau ($45 per person), and full-day rafting trips on the Class III and IV rapids of the **Blanchard** and **Tatshenshini Rivers** ($100 per person, including lunch). They also rent just about everything you might need to explore the park on your own, including tents, packs, and bear spray, and offer interpretive group hikes ($10-15 per person) and a certified guiding service for activities in the area. (Bikes $20 per day; $50 for 3 days. Canoes $25 per day. Guides $50 per half-day; $100 per day.)

HAINES JUNCTION AND THE SOUTH. The **Dezadeash River Loop** (DEZ-dee-ash) trailhead is downtown at the day-use area across from Madley's on Haines Rd. This flat, forested 5km trail will disappoint those craving vert, but it makes for a nice stroll and the first kilometer is wheelchair accessible. As always, use a noisemaker or belt out tunes to warn bears that you're coming. The more challenging 15km **Auriol Loop** has a primitive campground halfway along. The trail begins 7km south of Haines Junction on Haines Rd. and cuts through boreal forest, leading to a subalpine bench (elevation gain 400m/1300 ft.) just in front of the Auriol Range. This is a popular overnight trip, though four to six hours is adequate time without heavy packs. The 5km (one-way) **King's Throne Route** is a difficult but rewarding dayhike with a 1220m/4000 ft. elevation gain and a panoramic view (allow 4-10hr.). It begins at the Kathleen Lake day-use area at the campground (see **Accommodations,** above).

The **Alsek River Valley Trail,** which follows a bumpy old mining road for 14km from Alcan Km 1645 to Sugden Creek, is popular for **mountain biking.** The rocky road crosses several streams before gently climbing to a ridge with a stellar view of the Auriol Mountains. More insider tips on the park's bike-friendly trails are available from the good folks at PaddleWheel Adventures (see above).

For **winter use** of the southern portion of the park, call ahead for snow conditions (634-7250) and stop by the visitor center for free, detailed maps of at least five **cross-country ski routes.** The Auriol, Dezadeash, and St. Elias trails (see above) are all local favorites. Camping rules in the park are the same as in summer, and snowshoeing and dog-mushing are encouraged.

SHEEP MOUNTAIN AND THE NORTH. Excellent hiking awaits near **Sheep Mountain** in the park's northern section. An easy 500m jaunt up to **Soldier's Summit** starts 1km north of the Sheep Mountain Info Centre and leads to the site where the Alaska-Canada highway was officially opened on November 20, 1942. The site pays homage to the "grunts and doughboys" who labored over the massive project during WWII, and offers a nice view of Kluane Lake. The **Sheep Creek** trail, located down a short gravel access road just north of the visitor center, is a satisfying dayhike (5km one-way; 430m/1440 ft. elev. gain; 3-6hr. round-trip) up Sheep Mountain, and one of the better bets to see Dall sheep during the summer months. Only experienced backpackers should attempt the trek along the **Slims River** to the magnificent **Kaskawulsh Glacier.** Two rough routes along the either bank of the river are available, stretching 23 and 30km one-way (elev. gains of 910m/3000 ft. and 1340m/4400 ft., respectively) and requiring two to five days. Register and buy backcountry permits at the info center.

👁 🎵 SIGHTS AND ENTERTAINMENT

Those curious about **First Nations** history in the area can take a self-guided tour of the traditional Aishihik (AY-shak) salmon-fishing village of **Klukshu** (about 70km south on the Haines Cutoff), or visit the **Kwaday Dan Kenji** traditional camp (667-6375) of the Champagne people, recently constructed with the help of local elders. Kwaday Dan Kenji is a few minutes east of the village of Champagne, situated 70km west of Whitehorse and 88km east of Haines Junction on the Alcan. Camping facilities on a natural meadow have pit toilets and fresh water ($10), and there is a guided tour of the traditionally made shelters and animal traps ($7.50, children $5.25; small shop with artifacts and local crafts open daily May-Oct. 9am-7:30pm). The **Heritage Department** (634-2331) of the Champagne and Aishihik Administration Office houses archives, photos, and a knowledgeable and interested staff. Call ahead for hours and directions.

To reach the **Arctic Institute of North America** (841-4561) turn north off the Alcan at the sign 3km south of Sheep Mountain. This research facility studies ice cored from deep within glaciers and sediment samples taken from lake bottoms to assemble a record of ancient climate, pollutant, and vegetation changes. They maintain a self-interpretive center that is open when staff is about.

The usually quiet hamlet of Haines Junction vivifies itself once a year for what local Yukoners call "the function at the junction": music-loving rowdies from all over the area gather on the second weekend of June to hear northern artists perform at the **Alsek Music Festival** (634-2520; ask about the Kidzone for younger folk).

SHEEP MOUNTAIN TO ALASKA

The drive northwest from Haines Junction to the Alaska border is broken up by a smattering of pit stops. For several kilometers past **Sheep Mountain,** the highway winds along beside the gorgeous Kluane Lake. **Congdon Creek Campground,** at Km

1723 on the Alcan, is the nicest campground before the U.S. border, with a long stone beach for evening strolls (80 sites: $8 with Yukon camping permits only; water, pit toilets, firewood). The small town of **Destruction Bay**, at Km 1743 (Historic Milepost 1083), earned its name when, in 1952, the tremendous wind that tunnels down the valley and off Kluane Lake destroyed the first village. These days, it's home to a **gas station**, motel, and cafe (all built low to the ground). A nurse is on call 24 hours at the **health clinic** (841-4444; open M-F 9am-4:30pm). **Destruction Bay Lodge** (841-5332) is a convenient spot to rest the rig (hookups $18, sites $10; showers, toilets). Due to high winds, a strict **fire ban** is enforced in the town.

  Burwash Landing, 16km north, offers modest thrills at the **Kluane Museum of Natural History** (841-5561), home to the Yukon's largest wildlife display and a collection of Southern Tutchone artifacts and traditional clothing (open daily late May and early Sept. 10am-6pm; June-Aug. 9am-9pm; $3.75, seniors $3.25, children 6-12 $2). **Kluane First Nation's Dalan Campground** has a few roomy, secluded sites on the lake, with wood, water, and pit toilets (25 sites: $10). Tenting is free on the lawn of **Burwash Landing Resort** (841-4441; showers $3; hookups $15). The lakeside resort houses **Your Place** (soup and sandwich $5.50; open in summer daily 7am-4:30pm), and lets rooms with TV and private bath (singles $60; doubles $70). Another 39km up the road, at Km 1798 (Historical Mile 1118), **Kluane Wilderness Village** (841-4141) is a self-contained roadside vacation station, featuring gas (open 24hr.), tenting ($6), full hookups ($19.50 with satellite TV), private cabins (singles $50, $5 per additional person) and a cafe (open daily 6am-11:30pm; sandwiches $4.50-8).

  The most lively of all these roadside wonders, **Beaver Creek** at Km 1935, is the closest to the border on the Canadian side. If the oddly shaped historic church (on the Alcan just north of the town center) doesn't interest you, do as the locals do and hit the **Trapline Lounge** at the Westmark Inn (862-7501; open in summer 6pm until the party's over) then nurse a hangover with breakfast at **Ida's Hotel and Cafe** (862-7223). Ida's grills up eggs and toast ($5.75) or two hotcakes with eggs ($5.50); for lunch, $6.50 fetches a mushroom burger and fries (open daily 7am-8pm). A heated indoor **public pool** is open June-Aug. (call 862-7702 for hours). **Westmark RV** (862-7501) has a laundry (wash $1, dry 25¢ per 7min.) and is as good a spot as any to park for the night ($10; hookups $19; includes showers, tea/coffee, toilets).

  Past Beaver Creek, 20 mi. of highway and prime moose-viewing wilderness, separate U.S. and Canadian customs and immigration, although several signs and landmarks can be found at the official border on the 141st meridian. **Alaska time** is 1 hour behind **Pacific time**. Gas a few miles into U.S. territory is considerably cheaper than anything in Canada. From the border it's 80 mi. (1½hr.) to Tetlin Junction, where the Alcan meets the Taylor Highway (see p. 512) and 92 mi. (2hr.) to Tok (see p. 511). On the American side, both **Deadman Lake** (Alcan mi. 1249) and **Lakeview** (mi. 1257; wheelchair accessible) offer free camping with rudimentary facilities (pit toilets and potable water) on the edge of the Tetlin Wildlife Refuge.

THE CAMPBELL HIGHWAY, YT

If the Yukon were conceived as a body, the Campbell Highway (Hwy. 4) might be likened to the sensitive jugular vein of the territory's modern mining economy. The perversely risky livelihood of metal-seeking is alive and kicking along the highway, and especially strong in Faro, a bizarre jewel of an ex-lead and zinc resource town. Other roads off the Campbell service smaller mining and prospecting operations. From the tiny, largely native community of **Ross River** (originally a mid- to late-19th-century fur-trading post), a finger of road cuts off towards Northwest Territories (NWT) wilderness. (Drive even the Yukon stretch at your own risk—local operators of the ferry across the Pelly to the highway have been known to occasionally dump pickup trucks into the river's muddy waters.) Indeed, much of the activity and sparse settlement found along the Campbell seems to be dedicated to its maintenance; the 383km (4-4½hr.; no services on this stretch) of graded dirt road from

Watson Lake in the south (on the Alcan Hwy.) to Ross River runs through wilderness broken only by impressive year-round highway servicing camps.

WATSON LAKE TO KLONDIKE HWY. From the south the Campbell Hwy. runs 602km from Watson Lake to the modest-sized, picturesque town of Carmacks (8hr.). The route requires good tires and a spare, though the road improves after Ross River, the halfway point. There are no services along the southern stretch. Out of Watson Lake (see p. 368), the land is fairly flat with spruce forests in all directions. As you get closer to Ross River, you start to catch views of the velvet-puckered green Pelly Range to the south and strange, rounded, high dirt cliffs. On the way to Carmacks, the road continues on high bluffs and eventually follows the Yukon River with some nice views approaching town. Five government campsites ($8 permit camping only) lie on the route (Kms 80, 177, 376, 428 up towards Faro, and 517 near Little Salmon Lake), and three more on the short Frenchman Rd., which branches off the Campbell at Km 551, near Carmacks, and leads 60km to the Klondike Hwy.

ROSS RIVER. The first charming camping awaits just before Ross River, about 10km north of the highway, at **Lapi Canyon Territorial Campground** ($8; pit toilets, firewood, water), above the rushing little stream that flows between the sandy cliffs of the canyon. The log-cabin town of Ross River itself has most services: a general store with **groceries**, and a **service station** (969-3841; open daily 7am-7pm) that repairs tires. **Leprechaun Enterprises** dispenses hospitality and local lore out of a green house at the north end of town (near the Pelly River ferry). The **Hideaway Restaurant** (969-2905; open M-F 11am-8pm, Sa-Su 11am-7pm) serves sandwiches (from $8) on homemade bread with produce trucked in weekly and will rent you their pretty cabin ($75 sleeps 4; kitchen, continental breakfast included). Dirty apparel come clean at the **laundromat** at the Friendly Inn in the center of town (open daily 8am-7pm; wash $1.50, dry $1.50). **Public radio** is 990 AM or 90.5 FM. **Medical emergencies:** 969-4444. **Police:** 867-667-5555. From Ross River, you are 370km of gravel road and two campsites away from Watson Lake and the Alaska Highway. **Frances Lake** is 193km down the road, **Simpson Lake** lies 290km along ($8; pit toilets, water, firewood).

FARO. One hour northeast of Ross River and a jaunt down 10km of road will land you in the curious, almost-ghost-town of **Faro.** When active, the town's mine held the world's largest open-pit lead and zinc production complex. It was so big that attempts to reopen the mine today would drive world lead prices down below the unprofitable levels that forced it to close in 1997. Opened in 1968, it is reported that in the mine's glory days one out of six car batteries in the world contained Faro lead. Today, the houses that were home to 2000 souls lie dormant, but the mine is poised for reopening when lead prices recover, estimated to occur in seven years.

If you do make the trip to Faro, you will be rewarded with the gratitude of still-in-shock residents, some dang spectacular wilderness fit for good **fishing** and **hiking** at the crossing of the Pelly River and the Anvil Range mountains, blissfully (or eerily) deserted camping and RV sites, and perhaps a view of rare black-and-white **Fannin sheep** from one of the town's several specially constructed **viewing platforms** The closest platform to town is at the corner of Blind Creek Rd. and Lorna Blvd.; but ask at the visitor center for directions to others. The **Campbell Region Interpretive Centre** (994-2288), on the right as you enter town, provides great info on geology and mining, First Nation habitation and early fur-trading exploration of the area, and also serves as the community's **visitor center.** Here read the tale of Scottish-born Hudson Bay company pioneer Robert Campbell, who named almost every principal river in the Yukon and after whom the Campbell Highway was finally named upon its completion in 1968. Watch for special naturalist talks and presentations given at the center throughout the summer.

Camping can be found at the very private **John Connolly RV Park**, across from the visitor center ($10, hookups $15; toilets, hot showers $3 for non-guests). The **Johnson Lake Territorial Campground** lies 3.5km back toward the highway ($8; pit toilets, pump water, and firewood). Otherwise, several blocks down the road from the visitor center the owner of **Redmond's Hotel** (994-2430) might rent you a room indoors for $75 (doubles with bath $85) at the only hotel in town. **Hoang's** is the only restaurant in town (open M-Sa 10am-9pm, Su 5-9pm). **Public radio:** 105.1FM. **Nursing station:** just off Campbell St. **Police:** 994-5555 (take a left on McQueston Rd. as you enter Faro). **Post office:** just before the nursing station on Campbell St. (open M-F 8:30am-5:30pm, Sa 8:30am-12:30pm). **Car repair: Shell** (994-2538; 24hr. road service 994-3127 or 994-2364).

CARMACKS. Little Salmon Lake (camping requires $8 permit; pit toilets, firewood, water) lies a little before Carmacks. Signs from here will guide you down the Campbell's paved 180km (2hr.) to **Faro.** Stop at **Eagle's Nest Bluff,** about 30km along the road, to hear the aspens rustle and get a high, wide-ranging view of the wide and easy Yukon and surrounding lands. The final approach to Carmacks delivers beautiful **camping** along the Nordenskiold River at the popular **Tantalus Public Campground** ($12; pit toilets, water), and a meandering stretch of riverside boardwalk. Eat with local characters and work on becoming one at the **Gold Panner Cafe** (863-5221; open daily 6am-10pm; in winter 8am-8pm; pricey entrees), below the highway in the center of town. The **visitor center** (863-6330; open Tu-Su 9am-5pm) is beside the campground. Just north of town, the new **Tage Cho Hudan Cultural Centre** (863-5830) preserves the Tutchone culture and displays the world's only mammoth snare model (open daily 9am-5pm; donation requested). From **Carmacks,** the smooth **North Klondike Highway** (Hwy. 2) runs 175km south to Whitehorse or 360km north to Dawson City. **Police:** 863-5555. **Ambulance/health clinic:** 863-4444.

NORTHERN YUKON

DAWSON CITY

Gold! Gold! Gold! Of all the insanity ever inspired by the lust for the dust, the creation of Dawson City must be one of the wildest. For 12 glorious, crazy months, from July 1898 to July 1899, this was the largest Canadian city west of Toronto, known as "the Paris of the North." Perched on the doorstep of the Arctic Circle and 1000 miles from any other settlement, its 30,000 residents, with names like Swiftwater Bill, Skookum Jim, and Evaporated Kid, set out to make their fortunes. Each had lugged 1000 lb. of provisions over the treacherous Chilkoot Trail to the Yukon (see p. 375) and was determined to become filthy, stinkin' rich.

After a year of frenzied claim-staking and legend-making, most of the once-eager Sourdoughs (prospectors or, today, anyone who survives an Arctic winter) followed the Yukon River to Nome, and Dawson City fizzled almost as quickly as it had exploded. With the exception of a few who staked prime claims, most left Dawson empty-handed. In the early 1960s the Klondike Visitors Association and the Canadian government set out to return Dawson City to its gold-rush glory, restoring dirt roads, long boardwalks, wooden store fronts, and in the process transforming it into the lively RV and college student destination that it is today.

∄ ORIENTATION AND PRACTICAL INFORMATION

To reach Dawson City, take the **Klondike Hwy. (Hwy. 2)** 533km (about 6hr.) north from Whitehorse, or follow the majestic **Top-of-the-World Hwy. (Hwy. 9)** 108km east from the Alaska border (see **Taylor Hwy.,** p. 512).

Buses: Dawson City Taxi Courier Service (993-6687), from the Downtown Hotel or the corner of Front and King St. to Whitehorse (6½hr., June-Aug. daily 7am and 6pm, $62). Reservations recommended. **Alaska Direct** (800-770-6652) does some runs over the border via the Top of the World Hwy. (Hwy. 9), but requires at least 4 people.

Ferries: Yukon Queen II River Cruises (993-5599), on Front St. next to the Keno. Departs daily at 9am for Eagle, AK along the Yukon River. Includes hot meals and river narration (4-5hr. round trip). One-way standby US$117; CDN$158, round-trip US$205, CDN$277; returns canoes from Eagle for US$50 (see p. 386). Office open M-Sa 9:30am-5:30pm, Su noon-5:30pm.

Car Rental: Budget, 451 Craig St. (993-5644), in the Dawson City B&B. $55 per day, 19¢ per km after 100km. Free pick-up and delivery. Must be 21 with a credit card.

Auto Repair and Towing: Esso (993-5142) on the Klondike Hwy. (Hwy. 2) immediately before town. Open in summer 7am-11pm.

Visitor Information: (993-5566) at Front and King St. Movies and inexpensive **tours.** Open mid-May to mid-Sept. daily 8am-8pm. The **Northwest Territories Visitor Centre** (993-6167) opposite, knows the Dempster Hwy. Open May to Sept. daily 9am-8pm. The **Klondike Visitors Association** (993-5575; www.dawsoncity.com) has no office.

Banks: Canadian Imperial Bank of Commerce, at 2nd Ave. and Queen. St. The only bank and **ATM** (24hr.) in town. Open M-Th 10am-3pm, F 10am-5pm.

Equipment Rental: Dawson City River Hostel (see **Accommodations,** below). Bikes $20 per day, canoes $20 per day. Non-hostelers must use passport as deposit.

Library: (993-5571) in the school at 5th Ave. and Princess St. Open Tu-Th 10am-9pm, F-Sa 10am-5pm; in winter Tu-Th 1-9pm, F-Sa 12-5pm. Free 30min. **Internet access;** call ahead. **Public Radio:** 540 AM or 104.9 FM.

Bookstore: Maximilian's Goldrush Emporium (993-5486), on Front near Queen St. Open M-Sa 9am-8pm, Su 10am-8pm; in winter M-Sa 9am-6pm, Su noon-6pm.

Laundromat and Public Showers: The Wash House Laundromat (993-6555) on 2nd Ave. between Princess and Queen. Wash $2.50, dry 25¢ per 4min. Showers $1 per 4min., towels 50¢. Open daily 8am-9pm; in winter 10am-6pm.

Weather: 993-8367.

Police: (993-5555 or 867-667-5555), at Front St. and Turner St., in the southern part of town. **Ambulance:** 993-4444.

Medical Services: Nursing Station (993-4444), at 6th Ave. and Church. Open M-F 8:30am-5pm. **Crisis Line: Dawson Women's Shelter** (993-5086). 24hr.

Post Office: (993-5342) at 5th Ave. and Princess St. Open M-F 8:30am-5:30pm, Sa 9am-noon. The **Historical Post Office,** at 3rd and King St., gives historical service and is closer to downtown. Open daily noon-6pm. **Postal Code:** Y0B 1G0.

Internet Access: See **Library,** above. **Harper Street Publishing** (993-6671), on 2nd Ave. between Princess and Queen St. $6 per 30min. Open M-F 9:30am-5:30pm.

Area Code: 867.

▛ ACCOMMODATIONS AND CAMPGROUNDS

Contact the Northern Network of Bed and Breakfasts (993-5644; fax 993-5648; www.nnbandb.com) for that kind of thing. The hostel and the campground on the west side of town, across the Yukon River, are by far the cheapest options in the trap that is Dawson City tourism. The **ferry** to float you and your wheels across is free and runs 24 hours. Hop on at Front and Albert St., in the north end of town. The **tent city** in the woods next to the hostel is home to many of the town's summer college crowd, despite the $100 per person the government now charges.

🏚 **Dawson City River Hostel (HI)** (993-6823), across the Yukon River from downtown; take the 1st left off the ferry. The northernmost hostel in Canada and the best bargain in town. Bunks in log cabins, wood-heated "prospector's bath," outdoor kitchen, cozy lounge with wood stove and mini-library, and a hilltop view. Beds $13, nonmembers

$16; tent sites $9 for one person, $6.50 per extra person. Open mid-May to Sept.

■ **The Bunkhouse** (993-6164; fax 993-6051), on Princess at Front St. Conveniently located; clean wood-planked rooms. Singles $45, with bath $75; doubles $50, with bath $80; quads with bath $105. 10% senior discount. Open mid-May to mid-Sept.

■ **Dawson City Bed and Breakfast,** 451 Craig St. (993-5649; www.yukon.net/DawsonBB), on the south end of town. More like home than your own. Singles $75; doubles $85, both with shared bath; queen bed with private bath $95. Seniors and AAA members 5% discount. Winter discount $10. Make reservations at least a week in advance.

■ **Yukon River Campground,** on the 1st right off the ferry. Roomy, secluded sites are a haven for nature-lovers, who can peer at the peregrine falcons nesting across the river. Water and pit toilets. RVs welcome, but no hookups. Sites $8.

■ **Gold Rush Campground** (993-5247), at 5th and York St. Right downtown, this RV draw is always packed. Laundry (wash $3, dry $1.50), shower ($2 per 6min.), and dump station. Hookups $23, pull-through sites $14-21. Tent sites $15. Open May-Sept.

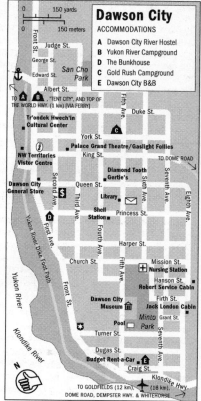

Dawson City

ACCOMMODATIONS

A Dawson City River Hostel
B Yukon River Campground
D The Bunkhouse
C Gold Rush Campground
E Dawson City B&B

⊙ FOOD

On Thanksgiving Day in 1898, a turkey in Dawson City cost over $100. Snag a butterball today at the **Dawson City General Store** (993-5475; open M-Sa 8am-8pm, Su 10am-8pm), on Front St.

Klondike Kate's (993-6527), at 3rd and King St., in one of Dawson's oldest buildings. Kate's breakfast special (served until 11am) would satisfy the hungriest Sourdough (2 eggs, bacon or sausage, home fries, and toast for $4). At lunch, kick back on the patio with a gyro or veggie wrap ($5). Open mid-May to mid-Sept. daily 7am-11pm.

River West Food and Health (993-6339), on Front and Queen St. A mean supergrain loaf, organic coffees, goodies and snacks, and perhaps the only hummus pitas in the Yukon ($6). Open M-Sa 8am-7pm, Su 9am-6pm; in winter M-Sa 10am-6pm.

Midnight Sun Hotel Restaurant (993-5495), 3rd and Queen St. Chinese entrees, created by chefs invited from Vancouver for the summer (from $11). Burgers and so on $5-8. Lunch smorgasbord on F ($10). Open Su-Th 6am-1am, F-Sa 6am-3am.

The Jack London Grill (993-5346), in the Downtown Hotel at 2nd and Queen St. Those too road-worn for the posh dining room can sip a little in the saloon (open daily 11am-1am; $3 pints 5-7pm). Sandwiches from $6, dinner from $10, shrimp caesar salad $10. Open Su-Th 6am-10pm, F-Sa 6am-11pm; in winter an hour shaved off either end.

⧉ ♫ SIGHTS, ENTERTAINMENT, AND EVENTS

The visitor center sells a **Parks Pass** ($15) that pays off if you want to see everything. The goldfields of **Bonanza** and **Eldorado Creeks** yielded some of the richest lodes discovered in the Klondike. Nearly 16km of maintained gravel road follow Bonanza Creek to the former site of **Grand Forks,** chewed up when the dredges came through. Along the way are **Gold Dredge #4,** a monster of a machine used to exhaust Bonanza Creek after the rush was over, and **Discovery Claim,** the site of the first discovery of gold in Dawson by George Carmack on August 16, 1896 (tours daily on the hour 9am-4pm except 11am; $5). **Bear Creek,** 13km south of town on the Klondike Hwy., is a ghost town of tools and machinery left behind when mining suddenly halted in 1966 (tours Su-F 1:30pm and 3pm; $5). **Goldbottom Mining Tours and Gold Panning** (993-5023), 30km south of town, offers a tour of an operating mine and an hour of panning (June to freeze-up daily 11am-7pm; $12). Anyone can pan for free at the confluence of the Bonanza and Eldorado Creeks with equipment (a pan) from a local hardware store. Panning anywhere else along the creeks could lead to a very unpleasant encounter with the owner/miner of the claim you're jumping.

Examine the traces of frontier literary genius at the **Jack London Cabin,** on 8th Ave. and Firth St., where the great Californian author's life and brief stint in the Yukon are described in lectures and photographs. (Open daily 10am-1pm and 2-6pm. 30min. tours daily 11:30am and 2:30pm. Exhibit by donation, talks $3.) Be sure to catch the animated **Robert Service readings** given at his nearby cabin. Authentic performances of witty ballads by the Yukon Bard, including "The Cremation of Sam McGee" and "The Shooting of Dan McGrew," are given in front of the cabin at 8th Ave. and Hanson St., where he penned them. (Shows daily June-Aug. at 10am and 3pm. $6, under 8 $3. Cabin free for viewing 9am-noon and 1-5pm.) For a broader, less lyrical historical perspective, check out the **Dawson City Museum** (993-5007), on 5th Ave. in Minto Park. Exhibits on the region's geography, natives, first settlers, and the gold rush complement special films, demonstrations, and a children's exhibit of family heirlooms. (Open daily 10am-6pm. $4, students and seniors $3, family $10. Wheelchair accessible.)

Diamond Tooth Gertie's, at 4th and Queen St., was Canada's first legal casino, and proves that Dawson is no movie set: for a $5 cover (or $20 season pass), gamblers can fritter away the night with roulette, blackjack, or Texas hold 'em against local legends such as Too-Tough Tanya or No Sleep Filippe. Free nightly floor shows at 8:30, 10:30pm, and 12:30am. (Must be 19. Open nightly 7pm-2am.) The **Gaslight Follies** (993-6217), a high-kicking vaudeville revue, is held in the **Palace Grand Theatre** on King St., between 2nd and 3rd St. (daily 8pm; box office open daily 11am-8pm; $16-18, under 12 $8). As the night winds down, karaoke winds up at the **Sun Tavern and Lounge** (993-5495), at 3rd St. and Queen St., where everyone ends up. Once Dawson's roughest bar, the Sun has since cooled down, but it's still no place to sip fruity drinks. (Pints $3.75. Open daily noon-2am.) **The Pit Tavern and Lounge** (993-5339 or 993-5463) at the old Westminster Hotel on 3rd, is a local watering hole with atmosphere as thick as the forest fire smoke that sometimes blankets Dawson. Barnacle Bob plays the tavern from 4pm, and the much-acclaimed country and blues house band plays the lounge Wednesday through Saturday at 10pm (tavern open 9am-11pm, lounge noon-2am; happy hour 4:45-5:45pm).

The **Tr'ondek Hwech'in Culture Centre** (993-6564) on Front St., celebrated for its architecture since its completion in 1998, is a striking and innovative home for exhibits on First Nation culture. The center is open for visitors (donations welcome) to browse displays, watch videos, or participate in various cultural activities and demonstrations (open Tu-Sa 10am-6pm).

Dawson is a jungle-gym for outdoorspeople. The Dawson City River Hostel sells topographical maps of the region ($12) and arranges four-day **canoe trips** to Eagle,

NO, MA'AM, THAT'S NOT AN OLIVE IN YOUR MARTINI

When some people run across amputated body parts, they take them to a hospital for surgical reattachment. But Capt. Dick Stevenson's discovery of a pickled human toe in a cabin in the Yukon meant one thing: a damn fine cocktail. The drink became famous and spawned the Sourtoe Cocktail Club, whose 14,000-plus members include a 6-month-old child and a 91-year-old toe-swallower. Aspiring initiates buy a drink of their choice and pay a small fee ($5) to Bill "Stillwater Willie" Holmes (Dick's replacement as keeper of the sourtoe), who drops the chemically preserved (er, pickled) toe in the drink. Then it's bottoms up, and the moment the toe touches your lips, you're in the club. "You can drink it fast, you can drink it slow—but the lips have gotta touch the toe." Listening to Stillwater Willie explain the club's sordid history and philosophize about life in the Yukon is itself worth $5, but the fee includes a certificate and membership card; a commemorative pin or a book relating the saga of the sourtoe can be purchased separately for $5 each. Sourtoe initiations are held from 9-11pm nightly (and Fridays from 5-7pm) in the Sourdough Saloon at the Downtown Hotel (993-5346) on the corner of Queen and 2nd. A word of warning for those who dare: Stillwater Willie may require that swallowed toes be replaced.

AK (US$110), or ten-day trips to Circle, AK (US$270). A trip up the **Midnight Dome,** 7km along Dome Rd., just past the Esso gas station on the way into town, is a tradition on the **summer solstice,** on which the sun dips below the horizon for just 20 minutes around 12:30am. Even for those who miss the solstice, the Midnight Dome makes for a panoramic picnic spot. The steep 4km trail ascends over 600m/1970 ft. The visitor center has photocopied maps.

During the third weekend of July, the **Dawson City Music Festival** (993-5584; www.dcmf.com) flies top-notch artists to the Yukon River's edge and floats them downriver to Dawson, where people from all over Canada await three days of fantastic music and atmosphere (July 21-23, 2000). Tickets to see 20-plus pop, rock, and folk bands engulf the town run about $70, go on sale in April, and usually sell out by mid-June. The ticketless can listen in from outside open venues and soak up the good feelings. Mid-August sees Dawson explode in Sourdough charm during **Discovery Days** (Aug. 18-21, 2000) with a parade, pancake breakfasts, and an entire town in gold-rush period costume. Labour Day visitors will not want to pass up their chance to behold the **Great International Outhouse Race** (Sept. 3, 2000). Teams of contenders tow occupied outhouses on wheels through the streets of Dawson (call the Visitor's Association, 993-5575, with questions and comments).

TOP OF THE WORLD HIGHWAY (HWY. 9)

This majestic 127km (1½hr.) highway truly deserves its name. Starting across the Yukon River from Dawson City, climbing for several kilometers and then following the spine of a series of mountains, the trip affords breathtaking views of the Southern Ogilvies and North Dawson range before connecting with the Taylor Highway at **Jack Wade Junction** in Alaska. Unmarked trails head into the bush from rest-stops. The road is open May through September, though the mountainous Yukon-Alaska border crossing at kilometer 108 is only open 9am-9pm Pacific (i.e., Yukon) time. The only services on the Canadian side are the links of the Top of the World Golf Course (867-667-1472), about 10 km past the ferry. The five-minute ferry runs from June to July, 24 hours (peak traffic 7-11am from Dawson and 2-8pm to town). While the Canadian road is well maintained (though slippery when wet), the potholed gravel on the American side will have you cursing Uncle Sam. Just over the border into the U.S., the **Boundary Cafe** sells snacks and will trade a gallon of gasoline for your soul (meaning US$2.50).

DEMPSTER HIGHWAY

Named after Inspector W.J.D. Dempster, one of the most courageous officers to wear the serge uniform of the Mounted Police, the Dempster Highway begins in the Yukon as Hwy. 5 and wends 741 spectacular kilometers toward Inuvik, becoming Hwy. 8 when it crosses into the Northwest Territories. In 1910, Dempster and his men went searching for four officers who had set out from Fort McPherson and never arrived in Dawson. With a dog sled team and native guide, Dempster found their dead bodies just 20 miles from the fort and brought the sad news to Dawson City in record time. Dempster completed his 475-mile patrol route countless times over the years, following roughly the same path that now bears his name. Construction of the highway began in the 1950s when oil and gas were discovered near the Arctic Circle at Eagle Plains, and was completed in 1979, finally providing road access to Canada's isolated Mackenzie River Delta towns of **Fort McPherson** (known as **Tetlit Zheh** by local Tetlit Gwich'in people), **Tsiigehtchic** (SIG-uh-chik, formerly known as Arctic Red River), and **Inuvik** (ih-NOO-vik). These communities along the highway are largely indigenous Inuvialuit and Gwich'in, and are quite welcoming of passing visitors. The highway begins 41km east of Dawson City on the Klondike Highway (Hwy. 2) at the **Klondike River Lodge**.

Like no other highway in North America, the Dempster confronts its drivers with real, naked wilderness, unmolested by logging scars or advertisements. Driving the Dempster can be a religious experience: those who brave it cross the Arctic Circle and the Continental Divide, pass more animals than cars, and stare into the geological beginnings of the continent—and then have the right to write "I did it!" in the dust coating their car. Despite the thrill, the Dempster is not to be taken lightly. While reasonably navigable and well maintained, it should be approached with careful planning. Services are limited, weather is erratic, and the dirt and gravel roads can give cars a thorough beating. Though a trip to Tombstone makes a pleasant overnight, the full drive takes at least 12 hours, though it deserves at least two days each way to be fully and safely appreciated. Most importantly, quick rainstorms or high winds can make portions of the route impassable (watch for flashing red lights that denote closed roads) and can disrupt ferry service for as long as two weeks, leaving unwitting travelers stranded in Inuvik for as long.

◪ **PRACTICAL INFORMATION.** The **Arctic Hotline** (800-661-0788 or 867-873-7200) and **Road and Ferry Report** (800-661-0752; in Inuvik 777-2678) provide up-to-date road info. The **NWT Visitor Centre** (see p. 383) in Dawson City has a free brochure on the highway. The ever-useful road guides *Along the Dempster* ($13) and *Western Arctic Travel* ($5) are sold at **Maxmillian's** in Dawson City.

A full tank of gas, dependable tires (6-ply or better), at least one good spare, and emergency supplies (food, clothes, a first aid kit, and a jerry can of gas) are necessary Dempster companions. The Klondike Lodge has full services, though Dawson City is just as good for preparations and sells cheaper gas. Bring a sure-fire bug repellent (and some form of netting if camping); the number of mosquitoes along the highway is staggering. If you lack wheels or doubt yours will survive the trip, **Arctic Adventures** (800-393-9055 or 867-668-2411; www.gowildtours.com) plans to restart a **van tour** twice weekly in the summer of 2000 for about $200 between Dawson, Tombstone, Eagle Plains, and Inuvik. **Area code:** 867.

⚑ ON THE ROAD AND OUTDOORS. The spectacular first 150km of the Dempster pass through the crags of the **Ogilvie Mountains,** renowned for their uncommon character and as such appropriately named for a revered surveyor and restorer of order to booming Dawson City. The dramatic peaks of the southern ranges gradually round out into the gentler, gravel-covered, unglaciated **Northern Ogilvies** near Engineer Creek (Km 194). The road then descends into forests and blankets of velvet tundra as it approaches the **Arctic Circle** (Km 405) and Inuvik. There are only a handful of settlements to distract drivers from the wonder of gazing. From Dawson some drivers make a beautiful overnight trip to Tombstone, where the **Interpretive Centre** at **Tombstone Campground** (Km 72) has an immensely wise staff, short trails, and expansive displays. For those continuing farther north, the center loans out a mile-by-mile written travelogue of the Dempster's natural history and wildlife: mountains and moraines, golden eagles, and the migrating **Porcupine caribou herd,** which, at 150,000 head, is the largest in North America. Several **government campgrounds** ($8) line the route north to Inuvik. Engineer Creek (Km 194) and Rock River (at particularly mosquito-infested Km 447) lie before **Nitainlii** (just before Ft. McPherson at Km 541) where there is an excellent Gwich'in **interpretive center** (open daily June-Sept. 9am-9pm). There are hookups only near Inuvik, at Chuk (777-3613; sites $12, electric $15; showers and toilets).

The mesmerizing landscape tempts **backcountry tripping** and demands the most vigilant take-nothing-leave-nothing ethic. The Ogilvie and Blackstone Rivers are favored by backcountry paddlers. *Paddling the Yukon* ($22, available at Maximillian's) is a comprehensive guide. Numerous mountain ridges that reach toward the road in the Northern Ogilvies are especially good for a straightforward manner of bushwhacking: following a ridge to the mountain. The tundra's spongelike, **hiker-unfriendly muskeg,** a lumpy surface of thawed permafrost, belies its deceptively long, flat, arid-looking appearance, but a handful of established paths access this wilderness. The road guide mentioned above, *Along the Dempster*, describes routes accessible from the highway in addition to the following highlights.

At Km 58, a small road behind the gravel pit at the garbage dump becomes the **Grizzly Valley** trail (3hr. one-way), which leads through spruce forest to an alpine ridge with a fine view. The hike to **Tombstone Mountain** (known in Gwich'in as **Ddhah Ch'aa Tat,** "among the sharp, ragged, rocky mountains") begins just north of the interpretive centre, takes 3-4 days, and requires self-reliance, a compass, and topo maps (available at the interpretive centre). For a day-long adventure in the Northern Ogilvies, at Km 154 the **Mt. Distincta trail** ("Windy Pass") heads over craggy boulders to one of the area's highest peaks (1800m/5600 ft.). From the highway, walk southeast across a narrow ribbon of tundra to the base of the ridge. Follow the ridge south 6km, past a radio tower, then up a slope to the west—this is the true summit. From here, hike north 6km and then descend back to the highway where you will emerge 5km west of the trailhead. This trail rises about 1000m/13300 ft. Sturdy boots are a must. **Sapper Hill,** with its distinct yellow-gray ridge, is one of the best half-day hikes along the highway. It begins just after Engineer Creek (Km 194), and takes about 4 hours. Avoid walking along the fishbone crest of the ridge—the chunky limestone near the summit can be tricky to navigate.

Halfway to Inuvik, at Km 363, gas, food, a coin laundry and showers, and accommodations are available at the well-kept **Eagle Plains Hotel** (993-2453), a paragon of monopoly pricing (singles $99, each extra person $11). Rocky, parking lot-style camping is available ($10, electrical $15). Car juice is something like 83¢ per liter, but what are you going to do? The next pump is 197km away. Food is of disarmingly good value. A Bushfire burger (onions, hot peppers and horseradish) with thick fries costs $7 (open daily 7am-9pm). The lounge and restaurant display fantastic, riveting photo-essays on the region's history: read about the tale of the "Mad

Trapper from Rat River," view his mortuary portrait, or admire snaps of the handsome Inspector Dempster (open daily 4:30pm-2am).

Just past Eagle Plains at Km 405, the Dempster crosses the **Arctic Circle.** Here there is an imaginary dotted line in the tundra and a sign to provide photographic proof that you've reached the true Land of the Midnight Sun.

Set your watch to Mountain Time when you enter the Northwest Territories at Km 465. From mid-June to mid-October, free **ferries** continuously cross the Peel River (daily 9am-1am) and the Arctic Red River (departs the south shore 25min. past the hour daily 9am-midnight), 191km and 141km south of Inuvik. In winter, cars can drive across the thick ice. No crossing is possible during the fall freeze or spring thaw. Call 800-661-0752 for ice status.

NORTHWEST TERRITORIES: INUVIK

Inuvik ("living place") has 3200 residents mostly from two separate Arctic peoples, the Inuvialuit of the Beaufort Sea coast and the Gwich'in of the Mackenzie River Delta. During the long winter, Inuvik's houses are flamboyantly painted with bright colors and the community is known for extravagant summer festivals.

Just about everything in town is on MacKenzie St., starting with the welcoming **Western Arctic Visitor Centre** (777-4727; open daily 9am-8pm). **Arctic Tire,** 80 Navy Rd. (777-4149; open M-F 9am-noon and 1-6pm), offers 24-hour road service. Both the **CIBC bank** and the **post office** have **24-hour ATMs.** The **public library,** 100 Mackenzie Rd. (777-2749), has free **Internet access** (open M-Th 11am-9pm, F 11am-6pm, Sa-Su 2-5pm). **Police:** 777-2935. **Inuvik Regional Hospital:** 777-2955. **Area code:** 867.

Affordable rooms are available at **Robertson's Bed and Breakfast,** 41 Mackenzie Rd. (777-3111; singles $70; doubles $80) and down the street at **Polar Bed and Breakfast** (777-4620; islc@permafrost.com; shared kitchen and free laundry; singles $75; doubles $85). The **Happy Valley Campground** (777-3652) is on Happy Valley Rd. off Union St. (wash and dry $2.75 each; free showers and toilets; sites $12, hookups $15). Dining in Inuvik lies on the north side of pricey. Try **The Backroom** (777-2727) for variety, from heaping plates of Chinese food (from $13.50), to the caribou burger ($12.50; open in summer daily 5-11pm). The **Cafe Gallery** (777-2888) serves nibblets and light lunches (lox on a bagel $7.50) in a sunny studio (open M-F 8am-8pm, Sa noon-6pm, Su noon-8pm). For an $8 breakfast and a nice view of the **Igloo Church,** try the **Sunriser Coffee Shop** (777-2861) at the Mackenzie hotel (open daily from 7am, breakfast M-F until 11am, Sa-Su until 2pm). On a late night (insert seasonal pun), hit the arctic's rowdy hotspot, **The Zoo,** in the Mackenzie Hotel.

Begun in 1989, The **Great Northern Arts Festival** (777-3536; fax 777-4445; www.greatart.nt.ca) brings over 100 artists and entertainers to Inuvik for performances and workshops (July 21-30, 2000). Though boating seems most appropriate in the sprawling Mackenzie Delta (the river drains 20% of Canada), one hiking trail is reasonably maintained in the area. The **Midnight Sun Tundra Nature Hike** begins at the visitor center and follows mountain ridges for 6km to 3 Mile Lake (2hr. one-way). The ridges are a perfect perch from which to watch the sun in its lowest arc and to survey the Richardson Range. To explore the Mackenzie Delta contact **Western Arctic Adventures and Equipment,** 38 Sprucehill Dr. (777-4542; fax 777-3103), for canoes, kayaks, air charters, and trip-planning help. **Arctic Nature Tours** (777-3300; fax 777-3400), beside the Igloo church, mobilizes outfitters and community contacts to lead 20-odd nature/culture tours: explore Inuvik (1hr., $20), cruise the Mackenzie River and visit an Inuvialuit camp for a BBQ (4½hr., $90), or fly to Herschel Island Territorial Park to see abandoned whaling towns and perhaps a musk ox or two (5hr., $275). **Aurora Research College Research Centre** (777-3838) offers a naturalist's canoe tour of the Delta (4hr.; $32; in summer M 6pm, Th 1pm). Stop by the research station at Duck Lake St. to peruse the arctic library (open M-F 8-30am-noon and 1-5pm), or catch a free slideshow on the region (45min., in summer Tu and F at 1:30pm). Still not north enough? **Beauford-Delta Tours** (777-3067) flies 40 minutes to ice-bound **Tuktoyak-tuk,** or "Tuk" to its friends, for a tour (7hr., $148). As with everything in Inuvik, call ahead.

SOUTHEAST ALASKA

ALASKA'S.... Capital: Juneau. **Population:** 607,800. **Area:** 586,412 sq. mi. **Motto:** "We're way bigger than Texas and have more oil!" **Real Motto:** North to the Future. **Bird:** Willow ptarmigan. **Flower:** Forget-me-not. **State Fish:** King salmon. **Tree:** Sitka spruce. **Mineral:** Gold. **Gem:** Jade. **Sport:** Dog mushing. **Holiday:** Alaska Day, Oct. 18. **Pay Phones:** Many phones will not return coins. Dial, wait until the party picks up, and then deposit coins. **Sales Tax:** None. **Drinking Age:** 21.

Southeast Alaska (also known as "the Panhandle" or "the Southeast") spans 500 miles from Misty Fiords National Monument, past the state capital of Juneau, to Skagway. The Southeast is accessible by boat or plane, separated from the interior by the snow-capped coastal range and divided by countless straits into thousands of islands, inlets, and fjords collectively known as the Inside Passage. Panhandle towns cling to narrow pockets of coast that provide little room for growth.

The region boasts a mild, wet climate year-round, fantastic salmon and halibut runs, and the Tongass National Forest, the largest old-growth temperate rainforest in the world. Fishing and logging are the primary industries, though tourism is king in summer. Nevertheless, while cruise ships, charter boats, and ferries clog the waterways, quiet beaches, mountains wrapped in clouds, and lush rainforest are never more than a short hike from town. Apart from the rain, snow, and cold, winter may be the nicest time to travel, as it's cheaper and you can avoid the crowds, though most businesses close down. Wilderness camping is always free anywhere within the Tongass, and remote, well-maintained Forest Service cabins are a steal (from $25 per night), though many of these, along with some of the region's most vaunted sights—Misty Fjords, the Stikine River, LeConte Glacier, Glacier Bay— require fly-in or boat-in service. (Such service can be expensive, but companies will often discount fares on single spaces that unexpectedly open up.)

Russian fur-traders and missionaries made the Southeast their headquarters in the 18th century. The United States bought the region from them in 1867, much to the chagrin of the British, who had also made claims to the land. Long before, the Southeast was home to the Tlingit, Haida, and Tsimshian peoples. Many of the region's towns and villages are built on old Native settlements, traditionally divided among geographical districts called *kwaans*, and native culture and activism are still very much alive. Innovative Tsimshian carvers in Metlakatla put a new spin on an old idea with their booming bentwood box drums, and the handiwork of Tlingit artists at the Southeast Alaskan Native Cultural Center in Sitka is in part an artistry of scale, from the deft carving of multi-story totem poles to the delicate weaving of palm-sized cedar baskets.

The Alaska Marine Highway's late-night departures, delays, and occasional long layovers require patience and flexibility. Mummy-bagged travelers camp on deck under the stars to avoid pricey accommodations, and daytime views are spectacular—the Southeast is home to more bald eagles than anywhere else in the world, and most of the humpback whales in the Pacific summer here.

HIGHLIGHTS OF SOUTHEAST ALASKA

- **Juneau** (see p. 411) has folk fests and fiddle jams, and blues at the Alaska Hotel.
- **Surfing** off or **sitting** on the black sands of **Yakutat** (see p. 433) is a treat and trek.
- The **Stikine River's** ice-choked sloughs and **Chief Shakes Hot Springs** are cold and hot, respectively, in a valley once called a "Yosemite that keeps going..." (See p. 407.)
- Make a forage into the interior from **Skagway** by foot on the **Chilkoot Trail**, by rail via the **White Pass & Yukon Route**, or by car along the **Klondike Hwy.** (see p. 428).

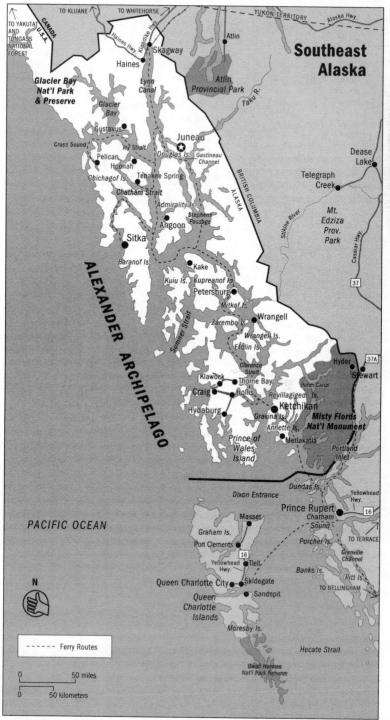

Southeast Alaska

TO KLUANE
TO WHITEHORSE
YUKON TERRITORY
Alaska Hwy.

TO YAKUTAT
AND
TONGASS
NATIONAL
FOREST

CANADA
U.S.A.

Haines Hwy.
Klondike Hwy.
Skagway
Atlin

Haines

Lynn
Canal

Atlin
Provincial Park

Taku R.

Glacier Bay
Nat'l Park
& Preserve

Glacier
Bay

Gustavus

Cross Sound

Pelican

Hoonah

Chichagof Is.

Icy Strait

Juneau

Douglas Is.
Gastineau
Channel

Dease
Lake

Telegraph
Creek

Tenakee Springs

Chatham Strait

BRITISH COLUMBIA

Stikine River

Mt.
Edziza
Prov.
Park

ALASKA

Admiralty Is.

Stephens
Passage

Angoon

Sitka

Baranof Is.

Kake

Cassiar Hwy.

37

Kuiu Is.

Kupreanof Is.

Petersburg

Mitkof Is.

Zarembo Is.

Wrangell

Wrangell Is.

Etolin Is.

Clarence
Strait

Hyder

37A

Stewart

Behm Canal

Klawock

Thorne Bay

Craig

Hollis

Revillagigedo Is.

Ketchikan

Hydaburg

Gravina Is.

Misty Fiords
Nat'l Monument

Annette Is.

Metlakatla

Prince of
Wales
Island

Portland
Inlet

Dundas Is.

Dixon Entrance

Yellowhead
Hwy.

Prince Rupert

16

Chatham
Sound

Masset

Porcher Is.

TO TERRACE

PACIFIC OCEAN

Graham Is.

Port Clements

Grenville
Channel

16

Yellowhead
Hwy.

Tleil

Banks Is.

Pitt Is.

Queen Charlotte City

Skidegate

Sandspit

TO BELLINGHAM

Queen
Charlotte
Islands

Moresby Is.

Hecate Strait

Gwaii Haanas
Nat'l Park Reserve

ALEXANDER ARCHIPELAGO

Summer Strait

N

- - - - - Ferry Routes

0   50 miles
0   50 kilometers

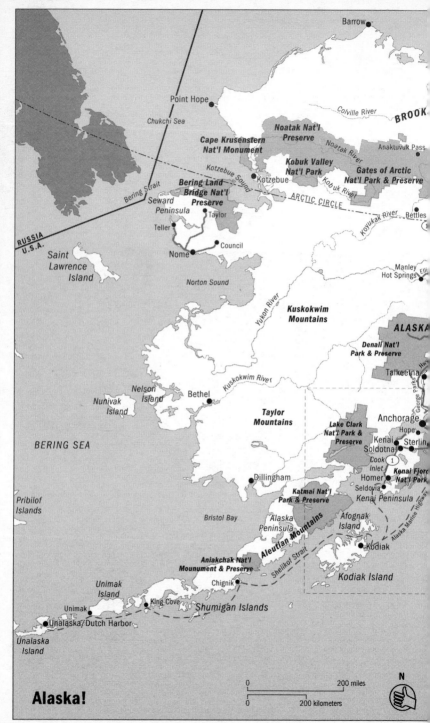

Alaska!

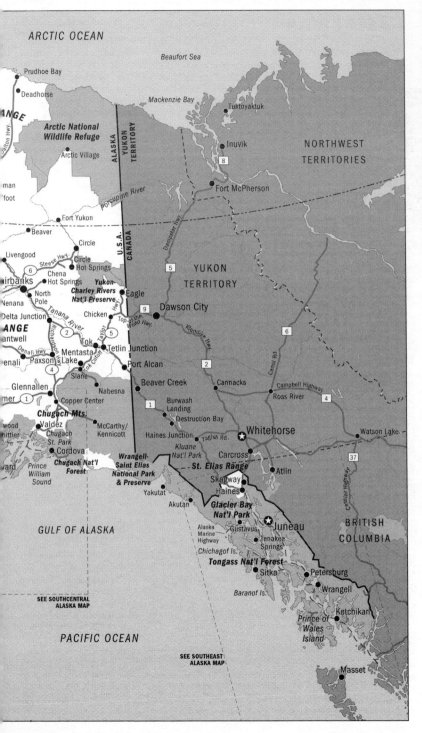

ARCTIC OCEAN

Beaufort Sea

Prudhoe Bay

Deadhorse

Mackenzie Bay

Tuktoyaktuk

Arctic National
Wildlife Refuge

ALASKA
YUKON TERRITORY

Inuvik

NORTHWEST
TERRITORIES

Arctic Village

8

man
foot

Fort McPherson

Porcupine River

Fort Yukon

Beaver

Circle

Livengood

Steese Hwy.

Circle
Hot Springs

6

Chena
Hot Springs

irbanks

Fairbanks

North
Pole

U.S.A.
CANADA

Dempster Hwy.

5

YUKON
TERRITORY

6

Nenana

Delta Junction

Tanana River

Yukon-
Charley Rivers
Nat'l Preserve

Eagle

9

Dawson City

ANGE
antwell

Chicken

2

Taylor

Top-of-the
World Hwy.

Klondike Hwy.

Denali Hwy.

Tok

Mentasta
Lake

5

Richardson Hwy.

Tetlin Junction

Port Alcan

Carmacks

Carol Rd.

Campbell Highway

enali

Paxson

4

Slana

Beaver Creek

Ross River

4

Glennallen

mer

1

Copper Center

Nabesna

Tok Cutoff Hwy.

1

Burwash
Landing

2

Alaska Hwy.

Tagish Rd.

Whitehorse

Watson Lake

wood
hitter

Valdez

Chugach
St. Park

McCarthy/
Kennicott

Destruction Bay

Haines Junction

Kluane
Nat'l Park

Carcross

37

Cassiar Highway

ard

Cordova

Prince
William
Sound

Chugach Mts.

Chugach Nat'l
Forest

Wrangell-
Saint Elias
National Park
& Preserve

Yakutat

St. Elias Range

Skagway

Atlin

BRITISH

COLUMBIA

GULF OF ALASKA

Akutan

Haines

Glacier Bay
Nat'l Park

Alaska
Marine
Highway

Gustavus

Juneau

Tenakee
Springs

Chichagof Is.

Tongass Nat'l Forest

Sitka

Petersburg

Baranof Is.

Wrangell

SEE SOUTHCENTRAL
ALASKA MAP

Prince of
Wales
Island

Ketchikan

PACIFIC OCEAN

SEE SOUTHEAST
ALASKA MAP

Masset

KETCHIKAN

Ketchikan is first stop in Alaska for cruise ships and would-be cannery workers, and is popular despite its notorious bad weather. An average of nearly 12½ ft. of "liquid sunshine" a year cannot deter visitors' delight in the town's rich culture or its fabulous proximity to Tongass National Forest (one third of which lies in the Ketchikan area) and the stunning Misty Fjords National Monument.

Three miles long and several hundred yards wide, Alaska's fourth largest settlement is stretched along the coast in typical Panhandle fashion. A revamped "historical district" is dressed for the tourists who support the newest growth industry, but much of Ketchikan remains economically and psychologically depressed. The adjustment to a tourism-based service economy has not been easy for some since salmon fishing and timber—the region's traditional industries—have fallen on increasingly hard times.

◪ ORIENTATION AND PRACTICAL INFORMATION

Ketchikan rests on **Revillagigedo Island** (ruh-VIL-ya-GIG-a-doe), 235 mi. southeast of Juneau and 90 mi. northwest of Prince Rupert, BC. If you're coming from Canada, **roll back your watch** an hour to Alaska Time. Ketchikan caters to the travel elite, as evidenced in the location of the cruise ship docks (downtown) and the ferry docks (2 mi. north of town). The town and its attractions are quite spread out and public transportation is inconvenient, so renting a bike is a good idea.

TRANSPORTATION

Airplanes: A small ferry runs from the **airport,** across from Ketchikan on Gravina Island, to just north of the state ferry dock (every 15min.; in winter every 30min; $2.50). **Ketchikan Airporter** (225-5429) shuttles between the airport and the ferries ($12.50). **Alaska Airlines** (225-2141 or 800-426-0333) makes daily flights around Alaska and to Juneau ($95-140). **Taquan Air** (225-8800; www.alaskaone.com/taquanair) and **Pro-Mech Air** (225-3845 or 800-850-3845) make regular flights to Metlakatla, Prince of Wales Island, and other regional destinations. Much of the surrounding wilderness can be reached only by boat or float plane, for hire through the Visitor Center. **Island Wings** (225-2444 or 888-854-2444; www.ktn.net/iwas) knows the worthwhile destinations.

Ferries: Alaska Marine Highway (225-6181 or 800-642-0066; www.akmhs.com), at the far end of town on N. Tongass Hwy., with bus access to town (see below). To: Wrangell (5½hr.; $24); Skagway (43hr.; $98) via Haines (40hr.; $92) via Juneau (30hr.; $74) via Sitka (18hr.; $54) via Petersburg (7½hr.; $38).

Public Transportation: The main bus route runs a loop between the airport parking lot near the ferry terminal and Dock and Main St. downtown. Stops about every 3 blocks. M-F every 30min. 5:15am-9:45pm. Sa 1 per hour 6:45am-8:45pm, Su 8:45am-3:45pm. $1; students, seniors, and children 75¢.

Taxis: Sourdough Cab, 225-5544. **Alaska Cab,** 225-2133. **Yellow Taxi,** 225-5555. All offer charter rates (about $26 per 30min.). From downtown to the ferry costs about $8.

Car Rental: Alaska Rent-A-Car, airport and in-town locations (225-5000 or 800-662-0007). Free local pick-up and delivery. $45 per day; unlimited mileage. Must be 22. **Southeast Auto Rental** (225-8778). Free delivery. $40 per day. Must be 21.

LOCAL SERVICES

Visitor Information: 131 Front St. (225-6166 or 800-770-3300; www.visit-ketchikan.com), on the cruise ship docks, offers maps, info on charter and touring companies, an ATM, public restrooms, and payphones. Open 8am-5pm year-round, and when the cruise ships are in. **Southeast Alaska Visitors Center (SEAVC),** 50 Main St. (228-6220), has beautiful exhibits on regional ecology and native history worth the $4 entry fee (free in the off-season). The invaluable trip planning room run by the U.S. Forest Service has a library, maps, brochures, and an extremely helpful staff to help you plan your dream trip. Information is available on wilderness destinations in throughout the Southeast and Alaska. Open Apr.-Sept. daily 8am-5pm; Oct.-Mar. Tu-Sa 8:30am-4:30pm.

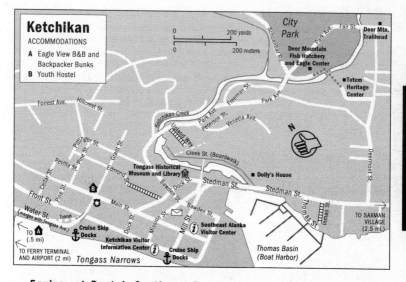

Ketchikan

ACCOMMODATIONS

A Eagle View B&B and
   Backpacker Bunks
B Youth Hostel

City Park

Deer Mtn. Trailhead

Deer Mountain Fish Hatchery and Eagle Center

Totem Heritage Center

Forrest Ave.

Hillcrest St.

Ketchikan Creek

Park Ave.

Peterson St.

Freeman St.

Venetia Ave.

Park Ave.

Prhinger St.

Pine St.

Revilla St.

Grant St.

Cedar St.

Pine St.

Edmond St.

Leland Way

Creek St. (Boardwalk)

Tongass Historical Museum and Library

Stedman St.

■ Dolly's House

Stedman St.

Deermont St.

Front St.

Main St.

Bawden Dock St.

Bawden St.

Dock St.

Mission St.

Mill St.

Thomas St.

Ihman St.

Water St. (merges with Tongass Ave.)

Tunnel

TO **A** (.5 mi)

Cruise Ship Docks

Ketchikan Visitor Information Center

Southeast Alaska Visitor Center

Cruise Ship Docks

TO FERRY TERMINAL AND AIRPORT (2 mi)

Tongass Narrows

Thomas Basin (Boat Harbor)

TO SAXMAN VILLAGE (2.5 mi)

0   200 yards
0   200 meters

N

SOUTHEAST ALASKA

Equipment Rental: Southeast Exposure, 515 Water St. (225-8829; www.southeastexposure.com), opposite the tunnel. Bikes $6 per hr., $14 per half day, $22 per day. Kayak rentals require a 1½hr. orientation class ($30). Singles $40 per day, $35 per day for 6+ days; doubles $50 per day, $45 per day for 6+ days. $200 damage deposit. Guided kayak tours available. Open daily May-Sept. 7am-5pm. **Southeast Sea Kayaks** (225-1258 or 800-287-1607; www.ktn.net/sea kayaks), in the visitor center. Singles $40 per day, $30 per day for 6+ days; doubles $50 per day, $40 per day for 6+ days. $200 damage deposit. Trip-planning service available. **The Pedalers** (225-0440), on the boardwalk around the corner from the SEAVC. Bikes $6 per hr., $15 for 4 hr., $22 per day. Open daily 8am-5pm. **Alaska Wilderness Outfitting,** 3857 Fairview Ave. (225-7335), rents camping kits that include a Coleman stove, lantern, mess kit, cooler, and extras ($20 per day). Call ahead daily 7am-10pm. Fishing licences are available at **Plaza Sports** (225-1587) in the Plaza Shopping Center.

Bookstores: SEAVC houses the **Alaska National History Association Bookstore** (228-6233), an authoritative source for Alaskana. **Parnassus,** 5 Creek St. (225-7690), and the **Village Source,** 807 Water St. (225-7600), serve hippies, hepcats, and healers.

Library: Ketchikan Public Library, 629 Dock St. (225 3331), south of Creek St. **Internet Access** available with a visitor's card ($5 with a $20 deposit). Open M-W 10am-8pm, Th-Sa 10am-6pm, Su 1-5pm.

Laundromat/Public Showers: Highliner Laundromat, 2703 Tongass Ave. (225-5308). Wash $2, dry 25¢ per 7min. Showers $2 per 10min. Open daily 6am-10pm. **Seamen's Center** (247-3680), on Mission St. next to St. John's. A warm, dry lounge for salty sailors. Wash and dry 75¢ each, showers $1. Open daily 5-8pm. **The Mat,** 989 Stedman St. (225-0628), ¾ mi. from downtown, offers TV, a play area, 10 lb. of laundry for $10, and showers $2.50 per 15min. Open daily 6am-11pm.

Public Pool: Kayhi Pool, 2160 4th Ave. (225-2010). Call for free swimming hours.

Public Radio: 105.9 FM.

Weather: 874-3232.

EMERGENCY AND COMMUNICATIONS

Emergency: 911. **Police:** 225-6631, at Main and Grant St. across from the hostel.

Pharmacy: Downtown Drugstore, 300 Front St. (225-3144). Open M-Sa 8am-6:30pm, Su 10am-6pm.

SOUTHEAST ALASKA

Hospital: Ketchikan General Hospital, 3100 Tongass Ave. (275-5171).

Post Office: (225-9601), next to the ferry terminal. Open M-F 8:30am-5pm. **Substations** at the corner of Race and Tongass Ave. (225-4153; open M-F 9am-6pm, Sa 9am-5pm) and in the Trading Post at Main and Mission St. (225-2349; open M-Sa 9am-5:30pm). **ZIP Code:** 99901.

Internet Access: See **Library,** above. **Soapy's Station,** 425 Water St. (247-9191), inside Sockeye Sam's by the tunnel, is open whenever there's a cruise ship in. $4 per 30min., $6 per hr. **Cyber by the Sea,** 5 Salmon Landing #217 (at the end of the cruise ship dock). $10 per hr., $6 minimum. $25 for 5 hr. Open M-Sa 9am-6pm, Su 10am-4pm.

Area Code: 907.

▞ ACCOMMODATIONS

There is little in the way of budget lodging in Ketchikan. The **Ketchikan Reservation Service** (800-987-5337; fax 247-5337) provides info on B&Bs (singles from $60). Because of boardwalk stairs, these accommodations aren't wheelchair accessible.

Ketchikan Youth Hostel (HI) (225-3319), at Main and Grant St. in the First Methodist Church. Busy, though the social scene is skimpy since the doors close at 11pm sharp. Bring a sleeping bag for the foam mats. Single-sex dorms and overflow in the sanctuary. Common area, 2 showers, kitchen, and free tea, coffee, and cookies every night. $8, nonmembers $11. 4-night max. stay when full. Lockout 9am-6pm. Lights out 11pm-7am. Call ahead if you're arriving on a late ferry, but make reservations. Open June-Aug.

Eagle View Bed & Breakfast and Backpacker Bunks, 2303 5th Ave. (225-5461). Take Jefferson Ave. uphill from Tongass, turn right on 5th Ave., a big brown house at the end of the street. Not as cheap as the hostel, but owner Dale gives guests free use of his kitchen, TV, sauna, BBQ, and hammocks. Laundry $2.50 per load. Less than a mile from the ferry docks, a long trudge up the hill rewards guests with a great view from the porch. Space for 10 with 2 doubles ($25), and two tent sites ($15 per person).

▞ CAMPGROUNDS

Ketchikan's campgrounds are really, really out of the way and you'll have to hike, hitch, or catch a cab since the bus doesn't go to any of these places.

Signal Creek Campground (USFS), 5¼ mi. from the ferry dock, mile 0.7 on Ward Lake Rd. Open Memorial Day to Sept. 24 sites: $8. Self-registration. Strict 7-day max. stay.

3 C's Campground (USFS), 5½ mi. from the ferry dock, mile 1 on Ward Lake Rd. Open mid-May to Sept. 4 sites: $8. Self-registration. Strict 7-day max. stay.

Last Chance Campground (800-280-2267), 7½ mi. from the ferry dock, mile 3 on Ward Lake Rd. 19 RV-friendly sites: $10. Self-registration. Reservations needed.

Settler's Cove, 16 mi. from the ferry dock, Mile 18.2 on the N. Tongass Hwy. 12 sites: $8. Self-registration. 7-day max. stay.

Clover Pass Resort (247-2234 or 800-410-2324), Mile 14 on N. Tongass Hwy. No tent sites. 30 Full hookups: $26. Reservations needed.

◖ FOOD

Most restaurants in town are mediocre, catering to cruise ship tourists. Restaurant hours vary with the ferry schedule, though the grocery stores are more consistent. **JR's,** closest to downtown at 407 Dock St., has a small selection (open daily 7am-11pm). **Tatsuda's IGA,** at the corner of Stedman and Deermont stocks groceries, liquor, and deli products (open daily 7am-11pm). **Carr's,** at the Plaza Shopping Center on Tongass near the ferry docks, is huge, has a pharmacy, and is open 24 hours.

The Pizza Mill, 808 Water St. (225-6646), through the tunnel, 2 blocks north of downtown. Personal pizzas with 2 toppings ($5.50). Split the "Generation X" with a disaffectedly hungry friend (12 in., $12). Open M-W and Su 11am-11pm, Th-Sa 11am-3am.

Linnie's Red Anchor Cafe and Deli, 1935 Tongass Ave. (247-5287). A healthy alternative to downtown seafood and burger joints, Linnie's serves homemade bread, sourdough pancake breakfasts, quiche, pies, and salads. Make-your-own sandwich/soup combo ($6). Open May-Oct. M-F 7am-3pm, Sa 8am-2pm; Nov.-Apr. daily 10am-3pm.

Burger Queen, 518 Water St. (225-6060), 1 block past the tunnel. The regal veggie burgers, chicken troika sandwiches, and guacamole cheddar burgers please the pickiest. Everything in 3 sizes ($2-8). Open in summer M-Sa 11am-8pm; in winter until 4pm.

Diaz Cafe, 335 Stedman St. (225-2257). This retro-style cafe offers an eclectic mix of Filipino, Chinese, and American food. Sandwiches ($5) come with fries or sticky rice with sweet-and-sour sauce. Dinner around $10. Daily specials. Open daily 10am-8pm.

◉ SIGHTS

Every summer day, thousands of travelers tumble down gangplanks into Ketchikan with little time to escape horse-drawn carriages and charter fishing boats. The official walking tour does little to improve the lot of disoriented tourists, but the town has much to offer. Ketchikan's primary cultural attraction is the **Saxman Totem Park,** 2½ mi. southwest of town on Tongass Hwy. (a short ride on the highway bike path or an $8 cab), home to Alaska's largest collection of totems. A Tlingit village founded in 1894, Saxman was only accessible by boat until a few decades ago. The community's longhouse is surrounded with recent and historic carvings up to 150 years old. The park is free and wheelchair accessible. Each pole's story is described in a $1 guide, available at the **Saxman Arts Co-op** down the hill. Local carvers work at the **Edwin C. Dewitt Carving Center** next door to the park.

At the **Totem Heritage Center,** 601 Deermont St. (225-5900), on the hill above downtown, a few poles are on display from the the largest collection of authentic pre-commercial totem poles in the U.S., brought here from Tlingit, Haida, and Tsimshian villages. (Open May-Sept. daily 8am-5pm, Oct.-Apr. Tu-F 1-5pm; $4, under 13 free. Wheelchair accessible.) A $7 combination ticket also provides

---

KNOW YOUR TOTEMS
Totem poles are everywhere in this part of the world—lurking in primeval forests, planted in local cemeteries, decorating cheap motels, even poking out from tourist-happy McDonald's. Many indigenous peoples have long used these intricate sculptures both to honor each other and to transmit over a thousand years of history and culture; some mortuary poles even contain ancestors' ashes. Each of the figures vertically stacked on the totem has a specific significance, depending on the artist's tribe. The following symbols represent local Haida and Tlingit myths:

Raven: The creator of humans and a trouble-making trickster, identifiable by his long, straight beak. When the world was dark, Raven stole the sun from an old chief, and is often depicted with an orb in his beak.

Eagle: The second most important mythological figure, signifying peace and friendship. His hooked beak distinguishes him from Raven.

Bear-Mother: With one cub between her ears and another between her legs, she links the tribes of Eagle and Raven.

Beaver: Distinguished by a flat tail and two large front teeth. Beaver is often associated with Eagle.

Bear and Wolf: Remarkably similar, with sharp teeth and a high forehead. Both caused a lot of trouble (and still do) in their relationships with humans.

Killer Whale: Often shown with a seal in its mouth, the large-finned and razor-toothed orca stands for strength.

admission to the **Deer Mountain Tribal Hatchery and Eagle Center** (225-6761) across the creek, run by the Ketchikan Indian Corporation (made up of Tlingit, Haida, and Tsimshian residents). Captive eagles swoop and catch king and silver salmon leaping their way upstream in an enclosed waterway. (Open daily May-Sept. 8:30am-4:30pm. Wheelchair accessible.)

The colorful stretch of houses perched on stilts along **Creek Street** make up "historic" Ketchikan, once a thriving red-light district where, as tour guides quip, sailors and salmon went upstream to spawn. Actresses in black fishnets beckon passersby into **Dolly's House,** 24 Creek St. (225-6329), a brothel-turned-museum. Antiques now sit in hideaways where Dolly once stashed money, bootleg liquor, and customers during police raids. (Typically open until 2:30 or 4:30pm. $4.) At the **Tongass Historical Museum,** 629 Dock St. (225-3331), in the same building as the library, old photos and films tell the story of Ketchikan's history as a Native fish camp, mining center, fishing port, timber town, cannery site, and transportation hub. (Open daily mid-May to Sept. 8am-5pm. $2. Wheelchair accessible.)

The distant **Totem Bight State Historical Park,** 10 mi. north of the ferry docks on the N. Tongass Hwy., shelters Tlingit and Haida totem poles and a beautifully painted longhouse. (Free. Wheelchair accessible.)

◪ ♫ NIGHTLIFE, ENTERTAINMENT, AND EVENTS

During the day most of Ketchikan moves to the rhythm of the cruise ships, but at night Ketchikan's bars belong solely to the locals and are great places to meet people. Be careful, though—bar brawls start pretty easily around here. At **The Potlatch** (225-4855) on Thomas St., at the docks off Stedman St. just south of downtown, uprooted railroad-car seats grant a place to sip a beer beneath the blackboard messages from one boat crew to another (open daily 11am-midnight or 2am, depending on the crowd). Younger drinkers gather at the **First City Saloon** (225-1494) on Water St. toward the ferry terminal, for Guinness and a variety of microbrews. Local bands play here (Th-Su). Drink first. (Open daily 9am-2am.) The hard-to-find **Hole in the Wall Marina,** 7500 S. Tongass Ave. (247-2296), is rich in local flavor, with more varieties of beer (18) than chairs (4). Fish off the dock and drink while your catch cooks (open when you get there).

Like Mom always said, you don't have to drink to have a good time. Among other works, Ketchikan's **First City Players** (225-4792) perform the bawdy *Fish Pirate's Daughter*, a super-melodrama about Prohibition-era Ketchikan, to sell out crowds at the Main St. Theatre, 338 Main St. (July-Aug. F 8pm; $15, students $12). The annual **Timber Carnival** enlivens a boisterous 4th of July with speed-chopping, axe-throwing, and other fantastic lumberjack feats. On the second Saturday in August, the **Blueberry Arts Festival** brings art, food, music, and wackiness to the streets, when locals compete in slug races and chewing gum competitions.

◪ OUTDOORS

The Ketchikan area wilderness offers boundless opportunities for the fisherman, hiker, or kayaker close to town. The SEAVC Trip Planning room (see p. 396) makes a great first stop. The U.S. Forest Service maintains **cabins** ($25-45 per night) and **shelters** in the Tongass National Forest that can be reserved at 877-444-6777 or www.reserveusa.com. Act quickly because these cabins fill up fast! USFS won't give you a prioritized list, but check in with Michelle at **Island Air** (see above) and she will fly you there (round-trip charters from $350 for 2 people).

From Ketchikan, a trail up 3001 ft. **Deer Mountain** makes a good dayhike. Walk up the hill past the city park on Fair St.; the marked trailhead branches off to the left just behind the dump. The ascent is steep but manageable, and on a rare clear day the walk yields sparkling views of the sea and surrounding islands. While most hikers stop at the 2½ mi. point, the trail continues above the treeline to the summit along an 8 mi. route that passes Blue Lake and leads over John Mountain to Little Silvis Lake and the Beaver Falls Fish Hatchery. This portion of the trail is poorly

COME CLOSER, AND LISTEN WELL... Though those who brave the bush usually fear only two animals—massive brown bears and vampire mosquitoes—if you pay heed to Tlingit stories told in hushed whispers around late-night fires, you will surely fear another. Anyone who's lived in the Southeast long enough isn't quick to dismiss their existence—or their danger. According to Tlingit tales, if you wander too close to the water or too far into the woods, the Kushtakas (KOOSH-ta-kuz)—land otters by day, humans by night—will snatch you and turn you into one of their own. Paddling in skate-skin canoes under cover of night, the Kushtakas rescue fishermen lost at sea, only to take them to the eerie land of the otter people, never to be seen again. Then, disguised as these lost men, the otter people come ashore to ensnare the fishermen's loved ones. Recognize a Kushtaka in otter form by its faint two-toned whistle, or in human guise by the fur between its fingers. Just don't stare too long, or you'll be overwhelmed by its numbing power...

marked, and snow and ice are common on the peaks even in the summer; only experienced and well-prepared hikers should attempt it. An A-frame cabin between Deer Mountain and John Mountain can be reserved through the Forest Service desk at SEAVC (see p. 396). The trail emerges 13 mi. from Ketchikan at the Beaver Falls power station parking lot.

A less strenuous, more family-oriented hike is the **Perseverance Lake Trail.** The trail begins approximately 100 ft. before the entrance to the Three C's Campground, and makes a leisurely 2¼ mi. climb to Perserverance Lake. The trail passes through muskeg, old-growth sitka spruce, hemlock, and cedar, and the lake is great for trout fishing. For cold swimming, a sandy beach, and picnic tables, head to **Ward Lake** at the Signal Creek Campground. A 1¼ mi. trail circles the grassy pond. Bikers can explore surrounding logging roads.

Defy the laws of rainy weather and gravity at **Kave Sport's indoor climbing gym,** 615 Stedman Ave. (225-5283; kavesp@hotmail.com). Over 2300 sq. ft. of climbing walls challenge beginners and expert climbers alike. (Open M-F 6am-10pm, Sa 8am-8pm, Su noon-6pm. $8 per day. Equipment rental up to $9.)

NEAR KETCHIKAN: METLAKATLA

Fifteen minutes by float plane from Ketchikan's cruise ship docks, Metlakatla, or "calm channel where the fog drifts in and out" in Tsimshian (SIM-she-an), is perched on the western flatlands of the Annette Islands Reserve. The Metlakatla Indian Community is the island's only settlement, founded in 1887 by an Anglican lay-minister and a group of Tsimshian natives who were given permission by President Grover Cleveland to escape white encroachment on the coast. Gently sloped beaches on the bay and a nearby waterfall made Metlakatla suitable for settlement, and the 86,000 bear-less acres of unspoiled lakes and mountains, and 700 mi. of shoreline, still beckon to visitors. A waterfront visitor information center is expected to be completed by the summer of 2000, and the Tourism Director at the **Municipal Office Building** (886-4441), on Upper Milton St., offers maps and info on cultural events and sites. The permit required to overnight on Annette Island is available here (open M-F 8am-4:30pm).

🔁 **PRACTICAL INFORMATION, CAMPGROUNDS, AND FOOD. Pro-Mech Air** (in Metlakatla 886-3845; in Ketchikan 225-3845; 800-860-3845) offers several 15-minute flights per day from Ketchikan to "Met"; frequency and number vary, so call ahead ($37 round-trip). **Taquan Air** (886-6868) offers comparable service at a slightly higher price. The **Alaska Marine Highway** (800-624-0066; www.akmhs.com) visits the island six times a week, twice on Saturdays (1¼hr.; $14). The ferry terminal is a short walk from town.

Overnight lodging is steep ($80-100 per night) though **camping** is free and generally acceptable out of sight of the road. Check with the Municipal Offices first and tell the Metlakatla police where you are going. South End, 2½ mi. down Airport

Road (at Nob Hill Rd.), has campsites in an old-growth forest area. Farther down Airport Rd. (10 miles out of town), camping is available at Davidson Point, the island's southernmost tip. Camping is also available at Scout Lake and beyond the cemetery at Pioneer Park (follow Western Ave. out of town until it becomes an unpaved road), though the underbrush is thick and the ground wet.

Ethel's B&B (886-5275) and **Uncle Fred's Cafe and Inn** (886-5007) are both on Western Ave. past the longhouse, and rent doubles for around $90 a night. Uncle Fred's (daily 11am-7pm) is also the closest thing in town to a sit-down restaurant, serving gourmet burgers ($7-10), salads, and daily specials that include homemade cheesecakes and chowder. The **Chester Bay Cafe** (886-5233) specializes in pizza. Other B&Bs are the **Annette Inn Bed and Breakfast** (886-5360) and **Bernita's Bed and Breakfast** (886-7563). The **Metlakatla Hotel and Suites** (886-3456, or 886-3458) offers singles and doubles for cheaper prices than the B&Bs, but without the charm. **Leask's Market,** close to the waterfront on Western Ave., has a full range of grocery items (open M-F 10am-6pm, Sa 10am-5:30pm, Su noon-5pm).

Metlakatla has no public transportation, but John and Fran Major offer a **taxi service** (886-5241, pager 228-3986), "$3 one-way, $5 round-trip anywhere." Hitching is reportedly easiest on the weekends when locals go out on picnics.

⚡ OUTDOORS AND SIGHTS. Bald eagles catch fish beyond the algae-speckled tidal flats beyond the cemetery and the boardwalk, picnic tables, and ropeswing of **Pioneer Park,** down the rocky beach that parallels Western Ave. The view from atop **Yellow Hill** (named for the unique color of its rusting iron ore deposits) offers splendid vistas of Annette Island and a glimpse of Ketchikan on a clear day. The boardwalk trail to it begins 2 mi. out of town on Airport Rd. Just past the ferry terminal at the other end of town, the water pipeline leads up **Purple Mountain.** From the dam at the top, numerous well-worn trails lead to the peak.

A visit to Metlakatla would not be complete without a tour of the community's **longhouse** on Western Ave. Four Metlakatla Tsimshian clans (Killerwhale, Wolf, Eagle, and Raven) have consented to sharing one longhouse. Dance groups practice and perform, and local artists practice, teach, and display their skills in the company of a collection of beautifully painted bentwood box drums, the only one of its kind in the world. Investigate the mural on the waterfront side of the building by local artist Wayne Hewson to see how many totems you can count in it (hint: there are more than three). The free **Duncan Museum** (in a bright yellow cottage near the waterfront) was once the home of William Duncan, one of the community's founders. The museum houses some of his personal effects, and photographs and curios from early Metlakatla. (These sites have no regular hours—see the Tourism Director at the Municipal Offices for permission to enter.)

MISTY FIORDS NATIONAL MONUMENT

The jagged peaks, plunging valleys, and dripping vegetation of **Misty Fiords National Monument,** 20 mi. east of Ketchikan, make biologists dream and outdoors enthusiasts drool. Only accessible by kayak, power boat, or float plane, the 2.3-million-acre monument offers superlative camping, kayaking, hiking, and wildlife viewing. Walls of sheer granite, scoured and scraped by retreating glaciers, rise up to 3000 ft. and encase deep saltwater bays. More than 12 ft. of annual rainfall and a flood of runoff from large icefields near the Canadian border feed the streams and waterfalls that empty into two long fjords, **Behm Canal** (117 mi. long) and **Portland Canal** (72 mi. long), on either side of the monument.

Seasoned **kayakers** navigate the harsh currents between Ketchikan and Behm Canal and paddle straight into the monument. Novices can contact **Alaska Cruises,** 220 Front St. (225-6044), to have themselves and their gear dropped off at the head of Rudyard Bay during one of four weekly sightseeing tours ($175 per person). Southeast Sea Kayaks (see p. 397) arranges similar transportation ($175-200 per person), books forest service cabins, and sells a trip-planning package with topographical maps for kayaking, fishing, and other activities ($14). If you want to do the planning yourself, the folks at SEAVC are a great resource (see p. 397). **Walker Cove, Punchbowl Cove,** and **Rudyard Bay,** off Behm Canal, are choice destinations for paddlers, though the waters are frigid and wide stretches of the coast lack good shelter or dry firewood. A slew of expensive charter operations offer trips from $125. Alaska Cruises offers an 11-hour boat tour with three meals ($155). Combination boat/flight tours last six hours ($195). **Island Wings** (see p. 396) has one of the best and cheapest flightseeing trips ($125). Call the Ketchikan Visitor Center for more info on local charters.

Camping is permitted throughout the monument, and the Forest Service maintains four free, first-come, first-served shelters and 14 cabins ($25). Write or call the **Misty Fiords Ranger Station** (907-225-2148) at 3031 Tongass Ave., Ketchikan, AK 99901, for information on these sites and reservations of the cabins, or ask the folks at the SEAVC trip planning room or Southeast Sea Kayaks.

PRINCE OF WALES ISLAND

Prince of Wales Island sits less than 30 mi. west of Ketchikan, beneath a thick rainforest canopy broken only by mountain peaks, patches of muskeg, and swaths of clear-cutting. Tongass National Forest and Native American tribal groups manage most of the island, which is criss-crossed with logging roads. Apart from these scars, a great deal of the island remains swaddled in virgin forest. You must allow at least a few days to access the wilderness and remote Forest Service cabins.

On an island this large, smaller only than Hawaii and Kodiak in the U.S., exploration requires a good set of wheels. The 1800 mi. of logging roads are perfect for mountain biking or tooling around in a 4x4 or all-terrain vehicle. Rentals on the island are expensive, so it's less taxing to bring a bike or truck over on the ferry. Pricey charter companies reel in fishermen, hunters, kayakers, and scuba divers, though independent travelers can set off on their own with maps and some help from the Forest Service (see below). Be sure to get permits for fishing and hunting, and to know where tribal lands end and National Forest begins.

There are three main towns on Prince of Wales: Craig, Klawock, and Thorne Bay. Craig is on the west side of the island with most of the tourist resources. Underinspiring Klawock lies 7 mi. east, while underwhelming Thorne Bay is 43 mi. farther east on the other side of the island. Hollis, where the ferry docks, is 31 mi. southeast of Craig and has no facilities to speak of, so come with a means of getting over to Craig or be ready to call a taxi service. There is only one paved road connecting these towns—stick to it and you can't get lost.

PRINCE OF WALES ISLAND: CRAIG

Craig, on the west coast of the Island, is home to most charter services, the district ranger station, a number of very nice and pricey hotels, and a couple of commendable restaurants. Apart from these niceties, there's little reason to linger. The surrounding area is clearcut and there are no convenient hiking trails.

◪ **PRACTICAL INFORMATION. Float planes** fly directly into Craig from Ketchikan, though schedules vary; call for more detailed information. **Promech Air** (826-3845 or 800-860-3845) flies the route for $74 or round-trip $140. **Taquan Air** (826-8800) flies for $91 or round-trip $182. The **Alaska Marine Highway** (800-642-0066; www.akmhs.com) runs from Ketchikan to Hollis (2¾hr.; about 1 per day in summer; $20, ages 2-11 $12, car $41). **Jackson Cab** (755-2557) runs between Hollis and Craig for about $25. **Klawock, Craig, Hollis Transporter** (826-3151, pager 755-3602) charges the same price for one person, but only $18 per person for two or more people. Call ahead for pick up. **Practical Rent-a-Car,** 250 Hilltop Dr. (826-2424), has 4x4s available for $50 per day and 30¢ per mi., or $75 per day with unlimited mileage. They also rent cars for use in the Craig/Klawock area only for $55 per day (unlimited mileage). You must be 21. (Open daily 8am-6pm.) At the same desk, **Holiday Rentals** rents fishing skiffs for $100 a day ($115 with trailer). **Wilderness Rent-a-Car,** 1 Easy St. (826-2205 or 800-949-2205), rents with 4x4s for $79 per day (unlimited mileage). You must be 25. At the same desk, **Log Cabin Sporting Goods** rents canoes and kayaks for $10 per day. (Open M-Th and Sa 8am-6pm, F 8am-7pm, Su 10am-3pm.) **Visitor information** is available at the **Craig Chamber of Commerce** on Easy St. (826-3870; www.princeofwalescoc.org; open M-F 10am-3pm). The **Forest Service Office** (826-3271), at 9th Ave. and Main St., gives the skinny on caves, camping, and 20 wilderness cabins and recreation sites on the Island. (Open M-F 7am-5pm.) The **Log Cabin** (826-2205) sells **fishing and hunting licenses.** (Open M-Th and Sa 8am-6pm, F 8am-7pm, Su 10am-3pm.) The **National Bank of Alaska** (826-3040), by the post office on Craig-Klawock St., has the only **ATM** in town. **Voyageur Bookstore** (826-2333), on Cold Storage Rd. in the Southwind Plaza, deals in cappuccino, books, and music. The owners sometimes wager coffee on games of chance. (Open M-F 7:30am-7pm, Sa 9am-7pm, Su 10am-5pm.) The **Library** (826-3281) is on 3rd St. (Open Tu-F 10-noon and 1-5pm; M-Th 7-9pm, Sa noon-3pm.) The **Seaview Medical Center** (826-3257) is on 3rd St. (Open M-F 9am-5pm, Sa 9am-2pm.) **Emergency:** 911. The **Police** (826-3330) are opposite the library. **State Police:** 755-2918. The **Post Office** (826-3298) is on Craig-Klawock St. beside the Thompson Supermarket. (Open M-F 8:30am-5pm, Sa noon-2pm.) **ZIP Code:** 99921. **Area Code:** 907.

⌐ ACCOMMODATIONS, CAMPGROUNDS, AND FOOD. Although most of the island falls within the free camping zone of Tongass National Forest, Craig is surrounded by private tribal lands where camping is prohibited. The **TLC Laundromat and Rooms** (826-2966), on Cold Storage Rd. behind the supermarket, offers affordable slumber space (singles $40; doubles $52). The laundromat (wash $2, dry 25¢) also has **showers** ($2.50 per 5min.; open M-Sa 7am-8pm).

Visits to **Tongass National Forest** may last up to one month, as long as campers spend no longer than two weeks at any one site. Contact the **Forest Service Station** in Craig (see above) or Thorne Bay (828-3304) for more information on the 20 **wilderness cabins** they maintain. Cabins are $25-45 per night. Advance reservations are required and can be made at 877-444-6777 or www.reserveusa.com. A few cabins are road/trail accessible, but most are only reachable by boat or float plane. The Forest Service also maintains two campgrounds on Prince of Wales Island: the newly built **Harris River Campground** halfway between Hollis and Craig, and the **Eagle's Nest Campground,** halfway between Craig and Thorne Bay. Both campgrounds have toilets, hand-pumped water, cooking grates, canoe launches, picnic tables, and RV parking. Sites cost $8 in summer.

There are several places to eat in town. **Donte's** (826-3880), at the corner of Third and Front St., serves burgers ($6), Chinese food (entrees $10) and breakfast. (Open Su-M 6am-4pm, Tu-Th 6am-7pm, F-Sa 4pm-8pm.) **Ruth Ann's** (826-3376), on Front St., has affordable breakfast and lunch options ($6-8), but dinner prices skyrocket upwards of $18. (Open daily 6am-10pm.) Perhaps the healthiest option in town is **T&K's Sub Marina** (826-3354), on Easy St., which offers a "healthy choice menu" and low-fat salads as well as standard greasy spoon options. (Soup and half-sub combo $7. Open daily 7:30am-6pm.) Groceries are at the **Thompson Supermarket** (826-3394), on Craig-Klawock St., where a salad bar and a deli complement a good spread of fruits and veggies (open M-Sa 7:30am-8pm, Su 9am-7pm).

◪ OUTDOORS AND UNDERGROUND. The **Craig Dive Center** (826-3481 or 800-380-3483), at 1st and Main St. in Craig, offers a two-tank dive for groups of four ($125 per person). Owner Craig lives in Craig—coincidence or destiny? **Island Adventures** (826-2710) rents kayaks for $20 per day. **Log Cabin** (826-2205 or 800-949-2205) rents canoes and kayaks for $10 per day. **Harris River Trading Co.** (530-7058) rents canoes on-site at the Harris River between Hollis and Craig. Before setting out, see the Forest Service for info on trails, cabins, and safe **hiking** and **biking** tips for local logging roads.

The most distinctive of the island's attractions is **El Capitan Cave**, North America's deepest cavern. The cave bores into the limestone bedrock of Prince of Wales and is adorned with striking marble outcroppings. Deep within the cave, speleologists (not to be confused with amateur spelunkers) have recently uncovered the remains of a 12,000-year-old grizzly bear. Free two-hour tours start behind the gate 150 ft. inside the cave, and require a hard-hat and flashlight. Make reservations with the Thorne Bay Ranger District (828-3304). The cave is about a three-hour drive from Craig or Thorne Bay. (Tours May-Sept. W-Su at noon, 1pm, and 3pm. Off-season tours available with 14-day advance notice.)

WRANGELL

Wrangell is the only part of Alaska to have been ruled by four different nations. In 1834, the Russian-American Company ousted a Tlingit village on an island near the mouth of the Stikine River to build a fort. Six years later, the British-owned Hudson Bay Company took out a lease on the Russian garrison. Then, in 1867, the U.S. purchased Alaska from Russia, and took control of the fort. During the three gold rushes of the next 40 years, the Stikine River became a crucial transportation corridor to Canada's interior. John Muir, the proto-ecologist responsible for the establishment of the first national parks in the U.S., called the 55-mile Stikine canyon "a Yosemite that just kept going and going."

Anyone emerging from heavily touristed Ketchikan or Juneau will find Wrangell a quiet and welcome respite. Logging and fishing are still the mainstays of this community of 2500 or so, and though they do get some cruise ship traffic, they have yet to import tourism wholesale and don't seem to miss it. (One recent mayoral candidate ran with the slogan, "It's a dirty little town and I aim to keep it that way.") The town's attractions are convenient enough for a brief visit during a ferry layover, but plentiful enough to merit a longer stay. Note that locals take their day of rest very seriously: almost everything is closed on Sunday.

▐ ORIENTATION AND PRACTICAL INFORMATION

Wrangell rests on the northern tip of 30-mile-long Wrangell Island, 85 mi. north of Ketchikan, and 150 mi. south of Juneau. The town is small and easily walkable. The **ferry** docks are at the north end of town; the **airport** is 1½ mi. east, over the hill.

Airplanes: Alaska Air (874-3308 or 800-426-0333) flies daily to: Petersburg ($78), Juneau ($132), and Ketchikan ($112). **Sunrise Aviation** (874-2319) offers flightseeing over the Stikine River ($285).

Ferries: Alaska Marine Highway (874-2021 or 800-642-0066), at Stikine Ave. and McCormack St. Frequent service to: Sitka (13hr., $38), Juneau (13-26hr., $56), and Ketchikan (6hr., $24). Open 2hr. before arrivals. Lockers 25¢.

Taxis: Star Cab (874-3622). $5 to the airport, $10 to the Rainbow Falls Trail.

Car Rental: Practical Rent-A-Car (874-3975; fax 874-3911), on Airport Rd. near the airport. Compacts $43 per day; vans $53 per day; unlimited mileage. Must be 21.

Visitor Information: Chamber of Commerce (874-3901; www.wrangell.org), on Front St. by the cruise ship docks. Open M-F 10am-4pm. A huge calendar across the street lists events.

Outdoor Information: District Forest Service Station, 525 Bennett St. (874-2323), ¾ mi. east of town. Maps and info on hiking, canoeing, kayaking. Reserves local Forest Service cabins (see p. 41). Open M-F 8am-5pm. **Alaska Department of Fish and Game** (874-3822), in the green Kadin Building on Front St. **Ottesen's True Value** (874-3377), on Front St., sells licenses.

Library: (874-3535), on 2nd St. Free Internet access. Open M and F 10am-noon and 1-5pm, Tu-Th 1-5pm and 7-9pm, Sa 9am-5pm.

Public Radio: 101.7 FM **KSTK** is a community-run radio station always in need of DJs. If you'd like to play a set, inquire at their office at the corner of Church and Michael St.

Laundromat and Public Showers: A curious abundance of laundromats. **Thunderbird Laundromat,** 233 Front St. (874-3322). Wash $2, dry 25¢. Open daily 6am-8pm.

Same laundry prices and showers ($2 per 8min.) at **Churchill Laundromat,** also on Front (open 7am-9pm).

Public Pool: (874-2444) at Wrangell High School on Church St. Hours vary; closed Sunday. Indoor pool, weight room, gym $2, under 18 $1.25; racquetball $6 per pair.

Emergency: 911. **Police:** (874-3304), in the Public Safety Building on Zimovia Hwy.

Pharmacy: Stikine Drug, 202 Front St. (874-3422). Open M-F 10am-5:30pm, Sa 10am-2pm.

Hospital: (874-3356) at Bennett St. and 2nd Ave.

Post Office: (874-3714), at the north end of Front St. Open M-F 8:30am-5pm, Sa 11am-1pm. **ZIP Code:** 99929.

Internet Access: See **Library,** above. **Seapac.net,** 208 Front St. $7.50 per hr., 30min. minimum. Open M-F 8:30am-5pm, Sa 11am-1pm.

Area Code: 907.

ACCOMMODATIONS AND CAMPGROUNDS

The chamber of commerce has a list of **B&Bs** in town. Closest to the ferry is **Fenimore's** (874-3012; www.seapac.net/~wrgbbb), with private entrances and baths, TVs, fridges, microwaves, and loaner bikes (singles $65, doubles $70). If you've got a car or other means of transportation, well-maintained, well-located, and free Forest Service campgrounds are a fine choice. **Shoemaker Bay,** 4½ mi. south of town, accommodates tenters and RVs. **Nemo,** 14 mi. south on Zimovia Hwy., has choice views of the water. The 28 area **Forest Service cabins** (see **Outdoor Information,** above), many of which are along the scenic Stikine, are a steal at $25-40 a night.

Wrangell Hostel, 220 Church St. (874-3534), 5 blocks from the ferry terminal in the Presbyterian Church; just look for the neon cross. Showers, kitchen, and spacious common room. 20 foam mats on the floor: $10. Blanket and pillows $1. Reception open daily 5pm-9am. 10pm curfew extended for late ferry arrivals. Closed in winter.

City Park, 1½ mi. south of town on Zimovia Hwy., immediately beyond the cemetery and baseball field. Picnic tables, shelters, drinking water, toilets, and a beautiful view of the water. 8 free sites. 1-day max. stay. Open Memorial Day to Labor Day.

Alaskan Water RV Park, 241 Berger St. (874-2378 or 800-347-4462; fax 874-3133), off Zimovia Hwy., ½ mi. from town. Clean and convenient, but gravelly and with scant privacy. 6 full hookups: $12. Showers $2.50. Open mid-Mar. to mid-Oct.

FOOD

Wrangell has very limited options for vegetarians or picky eaters; the standard in town is pizza and burgers. **Benjamin's IGA Supermarket,** 223 Brueger St. (874-2341), off Outer Dr., has groceries, a bakery, and a deli (open M-Sa 8am-8pm). For bulk health food, head to **Homestead Natural Foods** (874-3462), ½ mi. north of town on Evergreen Ave., on the way to the petroglyphs. Call first on nice days in case Rosemary decides to close up and go kayaking.

Ruby's Restaurant, 316 Front St. (874-2002), is the self-proclaimed "healthiest restaurant in town." Sandwiches, pitas, and salads for around $7. Huge breakfast buffet on Sunday $9. Arrive early for the best pickings. Open Tu-Sa 11am-8pm, Su 10am-2pm.

J&W's, 120 Front St. (874-2120). Good, messy burgers ($4) and fried mini-burritos ($2) at the window. Fries with that for $1. Creative alternatives include salmon and shrimp burgers ($5) and 13 flavors of shakes ($2.65). Open M-Sa 11am-7pm, Su noon-7pm.

Hungry Beaver Pizza/Marine Bar (874-3005), on Front St. just before the inner harbor. Where hard-drinking fishermen and high school grease-eaters mix. One-person pizzas from $5.50. Low-key waterfront bar is a last refuge for late-night diners. Kitchen open daily 4-10pm. Bar open daily 10am-2:30am. $3 showers and the requisite laundromat.

◼ SIGHTS

SHAKES ISLAND. If the ferry schedule gives you only 45 minutes in Wrangell, a walk out to **Shakes Island** is about your only option. Here you'll find a replica of turn-of-the-century Tlingit Chief Shakes's **longhouse**, built during the Depression by the Civilian Conservation Corps without the aid of a sawmill or a single nail, and surrounding **totem poles.** *(Follow Front St. to Shakes St., where a short bridge leads to the island. Tel. 874-3747. Open in summer whenever a cruise ship docks for 1hr., or by appointment for a donation of $20 or more. Regular donation $2.)*

PETROGLYPH BEACH. Faint, weather-worn stone carvings by some of the region's first inhabitants adorn the beach. Some are simple circles and spirals, while others illustrate complex facial patterns. Archaeologists are uncertain of the age of these petroglyphs, but local tradition maintains that they were in place before the Tlingit reached the harbor. Best viewing is at low tide. With new money acquired from the beach's recent designation as a State Historical Site, an interpretive center and wheelchair ramp are due by the summer of 2000. *(Three-quarters of a mile north of the ferry terminal on Evergreen Ave.)*

WRANGELL MUSEUM. Houses collections of Native American artifacts, a communications and aviation room, and an exhibit on the region's natural history. *(Temporarily in the basement of the community center on Church St. Tel. 874-3770. $2, under 16 free. Open in summer M-F 10am-5pm, Sa 1-5pm, Su for cruise ships; in winter Tu-F 10am-4pm.)*

◼ OUTDOORS

Wrangell's **Forest Service Station** offers free, guided day-long wildlife viewing excursions every Saturday during the summer, and is an invaluable trip-planning resource. Like many islands in the Southeast, Wrangell is criss-crossed with dozens of logging roads ideal for mountain biking.

The closest trail to town is the short (½ mi. round-trip), quiet **Mt. Dewey Trail,** which winds its way through hemlocks and cedars to the top of Mt. Dewey, overlooking the town and Zimovia Strait. Look for the sign on the right off Third St. To get to all the other trails around Wrangell you will need some sort of transportation. Three miles beyond City Park on Zimovia Hwy., the local favorite **Rainbow Falls Trail** starts on the cool, spongy floor of an old-growth rain forest, and climbs ½ mi. over boardwalk and stairs to a scenic view of the 100 ft. Rainbow Falls. Beyond that, the **Institute Creek Trail** follows a boardwalk for another 2¾ mi., paralleling a series of impressive waterfalls (1hr. from the trailhead) before breaking into several muskeg openings on a ridgetop overlooking Shoemaker Bay. A three-sided shelter, available for overnight use on a first-come, first-served basis, sits on the ridge at the end of the trail. The trailhead can be reached by taxi ($10) or by bike path. Marie at **Rainwalker Expeditions** (874-2549, marieo@seapac.net) will conduct guided tours of some of the island's better sites for around $10 per hour or $60 per day (includes transportation and bag lunch).

Kayakers, canoers, and sightseers will share John Muir's admiration for the **Stikine River.** The Stikine is one of the fastest navigable rivers in the region, and is crowded: only very experienced paddlers should attempt to run it. The Forest Service has maps and info. There are six Forest Service cabins throughout the Stikine Delta and two bathing huts at **Chief Shakes Hot Springs,** a few miles upriver. Unfortunately, besides paddling yourself, the only way to get to these and other attractions on the Stikine, such **Shakes Glaciers,** is by charter boat or plane. For a full listing of charter boat services (Wrangell has over 24) that serve these and other destinations, contact the Chamber of Commerce, which also provides info on **scuba-diving, whale-watching,** and **fishing** and **hunting** trips. Single travelers and small groups may have better luck getting a group together when a cruise ship is in town. **Breakaway Adventures** (874-2488; www.breakawayadventures.com) charges $135 per person for daytrips up the Stikine to the bear observatory or to the glaciers; **Stickeen Wilderness Adventures** (874-2085 or 800-874-2085; www.akgetaway.com), the town's longest-running charter service, runs the same trips for $155 per person (3 person minimum).

PETERSBURG

Drawing visitors and transient workers alike, the harbors of Petersburg teem with fresh salmon and generations of fisherfolk. Native Americans once had fish camps on the island but never settled permanently. In 1897, Norwegian immigrant Peter Buschmann saw opportunity in the natural harbor, abundant fish, and convenient glacier ice around Petersburg, and built a cannery. Now P-Burg claims one of the world's largest halibut fleets and a strong Scandinavian legacy. The tiny Wrangell Narrows that lead to Petersburg spare the fishing town from cruise-ship-induced touristification. The town has little in the way of cheap indoor accommodations, but plentiful summer work, some nice hiking, and a chance to see a Southeast fishing town at work can make it worth planting stakes.

🛈 ORIENTATION AND PRACTICAL INFORMATION

Petersburg is on **Mitkof Island.** If you're looking for **Nordic Dr., Main St.,** or **Mitkof Hwy.,** you're probably on it: the main drag goes by all three aliases. The ferry docks are a mere 1 mi. south of downtown. Cabs to town run about $4, to Tent City $6.

Airplanes: Alaska Airlines, 1506 Haugen Dr. (772-4255 or 800-426-0333), flies twice a day to Juneau ($114) and Seattle, WA ($346). Next door, **LAB** (772-4300) often beats these prices on its several flights per day to Juneau.

Ferries: Alaska Marine Highway, Mile 0.9 Mitkof Hwy. (772-3855 or 800-642-0066; www.akmhs.com), 1 mi. from the town center. To: Ketchikan (10hr., $38); Sitka (10hr., $26); Wrangell (3hr., $18); and Juneau (8hr., $44). Open 1½hr. before ferry arrivals.

Harbormaster: (772-4688) at North Harbor. VHF channel 16.

Taxis: City Cab (772-3003). Rates start at $4. Tent City residents are known to take the free Hammer & Wilkan supermarket shuttle bus (a.k.a. the **Hammer and Wilkan Taxi**) from their start point to the market and from the market to their destination, taking care of grocery shopping and transport in one go. (Call 776-2421, use one of their courtesy phones at South, Middle, and North Harbors, or stop by their satellite store at 218 N. Nordic Dr. to arrange a ride. Open M-Sa 7am-8pm, Su 7am-7pm.)

Visitor Information: (772-4636; www.petersburg.org) at 1st and Fram St. Houses a replica of the world-record 126½ lb. king salmon. Open in summer M-Sa 9am-5pm, Su noon-4pm; in winter M-F 10am-2pm.

Outdoor Information: Forest Service (772-3871), on 1st St., above the post office. Info and cabin reservations (see p. 41). Open M-F 8am-5pm. **Dept. of Fish and Game:** 772-3801, Sing Lee Alley. Licenses available at **The Trading Union** (772-3881) on N. Nordic Dr.

Equipment Rental: Northern Bikes (772-3978), next to the Scandia House. $4 per hr., $20 per day. Open M-Sa 11am-5pm, Su 10:30am-5pm. **Tongass Kayak Adventures** 106 N. Nordic Dr. (772-4600), rents kayaks. Singles $40; doubles $50 (3-day min.)

Public Showers: The harbormaster at North Harbor (772-4688) has what are rumored to be the hottest showers in all of Southeast AK ($1 per 7½min.). Also at **Glacier Laundry** ($2; towels $1), **Tent City, Twin Creek RV Park,** and **LeConte RV Park** (see below).

Library: (772-3265) at Haugen and Nordic Dr. above the Fire Hall. Free Internet access is very popular, but you can sign up the day before. Open M-Th noon-9pm, F-Sa 1-5pm.

Laundromat: Glacier Laundry (772-4400), at Nordic and Dolphin. Wash $2, dry 25¢ per 5min. Open daily 6am-10pm. Also at **Twin Creek** and **Leconte RV Parks** (see below).

Employment: Petersburg Employment Service (772-3791; www.labor.state.ak.us), at Haugen Dr. and 1st St. Petersburg is a great place to find temporary work in the canneries. Day labor is also often needed (see p. 64). Open M-F 10am-2pm.

Emergency: 911. **Police:** 16 S. Nordic Dr. (772-3838). **State Police:** 772-3100.

24hr. Refuge: At the **Homestead Cafe** (see **Food,** below).

Hospital: Petersburg Medical Center (772-4291), at Fram and N. 1st St.

Internet Access: At the **Library,** and **AlasKafe** (see Food, below) for $4 per 30min., $7 per hr.

Public Radio: 100.9 FM.

Post Office: (772-3121) at Haugen and Nordic Dr. Open M-F 9am-5:30pm, Sa 11am-2pm. Lobby with stamps open M-F 7am-8pm, Sa 8am-6pm. **ZIP Code:** 99833.

Area Code: 907.

ACCOMMODATIONS AND CAMPGROUNDS

Tent City, the only place near town for backpackers, is often crammed with summer cannery workers. The next nearest campground is Ohmer Creek, 22 mi. south of the ferries (water and pit toilets; $6). The Forest Service has info on free, unserviced campsites in the Tongass National Forest. The visitor center lists **B&Bs;** prices are high, thanks in part to a 10% accommodations tax.

Nordic House B&B, 806 Nordic Dr. (772-3620; fax 772-3673; www.nordichouse.net), ¼ mi. north of the ferry terminal. Three lovely rooms, shared kitchen and bath, and a sitting room with a view to cheer those pining for the fjords. Free continental breakfast, best eaten on the deck overlooking the docks. Singles from $65; doubles from $75. Reserve July-Aug.

Petersburg Bunk & Breakfast, 805 Gjoa St. (772-3632; ryn@alaska.net). New in town, close to both muskegs and the harbor. Bunks with shared bath in a private home $25, including light breakfast and taxes.

Tent City (772-9864), on Haugen Dr. past the airport, 2 mi. from the ferry. Established by the city as a cannery workers' homestead, this ramshackle collection of tarps and wooden platforms rests atop a muskeg swamp. The canneries have since built bunkhouses for their workers, but many still call Tent City home. They keep it tidy and safe in conjunction with the site manager, who stops in several times a day. The cannery workers are a gruff-looking lot, but if you sit down at their campfire, they'll take you in. Several sites are set aside for short-term visitors. Amenities include a pay phone, 3 hotplates, a communal shelter, fire pits stocked with wood, water, toilets, 4 showers (75¢), and soda machines. $5, $30 per week, $125 per month. Quiet hours 10pm-noon. Open May-Sept.

LeConte RV Park (772-4680), downtown at the corner of Fourth St. and Haugen Dr. Tent sites $7, hookups $25. Water, dump station, coin-operated showers and laundromat.

Twin Creek RV Park (772-3244), at Mile 7 of Mitkof Hwy. Steps away from foliage, fishing, and fun (hiking). Showers, laundry, fishing tackle. Full hookups $18.85.

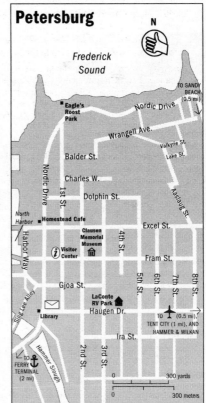

Petersburg

N

Frederick Sound

TO SANDY BEACH (0.5 mi)

Eagle's Roost Park

Nordic Drive

Wrangell Ave.

Valkyrie St.

Balder St.

Lake St.

Nordic Drive

Charles W.

Dolphin St.

Aaslaug St.

1st St.

North Harbor

Homestead Cafe

Excel St.

Clausen Memorial Museum

4th St.

Harbor Way

Visitor Center

Fram St.

5th St.

6th St.

7th St.

8th St.

Gjoa St.

LaConte RV Park

Sing Lee Alley

Library

Haugen Dr.

TO ✈ (0.5 mi), TENT CITY (1 mi), AND HAMMER & WILKAN

Ira St.

TO FERRY TERMINAL (2 mi)

Hammer Slough

2nd St.

3rd St.

0   300 yards

0   300 meters

FOOD AND NIGHTLIFE

Although swimming in fish, Petersburg still charges a whole lot for seafood. Grocery-shopping at **Hammer & Wikan,** 1300 Haugen Dr. (772-4246; open M-Sa 7am-8pm, Su 7am-7pm), earns a free shuttle ride (see **Taxis,** above).

Homestead Cafe (772-3900), on Nordic Dr. at Excel St., opposite the general store. The best diner in the Southeast bar none. Hear how the day's catch went or how the high school teams are doing. Just you try to finish a stack of their pancakes ($2.50), or the prodigious plate of biscuits and gravy ($5.50). Open M-Sa 24hr.

Alaskafe (772-5282), on Excel St. above Costal Cold Storage. Overdosing on Norse culture? The Fellini sandwich (mozzarella and gorgonzola cheeses, artichoke hearts, and sun-dried tomatoes; half $5.50, whole $7.75) should set you right. Live band, open-mic jam and poetry Sa nights. Open M-F 7:30am-5pm, Sa 7:30am-midnight.

Kito's Kave (772-3207), on Sing Lee Alley, is the liveliest place in town, providing fishermen and cannery workers after hours with sustenance (draft beers $3-4) and live music (W-Sa nights). Open M-F 10am-2am, Sa 10am-3am, Su noon-2am. **El Rincon** (772-2255), inside, serves $2 tacos. Open in summer M-Sa 11am-9pm, Su noon-8pm.

Helse-Health Foods and Deli (772-3444), on Sing Lee Alley off Nordic Dr. With flowers, little wooden stools, and cheerful owners, this quiet, friendly place has conversation and healthy food enough to go around. Soup and bread $5, "Cheese Breeze" (avocado, shrimp, mushrooms, and havarti) $7. Lots of juices. Open M-F 7:30am-3pm, Sa 10am-3pm.

Coastal Cold Storage (772-4177), at 306 N. Nordic Dr., houses a tasty seafood deli in addition to a fresh seafood market; see what looks good before you order. Creative entrees like the halibut enchilada run about $6.50. Open M-Sa 7am-6pm, Su 7am-5pm.

SIGHTS AND EVENTS

This is one of the best places on the Panhandle to see a fishing town at work. The heart of the year-round operations is down at **North Harbor,** near the middle of town on Excel Ave., where you can wander the docks, talk to local fishermen, read the bulletin boards, and savor the smells. Amateurs will discover that **jigging** for herring from the docks is alarmingly fun.

On the third full weekend in May, Petersburg joins in joyous celebration of Norway's 1905 independence from Sweden. During this **Little Norway Festival,** mock Vikings dance, sing, parade, hunt their own furs, wear horns, sail in longboats, and violently board an airplane in traditional Viking style. Memorial Day weekend brings the hallowed **Salmon Derby.** This search for the specially tagged fish—and its accompanying $10,000 prize—has sadly been unsuccessful in recent years. Stay away from open spaces on the **4th of July** in Petersburg: celebrations feature a **competitive herring toss.**

OUTDOORS

Only a handful of Petersburg's many trails are readily accessible by foot. The Forest Service has trail descriptions, maps of logging roads suitable for mountain biking, and makes reservations for cabins. The 4 mi. (one-way) **Raven's Roost Trail** leads to a very popular cabin by the same name ($25), offering glimpses of the Coast Mountains across Frederick Sound on clear days. Beware the many bears (see p. 44). The trail starts by the orange-and-white water towers behind the airport, about a mile out of town.

Several worthwhile trails begin at the state dock on neighboring **Kupreanof Island** (½ mi. across the Wrangell Narrows). Many charter operators in town ferry folks across the narrows and rent skiffs, but this can cost more than $100. You might try asking at the harbormaster's office about boats making the crossing with space for an extra passenger (a small number of commuters live on the island). To the west of the dock, the planked **Petersburg Creek Trail** runs 11½ mi. up to **Petersburg Lake,** through a wilderness area to a Forest Service cabin. If the tide is high, you can go up the creek a few miles by boat to cut the hike down to 6½ mi. The **Petersburg Mountain Trail,** which branches east from the dock, is a challenging 3½-mile trek ending with a steep climb to spectacular views from Narrows Peak.

Tongass Kayak Adventures (see above), rents sea kayaks and offers guided tours up Petersburg Creek (5hr. tours daily June-Aug.; $85 per person includes gear). **Pacific Wing** (772-4258) makes a one hour, $70 **flightseeing** tour of the Lakhanti Glacier.

JUNEAU

The gold deposits that spurred the founding of this town, now the state capital, were first shown to prospectors Richard Harris and Joe Juneau by Auke Bay Tlingits in 1880. The two named the new settlement Harrisburg, but miners arriving the next summer were so annoyed by Harris's habit of staking multiple claims that they took to calling their new home Juneau instead. Today's eclectic mix of politicians, artists, and fisherman lend the city an air of progressiveness not usually found in the fishing communities of Southeast Alaska. Accessible only by water and air, the city has happily avoided the urban sprawl that plagues Anchorage. The tourist industry, however, is firmly established: Juneau is the second busiest cruise ship port in the U.S. after Miami. Hundreds of thousands of travelers per year come to visit nearby Mendenhall Glacier and Glacier Bay, and locals and tourists alike make good use of area hiking trails. Be prepared to share the beauty.

■ ORIENTATION AND PRACTICAL INFORMATION

Juneau sits on the Gastineau Channel opposite Douglas Island, 650 mi. southeast of Anchorage and 900 mi. northwest of Seattle. **Franklin St.** is the main drag downtown. **Glacier Hwy.** connects downtown, the airport, the residential area of the Mendenhall Valley, and the ferry terminal. The ferry docks and the airport are both far from town (14 and 9 mi., respectively), and public transportation is inefficient.

TRANSPORTATION

Airplanes: Juneau International Airport, 9 mi. north of town on Glacier Hwy. **Alaska Airlines** (789-0600 or 800-426-0333) flies to: Anchorage ($114-236), Sitka ($98), Ketchikan ($140), and Gustavus ($42). The visitor center has schedules for other airlines. See **Buses,** below, for transport to and from the airport.

Ferries: Alaska Marine Highway, 1591 Glacier Ave. (465-3941 or 800-642-0066; fax 277-4829). Ferries dock at the Auke Bay terminal, 14 mi. from the city on the Glacier Hwy. To: Ketchikan (18-36hr., $74), Sitka (9hr., $26), Haines (4½hr., $24), and Bellingham, WA (2½ days; $226). Lockers 25¢ per 48hr. Open 3hr. before all departures.

Buses: Capital Transit (789-6901), runs about hourly from downtown to Douglas Island, Mendenhall Valley, and Auke Bay. From the airport, take the hourly express service from the northern end of the terminal (M-F 8:10am-5:10pm); evenings and weekends, catch the non-express from the Nugget Mall (a 10min. walk; ask at the airport for directions). The stop closest to the ferry dock is 2 mi. away, across from DeHart's General Store. Schedules available at municipal building, library, Davis Log Cabin, and on buses. $1.25, under 5 free; exact change only! Runs M-Sa 7am-10:30pm, Su 9am-6:30pm. **Island Waterways** (463-5321) runs to downtown hotels from the **airport** until 8:30pm. $5. **MGT Ferry Express** (789-5460), meets all ferries in big blue school buses, and drops off at the airport and some hotels ($5). Call 6-8pm a day in advance to reserve a ride from any major hotel to the airport or ferry. From the hostel, the Baranov is the closest hotel.

Harbormaster: 586-5255, Auke Bay 789-0819.

Taxis: Taku (586-2121). **Alaska** (780-6400). Approximate rates from downtown to: airport $15, ferry $20, Mendenhall glacier $15, brewery or hatchery $7.

Car Rental: Rent-A-Wreck, 9099 Glacier Hwy. (789-4111), next to the airport. $35 per day plus 15¢ per mi. after 100 mi. Must be 21. Free pickup. Open M-F 8am-6pm, Sa-

Su 9am-5pm. **Evergreen Ford** (789-9386), near the airport, rents cars for $40 per day. Free pickup. M-F 8am-6pm, Sa 9am-5pm.

VISITOR AND FINANCIAL SERVICES

Visitor Information: Davis Log Cabin Visitor Center, 134 3rd St. (586-2201 or 888-581-2201; fax 586-6304; jcvb@ptialaska.net), at Seward St. Open June-Sept. M-F 8:30am-5pm, Sa-Su 9am-5pm; Oct.-May M-F 8:30am-5pm. The **Capital City Weekly** (www.capweek.com), available at the center, has the lowdown on free local events.

Outdoor Information: Forest Service Information Center, 101 Egan Dr. (586-8751; fax 586-7928), in Centennial Hall. Trip-planning services and Forest Service cabin reservations (see p. 41). The $4 *Juneau Trails* booklet lists many 5-12 mi. hikes. Open M-F 8am-5pm. **Alaska Dept. of Fish and Game,** 1255 W. 8th St. (465-4112; licensing 465-2376), close to the bridge. Open M-F 8am-5pm. **Sportfishing Hotline** (465-4116).

Currency Exchange: Thomas Cook, 311 Franklin St. (586-5688). Also sells travelers checks. Open M-F 9am-5pm, Sa 10am-2pm.

American Express: 8745 Glacier Hwy. (800-770-2750). Open M-F 10am-7pm, Sa 10am-6pm.

LOCAL SERVICES

Outdoor Equipment: Mountain Gears, 126 Front St. (586-2575), opposite McDonald's. Mountain bikes $6 per hr., $25 per 24hr. Open M-F 10am-6pm, Sa 10am-5pm. **Juneau Outdoor Center** (586-8220), on Douglas Island, delivers kayaks anywhere in the area. Singles $35 per day; doubles $45 per day. **Alaska Paddle Sports** (463-5678), at 800 6th St., also rents kayaks (singles $40 per day, doubles $50), whitewater rafts ($75 per day), and dry suits ($15 per day). Gear for purchase is available at the high-end **Foggy Mountain Shop,** 134 N. Franklin St. (586-6780; open M-Sa 9am-6pm) and less expensive **Outdoor Headquarters,** 9131 Glacier Hwy. (800-478-0770 or 789-9785), near the airport. Open M-F 9am-7pm, Sa 9am-6pm, Su 10am-5pm; in winter closed Su.

Luggage Storage: $1 per bag at the hostel. Lockers at the ferry terminal (see above).

Bookstore: Hearthside Books, 254 Front St. (789-2750), caters to all tastes. Open M-Sa 9am-8pm, Su 10am-8pm. **The Observatory,** 235 2nd St. (586-9676), is a used and rare bookstore with many maps. Open M-F 10am-5:30pm, Sa noon-5:30pm.

Library: (586-5249) over the parking garage at Admiral Way and S. Franklin St. Free Internet access. Open M-Th 11am-9pm, F-Su noon-5pm. The **State Library,** on the 8th floor of the State Office Building (at the end of 4th St.), has net access with less of a wait. Open M-F 9am-5pm. The **Alaska Historical Library,** on the same floor, holds a large collection of early Alaskan photographs. Open M-F 1-5pm.

Gay/Lesbian Information: Southeast Alaska Gay and Lesbian Alliance (586-4297). Juneau has about the only "out" gay and lesbian community in Southeast Alaska. SEAGLA publishes *Perspective,* available at **Rainbow Foods.**

Laundromat and Public Showers: Dungeon Laundrette (586-2805), at 4th and Franklin. Wash $1.50, dry $1.50; free detergent. Open daily 8am-8pm. **Alaskan Hotel,** showers $3.

Weather: 586-3997. **Public Radio:** 104.3 FM, 103.4 FM, or 101.7 FM.

EMERGENCY AND COMMUNICATIONS

Emergency: 911. **Police:** 210 Admiral Way (586-2780), near Marine Park until Feb., 2000. New location TBA. Tourist permits available for 48hr. **parking** in a 1hr. zone.

Crisis and Suicide Prevention Hotline, 586-4357. Open M-F 9am-5pm.

Rape and Abuse Crisis Line (AWARE), 800-478-1090. 24hr.

Pharmacy: Juneau Drug, 202 Front St. (586-1233). Open M-F 9am-9pm, Sa-Su 9am-6pm.

Hospital: Bartlett Memorial, 3260 Hospital Dr. (586-2611), off Glacier Hwy. halfway between downtown and the airport.

Internet Access: See **Library,** above. **Myriad Cafe** (see **Food,** below), $8 per hr.

Post Office: 709 W. 9th St., 99801 (586-7987). Open M-F 9am-5:30pm.

Area Code: 907.

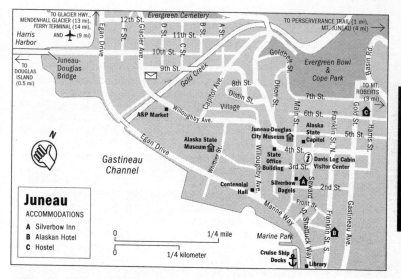

Juneau
ACCOMMODATIONS
A Silverbow Inn
B Alaskan Hotel
C Hostel

ACCOMMODATIONS AND CAMPGROUNDS

Affordable accommodations are limited; book ahead if possible. The **Alaska B&B Association** (586-2959; www.wetpage.com/bbaaip), can help you find a room (from $65). The two beautiful Forest Service campgrounds are easily accessible by car.

Juneau International Hostel (HI), 614 Harris St. (586-9559), at 6th St. atop a steep hill. A beautiful facility in a prime location with rigid rules. Do your chore or be swept out the door. Common area with comfy couches. 48 beds: $7, nonmembers $10. Kitchen; laundry (wash $1.25, dry 75¢); small charges for sheets, towels, soap, and detergent. Strict 9am-5pm lockout and 11pm curfew. 3-night max. stay if they're full. A $10 advance deposit by mail supplants phone reservations. No wheelchair access.

Alaskan Hotel, 167 Franklin St. (586-1000, in the Lower 48 call 800-327-9347), downtown. Meticulously restored 1913 hotel. Kitchenettes and TVs. Bar features live tunes and dancing. $67-84; less in winter. Laundry (wash and dry $1 each).

The Silverbow Guest Inn, 120 2nd St. (586-4146 or 800-586-4146; silverbo@alaska.net), just off Main St. Part B&B, part Euro-style urban *pension*. All rooms decorated in their own eclectic and cozy style. Cable TV, luxurious baths. Great free breakfast from the bagelry downstairs (see **Silverbow Bagels,** below). Doubles from $80, in winter half-price.

Mendenhall Lake Campground, on Montana Creek Rd. From town, take Glacier Hwy. north 9 mi. to Mendenhall Loop Rd.; take the right fork after 3½ mi. Bus drivers will stop within 2 mi. upon request (7am-10:30pm only). 6 mi. from the ferry. Stunning views of (and convenient trails to) the glacier. Firepits, water, toilets, showers, free firewood. 60 sites: $8, seniors $4. No reservations. 14-night max. stay. Open May 15-July 30.

Auke Village Campground (586-8800), 15 mi. from town on Glacier Hwy. (1½ mi. west of the ferry docks). 12 secluded sites near a scenic beach. Firepits, water, toilets, picnic tables. $8, seniors $4. No reservations. 14-night max. stay. Open May 1-Sept. 30.

FOOD

Juneau has the most varied food options in Southeast Alaska. **Juneau A&P Market,** 631 Willoughby Ave. (586-3101; open daily **24hr.**), near the Federal Building, is as good as it gets in these parts, grocery-wise, with an extensive salad bar ($3.30 per lb.) and jumbo deli sandwiches ($4.50). The healthy stuff is at **Rainbow Foods** (586-6476; open M-F 10am-7pm, Sa 10am-6pm, Su noon-6pm), at 2nd and Seward St.

RESTAURANTS

☒ **Armadillo Tex-Mex Cafe,** 431 S. Franklin St. (586-1880). A havén for locals, even in the heart of the cruise ship district. Southwest paintings and a few plastic armadillos watch over fast, saucy service and hot, spicy food. Heaping entrees $6-8. Mexican and home-brewed beers. Free chips and salsa. Open M-Sa 11am-10pm, Su 4-10pm.

The Back Room, 120 2nd St. (586-9866), behind the Silverbow Inn. No, this ain't New York, but they got the attitude. How's about Kielbasa and Pierogies ($10) for ya? Seriously folks, they got you and your vegetarian friends covered. A quiet spot for drinks on weekend nights. Theme movies on the big screen Tuesday and Thursday nights and Sunday afternoons ($3, including popcorn). Open for dinner Su-M 5-9pm, Tu-Th 5-10pm, F-Sa 5pm-midnight; lunch Tu-F 11:30am-2pm; and brunch Sa-Su 8am-2pm.

Myriad Cafe, 230 Seward St. (586-3433). All-organic, vegetarian- and vegan-friendly fare: the fish is macrobiotic, the meat hormone- and antibiotic-free, and even breakfast comes with tofu options. Salads and pasta from $6. Brown rice sushi $1.35, with seafood $1.75. Internet access $8 per hr. Open daily 9am-9pm, breakfast served until 5pm Sa-Su.

Thane Ore House Salmon Bake, 4400 Thane Rd. (586-3442). One of many cruise ship-oriented places a few miles out of town, but Mr. Ore will pick you up at your hotel. All-you-can-eat salmon, halibut, ribs, and fixings ($18.50). Open May-Sept. daily 11:30am-9pm.

CAFES

☒ **Silverbow Bagels,** 120 2nd St. (586-9866). The cheapest, best-smelling breakfast spot in town. The bagels are cheap (75¢) and good; the Super Cinnamon ($1.15) sates sweet-tooths. Hot drinks from espresso to chai. Soups ($3) and deli sandiches (from $4) for lunch. Open M-F 6:30am-5pm, Sa-Su 7:30am-3:30pm.

Valentine's Coffee House and Bakery, 111 Seward St. (463-5144). Mom's kitchen with a trendy feel and calico tablecloths. Fresh-baked calzones $6; burritos $6.25; salads $5; all sorts of breads. Open M-F 7am-6pm, Sa 8am-6pm, Su 9am-3pm.

◉ SIGHTS AND EVENTS

The excellent **Alaska State Museum,** 395 Whittier St. (465-2901), sets the standard for presenting and interpreting Native Alaskan art and artifacts. On the first floor, visitors are introduced to the history and culture of Alaska's four major native groups: Tlingit, Athabascan, Aleut, and Inuit. Exhibits on Alaska's maritime history and Russian Alaska, and contemporary art are upstairs. (Open May 18 to Sept. 17 M-F 9am-6pm, Sa-Su 10am-6pm; Sept. 18 to May 17 Tu-Sa 10am-4pm. $4, seniors and under 19 free.) The **Juneau Douglas City Museum,** on the corner of 4th and Calhoun St. (586-3572), houses hands-on exhibits on the gold rush days. (Open mid-May to Sept. M-F 9am-5pm, Sa-Su 10am-5pm; Oct to mid-May F-Sa noon-4pm and by appointment. $3 in summer, $2 in winter, seniors and under 19 free.)

The hexagonal, onion-domed 1894 **St. Nicholas Russian Orthodox Church,** on 5th St. between N. Franklin and Gold St., is home to a glorious altar. Services (Sa 6pm and Su 10am) are conducted in English, Old Slavonic, and Tlingit. (Open daily in summer 9am-5pm.) The **State Office Building (S.O.B.),** on Willoughby St., has an 8th-floor **observation platform** with a super view of Douglas Island and the channel. A large atrium on the same floor houses a totem pole and a massive pipe organ that gets fired up for occasional **free concerts** (see State Libary librarians for schedule).

Between mid-July and September, **Gastineau Salmon Hatchery,** 2697 Channel Dr. (463-5113 or 463-4810), is the place to be. The most impressive view of the spawning ladder and a brief talk are both available outside for free (open M-F 10am-6pm, Sa-Su noon-5pm; indoor aquarium $3; children $1). The **Alaska Brewing Co.,** 5429 Shaune Dr. (780-5866), gives free tours. Take the city bus to Lemon Creek, turn onto Anka Rd. from the Glacier Hwy., then make a right onto Shaune Dr. (Must be 21 or accompanied by a parent; tours every 30min. May-Sept. M-Sa 11am-4:30pm; Oct.-Apr. Th-Sa 11am-4:30pm.) The quiet, tree-shrouded **Shrine of St. Therese,** 23 miles north of town on the Glacier Hwy., on a small island connected by causeway to the shore, offers splendid views of the Chilkat Mountains. Beaches and the hike-accessible **Eagle Glacier** are this way, too, but no public transport is available.

Local musicians, from guitar-strumming folkies to African drum groups that get the whole crowd dancing, put on **free concerts** at Marine Park (on the waterfront by the cruise ship docks) on summer Friday nights from 7-8:30pm. The **Alaska Folk Festival** (364-2658; April 10-16, 2000) brings free, all-night jam sessions to Centennial Hall. **Juneau Jazz and Classics** (463-3378; May 19-28, 2000) enlivens various venues including a shipboard "blues cruise." The **Perserverance Theater** (364-2421), at 914 3rd St. on Douglas Island, puts on quality local theater, and plays work-shopped there have ended up on Broadway.

At the **Celebration 2000 Native Cultural Conference** (463-4844; June 1-3), native groups from across North America will share ideas and cultures. Arts and crafts exhibits, processions, and lectures will be open to the public.

🎵 NIGHTLIFE

The best bar in town is in the **Alaskan Hotel,** 167 Franklin St. It hosts frequent live Cajun and blues on weekend nights and is always packed on Thursdays for open mic, despite the shocking cost of beer ($5 pints; bar open daily noon-midnight). The **Red Dog Saloon,** 278 S. Franklin St. (463-9954), Juneau's most popular tourist trap, offers live music on weekends. Come winter, locals return to their customary stools between walls lined with bear pelts and tourist pelts (a.k.a. money). (Pints $4-5. Open Su-Th 10am-midnight, F-Sa 10am-1am; off-season Su-Th noon-midnight, F-Sa noon-1am.) Inebriated and frenzied flocks of hard-partying young things congregate at the city's only club, **Penthouse** (463-4141), on the 4th floor of the Senate Building. (F-Sa. $2 cover. Open Su-Th 9pm-1am, F-Sa 9pm-3am.) The **Hanger on the Wharf,** on Marine Way, is another youth magnet, with a huge selection of micro-brews. (Open M 4-11pm, Tu-W 11:30am-11pm, Th-Su 11:30am-1am.)

🏔 OUTDOORS

Juneau's trail system is extensive and crowded. To get the best view of the city, go to the end of 6th St. and head up the trail to the summit of **Mt. Roberts** (3576 ft.). It's a steep, 4 mi. climb, and higher elevations reveal panoramic views up the Gastineau Channel and west toward the Pacific, including nearby Mt. Juneau. A **tramway** also offers access to the vista but isn't worth the $20 round-trip. The much-vaunted **West Glacier Trail** begins off Montana Creek Rd., by the Mendenhall Lake Campground. The five- to six-hour walk yields stunning views of **Mendenhall Glacier** from the first step to the final outlook. The 3½ mi. (one-way) trail parallels the glacier through western hemlock forest and up a rocky cairn-marked scramble to the summit of 4226 ft. **Mt. McGinnis.**

A number of excellent trails start at the end of Basin Rd. The easy, wheelchair-accessible **Perseverance Trail** leads to the ruins of the Silverbowl Basin Mine and booming waterfalls. The end of the trail has been washed out, but should be open by the summer of 2000. Two miles along the Perseverance Trail, the more challenging **Granite Creek Trail** branches off and follows its namesake for 3¾ miles to a beautiful basin (1200 ft. elevation gain). The summit of Mt. Juneau lies 3 miles farther along a somewhat dangerous ridge run that offers terrific views of the Juneau icefield and the Chilkats. Attempt this run only with the proper gear and on a clear day. The shorter, steeper **Mt. Juneau Trail** is not recommended for the faint of heart or clumsy of feet: the path gets very slippery near the top, where there are no trees to grab hold of if you fall. The trail peels left from the Perseverance Trail about 1 mile from the trailhead (2 mi. one-way; elevation gain 3600 ft.). For more details on local hikes and trail safety, drop by the visitor center or any local bookstore to pick up *Juneau Trails* ($4). Rangers provide free copies of maps from this book at the Forest Service Information Center. Many trails in the area are well-maintained and excellent for **mountain biking.** Check with **Mountain Gears** for their difficulty rankings and suggestions. Biking off-road is sometimes prohibited. Whatever your mode of transport, be sure to keep the bears in mind (see p. 44).

The best excuse to spend money in town is on an incredible boat tour of **Tracy Arm**, a mini-fjord near Juneau. Known as "the poor man's Glacier Bay," Tracy Arm offers much of the same spectacular beauty and wildlife at well under half the cost. A typical tour includes sightings of humpback and killer whales, hundreds of seals, and bald eagles. The trip also passes by the **Sawyer Glaciers,** which frequently calve massive icebergs that glow blue in the sea. **Auk Nu Tours,** 76 Egan Dr. (800-820-2628), is the biggest tour company (8hr. tour $100, under 18 $60). The huge boats and resulting impersonality detract only slightly from the joy of the free lunch. **Wilderness Swift Charters** (463-4942; www.alaska.net/~tongass) might be worth the extra $25: their small boats take only 6 passengers, offer a smoked salmon lunch, and the chance to stop and listen to whales sing on an underwater microphone. **Adventure Bound,** 245 Marine Way. (463-2509 or 800-228-3875), whose mid-sized boat carries at most 28 passengers, strikes a happy medium with snacks and sandwiches ($100, under 18 $50. $20-off coupon in the Juneau visitor guide.)

Kayak Express, 4107 Blackberry St. (780-4591; www.adventuresports.com/asap/kayak/express), and **Alaska Discovery,** 5449 Shuane Dr. (780-6226 or 800-586-1911), provide rental kayaks, pickups and dropoffs in Glacier Bay and elsewhere, and **guided kayak tours** in about the same price range as the tour boats.

Southeast Alaska's only **ski area,** community-owned **Eaglecrest** (586-5284; www.juneau.lib.ak.us/eaglecrest), on Douglas Island, offers chutes, bowls, and marked runs. ($25 per day, high-schoolers $17, under 12 $12. Ski rental $20, children $14.) The Eaglecrest ski bus departs from the Baranov Hotel at 8:30am and returns from the slopes at 5pm on winter weekends and holidays (round-trip $6). In summer, the Eaglecrest **Alpine Summer Trail** is a good way to soak in the mountain scenery of virtually untouched Douglas Island.

TENAKEE SPRINGS

The largest town on the largely uninhabited Chichagof Island, Tenakee Springs' one street is a dirt path populated by children pushing grocery-laden wheelbarrows, older fisherman lolling outside the mercantile, and ATVs traveling under 10 mph. Residents thrive on the slow pace of this close-knit community of 100, and are quick to welcome visitors, even those heavy of pack and light of wallet. The few things to do here include sitting in the hot spring, talking to the locals, walking to Indian River, and sitting in the hot spring some more.

7 PRACTICAL INFORMATION. Both **Loken Aviation** (789-3331) and **Wings of Alaska** (736-2247) fly from Juneau almost daily (20min., $76). The state ferry *LeConte* makes a short stop in Tenakee on its route between Juneau and Sitka (7-8hr.; $22 either way). Residents adamantly oppose proposals to construct a road link with **Hoonah.** There are **no banks** in Tenakee and no one accepts credit cards.

The only public flush toilet in town is in the bakery (see below). There is one outhouse behind the bakery, and one behind the volunteer firehouse. The **library** (736-2248; open Tu and Th 11am-3pm, Sa noon-3pm) shares a building with the **city office** (736-2207). The **post office** (736-2236) is right off the dock (open M-F 7:30am-noon and 12:30-4:30pm, Sa 7:30-11:30am). **ZIP code:** 99841. **Area code:** 907.

ACCOMMODATIONS, CAMPGROUNDS, AND FOOD. There are two places to stay in town, and one of them costs thousands of dollars. The affordable option is to rent one of **Snyder Mercantile's** (736-2205) six cabins. Basic cabins sleep one to two comfortably; a larger cabin sleeps four to five (from $45 and $50; outhouses and cooking facilities, no bedding). A $70 cabin sleeps seven, with carpeting, fireplaces, and—my stars—a flush toilet. Reservations are essential in summer. **Camping** around Tenakee is bear-intensive; Chichagof Island has about one bear per square mile; only Admiralty Island has a denser population. Walking from the ferry dock, make a right turn on the dirt street. After about three-quarters of a mile, a boardwalk to the left leads to **Indian River.** Camping is not technically permitted along this trail, but there are tent sites, a shelter, and a picnic table. If there have been bear sightings, though, it isn't wise to camp near the river. In the event, locals generally don't mind if campers tent in the cleared-out woods or on the beach near the boat harbor at the far east end of the street.

Food options apart from the salmonberries along the main path include **Snyder Mercantile,** next to the ferry dock, which stocks a limited supply of groceries (open M-Sa 9am-noon and 1-5pm, Su 9am-2pm), and **Partytime Bakery** (736-2305), which bakes bread ($3.50) and cinnamon rolls ($2.50), and serves a diverse lunch menu, including spinach calzones ($2.50; open Th-M 8am-2pm). The **Blue Moon Cafe,** next to the bathhouse, is a Tenakee institution. If Rosie is there, and if she feels like cooking, she might cook ham and eggs ($7.50) or a chicken dinner ($9).

■ **THE HOT SPRING.** Tenakee's namesake and epicenter is a natural sulfuric hot spring that feeds the public bath house at the end of the ferry dock. You won't find this unglamorous blue building on any postcards, but miners and fishers have been soaking out aches and worries in these therapeutic 106°F (41°C) waters for more than a century, and the Tlingit maintained a winter settlement at the spring long before settlers arrived. Visitors can get in on the town gossip by bathing when the spring is busiest, at the start of each new gender shift. Bathers are required to be naked and reasonably clean. (Women-only 9am-2pm and 6-10pm; men-only 2-6pm and 10pm-9am; free, but donations are accepted at Snyder Mercantile.)

■ **SIGHTS AND OUTDOORS.** Tenakee's street extends several miles and is mostly closed off to motor vehicles. To the west, the road leads past a communal sawmill and small homesteads. Be careful to ask permission before entering private lands. A good distance from town, the path turns onto the shore of the inlet where smooth rocks make good footing for extended **beach walks.** In midsummer, silver salmon leap from the water. Use caution: bears travel this wide beach, too.

The rocks 15 minutes out from shore by kayak are home to dozens of **sea otters.** More seasoned paddlers ply **Tenakee Inlet,** at the end of which a 100-yard portage leads to **Port Frederick Inlet** and the town of **Hoonah.** This 40-mile trip offers unbroken shorelines, hidden coves, and local wildlife. Only the experienced should attempt it, however, since the waterways are often subject to squalls and bears are likely at beachside campsites. By the summer of 2000, **TK Custom** (736-2340) may have kayaks for rent, but you can also bring one across on the ferry for $9.

For **chartered expeditions** to fish, view wildlife, and learn about the area from someone who has been on the water around Tenakee all his life, contact **Jason Carter** (736-2311). Jason runs half- and full-day trips, and transports kayaks. Fishing and hunting licenses are available at **Snyder Mercantile.**

SITKA

Sitka's history suggests Alaska's in microcosm: for thousands of years a Tlingit settlement, it fell briefly and violently into Russian hands before becoming part of the U.S. After years of violent conflict between the Russians and the Tlingit at the close of the 18th century, "New Archangel," the capital of Russian America, emerged as a cultural and economic center. In 1867, Sitka was the site of the signing over of Russian Alaska to the U.S. The town has since regained its Tlingit name and strayed from its short-lived Russian heritage, despite the best efforts of tourism officials. College students, leather-faced fishermen, artists, cruise-ship passengers, a contingent of urbane ex-urbanites, and a still-thriving Tlingit community now share the town.

⛫ ORIENTATION AND PRACTICAL INFORMATION

Sitka is one of the westernmost cities in the Southeast. As in all Southeast Alaskan towns, the **ferry terminal** is a ways out of town—7 miles, to be exact. The **airport** is just a mile away across the O'Connell Bridge, on Japonski Island. The main drag is **Lincoln St.**, which connects the Sitka National Historical Park and Castle Hill.

Airplanes: Alaska Airlines (966-2422 or 800-426-0333; www.alaskaair.com). To: Juneau ($101-193); Ketchikan ($183-273); and elsewhere.

Ferries: Alaska Marine Highway, 7 Halibut Rd. (747-8737 or 800-642-0066; www.akhms.com), 7 mi. from town. To: Ketchikan (25hr., $54); Petersburg (10hr., $26); and Juneau (8¾hr., $26). Open 2hr. before arrival.

Local Transportation: Sitka Tours (747-8443) meets most ferries and planes ($3, round-trip $5); call ahead for a ride from town. **Tribal Tours** maintains a **Visitor Transit System** (747-7290) that services the major attractions, though most sights are within easy walking distance of one another. $5 per day.

Taxis: Sitka Taxi (747-5001) and **Arrowhead Taxi** (747-8888). About $13.50 from Sitka to the ferry, $6 to the airport; 50¢ per additional person.

Car Rental: A&A Car Rental (747-8228), on Sawmill Creek Hwy., has the lowest rates and a shuttle to the airport (free) and ferry ($10). $39 per day, unlimited miles. Must be 21.

Visitor Information: Sitka Convention and Visitors Bureau, 303 Lincoln St., suite 4 (747-5940; www.sitka.org). Open M-F 8am-5pm. A desk in the **Harrigan Centennial Building,** 330 Harbor Dr. (747-3225), is open daily in summer from 8am until the cruise ships leave.

Outdoor Information: Sitka Ranger District, 201 Katlian #109 (747-6671). Pick up the indispensable *Sitka Trails* ($4) and info on Forest Service cabins ($35-45 per night). Open M-F 8am-5pm. **Fish and Game Dept.,** 304 Lake St. #103 (fishing 747-5355, hunting 747-5449). **Mac's,** 213 Harbor Dr. (747-6970), sells licenses. Open M-Sa 8am-6pm, Su 9am-5pm. The **fire station,** 209 Lake St. (747-3233), loans **VHF radios** for use on extended backpacking and kayaking trips to those who file a trip plan.

Banks: On Lincoln St. behind the church: **Nations Bank of Alaska** (747-3226). Open M-Th 9:30am-5:30pm, F 9:30am-6pm. **24hr. ATM.**

Equipment Rental: Yellow Jersey Cycle Shop, 805 Halibut Pt. Rd. (747-6317), in the Pacific View Center, rents decent mountain bikes. $25 per 24hr., $20 per day for 2 or more days, $100 per week; call for hours. **Southeast Diving and Sports,** 105 Monastery St. (747-8279), rents clunky 5-speeds. $5 per hr., $20 per day; open M-Sa 10am-5:30pm. **Baidarka Boats** (747-8996; www.kayaksite.com), on Lincoln St. above Old Harbor Books. Single kayaks $25 per half-day, $35 per day; doubles $30 per half-day, $45 per day; less for longer rentals. Required 1hr. class for novices $30. Guided half-day ($50-100) and full-day ($70-150) tours. Open daily 8am-6:30pm; in winter shorter hours and closed Su. **Sitka Sound Ocean Adventures** (747-6375), in the big blue bus on the waterfront at Crescent Harbour, has similar rates and also rents skiffs from $85 per day.

Luggage Storage: The **fire station,** 209 Lake St., stores backpacks for free, as does the **Centennial Building,** 330 Harbor Dr. The **ferry terminal** has lockers (25¢ for 24hr.).

Bookstore: Old Harbor Books, 201 Lincoln St. (747-8808). Marine charts, **topographic maps,** and info on local arts events. Free copies of literary rags. Ecopolitical jeremiads on request. Open M-F 9am-6pm, Sa 9am-5pm, Su 9am-3pm.

Library: Kettleson Memorial Library, 320 Harbor Dr. (747-8708). Open M-Th 10am-9pm, F 1-6pm, Sa-Su 1-5pm. Great Alaskana and free Internet access.

Laundromats and Public Showers: Duds 'n' Suds Laundromat, 906 Halibut Point Rd. (747-5050), convenient to the hostel. Wash $1.75, dry 50¢ per 10min. Shower $2 per 10min. Open M-F 7am-8pm, Sa-Su 8am-8pm.

Hospital: Sitka Community Hospital, 209 Moller Dr. (747-3241).

Post Office: 338 Lincoln St., 99835 (747-8491). Open M-Sa 8:30am-5:30pm.

Internet Access: See **Library,** above. **Highliner Coffee** (747-4924), off Lake St. at the Seward Square Mall ($5.25 per 30min., $8.40 per hr.)

Area Code: 907.

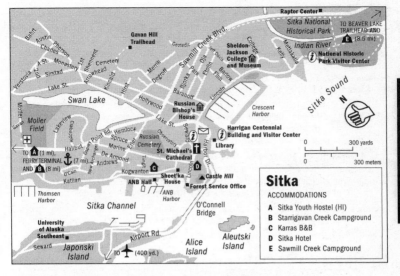

Sitka
ACCOMMODATIONS

A Sitka Youth Hostel (HI)
B Starrigavan Creek Campground
C Karras B&B
D Sitka Hotel
E Sawmill Creek Campground

ACCOMMODATIONS AND CAMPGROUNDS

Two recently renovated park service campgrounds are both far away. The visitors bureau has a list of Sitka's many **B&Bs** (from $50).

Sitka Youth Hostel (HI), 303 Kimshan St. (747-8356), in the United Methodist Church at Edgecumbe St. Find the McDonald's 1 mi. out of town on Halibut Point Rd., then walk 2min. up Peterson St. to Kimsham. 20 cots in basement dorms; no bedding. Kitchen, free local calls, and showers. $9, nonmembers $13. Lockout 9:30am-5pm. Curfew 11pm. 3-night max. stay. Open June-Aug.

Sitka Hotel, 118 Lincoln St. (747-3288; fax 747-8499; www.sitkahotel.com), downtown. Homey rooms with shared bath, cable, and free local calls. Coin laundry. Singles $50; doubles $55. Private bath $15 extra. Reserve 2 weeks in advance and request a view.

Karras Bed and Breakfast, 230 Kogwanton St. (747-3978). Bertha and Pete have been in the business a long time and know how to please, with huge breakfasts, laundry, private entrances, and big living rooms with views of the harbor. Good for large groups. Singles from $55; doubles from $70.

Sawmill Creek Campground, 8½ mi. south of town. Take Halibut Point Rd. to Sawmill Creek Rd. junction in Sitka. Follow Sawmill Creek Rd. to the pulp mill, then take the left spur for 1.4 mi. Trees, stream, solitude, picnic tables, fireplaces, pit toilets, and fishing in nearby Blue Lake. 11 sites. Free. Quiet hours 10pm-7am. 14-night max. stay.

Starrigavan Creek Campground, at the end of Halibut Point Rd., 1 mi. from the ferry, 8 mi. from town. Secluded RV and tent sites near a scenic estuary trail. Water, pit toilets. 30 sites: $8. 14-night max. stay. No vehicles 10pm-7am. Wheelchair accessible.

FOOD AND NIGHTLIFE

Find groceries, a pharmacy, and liquor at **Lakeside Grocery,** 705 Halibut Point Rd. (747-3317; open daily 6am-midnight). Pick up fresh seafood at the docks or ask nicely at **Seafood Producers Coop,** 507 Katlian Ave. (747-5811; open daily 9am-5pm), where unprocessed halibut and salmon run $2-3 per lb. **Evergreen Natural Foods,** 101 American Way (747-6944; open M-Sa 10am-6pm), sells granola ($2.50 per lb.).

Alaska Native Brotherhood (ANB) Hall (747-3359), 205 Katlian Ave. Since its founding by Christian Sitka natives in 1914, the ANB has stood for interracial understanding and native community development. Lunches of traditionally-prepared local fish and game are good and cheap ($5) and proceeds go to scholarships for local Native youth. Mouth-watering fry bread $1. Open in summer M-F noon-5pm.

The Backdoor, 104 Barracks St. (747-8856), behind Old Harbor Books. Popular hostelers' hangout with local art, unpredictable poetry readings, and occasional live accordion music. 12 oz. Buzzsaw (coffee with espresso) $2.25; homemade soup with bread $4; scones $1. Open M-Sa 7am-5pm and after-hours for performances.

The Mojo Cafe, 256 Katlian Ave. (747-0667), provides the food for the Backdoor. With an eclectic in-house bakery and over-achieving chef, you never know what smell will greet you at the door. Lunch specials are cheap ($3 pierogies) and vegetarian-friendly. A la carte dinner F and Sa $5-7. Open M-F 6:30am-2pm and F-Sa 5pm-8:30pm.

Mad Greek Bistro, 104 Lake St. (747-6818). One of Sitka's cheaper dinner options. A specialty pizza (like the Corinthian, with artichoke hearts, roasted peppers, goat and mozarella cheese; $16), and the Vegetarian Delight platter ($9), is more than enough for 3-4 people. Open M-Sa 11am-9pm, Su 4:30-9pm.

Ernie's Old Time Saloon, on Lincoln St. across from the Pioneer Home, has room enough for revelling fishermen and rowdy hostelers. Live hoe-down country sets everyone a-hoppin' Th-Su. 9pm-closing. Pool and darts, too. Pints $4. Open daily until 2am.

👁 SIGHTS AND EVENTS

Sitka is one of the few cities in Southeast Alaska with indoor attractions that serve as more than just an excuse to get out of the rain. The onion-domed **St. Michael's Cathedral,** built in 1848 by Bishop Innocent, hearkens back to Sitka's Slavic era. Services are open to the public and conducted in English, Tlingit, and Old Slavonic. (Hours vary with cruise ship schedules; generally open M-Sa 11am-3pm, Su noon-3pm. $1 donation.) Two blocks down Lincoln St., the meticulously refurbished **Russian Bishop's House** (747-6281) is one of four remaining Russian colonial buildings in America. (Open mid-May to Oct. 1 daily 9am-1pm and 2-5pm; call for off-season access. Tours every 30min. $3.) The magnificent chapel upstairs, dedicated to the Annunciation of the Virgin Mary, is adorned with gold and silver icons. At the east end of Lincoln St., formerly the site of Baranov's Castle, the seat of Russian administration in Alaska, **Castle Hill** provides an easily accessible view of the cathedral and the sound (open daily 6am-10pm).

The **Sheldon-Jackson Museum** (747-8981), on the tidy Sheldon-Jackson College campus at the east end of Lincoln St., is one of Alaska's best museums of Athabascan, Aleutian, Inuit, and Northwest Coast Native American culture. Pull-out drawers hold children's toys and the raven helmet worn by Chief Katlean, the Tlingit hero of the 1804 battle against the Russians. Summers see demonstrations from visiting Native artists. (Open daily 8am-5pm; in winter Th-Sa 10am-4pm. $3, under 18 free.) The **Sage Building,** also on the campus, houses local marine life in salt- and freshwater tanks. A "touch tank" facilitates close encounters of the slimy and prickly kind (open M-F 9am-5pm). At the **Sheet'ka Kwaan Naa Kahidi Community House,** at 200 Katlian St. next to the Pioneer Home, Sitka Tribal Enterprises, a branch of the local tribal government, has obtained permission to perform native dances, songs and stories from different clans for educational purposes ($6). Contact Tribal Tours (747-7290 or 888-270-8687; ttours@ptialaska.net) for more info.

The trails of the **Sitka National Historic Park** (747-6281), or "Totem Park," lie a few minutes' walk down Lincoln St., a half-mile east of St. Michael's. A one-mile shoreline loop passes 15 masterfully replicated totems and the site of the **Tlingit Fort** where the hammer-wielding Chief Katlean and his men nearly held off the Russians in the battle for Sitka. The park **visitor center** shows a film about the fight and houses the **Southeast Alaskan Native American Cultural Center** (747-8061; open daily 8am-5pm), where woodcarvers, costumers, and weavers demonstrate their crafts.

Eagles are to Sitka what pigeons are to Trafalgar Square. A good place to watch them is Thomsen Harbor when the fishing boats come in. Recovering bald eagles and owls are sheltered at the **Alaska Raptor Rehabilitation Center** (747-8662; open daily 8am-5pm) on Sawmill Creek Rd. ($10).

In 1972, the organizers of the **Sitka Summer Music Festival** (277-4852 or 747-6774; www.sitkamusicfestival.org), raised just enough private funds to buy one-way tickets to Sitka for performers and covered the return flights with their revenues. From June 2-17 2000, the festival, one of Alaska's most popular musical events, will draw about 15 of the world's best classical musicians for 8 chamber music concerts. (All shows $14, under 18 $7. Less-crowded **rehearsals** are free.) Other annual events include the **Russian Christmas** celebrations in January, the **Gathering of the People** in April (a cultural exchange that attracts native dance groups from across Alaska), and **Whalefest** in November. Call the visitor center for more info.

OUTDOORS

The Sitka area offers excellent **hiking** opportunities. Rain gear and a copy of *Sitka Trails*, $4 at the Forest Service office or Old Harbor Books, prove invaluable. The **Beaver Lake Trail**, a 2 mi. boardwalk that rises only 200 ft., is the easiest of the popular trails. Platforms overlooking the serene lake offer great fishing for grayling. The trail begins across the bridge over Sawmill Creek at the Sawmill Creek Campground. The **Indian River Trail** is a 5½ mile (one-way) riverside walk to the base of Indian River Falls. Take Sawmill Creek Rd. out of town and turn on Indian River Rd. before the bridge. The rocky Three Sisters Mountains can be seen from along the trail, as can spawning salmon in early fall.

Harbor Mountain/Gavan Hill Trail is a more strenuous hike but easier to access. The trailhead is near downtown, at the end of Baranof St. The majority of the 3-mile, 2500 ft. ascent is stairs, making the four- to five-hour hike reminiscent of a stairmaster workout. The perseverant are rewarded by a sensational view of the sound. Farther along, on Harbor Moutain, are the ruins of a WWII lookout. The **Mt. Verstovia Trail** provides an enjoyable hike with incredible panoramas. The trailhead is about 2 miles east of town, next to Rookie's Sports Bar and Grill on Sawmill Creek Hwy; look for the sign. (2½ mi. one-way. 2550 ft. elevation gain.)

The Forest Service maintains a number of **remote trails** in the Sitka region, most accessible only by boat or floatplane, and many leading to wilderness cabins ($25 per night). The **Mt. Edgecumbe Trail** is a full-day, 7-miles each way clamber to the crater of Sitka's very own dormant volcano. A shelter sits 3 miles up the trail, and the end of the hike offers stunning views and a close look at eonsold volcanic ash. The trailhead lies behind Fred's Creek Cabin, a half-hour skiff journey from Sitka.

Kayak and bicycle rental services, and over 30 **charter operators** vie to separate you from Sitka and your money. The visitor center has info on such options as deep-sea fishing, whale-watching, flightseeing, and wilderness drop-offs.

GUSTAVUS

The gateway to the gateway to Glacier Bay National Park, Gustavus is ignored by tourists on the way to Bartlett Cove, where trips into the Bay originate. Friendly locals are quick to reveal the secrets of the land, however, and their enthusiasm for the outdoors is infectious. The second graders of Gustavus Elementary School (and authors of the aptly-titled pamphlet *Gustavus, the Way to Glacier Bay*) advise thus: "In Gustavus there is no bank, no hospital, no toystore, no McDonalds, no other fast food places, and no zoo." Come prepared. To the list one could add liquor stores and ATMs, so bring your booze and money with you. Though last-minute food stuffs can be picked up at Bear Track Mercantile, if you're planning a trip here, bring your provisions with you. Besides the Fireweed Gallery (697-2325; open M-F 1-5pm and by appointment), most everything to see and do in Gustavus is outside and on the way to Glacier Bay. Wink from the boat dock at astonishing purple-gold sunsets and 360° of mountain vistas, register the logging roads for later bike exploration, and get to the fjords.

⛏ ORIENTATION AND PRACTICAL INFORMATION. Gustavus is situated on a crossroads called four corners, the intersection of Gustavus Rd. and State Ferry Rd. **Glacier Bay Lodge** and **Bartlett Cove,** the entrance to the park, lie 10 mi. west of four corners, the **airport** 2mi. east, and the ferry arrives 1½ mi. south. Gustavus is accessible only by boat or plane. The cheapest way to get there is via **Alaska Airlines** (800-426-0333; $42 one-way from Juneau). The company with the most frequent service from Juneau and Haines is **Haines Air** (877-359-2467; $62 one-way from Juneau, $91 one-way from Haines). Others include **Wings of Alaska** (800-478-9464), **Air Excursions** (697-2375), and **L.A.B.** (800-426-0543). On the two-hour ferry ride from Juneau, you can bring your kayak ($40) or bike ($10) with you. Contact **Auk Nu Tours** (800-820-2628; departs Auke Bay daily 11am; $45, round-trip $85). Once in Gustavus, A **bus** from the Glacier Bay Lodge (see p. 423) meets every Haines Airways and Alaskan Airlines flight, and rolls on to Bartlett Cove ($12). **TLC Taxi** (697-2239) charges $12 for one, $20 for two, and $8 per person if there are 3 or more of you, plus $5 per bike and $10 per kayak. TLC will lend you **white gas** for your stove if you leave a little left over. **Bud** (697-2403) rents midsize cars for $60 a day. There is no visitor center in Gustavus, but you can ask your questions of the **Gustavus Visitors Association,** P.O. Box 167 (697-2475; gustavusvisitors@hotmail.com), or the folks at **Glacier Bay Travel,** P.O. Box 103 (697-2239; fax 697-2475; www.glacierbaytravel.com). Otherwise, *Icy Passages* is the informative Gustavus paper and the community bulletin board is posted in front of **Bear Track Mercantile.** Should an elephant land on your toe or other injury arise, visit the **Gustavus Community Clinic** (697-3008). **Emergency:** 911. A voluntneer-run **library** (open M, W 7-9pm, Tu 1-5pm and 7-9pm, Th 10am-noon, Fr 1:30-3:30pm, Sa noon-4) sits right next to the **post office** (open M-F 8am-12:30pm and 1:30-4pm, Sa noon-2pm) on Gustavus Rd. near the airport. **ZIP Code:** 99826. **Area Code:** 907.

⛏ ACCOMMODATIONS AND FOOD. Gustavus's second graders might also have added that their town offers little in the way of budget accommodations. There are **no campgrounds** in Gustavus, though tenters sometimes crash on the beach near the ferry dock; the free campgrounds at Bartlett Cove aren't too far away and are the destination for most anyway. **Good River Bed and Breakfast** (697-2241; www.goodriver.com) lends bikes, fishing gear, and raingear and has a beautiful garden and cozy bedrooms with handmade quilts (singles $70; doubles $80). The **Bear's Nest** (697-2440) and **A Puffin's B&B** (697-2260) both maintain two cabins with kitchens that sleep four ($85 for two people, $10 per additional person). Both offer bikes, and shuttle service. Contact the Visitor Association for more cabins (from $85 per night). The most affordable food in Gustavus comes from **Bear Track Mercantile** (697-2358), a quarter of a mile south of four corners (open M-Sa 8am-6pm, Su 9am-5pm). The **Strawberry Point Cafe** next door should be up and running again in 2000 to serve homemade soups and the catch of the day. The **Bear's Nest Cafe** (697-2440), a quarter mile north of four corners, serves lasagna $8, enchiladas $9, and espresso $1.50 (open daily 11am-8pm).

⛏ OUTDOORS. **Wolf Track Expeditions** (697-2326) on State Ferry Road offers **bike rentals** for $35 per day and a combined bike rental and shuttle service to Couverden Point on Chicagof Island, across the Icy Straits, for $135) **Hikers** can walk the beach from Gustavus to Bartlett Cove in about a day. The trip is easiest at low tide though you may encounter bears (see p. 44). Kayakers can also depart Gustavus instead of Bartlett's Cove; contact **Sea Otter Kayaks** (697-3007; www.he.net/~seaotter). Singles $40 per day, doubles $50, including goodies like tide tables, dry bags, and boots. Hard-core golfers can tee off at the 9-hole **Mt. Fairweather Golf Course** (697-2214) year-round. Wow.

GLACIER BAY NATIONAL PARK

Glacier Bay was once referred to by explorer Jean François de Galaup de la Perouse as "perhaps the most extraordinary place in the world." Crystal monoliths, broken off from glaciers, float peacefully in fjords, while humpback whales maneuver the maze of the icy blue depths. Glacier Bay National Park encloses nine tidewater glaciers, as well as the **Fairweather Mountains,** the highest coastal range in the world. (Eat your heart out, Norway.) Charter flights, tours, and cruise ships all probe Glacier Bay, providing close encounters with glaciers, rookeries, whales, and seals. The bay itself is divided into two inlets: the westward **Tarr Inlet** advances as far as the **Grand Pacific** and **Margerie Glaciers,** while the eastward **Muir Inlet** ends at the **Muir** and **Riggs Glaciers.**

Glacier Bay provides a rare opportunity to see geological and ecological processes radically compressed. A mere two centuries ago, the **Grand Pacific Glacier** covered the entire region under a sheet of ancient ice. Severe earthquakes separated the glacier from its terminal moraine (the silt and debris that insulates advancing ice from the relatively warm surrounding seawater), and the glacier retreated 45 mi. in 150 years—light speed in glacial time. As a result, the uncovered ground is virgin territory, colonized by pioneering vegetation.

Getting to **Bartlett Cove,** the principle access point to the bay, is relatively easy: a plane or ferry takes visitors to **Gustavus** (see p. 421), and from there a taxi or shuttle (about $12) goes to **Glacier Bay Lodge** (697-2230 or 800-451-5952; open M-F 11:30am-2pm and 4-9pm) and the **Visitor Information Center,** both steps from the cove. The few ways to see the glaciers are expensive. Sightseers take one of a range of packages on a sightseeing cruise boat; backcountry travelers are dropped off by the same ship for their trips. Visitors should contact **Glacier Bay National Park** P.O. Box 140, Gustavus 99826 (697-2230; www.nps.gov/glba) for assistance in planning a backcountry trip. Glacier Bay is becoming *the* destination for extended kayak trips in the region. The only food available at Bartlett Cove is at the dining room in the Lodge (open daily 6-9am, 11:30-2:30pm, 4:30-10pm), which is rather expensive, so trippers bring provisions with them.

BOAT TOURS. The simplest is by boat tour. The *Spirit of Adventure* is owned by the lodge, and offers six **sightseeing packages** to the glaciers, ranging in price and niceties from a half-day whale-watching trip ($78) to a package with flights to and from Juneau, a night at the B&B, and an eight-hour glacier tour ($379). The basic "see the glaciers" daytrip runs from the lodge ($156). The park offers great opportunities for independent explorers. Because there are boat quotas in the summer, people with their own boats must call ahead to the **Information Station** (697-2627) to book a visit. Other cruise ships and charter flightseeing tours operate from outside the park boundaries—get a full list of these by writing to the **Superintendent** (907-697-2230), P.O. Box 140, Gustavus, AK 99826-0140.

CAMPING, HIKING, AND KAYAKING. Any visit to the park begins at the **Visitor Information Station** (697-2627), between Glacier bay Lodge and the tour boat dock in **Bartlett Cove,** 10 mi. north of the town of Gustavus, where rangers give a mandatory backcountry orientation, advise you of areas restricted by conservaton or bear activity, and distribute permits (open daily 7am-9pm). Additional maps and wildlife info are available at the information center on the second floor of the Glacier Bay Lodge.

Before entering the bay, backpackers and kayakers can stay in the free **campground** a quarter mile from the boat dock, which has 25 sites and is rarely full. Glimpses of orcas and humpback whales are common from the beachfront sites; whales sing the campers to sleep and their surfacing will wake them in the morning. Those without a tent can collapse in comfortable dorm beds at the **Glacier Bay Lodge** ($28). **Showers** ($1 per 5min.) and **laundry** ($2 wash, $1.25 dry) are available to all. Some visitors opt to stay in nearby **Gustavus,** and use it as their jumping-off point to the park.

Wilderness camping and **hiking** are permitted throughout the park, though there are no trails except the two near the lodge, and hiking is very difficult in most of the park because of thick alder brush. Backcountry hiking and kayaking is possible in the **Dry Bay** area (the northwest corner of the park), as is **rafting** down the

Alsek River. For info on these activities contact the Yakutat District Office of the National Park Service, P.O. Box 137, Yakutat, AK 99689 (784-3295).

Kayakers revel in the park's landscape and are welcomed heartily. From the four possible drop off points, the East arm is the least trafficked and avoids cruise ships venturing toward the West arm glaciers, which any traveler will see during their tour on the ship on the way in or the way out. Travelers should expect to come into contact with bears and will be provided bear cannisters for packing their supplies. Kayak rental is available at **Glacier Bay Sea Kayaks** (697-2257). Singles $40 per day, doubles $50, and multi day rates; double kayaks 3pm-7pm $35. Don't expect to make it out to the glaciers in a day—they're more than 50 miles away. **Sea Otter Kayaks** (967-3007; seaotter@he.net; www.he.net/~seaotter) rents at the same rates, and also provides rain gear, drybags, and charts. **Alaska Discovery** (800-586-1911; akdisco@alaska.net) offers guided one-day kayak trips from Bartlett Cove out to the **Beardslee Islands,** which are covered with birds and bird shit.

HAINES

Snowcapped mountains and crystal blue waters surround Haines with breathtaking beauty. Called "the sunny spot of the Southeast," Haines gets less than half the rain of nearby Juneau, and with locals quick to share stories and trail advice, Haines is unquestionably one of the most sublime towns in Southeast Alaska. Haines is also accessible, as a boat-bound traveler will attest at his or her first sight of RVs for weeks. The coastal town is connected to the interior in the manner of its neighbor, Skagway, by a mountain pass traditionally protected by the coastal Tlingit and interior Athabascans, and now paved and well-traveled by people from all over. Tlingit is still spoken in the streets of Klukwan (known as the "mother village" of the Tlingit people), north of Haines. A site of cultural importance to Tlingits throughout Southeast Alaska, Klukwan has cautiously begun to open its doors to tourism.

☷ ORIENTATION AND PRACTICAL INFORMATION

Haines lies on a thin peninsula between the **Chilkat** and **Chilkoot Inlets,** just southwest of Skagway on the Chilkoot Inlet. The Haines business district sits in the rectangle defined by **Main St.** and the **Haines Highway** and their perpendiculars, **2nd** and **3rd Avenues.** Fort Seward lies to the south. Below this peninsula, two inlets merge into **Lynn Canal.** There are U.S. (767-5511) and Canadian (767-5540) **customs offices** at Mile 42 of the Haines Hwy. (open daily 7am-11pm). Travelers must have at least $200 cash (not always enforced) and valid proof of citizenship to enter Canada. Rental cars are not always allowed across the border. (See **Customs,** p. 26.)

Airplanes: Wings of Alaska (766-2030; www.wingsofalaska.com) and **Haines Air** (766-2646 or 877-359-2467; www.haines.ak.us/hainesair) offer comparable rates to: Juneau ($70-75); Skagway ($85-110); and Glacier Bay ($85-110).

Buses: Make reservations for **Alaskon Express** (766-2000; 800-544-2206), in the lobby of the Hotel Hälsingland. Buses depart Tu, Th, and Su and stay overnight in Beaver Creek, YT, near the Alaskan border. To: Anchorage ($189); Fairbanks ($180); Whitehorse, YT ($86). Open daily 9am-8pm. **R.C. Shuttles** (877-479-0079; rcshuttles@aol.com) depart the Mountain View Motel Tu 9pm, for Fairbanks ($120), with stops in Tok ($80) and Delta Junction ($100).

Ferries: Alaska Marine Highway (766-2111 or 800-642-0066; www.akmhs.com). Terminal on Lutak Rd., 4 mi. from downtown. 1 per day to: Juneau (4½hr., $24) and Skagway (1hr., $14). Parking for ferry passengers $5 per day, $25 per week.

Taxis: The New Other Guy's Taxi (766-3257). $8 single fare between ferry or airport and downtown, or $5 per person.

Car Rental: Eagle's Nest Car Rental (766-2891 or 800-354-6009), at Eagle's Nest Motel, west of town on the Haines Hwy. $45 per day, plus 35¢ per mi. over 100 mi. Must be 18 with a credit card.

Car Repair: Charlie's Repair, 225 2nd Ave. (766-2494). Open M-F 8am-5pm.

Visitor Information: (766-2234 or 800-458-3579; fax 766-3155; www.haines.ak.us) on 2nd Ave. near Willard St. Open M-Th 8am-10pm, F 8am-8pm, Sa-Su 10am-6pm; in winter M-F 9am-4pm. Mobbed M-Th 7-10pm, when cruise ships are docked.

Outdoor Information: State Park Information Office, 259 Main St. (766-2292), above Helen's Shop between 2nd and 3rd Ave. Open Tu-Sa 8am-4:30pm, but call ahead. The **Fish and Game** folks are in the same building, open M-F 9am-5pm.

Bank: First National Bank of Anchorage, on Main St., is the only bank in town. Open M-Th 10am-4pm, F 10am-5pm. **ATM** open 24hr.

Equipment Rental: Sockeye Cycle (766-2869), on Portage St., above the cruise ship docks in Ft. Seward. Bikes $6 per hr., $20 for 4hr., $30 for 8hr. Helmets and locks included. From here the man who began the Kluane-Chilkat Bike Relay (see p. 427) guides trips. Open in the summer M-Sa 9am-6pm, Su 1-5pm. **Tanani Bay Kayak & Canoe Rentals** (766-2804), near the corner of Union and Front St. Single kayaks $18 per day, doubles $26; canoes $12 per day. Pickup and delivery; call for hours. **Alaska Sport Shop** (766-2441), sells fishing licenses. Open M-Sa 8:30am-6pm, Su 10am-4pm; in winter M-Sa 9am-5:30pm.

Bookstore: The Babbling Book (766-3356), on Main St. near Howser's Supermarket. Open M-Sa 9:30am-6pm, Su noon-5pm; call for winter hours.

Library: (766-2545) on 3rd Ave. Free Internet access; call ahead. Open M and W-Su 10am-9pm, Tu and Th 10am-4:30pm and 7-9pm, F 10am-4:30pm, Sa 1-4pm, Su 2-4pm.

Laundromat and Public Showers: Port Chilkoot Camper Park (766-2000), across from the Hälsingland Hotel. Wash $2, dry 25¢ per 7min. Showers $1.50. Open daily 7am-9pm. **Susie Q's** (766-2953), on Main St. near Front St. Wash $2, dry 50¢. Showers $2. Open daily 8am-8pm; in winter 8am-6pm. **Haines Quick Laundry,** behind the Outfitter on Haines Hwy. Wash $2.50, dry $1. Showers 25¢ per min. up to 15min.

Emergency: 911. **Police:** 766-2121, on Haines Hwy. between 2nd and 3rd Ave.

Rape and Abuse Crisis Line: 800-478-1090.

Medical Services: Health Clinic (766-2521), on 1st Ave. next to the visitor center.

Internet Access: See **Library,** above. **Mountain Market** (see below), $2 per 15min.

Post Office: On Haines Hwy., between 2nd Ave. and Front St. Open M-F 9am-5:30pm, Sa 1-3pm. **ZIP Code:** 99827.

Area Code: 907.

▉ ACCOMMODATIONS AND CAMPGROUNDS

The weather is better in Haines than almost anywhere else in Southeast Alaska, making camping a pleasure. In addition to private campgrounds, there are several state campgrounds (with water and toilets) around town. **Chilkat State Park,** 7 mi. south on Mud Bay Rd., has guided nature walks and good king salmon and halibut fishing (32 sites: $6). **Chilkoot Lake,** 10 mi. north of town on Lutak Rd., provides views and sockeye salmon (32 sites: $10). **Mosquito Lake,** 27 mi. north on Haines Hwy., earns its name in late summer (13 sites: $6). Call the State Park Information Office (766-2292; see **Practical Information,** above) for more info.

Bear Creek Camp and International Hostel (766-2259), on Small Tracts Rd., 2 mi. out of town. From downtown, follow 3rd Ave. out Mud Bay Rd. to Small Tracts. Convenient to nothing; call ahead for ferry terminal pickup. A ring of basic cabins, each with its own unique odor. Spartan furnishings—a roof and a foam pads on bunks. Beds $14; family cabins $38; tent sites $8. No curfew.

Hotel Hälsingland (766-2000, 800-542-6363, or 800-478-2525 in YT and BC; fax 766-2006). Old Ft. Seward officers' quarters, with original 30s decor that shows its age. Shared bath. Singles $49; doubles $59. Rooms with private bath cost twice as much. Open May-Sept and during Nov. for the Bald Eagle Festival.

Fort Seward Lodge (766-2009 or 800-478-7772), beyond the post office above Haines. A bit dark, but clean, with hand-finished furniture. Singles $45, with bath $60; doubles from $55, with bath from $75; Oct.-Apr. $10 less. Not wheelchair accessible.

Portage Cove, three quarters of a mile from town on Beach Rd. Backpackers and cyclists only. Scant privacy, pit toilets. 9 grassy sites overlook the water $6. 7-night max. stay.

Port Chilkoot Camper Park (766-2000 or 800-542-6363), opposite Hotel Hälsingland. Gravelly, well maintained; tall pines evoke a shady forest. Laundry (see above), and coin showers. 60 sites: $8; full hookups $19. Open Apr.-Sept.

Salmon Run RV Campground (766-3240), at Lutak Inlet, 1¾ mi. past the ferry terminal. Half the sites overlook the beach. Toilets. $10. Open year-round.

◐ FOOD

Creative sandwiches and burritos are beginning to replace steak and potatoes on Haines menus. Groceries are expensive; stock up in Juneau if you can. Visit **Howser's Supermarket** (766-2040), on Main St., for groceries (open daily 9am-8pm). You may find dungeness crab on the dock, but salmon ($5-7 per lb.) and prawns ($10-13 per lb.) are always at **Bell's Seafood** (766-2950), on 2nd Ave. under the Old City Jail and Firehouse sign (open Su-Tu and Th-Sa 9am-6pm, W 9am-10pm).

The Klondike (266-2477), in the Dalton City S.E. Fairgrounds on Haines Hwy. On the hokey-looking street where *White Fang* was filmed, local color meets trashy Western get-up. The result is sawdust, peanut shells, and slow service that is terribly polite. Delicious Tex-Mex entrees from $6. Pints $3.50. Horseshoe toss and frisbee golf. Frequent live music and jam sessions. Open daily 3pm-crowd leaves. Booze until 11pm.

Wild Strawberry, 138 2nd Ave. (766-3608), off Haines Hwy., tastes and looks like Mom's kitchen, if your momma was a gourmand. Loaded bagel sandwich $7. Grilled seafood specials fresh off the boat $9. Open M-F 7am-9pm, Sa-Su 8am-9pm.

Mountain Market (766-3340), at Haines Hwy. and 3rd Ave. Haines's health food grocery store and cafe serves overflowing sandwiches with soup ($6.50). Open M-Sa 7am-7pm, Su 7am-5pm; in winter daily 7:30am-6pm. Free Internet access (see above).

Grizzly Greg's (766-3622), on the corner of 2nd Ave. and Main St. A classic pizzeria, complete with red-and-white-checked decor. Pizza by the slice $2.50, enormous calzones $8. Open daily 11am-10pm. Will deliver to patrons at **The Fogcutter,** see below.

Bamboo Room (776-2800), on 2nd Ave. near Main St. Crowded until 3pm with fisherfolk downing buckwheat hotcakes and coffee ($4.25). Lunch specials $6-8; dinner specials $10-20. No bamboo in sight. Open daily 6am-10pm.

◉ ◫ SIGHTS, NIGHTLIFE, AND EVENTS

Fort William Seward, on the south side of town, was established in 1901 to assert American presence during a border dispute with Canada. With duties that included shoveling snow and watching for fires, the post quickly became known as a gentle assignment. "Even among men with the most modern arms, time is the hardest thing to kill," lamented one observer in a 1907 newspaper. After WWII, five veterans bought the 400-acre compound, intending to form a commune. Their utopian venture never succeeded, but most of these settlers became enterprising members of the community. Fort Seward's colonial-style buildings remain on display along with a replicated **Totem Village** (766-2160) and a tribal house where **salmon bakes** take place in the summer. The village is home to **Sea Wolf Studio-Gallery** (766-2540), where Tlingit artist Tresham Gregg carves masks (open M-F 9am until the last ship leaves). The **Chilkat Dancers** perform narrated Tlingit dances at the **Chilkat Center for the Arts.** (Usually at 8pm. Call Hotel Hälsingland at 766-2000 for tickets. $10, students $5, under 5 free.) The same building houses the **Alaska Indian Arts Center,** where carvers work in open workshops (766-2160; open M-F 9am-noon and 1-5pm).

The Sheldon Museum (766-2366), on Front St. in downtown Haines, exhibits historical artifacts from the collections of some of the town's oldest white families. Almost a quarter of Haines volunteers here. (Open daily 1-5pm; in winter Su, M, W 1-4pm, Tu, Th, F 3-5pm. $3.)

The well-meaning **American Bald Eagle Foundation Natural History Museum** (766-3094), at the intersection of Haines Hwy. and 2nd Ave., has a room full of stuffed Chilkat valley wildlife and screens a film on the November bald eagle occupation. (Open M-Th 9am-10pm, F 9am-5pm, Sa 10am-4pm, Su 1-4pm; in winter M, W, F 1-4pm. $2, ages 7-11 $1, under 7 free.)

The Klondike is home to the Haines music scene (see above). The three main watering holes in town are **The Fogcutter** on Main St., opposite the bank, **Harbor Bar,** by the small boat harbor, and the **Hälsingland Hotel Bar.** In a unique system, all of them open around 11am and close depending on where the drink specials and live music are: once the party-spot has established itself sometime after midnight, the favored barkeep calls the other two bars and they close up early. A good bet is to start at the Fogcutter for a wide selection on tap and 50¢ pool.

Haines becomes party central in early summer with a **Craft Beer and Home-Brew Festival** (May 19-20 in 2000), a **Bald Eagle Run** and **Harley Davidson Rodeo** (Memorial Day weekend), and an Alaskan **Mardi Gras** (the first weekend of June). If wheels are your thing, but hogs aren't, team up for the **International Kluane to Chilkoot Bike Relay** (June 17). The 153 mi. course covers the Haines Hwy. from Haines Junction, YT, to Haines, AK, with checkpoints every 20 mi. to relieve saddle soreness. Sockeye Cycle, above, has more info.

OUTDOORS

The **Haines Highway** winds 40 mi. from Haines into the **Chilkat Range** running north through the Yukon, with views guaranteed to blow you through the back of your Winnebago, were you to be driving such a vehicle. The world's highest concentration of bald eagles congregates each November in the **Chilkat Bald Eagle Preserve,** 19 mi. up the highway. The **American Bald Eagle Foundation Center** (766-3094) has more info.

Three main trails head into the wilderness around Haines, and all are detailed in the pamphlet *Haines is for Hikers*. Numerous points access the **Mt. Riley Trail,** which leads to a 1760 ft. summit with panoramic views of the Lynn Canal, the Chilkoot and Chilkat Inlets, and everything else within 30 miles. The primary trailhead is marked 3½ mi. from town, 1½ mi. down Mud Bay Rd. past the hostel. This trail is steep for most of its 2 miles and takes about two hours. **Mt. Ripinsky,** the 3920 ft. mountain looming over the north end of town, provides a challenging hike over two summits connected by an alpine ridge. On a clear day, the view from the ridge extends all the way to Juneau; shorter Mt. Riley even provides excellent views on cloudy days. To reach the Mt. Ripinsky trailhead, follow 2nd Ave. north to Lutak Rd., branch off Lutak onto Young St. at the hill, then turn right along the pipeline for 1 mile. After cresting the 3610 ft. **North Summit,** the trail dips down along the ridge and may be difficult to follow in poor weather. At the end of the ridge, it climbs again to a 3920 ft. peak, and descends steeply to its end at Mile 7 of the Haines Hwy. This strenuous 10 mi. hike makes for a long dayhike or a relaxed overnight trip. **Seduction Point Trail** offers 7 mi. (one-way) of birds, beaches, ocean bluffs, berry picking, wildflowers, and alluring views of **Rainbow** and **Davidson Glaciers.** Take Mud Bay Rd. out of Haines 7 mi. to Chilkat State Park, and time the last part of the hike along **David's Cove** to coincide with low tide.

A favorite swimming hole is **Chilkoot Lake,** 10 mi north on Lutak Rd. The Chilkat is a fabled late August salmon run, and the region is good for canoeing and kayaking. Call **Tanani Bay** or **Deishu Expeditions** for rentals and recommendations.

SKAGWAY

Five hundred miles from Skagway, in August 1896, a Tlingit man called Skookum Jim was washing a pan in a tributary of the Klondike River when he discovered strips of gold so thick they looked "like cheese in a sandwich." By October, 20,000 stampeders had set off for the site of Jim's discovery from Skagway, a valley settlement wedged near the trailheads of the Chilkoot and White Passes. As gold fields were exhausted, Skagway's shrunken population stayed on beside an empty port and the terminus of the hastily engineered White Pass railway.

Flights still connect out-trippers to nearby Glacier Bay via Gustavus, and the Chilkoot Trail continues to draw heavy backpacker traffic. But the railroad now carries tourists, and gargantuan cruise ships expand the town's population tenfold daily as 7000 passengers flood onto Broadway St., the town's renovated historic district. Most of the other streets and trails remain relatively uncrowded, however, and while you won't find Skagway serene during the weekdays of July and August (weekends are less busy), the town's fascinating past and arresting location make any visit worthwhile.

☑ ORIENTATION AND PRACTICAL INFORMATION

At the northernmost tip of the Inside Passage, Skagway is a terminus of the **Alaska Marine Hwy.** Skagway is also at the end of the **Klondike Hwy.** (Rte. 98 in AK and Hwy. 2 in YT), 113 mi. (2½hr.) south of Whitehorse and 66 mi. (1½hr.) south of Carcross. Canadian and U.S. **customs** are passable 24 hours a day, although the U.S. office is not staffed from midnight to 6am. There are no services between Skagway and Carcross. **Haines** is 15 mi. away by water, 360 mi. by land. Hitchers say they do better spending $17 on the ferry to Haines then thumbing the more heavily traveled **Haines Cutoff** to Kluane and Interior Alaska.

The **ferry** dock is at the southern end of downtown. Skagway's main drag, **Broadway St.**, runs inland from the docks with **Spring St.** on the right, and **State** and **Main St.** on the left. Numbered **avenues** intersect the streets, ascending from the water.

Skagway levies a 4% **city tax** on goods, food, and services, and 8% on lodgings.

TRANSPORTATION

Airplanes: Skagway Air Service (983-2218), on Broadway between 4th and 5th Ave. flies 8 times per day to: Haines (8min., $35); Juneau (45 min., $75); and Gustavus (1hr., $85); and tours Glacier Bay ($125). Open daily 7am-9pm; in winter, 7am-5pm.

Trains: White Pass and Yukon Route (983-2217 or 800-343-7373; www.whitepassrailroad.com), on 2nd Ave. One of North America's steepest and most scenic railroads. Round-trip excursions to the White Pass Summit or Bennett Lake. May 12 to Sept. 24 daily 8:30am and 1pm, Tu and W 4:30pm; from $78, ages 3-12 $39. Also accesses remote trailheads (see **Outdoors,** below). Train and bus service to Whitehorse, YT (5hr., daily at 12:40pm, $95, ages 3-12 $48). Buses may not be wheelchair accessible.

Buses: Alaska Direct (800-770-6652) runs vans by appointment from the ferry terminal, visitor center, and hostel to Whitehorse (3½hr., $35, round-trip $70). Connections on W, F, and Su to Fairbanks ($120) and Anchorage ($145) require an overnight stay in Whitehorse (accommodation not provided). **Alaskon Express** (983-2241 or 800-544-2206), in the Westmark Inn on 3rd Ave. between Broadway and Spring St., also runs in summer once daily to Whitehorse, YT (3hr., 7:30am, $45) and from mid-May to mid-Sept. Su, Tu, and Th to Anchorage ($209) and Fairbanks ($206). Both trips require an overnight stay in Beaver Creek, YT (about 23hr.; accommodation not provided).

Ferries: Alaska Marine Highway (983-2941 or 800-642-0066). 6 per week leave at 3:30pm to: Haines (1hr.; $17); Juneau (6½hr.; $32). Beware dockside ticket office's erratic hours (when the ferry is in, 1:30-3:30pm). **Water Taxi** (983-2083 or 888-766-3395) runs twice per day to Haines (1hr.; $19, round-trip with 4hr. stopover $32; under 12 half-price). Office open daily May-Sept. 7:30am-4:30pm. Buy tickets at Dijon Delights, on Broadway at 5th Ave.

Taxis: Frontier Excursions (983-2512), at 7th Ave. and Broadway, services Skagway and the Chilkoot trailheads. **Dyea Dave** (983-2731) runs tours, too. See **Outdoors,** below.

Car Rental: Sourdough Van & Car Rentals (983-2523, in AK 800-478-2529; rental@ptialaska.net), at 6th Ave. and Broadway. From $30 per day, plus 30¢ per mi. over 100 mi. Drop-offs at Haines and White-horse by arrangement ($100).

Auto Repair: Hoover's (983-2452), at 4th Ave. and Main St. Open daily 8am-7pm; in winter, 8am-5pm. Oil and lube about $30.

VISITOR AND LOCAL SERVICES

Visitor Information: Klondike Gold Rush National Historical Park (983-2921), at 2nd Ave. and Broadway. Free exhibits and 45min. walking tours 4 times per day; self-guided tour brochures available. Open June-Aug. daily 8am-7pm; May and Sept. 8am-6pm. **Skagway Convention and Visitors Bureau** (983-2854; www.skagway.org), on 5th Ave. off Broadway. Open May-Sept. daily 8am-6pm; Oct.-Apr. M-F 8am-5pm.

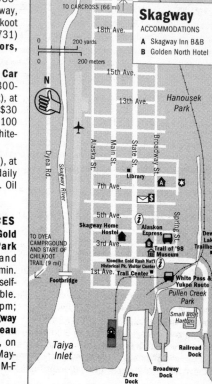

Outdoor Information: The joint-run U.S./Canada Parks **Trail Center** (phone/fax 983-3655) is on Broadway and sells **overnight permits** for the Canadian side of the Chilkoot trail. (CDN$35, under 16 CDN$17.50). Open late-May to mid-Sept. daily 8am-4:15pm.

Bank: National Bank of Alaska (983-2265), at Broadway and 6th Ave. Open M-F 9:30am-5pm. 24hr. **ATM.**

Equipment Rental: Sockeye Cycle (983-2851; www.haines.ak.us/sockeye/), on 5th Ave. off Broadway St. From $6 per hr. or $30 per day, with helmet and lock. Guided tours available. Open May-Sept. daily 9am-6pm. **Sourdough Van and Car Rentals** (see above) rents bikes, no frills, for $5 per hr. or $20 per day. **Skagway Hardware** (983-2233), on Broadway St. at 4th Ave., sells fishing permits ($10 per day) and some outdoor gear. Open mid-Apr. to Sept. M-Sa 8am-6pm, Su 10am-4pm; in winter M-Sa 8am-5pm. **The Sports Emporium** (983-2480), on 4th Ave. between Broadway and State, sells high-tech gear. Open May to late Sept. daily 9am-7pm; in winter M-Sa 10am-5pm.

Library: (983-2665) at 8th Ave. and State St. Free **Internet access** available (one terminal for research, one for email). Book ahead. Open M-F 1-9pm, Sa 1-5pm.

Laundromat: Services Unlimited Laundromat (983-2595), at 2nd Ave. and State St. Wash $2, dry 25¢ per 5min. Open daily 8am-8pm, last load 6:30pm; in winter F-Tu 9am-6pm. **Garden City RV Park** (983-2378), at State St. and 15th Ave. Wash $1.50, dry 25¢ per 5min. Open May-Sept. 7am-10pm.

Public Showers: Garden City RV Park (see **Laundromat,** above), 75¢ per 5min.

SOUTHEAST ALASKA

EMERGENCY AND COMMUNICATIONS

Emergency: 911. **Police:** (983-2232) on State St. towards the water past 1st Ave.

Hospital: Skagway Medical Service (983-2255; emergency 983-2418) on 11th Ave. between State and Broadway. Clinic open M-F 9am-noon and 1-5pm.

Local Radio: FM 103.7 (Skagway), FM 102.3 (Haines).

Post Office: (983-2330), at Broadway and 6th, next to the bank. Open M-F 8:30am-5pm. Lobby can serve as a **24hr. Refuge. ZIP Code:** 99840.

Area Code: 907.

ACCOMMODATIONS AND CAMPGROUNDS

The Skagway Home Hostel is reason enough to visit the town, and if it weren't, the Golden North Hotel and Skagway Inn B&B would take up the slack. Make reservations unless you're camping. Dyea, 9 mi. away, has the only available free tenting.

Skagway Home Hostel P.O. Box 231 (983-2131). On 3rd Ave. near Main St. Home sweet home invites you into their family. Shared kitchen. Up to 10 may sign up for dinner before 4:30pm ($5; free if you cook). Showers, kitchen, bike use, and plenty of Chilkoot Trail stories and advice. 21 beds $15; 1 double $40. Sheets and towels $1. Laundry $3. No credit cards. Chore required. Check-in 5:30-9pm. No lockout. Curfew 11pm (late ferries accommodated). Reservations advised (by mail only).

Golden North Hotel (983-2295), at 3rd Ave. and Broadway St. The classiest affordable hotel in Southeast Alaska and the oldest hotel in the state (est. 1898). Each room in a period style, with canopy beds and antique furniture. Ghost in Room 24. Singles $55, with bath $75; doubles $65, with bath $85.

Skagway Inn Bed and Breakfast (983-2289 or 888-752-4929; www.skagwayinn.com), on Broadway at 7th Ave. Built as a brothel in 1897 and now respectably refurbished, each room retains the name of one of the brothel's illustrious women. Divine full breakfast served in an elegant dining room. Pickup and drop-off to ferry and airport. Shared baths. Singles $95; doubles $115; winter rates $10 less.

Dyea Camping Area, 9 mi. northwest of Skagway on Dyea Rd., near the start of the Chilkoot Trail. 22 spacious, woodsy sites. Free. Pit toilets, fire rings, no showers. 14-night max. stay. Not recommended for RVs: the twisting, narrow dirt road takes a careful 20min. Shuttles will get you there and back without a hitch (see **Taxis,** above). Locals are reportedly sympathetic to hitchers on the way to town.

Pullen Creek RV Park (983-2768), on 2nd Ave. by the harbor. Small and noisy, but convenient, with a pretty, unobstructed view of the mountains. Bathrooms, coin shower. $10 ($5 extra for vehicle), hookups $20. No open fires.

FOOD

Skagway's status as a cruise ship magnet can make eating and shopping expensive. The **Fairway Supermarket** (983-2220), at 4th Ave. and State St., sells groceries (open M-Sa 8am-9pm, Su 9am-6pm; in winter M-Sa 9am-6pm, Su 10am-4pm). **You Say Tomato** (983-2784), on State St. at 9th Ave., sells dry, natural meals by the pound and groceries. 15% discount on bulk orders (open Apr.-Oct. M-Sa 10:30am-7:30pm, Su noon-5pm; call for winter hours).

Red Onion Saloon (983-2222), on Broadway between 2nd and 3rd Ave. At Skagway's classiest former bordello, have a Painted Lady (curried halibut salad sandwich, $7.50) or a Madam Jan personal pizza (jalapeno, pineapple, olive, onion, mushroom, $6.75). All you can eat dinner plus beer is about $10 (open May-Sept daily 10am-late).

Bonanza Bar and Grill (983-6214), on Broadway between 3rd and 4th Ave. As American as it gets, with basic sports grill fare and a game on the big-screen TV. Nachos grande, pizza, or sandwiches from $7. Pitchers from $10. Open May-Sept. daily 10am-midnight. Open-mic Wednesday nights with a young crowd out in full force.

Corner Cafe (983-2155), at 4th Ave. and State St. Where the locals head for basic grub and relaxed open-air seating that helps dissipate the smoke. Listen to that fryer sizzle! Stack of buttermilk pancakes $4, burgers $5.25-7. Open daily 6am-5pm.

Mabel G. Smith's, 342 5th Ave. (983-2609). Those avoiding Starbucks or the Love Boat stampede on Broadway get their caffeine here. Muffins and cookies $1.30. Open May-Sept. M-Sa 6am-6pm, Su 6am-4pm; in winter M-Sa 6am-5pm.

Stowaway Cafe (983-3463), on 2nd Ave. by the small boat harbor. Steps above the Broadway mayhem. Fresh seafood gumbo $16; veggie curry $13; unlimited bread made in heaven. Open May-Sept. daily 11am-10pm. Reservations suggested.

👁 🎵 SIGHTS AND ENTERTAINMENT

Many of the pristine buildings from the 1900s on Broadway St. are leased to local businesses by the Park Service as part of the **Klondike Gold Rush National Historical Park.** Polish up on gold rush trivia at the **Trail of '98 Museum** (983-2420), housed in the 1899 Arctic Brotherhood Hall, on Broadway between 2nd and 3rd Ave. The hall's driftwood-clad facade is the state's most photographed building. Among the museum's offerings is a magnificent mallard-throat robe. (Open in summer daily 9am-5pm. $2, students $1.) For ribald history, hit the **Red Onion Saloon** (983-2222), Skagway's first bordello and a popular bar with an enviable collection of bed pans. Come for live afternoon jazz (courtesy of cruise ship musicians) or the open jam (Th, Sa), and tour upstairs with Madame Spitfire. (Open May-Sept. daily 10am-late.) For less ambience and more taste, the **Skagway Brewing Company** in the Golden North Hotel serves up nine drafts from its in-house microbrewery. The Oosic Stout ($3.50) is named for the bone of a male walrus's nether regions. (Open May-Sept. daily 11am-midnight.) **Moe's Frontier Bar** (983-2238), on Broadway between 4th and 5th Ave., is worth a saunter in any night of the week. Check Wild Bill and his one-man show (W 8-11pm). Beer in a can is $2.75, in a bottle $3.25, mixed drinks $3. (Open April-Sept. 9am until closing; in winter 11am until closing.) Yee ha!

Skagway's history is nearly overshadowed by its souvenir shops. **Inside Passage Arts** (983-2585), at Broadway between 4th and 5th Ave., is an artist-run gallery that sells indigenous crafts. (Open May-Sept. daily 9am-7pm.) Bone carvings and fossil-

THE CLEANEST CON MAN IN THE NORTH

Skagway's most notorious ne'er-do-well, Jefferson Randolph "Soapy" Smith, got his name from his favorite scam, the "soap game." He would sit on a street corner selling a chance to pick a bar of soap from his collection for an outrageous $5. Each bar had some bill wrapped around it, with the bar and bill wrapped in cloth to obscure the denomination. With thousands of prospectors roaming the streets of Skagway any given day, it never took long before a crowd gathered, and some impetuous spenders would step forward to buy bars. As luck would have it, those first two or three invariably held very large bills and triggered a buying frenzy. Most purchasers ended up with only a bar of soap and a single greenback. The two or three lucky fellows (a.k.a. accomplices) would meet up with Soapy later and return the planted bills for a handsome payoff. Ultimately, Soapy Smith wasn't such a bad sort: he donated money to the community for a new church, started an adopt-a-dog program, and rarely robbed locals. In appreciation of his peculiar brand of philanthropy, the town named him a Marshal of the 4th of July parade in 1898. A few days later, Soapy died in a shootout, taking his adversary down with him. While Soapy was buried outside the limits of the town cemetery, the fickle public gave his killer a choice plot and a tombstone inscribed, "He gave his life for the honor of Skagway." Today, Soapy's spirit is celebrated each July at a debaucherous evening gathering called Soapy's Wake.

ized ivory fill the showroom and free museum at **Corrington Alaskan Ivory** (983-2580), at 5th Ave. and Broadway St. (Open May-Sept. daily 9am-6pm.)

The **Gold Rush Cemetery,** about 1½ mi. from town, retains an eerie serenity rare in other gold rush monuments. Take Main St. to the parking lot before the bridge and follow the dirt road. Soapy fans will have to pay their respects beyond the cemetery boundaries. A short trail from the cemetery leads to **Lower Reid Falls,** which cascades 300 ft. down the mountainside. **Dyea,** once the flourishing sister-city to Skagway, sinks beneath June's blooming fields of wild irises and chocolate lilies. **Dyea Dave** (see **Transportaton,** above) leads archaelogical tours of the site ($25), and Park Wardens give free, brief tours in the summer (W-Su at 2pm).

Those wanting to enjoy Soapy's exploits *sans* pamphlets can head to the **Skagway Days of '98** show in the Eagle's Hall (983-2545) at 6th and Broadway. The 70-year old vaudeville show features song and dance, play-money gambling, and audience-actor interaction, with raucous sincerity. (In summer daily: gambling 7:30pm; shows at 10:30am, 2, and 8pm. $14, children $7. Matinees $12, children $6.)

◣ OUTDOORS

Backpackers on the **Chilkoot Trail** (see p. 375) benefit from the Alaska National History Association's complete *Hiker's Guide to the Chilkoot Trail* ($2), available at the Trail Center. Hikers must register there to use any portion of the Chilkoot; in addition, hikers must contact Canadian customs in Fraser, BC, or Whitehorse, YT, (867-667-3493) upon completion of the route. Reservations for the Chilkoot are accepted one year in advance and are recommended July to August. Fifty people per day are allowed on the trail in summer and there is space for only eight walkons. Rangers are stationed at the Dyea trailhead and patrol the trail. (Registration CDN$5. Overnight permit CDN$10 per night, CDN$35 for the whole trail, CDN$17.50 for children. Reservations $10. In Whitehorse call 800-661-4086 or 867-667-3910; in Skagway 907-983-3655, 8am-4:30pm). There are a number of ways to get between Skagway or Carcross and the Chilkoot trailheads at Dyea and Bennett Lake. **Frontier Excursions** (983-2512) and **Dyea Dave** (983-2731) run taxis between Skagway and Dyea ($10) and between Skagway and Bennett Lake ($20; combined routes $25). **The White Pass & Yukon Route** (983-2217) runs trains between Skagway and Bennett Lake ($65). **Alaska Overland** (667-7896) runs buses between Bennett Lake, Carcross, and Skagway ($40-50). **Tutshi Charters** (821-4905) runs a water taxi between Bennett Lake and Carcross. Pack light. Don't lose your horse.

Although the Chilkoot Trail is the marquee name in Skagway hiking, shorter local trails have inspiring views and less traffic. Dayhikes are popular around **Bennett Lake,** accessible via rail (see above). The **Dewey Lake Trail System** provides some of the best nearby hiking, from a 2hr. stroll to a strenuous climb to alpine lakes at 3700 ft./1130m. To reach the trails, walk east along 2nd Ave. and follow the dirt path just before the railroad tracks to the left. Look for trailhead signs on the right. Narrow, tree-lined **Lower Dewey Lake** lies less than a mile up the trail. One trail branches to the lake (a 2 mi./3km hike), and another heads to **Icy Lake** and **Upper Reid Falls** (a 1½ mi./2.5km hike). Both walks are gentle, with little change in elevation. A third trail to **Upper Dewey Lake** branches off the Icy Lake trail near the northern end of Lower Dewey Lake. The first section of the 2¼ mi./3.5km trail is brutal until the climb mellows out into switchbacks to the site of the lake, in a stunning amphitheater of serrated peaks. The total ascent from town takes about three hours. A cabin with cramped space for four, newly renovated with bunks and cooking utensils, is available on a first-come, first-served basis. The best tenting sites are along the far shore. **Fishing** is available at both Dewey Lakes. The **Skyline Trail** leads up AB Mountain, named for the pattern created by spring meltwater on its face. Both the directions to the trailhead and the challenging trail itself are confusing; pick up a **Skagway Trail Map** at the Trail Center or at the Klondike Gold Rush National Historical Park Visitor Center. From town, it's about 5 mi. to the panoramic 3500 ft. summit; allow three to four hours for the steep ascent. A free **camping permit** is necessary in the Skagway area and is available at the police station.

Packer Expeditions (983-2544; packer@ptialaska.net) guides mountaineering trips and rents snowshoes and poles ($5 for the first day, $3 per each additional day) out of **The Mountain Shop,** on 5th Ave. just west of Broadway. (Open in summer daily 9am-8pm; in winter Tu-Sa noon-5pm.)

YAKUTAT

The most geographically isolated settlement in Alaska, this mostly Tlingit town of 800 is ringed by the highest coastal mountains in the world and flanked by alarmingly active ice. Hubbard Glacier to the north is the largest tidewater glacier in the world and has twice galloped across the mouth of Russell Fjord—once in 1986, and again in 1989—nearly transforming it into the world's largest glacial lake. While Yakutat's ocean-front weather isn't for the faint of heart (frequent storms bring up to 200 inches of rain and 200 inches of snow yearly), hardy surfers come here for some of the best surfing conditions in Alaska, and two canneries and hordes of sport fishermen do justice to Yakutat's reputation as fine fish-grounds. Wrangell-St.Elias National Park and Glacier Bay lie to the west and east, and much land around Yakutat is in the northernmost reaches of the Tongass National Forest. Rarely used Forest Service cabins and 22 miles of black sand beach beg attention. Nonetheless, Yakutat remains largely unexplored by backpackers. A flight to Anchorage stops here daily, however, and for a small charge well-equipped travelers bound farther north might generate a longer trip from this untrafficked gateway to the wilderness.

🔋 ORIENTATION AND PRACTICAL INFORMATION. Yakutat is the northernmost village in Southeast Alaska. It sits on Phipps Peninsula, enclosing Yakutat Bay, the only protected harbor on the Gulf of Alaska between the "mainland" and the Panhandle. The airport is 5 mi. south of the ferry dock and downtown, on Monti Bay. One road runs from the airport to the small boat harbor and another to the dump. Most folks in Yakutat give directions by landmarks, not street names. Yakutat is the smallest community in the world with daily jet service. **Alaskan Airlines** (784-3366 or 800-426-0333) flights #61 and 66 do the honors, stopping in on their way between Seattle and Anchorage. Once a month in summer, and then only if there's a vehicle reservation, the **Alaska Marine Highway** stops in on its way from Juneau to Valdez. **Sunset Taxi** (784-3612) grudgingly runs 24 hours. **Situk Leasing** (784-3316) meets flights and rents beat-up old trucks for $65 per day (unlimited mileage; in winter slightly cheaper; must be 18 with insurance and major credit card). The **Yakutat Chamber of Commerce** (784-3933 or 800-925-8828; www.yakutatalaska.com) has no office. The National Park Service has a **Ranger Station/Visitor Center** (P.O. Box 137; 784-3295; open M-F 8am-5pm, but call ahead) on Mallott Ave. that serves Wrangell-St. Elias and Glacier Bay National Parks. Reserve wilderness cabins at the **Yakutat Ranger District Forest Service** (784-3359; open M-F 8am-5pm), on Ocean Cape Rd. The **Alaska Dept. of Fish and Game office** (784-3255; open M-F 8am-5pm) is near the airport. **Yakutat Hardware** (784-3203; open M-Sa 10am-5:30pm), on Mallott Ave. downtown, sells licenses, hunting tags, gear, and supplies. **KeyBank** (784-3991; open M-Th 10am-3pm, F 10am-5pm), on Mallott Ave., is the only bank in town. **Monti Bay Foods** has the **ATM. Yakutat Lodge** has a coin laundry and charges $7 per shower. **Weather:** 800-662-6622. **Emergency:** 911. The **police** are in the hangar-shaped Public Safety Office on Max Italio Dr. The 24-hour **Health Center** (784-3275; open M-F 9am-noon and 1-4:30pm), dispenses from beneath the Forest Service office. The **post office** (784-3201; open M-F 9am-5pm, Sa 9am-1pm) is on Mallott Ave. **ZIP code:** 99689. **Area code:** 907.

🔋 ACCOMMODATIONS AND CAMPGROUNDS. Lodges and B&Bs cater to wealthy sports fishermen with packages in the winter, and have limited reservable lodging in the summer. Ask the chamber of commerce for a complete list of them. From April to August 15, **Yakutat Lodge** (784-3232; www.yakutat-lodge.com), next to the airport, rents spartan cabins with a shared bathhouse that sleep four ($25 per person). **Blue Heron Inn** (784-3287; blueheron@ptialaska.net), on Max Italio Dr. before the small boat harbor, rents clean, homey rooms and an apartment with kitchenette. (Breakfast and airport shuttle included. Rooms: Apr.-July $90 or $120 for 2 or more people; Aug. to mid-Oct., $60 per person for 3 or more; mid-Oct. to March $80.)

The only place near downtown suitable for **camping** is the field at the airport opposite Gulf Air. There are no bathrooms or faucets nearby. A 10-mile stretch of black sand perfect for running or beachcombing, **Cannon Beach,** near the airport, is frequented by bears, eagles, seals, and sea lions more than it is by humans. The old-growth forest running the length of the beach provides shelter from the weather. The Forest Service maintains a picnic shelter and pit toilets here, and is building pit toilets. Take a left a quarter mile from the airport onto the gravel road and follow it for 2 miles over the bridge, through the forest and onto the beach. Alternatively, find out where Native lands end and the National Forest begins, and camp on the (bear-frequented) public lands (see p. 44).

📷 **FOOD.** The **Glass Door Bar** (784-3331), on Mallott Ave., stays open nightly until folks clear out (pints $4-5) and is the only non-lodge bar in town. The **Yakutat Lodge** restaurant and bar is open daily 6am-10pm. **Mallott's General Store** (784-3355), on Max Italio Dr. a quarter mile from the turn-off after Monti Bay, is where locals get food, boots, and books. (Espresso window open from 6am. Store open daily 8am-8pm; in winter M-Sa 8am-7pm, Su 10am-3pm.) **Monti Bay Foods** (784-3395) on Mallott Ave. stays in business thanks to tourists and its ATM. (Open daily 7am-9pm.) Vegetarians make do with infrequent shipments of fresh fruits and vegetables. **Ret's Place** (784-3440), on Mallott Ave., fries the carnivorous spectrum. (Lunch specials $8. Summer special—"Fries, gravy, & a pop"—$4. Open daily 5am-5pm.) **The Landing Restaurant** (784-3592), at far end of the small boat harbor, is a family joint. (Sandwiches and burgers with fries $7-9. Open daily 11:30am-2pm, 6-10pm.) **Sunset Pizza** (784-3983), on Mallott Ave., serves big calzones ($9), small pizzas ($15) and smoothies ($3) with books to peruse. (Take-out Sa-Th 4-9pm, F 4-10pm.)

🏔 **SIGHTS AND OUTDOORS.** There are no tourist attractions in Yakutat. The five-clan **Mount St. Elias Dancers** perform when cruise ships are in town, or during holidays like **Fairweather Day** in August. Call the **Yakutat Tlingit Tribe** (784-3437) or the Native corporation, **Yak-Tat Kwaan Inc.** (784-3335), for details.

Worthwhile hikes and Forest Service cabins are accessible by foot from the **Dangerous River Road** which heads 30 miles east of Yakutat to the Dangerous River Bridge. If you do a single hike in Yakutat, be sure to visit **Harlequin Lake,** a three quarter mile easy hike from the end of the road. Crystal blue iceberg monoliths nudge the shore's edge and on a clear day the **Yakutat Glacier** is visible 6 miles away. Reserve the **Harlequin Lake Forest Service cabin** for an overnight stay. Beware that very big **bears** are known to roam these parts (see p. 44). Another relatively easy but no less beautiful hike close to town is the **Situk Lake Trail** (7 miles one-way), at the end of which there is a quiet lake and yet another Forest Service cabin. An easy additional 2 miles away is magnificent **Mountain Lake** in a silent, steep, lush valley.

Cannon Beach is 10 miles long and gorgeous. Surfers watch for rolling turquoise waves breaking off **Ocean Cape** or **Point Munoz** on Khantaak Island. Call Jack at **Icy Waves Surf Shop** (784-3983) to rent boards. Wetsuits are sold but not rented; you'll need 7-9mm for the 40-50°F water. Jack is also big cheese at the weather service and so knows what's coming.

Extensive waterways in the region are great for **kayaking** and **canoeing.** Consulting with the Forest Service can lead to some spectacular trips for experienced paddlers. Camping is permitted on some of the islands of Monti Bay, but experienced paddlers can venture farther afield. A long portage to **Russell Fjord** makes way for a trip up to **Hubbard Glacier.** The **Arhnklin, Dangerous,** and **Awke Rivers** run parallel to shore up to **Dry Bay,** the western end of **Glacier Bay National Park.** Some fishing charter services will transport backpackers and kayakers along the Puget Peninsula towards Hubbard Glacier, or across Yakutat Bay to the eastern end of **Wrangell-St. Elias National Park. Gulf Air** (784-3240) will fly backpackers and rafters to Wrangell-St. Elias, Glacier Bay, or the interior regions of the **Yakutat Forelands wilderness area** (about $250 per hr. for fly-ins and flightseeing). Contact the chamber of commerce for a list of charter operations, the Forest Service and the National Park Service have info on hiking and renting cabins in the region. Trippers bring their own gear and provisions.

The Yakutat region contains some of the richest salmon-producing streams in the world. The **Situk River** alone produces more fish than any other river of its size, and there are another 325 miles of rivers and streams to explore as well. The chamber of commerce runs high-end charters. **Hunting** in Yakutat yields moose, brown bear, black bear, mountain goats, an assortment of furry rodents, and all sorts of waterfowl. Whether you're out to shoot them or not, if you want to see some really big brown bears up close, you only need go as far as the Yakutat City Dump, where residents get out of their cars and go about their business seemingly without regard for the monster grizzlies roaming about.

SOUTHCENTRAL ALASKA

For **Road Conditions,** see p. 55. For **Alaska-wide** info, see p. 392.

For **Road Conditions,** see p. 55. For **Alaska-wide** info, see p. 392.

Anchorage, Prince William Sound, the Kenai Peninsula, and Kodiak Island are becoming more accessible as economic opportunities and an expanding network of well-maintained roads draw more and more escapees from the Lower 48. The cost of living slowly declines with the rise of telecommunications, and Alaska's isolation, while in little danger of disappearing, is gradually eroding in this region. Not all small communities have responded to tourism in the same way: several settlements, like Homer and Kenai, have retained a quiet, mellow feel. Alongside the beautiful paved routes dayhikes beckon, and in protected areas—like Chugach State Park or the Kenai Peninsula's parks and refuges—extended trips make for spectacular encounters with the wilderness. Not all the roads to the woods are so well serviced, as a trip toward the amazing Wrangell-St. Elias National Park will soon prove.

HIGHLIGHTS OF SOUTHCENTRAL ALASKA

■ Most travelers to Alaska pass through **Anchorage** (see p. 436), where goings-on at **Cyrano's** (see p. 443) and the fine **Museum of History and Art** (see p. 442) might temporarily distract them from the great state beyond.

■ Dayhike alongside Dall sheep on the pristine trails of **Chugach State Park** or undertake the gorgeous 22 mi. trip to Girdwood (see p. 445).

■ Diverse delights of the **Kenai Peninsula** (see p. 464) include the new **SeaLife Center** in **Seward** (see p. 467), overwhelming wildlife and glacier cruises in **Kenai Fjords National Park** (see p. 469), friendly folks in **Homer** (see p. 475) and laid-back **Kenai** (see p. 472), where the famed river of the same name is famed for its **fish.**

■ On **Prince William Sound** (p. 453), **Valdez** lies at the end of a gorgeous drive (see p. 458), while isolated **Cordova** hosts the calving **Childs Glacier** (see p. 461).

■ The massive glaciers and awe-inspiring scale of **Wrangell-St. Elias National Park** (see p. 448) can melt a person's mind.

ANCHORAGE

Alaska's foremost urban center and only metropolis, Anchorage is home to two-fifths of the state's population—a less-than-staggering 254,000 people. As far north as Helsinki and almost as far west as Honolulu, the city sprawls along highways and side-streets for almost 2000 sq. mi. The city achieved its size by hosting the headquarters of three enormous construction projects: the Alaska Railroad, WWII military development, and the Trans-Alaska Pipeline. Today, the world's largest and busiest harbor for tiny seaplanes lies near the Anchorage airport, itself a hugely busy cargo airport by virtue of its position on the great circle route between North America and Asia.

Anchorage may not be the next up-and-coming West Coast mecca, but outdoor cafes, street vendors, and hanging flower baskets on 4th Ave. downtown are certainly beautified for the arrival of summer tourists. The city serves as a starting point for most travelers, and as a good place to get oriented, prepare for a trip, and move on. Three of Alaska's 39 mountain ranges are visible from the city, and on a clear day, Denali (a.k.a. Mt. McKinley) can be seen from downtown. Although the city is far from architecturally pleasing, travelers can find plenty of entertaining activities within Anchorage and within reach.

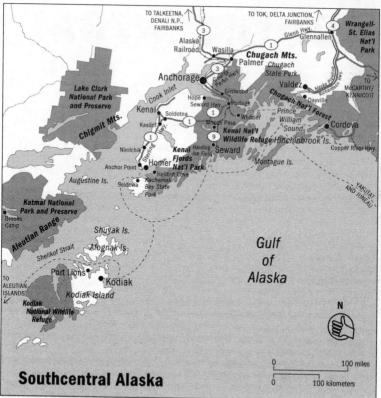

Southcentral Alaska

0 ——— 100 miles
0 ——— 100 kilometers

✳ ORIENTATION

Anchorage is the transportation hub of southcentral Alaska, 127 mi. (2½hr.) north of Seward on the Seward Hwy. (Rte. 9), 358 mi. (6hr.) south of Fairbanks on the George Parks Hwy. (Rte. 3), and 304 mi. (6hr.) west of Valdez along the Glenn Hwy. (Rte. 1) and Richardson Hwy. (Rte. 4). The city sprawls across some 50,000 acres of the Anchorage Bowl, framed by military bases **Fort Richardson** and **Elmendorf Air Force Base** to the north, the **Chugach Mountains** to the east, and the **Knik** and **Turnagain Arms** of the **Cook Inlet** to the west and south. Downtown Anchorage is laid out in a grid: numbered **avenues** run east-west, with addresses designated east or west from **C St.** North-south **streets** are lettered alphabetically to the west and named alphabetically to the east of **A St.** The rest of Anchorage spreads out along the major highways. The **University of Alaska** lies on 36th Ave., off Northern Lights Blvd. Buses run infrequently and the city is too spread out to walk everywhere. Renting a bike is a wise move, and several trails connect most of the city.

🄿 PRACTICAL INFORMATION

TRANSPORTATION

Airplanes: Anchorage International Airport (266-2437). Serviced by 8 international and 15 domestic carriers, including **Delta** (800-221-1212), **Northwest Airlines** (800-225-2525), **United** (800-241-6522), and **Alaska Airlines** (800-426-0333). Smaller airlines like **Reno Air** (800-736-6247), **Canada 3000** (888-336-3000), and **ERA Aviation** (800-866-8394) have cheap deals. Nearly every airport in Alaska can be reached from Anchorage, directly or via Fairbanks.

Trains: Alaska Railroad, 411 W. 1st Ave. (265-2494; outside AK 800-544-0552; www.akrr.com). 1 per day to: Seward (4hr., $50); Fairbanks (12hr., $154) via Talkeetna (3hr., $60) and Denali (8hr., $102). No service to Seward in winter. In summer, a flagstop train runs between Talkeetna and Hurricane (Th-Su; $25). The flagstop train will make unscheduled stops anywhere along this route; just wave it down with a white cloth and wait to be acknowledged with a whistle. In winter, a flagstop runs between Anchorage and Fairbanks. Bikes up to $20. Open M-F 5:30am-5pm, Sa-Su 5:30am-1pm. Tickets can be bought on board, but it's wise to book ahead.

Buses: Grayline Alaska (800-544-2206). Daily to: Seward (4hr., $40); Valdez (10hr., $66); Portage (2hr., $40). 3 per week to: Haines ($189); Skagway ($209); both with overnight in Beaver Creek. **Homer Stage Lines** (272-8644). To: Homer (daily M-Sa, $45). **Alaska Direct** (277-6652). To: Whitehorse, YT (3 per week, $145). **Parks Highway Express** (479-3065, in AK 888-600-6001). Daily to: Denali ($30); Fairbanks ($49). For Buses that run the George Parks Hwy., see p. 488.

Ferries: Alaska Marine Highway, 605 W. 4th Ave. (800-642-0066 or 800-642-0066; www.akhms.com), in the Old Federal Building. No terminal, but ferry tickets sold and reservations granted. Open daily 9am-5:30pm, M-F in the winter.

Public Transportation: People Mover Bus (343-6543), in the Transit Center on 6th Ave. between G and H St. **Free fare zone** bordered by 5th Ave., Denali St., 6th Ave., and L St. Runs hourly M-F 6am-10pm; restricted schedule Sa-Su, and off-schedule every time else. Fare $1, ages 5-18 50¢, over 65 25¢. Transit Center sells tokens (90¢), day passes ($2.50), schedules ($1), maps (50¢), and rents lockers ($2 per day); open M-F 8am-5pm.

Taxis: Yellow Cab, 272-2422. **Checker Cab,** 276-1234. **Alaska Cab,** 563-5353. About $15 from the airport to downtown; $8 to Spenard Hostel.

Car Rentals: Airport Car Rental, 502 W. Northern Lights Blvd. (277-7662). $45 per day with unlimited mileage or $40 and 22¢ per mi. after 150 mi. Must be 21; $5 per day extra if under 25. Cash deposit or credit card required. Free shuttle to, but not from, the airport. Open M-F 8am-8pm, Sa-Su 9am-6pm. **Affordable Car Rental,** 4707 Spenard Rd. (243-3370), opposite the Regal Alaskan Hotel. $56 per day, $336 per week; unlimited mileage. Must be 21 with major credit card. Free drop-off and pickup.

Ride Board: At the Anchorage Youth Hostel (see **Accommodations,** below).

VISITOR AND FINANCIAL SERVICES

Visitor Information: (274-3531; events 276-3200) on W. 4th Ave. at F St. A new building behind the cabin (274-2363) is typically less crowded and has more brochures. **Bike trails guide** 50¢. Open June-Aug. daily 7:30am-7pm; May and Sept. 8am-6pm; Oct.-Apr. 9am-4pm. Also at the airport (266-2437 or 266-2657), in the domestic terminal near the baggage claim, and in the international terminal at the central atrium.

Outdoor Information: Alaska Public Lands Information Center, 605 W. 4th Ave. (271-2737 or 271-2738; fax 271-2744; www.nps.gov/aplic/center), in the Old Federal Bldg. between F and G St. Here are the **Park Service, Forest Service, Division of State Parks,** the **Fish and Wildlife Service,** and the **Alaska Marine Highway** reservation desks under one glorious roof. Popular topographic maps, a computerized sportfishing map, and live presentations on Alaska's outdoor attractions. Open daily 9am-5:30pm.

Employment: Alaska Employment Service, 3301 Eagle St., P.O. Box 107024 (269-4800). Take bus #60 to get nearby. Open M-F 8am-5pm.

Currency Exchange: Thomas Cook, 311 F St. (278-2822 or 800-287-7362), next to the Hilton. Open in summer M-F 9am-5pm, Sa 10am-2pm.

LOCAL SERVICES

Equipment Rental: Downtown Bicycle Rental, 333 W. 4th St. (279-5293), between C and D St., 5 blocks from the Coastal Trail (see p. 445). Bikes $15 for 3hr., $19 for 5hr., $24 per day. Lock, helmet, map, and gloves included. Credit card required. Open daily 8am to 7 or 8pm. **The Bike Exchange,** 211 E. 4th (276-2453), between Barrow and Cordova. Bikes range in quality but are cheap. $10 for same day return, $15 per day with

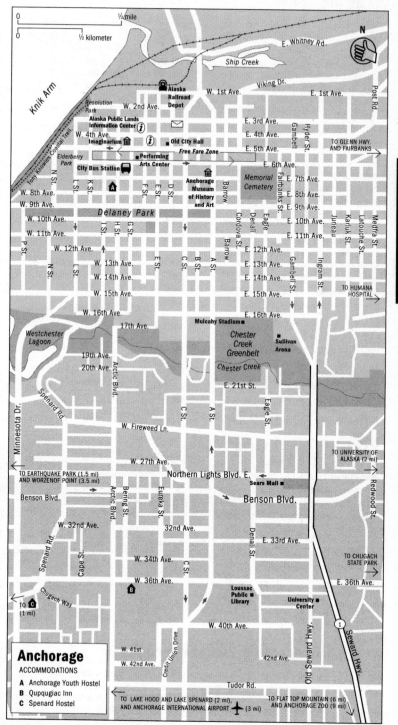

lock and helmet. Open M-F 11am-7pm, Sa noon-6pm. **Recreational Equipment, Inc. (REI),** 1200 Northern Lights Blvd. (272-4565), near Spenard. High-quality everything, plus rentals. Open M-F 10am-9pm, Sa-Su 10am-6pm. **Alaska Mountaineering and Hiking (AMH),** 2633 Spenard (272-1911; www.alaskamountaineering.com), between Northern Lights and Fireweed. Best selection, great advice, and a good network for finding hiking or climbing partners. Rentals, too. Open M-F 9am-7pm, Sa 9am-6pm, Su noon-5pm. **Army-Navy Store** (279-2401), on 4th Ave. opposite the Post Office Mall. Good prices for hunters and fishers. Open M-F 9am-8pm, Sa 9am-6pm, Su 9am-6pm. **Play It Again Sports** (278-7529), at 27th and Spenard near REI, buys and sells used equipment. Rents in-line skates for $15 for the first day, then $10 per day. Open M-F 10am-8pm, Sa 10am-6pm, Su 11:30am-5:30pm.

Bookstore: Cook Inlet Book Co., 415 W. 5th Ave. (258-4544), between D and E St. Claims the largest selection of Alaskana anywhere (open daily 8:30am-10pm; reduced hours in winter). For a dog-eared copy of *White Fang,* try **C&M Used Books,** 215 E. 4th Ave. (278-9394; open M-Tu and Th-F 10am-7pm, W and Sa 10am-6pm), between Barrow and Cordova, or **Title Wave,** 1068 W. Fireweed Ln. (278-2665 or 278-9283, www.wavebooks.com; open M-Sa 10:30am-6:30pm, Su noon-5pm).

Library: ZJ Loussac Library (261-2975), at 36th Ave. and Denali St. Take bus #2, 36, or 60. $40 million building devotes an entire wing to Alaskana. Free 1hr. Internet access; first-come first-served and 15min. limit on terminals. Open M-Th 11am-9pm, F-Sa 10am-6pm; in winter also Su noon-6pm.

Services for the Disabled: Challenge Alaska, 344-7399.

Gay and Lesbian Helpline: 258-4777. Open daily 6-11pm.

Laundromat: K-Speed Wash, 600 E. 6th St. (279-0731), at Fairbanks. Wash $1.50, dry 25¢ per 5min. Open M-Sa 7am-10pm.

Public Showers: Fairview Community Recreational Center, 1121 E. 10th St. (343-4130), between Karluk and Latouche, a 15min. walk from downtown. Untimed showers $2, ages 12-18 50¢. Open M-Sa 8am-9:45pm, Su 11am-5:45pm. Same prices at **Spenard Recreational Center,** 20 W. 48th Ave. (343-4160), next to the school at Northwood. Take bus #36. Open M-F 7:30am-10pm, Sa-Su 9am-10pm.

Weather: 936-2525. **Motorists' and Recreation Forecast:** 936-2626. **Road Conditions:** 273-6037. **Marine Weather:** 936-2727.

EMERGENCY AND COMMUNICATIONS

Emergency: 911. **Police,** 4501 S. Bragaw (786-8500). 24hr.

Rape Crisis Line: 800-478-8999 or 276-7273. 24hr. Office at 1057 W. Fireweed #230 at Spenard St., on bus #6, 7, and 60. Open M-F 8am-5pm.

Hospital: Columbia Alaska Regional Hospital, 2801 DeBarr Rd. (276-1131). 24hr. **Providence Hospital,** 3200 Providence St. (562-2211). 24hr.

Post Office: (800-275-8777) at W. 4th Ave. and C St. on the lower level of the banana-yellow mall. Open M-F 10am-5:30pm. **Stamp machine** 24hr. **ZIP Code:** 99510. The **state central post office** (266-3259), next to the airport, does not handle general delivery mail but is open 24hr.

Internet Access: See **Library,** above. **Surf City Cafe,** 415 L St. (279-7877), between 4th and 5th. 12¢ per min. Open M-F 7am-midnight, Sa-Su 10am-midnight. Swanky chairs.

Public Radio: 91.5 FM. Native American Band 90.3 FM.

Area Code: 907.

ACCOMMODATIONS AND CAMPGROUNDS

Anchorage has large hostels, each with its own drawback, and some quasi-hostels. Hotels and B&Bs are expensive, especially downtown. Cheap motels are less so (from $75). Try **Alaska Private Lodgings** (258-1717; open M-Sa 8am-7pm) or the **Anchorage reservation service** (272-5909) for out-of-town B&Bs (from $65).

Tenters have been known to try the gravel pull-outs on the western limits of Northern Lights Blvd. after it becomes a rural two-lane road, or to hike the coastal trail and camping in the woods. Pay campgrounds await in nearby **Chugach State Park** (354-5014). Two of the best are northeast of Anchorage along the Glenn Hwy. (Rte. 1). **Eagle River** is 12½ mi. from town ($15), and **Eklutna** (EE-kloot-nah) lies 26½ mi. along the Glenn and then 10 mi. east on Eklutna Rd. ($10). These secluded wooded spots are popular with locals. Show up early, especially on weekends.

■ **Spenard Hostel,** 2845 W. 42nd Pl. (248-5036). Take bus #36 or 7 from downtown, or #6 from the airport along Spenard to Turnagain Blvd. Go north on Turnagain then turn left onto 42nd Pl. About 4 mi. from downtown (20min. by bus or 30min. by bike) and 1½ mi. from the airport. Comfortable, clean, and welcoming. 3 lounges, 3 kitchens, and a big yard. Friendly hosts arrange weekly potlucks. 40 beds or tent space: $15. Free local calls and Denali Shuttle drop-off/pickup, Internet access ($5 per hr.), bike rental ($5), laundry, and lockers. Quiet hours, but no curfew or lockout. Chore requested, work exchange available. Check-in 9am-1pm and 7-11pm. 6-day max. stay.

Qupqugiaq Inn (koop-KOO-gee-ak), 640 W. 36th Ave. (563-5633), between Arctic Blvd. and C St. Take bus #9. Anchorage's only affordable non-hostel accommodations. Common lounge and kitchen, shared bathrooms, well-lit private rooms with locks, comfortable beds, and cable TV. Rooms face the street. Singles from $39; doubles $49. Includes a bagel and latte at the cafe downstairs and an alternative travel center with resources for travel, volunteering, and working. No smoking or alcohol. Common areas close at 10pm. Credit card reservations. Check-in noon-7pm or 10pm-2am.

International Backpackers Hostel, 3601 Peterkin Ave. (274-3870). The Parks Highway and Kachemak Bay Transit buses stop right in front every day. Take bus #45 from downtown to the Mountain View Carwash on Taylor Rd., turn left on Taylor and right at the stop on Peterkin. New owners and renovations should improve this hostel's reputation. Located in a residential neighborhood near downtown. Single-sex rooms and some curtained-off bunks. 30 bunks: $15. Tent space: $10. Free linens, towels $1, coin laundry, cable TV, bike rental ($10 per day, helmet $5), and free local calls. Quiet hours 10pm-6am, but no curfew or lock-out. Noon check-in and check-out. The **Borealis Shuttle** travels to and from the airport (15min.; $12 for 1, $15 for 2 people).

Anchorage International Youth Hostel (HI), 700 H St. (276-3635), at 7th St., 1 block south of the city bus station. You can't beat the location, but that's about all you can't beat. Plastic-covered floors, thin bunks. Kitchens, TV, balconies, lockers, laundry, and internet access ($10 per hr.). 91 bunks: $15, nonmembers $18. Lockout noon-5pm. Curfew 1am; watchman check-in until 2am. Chore requested. 5-night max. stay in summer. Filled to the rafters in summer; call ahead. Pay by 11am or lose your spot.

Centennial Park, 8300 Glenn Hwy. (333-9711), 15 min. drive north of town. Take Muldoon Rd. south off Glenn, left on Boundary, and left on Freeway Frontage Rd., or take bus #9 or 74 from downtown. Free toilets and showers, dumpsters, firepits, and water. 88 tent and RV sites $13, Alaskans or Golden Age Passport $11. 7-day max. stay. Quiet hours 10pm-8am. Noon check-out. Open May-Sept.

◘ FOOD

Anchorage presents travelers with the most affordable and varied culinary fare in the state. **Great Harvest Bread Company,** 570 E. Benson Blvd. (274-3331; open M-Sa 7am-6pm), in Metro Mall, stocks excellent fresh bread. Loaves run $4-6, but hefty slices are free. **New Sagaya,** 3700 Old Seward Hwy. (561-5173), at 36th, also at 13th and I St., is an international market with fine Asian food and fresh produce, also home to a coffee shop, Chinese take-out restaurant, and **L'Aroma Bakery** (see below). Take bus #2 or 36. (Open M-F 10am-9pm, Sa 9am-9pm, Su 10am-7pm.) **Carr's** (297-0200), at 13th and Gambell St., sells groceries 24 hours. Take bus #11; this neighborhood is somewhat unsafe for the six months of the year that it's dark.

■ **Moose's Tooth,** 3300 Old Seward (258-2537), take bus #2 or 36. Named for one of Denali's neighbors, this relaxed joint serves pizzas and brews as hearty as the climbers who tackle the peak. Small pizza $9. House-brewed raspberry wheat ale $3.50. Hot local bands usher in new brews on the first Thursday of every month. Open mic Monday 9pm-11pm. Open M-Th 11am-midnight, F-Sa noon-1am, Su noon-midnight.

Sweet Basil Cafe, 335 E St. (274-0070). The cafe's CEO is a black labrador retriever named Buba, but it's probably the owner-chefs who wake up bright and early to make the pastries, breads, and pastas. Killer vegetable and fruit juices (about $3), smoothies, and lunch. Their dinners are the most affordable gourmet options in town. Braised lamb in an orange tomato herb broth on fettucini $12.50. Open in summer from 7am 'til the sun goes down; winter hours vary.

Snow City Cafe, 1034 W. 4th St. (272-2489), at L St. Fine-art-bedecked and acoustically blessed by live music F-Sa (open mic Su). One of the best breakfasts in town is served until 5pm. Eggs benedict $7, interesting salads and big sandwiches $3-6, daily soup with fresh bagel $4.75. Open daily 7am-10pm; reduced winter hours.

Twin Dragon, 612 E. 15th Ave. (276-7535), near Gambell; take bus #11. Lures hungry travelers with the promise of great Mongolian barbecue. All-you-can-eat buffet of marinated meats and vegetables, hot off the giant grill. Lunch $7; BBQ and Chinese food buffet dinner combo $10. Open M-Sa 11am-midnight, Su 1pm-midnight.

M.A.'s Gourmet Dogs, at the corner of 4th and G St. PBS and *USA Today* called it one of the best hotdog stands in America. The people lined up around the block will back up that review. Hotdogs, polish sausage, or reindeer sausage $3.25. Open in summer.

Sawaddi Thai Restaurant, 300W. 36th St. (563-8335), 2 blocks east of the library, serves a delicious lunch buffet ($7; M-F 11am-2pm). Also at 219 Diamond Blvd. in the Kings Row Shoppes (522-3663) without the buffet. Both open daily 11am-10pm.

Muffin Man, 529 I St. (279-6836). Enjoy the fruits of a creative muffin mind. Blueberry banana nut or Oreo 75¢. Non-muffin options, too. Open M-F 6am-3pm, Sa 7am-2pm.

CAFES AND COFFEEHOUSES

Side Street Espresso, 412 G St. (258-9055). Political salons, acoustic music, a book exchange, and local writers. Thai iced-tea $1.50. Cappuccino $2.25. Open M-F 7am-7pm, Sa 7am-5pm, Su 8am-5pm.

Qupqugiaq Cafe and School, 640 W. 36th Ave. (563-5634). Named after a legendary 10-legged polar bear (koop-KOO-gee-ak) who rejected violence to create a community based on love and peace, this cafe offers free classes and wholesome food for hungry minds and stomachs. Herb-roasted chicken sandwich $6.50, latte $2.25. A bulletin board advertises local events. Live acoustic music most summer weekends. Open M-F 7am-8pm, Sa 9am-8pm, Su 9am-3pm. Inn upstairs (see **Accommodations,** above).

◉ SIGHTS

Watching over Anchorage from Cook Inlet is **Mt. Susitna,** known to locals as the "Sleeping Lady." Legend has it that this marks the resting spot of an Athabascan maid who dozed while awaiting her lover's return from war. When peace reigns in the world, the stories say, she will awake. Closer to town off Northern Lights Blvd., **Earthquake Park** recalls the 1964 Good Friday quake, the strongest ever recorded in North America, recently re-evaluated as a 9.2 on the Richter scale.

The ■ **Anchorage Museum of History and Art,** 121 W. 7th Ave. (343-4326), at A St., is hands-down the finest museum in town, and probably the state. Permanent exhibits of Native Alaskan artifacts and art mingle with national and international works. Once you're in, it's possible and advisable to spend the entire day here. (Open daily Su-F 9am-9pm, Sa 9am-6pm, Sept.-May Tu-Sa 10am-6pm, Su 1pm-5pm. Tours daily at 10, 11am, 1, and 2pm. $5, seniors $4.50, under 18 free.) The **Alaska Aviation Heritage Museum,** 4721 Aircraft Dr. (248-5325), affords a look at restoration work and 22 rare planes from 1928-52, some salvaged from the bush, and a film on aerial adventure and derring-do. To get there, take the Lake Hood Exit off International Airport Rd. and turn left onto Aircraft Dr. (Open daily 9am-6pm. $6; seniors $4.50; ages 7-12 $2.75; under 7 free; military and AAA members $4.50.)

If you don't see Alaska's animals in the wild—a challenge, indeed—you can spot them at the **Alaska Zoo** (346-2133 or 346-3242), Mile 2 on O'Malley Rd. Binky the Polar Bear mauled a tourist here in 1994 and became something of a local hero. The cub that survives him, Ahpun (ah-poon), will hopefully be just as popular. (*Let's Go* does not recommend attempting to endear yourself to locals by maiming tourists.) To get there, turn towards the mountains off the Seward Hwy. or take Minnesota which becomes O'Malley, or take bus #2 there and 91 back. (Open daily 9am-6pm. $7, seniors $6, under 3-12 $3.)

Children love the **Imaginarium**, 737 W. 5th St. (276-3179, www.imaginarium.org), between G and H St. downtown, and hands-on exhibits on dinosaurs, space, strange laws of physics, wetlands and forests; a touch tank, planetarium, and space ice cream ($2.75). The 19-foot Burmese python named Monty is not a hands-on exhibit. (Open M-Sa 10am-6pm, Su noon-5pm. $5, ages 2-12 and seniors $4.)

♫ ENTERTAINMENT

The visitor center provides a **calendar** of weekly events; call 276-3200 for more listings. ✪ **Cyrano's Off Center Playhouse**, at 413 D St. (274-2599; etc@alaskalife.net), between 4th and 5th, is a big supporter of young and local talent and center for all sorts of entertainment. It contains a cafe, a bookshop, a stage that is home to the **Eccentric Theatre Company,** and a cozy cinema that supports quirky festivals and screens foreign films. Storytellers spin Alaskan tales here on summer afternoons, and poetry readings, film discussion groups, and comedy keep things together. (Bookshop open daily 11am-9:30pm, but won't kick you out. Theater at 7pm, in summer F-Tu, in winter Th-Su. Tickets $12.50, students, seniors, and military $10. Stories $5, children $4. Films $6.50, matinees $3.)

Take bus #75 to the **Capri Cinema**, 3425 E. Tudor Rd. (561-0064), for screenings of art flicks and second-run mainstream films ($6, before 6pm $4). The **Alaska Experience Theater**, 705 W. 6th Ave. (276-3730 or 276-9076), shows "Alaska the Greatland," a 40-minute presentation of scenery, wildlife, and Alaskan culture projected

DOES THE WORD "MUSH" MEAN ANYTHING TO YOU?

The celebrated Iditarod dog sled race begins in Anchorage on the first weekend in March. Dogs and their drivers ("mushers") traverse a trail over two mountain ranges, along the mighty Yukon River, and over the frozen Norton Sound to Nome. State pride holds that the route is 1049 mi., in honor of Alaska's status as the 49th state, but the real distance is closer to 1150 mi.

The Iditarod ("a far-off place") Trail began as a dog sled supply route from Seward on the southern coast to interior mining towns. The race commemorates the 1925 rescue of Nome, when drivers ferried 300,000 units of life-saving diptheria serum from Nenana, near Fairbanks, to Nome. The first race, in 1967, was a 27 mi. jaunt; by 1973, the first full race was run in 20 days. Today, up to 70 contestants speed each year from Anchorage to Nome, competing for a $450,000 purse but surprisingly willing to help fellow mushers in distress. Susan Butcher has won four races, Rick Swanson clinched five, and Doug Swingley has made the fastest time (nine days, two hours).

The race has come under fire from animal rights activists because of the hardships borne by the dogs, some of whom die en route to Nome. Nevertheless, the dogs love to run, and Anchorage turns out in force for the ceremonial start downtown; the clock actually starts at Wasilla, north of the city. For more info, contact the Iditarod Trail Committee (376-5155; www.iditarod.com), Dept. M, P.O. Box 870800, Wasilla, AK 99687, or visit the Iditarod Headquarters (with museum, video presentations, gift shop, and free admission) at Mile 2.2 Knik Rd. in Wasilla.

on the inside of a hemispherical dome. (On the hour 9am-9pm. $7, ages 5-12 $4.) The theater's **earthquake exhibit** rumbles for a full 15 fun-filled minutes. (Every 20min. 8:50am-9:30pm. $5, ages 5-12 $4. Film and exhibit $10, ages 4-12 $7.) The **4th Avenue Theatre,** 630 4th Ave. (257-5635), one block west of the Log Cabin Visitor Center, has been restored its 1940s decor. The neon building contains a small grocery and gift shop, sponsors concerts and comedy, and shows a 45-minute **3D Alaska Gold Rush movie,** using the original, low-tech 3D glasses ($5).

Anchorage is no desert for the sports aficionado. The **Anchorage Bucs** (561-2827) and the **Anchorage Glacier Pilots** (274-3627) play baseball against teams like the Hawaii Island Movers and the Fairbanks Goldpanners in **Mulcahy Stadium,** at 16th and Cordova. This is a league of stars-to-be. Mark McGwire and Tom Seaver both played here before making it big. In the cold months, the **Anchorage Aces** and the **University of Alaska Anchorage** team play hockey. Call Carr's Tix for info, 263-2787.

🎵 NIGHTLIFE

The brewpub revolution has finally hit Anchorage, and microbrews gush from taps like oil through so many pipelines.

Bernie's Bungalow Lounge, 626 D St. (276-8808), at 7th St. Relax in one of many wingback chairs or couches as you sip your lemon drop martini ($5), puff on a cigar ($3-10), and play a round of croquet at Anchorage's newest hot spot. Frequented by the young and retro, with live music and an outdoor kitchen. Open M-Th 2pm-2:30am, F-Sa 2pm-3am, Su noon-2:30am; winter hours vary.

Humpy's (276-BEER/2337), at F Ave. and 6th St. Over 40 beers on tap: micros and out-of-state drafts $3.75, imports $4. Great selection of tequilas and scotches. Halibut tacos $7. Live music nightly, and so packed on weekends that you can barely see. Open M-W 11am-2am, Th-Sa 11am-2:30am, Su noon-2am.

Chilkoot Charlie's, 2435 Spenard Rd. (272-1010), at Fireweed; take bus #7. With cavernous dance floors and top 40/rock music, "Koots" is known as the place to dance late into the night. It's also known as a meat market. Dollar drink specials until 10pm. Escalating cover from 8pm ($2-5). Open Su-Th 10:30am-2:30am, F-Sa 11am-3am.

Blues Central, 825 Northern Lights Blvd. (272-1341), at the corner of Arctic St.; take bus #9. This smoky, sophisticated bar answers the cry for good live music. Live music daily at 9:30pm; jams on Sundays. Microbrews $4.50, gutter cocktails $3. Open M-F 11am-2am, Sa-Su 5pm-2am. Cover Tu-Th $2, F-Sa $3, Su free.

🛍 SHOPPING

Saturday Market, held on Wednesday and Saturday in the Lower Bowl parking lot at 3rd and E St. Made-in-Alaska products, as well as harvested-in-Alaska produce and fish. May to early Sept. Sa 10am-6pm. A slightly smaller **Wednesday Market** began last year and hopes to establish itself from 10am-8pm along 4th and 5th between C and F St.

Alaska Native Medical Center, 4315 Diplomacy Dr. (729-1122), off Tudor Rd. Take bus #75. The first-floor gift shop sells arts and handicrafts with which many Native Alaskans pay for medical services. Proceeds fund scholarships and aid for native communities. Open M-F 10am-2pm, and the first and third Saturdays of the month 11am-2pm.

The Rage Vintage Clothing, 423 G St. (274-7243), between 4th and 5th. Butterfly collars, smoking jackets, retro dresses for a bargain, though more expensive than a thrift store. Open M and W-F noon-7pm, Sa noon-6pm; Tu and Su and in winter, call ahead.

Salvation Army Thrift Store, 300 W. Northern Lights (561-5514), take bus #3 or 4. Hawks a wide range of cheap second-hand clothing. Open M-Sa 9am-8pm.

Mammoth Music, 2906 Spenard Rd. (258-3555), take bus #7, carries many, many, many new and used CDs. Open M-F 9am-10pm, Sa 10am-10pm, Su noon-6pm.

◢ OUTDOORS

From Anchorage both the north and south beckon. Just 30 minutes south along the Sterling Highway (Rte. 9), skiing awaits at Girdwood (see p. 462); the drive past the tidal bores of Turnagain Inlet shouldn't be missed (see p. 462). Two hours south on the Seward and across the Sterling, the Kenai River supports unstoppable fishing near Cooper Landing (see p. 470). Kenai National Wildlife Refuge lies within reach of Seward (see p. 468), a manageable overnight or daytrip from Anchorage. Hikes near Exit Glacier, flightseeing tours, and even a tour of the Kenai Fjords National Park are still more reasons to venture south (see p. 469). North of town Talkeetna offers access to the region of Denali above, and routes to and from Glennallen promise views of the Wrangell Mountains (see p. 447).

IN TOWN. Walk, skate, or bike to the **Tony Knowles Coastal Trail,** an 11 mi., wheelchair-accessible paved track that skirts Cook Inlet on one side and the backyards of Anchorage's upper crust on the other. The heavily traveled trail is one of the best urban bike paths in the country, groomed in winter for **cross-country skiing.** Pick up the trail on 2nd Ave. or Elderberry Park on the west edge of downtown.

CHUGACH STATE PARK. Within minutes, travelers can escape Anchorage for the serene 770 sq. mi. of **Chugach State Park,** which borders the city to the north, east, and south. The Public Lands Information Center (see **Practical Information,** above) provides a wealth of info on hiking and canoeing in the park. After inspecting the maps and pictures, call 800-280-2267 to reserve any of the park's **public use cabins** ($25 per night plus a $8.25 reservation fee), or seek more accessible camping (see **Accommodations and Campgrounds,** above). More info is available at the **Eagle River Nature Center** (694-2108; open in summer daily 10am-5pm; $3 parking fee), 12 miles up Eagle River Rd. off the Glenn Hwy. (Rte. 1); and at the **Potter Section House** (345-5014; open M-F 10am-noon and 1-3pm), 25 minutes south of Anchorage at Seward Hwy. Mile 110. For Seward Hwy. coverage, see p. 462.

Chugach has 25 established **dayhiking** trails, which leave from different points in Anchorage and along the Glenn Hwy. A 15-minute drive from the heart of the city, **Flattop Mountain** (4500 ft.) provides an excellent view of the inlet, the mountains of the Aleutian Chain, and on the rare clear day or evening, Denali. This is the most frequently climbed mountain in Alaska, with a steep and occasionally slippery 2-mile hike to its crowded summit. Unfortunately you need a car or a ride to get to the trailhead (parking $5; bus #92 drops you off at the foot of a 2000 ft. battle up the road to the trail). Take O'Malley, the continuation of Minnesota, toward the mountains off the Seward, turn right on Hillside, left on Upper Huffman for three-quarters of a mile, then turn right onto Toilsome and drive 2 miles to the flight of steps on the right side of the parking lot. Less crowded hikes branch off from the **Powerline Trail** through open taiga and tundra and a great mountain biking route begins here as well. The **Middle Fork Loop,** three-quarters of a mile up Powerline, leads a gentle 12 miles through spruce woods and open tundra.

Near the Eagle River Nature Center the **Old Iditarod Trail,** also known as **Crow Creek Pass,** begins its stellar 22-mile journey to **Girdwood** (see p. 462). The entire trip takes a good two or three days and requires one major stream crossing, but the first portion makes an excellent dayhike past waterfalls, beaver dams, and alpine lakes. A tremendous view of water shooting over the jagged walls of twin falls lies 5 miles along the lush valley. The trailhead for **Thunderbird Falls** is just off Glenn Hwy. at Mile 25; take the Thunderbird exit and follow signs for 1 mi. The gorge and falls are a leisurely mile-long walk. The beautiful **Albert Loop Trail** is a shorter and far easier 3-mile loop. It leaves right from the visitor center and nears the Eagle River, a real nice place to see a bear.

Chugach has several trails geared towards **cyclists.** The **Eklutna Lakeside Trail** extends 13 mi. one-way from the Eklutna Campground, off Mile 26 of the Glenn Hwy. (Rte. 1). A relatively flat dirt road, the trail follows the blue-green Eklutna Lake for 7 mi. before entering a steep river canyon, ending at the base of the

SOUTHCENTRAL ALASKA

Eklutna River. Kayakers and canoers relish the quiet waters of Eklutna Lake. **Nancy Lake State Recreation Area,** just west of the Parks Hwy. (Rte. 3) at Mile 67.3, and just south of **Willow,** is well known for its **canoeing.** The **Lynx Lake Loop** takes two days, weaving through 8 miles of lakes and portages, with designated campsites along the way. The loop begins at Mile 4.5 of the Nancy Lake Parkway, at the Tanaina Lake Canoe Trailhead. For **canoe rental** or **shuttle service** in the Nancy Lake area, call **Tippecanoe** (495-6688; open Th-Tu 9am-6pm; canoes $25 first day, $70 for 4-7 days; shuttle free for backpackers). **Lifetime Adventures** (746-4644), at the Eklutna Campground, rents **bikes** and **kayaks.** (Bikes $8 for 2hr., $15 for 4hr., $25 per day. Double kayaks from $25 per half-day, $45 per day.) **Class V Whitewater** (783-2004; www.alaska.net/~classv), runs kayaks and rafts down three different canyons on the stunning Sixmile River. (Class III $60, IV $85, V $125, must be 16 with prior experience.) **NOVA Riverrunners** (800-746-5753) runs whitewater rafting down the **Matanuska Valley** (4hr. Class III and IV trip $75).

WINTER. Skiing and **snowboarding trails** weave around Anchorage. **Alyeska Ski Resort** is a short drive away along the Seward Hwy. (Rte. 9; see **Girdwood,** p. 462). **Turnagain Pass** (see **Seward Hwy.,** p. 462) offers the best backcountry skiing and snowboarding in the region. At the end of Raspberry Road and the Tommy Knowles Coastal Trail lies **Kincaid Park,** the largest cross-country skiing area in the U.S. **Hatcher Pass,** north of **Wasilla** and **Palmer** on the Wasilla-Fishhook and the Palmer-Fishhook Roads, respectively, grooms cross-country trails; **Government Peak** and **Mile 16 Trail** are popular downhill skiing and snowboarding spots.

    Glacier tours offer one of the best opportunities in the state to witness the amazing spectacle of huge chunks of ice plummeting into the ocean. **Philips' 26 Glacier Cruise,** 509 W. 4th Ave. (276-8023 or 800-544-0529), actually departs from **Whittier,** a $52 train ride from Anchorage ($122, children $52, including halibut or chicken lunch). The five-hour voyage travels 110 mi. through **College** and **Harriman Fjords,** close by six tidewater glaciers (the other 20 are pined for from afar). A gaggle of other glacier tour companies have cruises that depart daily from Seward, 2½ hours south of Anchorage (see **Kenai Fjords National Park,** p. 469).

GLENN HIGHWAY (RTE. 1)

The Glenn Highway runs from Anchorage 189 mi. northeast to **Glennallen** (see p. 447), and from there to **Tok** and the **Richardson Hwy. (Rte. 4).** The first 37 mi. of the Glenn also begin the **George Parks Hwy. (Rte. 3)** to Denali and Fairbanks.

ANCHORAGE TO PALMER

The Glenn Highway runs from Anchorage 189 mi. northeast to **Glennallen** (see p. 447), and from there to **Tok** and the **Richardson Hwy. (Rte. 4).** The first 37 mi. of the Glenn also begin the **George Parks Hwy. (Rte. 3)** to Denali and Fairbanks.

    Leaving Anchorage on 6th Ave., the highway traces the western edge of **Chugach State Park** (for coverage of camping, hiking, biking, and canoeing in the park, see p. 445). At Mile 26, off the Eklutna (ee-KLOOT-na) Exit, is **Eklutna Historical Park** (688-6026, in Eagle River 696-2828), the remains of a Dena'ina village that dates back to 1620 and an example of the more recent confluence of Russian Orthodox and Athabascan traditions. The small log structure of **Old St. Nicholas Russian Church** was used for services until 1962 and remains the oldest standing building in greater Anchorage. The restored cemetery is home to 100 brightly painted **spirit houses.** The village is accessible through the gift shop ($3.50; children under 6 free). From there a pamphlet outlines a walking tour and a guided tour departs every hour (open mid-May to mid-Sept. daily 8am-6pm).

    From Eklutna, the Glenn Hwy. heads into the **Matanuska Valley,** where settlers watched in astonishment as the long summer daylight produced garden vegetables big enough to feed a ship. The valley is still famous for its produce, legal and illegal: those in the know claim that **Matanuska Valley Thunderfuck** is some of the world's best marijuana. (*Let's Go* does not recommend getting thunderfucked.)

PALMER

After passing the turn-off for the George Parks Hwy. (Rte. 3, see p. 488), the Glenn Hwy. (Rte. 1) rolls eastward into the agricultural hamlet of Palmer, home every August to the **Alaska State Fair** (745-4827 or 800-850-3247), which awarded ribbons to an 86.4 lb. cabbage and a 6.6 lb. carrot in 1998. Palmer's **visitor center,** 723 S. Valley Way (745-2880), provides standard info plus, in autumn, specimens of the region's freakishly big fruits and legumes—sorry, no pot (open May to mid-Sept. daily 8am-7pm). Four blocks from the visitor center is Palmer's artsy alternative to agriculture, **Vagabond Blues,** 642 S. Alaska St. (745-2233), with espresso, an entirely vegetarian menu, live music, and an open wall for upstart artists. (Live music F-Sa 8-10pm. Open M-Th 7am-9pm, F 7am-11pm, Sa 8am-11pm, Su 9am-5pm.)

The world's only **domesticated musk ox farm** (745-4151) flanks Archie Rd., a few miles from the Parks Hwy. turn-off at Mile 50.1 of the Glenn Hwy. Introduced from Greenland in 1934, Palmer's oxen are prized for their *qiviut* (KIV-ee-oot) or petal-soft fleece. (Open daily 9am-7pm. 30min. tours every 30min.; $8, students and seniors $6.50, ages 6-12 $5, under 6 free.) The musk oxen's ungulate cousins play their games at the **Reindeer Farm** (745-4000), on the Bordenburg Butte Loop Rd. off the Old Glenn Hwy., 11 miles from its southern junction with the main Glenn. Hand-feed the affable beasts, and learn that reindeer and caribou are practically the same animal. (Open daily 10am-6pm; $5, seniors $4, ages 3-11 $3.)

PALMER TO GLENNALLEN

The **Matanuska Glacier** is visible near Mile 100 as the highway becomes windy and narrow, and drivers divide their time between scanning the colored ridge lines for dall sheep, marveling at the glacier, and watching the road. The **Belanger Creek-Nelchina River Trailhead** at Mile 126.4 heads 1½ mi. to Eureka Creek, 8 mi. to Goober Lake, and 9 mi. to the Nelchina River. The highway climbs to its highest elevation at the **Eureka Summit** (3322 ft.), Mile 129, where the river unfolds in the valleys below, the **Chugach Mountains** loom to the south, and the **Talkeetnas** beckon from the northwest. Great hiking trails are marked with blue signs every few miles. The **Little Nelchina State Recreation Site** has free creek-side campsites, toilets, firepits, and a boat launch, but no water. The **Kamping Resort of Alaska** (822-3346), at Mile 153, is an all-purpose rest stop. Their restaurant and gas station are open daily 7am-10pm, and they have tent sites ($6), RV sites ($13-17), and cabins ($35-55). At Mile 160 the turn-off for **Lake Louise Recreation Area,** 19 mi. off the highway, leads to all services, including fishing licenses. This area is known for lake trout, cross-country skiing, and plump berries in late summer and early fall. Among these well-stocked lakes, **Ryan Lake,** at Mile 149, is known for grayling and rainbow trout. Big grayling await in the **Tolsona Creek** at Mile 173.

COPPER RIVER BASIN

GLENNALLEN

Glennallen isn't a destination in itself, but serves as a base for entering Wrangell-St. Elias National Park (see p. 448) and for fishing in decent rivers 20 miles north or 14 miles south of town; the marshy local land is better for hunting mosquitoes than for hiking, and much of it is privately owned. Glennallen stands 115 mi. (2½hr.) north of Valdez on the Richardson Hwy. (see p. 458) and 189 mi. (3½hr.) east of Anchorage on the Glenn Hwy., making it a stop for countless RVs. The two roads which lead into Wrangell-St. Elias are conveniently close. The **Nabesna Road** lies to the north (see p. 452), and the turn-off for **Edgerton Highway** (leading to the **McCarthy Road;** see p. 449) is south on the way to Valdez on the Richardson.

The **Wrangell-St. Elias Park Headquarters** (822-5234; www.nps.gov/wrst) is 8 mi. south of Glennallen off the Richardson Hwy. (open daily 8am-6pm; in winter 8am-4:30pm). A font of **Visitor Information** (822-5558) on Wrangell-St. Elias and the surrounding area, and pamphlets on lodging and fishing in the Copper River Valley, is flowing under a log cabin's sod roof at the intersection of the Glenn and Richardson Hwy., about a mile from Glennallen proper, which is on the Glenn Hwy. (open May 15 to Sept. 15 daily 8am-7pm). **Winter Visitor Information** (822-5558) is available at the Chamber of Commerce on the Richardson Hwy., in the Ahtna building (open daily 10am-4pm). A new visitor center is being built at Richardson Mile 106 to house an Ahtna museum with native historical and cultural exhibits. **National Bank of Alaska** has an **ATM** next to the post office, and at Hub Maxi Mart (both 24hr.). The **library** (822-5226), 1½ mi. from town on the Glenn Hwy., has free internet access (open Tu-Th 1-6pm, F 1-8pm, Sa 11am-6pm). The **laundromat** is next to Park's Place (open daily 6am-10pm). **Road Conditions:** 834-1039. **State Police:** 822-3263. The **Crossroads Medical Clinic** (822-3203) is 1 mi. from town on the Glenn. The **post office** (822-3273) is 2 mi. from the visitor center (open M-F 9am-5pm, Sa 9am-noon). **Public Radio:** 90.5 FM **ZIP Code:** 99588. **Area Code:** 907.

Native Americans own a large amount of land returned to them through the Alaska Native Claim Settlement Act of 1971. Since then, trespassing has been a significant problem. Much land which lines the Richardson Hwy. to the north and south of Glennallen, including some river access on the Gulkana, Klutina, and Copper Rivers, is Ahtna land, and some of it is not marked. Before camping or fishing, check in with the **Ahtna Inc. Headquarters,** (822-3476; www.ahtna-inc.com) across from the **visitor center** (open M-F 8am-5pm) or the **Bureau of Land Management** (827-3217; www.glennallen.ak.blm.gov), at mile 186.5 on the Glen Highway, (open M-F 8am-4pm). Both offices sell maps and have info on camping and river access.

Dry Creek State Campground, 4 mi. north of the visitor center on the Richardson Hwy., is a popular place with water, pit toilets, and 60 RV, tent, and walk-in sites ($10). The **Caribou Hotel** (822-3302 or 800-478-3302; fax 822-3711), behind the Caribou Cafe at Glenn Hwy. Mile 187, has reasonably priced annex rooms with shared bathrooms (singles $49; doubles $59). **Carol's B&B** (822-3594 or 822-3600; fax 822-3800) on the right side of Birch St. off the Glenn Hwy. about 2 mi. from the visitor center, serves a true Alaskan breakfast (singles $65; doubles $75). **Maranatha B&B,** 127 Terrace Dr. (822-3643; fax 822-5098; pmkildal@alaska.net), a right turn off the Glenn Hwy. about 1 mi. from the visitor center, also serves a continental breakfast in the heart of town (singles and doubles $65). The only supermarket around for park-bound trippers is **Park's Place Groceries** (822-3334), just west of town on the Glenn Hwy. (open daily 7am-11pm). There are several restaurants in town on the Glenn Hwy., all visible, none remarkable.

WRANGELL-ST. ELIAS NATIONAL PARK

In a state where the enormous is commonplace, Wrangell remains unique. The largest national park in the U.S., it is so big that six Yellowstone National Parks could fit within its boundaries. The Wrangell, St. Elias, Chugach, and Alaska ranges converge within its 13.2 million acres. Nine of North America's 16 tallest peaks can be found here, all towering over 14,000 ft., including Mt. St. Elias, the second-highest mountain in the U.S. (18,008 ft.), and Wrangell Mountain, a volcano that last erupted in 1900. Beyond towering peaks and extensive glaciers, Wrangell teems with wildlife. Bears, Dall sheep, caribou, moose, bison, sea lions, and a host of birds all make the park their home. With only two rough roads that penetrate its interior and almost no established trails, Wrangell keeps most tourists well away. Only a fraction of Denali's visitor load even makes it within park boundaries, much less into the mind-bogglingly beautiful backcountry. The land that surrounds the two roads into the park was prospected for copper and gold in the 1900s, and mining ruins, reeling railroad trestle bridges, and homesteaders' cabins still remain. Though hikers should inquire as to which lie on private property to avoid trespassing, those who venture farther into the back-country may find themselves quite literally where no one has walked before.

ORIENTATION AND GETTING THERE

Wrangell-St. Elias is in the southeast corner of Alaska's mainland, bordered by the **Copper River** to the west, the Yukon's **Kluane National Park** to the east (see p. 377), and **Yakutat Bay** to the southeast. The two routes to the park's interior are the **Nabesna Road** (see p. 452) which extends a grueling 46 miles from Slana into the park's northern portion, and the challenging **McCarthy Road** (see p. 450) which plunges 60 miles from Chitina (CHIT-nuh) to McCarthy.

Backcountry Connection (907-822-5292 or 800-478-5292) runs **buses** daily from Glennallen (4hr.; 7am; $65, round-trip $105) and Chitina (3hr.; 8:30am; $50, round-trip $90) to McCarthy. **Charter flights** from McCarthy, Nabesna, or Yakutat start at around $60 per person (one-way), and increase in price depending on the destination. Backpackers and dayhikers generally set out from points along the Slana-Nabesna or Chitina-McCarthy roads.

Mountaineers and climbers will revel in the park's many glaciers, icefields, and mountains. Most popular among the mountains are Sanford, Drum, Blackburn, and St. Elias. The Copper and Chitina rivers offer the best **rafting** opportunities in the park. **Kayakers** can navigate many of the inland rivers or streams, but the bays, inlets, and coasts in the Yakutat (see p. 433) and Icy Bay areas are perhaps the park's most beautiful and under-utilized waterways. **Crosscountry skiing** or **snowshoeing** is best in March, April, and May—after the winter's most severe cold weather, but before the snow has melted off the lowlands. **Mountain bikers** will thrill to the networks of wagon roads around McCarthy and Kennicott.

Camping is allowed anywhere in the park except on private property (check with ranger stations). For overnight trips, the rangers request a written itinerary. The park's few established trails are mostly uninspiring and muddy ATV trails; backcountry hiking is most rewarding. There are **ranger stations** in and around the park, (all open daily May-Sept., limited hours in winter). The **park headquarters** are in **Copper Center** (907-822-7261; open 8am-6pm), south of Glennallen. Additional outposts are **Chitina** (907-823-2205; open 10am-6pm), in the west; **Slana** (907-822-5238; open 8am-5pm), in the north; and **Yakutat** (907-784-3295; open 8am-5pm), in the east. An additional info booth at the park-run campground near **McCarthy** (see below; open daily noon-8pm) sells topographic maps ($9; quadrants $4).

Backcountry hikers in Wrangell will meet with untouched wilderness; they must be seasoned trippers with extensive experience in route-finding, stream-fording, glacier-crossing, and other survival skills. All hikers should be aware of Wrangell's large and active **brown and black bear populations** and should take precautions to avoid encountering them from anything but a safe distance (see p. 44). All backcountry trekkers should come prepared with wilderness first-aid knowledge. The closest **medical care** is in Glennallen to the west and in Yakutat to the east. Evacuations (even by air) difficult. Anyone entering the park should come ready with supplies, since services are limited in and near the park.

THE MCCARTHY ROAD

At the western gates of Wrangell-St. Elias lies **Chitina** (CHIT-nuh). Once the largest town in Alaska and heralded as its future capital, Chitina bucked the yoke of greatness. When the copper mines dried up in the 1930s, the town virtually disappeared, too. What's left is a flower child community of about 45 winter residents living in lopsided cabins. The town has a **ranger station** (823-2205; open 10am-6pm), a **post office** (823-2225; open M-F 8am-4pm, Sa 10am-2pm), the last **general store** (823-2211; open Su-Th 8am-9pm, F-Sa 8am-10pm) with fuel along the McCarthy Road, a **saloon** (823-2201; open daily 10am-2am), and the **It'll Do Cafe** (823-2244), which'll have to, since it's the only one in town (supposedly open Su-Th 6am-11pm and F-Sa 24hr. and closed in winter). Fifteen minutes' with the **public well** behind the firehouse costs 50¢. Penniless campers will delight in the spacious, free **campground** across the **Copper River** (pit toilets, no water), though winds in the canyon are intense and can blow poorly staked tents miles down the river.

Starting at Chitina, the McCarthy Road follows the old roadbed of the Copper River & Northwestern Railway for 58 miles to the **Kennicott River.** Roadwork in 1999 has improved what was once arguably the roughest state road in Alaska. Cars should take it slow (30mph is safe for most parts of the road) and carry at least one spare tire. The 2½-hour trip to McCarthy rewards unflappable drivers with amazing views of the Copper River Delta.

At Mile 13.5, a small wagon-wheel sign on the left marks the Nugget Creek/Kotsina Rd. The **Nugget Creek Trail** begins 2½ mi. up this road, immediately across Strelna Creek. This unremarkable 14-mile ATV route leads to a first-come, first-served **public-use cabin** at the foot of beautiful Mt. Blackburn and the Kuskulana Glacier. Dayhikes from here pursue the canyons of Nugget Creek and the mining ruins in the hills behind the cabin. The Nugget Creek/Kotsina Rd. will also lead you to the **Dixie Pass Trail** which follow Strelna Creek through pretty canyons and a narrow, breath-taking pass over the mountains. This route joins the **Kotsina Trail** which leads back to the road in a 45-mile loop.

At Mile 17, the Kuskulana Bridge passes 238 ft. above the raging **Kuskulana River.** Summer thrill-seekers can **bungee jump** from the bridge thanks to **Club Way North** (783-1335). One jump is $50, 2 jumps are $80, and jumps are free if you jump naked, but the rope burn... Call ahead. After jolting and rattling for 41 more miles, the road terminates on the western edge of the Kennicott River, where travelers must cross a footbridge and walk a half-mile into the town of McCarthy (see below). The National Park Service maintains a **free campground** (pit toilets, no water), **free parking** three-quarters of a mile before the river on the left, and a **Park Service information desk** (open mid-May through mid-Sept. daily noon-8pm), where all the rangers are local residents and give frank advice. Locals park on the right side of the road just before the first bridge. Some have been parking in the same spots for so long that they consider them their own. The lot at the Copper Point Tram Station beside the river charges $5 per day.

Before you even cross into McCarthy, a whole host of businesses are waiting to serve you. A half-mile before the bridge, the **Glacier View Campground** (554-4490; open Memorial Day to Labor Day) has campsites ($8), showers ($5), and serves nondescript barbecue food (burgers $6) all day long (7am-11pm). **Bike rentals** here are the area's cheapest ($10 per half-day, $20 per day). McCarthy's cheapest beds ($25 without linens, guest showers $5) await a quarter mile before the river at the **Kennicott River Lodge and Hostel** (554-4441; in winter 479-6822; www.ptialaska.net/ ~grosswlr). Great food is served at the **Roadside Potato Head** (554-1234; open daily 11am-9pm) in a colorfully decorated van (burgers and burritos $5-6; coffee $1). The **Copper Point Tram Station** (554-4401) houses the **Liberty Cafe** (lunch $5-6; espresso $3; open daily 7am-11pm). You can also park here, camp ($10), and rent high-end bikes ($20-30 per day).

MCCARTHY AND KENNICOTT

Deep in the heart of Wrangell-St. Elias National Park, abandoned log-hewn buildings and roads straying off to points unknown bear witness to the boom towns past of McCarthy and Kennicott. In the early 1900s, thousands of miners swarmed to the site of the purest copper ore ever discovered, a vein running between the Kennicott Glacier and McCarthy Creek. In its heyday the Copper River and Northwest Railway (CR&NW), jokingly dubbed the "Can't Run and Never Will," transported nearly $200 million of copper ore, but in 1938 the mine closed so abruptly that Kennicott residents had to pack up in hours to catch the last train out. McCarthy sprouted in the boom as a free-wheeling, sin-celebrating alternative to stick-in-the-mud Kennicott, a company town where strict rules of conduct were enforced.

■ **PRACTICAL INFORMATION. Backcountry Connection** buses (see above) run daily to McCarthy from Glennallen and Chitina. **Wrangell Mountain Air** (554-4411 or 800-478-1160; www.wrangellmountainair.com) flies to McCarthy twice daily from Chitina (9:05am and 2:45pm; $130 round-trip) and farther afield by arrangement.

Relatively regular traffic makes hitchhiking one possibility, though getting stranded is another. The road to town stops at the Kennicott River; carrying heavy gear across the footbridge is a self-evident hassle. Once in McCarthy, fill your water bottles at **Clear Creek,** the town's water source. The first building you'll pass houses the **McCarthy-Kennicott Historical Museum,** filled with mining pictures and artifacts. A walking tour map is available here. (Open in summer daily 9am-6pm. Suggested donation $1.) The **Nugget Liquor Store** (554-4412; open daily 9am-8pm) stocks snacks and camping gear. Kennicott is 4 miles north of McCarthy along the hiekable, bikeable **Old Wagon Trail** (see McCarthy Rd. campgrounds for rentals). Kennicott is the gateway to the **Root Glacier** and home to the spooky ruins of a **mill.** A **shuttle bus** runs the 5 mi. road between the towns (10am-8:30pm; round-trip $10).

▐▗▘ ACCOMMODATIONS, CAMPGROUNDS, AND FOOD. Cheap and convenient accommodations are on the McCarthy Road (see above). Since most of the land around McCarthy and Kennicott is privately owned, camping is prohibited in most areas east of the river. Six miles north of McCarthy and 2 miles north of Kennicott, a Park Service **campground** with no amenities except food storage bins overlooks the Root Glacier. The small tent sites on the hillside are hard to find but some have stunning views. In town, the **McCarthy Lodge** (554-4402; fax 554-4404) puts up guests in the **Ma Johnson Hotel** (singles $95; doubles $110). Non-guests can shower at the lodge ($5), breakfast (7-10am; $4-9), and sup (7-10pm; $15-20; reservations required) in the rustic dining room. The lodge is home to the **bar** with the only pool table around for hundreds of miles (open daily 5pm-closing time). The **▨ McCarthy Ice House** (open 8am-9pm) serves what could quite possibly be the best ice cream in Alaska. They blend the ingredients for you and serve scoops in a mouth-watering homemade waffle cone ($3.50, ice $2.25 per bag). The food at **Tailor-Made Pizza** (554-1155; open daily 10am-10pm) makes you wish their prices were off-the-rack (small pepperoni pie $13, calzones $9).

ORGANIZED ADVENTURE. If you go **flightseeing** anywhere in Alaska, do it here. Even a short flight to 16,390 ft. Mt. Blackburn and the surrounding glaciers offers magnificent views. **Wrangell Mountain Air** (see **Practical Information,** above), makes a 35-minute tour of the amazing icefalls of the Kennicott and Root Glaciers for $50 per person. The best bargain is a 70-minute trip up the narrow Chitistone Canyon to view the thundering Chitistone Falls, more than 15 glaciers, and five mountain peaks ($95 per person). There is a two-person minimum on all flights. **McCarthy Air** (554-4440 or outside AK 888-989-9891; www.mccarthyair.com) offers similar tours. **Copper Oar** (554-4453 or 800-523-4453; howmoz@aol.com) runs a two-hour **whitewater rafting** trip down the Class III Kennicott River ($45). **St. Elias Alpine Guides** (554-4445 or 888-933-5427 in Anchorage; stelias@ptialaska.net) and **Kennicott Wilderness Guides** (800-664-4537; fax 554-4444; www.alaskaone.com/k-mcguides) lead three-hour tours of Kennicott that give visitors their only chance to see inside the 14-story mill ($25). Both outfits lead hikes and fly-in adventures, though Kennicott Wilderness Guides favors smaller groups. A fully serviced trip will cost participants about $150 per day. A day of **ice climbing** and **glacier hikes** costs about $100.

▙▌ OUTDOORS. Wagon trails between McCarthy and Kennicott and into the bush are great for **mountain biking.** One good route is the semi-strenuous 9-mile ride along the wooded **Dan Creek Road** to Nizina River, where the broken Old Nizina River Bridge rests, a victim of glacial flooding. See above for bike rentals.

Two worthwhile **dayhikes** begin in Kennicott. The **Root Glacier Trail** runs alongside the Root Glacier for 4 miles past a Park Service campground (see above). Exercise extreme caution if you choose to climb onto the glacier where there is gravel covering it; snow-covered crevasses can swallow and drown hikers without warning. The steep **Bonanza Peak Trail** climbs 4000 ft. over 4 miles to a commanding view of the Kennicott and Root Glaciers and the Donoho Peak between them.

As is true of most parts of Wrangell-St. Elias, the best hikes in the McCarthy area are **backcountry hikes** along routes established by miners from decades past and by millennia of game. Accessible hiking trails depart town and the McCarthy Rd. At Mile 13½ of the McCarthy Rd., outside of Chitina, a small wagon-wheel sign on the left marks the Nugget Creek/Kotsina Rd. For a description of the **Nugget Creek Trails** and cabin and the 45-mile **Dixie Pass Trail-Kotsina Trail** loop which can be accessed from this point, see p. 450. The darling of backcountry McCarthy is the **Goat Trail,** an early miners' route from McCarthy to the Chisana gold fields. The trail starts at **Skolai Pass,** home to the Golden Horn and the Hole in the Wall glaciers, and traverses the ridge high above Chitistone Canyon and Falls, one of the park's most spectacular features. The route continues 25 miles to Glacier Creek with fantastic views of the Wrangell and St. Elias mountains. Round-trip fly-ins with a drop-off in Skolai and pickup at Glacier Creek start at $150 per person with a two-person minimum. Other fly-in hiking areas that come highly recommended (though without trails) are the **Nizina Valley,** with scenic highlights like the Mile High Cliffs, Chitistone Mountain, Regal Glacier, and Moonshine Creek; the **Upper Chitina Valley,** with extensive gravel bars fed by several Mt. Logan glaciers; and the **Tana,** a braided river valley with large sand dunes near the end of the river.

WRANGELL-ST. ELIAS: THE NABESNA ROAD

Underappreciated and underused, this second road into Wrangell-St. Elias National Park is shorter (1½hr.), more scenic, and slightly less bone-jarring than the McCarthy Road and offers access to nearly a dozen established trails of varying lengths and difficulties. The turn-off for the Nabesna Rd. is located at **Slana** (rhymes with "bandana"), 65 miles southwest of Tok (see p. 511) on the Tok Cutoff. Slana is the place to make last-minute preparations for a journey into the park, since **Nabesna,** at the end of the 46-mile road, is little more than a mining ghost town populated by one family. The gravel Nabesna Road is passable for most cars in summer; ask at the ranger station about the water levels of the three or four streams that cross the road. It's best to charge through low water at between 10 and 25mph to avoid getting mired in wet gravel.

The **Slana Ranger Station** (822-5238; open 8am-5pm, in winter by appointment), right off the Tok Cutoff, sells topographic maps ($9, quadrants $4) and provides info on weather and road conditions, bear behavior, and everything else. Call 911 for **emergencies,** or stop by the ranger station. Slana's **post office** is 1 mi. down the Nabesna Rd. (open M, W, F 10am-2pm). **ZIP code:** 99586. **Area code:** 907.

For everything you could wish for in Slana, there is Jim and Debbie of **Midway Services** (822-5877; open daily 8am-8pm), about 1 mi. northeast of the Nabesna Cutoff. Stop here for groceries, **free tent camping** (RV sites $10; a cabin for two from $35), showers ($2), coin laundry, **fishing permits** ($10 for a day, $20 for three days), minor car repairs, and unending hospitality. If you're not sleeping for free in the mountains and need to snooze in Slana, steeper **Doubletree RV Park** (822-3973), 1 mi. down the Nabesna Rd. next to the post office, has tent sites ($18), hookups ($20), and showers ($5). Nestled in the forest, family-run **Huck Hobbit's Homestead Retreat and Campground** (822-3196) rents cabin bunks ($15, with linens $20) and tent sites ($2.50). The secluded two- and six-person cabins sport trapping decor, are heated with wood-burning stoves, and are filled with relics from the last federal homestead. A fresh spring and solar showers provide cold and hot water respectively, and the friendly owners cook meals for guests with advance notice (breakfast $5; dinner $10), and rent **canoes** for use on the Slana River ($35 per day including drop-off and pickup). To get here, head south on the Nabesna Rd., turn left at Four Mile Rd., then take the first right; follow the signs to the trailhead and hike in three-quarters of a mile (or call ahead for an ATV lift). For gas, a meal, and a nightcap, **Duffy's Road House** (822-3133) lies 2 mi. northeast of Slana on the highway (open M-Sa 9am-8pm, Su 10am-7pm; bar open noon-10pm).

In infinitesimal Nabesna, the Ellis family charges $5 per day for the pleasure of parking on their property, and runs the **End-of-the-Road Bed and Breakfast** (822-5312, last-ditch messages 822-3426) with bunks ($20), singles ($55), and doubles ($65). Showers cost an extra $3, towels $2. The family also runs **horseback riding** and **hunt-**

ing trips (2-4 days, from $200 per person), and an **air taxi** (flightseeing $150 per hr. for 2 people, $235 per hr. for 3 people; round-trip fly-ins from $175 per person).

The Slana Ranger Station has a full list of **hikes** beginning at Nabesna or along the road. Most of these are ATV trails and are flat, wet, and muddy; they serve well as access points into the mountains along the road, but are not very scenic themselves. Be wary of bears in the brushy areas, and savor the rare opportunity to sing as loudly and as poorly as you want (see p. 44). The **Caribou Creek Trail,** at Mile 19.5, is an easy 4-mile walk through three shallow streams to a primitive mining cabin with first-come, first-served bunks. From this cabin you can forge your own trails into the surrounding mountains, some of which offer good views of Mt. Blackburn, Mt. Wrangell, and Mt. Sanford on clear days. Those comfortable with trackless ridge-walking can make a 16-mile loop starting from the **Lost Creek Trail** at Mile 31.2, and return on the redundantly named **Trail Creek Trail** at Mile 29.4, or vice-versa. The two are not directly connected; secure a detailed map and chat with the rangers before setting out. The **Skookum Volcanic Trail,** at Mile 36.8, recently cleared by the Sierra Club, runs 2½ miles (one-way) and rises about 3000 ft. up a forested alluvial fan, following rock cairns along a stream, then into the tundra-covered tussocks in the crater of Skookum Volcano. At the windy pass you can camp or continue alongside another creek down to the road again.

Like every place else in the Wrangells, the best, most pristine hiking around here is in the backcountry, where you will see few, if any, other people. Popular fly-in destinations in the Nabesna area are **Grizzly Lake, Jeager Mesa,** and **Cooper Pass;** climbers prefer **Mt. Gordon, Nabesna Glacier,** and **Copper Glacier.**

PRINCE WILLIAM SOUND

VALDEZ

Upon approach, Valdez seems set in a subarctic Garden of Eden. Lush vegetation laces the deep blue mountains, interrupted only by rushing waterfalls and sawtooth peaks. In town, the milk and honey of this land takes on a different hue: black. The northernmost ice-free port in Alaska, Valdez is the terminus of the Alaska pipeline, and oil runs the show.

Natural and human disaster has fixed Valdez in the popular imagination. The 1964 Good Friday earthquake, an 8.6 on the Richter scale, gathered hundred-foot tall waves that hammered the docks and flooded the town. Exactly 25 years later, disaster struck the relocated settlement again when the infamous Exxon *Valdez* tore open its hold on Bligh Reef; 11 million gallons spread across 1640 square miles of Prince William Sound, and over 1500 miles of shoreline, made casualties of some 2000 sea otters, 300 seals, 250 bald eagles, and 250,000 sea birds. The $2 billion dollar clean-up lasted over three years and tripled the town's population.

Disaster, however, has failed to mar the allure of Valdez. College-aged adventurers annually seek very small fortunes in canneries, or "slime houses," while sportsfishermen seek the catch outright. A handful of backpackers pass through, camping in the hills outside the city and exploring its misty forests and streams. An absurd amount of snow—330 inches on average—makes Valdez "The Snow Capital of Alaska," and draws the purest winter purists.

⚡ ORIENTATION AND PRACTICAL INFORMATION

Valdez lies in the northeast corner of Prince William Sound, 304 mi. (6hr.) east of Anchorage. From Valdez, the spectacular Richardson Hwy. (Rte. 4, see p. 458) runs 119 mi. north (2½hr.) to Glennallen, where it intersects with the Glenn Hwy. (Rte. 1, see p. 446) running southeast to Anchorage and northeast to Tok. The Richardson Hwy. enters Valdez on the east side of town, becoming **Egan St.,** the main drag. Most of downtown Valdez lies on **Egan St., Fairbanks,** and **Pioneer Dr.,** all of which run east-west between the north-south **Hazelet** and **Meals Ave.**

Airplanes: The airport is 4 mi. from town on Airport Rd. off Richardson Hwy. **ERA Aviation** (835-2636) flies to Anchorage (40 min.; M-Sa 3 times per day, Su twice; $88-114).

Buses: Gray Line (800-544-2206) departs the Westmark Hotel for Anchorage daily (10hr., 8am, $66).

Ferries: Alaska Marine Highway (835-4436 or 800-642-0066; www.akmhs.com), at the city dock at the end of Hazelet Ave. Service to: Bellingham, WA (3 days, $226, ages 2-11 $114) via Juneau (1½ days, $90, ages 2-11 $44).

Visitor Information: (835-2984, 835-4636, or 800-770-5954) at Fairbanks St. and Chenega. Open daily 8am-8pm; in winter M-F 9am-5pm. Free tour and lodging calls.

Outdoor Information: Parks and Recreation Hotline, 835-3200. Most fishing stores sell **fishing licenses. Crooked Creek Information Site** (835-4680), just east of town on the Richardson Hwy., operates a summer exhibit on spawning salmon and has info on fishing and hiking in the area. Open daily 9am-6pm.

Employment: Alaska Employment Service (835-4910; aesvldz@alaska.net), on Meals Ave. in the State Office Bldg. Open May-Sept. M-F 8am-noon and 1-4:30pm. See p. 64.

Equipment Rental and Sales: The Prospector (835-3838), beside the post office on Galena Dr., has an immense supply of outdoor gear. Open M-Sa 8am-10pm, Su 10am-7pm. **Beaver Sports** (835-4727), opposite the post office on Galena, carries high-quality backpacking and climbing gear. Cross-country ski, snowshoe, and **bike rentals.** Bikes $5 per hr., $10 per 6 hr., $20 per 24hr. Open M-F 10am-7pm, Sa 10am-6pm. **Fish Central,** 217 N. Harbor Dr. (835-5002; www.alaskanangler.net), rents boats and rods. **Anadyr Adventures** (835-2814 or 800-865-2925; anadyr@alaska.net), next to Fish Central, rents kayaks to competent kayakers, offers a $60 2hr. orientation and runs tours. Singles $45 per day for first 2 days, $35 per additional day; doubles $65 for first 2 days, $55 per additional day; $200-300 damage deposit or credit card required. **Phatz Ski Rental** (835-5378; phatz@pobox.alaska.net), at Richardson Mile 30, rents skis ($25 per day), snowboards ($30), and a safety gear package ($35).

Library: 200 Fairbanks Dr. (835-4632), beside the museum. Outstanding 3-floor library, with well-stocked Alaska Room and a selection of free books. Free 1hr. **Internet access;** call ahead. Open M and F 10am-6pm, Tu-Th 10am-8pm, Sa noon-5pm.

Laundromat and Public Showers: Like Home Laundromat, 121 Egan St. (835-2913). Wash $1.50, dry 25¢ per 7min. $4 for 10 min. shower with towel, soap, and shampoo. Open daily 8am-11pm. **Bear Paw RV Park** (see below), wash and dry $1.25 each. $4 for spotless private bathrooms and unlimited shower time. **Harbormaster,** 300 N. Harbor Dr. (835-4981). $4 for 12-14min.

Weather: 835-4505. **Time and Temperature:** 835-8463. **Public Radio:** 770 AM.

Emergency: 911. **Police:** 835-4560. **State Police:** 822-3263.

24hr. Crisis Line: 835-2999.

Pharmacy: Village Pharmacy (835-3737), in the same building as Eagle Quality Center at Pioneer and Meals. Open M-Th 9am-6pm, F 9am-7pm, Sa 11am-2pm.

Hospital: Valdez Community Hospital, 911 Meals Ave. (835-2249).

Post Office: (835-4449) at Galena and Tatitlek St. Open M-F 9am-5pm, Sa 10am-noon. **ZIP Code:** 99686.

24hr. Refuge: Eagle Quality Center (see **Food and Nightlife,** below).

Area Code: 907.

ACCOMMODATIONS AND CAMPGROUNDS

Finding a roof in Valdez is expensive and time-consuming. The visitor center provides non-prioritized options, brochures, and a phone. Next to the fast-filling hostel, the cheapest indoor options are B&Bs (from $55). The free **reservation center** (835-4988) arranges B&Bs (as well as glacier tours, rafting trips, and helicopter rides). Some B&Bs some of the time are sympathetic to tight budgets announced in person or over the phone. Valdez forbids camping in non-designated areas, but insolvent sojourners sometimes camp illegally along Mineral Creek, a 15-minute walk from downtown. To explore the beautiful canyon, take Mineral Creek Dr. from Hanagita St., stay straight as the road turns to gravel and cross the stream. Follow the left hand trail or stay on the road in the canyon. For free camping, most turn-offs at least 5 mi. out of town on the Richardson should be fair game (see p. 458).

HOSTELS AND B&BS

Valdez Hostel, 139 Atlanta St. (835-2155; www.alaska.net/~nckscs). This friendly, centrally located hostel is just getting started; rates, rules, and the number of beds may change. Slightly cramped, slightly chaotic accommodations, but by far the best deal in Valdez. Kitchen. 12 beds ($20). Towels and linen ($2), washer and dryer (75¢ each), free local calls. No lock-out or curfew. 10% HI discount.

Blessing House B&B (835-2259; www.valdezlink.com/bhousebb), at the corner of Meals and Dadina. Near downtown, the friendly hosts have 5 spacious rooms ($55-75) and offer continental breakfast and free use of the house, including a kitchen and a piano.

Anna's B&B, 1119 Ptarmigan St. (835-2202), has 3 brightly colored rooms with shared bath, and serves a commendable breakfast. Singles $55; doubles $65.

Alaskan Artistry B&B, 732 Copper Dr. (835-2542). A lovely place to stay. Large rooms with TV/VCR. Spacious and cozy lounge with a big-screen TV and a selection of videos and books. Mini-kitchen, toy room, and swing set. Singles from $70; doubles from $75.

CAMPGROUNDS

Blueberry Lake State Recreation Site, 24 mi. up the Richardson Hwy. from town, overlooks peaks and lakes near the top of Thompson Pass. Pit toilets and water. Sites: $10.

Valdez Glacier Campground (832-2282), look for a small sign on the left 5½ mi. from town and 1½ mi. past the airport. Slightly inconvenient, but the sites are many, big, chock-full o' trees, and quieter than those in town. Bears aplenty—keep a clean camp. Water and pit toilets. 101 sites: $10. 15-night max. stay. No reservations.

Bear Paw RV Park (835-2530), in the heart of downtown on Meals and N. Harbor Dr. Lounge with computer modem access, laundromat, and showers. Tent sites $15-17; full hook-up RV sites $22. Adult-only campground available for $3 extra.

◙ FOOD AND NIGHTLIFE

Low key drinking and eating abounds in Valdez. The **Sugar Loaf Saloon** (835-4600), on the corner of Meals and Egan St., is a good place to relax after a day on the road. Though neither particularly original nor Alaskan, it has good atmosphere, a huge TV, live music, and the most microbrews in town (drafts from $3; open daily 4pm-4:30am). **The Pipeline Club,** 321 Egan St. (835-4332), has a mellow feel, live music (Th-Sa), karaoke (Su and W), and bottled beer from $3.25 (open 11:30am until the bartender gets tired). The **Eagle Quality Center** (835-2100), at Meals Ave. and Pioneer Dr., peddles grocery store items 24 hours.

◙ **Mike's Palace** (a.k.a. **Pizza Palace**), 201 N. Harbor Dr. (835-2365). Good seafood and great pizza keep locals happy at the harborside. Greek, American, and Italian fare with great soup ($3), gyros ($7), halibut ($14), and pies ($18). Open daily 11am-11pm.

◙ **Lisa's Kitchen** (835-5633). Look or ask around for the current location of Lisa's trailer. The reward will be miraculous, tangy Mexican grub in a far northern seaport. Tamales $2.75; burritos $5.50. A *por favor* and *gracias* may earn Lisa's good graces and more salsa for your portion. Open May-Aug. M-Sa 11:30am-8pm.

Oscar's (835-4700), by Mike's. All-you-can-eat BBQ may be the biggest meal in town ($14). Mid-day menu has the same for less (11am-5pm). Open daily 5am-midnight.

No Name Pizza, 121 Egan St. (835-4419), serves an individual cheese pizza for $4, a decent deal in this town. Open daily 11am-2pm, M-Sa. 3pm-midnight, Sun. 3pm-11pm.

Egan St. Pub, (835-4485), on Egan St. across from the museum. The cheapest draft beers in town. Big burger and a pint $7. Open M-Sa 11am-1am, Su 2-10pm.

👁 🎵 SIGHTS, ENTERTAINMENT, AND EVENTS

The **Valdez Museum,** 217 Egan St. (835-2764), packs an impressive informational punch for its size with excerpts from prospectors' diaries and exhibits on the Good Friday disasters. (Open M-F 9am-6pm, Sa 8am-5pm. $3, seniors $2.50, ages 14-18 $2, under 14 free.) A free **1964 earthquake video** is shown daily at 4pm in the Totem Inn, 100 Totem Dr. (834-4443). **The Valdez Annex,** 436 S. Hazelet St. (835-5407), displays models of Valdez prior to the '64 earthquake (open daily 9am-4pm; $1.50). Yuk-hunting travelers hit **The Sugarloaf Saloon** (835-4600), at Richardson Hwy. and Meals Ave., on summer weekdays for an all-singin', all-dancin', *Waiting for Guffman*-style history of Valdez. The show is predictably hokey but surprisingly informative. (Shows Tu-Sa at 8pm. $15, ages 6-12 $10, under 5 free.)

At the business end of the 800-mile journey of the Alaska Pipeline from Prudhoe Bay (see p. 529), the **Valdez Marine Terminal** strikes a gusher in visitors' wallets with a dry two-hour tour. (4 tours daily depart from the airport. $15, ages 6-12 $7.50, under 6 free.) The **Pipeline Visitor Center** (835-2686) at the airport yields free pipelinalia and construction-related films.

The Prince William Sound Community College Theatre Conference (June 11-18, 2000), at the Civic Center (834-1612; www.uqa.alaska.edu/pwscc), sponsors workshops, performances, and five $1000 prizes for new playwrights. ($10 per day, $20 per show; week-long pass $135, students $35. Send plays to Dr. McDowell, PWSCC Theater Conference, Box 97, Valdez, AK, 99686.) **Gold Rush Days** (on the first W-Su in Aug.) are a feast for budget travelers. The visitor center hosts a free salmon and halibut fry, fashion show, dance, traveling jail bus, and **an ugly vehicle contest.**

Valdez makes the most of winter with the annual **Snowman Festival** (835-2330), on the first weekend in March. Amidst snowmen, a drive-in movie is projected onto a giant snowbank. Valdez's record for the largest snowman ever built has been broken in Japan, though without a movie projected onto its ample belly while kids skied through the screen. In late March, mad skiers and boarders from around the world migrate to Valdez for the **World Extreme Skiing Championship** (835-2108; www.alaska.net/~wizard/wesc.html) and the **King and Queen of the Hill Snowboard Competition** (337-5584; www.mcprodction.com/koth.htm). Competitors at the **Valdez Ice Climbing Festival** (248-5809), scale the frozen waterfalls of Keystone Canyon, and the 150-Mile **Quest for the Gold Sled Dog Race** lasts three days each winter. Call the visitor center for more info.

🏔 OUTDOORS

Fishing is the big draw for many of Valdez's summer visitors. Derbies boast big prizes all summer (call the Chamber of Commerce at 835-2330 and compare prices), but pink and silver salmon bite as close as the town docks through August. Ask at Fish Central (see **Practical Information,** above) for nearby hot spots.

Anadyr Adventures (see **Practical Information,** above) offers half-day **kayaking** tours twice daily ($55, children and seniors $50) and a popular trip to the calving Shoup Glacier ($140, children and seniors $125). Multi-day packages navigate inner channels to remote glaciers. River kayakers will thrill to the Class IV middle portion or the Class V upper stretch of the Tsaina River. **Keystone Adventures** (835-2606 or 800-328-8460; www.alaskawhitewater.com) leads kayaking and **rafting** trips, including a 4½ mi. (45min.; $35) route on the Lowe River through Class II and III rapids and past the vast Bridal Veil Falls, and a full day of adventure in the Tonsina River's Class III and IV whitewater ($85).

Local **hiking** is first rate. The **Solomon Gulch Trail** starts 150 yards northeast of the hatchery on Dayville Rd. near Valdez's hydroelectric plant. A mere 1¼ mi., this 2½-hour round-trip hike covers two steep inclines, ending at Solomon Lake with excellent views of Valdez Bay and the pipeline. The more rigorous **Goat**

TAKE THAT, FREUD Everything is big in Alaska—even the mosquitoes are the size of small predatory birds—and the 1968 discovery of oil in Prudhoe Bay was no exception, launching a massive technological effort to build the most specialized pipeline in the world. The oil may be crude, but the pipeline is not. The construction of the Trans-Alaskan Pipeline involved over 70,000 workers, $8 billion, the development of advanced insulation technologies and new roads, including the Dalton Highway. Unique supports suspend half the pipeline above tundra, a feature necessary since the oil's temperature could thaw permafrost and create unstable ground. In some places, the pipeline stands as high as 10 ft. to allow wildlife to pass underneath. Even the zig-zag construction (not the brainchild of an inebriated engineer) was specially designed to enable the pipeline to withstand an earthquake of up to 8.5 on the Richter scale. (Keep your fingers crossed on Good Fridays.) Oil first flowed through the pipe in 1977, a 6mph, five-day ooze from Prudhoe Bay. After traversing 800 mi., three mountain ranges, and over 800 rivers, the pipeline spills its precious fluid in Valdez at a rate of up to 75,000 barrels per hour (over 60 million gallons per day).

Trail, farther from the city, follows a Native Alaskan footpath, once the only route from Valdez to the interior. As it weaves through Keystone Canyon, the trail follows the Lowe River past glimpses of waterfalls. Look for the sign just past Horsetail Falls at Mile 13.5 to follow the dirt trail about a quarter of a mile from the Bridal Veil Falls at Mile 18.2. Just north of downtown, the first portion of the 5½ mi. **Mineral Creek Trail** is accessible by car. A footpath leads farther through the mountains past waterfalls and wildlife to the **Old Gold Mine.** The fairly level **Shoup Bay Trail** leads along the mountainside with views of the bay and distant mountains, but is a bit muddy and mosquito-infested in places. About six miles in, the trail crosses Gold Creek. A mile-long turn-off to the right leads to spectacular waterfalls. Another six miles along the trail leads to a pretty remarkable view of the distant Shoup Glacier. Inquire at the visitor center or Beaver Sports for more hike info.

By boat, helicopter, or plane, and for a hefty price, visitors can view Prince William Sound's most prized possessions: **Columbia** and **Shoup Glaciers.** The best budget option is the ferry (see **Practical Information,** above), which pauses in front of the face of the three-mile-wide **Columbia Glacier** for 10 minutes on its way to and from Whittier ($58). For private tours, the best first step is to call **One Call Does It All,** 241 N. Harbor Dr. (835-4988; www.alaska.net/~onecall), a free reservation and info service that will match you with trips with rates in your range. **Stan Stephens Charters** (835-4731 or 800-992-1297; ssc@alaska.net) offers an economy cruise to Columbia daily at 12:30pm (6½hr.; $65, ages 4-12 $45, under 3 free). **Captain Jim's Charter Company** (835-2282) also offers a five-hour Columbia Glacier trip, a nine-hour **Meares Glacier** trip, and wildlife cruises at similar prices. **The Chapel of the Sea** (800-411-0090) allows the pious and penniless aboard the *Lu-Lu Belle* for a one-hour, non-denominational church service in the sound. Show up Sunday by 7:30am (first-come, first-served) at the dock adjacent to the Westmark Hotel for an 8am departure; seats are limited. (Free, though offering is collected.)

Valdez's plentiful snowfall and prime coastal location, warming up to a balmy 25°F in January, make the town a **skier's paradise.** Experienced skiers and snowboarders charter helicopters to **Mt. Odyssey** and other prime spots, or drive, hitchhike, and "snow machine" (Alaskan for "snowmobile") to **Thompson Pass** to ski back to town. **Cross-country ski trails** lead to the left and right off Mineral Creek Rd. or along the road itself. Advanced runs are in the Tsaina Valley at the north base of Thompson Pass. Moderate trails begin at the Coast Guard Housing on Anchor Crest St. at the western end of town. For more details, pick up the free *Winter Guide* at the visitor center.

RICHARDSON HIGHWAY (RTE. 4)

Yet another route you may wish you could drive with camera and binoculars in hand, the Richardson Highway provides two paved lanes between Valdez and Glennallen. The trip to Anchorage (304 miles) can be made in about six hours, but frost heaves, construction, and worthwhile viewpoints every 1000 feet may slow you down. The mile markers for the Richardson Hwy. begin four miles out of Valdez, at the original townsite flattened by the 1964 earthquake. The highway winds through the **Keystone Canyon,** surrounded by towering mountains and overwhelmingly green vegetation, and passes untold numbers of waterfalls cascading down the rocks from hundreds of feet above. **Thompson Pass,** at Mile 26, affords a stunning above-treeline view of the mountains, the canyon, and wildflowers. Many say that this drive is the most scenic in the entire scenery-stuffed state. After 115 miles, the highway joins with the Glenn Hwy. in Glennallen (see p. 447).

CORDOVA

Surrounded by rugged mountains of volcanic rock and waters teeming with salmon, Cordova lures nature lovers and anglers. Accessible only by sea and air, the town has preserved blissfully uncrowded hiking, biking, skiing, bird-watching, and fishing opportunities. Bumper stickers reading "Keep the Copper River Delta Wild" display the community's opposition to the proposed connection of Cordova with the Interior's road network. Cruise ships were reluctantly permitted in Cordova's sheltered waters in 1998, but Cordovans publicly support low-impact ecotourism, a movement spearheaded by former mayor Kelley Weaverling who, until 1994, was the nation's highest elected Green Party official (he now owns the Orca Book Store). Cordova's only drawback is its weather. Many cloudy days and 150 in. of annual precipitation make this a damp paradise; June is the best month for staying dry. And Cordova has more seagulls than you have ever seen in your life.

◨ ORIENTATION AND PRACTICAL INFORMATION

Cordova, on the east side of Prince William Sound at **Orca Inlet,** starts at the shore and climbs up the steep hillside. **Railroad Ave.,** at water level, and numbered streets parallel the ocean. **First St.** is the downtown shopping district and leads out of town to the ferry terminal. Railroad Ave. becomes **Copper Bay Hwy.** out of town toward the airport and the Childs Glacier.

Airplanes: The **airport** is 13 mi. east of town on the Copper River Hwy. **Alaska Airlines** (424-3278 or 800-426-0333). To Juneau ($187) and Anchorage ($50-112). **Era Aviation** (800-866-8394) has 3 flights a day to Anchorage ($101). **JIM Air** (424-7745) will fly to Anchorage for under $100 one-way, or $165 round-trip. The **Airport Shuttle** (424-5356) meets flights and runs to town for $9. Call for pickup.

Ferries: Alaska Marine Highway (424-7333 or 800-642-0066; www.akmhs.com), 1 mi. north of town on Ocean Dock Rd. off 1st St. To: Valdez (5½hr., $30); Whittier (7hr., $58); Seward (11hr., $58); Homer ($138).

Taxis: Wild Hare Taxi Service (424-3939). **Bow 'n' Arrow Taxi** (424-5766).

Car Rental: Cordova Auto Rentals (424-5982; www.ptialaska.net/~cars), at the airport. $65 per day; unlimited free mi. Big cars $75 per day. Must be 21 with a credit card.

Visitor Information: Cordova Historical Museum, 622 1st St. (424-6665; fax 424-6666; cdvmsm@ptialaska.net). Open M-Sa 10am-6pm, Su 2-4pm. **Cordova Chamber of Commerce** (424-7260; www.ptialaska.net/~cchamber), on 1st Ave. opposite Cordova Realty. Open M-F 1:30-5:30pm (and mornings when cruise ships are in town).

Outdoor Information: Forest Service Cordova District Ranger Station (424-7661), on 2nd St. between Browning and Adams, on the 2nd floor. Reserve Forest Service **cabins**

here. Open M-F 8am-5pm. **Alaska Dept. of Fish and Game** (424-3215 or 424-7535), at Breakwater St. and Railroad Ave. **Fishing licenses** are available at **Davis' Super Foods** on 1st St. (open M-Sa 7:30am-9pm, Su 9am-8pm) and **A.C. Company** (424-7141) in the small boat harbor (open M-Sa 7:30am-10pm, Su 8am-9pm).

Equipment Rental: Cordova Coastal Outfitters (424-7424 or 800-357-5145; www.cdvcoastal.com), on the dock in the small boat harbor. Mountain bikes $15 per day. Single kayaks $35 per day, doubles $50. Canoes $30 per day. Skiffs (fishing gear and gas included) $85 per day. Inflatable Zodiacs $55 per day, with motor $85. Camping equipment, too. **Cordova Auto Rentals** rents canoes for $35 per day.

Bookstore: Orca Book Store (424-5305), on 1st St. Small but with ample room on the for reading. Open M-F 7am-5pm, Sa 8am-5pm. No credit cards.

Library: (424-6667) on 1st St. next to the museum. Open Tu-Sa 1-8pm. Free Internet access is veerry slow. **Public Radio:** 88.1 FM.

Laundromat and Showers: Club Speedwash, in the alley behind the Club Bar on 1st St. Wash $2, dry 25¢ per 15min. Showers $2.50 plus 25¢ per min. Open daily 8am-8pm. **Whirlwind Laundromat,** 100 Adams St. (424-5110), at 1st St. Wash $3.25, dry 25¢ per 5min. Open daily 7am-9pm; in winter 10am-6pm. **Harbormaster,** 602 Nicholoff Way (424-6400). $3 per 5min. Tokens available M-F 8am-5pm. Showers open 24hr.

Internet Access: See **Library,** above. **Laura's Liquor** (424-3144), on 1st St. by the library. 30¢ per min. Also has snacks, espresso, and smoothies, in addition to hooch.

Pharmacy: Cordova Drug Co. (424-3246), on 1st St. Open M-Sa 9:30am-6pm.

Hospital: 602 Chase Ave. (424-8000), off Copper River Hwy.

Emergency: 911. **Police:** (424-6100) beside the post office on Railroad Ave.

Post Office: (424-3564) at Council St. and Railroad Ave. Open M-F 10am-5:30pm, Sa 10am-1pm. **ZIP Code:** 99574.

Area Code: 907.

▚ ACCOMMODATIONS AND CAMPGROUNDS

The Chamber of Commerce has a complete list of B&Bs. The closest campsite to town is the **municipal campground,** a gravel parking lot. The residents of **Hippie Cove,** about 1½ mi. out of town past the ferry terminal, may help friendly backpackers find a place to tent down in the peaceful bay, even though camping there is illegal. The Forest Service has just put in a campground at **Childs Glacier** with a little room for RVs, almost 50 mi. out of town on the Copper River Hwy. Pit toilets, no water. ($5, 7-night max. stay.) It is also legal to camp on any land that falls within the Chugach National Forest—check with the Forest Service.

Alaskan Hotel and Bar (424-3299; fax 424-5276; hotelak@ptialaska.net), on 1st St. The cheapest rooms in town, and perhaps the most elegant...once upon a time. Simple rooms line the upper floors; those above the bar get noisy at night. Singles and doubles $35, with private bath $55. Add $10 for 3 or more people.

Northern Nights Inn (424-5356), at 3rd St. and Council Ave. Run by an enthusiastic and generous hostess in the meticulously restored home of a copper-era millionaire. Three of four rooms have kitchens. Private bath, cable TV/VCR. Singles $55, $5 per additional guest; 4-bunk rooms $80. Bikes $12 per day.

The Udder Inn (424-3895), 601 Lake Ave. Clean and comfy rooms with king-size bed, private bath, and TV/VCR. Shared kitchen and living room, and a big spread for breakfast. Videos and groceries in a shop downstairs. The only thing that takes some getting used to is the ridiculous amount of cow paraphernalia lying about. $65; in winter $55.

City RV Park (424-6200), on Whitshed Rd. 1 mi. from downtown. 4 RV sites and a few tent spots overlooking Orca Inlet. All gravel; bring tie-downs for tents. Toilets, showers, and water. Tent sites $3; RV hookups $12. 14-night max. stay. Pay the attendant or at the City Building downtown.

FOOD

By small-town Alaska standards, Cordova has a terrific variety of affordable lunch options, but finding a cheap dinner is dicey since many restaurants close by midday. The best selection of groceries is in the colossal **A.C. Company** (424-7141), on Nicholoff St., in the small boat harbor (open M-Sa 7:30am-10pm, Su 8am-9pm).

Killer Whale Cafe (424-7733), on 1st St. in the back of the groovy Orca Bookstore. Next to every other town's earthy espresso-steeped cafe, this is one of the better ones. Light-washed, wood-lined inside decks overlook the books in this hangout for all ages and origins. Homemade soup and croissant $3; killer sandwiches $5.50-8.50; cappuccino $2; chai $2.75. Open M-F 7am-4pm, Sa 8am-3:30pm.

Baja Taco (424-5599), in a red bus by the small boat harbor. A rolling taco stand with a permanent al fresco dining stage. Heads south of the border in winter for research and development. Chicken burrito $6.50; breakfast burrito $6.50; espresso 50¢. Open May-Oct., weather permitting, M-Sa 8am-4pm, Su 10am-4pm.

The OK Restaurant (424-3433), 616 1st St., is just that: OK Chinese, Korean, and American cuisine. All-you-can-eat lunch buffet M-F 11:30am-2pm is $9. Noodle dishes $7-10; seafood dishes $15. Open late. M-Sa 11:30am-11:30pm, Su 5-11pm.

SIGHTS, EVENTS, AND NIGHTLIFE

The **docks** are always bustling. Near Cordova Coastal Outfitters is a good place to see nets being mended, and you can see fish being processed at the canneries toward the ferry terminal. If it's raining (and it probably is), dry off in the **Cordova Historical Museum**, 622 1st St. (424-6665), in the same building as the library. The museum has living iceworms, the creatures that dwell inside the glaciers, plus Prince Willie, a leatherback turtle who strayed several thousand miles and wound up in a local fisherman's net. Check out the hilariously dramatic "Story of Cordova," shown daily at 3pm. The museum also boasts an old printing press, the reconstructed business end of a lighthouse, and a Native kayak. (Open M-Sa 10am-6pm, Su 2-4pm. $1 suggested donation.) **B Street Artworks** (424-5331), on Browning St., features local painting, pottery, sculpture, and design. (Open W, F-Sa 1-5pm.)

Locals flee rainy nights at the original 1906 oak bar of the **Alaskan Hotel and Bar** (424-3288). During the summer and holidays, blues and rock are live from 10pm until closing four nights a week, including Friday and Saturday. (Open M-Th 8am-2am, F-Sa 8am-4am, Su 10am-2am.) Since 1960, Cordova residents have held an **Iceworm Festival** in winter to relieve cabin fever and honor the semi-legendary squirmer. The celebration breaks loose the first weekend in February and includes a parading 100 ft. iceworm propelled by Cordova's children and the crowning of Miss Iceworm Queen.

OUTDOORS

Kayaking in Prince William Sound and Orca Inlet is spectacular and the weather is often nicer out at sea, away from the mountains behind Cordova that draw the rain out of the clouds. **Cordova Coastal Outfitters** (see above) offers guided tours of nearby waterways ($60 for 4hr.; $95 for 8hr.), drop-offs, gear rental, and advice.

Fishing in Cordova is also excellent, since all five species of Pacific salmon spawn seasonally in the Copper River. Fishing is best along Orca Inlet Rd., on the Eyak River, or at Hartney Bay. King salmon run in the winter, sockeye and dolly varden in summer and early fall, and coho salmon in late summer and fall.

Surfing in Cordova is warmer than in nearby Yakutat, though perhaps a little less spectacular. The best breaks can be found off of Hinchinbrook Island, Hook Point, and Strawberry Beach. You'll need to find a boat ride there, but can stay at the Hook Point Forest Service cabin. Call local board-shaper David Parsons of **Surfboards Alaska** (424-3524) for advice and gear.

The oldest chairlift in Alaska swings over a mere three runs at **Mt. Eyak Ski Area** (lift tickets $15). Excellent **Cross-country skiing** is free along the Mt. Tripod Trail and farther down the Copper River Highway at the Muskeg Meander Ski Trail. In the dark months the adventurous/foolhardy go **ice skating** on Lake Eyak and on Sheridan Glacier (see below).

NEAR CORDOVA. The **Copper River Delta** that parallels the Copper River Hwy. is the largest contiguous wetland area in the entire Western Hemisphere, and supports the largest accumulation of shore birds in the world during the first week of May, when birdwatchers flock to the annual **Shorebird Festival** (call the visitor center 424-6665, or the Orca Bookstore 424-5305, for details). Stunning vistas are visible from any vantage point, even the road, which turns to gravel after Mile 12 and provides access to hiking, biking, and camping.

Hiking in the delta is often wet and tough, but the neighboring **Chugach Mountains** provide well-maintained dry trails and excellent climbing opportunities. The popular and rewarding **Crater Lake Trail** is closest to town and takes around two hours each way (2.4 mi. one-way, 1500 ft. elev. gain). The trailhead is 1½ mi. down Lake Ave., past the city airstrip, on the shore of Lake Eyak. Half way up is a 1-mile connecting trail to the front side of Mt. Eyak, with access to the peak (2300 ft.) for aggressive hikers. For a strenuous hike, continue on from Crater Lake along a 5½ mi. ridge frequented by mountain goats to join the Power Creek Trail. This ridge route meets the trail midway on its 4 mi., 1500 ft. ascent to one of the most spectacular Forest Service **cabins** in the state (one of three in the area accessible by foot). The **Power Creek Trail** begins at the end of Power Creek Rd., 7 mi. from town. The loop combining the Crater Lake and Power Creek trails is a 12 mi. hike best completed over two days. Other, shorter trails branch off the Copper River Hwy.; check with the Forest Service for a great free pamphlet on hiking around Cordova.

The Copper River Hwy. provides access to shorter, easier trails, like the **Saddlebag Glacier Trail**, at Mile 25 of the highway, which climbs a mere 100 ft. over 3 mi. and ends with a beautiful view of the glacier across Saddlebag Lake. Another flat, 3 mi. trail, suitable for mountain biking, at Mile 21.6 of the highway leads to **McKinley Lake** and the Forest Service Cabin on its shores. The cabin can also be reached by paddling up **Beaver Creek,** which is an even shorter trip.

About 15 mi. from town, the **Sheridan Glacier** lets hikers get up close and personal with an icy monolith. Turn left off the Copper River Hwy. just past the airport, follow Sheridan Glacier Rd. to its end, then pick up the marked trail. Walking out onto the glacier is dangerous, and not all of the scores of death-courting tourists who venture onto it each summer return safely. Snow-covered crevasses can swallow hikers without a trace.

CHILDS GLACIER. At the end of the 50 mi. highway, **Childs Glacier** is one of the most stupendous road-accessible sights in Alaska, far more impressive than its famous cousin in Juneau, the Mendenhall. Under the heat of the summer sun, the glacier calves 20-story chunks of ice into the Copper River's silty waters hundreds of feet below. The largest calvings send 20 ft. waves over the observation area on the opposite bank of the river, a quarter mile away. Splintered trees and boulders strewn throughout the woods are testament to the power of these inland tsunamis. Although falls of this size are uncommon (occurring perhaps once per season), they are unpredictable and viewers should be prepared to run. It is also prohibited to harvest salmon flung into the woods by the waves. A popular local pastime is to wait for the glaciers to calve over a couple of beers.

The **Million Dollar Bridge,** only a few hundred yards from the viewing area, was considered an engineering marvel in 1910 because of its placement between two active glaciers. One has retreated, but Childs Glacier is now less than a half mile away. The bridge was heavily damaged in the 1964 earthquake, but a primitive patch job keeps it standing. Many drive across at their own risk. If you see an iceberg under the bridge's upstream side, then dash across, drop a penny onto its icy back when it emerges, and you'll be granted a wish.

The combined splendor of the delta and the glacier make the somewhat expensive trip worthwhile. If traveling with a group, rent a car, pack a lunch (there's no food anywhere on the highway), and make a glorious day of it. Hitchhikers have been known to get stranded since Childs is not a major tourist attraction. **Copper River and North West Tours** (424-5356), run by the folks at Northern Nights Inn, runs several all-day bus trips every week (call ahead for scheduling). Their Million Dollar tour lasts five to six hours, with a three-hour lunch stop at Childs ($35 per person, $40 with lunch). They'll also drop and pickup hikers anywhere along the highway for $1 per mile.

SEWARD HIGHWAY (RTE. 9)

ANCHORAGE TO PORTAGE

For heart-stopping scenery, cruise south on the Seward Hwy. from Anchorage. The road runs south between forested slopes laced with waterfalls and the **Turnagain Arm** of **Cook Inlet,** known for dramatic tidal fluctuations. Miles of the arm are uncovered at low tide, only to be inundated by 10 ft. **bores,** walls of water created as the 15 mph tide races in. The bore tides reach Turnagain Arm about two hours after low tide in Anchorage; consult the Daily News for a tidal report. Moreover, the Seward Hwy. is narrow and has many blind turns. Drivers stopping to view animals near the highway cause accidents.

> **! WHAT THE... NOBODY TOLD ME ABOUT THE QUICKSAND!**
> The area exposed at low tide turns into **extremely dangerous quicksand.** *Let's Go* does not, in all seriousness, recommend walking across it at low tide.

Potter Marsh, about 15 mi. down the arm (Seward Mile 117.4), is a tranquil bird sanctuary and a magnet for wildlife photographers. **The Chugach State Park Headquarters** (345-5014), at Mile 115.2, is a wise stop for southbound travelers choosing between the innumerable trails along the Seward (open M-F 10am-noon and 1-3pm). Dall sheep sightings are virtually guaranteed between **Beluga Point,** at Mile 110.4, and the turn-off across the road to the south. The 24-hour **Tesoro Gas Station** at the turn-off for **Girdwood** (see below) is at Mile 90, and is the last gas station for 83 miles. Immediately to the left off the turn-off is the **Chugach National Forest Glacier Ranger District Office** (783-3242). This is an office, not a visitor center, but if you missed the park headquarters or are coming from the south, rangers can still provide info on hikes within the national forest which stretches from just south of Anchorage to Prince William Sound (open M-F 7:30am-5pm). The turn-off for the nearest visitor center is another 10 mi. down the Seward Hwy. in **Portage** (see p. 463). There are well-marked trails at nearly every turn-off and a paved bike path which runs parallel to the highway. Kayakers are in luck in this creek-rich region. **Bird Creek,** at Mile 101.2, is a narrow Class V run. (Hike up the trail to put in, and take out at the highway). **Ingram Creek,** at Mile 75.2, is another Class V chute with gnarly waterfalls. **Class V Whitewater** (see **Girdwood,** below) offers rafting and kayaking trips and information on every bit of moving water around. With snow depths that can exceed 12 ft. in the winter, **Turnagain Pass,** at Mile 68.5, is a backcountry skiers' mecca. There are bathrooms and an emergency phone at the turn-off. **The Alyeska Resort** (see **Girdwood** below) grooms runs just off the highway.

GIRDWOOD

Nestled at the base of Mt. Alyeska, Girdwood is one of the great secrets of southcentral Alaska. Just three miles down the Alyeska Hwy. from Seward Mile 90, it has duped the swarms of RVs and remained undeveloped. You won't find souvenir shops in this town, only fine restaurants, great hiking and skiing, mountain vistas, and wonderful people. **Girdwood Ski and Cyclery,** (783-2453), on the Alyeska, rents **bikes** ($20 per day), snow shoes ($10 per day), and telemark and cross-country skis ($15-25 per day). **Class V Whitewater** (783-2004; www.alaska.net/~classv) leads moderate and truly intense rafting, kayaking, and fishing trips (from $50).

There is free **Internet access** at the **Municipal Library** (783-2565), in the school at the end of Hightower Rd., a left turn off the Alyeska Hwy. (open Tu 1-6pm, W 1-8pm, Th 10am-3pm, F-Sa 10am-6pm). Follow signs to the "new townsite" off Hightower Rd. for the **health clinic** (783-1355) and **post office** (783-2922; open M-F 9am-5pm, Sa 9am-noon). **Public radio:** 91.9 FM. **ZIP code:** 99587. **Area code:** 907.

The **Girdwood-Alyeska Home Hostel (HI)** (783-2099) is a rustic wooden cabin in a wide valley with mountains all around. From the Seward Hwy., drive 2½ mi. down the Alyeska Hwy. and turn right on Timberline Dr., and right again on Alpina until it turns into Alta. The hostel, on the right, has 11 beds ($10) and a sauna, but no hot showers. Showers, swimming, and a hot tub are available at the hotel ($5).

For produce and supplies, visit **Eagle Mercantile Grocery** (783-3900; open daily 7am-midnight). It's almost worth the detour into Alyeska just to visit the **Bake Shop** (783-2831) below the resort; turn left at the end of the Alyeska Access Rd. then turn right up the hill on Olympic. Folks state-wide sing the praises of its sourdough ($3), bottomless bowls of soup ($4), and amazing hanging pots of begonias and impatiens (open M-F and Su 7am-7pm, Sa 7am-8pm). **Chair 5 Restaurant and Bar** (783-2500), around the corner from the post office, serves the cheapest dinner in town, including small pizzas (from $7.50), burgers ($6.50), and steak or seafood entrees ($13). The bar boasts a perfect jukebox, 50¢ pool table, and many microbrews ($3.25). (Open daily 11am-10pm; bar open until 2am.) **Max's Bar and Grill** (783-2888), about a quarter mile up Crow Creek Rd., is the local bar of choice, featuring $3.50 drafts and all kinds of live music (open M-F at 5pm, Sa and Su 6pm; closing time varies). The **Double Musky Inn** (783-2822), a quarter mile up Crow Creek Rd. just past Max's, is called one of Alaska's best restaurants. A steep Cajun-style dinner ($18-30) shouldn't distract you from the Double Musky pie ($4) and the garden outside (open Tu-Th 5-10pm, F-Su 4:30-10pm).

Great **cross-country skiing** can be found at Moose Meadows, between the airstrip and the ski resort, and Winner Creek, just north of Moose Meadows. The **Alyeska Ski Resort** (754-7669), has seven chairlifts and a 3934 ft. vertical drop (open Nov.-Apr. for skiing; half-day $31, full-day ticket $44; ages 14-17 $22-26; ages 8-13 or 60-69 $19, under 8 and over 69 $7). A tram goes up in summer for lunch ($19; without lunch $16; child, student, military, and senior discounts). Intrepid hikers can ride the tram down for free, but no bikes are allowed on. The most spectacular short hike in Girdwood is the **Old Iditarod Trail** which climbs from the end of Crow Creek Rd. 3 miles to the base of Raven Glacier on the Crow Pass. The trail continues 19 miles past Crow Creek in Chugach State Park to the Eagle River visitor center (see p. 445).

PORTAGE

One might wonder why Portage is on the map, being little more than a train and bus stop 45 minutes from Anchorage, at Seward Hwy. (Rte. 9) Mile 80. Flattened by the 1964 Good Friday earthquake, the town has done little to rebuild itself. But the well-paved **Portage Highway,** beginning at Seward Mile 78.9, runs for 5 of its miles through the magnificent **Portage Valley.** Four roadside glaciers sit staunchly along the valley, periodically calving spectacular blue ice chunks into **Portage Lake.** Until the Portage Hwy. extends through the mountain to the small town of **Whittier,** now only accessible by train or ferry, the **Begich and Boggs Visitor Center** (907-783-2326), at the lakeside, is the end of the road. Ranger-led **iceworm safaris** to Byron Glacier in search of mysterious, miniscule, ice-dwelling, algae-eating beasts (May-Sept. Tu and Sa at 4pm), and a transparent observation tunnel in sight of water-bound and bizarrely blue glacial ice makes this visitor center one of the most kid-friendly around (open daily 9am-6pm; in winter Sa-Su 10am-4pm). Unfortunately, **Portage Glacier** has receded almost half a mile since the building's construction. **Gray Line** (907-277-5581) conducts hour-long boat-cruises within viewing range (May-Sept., 5 per day 10:30-4:30, $25, kids $12.50), and a seven-hour round-trip from Anchorage to the glacier, including stops at the Alyeska Ski Resort (see **Girdwood**, above) and the visitor center (May-Sept., daily 9am and noon, $60, kids $30).

Several short, worthwhile hikes depart the Portage Hwy. The wheelchair accessible **Moraine Nature Trail** is a quick half-hour loop with fine views of the glacier and lush, green valley. The 1¾ mi. **Byron Glacier Trail** is the most spectacular, beginning in an alder forest and continuing past the rushing Byron Creek to the foot of the glacier. **Middle Glacier** and salmon-spawning areas are accessible from **The Williwaw Nature Trail** that begins at the **Williwaw Campground;** ice fishermen set up on nearby Alder and Tangle Pond. Against the advice of the park service, people are known to skate right up to the glacier (which may yet calve and split the ice) when Portage Lake freezes solid. For more trail info, contact the Chugach National Forest Office (907-271-2500), 3301 C St., Anchorage 99503 (open M-F 8am-5pm).

The **Alaska Backpacker Shuttle** (907-344-8775 or 800-266-8625) runs between the Portage train station and Anchorage ($20). Hitchers report that rides are easy to find. In the national forest, camping is free anywhere that isn't an official campground or otherwise marked. About 4 mi. off the highway, two state-run campgrounds—**Black Bear** (tents only; $10) and **Williwaw** ($12-14)—have water, toilets, bear-proof food lockers, and views of the glacier. If you've ever wondered where all the hippies went, they're at the **Girdwood Forest Festival** (907-566-3039), a free three-day outdoor fair every July 4th weekend. Non-stop musical acts on two stages, crafts and artwork from local artists, tasty—if pricey—cuisine, and lots of beautiful people of all ages gather in the woods.

KENAI PENINSULA

Many visitors to Alaska spend their whole trip in the Kenai Peninsula, whether for the endless wildlife, the heart-stopping scenery, or the fantastic fishing. Just south of Anchorage, the Seward Highway (Rte. 9) runs to Seward and the Sterling Highway (Rte. 1) to Homer, skirting Chugach National Forest, Kenai Fjords National Park, and the Kenai National Wildlife Refuge, which protect most of the peninsula. On the western edge, snow-capped volcanoes reflect in the blue waters of Cook Inlet, while on the southern coast, glaciers reach out like enormous icy tongues from the Harding Ice Field to the sea.

SEWARD

Named for the Secretary of State who oversaw the purchase of Alaska from Russia in 1867, Seward was chosen as the terminus of the Alaska railroad for its ice-free, deep-water port. The lush alpine trails of Chugach National Forest and hulking tidewater glaciers of Kenai Fjords National Park see a massive wave of summer tourists that locals proudly welcome. Whale-filled emerald waters and abundant halibut and salmon draw still more visitors, and bald-eagles share the skies with exotic seabirds. Hikers, kayakers, sailors, and anglers: rejoice!

▶ ORIENTATION AND PRACTICAL INFORMATION

Seward is 127 mi. south of Anchorage on the scenic **Seward Highway** (Rte. 9). Most services and outdoor outfits cluster in the small-boat harbor on **Resurrection Bay.** (For information on tour companies in the harbor, see **Kenai Fjords National Park,** below). The more charming **downtown** is nine blocks farther south on the Seward Hwy. and one block east on 4th Ave., between Railroad and Madison Ave.

Airplanes: The airport is 2 mi. north of town on the Seward Hwy. **Era Aviation** (800-866-8394) flies twice a day M-Sa and once on Su to Anchorage (30min., $69). **Scenic Mountain Air** (288-3646 or 224-9152) offers charters.

Trains: Alaska Railroad (800-544-0552; www.akrr.com), at the north edge of town opposite the 3 renovated railroad cars. Trains leave in summer daily at 6:45am for Anchorage (4½hr., $50, ages 2-11 $25).

Buses: Seward Bus Lines, 1914 Seward Hwy. (224-3608). To: Anchorage (9am, $30, airport service $5). **Katchemak Bay Transit** (235-3795 or 877-235-6557) runs daily to Homer (5hr., $43); Soldotna, Kenai, Cooper Landing (1½-2½hr., $37); and Anchorage (3½hr., $37). **Moms's Express** (344-6667) runs daily service between Seward, Girdwood, Portage, the Hope turn-off, and points between for $50 round-trip.

Stage Line (224-3608) runs between Seward and Homer (M, W, F; 4hr.; $40).

Ferries: Alaska Marine Highway (224-5485 or 800-642-0066; www.akmhs.com), at 4th Ave. and Railway St. 3 per month in summer to: Kodiak (13hr., $54); Valdez (11hr., $58); Homer (25hr., $96).

Harbormaster: 1300 4th Ave. (224-3138; WFA 702).

Public Transportation: Seward's trolley has designated stops but will stop if flagged. $1.50, all day $3, ages 6-15 half-price. Runs daily 10am-7pm. Group tours available.

Taxis: Glacier Taxi (224-5678) and **Seward Independent** (224-3608).

Car Rental: U-Save (800-254-8728), rents compacts $60 per day, unlimited miles. Must be 21. Required under-25 insurance $8 per day. Major credit card or $250 deposit.

Road Conditions: 800-478-7675.

Visitor Information: Seward Chamber of Commerce (224-8051), at Mile 2 on the Seward Hwy. Pictures and prices of accommodations and free calls within Alaska (open M-F 8am-6pm, Sa 9am-5pm, Su 9am-4pm). Also at the corner of Jefferson and 3rd (open daily 9am-5pm). **The Harbor Train Station General Information** (224-8747; harbor@arctic.net), at Port and 4th. This privately run info center in a converted railcar has updated B&B vacancies and will reserve transportation, charters, and accommodations for free. Open in summer daily 9am-9pm; in winter reduced hours.

Outdoor Information: Kenai Fjords National Park Visitor Center (224-3175 or 224-2134; www.nps.gov/kefj), at the small-boat harbor. A short film on a ranger's crossing of the Harding icefield is shown every 2hr. 10am-6pm. Open daily 8am-7pm; in winter M-F 9am-5pm. The **Seward Ranger Station,** 334 4th Ave. (224-3374), at Jefferson St., has the skinny on cabins, reservable at 800-280-2267. Open M-F 8am-5pm.

Employment: Seward Employment Center (224-5276), 5th Ave. and Adams St., in the City Building. Lots of work. Open M-F 9am-noon and 1-4:30pm. See p. 64.

Bookstores: Northland Books and Charts, 234 4th Ave. (224-3102), at Adams St. Topo and other maps, guides, and Alaskana. Open M-F 9am-6pm, Sa-Su 10am-5pm.

Library: Seward Community Library (224-3646), at 5th and Adams. Free 30min. Internet access; call ahead. Open M-F noon-8pm, Sa noon-6pm.

Laundromat and Public Showers: Seward Laundry (224-5727), at 4th Ave. and C St, is the only laundromat in town gets very crowded. Wash $2, dry 25¢ per 5min. Showers $4 for 15min. with towel and soap. Open M-Sa 8am-8pm, Su noon-6:30pm. Showers are available 24hr. at the **harbormaster.** $2 per 7min.

Pharmacy: Seward Drug, 224 4th Ave. (224-8989). Open M-Sa 9am-6pm.

Equipment Rental: The Fish House (224-3674, www.alaskan.com/fishhouse), opposite the harbormaster, rent rods ($10). $100 cash or credit card deposit required. Tips and instructions free. Open daily 6am-10pm. **Bike rentals** are available from **Seward Bike Shop** (224-2448) in a converted rail car by the Harbor Train Station. Half-day $12-25, full day $19-38. Open daily 9am-7pm.

Emergency: 911. **Police:** (224-3338) at 4th and Adams. Provides a **24hr. refuge.**

Crisis Line: Seward Life Action Council, 224-3027 or 888-224-5257.

Hospital: Providence Seward Hospital (224-5205), at 1st Ave. and Jefferson St.

Post Office: (224-3001) at 5th Ave. and Madison St. Open M-F 9:30am-4:30pm, Sa 10am-2pm. **ZIP Code:** 99664.

Internet Access: See **Library,** above. **Grant Electronics,** 222 4th Ave. (224-7015). $2.50 per 30min. **Eagle Eye Photo,** 1401 4th Ave. (224-2022). $5 per hr.

Public Radio: 88.1 FM.

Area Code: 907.

■ ACCOMMODATIONS AND CAMPGROUNDS

Seward has a host of reasonable housing and camping options, and is a popular destination. The B&B board at the **Harbor Train Station Information Site** lists availability and rates. At Seward Hwy. Mile 29.5, the town of **Moose Pass** has four campgrounds with excellent fishing, pit toilets, and water: **Primrose** (Mile 17; $10) with river access and spacious sites in the trees; **Ptarmigan Creek** (Mile 23; $10); **Trail River** (Mile 24; singles $9, doubles $13); and **Tenderfoot** (Mile 46; $10; wheelchair accessible). To reserve a site call the **National Recreation Service** (877-444-6777; www.ReserveUSA.com). Free camping is 8 miles from town at the **Exit Glacier Campground,** on Exit Glacier Rd. at Seward Hwy. Mile 3.7. Nine secluded sites are a walk away from the massive glacier (water and pit toilets, 14-day max. stay).

Kate's Roadhouse (224-5888; fax 224-3081; katesroadhouse@hotmail.com), 5½ mi. outside town on the Seward Hwy. Huge continental breakfast with home-baking and a quietly sleeping pig in the sitting room. Free shuttle service, laundry, bedding, and towels. Shared baths. Clean dorms $17, private rooms $59, 4 private theme cabins with electricity, cable TV, and heat $29-49. No private baths.

Ballaine House Lodging, 437 3rd Ave. (224-2362), at Madison St. 2 blocks from downtown. In a bright house built by one of Seward's founding families. Made-to-order breakfast, a library with videos, and an accommodating owner. Singles $60, doubles $84; less for families or without breakfast. Free laundry with notice. Pick-up and drop-off.

Moby Dick Hostel (224-7072), at 3rd Ave. and Madison St. Avast! The cheapest indoors in town, conveniently located. Single-sex rooms, and a nice view of Mt. Marathon. Progressing renovations will expand narrow quarters. Smoke-free. Showers, kitchen, local calls, no lock-out or curfew. $17.50 or $16.50 cash; 2 private rooms $50.

Municipal Waterfront Campground, along Ballaine Rd. between Railway Ave. and D St. Showers and extra toilets at the harbormaster. Sites $6; RV sites $10, hookups $15. 2-week max. stay. Check-out 4pm. Open May 15-Sept. 30.

Miller's Landing (224-5739). Follow the Seward Hwy. to its end at the SeaLife Center, turn right, and follow coast for 3 mi. A $7 cab ride. Coastal hiking, fishing, and boating rentals, guided trips and drop-offs, and provisions. Grassy camping ($15, includes showers for 4), hookups ($20), and rustic cabins (2-13 people; $35-70; no bedding).

◖ FOOD AND NIGHTLIFE

Although affordable, Seward's food is not its forte. Stock up on groceries at the **Eagle Quality Center,** 1907 Seward Hwy. (224-3698; open 24hr.), at Mile 1.5. Reward yourself after the trek with a treat at the in-store soda fountain.

Miller's Daughter, 1215 4th Ave. (224-6091), on the waterfront across from the National Park center. The breads are organic, fat-free, and herbivore-friendly. Fresh vegetarian soup with bread ($4.50) and irresistible pastries. Open daily 7am-7pm.

Resurrect Art Coffee House Gallery, 320 3rd Ave. (224-7161), in a converted Lutheran church. Nondescript treats, but lattes so good they're nearly sinful ($2.25). Sip Italian soda ($1.50) at the altar-turned-art-display or play chess in the balcony-turned-loft. Books, live music, and readings. Open M-Th 7am-10pm, F-Sa 7am-midnight, Su 7am-6pm.

Ray's (224-5606), on 4th Ave., at the waterfront. A choice restaurant for a splurge at the bayside with fresher-than-fresh seafood (entrees from $18) and Seward's best chowder ($6). Salads that are meals in themselves ($8-12). Open daily 11am-10pm.

Red's, at 3rd and Van Buren St. The best burgers in town out of a kitchen in a white school bus fronted by picnic tables. Burger and fries $5. Open M-Sa 11am-8pm.

Oriental Garden, 311 4th Ave. (224-7677), between Church and Adams. All-you-can-eat buffet (until 2:30pm, $7), but no sushi. Open daily 11am-11:30pm.

The Pit (224-3006), Mile 3.5 on the Seward Hwy. Seward's late, late night spot. Get down and dirty from 8am-5am every day. Pints $3.75.

Yukon Bar (224-3063), at 4th Ave. and Washington St., draws a younger crowd. Pin a dollar to the ceiling lest you someday return with an empty wallet. Pool tables, micro-brew pints $3.50, open mic (M), and live music (W-Sa). Open daily noon-2am.

👁 SIGHTS AND ENTERTAINMENT

The **Alaska SeaLife Center** (224-6300 or 800-224-2525; www.alaskasealife.org), at the end of downtown on Railroad Ave. between 3rd and 4th Ave., was opened in 1998 to state-wide anticipation and has become one of Seward's prized attractions. Created in the black wake of the Exxon *Valdez* oil spill, the $56 million research center gives visitors a glimpse of underwater Alaska. While this is an active lab, not an ordinary aquarium, visitors can touch the starfish and watch tufted puffins, stellar sea lions, and harbor seals in large outdoor habitats. Visiting professors and resident biologists discuss current research, and kid-friendly programs include tours, films, sleep-overs in front of the tanks, and craft activities. (Open May-Sept. daily 8am-8pm; in winter W-Su 10am-5pm. $12.50, seniors $11.25, ages 7-12 $10.)

Next door, the **Chugach Heritage Center,** 501 Railway Ave. (224-5065), in a 1917 railroad depot, houses a theater and a gallery of Native Alaskan art. Thirty-minute performances, conceived by an Aleut director, include storytelling, singing, dancing, and authentic regalia made from sealskin and duck bellies. The fascinating performances represent one of the first attempts to present native oral tradition on a public stage. (Open Tu-Su 10am-6pm. $8, ages 4-16 $6.50.)

The self-guided **walking tour** of Seward passes turn-of-the-century homes and businesses (2-3hr.; brochure available at the visitor center). The **Resurrection Bay Historical Society Museum,** in the Senior Center at 3rd Ave. and Jefferson St., exhibits traditional Alaskan artifacts, including a fine collection of woven baskets. (Open Memorial Day to Labor Day daily 9am-5pm and when cruise ships are in. $2, ages 5-18 50¢.) Those feeling sedentary can get all shook up by the bona fide **1964 Earthquake Movie** at the library (mid-June to Sept. M-Sa at 2pm; $3 donation requested, under 13 free). **Liberty Theater,** 304 Adams St. (224-5418), screens mainstream flicks ($6; kids everyday, matinees and W $4).

EVENTS

Seward's principal insanity-inducing annual event is the 4th of July **Mountain Marathon** (224-8051). Alaska's oldest footrace (only the Boston Marathon is older in the U.S.) began after a sourdough challenged a barmate to get up and down Mt. Marathon (3022 ft.) in under an hour: the modern men's record is 43 minutes, the women's 50. Every year the governor and hundreds of competitors run, slide, fall, and bleed up and down the mountainside, and the pride is palpable as thousands of spectators line the streets to watch the pain-filled frenzy. Brave runners buy their tickets by the end of February, but a handful are auctioned off on July 3rd.

The annual **Silver Salmon Derby** (224-8051) creates a splash for nine days from the second Saturday in August. The elusive tagged fish is worth $100,000. No one has caught the slippery salmon since 1980, when Japanese tourist and lucky bastard Katsumi Takaku nabbed it from the city docks.

The annual **Seward Silver Salmon 10K Run** takes off over the Labor Day weekend, and the **Exit Glacier 5K and 10K Run** begins in mid-May (224-4054). Seward's truest test of physical endurance looms on the third weekend of January, when the three-day **Seward Polar Bear Jump** raises money for cancer research by plunging participants into the frigid waters of Resurrection Bay.

◣ OUTDOORS

HIKING

Hiking trails weave through the high alpine passes and lush valleys between Seward and its northern neighbor, **Portage** (see p. 463). Though many of these routes take days, some are easily accessible dayhikes. **Public cabins**, located throughout the forests and on several islands, sleep four to eight, and have tables and wood stoves, but no water, electricity, or mattresses. Call 800-280-2267 to reserve ($25 per night; $8.25 reservation fee). For more info, visit the **Ranger Station.**

Several wonderful trails of varying lengths and difficulties pass **Exit Glacier** in **Kenai Fjords National Park** (see below), 11 miles out of Seward. The local pick closer to town is a 7 mi. (one-way) **coastal trail** that weaves through **Caines Head State Recreation Area** at the mouth of Resurrection Bay near abandoned Fort McGilvary. The trailhead is at the end of 3rd Ave., after 2 miles of gravel. After 1½ mi., there is a 3 mi. stretch negotiable only at low tide. Most hikers stay overnight before returning in order to catch the next low tide. The last 2½ mi. follow the sand to South Beach. Consult visitor centers, the newspaper, or outfitters for tide information and a detailed map of the area as several attractions lie on side trails.

You don't *need* to be half-crazy to get to the top of **Mt. Marathon**; there is a far more pedestrian route that leads to a glorious view of the sea, the town, and the surrounding mountains. From 1st Ave. and Jefferson St., take Lowell St. to reach the trail, which begins with a steep ascent up a rocky stream bed. The more gradual switchbacks of a Jeep trail start up at 1st Ave. and Monroe St. Once above treeline, a network of trails continues up the rocky ledge to the left. Another route climbs through the scree to the right. Plan to make a two to three hour climb and a one-hour hop-and-slide back down.

The **Lost Lake Trail** makes a strenuous but extremely pretty dayhike or overnight trip. It begins at the end of a gravel road at Seward Hwy. Mile 5, and meanders above treeline for about half of its 7 miles. The trail, open to mountain bikers in the summer and cross-country skiers in the winter, offers dayhikers a wide-open view of glacially carved peaks. The **Primrose Trail**, which begins at **Primrose Campground**, 1½ mi. from Mile 17 on the Seward Hwy., moves through lakes and mountain passes. Though the first 4 of the trail's 8 miles pass through dense spruce forest, persistent trekkers can reach the glimmering **Porcupine Creek Falls,** which are off a spur trail at Mile 3. The last two or three miles of the Primrose Trail are steep as they rise beyond treeline. True to its name, the path is strewn with spectacular wildflowers.

Starting from Seward Hwy. Mile 34, the **Carter Lake Trail** gives grunting hikers another good survey of local terrain. The 3¼ mi. (one way) trail climbs steeply out of a hemlock forest, then flattens out into fields of wildflowers and low brush with striking views of surrounding peaks and sapphire lakes. From here, the **Crescent Lake Trail** continues for another 9 mi. Camping is available at Carter or Crescent Lakes. To reach the **Crescent Saddle Cabin**, 7.5 mi. from the Carter Lake trailhead, follow the poor trail along Crescent Lake to the south shore.

The true path to illumination, however, starts at Sterling Hwy. Mile 52. The **Resurrection Pass Trail** is a favorite among mountain bikers and weekend hikers—expect to see an eighth of Anchorage's population along this trail on any given Saturday. The 23 mi. **Johnson Pass Trail** serves as another fab route for a two- to three-day trip. The trail provides an ideal way to view different Kenai Peninsula ecosystems as it passes through a spruce forest, rises into shrubby sub-alpine regions, and finally extends into alpine tundra. The north trailhead starts at Seward Hwy. Mile 64; go south on a gravel road a quarter-mile to the trailhead. The south trailhead lies at Seward Hwy. Mile 32.5.

FISHING AND MUSHING

Salmon and halibut fill the bay, grayling and dolly varden can be hooked right outside of town, and fishing is free from the shore or docks. Charters are available for both halibut and salmon throughout the summer; prices start at $95, with all gear provided. Call **The Fish House** (800-257-7760), the largest charter-booking service in

Seward. Fish for salmon or watch them reel 'em in at the waterfall past the **SeaLife Center** on 3rd Ave. Head down to the harbor at the **B dock** behind the harbormaster at 5pm daily to watch the charters clean their huge catches.

To reach **IdidaRide Sled Dog Tours** (224-8607 or 800-478-3139), turn left on Exit Glacier Rd. at Seward Hwy. Mile 3.7, continue 3.3 mi., take a right on Old Exit Glacier Rd., and follow the signs for the next half-mile. Mitch Seavey competes in the Iditarod every year—he placed 4th in 1998—and you can help train his dogs in the summer by providing deadweight. (Full tour 1¼hr., 5 daily, $28.50, under 12 $15. Kennel tour $10, children $5. Call for reservations.)

KENAI FJORDS NATIONAL PARK

Seward serves as a gateway to the stunning waterways and yawning ice fields of Kenai Fjords National Park. The town's visitor center shares the small boat harbor with numerous charter companies offering glacier cruises. The park is largely inaccessible to novice kayakers, and is almost entirely blocked to hikers without mountaineering equipment, but the lay traveler can revel in the park's glory by foot, tour boat, kayak, or plane.

Hikes begin at **Exit Glacier**, the only road-accessible glacier in the park, 9 mi. west on a spur from Mile 3.7 of the Seward Hwy. A shuttle runs here four times per day from downtown Seward (224-8747; $10 round-trip), and the park entrance fee is good for a week ($5). From the **Ranger Station** at the end of the road, a leisurely three-quarter-mile stroll leads to the outlandishly blue glacier. The first half-mile is wheelchair accessible. Rangers lead free one-hour **guided walks** to the glacier (10am, noon, 2pm, and sometimes 4pm). The grueling but utterly worthwhile 3000 ft. climb to the top of Exit Glacier is a full day's scramble. The **Harding Ice Field Trail** begins at the parking lot on a paved trail, and continues 4 mi. to an astonishing view of the footprint-free **Harding Ice Field.** The glimmering 300 sq. mi. of ice is 3000-5000 ft. deep and the source of over 40 glaciers. The trail is often muddy or snow-covered. Good boots and a walking stick are recommended.

Boat cruises are the easiest and most popular way to see the park. All companies run basically the same trips, the difference being the size of boat and quality of food included. The longest and most expensive cruises access either **Aialik Bay** or the **Northwestern Fjord.** Both routes pass forested islands full of seabirds and coastal mountains striped with waterfalls and streams. **Kenai Fjords Tours** (224-8068 or 800-478-8068; www.kenaifjords.com) are informative and amusing. (To Northwestern Fjord; 9½hr.; $139, children $69. To Holgate Glacier; 6hr.; $99, children $49.) **Major Marine Tours** (224-8030 or 800-764-7300; www.majormarine.com) brings along a ranger and serves the best all-you-can-eat salmon and chicken buffet on the water for $10. (To Holgate Glacier; $99, kids $49.) Both companies also offer a variety of tours within Resurrection Bay, including overnighters, and it pays to shop around for just the right type of trip (the cheapest start at $49). **Renown Charters and Tours** (224-3806 or 800-655-3806) runs similar cruises for about the same prices. **Mariah Tours** (224-8623 or 800-270-1238) uses smaller boats to more intimate effect. (Max. 16 passengers. To Northwestern Fjord; 10hr.; $115, children $57) **Wildlife Quest** (888-305-2515) is the only outfit with speedy, smooth-riding catamarans. (To Holgate Glacier; 5½hr.; $99, children $49. Includes pass to SeaLife Center.) Pick up a list of charters at the chamber of commerce or **The Fish House** (see **Practical Information,** above).

Experienced kayakers can water taxi to islands and cabins. Contact the rangers in Seward for advice and resources. **Sunny Cove Sea Kayaking** (345-5339; www.sunnycove.com) offers a joint trip with Kenai Fjords Tours, including the wildlife cruise, a salmon bake, kayaking instruction, and a 2½-hour wilderness paddle (no experience necessary; 8hr., $139.). **Kayak and Custom Adventures Worldwide** (258-3866 or 800-288-3134) leads trips including paddling instruction ($75-95). **Miller's Landing** (see above) rents kayaks and leads full-day trips for the experienced. (Singles $30 for 1 day, $15 per additional day; doubles $55 per day, $45 per additional day. Guided trips $85. Lunch $10.)

Scenic Mountain Air (288-3646 or 224-9152) skims over the crevasses of the glaciers and soars high above the ice field. (1hr. tours from $110 per person, depending on the number of people). **Kenai Fjords Air Tours** (224-1060) runs similar tours; their planes seat three and cost between $150-200 per hour to rent.

STERLING HIGHWAY (RTE. 1)

The Sterling Highway begins 90 mi. south of Anchorage at the **Tern Lake Junction.** From here, the highway runs 66 mi. west to **Kenai** (see p. 472), past wonderful hiking, camping, and fishing in **Chugach National Forest** and the **Kenai National Wildlife Refuge** (see below). From Kenai, the highway runs south on the western side of the peninsula along **Cook Inlet** (see p. 474), ending after 75 mi. at the town of **Homer** (see p. 475). The Sterling passes through moose country, so drivers are advised to be especially cautious. Mile markers measure the distance from Seward.

COOPER LANDING

Shortly after its intersection with the Seward Hwy., the Sterling passes **Kenai Lake,** which stretches in a giant Z through the Chugach Range. **Kenai Lake Tackle** at Mile 47.1 (595-2248), sells licenses, supplies, rents gear and cabins, and guides trips. Laundry and showers are available at **WildWash** (495-1456), at Mile 47.5 (wash $2.25, dry $1.75 per 10min.; showers $3; open daily 8am-midnight). The highway then continues along the turquoise **Kenai River** to the town of Cooper Landing. Anglers rejoice: you have reached the Promised Land of **salmon fishing,** a land flowing with kings, silvers, reds, and pinks. For great dolly varden and free camping, turn left onto Snug Harbor Rd. after the Kenai River Bridge and drive 2½ mi. on the dirt road to the river. In another 10 mi. on Snug Harbor Rd. is trout-teeming **Cooper Lake** with more remote free camping. During the summer runs, Cooper Landing and surrounding campgrounds take on a carnival atmosphere, as fishermen line up on the banks of the Kenai River to try their luck. It's not unusual to see anglers standing shoulder-to-shoulder filling their baskets. **Licenses** are available at most grocery and fishing stores. **Fishing charters** in the $100 range abound. A cheaper option is the **ferry trip** to the opposite bank of the Kenai River, which yields comparable views and access to good fishing ($4, ages 3-11 $2.50). The boat uses cables and current to carry it across at Sterling Mile 55. Parking is $7, so take advantage of the gravel pull-outs just before and after the entrance.

The Kenai offers several places to **whitewater raft** without substantially risking life and limb. Some of these floats are as scenic as Class III river-running gets. Outdoor outfits generally supply lunch and gear on full-day trips, but anglers should buy their own licenses beforehand. **Alaska Wildland Adventures** (800-478-4100), in Cooper Landing, offers a variety of half- and full-day rafting trips ($45-195, children $29-69). The **Alaska River Company** (595-1226) offers rafting, fishing, and hiking tours; the most economical trip is a three-hour run through mild Class II waters ($42).

KENAI NATIONAL WILDLIFE REFUGE

From Cooper Landing, the Sterling Hwy. stretches 50 mi. to **Soldotna,** with services at Cooper and Sterling, alongside the Kenai River and through the two million acres of the Kenai National Wildlife Refuge. The peninsula is prime moose territory—the area was originally designated the Kenai National Moose Refuge in 1941—and makes for excellent hiking. There are great trails, fishing, canoe routes, and free camping everywhere, so it is wise to check out one of the visitor centers. The **Kenai National Wildlife Refuge Visitor Contact Station** is at Sterling Mile 58, close to many of the campgrounds and trailheads. This log cabin station sells maps ($3-4) and other outdoor literature, and has a lovely educational garden out front. (Open May-Sept. F-Sa 9am-7pm, Su-Th 9am-6pm.) The State Park **Headquarters** (262-5581; www.dnr.state.ak.us), off the Sterling Hwy. at Mile 85, 3.5 mi. toward the Morgan's Landing campsite, has info on cabins, campsites, and trails. (Open M-F 7am-5pm, Sa-Su 7am-10pm; in winter daily 8am-4pm.) The **Kenai National Wildlife Refuge Headquarters and Visitor Center** (262-7021) is off the Sterling Hwy. between Miles 96 and 97; turn left on Funny River Rd., then laugh all the way to Ski Hill Rd. *Refuge Reflections*, their free publication, gives detailed fishing, hiking, and canoeing tips. The center shows nature films daily and leads a host of hikes, talks, and kid-friendly exhibits. A 10-minute, wheelchair-accessible, self-guided nature walk also leaves from the center. (Open M-F 8am-5pm, Sa-Su 9am-6pm; in winter M-F 8am-4:30pm, Sa-Su 10am-5pm.)

The **Fuller Lakes Trail,** a 5.8 mi. round-trip hike at Mile 56.9, is one of the most strenuous established hikes in the region, with an elevation gain of 1400 ft. After a challenging first mile of steady ascent through dense forests, striking views highlight the glimmering Lower Fuller Lakes and the lush Kenai Mountains. The **Kenai River Trails** provide a moderate alternative to the Fuller Lakes Trail. To reach two of the trailheads, turn south on Skilak Lake Rd. at Mile 58. The **upper trail** starts at Mile 2.2 of Skilah Lake Rd. The 5.6 mi. round-trip trek (with a scant elevation gain of 260 ft.) provides impressive views of the turquoise waters off the Kenai coast. The **lower trail** (4.6 mi. round-trip) begins at Mile 3 of Skilak Lake Rd. Open meadows teem with wildflowers and, in late summer, blueberries. Plenty of **bears** in the area keep the moose company (see p. 44). The **Hidden Creek Trail** is a mild 2.6 mi. round-trip hike beginning at Mile 5.4 of Skilak Lake Rd., 1 mi. west of Hidden Lake Campground. A quick hike with only a 300 ft. elevation gain, the trail leads through forests to Skilak Lake and the mouth of not-so-Hidden Creek. If the water level is low, it's possible to hike around the lake.

The refuge, lying north of the Sterling Hwy., also boasts some of the best **canoeing** networks in Alaska. The **Swan Lake Route** has three different passages suitable for two- to four-day paddles. Over 30 lakes dot the wooded landscape, furnishing fishing and wildlife-viewing opportunities. The more challenging **Swanson River System** connects 40 lakes through marshy wetlands, offering several two-day routes and some that can last over a week. Because of its difficulty, this system is less popular with people and therefore more popular with wildlife. Only experienced paddlers should attempt this route.

Fish for Arctic char from the banks of Finger Lakes and Silver Lake. Dolly varden swim near the banks of Paddle Lake and the Kenai River. There are rainbows along the shores of Paddle, Forest, Eugumen, and Upper and Lower Ohmer Lakes. Red and silver Salmon ply the Kenai River.

Free **campgrounds** with boat launch, water, and toilets are at Dolly Varden Lake, Rainbow Lake, Engineer Lake, Lower Skilak Lake, Watson Lake, and Kelly Lake. (For info on these campgrounds, call the Soldotna visitor center at 252-7021.)

Winter recreation includes snowshoeing, cross-country skiing, snowmobiling (machining), and backcountry ice-fishing. Call the visitor center for resources.

SOLDOTNA

Soldotna spreads its strip mall tentacles for several miles along the northern stretch of the Sterling Hwy. An urban blemish on the face of the peninsula, the town supplies groceries and camping gear to travelers en route to elsewhere. **Wilderness Way** (262-3880), 2 mi. east of town, is well stocked with high-quality backpacking and canoeing gear (open M-Th 10am-6pm, F-Sa 10am-8pm, Su noon-5pm). The **Sports Den** (262-7491) sells gear and licenses and rents everything you need to catch the big one (canoes for $35 per day, $210 per week). They also run guided fishing and hunting trips and are a stellar source of outdoor info. (Open mid-May to Sept. 1 M-Sa 8am-7pm, Su 9am-6pm; in winter M-Sa 9am-5pm.)

Soldotna's **visitor center** (262-1337), just over the Kenai River on the way south to Homer, has pamphlets on fishing and recreation possibilities in the area, a phone for local use, and free canoe route maps (open daily 9am-7pm). **Winter road conditions:** 262-9228. **Hospital:** 250 Hospital Pl. (262-4404). **Post office:** on Binkley St. downtown (262-4760; open M-F 8:30am-5pm, Sa 10am-2pm). **ZIP code:** 99669. **Area code:** 907.

Camping is available pretty much everywhere along the Sterling Hwy., especially by **Skilak Lake Rd.** (see **Kenai Wildlife Refuge,** above). With the exception of the Kenai-Russian River, Upper Skilak Lake, and Hidden Lake Campgrounds ($5-10), camping within the refuge is free. Now for some even better news: the culinary gem of Alaska, land of otherwise expensive and bland food, shines in Soldotna. **Odie's** (262-5807), downtown on the Sterling, across from the Blazy Mall and next to the National Bank of Alaska (24hr. **ATM**), offers mouth-watering food at jaw-dropping prices. Odie prepares vast half-sandwiches on thick homemade bread ($3.75), acre-size cookies fresh from the oven (75¢), big cups of homemade soup with a roll ($2.25), short stacks of sourdough pancakes ($2.50), and untold other breads and sweets. (Open M-F 4am-10pm, Sa 4am-6pm.)

KENAI

Perched on a bluff overlooking the Kenai River where it empties into Cook Inlet, Kenai has a magical view of the Aleutian-Alaska Range and its prominent volcanoes, Mt. Redoubt and Mt. Augustine. First inhabited by the Dena'ina Indians, then colonized by Russian fur traders and missionaries at the end of the nineteenth century, and eventually fortified by the American military in the 1940s, Kenai culture bears the signs of its varied past. The fishing, oil, and tourism industries have left their respective stamps as well: a fishy smell along Kenai's beaches, drilling platforms offshore, and RVs everywhere. Alaskans swarm here to dip-net—the challenging and complex sport in which a net is placed in a stream until a fish swims into it. Kenai's large and rapidly growing population supports a refreshing variety of restaurants and services, but hurried expansion spares few traces of the city's history, and brings forgettable RV parks and low-rises in increasing numbers. Kenai lacks Seward's surroundings and Homer's hominess and can seem an overgrown pit stop. Nevertheless, the pristine Captain Cook State Recreation Site lies 30 mi. away, the Kenai Wilderness Refuge (see above) is full of free camping and great hiking, and the mouth of the Kenai River is a good place to catch salmon or watch beluga whales do the same.

▮ ORIENTATION AND PRACTICAL INFORMATION

Kenai, on the western Kenai Peninsula, is 158 mi. from Anchorage and 96 mi. north of Homer. The town can be reached via **Kalifornsky Beach Road,** which joins the Sterling Highway (Rte. 1) just south of Soldotna, or via the **Kenai Spur Road,** which runs north from Soldotna and west to Kenai. Kalifornsky mile markers measure distance from Kenai, while the Kenai Spur mile markers measure from Soldotna.

Airplanes: 1 mi. north of downtown. Take Kenai Spur Rd. to Willow St. and follow signs. **Alaska Airlines** (800-426-0333) has hourly service to Anchorage (30min., from $59).

Buses: Homer Stage Line (235-7847). To: Anchorage (4hr., 1 per day M-Sa around 10am, $35); Homer (1½hr., M and F, $30). **Kachemak Bay Transit** (235-3795) runs to Anchorage ($40) and Homer ($25).

Taxis: Inlet Cab, 283-4711. $1.50 base, $1.40 per mi.

Car Rental: Great Alaska Car Company (283-3469), from $45 per day, unlimited miles for multiple day rentals. Must be 21 with credit card.

Car Repair: Alyeska Sales and Service, 200 Willow St. (283-4821). Open M-F 8am-6pm, Sa 9am-5pm.

Visitor Information: Visitor and Cultural Center, 11471 Kenai Spur Hwy. (283-1991; fax 283-2230; www.visitkenai.com), just past the corner of the Spur Rd. and Main St. Hiking trail guide ($1), *Free and Inexpensive Things to Do in Kenai* (free), stuffed wildlife, traditional artifacts, and films on area development. Open M-F 9am-8pm, Sa 10am-7pm, Su 11am-7pm; in winter M-F 9am-5pm, Sa-Su 10am-4pm.

Outdoor Information: For info on **Lake Clark National Park and Preserve,** across Cook Inlet from Kenai, call the **superintendent** in Anchorage (271-3751), or the park ranger

(781-2218). **Lee's Alaska Booking Service,** 1000 Mission Ave. (283-4422 or 776-5608; lees_alaska@yahoo.com), provides info on local fishing, charters, tours, rents gear, and sells licenses. The **Kenai National Wildlife Refuge Headquarters** is 15min. away, in Soldotna (see above).

Employment: Alaska Employment Service, 283-2900. **Dial-a-Job,** 283-2924.

Library: 163 Main St. Loop (283-4378). Free Internet access. Open M-Th 8:30am-8pm, F-Sa 8:30am-5pm, Su noon-5pm.

Laundromat and Public Showers: Wash-n-Dry (283-8473), at Lake St. and Spur. Wash $1.75, dry 25¢ per 8min. Showers $4.20 untimed. Open daily 8am-10pm.

Crisis Line: 283-7257. 24hr. **Women's Services: Resource Center,** 325 S. Spruce St. (283-9479). Hotline and shelter. Open M-F 9am-5pm.

Hospital: Central Peninsula General Hospital, 250 Hospital Pl. (262-4404).

Emergency: 911. **Police:** 283-7879, at 107 S. Willow St.

Post Office: 140 Bidarka St., 99611 (283-7771). Open M-F 8:45am-5:15pm, Sa 9:30am-1pm.

Area Code: 907.

■ ACCOMMODATIONS AND CAMPGROUNDS

There are few inexpensive lodgings in Kenai; the numerous B&Bs begin at $70. **The B&B Association** (888-266-9091) has all the listings and rates. **Lee's Alaska Booking Service** (283-4422) arranges rooms at no charge. **Camping** is available on gravelly sites, with water and pit toilets, in the park at Kenai Spur Hwy. and Marathon Rd. Although camping down by the beach is illegal, squatters are reportedly not harassed; take Spruce Dr. from the Kenai Spur Hwy. People also camp right across from the visitor center on Main St. and Coho beside the baseball fields.

Katmai Hotel, 10800 Kenai Spur Hwy. (283-6101 or 800-275-6101), 1 block from downtown. Small rooms with nice decor and cable. Singles $83; doubles $92.

Beluga Lookout RV Park and Lodge, 929 Mission St. (283-5999). Take Main St. toward the water and go right on Mission St. Prime location. No tent sites. Scan the sea for belugas from the lounge. Full hookups $15-20, with view $25. Coin laundry. Showers $2.

◖ FOOD

Carr's Quality Center (283-6300), in the Kenai Mall at Kenai Spur Rd. and Airport Way, has a bakery, pharmacy, fruit, natural foods, and fast food (24hr. grocery).

■ **Veronica's Coffee House** (283-2725), at the end of Mission Rd. opposite the Russian church. In a historic building decorated with paintings and overlooking the inlet. Great veggie lasagna $5.25; amazing homemade desserts $3-4. Live folk F and Sa. Open M-Tu and Th 7am-7pm, W and F 7am-10pm, Sa 9am-10pm, Su 9am-7pm.

Old Town Village Restaurant (283-4515), 1000 Mission Ave. Housed in a restored 1918 cannery building, Old Town is known for its great seafood dinners (from $13), salad ($5), and hearty Sunday brunch (10am-2pm; $9). Many patrons from Beluga RV Park, a block away. Open M-Th 11am-9pm, F-Sa 11am-10pm, Su 10am-8pm.

New Peking, 145 S. Willow St. (283-4662), off Kenai Spur Rd. Savor the all-you-can-eat $6 lunch buffet (noon-2:30pm Su-F) in a lush Far Eastern setting. Dinner buffet $10 (daily 5-8:30pm). Open M-F 11am-10pm, Sa 3pm-10pm, Su 11am-9pm.

Little Ski-Mo's Burger-n-Brew (283-4463), on Kenai Spur Rd. across from the visitor center. A staggering array of burgers in a dimly lit, lodge-like interior, complete with fireplace. Twin Cities (egg, bacon, cheddar, and sprouts) $7; cheeseburger, fries, and large drink $6.25. Open M-Th 11am-10pm, F 11am-11pm, Sa 11am-10pm, Su 11am-7pm.

SIGHTS AND OUTDOORS

The visitor center provides a map of the half-mile, wheelchair-accessible walking tour of **Old Town Kenai.** The highlight of the tour is the **Holy Assumption Russian Orthodox Church,** on Mission St. off Overland St. Built in 1846, then rebuilt in 1896, this National Historic Landmark contains 200-year-old icons. Tours are given upon request; call 283-4122 for more info. (Open in summer M-F 11am-4pm. Public services Sa 6pm and Su 10am.)

Breathtaking **Cook Inlet** is framed by smooth sand, two mountain ranges, and volcanic **Mt. Augustine** and **Mt. Redoubt.** The beach at the end of Spruce Dr. is a great place to watch beluga, salmon, and eagles. The best time to see whales is two hours before or after high tide. If you coordinate with the arrival of the fishing boats, you may see a freeloading seal or sea lion as well.

The **Captain Cook State Recreation Area** lies at the northern end of the Kenai Spur Rd., 30 mi. from town. Premier views of the inlet and the Alaska-Aleutian Range make for a lovely picnic on a bluff or beach. Campsites here ($10) feature water and pit toilets. Bald eagle sightings are common, and a small caribou herd, often spotted trotting along Kenai Spur Hwy. or Bridge Access Rd., roams the flatlands between Kenai and Soldotna. You can swim at **Stormy Lake,** and the **Swanson River Canoe Trail** (see p. 471) begins nearby.

Fishing is what there is to do in town. Check at the visitor center or **Lee's** (see above) for **charter** info (prices are comparable to those in Soldotna). Anglers can do their thing on any public land along the **Kenai River,** where the majority of fishing takes place. Park at the end of Spruce Dr. and hike to the mouth. Beginners should ask at fishing shops for recommended locations to avoid accidentally damaging the banks of the river and jeopardizing fish habitat. **Licenses** are available at gas stations, groceries, or outfitters. **Swanson River** and **Stormy Lake,** in the Captain Cook Recreation Area, contain rainbow trout, silver salmon, and arctic char.

Nikiski, 12½ mi. north of Kenai at Mile 23.4 of the Spur Rd., is home to an alien spacecraft cleverly disguised as a geodesic-domed indoor pool (776-8472 or 776-8800), behind the Nikiski school. (Open Tu-F 1-5pm and 6-9pm, Sa-Su 1-5pm and 6-9pm. $3, seniors $2. Alaska's largest waterslides $6.) Near the pool, a hockey rink, ski- and paved-trail (wheelchair accessible), outdoor volleyball and tennis courts, and picnic area all await playful Earthlings.

The visitor center is hosting several events in the summer of 2000. **A Celebration of Wildlife Art** featuring 75 original works by some of the best known Alaskan artists will be on display May to July. Various programs continue during the summer.

NINILCHIK

From Kenai, the Sterling Highway (Rte. 1) winds through short, shoreline forest on a bluff overlooking the Cook Inlet. The route affords fantastic views across the inlet of Mt. Redoubt, and Mt. Iliamna; both volcanoes that rise over 10,000 ft. and have erupted in the last 50 years. The highway winds into the town of Ninilchik, a hamlet with spectacular fishing, fantastic scenery, a strong Russian heritage. *Do not* eat any shellfish harvested in the area without assurances from health authorities that they are free from toxins (see p. 34).

The **General Store** (567-3378), at Sterling Mile 137½, sells groceries and fishing supplies, and has the town's only **ATM** (open M-Th 7am-11pm, F 7am-midnight, Sa-Su 6am-11pm). The **Alaskan Angler RV Park** (800-347-4114; turn onto Kingsley at Mile 135 of the Sterling) rents clamming gear for $3 per day (tent sites $10, hookups $21; office open daily 9am-9pm.). Their **showers** ($2 for 10min., with towel) and **laundromat** (wash and dry each $1.50) are open 24hr. **Public radio** is on 91.9 FM.

For truly scenic dining, head to the **Boardwalk Cafe** (567-3388; take Mission off the Sterling and follow the signs for the beach and cannery). This seaside spot with outdoor tables serves huge pieces of homemade pie ($2) and sandwiches ($6.50), and great seafood soup in a bread bowl ($5.50; open May-Sept. daily 10am-

10pm). **Deep Creek Packing** (567-3396), at Mile 137, sells and gives **free samples** of different kinds of smoked fish. The **Inlet View** bar (567-3337) at Mile 134.5, is a laid-back local hangout that stays open real late (10am-5am; pints $3.50.)

The supremely pleasant ◪ **Eagle Watch Hostel (HI)** (567-3905) is 3 mi. east of town on Oil Well Rd., which starts just before the Chinook gas station. Although the building is spacious and clean, the hostel's highlight is outdoors. Always eagles (as advertised) and sometimes moose and bears can be seen from the deck, which overlooks a lush valley. A barbecue, showers, friendly hosts, phone, clam shovels, fishing rods, tree swing, new mattresses and playful dog seal the deal. The hostel is closed between 10am and 5pm, and enforces its 11pm curfew. ($10, nonmembers $13; linens $2, no sleeping bags; towels 50¢; cash and traveler's checks only).

The several **state campgrounds** near Ninilchik have water and toilets. Sites along the river are $8, along the beach $10. Superb spots in the **Ninilchik State Recreation Area** overlooking the inlet, are less than 1 mi. north of town. The nearby, beach-level **Deep Creek Recreation Area** (not the Deep Creek Campground) is one of the most popular campgrounds on the peninsula; turn west about ¼ mi. south of Deep Creek. Locals claim that the area has the world's best saltwater king salmon fishing; dolly varden and steelhead trout ply the waters, too ($10; day-use parking $5).

HOMER

In a state where the unique is commonplace and gorgeous settings are the norm, Homer's eclectic culture and idyllic setting stand out against the odds. The town's hiking and outdoor opportunities may be lackluster compared to neighboring Seward and Cordova, and the town may be a bit too spread out for foot travelers, but Homer's citizenry will not disappoint. Fisherfolk and aging counterculturalists share the streets with artists, several Russian Orthodox communities, and pop star Jewel's extended family. These diverse cultural elements mix against a spectacular backdrop: one end of town rises up on bluffs above Kachemak Bay, providing wide views of the blue mountains and pale glaciers across the water. Below these bluffs, Homer supports a theater group, scores of galleries, a fabulous public radio station and one of the best small newspapers in Alaska. Moderate temperatures and a mere two feet of annual rainfall put Homer in "Alaska's Banana Belt."

▣ ORIENTATION AND PRACTICAL INFORMATION

Surrounded by 400 million tons of coal, Homer rests on **Kachemak "Smokey" Bay,** named for the mysteriously burning deposits that first greeted settlers. The town is on the southwestern coast of Kenai Peninsula, on the north shore of the bay, and extending into the bay along an improbable 4½-mile tendril of sand, gravel, and RVs known as **the Spit.** The rugged, beautiful wilds and hiking trails of **Kachemak Bay State Park** lie across the bay, where the southern end of the **Kenai Mountains** reaches the sea. Also on the south side of the bay are the artist/fishing colony of **Halibut Cove,** the sparsely populated **Yukon Island,** the **Gull Island** bird rookery, and the Russian-founded hamlet of **Seldovia** (see p. 480).

The **Sterling Highway (Hwy. 1)** leads away from Homer across the Kenai Peninsula toward Anchorage, 226 mi. away. The heart of Homer lies in a triangle defined by the shoreside **Homer Bypass,** the downtown drag **Pioneer Ave.,** and the cross-cutting **Lake St.** Homer Bypass becomes the Sterling west of town, **Ocean Dr.** to the east and veers right to follow the Spit as **Homer Spit Rd.** The walk to the spit takes more than an hour, though shuttles run there. Reports say hitching is absurdly easy.

TRANSPORTATION

Airplanes: Follow signs from Ocean Dr. just before it becomes Spit Rd. to reach the airport. **Era Aviation** (800-866-8394) flies to Anchorage (7 per day, round-trip $142). **Homer Air** (235-8591) flies to Seldovia (15min., many per day, round-trip $55). **Smokey Bay Air,** 2100 Kachemak Dr. (235-1511), flies upon request to Seldovia (round-trip $50).

Buses: Homer Stage Line, 424 Homer Spit Rd. (235-2252). To: Soldotna (1½hr., 1 per day M-Sa, $25); Anchorage (5½hr., 1 per day M-Sa, $45); Seward (4hr.; M, W, F; $40). $5 extra for drop-off at Anchorage Airport. Runs Memorial Day to Labor Day.

Local Shuttle: Raven Transit (235-5550). From 2 miles up East End Rd. through downtown and to the Spit. Flag down the red-and-white bus. One ride $3, day pass $10. Runs May-September daily 6am-6pm.

Ferries: Alaska Marine Highway (235-8449 or 800-382-9229). Office and terminal just before the end of the Spit. To: Seldovia (1½hr., $18); Kodiak (9½hr., $48); Cordova ($138), and once per month to Dutch Harbor in the Aleutian Islands (4 days, $242). Open M-F 7am-4pm and when ferry is in.

Taxis: Chux Taxi, 235-2489. To downtown from the airport ($5) or ferry ($10). **Raven** (235-5550) is brand-new and cheaper.

Share-A-Ride: KBBI Public Radio, 890 AM (235-7721), is an on-air bulletin board, broadcasting requests for those both seeking and offering rides several times daily.

Car Rental: Polar (235-5998 until 9pm). $60 per day, 30¢ per mi. after 100 mi., 7th day free. $5 for unlimited mileage. Must be 21 with credit card. Open daily 8am-6:30pm.

VISITOR AND LOCAL SERVICES

Visitor Information: 135 Sterling Hwy. (235-5300; www.homeralaska.org), near Main St. Local and long-distance courtesy phone. Open June to Labor Day M-F 9am-8pm, Sa-Su 10am-6pm; Labor Day to May M-F 9am-5pm.

Outdoor Information: Alaska Maritime National Wildlife Refuge Visitor Center, 509 Sterling Hwy. (235-6961), next to the Best Western Bidarka Inn. Wildlife exhibits and helpful advice on Kachemak Bay backcountry. Leads 1hr. bird and tidepool walks twice a week. Open May-Sept. 9am-6pm. **Southern District Ranger Station** (235-7024), 4 mi. out of town on the Sterling Hwy. Great info on the park across the bay. Open W-Su 8:30am-4:30pm, call first in winter. **Fishing licenses** ($10 for 1 day, $20 for 3 days) available from local stores. **Alaska Department of Fish and Game,** 3298 Douglas St. (235-8191), near Owen Marine. Open M-F 8am-5pm.

Employment: Alaska State Employment Service, 601 E. Pioneer Ave. #123 (235-7791). Open M-F 8am-noon and 1-4:30pm. See p. 63.

ATM: Eagle Quality Center (24hr.; see **Food,** below). **Salty Dawg Saloon,** on the spit.

Equipment Rental: Homer Saw and Cycle, 1532 Ocean Dr. (235-8406). Top-of-the-line bikes $15 per half-day, $25 per day. Open M-F 9am-5:30pm, Sa 11am-5pm. **Chain Reaction** (235-0750), in the Lakeside Mall. Same rates. Open M-Sa 9am-6pm, Su noon-5pm, winter M-Sa 9am-6pm. Numerous outfits on the spit rent fishing gear and clamming rakes and shovels, including **Sportsman's Supplies** (235-2617), in the white building by the Fishing Hole. Open in summer daily 7am-9pm.

Bookstore: The Bookstore, 90 Sterling Hwy. (235-7496), next to the Eagle Quality Center. Open in summer M-Sa 10am-7pm, Su noon-5pm; in winter M-Sa 10am-6pm. **The Old Inlet** (235-1352), at the corner of Bunnell and Main St., stocks used books. Open M-Sa 11am-5pm, Su noon-5pm, closed Su-M in the winter.

Library: 141 Pioneer Ave. (235-3180), near Main St. Free Internet access (no email). Open M, W, F-Sa 10am-6pm, Tu, Th 10am-8pm.

Laundromat and Public Showers: Sportsman's Supplies (see **Equipment Rental,** above). Wash $2, dry $1. Showers $3.50 for 30min., towel 50¢.

EMERGENCY AND COMMUNICATIONS

Emergency: 911. **Police:** 4060 Heath St. (235-3150), off Pioneer Ave.

Women's Crisis Line: 235-8101, 24hr.

Hospital: South Peninsula Hospital, 4300 Bartlett (235-8101), off Pioneer St.

Internet Access: Free at the **Library** (no email), and at **K-Bay Cafe** 5941 East End Rd. (235-1551) 3½ mi. out of town in the Kachemak Building Center. Open M-F 8am-5pm,

Sa-Su 6am-6pm. **Surfin' Salmon,** 173 W. Pioneer (235-2627), next to the library. $5 per hr. Open M-F 8am-5pm, Sa-Su 6am-6pm.

Public Radio: 890 AM. Put away the mix tapes in this town.

Post Office: 3261 Wadell Rd., 99603 (235-6129), off Homer Bypass. Open M-F 8:30am-5pm, Sa 10am-1pm.

Area Code: 907.

ACCOMMODATIONS AND CAMPGROUNDS

Seaside Farm, 58335 East End Rd. (235-7850; seaside@xyz.net), 4½ mi. out of town. If you're young at heart, want to meet kind folk, like to drink and sing around a campfire, and can do without spotlessness and modern amenities, this is your rustic eden. A ways from town ($12 cab), but the hitching is easy. The hostel is not nearly as appealing as the clover field for camping which features one of Homer's finest views of the bay. Enjoy a covered outdoor common area, hammock, and seaside strolls. Bunks $15. Tent sites $6, with showers $9. Private cabins with propane burner and wood stove: singles $45; doubles $55. Discounts available for backpackers and extended stays. Lodging sometimes available in exchange for farm work. Open May-Labor Day.

Sunspin Guest House, 358 E. Lee Dr. (235-6677 or 800-391-6677; www.sunspin.com). From Pioneer Ave., take Kachemak Way toward the bluff to Lee Dr. on the right. Convenient to downtown. Clean and warm decor. Real beds, linens, and a continental breakfast. Beds $28; private rooms with shared bath from $55.

Old Town Bed and Breakfast, 106 W. Bunnell (235-7558, www.xyz.net/~oldtown), in the historic Old Inlet Trading Post, two blocks from both downtown and the beach. Rooms have big comfortable beds with Alaskan quilts, antique furniture, and great views. Full breakfast Sunday; $5 spree at the downstairs **Two Sisters Bakery** otherwise. Rooms $65, with bath $75, $5 less for singles. 20% discount Sept.-May.

Karen Hornaday Park, From Pioneer St., go uphill on Bartlett St., left on Fairview, right on Campground Rd. Within 1 mi. of downtown. Most sites grassy, secluded, and spacious. Water, pit toilets, a great playground, and a nice view of the bay. Tents $3; RVs $7.

Spit Municipal Camping, 3735 Homer Spit Rd. (235-2617), sites line the approach to the spit, but registration is at the booth across from the fishing hole. 2 areas for RVs; 1 for both tents and RVs. A giant gravel parking lot at seaside. Terrific views are often marred by crowds and tent-uprooting winds. Water, toilets. Tents $3, RVs $7.

FOOD

The huge 24-hour **Eagle Quality Center,** 90 Sterling Hwy. (235-2408), has pork chops and floor pie. Fine produce at **John's Market** (235-5494; open M-Sa 10am-7pm, Su noon-4pm), on Lake St. at Pioneer. **Smoky Bay Natural Foods,** 248 W. Pioneer Ave. (235-7252; open M-F 8:30am-8pm, Sa 10am-7pm), is opposite the Pratt Museum.

On the Spit, salmon bite at the **Fishing Hole.** Fresh seafood can be purchased directly from fishing boats or retail. **Katch Seafoods,** 765 Fish Dock Rd. (235-6241 or 800-368-7400; open 4:30am-4:30pm), lets its salmon and halibut go for $6.50 per lb. **Coal Point Trading Co.,** 4306 Homer Spit Rd. (235-3877 or 800-235-3877), will vacuum-pack and deep-freeze your catch for 70¢ per lb. (open 8am-8pm or later). Wash it down with free samples of locally brewed Broken Birch Bitter from the **Homer Brewing Company,** 1562 Homer Spit Rd. (235-3626; open M-Sa 11am-8pm, Su noon-6pm). Mmmm...beer. Escape indistinguishable chowder-shacks downtown.

Two Sisters Bakery, 106 W. Bunnell (235-2280), off Main St. near the water. A meeting place for artists, the wayward, and locals. Gooey cinnamon buns ($2.50) and salmon chowder ($5.50) tickle the senses; chatty locals excite the mind. Open M-Sa 7am-8pm.

Cafe Cups, 162 Pioneer Ave. (235-8330). The best of a big-city cafe hybridized with Homer's offbeat attitude. Unusual sandwiches and salad $7-8. $3 breakfast until 9:30am (2 eggs, toast, potatoes) is the cheapest in town. Open daily 7am-10pm.

Young's Oriental Restaurant, 565 E. Pioneer Ave. (235-4002). 20-foot buffet of Chinese and Japanese sends Young's shooting ahead in the race for all-you-can-eat Asian buffet champion ($6.50 from 11am-3:30pm; $9 from 3:30-9pm). Open daily 11am-10pm.

Pioneer Building Pizzeria, 265 E. Pioneer Ave. (235-3663), the all-you-can-eat pizza, salad, soft ice cream, soda, and coffee buffet ($8.50; 5pm-9pm) is an opportunist's delight. Open M-Th 11am-10pm, F-Sa 11am-11pm; closes at 10pm in the winter.

👁 SIGHTS AND EVENTS

The excellent **Pratt Museum,** 3779 Bartlett St. (235-8635; www.prattmuseum.org), houses a little of everything: local art, a saltwater aquarium, Kenai artifacts, and displays on homesteader cabins, arts of the Inuit and Denali peoples, and marine mammals, including the skeleton of the beaked Bering Sea minke whale. (Open daily 10am-6pm, Oct.-Dec. and Feb.-Apr. Tu-Su noon-5pm. $5, seniors and students with ID $4, under 18 $2. Wheelchair accessible.)

Homer's residents take art seriously—even the supermarket has a gallery. Pick up *Downtown Homer Art Galleries* for info on current exhibits. The **Bunnell Street Gallery,** 106 W. Bunnell (235-2662), features contemporary work from paintings to edible art. (Open in summer daily 10am-6pm; in winter M-Sa 11am-5pm.)

Homer is often billed the Halibut Capital of the World, and the **Homer Jackpot Halibut Derby** generates a whole lot of that hoopla. The competition runs from May 1 to Labor Day, and offers a grand prize in the neighborhood of $30,000. Tickets ($7) are available in local charter offices on the Spit. The **Homer Shorebird Festival** (235-7337), during the second week in May, brings birding tours, educational workshops, an arts fair, and 8-10,000 migrating birds. On a Sunday in July or August, KBBI (235-7721) stages the fabulous all-day **Concert on the Lawn** at the town commons, featuring blues, rock, and bluegrass. The annual **Winter Carnival** (235-7740), is held in the first week of February

🎵 ENTERTAINMENT AND NIGHTLIFE

Check the *Homer News* for live theater and other performance schedules. The **Homer Family Theater** (235-6728), at Main St. and Pioneer Ave., features current Hollywood blockbusters. ($6; seniors and under 12 $3. Mondays and matinees $3.)

The sun never sets on Homer summers, figuratively and almost literally. Nightlife ranges from beachcombing in the midnight sun to hanging at the combination tourist trap and local joint, the **Salty Dawg Saloon** (235-9990), under the log lighthouse near the end of the Spit. Long communal tables breed tall tales and arm wrestling competitions (open 11am-whenever). **Alice's Champagne Palace,** 196 Pioneer Ave. (235-7650), is a wooden barn that hosts varied live music W-Sa. See Alaska's pride, **Hobo Jim,** rock the packed house every Wednesday night as old and young dance like fools and yell along to down-home Alaskan tunes. (Pints $4; no cover; pool 75¢; open Tu-Sa 2pm-5am.)

THE ICICLE BURNED FOR A WEEK On July 1st, 1998, the Homer Spit suffered one of the worst disasters since it sank 30 feet in the '64 Good Friday quake. At Icicle Seafood's processing plant, an ammonia leak and a pilot flame combined to blow the roof 30 feet in the air. Luckily, there were no casualties, but the Spit was closed down for three days. Hundreds of cannery workers lost jobs they'd only had since the day before, leading to a massive party the night of the disaster. The plant has yet to be rebuilt, and the question of whether or not to do so will affect Homer in the coming years. Will a steady stream of young college students hard-up for cash still flock here? Will Jean the Eagle Lady be able to continue providing fish guts to her hundreds of bald eagles? Will t-shirts bearing "I survived Icicle '98" be the next best-selling piece of souvenir junk? Time will tell, and in the meantime, Homer's salmon and halibut will breathe that much easier.

OUTDOORS

Nearly everyone who comes to Homer spends some time on the **Homer Spit.** Don't expect sandy beaches: the 5-mile strip of land is fairly sinking under the weight of tourists, RVs, and the charter companies and gift shops that love them. The real reason to visit the spit is to take in (or take part in) the flurry of fishing activity. Between 5 and 6pm, the returning charters weigh in and display their massive catches, and successful fishers always appreciate an audience. A couple nights a week the commercial outfits pitch tons of salmon off their boats at the loading dock immediately on the left-hand side of Fishdock Rd. off Homer Spit Rd. Check with a charter company for showtimes.

As many as 90 halibut charter boats leave the Spit each day. Choosing one, like fishing itself, can be a crap shoot, though most charter companies are reputable businesses. Many of the boats are booked through **Central Charters** (235-7847 or 800-478-7847), near the middle of the Spit. Full-day trips start at $150, with all tackle and bait included, and a refund policy for foul weather. Odds are **The Bookie** (235-1581 or 888-335-1581) may be able to find a charter for as little as $135. It will also book kayak trips, flightseeing, and lodgings, all at no charge to you, the customer. (Open in summer daily 6am-9pm; phone service in winter.)

For those without the cash to chase after the big ones, there's always the **fishing hole** near the start of the Spit, where anyone who can hold a rod can probably catch a salmon. A stocking program plants fry in this lagoon. They return years later to spawn, but the lagoon is unsuitable for spawning, and pitiless anglers hook the fish that return. To actually get your own patch of sand, head to **Bishop's Beach;** take Main St. toward the water, and follow signs to the left on Bunnell Ave.

Views of the Kenai Mountains on the hilly **East Hill Rd.,** to the east of town off East End Rd., make for quite a drive. The best **hiking** is across the bay at **Kachemak Bay State Park** (see below). In and around Homer, take to the beach or the moderate 6.7 mi. **Homestead Trail** from any of three access points: take Roger's Loop Rd. off the Sterling across from the Bayview Inn to the marked trailhead sign; or take Diamond Ridge Rd. off West Hill Rd. to the trail sign; or drive past the reservoir on Skyline Dr. off West Hill to a parking lot and trail sign. A panoramic view of the bay can be had halfway between the Roger's Loop and Diamond Ridge access points at the memorial to legendary local walker, **Ruben Call.** Pick up a trail guide from the visitor center or the maritime center to better identify the arctic star flowers, marsh violets, green rein orchids, and other wildflowers blooming along the way.

For great birding, take the easy 1½-mile loop of the **Calvin and Coyle Trail;** turn right on Mariner Dr. from East End (1½ mi. from town). The trail leads to an observation deck from which shorebirds, waterfowl, and eagles are visible. The trail, which leads from behind the maritime center (see above) off the Sterling down to the water, also leads to some of Homer's finest tide pools.

The **Center for Alaskan Coastal Studies,** 708 Smokey Bay Way, off Lake St. across from Lakeside Mall (235-6667, www.xyz.net/~cacs) has a small exhibit room on marine life and issues. Seabird tours and free guided hikes through July on medicinal plants are among their other offerings. (Open M-F 10am-5pm.)

NEAR HOMER: KACHEMAK BAY STATE PARK

Locals are vocal in their praise of **Kachemak Bay State Park,** Alaska's first. One of the largest coastal parks in the country, the area contains about 375,000 acres of beaches, tide pools, mountains, and glaciers, and includes one of the northernmost temperate rainforests in the world. Stop by the **Southern District Ranger Station** (see **Practical Information,** above) for info on the park's myriad hiking and camping opportunities. There are some established campsites, but dispersed camping is more common, and all camping is free. The park's 40 miles of trails are described in the trail guide available at the Ranger Station. One popular destination is the Halibut Cove area, home to the **Halibut Cove Ranger Station** (235-6999), staffed by volunteers during most daylight hours in summer. **Inlet Charters** (235-6126 or 800-770-6126) on the Spit across from the harbormaster, books trips with several water taxi companies. **Mako's Water Taxi** (399-4133) may be the friendliest, and charges $49 for the round-trip. **Rainbow Tours** (235-7272) offers a 1½-hour cruise from the Spit to **Gull Island,** home to murres, cormorants, guillemots, and other beautiful birds with ungainly names, a few puffins, and about sixteen bijillion gulls (9am and 4:30pm; $20, seniors $15, under 12 $10). For a self-powered water adventure, consider a full-day kayak trip with **True North Kayak Adventures** (235-0708). The expensive tour comes with a great lunch and offers sea otter spotting ($125 includes round-trip water taxi).

NEAR HOMER: HALIBUT COVE

Yet another great way to spend an expensive afternoon in the Homer area is with **Danny J. Tours** (235-7847; booked through **Central Charters,** above) visiting the colorful artist/fishing colony of Halibut Cove and its few dozen residents. The quiet cove is scattered with homes up on stilts and is surrounded by towering mountains. There is no affordable lodging on the island. Early trips leave the Spit daily at noon and make a short visit to Gull Island (see above) before dropping passengers off at the village for 2½ hours (round-trip $42, seniors $34, children $21). The cheaper evening run (departure 5pm, return 10pm; $21) requires that you dine at **Saltry** (296-2223 for reservations; open 1-5pm and 6-9pm), the cove's only restaurant. Though pricey (salmon with raspberry chutney $17), the fresh fish served there is top-notch. All three art galleries stay open when the Danny J. is in. A raised boardwalk leads to the **Halibut Cove Experience Art Gallery's** collection of works by residents. At **Diana Tillion's Cove Gallery,** Diana works with ink extracted with a hypodermic needle from stranded octopi. Half a mile farther down the path, past the resident dock, a **six-foot-tall portrait of Alex Duff Combs' head** welcomes visitors to his gallery. World-traveled and acclaimed, Combs' pottery and painting is shown in a house filled with faded buoys and peacock feathers. The only established trail is the 1 mi. **Arch Trail,** a dirt path that departs from a staircase on the left of the boardwalk 150 yards past the Experience Gallery. The trail rambles along a ridge past intriguing rock formations to an overlook of the cove.

SELDOVIA

Virtually untouched by the tourist mania rampant on the rest of the Kenai Peninsula, this isolated hamlet combines maritime charm, slow-paced life, and funky ambience à la Homer. The Russians named Seldovia for its herring, which have long supported the town's economy. The town was also once an active fur trading post. Unique geological features, quiet coves, and desolate rocky beaches surround the town; Seldovia overlooks four active volcanoes: Augustine, Iliamna, Redoubt, and Spur.

⚡ PRACTICAL INFORMATION. Bring money to Seldovia; there are no banks, and few stores accept credit cards. The **airport** is less than 1 mi. out of town on Airport Ave. **Homer Air** (235-8591) flies nearly constantly to Homer ($29, round-trip $55). **Smokey Air** does the same for $25-50, and also flies on demand to Port Graham or Ninualack ($20, round-trip $40). **Great Northern Airlines** (800-243-1968) flies daily to Anchorage (1½hr., $100). The **Alaska Marine Highway** (235-8449, 234-7878, or 800-382-9229) chugs from Homer to Seldovia twice per week (Tu 12:30pm and Su 3am; one-way $18), lingering for only 4hr. before heading back. Two **tour boats** also cruise daily to Homer. **Rainbow Tours** (235-7272) offers the least expensive service (one-way $25, round-trip $40; seniors $36; youth $25). **Jakolof Bay Express** (235-2376, 235-0708) provides an eco-friendly and just plain friendly ferry ($40 round-trip) to the Jakalof dock, an 11-mile bike ride from "downtown" Seldovia. Bringing a bike costs $5, a kayak $10. Susan Springer, owner of **Herring Bay Mercantile** (234-7140), on Main St., and author of *Seldovia, Alaska*, is happy to share her great wealth of local knowledge. **The Buzz** (234-7479), just past the harbormaster's on Main St., **rents bikes** ($20 per day, $25 per 24hr.). Open Mar.-Sept. daily 7am-4:30pm. **Kayak'atak** (234-7425; www.alaska.net/~kayaks) with an office in Herring

Bay Mercantile on Main Street, rents kayaks (singles $50 per day; doubles $75 per day) and leads full-day trips ($110). Call between 8am and 10pm. The **library** on Seldovia St. near Main St. has free **Internet access**. (Open Tu 2-4:30pm and 7-9pm, Th 3:30-5:30pm and 7-9pm, Sa 11:30am-3:30pm.) **Laundromat and Showers: Harbor Laundromat** (see **Food,** below). **Emergency:** 911. **Police:** 234-7640. **Clinic:** (234-7825). Open M, W, F 9am-4pm. **Post office:** (234-7831) at Main and Seldovia St. Open M-F 9am-5pm. **ZIP code:** 99663. **Area code:** 907.

▓▓ ACCOMMODATIONS, CAMPGROUNDS, AND FOOD.

At the end of Main St. by the boardwalk, **Dancing Eagles Lodge** (234-7627) offers some small rooms (from $45), a beautiful private cabin ($125 for 2, $40 per additional person), a private extension of the town boardwalk, a hot tub, and a terrific view of the bay. **Gerry's Place B&B** is both less attractive and less expensive. Basic rooms with soft beds run $40 (for doubles $60). The best deal for groups of five or so are the pleasant, newly furnished, kitchenette-having **Seldovia Seaport Cottages,** 313 Shoreline Dr. (234-7483; chap@xyz.net; wheelchair accessible; up to 2 $70, each additional person $10). **Outside Beach,** 1 mi. from town, offers camping and close encounters with sea otters. An agent occasionally collects the $5 fee. Turn left off Jakolof Bay Rd. at the "Narrow Road" sign or hike the Otterbahn Trail (see below).

Seldovia Market (234-7633), on Main St., stocks a modest supply of groceries, hardware, tackle, liquor, and pharmaceuticals (open M-Sa 9am-8pm, Su noon-5pm). Frozen dairy treats, comforting hot showers, and laundry services mingle in bizarre but happy matrimony at the sparkling **Harbor Laundromat** (234-7420), also on Main St. (showers $4 per 10min., towel and soap included; wash $3.50-5, dry 25¢ per 5min.). Enjoy a delicious cone ($2) or milkshake ($4.50), or a variety of fried foods ($2-4) while toweling off or folding clothes (open daily 11am-8pm; call for winter hours; last shower 7:30pm; last wash 6:30pm). **The Buzz,** 231 Main St. (234-7479), serves coffee, espresso, and great food in a nice rainy afternoon loitering space. Calzones ($6.75), quiche ($4.75), and local art abound (open daily 7am-4:30pm Mar.-Sept.; credit cards accepted). The **Crab Pot Cafe** (234-7440), on Main St. next to the post office, is a small grocery and serves sandwiches on fresh-baked bread (from $5; open daily 10am-8pm, closed Jan.-Mar.).

▣ ▟ SIGHTS, OUTDOORS, AND ENTERTAINMENT.

Seldovia's quiet, colorful homes, friendly locals, and beautiful harbor make for lovely strolls. The Seldovia Native Association runs a tiny **museum** at 328 Main St. (234-7898; open M-Sa 8am-5pm, Su noon-5pm). The adjacent **Berry Kitchen/Museum Gift Shop,** whips up a mean blueberry jam (open M-Sa 10am-2pm, Su noon-5pm). **St. Nicholas Orthodox Church,** built in 1891, peers out over the town from a hilltop. The church is closed to the public except for scheduled tours. Check at the Mercantile for schedules.

The **Otterbahn Hiking Trail,** starting at the Susan B. English School near Winifred Ave., winds a moderate 1 mi. to the cliffs and tidal pools of Outside Beach, passing through old growth and floral meadows and granting a spectacular view of the volcanoes on clear days. A moderate 5 mi. hike, also good for mountain biking, leads up the bay on the dirt extension of **Rocky St.,** on the right 100 yards before the dump. A shorter trail leads from Airport Ave. before Fish Creek, up to the reservoir. The **Seldovia Native Corporation,** 328 Main St. (234-7637; open M-F 8am-5pm), owns much of the land above the reservoir and between the Jakalof dock and town. Hiking and camping in the area requires permits ($1 per day; they also allow berry-picking, from mid-August to mid-September). For indoor kicks, head to the **Linwood Bar** (234-9906; open in summer 10am-2am; in winter M-F 10am-midnight, Sa 10am-2am) or seek the brews and country music of the **Seldovia Lodge** (234-7693; open in summer daily 5pm-2am).

Seldovia triples in size on **Independence Day** (July 4). An old-fashioned celebration draws hundreds of visitors (a mob, in Seldovian terms) from all over the peninsula, and includes parades, the 5km Salmon Shuffle, games for all ages, and a pancake feed at the fire hall. The whole town sits on the breakwater to observe and cheer the canoe-jousters and log-rollers.

KODIAK ISLAND

In this century, Kodiak Island has been rocked by earthquakes, engulfed by *tsunamis*, coated in crude from the Exxon *Valdez*, and blanketed in nearly two feet of volcanic ash. But most of the island is still covered in thick spruce forests dripping with moss. Kodiak's peaks open up into wild, geranium-speckled meadows and provide views that rival most Alaskan vistas as tiny islands and rock outcroppings poke out of the whale-filled waters. Kodiak shelters the Kodiak National Wildlife Refuge, home to more than 3,000 Kodiak brown bears, the world's largest carnivorous land mammal. The refuge's 800 mi. of coastline encircle the island's sharp inland peaks, pushing Kodiak's human population onto the eastern shore. Rich surrounding waters have made the island's fishing fleet one of the most productive in the state, drawing young people each summer to work its canneries. Islanders take seafood seriously. Until recently, tourism has been only an afterthought.

KODIAK

Kodiak was the first capital of Russian Alaska before Alexander Baranof moved the Russian-American Company to Sitka. The glittering ladies of St. Petersburg dressed to the nines back in the colonial day, thanks to Russian enslavement of the native Alutiiq people, who were forced to hunt local otters to near extinction.

Nearby Novarupta Volcano in Katmai is anything but extinct. It erupted in 1912 with a force 10 times greater than the 1980 eruption of Mount St. Helens (see p. 517). In 1964, the Good Friday earthquake caused $24 million in damage and creating a tsunami that leveled most of downtown. When the swamped fishing port was rehabilitated by the Army Corps of Engineers, one 200-ft. vessel, *The Star of Kodiak*, was cemented into the ferry dock and converted into a cannery. But Kodiak is neither brusque about its industry nor hungering for tourists. Unlike most Alaskan ports, Kodiak hides its tourist charters and the **Alutiiq Museum** does a good job of sharing the community's rich native culture and history. A vibrant Russian Orthodox community remains proud that Kodiak was home to the first Russian Orthodox Church built in the new world.

▪ ORIENTATION AND PRACTICAL INFORMATION

The city of Kodiak is on the eastern tip of Kodiak Island, roughly 250 mi. south of Anchorage. Paved and rutted gravel roads run 100 mi. along the scenic coastlines north and south of the city. **Chiniak Rd.**, which heads south for 42 mi., makes an especially impressive trip. In town, the main drag is **Center St.**, which starts at the ferry terminal and heads inland, ending at the intersection with **Rezanof Dr.** to the left and **Lower Mill Bay Rd.** to the right. The cluster of downtown shops and most of the good restaurants are within a 5 minute walk from the ferry.

GETTING THERE AND GETTING AROUND

Airplanes: The **airport** is 5 mi. southwest of town on Rezanof Dr. **Era Aviation** (800-866-8394) flies to Anchorage (1hr., 6-7 per day, $115-150; round-trip $190-300). **Pen Air** (487-4014) flies to Karluk (30min., 2 per day, $75, round-trip $150); Port Lions (30min., 3 per day, $30; round-trip $60); Larsen Bay (30min., 3 per day, $60, round-trip $120), as does **Island Air** (486-6196 or 800-478-6196). Open daily 7am-5pm.

Ferries: Alaska Marine Highway (800-526-6731, 486-3800; fax 486-6166). Ferries depart Kodiak May-Sept. 1-3 times per week, and less frequently in winter. To: Homer (9hr., $48); Seward (13hr., $54); and Valdez (29hr., $98). 5-day round-trip to the Aleutian Islands (1 per month, $202). The terminal is next to the visitors bureau. Open M-F 8am-5pm, Sa 8am-4pm, Su 9-1, and when ferries are in. See p. 58 for discounts.

Taxis: A&B Taxi (486-4343) $3 base plus $2 per mi. $13 to the ferry or the airport.

Public Shuttle: Kodiak Area Transit System (KATS) (486-8308). 3 routes between the harbormaster, Kodiak College, and shop stops (M-Sa 6:45-8:10pm). Express from the harbormaster to the airport with shopping stops (M-Th 6:40am-9:30pm, F-Sa 6:40am-11:25pm, Su 12:30pm-5pm). $2, students and seniors $1, under 5 with adult free.

Car Rental: Rent-a-Heap (486-8550), at the airport. $29 per day, 29¢ per mi. Must be 25 with credit card. Open daily 6:30am-10pm. Also at Port Gifts. Open M-Su 9am-7pm. **Avis** (487-2264) rents to those 21 and under for $62 per day.

Car Repair: R.C., 2017 Mill Bay Rd. (486-8476). Open M-F 9am-6pm, Sa 10am-2pm.

VISITOR INFORMATION

Visitor Information: Kodiak Island Convention and Visitors Bureau, 100 Marine Way (486-4782; www.kodiak.org), in front of the ferry dock. Great hiking guides are $5 here, but free at the National Wildlife Refuge. Open daily 8am-5pm, and for most ferry arrivals; in winter M-F 8am-noon and 1-5pm, Sa-Su 10am-4pm.

Outdoor Information: Fish and Wildlife Service and **National Wildlife Refuge Visitor Center,** 1390 Buskin River Rd. (487-2600), just outside Buskin State Recreation Site, 4 mi. southwest of town on Rezanof Rd. Wildlife displays, stuffed brown bears, films, and info on Kodiak National Wildlife Refuge and its cabins. Excellent, free hiking guide. Summer kids programs, Sa 10am. Open M-F 8:30am-4:30pm, in summer also Sa-Su noon-4:30pm. **State Department of Parks,** 1200 Abercrombie Dr. (486-6339), at Fort Abercrombie. Info on state parks and campgrounds, as well as public-use cabins on Shuyak Island and Afognak Island. Open M-F 8am-noon, 1pm-4:30pm, Sa-Su hours vary. Free two- to three-hour **Audubon Hikes** on weekends mid-Apr. to mid-Sept. meet at the ferry dock and range from whale watching to strenuous climbs. For a free **Bunker Talks** just show up at Miller Pt. in the park on Tu, F, or Su 2:30-4pm.

Fishing Information: Alaska Department of Fish and Game, 211 Mission Rd. (486-1880, recorded run updates 486-4559). Open M-F 8am-4:30pm. **Licenses** are available at local sporting goods stores (1 day $10, 3 days $20, 7 days $30, 14 days $50).

Employment: Alaska State Employment Service, 309 Center St. (486-3105), in Kodiak Plaza. First stop for fish-canners. Open M-F 8am-5pm. See p. 64 for more info.

LOCAL SERVICES

Equipment Sales and Rental: 58° North, 1231 Mill Bay Rd. (486-6249; thowland@ptialaska.net) about 2 mi. from the ferry. Take Upper Mill Bay until it turns into Mill Bay. Rents bikes ($35 per 24hr.) and gear; great resource for hiking and biking trail info. **Russian Heritage Inn,** 119 Yukon (486-5657), three blocks from the ferry, rents road-worthy bikes ($25, same day return) **Mack's Sports Shop,** 117 Lower Mill Bay (486-4276), at end of Center Ave. Rods, guns, and tips. Open M-Sa 7am-7pm, Su 8am-6pm.

Library: 319 Lower Mill Bay Rd. (486-8686). Free 1hr. **Internet access.** Open M-F 10am-9pm, Sa 10am-5pm, Su 1-5pm.

Public Radio: 100.1 FM. Alutiiq word of the week Tu 9am, Sa 5pm, and Su 3pm.

Laundromat and Public Showers: Ernie's, 218 Shelikof (486-4119), opposite the harbor. Wash $3, dry 25¢ per 4min. Showers $4, towel $1. Open daily 8am-8pm.

EMERGENCY AND COMMUNICATIONS

Emergency: 911. **Police:** 217 Lower Mill Bay Rd. (486-8000).

Crisis Line: 486-3625. **Women's Crisis Line:** 486-6171.

Hospital: 1915 E. Rezanof Dr. (486-3281), on call 24 hr.

Post Office: 419 Lower Mill Bay Rd., 99615 (486-4721). Open M-F 9am-5:30pm. **Downtown Contract Station,** in the AC Grocery. Open M-Sa 10am-6pm.

Internet Access: See **Library,** above. **Sweets-N-More** (481-1630), next to McDonalds on Lower Mill Bay Rd. $3 per 30min. Open M-F 7am-7pm, Sa 10am-7pm, Su 10am-6pm.

Area Code: 907.

ACCOMMODATIONS AND CAMPGROUNDS

Kodiak has no hostels and no true budget accommodations. There are a couple of cheap motels close by and several nice, somewhat affordable B&B's farther out. Finding a room becomes almost impossible when the airport shuts down due to bad weather, and this happens often. Kodiak has a brutal 11% hotel tax in town, 6% outside of town. There is no free camping close to town. The state runs two nice **campgrounds** (see below), but on any trail outside of town camping is perfectly silent and free. About 2 mi. down Rezanof Dr. towards Fort Abercrombie, **Mill Bay** is a scenic lookout and picnic area with room in the woods for several tents. More remote are the meadows at the top of **Old Woman Mountain** (see below) or at the end of a gorgeous 1½-hr. drive down the Chiniak Hwy. to Pasagshak Bay Rd. Camp for free (though a fee may be levied in 2000) in the **Pasagshak State Recreation Site,** Pasagshak Bay Rd. Mile 9 (water, toilets; 7 sites) or continue 3½ mi. to Kodiak's best surfing beach, where whales rub their tummies right on shore.

Lakeview Terrace B&B, 2426 Spruce Cape Rd., (486-5135). Take Mission St. 2½ mi. northeast of town. It becomes Spruce Cape Rd. One big room with a big bed, cable TV, shared bath, breakfast, and a dog and cat. Single $45; double $55.

Shahafka Cove B&B, 1812 Mission Rd., (486-2409; www.ptialaska.net/~rwoitel/index.htm/), 1½ mi. from town opposite Uradahl Loop. Watch the bay from the hot tub after a multi-course breakfast. Single with shared bath $65 or $55 if multiple-night stay.

Shelikof Lodge, 211 Thorsheim Ave. (486-4141; fax 486-4116; www.ptialaska.net/~kyle), on a street to the right of McDonald's, three blocks from the ferry. Remodelled motel; green rooms with cable TV. Singles $60; doubles $65, triple $70. Courtesy airport shuttle M-F 8:30am-4:30pm.

Fort Abercrombie State Park (486-6339), 4 mi. northeast of town on Rezanof-Monashka Rd. WWII ruins, trails, a trout-filled fishing lake, spectacular sunsets, and whale watching. Water, shelters, and toilets. No RV hookups. 13 sites: $10. 7-night max. stay. Open to motor traffic in summer only; walk-ins year round.

Buskin River State Recreation Site (486-6339), 4½ mi. southwest of town, off Rezanof Dr. Water, pit toilets, RV dump station. Closer to the airport and the Buskin River, where over 50% of Kodiak's sport fish are caught. 15 sites: $10. 14-night max. stay.

FOOD AND NIGHTLIFE

The Chinese Deli at **Safeway,** 2685 Mill Bay Rd. (486-6811; open daily 6am-midnight; Deli open 10am-8:30pm), 2 mi. from town, is great. **Cactus Flats Natural Foods,** 338 Mission St. (486-4677; open M-Sa 10am-6pm), sells vitamins, too.

Monk's Rock Coffeehouse and Bookstore, 202 E. Rezanof, (486-0905), opposite of McDonald's. Refresh your body and spirit among decent folk as you partake of Kodiak's holiest cup of coffee ($1), or sip a glass of Thai iced tea ($2), both served by a sister. Russian Orthodox books and icons are for sale in an adjacent room. Free classic movies (F 7:30pm) with discussions following. Open M-F 2pm-10pm, Sa 2pm-midnight.

The Captain's Restaurant, 202 E. Rezanoff (486-4144), above Monk's Rock and run by the same good sorts. Serves Kodiak's best breakfast and lunch, with lots of good veggie and vegan options. Try one of their special home-fried potato concoctions (from $7) with a home-baked biscuit dreaming of the South. Open M-Sa 5:30am-2:30pm.

Harborside Coffee and Goods, 216 Shelikof (486-5862). Proximity to the harbor draws the summer fishing crowd. Soup and bread $4.50. Tea comes in a big, beautiful earthenware mug $1. Open M-Th 6:30am-9pm, F and Sa 6:30am-10pm, Su 7am-8pm.

El Chicano, 103 Center Ave. (486-6116). Pinkish stucco and guitar music play back up to black bean soup ($4.75) and huge burritos ($8.75). Open M-Sa 11am-10pm.

Henry's Great Alaskan Restaurant (486-8844), in the mall on Marine Way. All-you-can-eat pork ribs with lots of side dishes $13.50. A pint of Alaskan Amber costs $4.50, but order up when the bell rings: a friendly fisherman just bought the house a round. Open M-Th 11:30am-9:30pm, F-Sa 11:30-10:30pm, Su noon-9pm. Bar until 11pm.

Tony's Bar (486-9489), in the alley beside AC. Claims to be Kodiak's biggest navigational hazard with over a million drinks spilled. Bottled beer $3-4, cocktails $4, live rock music F and Sa, pool, darts, and a super bowling game. Open daily 11am-2:30am.

SIGHTS, ENTERTAINMENT, AND EVENTS

Housing displays and artifacts documenting the 7,500-year-old culture of the Alutiiq, The **Alutiiq Museum and Archaeological Repository**, 215 Mission Rd. (486-7004, www.ptialaska.net/~alutiiq2/), was built with restoration funds from the Exxon *Valdez* oil spill, and is supported by Alaska's native corporations. A 10-foot-tall stuffed bear watches over detailed exhibits on native lifestyles. There is a free weekly lecture series in August on Alutiiq culture and archeology. Visitors can volunteer to help on extensive archeological digs on Kodiak and neighboring islands during June and July. The museum sponsors an **Alutiiq Word of the Week** program in the local Friday paper, on their web page, and on 100.1 FM. "Looking Both Ways," an overview of the collection, will be on display from mid-May to mid-November, 2000. (Open M-F 10am-6pm, Sa 10am-4pm, Su 11am-4pm. $2, under 12 free.)

The **Baranov Museum**, 101 Marine Way (486-5920), is housed in a storehouse for sea otter pelts built in 1808, the oldest Russian structure standing in Alaska and the oldest wooden structure on the U.S. West Coast. The museum displays a collection of Russian and Native Alaskan artifacts and a walrus skull complete with tusks; the library has photos and literature ranging from the Russian period to the present. (Open Memorial Day to Labor Day M-Sa 10am-4pm, Su noon-4pm; Labor Day to Jan. and March to Memorial Day M-W and F 10am-3pm, Sa noon-3pm. $2, under 12 free.) The **Holy Resurrection Russian Orthodox Church** (486-3854), just behind the museum, serves the oldest parish in Alaska. Built in 1794 and rebuilt after a fire shortly before WWII, its elaborate icons date to the early 1800s. Vespers are open to the public (Sa and Th at 6:30). Another block past the church on Mission, **St. Herman's Theological Seminary** houses a small museum and library here, as well as a wonderful replica of the old chapel that used to stand down the road (open M-Sa 10am-4pm, Su 12-5). The **Chapel of St. Herman** is made entirely of wood, down to the pegs that hold it together. Services are open to the public, though the schedule varies. Tours given upon request; donation requested.

The **Kodiak Alutiiq Dancers**, 713 E. Rezanof Dr. (486-4449; tribe@ptialaska.net), at the Tribal Council, perform in fantastic regalia (shows June 1 to Sept. 1 daily at 2pm. $15). Modern animation and other films appear at the **Orpheum Theatre**, 102 Center Ave. (486-5449; 2 shows per night. $5.50).

The absurd **Pillar Mountain Golf Classic** (486-9489) is Alaska's answer to the Masters: one par-70 hole. The tee is at Tony's Bar, and the snowy green is atop Pillar Mountain (March 31-April 2, 2000). The **Old Harbor Whaling Festival** (286-9246) takes place during April and May as the whales migrate past America's last commercial whaling station at Port Hobron and Alaska's first Russian settlement on Three Saints Bay. Over the 4th of July, the **Bear Country Music Festival** brings bluegrass, country, folk, and world music to the Kodiak Fairgrounds, from noon-1:30am and around the campfire until dawn. (Tickets $10 per day, $25 for 3 days, camping $5 for the weekend.) Contact Jerimiah Myers (486-6117) of the Kodiak Lions Club for more info. The five-day **Kodiak Crab Festival** (486-5557), held just before Memorial Day, celebrates a bygone industry with parades, fishing derbies, and kayak, bike, foot, crab, and survival suit races. The festivities culminate with the **Chad Ogden Ultramarathon,** a superhuman race along 43 mi. of hilly roads from Chiniak to Kodiak. **St. Herman's Days** (486-3854), held on the weekend closest to August 9, honors the first saint of the Russian Orthodox Church in North America, canonized in 1970. On one of these days, depending on the weather, visitors are welcome to join the annual pilgrimage to St. Herman's former home on Spruce Island.

SOUTHCENTRAL ALASKA

◪ OUTDOORS

Hikers should pick up an area hiking guide for free at the National Wildlife Refuge Visitor Center for free, or purchase it for $5 at the visitor center in town.

Beautiful **Fort Abercrombie State Park** (486-6339), 3½ mi. north of town, was the site of the first secret radar installation in Alaska, plus a WWII defense installation. After Attu and Kiska in the Aleutian Islands were attacked and occupied by the Japanese in 1942, Kodiak became a staging area for the quiet North Pacific Campaign. Both installments are in severe disrepair; check them out from the park's beautiful **hiking trails.** Bunkers and other reminders of the Alaskan campaign are spread around the region; an old naval station lies 6½ mi. southwest of Kodiak.

On the rare clear day, hikers can take in a view stretching from the Kenai Peninsula to the Alaska Peninsula atop **Barometer Mountain.** To reach the trailhead, head west out of town on Rezanof Dr., then take the first right past the end of the airport runway, and go about 5 mi. from town; look for the trailhead on the left. After passing a stand of thick alders, the trail climbs steadily and steeply along a grassy ridge before arriving at the summit. Most hikers take about two hours to make the 5-mile climb to the top, and descend in half that time. The trail up **Pyramid Mountain** begins from the parking lot at the pass on Anton Larsen Bay Rd., about 11 mi. from town. At the top shoulder of alpine tundra, a nice view precedes the rugged final ascent. The hike covers 4 mi., and takes two to four hours. **Termination Point** pokes out into the ocean at the end of Monashka Bay Rd. Cross the creek and head to the beach, where hikers can either stroll in the sand or choose one of several paths that parallel the water for 3 mi. past a Russian Orthodox monastery. A return path detours to an old cabin at the edge of the forest, and then passes several mossy beaver ponds before arriving back at the parking lot.

If you have time for a longer hike, **Kashevaroff Mountain** is one of Kodiak's finest. The 6-mile round-trip offers views of the center of the island, the ocean, and Monashka Bay. From the peak, you can hike the ridge to many of the interior mountains. Drive past the airport around Women's Bay, park at the Salonie Creek Bridge, walk back 200 yards, and take the ATV trail up the hill. The trail opens up after 1.8 miles into spectacular alpine country.

The island's 100-mile road system gives access to several good **salmon streams.** In Kodiak, surfcasting into Mill Bay at high tide often yields a pink or silver. Red salmon, running from early June to early August, appear in the Buskin and Pasagshak Rivers. Pinks run up the Buskin, Russian, American, and Olds Rivers in astounding numbers from mid-July to mid-September. Better-tasting but scarcer silver salmon run up the same rivers from late August to early October. Dolly varden, the most frequently caught fish on Kodiak, can be hooked year-round from Pasagshak and Buskin Rivers.

Guided **sea kayaking** trips come eye-to-eye with sea otters, puffins, bald eagles, and, on lucky days, encounter giant Kodiak bears from a comfortable distance. **Wavetamer** (486-2604; wavetamer@gci.net), leads two-hour tours of Near Island and Mill Bay ($40), and five-hour coastal treks ($85). Gear is provided, and there is a two-person minimum. **Kodiak Kayak Tours** (486-2722; fish2live@aol.com) offers two daily trips, which explore much of the same territory for about three hours ($45). Trips typically start at 9am and 2pm. No experience is necessary; call at least a day ahead. **Mythos Expeditions** (486-5536, www.mythos-expeditions.com) runs similarly priced trips as well as more expensive trips to Shuyak and Afognak islands. They also rent kayaks and provide water taxi service.

If you have a vehicle, the 42-mile coastal drive to **Chiniak** presents beautiful seascapes of small offshore islets bathed in fog, and dozens of mufflers lying along the rough road. Pick up Kodiak's visitor guide magazine for mile-by-mile descriptions of several longer drives on the island, as well as a walking tour of downtown Kodiak. Take the turn-off for Pasagshak Bay Road at Mile 30 of the Chiniak for great hiking, fishing, and camping, and, at the end of the road, one of the prettiest bays on Kodiak. Mile 12.5 on Pasagshak Bay Rd. is Kodiak's best surfing spot with better breaks in the winter. If the potholes haven't rearranged your dental work, head back on the Chiniak Hwy. to procure a deluxe high-rise cheeseburger with fries ($6.25) at the **Road's End Restaurant and Bar,** 42 Road's End (486-2885).

Like all of Alaska's port towns, Kodiak offers a variety of fishing charter trips, but most of Kodiak's companies are operated out of people's homes or boats. The visitor center has the brochures, and the sporting goods stores can advise you.

KODIAK NATIONAL WILDLIFE REFUGE

Kodiak National Wildlife Refuge encompasses the western two-thirds of Kodiak Island. Since this is a refuge rather than a park, human recreational use is of secondary concern; no trails or roads lead into the region, and there are no official campgrounds. The refuge **visitor center** (see above) introduces this remarkable area with videos and stuffed bears.

Hiking into the refuge would demand a 20-or-more-mile trek crossing several mountains, though a round-trip flight to Larsen Bay ($110) will put you in range of the backcountry. While the refuge contains seven public use **cabins,** only three can be reached by boat; the others require an expensive float plane ride (around $450). The cabins with a kerosene heater and an adjacent pit toilet rent for $20 a night and sleep 4-5. They can be booked by mail through the refuge visitor center. Applications are processed in the first week of January for dates in April-June, the first week in April for July-Sept., and the first week in July for Oct.-Dec. Not all dates get booked, but it is wise to plan ahead; call the refuge visitor center for an application. **Pen Air** and **Island Air** (see Kodiak, above) both have reasonably priced flights to various locations in the refuge. The cabins would still be quite a hike, but this is some of Alaska's wildest terrain, majestic and virtually untouched by man.

Most visitors come to Kodiak to see the enormous bears. The numerous "guaranteed" brown-bear-viewing packages run $350-400 for a three- to four-hour float plane tour. Some of the prime viewing areas have visitor quotas, and reservations are made months ahead of time. Call the refuge visitor center or ask at the visitor center in town for permits and suggestions on how to get closest to the animals for cheapest. A worthwhile alternative is a similarly priced plane trip to Katmai (see p. 517), where bears can be seen at closer range in as remarkable a setting.

INTERIOR ALASKA

For **road conditions,** see p. 55. For **Alaska-wide info,** see p. 392.

Alaska's vast Interior sprawls between the Alaska Range to the south and the Brooks Range to the north, covering 166,000 sq. mi. of America's wildest and most stunning terrain. Most of the Interior alternates between flat forest and marshy, treeless tundra, punctuated by immense mountain ranges. Moose, grizzlies, wolves, caribou, Dall sheep, lynx, beavers, and hares roam the Interior's parks and wild country, while the Yukon River, the Tanana River, and hundreds of other waterways have created the sloughs, inlets, lakes, and bogs that sustain seasonal fish and a huge waterfowl population. The unofficial state bird, the mosquito, vastly outnumbers all other animals in summer. Outside of Fairbanks, Alaska's second-largest city, the region is sparsely populated. This landscape offers twilight hiking in summer, and spectacular Northern Lights viewing in winter.

In the late 19th and beginning of the 20th century, several gold rushes brought white settlers by the thousands to this region, until then sparsely inhabited by Athabaskans, who made encampments near rivers with large salmon runs like the Copper River. In more recent times, the discovery of oil to the north and, during the Cold War, the region's strategic proximity to Russia, have brought subsequent waves of settlement. Mining, oil dredging, and the military continue to drive the region's economy, though most visitors come to visit Denali National Park, the state's crown jewel. Bus service connects the major settlements along a trio of major highways: the Parks Highway from Anchorage to Fairbanks, the Glenn Highway from Anchorage east to the Yukon, and the Alaska Highway from the Yukon northwest to Fairbanks. The less well-maintained Denali Highway provides another, more scenic east-west route. The Alaska Railroad follows the path of the Parks Highway, and runs daily in summer, weekly in winter.

HIGHLIGHTS OF INTERIOR ALASKA

■ America's answer to an African game reserve, the vast and varied landscape of **Denali National Park's** (see p. 493) trail-less backcountry is splendid isolation.
■ The gravelly **Denali Highway** (see p. 515) is a beautiful alternative for east-west journeying south of the park.
■ Your search for character will end in ridiculously hospitable, folk-festival-blessed **Talkeetna** (see p. 489) or the remote outpost of **Eagle** (see p. 514).
■ Beyond containing a couple hundred "Northernmost" entities and some good bars, **Fairbanks** (see p. 500) hosts the excellent **University of Alaska Museum** (see p. 505) and provides access to far-off but fortifying **Circle** and **Chena Hot Springs** (see p. 510).
■ For hot water and hops and water, hit the **Alaskan Microbrew Festival,** held in early August at the Chena Hot Springs Resort (see p. 510).

GEORGE PARKS HIGHWAY

Thirty-five miles out of Anchorage, The George Parks Highway splits from the Glenn Highway (Rte. 1) and runs 323 miles north to Fairbanks, linking Alaska's two largest cities. A drive on "The Parks" is a visual feast: moose spottings, wolf crossings and spectacular views on the approach to Denali make it almost worthwhile trip in itself.

Its two lanes are paved and in great condition, except for a few frostheaves. Drivers heading north from Anchorage can stop in at the **Mat-Su Vistor's Center** (746-5000), at the junction of the Glenn Hwy. and the Parks, for some sweet birch candy and advice on where to stop along the way. (Open May-early Sept. daily 8:30am-6:30pm.)

Bluegrass and folk music festivals take place in towns up and down the highway at the end of July and beginning of August. Talkeetna's wild festival is complemented by the much quieter **Anderson Bluegrass Festival,** which takes place on the last weekend in July. It's a wonderful family affair: $20 buys music, camping, and drinking water for the weekend. For tickets or more information, contact Ken Terry at 338-3743 or kenterry@alaska.net.

WASILLA

Wasilla, at Mile 39.5, is home to the **Iditarod race headquarters and museum** (376-5155; ext. 108 for museum), 2.2 miles off the Parks on Knik Rd., where visitors can learn all about the famous race and take a short ride on a dog-drawn, if wheeled, sled. (Museum open June-Aug. daily 8am-7pm, Sept.-May M-F 8am-5pm, free; sled rides, June-Aug. only, $5 for about 5 min.). The race has always begun in downtown Anchorage (on Mar. 4, in 2000), but since 1980 the state Department of Transportation has refused to issue permits for the teams to travel the Glenn Hwy., so, after dogs and rider take an anticlimactic truck ride, the race "restarts" in Wasilla the morning after the first leg.

At the palatial ▧ **Wasilla Backpackers Hostel**, 3950 Carefree Dr. (357-3699; www.wasillabackpackers.com), off Campbell Dr. at Parks Hwy. Mile 39, an airy, carpeted solarium overlooks a manicured lawn made homely by a sled-dog team. Other features include flowers, a hammock, a living room with recliners and a fireplace, and kitchen with more counter space than you'll ever find use for. Bunks $23; private room with 1 double and 2 single beds $60 ($15 per extra person). Tenting $15. The owners have plenty of advice on nearby hiking/biking/canoeing opportunities and sometimes lead trips themselves. Mountain bikes are available for $20 per day. Laundry: wash $1, dry $1. Internet access $5 per hr.

Nancy Lake (mile 64) is one of the most picturesque of the many campgrounds along the Parks, with over 30 lakeside campsites ($10, pit toilets, running water). **Boat rentals** are available at Tippecanoe (mile 66; 495-6688; Th-Tu 9am-6pm).

TALKEETNA

Talkeetna (tah-KEET-nah) is a Tanaina word meaning "rivers of plenty" and an apt name for this eclectic settlement plunked at the confluence of the Talkeetna, Susitna, and Chulitna Rivers. A cluster of narrow dirt roads lined with log cabins and clapboard stores, Talkeetna is home to an off-beat population. The wayward traveler may meet a shopkeeper who believes fiddlehead ferns can help feed the world's hungry, a woman who boasts of having skinned and cleaned 27 moose in a single winter, or a young man who scaled Denali at age 12. In 1923, President Warren G. Harding died after stopping in Talkeetna to hammer in the golden spike that completed the railroad between Anchorage and Fairbanks. There was no evidence of foul play, but the rumor that President Harding was poisoned at the Fairview Inn is a perverse point of local pride.

Because of its proximity to Denali, only 60 mi. by air to the north, Talkeetna is a popular flight departure point for would-be climbers of the Mountain. Every year between April and June, over 1200 mountaineers from around the globe converge on Talkeetna, creating an unlikely international village and a run on accommodations. Most fly into the base camp on the Kahiltna Glacier, at 7200 ft.

▧ ORIENTATION AND PRACTICAL INFORMATION

Talkeetna lies at the end of the **Talkeetna Spur Rd.,** which runs 14 mi. east off the Parks Hwy. from Mile 98.5. The town is 113 mi. north of Anchorage, 139 mi. south of the Denali National Park entrance, and 260 mi. south of Fairbanks.

INTERIOR ALASKA

Trains: The **Alaska Railroad** station (800-544-0552; www.akrr.com) is a covered platform a half-mile south of town. Mid-May to mid-Sept., 1 per day to: Denali (4½hr., $60); Anchorage (4½hr., $60); Fairbanks (9hr.; $102). Purchase tickets on board. (See p. 52 for discounts.)

Buses: Travel time from the junction of the Parks and the Talkeetna Spur to Anchorage is about 2hr., to Denali 3hr., and to Fairbanks 6½hr. **Parks Highway Express** (888-600-6001; www.alaskashuttle.com) stops at the junction, but will drive in for 4 or more people (add $5 and 20min. each way to listed prices; call for pickup). Daily mid-May to late Sept. to: **Anchorage** (4:15pm, $25, round-trip $45), **Fairbanks** (11:15am, $35, round-trip $65) via **Denali** ($25, round-trip $45). Call for less frequent winter service info. **Talkeetna Shuttle Service** (733-1725 or 888-288-6008; www.alaska.net/~tshuttle) runs daily service to Anchorage right from town (late April-Aug.; 4:30pm, additional trips during climbing season, $40, round-trip $80). **Alaska Backpacker Shuttle** (344-8775 or 800-266-8625; www.alaska.net/~backpack) drops off in town only for groups of 4 or more during climbing season. To: **Anchorage** (6pm, $30, round-trip $55); and **Fairbanks** (10:30am, $45, round-trip $85) via **Denali** ($25, round-trip $45).

Visitor Information: Talkeetna Mountain Shop (733-1686), at Main St. and the Spur Rd. Info on air charters and walking tours. Open daily May to mid-Sept. 10am-5:30pm.

Outdoor Information: To reach the **Talkeetna Ranger Station** (733-2231; fax 733-1465; DENA_Talkeetna_Office@nps.gov), turn left at the terminus of Main St.; the station is on the left. With information in 8 languages and weather reports, the station is a great place to plan any kind of trip to Denali. Climbers must be registered 60 days in advance. Open mid-May to Aug. daily 8am-6pm; Sept. to mid-May daily M-F 8am-4:30pm.

Equipment Rental: see **Flightseeing and Outdoors,** below.

Banks: There are **no banks** in town, but there is an **ATM** ($2 surcharge) at the **Three Rivers Tesoro** gas station, on Main St. Open daily 8am-9pm.

Library: (733-2359), 1 mi. from town on the Spur Rd. Open Tu noon-8pm, W-F 11am-6pm, Sa 10am-5pm. **Public Radio:** 88.5 FM.

Laundromat and Public Showers: At the **Three Rivers Tesoro** gas station (733-2443). Wash $2, dry 25¢ per 6min. Showers $2 per 8min. Open daily 8am-9pm.

Emergency: 911. **State Police:** Parks Hwy. Mile 98 (733-2256).

24hr. Crisis Line: 733-1010. **Medical Services: Sunshine Community Health Clinic,** 9 mi. from town on the Spur Rd. (733-2273 or 24hr. emergency 733-2348), open M-Tu, Th-F, 9am-6pm, W 1-6pm, Sa 9am-5pm.

Post Office: (733-2275), in town on the Spur Rd. Open M-F 9am-5pm, Sa 10am-2pm. **ZIP Code:** 99676.

Area Code: 907.

▄ ACCOMMODATIONS AND CAMPGROUNDS

Talkeetna Hostel (733-4678; fax 733-4679; www.akhostel.com). Head towards the airport, left on "i" street; it's the 4th house on the right. A cheery home for people and sled dogs alike. Spacious lawn, BBQ, kitchen, free hot drinks in the morning, and a common area with TV and wood stove are all a bonus. One shared bath. Comfy bunks: $18. Private doubles $40. Laundry with soap, wash, and machine dry $4; hang-dry $2.50.

Talkeetna Roadhouse (733-1351; fax 733-1353; rdhouse@alaska.net), centrally located at Main and C St. The living room of this homey establishment features soft couches, old books, a guitar, and a piano. Shared bathrooms. Bunks $21; singles $47; doubles $63. During climbing season, reservations should be made well in advance.

Fairview Inn (733-2423), at the beginning of Main St. The alleged site of Harding's undoing. Four rooms with shared bath in a historic building. Singles $52; doubles $63.

Talkeetna River Adventures (733-2604). Turn right off the Spur Rd. at the airport, then turn left and follow the signs. Clean, quiet, and wooded area with water, outhouses, and easy river access. Beginning at the railroad tracks across from the waiting booth, several paths make a convenient shortcut to town. 40 sites: $12. Showers $3.

River Park Campground, at the end of Main St. Close to town, but as a popular late-night hangout for local teens it may not always be serene. $8, first-come, first-served.

⬤ FOOD

Nagley's Store (733-3663) on Main St. stocks groceries and sells a latte or hot dog for little more than $1 (open Su-Th 8am-10pm, F-Sa 8am-11pm; in winter closes 1 hr. earlier). The **Three Rivers Tesoro** gas station (see above), also sells groceries.

▓ **Talkeetna Roadhouse Cafe** (see **Accommodations & Campgrounds,** above), offers family-style dining, livened up with local banter and tall tales. Hearty breakfast and soup ($6). The cafe bakes bread, cookies, rolls, and blueberry muffins with a history, made with a sourdough starter dating back to 1902. Open Su-W 6am-4pm, Th-Sa 6am-10pm.

▓ **McKinley Grille** (733-1234), outside the deli at Main and C St. Everyone in town raves about the fresh halibut and salmon grilled in summer. Open Tu-Su 11am-7pm.

West Rib (733-3354), also on Main St., proudly serves tasty musk-ox burgers ($7.25) and fresh halibut dinners ($15), alongside great Alaskan beers ($3.75), in a pleasant beer garden. Open daily in summer 11am-2am; in winter 4pm-midnight.

Sparkey's (733-4141), a small hut on Main St., serves up speedy cheeseburgers ($5.25) and giant ice cream cones ($1.75). Open daily May-Sept. 11am-11pm.

▓ SIGHTS AND EVENTS

The **Talkeetna Historical Society Museum** (733-2487), off Main St. between C and D St., houses modest displays of Alaskana, the town's oldest cabin, and a dramatic scale model of the Mountain. (Open May-Aug. daily 10:30am-5:30pm; Apr. and Sept. F-Su 11am-5pm; Feb.-Mar. and Oct.-Nov. Sa-Su 11am-5pm; Dec.-Jan. Sa 11am-5pm. $1.) For life-size dioramas, authentic Alaskan noises, and updates on recent Bigfoot sightings, follow the moose tracks through the light-hearted **Museum of Northern Adventure** (733-3999), on the Spur Rd. near Main St. (Open in summer daily 11am-7pm, but flexibly; $2, seniors and under 12 $1, family $5.)

The second weekend in July brings Talkeetna's increasingly famous **Moose Dropping Festival.** Thousands flock here to enjoy live bagpipes, purchase various moose-nugget novelties, and compete in the moose dropping toss. Early December brings the **Wilderness Women Contest,** with such events as wood-chopping, salmon-fishing, target-shooting, and sandwich preparation, plus the associated **Bachelor's Ball. Miner's Day,** on the third weekend in May, promises tons of ore-related family fun. On the first weekend of August, Talkeetna is home to the huge **Talkeetna Bluegrass Festival** (561-2848 or 495-6718; akositz@world-net.att.net), held at a big lot at Mile 102 of the Parks Highway since it outgrew the town in the mid-1980's. Since then, there also hasn't been much true bluegrass music at the festival. Instead, folksy bands from across Alaska and the lower 48 come to this, the biggest "hippie event" in the state. Some come for the music, but most never make it past the parking lot party. The Hells Angels of Alaska keep the peace. ($35 includes 4 days of concerts and camping; drinking water and showers provided.)

◪ FLIGHTSEEING AND OUTDOORS

Even if you can't climb Denali, you can look at it. Talkeetna's **Denali overlook,** 1 mi. down the Spur Rd., boasts one of Alaska's best car-accessible views of the mountain. If the clouds cooperate, they'll unveil 3 mi. of rock and ice climbing straight to the sky. This perspective pales in comparison, however, to the vistas seen by plane. **Flightseeing** is worth the money: to see the world's tallest mountain (see p. 499) up-close amid other sheer peaks and glaciers is an incomparable experience. Flying around the mountain is called the closest thing on earth to orbiting another planet. Talkeetna's air services are actually closer to Denali than those at the park entrance, so trips from here are cheaper. Flights come in two standard flavors: a one hour flight approaching the mountain from the south, and an hour-and-a-half tour that circumnavigates the peak and allows you to take in all 14,000 ft. of Denali's north face, a.k.a. **Wickersham Wall,** the longest uninterrupted above-water slope in the world. The trips cost about $90 and $140 per person, respectively. A 15- to 30-minute stop-off on a glacier (often at a climbing base camp) costs an additional $20-35 per person. Many companies, including **Doug Geeting Aviation** (733-2366 or 800-770-2366; fax 733-1000; www.alaska.net/~airtours) offer significant discounts to groups of four or five. **Hudson Air Service** (733-2321 or 800-478-2321; www.alaskan.com/hudsonair), in operation more than 50 years, **K2 Aviation** (733-2291 or 800-764-2291; www.flyk2.com), **McKinley Air Service** (733-1765 or 800-564-1765; www.alaska.net/~mckair), and **Talkeetna Air Taxi** (733-2218 or 800-533-2219; fax 733-1434; www.gorp.com/flytat) offer the standard services, plus a variety of other specialized trips. Talkeetna Air Taxi provides free bunks to passenger on their flights. Be wary of companies offering landings far into July, when snow conditions can become unsafe. If you come to Talkeetna hell-bent on flightseeing, be prepared to wait a few days for the clouds to break, but call the flight outfits despite any foul weather in town: the mountains can bask in sun while clouds smother Talkeetna.

Fishing and **river tour** operations abound in the waterways around town. **Talkeetna River Guides** (733-2677 or 800-353-2677; talkeetnariverguides.com), in the only yurt on Main St., offers fishing tours and two-hour float trips with views of Denali and frequent wildlife sightings. (Fishing half-day $129, full-day $175. Float trip $46, under 10 $15.) **Mahay's Riverboat Service** (733-2223; uptz57a@prodigy.com), on Main St. just before downtown, also offers fishing charters, and leads tours geared more toward education, with a somewhat noisy 40-minute jet boat ride out interrupted by a calm 40-minute walk through the woods with a naturalist ($45, ages 2-12 $22.50). To head out solo, rent a canoe from Mahay's ($25 per day). **Tri-River Charters** (733-2400) runs fishing charters along the Talkeetna River and offers drop-off services and rentals. The **Talkeetna Outdoor Center** (733-4444), towards the end of town on Main St., sells mountaineering gear and some camping gear, provides outdoor information, and offers a fascinating walking tour full of native lore and geological history. (Open mid-Apr. to mid-Oct. daily 10am-6pm; open on demand in the off-season. $15.) **Crowley Guide Services** (733-1279; c.g.s2@worldnet. att.net), on Main St., sells, rents, and repairs mountain bikes, and offers tours and information. There isn't much hiking right out of town, save a 1¼ mi. loop starting at the scenic overlook 1 mi. up the Spur Rd.

TALKEETNA TO NENANA

From Talkeetna, the Parks Hwy. begins a gradual ascent into the Alaska Range, and offers some of the finest views of Mt. McKinley available from the ground. The **South Denali Viewpoint,** near the entrance to Denali National Park, offers a spectacular profile of the 20,320 ft. peak, and keeps rubberneckers from running off the road. The turn-off to the viewpoint is just a few miles from the **Ruth Glacier,** but may not be worth the trip when it's cloudy. Between 10pm and 4am is a good time to try for clear skies. **Denali State Park** (745-3975), Miles 132-168, offers plenty of hiking trails and more solitude than its big sib up the road. Two pleasant **campgrounds,** both with toilets and drinking water, are accessible from the highway: **Troublesome Creek** (Mile 137.2; 10 sites; $6) and **Byers Lake** (Mile 147; $12). The **Denali Viewpoint,** 10 minutes north of the state park, is yet another great photo op.

The road winds northward from here across the Alaska Range, passing over steep canyons and through **Broad Pass** (Mile 201), the scenic high point of the drive. **Denali National Park** (see below) is about 20 minutes past the turn-off for the **Denali Highway** (Rte. 8; see p. 515). North of the National Park, the highway follows the **Nenana River** for about 70 mi. to the town of the same name.

Nenana (ne-NAH-na), 53 mi. south of Fairbanks, has played host to the **Nenana Ice Pool** since 1917. Bored out of their skulls during the long winter, residents of Alaska and the Yukon bet on the precise minute when the Nenana River will thaw in the spring. The pot currently sits at $300,000. Call 832-5446, email tripod @ptialaska.net, or write P.O. Box 272, Nenana, 99760, to place a $2 bet. If waiting for the ice to break doesn't hold your interest, check out the free **Alaska State Railroad Museum** (832-5500), in the train depot at the end of A St., for exhibits on the construction of the Alaska Railroad (open in summer daily 8am-6pm). The museum is also home to the **Bed and Maybe Breakfast,** where rooms go for a flat rate of $65 (supposedly only $39 if you check in between 5-6pm), and breakfast the next morning is probable, but not guaranteed.

Nenana, meaning "place to camp between two rivers," is just that. **Nenana Valley RV Park** (832-5230), on the corner of 4th and C St., has large grassy sites (walk-ins $12.50, RV sites $14.50, hookups $18.50), laundry services (wash $2, dry $1), nice bathrooms, bike rentals, and free showers ($3 for non-guests). The **Two Choice Cafe** (832-1010), located on A St., has several; burgers $6, ice cream cones $1.50, and so on (open daily 7:30am-4pm).

DENALI NATIONAL PARK AND PRESERVE

With 9,000 square miles of snow-capped peaks, braided streams and glacier-carved valleys interrupted only by a lone gravel road, Denali is not a place made for humans. Visitors to the park are guests of the countless grizzly bears, moose, caribou, wolves, Dall sheep, raptors and wildflowers that thrive here. Every year, more than a million humans a year invite themselves, but there's nothing the crowds can do to take away from the glory of the park's crown jewel, Denali. Denali's 20,330 ft. make it the highest peak in North America. With 18,000 of those feet rising above the surrounding lands, it is the world's tallest mountain from base to peak. Although the U.S. Geological Survey names the peak Mt. McKinley, most Alaskans know it either as Denali or simply "the Mountain." A more specific description is unnecessary—the pure-white upper reaches of the Mountain, visible from as far away as Anchorage, dominate the park's skyline like a second sun. The Mountain is so big that it manufactures its own weather: when moist air from the Pacific Ocean collides with the cold mountaintop, sudden storms encircle the summit. As a result, Denali's face is only visible about 30% of the time in summer, and many visitors to the park will never actually see the peak.

Those who venture far from the park's few paths will find themselves in an often inhospitable land and climate. What the backcountry lacks in user-friendliness, however, it makes up for in splendor and solitude. Grizzly bears and golden eagles; Dall sheep and wolves; birds visiting each summer from as far away as Africa, Argentina, or Antarctica; and countless species of glorious wildflowers all motivated the park's establishment, and might even outshine its 20,320 ft. centerpiece, the largest mountain on earth.

In summer, especially between mid-June and mid-August, crowds and lines at the entrance are unavoidable. Shuttle buses into the park only run from late May until mid-September, so the window of relatively crowd-free access is small. Mid-to late August is an excellent time to visit—fall colors peak, berries ripen, mosquito season has virtually ended, and September's snows have not yet arrived. Whenever you go, though, the keys to enjoying Denali are planning, patience, and a desire to explore. Rules and permit limits that can seem so frustrating upon arrival make it possible to escape into the untrammeled wilderness, leaving the swarms of humanity behind.

PLANNING AHEAD AND FEES

Making advance reservations for campsites and shuttle buses will spare you a day or two of waiting for permits and tickets upon arrival at the park and will make you the envy of the unprepared hordes. Sixty-five percent of shuttle tickets and all of the campsites at Riley Creek, Savage River, Teklanika and Wonder Lake can be reserved from February up until the day before travel by calling 800-622-7275 or 272-7275 (open daily 7am-5pm). Permits for remaining sites are available two days in advance at the visitor center. Backcountry camping permits (free) are available on a first-come, first-served basis one day in advance only at the visitor center, so reserving a site at one of the campgrounds near the entrance and a shuttle ticket might still be a good idea: you can scope out the park from the bus, get to the ranger station bright and early, and avoid the unsightly red lines on your face associated with sleeping in your car out on the highway. The visitor center opens at 7am, and it goes without saying that the early bird gets the pick of the litter in this dog-eat-dog global economy. Campground reservations cost $4, and there's a $6 fee per site or bus ticket to change your reservations.

Buying a season pass to all U.S. National Parks (see p. 40), is the only way around the park entrance fee payable at the time of reservation ($5 per person for 7 days, $10 per family). Anyone with permission to overnight in the park can ride the flat-rate **camper buses** (see **Transportation within the Park,** below).

For each of four days in mid-September, 400 private cars are allowed to drive the park road. Contact the park HQ (683-2294) for info on the July mail-in ticket lottery. The park's comprehensive website (www.nps.gov/dena) has up-to-date prices and info on making reservations, including by mail and fax.

▐ GETTING THERE AND AWAY

The park is easily reached by road or rail. Anchorage lies 240 mi. (4hr.) south and Fairbanks 120 mi. (3hr.) north along the **George Parks Highway** (Rte. 3; see p. 488). The rough **Denali Highway** (Rte. 8; see p. 515) meets the Parks 27 mi. south of the park entrance at Cantwell, and extends 136 mi. east to Paxson. For info on shuttle buses, see **Transportation within the Park,** below.

Buses: Many of the buses that ply the Parks Hwy. will drop off and pick up at trailheads along the park's edge with advance notice. **Parks Highway Express** (479-3065 or 888-600-6001; www.alaskashuttle.com) and **Alaska Backpackers Shuttle** (344-8775 or 800-266-8625; www.alaska.net/~backpack) run daily to **Anchorage** (5hr., $35-40) and **Fairbanks** (3½hr., $20). **Alaska Tourquest** (344-6667; www.alaska-tourquest.com) makes the run daily from Anchorage for $25.

Trains: Alaska Railroad (683-2233 or 800-544-0552) stops at Denali Station, 1½ mi. from the park entrance (open daily 10am-5pm). Scenic ride to: **Fairbanks** (4½ hr., 3:45pm, $54, bikes $10) and **Anchorage** (8hr., noon, $102, bikes $20). Ages 2-11 50% off; under 2 free. Mid-Sept. to mid-May the train runs weekly at reduced rates.

▐ PRACTICAL INFORMATION

Summer Visitor Information:

Denali Visitor Center (683-2294; www.nps.gov/dena), a half mile from the Parks Hwy. The essential one-stop info and permit shop. Their free publication, the *Alpenglow*, contains park regulations, rates and history, and schedules of ranger-led events, including interpretive walks, sled-dog demonstrations, and campfire talks. A worthwhile 12min. **slide program** presents the history of Denali every hour. Most park privileges are distributed on a first-come, first-served basis. Lockers 50¢ per day. Open daily Memorial Day to Labor Day 7am-8pm; lines form for shuttle tickets by 6:30am. All references below are to this center.

Eielson Visitor Center, 66 mi. into the park, is accessible only by shuttle bus. Friendly rangers lead informative 45min. **tundra walks** daily at 1:30pm. No food is available here. None. Open daily in summer 9am-7pm, weather permitting.

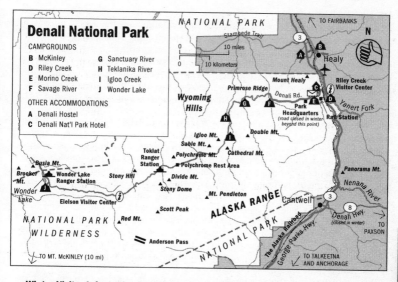

Denali National Park

CAMPGROUNDS

B   McKinley   G   Sanctuary River
D   Riley Creek   H   Teklanika River
E   Morino Creek   I   Igloo Creek
F   Savage River   J   Wonder Lake

OTHER ACCOMMODATIONS

A   Denali Hostel
C   Denali Nat'l Park Hotel

Winter Visitor Information: Before any winter travels in Denali, visit the **Park Headquarters** (683-2294) at Mile 3.2 on the left side of the park road. Open M-F 8am-4:30pm.

Mountaineering Information: Talkeetna Ranger Station, in Talkeetna (see p. 490).

Bank: None in the park or vicinity. **Wally's Service Station,** 11 mi. north of the park entrance in Healy, has a temperamental **ATM.** Most park services accept credit cards.

Equipment Rental: Denali Outdoor Center (683-1925), at Parks Mile 238.9, just north of the park entrance, rents bikes. Half-day $25; full-day $40; 5 or more days for $35 per day. **Denali Mountain Works** (683-1542), next door, rents and sells camping gear, including binoculars and compasses. Open daily in summer 9am-9pm.

Laundromat: McKinley Campground (683-2379), in Healy, 11 mi. north of the park entrance. Wash $2, dry $1. Tokens sold daily June-Aug. 8am-10pm; in winter 8am-8pm. Machines available 24hr.

Public Showers: At the **McKinley Campground** (see **Accommodations and Campgrounds,** below). $2.50 per 7½min. **McKinley Mercantile** (683-9246), 1½ mi. into the park. Unlimited showers $3 with $5 deposit. Open May-Sept. daily 7:00am-8:00pm.

Emergency: 911.

Medical Services: Healy Clinic (683-2211), 13 mi. north and a half-mile east of the park on Healy Spur Rd. Open M-F May-Sept. 9am-5pm, Oct.-Apr. 10am-3pm. Nurse on call 24hr.

Post Office: (683-2291) next to Denali Hotel, 1 mi. from the visitor center. Open May-Sept. M-F 8:30am-5pm, Sa 10am-1pm; Oct.-Apr. M-Sa 10am-1pm. **ZIP Code:** 99755.

Area Code: 907.

TRANSPORTATION WITHIN THE PARK

AT THE ENTRANCE

The free **Riley Creek Loop Bus** runs among the visitor center, the Denali Park Hotel, the Alaska Railroad station, the Horseshoe Lake trailhead, and the Riley Creek campground (30min., 6am-9pm). Chalet-owned **courtesy buses** run from the Denali Park Hotel to the chalet near Lynx Creek Pizza, and to McKinley Village, 6 mi. south of the park entrance, from 5am-midnight. **Caribou Cab** is at 683-5000; **Denali Taxi Service** at 683-2504.

IN THE PARK

In order to limit human impact on the land and wildlife, only the first 14 mi. of the park road are accessible by private vehicle (no special permit necessary. The remaining 75 miles can are open only to bicycles and park-run buses. In summer, two services plumb the park's interior in rehabilitated school buses.

Shuttle buses carrying talkative tour guides leave from the visitor center (daily 5am-6pm), stop when any passenger spots a large mammal or conspicuous-looking rock ("MOOOOOSE!"), and turn back at various points along the road. All travel times are round-trip; ages 13-16 50% off, under 13 free): **Toklat,** Mile 53 (6hr., $12.50); **Eielson,** Mile 66 (8hr., $21); **Wonder Lake,** Mile 85 (11hr., $27); and **Kantishna,** Mile 89 (13hr., $31). Most buses are wheelchair accessible. A ticket allows you to get on and off the bus as you please to take side hikes, naps, or photos. For those who don't make it into the backcountry, this is a great way to see the park, and wildlife sightings are all but guaranteed. **Camper buses** ($15.50), which transport only those visitors with campground or backcountry permits, have extra room for gear and **bikes,** and move faster than the shuttle buses. Camper buses leave the center daily at 6:40, 8:40, 10:40am, 2:40, and 4:40pm; a bus at 6:10pm goes only as far as **Polychrome,** Mile 37. The last bus stays overnight at Wonder Lake and returns at noon the next day. Both buses stop to pick up pedestrians anywhere along the road back. **Bicyclists** must keep to the road and only the road, though they can sometimes travel it even when it's closed to other vehicles. Backcountry travelers must leave bikes locked up at the racks provided at campgrounds.

Most shuttle tickets and campground spots can be (and are) purchased in advance by phone, though some are always available at the visitor center two days in advance (see **Planning Ahead and Fees,** above.) Two wise investments are the *Denali Road Guide* (available at the visitor center for $5) and **binoculars** (for rent at the hotel gift shop or at Denali Mountain Works for $6-7 per day).

■ ACCOMMODATIONS AND CAMPGROUNDS

INDOORS

Denali Hostel, (683-1295; fax 683-2106). Drive 9.6 mi. north of the park entrance, turn left onto Otto Lake Rd., and continue 1.3 mi. past the golf course (don't veer left); it's the 2nd house on the right, the log house with blue trim. Beautiful setting (oh, the sunsets!), international clientele, and helpful owners. Clean rooms, full kitchen, TV room, and showers. Morning shuttles to the park, daily pickups from the visitor center at 5 and 9pm, and from the Alaska Railroad (Anchorage train only). $23. Blankets $3 per stay. Check-in 5:30-10pm. No curfew. Reservations wise. Open May-Sept.

McKinley/Denali Steak and Salmon Bake (see **Food,** below) rents tent cabins. Singles and doubles $69, with bath $74; triples and quads $112, with bath $123.

OUTDOORS

Campers must obtain a **permit** from the visitor center, and may stay for up to 14 nights in park campgrounds. Sites at four of the seven campgrounds may be reserved in advance. Reservations are strongly recommended; without one, prepare to camp or stay outside the park for a night. Remaining sites are distributed at the visitor center two days in advance on a first-come, first-served basis. RV amenities are sparse in Denali: there are no hookups and only one dump station, at Riley Creek. RV drivers can pay $12 per night to park at **Riley Creek, Savage River,** or **Teklanika River,** or they can head to any of the RV parks near the park entrance. All campgrounds within the park are wheelchair accessible, except for Igloo Creek and Sanctuary River.

Riley Creek, Mile 0.4 Denali Park Rd. The only year-round campground in Denali (no water in winter). All sites assigned at the visitor center. Close to the highway and the visitor center, Riley Creek is louder and more congested than the other campgrounds. Piped water, toilets, and sewage dump keep campers from getting riled up. 100 sites: $12.

Morino Creek, Mile 1.9 Denali Park Rd., next to the train tracks. Sixty 2-person sites for backpackers without vehicles. Water, chemical toilets. No open fires. Nearest showers at the Mercantile, a quarter mile away (see **Practical Information,** above). Many backpackers stay here while they wait for permits and check out the park on the buses. $6.

Savage River, Mile 13 Denali Park Rd. High, dry country with easy access to popular Primrose Ridge. Complimentary shuttle to and from the visitor center. Toilets and water. Last area accessible by car without an access permit. 33 sites: $12.

Sanctuary River, Mile 23 Denali Park Rd. Quiet, wooded campsite with river and mountain views. Chemical toilets, no water, no fires. Accessible only by bus. 7 tent sites: $6.

Teklanika River, Mile 29 Denali Park Rd. Popular with members of the Winnebago tribe. Piped water and toilets. Accessible by shuttle bus or by vehicle with permit. 53 tent and RV sites: $12. 3-night min. for vehicle campers.

Igloo Creek, Mile 34 Denali Park Rd. On lower ground, and therefore more likely to invite swarms of mosquitoes, and thus *less* likely to invite swarms of tourists: quiet and secluded. Pit toilets, no water. No fires. Accessible only by bus. 7 tent sites: $6.

Wonder Lake, Mile 85 Denali Park Rd. You are a happy camper if you end up at Wonder Lake on a clear day. Spectacular, soul-searing views of the Mountain, a mere 27 mi. away. Piped water, toilets. No vehicles. A kabillion mosquitoes. 28 tent sites: $12.

FOOD

Food in Denali is expensive, and local grocery options aren't great. Wise is the traveler who stocks up in Fairbanks. **McKinley Mercantile** (683-9246), at Mile 2 on Denali Park Rd. (open daily 7am-9:30pm), the **Lynx Creek Park-Mart** (683-2548; open June-Sept. daily 7am-11:30pm), and **Denali General Store** (683-2920; open May-Sept. daily 8am-9pm), 1 mi. north of the park entrance, all stock similarly priced items. Once you board that park bus, there is no food available anywhere.

Black Bear Coffee House (683-1656), 1 mi. north of the park entrance. The coffee's hot and strong, the muffins are baked fresh on the premises, and the staff is all smiles. Tasty cappuccinos for $2.75, homemade cakes for $3.50, and a veggie sandwich with a hot cup of soup for $7 make this mellow log cabin the most affordable and fulfilling food stop near Denali. Open May-Sept. daily approximately 7am-10pm.

Denali Smoke Shack (683-7665), 1 mi. north of the park entrance. Real Alaskan barbecue. The Smoke Shack's hip young waitstaff, friendly dog, decently priced food, and large vegetarian menu make it a local favorite. Cajun chicken sandwich $8. Popular late-night scene with full bar and late hours. Open daily 8am-10:30am and noon-1am.

Denali Crow's Nest & Overlook Bar and Grill (683-2723), 1 mi. north of park entrance, on the right. High on a hill, the Crow's Nest affords eagle-eye views of Mt. Healy. Hefty burgers come with fries so greasy you may be able to see your reflection ($9). Draft beer from $3. Grill open daily 11am-11pm; bar open until 1am. Courtesy shuttle until 11pm.

Lynx Creek Pizza (683-2547), 1 mi. north of the park entrance. Cheese-heavy pizza with a great crust (14 in. pie from $16.75), and a lunch buffet with salad bar and soda ($10). More lodge decor! Open daily 11am-11pm. To get a beer with that, order to go and try the **Lynx Creek Pub** next door, open 11am-midnight.

McKinley/Denali Steak and Salmon Bake (683-2733), a rustic lodge just past the Crow's Nest. Serves quantity-over-quality fare such as an all-you-can-eat blueberry pancake breakfast ($5.50). Call for free shuttle. Open daily 5am-10pm.

Denali Park Hotel (683-2215), is the only sit-down dining option in the park. Dinner at the **Dining Room** runs $14-20. Open daily 7am-2pm and 5:30-10pm. The **Whistle Stop Snack Shop** vends pre-fab burgers ($6) and sandwiches ($5-7), but no fried green tomatoes. Open daily 5am-11pm. The **Espresso Station** sells muffins, cookies and espresso ($2). Open daily 6am-2pm.

⚠ HIKING

The shuttle bus affords excellent views and wildlife-sighting opportunities, but the real Denali lies beyond the road. Past Mile 14 there are **no trails.** The park's back-country philosophy rests on the idea that independent wandering creates more rewards and less impact than would a network of trails or routes. In an effort to disperse hikers as widely as possible, rangers will not recommend specific routes, although they will suggest areas that meet hikers' desires and abilities. Topographic maps are available at the visitor center.

DAYHIKING

You can begin dayhiking from anywhere along the park road by riding the shuttle bus to a suitable starting point and asking the driver to let you off. Don't feel obligated to get off at one of the designated rest stops (about every hour along the way); drivers will be happy to drop you off anywhere that isn't restricted. Once you've wandered to your heart's content, head back to the road and flag down a shuttle bus heading in your direction. The first couple of buses that pass may be full, but it's rare to wait more than half an hour or so for a ride. Many of the buses stop running fairly early, so be sure to check when the last buses will be passing your area. Stream crossings and bushwhacking are inevitable if you plan to get far from the road: good boots, long pants, and gaiters are all advisable. For details, see p. 43.

For those waiting on shuttle tickets, some great dayhiking is accessible from the Savage River campground. **Primrose Ridge,** at Mile 16 on the north side of the road, blooms with wildflowers and has spectacular views of the Alaska Range and the carpeted emerald valley below. A walk north from Mile 14 along the **Savage River** provides a colorful, scenic stroll through this valley. Deeper within the enormous and uniformly stunning park, recommendations become much harder to make, and much less useful: your best bet really is to spend a little time with the helpful staff and literature back at home base. A few easy-to-moderate trails are maintained around the park entrance. **Horseshoe Lake Trail** is a 1½ mi. round-trip walk with lovely mountain views. The lake itself is popular with moose. The **Rock Creek Trail** runs 2½ mi. from the hotel toward Park Headquarters, where the sled-dog demonstrations are held, but suffers from road noise. The more challenging **Mt. Healy Overlook Trail** starts from the hotel parking lot and climbs to an impressive view of the valley at 3400 ft. (5 mi. round-trip; 1700 ft. elev. gain; 3-4hr.) The particularly ambitious can continue up the ridge to the 5700 ft. summit.

Discovery hikes are guided three- to five-hour hikes, departing on special buses from the visitor center. Topics vary; a ranger might lead you on a cross-country scramble or a moose trail excursion, providing a comprehensive introduction to local wildlife, flowers, and geological formations. The hikes are free but require reservations and a bus ticket fee. More sedate 45-minute **tundra walks** leave from Eielson Visitor Center daily at 1:30pm, and many other talks and naturalist programs are posted at the visitor center.

EXPLORING THE BACKCOUNTRY

The road is hardly a scratch on this wilderness, and the wildlife doesn't seem quite so wild when seen through a bus window. With no major cities for 300 miles in every direction, camping in Denali's backcountry is an experience like no other. Only two to twelve backpackers can camp at a time in each of the park's 43 units. Overnight stays in the backcountry require a **free permit,** available no earlier or later than one day in advance at the **backcountry desk** in the visitor center. The **quota board** there reports which units are still available. Type-A hikers line up outside as early as 6:30am to grab permits for popular units. Some units may be temporarily closed after a fresh wildlife kill or a bear encounter. **Sable Pass,** a veritable bear bastion, has been off-limits for years. Talk to rangers and research your

MCKINLEY OR NOT MCKINLEY—THAT IS THE QUESTION

History has not been generous to William McKinley, the 25th president of the United States. Washington D.C. has no McKinley Memorial. Few have celebrated McKinley's birthday since he last marked the occasion himself in 1901. While Teddy Roosevelt, McKinley's Vice President and successor, is immortalized on South Dakota's Mt. Rushmore, McKinley doesn't even appear on a dime.

In Alaska, however, an attempt was once made to memorialize McKinley in a form that would dwarf puny Mt. Rushmore. In 1896, a Princeton-educated prospector named the highest mountain in North America "Mt. McKinley," and with a little pressure on Congress, the name was made official. Of course, the mountain had a name long before any Ivy-league Republicans laid eyes on it. Athabaskans of the interior had long called the 20,320 ft. giant Denali: "the Great One" or "the High One."

The mountain certainly deserves the title. At 18,000 ft. from base to summit, Denali has the greatest total altitude gain of any mountain in the world. Mt. Everest—originally Sagarmatha or Jomolungma—is higher above sea level but rises only 11,000 ft. from its base on the Plateau of Tibet. In 1980, an official effort to rename Mt. McKinley failed, but the land on which it stands was designated Denali National Park as a compromise. Today, almost everyone ignores the U.S. Geological Survey and uses the original name.

INTERIOR ALASKA

choices with the handy *Backcountry Description Guides* and *The Backcountry Companion*, available at the visitor center bookstore.

The park covers a variety of terrain, with varying implications for hiking. **River bars** are level and rocky, offering very good footing for hikers but potentially difficult stream crossings. **Low tundra,** in brushy, soggy areas above the treeline, is not easily navigable and makes for exasperating hiking under insect-infested conditions. **Alpine tundra,** or **dry tundra,** is higher and drier, meaning fewer mosquitoes. Generally, the southern reaches of the park contain dry tundra and river bars, opening wide vistas of the park. The northern reaches are brushier but include high points with incredible views of the Mountain. Some of the most enjoyable hiking and wildlife-viewing awaits in the middle of the park, near the Toklat River and Polychrome Pass.

Backcountry campers must stay within the unit for which they registered, pitching tents at least half a mile from the road, and out of sight. A compass (not available at the visitor center) is important; **topographical maps** ($4) are essential. Before they head out, campers receive a short introduction to bear management, and are required to spend some quality time with the center's interactive **backcountry simulator,** which allows virtual hikers to learn about a number of potentially dangerous wilderness situations. All but two zones require that food be carried in a 3 lb. plastic **bear-resistant food container (BRFC),** available for free loan at the backcountry desk. Be sure to leave space in your backpack (LSIYB). Backcountry hikers *will* cross streams, whack bushes, and battle mosquitoes: gaiters and head nets are luxuries to consider. Denali's backcountry provides the ideal conditions for **hypothermia**. With the park's cool, often drizzly weather and its many rivers, streams, and pools your feet *will* get wet, and hypothermia can set in quickly and quietly. Talk with the rangers about prevention and warning signs. (See **Environmental Hazards,** p. 33.)

◪ BIKES, RAFTS, KAYAKS, PLANES, AND DOG SLEDS

Unlike private vehicles, **bicycles** are permitted on the entire length of the park road, making them a perfect way to escape the shuttle-bus ticket blues. Park at Savage River and ride into the heart of Denali. Most of the road is unpaved, so thicker tires work best. Off-road biking is not permitted anywhere in the park. For bike rental info, see **Practical Information,** p. 495.

Several **rafting** companies run the Class III rapids of Denali's Nenana River. The stretch is swift, splashy, and scenic, but there are companies running with poor equipment and little experience. The **Denali Outdoor Center** (see p. 495) boasts the most experienced guides on the river, and is one of only two companies that provides drysuits—crucial safety gear in the 36°F (2°C) water. A canyon runs cost $55 per person, $75 for four hours. The DOC also runs guided **kayak** tours for $75, with no experience necessary.

Flightseeing tours are a wonderful way to see the Mountain, especially on a clear day, but the park is ironically not the best place to do this. **Denali Air** (683-2261) will take you up for one hour ($160), but the town of Talkeetna, south of the park, is closer to the mountain and has companies that offer cheaper trips (see p. 492).

Cross-country skiing, snowshoeing, and **dog-sledding** allow visitors to see the park during the winter. Despite 20-hour nights and temperatures below -40°F (-40°C), many people of perfect mental health consider winter the most beautiful time of year. If you plan to travel through Denali in the winter, you are *strongly encouraged* to visit the visitor center and inform them of your route.

FAIRBANKS

Had E.T. Barnette not run aground near the junction of the Tanana and Chena Rivers and not decided on the spur of the moment to set up a trading post, and had Felix Pedro, an Italian immigrant-turned-prospector, not unearthed a golden fortune nearby, Fairbanks might never have been born. But they did, and today, Fairbanks stands unchallenged as North American civilization's northernmost hub, home to such landmarks as the "World's Northernmost Woolworth's," "World's Northernmost Denny's," and "World's Northernmost Southern Barbecue." But the city's endless strip malls have original log cabins crammed between them, and even the omnipresent tourism industry can't hide the rough-and-ready flavor of this frontier town. Men noticeably outnumber women, the streets are filled with four-wheel-drive steeds, and the beer is devastatingly cheap. Outdoors opportunities are few though any road out of town leads into utter wilderness in minutes. Which is good for travelers itching to drive, fly, or float to the Arctic Circle, and a temptation for travelers turning back south.

🛈 ORIENTATION AND PRACTICAL INFORMATION

Fairbanks lies at the junction of three major routes: Prudhoe Bay lies 500 mi. north along the gravelly Dalton Hwy. (Rte. 11), Anchorage lies 358 mi. south along the George Parks Hwy. (Rte. 3), and Delta Junction lies 98 mi. southeast of Fairbanks along the Richardson/Alaska Hwy. Downtown proper is somewhat lost in urban sprawl, but almost every tourist destination lies within a square formed by four thoroughfares: **Airport Way** to the south, **College Rd.** to the north, **Cushman** to the east, and **University Ave.** to the west. The city center lies north of the intersection of Cushman and Airport Way. Fairbanks is a **bicycle-friendly** city with wide shoulders, multi-use paths, and sidewalks.

TRANSPORTATION

Airplanes: The airport is 5 mi. southwest of downtown on Airport Way. **Alaska Air** (452-1661) to: Anchorage ($91, round-trip $128) and Juneau ($185, round-trip $370). Other carriers include **Delta, Northwest, United,** and **Reno Air** (see p. 50). **Frontier Flyer Services** (474-0014) flies into the Bush. Fares change at the drop of a hat.

Trains: Alaska Railroad, 280 N. Cushman. (456-4155 or 800-544-0552; www.akrr.com), behind the Daily News-Miner building. An excellent way to see the wilderness. From mid-May to mid-Sept., 1 train per day to Anchorage (12hr.; $154) via Denali National Park (4hr.; $54). From mid-Sept. to mid-Oct. and from early Feb. to mid-May, a train leaves for Anchorage once per week ($120). Ages 2-11 half-price. Depot open M-F 7am-3pm, Sa-Su 7-11am, and for evening arrivals.

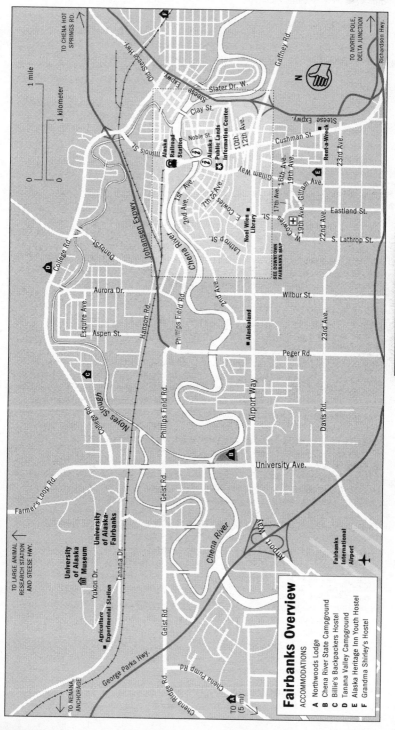

Fairbanks Overview

ACCOMMODATIONS

A Northwoods Lodge
B Chena River State Campground
C Billie's Backpackers Hostel
D Tanana Valley Campground
E Alaska Heritage Inn Youth Hostel
F Grandma Shirley's Hostel

Buses: Parks Highway Express (479-3065 or 888-600-6001; www.alaskashuttle.com) departs each day at 9am to Denali (3½hr., $20, round-trip $35) and Anchorage (9hr., $55, round-trip $100), and 3 times per week to Glenallen (2½hr., $45, round-trip $85) and Valdez (8hr., $60, round-trip $110). Pickup at the visitor center (see below), and Billie's Backpackers Hostel (see **Accommodations,** below), and elsewhere upon request. The **Alaska Backpacker Shuttle, Inc.** (344-8775 or 800-266-8625; www.alaska.net/~backpack/) runs a similar service. **Alaskon Express** (451-6835 or 800-544-2206) runs to Haines (overnight, 3 per week, $182), Skagway (overnight, daily, $206), and Valdez (overnight, daily, $150). **Alaska Direct** (800-770-6652) runs 3 buses per week to Tok (4½hr., $40) and Anchorage (12½hr., $65).

Public Transportation: Municipal Area Commuter Service (MACS) (459-1011), at 5th Ave. and Cushman St. $1.50; students, seniors, and disabled 75¢; under 5 free. Day pass $3. Schedules available at the visitor center and post office.

Taxis: King Diamond Taxi (455-7777), $1 base, $1.80 per mi. **Fairbanks Taxi** (452-3535), $1 base, $1.70 per mi. **Yellow Cab** (452-2121). 25 ¢ base, $2 per mi.

Car Rental: National companies offer free mileage, but won't allow driving on dirt roads; smaller companies charge hefty mileage fees. **Rent-a-Wreck,** 21055 Cushman St. (452-1606). $37 per day, 30¢ per mi. after 100 mi. Must be 21 with credit card. Local use as far as Denali. No gravel highways. **U-Save Auto Rental,** 3245 College Rd. (479-7060). $30 per day, 26¢ per mi. after 100 mi. Must be 21 with credit card or $250 cash deposit. Under 25 extra $3 per day plus $500 deposit.

Road Conditions: 800-478-7675; www.dot.state.ak.us.

VISITOR AND LOCAL SERVICES

Visitor Information: 550 1st Ave. (456-5774 or 800-327-5774), at Cushman. Free local calls. Open daily 8am-8pm; Labor Day-Memorial Day M-F 8am-5pm. **Fairbanks Information Hotline:** 456-INFO/4636.

Outdoor Information: Alaska Public Lands Information Center, 250 Cushman #1A (456-0527), in the basement of the Federal building at Cushman and 3rd. Info on Gates of the Arctic National Park or the Arctic National Wildlife Refuge. Thorough, indispensable tips. Open daily 9am-6pm; in winter Tu-Sa 10am-6pm.

Outdoor Equipment: Beaver Sports, 3480 College Rd. (479-2494), opposite College Corner Mall. Mountain bikes $16 for 6hr., $20 per day, $94 per week. Canoes $24 per day, $17 per day for 3-6 days, $12 per day for 7-10 days. In-line skates $13 per day. Open M-Sa 10am-7pm, Su 1-5pm. Large cash deposit or credit card required. **Rocket Surplus,** 1401 Cushman St. (456-7078), vends camping supplies. Open M-Sa 9am-6pm. **Apocalypse Design,** 101 College Rd. (451-7555), at Illinois. Speedy repairs on zippers and straps. Open M-F 9am-6pm, Sa 10am-4pm.

Bookstore: Gulliver's New and Used Books, 3525 College Rd. (474-9574), in the Campus Corner Mall, has free Internet access in its Second Story Cafe. Open M-Sa 9am-10pm, Su 9am-6pm. Gulliver's is also at the **Shopper's Forum,** 1255 Airport Way (456-3657). Open M-F 10am-8pm, Sa 10am-6pm, Su noon-6pm.

Libraries: Noel Wien Library, 1215 Cowles St. (459-1020), at Airport Way. Free Internet access. Open M-W 10am-9pm, Th-F 10am-6pm, Sa 10am-5pm. **University of Alaska Library** (474-7481), connected to the fine arts building on the eastern part of campus. Free Internet access. Open M-Th 7:30am-9pm, F 7:30am-6pm, Sa-Su noon-7pm.

Laundromat and Showers: B&C (479-2696), at University Ave. and College Rd., in Campus Mall. Wash $2, dry 25¢ per 8min. Showers $3, towels 50¢. Open M-Sa 8am-9:30pm, Su 9am-9:30pm. **B&L** (452-1355), at 3rd and Steese. Wash and dry each $1.50. Showers $3 per 20min. Open daily 8am-11pm. **Tanana Valley Campground,** see below, wash and dry $2 each.

Weather: 452-3553. **Public Radio:** 89.9 FM.

EMERGENCY AND COMMUNICATIONS

Emergency: 911. **Alaska Police Troopers:** 451-5333.

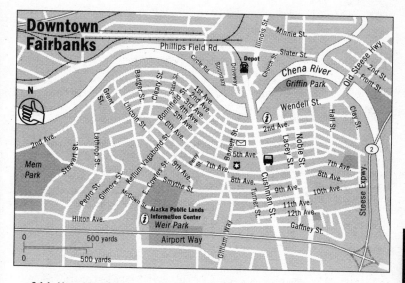

Downtown Fairbanks

Crisis Line: 452-HELP/4357. Provides info on **gay and lesbian groups.**

Rape Crisis: 452-7273 or 800-478-7273.

24hr. Refuge: Denny's, on Airport Way, will serve you a Grand Slam any hour all day.

Pharmacy: Payless Drugstore, 19 College Rd. (456-2151), at Steese, across from the Bentley Mall. Open M-F 9am-9pm, Sa 10am-7pm, Su 10am-6pm.

Hospital: Fairbanks Memorial, 1650 Cowles St. (452-8181), off Airport.

Post Office: 315 Barnette St., 99707 (452-3203). Open M-F 9am-6pm, Sa 10am-2pm.

Internet Access: See **Bookstore** and **Libraries,** above; **Grandma Shirley's Hostel,** below.

Area Code: 907.

ACCOMMODATIONS AND CAMPGROUNDS

Grandma Shirley's Hostel, 510 Dunbar St. (451-9816; www.mosquitonet.com/grandmashirleys). From the Steese Expwy., turn right onto Trainor Gate Rd., then left at E St., and right onto Dunbar St. Or take the purple bus to F St. Grandma takes the title of Fairbanks Überhostel. (The bear painted on the bathroom door put her over the top.) Bedding, spectacular kitchen, showers, a TV room, a big backyard, and free use of nearly 20 old but road-worthy bikes. Full-service laundry (wash, dry, and delivery) $4. Internet access $5 per hr., free local calls. Two co-ed rooms, 10 and 4 beds. $16.25.

Billie's Backpackers Hostel, 2895 Mack Blvd. (479-2034; fax 457-2034; www.alaskahostel.com). Take the red bus to Westwood and College, then walk a block off College to Mack Rd. Billie's maintains an abode somewhat cluttered with musical instruments and international travelers. Bikes $10 per half-day, $18 per day. Full breakfast $7. Occasional all-you-can-eat dinner $10. 3 rooms with 4 beds, hot shower, and kitchen $18 per person. Tent spaces $10 per person. Private double with jacuzzi $50.

Alaska Heritage Inn Youth Hostel, 1018 22nd Ave. (451-6587; kckoontz@alaska.net). Take Cushman to 22nd Ave., then go west to the large gray building on the right with the mean-looking dogs chained out front. Men's bunk room and facilities in the basement are a bit dim and cold. Women's room and facilities on the second floor are brighter.

Common room with TV, picnic area, showers $2.50. Beds $16.50, nonmembers $17.50. Tent spaces $11. Quiet hours from 11pm. No curfew.

North Woods Lodge (479-5300 or 800-478-5305; fax 479-6888). From town, take Chena Pump Rd. out about 5 mi., turn right onto Roland Rd., and then take another right onto E. Chena Hill Dr. The lodge is a quarter mile up on the right. A fair distance from Fairbanks; travelers will appreciate the quiet. Charming, clean wood cabins have electricity but no running water. Small kitchens, shared showers, and laundry (wash and dry $2 each). No bedding in loft. Free shuttles to the airport, bus, and train station. Nearby hiking trails. Cabins $40; double cabins $45; dorms $15. Tent sites $12-15.

Chena River State Campground, off Airport Way on University Ave. Landscaped, clean, and on a quiet stretch of the Chena River. 56 walk-in sites $10. 5-night max. stay per vehicle. $5 to use the dump station.

Tanana Valley Campground, 1800 College Rd. (456-7956), behind the farmer's market by the fairgrounds, near Aurora Ave.Noisy, but grassy and secluded in town. Breakfast ($5), dinner ($6-7), and staples. Haircuts $5. Showers $3 for non-campers. Laundry (wash and dry $2 each). RV sites $12; hookups $15; tent sites $8.

FOOD

On Airport Way and College Rd., the northernmost franchises of almost every fast-food chain in existence lure burger lovers to their artery-blocked doom. Pick up America's northernmost copy of *People* magazine and northernmost bag of frozen peas 24hr. at **Carr's**, 526 Gaffney (452-1121); at **Safeway** (479-4231), at University Ave. and Airport Way; and in the **Bentley Mall**, at 30 College Rd. (451-6870). If you're really stocking up, **Sam's Club**, 48 College Rd. (451-4800; open M-Sa 9am-8pm, Su 10am-7pm), lets nonmembers buy in bulk for an additional 5% of the low, low total price. The **Farmers Market** (456-3276; open W 11am-6pm, Sa 9am-4pm) at the fairgrounds at Aurora and College sells fresh produce.

RESTAURANTS

Lemon Grass, 388 Old Chena Pump Rd. (456-2200), in the mall behind the Red Fox. From town, take Geist Rd. past the Mitchell Expressway, then turn right after the gas station; or take the blue line and get off before the Pumphouse. Traditional instruments on the walls shake to Thai pop and hip hop and UAF students pack the house. *Tom kha* (chicken or shrimp simmered in coconut milk, with mushrooms, galanga, lemongrass, lime leaves, and roasted chili) $3.50. *Kang garee* (Thai yellow curry with vegetables and cucumber salad) $8. Open Tu-Su 11am-4pm and 5-9pm.

Gambardella Pasta Bella, 706 2nd Ave. (456-3417), at Barnette. Fresh flowers, an airy air, and excellent pasta make this classy family-run restaurant worth it. Subs $6-8, small pizzas $7-10. Stare down the "Mother of all Lasagnas" for $15. Open daily M-Sa 11am-10pm. Reservations and a seat outside recommended in summer.

The Cookie Jar, 1006 Cadillac Ct. (479-8319), behind Aurora Motors. Take Danby St. off Johanson or College Rd. Cookie jars line the walls, and sweets bar the door. Try Nolan's Own, a huge cinnamon roll dipped in batter, grilled, and dusted with powdered sugar, served with Virginia ham, $6.25. Or Beerock,: ground beef, onion, sauerkraut, and cheddar cheese wrapped in whole wheat dough, $6. Open M-Sa 6:30am-9:30pm, Su 8am-7pm.

The Whole Earth, 1157 Deborah St. (479-2052), behind College Corner Mall. This health food store and deli could well have been a joint venture by Rachel Carson and Jane Fonda. Southwestern art and maybe the only cacti in Alaska. Organic coffee and a variety of good-for-you foods like the giant No Bull Burger ($4.75) and Anna's Hummus Sandwich ($3.75). Open M-Sa 9am-8pm, Su 11am-6pm. Deli open M-Sa 11am-7pm.

The Pumphouse Restaurant and Saloon, Chena Pump Rd. Mile 1.3 (479-8452), last stop on the blue line. A 9 ft., 3 in. Kodiak brown bear welcomes you to the Fairbanks gold rush, when fine restaurants were decorated with mining equipment. Lunch buffet $10. The Saloon's burgers ($7-8) and appetizers ($6-8) are half-price 4-6pm and 10-11pm. Open daily 11:30am-12:30am.

Souvlaki, 310 1st Ave. (452-5393), a few blocks from the visitor center. You can almost get your fill on the heavenly aroma alone. Succulent stuffed grape leaves (3 for $1.25), falafel ($4.75), and sourdough cinnamon rolls the size of Alaska itself ($1.75). Take-out available. Open M-F 10am-9pm, Sa 10am-6pm; in winter M-Sa 10am-6pm.

BAKERIES AND COFFEEHOUSES

Wolf Run Dessert & Coffee House, 3360 Wolf Run (458-0636), just off University near Geist. Desserts, plush chairs, a stone hearth fireplace, a rocking chair, and a deck are a rustic sweet-tooth's dream. Blueberry or peanut butter pie $4.25. Espresso $1; latte $2.50. Open Tu-Th 11am-10pm, F-Sa 11am-midnight, Su noon-8pm.

Into the Woods, 3560 College Rd. (479-7701). Greenwich Village meets the Klondike in this log cabin coffeehouse. Relax in a wicker chair with a book you've bought or borrowed, and catch a poetry reading. Latte $2. Jazz (M) and Celtic (Su) jams. Open M 6-10pm, Tu-Th 11am-midnight, F-Sa 11am-2am.

👁 SIGHTS

One of Fairbanks's proudest institutions and main attractions is the **University of Alaska-Fairbanks (UAF),** at the top of a hill overlooking the flat cityscape. Bus routes stop at the **Wood Campus Center** (474-7034), located on Yukon Dr. across from the fire station, which has pool tables, flyers advertising campus goings-on, and enough video games to entertain all the little brothers of the world. (Open M-F 7am-7pm, Sa-Su 10:30am-6:30pm.) The **Student Activities Office** (474-6027), located in the Wood Center, has the skinny on movies, music, and campus activities during the school year. (Open M-F 8am-5pm.) Exhibits at the **University of Alaska Museum** (474-7505; www.uaf.alaska.edu/museum), a 10-minute walk up Yukon Dr. from the Wood Center, include displays on the aurora borealis, gold collections, a thorough look at the Aleut/Japanese evacuation during WWII, and indigenous crafts. Blue Babe, a 36,000-year-old steppe bison recovered from the permafrost, would be truly foolish to miss. (Open June-Aug. daily 9am-7pm; May and Sept. daily 9am-5pm; Oct.-Apr. M-F 9am-5pm and Sa-Su noon-5pm. $5, seniors $4.50, ages 7-17 $3, 6 and under free.) Free two-hour **campus tours** begin in front of the museum. (M-F at 10am, weather permitting.)

The search for a good picnic spot ends at the **Georgeson Botanical Gardens** (474-1944), on Tanana Dr. west of the museum. Tiptoe through the tulips (the best viewing time is late June through July) and enjoy the view of Fairbanks and the Alaska Range, including Denali on a clear day. Be sure to sit upwind of the university's **Large Animal Research Station** (474-7207), which offers a rare chance to see baby musk oxen and other Arctic animals up close. Take Farmer's Loop to Ballaine Rd. and turn left on Van Kovich; the farm is one mi. up on the right. (Tours June-Aug. Tu and Sa at 11am and 1:30pm, Th at 1:30pm; Sept. Sa 1:30pm. $5, students $2, seniors $4.) If you miss the tour, grab some binoculars and ogle the musk ox, reindeer, and caribou from the viewing stand on Yankovitch Rd.

Showcasing winners from the **International Ice Sculpting Competition,** the **Fairbanks Ice Museum** (451-8222), near the visitor center on 2nd Ave., demonstrates what a Fairbanks winter can do to your average under-stimulated sculptor. (Open daily 10am-6pm. $6, seniors $5, ages 6-12 $4, under 6 free.)

Alaskaland (459-1095), on Airport Way, is a small-scale, would-be Arctic Disneyland, but it just has a train, a merry-go-round, and no pixie-dust. Overrun by kids, Alaskaland is a tourist trap of woolly mammoth proportions. There's no general admission charge, though, and the gates are open from 11am to 9pm.

☒ NIGHTLIFE

This is a good town to get pined in. Not so many hikes, but lots of cheap beer.

■ **Howling Dog Saloon** (457-8780), 11½ mi. north of town on the Steese (Rte. 6) at the intersection of the Old and New Steese Hwys. Look for a colorful wooden structure in the middle of nowhere circled by pickup trucks. As the manager has it, the summer clientele is "rough, tough, and good-lookin'." Rough and tough volleyball, pool, and horseshoes. Live music W-Sa. Open May-Oct. Su-Th 4pm-2am, F-Sa 4pm-4am.

■ **Blue Loon Saloon,** 2999 Parks Hwy. (Rte. 3) (457-5666), 5 mi. south of town on the Parks Hwy., near **Ester.** There's always something cool happening at the Blue Loon. Music 4 nights a week, festivals in an outdoor amphitheater, 3 movies a week, and a mammoth dance floor. Cover $3. Open Tu-F 5pm-1:30am, Sa-Su 5pm-3am.

Club "G," 150 Farmer's Loop Ext. Rd. (451-7625), off the Steese Hwy. Past the school bus, techno and drag welcomes you to the city's only gay club and its hippest high-energy dance spot. Drink prices are steep; come steeped. Open F-Sa 9pm-3:30am.

The Marlin, 3412 College Rd. (479-4646; www.themarlin.net). Fairbanks's bar for live jazz and blues (F-Sa), open mic (Tu), and nightly live music. Smoky, low-lit, electric blue-tinged. Summer beer garden. Open M-Th 4pm-2am, F 4pm-3:30am, Sa 5pm-3:30am, Su 6pm-2am, shows after 9pm. $3 cover on weekends (free with college ID).

The Backdoor, behind Jeffrey's 24hr. Restaurant at the intersection of Trainer Gate Rd. and the Steese Hwy. Not so much atmosphere, but all draft beers (including Newcastle and Sam Adams) are $5 per pitcher. Tequila shots $1. Frequented by college kids and older drunks alike. Darts, nudie electronic games, foosball, and pool tables ensure that there's fun for everyone here. Open daily until 2am.

EVENTS

In mid-July Fairbanks citizens don old-time duds and whoop it up for **Golden Days,** a celebration of Felix Pedro's 1902 discovery that sparked the Fairbanks gold rush. Watch out for the traveling jail; without a silly-looking pin commemorating the event (sold at most businesses), an unknowing tourist may be taken prisoner and asked to pay to be sprung free. (The budget traveler might want to stay on board the paddywagon; it's a free ride and goes all over town.) Although its relation to the actual gold rush days is questionable, the **rubber duckie race** is one of the biggest events. For details, contact the visitors bureau or call 452-1105. Be warned that Fairbanks teems with tourists during Golden Days; make hotel reservations several months in advance.

The summer solstice inspires some wild activity in Fairbanks. The **Yukon 800 Marathon Riverboat Race** sends high-horsepower competitors in low-slung power-boats on an 800 mi. quest up the Tanana and Yukon Rivers to the town of Galena and back. On June 20th, thousands of people will join in the **10km Midnight Sun Run** (452-8351), to run, walk, or compete in the costume division. The Fairbanks Gold-panners play their annual **Midnight Sun Baseball Game** on the solstice itself (June 21, 2000). The game begins as the sun dips at 10:30pm, features a short pause near midnight for the celebration of the midnight sun, and ends at about 2am, in full daylight. The Goldpanners play more than 30 home games throughout the summer and have won five minor league national championships since 1970. Barry Bonds played here (perhaps the source for his massive taste for gold jewelry). Games are played at **Growden Memorial Park** (451-0095), near Alaskaland.

For a true sports spectacular, see the **World Eskimo-Indian Olympics** (452-6646), in mid-July. (Nightly pass $10, seniors and children $8. Season passes $20, seniors and children $15.) Native Alaskans from all over the state compete for three days in traditional tests of strength and survival. Witness the **ear pull,** for which sinew is wrapped around the ears of contestants, who then tug to see who can endure the most pain. *Ears have been pulled off in this event.*

The **Tanana Valley Fair** (452-3750), August 6-14, is a traditional country fair with rides, lots of food, and competitions for "biggest cabbage" and "cutest baby." (Tickets $7, seniors and ages 6-17 $3.) Suggestions for replacing them with "biggest baby" and "cutest cabbage" have so far been ignored. If you're lucky, you'll be chosen as a contestant in the **kiss the cow contest,** although the cow herself is unfairly prohibited from being the judge. The fairground is at the intersection of College Rd. and Aurora.

On September 18, Fairbanks hosts the annual **Equinox Marathon** (452-8531), one of the top five most rigorous in the nation. About 300 hearty competitors run 26.2 mi. up Ester Dome, sometimes in blizzard conditions, gaining 3500 ft. in elevation. They usually return so delirious that they blabber about impending Persians, then shout "Nike!" and collapse.

In winter, February's **Yukon Quest Dog Sled Race** runs between Fairbanks and Whitehorse, starting in Fairbanks on even years. The Quest is considered more extreme, colder, and dammit, more *Alaskan* than the famous Iditarod. There are fewer dogs, fewer stops, and less concern for human welfare. For information, contact the Yukon Quest Business Office, 558 2nd Ave. (452-7954).

OUTDOORS

Maps for **multi-use trails** are available at the Wood Center, in the UAF Student Activities Office. **Cross-country skiing trails** cross or near the UAF campus, and several begin and end at the University museum.

There are two mountains within a half-hour of Fairbanks open for **downhill skiing.** Twenty minutes northeast of town, **Moose Mountain** (479-8362; email moosemtn@polarnet.com) grooms over 20 trails. (Lift tickets $25; students, seniors, military, and ages 13-17 $20; ages 7-12 $15; under 6 and over 70 free. $5 off after 1pm or if the temperature is below 0°F.) **Mt. Aurora Ski Land,** 2315 Skiland Rd. (389-2314; email Mt.Aurora@worldnet.att.net) is 30 minutes north of Fairbanks. (Lift tickets $24, students and military $20, ages 13-17 and seniors $17, ages 7-12 $10, under 6 and over 70 $5.) Take a right onto Fairbanks Creek Rd. off the Steese Hwy. (Rte. 6) at Mile 20½, then turn left. Near Fairbanks, the **White Mountains National Recreation Area** has trails and cabins accessible from the Steese and Eliot Hwys. north of Fox, and the **Chena River State Recreation Area** (see **Near Fairbanks,** p. 507) has a variety of multi-use trails. Maps for both areas are available at the Alaska Public Lands Information Center (see p. 502).

NORTH OF FAIRBANKS

A short drive in any direction plunges travelers into genuine Alaskan wilderness. Within the vicinity of Fairbanks, you can soak your feet in hot-spring-fed lakes, look for wildlife in a river basin, or hike up a ridge to view the Brooks or Alaska Ranges, both over 200 miles away. Maps and detailed info on hikes are available at the Alaska Public Lands Information Center in Fairbanks (see p. 502). **Fishing** enthusiasts can find numerous places in and around Fairbanks to reel in a keeper.

CHENA RIVER AND ENVIRONS

Along the **Chena River,** graylings are common, and king salmon run in early July. The **Chatanika River,** which runs along the Steese Hwy. (Rte. 6) between Miles 29 and 39, teems with shellfish and northern pike. Would-be Bob Izumis stop at the visitor center (see p. 502) for licenses. Chena Hot Springs Road branches off the Steese Hwy. (Rte. 3) at Mile 5. The **Chena River State Recreation Area** (451-2695) spills across the road between Miles 26 and 51, encompassing almost 400 square miles of wilderness and offering outstanding fishing, hiking, canoeing, and camping. Tent sites (pit toilets, water; $8) convenient to Chena Hot Springs Rd. and fishing holes are available at the quiet, secluded **campgrounds** of **Rosehip** (Mile 27), **Tors Trail** (Mile 39), and **Red Squirrel** (Mile 42.8).

The **Granite Tors Trail,** across the road from Tors Trail Campground, begins in boreal forest at river level and climbs 2000 ft. every 7½ miles past the treeline to a peak topped by giant granite pillars ("Tors") and blessed with fantastic views of Chena Dome to the north and Flat Top Mountain to the west. There are also excellent views of the Alaska Range between miles 7 and 9 of the trail. In July and August, blueberries abound along the trail's first stretch. Rangers recommend taking the east trail (left) to do the 15 mi. loop clockwise. The **Angel Rocks Trail** (look for signs near Mile 49) follows the Chena River before turning for a 750 ft. climb alongside the Angel Rocks, prominent granite slabs that offer views of the river valley and the Alaska Range. This 3½ mi. loop through birch and boreal forest and wildflowers makes a wonderful family hike and has spawned numerous spur trails through the bush. Bring bug juice—this is mosquito country. The **Chena Dome Trail,** open to mountain bikers and equestrians, is the most spectacular trail in the park, a 29-mile adventure that follows the high, rocky rim of the Angel Creek Valley. The trailheads are at Mile 50½ and 170 yards past Mile 49 on the Chena Hot Springs Rd. The climb from either trailhead is a steep one, and park rangers advise backpackers planning on covering the entire (3-day) loop to begin at the northern trailhead. **Maps** and info on all these trails are available at the public lands office in Fairbanks, **Tacks' General Store** (open daily 8am-8pm; post office here too) at Mile 23 of Chena Hot Springs Rd., and at the Chena Hot Springs Resort.

Fifty-seven miles northeast of Fairbanks steams the bubbling pools of **Chena Hot Springs Resort** (907-451-8104, Fairbanks office 907-452-7867; www.chenahotsprings.com). In winter, scores shiver their way to the resort for prime northern lights viewing. In summer, Lower 48ers and Europeans (outer 39ers) are more frequent guests. **Rooms** are dear (in summer: doubles $105; suites $150), but **campsites** are available by the river (tent sites $15; RV sites $20; showers $3; water and dump station). Everyone pays to use the hot pools (open 24hr.; $8, seniors and ages 6-12 $6). The resort's **restaurant** serves standard expensive restaurant fare (lunch around $8, dinner from $15, burgers at the bar $6.75; open daily 7am-10pm). Nearby are hiking/biking trails, over 30 miles of cross-country skiing trails, and fine fishing (after the spring meltwater has run off). The resort rents bikes for $7.50 per hr., $25 per day. Early in August, the resort plays host to an annual **Alaskan microbrew festival,** where $20 buys you 5 beer coupons and free use of the hot pools all day.

ON THE 51ST DAY OF CHRISTMAS, MY TRUE LOVE GAVE TO ME...

The town of North Pole, AK, celebrates Christmas 365 days a year. Santa officially came to town in 1953, when the sleepy village of Moose Crossing changed its name to woo toy manufacturers. Town planners hoped that corporations would rush north for the privilege of displaying "made in the North Pole" on their products, but to no avail. The North Pole's 1700 residents, most of them military personnel stationed at nearby Fort Wainwright, have carried on nonetheless, transforming their town into a shrine to the jolly fat man. St. Nicholas Drive runs into Santa Claus Lane. Bus stops, lampposts, and shopping malls all reflect the Christmas theme. Holiday cheer is mandatory. The U.S. Postal Service even redirects Santa's mail—20,000 letters a year—to North Pole, and the merry old elf has recruited North Pole schoolchildren to help answer it.

When he's not finding out who's been naughty or nice, Santa moonlights as a North Pole entrepreneur. Eat Mexican at Santa's Tortilla Factory, do your duds at Santa's Suds, or hit the rides at Santaland Caravan Park. Best of all, anyone can get a personalized letter from Kris Kringle himself. Just send the recipient's name, age, sex, full mailing address, brothers' and sisters' names, favorite hobby, and anything special you would like Santa to write. The ruddy-cheeked old elf demands only $5 in return. His official address is 325 S. Santa Claus Lane, North Pole, AK 99705.

The resort is a good place to plan and amass info on a number of gerunds (snow-mobiling, dog sledding, rafting, fishing, horseback riding, ice skating, etc.), but it's not the only option for spending the night in the park. The **Angel Creek Lodge** (369-4128), at Mile 50 on the Chena Hot Springs Rd., provides more affordable accommodations. Its six rustic cabins sleep three to five people, have electricity and access to free showers and a sauna, and range in price from $45 to $100 a night. They'll let folks **camp** for **free** on their lawn, provided the guests use the outhouse, and not the indoor bathrooms (showers $3). A cafe, liquor store, and bar are open to anyone and everyone. The place really bustles in February as a checkpoint on the Yukon Quest Sled Dog Race (see p. 507).

STEESE HIGHWAY (RTE. 6)

The Steese Highway heads northeast out of Fairbanks and runs 162 mi. to the town of Circle on the **Yukon River.** Just 5 mi. outside Fairbanks, the Steese meets **Chena Hot Springs Road** (see p. 507), where a right turn brings you toward Chena River Recreation Area and the Chena Hot Springs. The **Elliot Highway (Rte. 2)** comes hard on the heels of the Chena Rd. at Mile 11 in **Fox.** Make a right turn at the intersection to stay on the Steese. Fox is the last place to fuel up for the next 117 miles of the Steese until the town of **Central** (and gas is far from cheap in Central). For the next 20 mi. past Fox, the highway winds through boreal forest, past two ski resorts, and into a region of stunted spruce and fir trees known as taiga. At Mile 16.5 is the **Felix Pedro Monument,** a plaque honoring Pedro's 1902 discovery of gold in the creek across the highway.

CAMPGROUNDS AND OUTDOORS

The **Upper Chatanika River Campground,** at Mile 39, provides secluded, woodsy campsites ($8). **Cripple Creek Campground,** at Mile 60, offers good fishing and recreational goldpanning (sites $6; walk-ins $3). Both campgrounds have access to the **Chatanika River Canoe Trail,** which parallels the Steese for nearly 30 miles. The easygoing stream is clear and Class II: its main treacherous obstacles are low water and overhanging trees. At Mile 45.4, soon after the road turns to gravel, the **Long Creek Trading Post** (389-5287) stands on the left side of the highway (open daily 9am-9pm). The Post runs a shuttle service for paddlers and their canoes ($1.50 per mile, $1 per mile after 15 miles; $10 minimum) and rents canoes ($30 per day). They also have a small general store and liquor store, and a bathhouse with laundry and an RV park with dump station is expected to be completed by the summer of 2000. Hiking trails to overlooks on the **Davidson Ditch** are gradual enough to handle even wheelchair traffic. At about Mile 70 the road begins to climb consistently into the highway's nicest scenery. The **White Mountain National Recreation Area** and the **Steese National Conservation Area** lie side-by-side to the north.

The trailhead for the **Pinnell Mountain Trail,** the most spectacular and popular hike in the vicinity of Fairbanks, is at Mile 86. The 27 mi. trail is rugged and exposed, and while it gains little elevation, it remains entirely above treeline and passes among alpine tundra flora. With proper timing, you can bask in the midnight sun (June 18-24, 2000), witness an explosion of wildflowers (late June), or watch caribou migration in the valleys below (Aug.-Sept.). Allow three days for the entire trip. Two cabins are well spaced along the trail for two nights' shelter, but the trail has no potable water. The trail ends on the highway at Mile 107; most hikers hitch back to their cars. Even if you don't have time to schlep 27 miles, a scramble up either end of the trail is worthwhile. For more info on this and other regional trails, call the Bureau of Land Management in Fairbanks at 474-2200.

Several entry points between Mile 94.5 and 147 lead to **Birch Creek,** which offers whitewater enthusiasts a varied 127-mile course including several Class III rapids at one extreme and glorified mud puddles at the other (be prepared for some portages). At Mile 108, the highway passes over **Eagle Summit** where the panoramic view of countless peaks and fragile tundra is well worth a stop.

CENTRAL AND CIRCLE HOT SPRINGS

Central (Mile 127), a pit-stop town of about 400 summer residents, is anything but central. The **Circle District Museum** displays beautiful native beadwork, a giant mammoth tusk and tooth, samples of local gold, and a playable pipe organ that was carried over the Chilkoot Trail and floated down the river to Circle (open Memorial Day-Labor Day daily noon-5pm; $1, children 50¢). The **Central Motor Inn** (520-5228; open daily 8am-close) serves nondescript meals (sandwiches $6, dinner from $8) and offers laundry (wash and dry $2 each) and shower facilities (showers $3). **Gas** is available here and at **Crabb's Grocery**, just down the street.

From Central, the road gets considerably worse, winding its way down towards the **Yukon River Flats Basin.** Unless you are planning to float the mighty **Yukon River** or urinate into its great waters—an activity inexplicably favored by some tourists—there is little reason to drive the highway's final 34 miles to **Circle.** Instead, follow the signs and veer right after downtown Central to the **Circle Hot Springs.** The springs are just 8 miles from Central, and provide a pleasant reward for those who make the long drive. The pool here is outdoors, and a day pass for non-guests at the **Arctic Circle Hot Springs Lodge** is $5 (open 8am-midnight). The lodge is charming, historic, boasts piping-hot spring-fed toilets, and is supposedly haunted by at least two ghosts—one is "a real prankster." The rooms are costly (singles $75; doubles $100), but the lodge has a hostel on the fourth floor next to its library. The hostel rooms are small and carpeted, with low ceilings and no beds, but those who stay there get free use of the pool (first person $20, each extra adult $15, under 9 $7.50; each room fits up to 4 people). Camping is also available (tent sites $5, RV sites $10, electrical $15). The dining room (open 7am-9pm) serves tasty sandwiches ($4-7) and dinner entrees ($10-16), and **Cold Rush** (open M-F 2-4pm and 6-9pm) offers an abundance of ice cream in a homemade waffle cone for $3.50.

THE ALASKA HIGHWAY (RTE. 2)

DELTA JUNCTION

Aptly named the Crossroads of Alaska, Delta Junction's function is to serve the intersection of the **Alaska Hwy. (Rte. 2),** which leads 108 miles southeast to **Tok** and the **Richardson Hwy. (Rte. 4)** which runs 100 miles northwest to Fairbanks and 270 miles south to Valdez (see p. 453). Moreover, the huge post in front of the **visitor center** (895-5069; open daily mid-May to mid-Sept. 8am-8pm) declares Delta Junction the terminus of the Alaska Hwy., though Fairbanks argues otherwise. For $1, you can buy a macho certificate of Alcan completion at Mile 1422. Across the street, the **Sullivan Roadhouse Historical Museum** (895-4415; open in summer daily 9am-6pm), formerly of the Valdez-Fairbanks Trail, displays a free collection of mining-era artifacts and photographs and chronicles the construction of the Richardson Hwy. and the arrival of the U.S. military. Eight miles north of town toward Fairbanks, **Big Delta Historic Park** is home to **Rika's Roadhouse** (895-4201; open daily 9am-5pm), a restored homestead and former trading post complete with barnyard and accompanying animals (free walking tour on request). A 1920s buffalo importation scheme is responsible for Delta Junction's free-ranging buffalo herd, the largest in the U.S. Glimpse the mighty bison from across the fence at the buffalo ranch 4 miles up Clearwater Rd. (7 mi. toward Tok on the Alcan, on your left).

Services are the last for miles: **Hendrick's Auto Parts and Garage** (895-4221; open M-Sa 9am-6pm and Su 9am-5pm), is at Richardson Hwy. Mile 269. **National Bank of Alaska** (895-4691), north on the Richardson Hwy., has a **24hr. ATM.** The **post office** (895-4601; open M-F 9:30am-5pm, Sa 10:30am-noon) is north of the visitor center. The **state police** (895-4344) are one mile south of the visitor center. **Emergency:** 911. **Health clinic:** 2360 Service Rd. (895-5100). **ZIP code:** 99737. **Area code:** 907.

Nearby state park areas have **camping** ($8; water and pit toilets), in addition to hiking, biking, canoeing, and fishing. **Delta State Recreation Site,** half a mile north,

A CASE OF THE RUNS France hosts the Tour de France, Boston the Boston Marathon, and Delta Junction the Great Alaskan Outhouse Race. The most exciting event at the Deltana Fair, held in late July and early August since 1987, the race pits locals in a contest to see which team can most swiftly push or pull an occupied outhouse through a 1½ mi. course. The commodes are hand-crafted to achieve the speediest, lightest design possible. During the race, four competitors struggle with the ungainly box while one lucky teammate rides the ceramic steering wheel, so to speak. Winners receive the exalted Golden Throne Award, a painted toilet with the team members' names engraved on the lid. The coveted Silver Plunger goes to the second place finishers, and the third place prize is the much-admired Copper Snake.

and **Clearwater Lake,** at the end of Clearwater Rd. off the Alcan toward Tok, are nearest. **Quartz Lake,** 10 mi. north on the Richardson, is called the top sport fishery in the Tanana River drainage. Laundry and showers are available in town at **Bergstad's RV Park and Camp Sites** (895-4856; tents $6, RV hookup $12).

Pizza Bella Restaurant (895-4841 or 895-4524; open Su-Th 11am-9:30pm, F-Sa 11am-10pm), opposite the visitor center, offers the town's highest nourishment-to-dollar ratio (half-sub $5). **Buffalo Center Drive-in** (895-4055; open M-Sa 11am-10pm, Su noon-8pm) fills Delta Junction's meat quota (buffalo burgers $6). Break into the **IGA Food Cache** (895-4653; open M-Sa 7am-10pm, Su 8am-8pm) up Fairbanks way.

TOK

With the Alaska Highway running through the heart of town, Tok (TOKE), at Mile 1314, calls itself "Mainstreet Alaska." Like many small towns along the highway, Tok is friendly, dull, and geared toward summer tourists: it is no place for the RV-shy. Those looking to kill some time in Tok can view yon Alaska Range from Tok's multi-use paved path, which runs for 13 mi. along the highway. Sandhill cranes and trumpeter swans are among the many species that use the nearby **Tetlin National Wildlife Refuge** as a migration corridor or nesting ground. There are no trails on the marshy land, so human disturbance of the 65,000 young born there each year is limited to flightseeing. Tok, named in honor of a U.S. Army battalion's pet husky shortly after the construction of the Alaska Hwy. during WWII, revives its affection for sled dogs every winter in late March with the **Race of Champions** (883-6874), the last major dog race on the Alaska circuit. In summer, the **Burnt Paw Shop** (883-4121) offers free dog team demonstrations (M-Sa 7:30pm).

🔢 ORIENTATION AND PRACTICAL INFORMATION. All roads lead to Tok. The town lies at the junction of the Alcan Highway and the Tok Cut-off, and is only 12 mi. east of the Alcan's intersection with the Taylor Highway (Rte. 5) at Tetlin Junction (see p. 512). Tok is 206 Alcan miles southeast of Fairbanks, and is the halfway point on the 600-mile drive from Whitehorse, YT, to Anchorage. **40 Mile Air** (883-5191), at Alcan Mile 1313, flies to **Fairbanks** on weekdays (1½hr., $130) and has less frequent scheduled service to many smaller towns. Reserve at least three days in advance. Hitchers have little luck with the RV's streaming through town. **Alaska Direct** (800-770-6652) buses leave from the front of **Northstar Cafe** beside **Northstar RV Park,** about half a mile east of the visitor center on the Alcan, at 2:30pm (W, F, and Su) to Fairbanks (4hr., $40), Anchorage (7hr., $65), and Whitehorse, YT (9½hr., $80). Reservations are recommended. The slower and pricier **Alaskon Express** (800-544-2206) leaves three times per week from the Westmark Inn (883-5174), at the junction, to even more destinations.

A spacious new **visitor center** (883-5775; www.tokalaskainfo.com), and the **Public Lands Information Center** (883-5666) are housed in the state's largest single-story log building, just east of the junction (open June to Labor Day daily 8am-8pm; in late May and mid-Sept. M-F 8am-4pm). The complex offers a trip-planning room, free coffee, and also houses the town **library,** which sells paperbacks for 25¢. Across the highway, the **Tetlin National Wildlife Refuge Headquarters** (883-5312) provides info on the waterfowl preserve (open M-F 8am-4:30pm). The Northstar RV Park (see above) houses a **laundromat** (wash $1.25, dry 25¢ per 7min.) and **showers** ($3.50). Call 800-472-0391 for a **weather report**. The **Health Clinic** (883-5855) is half a mile down the Tok Cut-off on the east side (open M-Th 8am-5pm, F 8am-noon). **Emergency:** 911. **Police:** 883-5111. **Internet access:** at **All Alaska Gifts** (883-5081), behind the visitor center ($2 for first 10min., then $3 per 30min.; open mid-May to mid-Sept. daily 7:30am-10pm). **Public radio:** 91.1 FM. **Post office:** at the junction (883-5880; open M-F 8:30am-5pm). **ZIP code:** 99780. **Area code:** 907.

⬛ ACCOMMODATIONS, CAMPGROUNDS, AND FOOD. The **Tok Youth Hostel (HI)** (883-3745) is 8 mi. from town in the woods. Going west on the Alcan, take Pringle Dr. on the left and follow it for three quarters of a mile until you see the hostel marker to the right. The hostel's dorm is an authentic medical tent from WWII, and satellite amenities include free laundry, hot showers, and a campfire circle with complimentary marshmallows ($10; open May-Sept.). In town, the **Golden Bear Motel & RV Park** (883-2561; fax 883-5950), on the west side of the Tok Cut-off half a mile south of town, has secluded tent sites ($15), firewood, showers, laundry (wash $1, dry $1.50) and a lounge with VCR and pool table. The **Tok River State Recreation Area Campground,** 4 mi. east of town, just across the Tok River on the north side of the highway, offers serene, woodsy riverside sites ($10, self-registration). A gas fill-up at **Saveway** (883-5389), next to the Golden Bear, earns free RV parking (no hookups) or a tent site with no facilities except for the bathroom in the 24-hour store. Rooms are also available (singles $55; doubles $60; room without TV or phone $38). At **Gateway Salmon Bake** (883-5555), on the Alcan at the east end of town, an all-you-can-eat dinner (king salmon $16.75; chicken $12) earns patrons a free RV or tent site with toilets, hot water and showers, but no hookups (open May 15 to Sept. 15 M-Sa 11am-9pm, Su 4-9pm; without dinner, sites $10).

Apart from the salmon, Tok serves up plenty of expensive, forgettable food. **Young's Cafe** (883-2233), with photos of historical Tok lining the walls, is definitely the venue with the most local atmosphere. Located across from the visitor center, it serves sandwiches ($4-7), sirloin steak ($14), and a sourdough pancake breakfast ($4-5; open daily May to mid-Sept. 6am-9pm). **Frontier Foods** (883-5195), next door, is the spot for reasonably priced bulk items and fresh fruit (open in summer daily 7am-11pm; in winter M-Sa 8am-9pm, Su 8am-7pm).

TAYLOR HIGHWAY (RTE. 5)

The Taylor proves that the term "highway" is used very loosely in the north. Following the track of an old horse and wagon trail, not much seems to have changed since the path's construction through the hilly wilderness of Alaska's richest and earliest (circa 1886) gold fields. With dirt or gravel roadbeds and countless hairpin turns, the Taylor Highway is definitely not for the high-strung. The road will, however, lead you to the remains and modern incarnations of the gold mining towns of Forty Mile, Wade Creek, and Chicken Creek, as well as historic dredges, some beautiful camping, and scenic rivers with fishing potential.

TETLIN JUNCTION TO EAGLE

Beginning at **Tetlin Junction,** 12 mi. east of **Tok** (see p. 511), the highway is initially pleasant, with wide, smooth lanes. At Mile 96, the highway intersects another gold route, the **Top-of-the-World Highway** (Hwy. 9; see p. 387), which continues 79 miles east to Dawson City, YT (see p. 383). The Taylor continues north 64 miles through worsening roads to the tiny town of **Eagle** (see below). The drive from Tetlin Junction to Eagle takes about 4½ hours. Camping overnight along the way or in Eagle would make for a comfortable two-day round-trip.

If you decide to cut off towards Dawson City, be prepared to cross the U.S./Canada border (open May-Sept. 8am-8pm Alaska time). Make sure to have proof of citizenship and of funds (see **Customs,** p. 26). No scheduled buses run the Taylor, although there is boat service between Eagle and Dawson City (see p. 383). Some car-less travelers hitchhike, but sparse RV traffic makes this difficult; most hitchers pack a good book and start early in the morning. Gas and food are available only at the **Boundary Cafe,** just west of the border, and **Chicken,** at Mile 66.

From **Mile 0,** the Taylor Hwy. gradually climbs to over 3500 ft. as it rolls toward 5541 ft. Mt. Fairplay. These first 50 miles are the easiest to drive and the most scenic. A sign at the rest stop just past the summit (Mile 35) explains the history of the highway. The woodsy **West Fork Campground** lies at Mile 49 (pit toilets, water; 25 sites: $6; 7 pull-throughs).

The megalopolis of **Chicken,** rumored to have received the name after local miners couldn't spell their first choice, "Ptarmigan," lies at Mile 66. Each summer, Chicken's population explodes with an influx of gold miners from its usual 25 to upwards of 100. The **Chicken Creek Saloon** throws the wildest pre-solstice, solstice, and 4th of July parties in the region and a free crab bake on Labor Day Saturday (open 8am-whenever). Free RV parking, pricey gas ($1.69 per gallon) and tire repair (hallelujah! about $20) can be found at the **Goldpanner,** on the Taylor south of the "downtown" turn-off (open May-Oct. daily 8am-8pm; V, MC accepted). Half-hour walking tours of old ghost-town Chicken leave three times per day (for groups of four or more) from in front of the store; they are the only way to see the original mining cabins (donations encouraged). The Goldpanner also loans out pans for free gold-panning at one well-panned stretch of water. Next to the Saloon, the pricey **Chicken Creek Cafe** serves up burgers and sandwiches from $7. Two weighty flapjacks ($4.75) or a wiener with potato salad ($6) are more reasonable deals (open daily 8am-6pm; cold food served in the bar until midnight). The cafe also hosts a nightly **Salmon Bake** (in summer daily 4-8pm, $15). Tenters and RVs can set up on the lot next to the cafe for free, although the site is less than ideal. The **Chicken Mercantile Emporium** pushes souvenirs aplenty and also sells gas for $1.59 per gallon (open summer daily 8am-8pm; Visa and Mastercard accepted).

Just past Chicken is a Bureau of Land Management **ranger station,** and an easy to moderate **hike** along Mosquito Fork River towards an old dredge. Take the mosquitoes seriously (2hr. round-trip). Another 8 miles north on the highway (Taylor Mile 82) will land you at **Walker Fork Campground,** with 20 riverside sites, water, pit toilets, and good fishing ($6). The **Jack Wade Dredge,** a huge machine used for placer mining, lies rusting away right next to the highway at Mile 86. The deteriorated dredge's safety is dubious, but that doesn't stop passersby from wandering around its eerie skeleton. From this point until Eagle, evidence of mining, large and small-scale, abounds. At Jack Wade Junction the road forks north for Eagle and east for Dawson via the Top-of-the-World. For the last 64 miles from the Eagle junction, the road tightropes and snakes along mountainsides and canyons of **Forty Mile River,** another popular, though difficult, spot for rafters to put in (see **Eagle,** below, for outfitters). This last portion of the highway can be an arduous, 2-hour test of drivers' grit, making them wonder if the tiny town at the end is really worth it. It is.

MY CAR'S STUCK 5 MILES UP THE ROAD. DO YOU HAVE AN ATM?

In the winter of 1905, the Norwegian explorer Roald Amundsen hiked several hundred miles across northern Canada into Eagle when his ship became locked in the ice floes of the Arctic Ocean. Amundsen used Eagle's new telegraph to cable his government for money, then mushed back to his ship and successfully completed the first journey from the Atlantic to the Pacific through the hitherto unthinkable Northwest Passage. Amundsen Park, on 1st St. at Amundsen, commemorates his voyage with a glistening silver globe etched in relief.

EAGLE

Many of Eagle's 240 residents say there's no place they'd rather live than this unpretentious wilderness town. Connected to the outside world only by sled dog or air, and, in summer, by the Taylor Hwy., Eagle is no tourist mecca, lacking both a town water and sewage system and a police department. Eagle's heyday was in 1899, when the Secretary of War established a military base here to keep the town's booming gold rush population in check. In 1901, Eagle became the Interior's first incorporated city. The military went south after the mining fizzled, but unlike other forts along the Yukon, several of Fort Egbert's buildings and paraphernalia remained untouched by marauding miners. Eager Eagle-ites have quick grins and plenty a tale about pioneer great-grandmothers to share with travelers passing through. They also have more enthusiasm for their town and way of life than perhaps any other northern community; during the long winters, when the only access is by plane, they proclaim: "We're not snowed in. You're snowed out!"

7 PRACTICAL INFORMATION. The Taylor Hwy. closes from mid-October until at least mid-May. **Tatonduk Air** (547-2249) flies twice a day except Sunday to Fairbanks (1¼hr.; $93). Ask at the **Eagle Trading Co.** for details. There is **no bank, no ATM,** and **nobody takes credit cards.** Bo Fay, the proprietor of **Telegraph Hill Services** (547-2261), on the Taylor Hwy., is an unofficial visitor center. He readily provides coffee, conversation, gas, car repairs, and an indispensable map (open daily 8am-6pm; in winter 9am-5pm). The real **visitor center** and the **Yukon-Charley Rivers National Preserve Headquarters** (547-2233; open in summer daily 8am-5pm) provides the lowdown on canoe trips to Circle and beyond, from the end of 1st St. (left off the main road toward the old airstrip). The **Eagle Trading Co.** (547-2220), on Front St. by the river, carries hardware, groceries, and supplies (open daily 8am-8pm in summer; in winter 10am-6pm). In an **emergency,** call the **Village Public Safety Officer** at 547-2300. **Public radio:** 91.7 FM. **Post office:** (547-2211) on 2nd St. at Jefferson (open M-F 8:30am-4:30pm). **ZIP code:** 99738. **Area code:** 907.

▮▯ ACCOMMODATIONS, CAMPGROUNDS, AND FOOD. The **Eagle Trading Co.** (547-2220), on Front St., has it all: gas, groceries, hot showers ($4), laundry (wash $4 per double load, dry 25¢ per 5min.), RV hookups ($15), and clean rooms with porches overlooking the river (singles $50; doubles $60; open in summer daily 8am-8pm; in winter 10am-6pm). Campers will rejoice upon finding the **Eagle BLM Campground,** a 1-mile hike past Fort Egbert, or the first left after Telegraph Hill Services. Several short hiking trails start here. Ask Bo—he knows (no water, pit toilets; sites $6, seniors $3). The **Riverside Cafe** (547-2250) serves the usual but with a view of the Yukon River (breakfast and lunch $4-5; open May-Oct. daily 7am-8pm).

▦ SIGHTS. No visit to Eagle is complete without the three-hour **walking tour** (547-2325), offered daily in summer by the **Eagle Historical Society and Museums.** The tour leaves at 9am from the **Courthouse Museum** at 1st and Berry St., and includes the courthouse and Fort Egbert, which can't be viewed otherwise. View well-preserved relics of frontier life, from a birch bark canoe to experimental (failed) horse snowshoes. ($5, under 12 free. Call to arrange an alternate time.)

Locals run yearly foot races up the copper-colored bluff above town and back down in 30 minutes. The line can be **hiked** in a more leisurely couple of hours. Follow the small road past the visitor's center, and then continue along the banks of the Yukon to Mission Creek; the creek must be forded several hundred feet upstream. It's all uphill from here, and good footwear is a must.

▨ FLOATING FROM EAGLE. The 1979-mile-long Yukon River is the fourth longest river in North America and has the fifth largest flow volume of any river on earth. No other American river is as undeveloped, and navigating its entire length has become a cult experience. The trip takes about three to four months and ends 1200 miles from Eagle near Nome at the Bering Sea. If four months sounds daunting, the 154-mile trip between Eagle and Circle (see p. 120) takes only four to six days. The river runs through the **Yukon-Charley Rivers National Preserve** and some of Alaska's wildest country, but remains relatively calm the whole way. Campers do their best to avoid bears and countless mosquitoes by pitching tents on the gravel bars along the river. For detailed info, visit the Eagle Visitor Center or write the National Preserve, P.O. Box 167, Eagle, AK 99738. **Eagle Canoe Rentals** (547-2203) will set you afloat for the five-day trip to Circle ($165; equipment return included). Getting back is up to you, but flights to Fairbanks are available from Eagle and Circle, as is the daily river trip from Eagle to Dawson City on the *M/V Yukon Queen* (5hr., US$117; canoe or kayak $20).

DENALI HIGHWAY (RTE. 8)

The breathtaking Denali Highway runs west from **Paxson**, 80 mi. (1¼hr.) south of Delta Junction on the Richardson Hwy. (Rte. 4), to **Cantwell**, 27 mi. (½hr.) south of the Denali National Park entrance. Along the way, it skirts the foothills of the Alaska Range amid countless lakes and streams teeming with trout and arctic char. Fortunately for solitary sorts, the highway's 115 mi. of gravel scare away most tour buses and RVs. This makes it a scenic road-less-traveled to Denali, while pristine free campgrounds and unique geological formations along the way make the road a destination in itself. Bullet-riddled road signs attest to the popularity of hunting in this area, but hikers, fishermen, bird-watchers, and archaeologists also frequent the region. The highway itself, and many of the trails that branch off it, particularly in the Tangle Lakes district (see below), are ideal for mountain biking. Glaciers and permafrost have been up to geological mischief, creating bizarre mounds, ridges, and basins all along the highway. For explanations of these features and general highway info, pick up *Denali Highway Points of Interest*, available at most local roadhouses, visitor centers, and pit stops. The Denali Highway is **closed** from October to mid-May. Except for the 21 mi. west of Paxson, it is entirely gravel. Most vehicles can expect to keep a pace of 30 mph. **Mile markers,** where they exist, measure the distance from Paxson. **Gas and services** are available at Mile 20 and Mile 82. **State Trooper:** 822-3263. **Ambulance:** 768-2982.

The **Tangle Lakes National Register District,** between Miles 17 and 37, serves as a base for mountain bikers, ATVers, and birders. Pick up the Bureau of Land Management's free *Trail Map and Guide to the Tangle Lakes* at the Tangle River Inn (see below) for details. Archaeological sites in the area contain evidence of some of the first human settlements in North America, some of which are at least 10,000 years old. For more info contact the **Bureau of Land Management** (822-3217; www.glennallen.ak.blm.gov). At Mile 21 is the **Tangle Lakes Campground** (toilets, water pump), and a quarter mile farther on is the **Tangle River Campground** (toilets, no water). Both are scenic and free, and provide easy access to the 30 mi., two- to three-day, **Delta River Canoe Route,** with one difficult stretch of Class III rapids and one portage. Take-out is at Mile 212.5 of the Richardson Highway. The **Upper Tangle Lakes Canoe Route** is an easier 9 mi. paddle beginning at **Tangle River** and ending at **Dickey Lake.** The helpful *Delta* brochure is available from the BLM and most estab-

INTERIOR ALASKA

PANNIN' FER GOALD: THEORY To make your fortune, you'll need a 12- or 18-inch pan, easily found at local stores, and an unclaimed stretch of beach or river. Look for tree roots, turns in the river, and upstream ends of gravel bars, where heavy gold may settle. Scoop up some promising-looking sand and gravel. Swirl water, sand, and gravel in the tilted gold pan, slowly washing materials over the edge. Be patient, dreaming of how you'll spend your riches. Eventually you'll be down to black sand, and—hopefully—gold. Gold is shinier than brassy-looking pyrite, or "fool's gold," and it doesn't break down at the touch like mica does.

PANNIN' FER GOALD II: PRACTICE Swish. Swish. Swish swish. "Nope." Swish swish swish. "Nope." Swish. Swish swish swish. Swish. Swish. "GO-ALD! It's goald, goald, I tells ya!"

lishments along the highway. The owner of the **Tangle River Inn** (822-7304 or 259-3970, in winter 895-4022; www.alaska.net/~tangle), at Mile 20 across the highway from the boat launch, homesteaded the area by dog sled before the highway was built. Private rooms ($45) and beds in a shared room ($25) with a common room with pool table, TV, and VCR are popular; book ahead. The inn offers a cafe, bar, gas, and canoe rental ($3 per hr., $24 per day). Birders, fishermen, and flora fans flock to the **Tangle River Lodge** (259-7302), at Mile 22, whose owners have the low-down on the area's wildlife and canoe routes. The area hosts 140 different species of birds, including the arctic warbler and Smith's longspur (see www.alaskan.com/tanglelakes/cklist.htm for a **birding checklist**), and some of the best car-accessible arctic grayling fishing in the state.

Spectacular mountain scenery lines the rest of the highway, interrupted by an occasional roadhouse or cafe. The trailhead at Mile 35 begins the short, level trail to the **Maclaren Summit** (4086 ft.), from which the **Maclaren River** is visible flowing from the **Maclaren Glacier,** with the Alaska Range and wildflowers all around. The scenic 8 mi. **Osar Lake Trail** begins at Mile 37 and is ideal for mountain biking. At Mile 80, the highway crosses the beautiful **Susitna River.** The turn-off at Mile 130, 5 mi. east of Cantwell, grants an excellent view of Denali on clear days. At Cantwell, the highway meets the more heavily traveled George Parks Highway (see p. 488); Denali National Park is 30min. north, and Anchorage is 3½hr. to the south.

THE BUSH

Pay Phones: Many phones will not return coins. Dial, wait until the party picks up, and then deposit coins. For motto, sales tax, and other **Alaska-wide info,** see p. 392.

The Bush, that is, anywhere you can't get by car, is home to some of Alaska's most remarkable terrain as well as some its most tenacious industries. At the end of the Aleutian archipelago stretching into the North Pacific and away from anything in the world except for Russia's most remote reaches, the natural deep harbor of Unalaska provides a haven for an extraordinarily profitable fishery. At another of Alaska's watery extremes, the Arctic Ocean is divided from the end of the Dalton Highway by the company-town responsible for sending Arctic oil down to Valdez and on to the lower 48. This is not to suggest that travelers can't get away from human settlement. Alaska's southwestern expanse includes the stunning sight of the Valley of Ten Thousand Smokes and bears that inhabit the Kenai peninsula; the flat, soggy terrain of the Yukon-Kushkowin delta; the mountainous Alaska Peninsula; and that volcanic archipelago with some of the worst weather on earth, the Aleutians. Northwest Alaska includes the Seward Peninsula, a treeless, hilly projection of tundra, where Nome and Kotzebue lie on the storm-lashed Bering Sea. In Arctic Alaska, the crowning Brooks Range stretches from the far northwest to the Canadian border, while its North Slope's flat expanses spread northward from the Brooks to the Arctic Ocean and Barrow. Polar bears ride ice floes and hundreds of thousands of caribou roam freely here. Native Alaskan settlements are few and far between, accessible only by plane, boat, or snowmobile. And the cannery workers and oil drillers that gather in these remote settlements know that the big money's theirs to save because there's nowhere to spend it.

Anyone who hopes to travel in the Bush must have a strong sense of adventure and self-reliance, or tons of money and trust in tour guides. Because all supplies must be flown in from Fairbanks, transportation in the Bush is expensive. Once in the Bush, tour outfitters abound, ready and willing to take visitors into the wilds to fish, hunt, hike, kayak, or canoe in some of the most remote real estate on earth.

HIGHLIGHTS OF THE BUSH

■ Any Bush destination we list would be the highlight of a trip. Except maybe Barrow.

SOUTHWESTERN ALASKA

KATMAI NATIONAL PARK

On June 1, 1912, all the birds, bugs, and mammals mysteriously fled the Katmai Valley. Sensing danger, the Sugpiak-Aeutiiq living in Katmai and Savonoski Villages followed a few days later. On June 6, this century's largest volcanic eruption began, and it didn't stop for 60 hours. A 20-mile-high column of ash shot violently out of the earth, and a wave of semi-molten rock, gas, and steam charged down the valley at 100 mph. No one was killed in the blast, nearly 40 times more powerful than the eruption of Mt. St. Helens, but in the blackness that enshrouded nearby settlements for days a lantern held at arms length couldn't be seen.

When Dr. Robert Griggs first visited the valley in 1916 on a National Geographic expedition, he proclaimed it to be "one of the most amazing visions ever beheld by mortal eye.... The whole valley as far as the eye could reach was full of hundreds, no thousands—literally tens of thousands—of smokes curling up from its fissured floor." Dr. Griggs believed that the fumaroles would steam interminably and that Katmai would surpass Yellowstone in geological intrigue, and he successfully convinced President Woodrow Wilson to declare Katmai a national monument in 1918. The smokes have all burned out, but now 4.2 million acres of Katmai have been protected as Katmai National Park and Preserve since 1980.

As amazing as the Valley of Ten Thousand Smokes is, many people come to Katmai without seeing it. They come instead to **Brooks Camp,** 23 miles from the valley, for the region's chief draw: brown bears. Katmai has nearly 2000 roaming within its boundaries, and many people see their first bear within minutes of their arrival to the park. The bears love Katmai for the same reason sport fishermen love it: the Brooks River, Naknek Lake, Lake Grosvenor, and the Coville River are teeming with sockeye salmon, rainbow and lake trout, arctic char and grayling. (The sockeyes run in July, but trout are best in June, and char and grayling fill the waters from June-Sept.) When the sockeyes are running in July, or after they have spawned and died in September, 900 lb. brown bears can be seen up and down the Brooks River regaining the 40% of their body weight lost during hibernation. The bear-viewing platform at Brooks Falls allows visitors to watch up to 20 bears at a time catching salmon. The facilities are open from June 1 to September 17.

Use of the backcountry is free, though a $10 **day-use fee** is required for visitors taking advantage of Brooks Camp bear-watching and camping facilities (see below). To find out more, stop at the Alaska Public Lands Information Center in Anchorage (907-271-2737; see p. 438). The visitor center in King Salmon is helpful, as is the ranger at Brooks Camp. Jean Bodeau's *Katmai* ($15), available at Cook Inlet Book Co. in Anchorage (see p. 440), and at the King Salmon visitor center, is a comprehensive guide to the park's trails, routes, and climbs.

KING SALMON

While King Salmon, 300 mi. from Anchorage and 20 mi. from Brooks Camp, is the gateway to Katmai National Park, most travelers don't spend even an hour here between their flights. Fishermen fill up the lodgings and book the flights in summer; the rivers and lakes in the region support several commercial fishing operations, based in nearby Bristol Bay. Services are spare and overpriced.

The **King Salmon Visitor Center** (246-4250), by the airport, is the town's best feature with a rich library, 60 wildlife videos, and a big screen television. (Open daily 8am-5pm May-Sept., M-F 9am-5pm Oct.-April.) The **King Salmon Mall** opposite the airport has a **24-hour ATM** in the National Bank of Alaska. **Trout Net** (246-7888) next door, provides espresso and **Internet access** for 20¢ per minute (open May-Sept. daily 7am-8pm). The trailer here houses a **laundromat** and **public shower** run by the **King Ko Inn** across the street (wash $2.50, dry 25¢ per 10min.; untimed showers $5 with soap and towel; open May-Sept. 24hr.). **Post office:** 2 mi. west of the airport (246-3396; open M-F 8am-4:30pm, Sa 9:30-11am). **Zip code:** 99613. **Area code:** 907.

BROOKS CAMP

Brooks Camp via King Salmon provides direct access to Katmai National Park. Several flight companies have packages to get you there. **Alaska Airlines** (800-426-0333) and **Pen Air** (800-448-4226) fly several times a day to King Salmon (1hr.; see below) and **Katmai Air** (800-544-0551) flies from there to Brooks Camp on a float plane (20min.). The package costs around $420 round-trip. **Reeve Aleutian** (800-544-2248) flies four times a week to King Salmon ($260 round-trip) and **Branch River Air** (246-3437) or **C-Air** (246-6318) goes on to Brooks Camp ($130 round-trip). Most charter companies charge 40¢ per lb. each way for bikes, kayaks, or bulky gear. **Katmailand Lodge,** in Brooks Camp, rents double kayaks ($7 per hr., $50 per day) and canoes ($6 per hr., $30 per day) with a cash deposit of $50 per day or $200. They also rent waders ($7 per day), spin and fly rods ($10 per day), and sell licenses ($10 per day, $30 per week).

Katmailand (243-5448 or 800-544-0551; www.katmailand.com) runs a grossly overpriced lodge and dining room at Brooks Camp, and rents **cabins** with bunks, toilets, and showers, for atmospheric sums, even for four people ($94 per person), but they are almost always full. **Brooks Campground** technically holds 60 people, but this may entail sharing a tent site with another group. The campground has water, outhouses, shelter, and an electrically fenced-in food and gear cache. Toilets and a **shower** are open 7am to 9pm ($5 for 10 min. and a towel). The campground can be crowded and noisy during the day, when float planes use the adjacent lake. Call or write for advance reservations ($5 per night) and to secure **day use permits** ($10 per day) at 800-365-2267 or **NPRS**, P.O. Box 1600, Cumberland, MD 21502.

The antler-adorned lodge has a large stone fireplace (open 7am-1am) and serves **buffet-style** breakfasts ($5-10), lunches ($10-12), and dinner ($10-22). The bar (open 4pm-1am) serves Alaskan Amber (pints $4.75). Hot beverages are free for lodge guests and $1 for the masses. The lodge **Trading Post** (July and Sept. open 8am-7pm, June and Aug. 7am-7pm) sells sodas, candy, and film at, yup, very high prices.

OUTDOORS IN THE PARK

THE VALLEY OF TEN THOUSAND SMOKES. Currently, the Katmailand **bus tour** ($79 with bagged lunch, $72 without, $42 one-way), is the only way to get to the valley. Trips fill up and should be booked ahead. The bus leaves daily at 9am (meet at lower platform on Brooks River at 8:30am) and returns at 4:30pm. Upon arrival, a knowledgeable park service ranger gives talks on area ecology and geology and leads a two- to three-hour hike into the valley. A 23-mile scenic dirt road continues into it, and Katmailand may start to rent out bikes. If you bring or rent a bike, ask a cooperative passenger to bring your pack on the bus or inquire about a baggage fee. There is an unlocked ranger cabin at the end of the road with emergency supplies, a bunk, and a scrapbook with great pictures and articles about the valley.

From the end of the bus ride, Katmai really needs several days to be fully appreciated. A trail leads into the Valley from the right side of the road a half-mile before the ranger cabin. It begins on a relatively steep decent through alders and willows until opening up into the great ashen valley. A shallow stream crossing of the **Windy River** is required. The flat trail through soft ash and pumice along the hauntingy beautiful **Lethe River** leads to a perfect camping spot at a large draw by a creek. Another 4 miles into the valley (the trail all but disappears, but the valley is wide open with clear peaks for orientation in good weather) lie the pristine **McGiek Lakes.** Ask the rangers about the crossing point of the Lethe River to get to the **Novarupta Volcano** or to access a small ranger cabin on **Baked Mountain.** If you only have a day in the valley, the **Ukak River Trail** is a 3 mi., 2½-hour, round-trip with 700 ft. elevation loss and gain. The trail leads to the canyons chiseled at the confluence of the Windy and Lethe Rivers and provides an excellent view of the valley. A short, flat, quarter-mile side trail leads to a waterfall. (The tour bus allows time for energetic hikers to check out both routes). If you're planning an extended stay in the valley, bring some eye protection and a handkerchief. Winds can be fierce and ash can kick up into black-outs, making hiking and tent set-up very difficult.

BEAR VIEWING AND HIKES FROM BROOKS CAMP. If you can't get to the valley, you could spend days at the bear-viewing platform (unless it is crowded and regulated). A trail leads from the Trading Post across a wooden bridge to the **Lower Platform;** check-in with a ranger who will radio ahead to the falls platform before you set out. (Be prepared: the region is almost as ranger intensive as bear intensive.) The road leads a quarter mile to a flat half-mile marked trail leading off on the right to the **Upper Falls Platform.** Let the viewing begin. Nowhere else in the world can you see so many bears from so close and still be safe. Learn each bear's fishing style as they catch or dive for sockeyes, swimming or jumping up the falls.

The moderate, 4 mi. **Mt. Dumpling Trail** leaving from the campground is the hike to do. A steep initial 1½ mi. through poplar forest with high brush cranberries (in late August) provides a panorama of Brooks Lake, Naknek Lake, and Iliuk Arm. On a clear day, the route through alders and willows into the open tundra (blueberries grow here in early Sept.) will reward you with a killer view of all the volcanic peaks in the valley all the way to King Salmon (a round-trip to the overlook takes 1½hr.; to the trail's end 5-6hr.). There is an easy **cultural walk** through old Dena'ina and Yupik pit dwellings to a reconstructed *inna* ("dwelling" in Sugpiak-Alutiiq), housed in an unlocked cabin.

FARTHER AFIELD. If you're blessed with a week in Katmai and have some paddling skills, consider the six- to seven-day **Savonoski Loop.** One of Alaska's finest kayak or canoe routes, it winds through remote and silent lakes and rivers. Boaters leave from Brooks Camp and can stay one night at **Fures Cabin,** a restored trapper's cabin with lots of memorabilia, bunks, and an outhouse. The cabin is reservable through the Park Office (246-3305 or 246-2100). From the cabin a moderately difficult one mile portage is required. But after that, it's smooth paddling through clear and clean waters full of pike and salmon. Camping is accessible on many tiny islands along the way, but is not wise along the bear-populated Savonoski River; ask rangers for recommendations. Periodic high winds make it wise to stay fairly close to shore and may lengthen trips unexpectedly.

ALEUTIAN ISLANDS

At the fiery boundary between two tectonic plates, the string of snow-capped volcanoes of the Alaska Peninsula and the Aleutian Islands stretches more than 1000 miles into the desolate North Pacific toward the coastal waters of Kamchatka, Russia. The Aleutians are one of the most remote locations on earth, and the lava-scarred cones on these green but treeless isles are abused by some of the world's most vicious storms. Recent findings on Hog Island, adjacent to Unalaska Island, support a hypothesis that the ancestors of today's Aleuts migrated here from Asia by moving into the northern Pacific island by island, rather than across the Bering Land Bridge formed later (see p. 526). In the 19th century, Russia, too, used the Aleutians as stepping stones into North America, and used the skilled Aleuts to expand their trade in valuable otter and seal skin. Enslavement, relocation, and armed conflict scarred these early communities, but Russian influence established an Orthodox Church presence still vibrant in the region today.

Another invasion came on June 3rd, 1942, when the Japanese, trying to divert American forces from the southern Pacific, began to bomb the islands and occupied Attu and Kiska. The U.S. responded by constructing the Alaska Highway and stationing nearly 60,000 soldiers on Unalaska, and the remains of their occupation—the last base is only now being gradually decommissioned—still mark the landscape. With as little as 24 hours notice, the U.S. Army evacuated Aleut residents from many of the islands, ostensibly in the interest of safety, though Caucasians were allowed to remain. In the inhumane conditions of their exile, up to 25% of the displaced Aleuts perished. Roughly 70% returned to find their property destroyed by American soldiers, and whole villages were abandoned. This is a little-known and shameful piece of American history, officially silenced until the passage of the Civil Liberties Act of 1988, when the Aleuts were offered an official apology and granted financial compensation.

These cliffs and emerald, treeless hills remain home to Aleut villages, Russian Orthodox churches, small abandoned military installations, and towns. While a modest fleet supports an enormously wealthy fishery, a handful of people venture here for the deep-sea sport-fishing, and a few hundred tourists more come each summer to explore the natural beauty of this volcanic wilderness.

┌ GETTING THERE

The only two ways of reaching the Aleutian Islands are alarmingly expensive. A one-way **flight** from Anchorage to Dutch Harbor, the largest town on the Aleutians, costs about $420. A one-way fare on the **Alaska Marine Highway** from Homer takes four days and costs $242 (children 2-11 $122, bikes/kayaks $39 extra; seniors 50% off one-way; an **AlaskaPass** might make the ferry trip more affordable, see p. 58). This route is serviced only seven times per year between April and September. Clear days promise unique panoramas, and an on-board naturalist gives regular presentations on the plants and wildlife visible from the ship. The ferry stops briefly at small towns, from fishing villages to prefabricated cannery quarters, before reaching Dutch Harbor. Unfortunately, it only stops here for about five hours before turning around and heading back. The boat has showers, water, and a dining room with limited hours and affordable food (breakfast $5-7, lunch $6-10, dinner $9-13); bringing provisions from Homer is a good idea, though campstoves may not be used on board. There is limited room in the enclosed lounge where you can grab a bench seat to sleep on. Otherwise passengers lay their sleeping bags and pitch their tents on deck. Call well in advance to rent a cabin. Stock up on Dramamine or another seasickness remedy before leaving, for while the weather is mildest in July, the *Tustumena* still weathers 5- to 15-foot seas—and is not called the "Vomit Comet" for nothing. The trip is popular with senior citizens, and a handful of families, students, anglers, and maniacal birdwatcher-types who run around with binoculars the size of small children screaming, "It's a whiskered auklet!"

UNALASKA AND DUTCH HARBOR

Isolated at the western limit of the Alaska Marine Highway's ferry service, Dutch Harbor and Unalaska (un-uh-LAS-ka) are as remote a community of 4100 as you'll find in North America. The name Unalaska comes from the original Aleut name for the area, "Agunalaksh." When the Russians came to the island, this evolved into "Ounalashka" and since 1890 the current name has persisted. Dutch Harbor is a port with its own post office and ZIP code. An Unalaskan suburb has been built on Amaknak Island, about 2 miles from downtown Unalaska, and is often called Dutch Harbor. The two islands are connected by the Bridge to the Other Side.

Unalaska has been the nation's top port, for pounds of seafood caught and value of fish and crab delivered, since 1988. Ninety percent of the community depends on the fishing industry. Two major fishing seasons run from January to March and August to November. During that time, 2000 workers staff the plants and thousands more work on-board vessels. Recreational fishing is also popular. A Fairbanks resident landed a 459-pound halibut here to set a new world record in 1996; a $100,000 prize awaits whomever can break it. While the treeless islands support no large game, countless bald eagles are known to fight over fish being reeled in, and occasionally attack humans from their posts atop masts, rooftops, and the domes of the Russian Orthodox Church.

Unalaska is not a haven for the budget traveler, due to its remoteness and unusually high incomes—over $130 million in seafood passes through this port annually. But the view of treeless, snow-capped, green mountains soaring thousands of feet from the bay's chilly blue waters may be a worthwhile investment.

◪ ORIENTATION AND PRACTICAL INFORMATION. Unalaska lies about 300 mi. from the tip of the Alaska Peninsula. It is in the same time zone as the rest of the state. The **airport** is about a quarter-mile from City Dock on the main road into town, and is served by **Pen Air** (581-1383 or 800-442-0333), **Alaska Airlines** (266-7700 or 800-426-0333), and **Reeves** (581-3382 or 800-544-2248) to Anchorage (about $420 one way). Planes sometimes don't fly in or out for a week at a time due to fog. The **Alaska Marine Highway** (800-526-6131) departs City Dock, 1½ mi. from Dutch Harbor and 2½ mi. from Unalaska, to Homer (4 days, about once a month, $242). **Parks Culture and Recreation Community Center** (581-1297), on 5th

St. around the corner from the post office, provides untimed showers with soap and shampoo, free local calls, a weight room and gym, free pool tables, and parlor games all for a $3.75 daily admission. (Open M-F 7am-10pm, Sa 8am-10pm, Su noon-9pm.) Taxi service is available from *five* companies—locals are as baffled by that number as we are. All run 24 hours (**Aleutian Taxi,** 581-1866). The ferry to town costs $12-14. **Visitor Information** (581-2612; www.arctic.net/~updhcvb) is available in the Grand Aleutian Hotel (open M-F 9am-5pm, potentially open Sa-Su 1-4pm). The **Ounalashka Corporation** (581-1276; www.ounalashka.com; open M-F 8am-noon and 1-5pm), in a low, orange-roofed building nearby, sells required **hiking and camping permits.** Jeff, at **Aleutian Adventure Sports** (581-4489 or 888-581-4489; www.arctic.net/~advsports), at 4th and Broadway, rents mountain bikes ($25 per half-day, $35 per day), kayaks ($45 per half-day, $65 per day), and cross-country skis ($20 per day) and gives advice. **Iliuliuk Family and Health Services** (581-1202; after-hours 581-1233; open M-F 8:30am-6pm, Sa 1pm-5pm) is in a big gray building around the corner from the police station. **Emergency:** 911. **Police:** 29 Safety Way (581-1233), on the Unalaska side. **Post office:** Unalaska, 99685 (581-1232); Dutch Harbor, 99692 (581-1657; both open M-F 9am-5pm and Sa 1-5pm). **Library:** (581-5060; free Internet access; open M-F 10am-9pm, Sa-Su noon-6) on Elanor Dr., past the post office. **Bank and ATM:** next to the Grand Aleutian. **Area code:** 907.

■■■ ACCOMMODATIONS, CAMPGROUNDS, AND FOOD. Once again: it ain't cheap. The visitor center keeps a list of accommodations. Ninety percent of the land is owned by native corporations, and a fee is required for access or camping (land-use $6 per day, camping $11 per night). If the Corporation (see above) is closed, purchase land-use permits from patrol trucks. **Summer Bay** is a popular, unserviced, camping spot, a 7-mile hike from the ferry. To camp closer to the town, hike up Bunker Hill near the WWII bunker. **The Bunkhouse** (581-4357) has rooms with shared baths, a lounge with TV, phone, fridge, and microwave (doubles $55). From the airport, follow the Airport Rd. past the Dutch Harbor post office and take the first left, about a half-mile down the road, on Gilman. The Bunkhouse is next to Peking restaurant. **Eagle Quality Center** (581-4040; open daily 7am-11pm), next to the Grand Aleutian, sells over-priced groceries, but their deli has some of the cheapest food in town.

■ SIGHTS. If it's sunny when you arrive, hastily see **Outdoors,** below. The brand new **Museum of the Aleutians** (581-5150; www.aleutians@arctic.net), just past the Ounalashka Corporation building on Salmon Way, provides a colorful and comprehensive history of the entire Aleutian chain and houses all sorts of interesting Aleut artifacts. (Open Sa-Th 10am-4pm, F 10am-7pm. Tickets $2.) Digs are ongoing, and visitors can frequently visit the sites and even volunteer to get down into the dirt. Packages may be available for longer, more remote projects. The **Qawalangin Tribal Council** hosts Culture Night, with free classes on Aleut doll-making and other crafts, at the senior center (May-Sept. M 7-9pm; call 581-5044 for details).

In Unalaska on Beach Front Rd., the impressive **Holy Ascension Orthodox Church,** built in 1824-27 and expanded in 1894, is the oldest standing Russian-built church in the U.S. This area was the thriving center of Orthodox missionary activity in Alaska, and the once-dilapidated church has recently been restored. Services (Sa 6:30pm and Su 10am) are open to the public and are conducted in English, Russian, and Aleut. Unless a service is in session, the only way to view the beautiful interior is through **A.L.E.U.T Tours** (581-0156 or 391-1747), led by a very knowledgeable Aleut guide. Tours during the ferry layover are $40 and take two to three hours. They fill quickly, so call ahead or talk to the Purser onboard the boat. The **Unalaska Cemetery** and **Memorial Park,** a mile past the church or 4 mi. from the City Dock, on the eastern edge of Unalaska, present a description of the Japanese air attacks of June 1942. If you haven't seen enough bald eagles, head to the landfill on Sommer Bay Rd. or the Westmark Cannery at Captains Bay.

◪ OUTDOORS. A **land-use pass** is required for venturing at all off the main roads. Purchase one at the visitor center or the Ounalashka Corporation ($6 per day). It's wise to rent a bike from **Aleutian Adventure Sports,** which often greets the ferry.

If you have the good fortune to have your ferry layover in Unalaska on a sunny day, make haste to hike to the top of **Mt. Ballyhoo,** just behind the airport, so named by author and temporary resident Jack London. The summit affords one of the most mind-bogglingly beautiful sights in the entire universe. Superlative overkill is not possible here. Amazing gold, red, and black rock formations jut out of a sheer cliff that drops 1634 ft. to the translucent green water of the ocean below, and 6880 ft. **Mt. Makushin Volcano** can be seen steaming on clear days. While the winners of the annual Ballyhoo Run make it to the summit in 26 minutes, a slightly saner pace takes 45 minutes to an hour, and a road on the mountain's far side, off Ulakta Dr., provides a mellow grade. Ferry passengers can walk along the ridge for another 20 to 30 minutes past the summit, and still easily return to catch the boat.

Just before the bridge to Unalaska (a 30min. walk from the ferry) sits **Bunker Hill,** which was heavily fortified during WWII. Following either the construction road clockwise from behind the hill or the beach counter-clockwise to reach the old trail, a quick but steep 420 ft. climb leads to a large concrete bunker affording a great view of the surrounding bays and mountains. Off Summer Bay Rd. is a small trail leading to the top of **New Hall.** The full hike takes about two hours, and the last stretch is mighty steep, but even climbing the first 30 or 45 minutes of the trail provides one of the best views of the Unalaska valley.

There are excellent longer hikes on Unalaska Island if you happen to miss your ferry back and have a month to play with. The **Ugadaga Bay Trail** is an easy-moderate, extremely scenic 2¼-mile trail that was an ancient trade route between Unalaska and the small outer islands by the Unangan people. In colder weather, it may require crossing a snowfield. The marked trailhead begins on the right side of a small pond at the top of Overland Dr. A perfect overnight would be to hike the **Agamgik Bay Trail,** which starts from Humpy Cove past Summer Bay. Cross the small bridge at Humpy Cove Creek on Summer Bay Rd., and the trailhead begins from the pull-off on the right. This flat and easy 4½-mile trail crosses to gorgeous Agamgik Bay on the other side of the island. The bay offers some wind-sheltered camping and a great view of Eagle Rock.

There will never be a better spot to go on a halibut charter. Companies all have comparable rates (half-day $90, full day $165), and can be booked through the visitor center or the Grand Aleutian gift shop. Trips are almost always full, so book well in advance. Fresh crab and fish can be bought straight from any of the seafood companies: **Alyeska** (581-1211); **Royal Aleutian** (581-1671); **Westward** (581-1660); or **Unisea** (581-3844). The kayaking from Unalaska is some of the finest you'll find in the Bering Sea. **Aleutian Adventure Sports** offers all sorts of trips ranging from four- to five-hour paddles to bird- and history-rich Hog Island to multi-day trips to survey the Akutan Volcano and hot springs.

AKUTAN

A day and a half in Akutan probably beats 5 hours in Dutch Harbor, but be sure that the ferry is stopping on the way back. There is no scheduled air service. A 45 minute stop on one leg is only long enough to walk the half-mile boardwalk through the town. The hike to the island's volcano begins about a mile from the ferry, and looks like a moderate hour to the base and a hard 4½hr. to the summit. The hot spring looks close to there.

The village was established in 1878 and the Akutan Corp. (698-2206) was founded in 1972. While both Akutan and Unalaska are nearly entirely owned by native corporations, Akutan doesn't require permits for land use. Eighty-nine people live here, but a Trident cannery brings in 900 or so employees for the two fishing seasons. The boss man built a very odd aluminum-sided "hopper-esque" grey church which is cold and futuristic against the solid green hill.

There is a small Russian orthodox chapel frequented by fledgling bald eagles, the **Grab-a-Dab Cafe,** a hotel—with rooms priced at $90 and 120 a night—a laundry service, a post office, police station, and a medical clinic, but no roads: everyone rides ATVs.

NORTHWEST ALASKA

NOME

Nome owes its existence to the "three lucky Swedes" who discovered gold on nearby Anvil Creek in 1898, and its name to the poor penmanship of a British sailor. Baffled as to what to call this barren, weather-beaten camp at the edge of the sea, he scribbled "Name?" on his map. Cartographers back in England got his vowels confused, and Nome's name was born. Nome is home to a population of 4000, half of which is Native Alaskan. Buildings are elevated on pilings to prevent the permafrosted ground from thawing beneath them, and most have ramshackle exteriors. Those who can afford to get here will find untamed wilderness accessible by road, refreshingly non-commercialized relics of mining history, and a culture centered around the Iditarod dog sled race and the Midnight Sun Festival.

■ PRACTICAL INFORMATION

Airplanes: The **airport** is about 2 mi. west of town. **Alaska Airlines** (800-426-0333) flies from Anchorage (round-trip $349 with 21-day advance purchase). **Alaska Airlines Vacations** (800-468-2248) offers circuit tours from Anchorage to Nome to Kotzebue.

Taxis: Checker Cab, 443-5211. **Nome Cab,** 443-3030. $3 in town, $5 to the airport. Both run 24hr.

Car Rental: Stampede (443-2985), on Front St. in the Aurora Inn. 2WD pickup $65 per day; 4WD pickup, Explorer, or van $75 per day; camper truck $125; unlimited mileage. Must be 25 with credit card or $100 cash deposit. **Gas** sells for an alarming $2 per gallon.

Visitor Information: (443-6624; www.nomealaska.org), on Front St. across from city hall. Open in summer and during Iditarod daily 9am-7pm; off-season 9am-6pm.

Outdoor Information: National Park Service (443-2522), on Front St. in the Sitnasuak Native Corp. Building. Info on Bering Land Bridge National Park and Preserve, all other Western Alaska national parks, and local hiking. Open M-F 8am-noon and 1-5pm.

Library: Kegoayah Kozga Library (443-6627), above the museum on Front St. Open M-Th noon-8pm, F-Sa noon-6pm. Free Internet access.

Laundromat: XYZ Senior Citizens Center (443-5238), next to the Courthouse.

Public Showers: Recreation Center (443-5431), at the northern edge of town on 6th Ave. Free with $4 admission. M-F 6am-10pm, Sa-Su 1-10pm. Closed Sa in Summer.

Radio: KICY 100.3 FM, 850 AM. **KNOM** 780 AM.

Weather: 443-2321. Otherwise, check the magic box outside the visitors bureau.

Emergency: 911. **Police:** 443-5262.

Hospital: Norton Sound Hospital (443-3311), at the end of Bering St.

Post Office: 240 E. Front St., 99762 (443-2401). Open M-F 9am-5pm.

Internet Access: See **Library,** above.

Area Code: 907.

ACCOMMODATIONS AND CAMPGROUNDS

Beds in Nome are costly, but **free camping** is permitted on the flat, sandy beaches, about 1 mi. east of town on Front St., past the sea wall. Gold miners dot the beaches; enjoy the company and hope to fall asleep despite the drone of their sluices. If you have a car, try **Salmon Lake State Campground**, at Mile 38 of the Taylor Hwy. (see **Outdoors**, below).

Betty's Igloo, (443-2419), at the eastern edge of town on 1st Ave. and K St. Clean and comfortable, with kitchen facilities, a spacious common room, and friendly hosts. Shared bath. Children not allowed. Singles $55; doubles $70; includes tax. Breakfast included. Reservations strongly recommended.

Weeks Apartments, 697 3rd. Ave. (443-3194), at G St. Clean inside. A mother lode of amenities: TV, maid service, kitchen, private bath, private washer and dryer. Singles $50-60; doubles $70-80. Call ahead.

FOOD

Stock up on groceries and supplies at **Hanson's Safeway** (443-5454), on Bering St. (open M-Sa 7:30am-10pm, Su 10am-7pm). The rowdy **bars** in town, grouped together on Front St., are always packed with locals.

Java Hut (443-3990), on Bering St. Nome's only flavorful food, with a young clientele and fresh atmosphere. Seawall Salmon Salad on a croissant $7.75; turtle cheesecake $2.50. Also serves cappuccino and espresso. Open M-Th 10am-7pm, F 10am-10pm, Sa 11am-10pm, and Su 11am-7pm.

Fat Freddie's (443-5899), next to the visitors bureau. A popular tour destination since it's clean, well-lit, and overlooks the ocean. Admire the blue expanses of the Bering Sea while chowing down on the soup and all-you-can-eat salad bar ($8). Fresh crab when it comes in to town. Breakfast omelettes $7. Open daily 6am-10pm.

Twin Dragon (443-5552), at the corner of Front St. and Steadman, has a bright, well-decorated interior. Extremely fresh vegetables—how'd they do that? Almond chicken or sweet and sour pork $12. Look for lunch specials. Open M-F 11am-11pm, Sa noon-11pm, Su 3-11pm.

Milano's (443-2924), on the corner of Front St. and Federal. Expensive pizza (medium $14) and Japanese fare (sushi dinner $15), with good service and a hint of dark ambience. Open M-Sa 11am-11pm, Su 3-11pm.

SIGHTS AND EVENTS

Isolation from the rest of the world makes people do strange things. The **Bering Sea Ice Golf Classic** is held on March 18, 2000 on the frozen ocean. Contestants use bright orange balls and face a number of unique hazards: ice crevasses, bottomless snow holes, and frosted greens. Course rules dictate: "If you hit a polar bear (Endangered Species List) with your golf ball, you will have three strokes added to your score. If you recover said ball, we will subtract five strokes." Two of the holes are in **Nome National Forest** (a "seasonal forest" consisting of donated Christmas trees frozen into holes drilled in the treeless tundra). The **Midnight Sun Festival** on June 17-18, 2000 celebrated the summer solstice with a parade, a barbecue, a simulated bank robbery, and a street dance, among other silliness. On Labor Day, the **Great Bathtub Race** sends wheeled bathtubs, filled with water, soap, and bather, hurtling down Front St. The biggest event of the year, however, is the **Iditarod** (800-545-6874; www.iditarod.com). On Memorial Day (ice permitting), everyone turns out for the **Polar Bear Swim.** The world's foremost dog sled race begins in Anchorage and finishes here around

March 19, 2000, beneath the log arch visible year-round by City Hall. Thousands of out-of-town spectators journey in for the finish, and local accommodations can be booked nearly a year in advance.

◤ OUTDOORS

Branching out into the surrounding wilderness, Nome's three highways are a godsend for the adventurous traveler. Though entirely gravel, all are generally well-maintained and navigable in a rental car. According to the visitors bureau, hitchers can usually find rides fairly easily up the Taylor or Council Highway on weekends, when many Nome residents head in that direction. There are excellent **fishing** rivers along the highways, including the **Nome** and **Pilgrim Rivers,** both accessible via the Taylor Hwy. Bring mosquito repellent or you will curse the day you ever heard of Nome.

Nome's outskirts are home to the remnants of abandoned **gold dredges.** The closest, **Swanberg's Dredge,** is about 1½ mi. from downtown on Front St., on the way to the Taylor Hwy. The **Taylor Highway** (also known as the Kougarok Rd.) heads north from Nome for 85 mi., then peters out without reaching any particular destination. Along the way is **Salmon Lake,** near Mile 38. Popular with locals, the lake offers fantastic fishing and primitive campsites. At Mile 53.6, an unmarked 7 mi. road leads to the **Pilgrim Hot Springs** area. The Catholic Church ran an orphanage here from 1917 to 1941, and many of the buildings are intact and undisturbed. This is private land, but the visitors bureau can provide the name and number of the caretaker for permission to soak in the hot springs. The **Kigluaik Mountains** are accessible via this highway, and offer some good hiking and wildflower viewing.

The **Council Highway** runs 73 mi. from Nome to **Council,** a ghost town and summer home for Nome residents, appealingly below the treeline, but only accessible by boat from the end of the road. En route, the highway goes around **Cape Nome,** passing beaches, fishing camps, and the fascinating **Last Train to Nowhere** at Mile 33, a failed railroad (with engine and cars) that sits rusting on the tundra. The **Nome-Teller Highway** winds west from Nome for 72 mi. to the tiny fishing village of **Teller,** home to the friendly Joe Garnie of Iditarod fame.

Nome is also one of two departure points for the **Bering Land Bridge National Park and Preserve.** Allegedly the least visited park in the United States, it encompasses the northern third of the Seward Peninsula, and contains lakes, lava fields, and ancient indigenous ruins. Stone tools, thousands of years old, rest untouched in a valley surrounded by granite spires. The most popular destination (relatively speaking) is the **Serpentine Hot Springs,** just inside the southern border of the park and about 30 mi. from the end of the Taylor Hwy. A primitive bathhouse contains the 140-170°F water and is open year-round. The most common way to get there is by snowmobile in the winter. In summer, a charter flight can be taken to **Taylor;** from there, Serpentine lies 8 mi. over the tundra. Contact the Park Service office (443-2522) for topographic maps and more info.

KOTZEBUE

On the tip of the **Baldwin Peninsula,** 160 mi. northeast of Nome and 25 mi. north of the Arctic Circle, Kotzebue (KOTZ-ih-boo) is principally a transportation and commercial hub for native settlements and other small communities in Alaska's Arctic Northwest. The wind-buffeted village has little to offer independent travelers except access to three remote and wild national parklands, all above the Arctic Circle (see **Northwest Alaska Areas,** below). The **Northwest Alaska Native Corporation (NANA)** has its headquarters here. It takes a ton of money to reach Kotzebue, and $20 more earns admission to the **NANA Museum's Iñupiaq Program** (info and reservations 442-3301), which teaches native dance and the ceremonial blanket toss.

The **airport** is on the west end of town, a 10-minute walk from Kotzebue's modest downtown. **Alaska Airlines** (442-3474 or 800-426-0333) flies four times per day to Anchorage (round-trip $386) and Nome (round-trip $320). **Yute Air** (243-1011; www.yuteair.com) also makes the trip. **Polar Cab** runs lucratively around town (442-2233). The **Visitor Center and National Park Service** (442-3760 or 442-3890) is two blocks from the Airport on 2nd Ave. (open daily 9am-6pm). The center is a stop-off for the busloads of tourists staying at the local expensive hotel, but also has maps and info about charter planes that fly into the three parks of the Noatak River region. There is no place to do laundry; do not besmirch yourself.

Camping is difficult in Kotzebue. Some visitors befriend locals and pitch tents in their backyards. Others make their way to the fish camps 1 mi. either way on the beach. **Ofreida's B&B,** 667 Caribou Dr. (442-3366), is a relatively reasonable indoor option. Ofreida rents two rooms with shared bath, homey decor, and a big breakfast (singles $65; doubles $75). She also lets folks pitch a tent in her backyard; call ahead. **Hanson's,** on Shore Ave., stocks the usual groceries, but be warned: a gallon of milk costs $5.50. **Bayside Restaurant,** on Shore Ave. (442-3600), is a decent place to eat, with windows overlooking the whitecaps.

NORTHWEST ALASKA AREAS

There are more than 14,000 sq. mi. of protected wilderness in Northwest Alaska; **Cape Krusenstern National Monument, Kobuk Valley National Park,** and **Noatak National Preserve** comprise 11% of all the land administered by the National Park Service. Local native people legally use the parks for subsistence hunting. This is wilderness at its wildest, and its remoteness all but guarantees that it will remain that way, accessible to only the most dedicated (and propertied) of outdoorspeople.

Cape Krusenstern National Monument was established primarily for archaeological reasons. Within its gravel, in chronological layers, lie artifacts from every known Inuit occupation of North America. The monument's marshy tundra borders the coastlines of the **Chukchi Sea** on the west and **Kotzebue Sound** to the south. Some hiking is possible in the rolling **Igichuk** and **Mulgrave Hills,** as is kayaking along the coast and in the numerous lagoons. The only way in is by charter plane from Kotzebue (about $250 per hr.).

The 2650 sq. mi. **Kobuk Valley National Park** occupies a broad valley along the central **Kobuk River,** 25 mi. north of the Arctic Circle. One of the park's more surprising features is the 25 sq. mi. **Great Kobuk Sand Dunes,** a small piece of the Sahara in Alaska's Arctic. The most popular park activity is floating the Kobuk. Popular put-in spots include the village of **Ambler** on the park's east edge, or at the river's headwaters in **Walker Lake,** deep in the Brooks Range. The sand dunes are accessible via a short overland hike from the Kobuk River, after floating within hiking range. The region is accessible via regularly scheduled flights from Kotzebue. **Yute Air** (442-3330) flies to Ambler from Kotzebue ($190 round-trip).

The 10,200 sq. mi. **Noatak National Preserve** contains the broad, gently sloping **Noatak River Valley.** This westward-flowing river drains the largest undisturbed watershed in North America. Most visitors see the area from the water, floating along the Noatak from the arboreal forest's northern edge into a treeless expanse of tundra. Wildlife abounds, especially members of the region's 400,000-strong caribou herd. Fewer than 100 visitors float the Noatak each season. The only way in is by (you guessed it) airplane; there are some scheduled flights between **Noatak,** an outlying town on the preserve's western boundary, and Kotzebue (around $80).

ARCTIC ALASKA

DALTON HIGHWAY (RTE. 11)

The Dalton Hwy. parallels the Alaska Pipeline from Fairbanks to the Arctic Circle, then reaches all the way to Deadhorse and the gates of Prudhoe Bay, an oil field on the Arctic Ocean. Before considering the drive, check your wallet to see if a tour is within your means. The **Northern Alaska Tour Company** (907-474-8600) offers a daytrip to the Arctic Circle boundary (departs 7am, returns 11pm; $109), and a three-day trip to Prudhoe Bay including everything but meals ($589). These pricey tours are the best way to view the area while preserving both your car and your sanity—and a flat tire halfway up the Dalton would be a far worse financial drain, anyway.

The entire Dalton Hwy. was opened to the public on January 1, 1995. Truckers predominate, spitting rocks and dust from their 36-wheel rigs. A tiny number of RVs, a handful of 4WD vehicles, and an occasional motorcyclist constitute the tourist traffic. Some hitchers proceed on the logic that nobody would leave a person stranded in the middle of nowhere, yet truckers almost always do. The road is passable in a standard passenger car at speeds under 45mph, but it's unwise to try it. The sharp gravel road is interrupted by rocks, boulders, and ditches, and most rental packages won't cover cars north of the Arctic Circle. The drive *is* breathtaking, though almost entirely without services. Bring two spare tires, a rabbit's foot or other superstitious talisman, and extra gas, tools, clothing, food supplies, and drinking water. Being towed back to Fairbanks costs around $7 *per mile*. The 498 mi. highway takes about four days round-trip. As in all of Alaska, seatbelts are required by law.

FAIRBANKS TO THE ARCTIC CIRCLE

A drive up the Dalton Hwy. begins with an 84 mi. jaunt from Fairbanks along the **Elliot Hwy.** to Mile 0 of the Dalton. Savor the pavement as you head out of Fairbanks—it's the blacktop last you'll see for almost 900 mi. The Dalton crosses the **Yukon River** at Mile 56, 140 mi. from Fairbanks. On the north side of the river is **Yukon Ventures** (907-655-9001), one of the highway's two (count 'em, two) service stations, which sells gas, rents rooms (singles $65; doubles $100; shared bath), and has a small cafe (open daily May-Nov. 7am-9pm).

As it gains elevation, the road winds through its first alpine region; at Mile 97.5, it passes **Finger Rock** to the east and **Caribou Mountain** to the west. The **rest area** just past Finger Rock is an ideal place to calm pothole-jarred nerves and enjoy views of the Brooks Range. Next comes the **Arctic Circle** (Mile 115), the southernmost point at which the sun does not set on the longest day of the year. A recently constructed pull-off has several picnic tables and presents four displays on the Arctic seasons (summer, winter, winter, and winter). Thousands hunger for the enormous Arctic Circle sign photo-op, and the spot offers good, free camping. Most folks are satisfied with merely reaching the Arctic Circle, and quickly retreat to Fairbanks. From here, the road only gets worse.

ARCTIC CIRCLE TO DEADHORSE

Continuing north over Gobblers Knob (1500 ft.), the Dalton rattles past Prospect Camp and Pump Station No. 5, then over the Jim River and the South Fork of the Koyukuk River. A popular rafting trip is the middle fork of the Koyukuk River; many put in at **Coldfoot**, leaving their cars by the airstrip and arranging to be picked up 90 miles downriver in Bettles and flown back (contact the Coldfoot visitor center for more info; for Bettles charters and outfitters, see p. 531). Coldfoot has the last services before Prudhoe Bay, 240 mi. away. A mining town that once boasted a gambling hall, two road houses, seven saloons, and ten prostitutes, Coldfoot was named for the group of prospectors who briefly considered wintering above the Arctic Circle, and then headed south again. Just north of town, the **Coldfoot visitor center** (678-5209) is a resource for travelers eyeing the Brooks Range (open daily 10am-10pm; daily slide presentations 8:30pm). Otherwise the settlement is "the northernmost truck stop in North America." Gas flows 24 hours a day, the tire shop is on call, and the **Coldfoot Cafe** (678-5201) serves hot, expensive food around the clock in summer. The **Slate Creek Inn** (678-5224) rents RV sites (hookups $25) and has pay **showers** ($5). Eight miles north, the **Marion Creek Campground** rents sites in muskeg forest (water and pit toilets, $6). Out of the way of Alaska access roads, **camping** is free. Send news of your journey from the **post office** (678-5204; open M, W, and F 10am-6pm; in winter 1:30-6pm; **ZIP code** 99701). **Area code:** 907.

Twelve miles north of Coldfoot, a turn-off at Mile 188.6 leads 3 miles to the intact gold-mining village of **Wiseman,** subject of Robert Marshall's 1933 work, *Arctic Village.* Perhaps the wildest road-accessible frontier town in Alaska, Wiseman is home to many of the canine stars in the movie version of *White Fang*—including W.F. himself. There is a modest **museum** here (open in summer daily 9am-noon and 1-5pm). Contact the Coldfoot visitor center for info on renting rooms in a **cabin** (singles $50, doubles $70). From Wiseman, the highway continues into the heart of the **Brooks Range,** a region frequented by moose, Dall sheep, bear, caribou, and hawks. At Mile 235, the last tree along the highway—a majestic, surprisingly tall spruce—marks the beginning of the steep and awe-inspiring ascent toward **Atigun Pass** (4752 ft.). The highway cuts steeply into the mountainside as it approaches the snow-covered pass, granting spectacular views of the Dietrich River Valley. Over the mountains lies the long descent toward the Arctic Ocean.

The mountains gradually flatten into tundra, perpetually brown except during a short flourish in July and August. Its surface of bumps and lumps of moss, called tussocks, is underlaid by water trapped beneath the frozen ground. The terrain is wet, soggy, and makes for difficult walking, though it supports wildlife not found below the Brooks Range: musk oxen, arctic fox, snow owls, and tundra swans. Even in summer, the temperature rises to only 43°F (5°C).

Ten miles from the highway's end, coastal fog enshrouds the sun and the temperature plummets. Deadhorse appears on the horizon and, 3 miles later, Prudhoe Bay. And then you're there. The Arctic Ocean. The northernmost point accessible by road in North America. Fun, wasn't it? Now you just have to get back.

DEADHORSE AND PRUDHOE BAY

Deadhorse, on the southern perimeter of Lake Colleen, got its name from the motto of the company that shipped the road-building materials north, "We'll haul anything, even a dead horse." The airstrip here is serviced by **Alaska Airlines** (800-

> # OLD PILOTS AND BOLD PILOTS, BUT NO OLD, BOLD PILOTS Alaska has the highest per capita ownership
> of small planes, the greatest number of pilots, the highest number of float planes, and one of the nation's busiest airports (in Anchorage). Throughout much of the Interior, small planes aren't simply the best way to get there; they're the only way. Some of the state's most colorful lore is steeped in aviation—like the story of Alaska's third governor, who broke both ankles crash-landing his small plane to avoid endangering the children playing on the airstrip. Tales of unusual landings are as common as tales of unusual cargo: bush pilots have been known to transport canoes, beer, furniture, pizza, and even moose to the farthest reaches of the state.

225-2752; from Fairbanks $285 each way). Gas stations are open daily 7am to 5:30pm, but petrol flows for credit non-stop. Staples are sold in the **Arctic Caribou Inn** (659-2368) from 10:30am to 9pm. Register at the hotel for rooms (from $90) and tours of **Prudhoe Bay,** the area of company-owned oil fields that flank the Arctic Ocean, otherwise inaccessible to the public. The 2½-hour tour (daily at 8:15am and 1:30pm, $60) brings visitors to Mile 0 of the pipeline at Pumpstation No. 1 and the shore of the Arctic Ocean for 20 minutes. A shortened version passes through the oil fields en route to the ocean (80min.; 11am, 4:30pm, and 6pm; $25). Be aware that this is a dry "community." In an **emergency,** call the ARCO operator at 659-5300; there are no public emergency services. Mail another letter from the **post office** (659-2669; open daily 1-3:30pm and 6:30-9pm). **ZIP code:** 99734. **Area code:** 907.

BROOKS RANGE

The magnificent Brooks Range makes a great semicircle from the Bering Strait in the west, through the **Noatak National Preserve** and **Gates of the Arctic National Park,** to the **Arctic National Wildlife Refuge (ANWR)** and the Canadian border in the east. This is the northern terminus of the Rocky Mountains and remains one of the last stretches of truly untouched wilderness in the U.S. Accessing the Brooks Range and the parks that protect it is difficult and expensive. It's possible to hike into the mountains from the Dalton Hwy. near Wiseman (see p. 528), but a plane is required to venture deep into the best parts of the range. Talk to park officials before planning a trip into the Brooks. The headquarters for both ANWR and the Gates are in Fairbanks (see p. 502), and the Coldfoot visitor center (see p. 529) can give specific info on where to hike into the range from the Dalton Hwy.

ANAKTUVUK PASS

Many travelers heading into Gates of the Arctic National Park and Preserve fly to Anaktuvuk Pass, the only break in the 1000-mile Brooks Range. Literally translated, "Anaktuvuk" (AN-ak-TOO-vuk) means "caribou shit." Thousands of caribou migrate through the pass every year. Though Anaktuvuk is within the park and protected by U.S. law, it is private land owned by the Nunamiut (NOON-ah-myoot). These inland Inuit have only begun to make permanent settlements in the last 50 years, and continue traditional land-use—hunting and trapping—with modern equipment and vehicles. Until recently, the Nunamiut had been wary of allowing free use of their land. Visitors are expected to practice low-impact camping and low-profile tourism, and to absolutely never take pictures of locals without permission. The **Simon Paneak Memorial Museum** (661-3413) has informative displays on Nunamiut culture and houses the **Hans van der Laan Brooks Range Library,** an interesting collection of material on the people and land of Alaska's far north (both open daily 8:30am-5pm; $5).

Larry's Flying Service (474-9169) is one of the most respected of several bush airlines that fly to Anaktuvuk Pass from Fairbanks (Tu, F, $246 round-trip). The flight over the Brooks Range is probably worth the money—wilderness this pristine and beautiful exists few places on earth. Anaktuvuk has no rooms for rent, but visitors can **camp** anywhere just outside of town. The hills on the other side of the **John River** have desirable sites. The **Nunamiut Corporation Store** (661-3327) sells groceries at prices as steep as the mountains (open M-F 10am-7pm, Sa noon-6pm). The **Nunamiut Corporation Camp Kitchen** (661-3123), a hole-in-the-wall restaurant on the south end of town, serves breakfast ($6) and burgers ($7; open daily 6:30-9am, 11am-1pm, and 3-7pm). The **Washeteria** (661-9713), next to the enormous blue-roofed school, has **laundry** facilities and free **showers. Emer-**

gency: 911. **Police:** 661-3911. **Health clinic:** 661-3914. The **post office** (661-3615) is next to the airstrip (open M-F 8:30-11:30am and 12:30-5:30pm). **ZIP code:** 99721. **Area code:** 907.

GATES OF THE ARCTIC NATIONAL PARK AND PRESERVE AND THE ARCTIC NATIONAL WILDLIFE REFUGE

Established in 1980, Gates of the Arctic National Park and Preserve protects over 13,000 sq. mi. of the central Brooks Range, a heavily glaciated wilderness of grand U-shaped valleys and rivers. The park's remote setting and untouched interior draw the most dedicated explorers for extended hikes and floating trips on six National Wild and Scenic rivers. Covering a vast swath of the northeast, the isolated 31,100 sq. mi. of the **Arctic National Wildlife Refuge (ANWR)** encompass the calving grounds of the teeming Porcupine caribou herd and the Brooks Range's highest mountains. The presence of oil companies, however, may soon alter this region forever.

The park and refuge are most accessible to the powerfully determined and decidedly wealthy. In a long and uncertain journey, budget backpackers sometimes hitch up the Dalton Hwy. and hike in from several access points along the road. Commercial flights service **Anaktuvuk Pass** (see above), from which the refuge is significantly nearer. Those with still more cash to burn can charter a plane and truly isolate themselves. The town of **Bettles** lies south of the mountains on the Middle Fork of the **Koyukuk River**, and is the jumping-off point for plane charters. Several companies offer charter service; ask around for the best deal but expect to pay several hundred dollars per hour. **Brooks Range Aviation** (692-5444 or 800-692-5443) does fly-ins from $300 one-way.

The **Alaska Public Lands Information Center,** 250 Cushman #1A (907-456-0527), in Fairbanks, suggests that only travelers with extensive backpacking background, wilderness survival skills, and experience in Alaskan parks should enter Gates. For more info, contact **Park Headquarters,** 201 1st Ave. (907-456-0281), in Fairbanks. The Park Service also operates the helpful **Gates of the Arctic Field Station** (692-5494; open daily 8am-5pm) in Bettles. **Sourdough Outfitters** (692-5252; fax 692-5557; www.sourdoughoutfitters.com), also in Bettles, rents gear including canoes (inflatable canoes $35 per day) and cabins with kitchens that sleep four ($80-100). Its guides are extremely knowledgeable about the park. (Open M-F 9am-6pm, Sa 10am-6pm.) **Post office:** (692-5236; open M-F 8am-noon and 1-5pm, but sometimes closes early; Sa 1-4pm). **ZIP code:** 99726. **Area code:** 907.

Ask around for good places to pitch a tent. The **Bettles Lodge** (692-5111 or 800-770-5111) has a bunkhouse ($15, sleeping bag required), private rooms (singles $95; doubles $115), showers ($3.50; towel $1), laundry ($7.50 per load), and a restaurant with good cheeseburgers ($7; open daily 8-10pm). At the lodge, the **Bettles Trading Post/Sourdough Outfitters** (see above) sells expensive groceries.

BARROW

Huddled on flat brown tundra next to the icy waters of the Chukchi Sea, Barrow endures some of the harshest conditions in the world: temperatures below -60°F (-51°C) and months of unending twilight. Barrow is the northernmost point on the North American mainland, almost 330 mi. north of the Arctic Circle. Even more remarkable than the pluck it takes for locals to withstand nature's aggressions is how long Barrow natives have been doing so. As early as 2000 BC, the native Iñupiat roamed the area; by 1200 AD, Barrow had become their permanent home. Today, 60% of the 4000-person population is Iñupiat. As in ancient times, bowhead whaling remains an economic mainstay, with extensive hunts in the fall and spring. The native Iñupiat language is spoken as much as English, and ancient and modern customs co-exist. Fresh seal meat and bear hides hang out to dry beside $30,000 cars, all across the street from the local espresso shop. This blend gives Barrow a distinct flavor and smell, attracting the smattering of tourists who visit each year. After dipping their toes in the chilly arctic water and taking several pictures of Iñupiat dancing, however, most travelers content themselves with the fact that they've been to the "top of the world," and then head back south, leaving the persistent town to face a winter world of permafrost and pervasive gray.

▼ ORIENTATION AND PRACTICAL INFORMATION

As with all true Bush communities, Barrow is only accessible by plane, and at quite a price. Buy a ticket far in advance; the earlier the reservation, the cheaper. Barrow itself is infinitely walkable.

Airplanes: The **airport** is downtown, a few blocks from the water on Ogrook St. **Alaska Airlines** (800-426-0333) flies several times per day from Anchorage ($378 round-trip).

Public Transportation: Buses depart across from the airport, and swing around town every 20min. Flag one down anywhere along the route. 50¢, seniors free.

Taxis: City Cab, 852-5050. **Arctic Cab,** 852-2227. Rides around Barrow $5, each additional person $1. Both run 24hr.

Car Rental: UIC Car Rental (852-2700). $75 per day, $20 extra if uninsured. Must be 25. Credit cards accepted.

Visitor Information: Top-of-the-World Hotel, at the corner of Stevenson and Agvik St. (see **Accommodations,** below), is the best source of local info, with walking maps of town. Lobby open 24hr. For employment and general info, contact the **North Slope Borough Public Information Office,** P.O. Box 69 (852-0215).

Tours: A package tour can actually be the cheapest way to see Barrow. Several companies offer 1-day and overnight packages that include guided tours and cost less than an independent ticket and hotel accommodation. **Alaska Airlines Vacations** (800-468-2248) offers 2 tours in conjunction with **Top-of-the-World Hotel.** Trips run mid-May through mid-Sept. Daytrip from Fairbanks $395. Overnight package includes accommodations at the Top-of-the-World Hotel ($438). To or from Anchorage, add $85.

Library: See **Heritage Center,** below.

Emergency: 911. **Police:** (852-0311), across from the Top-of-the-World Hotel.

Crisis Line: 852-0267. 24hr.

Hospital: (852-4611), at the end of Agvik St., by the Middle Lagoon.

Post Office: 601 Cunningham St., 99723 (852-6800). Open M-F 10am-5pm, Sa 9am-1pm.

Area Code: 907.

▶ ACCOMMODATIONS AND CAMPGROUNDS

Accommodations in Barrow are outrageously expensive; if you're planning to stay the night, be prepared to pay an arm and a leg. Harsh weather makes camping a purgatory, but die-hard tenters can ask permission to camp on the beach outside the Top-of-the-World Hotel.

Top-of-the-World Hotel, (800-882-8478, in AK 800-478-8520) 1200 Agvik St. The most prominent hotel in town, with full-service accommodations. Clean, bright rooms, with cable and refrigerators, brighten up the tundra-intensive view just outside the window. Many rooms overlook the icy waters of the Arctic Ocean. Singles $159; doubles $179.

Airport Inn, P.O. Box 933 (852-2525). Friendly and informative staff. Cheerful but plain 70s decor suggests a Motel 6 a loooong way from the Interstate. The prices do not. Singles $115; doubles $125. Kitchenettes available for no extra charge.

📍 FOOD

Although costly, Barrow's food options are surprisingly good. Economy-minded travelers hunting groceries can mush to **Alaska Commercial** (852-6711), one block from Top-of-the-World Hotel on Agvik St. (open M-F 7am-11pm, Sa-Su 7am-10pm).

Arctic Pizza (852-4222 or 852-4223), at Ogrook and Apayauk St. A local favorite, this spacious oceanside restaurant serves a variety of seafood, Italian, and Mexican chow. Ignore the name and order Shrimp à la Arctic, Halibut à la Arctic, or Scallops à la Arctic (around $16). Hamburgers $6.50. Open M-Th 11:30am-10:45pm, F-Sa 11:30am-11:45pm, Su 4-10:45pm.

Polar Haven Coffee Company (852-2326), across from the Top-of-the-World Hotel. A town with 85 straight days of darkness had better have some damn good coffee. Thanks to Polar Haven, Barrow does. Steaming hot lattes (tall $3.25) and cocoa ($1.75) in a country-style cafe, with bright decor and art books. Bagels with salmon $4.25; coffee shakes from $4. Open M-F 7am-6pm, Sa 8am-6pm.

Pepe's North of the Border Restaurant (852-8200). Prices are high at the world's northernmost Mexican restaurant. A la carte burritos $4.25; entrees around $15. The food is decent, but the ambience is far (4000 mi.) from authentic. Open M-Sa 6am-10pm, Su 8am-10pm.

Teriyaki House (852-2276), around the corner from the airport. The Bering Land Bridge is gone, but the Asian influence holds on in this modest downtown restaurant, which serves a host of Chinese and Japanese options (sushi from $6). Lunch specials like Kung Pao chicken with fried rice, egg roll, and soup ($8.50) offered M-F 11:30am-2pm. Open daily 11:30am-11:30pm.

👁 SIGHTS AND EVENTS

The most obvious sight in Barrow is **Point Barrow,** the northernmost tip of the North American continent, a 2-mile walk from Stevenson St. north. Very easy to get to, all things considered. Those nostalgic for the days of Mutual Assured Destruction (or *Dr. Strangelove* fans) might appreciate a trip across town to the **DEW Line,** the Distant Early Warning system designed to detect Soviet missiles flying over the Arctic.

Across the street from Arctic Pizza at Apayauk and Ogrook St. are the **Mounds,** the site of Barrow's original Iñupiat settlement. Today, the ancient sod buildings lie below a grassy knoll and offer little to see, but in 1982, five 650-year-old bodies were discovered here. The two women and three children, well preserved by permafrost, were dubbed the **Frozen Family.** In 1994, an even older body was discovered—a girl, still dressed in a hooded parka, from around 1200 AD.

The **jaws of a giant bowhead whale** sprout up from the ground on Eben Hopson St. Next to the whale-bone arch is **Brower's Store,** Barrow's original whaling station and the oldest wooden structure in the Arctic. The **Iñupiat Heritage Center,** across from the Alaska Commercial Company Store about 1 mi. from town, opened in the fall of 1998. The center includes historical displays, traditional arts, and a library. For more info, call the **Commission on Iñupiat History, Language, and Culture** (852-2611; open daily 9am-6pm).

The **Nalukatag,** or "blanket toss festival," celebrates the end of a successful whaling season every June around the 10th. In this important Iñupiat ritual, children are thrown high into the frigid air from hide blankets. In early August, on the first day that the sun sets, self-punishing travelers can take a short and ceremonial plunge into the icy arctic water.

INDEX

Next time, make your *own* hotel arrangements.

Yahoo! Travel

READER QUESTIONNAIRE

Name: _____

Address: _____

City: _____ **State:** _____ **Country:** _____

ZIP/Postal Code: _____ **E-mail:** _____ **How old are you?** ____

And you're...? in high school   in college   in graduate school

employed   retired   between jobs

Which book(s) have you used? _____

Where have you gone with Let's Go? _____

Have you traveled extensively before? yes   no

Had you used Let's Go before? yes no   **Would you use it again?** yes no

How did you hear about Let's Go? friend   store clerk   television

review   bookstore display

ad/promotion   internet   other: _____

Why did you choose Let's Go?   reputation   budget focus   annual updating

wit & incision   price   other: _____

Which guides have you used?   Fodor's   Footprint Handbooks Frommer's $-a-day

Lonely Planet   Moon Guides   Rick Steve's

Rough Guides   UpClose   other: _____

Which guide do you prefer? Why? _____

Please rank the following in your Let's Go guide: (1=needs improvement, 5=perfect)

packaging/cover	1 2 3 4 5	food	1 2 3 4 5	maps		1 2 3 4 5
cultural introduction	1 2 3 4 5	sights	1 2 3 4 5	directions		1 2 3 4 5
"Essentials"	1 2 3 4 5	entertainment	1 2 3 4 5	writing style		1 2 3 4 5
practical info	1 2 3 4 5	gay/lesbian info	1 2 3 4 5	budget resources	1 2 3 4 5
accommodations	1 2 3 4 5	up-to-date info	1 2 3 4 5	other: _____	1 2 3 4 5

How long was your trip? one week   two wks.   three wks.   a month   2+ months

Why did you go? sightseeing   adventure travel   study abroad   other: _____

What was your average daily budget, not including flights? _____

Do you buy a separate map when you visit a foreign city? yes   no

Have you used a Let's Go Map Guide? yes   no **If you have, which one?** _____

Would you recommend them to others? yes   no

Have you visited Let's Go's website? yes no

What would you like to see included on Let's Go's website? _____

What percentage of your trip planning did you do on the web? _____

What kind of Let's Go guide would you like to see? recreation (e.g., skiing)   phrasebook

spring break   adventure/trekking   first-time travel info   Europe altas

Which of the following destinations would you like to see Let's Go cover?

Argentina   Brazil   Canada   Caribbean   Chile   Costa Rica   Cuba

Morocco   Nepal   Russia   Scandinavia   Southwest USA   other: _____

Where did you buy your guidebook?   independent bookstore   college bookstore

travel store   Internet   chain bookstore   gift   other: _____